THE OXFORD HANDBOOK OF

BUSINESS GEOGRAPHY

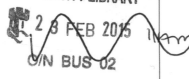
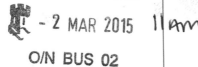

THE OXFORD HANDBOOK OF

BUSINESS GROUPS

Edited by

ASLI M. COLPAN, TAKASHI HIKINO,

and

JAMES R. LINCOLN

OXFORD

UNIVERSITY PRESS

OXFORD
UNIVERSITY PRESS

Great Clarendon Street, Oxford OX2 6DP

Oxford University Press is a department of the University of Oxford.
It furthers the University's objective of excellence in research, scholarship,
and education by publishing worldwide in

Oxford New York

Auckland Cape Town Dar es Salaam Hong Kong Karachi
Kuala Lumpur Madrid Melbourne Mexico City Nairobi
New Delhi Shanghai Taipei Toronto

With offices in

Argentina Austria Brazil Chile Czech Republic France Greece
Guatemala Hungary Italy Japan Poland Portugal Singapore
South Korea Switzerland Thailand Turkey Ukraine Vietnam

Oxford is a registered trade mark of Oxford University Press
in the UK and in certain other countries

Published in the United States
by Oxford University Press Inc., New York

© Oxford University Press 2010

British Library Cataloguing in Publication Data

Data available

Library of Congress Cataloging in Publication Data

Data available

Typeset by SPI Publisher Services, Pondicherry, India
Printed in Great Britain
on acid-free paper by
Ashford Colour Press, Gosport, Hampshire

ISBN 978–0–19–955286–3 (hbk.)
ISBN 978–0–19–966052–0 (pbk.)

1 3 5 7 9 10 8 6 4 2

ACKNOWLEDGEMENTS

the many individuals and organizations
First and foremost, we are deeply indebted
e generous contribution to the Graduate
ѕity provided the financing that carried the
ɡes to the preparation and publication of
highly academic enterprise demonstrates
1 of the value of international business

 University's Graduate School of Manage-
e for Technology, Enterprise and Competi-
tional conference in the fall of 2007, which
olume together in a stimulating exchange of
ɪrovided the foundation on which this book

wledge the many individuals who contrib-
me, we do wish to give explicit recognition
ɛr, Michael Carney, Will Mitchell, Keetie

ѕistance supplied by the team of editorial
s who oversaw the compilation, editing,
me. We particularly thank the leader of
d Musson, the Business and Management
ɪject, his skill and diligence in coordinating
its many facets, and his patient and thoughtful encouragement along the
way. His commitment and support were absolutely critical to this book becoming
a reality.

Others on the OUP team who deserve mention include Matthew Derbyshire and
Emma Lambert, Assistant Commissioning Editors at OUP, and Abigail Coulson and
Carol Bestley, Production Editors, who led us through the many logistical complexities of the publication process. Hilary Walford deserves special credit and apprecia-
tion for her professional handling of the challenging task of copy editing the
individual chapters. Rendering smooth, readable, and stylistically consistent the
prose of authors whose first language was in many cases not English and whose
topics spanned a good deal of regional, institutional, and disciplinary esoterica was
no small feat.

Finally, we wish to express our gratitude to the many scholars from all over the world who contributed chapters to the volume. Their patient, careful, and timely responses to our critical comments and requests for changes made our job as editors much more pleasant and manageable. We thank them all for their participation in the project, and their contributions to the Handbook, which we hope will prove to be a useful contribution to the scholarly understanding of business groups.

Asli M. Colpan
Takashi Hikino
James R. Lincoln

Contents

Group 2. Latin America

Group 3. The Middle East, Eastern Europe, and Africa

PART III. ECONOMIC, SOCIOPOLITICAL, AND MANAGERIAL UNDERPINNINGS OF BUSINESS GROUPS

List of Figures

LIST OF TABLES

Abbreviations

AAIT	Anglo American Investment Trust
ADA	Anil Dhirubhai Ambani
ADR	American depository receipt
AFTA	ASEAN Free Trade Area
ANC	African National Congress
ASEAN	Association of South East Asian Nations
BAT	British American Tobacco
BEE	Black Economic Empowerment
BEEC	Black Economic Empowerment Commission
BGT	*Business Groups in Taiwan*
BIBF	Bangkok International Banking Facilities
BIS	Bank of International Settlements
BMB	Bangkok Metropolitan Bank
BMV	Mexican Securities Exchange
BNDE	Banco Nacional de Desenvolvimento Econômico
BNDES	Banco Nacional de Desenvolvimento Econômico e Social (National Bank for Economic and Social Development)
BOI	Board of Investment
BOT	Bank of Thailand
CCIS	China Credit Information Service
CDRAC	Corporate Debt Restructuring Advisory Committee
CEO	chief executive officer
CMHN	Consejo Mexicano de Hombres de Negocios (Mexican Council of Businessmen)
CMPC	Compania Manufacturera de Papeles y Cartones
COPEC	Compañía de Petróleos de Chile SA
CPO	Certificados de Praticipación Ordinarias
CRC	Central Retail Corporation
CSMAR	China Stock Market and Accounting Research Database
CSN	Companhia Siderúrgica Nacional
CUL	Cambridge University Library
CVM	Comissão de Valores Imobiliários
DBCM	De Beers Consolidated Mines
EAEA	East Asian Economic Association
EGAT	Electricity Generating Authority of Thailand
EU	European Union
FASB	Financial Accounting Standards Board
FDI	foreign direct investment

FIG	financial–industrial groups
FVB	Federale Volksbeleggings
GDP	gross domestic product
GHQ	General Headquarters
GHL	Guildhall Library
GTC	general trading company
HCI	heavy and chemical industries
HCLC	Holding Company Liquidation Commission
HHI	Herfindahl–Hirschman index
IASC	International Accounting Standards Committee
IC	integrated circuit
IDC	Industrial Development Corporation
IMF	International Monetary Fund
IPO	initial public offering
ISA	Israel Securities Authority
ISI	import substitution industrialization
ISIC	International Standard of Industrial Classification
ITRI	Industrial Technology Research Institute
JEL	*Journal of Economic Literature*
JMA	Jardine Matheson Archives
JSE	Johannesburg Stock Exchange
KMT	Kuomintang
LG	Lucky-Goldstar
LSE	London Stock Exchange
M&A	mergers and acquisitions
MAS	Monetary Authority of Singapore
MBR	market to book value ratio
MERCOSUR	Mercado Común del Sur
MNE	multinational enterprise
MRTP	Monopolies and Restrictive Trade Practices (Act)
NAFTA	North American Free Trade Agreement
NDVR	Non-Voting Depository Receipts
NEDB	National Economic Development Board (later NESDB)
NEIO	New Empirical Industrial Organization
NLI	Nippon Life Insurance
NSBC	National Statistics Bureau of China
OBM	own brand manufacture
ODFI	outward direct foreign investment
ODM	own design and manufacture
OEC	Organization for Economic Cooperation and Development
OEM	original equipment manufacture/manufacturer/manufacturing
PACs	Persons Acting in Concert
PEIF	private equity investment fund
POSB	Post Office of Singapore Bank
PPVA	post-production value added
PTT	Petroleum Authority of Thailand
R&D	research and development

RDP	Reconstruction and Development Program
ROA	return on assets
SAIC	State Administration for Industry and Commerce
SASAC	State-Owned Assets Supervision and Administration Commission of the State Council
SBDC	Small Business Development Corporation
SCAP	Supreme Command of the Allied Powers
SFE	stochastic frontier estimation
SIC	Standard Industrial Classification
SME	small and medium enterprise
SOAS	School of Oriental and African Studies
SOE	state-owned enterprise
SSRN	Social Science Research Network
SVS	Chilean Superintendence of Securities
TASE	Tel Aviv Stock Exchange
TEV	township and village enterprise
TNC	transnational corporation
TSD	Thailand Securities Depository (TSD)
TSMC	Taiwan Semiconductor Manufacturing Corporation
UAC	United Africa Company
UERT	Unión Explosivos Río Tinto
UMC	United Microelectronics Corporation
VGG	*Valor Grandes Grupos*
WSOE	wholly state-owned enterprise
WTO	World Trade Organization

Notes on Contributors

Dante M. Aldrighi is Associate Professor of Economics at the University of São Paulo and Researcher at the National Counsel of Technological and Scientific Development, Brazil. His research interests include corporate governance and corporate finance. He has published in journals such as *Revista Brasileira de Economia, Brazilian Journal of Political Economy,* and *Estudos Econômicos.* He was also one of the contributors to the Global corruption Report 2009.

Brian K. Boyd is Chair Professor of Strategic Management and also Chair of the Management Department at City University of Hong Kong. His primary interests include corporate governance, strategy implementation, and research methods. He has been Associate Editor at both *Organizational Research Methods* and *Corporate Governance: An International Review,* and also served as guest editor of several special issues. He presently serves on the Editorial Boards of *Strategic Management Journal, Journal of Management Studies,* and *Management & Organization Review,* and has previously held a number of other editorial board appointments. In 2011, he received the Sage/Robert McDonald Award for outstanding contribution to organizational research methods. He has also held elected positions in both the Academy of Management and Strategic Management Society.

Chi-Nien Chung is Associate Professor in the Department of Management and Organization at the NUS Business School, National University of Singapore, Singapore. His research interests include strategies and structure of business groups in East Asia, organization theory, economic sociology, networks, and organizations. He has published in such journals as *Administrative Science Quarterly, Organization Science, Journal of International Business Studies, Journal of Management Studies, and Organization Studies.* He serves on the editorial board of *Strategic Management Journal.*

Asli M. Colpan is Associate Professor of Corporate Strategy and holds the Mizuho Securities Chair at the Graduate School of Management, Kyoto University, Japan. She is also Adjunct Associate Professor at Kyoto Consortium for Japanese Studies of Columbia University. Her research interests include corporate strategy, corporate governance, and especially the evolution of large enterprises in industrial and emerging economies. Her work has been published in such journals as *Industrial and Corporate Change, Journal of Management Studies,* and *Asia Pacific Journal of Management.* In 2010 she was awarded the Tachibana prize for the most outstanding female scholar at Kyoto University.

Andrew Delios is Professor in the Department of Strategy and Policy, NUS Business School, National University of Singapore, Singapore. His research interests include corporate strategy, international management, and especially foreign direct investment and global competition issues in emerging economies and international strategies of Japanese multinational corporations. His research has been published in such journals as *Strategic Management Journal, Academy of Management Journal, Administrative Science Quarterly,* and *Asia Pacific Journal of Management.*

Eduardo Fracchia is Associate Professor of Economics at IAE Business School, Argentina. His current research interests include national and business competitiveness, macroeconomics in Latin America, industrial policy, and business groups. His research on business groups in emerging economies has been published in *Management Research.* He also wrote a chapter on business groups in the volume *Can Latin American Firms Compete?* (Oxford University Press, 2007). He analysed the determinants of strategic decisions of business groups in Argentina during the 1990s in his doctoral thesis in the IESE, and has also written a book about applied macroeconomics and collaborated with four of the cases in the forthcoming volume *The Two Shores.*

Andrea Goldstein is Deputy Director of the Heiligendamm Dialogue Process Support Unit at the OECD, France (at the time of writing he was a Senior Economist at the OECD Directorate for Financial and Enterprise Affairs). His research interests include regulatory reform in network industries, the impact of the emergence of China and India on other developing countries, and multinationals from emerging, transitional, and developing countries. He has published in several journals including *Asian Development Review, Cambridge Journal of Economics, Industrial and Corporate Change, Journal of World Business,* and *World Economy.* He is also the author of *Multinational Companies from Emerging Economies: Composition, Conceptualization and Direction in the Global Economy* (Palgrave, 2007).

Mauro F. Guillén is the Dr Felix Zandman Professor of International Management at the Wharton School of the University of Pennsylvania in the United States where he is also Director of the Joseph H. Lauder Institute for Management and International Studies. His research deals with globalization, the diffusion of practices, and cross-border financial services. His most recent books are *The Taylorized Beauty of the Mechanical* (Princeton, 2006) and *Building a Global Bank: The Transformation of Banco Santander* (Princeton, 2008).

Sergei Guriev is Morgan Stanley Professor of Economics and the Rector of the New Economic School in Moscow, Russia. He is also the President of the Center for Economic and Financial Research at the New Economic School and a Research Affiliate at the Centre for Economic Policy Research, London. His research interests include contract theory, corporate governance, political economy, and labour mobility. He has published in international refereed journals including *American Economic Review, Journal of European Economic Association,* and *Journal of Economic Perspectives.*

Takashi Hikino is Associate Professor of Industrial and Business Organization at the Graduate School of Economics and the Graduate School of Management at Kyoto University, Japan. His recent publications include *Big Business and Wealth of Nations* (Cambridge University Press, 1997) (co-edited with Alfred D. Chandler and Franco Amatori), *Policies for Competitiveness: Comparing Business–Government Relationships in the 'Golden Age of Capitalism'* (Oxford University Press, 1999) (co-edited with Hideaki Miyajima and Takeo Kikkawa), and *The Global Chemical Industry in the Age of the Petrochemical Revolution* (Cambridge University Press, 2006) (co-edited with Louis Galambos and Vera Zamagni).

Mike Hobday is Professor of Innovation Management at CENTRIM (Centre for Research in Innovation Management), Brighton University, UK. His research interests include innovation processes in East and South East Asia focusing on technological progress and strategy within local firms and multinational corporations. He also works on project-based innovation in high-value complex products and systems. Besides many journal publications, he is the author of *Innovation in East Asia: The Challenge to Japan* (Edward Elgar, 1997); co-author (with Andrew Davies) of *The Business of Projects: Managing Innovation in Complex Products and Systems* (Cambridge University Press, 2005); and co-editor (with Andrea Prencipe and Andrew Davies) of *The Business of Systems Integration* (Oxford University Press, 2003).

Taeko Hoshino is Research Fellow of the Area Studies Center, Institute of Developing Economies, Japan. Her research interests include the Mexican economy, Mexican business groups, and the business history of developing countries. She has published in such journals as *Developing Economies* and *Ajia Keizai*. She is the author of *Industrialization and Private Enterprises in Mexico* (Institute of Developing Economies, 2001), and also the editor of *La restructuración industrial en México, el caso de la industria de autopartes* (El Colegio de México, 1993), and *The Transformation of the Business Sector under Economic and Political Reforms: The Case of Mexico* (Institute of Developing Economies, 1997).

Robert E. Hoskisson currently holds the George R. Brown Chair of Management at the Jesse H. Jones Graduate School of Management at Rice University, United States. His research focuses on: corporate and international diversification strategies; governance and innovation, and entrepreneurship; acquisitions and divestitures; business groups and strategies of emerging economy firms; and cooperative strategy. Professor Hoskisson's research has been published widely in top management journals and he has co-authored over twenty books. He is currently an Associated Editor of the *Strategic Management Journal* as well as serving in a number of other editorial roles or as a board member at other journals. He is a Fellow of the Strategic Management Society and the Academy of Management.

Geoffrey Jones is Isidor Straus Professor of Business History, Harvard Business School, United States. He is the author and editor of many books and articles on the history of international business, including *British Multinational Banking 1830–1990* (Oxford University Press, 1993), *Merchants to Multinationals* (Oxford University Press, 2000), *Multinationals and Global Capitalism* (Oxford University Press, 2005), *Renewing Unilever* (Oxford University Press, 2005), and *Beauty Imagined: A History of the Global Beauty Industry* (Oxford University Press, 2010). He is a former President of both the European Business History Association and the Business History Conference of the United States, and is co-editor of the journal *Business History Review*. In 2010 he was elected a Fellow of the Academy of International Business.

Young-Sam Kang is Postdoctoral Fellow at the Department of Economics, Seoul National University, South Korea. His research interests include economic development and business economics. He has published in journals such as the *Seoul Journal of Economics* and *Area Studies Review*.

Shinya Kawamoto is Assistant Professor of Social Science at the Waseda Institute for Advanced Study, Waseda University, Japan. His research interests include corporate governance, Japanese economy and business economics. He is the co-author (with Takashi Saito) of "Divestment Management Buy-Outs in Japan: Performance, Governance, and Business Strategies of Seller Firms", *Corporate Ownership and Control*, 7(2), 2009, and (with Hideaki Miyajima, Yusuke Omi, and Nao Saito) of "Corporate Ownership and Performance in Twentieth Century Japan" in Youssef Cassis and Andrea Colli (eds.), *Corporate Performance in the Twentieth Century* (Cambridge University Press, forthcoming).

Tarun Khanna is the Jorge Paulo Lemann Professor at the Harvard Business School, United States, where he has studied companies and organizations in emerging markets worldwide since 1993. His book *Billions of Entrepreneurs: How China and India are Reshaping their Futures, and Yours*, was published in 2008 by Harvard Business Press, and has been translated into several languages. In 2007 he was elected a Young Global Leader (under 40) by the World Economic Forum. In 2009 he was elected a Fellow of the Academy of International Business. He serves on several publicly traded and privately held corporate boards, mentors start-up ventures, and volunteers time with non-profits, especially in Asia.

Hicheon Kim is Professor of Strategy and Organization at Korea University Business School, South Korea. His research interests include business groups, diversification and restructuring, corporate governance, and corporate venturing. His work has been published in leading journals, including *Academy of Management Journal, Strategic Management Journal, Organization Science*, and *Journal of Management*.

Konstantin Kosenko is Economist in the Research Department of the Bank of Israel, Israel. His research interests include corporate governance, corporate finance, financial intermediation, and the role of information in financial markets. He has written several articles on the financial system in Israel, including a paper on conflicts of interest in analyst recommendations that resulted in regulatory changes. His current research focuses on the evolution, performance, and economic impact of business groups in Israel.

Richard N. Langlois is Professor of Economics at the University of Connecticut, United States. His research interests include the economics of organization, the economics of social institutions, and business history. He is the author of *Firms, Markets, and Economic Change: A Dynamic Theory of Business Institutions* (with Paul L. Robertson) (Routledge, 1995) and *The Dynamics of Industrial Capitalism: Schumpeter, Chandler, and the New Economy* (Routledge, 2007).

Keun Lee is Professor at the Department of Economics, and Director of the Center for Economic Catch-up, and also former director of the Institute for China Studies, Seoul National University, South Korea. His research topics include economics of catch-up, corporate governance and growth, and technology policy. He has published in these fields in such journals as *Industrial and Corporate Change, Research Policy, Cambridge Journal of Economics, World Development,* and *Journal of Comparative Economics.* He has edited a volume on *Power and Sustainability of the Chinese State* (Routledge, 2009). He is also editor of *Seoul Journal of Economics.*

Fernando Lefort is Professor and Dean of the Business-Economics School at Universidad Diego Portales. He is also a member of the Chilean National Council of Innovation, the Self-Regulatory Committee of the Chilean Mutual Fund Association, and Vice-Chairman of the Chilean National Unemployment Fund (AFC Chile). His main research interests include corporate finance and governance, and economic growth. He has published several academic articles and books on corporate governance in Chile and Latin America. His research appeared in such journals as *Journal of Business Research, The Developing Economies,* and *Journal of Economic Growth.*

James R. Lincoln is Mitsubishi Bank Professor of International Business and Finance in the Walter A. Haas School of Business, University of California at Berkeley, United States. His primary research interests include organizational design and innovation, Japanese management, and interorganizational networks. He is the co-author (with Arne L. Kalleberg) of *Culture, Control and Commitment: A Study of Work Organization and Work Attitudes in the US and Japan* (Cambridge University Press, 1990), and (with Michael L. Gerlach) of *Japan's Network Economy: Structure, Persistence and Change* (Cambridge University Press, 2004).

Xufei Ma is Assistant Professor in the Department of Management, Chinese University of Hong Kong, Hong Kong. His research interests include strategic management and international business, especially multinational firms' strategies in emerging markets, the internationalization of Chinese firms, and the strategy and governance of Chinese business groups. His research has been published in such journals as *Academy of Management Journal, Journal of International Business Studies, International Business Review, Journal of Business Research,* and *Asia Pacific Journal of Management.*

Ishtiaq P. Mahmood is Associate Professor at the NUS Business School, National University of Singapore, Singapore. His current research interests include innovation in the context of multi-business firms and the role of institutional contexts in shaping business strategy. His research appeared in such journals as *Academy of Management Journal, Management Science, Academy of Management Review, Research Policy, Organization Science, Industrial and Corporate Change, and Journal of Economic Behavior and Organization*. Professor Mahmood won the Haynes Prize from the Academy of International Business for the most prominent scholar in international business under the age of 40.

Luiz Mesquita is Associate Professor of Strategy and Organization, at the W. P. Carey School of Business, Arizona State University, United States, with a joint appointment at the Insper Institute of Education & Research. His research centers on issues of multi-party coordination in contexts of simultaneous cooperation and competition. His publications have appeared in outlets such as the *Academy of Management Journal, Academy of Management Review, Strategic Management Journal*, and *Harvard Business Review*, among others. He is also the co-editor (with Robert Grosse) of *Can Latin American Firms Compete?* (Oxford University Press, 2007), and (with Arnold Cooper, Sharon Alvarez, Aljandro Carrera, and Roberto Vassolo) of *Entrepreneurial Strategies: New Technologies and Emerging Markets* (Blackwell Publishing, 2006).

Hideaki Miyajima is Professor of Japanese Economy in the Graduate School of Commerce, Waseda University, Japan, and Faculty Fellow of RIETI. His primary research interests include corporate governance, corporate finance, institutional change, and their effects on economic growth. He is the co-author (with Masahiko Aoki, and Gregory Jackson) of *Corporate Governance in Japan: Institutional Change and Organizational Diversity* (Oxford University Press, 2007), (with Javed Maswood, Geffrey Graham) of *Japan Change and Continuity* (Routledge Curson, 2002) and (with Takeo Kikkawa and Takashi Hikino) of *Policies for Competitiveness: Comparing Business–Government Relationships in the 'Golden Age of Capitalism'* (Oxford University Press, 1999).

Randall Morck is University Professor of Business and Jarislowsky Distinguished Professor of Finance at the University of Alberta School of Business, Canada, and Research Associate at the National Bureau of Economic Research in Cambridge, Massachusetts, United States. He has published on corporate governance, corporate ownership, and corporate finance in such academic journals as the *American Economic Review, Journal of Finance*, and *Journal of Financial Economics*. He is also the editor of *Concentrated Corporate Ownership* (National Bureau of Economic Research and the University of Chicago Press, 2000) and *The History of Corporate Governance around the World: Family Business Groups to Professional Managers* (National Bureau of Economic Research and the University of Chicago Press, 2005). Parts of the chapter in this volume were written while Professor Morck served as Schoen Visiting Professor of Finance at Yale University.

Fernando A. S. Postali is Professor of Economics at the Department of Economics, University of São Paulo, Brazil. His current research interests include corporate governance and investment and regulation policy, with special attention to the oil and gas sector. His research has been published in such journals as *Energy Economics* and *Pesquisa e Planejamento Econômico*.

Juan Quiroga is Assistant Professor of Business Policy at IAE Business School, Argentina. His current research interests include the way ownership and corporate governance impact decision-making in organizations in emerging economies. His research has been published in such journals as the *Academy of Management Executive*. He is currently a doctoral student specializing in the strategy field at INSEAD.

Jayati Sarkar is Associate Professor at the Indira Gandhi Institute of Development Research, India. Her current research interests include ownership and corporate governance in India and emerging economies. Her research has been published in such journals as *International Review of Finance*, *Journal of Comparative Economics*, and *Economics of Transition*. She is also the co-author (with Subrata Sarkar) of "Ownership and Firm Performance," in Kaushik Basu (ed.), *Oxford Companion to Economics in India* (Oxford University Press, 2007).

Ben Ross Schneider is Professor of Political Science at the Massachusetts Institute of Technology, United States. His books include *Reinventing Leviathan: The Politics of Administrative Reform in Developing Countries* (Lynne Riener, 2003) and *Business Politics and the State in 20th Century Latin America* (Cambridge University Press, 2004). He has also written on economic reform, democratization, technocracy, the developmental state, comparative bureaucracy, and corporate governance.

Masahiro Shimotani is Professor at the Faculty of Economics, Fukui Prefectural University, and Emeritus Professor at the Faculty of Economics, Kyoto University, Japan. His research interest is mainly in the history and structure of business groups in Japan. Recently he has devoted himself to analyzing the holding company issues in Japan. He is the author of several books on the Japanese *zaibatsu*, business groups, and holding companies. He is also the co-editor (with Takao Shiba) of *Beyond the Firm: Business Groups in International and Historical Perspectives* (Oxford University Press, 1997).

Akira Suehiro is Director of and Professor at the Institute of Social Science, The University of Tokyo, Japan. His research interests include industrial development, corporate management, regional cooperation and welfare system in East Asian countries. His major works include *Capital Accumulation in Thailand 1885–1985* (UNESCO, 1989), *Family Business: Agents in Late-Industrializing Countries* (Nagoya University Press, 2006) (in Japanese), *Catch-up Industrialization: The Trajectory and Prospects of East Asian Economies* (National University of Singapore Press, 2008), and *Thailand: Alternatives for a Mid-Income Country* (Iwanami Publisher, 2009) (in Japanese).

Lai Si Tsui-Auch is Associate Professor at Nanyang Business School, Nanyang Technological University of Singapore, Singapore. Her research focuses on business groups, state–capital relations, corporate governance reforms, and multinational corporations in emerging economies. Her research has been published in such journals as *Organization Science, Journal of International Business Studies, Organization Studies, Journal of Management Studies, Management Learning, Journal of Asian Business, Best Paper Proceedings of the Academy of Management, International Sociology, International Journal of Urban and Regional Research,* and *Development and Change.* She won the Carolyn Dexter Best International Paper Award at the Academy of Management Conference in 2007.

Behlül Üsdiken is Professor at the School of Management, Sabancı University, Turkey. His interest areas include organization theory, history of management thought, and management education. He has published in such journals as *Business History, Organization Studies, British Journal of Management,* and *Strategic Management Journal.* He is the co-editor (with Ayşe Buğra) of *State, Market and Organizational Form* (Walter de Gruyter, 1997), and co-author (with Mattias Kipping) of "Business History and Management Studies," in Geoffrey Jones and Jonathan Zeitlin (eds.), *The Oxford Handbook of Business History* (Oxford University Press, 2008).

Natenapha Wailerdsak is Visiting Research Fellow at the Faculty of Economics, University of the Philippines, Philippines. She has published in English, Japanese, and Thai on business groups, human resource management, and corporate management and governance in Thailand, in academic journals such as *ASEAN Economic Bulletin, Journal of International Human Resource Management, Asian Business & Management,* and *Journal of Asian Business.* Her books include *Managerial Careers in Thailand and Japan* (Silkworm Books, 2005) and *Business Groups and Family Business in Thailand before and after the 1997 Crisis* (BrandAge Books, 2006) (in Thai).

Yishay Yafeh is Associate Professor at the School of Business Administration, The Hebrew University, Israel, and Research Fellow at Centre of Economic Policy Research (CEPR) and the European Corporate Governance Institute (ECGI). He is co-author (with Paolo Mauro and Nathan Sussman) of *Emerging Markets and Financial Globalization: Sovereign Bond Spreads in 1870–1913 and Today* (Oxford University Press, 2006). He has published in many journals, including *Journal of Finance, Quarterly Journal of Economics, Economic Journal, Journal of Business,* and *Journal of Industrial Economics.*

Toru Yoshikawa is Associate Professor of Strategic Management at Lee Kong Chian School of Business, Singapore Management University. His main research interest is corporate governance, especially its relation to corporate strategy and performance in large publicly listed firms and in family-owned firms. His research has been published in such journals as the *Academy of Management Journal, Strategic Management Journal, Organization Science, Journal of Management, Organization Studies,* and *Journal of Business Venturing.*

CHAPTER 1

··

INTRODUCTION

··

ASLI M. COLPAN

TAKASHI HIKINO

JAMES R. LINCOLN

THIS *Handbook* brings together an array of state-of-the-art research on the distinctive form of economic institution known as "business groups." The volume seeks to strengthen both scholarly and policy-oriented understanding of the business group phenomenon, which is particularly prominent in emerging markets but also in some mature industrial economies. We see the volume making two primary and related contributions. First, the nation-focused chapters provide detailed analytical and historically grounded empirical treatments of business groups in many nations. Secondly, the cross-national subject-focused chapters offer theoretically based discussion of how those nations compare to one another and fit into a global context. The combination of these perspectives—the empirically specific with the conceptually and comparatively general—gives the volume a broad handle on the diverse and complex evolutionary paths followed by the world's business groups.

Despite their high profiles in numerous countries and their prevalence and importance in the global economy as a whole, business groups remain an understudied phenomenon, although scholarly interest has intensified since the late 1990s. We see three primary reasons for this relative paucity of systematic research and the slowness until recently with which scholars have taken up the topic. The first is that researchers interested in business organization have tended to frame the problem in ways consistent with the study of mature industrial economies. For example, the influential classification by Chandler (1977, 1990) and Williamson (1975, 1985) of the organizational forms of large US corporations in the twentieth century (as functional, multidivisional, conglomerate, and holding company) makes no mention of "business group," a distinct form often associated with developing economies that resembles the Chandler–Williamson "M" or multidivisional form in some respects while differing sharply in others. Secondly, accurate firm-level data are difficult to obtain in emerging nations, where regulatory rules governing the disclosure of even the most basic financial and operational information typically remain weak. Thirdly, the family-owned and otherwise closely held nature of group-affiliated companies (especially the holding company positioned at the apex) often relieves groups of the reporting requirements to which publicly listed and widely held companies are subject.

The extant scholarly literature on the governance, strategies, structures, and performance of business groups in the developing world deals predominantly with particular national and regional cases, more often than not in East and South East Asian venues (see, e.g., Chang 2006). These regions were home to the "Japanese miracle" and the four "Asian Tigers" (Hong Kong, Singapore, South Korea, and Taiwan), all postwar developers in whose remarkable drives to global competitive success business groups figured prominently. The few truly comparative studies tend to juxtapose the high-achieving Asian groups with their generally underperforming Latin American counterparts. The Korean *chaebol*, for example, are generally portrayed as aggressive and effective agents of that dynamic economy's export-led strategy, whereas the fragmented family-based groups of Argentina appear cumbersome and inefficient entities whose viability depended on the protective cloak of important substitution policy. This *Handbook*, therefore, is intended to fill some of the empirical as well as theoretical gaps in the scholarly literature on business groups, while providing a bridge between past and future examinations of the topic.

ORGANIZATION OF THE VOLUME

The variety of economic, political, and sociocultural settings surveyed in the volume's nation-specific case studies is wide. The world regions covered in the volume range from Asia to Latin America, the Middle East, and Africa. Consistent with a view of business groups as the prototypical large-enterprise form in such settings, the emphasis is on "late-industrializing" nations, which achieved a critical path of "modern economic growth" in the twentieth century, especially after the Second World War (Amsden 1989, 2001). Table 1.1 illustrates the impressive rates of growth of several late-industrializing nations from the early post-Second World War period to the present. For purposes of comparison, a number of early industrializing nations are included as well. As business groups were integral and critical agents in the late-industrializing economies represented in Table 1.1, it is hard to avoid the conclusion that they often had a hand in those trajectories of growth.

Given the prominence of business groups in industrializing economies since the early decades of the twentieth century, this volume focuses on the evolution and contributions of that form of economic institution in the context of representative

Table 1.1 Levels of per capita GDP in late and early industrializing economies, 1820–2006 (1990 international Geary-Khamis dollars)

Country	1820	1870	1913	1950	1960	1970	1980	1990	2000	2006
Japan	669	737	1,387	1,921	3,986	9,714	13,428	18,789	20,738	22,462
South Korea	600	604	869	854	1,226	2,167	4,114	8,704	14,375	18,356
Taiwan	550	550	747	924	1,492	2,980	5,869	9,886	16,835	19,860
China	600	530	552	448	662	778	1,061	1,871	3,421	6,048
Thailand	570	608	841	817	1,073	1,694	2,554	4,633	6,398	8,215
Singapore	683	682	1,279	2,219	2,310	4,439	9,058	14,220	22,518	26,162
India	533	533	673	619	753	868	938	1,309	1,892	2,598
Argentina	N.A.	1,311	3,797	4,987	5,559	7,302	8,206	6,433	8,581	9,679
Brazil	646	713	811	1,672	2,335	3,057	5,195	4,920	5,532	5,835
Chile	694	1,290	2,988	3,670	4,270	5,231	5,680	6,401	10,309	12,516
Mexico	759	674	1,732	2,365	3,155	4,320	6,320	6,085	7,275	7,753
Israel	N.A.	N.A.	N.A.	2,817	4,663	8,101	10,984	13,067	16,172	16,997
Turkey	643	825	1,213	1,623	2,247	3,078	4,022	5,399	6,446	7,717
Russia	688	943	1,488	2,841	3,945	5,575	6,427	7,779	5,277	7,831
South Africa	415	858	1,602	2,535	3,041	4,045	4,390	3,834	3,890	4,543
USA	1,257	2,445	5,301	9,561	11,328	15,030	18,577	23,201	28,467	31,049
Canada	904	1,695	4,447	7,291	8,753	12,050	16,176	18,872	22,488	24,951
Belgium	1,319	2,692	4,220	5,462	6,952	10,611	14,467	17,197	20,656	22,729
France	1,135	1,876	3,485	5,186	7,398	11,410	14,766	17,647	20,422	21,809
Germany	1,077	1,839	3,648	3,881	7,705	10,839	14,114	15,929	18,944	19,993
Italy	1,117	1,499	2,564	3,502	5,516	9,719	13,149	16,313	18,774	19,802
Sweden	1,198	1,662	3,096	6,739	8,688	12,716	14,937	17,609	20,710	24,204
UK	1,706	3,190	4,921	6,939	8,645	10,767	12,931	16,430	20,353	23,013

Source: Compiled from Maddison (2009).

late-industrializing nations. Business groups of varied types are still influential in the early twenty-first century in a considerable number of mature industrial nations. In many other such nations, where groups no longer have a significant presence, they were nonetheless important at earlier historical stages. Chapter 3 by Jones and Colpan, for instance, provides an analytical summary of the diversified business groups with pyramidal characteristics organized by British trading houses well into the twentieth century (see also Jones 2000). Chapter 21 by Morck explains the demise of pyramidal business groups in the USA and UK in the 1930s and late 1960s, respectively. Morck sees the Anglo-American experience as exceptional, however, and finds business groups persisting even today in numerous advanced economies (Morck 2005). That persistence, he argues, derives from path-dependent historical factors, such that, compared to their emerging economy counterparts, they are less comprehensible in terms of current market conditions.

The volume comprises twenty-eight chapters divided into three distinct parts. Part I provides an overview of the emergence, evolution, and consequentiality of business groups in theoretical, comparative, and historical perspective. Part II contains sixteen chapters, each analyzing a country-specific pattern of business group organization and behavior. The authors of these chapters examine the degree to which and how the economic, political, and sociocultural arrangements particular to these national settings provided the soil in which groups took root while constraining and channeling the forms they adopted, the paths they followed, and how they meshed with local and international institutions.

Part II's nation-focused chapters also address the competitive strategic goals and actions of business groups: the economic sectors that spawned them; how they diversified in expanding into new domestic industries as well as international markets and the strategic logic of that diversification. They further take on the all-important questions of governance: how are ownership and control distributed within groups; what are the consequences in terms of shareholder interest; and the issues of transparency, quality of monitoring, managerial professionalism, and the like. The chapters further investigate the competitive capabilities that business groups in different countries sought and acquired and that enabled them with varying degrees of success to adapt to shifting economic and political environments.

The nation-specific case studies are followed in Part III by a set of theoretical and comparative treatments of business groups in international perspective. Nine chapters are organized by broad substantive topic. The first three chapters in Part III represent economic analyses of business groups. While sharing a common economics underpinning, those chapters take distinct perspectives on varied facets of business group organization and circumstance such as product portfolio, ownership and governance, and institutional boundaries. The fourth chapter moves to politics and policy, addressing from a political-economy perspective such often-sensitive issues as the connection between industrial policy and group diversification strategy and other close cooperation between business groups and the state. The remaining five chapters all concern the internal functioning of business groups, from corporate governance and leadership to strategy and competitive capabilities. The chapters addressing such management and organization questions place particular emphasis on the international perspective, thus placing the unique and country-specific attributes of groups in broader comparative context.

The diversity of conceptual frames applied in these chapters is a distinguishing feature of this *Handbook* and, we believe, an important strength. Business groups in emerging economy settings are complex, multifaceted (political and cultural as well as economic) entities. Indeed, it is safe to characterize business groups as socially embedded and molded to a degree considerably greater than that of "M-form" and other corporate structures in mature industrial economies such as the United States. In most development theory, such embeddedness both explains and reflects inefficiency. Modes of economic organization that are tightly aligned with local institutions and cultures will in general lag behind the efficiency of modes that instead are attuned to worldwide "best practice." When business groups in developing nations do well in economic terms, is it because they are efficient in the usual economic sense, or is it because they have adapted successfully to a highly localized and idiosyncratic institutional environment? That question comes up repeatedly in these pages.

VARIED DEFINITIONS OF BUSINESS GROUPS

One of the challenges in producing a book on the topic of business groups in a globally comparative context is the diverse use of the term in scholarly writing. Sociologists like Granovetter (1995, 2005) favor a fluid, network conception that highlights the multiplex (many types of ties) and porous organization of groups and their mesh with sociocultural systems. To development economists, groups are a form of big business distinguished chiefly by the technologically unrelated market portfolios characteristic of emerging economies. Khanna and Yafeh's much-cited review article (2007), for example, sees groups operating in multiple, often unrelated, markets (see also Khanna and Palepu 1997; Guillén 2000). Finance scholars, in turn, tend to view business groups as a device used by controlling shareholders to disenfranchise and expropriate value from minority shareholders (La Porta et al. 1999; Morck et al. 2005). The iconic business group with a pyramidal structure, wherein a peak shareholder, often a founding family, exercises effective control over a cluster of affiliate companies through a chain of equity ties, is often argued to be an effective mechanism for such expropriation.

Still other definitions and conceptualizations of business groups derive from the conventions of regulatory bodies and economic journalism. In order to guide the reader through the definitional thicket, we summarize in an Appendix to this Introduction all the working definitions employed in the nation-focused chapters of the *Handbook*. The use of the term business group in a specific nation (for example, the Chilean case) may emphasize one attribute—for example, the pyramidal form—but not another—for example, unrelated diversification. In a different case (for example, India), unrelated product portfolio is emphasized, while public listing of member companies is not. Still other chapters (for example, on China and Thailand) discount diversified portfolio or pyramidal structure as defining attributes. Loosely structured network-type business groups that lack a controlling unit at the apex (family, headquarters entity, or holding company) are best represented in the *keiretsu* groupings that emerged and played important roles in the postwar Japanese economy. Chapter 5 by Lincoln and Shimotani on the postwar *keiretsu* draws attention, as do some of the conceptual/comparative chapters, to how the horizontal *keiretsu* (Mitsubishi, Mitsui, Sumitomo, and so on) derived their cohesion from webs of relatively small cross-shareholdings and occasional executive transfers such that each affiliated firm was somewhat controlled by the group, but no one firm, holding company, or family did much of the controlling.

Such variations in definition do not, however, mean that the cross-national study of business groups necessarily devolves to a survey of altogether unique and dissimilar cases. While readers of these pages will indeed encounter variety in how groups are defined and how they compare to other modes of business organization, the contributors of our nation-focused chapters share a broad understanding of groups as clusters of coordinated activities carried out by interlinked but legally independent enterprises. The "legal independence" of a business group's constituent companies is a definitional criterion on which general agreement exists. Hence, a large corporation's internal product or market divisions do not constitute a "group" in this sense, as they stand collectively as a single corporate entity.

Another commonality across our chapters is the focus on the *largest* business groups in each of the national economies considered. It is the distinguishing features and impact of large groups that in most observers' minds define this particular economic institution. While a restriction of the *Handbook*'s purview risks neglecting some examples of the form that might be interesting and warrant attention, this narrowing of focus seems justified. First, as noted, large groups are the conspicuous and consequential ones and thus those to which scholarly, policy, and journalistic attention is mostly paid. Secondly, several important, even definitive, attributes of business groups are highly correlated with size. Only groups above a certain scale, for example, can encompass a significant number of companies, each of which is itself of reasonable size and often publicly listed; can be widely diversified; can be organized in tall pyramids or bound together by cross-shareholdings; will be noteworthy for their market power, relations with the state, and so on. The very concept of a "business group," then, would seem to imply a relatively large cluster of well-established, legally independent affiliated companies.

Colpan and Hikino (Chapter 2, this volume) deal at greater length with the definitional and conceptual labyrinth that surrounds the topic of business groups. They provide a taxonomy identifying distinct business group forms and distinguishing them from such other organizational forms as the multidivisional and conglomerate types that have drawn so much attention in the business academic literature on advanced industrial economies.

THE VIABILITY OF THE BUSINESS GROUPS

Because of their identification with emerging markets but also because their owner-ship, governance, and other organizational features appear to outside observers personalistic and opaque, business groups are often criticized as inefficient, some-times corrupt, "crony capitalist" institutions. For some realizations of the form, the negative reviews are certainly deserved. Yet, thanks to some new strains of organiza-tional theory and recent empirical research, more and more observers have come to see business groups playing useful roles especially in economic systems that have yet to acquire the well-functioning markets and supportive institutions critical to efficient capitalist economies.

What specifically is it about business groups that explains the part they seem to play in economic growth? An answer offered frequently by the authors of this *Handbook* is that business groups internalize functions for which no external market or supporting institution exists. An even larger role in the advancement of those economies is suggested by Morck's chapter: business groups, largely via their broadly diversified investments, supply the "Big Push" that a developing economy requires in order to jump start its industry sectors and move them simultaneously up trajec-tories of growth. While, in most cases, extreme and unrelated diversification has been shown an unprofitable and dysfunctional strategy when practiced by large corpora-tions in mature economies, it appears to pay systemic (as well as company-level and group-wide) dividends in emerging markets.

If market imperfection explains the emergence and growth of diversified business groups, as most scholars recognize, the global shift since the 1980s toward liberalized markets and more accountable governance practices should, by this logic, undermine the groups' *raison d'être*. Business groups of the pyramidal variety are unlikely to thrive in the presence of accounting and regulatory supervision that demands transparency and safeguards against abuses such as the "tunneling"—expropriation of minority shareholder wealth—often attributed to business groups. Economic maturation thus breeds an environment conducive either to the wholesale demise of the business group form or, short of that, to the focusing of their portfolios, the simplification of their ownership networks, and the professionalization of their boards and executive teams. As business groups are frequently cast as a kind of immature or emergent multidivisional "M-form" corporate organization, it is useful and interesting to speculate on their possible evolution into that form, as defined by related diversification, internal divisionalization, and professional control in the service of long-term strategic goals (Chandler 1977, 1990).

However, the evidence that business groups the world over have been undergoing such simplification, focusing, or at the extreme, total collapse is on the whole scant. Major groups lacking those attributes do not appear to be unraveling or otherwise becoming less important to their national and regional economies. One might suppose that the rising global pressures over recent decades for economic liberaliza-tion and, especially, the financial stresses and economic turbulences since the 1990s would have eroded the institutions supporting business groups in those regions. While several groups in particular countries did decline and even disappear (for example, the Daewoo *chaebol* in Korea), for the most part the developing world's groups survived such selection pressures and emerged largely unscathed and sometimes even strengthened. For example, offsetting Daewoo's demise following the 1997 Asian financial crisis and the International Monetary Fund's draconian reforms was the re-emergence of the Samsung and Lucky-Goldstar (LG) groups as reinvigorated global competitors.

The persistence and continuity of business groups around the world suggest strongly that this distinctive form of business organization cannot be reasonably reduced to a second-best functional substitute for the Anglo-American multidivisional enterprise and therefore may move down its own unique evolutionary path. Nor is the groups' general adaptability in emerging economies easily dismissed as symptomatic of those countries' premodern and crony-esque institutional environments. Even in some advanced economies, pyramidal business groups have survived in the presence of investor protections that effectively prevent the "tunneling" of wealth from minority to controlling shareholders. Moreover, while business groups are often accused of surviving on political rents (which, indeed, they are often well positioned to extract), the evidence presented in the chapters to follow is that, depending on the type of group, the stage of development, the region, and so on, the rents that groups seek and extract are mostly of the economic sort. When groups enjoy extraordinary returns, the reasons, as suggested by the authors of many of our chapters, lie in the competitive capabilities in which they invested. While generalizations of this sort are always hazardous, the thrust of the evidence that the authors of this volume have garnered is that in many instances business groups have successfully adapted, not only to the political and cultural realities of the countries in which they are located, but to the economic realities, local, regional, and global, as well. Those capabilities and adaptations in large measure constitute the subject matter of this *Handbook*.

REFERENCES

AMSDEN, A. H. (1989). *Asia's Next Giant: South Korea and Late Industrialization.* New York and Oxford: Oxford University Press.

AMSDEN, A. H. (2001). *The Rise of "the Rest": Challenges to the West from Late-Industrializing Economies.* Oxford: Oxford University Press.

CHANDLER, A. D., JR. (1977). *The Visible Hand: The Managerial Revolution in American Business.* Cambridge, MA: Belknap Press.

CHANDLER, A. D., JR. (1990). *Scale and Scope: The Dynamics of Industrial Capitalism* Cambridge, MA: Belknap Press.

CHANG, S. J. (ed) (2006). *Business Groups in East Asia: Financial Crisis Restructuring, and New Growth.* Oxford: Oxford University Press.

COLPAN, A. M., and HIKINO, T. (2008). "Türkiye'nin Büyük Şirketler Kesiminde Işletme Gruplarının Yeri ve Çeşitlendirme Stratejileri" (Diversifying to be the Leading Developmental Agent: Business Groups in Turkey's Large-Enterprise Economy), *Yönetim Araştırmaları Dergisi (Management Research Journal)*, 8/1–2: 23–58.

GRANOVETTER, M. (1995). "Coase Revisited: Business Groups in the Modern Economy," *Industrial and Corporate Change*, 4/1: 93–130.

GRANOVETTER, M. (2005). "Business Groups and Social Organization," in N. Smelser and R. Swedberg (eds.), *The Handbook of Economic Sociology*. 2nd edn. Princeton: Princeton University Press, 429–50.

GUILLÉN, M. F. (2000). "Business Groups in Emerging Economies: A Resource-Based View," *Academy of Management Journal*, 43/3 (June 2000): 362–80.

JONES, G. (2000). *Merchants to Multinationals: British Trading Companies in the Nineteenth and Twentieth Centuries*. Oxford and New York: Oxford University Press.

KHANNA, T., and PALEPU, K. (1997). "Why Focused Strategies May be Wrong for Emerging Markets," *Harvard Business Review*, 75/4 (July–Aug.), 41–51.

KHANNA, N., and RIVKIN, J. (2001). "Estimating the Performance Effects of Business Groups in Emerging Markets," *Strategic Management Journal*, 22: 45–74.

KHANNA, T., and YAFEH, Y. (2007). "Business Groups in Emerging Markets: Paragons or Parasites?" *Journal of Economic Literature*, 45/2: 331–72.

LA PORTA, R., LOPEZ-DE-SILANES, F., and SHLEIFER, A. (1999). "Corporate Ownership around the World," *Journal of Finance*, 54/2: 471–517.

MCGREGORS (various years). *Who Owns Whom in SA*. Johannesburg: McGregors.

MADDISON, A. (2009). "Statistics on World Population, GDP and Per Capita GDP, 1–2006 AD." www.ggdc.net/maddison

MORCK, R. (2005). "How to Eliminate Pyramidal Business Groups: The Double Taxation of Intercorporate Dividends and Other Incisive Uses of Tax Policy," *Tax Policy and the Economy*, 19: 135–79.

MORCK, R., WOLFENZON, D., and YEUNG, B. (2005). "Corporate Governance, Economic Entrenchment, and Growth," *Journal of Economic Literature*, 43/3: 655–720.

Valor Grandes Grupos (2008). Supplement of *Valor Economico*.

WILLIAMSON, O. E. (1975). *Markets and Hierarchies: Analysis and Antitrust Implications*. New York: Free Press.

WILLIAMSON, O. E. (1985). *The Economic Institutions of Capitalism*. New York: Free Press.

World Bank (2004). *From Transition to Development: A Country Economic Memorandum for the Russian Federation*. Moscow: World Bank.

Appendix: Working definitions and analytical coverage of business groups in individual national economies

Nations	Definition
Prewar Japan	"[A] set of legally independent firms that were wholly or partly owned by a holding company or a parent firm." They had family-led characteristics in that family or entrepreneurs kept effective control, and were diversified into multiple sectors. (Chapter authors' definition.)
Postwar Japan	"[A cluster] of independently managed firms whose intertwined activities were reinforced by governance mechanisms such as presidents' councils, partial cross-ownership, and personnel exchanges." (Chapter authors' definition.)
South Korea	"[A] set of firms which, though legally independent, are bound together by a constellation of formal and informal ties and are accustomed to taking coordinated action" (Khanna and Rivkin 2001: 47–8). In principle, any organization with more than two affiliated firms can be classified as a business group. (List of groups comes from Korean Fair Trade Commission.)
Taiwan	"[A] coherent business organization including several legally independent enterprises." Database is constructed by examining interorganizational relationships such as shared identity, cross-shareholding, and interlocking directorates among firms. (Biennial directory, "Business Groups in Taiwan," compiled by China Credit Information Service in Taipei.)
China	"[A] collection of legally independent entities that are partly or wholly owned by a parent firm and registered as affiliated firms of that parent firm . . . the core company of a business group in China, *qiye jituan*, should have a registered capital of over 50 million yuan plus at least five affiliated companies, and the business group should have a total registered capital (including the core and other affiliated companies) of over 100 million yuan." (The National Statistics Bureau of China (NSBC), and State Administration for Industry and Commerce.)
Thailand	"[A] business organization that owns and operates two or more firms under single ownership (particular family, corporate, or state-sponsored company). The fact that a listed company is included in a group is not essential to this definition." (Chapter authors' definition and compilation.)
Singapore	"[A] set of legally separate firms linked together in formal and/or informal ways." (Chapter authors' definition adopting Granovetter 2005; own compilation.)
India	"[A]n agglomeration of privately held and publicly traded firms operating in different lines of business, each of which is incorporated as a separate legal entity, *but* which are collectively under the entrepreneurial, financial, and strategic control of a common authority, typically a family, and are interlinked by trust-based relationships forged around a similar persona, ethnicity, or community." (Chapter author's definition, based on various sources, including the corporate database Prowess.)

Nations	Definition
Argentina	A business entity that owns and operates two and more firms under the single ownership, that are "(1) family owned, in that a family (or a group of families) has the power to make strategic decisions; (2) large, in that they have revenues above US$100 million (as per the exchange rate of 2007); and (3) diversified, as the firms integrating each business group are either involved in more than one industry or have a predominant role in a business to which activities belonging to different links in a single value chain are associated." (Chapter authors' definition and compilation.)
Brazil	"[A] group of firms that, in addition to being strictly controlled by the same entity, either embraces at least one listed firm (what we call a 'listed-firm business group') or is diversified into at least three industries (what we dub a 'diversified business group')."(Chapter authors' definition. List of groups comes from Valor Grandes Grupos, a report annually published by the Brazilian business-specialized newspaper *Valor Econômico*.)
Chile	"[T]wo or more listed companies that are controlled by the same shareholder (or group of shareholders), even when one of the companies is just an investment company holding shares of a single operating firm." (The Chilean Superintendence of Securities.)
Mexico	A constellation of "large companies that are under the common control of an owner family [often forming] a hierarchical shareholding structure with a holding company at its apex that is generally listed on stock exchanges." (Chapter author's definition and compilation.)
Israel	A set of firms "where at least three public companies are controlled by the same (ultimate) shareholder." (Chapter authors' definition and compilation.)
Turkey	An agglomeration of "legally independent, privately held and publicly owned, companies operating in multiple industries, which are controlled through a top holding company with various equity and non-equity arrangements." (Chapter author's definition based on Khanna and Yafeh 2007 and Colpan and Hikino 2008; own compilation.)
Russia	"[L]egally independent firms linked together in formal and informal ties." Whether a listed company is included in a group or not is not essential in the definition taken in this chapter. (Chapter author's definition adopting Khanna and Yafeh 2007. List of groups is based on World Bank 2004.)
South Africa	Group of firms "where two or more listed companies are controlled by the same ultimate shareholder." (Chapter author's definition and compilation based on McGregor, *Who Owns Whom in South Africa*.)

PART I

THEORETICAL AND HISTORICAL OVERVIEW

....

CHAPTER 2

FOUNDATIONS OF BUSINESS GROUPS: TOWARDS AN INTEGRATED FRAMEWORK

....

ASLI M. COLPAN

TAKASHI HIKINO

2.1 INTRODUCTION

....

FOR all their rising recognition in academic disciplines as well as in business journalism, business groups have incurred both frustrating confusion as well as heated discussion regarding their organizational nature and economic contributions. This controversy has frequently stemmed from the very concept of "business groups," as that designation implies somewhat different organization models and business arrangements to individual scholars belonging to diverse academic traditions. In

We are indebted to Geoffrey Jones, James R. Lincoln, and Ben Ross Schneider for insightful comments, and especially to Randall Morck for invaluable correspondence and helpful suggestions. We also thank the participants at the Kyoto International Conference on Evolutionary Dynamics of Business Groups in Emerging Economies, Academy of Management Conference in Anaheim, the Asia Academy of Management Conference in Taipei, and the Strategic Management Conference in Washington.

addition to the conceptual discrepancies regarding business groups that different academic disciplines target and examine, even the definition of business groups that is customarily employed varies across nations and regions. All in all, then, these circumstances have hindered the balanced, systematic, and comprehensive under-standing of this important yet elusive economic institution.

This confusion amid surging academic and popular interest is regrettable, as the business group organization has been the pre-eminent form of large enterprises, especially in emerging markets, since the early decades of the twentieth century. Multidivisional enterprises exhibiting wide yet related product portfolios have not become representative in those developing economies. At one time state-owned enterprises with a focus on specific industries emerged and flourished as another prominent variety of large enterprises, but their economic presence has been in relative decline in many economies, especially since the 1980s. Business groups, by contrast, have remained a core of the large enterprise sector with their characteristic wide and unrelated product portfolio, often combined with the "pyramidal" struc-ture of ownership. Moreover, usually families have kept their ownership and control of business groups.

It is thus the combination of these three factors that has attracted scholarly and popular attention: unrelated product portfolio, pyramidal ownership structure, and family ownership and control. Interestingly, none of the three provides an overall positive connotation. Product domains should be technologically related, it has been argued in strategy literature, so that an enterprise can exploit the benefits of accu-mulated intra-organizational knowledge, which can then be transferred to related product categories, ensuring the lower-than-market cost of production. Unrelated diversification encounters the "conglomerate discount" problem—that is, the market value of the entire group as a whole is lower than that of the sum of the individual operating companies. A pyramidal structure of ownership harms both the investing public and the economy as a whole, because controlling shareholders can "tunnel" the economic benefits of ownership from minority shareholders to themselves and come to exercise economy-wide power disproportionate to the small ownership stakes they actually hold. When that power falls into the hands of a few elite business families, even a democratic society can ultimately be disturbed, as the families may mobilize economic wealth for social influence and political clout.

The overall negative undertone that is attached to business groups, however, need not hinder the systematic examination of this business organization. Nor do the variations in national conventions as well as in academic disciplinary orientations regarding the definition of business groups mean that business groups cannot be examined coherently in different nations across time periods. Rather, these suggest a need to classify the primary "business group" forms and to clarify the critical issues pertaining to that organization model before research advances any further. This task is what this chapter aims to accomplish.

2.2 THE "BUSINESS GROUP" AS AN
ORGANIZATION MODEL

Business groups in their broadest sense characterize an economic coordination mechanism in which legally independent companies utilize the collaborative arrangements to enhance their collective economic welfare. Business groups as a collaboration mechanism should then be contrasted with pure arm's-length market coordination in which the firm follows price signals in competitive settings. In the case of business groups, the behavioral principle governing coordination among companies is a collaborative arrangement, rather than a competitive rivalry. Within this fundamental understanding of business groups as a collaboratively coordinated set of *legally independent companies*, several categories of business groups have been detected from different analytical perspectives. Table 2.1 gives a taxonomy of business

Table 2.1 Stylized characteristics of the three major categories of business groups

Characteristics	"Alliance" principle	"Authority" principle	
	Network-type business groups	Hierarchy-type business groups	
		Diversified business groups *Development and strategy perspectives*	Pyramidal business groups *Finance and governance perspectives*
Ownership	No single controlling owner	Mostly family	Mostly family
Control unit	None	Mostly holding company	Mostly holding company
Top management	Not applicable	Mostly family	Mostly family
Administrative control	Inter-firm coordination	Strategic and /or budgetary control	"Ultimate control"*
Operating units	Stand-alone enterprises	Subsidiaries and affiliates	Tiers of listed group companies
Growth pattern	Proliferation of clustering enterprises	Organic growth and acquisitions	Formation of listed affiliates
Product portfolios	Related or unrelated	Unrelated	Related or unrelated

Note: The above characterization of business groups is based on various chapters of this volume. For diversified business groups refer to Chapter 20; for pyramidal business groups Chapter 21; and for network-type business groups in the postwar Japanese context Chapter 5.

*"Ultimate control" here means "in a position to control, or materially to influence, the management of one or more other companies by virtue, in part at least, of its ownership of securities in the other company or companies" (Bonbright and Means 1932: 10).

groups and identifies the significant characteristics of the major categories of business groups, classified according to their behavioral principles as well as from the perspectives of finance and governance, and development and strategic conduct.[1] Note that such perspectives focus on somewhat separate aspects of different organizational arrangements under the single rubric of "business groups." This further complicates the systematic understanding of business group categories. Employing the table as a general guide, below we examine the classification and critical categories of business groups.

2.2.1 Categorical classification of business groups

The classifications of business groups and their relationships to each other are illustrated in Fig. 2.1. We identify two basic and distinct types of business groups at the outset: the network-type business groups, in which the constituent companies adopt the behavioral principle of *alliance*; and the hierarchy-type business groups,

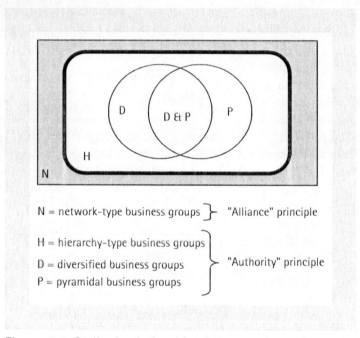

Figure 2.1 Stylized relationships between the major categories of business groups

Note: See the text for the definition and explanation of each category.

---

[1] See, among others, Goto (1982), Granovetter (1995, 2005), Feenstra and Hamilton (2006), Fruin (2008), Khanna and Yafeh (Chapter 20, this volume), Schneider (Chapter 23, this volume), and Boyd and Hoskisson (Chapter 24, this volume) for alternative and complementary approaches and classifications.

which are organized by the *authority* principle. Neither of them represents arm's-length market transactions, as has been argued above. As distinctive as they are, the network-type business groups stand between the polar modes of the market and the firm. They thus differ from a classic firm that internally coordinates its economic activities through administrative instruments. The hierarchy-type business groups, by contrast, *theoretically* come close to, or even are identical to, *the firm* itself in the economics sense, depending on how constituent companies are integrated and controlled in terms of their strategic decision-making and budget allocation. Note that, in this context, "hierarchy-type" broadly designates administrative layers that are organized successively, with each level subordinate to the one above in terms of its authority.[2]

2.2.1.1 *"Alliance" principle: Network-type business groups*

The "alliance" principle designates the business group form as a constellation of legally independent companies that cooperate for common long-term goals. The identifiable characteristics of business groups here are that they are "loose coalitions of firms which have no legal status and in which no single firm or individual holds controlling interests in the other firms" (Granovetter 1995: 96).[3] In other words, these are the "network-type business groups," where no single firm, organization, or individual exercises the dominant control over strategic and budgetary decision-making for the entire group. Depending on the nature and degree of independence and autonomy of constituent companies, however, several varieties of the network-type business groups can be detected.

Included under the designation of network-type business groups is, therefore, a heterogeneous set of business organizations, as long as we follow the lead of Mark Granovetter (1995). The groups designated by this principle actually encompass Japanese inter-market coalitions, such as the Mitsubishi corporate group (*kigyo shudan* or the horizontal *keiretsu*) after the Second World War; regional clusters or industrial districts, such as Silicon Valley and the Third Italy, which exhibit related products; and long-term strategic alliances, such as international airline networks Star Alliance, Oneworld, and SkyTeam Alliance, which are product-focused. As diverse as the network-type of business groups is, the scholars who have studied these economic institutions thus usually consider them as *business networks*, rather than as business groups (Fruin 2008; Lincoln and Shimotani, Chapter 5, this volume; Langlois, Chapter 22, this volume). In order to keep the robustness of analytical concepts, therefore, we will concentrate on the second category, the hierarchy-type business groups, in this chapter. (For the in-depth theoretical and empirical analyses of these network forms of organizations in general, see, among others, Powell 1990;

---

[2] This employment of the term "hierarchy" differs from the one adapted by Williamson (1975), who employs that term as the internal structure unique to the firm.

[3] These loosely bound collections of enterprises are included in Granovetter's definition of business groups as "sets of legally separate firms bound together in persistent formal and/or informal ways" (Granovetter 2005: 429).

Gerlach 1992; Gulati 1995; Smith-Doerr and Powell 1995; Podolny and Page 1998; Lincoln and Gerlach 2004; and Child et al. 2005.)

2.2.1.2 'Authority' principle: Hierarchy-type business groups

The "authority" principle likens business groups to a coherent organization model in which, customarily, a holding company at the helm of the hierarchy owns and controls legally independent operating units, which are usually organized as sub-sidiaries and affiliates through equity ties and other economic means such as inter-locking directorates, budget allocation, and intra-group transactions. Often a family or an entrepreneur owns and controls the apex holding company, but sometimes the family or the entrepreneur directly owns the operating companies underneath, without incorporating or formalizing the apex control unit. This authority principle thus focuses on the hierarchical design of business groups, or "hierarchy-type business groups," with their group headquarters unit or central office exercising control over operating companies. This illustrates a sharp contrast to the network-type business groups based on the alliance principle, in which individual enterprises hold their own autonomy in terms of basic strategic and budgetary decisions.

Hierarchy-type business groups theoretically connote two interrelated yet distinct categories that reflect separate perspectives and also represent different business arrangements: diversified business groups and pyramidal business groups.

Diversified business groups.   In development economics and strategy research, the emphasis lies mostly in the characteristic product portfolio of business groups that exhibit a predominant pattern of unrelated diversification. In a classic definition by Nathaniel Leff (1978: 663), for instance, "the group is a multicompany firm which transacts in different markets but which does so under common entrepreneurial and financial control." In a more recent definition, diversified business groups are "legally independent firms, operating in multiple (often unrelated) industries, which are bound together by persistent formal (e.g., equity) and informal (e.g., family) ties" (Khanna and Yafeh 2007: 331). The basic interest in this variety of business group originates in its contrast to other organizational forms, especially the multidivisional structure with a related product portfolio, which is commonly found in large enterprises of mature industrial economies (Chandler 1990a; Fligstein 1990). Multi-divisional enterprises are often cast as mature economic institutions, in contrast to diversified business groups, which, it is argued, represent an opportunistic response to "imperfect" market environments. Fig. 2.2 shows an archetypal structure of a diversified business group.

Pyramidal business groups.   In the finance and governance literatures, by contrast, the issues of ownership structure, especially those related to the "pyramidal" ar-rangement within business groups, occupy the center of analytical attention. The research focus here is on business groups with listed affiliated companies, which are defined as "two or more listed firms under a common controlling shareholder, presumed to be the largest blockholder voting at least 20 percent or, alternatively,

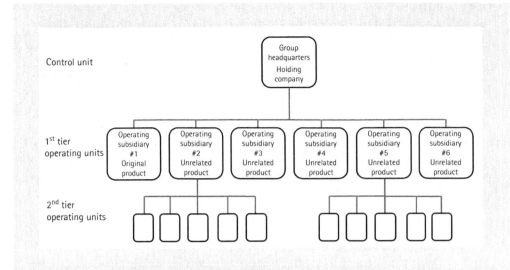

Figure 2.2 Archetypal structure of a diversified business group

10 percent" (Morck, Chapter 21, this volume: 603). The listed companies under common control may be organized under dissimilar ownership structures such as direct (or horizontal) ownership and other complex structures utilizing such control instruments as dual-class shares and supervoting stocks (Almeida and Wolfenzon 2006). Yet, in the bulk of finance and governance literature, the center of attention is on the "pyramidal business groups" that are formed when "one listed group firm is a controlled subsidiary of another" (Morck, Chapter 21, this volume: 603). This stems mainly from the acute concern that has focused, since the classic study by Adolf Berle and Gardiner Means (1932), on the gap between the small proportion of equity ownership and the eventual exercise of the dominant control of tiers of listed companies by the largest blockholder. This discrepancy—the separation of control rights from cash-flow rights—has alarmed finance economists for its potential harm (via 'tunneling' of profits) to minority shareholder interests and ultimately to the economy as a whole. Fig. 2.3 shows an archetypal structure of a pyramidal business group.

Two critical points should be highlighted regarding the two approaches to hierarchy-type business groups: developmental and strategic research, and finance and governance perspectives. First, they do not examine the identical organizational arrangements, even when "business groups" are the focus of their analyses. The developmental and strategy approach aims to clarify the relationships between unrelated product portfolio and organizational and economic efficiency, while the finance and governance approach targets the unique ownership structure and ensuing economic consequences. Second, however, the two approaches hold a common ground in recognizing business groups as a second-best institution that represents

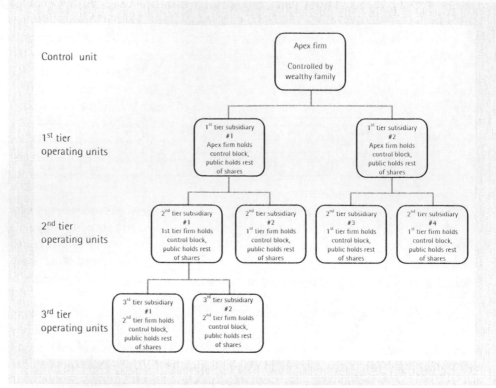

Figure 2.3 Archetypal structure of a pyramidal business group

Source: Reprinted from Morck and Nakamura (2007: 570) with some additions.

the effective yet opportunistic reaction to market imperfections and immaturity, which should result in a suboptimal allocation and utilization of resources in the relevant economies. Developmental and strategic research actually shares a critical interest with finance and governance perspectives in ultimately focusing on the intersection of the two approaches: diversified business groups with a pyramidal structure of ownership. Coupled often with the family ownership and control that integrate the entire group structure, it is this particular organization model that has attracted much attention for its dominant influence in individual national economies. As such, it will now be explored in further detail.

2.2.2 Business groups versus alternative organization models

One critical task in categorizing and examining business groups is to separate them from alternative forms of organization models. This task is quite daunting, because the organizational structures that are discussed as their alternatives are often loosely and inconsistently defined in business and economics literature. Furthermore, those alternatives are not the same for diversified business groups and pyramidal business groups, because diversified business groups mostly relate to the issue of administrative arrangements and strategic choices, while pyramidal business groups are concerned with ownership arrangements and the control apparatus. For diversified business groups, therefore, comparable structures are mainly multidivisional enterprises, conglomerate enterprises, and holding company organizations. For pyramidal business groups, on the other hand, the immediate theoretical alternative is the ownership structure that Heitor Almeida and Daniel Wolfenzon (2006) call "horizontal business groups," where controlling owners consecutively establish new listed companies by directly holding their shares. The two concepts of diversified business groups and pyramidal business groups therefore represent different dimensions, in that diversified business groups may actually adopt pyramidal, horizontal, or other complex ownership structures.

Below we will focus on the comparative examinations of diversified business groups, as the categorical confusions are especially profound regarding this organizational form. We will leave issues relating to pyramidal ownership structures to Section 2.4.2. In order to give a general perspective on this complicated issue concerning diversified business groups, Table 2.2 first summarizes the stylized characteristics of the major comparable organizational forms.

The diversified business groups and comparable organizational forms are all classified under the general category of "multi-unit" enterprises, as coined originally by Alfred Chandler (1977). The multi-unit enterprises consist of a headquarters unit and operating units, which illustrate the basic division of labor between the task of administrative control and the actual production of goods and services. The way a headquarters unit exercises administrative control over operating units remains the analytical focus of the Chandlerian classification of large industrial enterprises (Chandler 1962). In diversified business groups, then, similar to the case of Chandlerian multidivisional enterprises, the headquarters unit of business groups is typically responsible for the long-term allocation of resources and the monitoring performance of the operating units, which are organized as legally independent subsidiaries and affiliates.

The broad categories of multi-unit enterprises naturally bear some resemblance to each other, owing to their general characteristics of hierarchical structures and administrative control. Conceptual clarification and categorical reclassification are thus necessary to distinguish one form from another. A key to solving this conundrum lies in highlighting and examining the distinctive characteristics of each structure. In order to characterize the critical differences and distinguishable features between the analytical categories of multi-unit enterprises, Table 2.2 includes the major stylized characteristics of the business organizations, which will be used as a general guide.

2.2.2.1 *Multidivisional enterprises*

First, we consider the multidivisional organizational structure, because that business organization model represents large enterprises in mature economies, in contrast to diversified business groups, which have long been assumed to be a typical form of big

Table 2.2 Stylized characteristics of comparable organization models

Characteristics	Multidivisional enterprises		Conglomerate enterprises		Holding company organization	
	Chandler	Williamson *M-form Type D1*	Williamson *M-form Type D2**	Berg	Chandler; Williamson	Bonbright and Means
Ownership	Mostly public	Mostly public	Mostly public	Mostly public	Mostly public	Family or public
Control unit	Corporate office or holding company	General office or holding company	General office or holding company	Holding company	"Holding company"	Holding company
Top management	Salaried managers	Salaried managers	Salaried managers and/or entrepreneurs	Salaried managers and/or entrepreneurs	–	Entrepreneurs/ family or salaried managers
Administrative control	Strategic planning or strategic control	Extensive internal control	Not extensive internal control†	Budgetary control	Limited and unsystematic internal control	"Ultimate control"†‡
Operating units	Internal divisions and/or subsidiaries	Internal divisions and/or subsidiaries	Internal divisions and/or subsidiaries	Subsidiaries	Autonomous subsidiaries	Tiers of listed group companies
Growth pattern	Organic growth and acquisitions	Organic growth and acquisitions	Organic growth and acquisitions	Acquisitions and sell-offs	Acquisitions and sell-offs	Formation of listed affiliates
Product portfolios	Related	Related	Diversified	Unrelated	Related	Related

Note: See the text for the above characterization. Refer to Bonbright and Means (1932), Chandler (1962, 1977, 1982); Berg (1969); Williamson (1975, 1985).

*While in the original Williamson classification (1975, 1985), conglomerate enterprises are classified under the general category of multidivisional enterprises, the two subcategories of his classifications, types D1 and D2, are separated here in order to clarify the characteristics of those two organizational structures.

†Less extensive internal control apparatus relative to the original case of multidivisional form of type D1 (Williamson 1975: 153).

‡"Ultimate control" here means "in a position to control, or materially to influence, the management of one or more other companies by virtue, in part at least, of its ownership of securities in the other company or companies" (Bonbright and Means 1932: 10).

business, especially in emerging economies. These are the two business organizations that are most often compared with each other in development and strategy literature. The multidivisional structure in the Alfred Chandler–Oliver Williamson line of classification is defined as "the divisionalized enterprise in which a separation of operating from strategic decision-making is provided and for which the requisite internal control apparatus has been assembled and is systematically employed" (Williamson 1975: 152). Note that Williamson further divides this category into two varieties, D1 and D2. The former represents "common" product categories, suggesting related lines. The latter denotes "diversified" categories, encompassing unrelated domains that eventually point to conglomerate enterprises, which will be examined in the next section. While Williamson takes Chandler's historical descriptions of multidivisional enterprises to formulate his own theoretical examinations of M-form structures, their conceptualizations actually differ, which has often resulted in categorical confusion. Chandler takes up product-market issues, with product-specific knowledge accumulated within large industrial enterprises functioning as a competitive resource that will be spilled over to related product categories. By contrast, Williamson mainly focuses on capital market imperfections, which theoretically yield various concerns related to transaction costs. While acknowledging the product-related externalities, Williamson's interest remains within transaction-related concerns that are non-product specific. As such, several scholars to date have taken Williamson's D2 form as the typical Williamsonian M-form structure (Kock and Guillén 2001), whereas some other scholars attempt to reformulate the M-form thesis to be analytically operational (Hoskisson et al. 1993). In order to avoid further complications we employ his D1 form as the multidivisional form that is comparable to Chandler's classic category.

A distinguishing aspect of the multidivisional structure relative to diversified business groups relates to the legal status of the headquarters or operating units. Whereas within business groups each company is legally independent, the multidivisional structure is not that sensitive to the matter of legal status. This characterization may sound odd, as many scholars have assumed that a multidivisional structure necessarily means internal divisions, *not* legally independent companies as far as operating units are concerned. It is thus critical to recall that, in his classic study of "multidivisional structure," Chandler was concerned solely with "administrative structure" in which "general executives and staff specialists coordinate, appraise, and plan goals and policies and allocate resources for a number of quasi-autonomous, fairly self-contained divisions" (Chandler 1962: 9).

In this proposition, while discussing the functional division of labor in which top management specializes in an executive role such as monitoring and administering the operating divisions, Chandler never explicitly or systematically examined the legal status of operating units. In his description he actually mentioned the names of numerous subsidiaries as well as internal divisions, but he did not weigh up the significance of the differences in terms of their legal status. His sole concern remained the "administrative structure," which comes close to organizational design in today's management terms. In other words, operating units may well be organized as legally independent subsidiaries, as long as they are administered as divisions within the enterprise.

The now-classic four cases of Du Pont, General Motors, Standard Oil (New Jersey), and Sears, Roebuck, which Chandler (1962) studied in detail as the representative cases of multidivisional enterprises, actually exemplify this oft-misunderstood point that, from a legal point of view, large enterprises with a multidivisional form often adopted the holding company-operating subsidiary structure. The first two examples, Du Pont and General Motors, may come close to the textbook description of a multidivisional structure whose major operating units are organized as internal product divisions. After all, Du Pont exemplified one of the critical pioneering cases of the adoption of the multidivisional structure when in August 1921 the company introduced a "new structure for new strategy," with operating units organized as internal product "departments" and their subcategory as "divisions" (Chandler 1962: 104–13). Still, it is important to recall that, as late as 1937, at the height of the anti-holding company policy introduced by the Roosevelt administration, that company, apart from all its foreign affiliates, which were inevitably organized as legally independent international subsidiaries and associates, still owned several important domestic subsidiaries such as American Zinc Products (100% owned and administered as a division) and Remington Arms (60% owned and administered as a department). In the same year, General Motors, which in 1917 had reorganized a holding company organization into a divisionalized structure along its major automobile product lines such as Cadillac, Buick, Oldsmobile, Pontiac, and Chevrolet, continued to keep legally independent yet important subsidiaries and affiliates such as A. C. Spark Plugs (100% owned), General Motors Acceptance Corp. (100% owned), Bendix Aviation (23.8% owned), and Yellow Truck & Coach Manufacturing, which would become Hertz (50.3% owned). Sears, Roebuck, too, organized such important operating units as Allstate Insurance Co., Sears Finance Corp., and Encyclopedia Britannica as legally independent subsidiaries. An extreme case could well be Standard Oil Company (New Jersey), which remained "a holding company solely, owning stock in subsidiaries and other corporations, bonds and other securities" (Moody's 1938: 2972). This structure basically remained unchanged well into the post-Second World War decades. The headquarters unit of multidivisional enterprises could, therefore, well be an operating holding company or a pure holding company as well as the internal corporate office.

By definition, the categorical differentiation of multidivisional enterprises with internal divisions from business groups is thus clear cut, because business groups own legally independent operating units. For multidivisional enterprises with major businesses set up as legally independent subsidiaries, this differentiation is possible only when two independent criteria of product portfolio and administrative structure are included. The product portfolio is diversified yet *related* for Chandlerian multidivisional enterprises, while it is diversified and *unrelated* for diversified business groups. This point related to the strategic decision in terms of product portfolio is critical, as the choice of "structure [organizational form] follows strategy" (Chandler 1962). The headquarters units of multidivisional enterprises most often utilize *strategic* means to influence operating divisions, in terms of administrative instruments used by the corporate headquarters. Employing the detailed classification by Michael Goold and Andrew Campbell (1987), the headquarters adopts either the "strategic planning" or the "strategic control" models. The strategic planning models imply the headquarters working "with the business unit managers to develop strategy," while in the strategic control models the headquarters "prefers to leave the initiative in the development of plans to business unit managers . . . Targets are set for strategic objectives as well as financial performance, and [business unit] managers are expected to meet the targets." Unless product portfolio is diversified into unrelated categories, they seldom adopt the "budgetary control" models in which the headquarters' influences are "exercised through the budget process" (Goold and Campbell 1987: 42–3).

The emphasis on the "strategic planning" and "strategic control" models derives from the technologically related nature of a product portfolio, which makes the senior management within the headquarters unit directly or indirectly involved in the product-focused decision-making that remains within the boundaries of its capability. That involvement is critical in making inter-product spillovers of knowledge possible between individual product divisions, as capturing that synergy becomes a critical source of competitive advantage. Thus, multidivisional enterprises "with differentiated but otherwise common final products [need] a more extensive internal control apparatus to manage spillover effects" (Williamson 1975: 153). For business groups, by contrast, the headquarters unit may actually combine the moderate "strategic control" means with basic "financial control" characteristics, thanks to their characteristic product portfolio with widely diversified and unrelated categories—as the cases of the Koç and Sabancı groups in Turkey (described in Chapter 17 of this volume) suggest.

2.2.2.2 *Conglomerate enterprises*

As we further develop the Chandler–Williamson line of examination of multi-unit enterprises that resemble business groups, conglomerate enterprises should actually be the most significant category. According to Williamson, in terms of product portfolio and ensuing structure, conglomerate organizations represent "a logical outgrowth of the M-form [multidivisional] mode for organizing complex economic affairs . . . [that are] less closely related" (Williamson 1985: 288). Their internal control apparatus is thus less extensive, because multi-product spillovers remain marginal relative to the case of classic multidivisional enterprises with a related product portfolio (Williamson 1975: 153). While some variation of this particular definition of conglomerate enterprises includes those with internal divisions only, most others also include the structure with parent corporations controlling fully owned subsidiaries, as most of the original "conglomcrate" enterprises in the United States have historically adopted this holding company-operating subsidiary form. Extending this line of argument, the term "conglomerate" has been popularly employed in recent literature to mean enterprises in general that are active in multiple product categories. The current popular use is not principally sensitive to the nature of the product portfolio, as it can be related or unrelated, as long as it is widely diversified into multi-industries. As such, classic multidivisional enterprises such as GE, Du-Pont, and 3M are symbolically labeled as "fully-blown imperial conglomerates" (Dugger 1979: 218).

The term "conglomerate," however, was originally and, in a sense, more robustly employed to describe "a company that has become highly diversified quickly, through a series of recent acquisitions and mergers, in more-or-less unrelated areas" (Berg 1969: 112). In this definition, the conglomerate organization basically consisted of a holding company and a wholly owned subsidiary structure, which included such enterprises as ITT, LTV, Litton, and Textron, whose acquisitive behavior and the welfare consequence of an extensive product portfolio became a public-policy issue in the 1960s and 1970s. Contemporary popular examples here may well be Tyco International and Berkshire Hathaway, although their records of acquisitions and divestitures are markedly different. The latter has wholly owned legally independent subsidiaries "that engage in a number of diverse business activities including property and casualty insurance and reinsurance, utilities and energy, finance, manufacturing, services and retailing" (Berkshire Hathaway 2008: inside front cover). These are, therefore, different from "a [multidivisional] company that has become highly diversified over a long period, primarily through internal expansion into related areas" (Berg 1969: 112).

This description by Norman Berg of conglomerate enterprises actually poses the most difficult challenge among the various classifications of multi-unit enterprises that have been examined above, as it comes close to the basic characteristics of diversified business groups. Except for the contrasting general environmental settings—most often mature industrial economies for conglomerates, and usually emerging economies for diversified business groups—both categories exhibit a diversified and unrelated product portfolio and mostly adopt the "holding company" structure in the broad sense given by James Bonbright and Gardiner Means (1932).

In separating out the categories of conglomerate organizations from those of diversified business groups, there are, then, four issues that are particularly delicate and confusing: the ownership and control of the apex unit; the top management of that unit; the public-trading status of operating companies; and the administrative control apparatus. For diversified business groups, the controlling and often exclusive owners of the apex holding company or equivalent entities are usually the family, as the national chapters in this volume amply illustrate. By contrast, their counterparts for conglomerate enterprises are not confined to families. In fact, the headquarters organization of representative US conglomerates has usually been a publicly held corporation whose ownership is widely scattered. Even Royal Little, "the man who started the whole conglomerate movement" with Textron, ceased to be a controlling shareholder as his company grew substantially, thanks to aggressive acquisitions in the 1950s. Reflecting the nature of share ownership, professional salaried management carries out the basic decision-making in terms of resource allocation and performance monitoring for most conglomerate enterprises. "Conglomerate kings" such as Harold Geneen of ITT and Charles Bluhdorn of Gulf +

Western were salaried professionals, however famous they had become thanks to the corporate empires they had created (Sobel 1999). By contrast, family members bear the responsibilities of that critical decision-making role at the apex headquarters in case of diversified business groups. Conglomerates, then, customarily own operating units as fully owned subsidiaries, and as such listing the shares of operating subsidiaries is irrelevant. For diversified business groups, shares of operating companies are often listed and publicly traded. This is the necessary condition for possible tunneling profits, about which financial economists have been arguing (Morck, Chapter 21, this volume). Finally, administrative control exercised by the headquarters organization is often different between diversified business groups and conglomerate enterprises. For conglomerate enterprises, the basic means of internal coordination remain budgetary. The case of Berkshire Hathaway provides an extreme example: "Operating decisions for the various Berkshire businesses are made by managers of the business units. Investment decisions and all other capital allocation decisions are made for Berkshire and its subsidiaries by Warren E. Buffett, in consultation with Charles T. Munger. Mr Buffett is Chairman and Mr Munger is Vice Chairman of Berkshire's Board of Directors" (Berkshire Hathaway 2008: inside front cover). For diversified business groups, however, the families may still hold to the "strategic control" of operating subsidiaries while incorporating some characteristic of "financial control."

2.2.2.3 *Holding company organization*

The legal and administrative issues regarding the relationships between the head-quarters unit and the operating units exhibit themselves more directly in another classification of multi-unit enterprises: the holding company organization. The comparison of this category with the diversified business groups is actually the most bewildering and misleading.

The classification of the holding company organization adopted in strategy re-search has usually followed the definition using the "loose-federation" model that the British holding company employed from the late nineteenth century. Chandler actually cites several examples of this "loose-federation" variety of holding company structure, especially in his *Scale and Scope* (1990a), in which he points to a horizontal combination of family-owned enterprises such as Imperial Tobacco and the Calico Printers' Association. These holding company organizations sought national market control through cooperative arrangements. In that organization, the "parent company's central office was usually little more than a meeting place for a board of directors...legal consolidation [did not] bring administrative centralization, new investment in production and distribution facilities, or the recruitment of salaried top and middle managers" (Chandler 1990a: 288). Using this historical generalization, Williamson (1975: 143) defines the holding company as "a loosely divisionalized structure in which the controls between the headquarters unit and the separate operational parts are limited and often unsystematic." Williamson, then, describes the holding company organization as being a "weak executive structure" that "represents divisionalization of a very limited sort" that corresponds to its narrow and related product portfolio. As such, Williamson (1975: 144) concludes: "Holding companies certainly cannot be expected reliably to yield results that compare favorably with . . . the M [multidivisional]-form structure." This recognition of the holding company structure as a *weak* organizational form, however, compounds categorical confusion in clarifying the unique characteristics of business groups, in that the holding company structure in its legal sense is broadly identical to the hierarchy-type business groups, as has been argued above.

The categorical issue of the holding company organization is actually more complicated, as it was originally theorized by Bonbright and Means (1932) in the 1930s based on the interest that was almost identical to the category of pyramidal business groups that is employed by today's finance economists and discussed in detail by Randall Morck in Chapter 21. According to Bonbright and Means (1932: 1), a holding company is "any company, incorporated or unincorporated, which is in a position to control, or materially to influence, the management of one or more other companies by virtue, in part at least, of its ownership of securities in the other company or companies." In their analysis, however, Bonbright and Means (1932: 12) go further into the issue of control in pointing out a rationale in forming such a business organization: "to pyramid the voting control so as to give to the organizers of the holding company control over the subsidiaries with a minimum amount of investment." Why is that pyramiding so important for controlling shareholders? One of the reasons cited by Bonbright and Means (1932: 153–4) is that they can "milk" the operating companies. While Bonbright and Means did not quite employ the term "tunneling" of profits, as modern finance economists do, they eventually detected a similar reasoning for the holding company structure.

After all, unlike other business structures such as multidivisional enterprises and conglomerate enterprises, the holding company organization has basically been a legal device or an ownership instrument that can be employed by any of the business organizations examined here and can thus be included in any of the hierarchical varieties of business groups, or even in multidivisional structures and conglomerates, for that matter. As such, the employment of the category of holding company organization can be misleading, unless that classification is clearly defined in the explicit context of specific organizational structures.

2.3 CONTOURS OF BUSINESS GROUPS IN LATE INDUSTRIALIZING NATIONS

Business groups with a diversified product portfolio and the characteristics of a pyramidal ownership structure play a particularly significant role in "late-industrializing" nations that started experiencing the structural transformation into modern industrial economies in the twentieth century, and especially after the Second World War (Amsden 1989, 2001). Yet, business groups are also prevalent in some early industrializing economies as well. Table 2.3, which lists the largest economic players in late industrializing nations in around 2007, illustrates the critical importance of business groups in contemporary emerging economies. Out of the 78 economic players listed in that table, we find 53 units that are classified as business groups. A close look at the controlling ownership of large enterprises in general in those countries shows the dominance of family as well as government control. Of the economic players, 26 are controlled by the family, and 42 by the government.

In terms of industry distribution and product diversity, the dominant pattern is diversified product portfolio in technologically unrelated categories, represented by 27 economic units. Next are petroleum-related industries: 18 economic units operate in that product category, which requires huge investment in capital-intensive facilities. A further breakdown illustrates that, among the 26 family-controlled agents, 20 are active in diversified businesses. By contrast, among the 42 government-controlled units, 19 are in petroleum-related businesses, 9 in financial services such as banking and/or insurance, and only 5 have a diversified product portfolio. With respect to the publicly trading status of operating companies, we detect that 50 out of the total 78 economic units have two or more publicly listed subsidiaries, which indicates the prevalence of business groups with pyramidal characteristics in those economies.[4]

If we focus just on the business group category in the list, China occupies a disproportionate significance, having 17 cases among the total of 53 business groups in the list. China, however, also stands out as an anomaly, since all Chinese groups in Table 2.3 are government owned, *not* diversified in terms of their product portfolio, and about only half have two or more listed subsidiaries. The exceptional situation in China has resulted from the restructuring and revitalization of the state-owned enterprises in that economy after the mid-1980s, in which governmental forces played a substantial direct role in terms of industrial organization and corporate behavior (see Lee and Kang, Chapter 8, this volume).

If we put the Chinese case aside, a closer look at the remaining business groups in the list shows that they share significant characteristics. The business groups in all the remaining national economies consist of legally independent companies, often with diversified and an unrelated product portfolio. We find that, among the 36 business groups representing a diverse set of national economies, 23 are diversified in technologically unrelated fields. While these business groups often illustrate family ownership (25 business groups are family owned), the majority (30 business groups) controls two or more listed subsidiaries with a group-level headquarters unit

---

[4] We could not, however, differentiate pyramidal from other types of business groups with listed affiliates because of the lack of systematic data. Detecting pyramidal business groups is difficult, as actual business groups of that category often adopt a complex structure of organizations and ownership (Khanna and Yafeh 2007).

Table 2.3 The largest economic players in late-industrializing countries (except Japan), 2007

Rank	Enterprise/group name	Revenues (US$ m.)	Country	Year	Controlling owner	Industry*	Has two or more listed subsidiaries?	Business group?†
1	Samsung	161,780	South Korea	2007	Family	Diversified	Yes	BG
2	China Petrochemical Co. (Sinopec)	159,260	China	2007	Government	Petroleum, natural gas and petrochemicals	Yes	BG
3	State Grid. Co. of China	132,885	China	2007	Government	Electric power	No	BG
4	China National Petroleum Co.	129,798	China	2007	Government	Petroleum, natural gas and petrochemicals	No	BG
5	Petrobras	112,046	Brazil	2007	Government	Petroleum, natural gas and petrochemicals	No	BG
6	Pemex	103,961	Mexico	2007	Government	Mining and petroleum	No	x
7	Gazprom	98,642	Russia	2007	Government	Gas and energy	Yes	x
8	Hyundai Motor	83,392	South Korea	2007	Family	Diversified	Yes	BG
9	SK	75,784	South Korea	2007	Family	Diversified	Yes	BG
10	LG	71,498	South Korea	2007	Family	Diversified	Yes	BG
11	Lukoil	67,205	Russia	2007	Family	Petroleum, natural gas and petrochemicals	No	BG
12	Petronas	66,218	Malaysia	2007	Government	Petroleum, natural gas and petrochemicals	Yes	na
13	Tata Group	62,500	India	2008	Family	Diversified	Yes	BG
14	Indian Oil	57,427	India	2007	Government	Petroleum	Yes	x
15	Temasek Holding	54,000	Singapore	2008	Government	Diversified	Yes	BG
16	Industrial & Commercial Bank of China	51,526	China	2007	Government	Commercial banking	No	x
17	Carso	51,199	Mexico	2006	Family	Diversified	Yes	BG

Rank	Enterprise/group name	Revenues (US$ m.)	Country	Year	Controlling owner	Industry*	Has two or more listed subsidiaries?	Business group?†
18	PTT	51,193	Thailand	2007	Government	Petroleum, natural gas and petrochemicals	Yes	BG
19	Korea Electric Power	50,271	South Korea	2007	Government	Electric power	Yes	BG
20	Formosa Plastics	49,519	Taiwan	2006	Family	Diversified	Yes	BG
21	Hon Hai	47,571	Taiwan	2006	Family	Diversified	Yes	BG
22	China Mobile Telecommunications Co.	47,055	China	2007	Government	Telecommunications	No	BG
23	China Life Insurance	43,440	China	2007	Government	Insurance	No	x
24	China Construction Bank	41,307	China	2007	Government	Commercial banking	No	x
25	Koç Holding	39,392	Turkey	2007	Family	Diversified	Yes	BG
26	BHP Billiton Plc	39,210	South Africa/ Australia	2007	Institutional shareholders	Mining and refining, petroleum and natural gas	Yes	BG
27	Bank of China	38,904	China	2007	Government	Commercial banking	No	x
28	Bradesco	38,264	Brazil	2007	Family	Diversified	Yes	BG
29	Russian Railways	38,139	Russia	2007	Government	Railways	No	x
30	Rosneft Oil	36,184	Russia	2007	Government	Petroleum, natural gas and petrochemicals	No	x
31	Reliance Group	35,915	India	2007	Family	Diversified	Yes	BG
32	Vale (CVRD)	34,080	Brazil	2007	Pension funds	Diversified	Yes	BG
33	Agricultural Bank of China	34,059	China	2007	Government	Commercial banking	No	x

(continued)

Table 2.3 Continued

Rank	Enterprise/group name	Revenues (US$ m.)	Country	Year	Controlling owner	Industry*	Has two or more listed subsidiaries?	Business group?†
34	Old Mutual	33,917	South Africa/UK	2007	Policy-holders	Insurance, asset management and commercial banking	Yes	BG
35	China Southern Power Grid	33,861	China	2007	Government	Electric power	No	BG
36	Sabic	33,678	Saudi Arabia	2007	Government	Petrochemicals and metals	Yes	na
37	GS	33,478	South Korea	2007	Family	Diversified	Yes	BG
38	Posco	31,163	South Korea	2007	Institutional shareholders	Steel	Yes	BG
39	Lotte	31,070	South Korea	2006	Family	Diversified	Yes	BG
40	Sinochem Group	30,204	China	2007	Government	Diversified	Yes	BG
41	Baosteel Group	29,939	China	2007	Government	Diversified	Yes	BG
42	Anglo American	29,532	South Africa/UK	2007	Institutional shareholders	Diversified	Yes	BG
43	Aditya Birla Group	29,200	India	2008	Family	Diversified	Yes	BG
44	Itausa	28,961	Brazil	2007	Family	Diversified	Yes	BG
45	Shinhan Financial Group	28,729	South Korea	2007	Institutional shareholders	Universal banking, life insurance and asset management	Yes	x
46	Woori Finance Holdings	28,679	South Korea	2007	Government	Universal banking, life insurance and asset management	Yes	x
47	Banco do Brasil	28,449	Brazil	2007	Government	Universal banking	No	BG

Rank	Enterprise/group name	Revenues (US$ m.)	Country	Year	Controlling owner	Industry*	Has two or more listed subsidiaries?	Business group?†
48	Hutchison Whampoa	28,035	Hong Kong	2007	Family	Diversified	Yes	BG
49	Bharat Petroleum	27,873	India	2007	Government	Petroleum	Yes	x
50	China Telecommunications	27,856	China	2007	Government	Telecommunications	No	BG
51	Hindustan Petroleum	27,718	India	2007	Government	Petroleum	No	x
52	Flextronics International	27,558	Singapore	2007	Institutional shareholders	Electronics	Yes	x
53	Cathay Financial Holdings	26,811	Taiwan	2007	Family	Universal banking and insurance	Yes	x
54	Base Element	26,800	Russia	2007	Family	Diversified	No	BG
55	China FAW Group	26,391	China	2007	Government	Automobiles	Yes	BG
56	TNK–BP Holding	24,940	Russia	2007	Alfa, Access-Renova groups and British Petroleum	Petroleum	No	Part of BG
57	CPC	24,808	Taiwan	2007	Government	Petroleum and natural gas	Yes	x
58	Oil & Natural Gas	24,032	India	2007	Government	Petroleum and natural gas	Yes	x
59	China Railway Group	23,732	China	2007	Government	General construction, fabricated metals and property development	No	BG
60	Quanta Computer	23,665	Taiwan	2007	Family	Computer and peripheral equipment	Yes	BG
61	Noble Group	23,497	Hong Kong	2007	Family	Diversified	No	BG

(continued)

Table 2.3 Continued

Rank	Enterprise/group name	Revenues (US$ m.)	Country	Year	Controlling owner	Industry*	Has two or more listed subsidiaries?	Business group?†
62	China Railway Construction	23,335	China	2007	Government	General construction, fabricated metals and property development	No	BG
63	Surgutneftegas	23,302	Russia	2007	Family	Petroleum, natural gas and petrochemicals	No	BG
64	Asustek	22,993	Taiwan	2007	Family	Computer and peripheral equipment	Yes	BG
65	Shanghai Automotive (SAIC Group)	22,607	China	2007	Government	Automobiles	No	BG
66	Hanwha	22,496	South Korea	2007	Family	Diversified	Yes	BG
67	State Bank of India	22,402	India	2007	Government	Commercial banking	Yes	x
68	China State Construction	22,128	China	2007	Government	General construction and property development	No	BG
69	Techint	22,000	Argentina	2007	Family	Diversified	Yes	BG
70	Cemex	21,658	Mexico	2007	Family	Cement manufacturing and wholesale trade	Yes	BG
71	COFCO	21,202	China	2007	Government	Diversified	Yes	BG
72	KT	21,131	South Korea	2007	Institutional shareholders	Telecommunications	Yes	BG
73	Telefonica	21,100	Brazil	2007	Foreign	Telecommunication and information technology	No	x

Rank	Enterprise/group name	Revenues (US$ m.)	Country	Year	Controlling owner	Industry*	Has two or more listed subsidiaries?	Business group?†
74	China Ocean Shipping	20,840	China	2007	Government	Shipping and auxiliary services	Yes	BG
75	Sberbank	20,785	Russia	2007	Government	Commercial banking	No	x
76	CFE	20,658	Mexico	2007	Government	Electric power	No	x
77	China National Offshore Oil	20,637	China	2007	Government	Petroleum, natural gas and petrochemicals	Yes	BG
78	China Minmetals	20,517	China	2007	Government	Diversified	Yes	BG

Note: Economic agents with revenues of more than US$ 20,000 m. are listed.

*Diversified means operating in three or more unrelated businesses.

†Business groups as defined in individual national chapters.

Source: Compiled from Fortune's "Global 500" (2008); annual reports and homepages of relevant enterprises/groups; and national chapters of this volume. Assistance of and consultation with the authors of national chapters are gratefully acknowledged.

organized as a holding company. Product-diversified and family-owned business groups with pyramidal ownership characteristics and several listed subsidiaries are, therefore, at the core of the business groups in the late-industrializing economies represented in the list.

The resilience of the diversified and family-owned business groups is clearly evident when we look at the largest economic players of late industrialization from a long-term perspective. Table 2.4 compares the largest 25 "private" industrial economic agents in 1987 and 2007. Out of the 25, almost all were diversified and family controlled in both years. In 1987 we see 21 diversified and 21 family-owned groups, while for 2007 there are 20 diversified and 20 family-owned groups.

In terms of the continuing presence of individual enterprises and groups, 10 are listed for both years. Two of the groups on the 1987 list, Daewoo and Sangyong, both from South Korea, were dismantled after the 1997 Asian financial crises. While all the others were still active in business in 2007, by that year they had been replaced on the list by newer groups. Despite these fluctuations in the fortunes of individual groups, diversified and family-controlled groups have collectively remained as the core of the big business economy in the late-industrializing economies.

2.4 EXPLAINING THE *RAISON D'ÊTRE* OF BUSINESS GROUPS

The formation of business groups has been explained from several perspectives. These arguments have mostly explained the development of the business group as a single identifiable business organization without distinguishing the specific varieties of groups. This has led to a conceptual and theoretical confusion regarding the fundamental rationale for the existence of business groups. Here we classify and explain the economic foundations of business groups by distinguishing two subcategories: diversified business groups and pyramidal business groups. Although these two often overlap with each other, the dynamics that explain their *raison d'être* are different.

2.4.1 Approaches to "diversified business groups"

Here we explain approaches to the research on diversified business groups that fall into two broad analytical frameworks: the first emphasizes causal exogeneity—the primacy of environmental factors; the second stresses endogeneity—the dynamics of intra-group structure and processes.

Table 2.4 The largest private industrial economic agents in late-industrializing countries (except Japan), 1987 and 2007

	1987					2007*				
Rank	Name	Revenues (US$ m.)	Country	Control	Industry	Rank	Name	Country Revenues (US$ m.)	Revenues (US$ m.) Country	Control	Industry

Rank	Name	Revenues (US$ m.)	Country	Control	Industry	Rank	Name	Country	Revenues (US$ m.)	Control	Industry
1	Hyundai	25,243	South Korea	Family	Diversified	1	Samsung	161,780	South Korea	Family	Diversified
2	Samsung	21,053	South Korea	Family	Diversified	2	Hyundai Motor	83,392	South Korea	Family	Diversified
3	Lucky Goldstar (later LG)	14,422	South Korea	Family	Diversified	3	SK	75,784	South Korea	Family	Diversified
4	Daewoo	13,437	South Korea	Family	Diversified	4	LG	71,498	South Korea	Family	Diversified
5	Barlow Rand	7,617	South Africa	Prof.[+]	Diversified	5	Tata Group	62,500	India	Family	Diversified
6	Sunkyong (later SK)	6,781	South Korea	Family	Diversified	6	Carso	51,199	Mexico	Family	Diversified
7	Tata Group	4,866	India	Family	Diversified	7	Formosa Plastics	49,519	Taiwan	Family	Diversified
8	Koç Holding	4,738	Turkey	Family	Diversified	8	Hon Hai	47,571	Taiwan	Family	Diversified
9	Ssangyong	4,582	South Korea	Family	Diversified	9	Koç Holding	39,392	Turkey	Family	Diversified
10	Sabancı Group	4,582	Turkey	Family	Diversified	10	BHP Billiton Plc	39,210	South Africa/ Australia	Institutional shareholders	Petroleum and resources
11	Korea Explosives (later Hanhwa)	3,563	South Korea	Family	Diversified	11	Bradesco	38,264	Brazil	Family	Diversified
12	Hyosung	3,257	South Korea	Family	Diversified	12	Reliance Group	35,915	India	Family	Diversified
13	De Beers	3,091	South Africa	Family	Diversified	13	Vale (CVRD)	34,080	Brazil	Pension funds	Diversified
14	Formosa Plastics	2,955	Taiwan	Family	Diversified	14	GS	33,478	South Korea	Family	Diversified
15	Birla Group	2,932	India	Family	Diversified	15	Posco	31,163	South Korea	Institutional shareholders	Steel
16	Swire Pacific	2,585	Hong Kong	Family	Diversified	16	Lotte	31,070	South Korea	Family	Diversified

(continued)

Table 2.4 Continued

Rank	Name	1987				Rank	Name	2007*			
		Revenues (US$ m.)	Country	Control	Industry			Country	Revenues (US$ m.)	Control	Industry
17	Koor Industries	2,571	Israel	Union††	Diversified	17	Anglo American (includes De Beers)	29,532	South Africa/UK	Institutional shareholders	Diversified
18	Jardine Matheson	1,628	Hong Kong	Family	Diversified	18	Aditya Birla Group	29,200	India	Family	Diversified
19	AECI	1,607	South Africa	Family	Chemicals	19	Itausa	28,961	Brazil	Family	Diversified
20	Copersucar	1,512	Brazil	Coop.§	Food	20	Hutchison Whampoa	28,035	Hong Kong	Family	Diversified
21	Doosan	1,478	South Korea	Family	Diversified	21	Flextronics International	27,558	Singapore	Institutional shareholders	Electronics
22	Sasol	1,417	South Africa	Govt.¶	Chemicals	22	Quanta Computer	23,665	Taiwan	Family	Computer
23	Alfa	1,380	Mexico	Family	Diversified	23	Noble Group	23,497	Hong Kong	Family	Diversified
24	Tatung	1,248	Taiwan	Family	Electronics	24	Asustek	22,993	Taiwan	Family	Computer
25	Modi Group	1,070	India	Family	Diversified	25	Hanwha	22,496	South Korea	Family	Diversified

For 2007 figures, exact years of individual firm/group data may be different (please see Table 2.3 for precise years).

†Publicly owned, professionally managed.
††Owned by Israeli trade union federations.
§Cooperative.
¶Government holds controlling influence.

Sources: 1987 data: adopted from Amsden and Hikino (1994: 188); 2007 data: based on Table 2.3. To make the two tables comparable, we first listed private economic agents and excluded the ones operating in service sectors only. Russia is also excluded, as the1987 data do not include planned economies.

2.4.1.1 *Exogenous-force explanations*

Among economists in particular, the emphasis in explanations has been placed on the significance of exogenous factors, and especially on demand conditions that have functioned as instrumental mechanisms to support the formation and development of business groups. In these explanations, exogenously given factors on both demand and supply sides, such as market conditions and government policies, facilitate the continuous investment in diversified product categories. We can mention two demand–pull factors in particular: unfulfilled demand as a symptom of imperfect market conditions in underdevelopment; and government actions that artificially create and secure demand through import-substitution policies and public investments, especially in infrastructure. In addition, the government actions actually include a supply–push mechanism that individual enterprises internalize through various incentives brought about by industrial policy apparatus.

Market imperfection approaches. An extensive body of work explaining diversified business groups focuses on the economics concept of market imperfections and failure and the associated transaction costs in developing economics (Leff 1976, 1978; Ghemawat and Khanna 1998). Theoretically, transactions are costly when markets and their supporting institutions, such as regulatory systems, contract enforcing mechanisms, and rules for information disclosure and transparency, are immature and weak. From this point of view, business groups are seen as responses to imperfections in capital, product, labor, and other markets and institutions that are particularly commonplace in emerging markets (Khanna and Palepu 1997; Khanna and Rivkin 2001). Arguments for the emergence of business groups then rest on how business groups fill in the "gaps" in the institutional as well as the market infrastructure of those economies.

Product markets, for instance, may not be functioning well because of a lack of qualified market participants, despite sufficient demand. The oft-cited case of South Korea's Lucky-Goldstar (see Kim, Chapter 6, this volume) illustrates how an absence of suppliers in the market led that group to fill the gap by diversifying into several unrelated product lines. Weak contract enforcement may then lead to the group's investing in several businesses rather than trusting external parties that might behave opportunistically. Given the inadequacy of information in developing economies, a reliable umbrella brand can also facilitate the group's entry into several, even unrelated, businesses (Khanna and Palepu 1997; Khanna and Rivkin 2001).

Diversified business groups may also be an effective substitute for the imperfect capital markets that typify emerging economies. A group can create an internal capital market by transferring capital inside the group to invest in existing lines of businesses and to enter into new fields. As outside providers of capital will be reluctant to invest in new companies, thanks to the absence of reliable information and to poor protective measures for those investors, diversified business groups with a well-established reputation will also be in a favorable position to access capital markets (Khanna and Palepu 1997). While mutual insurance or risk-sharing has also been suggested as a function of diversified business groups in compensating for underdeveloped financial markets, Tarun Khanna and Yishay Yafeh (2005) find no strong evidence of this in any nations other than Japan, Korea, and Thailand.

Labor markets are also inefficient in emerging economies, as there is a scarcity of qualified employees and of reliable certification of an employee's abilities. The establishment of an internal labor market and rotating personnel among group-affiliated companies may then become more effective compared to the external market (Khanna and Rivkin 2001). For that purpose, business groups can found their own training facilities, management programs, and other educational facilities to nurture well-trained employees, whom they can later deploy to their other businesses as needed.

Political-economy approaches.   The state and its relationships to business have been suggested as another critical factor in the formation of diversified business groups in emerging economies. The main argument of this particular view is that the government has targeted a few industries and has supported selected entrepreneurs and provided them with favors as a way of promoting industrialization. This, in turn, facilitated those entrepreneurs to proliferate their businesses. The experience of South Korea provides a good example for this. In South Korea, General Park Chung Hee's policies targeted certain industries and selected a few enterprises. The government provided these selected enterprises with the necessary funds, with interest charged at rates that were lower than the market level, as well as with favorable access to international technology sources, direct subsidies, and domestic market protection. As the policy of the government moved on and targeted industries in more advanced fields, businesses collaborating with the government on developmental schemes upgraded their capabilities and ultimately diversified their product portfolios. This ultimately led to the building of diversified business groups (Amsden 1989; Evans 1995; Kim, Chapter 6, this volume).

Governmental support of and favors to business groups, however, have often been associated with political rent-seeking and crony capitalism. Political connections can lead to favorable treatments that can privately benefit business groups but may be socially detrimental (Khanna and Yafeh 2007; Schneider, Chapter 23, this volume). Political and economic influences exercised by large business groups can cause "economic entrenchment" by distorting government policy concerning the protection of property rights and the capital markets and other economic organizations (Morck et al. 2005).

These irregularities are not quite unique to business groups, needless to say. They are more or less the symbolic relationships between large enterprises in general, or their owning families, and the government. Further, cozy business–government relationships and entrenchment may not hold true at all times. Russia provides a good example of how the government can actually harm business groups. Business groups, or the so-called oligarchs in the Russian context, have been facing the risk of expropriation by the government for forced nationalization, as politicians can appeal to the populist sentiment on the part of the general public, who have felt injustice in the process of the privatization drive since the early 1990s (Guriev and Rachinsky 2005; Guriev, Chapter 18, this volume). As for India, the high turnover of large business groups since independence, thanks to the ever-changing policies adopted by an often-hostile socialist government, has challenged the strong en-trenchment argument (Khanna and Palepu 2005; Khanna and Yafeh 2007; Schneider, Chapter 23, this volume).

2.4.1.2 *Endogenous-force explanations*

Endogenous-force explanations of business groups elucidate the rise of diversified business groups by looking at the internal competitive resources and capabilities underlying diversified growth. The main argument to explain the appearance of diversified business groups in late-industrializing nations comes from the absence of proprietary technology to enter into technologically related fields and the profit opportunities in several pre-modernized industries in those nations (Amsden and Hikino 1994). In the absence of such technological capabilities, it has been argued that "contact capabilities" with the state and also with foreign multinationals, followed by "project execution capabilities," might explain the necessary skills for the repeated industry-entry patterns of business groups (Amsden and Hikino 1994; Guillén 2000; Kock and Guillén 2001). Those project execution capabilities specifi-cally refer "to the skills required to establish or expand operating and other corporate facilities, including undertaking preinvestment feasibility studies, project manage-ment, project engineering (basic and detailed), procurement, construction and start-up of operations" (Amsden and Hikino 1994: 129).

In these views, business groups diversify into several unrelated industries rather than focus on one specific industry, or enter into related businesses because of the generic characteristics of the above-mentioned capabilities. As a new plant is established and starts operating, the contact and project-execution capabilities become idle assets within business groups; this encourages further entry into new and different industries (Guillén 2000). Mauro Guillén (2000; and Chapter 27, this volume) argues that these generic capabilities alone are not adequate for business groups to sustain their competitive advantages. Those capabilities can become valuable and rare "only under asymmetric foreign-trade and investment conditions with the rest of the world—that is, when the development path is either open to exports and outward foreign investment but not to imports and inward investment, or vice versa" (Guillén, Chapter 27, this volume). The generalization Guillén pro-posed, however, has been questioned in some studies, as business groups far predated such public policies (Jones and Khanna 2006).

Despite the debate on the value of these capabilities under different environmental contexts, the significance of contact and project-execution capabilities has been widely recognized as the competitive asset of business groups in emerging economies with imperfect markets and weak institutions. As the functioning of markets improves, a straightforward economic argument claims that, to stay competitive, business groups are pressured to focus on core domains and technologically related activities. Guillén (2001), for instance, argues for the need of relatedness and the value of organizational and technological capabilities as the environment shifts toward mature markets.

Carl Kock and Guillén (2001) give a good example to illustrate this point. They cite two cases of South Korean and Argentinian business groups, Hyundai and Techint, respectively, which had made transitions to technological and organizational cap-abilities in *certain* industries by the 1990s. The same can be said for several other business groups covered in this volume, which made shifts toward such technological capabilities. Turkey's Koç group, spearheaded by its consumer durable goods company Arçelik, was ranked the third largest in Europe and the sixth largest in the world in household-appliance manufacturing in 2008, thanks to its continuous investment in research and development (R&D) (Bonaglia et al. 2008). Most prominent of all, Samsung of South Korea has long established a well-known global brand with a significant technological competence in the electronics industry.

Yet, the overall portfolio of these business groups shows that they have largely remained diversified, without transforming into tightly integrated multidivi-sional organizations. The persistence and resilience of such diversified business groups have been conventionally justified by the continuing significance of contact capabilities as well as the prevailing inefficient markets and ineffective market inter-mediaries (Khanna and Palepu 1999; Guillén, Chapter 24, this volume). A more positive reasoning we suggest here is related to the building of "trans-product" capabilities at the group level. Accumulated "functional areas of learned capabilities and the resulting nature of shareable knowledge" (Amsden and Hikino 1994: 139) may become a source of sustainable advantages even in competitive markets, despite the fact that the resource-based view often undervalues the importance of such functional competencies by stressing product-specific or product-related capabilities. The headquarters, then, may continue to function as a planning and coordination office whose competence encompasses functional capabilities such as administration, finance, human resources, and marketing. As long as a coordination mechanism in the corporate office can be established and positive spillovers of "fungible" capabil-ities across individual operation units are generated, the organization model of diversified business groups shall continue to prove a competitive asset. These issues will be further explored in the discussion section.

2.4.2 Approaches to "pyramidal business groups"

A critical issue regarding the formation of pyramidal business groups has to do with the problematic concern of control rights that exceed cash flow rights. Pyramidal forms of group organization allow controlling shareholders at the top of the hierar-chical structure to control directly the immediate company and also numerous companies underneath as well (Morck et al. 2005). Even with partial ownership, controlling shareholders can exercise undisputed control over operating affiliates, having eventually been insulated from institutional investor pressure or takeover threats (Khanna and Yafeh 2007). The controlling shareholders can, therefore, expand their domain of control by "pyramiding" publicly held corporations as long as general shareholders take up the remaining part of share ownership. Such control may, of course, be achieved by other mechanisms, such as dual-class shares and multiple voting stocks, and pyramiding may actually be used together with those instruments to achieve control over even larger corporate assets (Morck, Chapter 21, this volume). The controlling shareholders can ultimately maintain huge corporate assets under their control without comparable levels of equity stake.

Control pyramids are one of the most important control mechanisms used by business groups, and we can observe the pyramidal arrangement of ownership in varying degrees in many developed as well as emerging economies. In two major economies, however, the United States and the United Kingdom, historical developments have resulted in legal and regulatory regimes in which the pyramidal control of business groups has become impractical or outright impossible. In the United States, reflecting the mounting anti-monopoly sentiment of the 1930s, the administration of Franklin D. Roosevelt introduced a series of tax policies that ultimately forced controlling shareholders to convert their holding stake of pyramided operating companies to a much higher level, often to the level of full ownership (Hawley 1966; Leff 1984; Morck, Chapter 21, this volume). In the United Kingdom, the 1968 Takeover Rule formulated by the London Stock Exchange turned out to be a pivotal move. That rule mandated that a shareholder who acquires 30 percent or more of the stocks of a listed company should buy the entire stock (Franks et al. 2005). Either way, pyramidal arrangements could not be sustained as an ownership structure in these two nations (Morck, Chapter 21, this volume).

The central question for the controlling shareholders and the regulating government institutions is why pyramiding is so important. The general benefit of undisputed control that comes with limited capital investment should derive from the tunneling of profits. The controlling shareholders extract at least a part of the economic income that publicly traded companies earn within their pyramid, which many economists have emphasized as a main *raison d'être* for pyramidal business groups (Morck and Nakamura 2007). It is thus argued that, by exploiting the separation between cash flow rights and control rights, the controlling shareholders siphon earned profits to their own private benefits at the cost of minority shareholders of controlled companies. Theoretically, then, pyramidal business groups should thrive in *developing* economies, where investor protection is weak and/or the enforcement of contract law remains inadequate.

Morck, in Chapter 21 of this volume, differentiates himself in two critical ways from the standard argument of the tunneling and expropriation of shareholders' wealth summarized above. First, while citing a classic argument by Michael Jensen and William Meckling (1976), he claims that, as long as general shareholders expect the probability of profit diversion by controlling shareholders, share prices of that company should be rationally discounted in the market. Minority shareholders are thus not directly affected in a negative sense. While relegating the significance of private cost on the part of minority shareholders, Morck focuses on the societal cost of pyramidal structure of ownership. Once tunneling has become a rule of the investing game in an economy, he emphasizes, the development of capital markets continues to suffer, as the investing public justifiably press for and get a discount for the listed stocks of the affiliated companies within pyramidal business groups. Not only do capital markets in general get deterred, but also negative spillovers of possible tunneling behavior further harm honest entrepreneurs, whose capital costs are set to higher-than-competitive market rates.

Still, as Morck emphasizes as his second point, society needed someone indisputably in control to coordinate the "Big Push" growth mechanism in the early phase of industrialization, originally proposed by Paul Rosenstein-Rodan (1943) for state-coordinated economic growth. The emergence of pyramidal business groups thus seems relevant in emerging economies, as the pyramidal ownership structure helped several significant industries to flourish, when profitable group companies subsidized nascent businesses or unprofitable member companies for the sake of the group's collective prosperity. Large pyramidal business groups are thus a private mechanism "of planned industrialisation comprising a simultaneous planning of several complementary industries" (Rosenstein-Rodan 1943: 204). In Japan, for instance, rapid economic growth followed after the Meiji government privatized state-owned enterprises that had been established as a pillar of state-run industrialization schemes. Replacing the poorly managed public enterprises, the then-emerging family-controlled business groups, the *zaibatsu*, which acquired those privatized properties in various industries, became a driving force in the industrial development of that nation (Morck and Nakamura 2007).

From the above-mentioned arguments, it can be seen that pyramidal business groups could be useful as an instrumental mechanism in the early phase of the modern economic growth of individual nations. But, in the long run, the societal cost ensuing from the eventual transfer of income from minority shareholders through profit tunneling, the less-than-optimal development of capital markets, and the exercise of economic power by a few wealthy business families would start exceeding the short-run need for the large-scale coordinating institution of the "Big Push." Given the long-run cost of "entrenchment," as in the cases of the United States and the United Kingdom pyramidal business groups should theoretically disappear as an economy reaches a mature phase in which minority shareholder protection becomes a rule of the capital market.

Interestingly, however, pyramidal business groups remain widespread in mature market economies that are equipped with strong legal as well as market institutions supporting the functioning of capital markets. Morck admits that this is "a mystery" (Chapter 21, this volume). But he continues to argue that, even without the direct economic benefits of profit tunneling, controlling shareholders may extract social and political as well as economic private gains, resulting from invisible assets such as group reputation and prestige or even political connections, all of which would be lost once the control of the companies is given away. In fact, several national chapters in this volume illustrate various forms of those pecuniary benefits, such as tax advantages, direct subsidies, and favorable transactions related to privatizing state-owned enterprises.

Certainly, those irregularities could happen between pyramidal business groups, or any large enterprises in general, or their owning families for that matter, and the government, as mentioned earlier. For all of the private as well as the societal costs that have been universally emphasized to date, however, it is somewhat strange that on the benefit side only the private interest of controlling shareholders and the societal gains resulted from the "Big Push" mechanism have been singled out. No private benefits on the part of minority shareholders have been seriously examined, as Khanna and Yafeh (2007) pointed out. Even with the threat of serious profit tunneling exercised by controlling shareholders, combined with the possibility of economic entrenchment that is harmful to societal economic welfare, why do minority shareholders commit to invest extensively in the companies that involve a pyramidal arrangement? After all, the pyramidal ownership structure can be sustained as an ongoing two-party game only when both parties, controlling shareholders and minority shareholders as well, find some positive incentives to participate. What is urgently needed now are theoretical examination and empirical testing systematically to identify the economic benefits to, and the costs incurred by, majority and minority shareholders and possibly the national economy associated with pyramidal arrangements of ownership.

2.5 BUSINESS GROUPS IN LATE VERSUS EARLY INDUSTRIALIZING ECONOMIES

Business groups may be commonly found in contemporary emerging markets, but they have in fact been active in many regions and nations since the early phase of the modern economy. Explaining their historical experiences in a comparative context should reveal the competitive nature of business groups in different evolutionary environments of modern economies.

2.5.1 The historical legacy of business groups in multinational activities

Family-owned business groups with the characteristics of a diversified product portfolio and pyramidal ownership structures were present as early as the beginning of the nineteenth century. The British overseas merchants, merchant bankers, and agency houses are the well-known cases that illustrate the presence of such business groups from the embryonic phase of modern economic growth, as detailed in Chapter 3 of this volume. We can actually cite many *individual* cases of business groups with a history of a diversified product portfolio. For example, Hudson's Bay Company (chartered in 1670) has been active in diversified industries in Canada since the early days of that territory. In a similar historical setting, Australia has had its own share of diversified business groups: Broken Hill Proprietary has remained one of the largest and most prominent enterprises in that economy.

These historical business groups should not, however, be labeled solely as a British mercantile heritage. After all, one of the first large enterprises of the modern world, the Medici Bank of Renaissance Florence, was a family-owned business group operating in trading, distribution, and manufacturing as well as in various financial services. In the sixteenth century the Fugger family of Augsburg made a vast fortune in trading, mining, banking, and other business activities, with its subsidiaries spread out throughout Europe; the patriarch of the family was called Jakob Fugger the Rich. The Rothschild family of Frankfurt am Main expanded its diversified operations in all major European cities, including Vienna, London, Naples, and Paris, from the eighteenth century. Although not quite family owned, the East India Company entities, based in the Netherlands (established in 1602) and France (since 1664), like the British East India Company (founded in 1600), had diversified businesses around their trading activities.

The history of the New World also had its share of diversified business groups. The renowned Boston Associates resembled the business groups of the network variety with their extensive business portfolios from mercantile to manufacturing activities, if we take that business investing community as a whole. The infamous United Fruit Company had the nickname *el pulpo*, or the octopus, because of its vast geographical scope and wide-ranging business activities in Latin America. Also in Latin America, W. R. Grace and Co. was once committed to extensive businesses such as shipping, airline, agriculture, and mining besides its main products of fertilizers and chemicals (Jones 2005). The now-forgotten "Big Five" (Castle & Cooke, Alexander & Baldwin, Amfac, Theodore H. Davies, and C. Brewer) that represented the US large enterprises in Hawaii ruled all the major aspects of economic life on the islands.

2.5.2 Business groups and inter-regional market imperfections

All in all, in the embryonic phase of modern industrialization and internationalization, business groups—and especially those functioning in overseas activities—played a significant role in the large enterprise sector in all the major economies that would later become industrial powers of the modern global economy. In terms of their pure scale, these international trading concerns actually represented the first big business of the early industrializing nations. Geoffrey Jones and Khanna (2006: 459) in their influential article thus came up with the following proposition: "we see that intra-country market failures in an array of contemporary contexts result in certain patterns regarding the structure and effects of business groups. The historical context, focused on inter-country market imperfections, also yields the same pattern." This is certainly a neat market-imperfection argument to single out overseas trading companies as the origin of business groups.

Those inter-regional market imperfections aside, acute market imperfections in product, capital, and labor historically engulfed any one economy. In exploiting those imperfections within the British domestic economy, why did not British textile companies or iron manufacturers diversify into unrelated product categories in the eighteenth and nineteenth centuries? Furthermore, if *inter-regional* or *inter-economy* market imperfections are the major reason for widely diversified activities, today's large multinational enterprises coming from mature economies should find more profit opportunities in emerging markets, relative to their predecessors in the nineteenth century. This is because the extent of market imperfections *across* the countries (roughly illustrated in income disparity between OECD-type economies and emerging markets) has widened, not narrowed (Hikino and Amsden 1994; Maddison 2009). Do those multinational enterprises active in developing economies, then, enjoy more diversification opportunities to form business groups today? Evidence gathered in much of the research on multinational enterprises seems to refute this conclusion, as, apart from those of the small developed nations of northern Europe, enterprises usually concentrate on the product categories to which they have been committed in their home countries (Dunning and Lundan 2008: ch. 15).

2.5.3 Business groups in the development of national economies

Historically, diversified business groups were not actually confined to those economic entities engaging in international activities, which surely exhibited the economic characteristics of *inter-economy* market imperfections. Interestingly, in continental Europe, several prominent business families held onto their economic power by diversifying their business portfolio into multiple industries and adopting the business group structure to integrate them. The Wallenbergs' holdings in Sweden and other Old Wealth entities may well be prominent cases of diversified business groups that have successfully survived in matured industrial economies. Family business groups individually have also appeared in maturing or matured economies, including extensively diversified business entities such as Hugo Stiness, Germany's "Business Kaiser," who owned and controlled more than 4,000 companies in mining, steel, public utilities, finance, newspapers, and chemicals in multiple countries at his death in 1924. The Quandt family of Brandenburg followed suit by establishing a diversified business group with around 200 businesses in batteries, metals, textiles, and chemicals after the First World War and were subsequently to have a substantial interest in BMW and Daimler-Benz after the 1950s. But by the end of the twentieth century the Agnelli family of Italy may actually have been the most notable business dynasty, having diversified from its flagship company in automobiles, Fiat, into food, agriculture, real estate, cement, hotel and tourism, finance and insurance, and publishing.

In addition to the business families, universal banks became a core of industrial combinations. Such mega-banks as Deutsche Bank, Commerzbank, and Dresdner Bank functioned as an eventual apex organization that controlled large operating companies scattered across diverse sets of industries. As universal banks, they were in charge of debt and equity financing and exhibited an extensive network of interlocking directorates. As such, the bank-centered groups in interwar Germany appear to have been more like the hierarchy-type business groups. This extensive involvement makes a sharp contrast to the "main bank" system or the bank-enterprise ties through debt financing (*yushi keiretsu*) of postwar Japan, in which large commercial banks held long-term ties based mostly on debt financing relationships with diverse operating companies, but the banks usually distanced themselves from committing to strategic as well as budgetary decision-making.

Even in the United States, where competitive market settings are not supposed to be conducive to diversified product portfolio, the Pritzker family of Chicago has remained one of the richest business families, with its holdings in hotels, manufacturing, services, and finance. Similar to those who interpreted the interwar economy of Germany, some US authors, such as George Edwards, who was critical of contemporary economic organizations, came up with a theory of finance capitalism according to which bank-centered business groups had started to control the whole economy (Edwards 1938). The Hees–Edper corporate group, which is connected to the Bronfman fortune in Canada, has established a sizable business group with a diversified product portfolio and pyramidal ownership structure, as Morck tellingly illustrates in Chapter 21 of this volume. Does this historical regularity mean that the evolutionary experiences of diversified business groups in emerging markets, especially since the Second World War, do *not* fundamentally differ from those of today's mature industrial economies? We suggest that this is not quite the case, an issue which we turn below.

2.5.4 Business groups in early versus late industrialization

The key question that should be asked is: why do we find the *prominence* of diversified business groups mostly in late-industrializing nations, which transformed themselves into the modern economy in the twentieth century? To put it another way, why do we *not* detect the predominance of diversified business groups in many of today's mature economies, which experienced the initial phases of industrialization in the eighteenth and nineteenth centuries? After all, market imperfections, which are assumed to be the prime factor for the rise and development of diversified business groups, were more acute if we go back to the earlier periods of economic growth.

While *individually* diversified business groups may historically have been active even in today's mature industrial economies, *collectively* they have mainly remained secondary players in those economies next to the small and medium-sized enterprises with a focused product portfolio or the large industrial enterprises that exhibit technologically related diversification. The UK and the USA, for instance, which have driven industrial development on a global scale since the late eighteenth century, certainly had a large enterprise sector, in which diversified business groups, especially those engaging in international trade, played a critical role in the early phase of modern economic growth. But that embryonic large enterprise sector did decline *relatively* in most early industrializing nations, once the modern industrial economy had become firmly established, with the philosophy of laissez-faire and free competition, in the early part of the nineteenth century. The economy in that liberal phase was characterized by mostly small and medium-sized enterprises, although many business groups with a diversified product portfolio might have survived *individually*. That liberal competitive economy gave way to another wave of emerging large enterprises, which illustrated the characteristic product portfolio of related categories. Ultimately, we now observe the mature industrial economy in which large enterprises with a related product portfolio *collectively* play a critical role.

In most of the early industrializing economies, therefore, the large enterprise sector experienced two historic waves of developments. In the first the business groups exhibited a diversified product portfolio in the early phase of industrial growth; after that wave had *relatively* calmed down, the second one appeared in the form of the Chandlerian *modern industrial enterprise*, with a related product portfolio in the maturing phase of economic development. Most economies of early industrialization broadly followed this general pattern, although we should certainly acknowledge several national exceptions, such as Sweden, where a family-owned group has historically played a critical economic role, and Belgium, where bank-centered groups have occupied a significant portion of the national economy.

By contrast, in most of the economies, spearheaded by Japan, that experienced late industrialization, the large business groups appeared in the early phase of industrial development, and those very groups have collectively and individually remained the prime and leading business organizations in the relevant economies up to the twenty-first century. This discontinuity and continuity in terms of the leading role played by the business groups with diversified product categories make the sharpest dissimilarity between the early and late-industrializing economies. Note that this historical legacy of industrialization experiences remains a critical factor in terms of the prime position that diversified business groups occupy in individual economies. Some late-industrializing nations, such as South Korea and Israel, still exhibit a corporate structure in which diversified business groups play a significant role, despite the maturing state of economic development and the resultant high level of per-capita income.

One of the most intriguing topics that has not been explored systematically is, therefore, the *non-representativeness* of diversified business groups in national economies that embarked upon their modern economic growth in the global wave of the First Industrial Revolution of the late eighteenth and early nineteenth centuries. In spite of the extensive activities of business groups in the embryonic phases of respective industrialization processes, why have they not ultimately grown to become the typical and dominant big business model in those national economies? Scholars often forget to ask why diversified business groups did *not* become a representative form of modern big business in most nations in North America and Western Europe. In spite of widespread imperfections in capital as well as product markets in the historical setting of corporate growth, which economists have often cited as the major reason for the emergence and growth of business groups, business models with an initial commitment to product specialization and subsequent related diversification were the ones that would eventually have dominated those early industrializing economies once they had gone through the embryonic phase of industrialization.

2.5.5 Contrasting competitive assets of business groups

The key mechanism to understand the dichotomy between the prevalence of product-related corporate growth in early industrialization and the representativeness of product-unrelated business groups in late-industrializing economies is the contrasting nature of internal capabilities between business groups and the other forms of business and organization models. As today's mature economies historically industrialized extensively, business groups in those economies faced competitive pressure coming from other business and organization models: product-centered and functionally organized enterprises as well as technologically related and multidivisional enterprises. As these large enterprises with technological, marketing, and managerial capabilities became the mainstay of the national and then international economy, they eventually undermined the organization model of diversified business groups altogether.

Most business groups that historically appeared in early industrializing economies, after all, could not establish either product-specific competitive assets or generic and functional capabilities that transcend product and industry boundaries. All the East India Company entities as well as the Bank of Medici and the Fugger fortune thus collapsed completely. Did the business group model of Jardine Matheson or Harrisons & Crosfield become a standard and representative entity of the British large enterprises operating in and beyond the UK markets? Their economic contributions were surely noteworthy as one type of British multinational enterprises and were significant in the host regions such as Hong Kong and the Malay Peninsula where they actually functioned. The groups were yet overshadowed in the long run by mainstream industrial and service enterprises that had gradually developed from the specialized company with focused product and service capabilities to the large enterprise diversified around proprietary knowledge or core competencies. For the sake of its survival, Harrisons & Crosfield therefore transformed itself into a specialty chemical company. Hudson's Bay Company is now a department store, after the company had exited from all the extensive yet uncompetitive activities. Broken Hill Proprietary mostly concentrates on oil exploration and mining activities. Both United Fruit and Castle & Cooke, after experiencing so much turmoil in individual businesses and as a corporation, still produce the Chiquita and Dole brands of bananas, respectively, although both of them have been acquired by outside interests.

After all, among the Big Five of Hawaii, only Alexander & Baldwin had remained an independent company by the late twentieth century. W. R. Grace does not produce anything but chemicals. Certainly, in the meantime, Swire-Pacific has grown to be an international giant while keeping its extensive industry portfolio, but it has remained a Hong Kong-based company. The case of Unilever and other British enterprises that once exhibited the historical characteristics of business groups can be understood in this context of strategic reorientation in the long run. While several family-owned business groups *individually* remain prominent, as has been pointed out, enterprises with a business group heritage *in mature economies* have mostly survived only through the reconcentration of their product and industry portfolio into businesses where they possess product-specific competitive capabilities.

Business groups in today's dynamic emerging markets beg to differ in terms of the way they have weathered the competitive pressure of local specialized businesses and multinational enterprises. To date, the business groups that are examined in our volume have fared relatively well in terms of maintaining an extensive product and industry portfolio and keeping reasonable profitability. In all the nations that are represented in this volume, business groups are not only common and widespread but also representative and dominant as the developmental agent. Accumulated capabilities that have been nurtured in operating and developing complicated organizations have functioned instrumentally in keeping the business groups resilient and viable, even in the increasingly competitive economic environment of the twenty-first century. It is the ownership and managerial decision-making that promotes or withholds competitive assets related to intangible resources such as administrative skills, financial capabilities, human resource management, and marketing knowledge at the group level and product-specific capabilities at the level of operating companies. This commitment to resources and capabilities and their utilization will ultimately determine the economic contributions of business groups as developmental agents.

All the historical and empirical descriptions regarding the organizational model of business groups so far have been related eventually to *diversified* ones. This focus on diversified business groups resulted from two reasons. First, this variety of business groups has invited coherent theoretical interpretations mostly with the organized frameworks of market imperfections and intra-firm capabilities. Second, ample empirical research on individual economies has been available since the 1970s for an integrated historical synthesis. By contrast, *pyramidal* ownership structure, another variety of business groups, has invited extensive scholarly attention from historical and comparative perspectives only since the 1990s and has thus accumulated relatively less research outputs.

2.5.6 Historical accounts of the pyramidal structure of ownership

Minority shareholder protection and profit tunneling may well be the key concepts to integrate all the directions of research on pyramidal business groups. And the principle of investor protection is broadly and positively related to the level of market maturity. Yet, that relationship has not been that concretely or universally detected, because such non-market institutional forces as legal convention and historical contexts have always played a significant role in determining investor protection and other capital market arrangements (La Porta et al. 1999). As such, the emergence and subsequent development of pyramidal business groups remain more embedded in the specific institutional conditions and contexts of relevant economies.

Empirically, on the other hand, Morck and Nakamura (2007: 569) suggest: "By the late nineteenth century, pyramids existed in the United States, Canada, Europe, and elsewhere. By the 1920s, they were a preferred structure for big businesses throughout the world." At the end of the twentieth century, then, widely held corporations still remained an exception as the ownership structure of large enterprises in the global economy. Rather, wealthy families and to a lesser extent the state dominated as the controlling shareholder. These characteristics can even be applied to several high-income economies in the 1990s and thereafter (La Porta et al. 1999). While this broad picture may reflect the stylized characteristics of the large enterprise economy in general, evolutionary trajectories of individual nations significantly differ from each other. In Germany, for instance, the pyramidal structure of ownership became prominent after the Second World War, as dual class shares, one of the alternative control means, were banned. By contrast, pyramidal ownership was prominent in the US large enterprises before the New Deal regulations eventually severed that control arrangement in the 1930s. As Morck summarizes in Chapter 21 of this volume, large enterprises and their controlling owners had often employed the organizational form of pyramidal business groups before that decade. In sum, it is not simply the direct reflection of the degree of market imperfections corresponding to the level of economic development that critically influences the employment of the pyramidal structure of ownership. Rather, relatively independent of market factors, institutional forces have significantly affected the adoption of this particular form of ownership structure.

The US experiences with pyramidal ownership structures further highlight two important concerns. First, the distribution of this business group organization was skewed toward certain industries such as public utilities and other infrastructure-related sectors. In the manufacturing sector, by contrast, large enterprises frequently adopted the holding company organization, in which operating units were legally structured as subsidiaries, rather than internal divisions, but the systematic use of pyramiding those subsidiaries was not extensive (Bonbright and Means 1932). This skewed distribution implies that pyramidal ownership structure may not be solely motivated and actually arranged by the universal intent of controlling shareholders for tunneling profits alone. Second, before the eventual disappearance of pyramidal ownership structures in the USA in the 1930s, this particular form of business groups had exhibited its prominence only after the New Jersey corporation law in 1888 as a general principle permitted business corporations to own other corporations' securities. To put it another way, until 1888 controlling shareholders could not utilize this particular ownership arrangement to control a huge corporate empire with a disproportionately small equity holding and to tunnel the profits from group affiliates.

Pyramidal ownership structure was thus immediately conditioned by legal institutional forces, even if it exhibited indirect links to the maturity of the market economy. Note that, by the late nineteenth century, the US economy had long passed the early phase of modern economic growth to have already formulated mature economic organizations. For the US economy, therefore, the pyramidal ownership structure was not a substitute for the imperfect functioning of various market institutions. It was rather the active conduct of such businessmen as Samuel Insull and S. J. Mitchell to create a monopolistic entity that would deliberately distort competitive market prices. Market imperfections were therefore more of an intended outcome, rather than an exogenously given precondition, of pyramidal ownership structure.

2.6 Discussions and implications

Market immaturity has been broadly credited as the suitable settings for the organization model of business groups. Does this imply the slow decline of business groups in forthcoming years, as markets become competitive and "unfulfilled demand" disappears on a global scale as well as in individual economies? Are we actually observing the secular trend toward the dissolution of the family-based, state-supported diversified business groups that often utilize the pyramidal structure of ownership? Or, as has been theoretically assumed, are those groups facing a restructuring that will bring about a focused business portfolio in the product categories where they possess competitive capabilities? The controlling families may also have to re-examine the way they control and manage their pyramidal structure, as liberalized markets bring more accountable governance practices with accounting and regulatory supervision that demands transparency and safeguards.

If such governance, strategic, and managerial modifications become prerequisite, then the organization model and the market behavior of business groups should eventually converge into those of the classic Chandlerian multidivisional enterprises. Yet, the fact remains that this scenario of the decline or conversion of business groups has not appeared as a clear or dominant trend, as the many national cases in this volume illustrate.

2.6.1 Market dynamics of product-specific and industry-transcending capabilities

How have diversified business groups allegedly marked by unrelated product diversification, subpar corporate governance systems, and frequent lack of professional management remained a viable and representative organization model in many economies? One answer that comes mainly from straightforward economics perspectives refers to the short time span that has passed since the market liberalization drive was institutionalized in the early 1980s (Khanna and Palepu 1999). Institutional rigidities have certainly prevented the full blossoming of competitive market forces to be materialized. If we follow this line of thinking, diversified groups will surely disappear as the dominant business organization, as societal economic institutions will be more market supporting and thus competitive forces will function to make diversified business groups less effective and then obsolete.

Another explanation comes from a firm-level behavioral perspective that focuses on the investment behavior on the part of business groups. Different from a straightforward economics explanation that deals with a supply-side response to an unfilled demand as the *aggregate behavior,* this perspective looks at the *individual behavior* that specific enterprises or groups strategically adopt. In an examination of the long-run competitive dynamics of the business group model, individual entry behavior that seeks the entrepreneurial rent derived from Schumpeterian market innovations will be critical. This is because a single enterprise or group alone rarely captures the monopoly profits by fulfilling the demand in any product market, however acute market imperfections may be in emerging markets. As is amply illustrated in the national cases in this volume, a few enterprises or groups simultaneously or consecutively enter the particular market as entrepreneurial profits captured by the original entrant motivate others to make a similar move into the same product market, as was originally theorized by Izrael Kirzner (1973).

The ensuing market structure then becomes that of oligopoly for individual industries, with the enterprises or business groups usually competing against each other for survival and growth. The product market is, therefore, not dominated by a single enterprise or group extracting monopoly rents, to the welfare loss to the whole economy. The industry structure becomes particularly dynamic when multinational enterprises participate in the oligopoly game in the domestic market or those local enterprises start competing in the international markets. As they then have to invest in cost-lowering facilities and productivity-enhancing technologies, the enterprises and groups involved usually become dynamic innovators, not sleepy giants or hungry predators. This is the usual game of oligopolistic competition, through which enterprises and groups accumulate *product-specific* proprietary resources and competitive capabilities.

As business groups have been active in various product categories in response to a growing demand in a diverse set of markets, their competitive resources and capabilities concurrently have become non-industry specific, as their proprietary assets are not confined to specific products and industries. Through repeated entry into unrelated categories of products and a diverse set of industries, those groups gradually establish "trans-product" or *industry-transcending* capabilities. The ensuing knowledge that can then be shared within the groups exhibits the characteristics of a *natural monopoly* that, in economics terms, functions as a non-rival public goods within the particular business group. As such, it becomes the source of a sustainable competitive advantage even in maturing markets, although the resource-based view of the firm has not conventionally valued the significance of such industry-trans-cending competencies and their operational outcomes.

As long as the group headquarters continues to take the primary role of effective administrative coordination, it can realize positive spillovers of "fungible" capabil-ities across individual operational affiliates. The business group form may then prove a competitive asset, with its accumulated knowledge in administrative skills, financial capabilities, human resource management, and marketing expertise that the groups acquire through consecutive entries.

In sum, market imperfections may well be the general environmental setting for the emergence and growth of diversified business groups, but the intra-group resources and capabilities represent the prime source for the survival and resilience of specific individual groups. While we should not underestimate the extent of collusion between the business groups or cozy "crony" relationships with the gov-ernment, the dynamics of inter-group multi-industry rivalry and repeated unrelated-diversifying investments that ensure industry-transcending generic capabilities with-in the groups constitute their sources of competitiveness and ultimately a driving force of economic development in relevant nations.

2.6.2 Market dynamics of controlling and minority shareholders

While the principles of investor protection, governance arrangements, and other capital market institutions should broadly and positively match the progress of market maturity, that relationship has not been concrete or universal, because such non-market forces as legal systems, political dynamics, and historical contexts have always played a critical role in determining the law and regulation regarding capital market arrangements. As long as the presence and resilience of pyramidal business groups remain more embedded into specific institutional conditions of relevant economies, long-run shifts toward a mature and competitive market structure do not immediately result in the wholesale protection of shareholder rights, which may lead to the disappearance of the pyramidal structure of ownership.

In reality, however, the pyramidal structure of ownership is not only still alive but also relatively well in many economies. This is possibly because controlling shareholders may have some positive and direct incentives other than "tunneling" to keep the pyramidal ownership structure. For instance, they should find some benefits in controlling the vast economic wealth that is much larger than the actual holding, because they may leverage the size of that wealth for economic gains like favorable business transactions. Further, even if keeping the pyramidal structure of ownership incurs some governance and administrative cost, controlling shareholders may hold on to that structure as long as they value the non-economic benefits of the wealth, such as political power and social prestige. Many economists, including Morck in this volume, are justifiably concerned with these broad issues of "economic entrenchment," although the magnitude of the societal cost in economic welfare incurred from this problem still remains to be explored.

The pyramidal structure of ownership, on the other hand, may function as a mechanism to reduce and isolate market risks for controlling shareholders, which in turn may benefit other concerned parties. For instance, when uncertainty is prohibitively high in the market for a potentially innovative product to deter the controlling shareholders from committing to that particular market, the infusion of external capital to a group operating company within the pyramidal structure may lower the amount of risk associated with the market entry taken by controlling shareholders. This risk-sharing arrangement should give a positive incentive to the controlling shareholders to make a commitment into that product market. While the mechanism of reducing market risks can naturally be arranged in different ways, the pyramidal structure of ownership possesses a distinctive advantage. By holding individual operating units legally independently, controlling shareholders can *isolate* those risks. Given the limited liability that these operating companies enjoy, risks associated with the market entry should be contained within the operating company. If that company fails, the controlling shareholders, the minority shareholders, and the general creditors, including the society, will bear the cost. When it comes up with an innovative product, the rewards of that innovation should be captured by the controlling shareholders and the minority shareholders. While the society should benefit indirectly from the innovation, needless to say, immediate profits will be divided between the two groups of shareholders alone. This asymmetry of cost-bearing and reward-sharing, resulting from the pyramidal structure of ownership, can be a significant incentive for the controlling shareholders to hold on to that structure, even when profit tunneling has become impossible.

While the negative consequence of the pyramidal structure of ownership has been overwhelmingly emphasized to date, the persistence of pyramidal business groups in mature markets in which shareholder rights are well established should, therefore, be further investigated by incorporating the positive as well as the negative implications of that ownership structure. After all, a paradox remains about both Sweden, in which one family-owned group has reigned the entire economy, and Canada, where the pyramidal arrangement of ownership has stretched to an amazing extent. For all the hypothesized negative consequences, those nations actually represent two of the most highly developed economies.

2.6.3 Toward an effective organization model

Business groups have been searching for an organization model of their own to sustain and enhance their competitiveness. This is particularly true among the family-owned and -controlled business groups with a diversified product portfolio that still dominate the large enterprise sector in contemporary emerging economies. As long as the families aim to keep that diversified portfolio, they naturally encounter serious information, control, and capability troubles of all sorts. It is difficult enough to overcome the usual asymmetry of information between the owning families making decisions at the group-headquarters level and the senior management executing the decisions at the level of operating affiliates. This generic trouble of intra-organizational asymmetry is compounded by the amount, difficulty, diversity, and complexity of information that the members of the owner families have to process to come up with a coherent mix of effective internal coordination mechanisms. Even with the assistance of capable line staffs in the group headquarters or the advice given by competent external consultants, the total amount and basic nature of information to be processed by family members far exceed the resources and capabilities that the family directors in the group headquarters can personally or collectively mobilize.

This pressing environment is somewhat analogous to the historical setting of the organizational innovation of the classic multidivisional structure, as summarized by Chandler:

[T]he overload in the decision making at the top was indeed the reason for creating the new structure. But the need did not result from the larger size of the enterprise *per se*. It came rather from the increasing diversity and complexity of decision that senior managers had to make. (Chandler 1990b: introduction)

In the case of the Chandlerian multidivisional structure, naturally, product categories were technologically related, so that the top management instituted the administrative principle of strategic planning or control to maximize the inter-product spillovers of technological know-how that had been pooled as a shareable resource to be utilized within the firm. This remains one of the significant sources of competitiveness exhibited by multidivisional enterprises.

While the "overload in the decision-making at the top" can well be the reason why diversified business groups have to formulate an effective organization model, two critical differences should be pointed out between the historic precedence of the multidivisional enterprises and the current struggles of the diversified business groups. First, needless to say, the product portfolio is different, with classic multidivisional enterprises possessing technologically related categories and contemporary diversified business groups exhibiting unrelated ones. Second, the top management in charge of basic decision-making was comprised of salaried professionals for multidivisional enterprises, while it is family members for diversified business groups.

These contrasting characteristics make a critical difference in terms of the configuration of an effective organization model. As long as the business groups continue to commit themselves to product categories that are growing and profitable, then they cannot avoid some industries with a high knowledge content, such as advanced electronics, pharmaceuticals, and finance. If one group shuns those products and industries, because owning families and their associates and supporting staff possess little technical expertise, domestic rivals and multinational enterprises will eventually crowd that particular group out of the product market. Although this survival game among oligopolistic rivals was originally formulated with large enterprises with a *related* product portfolio in mind (Knickerbocker 1973), a similar behavioral principle can easily be applied to unrelated diversification.

As market rivalry thus compels the family directors of diversified business groups to commit consecutively to knowledge-intensive industries, they increasingly face alien markets that are unrelated, sophisticated, and complex. The information and knowledge barriers in terms of technology and markets become prohibitively high, given the limited expertise of those family directors. After all, even for professional experts controlling and managing diversified businesses, the challenges are daunting, as has often been detected in the cases of conglomerate enterprises and private equity funds.

A new effective organization model for business groups thus should balance idiosyncratic internal resources and capabilities with the growth and profit

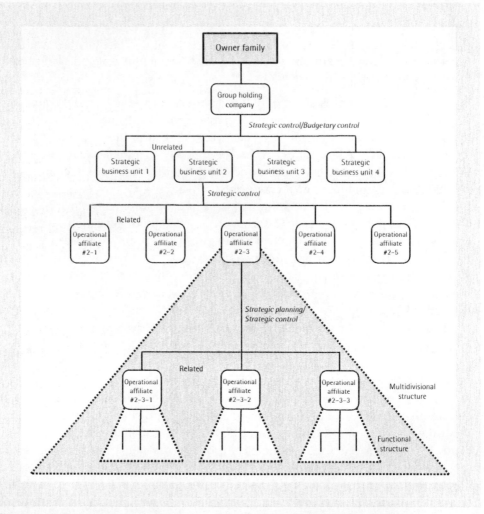

Figure 2.4 Emerging organization model of diversified business groups

opportunities provided in external markets. For one thing, the organization model should still incorporate an internal mechanism to enhance competitive capabilities for each product and industry category. These product- and industry-specific assets constitute the primary basis of market competition, after all. On the other hand, however, the business groups have to exploit the above-mentioned industry-transcending knowledge in such generic functions as administrative skills, financial capabilities, human resource management, and marketing knowledge. They are assumed to be the critical source of competitive advantages for business groups. Above all, then, the whole business group organization must have structural and administrative coherence to enable such characteristic knowledge and capabilities to be systematically spilled over into all the parts within the groups.

Constructing effective organization models that meet all of these conditions should be an interesting intellectual exercise to economics and management research. It will also be a difficult yet rewarding challenge to the controlling families themselves. In one stylized model, illustrated in Fig. 2.4, the controlling families continue to keep the diversified portfolio in unrelated products to reduce product-related risks and to keep them integrated through coherent control mechanisms. Modeled after the actual structure and operation of such large and influential groups as the Tata group in India and the Koç group in Turkey, the organization model aims to meet the general conditions that have been specified above. First, that business group model accomplishes the goal of technology and knowledge enhancement by organizing a constellation of affiliated companies with similar product categories into multidivisional structures. Further, given the large size and diversified portfolio of business groups, the number of those product-based divisions should be high enough to warrant the adoption of the strategic business unit organization. So, as is usual with the enterprises with strategic business units, the business groups achieve two goals simultaneously: enhancing technology and knowledge competence at the product and industry levels through spillovers from related products as well as by consecutive investments; and maintaining an effective internal coordination over multidivisional enterprises through strategic business units.

Ultimately, then, the family directors in the group holding company choose and combine the internal coordination mechanisms that administer those strategic business units. Theoretically, budgetary, rather than strategic, control apparatus may function more effectively from governance and finance perspectives. Based on the principle of division of labor, the apex holding company owned and controlled by the families concentrates on the portfolio management of the diversified corporate assets and do not get involved in any aspects of strategic decision-making that is to be carried out by the operational affiliates underneath. Thus, that group headquarters does not pursue the synergies or spillovers *between* strategic business units. The synergies and spillovers remain industry- or product-specific *within* strategic business units and multidivisional operating affiliates underneath. The family directors are free from all the diverse industry- and product-specific information and knowledge that remains far beyond their bounded capacity. Further, the controlling families can save a lot of financial resources in not maintaining a massive group headquarters with highly paid salaried executives and staff. Those expenses are required as long as they commit to the *strategic* control of operating affiliates.

Little agency costs get involved in terms of the selection, combination, and ultimate scope of corporate portfolios, because the group holding company owned and controlled by the families makes the decisions according to their own preferences. Following these administrative approaches, the intra-group coordination exercised by the apex holding company comes close to the operational principle adopted by acquisitive conglomerates and private-equity organizations. For the owning families, managing the entire group organization eventually becomes synonymous with the choice and combination of corporate portfolios. Then, the family directors should collectively excel in the management of business portfolios, not in product-specific knowledge or technological expertise.

A critical dilemma still lingers with the straightforward business portfolio management of diversified groups, though. What constitute the basic competitive advantages of this particular organization model? As long as the owning families govern the business groups with budgetary control apparatus by employing financial principles alone, the value of the whole business group organization theoretically remains the simple sum of the composite value of individual operating affiliates. If portfolio management is the coordination principle for the entire group, after all, why do they need a sizable and stable headquarters unit to integrate the entire business group structure? Theoretically, they do not.

As long as the owning families aim to realize and maximize the competitive potential of the business group organization, they have to exploit the economic rent derived from all the generic industry-transcending resources and capabilities that the group headquarters has accumulated. While the families can certainly utilize financial expertise, they should not overlook the potential strategic deployment of competitive assets in administration and management, production and operations, marketing and human resources. With the strict portfolio approaches to group control, these intangible competitive assets will be unused altogether. Quite often the families controlling the major diversified business groups instinctively recognize and value those assets, so that they hesitate to shift swiftly toward the financial means of control. The family directors frequently sit on the board of operating affiliates to exercise the control and monitoring of strategic decision-making that is in line with the overall group-level strategic plan that they themselves formulate at the board meeting of the group holding company. As they acknowledge the merits of budgetary principles, in the end, the directors representing the controlling families deliberately or unconsciously combine the different approaches to internal coordination mechanisms. With this hybrid approach, understandably, they often face all the problems of a patchwork. How do the controlling families systematically integrate the different and often conflicting principles of strategic and budgetary controls so that they exploit those competitive assets to their full advantage? Or should they rather look for a new principle that differs from strategic and budgetary instruments? That critical task for the families is also vital for the whole society, whose economic welfare often depends on the viability of business groups as a core economic institution.

REFERENCES

ALMEIDA, H., and WOLFENZON D. (2006). "A Theory of Pyramidal Ownership and Family Business Groups," *Journal of Finance*, 61/6: 2637–80.

AMSDEN, A. H. (1989). *Asia's Next Giant: South Korea and Late Industrialization*. New York and Oxford: Oxford University Press.

AMSDEN, A. H. (2001). *The Rise of "The Rest": Challenges to the West from Late-Industrialization Economies*. New York: Oxford University Press.

AMSDEN, A. H., and HIKINO, T. (1994). "Project Execution Capability, Organizational Know-How and Conglomerate Corporate Growth in Late Industrialization," *Industrial and Corporate Change*, 3/1:111–47.

BERLE, A., and MEANS, G. (1932). *Modern Corporation and Private Property*. New York: Commerce Clearing House.

BERG, N. A. (1969). "What's Different about Conglomerate Management?" *Harvard Business Review*, 47/6: 112–20.

Berkshire Hathaway (2008). Annual Report.

BONBRIGHT, J., and MEANS, G. (1932). *The Holding Company: Its Public Significance and its Regulation*. New York: McGraw-Hill.

BONAGLIA, F., COLPAN, A. M., and GOLDSTEIN, A. (2008). "Innovation and Internationalization in the White Goods GVC: The Case of Arcelik," *International Journal of Technological Learning, Innovation and Development*, 1/4: 520–35.

CENDROWSKI, H., MARTIN, J. P., and PETRO, L. W. (2008). *Private Equity: History, Governance, and Operations*. Hoboken: John Wiley & Sons.

CHANDLER, A. D., JR. (1962). *Strategy and Structure: Chapters in the History of the American Industrial Enterprise*. Cambridge, MA: MIT Press.

CHANDLER, A. D., JR. (1977). *The Visible Hand: The Managerial Revolution in American Business*. Cambridge, MA: Belknap Press.

CHANDLER, A. D., JR. (1990a). *Scale and Scope: The Dynamics of Industrial Capitalism*. Cambridge, MA: Belknap Press.

CHANDLER, A. D., JR. (1990b). *Strategy and Structure: Chapters in the History of the American Industrial Enterprise*. Reprint edn. with new introduction. Cambridge, MA: MIT Press.

CHILD, J., FAULKNER D., and TALLMAN S. (2005). *Cooperative Strategy: Managing Alliances, Networks, and Joint Ventures*. New York: Oxford University Press.

DUGGER, W. M. (1979). "An Institutional Analysis of Economic Power," in M. R. Tool and W. J. Samuels, *The Economy as a System of Power*. New Brunswick, NJ: Transaction Books.

DUNNING, J. H., and LUNDAN, S. M. (2008). *Multinational Enterprises and the Global Economy*. 2nd edn. Cheltenham: Edward Elgar.

EDWARDS, G. W. (1939). *The Evolution of Finance Capitalism*. New York: Longmans, Green, and Co.

EVANS, P. (1995). *Embedded Autonomy*. Princeton: Princeton University Press.

FEENSTRA, R. C., and HAMILTON, G. G. (2006). *Emergent Economies, Divergent Paths: Economic Organization and International Trade in South Korea and Taiwan*. Structural Analysis in the Social Sciences series, vol. 29. Cambridge and New York: Cambridge University Press.

FLIGSTEIN, N. (1990). *The Transformation of Corporate Control*. Cambridge, MA: Harvard University Press.

FRANKS J., MAYER, C., and ROSSI, S. (2005). "Spending Less Time with the Family: The Decline of Family Ownership in the United Kingdom," in R. K. Morck (ed.), *A History of Corporate Governance around the World*. Chicago and London: University of Chicago Press.

FRUIN, W. M. (2008). "Business Groups and Interfirm Networks," in G. Jones and J. Zeitlin (eds.), *The Oxford Handbook of Business Groups*. Oxford: Oxford University Press.

GERLACH, M. L. (1992). *Alliance Capitalism: The Social Organization of Japanese Business*. Berkeley and Los Angeles: University of California Press.

GHEMAWAT, P., and KHANNA, T. (1998). "The Nature of Diversified Business Groups: A Research Design and Two Case Studies," *Journal of Industrial Economics*, 46/1: 35–61.

GOOLD, M., and CAMPBELL, A. (1987). *Strategies and Styles: The Role of the Centre in Managing Diversified Corporations*. Oxford: Blackwell.

GOTO, A. (1982). "Business Groups in a Market Economy," *European Economic Review*, 19: 53–70.

GRANOVETTER, M. (1995). "Coase Revisited: Business Groups in the Modern Economy," *Industrial and Corporate Change*, 4/1: 93–130.

GRANOVETTER, M. (2005). "Business Groups and Social Organization," in N. Smelser and R. Swedberg (eds.), *The Handbook of Economic Sociology*. 2nd edn. Princeton: Princeton University Press, 429–50.

GUILLÉN, M. F. (2000). "Business Groups in Emerging Economies: A Resource-Based View," *Academy of Management Journal*, 4/3: 362–80.

GUILLÉN, M. F. (2001). *The Limits of Convergence: Globalization and Organizational Change in Argentina, South Korea, and Spain*. Princeton: Princeton University Press.

GULATI, R. (1995). "Social Structure and Alliance Formation Patterns: A Longitudinal Analysis," *Administrative Science Quarterly*, 40: 619–52.

GURIEV, S. M., and RACHINSKY, A. (2005). "The Role of Oligarchs in Russian Capitalism," *Journal of Economic Perspectives*, 19/1: 131–50.

HAMILTON, G. G., and BIGGART, N. W. (1988). "Market, Culture and Authority: A Comparative Analysis of Management and Organization in the Far East," *American Journal of Sociology*, 94: S52–S94.

HAWLEY, E. W. (1966). *The New Deal and the Problem of Monopoly: A Study in Economic Ambivalence*. Princeton: Princeton University Press.

HIKINO, T., and AMSDEN, A. H. (1994). "Staying Behind, Stumbling Back, Sneaking Up, Soaring Ahead: Late-Industrialization in Historical Perspective," in W. J Biumol, R. R. Nelson, and E. N. Wolff (eds.). *Convergence in Productivity: Cross-Country Studies and Historical Evidence*. New York and Oxford: Oxford University Press.

HOSKISSON, R. E., HILL, C. W. L., and KIM, H. (1993). "The Multidivisional Structure: Organizational Fossil or Source of Value?" *Journal of Management*, 19: 269–98.

JENSEN, M., and MECKLING, W. (1976). "Theory of the Firm: Managerial Behavior, Agency Costs and Ownership Structure," *Journal of Financial Economics*, 3/4: 305–60.

JONES, G. (2000). *Merchants to Multinationals: British Trading Companies in the Nineteenth and Twentieth Centuries*. Oxford: Oxford University Press.

JONES, G. (2005). *Multinationals and Global Capitalism*. Oxford: Oxford University Press.

JONES, G., and KHANNA, T. (2006). "Bringing History (back) into International Business," *Journal of International Business Studies*, 37: 453–68.

KHANNA, T., and PALEPU, K. (1997). "Why Focused Strategies May Be Wrong for Emerging Markets," *Harvard Business Review*, 75/4: 41–51.

KHANNA, T., and PALEPU, K. (1999). "Policy Shocks, Market Intermediaries, and Corporate Strategy: The Evolution of Business Groups in Chile and India," *Journal of Economics and Management Strategy*, 8/2: 271–310.

KHANNA, T., and PALEPU, K. (2005). "The Evolution of Concentrated Ownership in India: Broad Patterns and a History of the Indian Software Industry," in R. Morck (ed.), *A History of Corporate Governance around the World: Family Business Groups to Professional Managers*. Chicago: University of Chicago Press, 283–320.

KHANNA, N., and RIVKIN, J. (2001). "Estimating the Performance Effects of Business Groups in Emerging Markets," *Strategic Management Journal*, 22: 45.

KHANNA, T., and YAFEH, Y. (2005). "Business Groups and Risk Sharing around the World," *Journal of Business*, 78/1: 301–40.

KHANNA, T., and YAFEH, Y. (2007). "Business Groups in Emerging Markets: Paragons or Parasites?" *Journal of Economic Literature*, 45/2: 331–72.

KIRZNER, I. (1973). *Competition and Entrepreneurship*. Chicago: Chicago University Press.

KNICKERBOCKER, F. T. (1973). *Oligopolistic Reaction and Multinational Enterprise*, Cambridge, MA: Harvard University Press.

KOCK, C., and GUILLÉN, M. F. (2001). "Strategy and Structure in Developing Countries: Business Groups as an Evolutionary Response to Opportunities for Unrelated Diversification," *Industrial & Corporate Change*, 10/1: 1–37.

LA PORTA, R., LOPEZ-DE-SILANES, F., and SHLEIFER, A. (1999). "Corporate Ownership around the World," *Journal of Finance*, 54/2: 471–517.

LEFF, N. H. (1976). "Capital Markets in Less Developed Countries: The Group Principle," in R. McKinnon (ed.), *Money and Finance in Economic Growth and Development: Essays in Honor of Edward S. Shaw*. New York: Decker Press, 97–122.

LEFF, N. H. (1978). "Industrial Organization and Entrepreneurship in the Developing Countries: The Economic Groups," *Economic Development and Cultural Change*, 26/4: 661–75.

LEFF, M. H. (1984). *The Limit of Symbolic Reform: The New Dear and Taxation, 1933–1939*. Cambridge: Cambridge University Press.

LINCOLN, J. R., and GERLACH, M. L. (2004). *Japan's Network Economy: Structure, Persistence, and Change*. New York: Cambridge University Press.

MADDISON, A. (2009). "Statistics on World Population, GDP and Per Capita GDP, 1-2006 AD." www.ggdc.net/maddison

MAMAN, D. (2002). "The Emergence of Business Groups: Israel and South Korea Compared," *Organization Studies*, 23/5: 737–58.

Moody's (1938). *Moody's Manual of Investments*. New York: Moody's Investors Service.

MORCK, R. (2005). "How to Eliminate Pyramidal Business Groups: The Double Taxation of Intercorporate Dividends and Other Incisive Uses of Tax Policy," *Tax Policy and the Economy*, 19: 135–79.

MORCK, R., and NAKAMURA, M. (2007). "Business Groups and the Big Push: Meiji Japan's Mass Privatization and Subsequent Growth," *Enterprise and Society*, 8/3: 543–601.

MORCK, R., and YEUNG, B. (2004). "Special Issues Related to Corporate Governance and Family Control." World Bank Policy Research Working Paper 3406.

MORCK, R., WOLFENZON, D., and YEUNG, B. (2005). "Corporate Governance, Economic Entrenchment, and Growth," *Journal of Economic Literature*, 43/3: 655–720.

PODOLNY, J. M., and PAGE, K. L. (1998). "Network Forms of Organization," *Annual Review of Sociology*, 24: 57–76.

POWELL, W. W. (1990). "Neither Market nor Hierarchy: Network Forms of Organization," in B. M. Staw and L. L. Cummings (eds.), *Research in Organizational Behavior.* Greenwich, CT: JAI Press, xii. 295–336.

PUTHUCHEARY, J. J. (1960). *Ownership and Control in the Malayan Economy.* Singapore: Eastern University Press.

ROSENSTEIN-RODAN, P. (1943). "Problems of Industrialization of Eastern and South Eastern Europe," *Economic Journal,* 53: 202–11.

SHIBA, T., and SHIMOTANI, M. (eds.) (1997). *Beyond the Firm: Business Groups in International and Historical Perspective.* New York: Oxford University Press.

SMITH-DOERR, L., and POWELL, W. W. (1995). "Networks and Economic Life," in N. J. Smelser and R, Swedberg (eds.), *The Handbook of Economic Sociology.* Princeton: Princeton University Press.

SOBEL R. (1999). *The Rise and Fall of the Conglomerate Kings.* 2nd edn. New York: Beard Books.

WILKINSON, B. (1996). "Culture, Institutions and Business in East Asia," *Organization Studies,* 17/3: 421–47.

WILLIAMSON, O. E. (1975). *Markets and Hierarchies: Analysis and Antitrust Implications.* New York: Free Press.

WILLIAMSON, O. E. (1985). *The Economic Institutions of Capitalism.* New York: Free Press.

CHAPTER 3

BUSINESS GROUPS IN HISTORICAL PERSPECTIVES

GEOFFREY JONES

ASLI M. COLPAN

3.1 INTRODUCTION

THIS chapter explores the evolutionary dynamics and organizational characteristics of the diversified business groups built up by the UK-based trading companies from their nineteenth-century origins. It examines firms such as Jardine Matheson and Swire, which remain important components of the Asia Pacific economy into the twenty-first century, and other firms such as Inchcape and the United Africa Company (UAC), which were once major regional players—UAC employed around 70,000 in West Africa in the 1960s, and was the largest modern business enterprise in the region—but which for one reason or another no longer exist, at least in their original form. The chapter concentrates on the British trading firms because of their extensive scale and distinctive scope, although there were many similarities in terms of adopted business models between the British and the Dutch, Danish, French, and other European trading companies of this era.

This chapter illustrates that conclusions reached by the literature on contemporary emerging market business groups are remarkably similar to independently reached

This chapter is based on Jones (2000), and Jones and Khanna (2006), and has been revised by Asli M. Colpan and Geoffrey Jones for inclusion in this volume.

conclusions about a very similar organizational form that was ubiquitous in the age of empire. Historical evidence presented in this chapter is of critical importance in that it avoids spurious labeling of the business groups phenomena as "new," and by doing so challenges current explanations of their determinants. This historical experience of business groups had long been forgotten, or at least de-emphasized. Guillén (2000, and Chapter 27, this volume), for example, presents a view of diversified business groups as being the consequence of the interaction of specific inward and outward investment policies pursued in the postwar era. Although this may have been a factor during the time period of his study, the fact remains that such groups far predate this time period and such public policies. Business groups—collections of legally independent businesses, often extensively diversified, and interconnected by a medley of economic and social ties—are therefore more important than one would believe simply by examining contemporary settings.

A central theme of this chapter is to examine how the British trading companies faced the challenge of organizing increasingly complex businesses as they diversified. In the late-nineteenth-century United States, firms grew in size, and the manufacture of different products in different countries was undertaken within the boundaries of a firm. To handle diversity, a new type of organizational form—the multidivisional structure (M-form)—appeared in the interwar years, which separated planning and coordination from operating divisions. The M-form has become widely accepted as the most appropriate organization form to manage such diversified firms (Chandler 1962; Williamson 1975). The British trading companies organized their diversified operations in different ways. Not only was there little attempt at divisionalization at least until the 1960s, but often full internalization was avoided. Instead, as in many developing countries and Japan, business groups emerged consisting of constellations of companies linked by various forms of binding, including ownership relations, interlocking directorships, contacts, and ethnic ties (Granovetter 1995).

The next section examines the strategies of British trading companies from the late eighteenth century into the twenty-first. Section 3.3 analyzes the ways that trading companies organized their activities as they diversified in terms of geography and product. The fourth section considers the competences of those companies. A final section before the conclusion discusses the similarities of business groups in history and today.

3.2 TRADERS AS BUSINESS GROUPS

3.2.1 Emergence of business groups

The growth of the first global economy provided unprecedented opportunities for British merchants. British trading companies grew rapidly to exploit commercial links between their home country and the colonies as well as other emerging markets.

In the nineteenth century, the weakness in infrastructure and local entrepreneurship in developing countries meant, first, that trading companies had to make investments themselves rather than rely on others to create complementary businesses, and, secondly, that there were numerous profitable opportunities that could be exploited as the borders of the international economy and of empires advanced. In particular, they perceived and could exploit the large profits to be earned from the development of, and trade in, natural resources. By 1914 a number of these British trading firms had become multinational business groups with diversified operations on several continents.

A closer look at the British trading firms shows that the general pattern of diversification before 1914 was from trade to related services such as insurance and shipping agencies, foreign direct investment (FDI) in resources, and processing in developing host economies. The British trading companies made the largest investments in tea, rubber and sugar plantations, and teak. Chilean nitrates, Indian coal, and petroleum were also the recipients of considerable investment. As merchants, they were less interested in locking up capital in manufacturing, but during the second half of the nineteenth century and later they did make substantial investments in cotton textile and jute manufacture, sugar refining, and flour milling.

A classic pattern can be seen in the case of Harrisons & Crosfield. Founded as a Liverpool-based partnership engaged in tea trading, buying tea in India and China and selling it in Britain, from the 1890s the firm opened branches outside Britain in Sri Lanka, India, Malaya, the Dutch East Indies (Indonesia), the United States, Canada, Australia, and New Zealand. These branches were usually established to trade in tea, but soon acquired a wider range of import and export business, and began acting as agents for insurance and shipping companies. Tea trading led to the purchase of tea estates in South Asia from 1899 onwards, and then the development of distribution facilities in tea-consuming countries in Britain and North America. After 1903 the firm diversified into rubber plantations. During the interwar years, Harrisons & Crosfield deepened its involvement in South East Asia through investment in logging in Sabah, while in Malaya it diversified from rubber plantations into rubber manufacture. These tea and rubber plantations were all placed in publicly quoted companies in which Harrisons & Crosfield retained some equity (Jones and Wale 1999).

Four factors exercised systematic influences on the diversification strategies of the British companies in this era. The first was the opportunities to exploit scope economies and the incentive to reduce transaction costs. Like the diversified business groups active in many developing countries today, British merchants had established extensive contacts with (often colonial) governments and other resource owners, which created asymmetries of information and access between them and other foreign firms, and provided considerable potential for diversified entry (Kock and Guillén 2001). Trading companies could thus economize on information costs in a world characterized by uncertainty and risk because of distance and poor communications. Their information and expertise about the regions, marketing channels and products involved, then, gave them the experience and know-how further to diversify their activities.

A second determinant was the boom in commodity prices. Industrialization in Europe and the United States stimulated a worldwide search for new sources of supply of the raw materials such as coal and oil and the foodstuffs including tea, coffee, sugar, and tropical fruits that had been luxuries to previous generations. By 1870 the British trading companies were already trading in primary commodities or were at least established in countries that were probably candidates to become major producers. They were consequently well positioned to diversify into production.

A third influence was the further expansion of imperial frontiers. In Asia, British political influence was extended over the whole of the Malayan peninsular from the 1870s, while the annexation of Upper Burma in 1886 brought the rest of that country under British control. Also during the late nineteenth century large regions of tropical Africa were incorporated in the European, especially British and French, colonial empires during the "scramble for Africa." As the imperial frontiers expanded, so the trading companies followed in their wake.

A final determinant of the diversification of the British trading companies in particular was the availability of capital arising from Britain's booming capital exports from the 1870s. In this period they made good use of the British capital markets and the availability of limited liability to raise finance for the new business opportunities that appeared. They functioned in part as venture capitalists, identifying opportunities and placing potential British investors in touch with those opportunites. For the most part this was achieved not by opening up the shareholding of the parent trading company, but by floating separate "free-standing" firms on the British capital markets, which the merchant houses continued to control through management contracts and other means in the established tradition of "agency houses."[1]

The upshot was the creation of diversified business groups around the British merchant houses. The merchant house acted as the core firm within each group, usually responsible through its overseas branches for trading and agency business, while separately quoted or incorporated affiliates—often not wholly owned—were engaged in plantations, mines, processing, and other non-trading operations. Consequently, although reinvested profits continued to be an important source of funds for the British merchant groups, after 1870 the groups also drew substantially on outside funds to finance expansion into new activities. Partners and directors of the merchant houses did not generally provide large amounts of new capital themselves

---

[1] In the business history literature, "free-standing firms" is a term coined by Mira Wilkins (1986: 80–95; 1988) to describe the numerous European firms (in particular) that were established with the primary intention of pursuing international investment opportunities. She considered them to be "the most typical mode of British direct investment before 1914." These firms, the numbers of which she and others observed ran into thousands, were registered in Britain "to conduct business overseas, much of which, unlike the American model, did not grow out of the domestic operations of existing enterprises that had headquarters in Britain." Jones (1998) suggests that the term might be a misnomer, as many such companies were parts of business groups or other types of networks.

Table 3.1 Multi-regional business groups by 1914

Trading company	Major host regions	Outposts
Inchcape/ Mackinnon	India; Gulf; East Africa; Australia	
Grahams	India; Portugal	
James Finlay	India; UK	Ceylon; USA; Canada; Russia
Harrisons & Crosfield	Malaya; Dutch East Indies; India	Ceylon; USA; Canada; Australia; New Zealand
Jardine Matheson	China	Japan; USA; South Africa; Peru
Dodwells	China; Canada; USA	Ceylon; Japan
Antony Gibbs	Chile; Australia	Peru; USA
Balfour Williamson	Chile; USA	Peru; Canada
Alfred Booth	Brazil; UK; USA	
Ocean Coal & Wilsons	Brazil; UK	Argentina; North and West Africa

in this period. Table 3.1 lists some of the business groups with extensive presence in different parts of the world by 1914.

3.2.2 Diversification and reinvention before and after the Second World War

The interwar years meant more constrained diversification by function or geography for the British trading companies. While some firms extended the range of activities they conducted in particular countries, others transferred their established expertise in one product to other countries. There was an evident financial constraint on diversification. The shock of the post-1919 recession and the continuing liquidity problems of many firms exercised a strong dampening effect on firms that relied heavily on reinvested earnings. In other cases, firms may have been performing sufficiently well in their traditional activities to reduce enthusiasm for new departures.

The most noteworthy aspect of this period was that, despite the many external shocks, including major trade depressions, the collapse of primary commodity prices, and the growth of trade barriers and exchange controls, merchant firms survived with only a limited number of fatalities. Their survival indicated that their organizational structures and management systems—which had changed little from those prevailing before 1914—were robust. There were, nevertheless, also other elements in their survival. Family and other shareholders sustained companies paying low or no dividends, while Unilever's shareholders underwrote British trading interests in West Africa. Many of the groups had all or most of their business within the sheltered confines of the British Empire. They sometimes still benefited from fiscal and other privileges from colonial governments, while collusive cartels were permitted and usually supported.

After 1945 the British trading companies continued to diversify and reinvent themselves. There were new investments in tropical hardwoods in Borneo, in oil palm in Papua New Guinea, and in textiles and brewing in Africa. General and produce trading gave way to more specialized trading and sales agencies. Firms diversified geographically: the Inchcape group relocated itself out of India towards the faster-growing and more open economies further east. In the postwar decades, constraints were often more political than financial. Leaving aside such havens as Hong Kong, the general thrust of public policy in most developing host economies was to restrict or prohibit FDI, especially in natural resources and services. Among the most successful trading companies were firms that had suffered traumatic shocks as a result of the Pacific War and the Chinese revolution. The British merchants in the Far East and South East Asia acquired new premises and facilities, which probably improved their efficiency compared with the prewar period, but more importantly their losses seem to have stimulated an entrepreneurial urge to rebuild and renew their businesses. Motivation of this type was perhaps lacking among the British firms that were active in India and South America, where owners and managers often seemed resigned to slow decline.

The fate of firms was thus in part correlated with their main host regions. The British traders were heavily embedded in specific countries, where their contacts and knowledge were major sources of competitive advantage, and where they owned large fixed assets. This became a source of competitive disadvantage if, as happened after 1945, some host regions became hostile to foreign firms or imposed penal rates of taxation. This happened to the British firms in South Asia and Latin America— and more especially, for a period at least, in the southern cone countries of Chile and Peru. East and South East Asia and West Africa—at least through to the 1970s— offered much greater prospects. From the 1950s, Hong Kong, which combined fast economic growth with low taxes and a British legal system, offered especially favorable conditions.

Managerial discretion, however, meant that the fate of firms was not wholly dependent on their host economies. Swire's and Jardine's survived the loss of their Chinese investments in 1949. Inchcape and Booker McConnell both successfully escaped from difficult host countries to more attractive areas. And, while overall political and economic conditions in Africa deteriorated from the perspective of Western firms from the 1960s, Lonrho developed as a large hybrid trading company in this period. Conversely, British mercantile interests in Chile were wound down during the 1970s, despite the fact that the Pinochet coup in 1973 once again made it a profitable and hospitable environment for foreign firms.

The fate of the firms was also related to the stability of their shareholding structure. In a considerable number of cases, the decision by family shareholders to sell their shareholding was the catalyst that ended the independent existence and/ or British ownership of firms. These decades saw many founding family shareholders sell out. The problem was that, for a number of reasons, many firms were not well enough equipped to retain their independence once the family shareholding had gone. This was partly because of the risky nature of international trading and investments in developing countries. In some cases it was because good franchises were not well managed. Coincidently, the development of a more fluid market for corporate control in Britain from the 1950s meant that the vulnerability of firms to a takeover was much greater.

Against this background, diversification strategies between the 1960s and 1980s were heavily focused on redeployment from high-risk developing countries to developed countries such as the Commonwealth countries, including Britain, followed by the United States. This often also meant a functional redeployment, as firms pursued opportunities in manufacturing and financial services. Dutch and other European trading companies pursued similar strategies in response to political risk. In retrospect, it is apparent that British firms exaggerated the risks caused by political change in the developing world, while firms also misjudged their core competences by acquiring firms in new industries and countries where they had no advantage and could add no value. However, in the case of some firms, successful transitions were made from traders and plantation owners in developing economies to manufacturers or distributors in developed countries.

Overall, the post-Second World War decades saw the British traders continuing to reinvent themselves. The handling of host regions by commodity exports declined in importance or disappeared altogether, while firms refocused on importing more specialized products to which they could add value. Providing mere access to overseas markets was no longer a sufficient competitive advantage. The British merchant houses in the Far East and South East Asia rose from the ashes of the wartime destruction of their assets and built vibrant new businesses, becoming large-scale automobile distributors and even the owner of a major airline. However, the British trading companies in India and Latin America were notably unsuccessful in finding new strategies to fit changing circumstances. Many of the attempts by firms to invest in developed countries appeared misconceived, either because firms lacked the capabilities or because the strategies employed were faulty. In some cases the cost of attempting to build a presence in Britain or elsewhere was the neglect of potential opportunities in host developing countries.

3.2.3 Demise of the British trading companies

At the beginning of the 1980s the successors to the British trading companies that had originated in the eighteenth and nineteenth centuries were alive and active as large and complex multinational business enterprises. Two decades later some had disappeared altogether, while others had focused on becoming food companies, automobile distributors, or chemical companies. In other cases, substantial and successful businesses continued but were no longer British owned. Of the surviving British trading companies, Lonrho (formerly Lonrho Africa, which had been carved out of the once vast Lonrho business when the mining interests were formed into a separate company in 1998) remained as a residual of the great merchant empires in Africa, while in Asia Pacific Swire's and Jardine Matheson continued in business as large and ultimately British-controlled multinational enterprises. John Swire & Sons and Jardine Matheson were thus the two really substantial survivors from the nineteenth century to enter the twenty-first century, employing 113,000 and 240,000 persons, respectively, in 2008.

The demise of so many of the old British trading companies was curious, given that the world political economy appeared once again to be offering prospects for their skills, as economies were liberalized and opened to foreign trade and investment. So what caused the decline of British trading companies in this era?

The first challenge arose from further changes in the economic and political environment of important host economies. The trading companies, as regional specialists, were always vulnerable to adverse changes in their host economies. In the postwar period the demise of most British traders in Latin America and South Asia reflected the difficult economic, fiscal, and political environment faced by all foreign firms—especially ones involved in services and resources—in those areas. Jardine Matheson and Swire's, most obviously, continued to draw enormous advantage from their position in Hong Kong, while—conversely—UAC's fate was all but sealed by the decline of the West African, and especially the Nigerian, economies from the 1970s, as well as the growing level of corruption that was increasingly difficult for its parent Unilever to control (Jones 2005: 96, 191–7).

Secondly, the firms fell victim to their failed attempts to diversify into regions and industries where they lacked expertise. The merchant-adventurer ethos and the desire to escape from their traditional developing-country hosts had led firms in some cases far away from core competences, however widely defined. During the 1980s many of these diversification strategies ran into great difficulties. The consequences of failed diversification strategies were the most fatal for UAC. During the 1970s, redeployment had been a central strategy for UAC to protect itself should its traditional African business collapse. This strategy had rested on an underlying assumption that UAC's skills were transferable elsewhere, but this proved largely not to be the case. The competence in region-specific knowledge and know-how was thus both a competitive advantage and a competitive disadvantage for the trading firms, in that it provided a constraint on diversification options outside the host region. Extensive diversification outside core activities also proved to be detrimental, thanks to the escalating costs from managerial constraints and diminishing benefits from the exploitation of established and proven expertise.

The final and the ultimate arbiter of the fate of the diversified trading companies in the late twentieth century was, however, the British capital markets. The capital markets, which had made the creation of the diversified business groups possible before 1914, were to prove their nemesis in the 1990s. It was the declining share price of the publicly quoted firms that led to their ultimate demise as diversified trading companies. The changed nature of British equity holders, which was different from before 1914 as individuals had been largely replaced by financial institutions, played a major role in that end. While the individual shareholders before 1914—and indeed much later—were passive and often long-term holders of stock, the financial institutions viewed shares as short-term investment vehicles. They were responsible to the owners of the funds that they invested, and as such had a duty to maximize investment returns. Consequently, the main preoccupation of the institutions was short-term financial performance and share prices.

Diversified conglomerates were not favored by institutional investors in Britain, who held diversified portfolios themselves and preferred individual firms to focus on their core areas, enabling their performance and prospects to be more efficiently monitored. During the second half of the 1990s Britain's once large industrial conglomerates—Hanson Trust, BTR, Tomkins, and Suter—were dismantled, focused on a core business, or acquired by other firms. Diversified trading companies were especially unfashionable in such a context, as the evident difficulties of many diversification strategies only reinforced the poor reputation of diversified conglomerates. Interestingly, therefore, in the final years of the twentieth century, it was only the family-owned firms that survived. Not surprisingly, therefore, it was the family control of Swire's and Jardine Matheson that would ensure their survival.

3.3 TYPES OF BUSINESS GROUPS

As British trading companies diversified over the course of the nineteenth century and especially after 1870, they organized their activities in a number of ways. Table 3.2 offers a typology identifying three organizational forms.

Three organizational patterns were employed between the 1870s and the 1970s. In the "unitary" business groups, activities were wholly owned, although this did not mean that they were integrated in the sense of a modern corporation. The second, "network," form consisted of a core trading company with multiple wholly owned branches surrounded by a cluster of partly owned firms linked not only by equity, but also by debt, management, cross-directorships, and trading relationships. It is this type that most resembles the business groups in today's emerging economies. It is also this type of business group that has been most discussed in the literature, and whose alleged rent-seeking and weak organizational capabilities have been the object of debate. A variant of the type, called a "loose network" here, had no corporate core beyond family shareholdings.

The choice of organizational form was determined in part by the business portfolios of companies. Trading operations and acting as agents for shipping, insurance, and manufacturing firms were generally internalized. These activities required either a large knowledge base on the part of firms, or the maintenance of a sound reputation among actual or potential clients. Within network-type business groups, these activities were the responsibilities of wholly owned branches. Trading companies

Table 3.2 Typology of the business groups around British trading companies, c.1870s–c.1970s

Organizational form	Examples
Unitary	UAC; Booker Brothers, McConnell; Dodwells; Wilson, Sons
Network	Swire's; Jardine Matheson; James Finlay; Harrisons & Crosfield; Balfour Williamson
Loose network	Grahams; Inchcape family

Note: The unitary and network forms correspond to the hierarchy-type business groups described in Chapter 2. The unitary form can be classified as a diversified business group with wholly owned subsidiaries, while the network form is a diversified business group with a pyramidal ownership structure. The loose-network form falls somewhere in between the hierarchy-type business groups and the network-type business groups identified in Chapter 2.

whose business consisted primarily of trading and shipping agency and other agency work were mostly organized on a unitary basis.

In contrast, network-type business groups were those that had diversified into plantations, mines, processing, and in some cases the ownership of shipping companies. Merchants made their profits from commissions on trade and agency business. As a result, they sought access to trade flows and information, and to prevent being denied access by being bypassed by parties they had brought together. Outright ownership of mines and plantations was, as a result, unnecessary. These network groups, therefore, placed their activities into separate partly owned firms, through which sufficient access was secured by non-equity modes.

If ownership of non-core activities could be shared, there were other advantages. It limited the risks of the parent trading companies, while enabling outside capital to be bought into ventures. This permitted the use of other people's money to undertake entrepreneurial investments designed to generate new sources of income for them through commission and fees. Moreover, merchants' desire to use other people's money was married to the desire of individual investors to reduce the risks of their portfolio (Hennart 1998: 71–2). This was because potential investors had little information on whether such ventures were well managed or even honest. Many resource and commodity investments carried inherent risks, which the state of company law did little to modify. Companies operated in a veil of secrecy, even from their shareholders. It was not until the Companies Act of 1929 that it was stipulated in the case of British public companies that balance sheets should be sent to all shareholders prior to the annual general meeting, and not until 1948 that it was stipulated that the profit and loss account also had to be circulated. The association of a reputable trading company with a new company provided an assurance to investors of honest and competent management.

The other major influence on choice of organizational structure was the preference of the owners of the firm. A number of the family-owned businesses were especially concerned not to permit outsiders access to their affairs. Dodwells' tea-trading and shipping-agency business was conducted by branches, but it also organized its salmon canneries, flour mills, and plantations in this way. Antony Gibbs also preferred to control most of its business through its interlocking partnerships, except its operations in Australia, where a number of partly owned ventures owning ranches, mines, and a wire-netting manufacturer were limited companies. The three organizational forms are examined in more detail below.

3.3.1 Unitary form

In West Africa the British companies were largely concerned with trading and related activities, which they conducted through their wholly owned branches. Only the rather modest ventures beyond this core business were placed in separate limited companies. This was the case of the tin-mining companies promoted by the Niger Company. This firm also established a separate French subsidiary, Compagnie du Niger Français, in 1913 to operate in French West Africa. The general preference of these firms was for full control. When John Holt established its own steamship line, it was fully internalized within the firm.

After 1914 the West African trading firms continued to favor a more unitary approach. During the 1920s the diversification strategies of African & Eastern and, to a lesser extent, the Niger Company bequeathed the UAC on its formation a considerable collection of subsidiary firms, mostly related to trade in West Africa, but also in East Africa, the Mediterranean, the Middle East, and Singapore, plus some small industrial firms in Britain. Although many of these were retained by UAC, they were organized as wholly owned subsidiaries. This reflected the overall Unilever policy that it should wholly own all its businesses (Fieldhouse 1994: 622–3). In this respect, UAC did not employ a network form of organization. On the other hand, it was not a single integrated business either, as UAC's London headquarters presided over a complex of semi-autonomous (if wholly owned) enterprises, often using their original names, such as G. B. Ollivant, and registered in Britain, France, or Belgium (Fieldhouse 1994: 26–30). Ollivants continued through the 1960s and 1970s to function almost independently of UAC, and competed directly with UAC in some of its trading business (Fieldhouse 1994: 157–9).

During the postwar decades the unitary forms of business group came under two kinds of pressure. The first was that firms that wished to diversify into manufacturing in particular needed joint ventures to access technical expertise. UAC began to move beyond full ownership of its businesses after the Second World War as the firm used joint ventures to develop non-trading interests in West Africa. Secondly, in the immediate post-colonial period, as many governments sought to curtail or limit foreign investments in their economies, they encouraged local participation in shareholdings, and in some cases made it obligatory. Consequently, the trading companies came under considerable pressure in many host economies to form locally registered companies with local equity participation. The wholly owned structure of UAC, for instance, was eventually broken up by host-government pressure for localization in West Africa, and especially in Nigeria. In the latter case, because of Nigerian government pressure, 40 percent of UAC's business in Nigeria was sold to the public in 1974. The price was set by the government and considerably undervalued the company, while half of the proceeds had to be reinvested in Nigeria. Further government legislation in 1977 then reduced the UAC shareholding in UAC (Nigeria) to 40 percent, which eventually changed the nature of UAC's organization.

3.3.2 Network form

While some of the largest trading companies preferred full ownership of their business groups, most of the hybrid trading companies used network forms of organization. By 1870 use of networks of partly owned affiliates was well established, especially in the Indian managing agencies, but was not well developed. However, over the following decades, large and complex business groups organized as networks developed, as the trading companies diversified their activities and took full advantage of the capital availability in Britain by floating new "free-standing" companies on the British or colonial capital markets. Both trading companies that retained the partnership form and those that had incorporated adopted this organizational form.

The scale and complexity of the business groups organized around trading companies varied considerably by 1914. Table 3.3 shows the organization of John Swire & Sons around 1914.

The headquarters of John Swire & Sons was in London after 1870. The head office provided agency services for its affiliated firms and for Alfred Holt's Ocean Steamship Company. Among other tasks, the London office recruited the expatriate staff for the Far East and the affiliated companies, and handled contracts for the building of new vessels for its fleets. In the East the firm operated under the name of Butterfield & Swire—in practice they were one firm—which was jointly headquartered in Hong Kong and Shanghai. Butterfield & Swire had a network of wholly owned branches in China and two in Japan.

John Swire & Sons held shareholdings in all its affiliated firms. The China Navigation Company was established with most of the initial capital put up by the Swires and their close associates, and in 1911 the firm "and [its] retired partners" still held "the largest stake in the Company."[2] The Taikoo Sugar Refinery was also established in the same fashion, but more capital may have been sold to outsiders over time. In 1934 the firm held a 17 percent stake.[3] The Taikoo Dockyard and Engineering Company was majority owned. When the company was founded, John Swire & Son received a large percentage of the shares and debentures as a consideration for the expenditure it had incurred in setting up the Hong Kong shipyard earlier in the 1900s, but thereafter outside capital was also attracted. The Tientsin Lighter Company was a joint venture between Swire's and Alfred

---

[2] J. D. Scott to J. Bruce Ismay, May 29, 1911, Swire Archives, JSSI/1/15, School of Oriental and African Studies, University of London (hereafter SOAS).

[3] John Swire & Sons to V. Grayburn, Nov. 9, 1934, Swire Archives, JSSI/4/13, SOAS.

Table 3.3 John Swire & Son group, c.1914

Wholly owned branches	Date opened	Principal activities in addition to imports, shipping, and insurance agencies
United Kingdom		
London	1870*	Head office of John Swire & Sons; management services for affiliated companies; London agency of Ocean Steamship Company
China		
Shanghai	1867	Head office for Butterfield & Swire
Hong Kong	1870	Head office for Butterfield & Swire
Foochow	1872	
Swatow	1882	
Kiukiang	1886	
Tientsin	1886	
Hankow	1887	
Canton	1892	
Amoy	1896	
Tsingtao	1890s	
Japan		
Yokohama	1867	
Kobe	1888	

Principal affiliates	Date started/ acquired	% equity held	Place of registration	Principal activity
China Navigation Co.	1872	'Largest stake'	London	Shipping; 50 % of Tientsin Lighter; 33 % of Luen Steamship Co.
Taikoo Sugar Refining Co.	1881	?17%	London	Sugar refining
Tientsin Lighter Co.	1904	50% CNC	London	Lighter services
Taikoo Dockyard and Engineering Co.	1908	Majority	London	Dockyards

Note: *Established in Liverpool 1832, head office moved to London in 1870.

Sources: Swire Archives, SOAS; Sugiyama (1987).

Holt designed to serve the China Navigation Company, and it was jointly owned by the two firms. The equity relationship formed an important component of the binding between Swire's and its affiliates, but as important were the agency agreements, cross-directorships, and flows of funds between the parent and the affiliate.

A second example of a network form of a business group before 1914 can be provided by Harrisons & Crosfield. This firm had a different business profile from Swire's, and this was reflected in the different organizational structure, as shown in Table 3.4.

As in the case of Swire's, the London head office presided over a network of wholly owned branches and affiliated companies. The branches traded in teas and later other commodities, acted as agents for shipping and insurance companies, and provided plantation management services. The firm's diversification into tea plantations in Ceylon and later India after 1899, and rubber plantations in Malaya from 1903, was made by establishing separate plantation companies. Although Harrisons & Crosfield's interests spanned a number of countries, the affiliates specialized in one country. Harrisons & Crosfield's share of the equity of these companies in 1914 varied from under 1 percent to over two-thirds. Shareholdings were held by the firm itself, or through the Rubber Plantations Investment Trust, which Harrisons & Crosfield controlled through a large but not majority shareholding (Brown 1994: 57–8). The plantation companies were formed and floated on the London market, but another component of the group, Irwin-Harrisons & Crosfield Inc., was registered in the USA. This was formed in 1914 by a merger of the firm's New York tea-importing affiliate, Harrisons & Crosfield Inc., and A. P. Irwin & Co. of Philadelphia. Harrisons & Crosfield held 20 percent of the shares—and half the seats on the board—while over two-thirds of the capital was taken by the Irwin family.

Contracts and cross-directorships bound the group together. Harrisons & Crosfield acted as secretaries and/or agents to almost all the plantation companies in which it held equity shares. In most cases, it acquired those functions at the company's formation. The secretarial function was performed in Britain and included the provision of management support to the board of an individual plantation company. The overseas branches performed the agency function, which involved the management of the business on the spot, and the collection and transmission to individual company boards in Britain of all relevant information to assist in decision-making. Each agency agreement would put one or two of Harrisons & Crosfield's own directors on the plantation company's board.

For the most part, the basic organizational pattern of the network form of business groups, as they had developed by the early twentieth century, remained in place until at least the 1960s. The creation of new affiliate firms to undertake non-trading activities continued, and in the 1920s a new generation of partly owned free-standing companies was floated on the British capital market. After 1929, British exchange controls on investments outside the sterling area as well as the perceived risks of international investment effectively ended the flotation of new firms on the British capital markets. However, well before then the trading companies had begun to make more use of locally registered firms or other types of institutional arrangement. The growing burden of British taxation on companies whose profits were earned largely abroad during and after the First World War was initially an important consideration, and this led to the registration of several affiliated firms being shifted.

Table 3.4 Harrisons & Crosfield group, c.1914

Wholly owned branches	Date opened	Principal activities in addition to import, shipping, and insurance agencies
United Kingdom		
London	c.1845*	Head office: secretarial services to plantation companies
South East Asia		
Kuala Lumpur, Malaya[†]	1907	Rubber export, plantation management
Medan, Sumatra, Dutch East Indies[†]	1910	Rubber export, plantation management, engineering workshops
Batavia, Java, Dutch East Indies[†]	1911	Tea and rubber export, plantation management
South Asia		
Colombo, Ceylon[†]	1895	Tea and rubber export, plantation management
Calcutta, India[†]	1900	Tea export, plantation management
Quilon, India[†]	1912	Tea and rubber export, plantation management, engineering workshops
Elsewhere		
New York, USA	1904	Tea import and distribution
Montreal, Canada[†]	1905	Tea and rubber import, chemicals distribution
Melbourne, Australia	1910	Tea and rubber import, general distribution
Wellington, New Zealand	1910	Tea and rubber import, general distribution

Principal affiliates	Date started	% of equity held	Place of registration	Principal activities
c.40 plantation companies	1903–14	<1%–70%	London[‡]	Rubber and tea plantations
Rubber Plantations Investment Trust Ltd.	1908	?30–50%	London	Holding shares in plantation companies
Irwin-Harrisons & Crosfield Inc.	1914	?20%	New York	US tea trading

Notes: *The first office was opened in Liverpool in 1844, but the partnership early established a second office in the City of London, which soon became the centre of the firm's operations.

[†]In these countries Harrisons & Crosfield had branch offices in a number of locations in addition to the main offices listed here.

[‡]In the case of several companies with plantations in Java, the London-registered company was merely a holding company for a wholly owned and locally registered operating company.

Sources: Harrisons & Crosfield (1944); annual reports and board minutes of individual plantation companies; Harrisons & Crosfield lists of shareholdings in 'secretarial' companies; all in Harrisons & Crosfield Archives, Guildhall Library, London.

Table 3.5 shows the organizational pattern of the Jardine Matheson group at the end of the 1930s, and reveals a structure very similar to that prevailing in 1914.

Jardine Matheson's head office and place of registration was in Hong Kong. It owned and controlled Matheson & Co. in London, though, in practice, ultimate control lay with the proprietors in Scotland. In 1938 Jardine Matheson had a dozen or so wholly owned branches in China and one in Japan, the branch in New York having been closed in 1931. Its affiliated companies, for most of which it acted as agents and secretaries, were mainly registered in Hong Kong. Before 1914 they generally took the form of public limited companies in which only a share of the equity was held. However, the new investments made in the interwar years remained wholly owned private companies. Jardine's was interested in floating such companies, but their poor profitability in the interwar years did not provide suitable circumstances.[4]

During the 1950s the organizational structures of the network business groups remained in place, but from the 1960s there were considerable pressures for change. In some countries, the managing-agency system came to be regarded as politically unacceptable. It was made illegal in India in 1967. At the same time, its original rationale disappeared. Improvements in corporate reporting and the emergence of organized capital markets in many countries meant that investors no longer needed the brand of a British trading company to guarantee that their savings would be safe. Indeed, complex groups with cross-shareholdings and internal transfers of commission and fees within the group were no longer attractive, as shareholders changed from being atomistic individuals to institutional investors (in Britain) or powerful business elites (in Asia and elsewhere).

From the 1960s there was a general trend either to take full ownership of affiliates or—as in the case of most of the Indian managing agencies—to sell out altogether. Harrisons & Crosfield, for instance, purchased the outstanding equity of its major plantation affiliates—becoming for the first time an owner rather than a manager and selling agent.[5] Government pressures for localization rapidly ended the brief moment of internalization, nevertheless. In 1982 the majority of the equity of Harrisons Malaysian Estates was sold to a state-owned company, Harrisons & Crosfield retaining a 30.3 percent interest in the successor company. In the same year, the firm was obliged to sell 34 percent of its equity in its Indian plantations company to Indian nationals, reducing its shareholding to 40 percent. In 1989 the remaining shareholding in the Malaysian company was sold.

In the 1980s it was only the Hong Kong-centered British trading firms that retained the network form of organization, as the British firms in Hong Kong continued to be sheltered from governmental pressures for localization. Both Jardine Matheson and Swire's thus retained a network form of organization. The former was attacked on several occasions. In 1980 Hong Kong entrepreneurs bought into and took control of one of Jardine's associated property companies, the Hong Kong and Kowloon Wharf

---

[4] J. J. Paterson to D. G. M. Bernard, Dec. 10, 1936, S/O Hong Kong to London, 1936, Jardine Matheson Archives, Cambridge University Library (hereafter CUL).

[5] Chairman's statement, Harrisons & Crosfield Annual Report, 1978.

Table 3.5 Jardine Matheson group, c.1938

Wholly owned branches	Date opened	Principal activities
United Kingdom		
Matheson & Co.	1848	Banking, insurance, secretarial services, tea and egg imports
China Coast		
Jardine Matheson		
Canton	1832/43	
Hong Kong	1844	Head office
Shanghai	1844	
Foochow	1854	
Peking	1861	
Swatow	1861	
Tientsin	1861	
Hankow	1860s	
Chung King	1860s	
Tsingtao	1860s	
Taipei	1860s	
Japan		
Kobe	1890s	

Principal affiliates	Date started/ acquired	% of equity held	Place of registration	Principal activities
Canton Insurance Office	1836	?	Hong Kong	Marine, fire, accident insurance
Hong Kong Fire Insurance	1868	?	Hong Kong	Marine, fire, accident insurance
Shanghai & Hongkew Wharf	1875	?	Hong Kong	Shanghai wharves and warehouses
Hong Kong & Kowloon Wharf & Godown	1886	7	Hong Kong	Hong Kong wharves and warehouses
Indo-China Steam Navigation Co.	1881	?	UK	Ocean shipping
Hong Kong Land Company	1889	?	Hong Kong	Hong Kong real estate
Lombard Insurance Co.	1895	100	UK	Formerly reinsurance; mostly investments
Ewo Yuen Press Packing Co.	1919	100	Hong Kong	Packing in Shanghai
Ewo Cold Storage Co.	1920	100	Hong Kong	Manufacture and export of dried eggs, Shanghai
Ewo Cotton Mills Ltd.	1921	12	Hong Kong	Shanghai cotton mills
Jardine Engineering Corporation	1923	100	Hong Kong	Engineering agencies in China
Ewo Breweries	1936	100	Hong Kong	Shanghai beer brewing
Various East African companies	1936	?	East Africa	Plantations; mines in East Africa

Sources: Jardine Matheson Archives, CUL; Le Fevour (1968).

and Godown Company. Jardine's, however, increased its shareholding in the second major local company, Hongkong Land Company, and secured 40 percent of the equity. In 1981 Hongkong Land took a 40 percent stake in Jardine Matheson (Keswick 1982: 234–5).

Swire's undertook a limited consolidation. In 1974 Swire's placed most of its Hong Kong affiliates into the partly owned but publicly quoted holding company, Swire Pacific, which in turn held equity in the principal Hong Kong affiliates, including Cathay Pacific and Swire Properties.[6] At that time John Swire & Sons directly held 50 percent of the China Navigation Company, the major shipping subsidiary that was British registered, and in 1976 the firm acquired the remaining 50 percent of the equity. Most of the other affiliates remained partly owned, different classes of shareholding meaning that full control remained in the hands of John Swire & Sons, itself still wholly owned by the founding families.

3.3.3 Loose network form

A variant of the network form of organization employed by British trading companies can be termed the "loose network." In the first part of the nineteenth century merchant firms typically took the form of interlocked but independent partnerships lacking an overall corporate center or parent, but this form tended to evolve into the network form with a parent merchant firm (or partnership) bound to affiliates. However, in some instances loose networks persisted. The Graham group's network of interlocked partnerships was not consolidated until the 1920s, and then as a result of the group's bankruptcy and reconstruction.

A more durable instance of the loose network organization was the large cluster of companies in which the Inchcape family held shares. This lacked a parent trading company and was dependent on Inchcape family shareholdings to provide some coherence. During the 1920s the Inchcape group appeared to be evolving into a network form of business group, with relationships other than family shareholdings to bind different parts. There was an attempt to develop more synergies inside the group. For example, the different companies made diverse insurance arrangements, and attempts were made to encourage firms to use the Inchcape-controlled Gray Dawes as brokers.[7] In 1920 Inchcape established a bank, the P&O Banking Corporation, to develop the private banking business of the P&O Steam Navigation Company (Jones 1993: 158).

The coordination of business services within the Inchcape network proved difficult to achieve. The P&O Bank was unable to attract the custom of many Inchcape companies, which stayed loyal to their old bankers, leading the bank to seek more risky business, which in turn caused bad debts. In 1927 Inchcape sold three-quarters

---

[6] Annual Report, John Swire & Sons, 1974.
[7] Memorandum for Lord Inchcape, Nov. 8, 1923, Gray Dawes Archives, MS 27605, Guildhall Library, London.

of the shares in the bank to the Chartered Bank, and some years later it was totally absorbed by the latter, having never established a viable business (Jones 1993: 159). The allocation of resources within the group was distorted by Lord Inchcape's determination to support his financially troubled shipping companies, while Inchcape himself was too immersed in details and too involved with past tradition and practices to develop a coherent business group further.

After Lord Inchcape's death in 1932, the group persisted through the 1930s as a large but amorphous collection of trading and shipping companies, focused especially on India, but extending to the Gulf, East Africa, and Australia. It was not until the third earl became the Senior in the firm in 1948 that the consolidation and reconstruction of this structure began, culminating in the formation of Inchcape & Co., a public limited company, in 1958.

3.4 COMPETENCES OF BRITISH TRADING COMPANIES

British trading companies created and sustained complex diversified businesses using managerial methods and organizational forms radically different from textbook models. It is the robustness of the traders and their ability to sustain reinvention strategies that is so striking.

The competences of the trading companies rested on the locational advantages of their home economy. They developed at a time when Britain dominated world trade flows and, by the late nineteenth century, world capital flows. They were able to access the world's largest equity markets. Many of their investments were located within the British Empire or parts of Latin America under British informal influence. In the interwar years the merchant firms were able to protect their business through extensive collusive cartels supported by the colonial authorities. Although Britain's relative importance in the world economy began to decline from the late nineteenth century, the British trading companies in Asia and Africa continued to benefit from the umbrella of British colonial rule through until the 1950s and even later. The continued colonial status of Hong Kong until 1997 forms one of the central explanations for the growth and survival of Swire's and Jardine Matheson compared to the firms whose business was centered on Latin America.

The historical longevity of the trading companies in their host regions and the colonial status of many of these countries resulted in multiple contacts, which provided a major competitive advantage. British colonial officials were frequently critical of the merchant firms, and certainly did not protect them against competitors. The interwar decline of the Calcutta agency houses, or the failure of the West African traders to prevent the creation of marketing boards after the Second World

War, illustrate this point. But, if colonial administrations had their own agendas, they were still sufficiently close to the merchant firms in their ideological and cultural outlook to provide an immensely supportive context. However, the trading companies also established long-standing contacts with local business elites in Asia, Africa, and Latin America, which gave them a quasi-local status, akin to indigenous business groups today. Such contacts were renewed in successive generations and provided the basis for a sustained competitive advantage in these host economies.

The importance of the British economy and Empire in some respects makes the role and longevity of British trading companies more understandable than those of, say, Swiss or Danish trading companies. However, British firms were not simply free-riders on the British economy or Empire. There were core competences centered around the areas of knowledge, information, and external relationships. Management systems that involved staff and directors spending their entire careers abroad generated extensive tacit knowledge about regions, products, and marketing channels. The upshot was the creation of a generalist managerial cadre able to provide senior management that could control a surprisingly wide range of businesses. Site-specific learning was enhanced by systems and routines to control flows of information. The requirements for motivating staff while preventing opportunism were dealt with by remuneration systems combining commission payments with strong moral cultures (Connell 2004).

These managers had sufficient skills to undertake all sorts of trading and distribution, run shipping companies and dockyards, and manage large plantation companies and eventually, in one case, a major airline. They were able to sustain long-term investments in the processing of locally produced commodities. There were more problems for the firms from the interwar years, when they might have invested further in manufacturing if they had possessed the skills. The use of joint ventures was an obvious answer, and this was employed successfully in the 1960s and 1970s, in West African brewing and textiles, and in Malaysia. However, the opportunities for trading companies to pursue this strategy more extensively, even if they had wished to do so, were constrained by the desire of British manufacturing firms to integrate themselves forward if market volumes justified it.

The persistence of family ownership and control was a striking feature in the management of the trading companies, although some of the largest had no family influence. There is little evidence that family control was necessarily a disadvantage for a trading company, provided it could be combined with a willingness to allow sufficient outside capital into the business to permit growth. Family control could provide an element of continuity to firms that engaged in risky businesses and reinvented themselves. Reputations for probity, competence, and durability are major assets for trading companies, and these could be enhanced by sustained family ownership. Especially after 1945, continuing family ownership was an important key to the continued independence of firms. Few firms made a successful transition from a family to a managerial business. The sale of family shareholdings usually triggered a period of shareholder instability, followed by acquisition or dissolution.

The internal architecture of the trading companies was robust. The constellation of firms around the trading companies was tied with multiple institutional and contractual modes, with flows of managerial, financial, and trading relationships among those. The business groups possessed real advantages related to imperfections in capital, labor, and product markets and in the area of property-rights enforcement. There were numerous conflicts of interest and potential for opportunist behavior, but in practice rent-seeking was restrained.

The external relationships surrounding the trading companies were also important elements of their architecture. These networks often relied on trust rather than contracts and were extremely durable. British merchants emerged from hubs such as London, Liverpool, and Glasgow and clustered in hubs overseas, and this provided one support for the high trust levels that facilitated such networks. Long-term relationships with banks provided a source of credit for routine operations. At times of crisis, banks supported trading companies that experienced serious financial problems, occasionally becoming involved in the reconstruction of firms. Long-term relationships with shipping and insurance companies, and even some manufacturers, provided important elements in the business of the trading companies.

3.5 BUSINESS GROUPS IN HISTORY AND TODAY

The British trading companies discussed above illustrate many similarities to today's emerging-market business groups, as both of those economic agents operate in similar environments of market imperfections. Incentives to reduce transaction costs that arise from information and contracting problems, for instance, were a major influence on the diversification strategies of British trading companies. As discussed in Section 3.3 in detail, corporate information was largely inaccessible even to shareholders in nineteenth-century Britain. In a similar fashion, Chang et al. (2001), in a study of analysts' behavior around the world using contemporary data, also show the difficulty of gaining access to accurate, unbiased information on corporate activity around the world, and especially in emerging markets.

Evidence of contracting difficulty also abounds. Extreme examples perhaps illustrate this best. Jardine's and Swire's were subjected to forced divestment of their assets by the Communist regime in China after 1949. In only slightly less draconian fashion, India's post-independence socialist government confiscated some prized assets of the Tata Group, India's oldest and most celebrated business house (including airlines and insurance companies). Thus the grabbing hand (Shleifer and Vishny 1998) of government has been evident cross-sectionally both in history and today.

British trading companies historically and contemporary business groups in emerging markets operate in environments of scarcity of talent. The responses of the groups are remarkably parallel. Samsung runs a de facto business school, a training center, where it attempts to capture expertise from its various businesses and channel it to other (often very different) businesses. Tata runs the Tata Administrative Services, which seeks to develop an elite cadre of managers who are rotated across again very diverse businesses. This de facto business school function is valuable in an environment where the nurturing of commercial talent is in short supply, relative to demand (Khanna and Palepu 1997). A similar elite corps of managers was evident in Jardine's and Swire's, recruited initially from particular communities and educational backgrounds. For several generations Jardine Matheson recruited most of its managers not only from Scotland, but from a discrete region of Scotland: the county of Dumfriesshire (Jardine Matheson 1947). When it began to experiment with recruiting university graduates during the 1930s, it much preferred them to have attended Scottish universities. Swire's, in contrast, recruited from the leading English universities of Oxford and Cambridge.

The organization of the diversified businesses of these British trading firms had even more parallels with that seen in contemporary emerging markets. Whereas trading operations and certain agency businesses were wholly owned, diversified activities in ownership of plantations and mines were placed in partially owned firms, which were often floated on the equity market. Harrisons & Crosfield had floated around forty plantation companies by 1914, with shares in the equity of between 1 and 70 percent. Equity provides only one link within these business groups, and rarely the most important ones. Hennart and Kryda (1998: 213–27) assert that the establishment and maintenance of trade relationships were the goal, and equity, debt, and cross-directorships were the means, in these British business groups. Similar ties hold business groups together today. Indeed, it is not even clear that the equity ties are the most salient. In a contemporary study of Chilean business groups, Khanna and Rivkin (2000) argue that equity ties are not the most salient delineators of business group boundaries.

In much of the older literature the organizational forms employed by the British trading firms in South and South East Asia were looked upon with the greatest suspicion. The complexity and costs of interest within such groups appeared costly and inefficient. Outside shareholders looked vulnerable to exploitation compared with the owners of the core trading firms, which were often families (Bauer 1948). However, the historical findings in this chapter suggest that there were also real benefits from these groups. They functioned as venture capitalists in countries where capital markets were highly undeveloped. They could recruit far better management than lots of atomistic small firms, as they could offer far better career prospects. They facilitated the international marketing of products, and provided a mechanism for spreading information and knowledge between firms. Thinking of these business groups purely as investment groups drastically understates their true role and function—they performed a wide range of market intermediation functions in the face of an equally wide range of market imperfections. The study of contemporary business groups documents the same patterns (Khanna 2000) and similar skepticism regarding minority shareholder exploitation (La Porta et al. 1999). The extreme view of the skeptic's school was mistaken then, and is mistaken now. A nuanced approach, emanating from an understanding of the contextual environment, remains the more sensible interpretation.

Consider also the longevity of the business group organizational form. Again, the studies on today's emerging economies and the British trading companies from the nineteenth century yield the same conclusion. European trading companies lasted well beyond the initial circumstances in the nineteenth century that encouraged and facilitated their roles as trade intermediaries, especially the poor state of transport and communications, which gave rise to a high degree of information asymmetry, and the spread of colonialism, which provided a favorable political context for direct investment.

In practice, European trading companies and their business groups proved robust. They survived radical improvements in the information environment—which occurred in stages, with the progressive introduction of the telegraph (1860s), telephones, faxes, and the Internet. They also survived momentous shifts in the political environment—associated with the end of Empire and widespread nationalizations, as in China—and in technological paradigms. The companies frequently reinvented themselves to suit the evolution of context, but always outperforming sensible comparable companies. As sea transportation gave way to air travel after the Second World War, Swire's—which had owned a large commercial shipping fleet since the late nineteenth century—established Cathay Pacific, which remains one of Asia's leading airlines today, still controlled by Swire's. British trading companies such as Harrisons & Crosfield and Inchcape functioned as highly diversified general trading companies with striking resemblances to Japan's *sogo shosha*. In the early 1980s Inchcape operated in 44 countries and marketed the products of 2,750 manufacturers. Its business group included general merchandising, shipping, port operators, tea producers, and manufacturing.

It was only during the 1980s that capital market pressures, arising from the growing preference among investment analysts and consultants for focused rather than diversified businesses, resulted in the restructuring of Harrisons & Crosfield and Inchcape into core businesses (Butler and Keary 2000). Similarly, Khanna and Palepu (1999, 2005) demonstrate that contemporary Chilean and Indian groups respond to dramatic improvements in ambient information and dramatically higher levels of competition, not by disbanding but by reinventing themselves and seeking out newer areas of business.

3.6 CONCLUSION

This chapter has examined the evolution of the diversified business groups organized around British trading companies from the late eighteenth century to the start of the twenty-first century. A major contribution of this chapter to the research on today's business groups is to demonstrate the similar forms of diverse and complex organizations in the past, and to challenge theories and models based on contemporary experiences to explain such diversity. In the now-burgeoning business groups literature in which contemporary emerging economies remain a central preoccupation, this study has thus focused instead on a group of service sector firms with nineteenth-century origins. It has shown how organizational forms of business groups were employed over long time periods to control large and diversified multinational complexes and identified competitive advantages and management skills residing in contacts, knowledge, information, and relationships.

While not the creators of major technological breakthroughs through innovation or the application of science to manufacturing, British trading companies played an innovative role in developing new sources of supply of resources and opening new markets, especially before 1914. They not only intermediated for trade, but mobilized capital flows and directed them toward expanding supplies and markets in the emerging global economy. They were entrepreneurial firms that pioneered new industries, from jute manufacture in India and cotton-textile manufacture in China, to the oil industry in California. They were not portfolio investors in these activities, but employed and transferred specific organizational and technological skills and competences. In the twentieth century, then, their roles as agents of economic growth looked less heroic. They were supplanted over time by locally owned firms or other types of multinational enterprise. However, they continued to innovate in the production of commodities such as tea, rubber, and palm oil, and during the 1950s and 1960s were significant in the industrialization of a range of developing countries. In some countries they remained large-scale business enterprises that continued to innovate, to open new marketing and distribution channels, and to offer employment well into the 1970s and in some cases into the twenty-first century.

This chapter has thus cast the business groups in a more dynamic light than as mere rent-seekers serving the interests of the controlling family, or fragile forms of governance unable to sustain complex enterprises over the long term (Chapman 1985, 1992; Wilkins 1998). It has shown that British trading groups had a wider range of functions related to imperfections in capital, labor, and product markets and to the need for property-rights enforcement. They possessed competences that sustained long-lasting and relatively successful international businesses and that gave them genuine efficiency-enhancing roles. This debate finds strong resonances in interpretations of the contemporary diversified business organizations in emerging economies. The existence of business groups in developing countries has often been explained in terms of rent-seeking behavior, a view reinforced by the Asian financial crises of the late 1990s. If any capability was identified, it was one of the financial intermediation in conditions of capital market imperfection. Nonetheless, more recently, as is typically illustrated in the several chapters of this *Handbook*, important resources and capabilities such as contacts, local knowledge, human resources, finance, and organization have been stressed.

To conclude, for all the different economic, social, and political environments surrounding business groups in history and at present, this chapter has provided critical hints for a wider and deeper understanding of business groups active today. Historical perspectives open the way to a better grasp of the strategy and performance of firms and are thus an indispensable part of the balanced understanding of the role and the functioning of business groups now and in the future.

REFERENCES

BAUER, P. T. (1948). *The Rubber Industry.* London: Longman.

BROWN, R. A. (1994). *Capital and Entrepreneurship in South-East Asia.* London: Macmillan.

BUTLER, C., and KEARY, J. (2000). *Managers and Mantras.* Singapore: John Wiley.

CHANDLER, A. D., JR. (1962). *Strategy and Structure.* Cambridge, MA: MIT Press.

CHANG, J., KHANNA, T., and PALEPU, K. (2001). "Analyst Activity around the World." Harvard Business School Working Paper.

CHAPMAN, S. (1985). "British-Based Investment Groups before 1914," *Economic History Review,* 38: 230–51.

CHAPMAN, S. (1992). *Merchant Enterprise in Britain.* Cambridge: Cambridge University Press.

CONNELL, C. M. (2004). *A Business in Risk: Jardine Matheson and the Hong Kong Trading Industry.* Westport, CT: Praeger.

FIELDHOUSE, D. K. (1994). *Merchant Capital and Economic Decolonization.* Oxford: Clarendon Press.

GRANOVETTER, M. (1995). "Coase Revisited: Business Groups in the Modern Economy," *Industrial and Corporate Change,* 4: 93–150.

GUILLÉN, M. (2000). "Business Groups in Emerging Economies: A Resource-Based View," *Academy of Management Journal,* 43/3: 362–80.

Harrisons & Crosfield (1944). *One Hundred Years as East India Merchants: Harrisons & Crosfield 1844–1943.* London: the firm.

HENNART, J. F. (1998). "Transaction Cost Theory and the Free-Standing Firm," in M. Wilkins and H. Schröter (eds.), *The Free-Standing Company in the World Economy 1830–1996.* Oxford: Oxford University Press.

HENNART, J. F., and KRYDA, G. M. (1998). "Why do Traders Invest in Manufacturing?" in G. Jones (ed.), *The Multinational Traders.* Routledge: London.

JARDINE MATHESON (1947). *Jardine's and the Ewo Interests.* New York: Charles A. Phelps.

JONES, G. (1993). *British Multinational Banking 1830–1990.* Oxford: Clarendon Press.

JONES, G. (1998). "British Overseas Banks as Free-Standing Companies 1830–1994," in M. Wilkins and H. Schröter (eds.), *The Free-Standing Company in the World Economy, 1830–1996.* Oxford: Oxford University Press.

JONES, G. (2000). *Merchants to Multinationals: British Trading Companies in the Nineteenth and Twentieth Centuries.* Oxford: Oxford University Press.

JONES, G. (2005). *Renewing Unilever: Transformation and Tradition.* Oxford: Oxford University Press.

JONES G., and KHANNA, T. (2006). "Bringing History (back) into International Business," *Journal of International Business Studies*, 37: 453–68.

JONES, G., and WALE, J. (1999). "Diversification Strategies of British Trading Companies: Harrisons & Crosfield, *c.*1900–*c.*1980," *Business History*, 41/2: 69–101.

KESWICK, M. (ed.) (1982). *The Thistle and the Jade*. London: Octopus.

KHANNA, T. (2000). "Business Groups and Social Welfare in Emerging Markets: Existing Evidence and Unanswered Questions," *European Economic Review*, 44/4–6: 748–61.

KHANNA, T., and PALEPU, K. G. (1997). "Why Focused Strategies may be Wrong for Emerging Markets," *Harvard Business Review*, 75/4: 41–51.

KHANNA, T., and PALEPU, K. G. (1999). "Policy Shocks, Market Intermediaries, and Corporate Strategy: The Evolution of Business Groups in Chile and India," *Journal of Economics and Management Strategy*, 8/2: 271–310.

KHANNA, T., and PALEPU, K. G. (2005). "The Evolution of Concentrated Ownership in India: Broad Patterns and the History of the Indian Software Industry', in R. Morck (ed.), *The History of Concentrated Corporate Ownership*. NBER. Chicago: University of Chicago Press, 283–324.

KHANNA, T., and RIVKIN, J. (2000). "Ties that Bind Business Groups: Evidence from an Emerging Economy." Harvard Business School Working Paper Series, No. 00-068, Boston: Harvard Business School Publishing.

KOCK, C., and GUILLÉN, M. F. (2001). "Strategy and Structure in Developing Countries: Business Groups as an Evolutionary Response to Opportunities for Unrelated Diversification," *Industrial and Corporate Change*, 10/1: 77–113.

LA PORTA, R., LOPEZ-DE-SILANES, F., and SHLEIFER, A. (1999). "Corporate Ownership around the World," *Journal of Finance*, 54/2: 471–517.

LE FEVOUR, E. (1968). *Western Enterprise in Late Ch'ing China*. Cambridge, MA: East Asian Research Center.

SHLEIFER, A., and VISHNY, R. W. (1998). *The Grabbing Hand: Government Pathologies and Their Cures*. Cambridge, MA: Harvard University Press.

SUGIYAMA, S. (1987). "A British Trading Firm in the Far East: John Swire & Sons, 1867–1914," in S. Yonekawa and H. Yoshihara (eds.), *Business History of General Trading Companies*. Tokyo: University of Tokyo Press, 1987).

WILKINS, M. (1986). "Defining a Firm: History and Theory," in P. Hertner and G. Jones (eds.), *Multinationals: Theory and History*. Gower: Aldershot.

WILKINS, M. (1988). "The Free-Standing Company, 1870–1914: An Important Type of British Foreign Direct Investment," *Economic History Review*, 41/2: 259–85.

WILLIAMSON, O. M. (1975). *Markets and Hierarchies*. New York: Free Press.

PART II

NATIONAL EXPERIENCES OF BUSINESS GROUPS

Group 1. Asia

CHAPTER 4

....

BUSINESS GROUPS IN PREWAR JAPAN: HISTORICAL FORMATION AND LEGACY

....

HIDEAKI MIYAJIMA
SHINYA KAWAMOTO

4.1 INTRODUCTION

....

THE objective of this chapter is to examine the evolution and economic function of business groups, often referred to as *zaibatsu*, in prewar Japan. Japan is the only country outside Europe and North America to have industrialized successfully before the Second World War. During Japan's industrialization process, business groups emerged as a prominent form of corporate organization.

It should be noted, however, that, in spite of the prominence of the *zaibatsu* as economic actors, the share of business groups in the prewar economy was not as high

We would like to thank Asli Colpan, Takashi Hikino, and Masao Nakamura for helpful suggestions. We also owe a lot to valuable discussions with Julian Franks and Colin Mayer. The database used for this chapter was constructed as part of the Centre of Excellence Programme at the Ministry of Education in Japan. Miyajima has received a science research grant (proj. no. 19203017) from the Japan Society for the Promotion of Science. Kawamoto has received a grant (proj. no. 21730322) from the same organization.

as is often assumed. In fact, when compared to business groups in other developing countries such as Korea or Thailand, in the USA or the UK in the early twentieth century, or in postwar Japan, where bank-centered business groups were predominant, business groups in prewar Japan had a much lower share of overall economic activity. According to the Holding Company Liquidation Commission (HCLC 1951), the largest nine *zaibatsu* accounted for 19 percent of total paid-in capital in 1937, while all business groups accounted for 35 percent of the largest 100 industrial firms (asset base) in the same year. While the share of business groups in an economy will vary depending on definitions of business groups and dates of estimation, their prewar share was also modest when compared to the shares of their counterparts in developing economies (Khanna and Yafeh 2007). In prewar Japan, most large firms operated as stand-alone entities, and most of them were listed on the stock exchange. To put it differently, the prewar Japanese economy was not dominated by business groups, but instead was characterized by the coexistence of business groups and stand-alone (independent) firms.[1]

Prewar business groups are defined as a set of legally independent firms that were wholly or partly owned by a holding company or a parent firm. Family or entrepreneurs, sometimes exclusively, owned the holding or parent company, and kept effective control over group firms. The holding or parent company organized the multi-tiered subsidiary businesses, which commonly diversified into multiple sectors, in either a pyramidal structure (where some of the subsidiary firms were listed) or a hierarchical one (where most of them were unlisted).[2] Although they shared these traits, prewar business groups showed non-trivial differences. Fig. 4.1 is a three-dimensional rendering of the differences in the characteristics of the various types of business groups as reflected in three criteria: whether groups had a holding company at the apex or not, whether the apex and group firms were held privately or publicly, and the extent of diversification. The size of the balloons for each business group type varies to reflect differences in the aggregate percentage shares of the assets of the 100 largest firms in 1937 held by the groups and subsidiary firms within each group category.

The first type of business group (Type I) was comprised of the three established *zaibatsu* (Mitsui, Mitsubishi, and Sumitomo). These were family-controlled pyramidal groups, with private holding companies at their apex and widely diversified subsidiaries ranging from finance and trading to manufacturing and mining. They held the largest share of the assets of the top 100 industrial firms at nearly 19 percent. Type II business groups consisted of the smaller *zaibatsu*, which shared traits with Type I such as family ownership and private holding companies at the apex, but their systems of control were less elaborate. Their group structure was hierarchical in

---

[1] See Shibagaki (1965) and, more recently, Okazaki (1999a, b). Franks et al. (2009) also document the coexistence of business groups and stand-alone firms, focusing on ownership structures.

[2] The term "hierarchical" is employed here to imply a control structure where most of the subsidiaries in a business group are unlisted. Although the term "hierarchical" normally encompasses pyramidal structures with listed subsidiaries, it has been used here to imply non-pyramidal business groups. This division has been necessary to distinguish groups where control is disproportionate to the ownership.

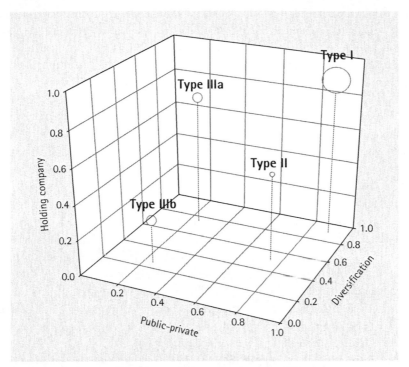

Figure 4.1 Types of business groups in Japan, 1937

Note: The Holding company axis denotes whether groups have a holding company at the apex or not. The *Public-private* axis denotes whether apex and group firms are private or public. The Diversification axis denotes the extent of diversification. The size of the balloons are an indication of the relative difference in percentage shares of the assets of the top 100 industrial firms in 1937 for each business group type.

Sources: The authors' calculations from *Kabushiki kaisha Nenkan*, Toyo Keizal shinposha; *Honpo Jigyo Seiseki Bunseki*; Mitsubishi Economic Research Institute, HCLC (1951) and other sources.

some cases, and their level of diversification was much more modest. The Type II business group share of the assets of the top 100 industrial firms declined dramatically during the interwar period from 16 percent in 1921 to 3 percent in 1937 because of the bankruptcy of some groups. The Type III business groups had publicly held firms at their apex and were led by distinguished entrepreneurs. Among them, Nissan was unique, with a publicly held holding company at its apex with a pyramidal structure (Type IIIa in Fig. 4.1). Nissan had diversified its businesses widely, even though it did not establish financial and trading firms, and had emerged as the third largest business group in 1937 with a 7 percent share of the assets of the top 100 industrial firms. Other corporate groups are categorized as Type IIIb groups, because they shared with Nissan features such as entrepreneurial founders and public ownership but did not have a holding company at their apex. Type IIIb business groups attempted only limited diversification, primarily vertically at high-tech sectors, and thus were often referred to as industrial business groups (establishing a model for the postwar vertical *keiretsu*).[3] Most Type I and II groups can trace their beginnings to the mass privatization drive of the mid-1880s, while Type III groups emerged or expanded in the 1930s against the backdrop of the stock-market boom.

Focusing on the three established *zaibatsu* and Nissan, this chapter examines how business groups evolved in prewar Japan, and what functions they served. To support our analysis, we constructed a micro database on ownership, capital composition, and performance for the prewar period. It is comprised of the 159 manufacturing and mining firms that appeared on the list of the top 100 firms at least once during 1921, 1928, and 1937.

The next section provides an overview of the emergence of prewar business groups. Section 4.3 summarizes the ownership, organization, and business portfolios of the various business group types. Section 4.4 addresses the competitive capabilities of business groups, and the hypothesis put forth in earlier research that emphasizes the positive features of business groups: the scale and scope of economies, the synergy and spillover effects, the financial role of internal markets, and the effective monitoring of subsidiary firms. Section 4.5 examines their negatives traits, including phenomena such as entrenchment and tunneling, and over- and underinvestment. Section 4.6 shows how the various types of business groups affect performance. In the last section, we compare prewar business groups with postwar business groups in Japan as well as with business groups in currently emerging economies.

4.2 EMERGENCE AND EVOLUTION
OF BUSINESS GROUPS

In contrast to the postwar Japanese economy, the prewar Japanese economy was basically liberal and open from the time of the establishment of a modern capitalist system in the Meiji period. Tariffs were generally set very low, which was due partly to the unequal treaties with the developed countries (Japan did not acquire full tariff autonomy until 1911), and partly to a careful consideration of the benefits of trade. Up to the early 1930s, there were few restrictions on inflows and outflows of capital, and foreign direct investment played a crucial role, especially in the high-tech area. A legal framework for corporations had been established and property rights were well protected, but economic activities were only loosely regulated, and there were no regulations explicitly governing the shareholding of firms and banks. A modern corporate law was enacted in 1899, modeled on German civil law. An application of the recent law and finance framework (La Porta et al. 1998) shows that investor protections earn a low score of only one out of a maximum score of six (Franks et al. 2009). Given the relatively liberal economic environment, and limited

---

[3] Among them were the local *zaibatsu*, whose business coverage was limited to a specific geographical area. See Morikawa (1985) for a more detailed description.

investor protections, business groups and publicly held stand-alone firms chose to organize themselves in a variety of ways. Let us begin with a brief overview of the events that are signposts in the evolution of business groups in Japan (outlined in Table 4.1).

4.2.1 Establishment and spurt: Privatization of state-owned firms

Many business groups in prewar Japan can trace their origins to the mass privatization drive that was implemented in the mid-1880s. The new modern factories and facilities that the Meiji government established after the Meiji Restoration frequently encountered operational difficulties and financial troubles. The Minister of Finance, Masayoshi Matsukata, decided to sell off state-owned enterprises (SOEs) in almost all areas except munitions. As a result, coal- and metal-mining companies, machinery manufacturers, and shipbuilding and textiles firms were transferred into private hands. By 1896 the state had privatized twenty-six large SOEs.

The buyers were wealthy families such as the Mitsui, and emerging entrepreneurs such as Iwasaki (later Mitsubishi), Yasuda, Asano, Furukawa, and others. The firms were purchased at prices much lower than their book values.[4] But this was not surprising, because many of the SOEs had performed poorly and were operating at a loss. The families and entrepreneurs that acquired the former SOEs succeeded in bringing them into the black through transfers of business know-how and management skills. As a result of the state's sell-off of SOEs, the *zaibatsu* acquired enterprises that later became cash cows. Mitsui, for example, bought Miike Mining, which became one of its core businesses during its early growth stages, while Mitsubishi acquired Nagasaki Shipyard, and the Takashima and other mining operations, all of which became major profit centers.

4.2.2 Industrialization and the First World War boom, 1890–1919

Japan's modern economic growth began around the turn of the twentieth century.[5] The three established *zaibatsu*—Mitsui, Mitsubishi, and Sumitomo—continued to grow as they entered their next phase of development. Mitsui, whose core businesses were originally in mining, trading, and banking, diversified into businesses ranging from paper to textiles, with the Mitsui Bank playing a leading role. In

---

[4] Mitsubishi (Iwasaki) bought Nagasaki Shipyard, whose book value was 1,130,949 yen, for 459,000 yen. See Kobayashi (1977) and Morck and Nakamura (2007) for more details. Sumitomo was reluctant to purchase SOEs, because it was wary of the political risks.

[5] There is a broad consensus among Japanese economic historians that Japan's industrial revolution began sometime between the 1890s and 1900s. Rostow (1956) also suggests that the takeoff of the Japanese economy into modern economic growth began by 1900, and by 1914 at the latest.

Table 4.1 Evolution of business groups in Japan

Year	Political events	Business group developments
1590		Sumitomo founds copper business
1673		Mitsui opens for business
1868	Meiji Restoration	
1876		Mitsui establishes banking business
1886	Privatization of state-owned Enterprises begins	
1886	Bank of Japan established	
1890	Original Company Law introduced	
		Mitsui Trading and Mitsui Bank (limited partnership) are incorporated
1893		Mitsubishi Company formed after dissolving Mitsubishi partnership
1894–5	Sino-Japanese War	
1895		Mitsubishi enters into banking business through acquisitions
		Sumitomo reorganizes financial business into bank
1899	Commercial Code revised.	
1904–5	Russo-Japanese War/Tax reforms (introduction of income tax created tax advantages for corporations)	
1909		Mitsui Partnership established
1912		Yasuda Partnership established
1914–18	World War I	
1917		Mitsubishi holding company (limited partnership) with spins off former divisions Furukawa Unlimited Partnership established Okura Limited Partnership established
1918		Asano Family Holding Ltd established (reorganization of Asano limited partnership formed in 1914)
1920	Tax reforms (Give advantages to holding companies)	
1921		Sumitomo Limited Partnership established, Furukawa Trading de facto bankruptcy; merges into Furukawa Mining
1923	Kanto Earthquake	
		Suzuki Unlimited Partnership established
1927	Showa Financial Crisis	
		Suzuki Shoten goes bankrupt, Kawasaki Shipbuilding goes bankrupt
1928		Ayukawa organizes Nippon Sangyo
1929	Showa Depression	
1931	Manchurian Incident	
		Furukawa Bank liquidated

Year	Political events	Business group developments
1932	May 15 Incident	
		Hitachi, and Nippon Mining (Nissan Group) go to public
1934	Accounting statement guidelines adopted	
		Mitsubishi Limited Partnership sells Mitsubishi Heavy Industries
		Nippon Soda goes to public
1936	Feb. 26 Incident	
1937	Sino-Japanese War erupts	
		Mitsubishi, Sumitomo Limited Partnership reorganized into joint stock companies.
1938	Enactment of State Mobilization Law and revision of the Commercial Code	
1939	World War II breaks out Corporate Profit Dividend and Capital Distribution Directive promulgated	
1940		Mitsui partnership merges with Mitsui & Co. (trading company)
		Mitsubishi Company holds initial public offering
1941	Asia-Pacific War begins	
1943	Munitions Company Law introduced	
1945	War ends	
1946	Corporate Reorganization Law enacted Holding Company Liquidation Commission Directive promulgated, zaibatsu dissolution begins	
1951	Holding Company Liquidation Commission disbanded (zaibatsu dissolution ends)	

Sources: Morikawa (1992); Hashimoto and Takeda (1992); and other sources.

1895 Mitsubishi added banking to its business portfolio by merging local banks, and it built a vast business group that encompassed a wide variety of businesses ranging from mining and shipbuilding to finance. The Sumitomo *zaibatsu*, whose core businesses were copper mining (Besshi Copper Mining) and banking, began to expand through diversification into related businesses. Sumitomo acquired downstream industries such as copper refiners, processors, and smelters. In this phase, mergers and acquisitions (M&A) played a central role in growth strategies, and the three *zaibatsu* grew steadily. In our rough estimation, the total assets of the three *zaibatsu* in 1914, before the outbreak of the First World War, accounted for 18.3 percent of the aggregate assets of the top 100 industrial firms.[6]

As a result of active diversification, the three *zaibatsu* gradually devised their own group structures, and thus established their business portfolio. Motivated by the tax reform instituted during the 1904–5 Russo-Japanese War (which made the legal entity preferable to personal business and also made the joint stock company preferable to other forms in terms of corporate tax,), in 1909 Mitsui, the largest business group at the time, chose to incorporate its headquarters (Mitsui Omotokata) into a holding company in the form of a legal partnership with limited liabilities, and its first-tier firms into joint stock companies. Mitsubishi followed this organizational innovation in 1918 by spinning off its multidivisional units, while Sumitomo established its holding company in 1921 and spun off its in-house divisions in stages. Other second-rank family groups also established holding companies in 1917 and 1920 (see Table 4.1).

The industrialization process, which was initially driven by the textile, railway, and electricity industries, was given an added fillip with the establishment of heavy industries after the Russo-Japanese War. Following in the footsteps of the three established *zaibatsu* and other family business groups, a second generation of entrepreneurs emerged during this new incorporation boom. Suzuki Shoten, which had originally been established as a sugar merchant, gradually enlarged its business. Nippon Chisso (a chemical firm), and Kuhara Mining, the forerunner of the later Nissan group, were also established in the early 1900s. The First World War provided a big boost to the new entrepreneurial firms, enabling them to expand their business networks further. Particularly active were Suzuki, Kuhara, and Kawasaki, which are often referred to as the "Taisho" (the name of an era from 1912 to 1926) *zaibatsu*. Suzuki, for example, expanded into shipping, iron and steel, and synthetic fiber (Teikoku Rayon), utilizing its huge profits from wartime trading. By 1920 the Suzuki group was almost as large as Mitsui. Kuhara Mining entered into trading (Kuhara Trading), shipping (Nippon Steamship), and shipbuilding (Osaka Iron Works), while the Kuhara group incorporated and spun off its former in-house electric machine division (Hitachi Seisakusho). Table 4.2 shows the number of business group firms and their percentage share of the assets of the top 100 firms in the mining and manufacturing sectors in 1921–42. (The comprehensive list of the largest firms was constructed from Fruin (1992: apps. A1 and A2) for 1918 and 1930, and from the Mitsubishi Research Institute for 1937; see Miyajima et al. (forthcoming) for details of the dataset construction.) In 1921 the three established *zaibatsu* had 9 firms

---

[6] In 1914 Mitsui Gomei had total assets of 78 million yen, Mitsubishi Goshi 49 million yen, and Sumitomo 41 million yen. The assets of their three holding companies were added to the denominator. Note that, since the assets of holding companies include non-manufacturing businesses, this share is not strictly comparable to the data in Table 4.2.

Table 4.2 The proportion of group firms among the largest 100 industrial firms in Japan, 1921–42

Panel A: Number of firms

Business group type	1921	1928	1937	1942
I	9	14	17	13
II	9	7	5	7
III	4	5	8	12
(IIIa)	(3)	(3)	(4)	(5)
(IIIb)	(1)	(2)	(4)	(7)
All types	22	26	30	32

Panel B: Aggregated assets of business groups (million yen)

Business group type	1921	1928	1937	1942
I	543	673	1,482	5,283
II	450	261	250	923
III	165	264	1,068	3,935
(IIIa)	(140)	(177)	(537)	(2,088)
(IIIb)	(24)	(88)	(531)	(1,846)
All types	1,158	1,199	2,800	10,140
100 firms total	2,891	4,441	7,839	20,600

Panel C: Percentage share of top 100 industrial firm assets held by business groups

Business group type	1921	1928	1937	1942
I	18.8	15.2	18.9	25.6
II	15.6	5.9	3.2	4.5
III	5.7	6.0	13.6	19.1
(IIIa)	(4.9)	(4.0)	(6.8)	(10.1)
(IIIb)	(0.8)	(2.0)	(6.8)	(9.0)
All types	40.1	27.0	35.7	49.2
100 firms total	100.0	100.0	100.0	100.0

Notes: This table presents trends in the percentage shares of the top 100 industrial firms held by each type of business group. We constructed a comprehensive list of the largest firms from Appendix A-1 and A-2 in Fruin (1992) for 1918 and 1930, and *Honpo Jigyo Seiseki Bunseki* for 1937. For details on data set construction, see Miyajima *et al.* (forthcoming). Group types correspond to those in Figure 4.1, **Type I** denotes the Mitsui, Mitsubishi, and Sumitomo groups. **Type II** denotes the Yasuda, Furukawa, Okura, Asano, Suzuki, and Kawasaki groups. **Type IIIa** denotes Kuhara and Nissan, and **IIIb** denotes Nihon Chisso, Nihon Soda, Mori, and Riken.

Sources: Mitsubishi Research Institute (annual); Toyo keizai (annual); HCLC (1951); and companies' annual reports.

among the top 100 industrial firms, which accounted for 18.8 percent of the total assets of the top 100, while other types of groups had 13 firms and accounted for a share of 21.3 percent of the top 100 total assets.

4.2.3 Interwar period: The stable growth of the three established *zaibatsu* and the emergence of new *zaibatsu*, 1920–37

The post-First World War boom ended in March 1920, after which the Japanese economy entered into a deflationary period that continued for more than a decade and exerted severe pressure on some family-controlled groups. Suzuki Shoten and Kawasaki Shipbuilding had been highly dependent on leverage for their growth during the First World War, and were hit hard by the economic shock of declining prices and shrinking demand. In 1927 both companies faced serious financial distress and had to be reconstructed under bank control. The family owners were forced to retire, and Suzuki Gomei was dissolved. As a result, the share of Type II groups declined from 15.6 percent in 1921 to 3.2 percent in 1937.

By contrast, the three established *zaibatsu* adhered to a conservative strategy during the deflationary period, and adapted their businesses to shrinking demand by rationalizing their businesses and balance sheets. Although their diversification into manufacturing slowed, they entered other areas of finance, including the trust business and insurance (Hashimoto and Takeda 1992: ch. 2).

After the gold standard had been abolished in December 1931, the Japanese economy rebounded more rapidly than most other countries experiencing the Great Depression. Low interest rates, government fiscal policy, the Manchuria Incident, and a stock-market boom contributed to the early economic recovery. This stock-market boom was exceptional, bucking the global trend of depressed stock markets (Rajan and Zingales 2003). Taking advantage of this economic boom, the three established *zaibatsu* began to turn to external funds for financing in the 1930s, and took their first- and second-tier subsidiary firms public.

But the Type III groups led by new entrepreneurs were even more aggressive in utilizing these favorable macroeconomic conditions. Nissan, Nippon Soda, and Nippon Chisso came to be known as the "new" *zaibatsu*. Their talented entrepreneurs made the decision to expand into high-tech sectors such as electronics, chemical, and aluminum. They enlarged their businesses very rapidly through initial public offerings (IPOs), new seasoned issues, and M&A through exchanges of stock that was highly valued by the stock market. Their growth could indeed be described as stock-market driven. The share of Type III groups increased from 5.7 percent in 1921 to 13.6 percent in 1937.

4.2.4 Expansion of business groups during the Second World War, 1937–45

The growth of business groups was accelerated by the wartime planned economy, which triggered a decentralization of governance structure. The war had a twofold impact on the evolution of business groups. First, government policy influenced the organization and strategy of business groups. Some reformist military officers and government officials were highly critical of shareholders in general, and *zaibatsu* families in particular. The enactment of the State Mobilization Law in 1938 enabled the government to intervene in important corporate decisions. The government used the new law to restrict dividend payments and compensation for firms from 1939. The Munitions Company Law in 1943 made it possible for the government to appoint the chief executive officer (CEO) of designated companies, and to suspend the decision-making of general shareholder meetings if necessary. These procedures gradually restricted the ability of families to exercise effective control over their subsidiary firms (Okazaki 1999a; Hoshi and Kashyap 2001; Miyajima 2004: ch. 6).

Secondly, although anti-*zaibatsu* sentiment was widespread, wartime realities were such that the economy could not operate smoothly without the active involvement of *zaibatsu*-affiliated firms. Consequently, resource allocation by the planning agency tended to give priority to the *zaibatsu*-affiliated firms, especially from 1939. On the other hand, firms had a strong incentive to organize their own networks, because the supply of materials was increasingly constrained, and their systems for distributing resources were efficient. The planned economy provided an advantage to internal transactions (within groups) and put external transactions (through distribution agencies) at a disadvantage, thus serving to promote a slew of M&A, and alliances with other firms (Hashimoto and Takeda 1992: ch. 3; Miyajima 2004: ch. 6).

Consequently, business groups increased their share of the economy. Firms affiliated with the three established *zaibatsu* firms accounted for 25.6 percent of the assets of the top 100 firms in 1942, while the other types of groups also grew rapidly (Table 4.2).[7] The new Type III business groups, whose main businesses were closely tied to wartime demand, also expanded, and strengthened their vertical group networks. Along with existing business groups, other entrepreneur firms (Matsushita Electric and Toyota Motor) and managerial firms (Nippon Iron and Steel, Kanegafuchi Spinning) also began to organize vertical networks. Further, *zaibatsu*-affiliated firms (first- and second-tier firms) also organized their own vertical organizations. For instance, Hitachi, which was a first-tier firm of Nissan, set up its own vertical group network with its main supplier (Shimotani 1993).

Postwar reforms initiated by the General Headquarters (GHQ) of the Supreme Commander of the Allied Powers targeted these expanded business groups. As its main targets, GHQ designated 56 families of 10 *zaibatsu* as well as 83 holding

---

[7] At the end of the war, the four largest and the ten largest *zaibatsu* accounted for 25%, and 35% of paid-in capital respectively (Hadley 1970; Hoshi and Kashyap 2001: 69).

companies—23 pure holding companies and 60 business enterprises with holding company traits. The designated families, holding companies and *zaibatsu* firms, were instructed to transfer their stockholdings to the Holding Companies Liquidation Commission, which liquidated them in sales to the public with strict priority rules. GHQ also dissolved pure holding companies, and banned their future establishment (Article 9 of the Anti-Trust Law). By GHQ's order, the incumbent top managers who had been appointed by the designated holding companies (so-called *zaibatsu* appointees) were thoroughly purged from the business world. Subsequently, young salaried managers were promoted from within the firms to take over their positions. Thus, these postwar reforms gave rise to a highly dispersed ownership structure with insider boards (Hadley 1970; Miyajima 1994).

4.3 STRUCTURE AND STRATEGY

4.3.1 Ownership, capital composition, and governance

4.3.1.1 *Three established* zaibatsu: *Concentrated ownership, low leverage, and strict monitoring*

The three established family-controlled groups had similar ownership, capital, and organizational structures. To illustrate how they were organized, we will examine the structure of Mitsui, the largest *zaibatsu*.

Each of the three established *zaibatsu* had a holding company, organized in the form of a partnership, at its apex. Mitsui Gomei took the form of a partnership with unlimited liability in 1909, while Mitsubishi Goshi followed in 1918 and Sumitomo Goshi in 1921 by forming partnerships with limited liability. The partnerships were comprised exclusively of members of the controlling families. In the Mitsui group, eleven families jointly held the shares of Mitsui Gomei and were not allowed to sell them. The partnership form was maintained until the inheritance and dividend income tax was revised in 1937, forcing the group to reorganize its partnership into a joint stock company.[8] In spite of the dominance of family members on the board of directors of the holding company, the three established *zaibatsu* delegated professional managers (*riji*) to run their holding companies.[9] The members of its professional board of directors were usually recruited from its first-tier subsidiaries (Bank, Trading Co., and Mining), so that they had sufficient knowledge of subsidiary operations.

---

[8] See Morck and Nakamura (2005) for a brief summary and Morikawa (1992) for a detailed description. The Mitsubishi holding company raised capital from the public for the first time in 1940.

[9] This delegation could be traced back to the early Edo period (seventeenth century) for Mitsui and Sumitomo.

Table 4.3 Ownership structure and capital composition of business groups in Japan, 1921–37

Panel A: Ownership structure

Business group type	Year	N	C1		C5	
			Mean	Std. dev	Mean	Std. dev.
I	1928	13	0.655	0.301	0.831	0.274
	1937	16	0.400	0.202	0.607	0.196
II	1928	7	0.378	0.331	0.624	0.347
	1937	5	0.334	0.301	0.514	0.356
III	1928	5	0.310	0.262	0.526	0.309
	1937	8	0.408	0.326	0.526	0.289
Stand-alone	1928	70	0.123	0.159	0.235	0.194
	1937	63	0.140	0.177	0.256	0.190

Panel B: Capital composition; debt–asset ratio, 1921–37

Business group type	N	Mean	t-value	Std. dev.	F-value
I	202	0.327	2.179**	0.168	1.526***
II	122	0.462	−5.162***	0.187	1.229
III	86	0.391	−1.330	0.137	2.291***
All types	410	0.381	−1.731*	0.177	1.366***
Stand-alone	1,183	0.361	·	0.207	·

Notes: Panel A describes the ownership structure, using a sample smaller than the top 100 industrial firms due to data availability. C1 is the percentage share held by the largest shareholder, C5 is the cumulative percentage share held by the five largest shareholders. The definition of business group types is based on Figure 4.1. Panel B describes the capital composition. The statistical significance of the difference of means and standard deviations between business groups and stand-alone firms are also reported. Significance at the 10%, 5%, and 1% level are indicated by *, **, and *** respectively.

Sources: Mitsubishi Research Institute (annual); Toyo Keizai (annual); HCLC (1951); and companies' annual reports.

The ownership structure of the subsidiary was designed to ensure that it remained under the exclusive control of the holding company. Banks and other financial institutions were the exception, however. The controlling families were aware of the quasi-public traits of such companies, and thus allowed them to go public at an early stage. However, the other manufacturing and mining firms that were spun off in the 1910s and 1920s were initially owned exclusively by their holding companies. These firms did not go public until the 1930s, and even then the holding companies carefully maintained majority control through cross-shareholdings among group firms. Of the thirteen firms of Type I groups, the average percentage share held by the largest shareholder (C1), which is in fact identical to the share held by the holding company, was 65.5 percent in 1928 and 40.0 percent in 1937 respectively (Table 4.3, Panel A). The cumulative share held by the five largest shareholders (C5) accounted for 83.1 percent of all shares in 1928 and still for 60.7 percent in 1937. As long as the business group firms of the "big three" were less reliant on financing from the public, the wedge between control rights and cash-flow rights remained relatively small.

The capital structure of the first-tier firms in the established three shows that they relied on a low level of leveraging. The families of the three *zaibatsu* had a strong preference for a healthy capital composition, so the average debt–asset ratio of group firms was significantly lower than that of stand-alone firms (Table 4.3, Panel B). The average debt–asset ratio of the fourteen first- and second-tier firms of the three established *zaibatsu* (Type I) in 1921–37 was 32.7 percent, which was comparable to the 36.1 percent of stand-alone firms, but considerably lower than the 46 percent plus for firms in Type II groups. In Miyajima and Kawamoto (2010) we show the estimated results, which regressed the debt–asset ratio for the top 100 firms on some control variables (size, capital intensity, year dummy) and for a *zaibatsu* dummy to avoid possible bias caused by other factors that affected the debt–asset ratio. We find that in Type I (the established three) the group dummy is significantly negative, and the estimated coefficient suggests that their debt–asset ratio is 5.5 percent lower than that of stand-alone firms. This result suggests that the characteristics of business groups affected their capital decisions.

Given these ownership and capital structures, the corporate governance of the three established *zaibatsu* was characterized by the strict monitoring of subsidiary firms by the holding company. Applying standard terminology of agency theory, we can describe the investment projects of each subsidiary as being initiated by professional managers, whose proposed projects were then ratified by the holding company after it had considered the financial implications. After obtaining ratification by the holding company, the top management of the first-tier firms implemented the investment projects. The holding company would then evaluate the performance of the projects, and take necessary action if performance was substantially lower than originally planned.

We would like to point out two aspects of the relationship between the holding company and subsidiaries. On the one hand, the top managers of each subsidiary were guaranteed a greater degree of autonomy compared to that afforded to them in their former multidivisional organizations. With the provision of legal status to the former divisions, the discretion or autonomy (in the sense of Burkart et al. 1997) of salaried managers was substantially enhanced.

On the other hand, ratification by the holding company was not a mere rubber stamp, but rather a substantive process. On occasions, the holding company overruled or modified projects proposed by professional managers, as was the case with Sumitomo Fertilizer's plans to enter into the ammonia/nitrogen fertilizer sector in the late 1920s. The top management of this company initiated an adventurous investment plan with an eye to economies of scale. However, its holding company, Sumitomo Goshi, strictly vetted the plan, and encouraged Fertilizer to modify it to reduce the technological risks. The plan that was ultimately implemented was based upon the introduction of technology from a foreign partner with a cost that far exceeded the original budget, so the holding company criticized the top manager of Fertilizer, and finally dismissed him. Sumitomo Goshi did not approve subsequent investment plans during the Showa Depression either, insisting that any investments should be suspended under such uncertain conditions (Hashimoto and Takeda 1992:

120: Miyajima 2004: 187). This example shows that real authority, as this concept is used by Aghion and Tirole (1997), was wielded by the holding company.

As illustrated by the above example, the main tools for wielding control over first-tier firms were personnel appointments, and the allocation of financial resources. The CEO of the first-tier firm was appointed by the holding company; CEOs were often rotated among subsidiary firms. Personnel management was fully centralized in the established three.[10] On the other hand, the holding company also exercised strict financial control over affiliated firms. Budgets, settlements, and dividend payments required ratification from the holding company. Affiliated firms were also required to submit detailed financial statements to the holding company every half year. Investment plans that exceeded internal funding capacity required ratification by the holding company, so the top management of the first-tier firms did not have autonomy over capital decisions. Furthermore, it is documented that, at Mitsubishi, temporal surpluses associated with operations were deposited at the holding company during the 1920s (Asajima 1986). Such strict financial controls may have enabled the holding company to mitigate the free cash-flow problem at subsidiary firms.

4.3.1.2 *Nissan and other groups*

Unlike the three established *zaibatsu* (Type I), the medium-sized family groups (Type II) did not have well-organized holding companies, and were less likely to delegate professional managers to operate group firms. Since these families had a strong incentive to maintain at least a controlling majority over their subsidiaries, they tended to raise funds through external sources in the form of debt; consequently, their organization was sometimes a hierarchical structure rather than a pyramid (see Table 4.4). Panel B of Table 4.3 shows that the debt–asset ratio of Type II firms was significantly higher than that of Type I and stand-alone firms.

Nissan was a unique business group in prewar Japan because the holding company at its apex was publicly held, and it had a highly dispersed ownership structure. Kuhara Mining, the forerunner of Nissan, already had 14,277 shareholders in 1921, with a C5 of 36.1 percent. In 1926 Kuhara Mining faced financial difficulties because of failed speculation in a trading business that was newly established during the First World War. Fusanosuke Kuhara asked his brother-in-law, Yoshisuke Ayukawa, to take over as CEO of this company. His basic scheme for drastic corporate restructuring was to establish Nippon Mining as the new operating company and to transfer Kuhara Mining's fixed assets to Nippon Mining through exchange of stock. Kuhara Mining, which had now become a pure holding company, changed its name to Nippon Sangyo (Nissan is its abbreviation).

Ayukawa (1934) had a clear strategy that viewed the holding company as a vehicle for raising money from public investors. The Nissan group, whose size was modest at

---

[10] See Morikawa (1980) for Mitsui, Asajima (1986) for Mitsubishi, and Asajima (1987) for the three *zaibatsu*. Miyajima (2004: ch. 4) also provides a brief description. Kawamoto and Miyajima (2008) show that the turnover of presidents of *zaibatsu* firms was less sensitive to corporate performance compared to stand-alone firms, suggesting that holding companies rotated top managers among their group firms.

Table 4.4 Diversification of business groups in Japan, 1890–1937

Business group type	Business group name	Structure	Mining	Food	Fiber	Metal	Paper	Cement	Chemicals	Shipyard	Electric machines	Automobile	Aircraft	Real estate, Warehouse	Trading	Shipping	Bank	Insurance
I	Mitsui	P	○	○	○	○	△		○	○	○			○	○	○	○	○
	Mitsubishi	P	○	○	○	○	○	○	○	○	○			○	○	△	○	○
	Sumitomo	P	○			○		○	○		●		○	○			○	○
II	Yasuda	P	×						○		○			○	×		○	○
	Furukawa	P	○			○			○		○			○	○		×	
	Okura	H	○	×		○											×	
	Asano	P				○		○	○		○			○	○			○
	Suzuki	P	○	○		○				○	○			○	○	○		
	Kawasaki	H				○			○	○	○			○		○	○	○
IIIa	Nissan	P	○	●		●			●		●	●	○	○	×			
IIIb	Nippon Chisso	H			○				○									
	Nippon Soda	P		●		●			○									
	Mori	P		●		●			○		●							
	Riken	H				●					●							

This table presents the business portfolios of business groups around 1937. P in column Structure denotes that multi tiered subsidiary firms were largely listed and organized pyramidically. H denotes that multi tiered subsidiary firms were basically unlisted and organized hierarchically. This notation is roughly based on the structure in 1937, except Suzuki and Kawasaki. ○ denotes that group firms entered into this sector before 1930. ● denotes that a group entered into this sector after 1930. △ denotes that group firms in the sector became independent because holding company sold their holding stocks. × denotes group exit from this sector due to low performance (financial distress) before 1937. Group affiliation is basically identified if a majority (over 50%) of shares was held by the holding company and other group firms. The business portfolios and structure of the Suzuki and Kawasaki groups present their profiles around 1927 just prior to their bankruptcies.

Sources: Hashimoto and Takeda (1992); Kikkawa (1996); Okazaki (1999b); Udagawa (1984); and others.

the end of 1920s, grew rapidly through M&A and IPOs in the 1930s, in tandem with the stock-market boom. In 1932 Nissan decided to hold IPOs for its subsidiaries (Hitachi and Nippon Mining), while Nissan itself also issued new stock for the purpose of investing in existing subsidiaries and acquiring firms in new areas such as foods, chemicals, and fisheries (Wada 1937; Udagawa 1984).

As a result, the ownership structure of Nissan in 1937 was completely dispersed, with 51,804 shareholders, and a C5 of 7.2 percent, while Ayukawa held only 3.1 percent of Nissan shares. Nissan as a holding company had a majority stake in its first-tier firms, which in turn held a controlling majority in the second-tier firms. In this sense, the Nissan group was publicly financed and its pyramidal structure was accompanied by a large wedge between control rights and cash-flow rights (Morck and Nakamura 2005). Nissan exercised less control over subsidiary firms and had a more decentralized structure than the three established *zaibatsu*.

4.3.2 Group structure and business portfolio

4.3.2.1 *Three established* zaibatsu

Table 4.4 illustrates the group structure and the business portfolios of groups in 1937. Using the pyramidal structure, the three established *zaibatsu* diversified into almost all sectors except textiles. They all had influential banks, insurance companies, and mining firms in their first tier. Mitsui and the Mitsubishi group also had their general trading firms.[11] These first-tier firms formed the core of each group, and were highly profitable cash cows for most of the prewar period. Obviously, the banking, trading, and mining companies operated in unrelated sectors, so diversification contributed to the stabilization of *zaibatsu* profitability as a whole.

On the other hand, once these first-tier core companies had been spun off around the time of the First World War, they become the main drivers of further diversification. For instance, one of the most active players was the general treading company Mitsui & Co., which founded a shipbuilding company in 1917, purchased an iron and steel firm in 1924, and established Toyo Rayon to enter into synthetic textiles in 1926. In 1937 Mitsui & Co. held a majority stake in twenty-two subsidiaries and held 76.3 million yen in securities, which accounted for 13.9 percent of total assets (HCLC 1951; Mitsui Bunko 1994).

After the First World War, the first-tier firms diversified mainly into related fields, and did so through internal growth rather than through M&A. For instance, the mining companies of the big three *zaibatsu* diversified into chemicals (dyestuffs or fertilizers), using their knowledge of coal mining, and spun-off companies. Mitsubishi Shipbuilding spun out its former in-house electric machine division in an alliance with Westinghouse, and entered into the aviation sector, using its engine technology. In the 1920s, the three established *zaibatsu* hardly ever merged with or

---

[11] Sumitomo had its sales division within its holding company, which was spun off during the postwar *zaibatsu* dissolution program.

acquired other firms, except when they were involved in restructuring efforts. The low level of M&A activity can be attributed to the limited supply of potential targets in the new high-tech industries, and concerns about the organizational costs associated with mergers and acquisitions. The *zaibatsu* firms had elaborate promotion and training systems, which enabled them gradually to accumulate organizational assets, so they may have been reluctant to acquire other firms that could bring high adjustment costs.

4.3.2.2 *Nissan and other groups*

In both smaller family groups (Type II) and new business groups (Type III), with either a pyramidal or a hierarchical structure of group firms, the scope of diversification was relatively narrow, as shown in Table 4.4. Some business groups diversified primarily into finance (Yasuda), and others (Suzuki, Kawasaki, and Nippon Chisso) did not have their own financial institutions, but some (Furukawa and Asano) entered into these businesses only to fail. Furukawa diversified its business from copper into wiring and electronics. Kawasaki entered iron and steel, and aviation, using its windfall earnings during the First World War. In all these cases, the diversification was directed toward related areas.

Among the Type II and III groups, Nissan was unique in its decision to adopt an unrelated diversification strategy. Ayukawa (1934) thought that one of the advantages of establishing a holding company system was the ability to stabilize profits (see also Morck and Nakamura 2007). He also strongly believed that businesses that catered to the lifestyles of the expanding middle class had tremendous potential. His belief prompted Nissan to enter into the automobile field as well as to establish the largest fishery and seafood processing firm (Nippon Suisan) through M&As. As a result, Nissan became the third largest group in Japan in 1937, with first- and second-tier firms in mining, manufacturing, distribution, and insurance.

4.4 COMPETIVIVE CAPABILITIES OF PREWAR BUSINESS GROUPS

4.4.1 Scale and scope of economy: Synergy and spillover

Given the unique characteristics of prewar business groups described above, what kind of competitive capabilities did they bring to the table? And what role did they play in spurring economic growth in Japan?

First, as first movers, the *zaibatsu* possessed managerial skill, know-how, accounting standards, and monitoring systems that provided them with real advantages,

given the imperfections in the managerial, labor, and capital markets.[12] At the
beginning of Japanese industrialization, the *zaibatsu* sustained a dominant position
in their core businesses. This dominance made it possible for them to collect large
quasi-monopolistic rents, enabling them to rely on their internal capital markets to
innovate continuously. Furthermore, the sustained profits provided job security and
relatively high compensation to corporate insiders, and allowed them to invest in
firm-specific human capital. These factors enabled the *zaibatsu* to become major
technology innovators (Odagiri and Goto 1996).

Mitsui Mining's entry into the dyestuffs market illustrates how the *zaibatsu* used
their advantages. In the prewar period, the dyestuffs market had been dominated by
German oligopoly firms (later merged into IG Farben). Once the First World War
had erupted, and imports had stopped, the price of dyestuffs soared. However,
dyestuffs were considered high-tech goods at the time, and dyestuff patents were
monopolized by the German oligopoly. Mitsui Mining's resources, however, allowed
it to provide substitutes for foreign imports (Miyajima 2004: ch. 3).

Secondly, given serious market imperfections in the prewar era, business groups,
and especially general trading companies, filled a crucial role. Mitsui & Co. was the
sole sales agent of Mitsui Mining, and helped to increase the volume of coal sales and
to reduce transaction costs. The company also helped group firms to introduce new
technology from foreign firms, lowering the cost of searching for technology, and
intermediating transactions between foreign and groups firms. Furthermore, Mitsui
& Co. played a significant role in importing cotton-spinning machines from Pratt
Brothers, for example. It arranged technology deals, not only for firms within the
Mitsui group but also for other spinning firms, and also played an intermediary role
in supplying locomotives to railways and chemical machines for nitrogen production. The activities of trading firms such as Mitsui & Co. had a positive influence on
group firms as well as on the economy as a whole.[13]

Thirdly, the trust and reputations that were built during the growth stage were also
important to their competitiveness. Around 1900 the word *zaibatsu* began to be used
in journalism to refer to the family groups as a way of acknowledging their unique-
ness and dominance. But the name of each *zaibatsu* also began to acquire its own
brand value. The brand name provided strong advantages in their businesses under
imperfect market conditions, as emphasized in Khanna and Yafeh (2007). When
foreign companies sought to invest directly in Japan by alliance or joint ventures,
Mitsui, Mitsubishi, Sumitomo, and Furukawa were among the handful of firms that
could be trusted without having to invest in substantial search and monitoring costs.
For ordinary transactions, goods supplied by Mitsui & Co. were considered reliable

[12] The *zaibatsu* recruited top managers and technicians with high salaries, which might have affected
the allocation of talent, and possibly discouraged talented people from seeking careers in government
(Morikawa 1980: 16–19). On the other hand, by the turn of the century at the latest, the *zaibatsu* had
become a supplier of managerial talent (Hashimoto and Takeda 1992: ch. 1).

[13] Morck and Nakamura (2007) emphasize that *zaibatsu* served to provide a Big Push, and were a
substitute for active government industrial policies by the First World War.

and trustworthy. Furthermore, the enhanced brand value of *zaibatsu* also provided them with an advantage in recruiting talented employees.

The *zaibatsu* carefully managed their brand names to maintain their reputations. For example, the Mitsui Group bestowed the Mitsui name on its first-tier firms, but gave the name Toyo to second-tier firms engaged in riskier businesses. Even dividend payments to minority shareholders were used to burnish the brand name. Mitsubishi Mining, which was one of the first *zaibatsu* firms to go public at the beginning of 1920s, earned very low profits and only a 3–4 percent return on equity from 1921 to 1924. Though Mitsubishi Goshi, the holding company of the Mitsubishi, held 58 percent of Mitsubishi Mining stock, it declined to receive dividends, even though Mitsubishi Mining continued to pay out the same level of dividends to other shareholders (Miyajima 2004: ch. 5). By maintaining their trust and reputations, the *zaibatsu* could benefit in other ways, such as by earning premiums on new share issues (Franks et al. 2009).[14]

4.4.2 Internal capital markets

Business groups in prewar Japan also possessed another competitive capability: an advantage in capital allocation. It is commonly understood that internal capital markets played a significant role under market imperfections (Khanna and Yafeh 2007). In the case of prewar Japan, massive investment and new entries into the high-technology sectors were supported by the internal capital markets of business groups (Takeda 1993; Okazaki 1999b). For the three established *zaibatsu*, internal capital markets were particularly important during the early phase of industrialization. They invested their high profits from mining (a cash-cow sector) into growth sectors such as chemicals and electric machinery.

In the 1920s, outsider money was not often channeled to firms (divisions) with high growth opportunities, because the holding company imposed a strict budget constraint on its subsidiaries. In the 1930s, however, the three established *zaibatsu* decided to allow their first-tier firms to go public, so internal capital markets began to play a role in reallocating funds that had been raised externally. The three *zaibatsu* firms could raise capital for subsidiary firms through rights issues. The holding company paid the face value of the stock to the subsidiary and then sold the shares to the public at a higher offer price. For example, shares were created in Mitsubishi Heavy Industries in August 1934 with a face value of 50 yen per share. The shares were then sold to the public for 65 yen. This premium was used for donations, responding to the soaring anti-*zaibatsu* sentiment in the early 1930s, and only a limited portion of it

---

[14] Another reason for their high reputation is that *zaibatsu* were regarded as having good monitoring capabilities. In the late 1920s, when some firms with dispersed ownership and interlocking directorships faced financial distress, *zaibatsu*-affiliated firms continued to turn in stable performances. Observers at the time criticized firms with dispersed ownership and interlocking outside directors, and recommended that small investors should invest in *zaibatsu*-related firms (Takahashi 1930; Okazaki 1999b).

was used to purchase newly issued shares of group firms (Takeda 1993). In sum, the mechanism for channeling external funds to affiliated firms suggested by Morck and Nakamura (2005) was rarely tapped by the three established *zaibatsu*.

4.4.2.1 *Supplying patient capital and risk sharing*

The three established *zaibatsu* also played an important role as a supplier of "patient capital" during business downturns. After the First World War boom had ended, most firms that had entered growth sectors such as shipbuilding, mining, iron and steel, and chemicals faced financial troubles under serious international competition, and had to reconstruct their businesses. Some stand-alone firms went bankrupt, and others were downsized. Even within the three established *zaibatsu*, there were serious internal arguments over whether to continue with the new businesses. For example, Asahi Glass, which had entered into soda ash (Solvey Methode) production, faced serious competition from international giants (later integrated into Imperial Chemical Industries) after the First World War had ended, and considered leaving this market. However, Asahi Glass decided to continue the business, and even added investment to achieve the minimum optimal plant size. Similar scenarios unfolded in the iron and steel (Mitsubishi and Mitsui) and dyestuffs (Mitsui) markets in the 1920s (Miyajima 2004: ch. 2).

4.4.2.2 *Channeling external funds to growth sectors*

On the other hand, Type II and III groups utilized both internal and external capital markets on a large scale to exploit new business opportunities. During the First World War, Type II business groups raised loans externally and distributed the funds to group firms through internal markets. For instance, Suzuki Shoten and Kawasaki Shipbuilding invested their high profits in new industries, in combination with new money raised through borrowing (Tsurumi 1974).

In the 1930s, Type III groups, and Nissan in particular, actively turned to the external market, using the proceeds from new share issues to invest in new businesses. For instance, Nissan sold shares in its first-tier firms (Hitachi and Nippon Mining) and invested the new money in the automobile industry. Since even the smallest automobile plant had to be quite large to optimize output, this industry could not be entered into without a large amount of premium. Thus, Nissan assumed a role in Japan's development that resembled that of venture capital firms in the United States (Morck and Nakamura 2005: 397).

Nissan also used its internal capital market and its reputation to engage in M&A and IPOs. Ayukawa regarded food-related businesses as a growth area, and looked for appropriate targets in the early 1930s. Nissan purchased the Nippon Ice Companies, a listed company, through exchange of stocks (Wada 1937). After reconstructing the business, Nissan spun off the firm as a separate legal entity, and let it go public through an IPO at a substantial premium. In this case, it played the role that buyout firms fill today.

4.5 COST OF PREWAR BUSINESS GROUPS

4.5.1 Underinvestment by strict monitoring

Prewar business groups also exacted costs. One of these costs was excessively strict monitoring of subsidiaries (mainly first-tier firms) by the holding company. This cost, which is common to monitoring by large shareholders, as Shleifer and Vishny (1997) suggest, applied mainly to the three established *zaibatsu* (Type I) groups.

When a holding company exercises strict monitoring and applies a hard budget constraint on its subsidiaries, the investment level of its firms is likely to be lower than that of stand-alone firms, especially during business upturns. It has been documented that the investments of Mitsubishi Shipbuilding were much more modest than those of other shipbuilders during the First World War, and the investments of both Mitsui and Mitsubishi Mining in the 1930s were also much more modest than their industrial rivals (Morikawa 1980; Hashimoto and Takeda 1992; Miyajima 2004: ch. 4). Their reluctance to enter into high-tech industries such as chemicals and automobiles is further evidence of their conservatism. In spite of frequent urging by the government and military authorities, the three established *zaibatsu* decided not to enter those industries (Morikawa 1980). In general, the professional managers of subsidiary firms were seemingly hesitant to initiate risky investment projects, in the light of strict monitoring and a desire not to be overruled by the holding company.

Miyajima (2004: ch. 5) estimates the standard investment function for testing whether internal funds and default risks (proxied by the debt–asset ratio) constrained the investment of groups firms.[15] Although the results are highly tentative because of limitations in the availability and reliability of data, the investments of three *zaibatsu* firms were much more sensitive to cash flow than those of other firms. Miyajima also found that the investments of the three *zaibatsu* firms were much more negatively sensitive to debt–asset levels. Higher leverage was likely to produce lower investment than in stand-alone firms. Overall, the results are consistent with the understanding that the group firms of the three *zaibatsu* were constrained by their internal funds and capital structure.

4.5.2 Entrenchment, tunneling, and overinvestment

Prewar business groups in Japan were also accompanied by other costs, including the tunneling and overinvestment effects that are part and parcel of business groups around the world (Morck *et al.* 2005).

---

[15] Using sixty-eight large firms as a sample, Miyajima (2004) estimates the investment behavior of firms in the 1920s and 1930s. Since most *zaibatsu* firms were not listed, the real growth rate of sales (or revenues) was used as a proxy for business opportunity.

In general, the pyramidal structure of business groups entrenched the controlling families or entrepreneurs, shielding them from outside investors, and leading to various forms of tunneling, such as excessive compensation, loan guarantees, dilutive share issues, insider trading, and other financial transactions that discriminated against minority shareholders (Johnson *et al.* 2000). Tunneling in this sense was observed in prewar business groups. For example, there was a considerable amount of price discrimination in the new issues among the three established *zaibatsu*.[16] However, tunneling was not a serious issue among them, because the ownership structure of Type I groups was highly concentrated, and debt was used carefully as a financial resource.

Tunneling was much more severe in Type II and III business groups, however. A typical case was the Suzuki group, whose holding company, Suzuki Gomei, used subsidiary assets (Kobe Steel and Teikoku Rayon) as loan collateral. When Suzuki Gomei went bankrupt in 1927, these two firms were under bank control. Another example involved high dividend payments from subsidiary firms to the holding company. Furukawa Electric Metal paid over 70 percent of its earnings as dividends to Furukawa Gomei (the holding company), which used the dividends to compensate losses at its trading businesses. The pyramidal structure of family-owned business groups made it possible to entrench managers away from the pressure of outside investors or effective monitors, and induced overinvestment, or asset substitution. This was often the case for Type II groups, and their overinvestment was supported by their exclusive relationship with banks (the so-called organ bank system).

The de facto bankruptcies of Suzuki and Kawasaki were glaring examples of the *zaibatsu* dysfunction. They faced serious financial trouble when the wartime boom ended. However, instead of launching early efforts to reconstruct their businesses, both companies adjusted their balance sheets through additional borrowing from related banks (often called organ banks). The Suzuki and Kawasaki groups had close ties with the Taiwan Bank and the Dai Jugo (Number 15 National) Bank respectively. Since these banks were heavily committed to both companies, they could not withdraw their loans, and instead supplied additional loans, even though both banks were aware that drastic balance-sheet improvements were essential. The lack of a credible threat induced morally hazardous behavior in both companies typical of soft budget constraint situations. Finally, these firms and their banks went bankrupt in the financial crisis of 1927.

Miyajima (2004: ch. 5) supports the understanding that Type II and III groups are likely to be entrenched from outside investors. It reports that the investments of either Type II or III business groups or firms with high managerial ownership are less sensitive to internal funds, and, somewhat surprisingly, positively sensitive to the debt–asset ratio in the 1920s. The lower sensitivity to cash flow in the 1920s indicates that Type II and III group firms tended to invest more (or even to undertake a discretionary re-evaluation of their fixed assets), whereas the positive sensitivity of investment to the debt–asset ratio implies that these family firms tended to invest (or re-evaluate their assets) more when their leverage

---

[16] Franks et al. (2009) document the price discrimination in the case of Toyo Rayon, a second-tier subsidiary of the Mitsui *zaibatsu*.

was high. In sum, there is some evidence that some types of Japanese business groups tended to overinvest because of entrenchment from appropriate outside monitors.

4.6 PERFORMANCE OF BUSINESS GROUPS IN PREWAR JAPAN

As mentioned earlier, business groups in prewar Japan, like those of other countries, had both positive and negative traits. We have examined whether the positive traits outweighed, or were overwhelmed by, the negative ones, and identified the differences in performance between the three types of business groups.[17]

Panels A and B of Table 4.5 summarize the performance (ROE and annual asset growth rate ΔA) of business groups and stand-alone firms from 1920 to 1937. The ROE of group firms was not higher than that of stand-alone firms, while group firms showed significant rapid growth in Panel B. This result is also supported by the conditional estimates in Miyajima and Kawamoto (2010), where ROE and the annual growth rate of assets are regressed on a group dummy, and an industry and year dummy. Even when we include size (assets) and the debt–asset ratio in the estimation, all dummy types still had no effect.

However, interestingly, when we divided business groups into three types, we found significant differences in performance between them. First, the ROE and annual growth rate of the three established *zaibatsu* (Type I) groups are at almost the same level as those of stand-alone firms. These results are also supported by the conditional estimates (Miyajima and Kawamoto 2010). Note that the results are not contrary to the understanding that Type I firms performed better, because ROE is significantly positively correlated to firm size and negatively to leverage in the prewar period, and they were already dominant and had a healthier capital composition at the beginning of the interwar period. The results just show that there is no evidence that group affiliation had any actual effect on their performance except in terms of economies of scale or capital cost advantages.

Second, Type II groups were low performers, while Type III groups were high performers in terms of both ROE and annual growth rates of assets (Table 4.5). This result remains unchanged after considering other control variables. According to Miyajima and Kawamoto (2010), ROE and the annual growth rate of Type III is 2.4 percent and 12.1 percent higher than that of stand-alone firms respectively. Business groups with a public apex and entrepreneurs performed better during the interwar

---

[17] Although the sample coverage, estimation period, and definition of *zaibatsu* vary, Frankl (1999) reports that new *zaibatsu* had high growth rates, while Okazaki (2001) shows that the *zaibatsu* performed relatively better than stand-alone firms. Miyajima et al. (forthcoming) expected but could not find high performance of *zaibatsu* firms, while reporting the U-shape of managerial ownership and performance.

Table 4.5 Performance indexes and business groups in Japan, 1921–37

Panel A: ROE

Business group type	N	Mean	t-value	Std. dev.	F-value
I	202	0.072	0.044	0.072	1.845***
II	122	0.056	1.729*	0.111	0.774**
III	86	0.089	−1.500	0.069	1.989***
All types	410	0.071	0.299	0.086	1.305***
Stand-alone	1,183	0.073	·	0.098	·

Panel B: Asset growth

Business group type	N	Mean	t-value	Std. dev.	F-value
I	202	0.090	−1.308	0.216	1.108
II	122	0.040	1.309	0.170	1.790***
III	86	0.185	−4.491***	0.324	0.491***
All types	410	0.095	−2.093**	0.236	0.923
Stand-alone	1,183	0.067	·	0.227	·

Panel C: Performance variability (ROE) by periods

Year	All types	I	II	III	Stand-alone
1921–7	0.095	0.090	0.104	0.078	0.113
N	148	59	63	26	515
1928–32	0.082	0.046	0.128	0.067	0.097
N	125	68	34	23	346
1933–7	0.058	0.047	0.078	0.045	0.050
N	137	75	25	37	322
1921–37	0.086	0.072	0.111	0.069	0.098
N	410	202	122	86	410

Notes: Panel A and B show the average of ROE and annual growth rates of assets between stand-alone and group firms from 1921–37. The definitions of group types are the same as Figure 4.1. The statistical significance of the difference of means and the variance deviations between business groups and stand-alone firms are also reported. Significance at the 10%, 5%, and 1% levels are indicated by *, **, and *** respectively. Panel C reports the standard deviation of ROE by sub-periods. Bold denotes when the null hypothesis that variance of performance for each group is the same as that of stand-alone firms is rejected at the 10% significance level.

Sources: Mitsubishi Research Institute (annual); Toyo Keizai (annual); companies' annual reports.

period. Accordingly, the low effect of all business groups on ROE is a result of the high ROE of Type III groups being offset by the low ROE of Type II. Furthermore, the high growth rates of business groups that have been observed apply primarily to Type III groups.

Table 4.5 also tests whether business groups had a stabilizing effect of performance. It is clear that business groups, especially the three established *zaibatsu* (Type I) groups, were associated with low variance of ROE compared to stand-alone firms. Statistical tests in Panel A of Table 4.5 support this difference in variance at the 1 percent significance level. This is the same pattern that was observed for the postwar period (Yafeh 2003) and for business groups in other emerging economies (Khanna and Yafeh 2005). According to Panel C, where the interwar period is divided into three subperiods (from the collapse of the boom to the financial crisis of 1921–7; the Showa Crisis period of 1928–32; and the boom period of 1933–7), the stabilizing effect of groups on performance was remarkable in the deflationary period rather than in the boom period. During the Showa Crisis Type I groups most clearly performed such a stabilizing function. This stability might be partly due to the result of risk sharing among group firms, but, in our understanding, was mainly caused by the strict monitoring of affiliated firms by the holding company. Other types of business groups, especially Type II, did not have such a stabilizing effect, and rather showed high variance in ROE (Type II) and growth rates (Type III).

4.7 WHAT ARE THE UNIVERSAL AND THE UNIQUE CHARACTERISTICS OF PREWAR BUSINESS GROUPS?

Business groups in prewar Japan shared common features with those of other countries in the sense that they were family owned, and had pyramidal or hierarchical structures with highly diversified business portfolios. They emerged as a response to market failures in the industrialization process. They also reaped advantages from internal markets, while they shared negative traits such as the entrenchment of managers beyond the reach of outside investors. Prewar business groups, especially the three established *zaibatsu*, showed a low variance in performance, which was also common to the postwar period. What, then, are the unique characteristics of the prewar business groups that are relevant to both postwar Japanese and emerging economies?

One of the characteristics of prewar business groups is the diversity of internal structures and behaviors, as illustrated by the three types introduced in this chapter. This organizational diversity distinguished them from the postwar bank-centered business groups, whose structures and behaviors were homogeneous, partly because of the economic reforms of the postwar period and subsequent regulations.

The three established *zaibatsu* (Type I), which were the first movers, assumed a dominant position among business groups in prewar Japan. Their structure was relatively similar to family firms in the European continent, in that they delegated professional managers to run their businesses at the operational and partly strategic level. However, families exercised ultimate control, and imposed a significant conservative bias on investment and financial policies. The function of the Type I groups was quite different from that of postwar bank-centered business groups, which encouraged high investment and high leverage. They were also reluctant to take their subsidiary firms public. It is also worth noting that families put their banks at or near the apex (Morck and Nakamura 2005), and required them to pursue sound banking policy. These banks were never required to finance groups' firms in the prewar era, so they were relatively free from tunneling issues.

The Type II and III business groups, the Taisho *zaibatsu* and new *zaibatsu* respectively, were relatively small and latecomers. Their structure was rather similar to family firms in emerging economies in that families or entrepreneurs exercised effective control, and were likely to depend on external financing (either equity or debt) to maximize growth. Pyramidal and hierarchical group control structures allowed them to entrench themselves from outside investors, and sometime induced tunneling, resulting in volatile performances. They also established a blueprint for postwar business groups to take high risks using external financing, making it possible for affiliated firms to be less constrained by cash flow and default risk. However, unlike bank-centered business groups in postwar Japan, some groups preferred equity financing, and other groups depended on debt but were not subject to effective monitoring by banks.

We should conclude by making a few additional comments on the characteristics of prewar business groups. First, prewar business groups were relatively free from the so-called Carnegie Effect, which has been quite common in business groups in emerging economies.[18] Since the three established *zaibatsu* delegated their businesses to professional managers from the beginning of industrialization, family succession had less of an impact on managerial capabilities. The effective control of new *zaibatsu* (Type III) resided mainly in the hands of talented entrepreneurs, so that, once they had died, the group ties were likely to be relaxed rapidly. For example, the Nippon Chisso group lost its group integrity after the founder, Shitagau Noguchi, died in 1940. Family succession remained a significant issue just for Type II groups (such as Furukawa or Asano), where family members still had real control.

Secondly, the relation between the three established *zaibatsu* and other types of groups could be characterized as complementary, especially after the First World War family-owned (Type II) groups and entrepreneur-type groups (Type III) firms had spurts in the boom periods (the First World War and the 1930s) and assumed enormous risks to enter into new industries (nitrogen fertilizer, aluminum, and automobiles). These Type II and III business groups established many of the new high-tech firms in prewar Japan. They were a good substitute for the three established *zaibatsu*, which were potential innovators but often tended to avoid risk. However, these Type II and III groups sometimes engaged in overinvestment with high leverage, and faced financial difficulty. The three *zaibatsu* played a

---

[18] The Carnegie Effect refers to the fact that each successive generation of controlling shareholders is sometimes less able than the first generation (the founders). Hence, corporate control by heirs adversely affects corporate decision-making, as they are prone to being less hard-working and ethical than the self-made founders.

complementary role in two ways: (1) they supplied long-term capital to their affiliates, allowing them to survive the depression period; and (2) at times they took the initiative in corporate restructuring through M&As. Mitsui & Co. acquired a capital stake in Nippon Flour Mills, and Mitsui Mining acquired two former Suzuki chemical firms (nitrogen fertilizers).

Lastly, we can cite the political stance of the prewar *zaibatsu* as an additional unique feature. It is true that government support contributed to the growth of business groups by the early twentieth century (Morikawa 1992; Khanna and Yafeh 2007: table 4). However, as groups became larger and matured, business groups were relatively independent from the government. During the interwar period, representatives of the three established *zaibatsu* were normally advocates of free trade and laissez-faire. Members of business groups rarely indulged in political rent-seeking. Rather, the three established *zaibatsu* manipulated their country's political system to entrench themselves. It has been documented that *zaibatsu* members tried to minimize government intervention in their activities, while the families of the three *zaibatsu* adopted house rules and constitutions requiring company members to avoid involvement in political affairs.[19]

REFERENCES

AGHION, P., and TIROLE, J. (1997). "Formal and Real Authority in Organizations," *Journal of Political Economy*, 105: 1–29.

ASAJIMA, S. (1983). *Senkanki Sumitomo Zaibatsu Keieishi* (The Business History of Sumitomo Zaibatsu during the Interwar Period). Tokyo: University of Tokyo Press.

ASAJIMA, S. (1986). *Mitsubishi Zaibatsu no Kinyu Kozo* (The Financial Structure of Mitsubishi Zaibatsu). Tokyo: Ochanomizu Shobo.

ASAJIMA, S. (eds.) (1987). *Zaibatsu Kinyu Kozo no Hikaku Kenkyu* (Comparative Studies on the Financial Structures of Zaibatsu). Tokyo: Ochanomizu Shobo.

AYUKAWA, Y. (1934). *Shinshihonshugi to Mochikabukaisha* (New Capitalism and Holding Companies). Tokyo: Tokyo Ginko Shukaijo.

BURKART, M., GROMB, D., and PANUNZI, F. (1997). "Large Shareholders, Monitoring and the Value of the Firm," *Quarterly Journal of Economics*, 112: 693–728.

FRANKL, J. (1999). "An Analysis of Japanese Corporate Structure, 1915–1937," *Journal of Economic History*, 59: 997–1015.

FRANKS, J., MAYER, C., and MIYAJIMA, H. (2009). "The Equity Market and Institutions: The Evidence from Japan." Mimeo.

FRUIN, W. M. (1992). *The Japanese Enterprise System: Competitive Strategies and Cooperative Structures*. Oxford: Oxford University Press.

---

[19] The *zaibatsu* were not enthusiastic supporters of the Important Industries Control Act of 1931 (see Miyajima 2004: ch. 3). And it is well known that, when the chairman of Mitsubishi Heavy Industries, Kiyoshi Goko, accepted a post as adviser to the Cabinet in 1943, the holding company of Mitsubishi required him to resign his Mitsubishi position on the grounds that it violated the house rule against involvement in politics (Miyajima 2004: 314, 18).

HADLEY, E. (1970). *Antitrust in Japan.* Princeton: Princeton University Press.

HASHIMOTO, J., and TAKEDA, H. (eds.) (1992). *Nippon no Keizai Hatten to Kigyo Shudan* (Japanese Economic Development and Business Groups). Tokyo: University of Tokyo Press.

HCLC (Holding Company Liquidation Commission) (1951). *Nippon Zaibatsu to Sono Kaitai* (Japanese Zaibatsu and their Dissolution) Tokyo: Mochikabu-kaisha Seiri-iinkai.

HOSHI, T., and KASHYAP, A. (2001). *Corporate Financing and Governance in Japan: The Road to the Future.* Cambridge, MA: MIT Press.

JOHNSON, S., LA PORTA, R., LOPEZ-DE-SILANES, F., and SHLEIFER, A. (2000). "Tunneling," *American Economic Review,* 90: 22–7.

KAWAMOTO, S., and MIYAJIMA, H. (2008). "Senzenki Nippon ni okeru Kigyo Tochi no Yukosei" (The Effectiveness of Corporate Governance in Prewar Japan), in H. Miyajima (ed.), *Kigyo Tochi Bunseki no Furontia* (The Frontiers of Corporate Governance Analysis). Tokyo: Nippon Hyoronsha.

KHANNA, T., and YAFEH, Y. (2005). "Business Groups and Risk Sharing around the World," *Journal of Business,* 78: 301–40.

KHANNA, T., and YAFEH, Y. (2007). "Business Groups in Emerging Markets: Paragons or Parasites," *Journal of Economic Literature,* 45: 331–72.

KIKKAWA, T. (1996). *Nihon no Kigyo Shudan (Corporate Groups in Japan).* Tokyo: Yuhikaku.

KOBAYASHI, M. (1977). *Nippon no Kogyoka to Kangyo Haraisage* (Japan's Industrialization and Privatization of Government Enterprises). Tokyo: Toyo Keizai Shinposha.

LA PORTA, R., LOPEZ-DE SILANES, F., SHLEIFER, A., and VISHNY, R. (1998). "Law and Finance," *Journal of Political Economy,* 106: 1113–55.

Mitsui Bunko (1994). *Mitsui Jigyoshi Honpen Dai 3 Kan* (The History of Mitsui Business, Vol. 3). Tokyo: Mitsui-bunko.

Mitsubishi Economic Research Institute (annual). *Honpo Jigyo Seiseki Bunseki (Analysis of Corporate Performance in Japanese Firms).* Tokyo: Mitsubishi Economic Research Institute.

MIYAJIMA, H. (1994). "The Transformation of Zaibatsu to Postwar Corporate Groups: From Hierarchical Integrated Groups to Horizontally Integrated Groups," *Journal of Japanese and International Economies,* 8: 293–328.

MIYAJIMA, H. (2004). *Sangyo Seisaku to Kigyo Tochi no Keizaishi Nippon Keizai Hatten no Mikuro Bunseki* (Economic History of Industrial Policy and Corporate Governance: Microanalysis of the Development of the Japanese Economy). Tokyo: Yuhikaku.

MIYAJIMA, H., and KAWAMOTO, S. (2010). "The Competitive Capabilities and Cost of Prewar Business Groups." Discussion paper series, No. 2009–006; Waseda Institute for Advanced Study.

MIYAJIMA, H., KAWAMOTO, S., OMI, Y., and SAITO, N. (forthcoming). "Ownership and Corporate Performance in Twentieth-Century Japan," in Y. Cassis and A. Colli (eds.), *Corporate Performance in the Twentieth Century* (tentative). Cambridge: Cambridge University Press.

MORCK, R., and NAKAMURA, M. (2005). "A Frog in a Well Knows Nothing of the Ocean: A History of Corporate Ownership in Japan," in R. Morck (ed.), *A History of Corporate Governance around the World: Family Business Groups to Professional Managers.* Chicago: Chicago University Press.

MORCK, R., and NAKAMURA, M. (2007). "Business Groups and the Big Push: Meiji Japan's Mass Privatization and Subsequent Growth," *Enterprise and Society,* 8: 543–601.

MORCK, R., WOLFENZON, D., and YEUNG, B. (2005). "Corporate Governance, Economic Entrenchment and Growth," *Journal of Economic Literature*, 43: 655–720.

MORIKAWA, H. (1980). *Zaibatsu no Keieishiteki Kenkyu* (Business History of Zaibatsu). Tokyo: Toyo Keizai Shinposha.

MORIKAWA, H. (1985). *Chiho Zaibatsu* (Local Zaibatsu). Tokyo: Nippon Keizai Shinbunsha.

MORIKAWA, H. (1992). *Zaibatsu: The Rise and Fall of Family Enterprise Groups in Japan.* Tokyo: University of Tokyo Press.

NAKAMURA, S. (1976). *Wagakuni Daikigyo no Keisei Hattenkatei* (The Emergence and Development of Large Firms in Japan). Tokyo: Sangyo Seisaku Kenkyujo.

ODAGIRI, H., and GOTO, A. (1996). *Technology and Industrial Development in Japan: Building Capabilities by Learning, Innovations, and Public Policy.* Oxford: Oxford University Press.

OKAZAKI, T. (1999a). "Corporate Governance," in T. Okazaki and M. Okuno-Fujiwara (eds.), *The Japanese Economics System and its Historical Origins.* Oxford: Oxford University Press.

OKAZAKI, T. (1999b). *Mochikabu-kaisha no Rekishi* (History on Holding Company). Tokyo: Chikuma Shobo.

OKAZAKI, T. (2001). "The Role of Holding Companies in Prewar Japanese Economic Development: Rethinking Zaibatsu in Perspectives of Corporate Governance," *Social Science Japan Journal*, 4: 243–68.

RAJAN, R., and ZINGALES, L. (2003). "The Great Reversals: The Politics of Financial Development in the Twentieth Century," *Journal of Financial Economics*, 69: 5–50.

ROSTOW, W. (1956). "The Take-off into Self-Sustained Growth," *Economic Journal*, 66: 25–48.

SHIBAGAKI, K. (1965). *Nippon Kinyu Shihon Bunseki* (An Analysis of Financial Capital in Japan). Tokyo: University of Tokyo Press.

SHIMOTANI, M. (1993). *Nippon no Keiretsu to Kigyo Group: Sono Riron to Rekishi* (Keiretsu and Corporate Groups in Japan). Tokyo: Yuhikaku.

SHLEIFER, A., and VISHNY, R. (1997). "A Survey of Corporate Governance," *Journal of Finance*, 52: 737–83.

TAKAHASHI, K. (1930). *Kabushiki Gaisha Bokokuron* (The Joint Stock Company: A Cause of National Decay). Tokyo: Banrikaku Shobo.

TAKEDA, H. (1993). "Zaibatsu to Naibu Shihon Shijo" (Zaibatsu and Internal Capital Markets), in A. Okochi and G. Takada (eds.), *Kigyosha Katsudo to Kigyo Shisutemu* (Entrepreneurship and Corporate Systems). Tokyo: University of Tokyo Press.

Toyo Keizai (annual). *Kabushiki Gaisha Nenkan (Handbook on Joint Stock Campany).* Tokyo: Toyo Keizai Shinposha.

TSURUMI, S. (1974). "Dai Ichi-ji Taisen-ki Jukagaku Kogyo ka to 'Shinko' zaibatsu no Shikin Chotatsu-kiko" (The Corporate Financing Pattern of "emerging zaibatsu" during World War One), *Keizai-Shirin*, 42/3: 115–57.

UDAGAWA, M. (1984). *Shinko Zaibatsu* (New Zaibatsu). Tokyo: Nippon Keizai Shinbunsha.

WADA, H. (1937). *Nippon Konzern Dokuhon Nissan* (The Guidebook to Japanese Konzern: Nissan). Tokyo: Shunjusha.

YAFEH, Y. (2003). "An International Perspective of Corporate Groups and their Prospects," in M. Blomström, J. Corbett, F. Hayashi, and A. Kashyap (eds.), *Structural Impediments to Growth in Japan.* Chicago: University of Chicago Press.

CHAPTER 5

....

BUSINESS NETWORKS IN POSTWAR JAPAN: WHITHER THE *KEIRETSU?*

....

JAMES R. LINCOLN

MASAHIRO SHIMOTANI

5.1 INTRODUCTION

....

THE title of this volume and the chapters that fill it concern business "groups," a term suggesting an identifiable collection of actors (here, firms) within a relatively clear-cut boundary. The Japanese postwar *keiretsu* have been described in similar terms, yet, compared to business groups in other countries (for example, the Korean *chaebol*), the term "group" is misapplied in the *keiretsu* case. The *zaibatsu*, the prewar progenitor of the *keiretsu*, could fairly be described as groups, and, in their relatively sharp boundaries, hierarchical structure, family control, and linkage to the state, they were structurally similar to the *chaebol* and business groups elsewhere in the world. With the break-up by

The research support of the Mitsubishi Chair in International Finance and the Twenty-First Century Center of Excellence Program of the Japan Ministry of Education are gratefully acknowledged.

the US occupation of the largest member firms, the purging of their executives, and the outlawing of the holding company structure coordinating them at the top, the *zaibatsu* were transformed into quite different entities, which we and other authors call "network forms" of organization (Miyajima 1994; Podolny and Page 1998).

Our purpose in this chapter is to discuss the postwar Japanese *keiretsu*. It is our view, supported by wide-ranging and consistent evidence, that they are mostly things of the past. In the face of powerful forces of institutional and economic change, the groups have "withered away," such that they no longer constitute a significant topographic feature of the Japanese economic landscape, despite having been one from the 1950s to the early 2000s. While our colleagues' chapters treat business groups in other, mostly emerging, economies as in general "alive and well," our review of the *keiretsu* is largely retrospective.

The layout of the chapter is as follows: we give an overview of the horizontal and vertical *keiretsu*; how they differed from business groups in other countries; where they came from; how they were structured; their benefits and liabilities for individual firms and the Japanese economy as a whole; why they have largely died out; and whether they—the vertical groups in particular—might be revived.

5.2 WHAT ARE THE *KEIRETSU* AND WHERE DID THEY COME FROM?

The term *keiretsu* has been applied to a variety of Japanese enterprise forms. All are clusters of independently managed firms whose intertwined activities were reinforced by governance mechanisms such as presidents' councils, partial cross-ownership, and personnel exchanges.

The two principal *keiretsu* types that have garnered the most attention from scholars, business journalists, and practitioners are, first, the "horizontal" *keiretsu* (also called financial *keiretsu* and enterprise groups); and, secondly, the vertical manufacturing *keiretsu* composed of a manufacturer and its affiliated suppliers.

Less analyzed and discussed have been the distribution *keiretsu*—the dedicated retail networks of large manufacturers such as Matsushita, Shiseido, and Fuji Photo Film (Shimotani 1995). Other corporate clusters sometimes referred to as *keiretsu* are department stores linked with railroads and amusement parks, and bank/non-bank financial groupings.

We begin with some historical consideration of how the postwar *keiretsu* groupings evolved from the prewar *zaibatsu*. The reader should see the chapter by Miyajima and Kawamoto (Chapter 4, this volume) for a much more complete account of the history, organization, and operation of the *zaibatsu*.

5.2.1 From *zaibatsu* to *keiretsu*

The *zaibatsu* were multi-layered and industrially diversified business entities coordinated from the top by a family-controlled headquarters or holding company. Like the business groups still prevalent in the developing world, the prewar *zaibatsu*, beginning around 1910, acquired pyramidal structures, such that, through chains of cascading equity ties, a small number of family owners acquired control over large segments of the Japanese economy. The most prominent prewar *zaibatsu* were Mitsui, Mitsubishi, and Sumitomo. Originating as integrated firms, they expanded rapidly after the Meiji Restoration—the *coup d'état* that deposed the shogun and ended 200 years of Tokugawa feudalism—and expanded again with the military build-up in the twentieth century.

These spurts of growth contributed to the companies' evolution into the distinctive *zaibatsu* business group form. The Mitsubishi *zaibatsu*, for example, began spinning off its internal divisions of shipbuilding, mining, banking, insurance, and the trading company into separate legal corporations between 1917 and 1920. It was thus transformed from a single integrated corporation into a business group with a pyramidal structure. The *zaibatsu* headquarters owned and controlled the capital stock of multiple affiliated firms and was in turn wholly owned by the Iwasaki family. With close ties to the state and leading politicians, they and the other *zaibatsu* families were also an integral part of the prewar power structure.

By 1937, the "big three" *zaibatsu* were in control of 12 percent of total corporate capital in Japan, rising to 23 percent by the end of the war. The ten largest *zaibatsu* then accounted for 35 percent.

5.2.2 The postwar era: The emergence of the horizontal *keiretsu*

As part of its general program of economic democratization, the Supreme Command of the Allied Powers (SCAP) under General Douglas MacArthur widely redistributed the stock of the component companies of the confiscated former *zaibatsu*. In this relatively brief period of dispersed shareholding in the Japanese economy, a number of enterprises fell prey to hostile takeover. That experience spurred the member enterprises of the big three former *zaibatsu* to weave a defensive circle-like web of cross-shareholdings, which, being similar in function to the prewar holding company structure, guaranteed that the group held the majority of an affiliated firm's stock, providing a buffer against takeover that remained in place over most of the postwar era.

Linked together by cross-shareholdings, executive transfers, preferential trade and lending, and the regular encounters of chief executives in *shacho-kai* or presidents' councils, the member firms of the former Mitsubishi, Mitsui, and Sumitomo *zaibatsu* were reunited. The modern horizontal *keiretsu* came into being when the former *zaibatsu* were joined in the 1960s and early 1970s by the looser-knit bank-centered groups revolving around Fuji, Dai-Ichi Kangyo, and Sanwa banks. One such group subsumed the prewar Yasuda *zaibatsu*. Following the break-up in 1948 of the *zaibatsu* by SCAP, Yasuda Bank in 1948 changed its name to Fuji (for Mount Fuji) and rejoined other Yasuda financial institutions in a diversified cluster that further included the Nissan and Nippon Steel vertical groups.

In common economics parlance, "horizontal" refers to relationships among competitors within an industry. The "horizontal" or *yoko* (meaning lateral or non-vertical) *keiretsu* were diverse in industry make-up owing to the "one-set principle" that guided their prewar *zaibatsu* design. In contrast to the hierarchical ordering of the vertical *keiretsu*, the horizontal groups were more or less communities of equals. They had their leaders: large commercial ("city") banks served as nerve center and general coordinator of group affairs. The bank hosted the monthly *shacho-kai* meeting and monitored and orchestrated the member firms' activities through its lending, equity, and board connections. The general trading companies (*sogo shosha*) had similar leadership responsibilities in the early postwar decades, but, as their role in the economy as broker of commodity flows declined, so did their influence over group affairs (Yoshino and Lifson 1986). A major manufacturer such as Mitsubishi Heavy Industries provided the third branch of a leadership triumvirate.

5.2.2.1 *The presidents' council* (shacho-kai)

The one formal governance structure associated with each horizontal *keiretsu* was the *shacho-kai*, or presidents' council, a regularly convening association of the presidents (*shacho*) of the member firms. Emerging soon after the SCAP break-up of the *zaibatsu* and purge of senior management, the *shacho-kai* provided an information-sharing and mutual support network for the new generation of executives at the helms of former *zaibatsu* firms. The councils were extraordinarily stable until the turbulent mid-1990s, when membership turnover increased markedly.

While lists of *shacho-kai* members have been publicly available (see Table 5.1 for the 1993 list), the internal deliberations of the councils were not divulged. Participants painted them as purely social gatherings or, at most, forums for the discussion of broad economic issues—in no way were they portrayed as governance or management devices for coordinating strategy or monitoring member firms. Yet council membership marks a company as centrally positioned in its horizontal group. Research also shows the councils having significant effects on the performance of member firms (Lincoln and Gerlach 2004: ch. 5).

5.2.3 The vertical *keiretsu*

The second major *keiretsu* form was the manufacturing groups: suppliers and sub-contractors organized in a vertical division of labor around a large industrial firm such as Matsushita, Nippon Steel, or Toyota.

There is no counterpart to the *shacho-kai* in the vertical *keiretsu*. The "cooperative associations" (*kyoryoku-kai*) of suppliers maintained by manufacturers are some-times cast in that role (Sako 1996; Miwa and Ramseyer 2006), but these are very loose

Table 5.1 Member companies of presidents' councils (*shacho-kai*) of six major horizontal *keiretsu* groups in Japan, 1993

Industry	Mitsui Nimoku-kai: 1980:24 firms 1993:26 firms	Mitsubishi Kinyo-kai: 1980:28 firms 1991:29 firms	Sumitomo Hakusui-kai: 1980:21 firms 1991:20 firms	Fuyo Fuyo-kai: 1980: 29 firms 1991:29 firms	Sanwa Sanwa Sansui-kai: 1980:40; 1991:44 firms	DKB Sankin-kai: 1980: 43 firms 1991: 45 firms 1993: 46 firms
Finance	Mitsui Bank Mitsui Trust Mitsui Mutal Life Taisho Marine & Fire	Mitsubishi Bank Mitsubishi Trust Meiji Mutual Life Tokio Marine & Fire	Sumitomo Bank Sumitomo Trust Sumitomo Mutual Life Sumitomo Marine & Fire	Fuji Bank Yasuda Trust Yasuda Mutual Life Yasuda Fire & Marine	Sanwa Bank Toyo Trust Nippon Life	Dai-ichi Kangyo Bank Asahi Mutual Life Fukoku Mutual Life Nissan Fire & Marine Taisei Fire & Marine Nippon Kangyo Kakumarau Securities
Commerce	Mitsui & Co. Mitsukoshi Department Store	Mitsubishi Corp.	Sumitomo Corp.	Marubeni	Nichimen Nissho Iwai Iwatani International Takashimaya	Itochu Nissho Iwai Kanematsu Kawasho Seibu Department Store Itoki (post 1991)
Forestry			Sumitomo Forestry			
Mining	Mitsui Mining Hokkaido Colliery & Steamship		Sumitomo Coal Mining			
Construction	Mitsui Construction Sanki Engineering	Mitsubishi Construction	Sumitomo Construction	Taisei	Obayashi Toyo Construction Sekisui House Zenitaka (post 1980)	Shimizu

(continued)

Table 5.1 Continued

Industry	Mitsui Nimoku-kai: 1980:24 firms 1993:26 firms	Mitsubishi Kinyo-kai: 1980:28 firms 1991:29 firms	Sumitomo Hakusui-kai: 1980:21 firms 1991:20 firms	Fuyo Fuyo-kai: 1980: 29 firms 1991:29 firms	Sanwa Sanwa Sansui-kai: 1980:40; 1991:44 firms	DKB Sankin-kai: 1980: 43 firms 1991: 45 firms 1993: 46 firms
Foodstuffs and beverages	Nippon Flour Mills	Kirin Brewery		Nissin Flour Milling, Nichirei, Sapporo Breweries	Itoham Foods, Suntory (post 1980)	
Textile products				Nisshinbo Industries, Toho Rayon	Unitika	
Paper and pulp	Oji Paper			Sanyo-Kokusaku Pulp		Honshu Paper
Chemical products	Mitsui Toatsu, Mitsui Petrochemical, Toray Industries, Denki Kagaku Kogyo (post 1991)	Mitsubishi Kasei, Mitsubishi Gas Chemical, Mitsubishi Petrochemical, Mitsubishi Monsanto	Sumitomo Chemical, Sumitomo Bakelite	Showa Denko K K, Kureha Chemical, Nippon Oil & Fats	Teijin, Tokuyama Soda, Sekisui Chemical, Ube Industries, Hitachi Chemical, Tanabe Seiyaku, Fujisawa Pharmaceutical, Kansai Paint	Denki Kagaku Kogyo, Kyowa Hakko Kogyo, Nippon Zeon, Asahi Denka Kogyo, Sankyo, Shiseido, Lion, Asahi Chemical

Industry	Mitsui Nimoku-kai: 1980:24 firms 1993:26 firms	Mitsubishi Kinyo-kai: 1980:28 firms 1991:29 firms	Sumitomo Hakusui-kai: 1980:21 firms 1991:20 firms	Fuyo Fuyo-kai: 1980:29 firms 1991:29 firms	Sanwa Sansui-kai: 1980:40; 1991:44 firms	DKB Sankin-kai: 1980:43 firms 1991:45 firms 1993:46 firms
		Mitsubishi Plastics Mitsubishi Rayon				
Petroleum refining		Mitsubishi Oil		Toden	Cosmo Oil	Showa Shell Sekiyu
Rubber products		Asahi Glass			Toyo Tire & Rubber	Yokohama Rubber
Ceramic, stone, clay & glass products	Onoda Cement	Mitsubishi Mining & Cement	Nippon Sheet Glass Sumitomo Cement	Nihon Cement	Osaka Cement Kyocera	Chichibu Cement
Iron and steel	Japan Steel Works	Mitsubishi Steel Mfg	Sumitomo Metal	NKK	Kobe Steel Nisshin Steel Nakayama Steel Works Hitachi Metals	Kobe Steel Kawasaki Steel Japan Metals & Chemicals
Non-ferrous metals	Mitsui Mining & Smelting	Mitsubishi Metal Mitsubishi Aluminum Mitsubishi Cable	Sumitomo Metal Mining Sumitomo Light Metal Sumitomo Electric		Hitachi Cable	Nippon Light Metal Furukawa Furkawa Electric

(continued)

Table 5.1 Continued

Industry	Mitsui Nimoku-kai: 1980:24 firms 1993:26 firms	Mitsubishi Kinyo-kai: 1980:28 firms 1991:29 firms	Sumitomo Hakusui-kai: 1980:21 firms 1991:20 firms	Fuyo Fuyo-kai: 1980: 29 firms 1991:29 firms	Sanwa Sanwa Sansui-kai: 1980:40; 1991:44 firms	DKB Sankin-kai: 1980: 43 firms 1991: 45 firms 1993: 46 firms
Gen'l machinery & apparatus		Mitsubishi Kakoki	Sumitomo Heavy Industries	Kubota Nippon Seiko K K	NTN	Niigata Engineering Iseki Ebara
Electric machinery and apparatus	Toshiba	Mitsubishi Electric	NEC	Hitachi Oki Electric Industry Yokogawa Electric	Hitachi Iwatsu Electric Sharp Nitto Electric	Hitachi Fuji Electric Yasukawa Electric Fujitsu Nippon Columbia
Transportation and equipment	Toyota Motor Mitsui Engineering & Shipbuilding Ishikawajima-Harima (post-1991)	Mitsubishi Heavy		Nissan Motor	Hitachi Zosen Shin Meiwa Industry Daihatsu Motor	Kawasaki Heavy Ishikawajima–Harima Isuzu Motors
Precision machinery		Mitsubishi Motors Nikon		Canon	Hoya (post 1980)	Asahi Optical
Real estate	Mitsui Real Estate Development	Mitsubishi Estate	Sumitomo Realty & Development	Tokyo Tatemono		

Industry	Mitsui Nimoku-kai: 1980:24 firms 1993:26 firms	Mitsubishi Kinyo-kai: 1980:28 firms 1991:29 firms	Sumitomo Hakusui-kai: 1980:21 firms 1991:20 firms	Fuyo Fuyo-kai: 1980: 29 firms 1991:29 firms	Sanwa Sansui-kai: 1980:40; 1991:44 firms	DKB Sankin-kai: 1980: 43 firms 1991: 45 firms 1993: 46 firms
Railways and road transport				Tobu Railway Keihin Electric Express	Hankyu Nippon Express	
Water transport	Mitsui O S K Lines	Nippon Yusen		Showa Line	Navix Line	Kawasaki Kisen
Warehouse	Mitsui Warehouse	Mitsubishi Warehouse	Sumitomo Warehouse			Shibusawa Warehouse
Services					Orix	Orient Co. (post 80)
Other					Nittsu (pre 1991)	Korakuen Stadium Co. Nittsu (pre 1991)

Source: Japan Fair Trade Commission (1993).

organizations that encompass *keiretsu* and independent suppliers alike (Guillot and Lincoln 2005).

Otherwise, the ties binding firms within the horizontal and vertical *keiretsu* are generally the same: cross-shareholding, personnel transfers, and preferential lending and trade. Given the groups' vertical supply-chain structure, the personnel flows have been of broader scope and a greater contributor of cohesion than in the horizontal groups. Exchanges of engineers and other trained personnel enabled coordination of development and production processes between customer and supplier. Oft-noted, in addition, are the *shukko* transfers from higher- to lower-tier firms that served to reduce the former's redundant labor stock while enabling it to claim (titular) adherence to lifetime employment norms.

Much scholarly and journalistic writing on the Japanese vertical *keiretsu* sees the close, cooperative, and flexible relations endemic to these networks facilitating responsiveness, reliability, and learning among affiliate firms. Unlike the arm's-length and adversarial supplier relations historically typical of the American auto industry, *keiretsu* suppliers supported one another by, for example, assisting in the development of products, parts, processes, and people (Helper and Sako 1995). Although an older school of Japanese "dual-economy" thought painted the parent manufacturers as exploiting the smaller up- and downstream firms as risk buffers, later scholarship based on better evidence described the supplier and assembler tie as one of risk-sharing: each party supports the other by absorbing some of its costs and risks (Asanuma and Kikutani 1992; Okamuro 2001).

5.2.4 The horizontal and vertical *keiretsu* as overlapping networks

Often portrayed as quite distinct business entities, the horizontal and vertical *keiretsu* are better cast as intertwined and overlapping networks, as Fig. 5.1 depicts. The Toyota group is a vertical *keiretsu* aligned with the Mitsui *kigyo shudan*, as is Nissan with Fuyo, NEC with Sumitomo, Furukawa with DKB, and so on. By a similar organizational logic, when a vertical *keiretsu* overlay two horizontal groups, it thereby bridged or tethered them. Toyota Motor was a Mitsui *Nimoku-kai* member (technically an "observer"). Daihatsu, however, is a Toyota *keiretsu* affiliate that held a seat on the Sanwa *Sansui-kai*. Similarly, Hitachi's membership on the Fuyo, DKB, and Sanwa councils supplied a "gravitational pull" that drew those clusters together in the corporate network space. Indeed, much of the definition of the least cohesive horizontal groups (DKB and Sanwa) derived from the vertical groups within them, patterns apparent from the blockmodel (network clustering) analyses conducted by Lincoln and Gerlach (2004: ch. 3). DKB contains the Furukawa manufacturing group (Furukawa Electric, Fujitsu, Fuji Electric), while the Sanwa group owes its structure largely to its bank and trading ties to the Hitachi and, to a lesser degree, Toyota vertical *keiretsu*. Of the four horizontal *keiretsu* (or *kigyo shudan*) with prewar

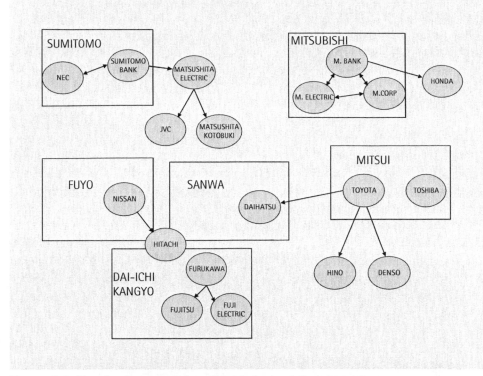

Figure 5.1 How horizontal and vertical *keiretsu* interconnect

Note: Firms within a rectangle are shacho-kai members.
Source: Lincoln and Gerlach (2004).

zaibatsu histories, the less cohesive two, Fuyo and Mitsui, are defined in large measure by the vertical groups they subsume (Hitachi and Nissan in Fuyo; Toyota in Mitsui). By contrast, the most cohesive of the former *zaibatsu*—Mitsubishi and Sumitomo—are relatively unstructured by vertical *keiretsu*. In our view, such over-lapping of the horizontal and vertical principles argue against the kind of sharp delineation of the two made in much of the *keiretsu* literature. Consequently, the discussion that follows does not keep horizontal and vertical *keiretsu* clearly separate, but rather treats relationships, governance mechanisms, and instances of collective action (for example, risk-sharing intervention) as characteristic of a general *keiretsu* form.

5.2.5 Identifying the members

Given the fluid network structuring of the *keiretsu*, a complete census of affiliate firms—a relatively straightforward exercise in some countries—is near impossible in Japan. That has not stopped scholars, consultants, and journalists from trying. Published classifications and directories abound—many produced by for-profit marketing and investment-rating firms (see citations to Dodwell Marketing Consultants; *Kaisha nenkan*; *Keiretsu no kenkyu*; and *Kigyo keiretsu soran* in the References). Miwa and Ramseyer (2006) have rightly criticized *keiretsu* research for its over-reliance on such listings, which typically impose arbitrary cut-offs on such continua as equity or bank debt relationships in order dichotomously to separate "member" from "non-member" firms.

For the horizontal *keiretsu*, such directories generally begin with *shacho-kai* lists, adding firms whose equity, banking, trade, and other ties signified close associations with the council members. By such criteria as bank borrowing, some non-council firms displayed tilts toward a particular group (for example, Matsushita toward Sumitomo). Others by the same criteria were much more weakly so aligned (for example, Honda toward Mitsubishi). Portraits of the *keiretsu* as peaks and valleys in an undulating sea of corporate ties capture such subtle variations. The "group" concept really cannot.

If it is difficult to determine exactly what firms belong to which, if any, groups, it is equally difficult to estimate the shares of the Japanese economy those groups control. Consequently, estimates varied widely, and all are suspect. Ito (1992: 188) calculated that the horizontal groups in the 1980s accounted for 5 percent of the Japanese labor force and 16 percent of total sales. Pempel (1998: 70) put them at 0.1 percent of all Japanese companies but 25 percent of postwar GNP and 75 percent of the value of shares on the Tokyo Stock Exchange for the same period.

5.2.5.1 Keiretsu *as clusterings of the Japanese corporate network*

An alternative to the directory classifications is an empirical cluster analysis of the ties that connect companies economy-wide. Several analysts have used network clustering algorithms to infer groupings in the Japanese corporate network (Scott 1986; Gerlach 1992b). Fig. 5.2 presents the results of Lincoln and Gerlach's application (2004: ch. 3) of the CONCOR algorithm to data on trade, lending, equity, and director transfer ties among the 50 largest financials, 200 largest industrials, and 7 largest trading companies in the Japanese economy in 1978. In this methodology, *keiretsu* materialize as blocks or clusters of firms occupying structurally equivalent positions in the network. We present the 1978 results because, of blockmodels generated by Lincoln and Gerlach every 3–4 years from 1978 to 1998, the earliest year gives the clearest picture of distinct *keiretsu* clusterings. In each succeeding period, the empirically derived groups were less sharply drawn and corresponded less well to such external criteria as *shacho-kai* affiliation. By the mid- to late 1990s, the CONCOR map of the large-firm network reveals general *keiretsu* dissolution, whether of the big-six horizontal groups or such historically prominent vertical groups as Hitachi, Matsushita, Nissan, Nippon Steel, and Toyota.

5.2.6 Processes of *keiretsu* formation

Apart from their evolution from the prewar *zaibatsu*, the *keiretsu* emerged from a confluence of centrifugal and centripetal processes. Independent firms fell into the

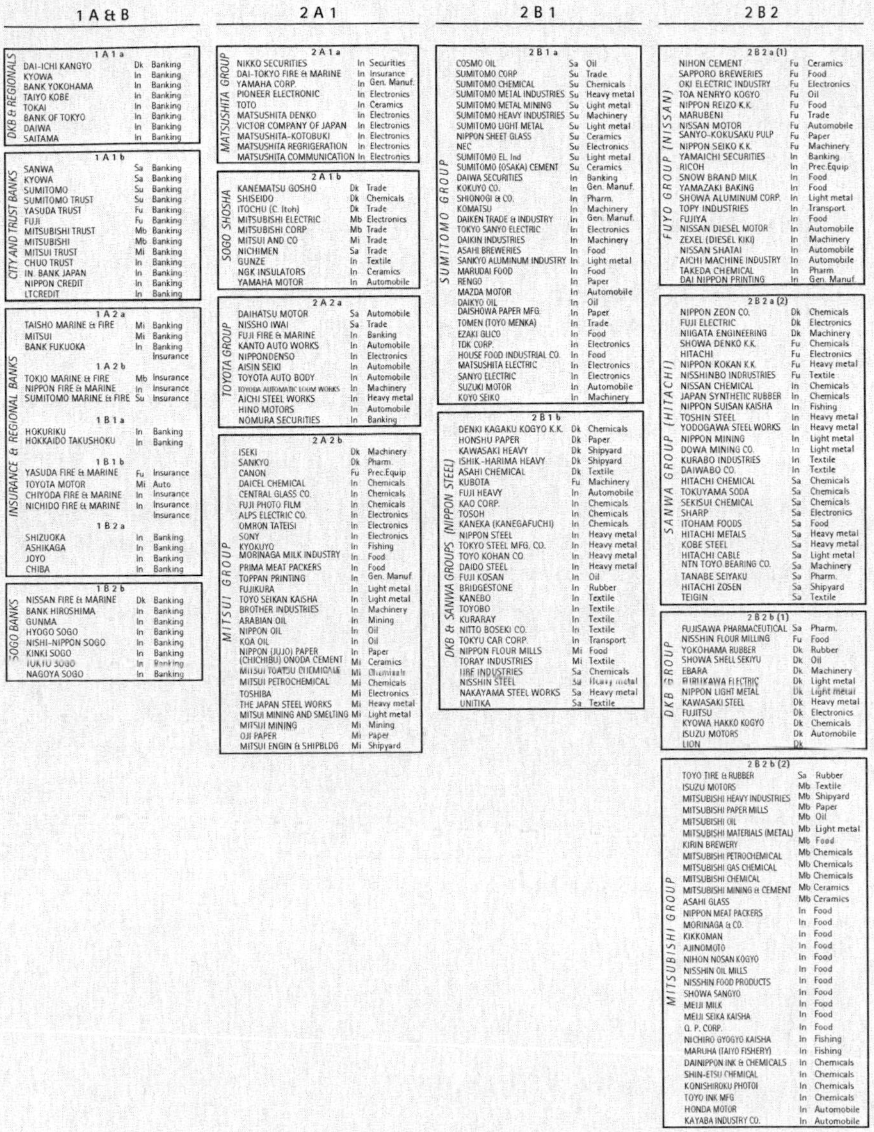

1 A & B

1A1a *(DKB & REGIONALS)*

DAI-ICHI KANGYO	Dk	Banking
KYOWA	In	Banking
BANK YOKOHAMA	In	Banking
TAIYO KOBE	In	Banking
TOKAI	In	Banking
BANK OF TOKYO	In	Banking
DAIWA	In	Banking
SAITAMA	In	Banking

1A1b *(CITY AND TRUST BANKS)*

SANWA	Sa	Banking
KYOWA	Sa	Banking
SUMITOMO	Su	Banking
SUMITOMO TRUST	Su	Banking
YASUDA TRUST	Fu	Banking
FUJI	Fu	Banking
MITSUBISHI TRUST	Mb	Banking
MITSUBISHI	Mb	Banking
MITSUI TRUST	Mi	Banking
CHUO TRUST	In	Banking
IN. BANK JAPAN	In	Banking
LTCREDIT	In	Banking

1A2a

TAISHO MARINE & FIRE	Mi	Banking
MITSUI	Mi	Banking
BANK FUKUOKA	In	Banking / Insurance

1A2b

TOKIO MARINE & FIRE	Mb	Insurance
NIPPON FIRE & MARINE	In	Insurance
SUMITOMO MARINE & FIRE	Su	Insurance

1B1a *(INSURANCE & REGIONAL BANKS)*

HOKURIKU	In	Banking
HOKKAIDO TAKUSHOKU	In	Banking

1B1b

YASUDA FIRE & MARINE	Fu	Insurance
TOYOTA MOTOR	Mi	Auto
CHIYODA FIRE & MARINE	In	Insurance
NICHIDO FIRE & MARINE	In	Insurance

1B2a

SHIZUOKA	In	Banking
ASHIKAGA	In	Banking
JOYO	In	Banking
CHIBA	In	Banking

1B2b *(SOGO BANKS)*

NISSAN FIRE & MARINE	Dk	Banking
BANK HIROSHIMA	In	Banking
GUNMA	In	Banking
HYOGO SOGO	In	Banking
NISHI-NIPPON SOGO	In	Banking
KINKI SOGO	In	Banking
TOKYO SOGO	In	Banking
NAGOYA SOGO	In	Banking

2 A 1

2A1a *(MATSUSHITA GROUP)*

NIKKO SECURITIES	In	Securities
DAI-TOKYO FIRE & MARINE	In	Insurance
YAMAHA CORP	In	Gen. Manuf.
PIONEER ELECTRONIC	In	Electronics
TOTO	In	Ceramics
MATSUSHITA DENKO	In	Electronics
VICTOR COMPANY OF JAPAN	In	Electronics
MATSUSHITA-KOTOBUKI	In	Electronics
MATSUSHITA REGRIGERATION	In	Electronics
MATSUSHITA COMMUNICATION	In	Electronics

2A1b *(SOGO SHOSHA)*

KANEMATSU GOSHO	Dk	Trade
SHISEIDO	Dk	Chemicals
ITOCHU (C. Itoh)	Dk	Trade
MITSUBISHI ELECTRIC	Mb	Electronics
MITSUBISHI CORP	Mb	Trade
MITSUI AND CO	Mi	Trade
NICHIMEN	Sa	Trade
GUNZE	In	Textile
NGK INSULATORS	In	Ceramics
YAMAHA MOTOR	In	Automobile

2A2a *(TOYOTA GROUP)*

DAIHATSU MOTOR	Sa	Automobile
NISSHO IWAI	Sa	Trade
FUJI FIRE & MARINE	In	Banking
KANTO AUTO WORKS	In	Automobile
NIPPONDENSO	In	Automobile
AISIN SEIKI	In	Automobile
TOYOTA AUTO BODY	In	Automobile
TOYODA AUTOMATIC LOOM WORKS	In	Machinery
AICHI STEEL WORKS	In	Heavy metal
HINO MOTORS	In	Automobile
NOMURA SECURITIES	In	Banking

2A2b *(MITSUI GROUP)*

ISEKI	Dk	Machinery
SANKYO	Dk	Pharm.
CANON	Fu	Prec.Equip
DAICEL CHEMICAL	In	Chemicals
CENTRAL GLASS CO.	In	Chemicals
FUJI PHOTO FILM	In	Chemicals
ALPS ELECTRIC CO.	In	Electronics
OMRON TATEISI	In	Electronics
SONY	In	Electronics
KYOKUYO	In	Fishing
MORINAGA MILK INDUSTRY	In	Food
PRIMA MEAT PACKERS	In	Food
TOPPAN PRINTING	In	Gen. Manuf.
FUJIKURA	In	Light metal
TOYO SEIKAN KAISHA	In	Light metal
BROTHER INDUSTRIES	In	Machinery
NIPPON OIL	In	Mining
KOA OIL	In	Oil
NIPPON (JUJO) PAPER	In	Paper
(CHICHIBU) ONODA CEMENT	Mi	Ceramics
MITSUI TOATSU CHEMICAL	Mi	Chemicals
MITSUI PETROCHEMICAL	Mi	Chemicals
TOSHIBA	Mi	Electronics
THE JAPAN STEEL WORKS	Mi	Heavy metal
MITSUI MINING AND SMELTING	Mi	Light metal
MITSUI MINING	Mi	Mining
OJI PAPER	Mi	Paper
MITSUI ENGIN & SHIPBLDG	Mi	Shipyard

2 B 1

2B1a *(SUMITOMO GROUP)*

COSMO OIL	Sa	Oil
SUMITOMO CORP	Su	Trade
SUMITOMO CHEMICAL	Su	Chemicals
SUMITOMO METAL INDUSTRIES	Su	Heavy metal
SUMITOMO METAL MINING	Su	Light metal
SUMITOMO HEAVY INDUSTRIES	Su	Machinery
SUMITOMO LIGHT METAL	Su	Light metal
NIPPON SHEET GLASS	Su	Ceramics
NEC	Su	Electronics
SUMITOMO EL. Ind	Su	Light metal
SUMITOMO (OSAKA) CEMENT	Su	Ceramics
DAIWA SECURITIES	In	Banking
KOKUYO CO.	In	Gen. Manuf.
SHIONOGI & CO.	In	Pharm.
KOMATSU	In	Gen. Manuf.
DAIKEN TRADE & INDUSTRY	In	Gen. Manuf.
TOKYO SANYO ELECTRIC	In	Electronics
DAIKIN INDUSTRIES	In	Machinery
ASAHI BREWERIES	In	Food
SANKYO ALUMINUM INDUSTRY	In	Light metal
MARUDAI FOOD	In	Food
RENGO	In	Paper
MAZDA MOTOR	In	Automobile
DAIKYO OIL	In	Oil
DAISHOWA PAPER MFG.	In	Paper
TOMEN (TOYO MENKA)	In	Trade
EZAKI GLICO	In	Food
TDK CORP.	In	Electronics
HOUSE FOOD INDUSTRIAL CO.	In	Food
MATSUSHITA ELECTRIC	In	Electronics
SANYO ELECTRIC	In	Electronics
SUZUKI MOTOR	In	Automobile
KOYO SEIKO	In	Machinery

2B1b *(NIPPON STEEL)*

DENKI KAGAKU KOGYO K.K.	Dk	Chemicals
HONSHU PAPER	Dk	Paper
KAWASAKI HEAVY	Dk	Shipyard
ISHIK.-HARIMA HEAVY	Dk	Shipyard
ASAHI CHEMICAL	Dk	Textile
KUBOTA	Fu	Machinery
FUJI HEAVY	In	Automobile
KAO CORP.	In	Chemicals
TOSOH	In	Chemicals
KANEKA (KANEGAFUCHI)	In	Chemicals
NIPPON STEEL	In	Heavy metal
TOKYO STEEL MFG. CO.	In	Heavy metal
TOYO KOHAN CO	In	Heavy metal
DAIDO STEEL	In	Heavy metal
FUJI KOSAN	In	Oil
BRIDGESTONE	In	Rubber
KANEBO	In	Textile
TOYOBO	In	Textile
KURARAY	In	Textile
NITTO BOSEKI CO.	In	Textile
TOKYU CAR CORP.	In	Transport
NIPPON FLOUR MILLS	Mi	Food
TORAY INDUSTRIES	Mi	Textile
IIRE INDUSTRIES	Sa	Chemicals
NISSHIN STEEL	Sa	Heavy metal
NAKAYAMA STEEL WORKS	Sa	Heavy metal
UNITIKA	Sa	Textile

(Left margin: DKB & SANWA GROUPS (NIPPON STEEL))

2 B 2

2B2a(1) *(FUYO GROUP (NISSAN))*

NIHON CEMENT	Fu	Ceramics
SAPPORO BREWERIES	Fu	Food
OKI ELECTRIC INDUSTRY	Fu	Electronics
TOA NENRYO KOGYO	Fu	Oil
NIPPON REIZO K.K.	Fu	Food
MARUBENI	Fu	Trade
NISSAN MOTOR	Fu	Automobile
SANYO-KOKUSAKU PULP	Fu	Paper
NIPPON SEIKO K.K.	Fu	Machinery
YAMAICHI SECURITIES	In	Banking
RICOH	In	Prec.Equip
SNOW BRAND MILK	In	Food
YAMAZAKI BAKING	In	Food
SHOWA ALUMINUM CORP.	In	Light metal
TOPY INDUSTRIES	In	Transport
FUJIYA	In	Food
NISSAN DIESEL MOTOR	In	Automobile
ZEXEL (DIESEL KIKI)	In	Machinery
NISSAN SHATAI	In	Automobile
AICHI MACHINE INDUSTRY	In	Automobile
TAKEDA CHEMICAL	In	Pharm.
DAI NIPPON PRINTING	In	Gen. Manuf.

2B2a(2) *(HITACHI)*

NIPPON ZEON CO.	Dk	Chemicals
FUJI ELECTRIC	Dk	Electronics
NIIGATA ENGINEERING	Dk	Machinery
SHOWA DENKO K.K.	Dk	Chemicals
HITACHI	Fu	Electronics
NIPPON KOKAN K.K.	Fu	Heavy metal
NISSHINBO INDRUSTRIES	Fu	Textile
NISSAN CHEMICAL	In	Chemicals
JAPAN SYNTHETIC RUBBER	In	Chemicals
NIPPON SUISAN KAISHA	In	Fishing
TOSHIN STEEL	In	Heavy metal
YODOGAWA STEEL WORKS	In	Heavy metal
NIPPON MINING	In	Light metal
DOWA MINING CO.	In	Light metal
KURABO INDUSTRIES	In	Textile
DAIWABO CO.	In	Textile
HITACHI CHEMICAL	Sa	Chemicals
TOKUYAMA SODA	Sa	Chemicals
SEKISUI CHEMICAL	Sa	Chemicals
SHARP	Sa	Electronics
ITOHAM FOODS	Sa	Food
HITACHI METALS	Sa	Heavy metal
KOBE STEEL	Sa	Heavy metal
HITACHI CABLE	Sa	Light metal
NTN TOYO BEARING CO.	Sa	Machinery
TANABE SEIYAKU	Sa	Pharm.
HITACHI ZOSEN	Sa	Shipyard
TEIGIN	Sa	Textile

(Left margin: SANWA GROUP (HITACHI))

2B2b(1) *(DKB GROUP)*

FUJISAWA PHARMACEUTICAL	In	Pharm.
NISSHIN FLOUR MILLING	Fu	Food
YOKOHAMA RUBBER	Dk	Rubber
SHOWA SHELL SEKIYU	Dk	Oil
EBARA	Dk	Machinery
SHIRAIKAWA ELECTRIC	Dk	Light metal
NIPPON LIGHT METAL	Dk	Light metal
KAWASAKI STEEL	Dk	Heavy metal
FUJITSU	Dk	Electronics
KYOWA HAKKO KOGYO	Dk	Chemicals
ISUZU MOTORS	Dk	Automobile
LION	Dk	

2B2b(2) *(MITSUBISHI GROUP)*

TOYO TIRE & RUBBER	Sa	Rubber
ISUZU MOTORS	Mb	Textile
MITSUBISHI HEAVY INDUSTRIES	Mb	Shipyard
MITSUBISHI PAPER MILLS	Mb	Paper
MITSUBISHI OIL	Mb	Oil
MITSUBISHI MATERIALS (METAL)	Mb	Light metal
KIRIN BREWERY	Mb	Food
MITSUBISHI PETROCHEMICAL	Mb	Chemicals
MITSUBISHI GAS CHEMICAL	Mb	Chemicals
MITSUBISHI CHEMICAL	Mb	Chemicals
MITSUBISHI MINING & CEMENT	Mb	Ceramics
ASAHI GLASS	Mb	Ceramics
NIPPON MEAT PACKERS	In	Food
MORINAGA & CO.	In	Food
KIKKOMAN	In	Food
AJINOMOTO	In	Food
NIHON NOSAN KOGYO	In	Food
NISSHIN OIL MILLS	In	Food
NISSHIN FOOD PRODUCTS	In	Food
SHOWA SANGYO	In	Food
MEIJI MILK	In	Food
MEIJI SEIKA KAISHA	In	Food
Q. P. CORP.	In	Food
NICHIRO GYOGYO KAISHA	In	Fishing
MARUHA (TAIYO FISHERY)	In	Fishing
DAINIPPON INK & CHEMICALS	In	Chemicals
SHIN-ETSU CHEMICAL	In	Chemicals
KONISHIROKU PHOTO	In	Chemicals
TOYO INK MFG	In	Chemicals
HONDA MOTOR	In	Automobile
KAYABA INDUSTRY CO.	In	Automobile

(Left margin: MITSUBISHI GROUP)

Figure 5.2 CONCOR partitioning of 259 Japanese firms, 1978

Note: Each panel is a cluster of firms identified at a given CONCOR iteration. The alphanumeric label (1A, etc.) indicates the CONCOR iteration that yielded the cluster; i.e., iteration 1: 1, 2; iteration 2: 1A, 1B, 2A, 2B; iteration 3: 1A1, 1A2, ... 2B1, 2B2, iteration 4: 1A1a, ..., 2B2b; iteration 5: 1A1a(1), ..., 2B2b iteration 6: 1A1a(1b), ... 2B2b(2b). Group identifiers are: Mi=Mitsui Mb=Mitsubishi Su=Sumitomo. Fu=Fuyo, Sa=Sanwa, Dk=DkB, In=Council independent. Vertical group names are in parantheses (e. g. Hitachi).

Source: Lincoln and Gerlach (2004).

orbit of a group through banking and trading relationships that grew tighter over time. Regional proximity also fostered *keiretsu*-ization. Manufacturers in Aichi Prefecture inhabited a Toyota-centric world. Matsushita's lean toward Sumitomo derived in part from common Osaka location. Sometimes a bank- or customer-led bailout of an independent company brought it into the *keiretsu* web of exchange and control. Daihatsu was an independent maker of minicars drawn into the Toyota *keiretsu* after a rescue and turnaround by Toyota in 1967. Stand-alone firms were also occasionally anointed *keiretsu* members chiefly to serve as *ukezara* (saucers), catching the "overflow" of redundant affiliated firm employees (Lincoln and Ahmadjian 2001).

The centrifugal process of group formation is that of an integrated firm divesting internal divisions as independently managed but affiliated satellite companies. Such spin-offs were at times coerced—as, for example, SCAP's break-up of the prewar *zaibatsu* and their subsequent reconstitution as horizontal *keiretsu*. Another example is Toyota's spin-off in the late 1940s of its (then) Nippondenso and Toyota Motor Sales divisions as a downsizing response to financial distress and pressure from its principal banks (Ito 1995; Sako 2006: 100).

Another genre of divisional spin-off highlights the interface between the *keiretsu* system and the postwar Japanese economy's distinctive patterns of innovation and entrepreneurship (Gerlach and Lincoln 2001). Many *keiretsu* expanded through a process of established firms generating new product ideas, setting up divisions to commercialize them, then hiving off the divisions as separate companies charged with growing and thriving on their own, all the while maintaining a measure of parent firm support and control. The strong cultures and tight organization of the Japanese corporation denied the internal division the kind of autonomy afforded its counterparts in a Hewlett Packard or Johnson & Johnson (Yoshihara et al. 1981; Itoh 1995; Sako 2006). The spin-off of the division as a *keiretsu* satellite created a substitute "quasi-intrapreneurial" business environment from which parent and spin-off alike derived benefit. Such *keiretsu*-ization of enterprise creation, however, has been criticized in recent years as one of several causes of Japan's failure to build a strongly entrepreneurial environment (Chesbrough 2006).

5.2.7 The scope of firm and group: Diversification strategy and the *keiretsu*

A defining strategic attribute of business groups in emerging economies, product-line diversification distinguishes the post-war *keiretsu* as well, but in ways that differ markedly between the horizontal and vertical groups (on Japanese diversification strategy, see Yoshihara et al. 1981; Odagiri 1992; Sako 2006). The prewar *zaibatsu*, as noted, were crafted in accordance with a "one-set principle": each group draws one large firm from every major sector—financial, distribution, extractive, and the leading manufacturing industries. In the tightest-knit former *zaibatsu* (Mitsubishi and Sumitomo), less so in less cohesive Mitsui, and much less so in the bank-centered groups (Fuyo, Dai-ichi Kangyo, Sanwa), adherence to the one-set rule mostly excluded industry competitors.

The interplay between internal organization and diversification strategy is particularly notable in the vertical groups. Usually identified as upstream suppliers and downstream distributors to a large manufacturer, the ancillary firms of the vertical *keiretsu* also at times expanded the manufacturer's product market scope. The Toyota group is a case in point. Toyota Motor has been a relatively small corporation specializing in the assembly of sedans. It thus stood in sharp contrast to the huge and broadly diversified General Motors. But, through its *keiretsu* partnerships, Toyota expanded its product line to include trucks (produced by Hino), minicars (produced by Daihatsu), and other specialty vehicles (Shioji 1995). This pattern was just one of several ways in which the *keiretsu* took on some of the strategic and operational functions that in the USA and elsewhere were the province of integrated and diversified individual firms.

5.3 THE ECONOMIC CONSEQUENCES OF *KEIRETSU*

The question of economic consequences can be addressed at two levels: (1) the functions, benefits, and liabilities of the *keiretsu* system for the Japanese economy as a whole; (2) the effects of *keiretsu* on the competitive strategies and financial performance of affiliated firms. Most of our attention is directed at the second question. However, it is useful to begin with some consideration of an issue often raised concerning business groups in emerging economies: did they emerge to fill gaps caused by market imperfections and undeveloped institutional infrastructure?

5.3.1 The filling of holes: The functions of the *keiretsu* in the developing postwar economy

As in other economies, Japan's business groups initially functioned to remedy certain market and institutional deficiencies. High dependence for investment capital on bank loans supplied by group commercial banks or trade credits provided by trading partners endowed groups with an "internal capital market" function. The affiliated *shosha*'s (trading company) brokerage and procurement roles afforded scale and coordination economies in Japan's balkanized and convoluted distribution system. The absence in the 1950s of mature producer goods markets and supply-chain infrastructure forced manufacturers to found and support vendors of critical components and materials (Odaka et al. 1988). As noted, a general absence of venture capital and other facilitating structures and culture of entrepreneurship was offset by the *keiretsu* internalization of innovation and entrepreneurship. New product divisions within established firms were then spun off as independently managed affiliates (Gerlach and Lincoln 2001).

Most students of business groups are ultimately interested in the impact on the performance of member firms. Much discussion of the question appears in the *keiretsu* literature. Three competing positions can be identified: (1) the *keiretsu* do nothing; (2) the *keiretsu* have positive effects; (3) the *keiretsu* have negative effects.

5.3.2 Micro-economic effects: *Keiretsu* affiliation and the financial performance of firms

5.3.2.1 *The performance of horizontal* keiretsu *firms*

The claim that the horizontal *keiretsu* have been of little economic consequence in the postwar Japanese economy has often been made. In this camp, if public statements be any guide, was a multitude of Japanese businesspeople and politicians. Such assertions were heard with particular frequency at the pinnacle of Japanese economic ascendancy—the late 1980s—when the *keiretsu* phenomenon was eyed suspiciously by the West as a "structural" (non-tariff) but nonetheless pernicious impediment to trade with and investment in Japan (see Imai 1990).

A more scholarly story of the irrelevance of the postwar horizontal groups treats them as historical and cultural residues: the *zaibatsu* names persisted, as did the *shacho-kai* meetings, but the economic and political significance had long ago ebbed away. Moreover, Japan's Anti-Monopoly law, it was said, precluded *shacho-kai* involvement in the business affairs of member firms. Tempting as it was to view the presidents' councils as group-wide "boards of directors" or "control towers" akin to the prewar *zaibatsu* holding companies, Western scholars by and large accepted the Japanese view of the *shacho-kai* as largely a ceremonial or, at most, information-sharing, device (Caves and Uekusa 1976).

Yet sizable qualitative as well as quantitative bodies of evidence demonstrate the real corporate performance consequences of *keiretsu* affiliations. Early treatments by industrial organization economists (Hadley 1970; Caves and Uekusa 1976), viewing the problem through an antitrust lens, interpreted the horizontal groups as colluding oligopolists. Caves and Uekusa argued that in their intra-group trade and lending *keiretsu* firms practice efficient pricing but in their business dealings with outsiders they collectively exploit their market dominance. Yet the consistent evidence that *kigyo shudan* firms both were less profitable and grew more slowly than independent counterparts was hard to reconcile with such reasoning. As a consequence, apart from Japan's peculiar tradition of Marxist economics, few scholars since have framed the *keiretsu* problem in monopoly/oligopoly terms (Miwa and Ramseyer 2006).

The evidence of financial underperformance of horizontal *keiretsu* firms was also at odds with a crop of 1980s theories that attributed transaction and agency cost economies to business groups and networks (Goto 1982; Dore 1983; Imai and Itami 1984; Aoki 1988; Thurow 1993). In the terminology of Oliver Williamson (1985), groups were "hybrid" forms: they economized both on market (weak or absent price mechanisms) and organizational failures (for example, bureaucratic rigidities).

Stable cross-shareholding and monitoring by *keiretsu* partners were claimed to yield higher-quality corporate governance compared to the US system of dispersed stock ownership. Although the proportion of one affiliate's stock owned by any one other was typically small (ownership by banks being limited by law to 5 percent until 1997), the holdings of the group as a whole were often substantial—large enough to prevent a predator from amassing a controlling stake. Moreover, banks and trading companies were perceived to act as group-assigned "delegated monitors," scrutinizing and intervening in the behavior of client firms to a degree disproportionate to their transaction volumes or ownership rights (Sheard 1994).

There is a general consensus among scholars that what the horizontal groups really do is risk-sharing and resource-shifting. Interventions by the horizontal *keiretsu* in the affairs of affiliated firms to realign financial fortunes, alter strategic orientation, and restructure managements are well documented by a rich case-study and journalistic literature. In the 1970s Sumitomo Bank orchestrated a rescue of the ailing Mazda Motors. Sumitomo Bank provided new loans, dispatched managers, lobbied other firms to keep their Mazda shares, negotiated lower prices for steel and other inputs, and even pressured Sumitomo executives to buy Mazda cars (Pascale and Rohlen 1983; Hoshi and Kashyap 2001). A decade later and using similar methods, the Mitsubishi group rescued member Akai Electric from bankruptcy (Kester 1991). In 1982 members of the Mitsui group stepped in to avert an embarrassing scandal at the group department store, Mitsukoshi. The retired CEO of Mitsui Bank, a Mitsukoshi board member, led the charge to oust Mitsukoshi's president, Shigeru Okada, and so restore Mitsukoshi's reputation and profitability (Gerlach 1992a).

It is noteworthy that in neither the Akai nor the Mazda case was the company targeted a *shacho-kai* member. Yet each had banking and trading relationships that brought them within the "gravitational fields," respectively, of the Mitsubishi and Sumitomo groups. Table 5.2's blockmodel analysis clusters Mazda with Sumitomo in 1978, an association maintained in later years (Lincoln and Gerlach 2004: ch. 3). These and similar examples support the point that, while the formal membership of *shacho-kai* delineates the horizontal group's central core, its boundaries—its gravitational field—extends much farther. Moreover, as Kester (1991) and Lincoln and Gerlach (2004: ch. 5) document in the Akai bailout and Pascale and Rohlen (1983) do for the Mazda case, the respective Mitsubishi and Sumitomo interventions, while spearheaded by the banks, were bona fide group affairs in which affiliated manufacturers were actively involved. Indeed, as a consequence of its bailout, Akai became a subsidiary of Mitsubishi Electric.

A significant body of quantitative evidence likewise shows that *keiretsu* and main bank interventions are effective in averting bankruptcy and restoring troubled affiliates to growth and profitability. A pioneering study of a sample of financially distressed firms found such ties contributing to faster recovery (Hoshi et al. 1991). Complementary studies by Kaplan and Minton (1994), Kang and Shivdasani (1995), and Morck and Nakamura (1999) document that shortfalls in performance on the part of client firms generally trigger transfers of executives from *keiretsu* banks to the client firm's board and that, following such transfers, the target experiences improvements in profitability, growth, and other performance outcomes.

Yet Lincoln, Gerlach, and Ahmadjian (1996; see also Lincoln and Gerlach 2004: ch. 5) show that horizontal group affiliations benefit poor-performing companies at the expense of their high-performing counterparts. Their result is consistent with a number of arguments for the economic functionality of the groups. Nakatani (1984) and Aoki (1984) proposed a risk-pooling or insurance rationale for the existence of *keiretsu*: member firms pay a premium or agency fee, which supplies the funds from which bailouts and turnarounds are financed. The charge, however, might better be described as a tax, for it falls primarily, not on the firms most at risk of failure and thus in need of rescue, but on their healthiest brethren.

During the post-bubble 1990s, when Japan seemed wholly incapable of getting its economic house in order, such *keiretsu* and main bank interventions (sometimes orchestrated through a private-sector "convoy" set up by government ministries) were strongly criticized. They were seen to have spawned a legion of unfit "zombie" companies, forestalling the recovery of fit firms and banks and weakening the economy as a whole (Katz 1998; Sugawara 1998; Caballero et al. 2006).

5.3.2.2 *Vertical* keiretsu *and the performance of firms: All upside?*

Quantitative evidence on the performance consequences of the vertical *keiretsu* is less plentiful than that regarding the horizontal *keiretsu*, the likely reason being lower published data availability. Nonetheless, numerous case and survey studies hail the advantages in efficiency and innovation terms of the close, stable, and collaborative buyer–supplier relationships typical of Toyota and other vertical industrial groups (Asanuma 1989; Womack et al. 1990; Dyer 1996).

Indeed, much more so than the horizontal *keiretsu*, the vertical *keiretsu* have been widely celebrated as economically rational business clusterings, not mere holdovers from Japan's economic "adolescence" (Katz 1998). Invoking Williamson's transaction-cost theory, Asanuma (1989) and others argued that the high-trust, tacit knowledge-sharing, implicit contracting styles found within vertical *keiretsu* play an efficient governance role in the presence of relationship-specific investments—the product or process is relatively customized to and embedded in the transaction partnership. A study by Nagaoka, Takeishi, and Noro (2008) shows that Japanese automakers are most likely to choose *keiretsu* suppliers over independent suppliers when the complexity and specificity of the part sourced are high.

Have Japan's vertical *keiretsu* performed what arguably was *the* primary function of the horizontal *keiretsu*—like business groups around the world—to share or pool risks of member firms (Khanna and Yafeh 2005)? Both qualitative and quantitative evidence says they did. By extending trade credits and setting price and volume in purchases of materials and components, a large manufacturer can easily manipulate the earnings and profits of a dependent supplier (Okamuro 2001; Lincoln and Gerlach 2004: ch. 5; Schaede 2008). The steep annual price reductions that Toyota imposed on its suppliers over the life of a vehicle model have been much noted (Womack et al. 1990). Also noted, however, is Toyota's practice of working closely with its suppliers to ensure that they can meet its demands and still succeed in business. Toyota's interventions to discipline the management and improve the performance of its suppliers are legend (Ahmadjian and Lincoln 2001). A careful quantitative study by Okamuro (2001) finds that the suppliers to all the major Japanese auto assemblers are buffered from the demand fluctuations that the assemblers must absorb. The variance he calculates in the suppliers' earnings is consistently lower than the assemblers', and, the greater the dependence of the supplier and equity ownership by the assembler, the more this is true.

5.3.3 Main bank versus *keiretsu* interventionism

As our focus is the *keiretsu*, we have implied that the Japanese "main-bank" relation is a kind of *keiretsu* tie. For reasons of space, we do not examine separately the nature and consequences of main bank, ministry guidance, and other distinctive interorganizational relations in the Japanese economy that overlap with and constrain and augment *keiretsu* networks but are also distinct from them (Aoki 1988). Some literature on the Japanese economy addresses the main bank relationship with little or no reference to the *keiretsu* phenomenon. Other authors' inattention to the interface between the two leads them into some confusion. Miwa and Ramseyer (2006), for example, assert on mostly logical grounds that Japanese banks do not intervene to bail out and restructure their industrial clients, because bankers know little of manufacturing management. That such bank interventions are often *keiretsu* affairs in which, as in the Akai and Mazda cases, the bank's entourage of manufacturers and trading companies gets involved seems to have eluded them. Sheard's view (1994) of main banks as "reciprocal delegated monitors" resolves the problems. He sees Japanese banks launching interventions not on their own behalf or proportionate to their own small equity stakes but rather as the agent of a network of creditors and trading partners.

The best available empirical work examines the parallel and interactive effects of main bank and *keiretsu* relationships. Hoshi, Kashyap, and Scharfstein (1991), for example, find that main bank and horizontal group affiliations contribute similarly to Japanese firms' recovery from financial distress. Lincoln and Gerlach's effort (2004: ch. 5) to tease out the unique effects of horizontal group banking, trading, equity, and board ties does likewise. They find the risk-sharing intervention effects of banking relationships disappearing in the early 1990s, although those of other ties (*shacho-kai*, trading partnerships, board interlocks) persisted longer. A Morck and Nakamura (1999) study may best untangle the overlap between the main bank and *keiretsu* phenomena and its implications for client and affiliate firms. When main bank ties are embedded in and augmented by *keiretsu* linkages, they are mobilized earlier, more aggressively, and in response to weaker signals as compared with bank interventions that lack a *keiretsu* context.

5.4 THE "WITHERING-AWAY" OF THE *KEIRETSU*

The evidence of *keiretsu* breakdown since the 1980s is substantial. Lincoln and Gerlach (2004) performed a series of blockmodel analyses of the largest 259 financials, industrials, and trading companies in the Japanese economy every two to three years from 1978 to 1998. In the first period, as earlier noted, they observe sharply etched clusterings that correspond well to the usual intuitive images and classifications of horizontal and vertical groups (for example, by presidents' council or commercial directory classification). By the late 1990s, however, identifiable *keiretsu* clusters are much more difficult to discern, and companies linked by name (Mitsubishi) or presidents' council are no longer adjacent in the network space but are often far apart. Analyses of specific ties—equity, in particular—likewise document the unraveling of the *keiretsu*. The sell-off of cross-shareholdings by major banks and insurance companies and their replacement with foreign institutional shareholders did significant violence to the cohesion and definition of the groups (Ahmadjian and Robinson 2001). By the end of the 1990s, long-standing vertical groups formed around older firms in declining industries were essentially nonexistent: Nippon Steel most conspicuously, Hitachi to a lesser degree.

Fine-grained dyad-based regression analyses done by Lincoln and Gerlach (2004: ch. 4) likewise show a fraying of intercorporate ties through this period and accelerating in the latter 1990s. They finally report substantial evidence of *keiretsu* risk-sharing activity diminishing as the 1990s progressed. Lincoln and Guillot (2008), furthermore, find *keiretsu* affiliation figuring less and less in Japanese electronics firms' choices of domestic strategic alliance partner, particularly when the alliance goal was R&D.

5.4.1 Why the decline?

What reasons lie behind the unraveling of the Japanese groups? There are more than we have space to address. Treatments of the subject can be found in Lincoln and Gerlach (2004) and Schaede (2008). We focus on the following forces: banking consolidation, accounting rule change, corporate governance reform, technological change, and cultural and political delegitimation.

5.4.1.1 *Banking consolidation*

The wave of Japanese bank consolidations at the end of the 1990s wrought a dramatic and sweeping change in the country's financial service landscape. Bank mergers have a lengthy history in Japan, but what was distinctive in the late 1990s merger wave was the scale of the institutions involved and the enormity of their problems. Early in the decade two important bank mergers had taken place: Mitsui Bank joined with Taiyo-Kobe Bank in 1990 to form Sakura, and Mitsubishi merged with Bank of Tokyo in 1996. A later series of mergers linked the trust banks of the big-six groups to their counterpart city banks. These were dwarfed, however, by a succession of mega-mergers in the late 1990s that fundamentally altered the structure of Japanese banking and its interplay with the horizontal groups.

In August 1998 three of Japan's largest banks (Fuji, Dai-ichi Kangyo, and Industrial Bank of Japan), the first two at the helms of major horizontal groups, announced plans to merge into Mizuho Bank, a financial behemoth whose 140 trillion yen in assets made it half the size again of the world's next largest institution, Deutsche Bank. In October 1999 followed the news that Sumitomo Bank and Sakura (Mitsui) would merge. The implications for Japan's postwar horizontal *keiretsu* were huge: together, these two bank mergers reduced from six to four the commercial "city" banks, which had long provided the institutional leadership and public face of the *kigyo shudan*.

On the heels of the bank mergers came a parallel consolidation of their *keiretsu* industrial partners. Kawasaki Steel of the DKB group and Nippon Kokan (NKK) of Fuyo announced in 2000 an alliance in distribution, maintenance, and materials purchasing. A month later, Fuyo trader Marubeni joined with DKB counterpart Itochu in announcing a consolidation of steel operations in China, prompting rumors that merger plans were afoot. Tie-ups between Mitsui and Sumitomo industrial companies also surfaced. Mitsui Chemical and Sumitomo Chemical announced a merger in the fall of 2001, labeled by the business press "the first alliance on such a scale beyond the boundaries of *zaibatsu* business groups in the manufacturing industry."

5.4.1.2 *Accounting rule change*

Revision of financial reporting requirements was another reform initiative aimed at increasing the transparency of Japanese firms and forcing responsiveness to shareholder interests. In their financial reports for 1999 public firms were required for the first time to provide consolidated accounts that included results from affiliates over which they had de facto control, even when the equity stakes were small. Under the old accounting rules, companies were able to hide both liabilities and assets in partner firms (the "tunneling" ascribed to business groups around the world). The accounting change curtailed such *keiretsu* practices as transferring personnel (*shukko*) to affiliates or the bailouts and restructurings that further utilize clandestine resource transfers.

A major spur to the unraveling of a signature *keiretsu* tie was an April 1, 2001 accounting rule change that required corporations to report assets at market, rather than book, value. The new rules showed many banks to be much worse off than they had appeared and insufficiently capitalized to support their lending. In anticipation of the change, banks rushed to dump cross-held shares. The impact on the *kigyo shudan* was substantial. Fig. 5.3 is taken from the Nippon Life Insurance (NLI) Research Institute report on cross-shareholding trends within the horizontal *keiretsu* (Kuroki 2001). While intra-group equity ties were relatively stable up to 1999, marked declines are evident from 1999 to 2000 (particularly steep in the case of Mitsubishi).

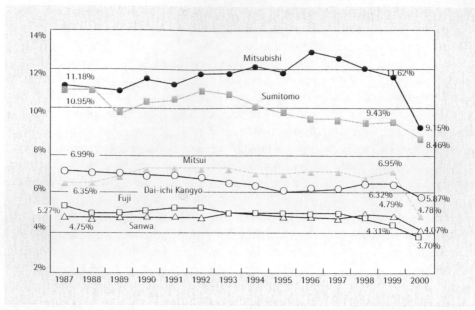

Figure 5.3 Trends in cross-shareholding within Japan's big six horizontal groups, 1987–2000

Source: Kuroki (2004).

5.4.1.3 *Corporate governance reform*

Also geared to improving managerial accountability were proposals to change the structure and composition of boards of directors (Ahmadjian 2003). An amendment to the Commercial Code in 1994 required the addition of an outside auditor to the board to ensure independent oversight of corporate finances. Another amendment in 1997 removed legal strictures on stock options, thereby making available an incentive mechanism popular in the USA and thought to be effective in aligning the interests of management with those of shareholders.

Beyond these regulatory changes, a number of large companies announced plans to reduce the size of their boards in order to speed decision-making and end the practice of routinely granting director status to high-ranking executives. Under the new rules implemented in the commercial code in April 2003, firms could choose between the traditional system of internal auditors or the US model of outside directors and an audit committee. Sony, having reduced its board from 38 to 10 in 1997, switched to the US system and increased its outside directors from three to five. Large boards had played an integral role in the *keiretsu* system of executive exchanges and interlocking directorates. Small boards and tighter rules on directors' participation in operating management rendered Japanese companies' corporate governance structures less conducive to the *keiretsu* practice of seconding bank and trading partner personnel to director (and, therefore, executive) roles in affiliate firms.

5.4.1.4 *Technological change*

The vertical *keiretsu* were weakened by the forces identified above and more. Foreign investors pressed companies to dispose of shareholdings in affiliates. Vertical *keiretsu* experience—and Japanese-style supply-chain management more broadly—had been seen as a "relational" capability, leveraged by Japanese manufacturing firms into superior efficiency, quality, reliability, flexibility, and development speed (Womack et al. 1990; Nishiguchi 1994; Dyer 1996). The Japanese global competitive advantage provided by *keiretsu*-style supply management faded in the 1990s. One reason was the advent of modular manufacturing, which requires less integration/articulation/customization of production stages (Sturgeon 2005). To lower costs, Japanese automakers shifted to a practice of installing in multiple models standardized parts and assemblies sourced from fewer and large suppliers, including one another. Moreover, supply-chain management software and online procurement systems enabled companies to automate some of the hands-on and face-to-face communication and monitoring tasks that under the *keiretsu* system had bound customer to supplier in close and enduring relations. The globally conspicuous success of the Japanese "lean-production" paradigm, comprising just-in-time, continuous improvement, total quality, *and* tight supply-chain coordination, was itself a factor in vertical *keiretsu* decline. For decades, Japan's competitors had been absorbing the lessons of that model, such that Japanese-style operations management had evolved into the global standard and so afforded Japanese manufacturers less competitive advantage than in the past.

Finally, exchange-rate fluctuations, labor and transportation costs, and local content rules together drove Japanese manufacturers to move production abroad and in so doing abandon domestic *keiretsu* suppliers for new-found foreign ones. Manufacturers like Toyota found they could transfer their home-grown *keiretsu* capabilities in cultivating high-trust, long-term partnerships with foreign suppliers.

5.4.1.5 *Delegitimation*

Less easily documented is the general cultural and political "delegitimation" of the *keiretsu* phenomenon that picked up speed in the late 1990s. When Renault executive and Nissan CEO Carlos Ghosn undertook to dismantle the Nissan supply *keiretsu*, he was criticized in the Japanese press and by politicians for his harshly "un-Japanese" tactics. But, as the turnaround of Nissan succeeded, Ghosn's methods were vindicated, public opinion shifted, and "wet" *keiretsu*-style supplier relations became less a sacred cow in Japanese business culture.

A related shift in the winds was that banks and trading partners that refused to bail out distressed affiliates found themselves rewarded, not punished as in the past, by the stock market (Lincoln and Gerlach 2004: ch. 5). Inspired, perhaps, by Prime Minister Junichiro Koizumi's reform efforts at the national level, even local government came around. In 2002 the Nagoya Regional Tax Bureau presented Toyota Motor with a tax bill for undeclared income. The Bureau ruled that the extraordinarily high prices Toyota had paid a struggling supplier, Toyota Boshoku, were transparent subsidies, not operating expenses. In an earlier era, government agencies, whether local or national, would have tolerated, if not tacitly supported, *keiretsu* risk-sharing interventions of this sort.

5.4.1.6 Keiretsu *redux?*

There have been press reports in recent years that the vertical *keiretsu* have been coming back in the 2000s (Web Japan 2005). Chiefly these call attention to the formation of new cross-shareholdings between some manufacturers and their suppliers. Most surprising, given the company's complete elimination of *keiretsu* ties during Carlos Ghosn's restructuring drive, was the news that Nissan was again taking equity stakes in its suppliers. Even Honda, famous among Japanese automakers for its diverse supplier base and lack of vertical *keiretsu,* was forging equity bonds with leading suppliers. Toyota, too, was hiking stakes in affiliate companies, as discussed in detail below.

The primary reason for the recent upturn in vertical cross-shareholdings is manufacturers' fear that strategically important suppliers might succumb to foreign ownership and control. With rising foreign investment and general liberalization of M&A rules, Japanese companies were turning, as in the early postwar period, to the cross-shareholding defense. Companies also rationalized the new cross-shareholdings on the ground that tighter coordination with partner firms was required for survival in an increasingly competitive global economy (Ahmadjian and Lincoln 2001).

Perhaps the return of defensive cross-shareholding is a first step toward reviving the vertical *keiretsu,* whose claim to economic rationality was always stronger than the horizontal groups', and which had yet to "wither away" to the same degree. But a closer look at the moves in this direction on the part of two prominent companies inspires doubt. In the early 2000s, Toyota Motor, as earlier noted, and Matsushita Electric (now Panasonic) hiked their equity stakes in several closely affiliated firms. Toyota converted three of its affiliates—Daihatsu, Hino, and Kanto Auto Works—into formal subsidiaries or *kogaisha* (parent company ownership of more than 50 percent). Again, Toyota's concern was foreign takeover, a possibility made greater by the sell-off in the late 1990s of Toyota group shareholdings by the group's principal banks, Mitsui, Sanwa, and Tokai. In addition, some Toyota affiliates—Daihatsu and Hino—had been performing sub par, and Toyota wanted a freer hand in turning them around (Shirouzo 1999).

Matsushita went farther, converting five out of six of its affiliated Matsushita group companies into wholly owned subsidiaries while maintaining a controlling 52.4 percent stake in JVC (Naito 2002). President Kunio Nakamura, widely credited with having turned around a troubled Matsushita in an aggressive restructuring drive, told the press that, while competition among the seven Matsushita companies had in the past made the group more competitive, slow economic growth and fierce price competition in the electronics industry had rendered the *keiretsu* model of independently managed overlapping businesses unaffordably costly.

We submit that the actions taken by Toyota and Matsushita were steps toward the *destruction* of the *keiretsu* form, not the reinforcement or recreation of it. *Keiretsu* organization is by definition network organization—a web of overlapping, reciprocated, direct and indirect ties that facilitates loose but significant coordination of a set of formally independent firms. While some vertical *keiretsu* were giving way to arm's-length procurement markets, the Toyota, Matsushita, and other groups were evolving in the opposite way: toward centrally managed, vertically integrated, and internally divisionalized corporate organization.

5.5 CONCLUSIONS

Japan's horizontal and vertical *keiretsu* postwar business groups have been organized in network fashion, a configuration quite different from the sharply bounded and centrally coordinated structures of business groups elsewhere, such as the Korean *chaebol*. Despite that loose organization, the groups were capable of concerted action, which in the early postwar period and ensuing high-growth era seemed beneficial in filling gaps in Japan's still-maturing economy, monitoring and sharing risks of member firms, and, in the vertical groups, achieving a degree of efficient supply-chain coordination that became the envy of manufacturers worldwide. Now, as the first decade of the twenty-first century draws to a close, the horizontal groups, as a consequence of globalization, restructuring and re-regulation, financial consolidation, and other forces, are for most intents and purposes defunct. The vertical manufacturing *keiretsu*, too, despite always having had a superior economic rationale, have mostly faded away. True, the 2000s have seen some restoration of equity ties and other cooperative pacts between parent and affiliate manufacturers, but in the most prominent of those cases the equity ownership reached levels that constituted acquisition, not "*keiretsu*." Japan today is less a network economy than it was in the 1970s and 1980s, for its industrial organization has moved down two divergent paths: toward (1), on the one hand, more arm's-length market-like relations; and (2), on the other, greater internalization of business functions, stages, and products within a hierarchically coordinated firm. The Japanese economy retains distinctive features, to be sure, but in the structuring and management of its corporate organizations it has become more similar to the Anglo-American West.

REFERENCES

AHMADJIAN, C. L. (2003). "Changing Japanese Corporate Governance," in U. Schaede and W. Grimes (eds.), *Japan Changes: The New Political Economy of Structural Adjustment and Globalization*. New York: M. E. Sharpe.

AHMADJIAN, C. L., and LINCOLN, J. R. (2001). "Keiretsu, Governance, and Learning: Case Studies in Change from the Japanese Automotive Industry," *Organization Science*, 12: 683–701.

AHMADJIAN, C. L., and ROBINSON, P. (2001). "Safety in Numbers: Downsizing and the Deinstitutionalization of Permanent Employment in Japan," *Administrative Science Quarterly*, 46: 622–54.

AOKI, M. (1984). "Risk-Sharing in the Corporate Group," in M. Aoki (ed.), *The Economic Analysis of the Japanese Firm*. Amsterdam: North-Holland, 259–64.

AOKI, M. (1988). *Information, Incentives, and Bargaining in the Japanese Economy*. New York: Cambridge University Press.

AOKI, M., and PATRICK, H. T. (1994). *The Japanese Main Bank System: Its Relevance for Developing and Transforming Economies*. New York: Oxford University Press.

ASANUMA, B. (1989). "Manufacturer–Supplier Relationships in Japan and the Concept of Relation-Specific Skill," *Journal of the Japanese and International Economies*, 3: 1–30.

ASANUMA, B., and KIKUTANI, T. (1992). "Risk Absorption in Japanese Subcontracting: A Microeconometric Study of the Automobile-Industry," *Journal of the Japanese and International Economies*, 6: 1–29.

BERGLOF, E., and PEROTTI, E. (1994). "The Governance Structure of the Japanese Financial Keiretsu," *Journal of Financial Economics*, 36: 259–84.

BERTRAND, M., MEHTA, P., and MULLAINATHAN, S. (2002). "Ferreting out Tunneling: An Application to Indian Business Groups," *Quarterly Journal of Economics*, 117: 121–48.

BORGATTI, S. P., and EVERETT, M. G. (1992). "Notions of Position in Social Network Analysis," *Sociological Methodology*, 22: 1–35.

BRANSTETTER, L. (2000). "Vertical Keiretsu and Knowledge Spillovers in Japanese Manufacturing: An Empirical Assessment," *Journal of the Japanese and International Economies*, 14: 73–104.

CABALLERO, R. J., HOSHI, T., and KASHYAP, A. K. (2006). "Zombie Lending and Depressed Restructuring in Japan," *American Economic Review*, 98: 1943–77.

Career Development Center (Kyarya Deberopmento Senta) (2002). *Kigyo Gurupu to Gyokai Chizu* (Enterprise Groups and the Map of the Business World). Tokyo: Takabashi Shoten.

CAVES, R., and UEKUSA, M. (1976). *Industrial Organization in Japan*. Washington: Brookings Institution.

CHESBROUGH, H. W. (2006). "The Open Innovation Model: Implications for Innovation in Japan," in D. Hugh Whittaker and R. E. Cole (eds.), *Recovering from Success: Innovation and Technology Management in Japan*. New York: Oxford University Press, 129–44.

COLE, R. E., and RTISCHEV, D. (2003). "The Role of Organizational Discontinuity in High Technology: Insights from a US–Japan Comparison," in J. Bachnik (ed.), *Roadblocks on the Information Highway*. Lanham, MD: Rowman Littlefield.

Dodwell Marketing Consultants. Various years. *Industrial Groupings in Japan*. Tokyo: Dodwell.

DORE, R. P. (1983). "Goodwill and the Spirit of Market Capitalism," *British Journal of Sociology*, 34: 459–82.

DVORAK, P., GUTH, R. A., S.INGER, J., and ZAUN, T. (2001). "Recession Frays Japan Inc.'s Tradition of Loyal, Long-Term Corporate Alliances," *Wall Street Journal*, Mar. 2.

DYER, J. H. (1996). "Does Governance Matter? Keiretsu Alliances and Asset Specificity as Sources of Japanese Competitive Advantage," *Organization Science*, 7: 649–66.

Fair Trade Commission (*Kosei torihiki iinkai*) (1992). *The Outline of the Report on the Actual Conditions of the Six Major Corporate Groups*. Tokyo: Executive Office, Fair Trade Commission.

GAO, B. (2001). *Japan's Economic Dilemma: The Institutional Origins of Prosperity and Stagnation*. New York: Cambridge University Press.

GERLACH, M. L. (1992a). *Alliance Capitalism: The Social Organization of Japanese Business.* Berkeley and Los Angeles: University of California Press.

GERLACH, M. L. (1992b). "The Japanese Corporate Network: A Blockmodel Analysis," *Administrative Science Quarterly*, 37: 105–39.

GERLACH, M. L., and LINCOLN, J. R. (2001). "Economic Organization and Innovation in Japan: Networks, Spinoffs, and the Creation of Enterprise," in I. Nonaka, G. von Krogh, and T. Nishiguchi (eds.), *Knowledge Creation: A New Source of Value.* London: Macmillan, 151–98.

GOTO, A. (1982). "Business Groups in a Market-Economy," *European Economic Review*, 19: 53–70.

GRANOVETTER, M. (2003). "Business Groups and Social Organization," in N. Smelser and R. Swedberg (eds.), *Handbook of Economic Sociology.* 2nd edn. Princeton: Princeton University Press.

GUILLEN, M. F. (2000). "Business Groups in Emerging Economies: A Resource-Based View," *Academy of Management Journal*, 43: 362–80.

GUILLOT, D., and LINCOLN, J. R. (2005). "Dyad and Network: Models of Manufacturer–Supplier Collaboration in the Japanese TV Manufacturing Industry," in Allan Bird and Thomas Roehl (eds.), *Advances in International Management: Special Issue on Changing Japan.* Greenwich, CT: JAI Press.

HADLEY, E. (1970). *Antitrust in Japan.* Princeton: Princeton University Press.

HELPER, S. R., and SAKO, M. (1995). "Supplier Relations in Japan and the United States: Are They Converging?" *Sloan Management Review*, 36: 77–84.

HOSHI, T., and KASHYAP, A. (2001). *Corporate Financing and Governance in Japan.* Cambridge, MA: MIT Press.

HOSHI, T., KASHYAP, A., and SCHARFSTEIN, D. (1991). "The Role of Banks in Reducing the Costs of Financial Distress in Japan," *Journal of Financial Economics*, 27: 67–88.

IBISON, D. (2003). "Business Links Make a Return in Japan," *Financial Times*, Jan. 21.

IMAI, K. (1990). "Japanese Business Groups and the Structural Impediments Initiative," in Kozo Yamamura (ed.), *Japan's Economic Structure: Should It Change?* Seattle: Society for Japanese Studies.

IMAI, K., and ITAMI, H. (1984). "Interpenetration of Organization and Market," *International Journal of Industrial Organization*, 2: 285–310.

ITO, T. (1992). *The Japanese Economy.* Cambridge, MA: MIT Press.

ITO, K. (1995). "Japanese Spinoffs: Unexplored Survival Strategies," *Strategic Management Journal*, 16: 431–46.

ITOH, H. (2003). "Corporate Restructuring in Japan, Part I: Can M-Form Organization Manage Diverse Businesses?" *Japanese Economic Review*, 54: 49–73.

Japan Fair Trade Commission (*Kosei torihiki iinkai*) (1995). *The Outline of the Report on the Actual Conditions of the Six Major Corporate Groups.* Tokyo: Executive Office, Fair Trade Commission.

Kaisha nenkan (Company Annual) (various years). Tokyo: Nihon Keizai Shimbun-sha.

KANG, J. K., and SHIVDASANI, A. (1995). "Firm Performance, Corporate Governance, and Top Executive Turnover in Japan," *Journal of Financial Economics*, 38: 29–58.

KAPLAN, S. N., and MINTON, B. A. (1994). "Appointment of Outsiders to Japanese Boards: Determinants and Implications for Managers," *Journal of Financial Economics*, 36: 225–58.

KATZ, R. (1998). *Japan: The System that Soured.* New York: M. E. Sharpe.

Keiretsu no kenkyu (Keiretsu Research). (Various years). Tokyo: Keizai Chosa Kyokai.

KESTER, W. C. (1991). *Japanese Takeovers: The Global Contest for Corporate Control*. Boston: Harvard Business School Press.

KHANNA, T., and RIVKIN, J. W. (2001). "Estimating the Performance Effects of Business Groups in Emerging Markets," *Strategic Management Journal*, 22: 45–74.

KHANNA, T., and YAFEH, Y. (2005). "Business Groups and Risk-Sharing around the World," *Journal of Business*, 78: 310–40.

Kigyo keiretsu soran (Enterprise Keiretsu Survey) (various years). Tokyo: Toyo Keizai Ltd.

KUROKI, F. (2001). *The Present Status of Unwinding of Cross-Shareholding: The Fiscal 2000 Survey of Cross-Shareholding*. Tokyo: NLI (Nippon Life Insurance) Research Institute Financial Research Group.

LINCOLN, J. R., and AHMADJIAN, C. (2001). "Shukko (Employee Transfers) and Tacit Knowledge Exchange in Japanese Supply Networks: The Electronics Industry Case," in I. Nonaka and T. Nishiguchi (eds.), *Knowledge Emergence: Social, Technical, and Evolutionary Dimensions of Knowledge Creation*. New York: Oxford University Press, 151–98.

LINCOLN, J. R., and GERLACH, M. L. (2004). *Japan's Network Economy: Structure, Persistence, and Change*. New York: Cambridge University Press.

LINCOLN, J. R., and GUILLOT, D. (2008). "Innovation and Change in Strategic Alliance Formation in the Japanese Electronics Industry." Paper presented to the annual meetings of the Asian Academy of Management, Taipei, Dec. 13–14.

LINCOLN, J. R., GERLACH, M. L., and AHMADJIAN, C. L. (1996). "Keiretsu Networks and Corporate Performance in Japan," *American Sociological Review*, 61: 67–88.

MIWA, Y., and RAMSEYER, J. M. (2006). *The Fable of the Keiretsu: Urban Legends of the Japanese Economy*. Chicago: University of Chicago Press.

MIYAJIMA, H. (1994). "The Transformation of Zaibatsu to Postwar Corporate Groups: From Hierarchically Integrated Groups to Horizontally Integrated Groups," *Journal of the Japanese and International Economies*, 8: 293–328.

MORCK, R., and NAKAMURA, M. (1999). "Banks and Corporate Control in Japan," *Journal of Finance*, 54: 319–39.

MORIKAWA, H. (1993). *Zaibatsu: The Rise and Fall of Family Enterprise Groups in Japan*. Tokyo: University of Tokyo Press.

NAGAOKA, S., TAKEISHI, A., and NORO, Y. (2008). "Determinants of Firm Boundaries: Empirical Analysis of the Japanese Auto Industry from 1984 to 2002," *Journal of the Japanese and International Economies*, 22: 187–206.

NAITO, M. (2002). "Matsushita Electric to be Reborn," *Nikkei Net Interactive*, Apr. 29.

NAKATANI, I. (1984). "The Economic Role of Financial Corporate Grouping," in M. Aoki (ed.), *The Economic Analysis of the Japanese Firm*. Amsterdam: North-Holland, 227–258.

Nikkei Net Interactive (2002). "Matsushita Electric will not Turn JVC into Wholly-Owned Unit," Jan. 11.

NISHIGUCHI, T. (1994). *Strategic Industrial Sourcing: The Japanese Advantage*. New York: Oxford University Press.

ODAKA, K., ONO, K., and ADACHI, F. (1988). *The Automobile Industry in Japan: A Study of Ancillary Firm Development*. Tokyo: Kinokuniya.

ODAGIRI, H. (1992). *Growth through Competition, Competition through Growth: Strategic Management and the Economy in Japan*. New York: Oxford University Press.

OKAMURO, H. (2001). "Risk Sharing in the Supplier Relationship: New Evidence from the Japanese Automotive Industry," *Journal of Economic Behavior & Organization*, 45: 361–81.

PASCALE, R. T., and ROHLEN, T. (1983). "The Mazda Turnaround," *Journal of Japanese Studies*, 9: 219–63.

PEMPEL, T. J. (1998). *Regime Shift: Comparative Dynamics of the Japanese Political Economy.* Ithaca, NY: Cornell University Press.

PODOLNY, J. M., and PAGE, K. L. (1998). "Network Forms of Organization," *Annual Review of Sociology*, 24: 57–76.

POWELL, W. W. (1990). "Neither Market nor Hierarchy: Network Forms of Organization," in B. M. Staw and L. L. Cummings. (eds.), *Research in Organizational Behavior*, xii. 295–336.

SAKO, M. (1996). "Suppliers' Associations in the Japanese Automobile Industry: Collective Action for Technology Diffusion," *Cambridge Journal of Economics*, 20: 651–71.

SAKO, M. (2006). *Shifting Boundaries of the Firm.* Oxford: Oxford University Press.

SAKO, M., and HELPER, S. (1998). "Determinants of Trust in Supplier Relations: Evidence from the Automotive Industry in Japan and the United States," *Journal of Economic Behavior & Organization*, 34: 387–417.

SCHAEDE, U. (2008). *Choose and Focus: Japan's Business Strategies in the 21st Century.* Ithaca, NY: Cornell University Press.

SCOTT, J. (1986). *Capitalist Property and Financial Power.* Brighton: Wheatsheaf Books.

SHEARD, P. (1989a). "The Main Bank System and Corporate Monitoring and Control in Japan," *Journal of Economic Behavior and Organization*, 11: 399–422.

SHEARD, P. (1989b). "The Japanese General Trading Company as an Aspect of Interfirm Risk-Sharing," *Journal of the Japanese and International Economies*, 3: 308–22.

SHEARD, P. (1994). "Reciprocal Delegated Monitoring in the Japanese Main Bank System," *Journal of the Japanese and International Economies*, 8: 1–21.

SHIBA, T., and SHIMOTANI, M. (1997) (eds.). *Beyond the Firm: Business Groups in International and Historical Perspective.* New York: Oxford University Press.

SHIMOTANI, M. (1987). "Jigyobusei to bunshasei: Matsushita Denki Sangyo no keesu" (The System of Product Divisions and Spin-offs: The Case of Matsushita Electric Industrial), in K. Sakamoto and M. Shimotani (eds.), *Gendai Nihon no Kigyo Gurupu* (Corporate Groups in Contemporary Japan). Tokyo: Toyo Keizai Shinposha.

SHIMOTANI, M. (1993). *Nihon no keiretsu to kigyou gurupu: sono rekishi to riron* (Japan's Keiretsu and Enterprise Groups: History and Theory). Tokyo: Yuhikaku.

SHIMOTANI, M. (1995). "The Formation of Distribution keiretsu: The Case of Matsushita Electric.," in E. Abe and R. Fitzgerald (eds.), *The Origins of Japanese Industrial Power: Strategy, Institutions, and the Development of Organisational Capability.* London: Routledge, 54–69.

SHIMOTANI, M. (1998). *Matsushita Gurupu no Rekishi to Kozo* (The History and Structure of the Matsushita Group). Tokyo: Yūhikaku.

SHIOJI, H. (1995). "Itaku Automotive Production: An Aspect of the Development of Full-Line and Wide-Selection Production by Toyota in the 1960s," *Kyoto University Economic Review*, 66: 19–42.

SHIROUZU, N. (1999). "Toyota Is Tightening Control of Key Suppliers in Bid to Block Encroachment by Foreign Firms," *Wall Street Journal*, Aug. 3, p. A18.

STURGEON, T. (2005). "Modular Production's Impact on Japan's Electronics Industry," in D. Hugh Whittaker and Robert E. Cole (eds.), *Recovering from Success: Innovation and Technology Management in Japan.* New York: Oxford University Press, 47–69.

SUGAWARA, S. (1998). "In Japan Ties Meant to Bind Now Strangle: Powerful Keiretsu System Stalls Nation's Recovery," *Washington Post*, Oct. 16.

THUROW, L. C. (1993). *Head to Head: The Coming Economic Battle among Japan, Europe, and America*. New York: Warner Books.

Web Japan (2005). "Keiretsu Comeback: Conglomerates are Back in Fashion," Sept. 5. http://web-japan.org/trends/business/bus050905.html

WEINSTEIN, D. E., and YAFEH, Y. (1995). "Japan's Corporate Groups: Collusive or Competitive? An Empirical Investigation of Keiretsu Behavior," *Journal of Industrial Economics*, 43: 359–76.

WILLIAMSON, O. E. (1985). *The Economic Institutions of Capitalism*. New York: Free Press.

WOMACK, J. P., JONES, D. T., and ROOS, D. (1990). *The Machine that Changed the World*. New York: Rawson.

YOSHIHARA, H., SAKUMA, A., ITAMI, H., and KAGONO, T. (1981). *Nihon kigyo no tayo-ka senryaku: keiei shigen apurochi* (The Diversification Strategy of Japanese Firms: A Managerial Resource Approach). Tokyo: Nihon Keizai Shinbunsha.

YOSHINO, M. Y., and LIFSON, T. B. (1986). *The Invisible Link: Japan's Sogo Shosha and the Organization of Trade*. Cambridge, MA: MIT Press.

CHAPTER 6

....

BUSINESS GROUPS IN SOUTH KOREA

....

HICHEON KIM

6.1 INTRODUCTION
....

FEW economies in the world have matched the phenomenal economic development of Korea in industrialization. Korea's per capita gross domestic product (GDP) increased from less than US$100 in 1961 to US$18,373 in 2006. By 1996 Korea had emerged as the world's eleventh largest economy and as a major global player in many industries ranging from shipbuilding and steel to semiconductors and automobiles, becoming the second Asian country after Japan to join the Organization for Economic Cooperation and Development (OECD). At the heart of Korea's rapid and successful industrial transformation have been the family-controlled, diversified business groups known as *chaebol*, which have at times been praised and at other times criticized.

In the 1960s, the state took initiatives to jump start industrialization by designing and implementing a series of five-year economic development plans. In the early stages of industrialization, it was exceedingly difficult to secure the financial capital, human resources, and foreign technologies necessary to build modern enterprises. By serving as partners in implementing the state's development strategy, *chaebol* were able to overcome resource constraints and diversify their business portfolios. *Chaebol* also pooled and shared scarce resources among group member firms to support

I thank Kee Yup Lee for able research assistance. I also thank the editors and the participants at the Kyoto International Conference on evolutionary dynamics of business groups in emerging economies for helpful comments and suggestions.

their rapid growth. By 1996, the thirty largest *chaebol* accounted for 40 percent of Korea's total output (Ungson et al. 1997). Leading *chaebol*, such as Samsung, Hyundai, Lucky-Goldstar (LG), and Daewoo, had over eighty affiliated companies, each participating in a wide range of industries, including semiconductors, consumer electronics, construction, shipbuilding, automobiles, trading, and financial services. By successfully transforming themselves over the previous two decades from exporters of cheap products into major global players, *chaebol* had come to be regarded as the drivers behind the unprecedented success of the Korean economy (Amsden 1989; Ungson et al. 1997).

But the perception of these large and diverse business groups changed dramatically as Korea suffered its worst economic crisis in late 1997. Hard hit by the Asian financial crisis, which spread rapidly from Thailand, Korea had no choice but to seek a record US$58 billion emergency rescue fund from the International Monetary Fund (IMF) and the World Bank. The Korean economy was described as hopelessly squeezed by two giants: Japan, equipped with advanced technological capabilities, and China, equipped with low wages. *Chaebol* were blamed of causing the nation's worst and most humiliating economic crisis, and were accused of being excessively diversified, globally non-competitive, and poorly managed conglomerates. In response, the state initiated a *chaebol* reform policy, with some scholars even arguing for their break-up (Bremner and Moon 2002). In fact, about half of the thirty largest *chaebol* in 1996 underwent bankruptcy proceedings or bank-sponsored restructuring programs. For instance, Daewoo, which ranked number four in 1996, was literally broken up and no longer exists. Other *chaebol* also voluntarily undertook their own restructuring efforts, often on a large scale.

But the recession did not last long. By 2002, Korea's GDP had surpassed that of 1996 and continues to grow rapidly today. Furthermore, many *chaebol* appear to have regained their lost fame and re-emerged as more competitive and stronger global players. Until the 1990s, Samsung Electronics and LG Electronics were known as makers of cheap knock-offs of foreign brands, notably Sony. Thanks to aggressive investments in R&D and design, both have evolved into leading multinationals in the consumer-electronics industry with a reputation for making trendy and sophisticated mobile handsets, MP3 players, televisions, digital cameras, and more. As of 2008, Korea was home to the world's biggest maker of flash memory (Samsung Electronics), the two biggest makers of DRAM chips (Samsung Electronics and Hynix), the third-largest steelmaker (POSCO), the fifth-largest carmaker (Hyundai Motor), and the world's three biggest shipbuilders (Hyundai Heavy Industries, Samsung Heavy Industries, and Daewoo Shipbuilding & Marine Engineering) (*The Economist* 2008).

The rise, fall, and re-emergence of the *chaebol* pose an intriguing question for scholars and public policy-makers alike. This chapter starts with a brief historical overview of the genesis and subsequent evolution of the *chaebol*. We will then discuss their diversification, globalization, and corporate governance, and finally conclude with their theoretical, practical, and public policy implications.

6.2 THE GENESIS AND EVOLUTION OF THE *CHAEBOL*: A BRIEF OVERVIEW

Before we analyze the genesis and evolution of the *chaebol*, consider Table 6.1, which lists the thirty largest business groups in Korea as of 2006.[1] The top four *chaebol* are Samsung, Hyundai Motor, SK, and LG. Samsung, SK, and LG also belonged to the top five in 1996. Spun off from the Hyundai group in 2000, Hyundai Motor Group has diversified into the areas reinforcing and complementing the automobile business, transforming itself into a comprehensive automobile group providing the end-to-end solution including auto purchase, insurance, financing, and information.

6.2.1 The genesis of the *chaebol*, 1960s and 1970s

Korea provides an illuminating case of state intervention to promote economic development (Amsden 1989; Wade 1990; Evans 1995, 1998). Upon becoming president in 1962 through a military coup, General Park Chung Hee gave top priority to economic development. In 1962 the Korean economy was based primarily on agriculture and mining. There were still enormous poverty and unemployment, per capita income was lower than it had been in 1945, and the economic infrastructure remained devastated from the Korean War. Lacking adequate resources, market institutions, and experience, the state embraced a policy of targeting industries and partnering with a select few entrepreneurs by launching a series of five-year economic development plans (see Table 6.2). The state first picked the "strategic sectors" that it deemed critical to economic development; it then selected a few firms as partners and provided them with low-interest funds, access to foreign technologies, state subsidies, and domestic market protection.

Enrepreneurs entering into these new industries in response to the state's development strategy could readily secure capital and foreign technologies and enjoy monopolistic rents in domestic markets. Furthermore, as the state's focus sequentially moved on to more advanced industries, entrepreneurs who continued to work with the state on national developmental projects were able to upgrade and diversify their business portfolios and build diversified business groups. By contrast, firms that did not receive state incentives and stuck to their core businesses failed to evolve into modern industrial enterprises (Amsden 1989).

---

[1] Business groups are described as "a set of firms which, though legally independent, are bound together by a constellation of formal and informal ties and are accustomed to taking coordinated action" (Khanna and Rivkin 2001: 47–8). The Korean government annually identifies the top thirty business groups in asset size for regulatory purposes. In principle, any organization with more than two affiliated firms can be classified as a business group. However, "small" *chaebol* are very limited in generating the benefits and costs associated with business groups. Thus, following previous studies (e.g., Chang et al. 2006), we classify only the firms belonging to the top thirty *chaebol* as group-affiliated firms.

Table 6.1 The top thirty business groups in Korea, 2006

Ranking	Group name	No of affiliates	Assets (billion Korean won)	Sales (billion Korean won)	Debt/ equity (%)	Family ownership (%)	Affiliate ownership (%)
1	Samsung	59	115,924	142,570	176.7	0.55	48.44
2	Hyundai Motor	40	62,235	73,769	137.8	1.03	41.90
3	SK	56	54,808	64,520	126.6	0.34	60.10
4	LG	30	54,432	64,033	87.9	3.97	32.19
5	Lotte	43	32,961	27,651	81.7	2.65	53.16
6	Posco	21	30,183	31,034	33.2	0.00	9.12
7	GS	50	21,827	27,614	97.2	19.44	35.49
8	Hanjin	22	20,702	15,135	184.9	3.50	29.44
9	Hyundai Heavy Industries	7	17,267	14,225	237.3	0.58	44.47
10	Hanwha	31	16,526	20,558	534.6	0.61	39.01
11	Doosan	18	13,659	11,504	200.5	3.02	44.13
12	KumhoAsiana	23	12,982	10,900	286.4	3.99	47.31
13	Hynix	5	10,358	5,888	66.1	0.00	0.00
14	Dongbu	22	8,651	10,049	351.5	4.90	42.08
15	Hyundai	9	7,125	6,524	187.1	1.36	16.96
16	Shinsaegye	14	7,030	8,995	125.8	8.76	49.09
17	CJ	56	6,797	6,030	91.4	1.34	49.75
18	LS	19	6,591	9,648	124.1	9.53	38.63
19	Daelim	13	6,527	7,683	91.6	2.44	45.19
20	GM-Daewoo	3	6,492	7,569	178.3	0.00	0.00
21	Hite Beer	13	6,027	1,743	238.3	0.21	40.78
22	Daewoo Construction	11	5,978	5,140	126.1	0.00	0.00
23	Dongkuk Steel	12	5,702	5,212	102.5	6.67	35.15

Ranking	Group name	No of affiliates	Assets (billion Korean won)	Sales (billion Korean won)	Debt/ equity (%)	Family ownership (%)	Affiliate ownership (%)
24	Daewoo Shipbuilding & Marine Engineering	5	5,370	4,941	257.1	0.00	0.00
25	STX	10	4,907	6,468	168.8	6.00	49.83
26	Dongyang	15	4,611	4,127	719.3	2.08	57.30
27	Hycsung	17	4,487	5,718	222.4	16.57	24.76
28	Hyundai Oilbank	2	4,445	8,180	191.3	0.00	0.00
29	Hyundai Department Stores	23	4,404	2,688	68.1	5.79	50.18
30	Kolon	23	4,380	4,683	215.1	2.81	57.57

Source: Korean Fair Trade Commission.

Table 6.2 Goals and achievements of the five-year economic development plans, 1962–81

Five-year plans	Years	Strategic sectors	Real GNP growth (%)	Export growth (%)
First plan	1962–6	Import substitution industries (fertilizer, food-processing, oil-refining)	7.8	36.8
Second plan	1967–71	Labor-intensive industries (textiles and clothing)	9.7	33.8
Third plan	1972–6	Labor-intensive industries; establishment of general trading companies	10.1	32.7
Fourth plan	1977–81	Chemicals and heavy industries	5.5	10.5

Source: Economic Planning Board.

Once diversified, the *chaebol* came to pool and share scarce resources such as financial capital, human talent, and intermediate products among the group member firms, thereby internalizing the roles of external markets and overcoming market imperfections (Khanna and Palepu 1997; Kim et al. 2004). For instance, in establishing a new subsidiary to start up an entrepreneurial venture, the *chaebol* often raised money from existing group members; in turn, the new subsidiary assumed equity stakes in other group members. Additionally, the *chaebol* manipulated the transfer prices of intra-group transactions, thereby shifting money from cash-rich subsidiaries into cash-starved ones (Chang and Hong 2000). Unlike their counterparts in Japan (the *keiretsu*), the *chaebol* were prohibited from owning commercial banks, but they were allowed and were eager to diversify into non-banking financial institutions in order to expand the capacity and flexibility of their internal capital markets. Given a shortage of capital, internal financing capabilities were essential to funding the rapid growth of the *chaebol*.

Facing a shortage of well-trained people, the *chaebol* also internalized the role of labor markets. Instead of having each member firm recruit and train its own employees, *chaebol* recruited and trained people at the group level and shared them among group members. Such group-level recruiting, training, and sharing helped *chaebol* economize on the costs of human resources development and increased their flexibility in mobilizing human resources. For instance, *chaebol* could easily staff new ventures by transferring employees from other group members. A study based on five *chaebol* (Hyundai, Samsung, Daewoo, LG, and SK) documented that, when starting up a new venture, these *chaebol* would fill managerial positions by transferring employees from their existing group members (Korea Economic Research Institute 1995). Given a shortage of well-trained people, the ability to develop and share necessary human talent at the group level was crucial to staffing the rapid growth of the *chaebol*.

Many *chaebol* invested in building group brands. Developing a credible brand is more difficult in emerging than in developed economies. In emerging economies, the communications infrastructure, certification organizations, and regulatory bodies— which provide reliable information and redress mechanisms to consumers— are poorly developed (Khanna and Palepu 1997). A firm with excellent products often has difficulty communicating product information in a credible, efficient way and building a brand around the product. Thus, developing a brand takes longer and requires greater investment in emerging economies. The group brand in Korea is a case in point. By building group brands such as Samsung and LG, *chaebol* were able to economize on the time and the costs of developing individual brands. For instance, at the start of a new business, being able to use a reputable group brand signaled images of reliability, quality, and credibility to prospective customers, suppliers, and other business partners. Given a shortage of reliable firm-specific and product-specific information, the ability to develop and share group brands was crucial to gaining customer and supplier support during the rapid growth of the *chaebol*.

In sum, during the early stages of economic development, Korean entrepreneurs faced both opportunities and challenges. On the one hand, external markets were non-existent or underdeveloped. Financial and human resources were in short supply, and market-supporting institutions were poorly developed. But, on the other hand, there was an abundance of new business opportunities. *Chaebol* exploited these opportunities while securing scarce resources by partnering with the state over national development projects and by pooling and sharing financial capital, human talent, intermediate products, and group brands.

6.2.2 Liberalization and the *chaebols*: The 1980s to the Asian financial crisis

In the late 1970s the state set out to develop heavy industries such as steel and chemicals with the same policy of targeting industries and choosing partners that it had applied to other sectors in the 1960s and 1970s. But the domestic heavy industries experienced serious excess capacity and financial problems that continued into the 1980s. Criticism was mounting that the state's development strategies for heavy industries were poorly crafted and overly optimistic, leading to a serious misallocation of resources. This invoked skepticism over the viability of the state's interventionist policies in promoting more advanced industries. Furthermore, major trading partners asked for economic liberalization, including reducing state subsidies and import barriers. In response, starting with the fifth economic development plan (1982–6), the state shifted its role from a "developmental" to a "regulatory" one, focusing on building market-oriented institutions rather than playing an active role in allocating resources for economic development (E. M. Kim 1997).

To reduce its role in allocating credit and to build autonomous financial-service sectors, the state gradually eliminated policy loans with preferential low interest rates. Such loans had played a dominant role in inducing firms to engage in the national projects of developing strategic sectors. Indeed, most investments in heavy industries were made in the form of policy loans, and *chaebol* were the largest beneficiaries of such loans (Moon 1998). The state also privatized commercial banks, which it owned and had used as a major policy instrument to support firms investing in strategic sectors over the previous two decades. But the *chaebol* were prohibited from acquiring commercial banks to prevent them from becoming too powerful.

On the other hand, financial liberalization and the subsequent development of the financial-services sector, along with economic development, increased the supply of financial resources available in the capital markets. But information imperfections and weak governance remained serious barriers to efficient resource allocation in these markets. In the absence of reliable corporate information and credit-rating capabilities, banks often asked financially strong group members to guarantee the debt repayment of other group members. The "too-big-to-fail" image, along with the availability of debt guarantees and group-level diversified business portfolios, made *chaebol*-affiliated firms attractive borrowers in the eyes of the banks. As a consequence, the elimination of policy loans and subsequent financial liberalization increased—rather than decreased—the advantages enjoyed by the *chaebol* in mobilizing financial resources.

Owing to heavy investments in education, the supply of a well-educated workforce also increased dramatically. In 1960 about 28 percent of the population was illiterate, but illiteracy virtually disappeared after the mid-1970s (L. Kim 1997). Between 1960 and 1980, school enrollment ratios on the secondary and tertiary education levels as a percentage of the corresponding age groups more than tripled. But, despite this increase in education levels and the corresponding supply of human talent, the labor market for experienced managers and engineers remained inflexible. Firms were reluctant to hire mid-career employees from outside; instead, they continued to recruit employees at the entry level and develop and share them within. Not only did *chaebol* provide ample training opportunities, but they also offered more opportunities for promotion and career development, as they kept expanding into more advanced industries (Amsden 1989). In the absence of a well-developed external labor market, prospective employees preferred to join *chaebol* whose internal labor markets were expected to grow and expand into promising areas. As a consequence, the increased supply of a well-educated labor force amplified—rather than decreased—the advantages of the *chaebol* in human resources.

To promote competition in the product markets, the state privatized state-owned enterprises and reduced the regulations and restrictions associated with market entry. In seeking growth opportunities, *chaebol* were also eager to acquire state-owned enterprises that were being privatized. For instance, SK emerged as a major business group by acquiring the state-owned refinery and the state-owned telecommunications service provider. In restructuring troubled industries, the state often turned to *chaebol* for acquiring and revamping a financially troubled firm. Daewoo, which was founded as a small textile trading company with four employees, grew into one of the big four *chaebol* by taking over ailing firms and turning them around, often at the state's request (Steers et al. 1989). It was the *chaebol*, then, that were able to mobilize the financial and human resources and the management skills necessary to make such acquisitions. As a consequence, the *chaebol* grew even bigger by reducing entry barriers and privatizing state-owned enterprises.

In sum, starting in the 1980s, state policy shifted its emphasis to liberalization and the building-up of market-oriented institutions. Although the supply of financial capital and human talent increased substantially, market institutions supporting the efficient allocation of capital and labor remained poorly developed, suffering from various imperfections. In the absence of well-functioning market-supporting institutions, *chaebol* were poised to become the beneficiaries of the increased supply in financial and human resources, further increasing their size and business scope.

6.2.3 The Asian financial crisis and the *chaebol*

More fundamental changes to market-supporting institutions came with the financial crisis in late 1997. The news of the collapsing Thai baht caused a massive exodus of foreign capital from Asian countries like Korea, Malaysia, and Indonesia. As foreign financial institutions called in their loans, many Korean firms went bankrupt, and the entire Korean economy was in a state of panic. Of the thirty largest *chaebol* in 1996, about half went bankrupt or were under bank-sponsored work-out programs (Kim et al. 2004). Finally, the "too-big-to-fail" fallacy was dispelled, and the survival of major *chaebol* came into question. At the same time, foreign-exchange rates soared from 864 won per dollar in January 1997 to 1,695 won per dollar by December 1997, while the Korean stock-exchange index dropped from 669 to 390 (Chang 2006).

Viewing the reckless expansion of the *chaebol* as a major contributor to the financial crisis, the state initiated a '*chaebol* reform policy' that included eliminating debt guarantees between affiliates, reducing debt-to-equity ratios to below 200 percent, and banning both cross-shareholdings and unfair trade between affiliates (Jang 2002). The government also took a series of regulatory actions to reform the corporate governance of the *chaebol* and to enhance their transparency and accountability (Chang 2006; Park and Kim 2008).

In response to the state's initiatives and to survive the financial crisis, the *chaebol* substantially improved their financial structure and transparency by reducing debt–equity ratios and eliminating almost all debt guarantees. They also restructured their business portfolios by divesting poorly performing, unrelated, and debt-ridden business units or group member firms (Choe and Roehl 2007). Later they resumed expansion and increased the number of group member firms, but they tended to focus on expanding into related areas that complemented their core businesses (Kim et al. 2004). Furthermore, for the first time in their history, the *chaebol* breached their time-honored lifetime employment practice, engaging in massive lay-offs and transforming organizations by adopting a merit-based pay system and a team-based structure (Park and Yu 2002). Although some *chaebol* failed to weather the financial crisis, others went through a painful financial, strategic, and organizational restructuring and re-emerged as more competitive players (Park 2007).

6.3 The strategy, structure and governance of business groups

6.3.1 Diversification

Chaebol have often pursued unrelated diversification on the group level. During the early stages of economic development, finding qualified suppliers of necessary parts and services was exceedingly difficult. Thus, *chaebol* often had no choice but to diversify into these related areas through vertical integration. According to former chairman Koo Cha-Kyung of the LG Group (Aguilar and Cho 1985: 3):

My father and I started a cosmetic cream factory in the late 1940s. At the time, no company could supply us with plastic caps of adequate quality for cream jars, so we had to start a plastics business. Plastic caps alone were not sufficient to run the plastic molding plant, so we added combs, toothbrushes, and soap boxes. This plastics business also led us to manufacture electric fan blades and telephone cases, which in turn led us to manufacture electrical and electronic products and telecommunication equipment. The plastics business also took us into oil refining, which needed a tanker shipping company. The oil refining company alone was paying an insurance premium amounting to more than half the total revenue of the then largest insurance company in Korea. Thus, an insurance company was started. This natural step-by-step evolution through related businesses resulted in the Lucky-Goldstar group as we see it today.

Diversifying from the cosmetic to the plastic business, from plastics to the oil-refining business, and from oil-refining to the insurance business would be considered "unrelated" diversification in the context of advanced countries. But without qualified suppliers, such diversification was often necessary and constituted a "natural step-by-step evolution through related businesses."

Furthermore, the lack of qualified suppliers in and of itself represented lucrative new business opportunities. Many modern industrial sectors simply did not exist, and demand often surpassed supply. Competent entrepreneurs—if arranged with the necessary resources and foreign technologies—could succeed with almost any business. With state subsidies and/or with their own internal-market capabilities for financial capital, human talent and intermediate products, *chaebol* were able to organize the necessary resources and pre-empt lucrative business opportunities.

With the rapid growth in their size and scope, *chaebol* established group head-quarters in their efforts to craft group-level strategies and manage group members. Samsung, for instance, established its group headquarters in 1959; LG, SK, and Hyundai followed suit in 1966, 1974, and 1979, respectively (Chang 2006). Although these *chaebol* pursued unrelated diversification, they adopted strategic control systems. Even if the group headquarters delegated decision-making authority on operational issues to its group members, it retained control over important strategic decisions such as the launch of new businesses, overseas expansion, large-scale investments, and the appointment of key executives. Intervention and coordination by the group headquarters were often necessary for rapidly mobilizing financial and human resources among group members in response to emerging entrepreneurial opportunities. For example, in entering the shipbuilding industry, the Hyundai group claimed that shipbuilding and its then core business, construction, were similar in "building things" (Amsden 1997). Indeed, its accumulated experience in project feasibility studies, project task force formation, access to foreign technical assistance, training, equipment purchase, new plant design and construction, and the operation of project start-ups in the construction business helped Hyundai to set up its new shipbuilding business (Amsden and Hikino 1994). It was the group head-quarters that would orchestrate the transfer and sharing of resources and expertise between two group members.

As Fig. 6.1 shows, the *chaebol* kept expanding their business scope until the financial crisis in late 1997. But, in the process, their advantages in pursuing unrelated diversification might have been overstretched. As major *chaebol* continued to expand their business scope, they began competing fiercely against one another, as a result of which their internal-market advantages in mobilizing generic resources (for example, financial and human resources) lost much of their significance. Instead, more industry-specific resources (technological and marketing capabilities) became the defining sources of competitive advantage in the domestic market. In addition, as *chaebol* moved into the higher-end segments of the global industry after their initial success in exporting low-end products, the significance of their industry-specific capabilities increased. Furthermore, the challenges from less-developed countries such as China and other South East Asian countries as well as the sharp increase in domestic labor costs during the 1980s and 1990s made the global cost leadership of the *chaebol* obsolete. The competitive landscape, both domestic and global, indicated a shift in their competitive basis from generic to industry-specific capabilities. The *chaebol* had maintained their internal-market advantages and group-level resource advantages, but might have failed to convert them into industry-specific capabilities.

The reckless expansion of the *chaebol* was challenged in the wake of the 1997 financial crisis. In response, they refocused their business portfolios. Among the top thirty *chaebol*, the average number of 4-digit Korean SIC codes was about 15 in 1987, increased to more than 23 in 1997, and had fallen to about 14 in 2006. During this

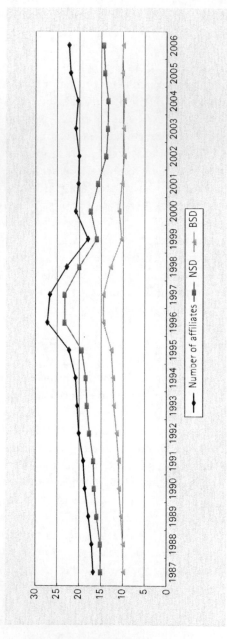

Figure 6.1 Diversification of the top thirty chaebols, 1987–2006

Note: Figures include non-financial sectors only.

NSD (Narrow Spectrum Diversificaion): number of 4-digit SIC segments.
BSD (Broad Spectrum Diversification): number of 2-digit SIC segments.

Source: Korea Investors Service.

period, the average number of 2-digit Korean SIC codes shifted from 9.9 in 1987, to 14.5 in 1997, to 10 in 2006. Although the *chaebol* have remained unrelated diversified firms, they have somewhat improved their focus.

6.3.2 Globalization

Chaebol have been leaders in globalization (E. M. Kim 2000). For instance, Table 6.3, which ranks the major Korean multinational firms according to the number of their foreign subsidiaries, shows that most of them are group-affiliated firms. Likewise, of the ten Korean firms listed among the *Business Week* Global 1,000 companies in 2004, all except four of the enterprises that were state owned, either formerly or at that time, belonged to major *chaebol* (Samsung Electronics, SK Telecom, Hyundai Motor, LG Electronics, SK Networks, and SK Corp.).

From the early days of industrialization, the Korean government pursued a strategy of export-led growth (Haggard 1990; Westphal 1990). Although the initial five-year economic plan (1962–6) focused on import substitution, the emphasis quickly switched to export promotion. Exports were promoted, not only as a way to earn foreign exchange to pay off foreign debt incurred during the 1950s and early 1960s, but also as a requisite to justify investing in large-scale manufacturing facilities, given the small domestic market. Thus, a commitment to and the capability for export promotion became major requirements for becoming a strategic partner on developmental projects.

During the third five-year plan (1972–6), the state established general trading companies (GTCs), modeled after Japan's *sogo shosha*, and used all sorts of measures to promote their exports. It provided low-cost financing for each dollar exported, which often more than compensated for losses incurred in export transactions. It also recognized excellence in exports in various forms, including prizes, citations, and medals. Furthermore, it annually increased the minimum amount of exports that the GTC needed to reach to maintain its GTC status that came with the state's preferential treatment. In response, GTCs made strenuous efforts, often vying fiercely against one another, to increase exports, thereby playing a key role in export promotion (Cho 1987). The state granted licenses to thirteen GTCs, twelve of which belonged to large *chaebol* and only one of which was established specifically to coordinate the export activities of stand-alone small- and medium-sized firms. As a consequence, the large *chaebol*, which already enjoyed advantages in size and scope, received an additional boost with the licensing of GTCs and became leading players in exports. But, as the composition of exports shifted from primary products to manufactured products, from labor-intensive products to more capital-intensive products, and from low-tech products to more advanced products, the role of the GTCs in promoting exports declined. Nonetheless, the state's development strategy of export-led growth gave a significant head start to major *chaebol* in looking for foreign-market opportunities and gaining international experience.

Table 6.3 Leading Korean multinational firms, 2003

Company name	Group name	Sales (thousand Korean won)	No. of subsidiaries	No. of countries	No. of regions*
LG Electronics	LG	20,176,910,000	92	46	6
Samsung Electronics	Samsung	43,582,016,000	85	33	6
LG Chem Investment	LG	357,545,000	44	15	4
Youngone		509,063,198	27	10	3
Hyundai Motor	Hyundai Motor	24,967,265,000	25	13	5
CJ	CJ	2,405,508,191	24	11	3
Hyundai Heavy Industries	Hyundai Heavy Industries	8,153,499,952	20	13	4
LG Ind. Systems	LG	868,341,299	19	10	3
Samsung Electro-Mechanics	Samsung	2,591,349,149	18	11	4
Hyosung	Hyosung	4,218,696,022	18	10	4
Daerim	Daerim	251,247,706	17	11	4
Hanwha	Hanwha	2,200,754,856	17	10	5
Trigem Computer		2,226,231,283	17	8	3
Hyundai Mobis	Hyundai Motor	5,306,638,804	15	7	3
SKC Ltd	SK	1,331,344,373	15	5	3
Hankook Tire		1,684,227,069	14	12	3
Doosan	Doosan	2,016,093,051	13	6	3
Pacific		1,119,838,216	12	8	3
Kia Motors	Hyundai Motor	12,839,881,000	11	7	3
LG Cable & Machinery	LG	1,939,661,763	11	5	2
Ssang Bang Wool		217,760,728	11	4	2
Poongsan		65,089,348	10	8	2
Samsung SDI	Samsung	4,779,221,417	10	8	5
Kolon Ind.	Kolon	1,250,484,776	10	7	3
Partsnic Co. Ltd		210,024,100	10	6	4
Taihan Electric Wire		1,246,135,399	9	8	3
Cheil Ind.	Samsung	2,086,253,452	9	6	3
Zinus		107,769,728	9	6	2
Kumho Industrial	Kumho	1,806,081,908	8	7	3
Dongsung Chemical		90,066,124	8	5	2
SK Chemicals	SK	852,970,322	8	5	3

Note: * To calculate the number of geographic regions, host countries are categorized into six regions: Asia and the Pacific, the Middle East, Europe, North America, South America, and Africa.

Source: Korea Investors Service and Export-Import Bank of Korea.

The internal-market advantages of the *chaebol* have also contributed to pursuing international expansion. Given that global expansion often requires a serious commitment of financial and human resources, the ability of the *chaebol* to pool and share these resources has played an important role in promoting foreign expansion. Such internal-market advantages are often converted into firm-specific advantages such as technological and marketing capabilities, which can be transferred into foreign markets. For instance, group-affiliated firms enjoy several advantages over stand-alone firms in building technological capabilities (Chang et al. 2006). *Chaebol* can secure the necessary scientists and engineers by relying on group internal labor markets. In economies with an acute scarcity of qualified scientists and engineers, attracting, developing, and sharing talented scientists and engineers within a group provides substantial advantages. *Chaebol* sometimes establish group-level research laboratories, which focus on basic research and long-term projects, to complement and extend the technological capabilities of their group member firms. Advantages in technological capabilities provide a higher incentive and facility for *chaebol*-affiliated firms to pursue international expansion.

In addition, *chaebol* often seek to replicate internal-market advantages in foreign markets as well. In entering into a foreign market, other group member firms may constitute reliable, trustworthy partners that often design specialized components and provide just-in-time delivery. Since prior relationships and geographic proximity increase the efficiency of such collaboration, *chaebol*-affiliated firms have incentives to co-locate their foreign operations (Martin et al. 1998; Shaver and Flyer 2000). For example, Samsung Electric entered Portugal to supply TV tuners and FBTs for Samsung Electronics' three plants located in England, Spain, and Hungary (Jun 1995). The entry into China by group member firms of the Samsung group is another case in point (Chang and Park 2005). If Samsung Electronics is located in Tianjin, other group members such as Samsung Corporation and Samsung SDI are more likely to locate in Tianjin than in other regions of China. In doing so, they can learn from Samsung Electronics about the local environment, do business with Samsung Electronics, and benefit from its reputation. Indeed, using a sample of Korean firms' foreign direct investments in China, Guillén (2002) and Chang and Park (2005) found strong evidence that *chaebol*-affiliated firms tended to be clustered in a similar region. By co-locating and coordinating foreign operations, such firms can replicate group-level resource advantages in foreign markets.

6.3.3 Corporate governance

Most Korean firms are family firms, and *chaebol* are not exceptions. The Samsung Group is controlled by the Lee family, the LG group by the Koo family, the Hyundai group by the Chung family, and the SK group by the Chey family. Although the equity holdings of the controlling families have declined as group member firms have grown in number and volume, the families still maintain tight control over the firms

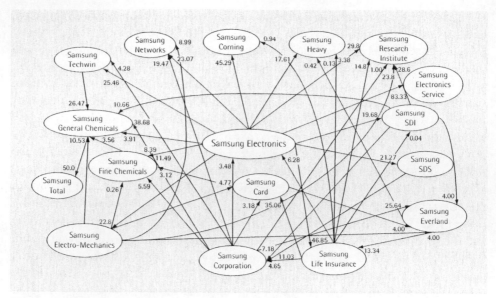

Figure 6.2 Ownership structure of the Samsung group, 2006

Note: Figures are percentages.

Source: Korea Investors Service.

through cross-shareholdings among group members (see Fig. 6.2 for the ownership structure of the Samsung group).

Controling families have substantial incentives to maximize firm performance, hoping to pass control of the firm to their descendants rather than consume the wealth during their lifetime (Casson 1999). Furthermore, the families are strongly identified with their business groups; consequently, failing in business often means disgrace for their family names as well as economic disaster. Thus, family ownership and control have contributed to the rapid growth and long-term success of the *chaebol*.

But, on the other hand, because families have complete control of the *chaebol* despite their small ownership stakes in the group member firms, they are able to pursue private gain, often to the detriment of minority shareholders. Bae, Kang, and Kim (2002) and Baek, Kang and Lee (2006) reported that *chaebol* family members tunnel profits out of member firms where they have low cash-flow rights to member firms where they have high cash-flow rights, thereby increasing their private gains and expropriating wealth from outside investors. Chang (2003) also provided strong evidence that controlling families exploit insider information to take both direct and indirect equity stakes in profitable or promising member firms in order to maximize their private gains. Thus, family ownership and control have both a bright and a dark side in the context of *chaebol*. On the one hand, family ownership and control provide adequate incentives and long-term orientation in the value-creation process, but they also allow the families to expropriate minority shareholders.

Such inadequacies in corporate governance have been brought to light since the financial crisis, leading to serious efforts to build market-oriented economic institutions. Viewing the inefficiencies and reckless expansion of business groups as the root cause of the financial crisis, the post-financial crisis reform has focused on improving the institutional support of external markets and corporate governance to discipline the *chaebol* (Park and Kim 2008). To improve transparency and accountability, major *chaebol* have been required to prepare combined financial statements. To improve the independence and accountability of the boards, all listed firms are now required to fill at least 25 percent of their board seats with outside directors; the minimum requirement is even higher at 50 percent for large firms with an asset size of more than two trillion Korean won (Choi et al. 2007). Before the financial crisis, domestic institutional investors were allowed to exercise their voting rights only through shadow voting, thereby seriously limiting their monitoring role. Since the financial crisis, those constraints have been eliminated. In addition, to protect minority shareholders and promote fair competition, the government has carefully examined intra-group transactions.

Before the financial crisis, foreign investors were not allowed to own more than 7 percent of shares in a domestic Korean firm. But such barriers have now been lifted, as a result of which foreign ownership in Korea increased from 13 percent of publicly listed firms in 1997 to 42 percent in 2006 in terms of market capitalization (*Business Week* 2006). For some large companies, foreign ownership was even higher: 85.7 percent in Kookmin Bank, one of the largest banks in Korea; 68 percent in POSCO, the renowned steel maker; and 54 percent in Samsung Electronics. The increasing presence of foreign investors has also ushered in the notion of "shareholder capitalism" and led to greater shareholder activism. For instance, the Dubai-based investment company Sovereign Asset Management became the largest shareholder of SK Corp. by acquiring 14.9 percent of shares in 2002. Sovereign Asset Management then declared that it intended to influence and discipline management for the benefit of minority shareholders. Indeed, it attempted to oust Chey Tae Won, the CEO and group chairperson, who was convicted of accounting fraud. Even though the attempt failed, Sovereign Asset Management brought concerns over corporate transparency, shareholder rights, and corporate governance to public attention.

In sum, as family-controlled diversified business groups, *chaebol* entail both advantages and disadvantages of family ownership and control. The entrepreneurial spirit, strong incentives, and long-term horizons by controling families have played an important role in the rapid growth of the *chaebol*. But excessive family control much beyond its cash-flow rights sometimes leads to the expropriation of minority shareholders. Since the financial crisis, corporate governance reforms have been implemented to improve transparency and accountability.

6.4 Discussion and conclusion

The genesis and evolution of the *chaebol* agree well with extant theories about business groups. The political economy perspective has examined the role of the state in the formation of business groups to facilitate economic development (Amsden 1989; Wade 1990; Evans 1995; Feenstra and Hamilton 2006). In the early stages of economic development, developmental states with the ability to allocate capital and other scarce resources often encourage a few entrepreneurs to enter new industries that are deemed crucial to economic development, thereby facilitating the proliferation of business groups. Korea is a case in point. In implementing a series of five-year economic development plans, the state designated "strategic sectors", selected a few firms as partners, and arranged generous support, including low-interest funds, access to foreign technologies, state subsidies, and domestic market protection. With support came discipline as well. The state demanded high performance in return for generous support; if a selected firm failed to meet performance expectations, it ceased to be subsidized. In the absence of adequate resources and institutions, the state's "disciplined" support contributed significantly to the formation of the *chaebol* and Korea's rapid economic development instead of to "cronyism" in resource allocation (Evans 1995; Amsden 1997).

While the political economy perspective focuses on the business–state coalition as a cause of the emergence of business groups, the market-failure perspective views business groups as an organizational "innovation overcoming—and reaping from—imperfect markets in the less developed countries" (Leff 1978: 668). In other words, business groups can overcome the disadvantages of market imperfections and the institutional backwardness of emerging economies by internalizing the roles of markets for financial capital, human talent, and intermediate products (Khanna and Palepu 1997; Feenstra and Hamilton 2006). In fact, *chaebol*—facing a shortage of financial capital, human talent, and qualified suppliers during the early days of industrialization—pooled and shared scarce resources among group members, thereby creating group-level resource advantages that played a crucial role in their early success. In addition, as the supply of financial capital and human talent increased over time without the concomitant development of well-functioning market-supporting institutions, *chaebol* were also better positioned to mobilize these resources in the external markets, thereby amplifying their resource advantages further. Indeed, *chaebol* have often succeeded in transforming such resource advantages into firm-specific competitive advantages, evolving into major players in the domestic markets and into leading Korean multinational firms.

But since the 1990s this dominance of business groups in the Korean economy has come to be seen as a major obstacle to developing efficient external markets (Almeida and Wolfenzon 2006). The rankings among information technology service firms closely resemble those among the *chaebol*. The reasons are that each major *chaebol* has its own information technology service firm, and all the group members tend to do business with this firm in the same business group. The availability of such captive customers offers a valuable edge to *chaebol*-affiliated firms in seeking new market opportunities and increasing market share. But the prevalence of *chaebol* and intra-group transactions inhibits fair competition and the emergence of specialized players. In a similar vein, the *chaebol* are believed to inhibit the formation and growth of small entrepreneurial firms. For instance, in the USA, small, agile start-ups usually dominate in the emerging Internet industry, but in Korea the market is still tilted toward *chaebol* (Einhorn et al. 1999). *Chaebol* have unique advantages in financial resources, specialized manufacturing capability, access to distribution channels, service networks, and complementary technologies that are necessary to commercialize and profit from an innovation. As a consequence, while start-ups encounter difficulties in raising equity capital and cracking protected markets, *chaebol*-affiliated firms—strong in brand names, distribution channels, customer bases, and financial resources—enjoy distinct advantages in pursuing new opportunities. In short, *chaebol* came into existence as a response to market imperfections, but their success and dominance in the Korean economy now make them a source of market imperfection and an obstacle to the development of efficient external markets.

Since the financial crisis of 1997, the Korean economy has gone through rapid liberalization and market-oriented institutional transitions. To the extent that *chaebol* overcome market imperfections and create group-level resource advantages by pooling and sharing resources through internal-market operations, liberalization and market-oriented institutional transitions may be expected to make such internal-market advantages less relevant, thereby reducing the competitive advantages of the *chaebol* (Kim et al. 2004; Chang 2006). Indeed, some *chaebol* have gone bankrupt since the financial crisis. But many of them appear to have made impressive turnarounds and have become stronger rather than weaker since the crisis (Choo et al. 2009). In fact, there are some reasons to believe that market-oriented institutional transitions would not instantaneously eliminate the advantages of the *chaebol* and their internal markets. Although market and trade barriers can be eradicated instantaneously, well-functioning market-supporting institutions cannot be built overnight (Khanna and Palepu 2000). The development of a new, properly functioning institution often requires developing other complementary institutions. Such interrelationships among institutions make introducing new institutions difficult and time-consuming. Thus, although the value-creating potentials of the *chaebol* may increasingly require better internal markets predicated upon a larger pool of businesses, they may not disappear immediately. And so, large and well-diversified business groups like the major *chaebol* appear to be retaining their competitive advantages (Hoskisson et al. 2004).

In addition, corporate governance reform since the financial crisis may also induce *chaebol* to run internal-market operations with a stronger emphasis on efficiency and value creation. When external markets are underdeveloped, the internal markets of business groups, despite their value-adding potential, suffer from agency conflicts and inefficiencies, thereby giving rise to resource misallocation and value destruction. For instance, business groups may allocate resources among their member firms by the "norms of equity and common welfare," rather than by the attractiveness of investment opportunities (Lincoln et al. 1996: 71). Controlling families may shift resources among group members to maximize their private benefits (Johnson et al. 2000). But advances in external-market institutions and corporate governance systems may also mitigate such value-destroying aspects of internal markets. With increasing market competition, business groups would have heightened incentives to operate their internal markets with an increased emphasis on enhancing efficiency and competitive advantages. Likewise, increased transparency and managerial accountability would curb controling families from distorting intra-group transactions for their own private benefit. Thus, by mitigating the agency conflicts and inefficiencies embedded in internal markets, the development of external markets may increase, rather than decrease, the benefits of the internal markets and business groups accordingly.

Indeed, recent studies have suggested that business groups became more efficiency-oriented after the financial crisis (e.g. Chang and Shin 2006; Choo et al. 2009). Choo et al. (2009) reported that *chaebol*-affiliated firms were no more efficient than stand-alone firms before the financial crisis but became significantly more so in the post-crisis period. In a similar vein, Chang and Shin (2006) also provided evidence that the financial crisis induced *chaebol* to operate their internal labor markets with a greater emphasis on efficiency. They found that, before the financial crisis, CEO turnover was unrelated to firm performance among *chaebol*-affiliated firms and stand-alone firms alike, but that, since the crisis, poor performance has significantly increased the likelihood of CEO turnover among *chaebol*-affiliated firms but not among stand-alone firms. These findings indicate that, since the crisis, *chaebol* have operated their internal labor markets more efficiently, which may explain in part their post-crisis re-emergence. As a consequence, the advancement of market-supporting institutions and corporate governance since the financial crisis may have quite different implications for established major *chaebol* and for the formation of new business groups. Major *chaebol* that already have well-diversified business portfolios are likely to retain their internal-market advantages. But the advancement of market-supporting institutions would make it increasingly difficult to build a new business group from scratch.

In conclusion, this chapter has addressed how Korean *chaebol* got started and evolved over time with special emphases on product diversification, globalization, and corporate governance. The Korean experience suggests that state policy, entrepreneurs, and competitive and institutional environments all play important roles in dictating the evolutionary paths and competitive strategies of business groups. Business groups entail both a bright and a dark side. They are organizational arrangements designed to overcome market imperfections in emerging economies, producing global players in the process. By contrast, intra-group trading and a lack of transparency and accountability allow business groups to breed "cronyism" in both resource allocation and the expropriation of minority shareholders. The excessive success and dominance of business groups may make the formation of small- and medium-sized firms and the development of efficient external markets difficult.

Such a duality of business groups presents difficult challenges to scholars, managers, and public policy-makers alike. The Korean experience both before and after the financial crisis presents an excellent opportunity to enhance our understanding of the various issues associated with business groups.

REFERENCES

AGUILAR, F. J., and CHO, D. S. (1985). *Gold Star Co. Ltd. Case no. 9-385-264.* Boston: Harvard Business School.

ALMEIDA, H., and WOLFENZON, D. (2006). "Should Business Groups be Dismantled? The Equilibrium Costs of Efficient Internal Capital Markets," *Journal of Financial Economics*, 79: 99–144.

AMSDEN, A. H. (1989). *Asia's Next Giant.* New York: Oxford University Press.

AMSDEN, A. H. (1997). "South Korea: Enterprising Groups and Entrepreneurial Government," in A. D. Chandler, Jr., F. Amatori, and T. Hikino (eds.), *Big Business and the Wealth of Nations.* New York: Cambridge University Press.

AMSDEN, A. H., and HIKINO, T. (1994). "Project Execution Capability, Organizational Know-how and Conglomerate Corporate Growth in Late Industrialization," *Industrial and Corporate Change*, 3: 111–47.

BAE, K.-H., KANG, J.-K., and KIM, J.-M. (2002). "Tunneling or Value Added? Evidence from Mergers by Korean Business Groups," *Journal of Finance*, 57: 2695–740.

BAEK, J. S., KANG, J. K., and LEE, I. (2006). "Business Groups and Tunneling: Evidence from Private Securities Offerings by Korean *chaebol*," *Journal of Finance*, 61: 2415–49.

BREMNER, B., and MOON, M. (2002). "Cool Korea: How it Roared back from Disaster and Became a Model for Asia", *Business Week*, June 10, pp. 54–8.

Business Week (2006). "An Unruly Guest from the West," Feb. 27.

CASSON, M. (1999). "The Economics of the Family Firm," *Scandinavian Economic History Review*, 17/1: 10–23.

CHANG, J., and SHIN, H.-H. (2006). "Governance System Effectiveness Following the Crisis: The Case of Korean Business Group Headquarters," *Corporate Governance*, 14/2: 85–97.

CHANG S. J. (2003). *The Rise and Fall of Chaebol: Financial Crisis and Transformations of Korean Business Groups.* Cambridge: Cambridge University Press.

CHANG S. J. (2006). "Korean Business Groups: The Financial Crisis and the Restructuring of *chaebol*," in S. J. Chang (ed.), *Business Groups in East Asia: Financial Crisis, Restructuring, and New Growth.* Oxford: Oxford University Press, 52–69.

CHANG, S. J., and HONG, J. (2000). "Economic Performance of Group-Affiliated Companies in Korea: Intragroup Resource Sharing and Internal Business Transactions," *Academy of Management Journal*, 43: 429–48.

CHANG, S. J., and PARK, S. (2005). "Types of Firms Generating Network Externalities and MNCs' Co-Location Decisions," *Strategic Management Journal*, 26: 595–615.

CHANG, S. J., CHUNG, C. N., and MAHMOOD, I. (2006). "When and how does Business Group Affiliation Promote Firm Innovation? A Tale of Two Emerging Economies," *Organization Science*, 17: 637–56.

CHO, D. S. (1987). *The General Trading Company: Concepts and Strategy.* Lexington, MA: Lexington Books.

CHOE, S., and ROEHL, T. W. (2007). "What to Shed and what to Keep: Corporate Transformation in Korean Business Groups," *Long Range Planning*, 40: 465–87.

CHOI, J. J., PARK, S. W., and YOO, S. S. (2007). "The Value of Outside Directors: Evidence from Corporate Governance Reform in Korea," *Journal of Financial and Quantitative Analysis*, 42: 941–62.

CHOO, K., LEE, K., RYU, K., and YOON, J. (2009). "Changing Performance of Business Groups over Two Decades: Technological Capabilities and Investment Inefficiency in Korean *Chaebols*," *Economic Development and Cultural Change*, 57: 359–86.

The Economist. (2008). "The Export Juggernaut," Sept. 27.

EINHORN, B., SHARI, M., and VEALE, J. (1999). "Company Size does Matter in Asia's Cyber Race from Singapore to Taipei," *Business Week*, May 17.

EVANS, P. (1995). *Embedded Autonomy.* Princeton: Princeton University Press.

EVANS, P. (1998). "Transferable Lessons? Re-Examining the Institutional Prerequisites of East Asian Economic Policies," *Journal of Development Studies*, 34/6: 66–86.

FEENSTRA, R. C., and HAMILTON, G. G. (2006). *Emergent Economies, Divergent Paths: Economic Organization and International Trade in South Korea and Taiwan.* New York: Cambridge University Press.

GUILLÉN, M. (2002). "Structural Inertia, Imitation, and Foreign Expansion: South Korean Firms and Business Groups in China, 1987–95," *Academy of Management Journal*, 45: 509–25.

HAGGARD, S. (1990). *Pathways from the Periphery.* Ithaca, NY: Cornell University Press.

HOSKISSON, R., KIM, H., WHITE, R., and TIHANYI, L. (2004). "A Framework for Understanding International Diversification by Business Groups from Emerging Economies," in M. Hitt, and J. L. Cheng (eds.), *Advances in International Management.* Oxford: Elsevier/JAI Press, 137–63.

JANG, H. (2002). "After the Economic Crisis: An Analysis of the Effects of Corporate Restructuring," in Z. Rhee and E. Chang (eds.), *Korean Business and Management: The Reality and the Vision.* Seoul: Hollym.

JOHNSON, S., LA PORTA, R., LOPEZ-DE-SILANES, F., and SHLEIFER, A. (2000). "Tunneling," *American Economic Review*, 90/2 (May), 22–7.

JUN Y. (1995). "Strategic Responses of Korean Firms to Globalization and Regionalization Forces," in D. F. Simon (ed.), *Corporate Strategies in the Pacific Rim: Global versus Regional Trends*: London: Routledge, 166–90.

KHANNA, T., and PALEPU, K. (1997). "Why Focused Strategies may be Wrong for Emerging Markets," *Harvard Business Review*, 75/4: 41–51.

KHANNA T., and PALEPU, K. (2000). "The Future of Business Groups in Emerging Markets: Long Run Evidence from Chile," *Academy of Management Journal*, 43: 268–85.

KHANNA, T., and RIVKIN, J. (2001). "Estimating the Performance Effects of Business Groups in Emerging m Markets," *Strategic Management Journal*, 22: 45–74.

KIM, E. M. (1997). *Big Business, Strong State.* Albany, NY: State University of New York Press.

KIM, E. M. (2000). "Globalization of the South Korean *Chaebol*," in S. S. Kim (ed.), *Korea's Globalization.* New York: Cambridge University Press, 102–25.

KIM, H., HOSKISSON, R., TIHANYI, L., and HONG, J. (2004). "The Evolution and Restructuring of Diversified Business Groups in Emerging Markets: The Lessons from *chaebol* in Korea," *Asia Pacific Journal of Management*, 21: 25–48.

KIM, L. (1997). *Imitation to Innovation.* Boston: Harvard Business School Press.

Korea Economic Research Institute (1995). *Business Groups in Korea* (in Korean). Seoul: Korea Economic Research Institute.

LEFF, N. H. (1978). "Industrial Organization and Entrepreneurship in the Developing Countries: The Economic Groups," *Economic Development and Cultural Change*, 26: 661–75.

LINCOLN, J. R., GERLACH, M. L., and AHMADJIAN, C. L. (1996). "Keiretsu Networks and Corporate Performance in Japan," *American Sociological Review*, 61: 67–88.

MARTIN, X., SWAMINATHAN, A., and MITCHELL, W. (1998). "Organizational Evolution in the Interorganizational Environment: Incentives and Constraints on International Expansion Strategy," *Administrative Science Quarterly*, 43: 566–601.

MOON, C. (1998). "The Demise of a Developmentalist State? Neoconservative Reforms and Political Consequences in South Korea," *Journal of Developing Societies*, 4: 67–84.

PARK, C. (2007). "Radical Environmental Changes and Corporate Transformation: Korean Firms," *Long Range Planning*, 40: 419–30.

PARK, C., and KIM, S. (2008). "Corporate Governance, Regulatory Changes, and Corporate Restructuring in Korea, 1993–2004," *Journal of World Business*, 43: 66–84.

PARK, W. S., and YU, G. C. (2002). "HRM in Korea: Transformation and New Patterns," in Z. Rhee and E. Chang (eds.), *Korean Business and Management: The Reality and the Vision*. Elizabeth, NJ: Hollym, 367–91.

SHAVER J. M., and FLYER, F. (2000). "Agglomeration Economics, Firm Heterogeneity and Foreign Direct investment in the United States," *Strategic Management Journal*, 21: 1175–93.

STEERS, R. M., SHIN, Y. K., and UNGSON, G. R. (1989). *The Chaebol: Korea's New Industrial Might*. New York: Harper & Row.

UNGSON, G. R., STEERS, R. M., and PARK, S. (1997). *Korean Enterprise*. Boston: Harvard Business School Press.

WADE, R. (1990). *Governing the Market*. Princeton: Princeton University Press.

WESTPHAL, L. E. (1990). "Industrial Policy in an Export-Propelled Economy: Lessons from South Korea's Experience," *Journal of Economic Perspective*, 4/3: 41–59.

CHAPTER 7

BUSINESS GROUPS IN TAIWAN

CHI-NIEN CHUNG

ISHTIAQ P. MAHMOOD

7.1 INTRODUCTION

THIS chapter examines the formation and evolution of the 100 largest business groups in Taiwan from the 1970s to the 2000s. We first provide a brief description of the formation process of business groups in Taiwan. Specifically, we refer to the three main arguments related to the emergence of business groups in the literature, market power, state and policy targeting, and persistent social systems (Hamilton and Biggart 1988). We next investigate the strategy and structure of Taiwanese business groups. We develop indicators and study the trends of product diversification and internationalization of the groups. We also review key studies that explain the diversification patterns of the top 100 groups in Taiwan. In terms of group structure, we discuss inter-firm ties among affiliates within the groups and how the diversification strategy and inter-firm ties have co-evolved. The third area of discussion concerns the governance structure of the group. We examine the background of the shareholders and their respective shareholding in the group firms. We also analyze the composition and professional and social background of the top management. Finally, we consider the competitive capabilities of the group. We discuss the core competences, such as the technological innovation and marketing capabilities, of the groups.

This chapter is the one of the few large-scale empirical studies to investigate the evolution of the strategy, structure, governance, and core competence of Taiwan's top

100 groups. Unlike previous studies, which have examined a single or a few groups (Takao 1989; Numazaki 1993) or the top 100 groups in a single year (Hamilton 1997), this chapter examines the largest 100 groups over thirty years. The scale and scope of our analysis not only contribute to the understanding of Taiwanese groups but also shed light on how business groups respond to environmental changes in general.

The rest of the chapter is organized as follows. In Section 7.2 we discuss Taiwan's early industrialization in the 1960s and 1970s, the institutional transition in the late 1980s, and recent developments in the 1990s and 2000 onwards. We consider the environmental factors that have affected the formation and transformation of Taiwan's business groups. In Section 7.3 we describe our data sources and coding procedures. In Section 7.4 we portray the growth of Taiwanese business groups from the 1970s to the 2000s. We then turn to the evolution of strategy and structure of the top 100 groups in Section 7.5. We move on to group governance in Section 7.6 and examine the composition and top executives. In Section 7.7 we investigate the innovation capabilities and performance (such as number of patents) of business groups. Section 7.8 is our conclusion, in which we summarize the growth of Taiwanese business groups over the period 1970s–2000s and project their possible future development.

7.2 INDUSTRIALIZATION, INSTITUTIONAL CHANGES, AND BUSINESS GROUPS IN TAIWAN, 1960S–2006

In our research we adopted an integrative institutional perspective to analyze the formation and evolution of Taiwanese business groups.[1] This view regards a nation's pre-existing arrangements, particularly those among the nation's sociocultural environment, its state government, and its market conditions, as the path-dependent context that guides how individual firms, business groups, and governments respond to the external opportunities and constraints (e.g. Chang 2006). In other words, it sees the firms and the groups as operating on a complex set of variables that differs from one context to another.

7.2.1 Industrialization in the 1950s–70s

Taiwan's initial industrialization started in the late 1950s. The Kuomintang (KMT) government provided ample tax incentives to attract foreign investment to produce

---

[1] See Section 7.3 for the detailed definition of business groups in Taiwan.

goods for export. This export-oriented strategy was spearheaded by licensing agreements, sometimes called original equipment manufacturers (OEMs) by scholars (Hobday 1995). Under OEM, Taiwanese firms paid for the right to manufacture products, and foreign multinationals transferred the necessary manufacturing know-how. The government also set up research facilities such as the Industrial Technology Research Institute (ITRI) to conduct risky, expensive research and development (R&D) and to transfer technological knowledge to domestic firms. The developmental model adopted by KMT was thus different from that of other East Asian countries such as Korea, which allocated bank credit and directed monetary policies (Cheng 2001). This model not only shaped Taiwan's economic structure but also affected Taiwan's business organizations. Certain regulations and policies that accompanied this developmental model directly affected Taiwan's business groups. Chung (2001) suggests that regulatory institutions were central to the formation of Taiwan's large groups, especially the Statute for Encouragement of Investment, which was enacted in 1960. Its original intent was to prompt Taiwan's initial industrialization (Li 1988: 16–17).

For the policy planner, this statute influenced business groups' activities in unintended ways. In the 1960 ordinance, new investments (new firms) had income-tax relief for five years. For firms with increased production capacity, this tax holiday applied only when the capacity was 30 percent greater than that of the original firm (Li 1988). Under this regulation, it was more attractive to establish new firms to capitalize on the tax holiday and establish a group than it was to expand the original firm and form a multiunit enterprise. When the KMT regime removed restrictions on new establishments in most industries in 1964 because of the change of orientation of economy policy from import substitution industrialization (ISI) to export growth (Cheng 2001), Taiwanese entrepreneurs responded by setting up many business groups. Chung (2001) found that more than half of the 150 groups in his sample established their second firms between 1964 and 1968, while less than 5 percent of the groups set up their second firms after 1969.

As well as citing local industrial and tax policies, recent studies have also highlighted the influence of global markets on the development of Taiwanese business groups (Feenstra and Hamilton 2006). We believe that both international and local forces contributed to the formation of Taiwanese groups. In fact, our integrative institutional framework, which incorporates global markets, local states, and social and cultural factors, has given us a better understanding of the formation process of Taiwanese groups (Chung and Mahmood 2006).

Taiwan's experience shows that market expansion prepared the necessary template for firms to grow, the strong motivation from Chinese familism drove the entrepreneurs to catch the opportunity and expand their enterprises, and then the institutional incentive led the enterprise system toward a group form (Chung 2001). Table 7.1A shows that the thirty largest groups had already participated in quite a few unrelated industries in the early 1970s. Longitudinal and comparative case studies indicate that political ties to the KMT regime helped connected groups to move into regulated industries, shaping the diversification profile of Taiwanese

Table 7.1A Top thirty Taiwanese business groups, 1973

Rank	Group name	Year of establishment	Main industry	Number of industries	Sales (US$ m.)
1	Formosa Plastics	1954	Plastic products	7	397
2	Far Eastern	1954	Textiles	5	146
3	Tainan Spinning	1953	Textiles	9	143
4	Cathay	1961	Plastic products	7	128
5	Tatung	1918	Machinery	17	117
6	Yulon	1953	Transportation equipment	5	112
7	Hsiao's Brothers	1956	Chemical materials	3	102
8	Wei Chuan	1947	Food products	5	91
9	Shin Kong	1952	Chemical materials	5	85
10	Lai Ching Tien	1952	Chemical materials	2	75
11	Pacific Electric Wire & Cable	1950	Electrical & electronic products	5	71
12	China General Plastics	1955	Plastic products	5	64
13	Yuen Foong Yu	1950	Pulp & paper products	7	64
14	Sampo	1962	Electrical & electronic products	2	63
15	Tai Yu	1954	Food products	2	55
16	Tuntex	1959	Textiles	6	55
17	Kao Hsing Chang	1951	Basic metal	7	54
18	Cheng He Fa	1949	Food products	8	49
19	All Sincere	1966	Food products	4	49
20	Jang Dah Fiber	1962	Chemical materials	2	48
21	Tai Ling Textile	1955	Chemical materials	3	47
22	Kou Feng	1955	Textiles	7	46
23	Pao Tung	1958	Pulp & paper products	7	45
24	Lee Chang Yung	1959	Lumber & wood products	3	40
25	Jung Hsing	1951	Textiles	4	39
26	Taiwan Plywood	1959	Lumber & wood products	3	37
27	Chi Mei	1960	Chemical materials	5	34
28	Hung Chow	1957	Textiles	2	32
29	Ve Wong	1951	Food products	2	32
30	Kwang Yang	1963	Transportation equipment	3	32

Note: The number of 2-digit industrial sectors according to the Standard Industrial Classification (SIC) system published by the Taiwanese government in 2006.

Source: Compiled from the directory Business Groups in Taiwan, see the data section of the text for details.

groups in the early stage. For example, both Far Eastern and Tainan Spinning groups started their businesses in the textile industry and then moved into the cement industry, which at that time was restricted, with the assistance of their political networks (Chung 2006).

By the early 1970s Taiwanese society widely accepted and understood the group form as a popular way to organize business. Reflecting the importance of business groups in Taiwan, the first version of the directory *Business Groups in Taiwan* (*BGT*) was published by the China Credit Information Service (CCIS) in Taipei during this period. In other words, Taiwanese business groups had become a legitimized organizational form.

7.2.2 Economic liberalization in the 1980s and recent development

In the late 1980s Taiwan experienced the largest wave of economic liberalization in its modern history. The market-centered transition opened up product markets, financial markets, and labor markets far more than they had been before. These changes were so significant that scholars labeled them the "Great Transition" (Tien 1989).

Before the late 1980s the Taiwanese state (that is, the KMT) had dominated Taiwan's politics and economy (Amsden 1985; Gold 1985). Although it pushed economic growth through an export-oriented strategy and technological R&D, the state dominated most financial industries, public utilities, transportation, and other key manufacturing sectors (Wade 1990). The situation did not change until the mid-1980s, when the KMT faced US pressure for fair trade practices, as well as internal challenges such as political opposition, social movements, and dissatisfied capitalists. Economic liberalization was accompanied and accelerated by the political democratization that started in 1987, one year before the death of President Chiang Ching-Kuo (the son of Chiang Kai-Shek). Martial law was lifted, and labor protests and private mass media were allowed. Within a short period, not only were more open administrative policies initiated, but more liberal additions and amendments to the legal framework were also inaugurated (Luo and Chung 2005).

With these changes, key industries previously monopolized by state enterprises, such as banking, telecommunications, and electricity, were opened to the private sector. Business groups had many opportunities to expand into new markets. The recent changes of institutions from 2000 onward can be conceived as a continuation of the institutional deregulation started in the late 1980s. Taiwan was relatively less affected by the Asian financial crisis of 1997–8. Many factors, such as the KMT's developmental strategy, a large trade surplus, heavy restrictions on currency trading, and relatively low ratios of corporate debt and non-performing loans, contributed to this exceptional case (*The Economist* 1998). Thus, in contrast to other East Asian countries, which reformed their financial sectors because of the financial crisis, Taiwan's enactment of the Financial Institutions Consolidation Law (2000) and the

Act of Financial Holding Companies (2001) was triggered by the proliferation of banks and other financial service firms that followed the financial-sector liberalization in the early 1990s (*Far Eastern Economic Review* 2001). The first law opened up the banking sector to mergers and acquisitions, permitted the government to force the merger of weak institutions, and allowed asset management companies to take over bad loans (*Far Eastern Economic Review* 2000). The second law allowed affiliated firms of a financial holding company to consolidate their sales and marketing strategies and to cross-promote their services and products to each other's customers. To a large extent, these two legal institutions broadened the financial-sector liberalization of the early 1990s and provided a new venue for business groups to diversify and grow. Many groups with financial arms consolidated and expanded their financial services. Other financial groups grew aggressively by merging with or buying other financial institutions.

7.3 DATA

Our analysis is based upon data of the 100 largest groups in eight periods, from 1973 to 2006 at four-year intervals.[2] Our primary data source is the biennial directory *Business Groups in Taiwan* (*BGT*), compiled by the CCIS in Taipei, the oldest and most prestigious credit-checking agency in Taiwan and an affiliate of Standard & Poor of the United States. This directory collects sales information for the top 100 groups and is confined to groups whose core firms are registered in Taiwan. Consistent with our definition, the CCIS defines a business group as "a coherent business organization including several legally independent enterprises." The CCIS constructs a database of business groups by examining interorganizational relationships such as shared identity, cross-shareholding, and interlocking directorates among these firms. In addition to self-identification, firms have to meet one of several objective criteria to be considered as member firms, including having overlaps of shareholders, directors, auditors, or decision-makers with the core firm and having a substantial proportion of their shares held by other group members. This directory is the most comprehensive and reliable source for business groups in Taiwan and has been used in previous studies (Hamilton and Biggart 1988; Claessens et al. 2000; Chung 2001; Khanna and Rivkin 2001; Luo and Chung 2005; Chung and Luo 2008a, b).

We also supplemented the *BGT* directory with other sources. We adopted the Standard Industrial Classification (SIC) system published by the Taiwanese government (2006 version) to build our diversification measures. To figure out who

---

[2] As can be seen in Table 7.2, *BGT* did not collect data on the *exact* 100 largest groups. This discrepancy is due to various conditions for data collection in different periods. For 1986, some targeted groups refused to provide data, which resulted in a smaller sample.

the main shareholders and top executives of group firms are, we referred to both the family trees presented in the *BGT* and other biographical directories.

We examine the top 100 groups reported in the directory from 1973 to 2006. We believe that the thirty-three-year research period covers important stages of Taiwan's economic growth and transition in industrial structure.

7.4 THE GROWTH OF TAIWANESE BUSINESS GROUPS

Tables 7.1A and 7.1B list the year of establishment, the main industry, the 2-digit industries in which they participated, and the annual sales of the thirty largest Taiwanese business groups in 1973 and 2006. We see from Table 7.1A that more than two-thirds of the large business groups established their first business units in the 1950s, and many of them operated in industries that characterize Taiwan's first wave of industrialization such as chemicals, food, plastics, and textiles. The average size of these groups in terms of annual sales is relatively small as compared to large firms in more developed countries. These are the prototype of Taiwanese groups, and their formation and evolution illustrate the influence of global markets and trade networks as well as local institutions and social structure to Taiwanese corporations during the 1950s and 1960s (Hamilton and Biggart 1988; Chung 2001; Feenstra and Hamilton 2006).

After more than three decades of development, we see a different profile of the top business groups in Taiwan in 2006. While around one-third of the top thirty groups were the original prototypes, the "second-generation" Taiwanese groups emerged around the 1970s and 1980s, and almost all of them operated in the electronic sector. A few financial holding groups joined the elite club around 2001 and 2002, after the new regulations of the financial industry had been inaugurated. The industrial profile of the top thirty groups corresponds largely to the trajectory of Taiwan's economic development and industrial restructuring in the 1970s and 1980s. The annual revenues of these large groups, according to our data source, *Business Groups in Taiwan*, were comparable to other leading corporations around the world. For example, the Formosa Plastics Group, with annual sales of US$4.9 billion, would have been ranked 122 in *Fortune*'s "Global 500" list for 2007, and Quanta Computer would have been ranked 449 if included. We discuss in the next section how the growth of the top 100 business groups as a whole is embedded in the process of Taiwan's political and economic development.

The top 100 Taiwanese groups as a whole experienced steady growth betweeen the 1970s and the 2000s. Moreover, deregulation and privatization in domestic institutional contexts in the 1980s and the 1990s, as well as the expansion of globalization of markets over the same time period, contributed to fast growth and the emergence of certain gigantic groups at the beginning of the twenty-first century.

Table 7.1B Top thirty Taiwanese business groups, 2006

Rank	Group name	Year of establishment	Main industry	Number of industries	Sales (US$ m.)
1	Formosa Plastics	1954	Plastic products	30	49,519
2	Hon Hai	1974	Electrical & electronic products	15	47,571
3	Asustek	1990	Electrical & electronic products	11	17,200
4	Kinpo	1973	Electrical & electronic products	10	16,993
5	Quanta Computer	1988	Electrical & electronic products	4	16,498
6	Lien Hwa-Mitac	1955	Electrical & electronic products	16	16,282
7	Benq	1984	Electrical & electronic products	10	15,967
8	Acer	1979	Electrical & electronic products	11	15,785
9	Inventec	1975	Electrical & electronic products	5	11,385
10	Far Eastern	1954	Textiles	34	10,781
11	President	1967	Food products	35	10,755
12	Chi Mei	1960	Chemical materials	17	9,968
13	TSMC	1987	Electrical & electronic products	5	9,739
14	Evergreen	1968	Transport	20	9,458
15	Walsin Lihwa	1966	Electrical & electronic products	15	8,601
16	China Steel	1971	Basic metal	20	8,546
17	Liton Electronic	1989	Electrical & electronic products	16	7,782
18	Wistron	2001	Electrical & electronic products	6	7,528
19	Chinatrust Financial Holding	2002	Financing	21	7,189
20	Yulon	1953	Transportation equipment	28	6,926
21	United Microelectronics	1980	Electrical & electronic products	8	6,605
22	Fubon Financial Holding	2001	Financing	16	6,342
23	Chunghua Telecom	1979	Telecommunication	5	6,204
24	Tatung	1950	Electrical & electronic products	21	5,999
25	Ho Tai	1955	Electrical & electronic products	12	5,826
26	Yieh Loong	1978	Basic metal	13	5,818
27	Pou Chen	1969	Textiles	17	5,807
28	Ruentex	1976	Retailing	18	5,351
29	Shin Kong Financial Holding	2002	Financing	31	4,781
30	Advanced Semiconductor	1984	Electrical & electronic products	12	4,765

Note: The number of 2-digit industrial sectors according to the SIC system published by the Taiwanese government in 2006.

Source: Compiled from the directory Business Groups in Taiwan, see the data section of the text for details.

Table 7.2 Economic significance of the top 100 Taiwanese business groups, 1973–2006

Economic significance	1973	1977	1981	1986	1990	1994	1998	2002	2006
Number of member firms	724	651	719	746	815	1,021	1,362	4,825	6,038
Group sales (A) (US$bn.)	3.5	6.3	13.4	23.7	62.3	102.1	150.6	248.9	468.1
National GDP (B) (US$bn.)	10.8	21.8	46.9	80.5	158.9	246.3	277.4	282.2	363.9
Percentage (A/B) (%)	32.4	28.8	28.6	29.4	39.2	41.5	54.3	85.4	128.9
Number of group employees (000) (C)	272	306	318	335	396	467	730	894	2,438
Number of population employed (D)	5,327	5,980	6,672	7,733	8,283	8,939	9,289	9,454	10,111
Percentage (C/D) (%)	5.1	5.2	4.8	4.3	4.8	5.2	7.9	9.5	24
Group sales growth (%)	N.A.	23.5	10.9	18.1	10.8	20.6	27.8	1.13	14
Group return on assets (%)	N.A.	5.2	2.5	6.9	4.9	6.1	3.5	0.6	3.8
Number of groups	100	100	100	97	100	100	100	100	100

Note: The conversion rate for NT$ to US$ is 37.9 (1973), 37.95 (1977), 17.79 (1981), 35.45 (1986), 27.11 (1990), 26.24 (1994), 32.22 (1998), 34.5 (2002), and 32.59 (2006). N. A. = not available. The values of GDP and number of employed population: Council for Economic Planning and Development (2007).

Source: Compiled from the directory Business Groups in Taiwan, see the data section of the text for details.

First, Table 7.2 demonstrates that the number of member firms in the top 100 business groups increased steadily from 1973 through 1998 and jumped up substantially between 2002 and 2006. Meanwhile, the variation among the top 100 groups also widened. The standard deviation of the number of member firms ranged between 4 and 8 during 1973 and 1998, but was 42 and 61 respectively in 2002 and 2006. Large groups such as the President Food Group operated more than 250 affiliates in 2006, and some small groups had only 4 constituents. While the increase in scale between 1998 and 2002 partially reflects the change of legal regulations of Taiwanese groups and the subsequent enhanced information disclosure during 2000 and 2001,[3] the upward trend since the 1970s indicates that the top 100 groups had been growing progressively. This trend is also supported by the escalating group sales. In 2006 the total sales generated by group affiliates, both in Taiwan and overseas, surpassed the value of gross domestic product (GDP) and reached US$468 billion. One of the contributing factors was the success of electronic groups such as Asustek, Kinpo, and Quanta. Eight of the top ten groups in terms of sales in 2006 were groups specializing in computer and related products. A 2005 special report on Taiwan's technology firms (*Business Week* 2005) indicates that Taiwanese high-tech companies manufactured thousands of items that are essential to the global digital economy. Taiwan was the first or second provider for more than ten key products, such as computer chips, LCD monitors, notebook, PDAs, and LAN equipment in the global markets. What the report does not mention,

[3] During 2000 and 2001, a new chapter of company laws was added. The incomes of overseas affiliates were included in the annual reports.

however, is that many of the high-tech firms were actually affiliates of business groups. On the list of the major technology firms introduced by the *Business Week* report (2005: 20–1), all but one were member firms of the top 100 business groups in 2006 according to the directory *Business Groups in Taiwan*.

Nevertheless, the electronic groups were not the whole story. Certain groups focusing on "traditional" industries such as plastics, chemicals, or textiles were also expanding. For example, the largest group in terms of sales in both 1973 and 2006, Formosa Plastics, diversified into the steel industry in 2007 and initiated a large investment project of steel mills in Vietnam. The total amount of the investment was US$6 billion and it will take about nine years to finish the project. When it is completed, the total output of Formosa Plastics Group is estimated to reach roughly 40 percent of Taiwan's GDP (*Business Weekly* 2008: 72–5).

The third reason for the growth of the top 100 groups is that quite a few large financial holding groups, such as Cathay Financial Holding and China Trust Financial Holding, by merging various banks and other financial institutions, had become very large in scale. There was even a newly formed financial holding group named "Mega" Financial Holding. The newly passed Act of Financial Holding Companies, which facilitates mergers and acquisitions, made giant financial holding groups feasible.

The second indicator for the significance of Taiwanese business groups is the proportion of the population employed by the top 100 groups. Before 1994 only about 5 percent of the employed labor force above age 15 worked for business groups; the number grew to 7.9 percent in 1998, 9.5 percent in 2002, and 24 percent in 2006. This shows the centralization of Taiwan's economic activities around large business groups during the 1990s and 2000s. The large business groups control not only the majority of capital, technology, and production capacity but also the majority of the labor force in Taiwan. For example, the Honhai Group (Foxconn) alone hired 469,906 people in 2006. This is more than the total number of employees hired by all the top 100 groups before 1994. This development modifies the traditional view on Taiwan's "dual" economic structure: Large business groups hold capital and technology, and small subcontracting firms employ the majority of the labor force (Hamilton 1997; Cheng 2001). Starting from the late 1990s, more and more people were employed by large business groups. The concentration of employees in large business groups made Taiwan's economic structure, centering around large business groups.

7.5 STRATEGY AND STRUCTURE OF THE GROUP

7.5.1 Diversification strategy of the group

Tables 7.1A, 7.1B, and 7.2 demonstrate the clear and consistent pattern of growth of Taiwanese business groups since Taiwan started industrializing in the 1950s and 1960s. One of the key strategies that the large groups adopted for expansion was industrial diversification and timely adjustment of industrial portfolios when the markets shifted. Systematically to examine industrial diversification of business groups, we constructed two measures: (a) entropy value (Palepu 1985); and (b) a simple count of industrial sectors. Following Khanna and Palepu (2000), we constructed a group-level entropy value according to the product information of each member firm. Assuming a group operates in N industry segments, if P_i is the share of the ith segment in the total sales of the group, the entropy measure of total diversification DT is defined as follows:

$$DT = \sum_{i=1}^{N} P_i \log \left(\frac{1}{P_i}\right)$$

This measure takes into account two elements of diversification: (a) the number of segments in which a group operates; and (b) the relative importance of each segment. We used 2-digit and 4-digit Standard Industrial Classification (SIC) codes to calculate the entropy index.[4] The SIC system we adopted, which is the 2006 version of the Taiwanese SIC system, has 19 1-digit industries, 89 2-digit industries, 253 3-digit industries, and 557 4-digit industries. We calculated group-level entropy by taking the weighted average of firm sales across industry codes.

Table 7.3 presents the value of entropy and the number of 2-digit SIC industries that on average the top 100 groups operated between 1981 and 2004. A steadily diversifying profile appears in both indicators of the entropy value and the simple counts of broad industrial sectors. Since the 2006 Taiwanese SIC system has only 89 2-digit industries, spanning across 2-digit industries represents participation in distinct manufacturing and service-providing activities that require additional capital investment and divergent firm resources such as production technology, project-execution capabilities, organizational routines, managerial know-how, and skilled labor (Amsden and Hikino 1994).

The relatively large scale of diversification since the late 1990s corroborates the effects of privatization of many state-owned firms and the deregulation of monopolized sectors since the late 1980s and early 1990s. By 1987 there were still forty-two industries in which entry "permits" were needed (Chu 2001). By the next decade, industries such as aviation, banking, insurance, public transportation, publishing, securities, shipping, telecommunications, and television were deregulated. Since then business groups have steadily acquired and merged with these previously state-owned firms and participated in sectors that were previously monopolized by

---

[4] Unlike most US data, there is no ready-to-use industry coding in the *BGT* directory. Also, the directory did not provide a digital format until 2000. We therefore examined the paper directory and manually assigned a SIC code to each member firm.

Table 7.3 Industrial diversification of the top 100 Taiwanese business groups, 1981–2004

	1981	1983	1986	1988	1990	1992	1994	1996	1998	2000	2002	2004
Total diversification	0.84	0.89	0.82	0.86	0.89	0.93	0.97	0.94	1.04	1.17	1.19	1.23
SD	0.46	0.47	0.45	0.44	0.43	0.45	0.49	0.48	0.54	0.64	0.59	0.56
2-digit SIC counts	4.65	5.12	5.0	5.5	5.44	6.0	6.2	6.56	7.43	11.42	11.63	11.51
SD	3.12	3.40	3.54	3.38	3.26	3.80	3.65	4.0	4.48	7.66	7.77	7.42
Industries entered	n.a.	1.26	1.45	1.53	1.43	1.62	1.77	1.75	2.57	7.54	3.02	2.01
SD		1.54	1.69	1.53	1.40	1.57	1.59	1.53	1.86	5.14	2.35	1.60
Industries exited	n.a.	0.95	1.12	1.28	1.49	1.25	1.45	1.41	1.61	1.52	2.33	2.33
SD		1.09	1.50	1.47	1.50	1.34	1.52	1.33	1.44	1.45	1.93	3.02
Number of groups	100	95	97	100	100	100	100	100	100	100	100	100

Notes: SD = standard deviation. Industries entered and exited are the average of the total number of 2-digit SIC industries that a group entered and exited between T1 and T2—e.g., 1981 and 1983. A group needs to be included in the top hundred list for at least two consecutive years for calculation of these values. The number of groups included is less than 100. N. A. = not available.

Source: Compiled from the directory Business Groups in Taiwan, see the data section of the text for details.

state-owned firms. The average number of 2-digit SIC industries operated by large groups hence grew from 6 in 1992 to 7.4 in 1998 and 11.4 in 2002.

During the same period, the variation of diversification level among the top 100 groups also increased. The standard deviation of the number of 2-digit industries grew from 3.12 in 1981 to 4.48 in 1998 and 7.42 in 2004. Research has shown that, on top of firms' various resources, political connections between business group leaders and politicians facilitate industrial diversification and help explain the various diversification levels among groups (Chung 2006). This is because these political ties offer privileged access to information and resources that firms can use to pursue new business opportunities (Kock and Guillén 2001). The effects of political ties are particularly explicit during and immediately after institutional transition. Network ties play an even more important role after economies have undergone deregulation and privatization, because it takes time for economies to build an effective institutional infrastructure (Ghemawat and Khanna 1998). In the case of Taiwanese business groups, Chung, Mahmood, and Mitchell (2006) show that about 30 percent of the top 100 business groups had formal interlocking ties with government agencies, the parliament, and political parties in the 1990s. In other words, 30 percent of the large groups had top executives, directors, or shareholders who simultaneously held official positions in various political institutions. Their research also shows that politically connected groups were more diversified then non-connected groups in terms of both number of 2-digit SIC codes and entropy value. Connected groups on average participated in three more 2-digit industries than non-connected groups.

The diversification level of business groups presented in Table 7.3 is an aggregation of entries into new industries and exits from current industries. A dynamic analysis of industrial restructuring, which distinguishes entries from exits, shows that Taiwanese groups become more diversified mainly by entering into new industries, particularly in the years 1998 and 2000. Recent research (Zhu and Chung 2008) confirmed that political ties have a positive and significant influence on entries into unrelated industries, because of information advantage, resource access, and legitimacy and preferential treatment from the political power.

However, what is interesting is that large business groups seem to be relatively slower in exiting industries, which helps explain the total increase of diversification level. While, in 2000, groups on average entered 7 industries but only exited 1.6 industries, this was not very different from the exit rate of the previous years. It seems that regulatory changes such as deregulation and privatization and the new opportunities that followed did not have a significant impact on industries' exit patterns. Empirical research has shown that, among the top 100 groups, those with more family ownership were less likely to divest of unrelated businesses than groups less dominated by the family, probably because of the institutionalized practice of the equal inheritance pattern of family assets, concerns of family reputation and status, and other family interests (Chung and Luo 2008b).

Table 7.4 Internationalization of the top 100 Taiwanese business groups, 1981–2002

Internationalization	1981	1986	1990	1994	1998	2002
Proportion of group affiliates in all foreign countries (%)	2	3	4	9	16	49
Proportion of group affiliates in China (%)	0.1	0.2	0.4	4.0	7.0	17
Proportion of group sales from all foreign affiliates (%)	0.1	0.1	0.8	2.0	6.0	20
Proportion of group sales from affiliates in China (%)	0.1	0.1	0.1	0.6	3.0	6.0
Number of groups	100	97	100	100	100	100

Source: Compiled from the directory Business Groups in Taiwan, see the data section of the text for details.

7.5.2 Internationalization of the group

The other way the groups grow is through international expansion. In order to get a clear picture of internationalization of Taiwanese business groups between the 1970s and the 2000s, we checked the address of each of the group affiliates in our database and assigned each affiliate a code of country (or geographical area). Because of the huge amount of time and human power needed for this task, we managed to code data only for six time periods with four-year intervals. We present the results in Table 7.4. In 1981, it was rare for Taiwanese groups to have set up subsidiaries overseas. The situation was maintained until the second half of the 1990s, when we observe substantial international expansion. In 1998, on average, 16 percent of the affiliates of the top 100 groups were located in another country. This trend corresponds to the considerable changes in the domestic environment in the late 1990s, such as rising land and labor costs, tightening regulations on environmental pollution, and intensified labor protests, as well as the increased attractiveness of investment conditions in other countries such as China. As a result, around 20 percent of the group sales in 2002 were generated by foreign affiliates.

Further analysis of the countries in which group affiliates were located demonstrates revealing evidence. We examined the top ten countries where most of the group firms (86 percent) operated and found that China (including Hong Kong) topped the list in 2002. For all foreign group affiliates, 35 percent were in China. Furthermore, another 24 percent were located in the British Virgin Islands and the Cayman Islands, two offshore financial centers with favorable regulations on corporation registration and capital movement. Anecdotal evidence indicates that Taiwanese business set up subsidiaries in these two islands to avoid the domestic regulations on investment into China.[5] In other words, the Taiwanese companies

---

[5] There is a limit for investment into China that a listed company in Taiwan can make. It was 40% of capital during our research period.

invested in China via their subunits in these two areas. If that is the case, about 60 percent of the business group affiliates operating in foreign countries were actually either located in China or have investment in (or capital movement to) China. This reflects the importance of cultural and language affinity in the location choice of foreign expansion of Taiwanese business groups. The other countries in the top ten list for 2002 included USA (12%), Singapore (5%), Malaysia (3%), and Japan (2%).

As far as we know there is as yet no large-scale empirical studies on the internationalization of Taiwanese business groups. One interesting angle would be to investigate the correlation between product (industry) diversification and geographical diversification. Whether geographical diversification is a substitute for or a complement to industrial diversification, or under what contingencies it becomes a substitute or a complement, or whether industrial and geographical diversification has no systematic relationship, the one with the other, has been discussed in the literature. We use the number of 2-digit SIC industries and the number of countries in which a business group operated to test these ideas. Our examination of the data for the six time periods shows that the correlation ratio between industrial and geographical diversification was 0.45, with a significance level higher than 0.001. This indicates that in general Taiwanese business groups tended to be more geographically diversified when they were more industrially diversified, or vice versa. Industrial diversification and geographical diversification hence complement each other in our context. While this observation maintains when we investigate the correlation ratios by individual years, there are some nuances. The correlation ratio gradually declined from 0.48 in 1981 to 0.40 in 1990, and finally to 0.25 in 2002, while the significance levels were all above 0.01. What it demonstrates is that the complementarities between industrial and geographical diversification mollify when both types of diversification escalate, although there is still no sign of substitution between types of diversification.

7.5.3 Diversification, internationalization, and inter-firm network structure

After discussing the expansion through product diversification and internationalization of Taiwanese business groups, we now turn to group structure and examine how diversification strategy and group structure co-evolved. Theoretical works have proposed conceptualizing business groups as a network form of organization (Powell and Smith-Doerr 1994). Member firms of business groups are legally independent and yet coordinated through inter-firm ties and operate with a substantial degree of interdependence and coordination (Granovetter 1995). In addition, the inter-firm ties are more stable than those in conventional holding companies and conglomerates (Davis et al. 1994), probably because of a pre-existing social structure such as family. Business groups thus function as networks of loosely coupled firms, linked by formal and informal ties (Powell and Smith-Doerr 1994; Granovetter 1995). The ties that connect group firms range from formal economic arrangements such as equity cross-holdings, director interlocks, mutual loans, and buyer–suppler agreements (Gerlach 1992) to informal ties based on family, friendship, religion, language, and ethnicity (Granovetter 1995; Luo and Chung 2005). We focus on formal ties in this section. Specifically, we will examine the inter-firm ties that are closely related to group diversification such as ownership and operation (buyer–supplier) ties.

Fig. 7.1 presents the evolution of the density of ownership ties and operation ties within the top 100 Taiwanese groups between 1973 and 1998. Density is defined as the ratio of actual number of ties within a given network to the total number of potential ties that organizations could forge within that network (Wassermann and Faust 1994). Ownership within Taiwanese business groups is maintained through complex, intertwined, and multi-layer shareholding networks (Chung 2004). Fig. 7.1 indicates a stable (or minor upward) trend of ownership density over the years. This is noticeable, given the significant increase in the number of member firms as well as in industrial and geographical diversification during the same period. This suggests that maintaining ownership is a one of the top priorities when Taiwanese business groups grow in scale and scope. The significance of stable ownership tie density manifests when it is contrasted with the decline of operation tie density. The operation linkages among group member firms weaken when firms pursue

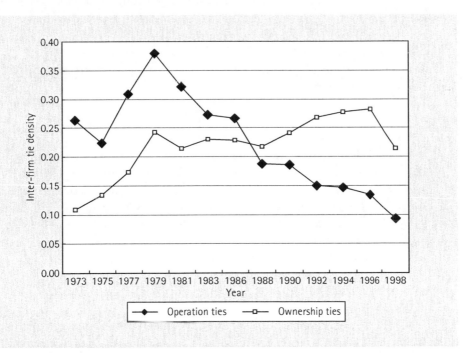

Figure 7.1 Density of operation and ownership networks of top 100 Taiwanese business groups, 1973–98

Source: Compiled from the directory Business Groups in Taiwan, see the data section of the text for details.

opportunities in distinct and multiple industrial sectors. For example, the average operation tie density of the top 100 groups was 0.32 in 1981, when the average number of 2-digit industries the groups participated in was 4.6. The density, however, dropped to 0.09 when the number of industries rose to 7.43 in 1998. Our findings suggest that heterogeneity in production and service-providing activities within business groups tended to decrease operational cohesion of the group.

7.6 COMPOSITION OF OWNERSHIP AND TOP MANAGEMENT OF THE GROUP

In terms of governance structure, we discuss ownership and top management of business groups. For ownership, we coded and examined the ownership data of group firms between 1988 and 1998,[6] the period when groups expanded extensively. We first recorded the major shareholders and the percentage of their shareholding for each member firm. We then assigned one of five categories to each of the shareholders: family, affiliate, government, foreign, and institutional. *Family ownership* is the proportion of firm shares owned by family members. *Affiliate ownership* is the portion owned by other units in the same group. *Government ownership* is the proportion of shares owned by governmental agencies. *Foreign ownership* is the percentage of shares owned by foreign companies and individuals that are not affiliated with the group. *Institutional ownership* is the part of firm shares owned by financial institutions such as commercial banks, insurance companies, investment companies, mutual funds, and venture capital. In total, we coded shareholder data for 9,841 cases of firm-year, with an average of 5.1 shareholders per firm.

Fig. 7.2 shows the ownership composition of the group firms between 1988 and 1998 at two-year intervals. Since *BGT* listed only major shareholders, the aggregate percentage was around 76 percent. On the surface, the controlling power of the family seems to have been declining, since family ownership dropped from 23 percent to 4 percent in a decade. At the same time, affiliate ownership rose from 35 percent to 53 percent. Other categories maintained more or less the same proportions.[7] However, examining the background of owners we found that many of the ultimate owners of group affiliates were in fact private holding companies and investment companies that were controlled by the family. Hence, our finding is consistent with previous research that groups often use a "pyramidal structure" to organize their ownership (Chang and Hong 2000; Claessens et al. 2000; Chung 2004). The findings

[6] We were not able to collect shareholder information before 1988, since the *BGT* did not report the percentage of shareholding until that time.

[7] The percentage of government ownership was between 0.17% and 0.3% between 1988 and 1998, hence we cannot depict this component clearly in the bar chart.

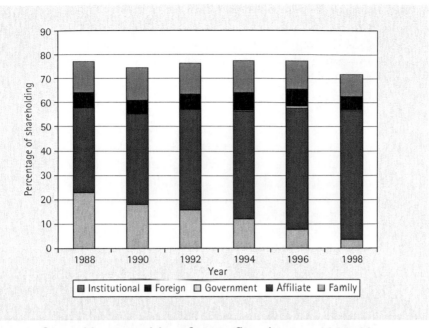

Figure 7.2 Ownership composition of group firms by year, 1988–98

Source: Compiled from the directory Business Groups in Taiwan, see the data section of the text for details.

on ownership composition corroborate the findings of stable ownership network density that we discussed earlier.

The pyramid is a multiple-level ownership network constructed by chains of interorganizational shareholding. It is often structured with a control center such as the core firm or holding company at the top, a few intermediary firms in the middle, and many subordinate firms at the bottom. Through this mechanism, the controlling family can control the whole group by maintaining sufficient equity only in the controlling center. Studies by finance scholars (La Porta et al. 1999; Claessens et al. 2000) indicate that the pyramidal structure allows the ultimate controller to own significant voting rights with minimal cash. At the same time, by creating separation between ownership and control, pyramids provide controlling families with opportunities to expropriate minority shareholders (Morck et al. 2005). Claessens et al. did not find a significant relationship between ownership structure and corporate value in Taiwan, but more recent research by Yeh, Ko, and Su (2003) and Yeh and Woidtke (2005) found evidence of expropriation. Taiwan's remaining unscathed by the Asian financial crisis allowed groups to avoid tightened regulations and shareholder activists' aggressive scrutiny.

In terms of the control and management of Taiwanese business groups, family-controlled holding companies or investment companies are not necessarily involved in the decision-making and administration of the whole group. Unlike group headquarters seen in the business groups of most other economies, like the one in the Korean *chaebol* that rule all group affiliates, the main function of the top organization here is to hold the shares of the affiliated firms. The overall planning of the whole group, then, relies on a set of socially related top executives (Hamilton 1997). This set of leaders occupies commanding positions in member firms and sets the course of planning and development for the whole group; and the leaders have different types of social relationships with the key leader (who is often the founder or his son). Following Thompson (1967), Hamilton and Kao (1990) use the term "inner circle" to refer to this set of leaders, who possess the greatest decision-making power. Luo and Chung (2005) focus on the dyadic ties between the key leader and other top executives in the inner circle and find that the social relationships within the inner core have a significant impact on the strategies and performance of the group. For example, family ties in general would have a positive influence on group financial performance, since these strong ties facilitated internal transactions among member firms within the group. However, the positive contribution of family members would rise up to a threshold, after which additional family members tended to derail group performance due to information redundancy and legitimacy discount (Uzzi 1997).

With the importance of family ties in mind, Table 7.5 shows that, on average, in the top 100 groups, family members constituted between 60 percent and 50 percent of the inner circle between 1981 and 1998, but that the proportion declined during these years.. During the same period, the educational level of the inner-circle members was on the rise, with 62 percent of the members owning a university degree (or above) in 1998. In addition, more and more inner-circle members possessed advanced degrees such as an MBA from a top American business school. The percentage of US MBA holders within the inner circle increased from 13 percent in 1981 to 25 percent in 1998. Much of the increase came from the participation of the second-generation

Table 7.5 Characteristics of the inner circle of the top 100 Taiwanese business groups, 1981–98

Characteristics of the inner circle	1981	1983	1986	1988	1990	1992	1994	1996	1998
Proportion of family members (%)	61	59	64	64	58	57	55	58	53
Proportion with university degree (or above) (%)	47	53	48	51	57	58	61	58	62
Proportion with overseas working experience (%)	6.0	5.0	5.0	6.0	6.0	5.0	7.0	5.0	5.0
Proportion with US formal education (%)	13	17	16	19	20	22	24	20	25
Number of groups	100	95	97	100	100	100	100	100	100

Source: Compiled from the directory Business Groups in Taiwan, see the data section of the text for details.

descendants in the inner circle. For example, Douglas Hsu of the Far Eastern group (the second largest group in 1973 and the tenth in 2006), who is the son of the group founder, earned an MBA degree from the University of Notre Dame and a master's degree in economics from Columbia University. While such a degree enhances the reputation and skills of potential leaders, the *content* of the MBA program may also serve as an important channel for transferring different models of governance, strategy, and structure (Sahlin-Andersson and Engwall 2002). Chung and Luo (2008a) found that, when the US-educated second-generation successors become the key leaders within the inner circle, they are more likely to reduce the proportion of family members in the inner circle, particularly when the environment is turbulent and the group is highly diversified. Their findings help explain the negative correlation between the proportion of family members in the inner circle and the proportion of inner-circle members with US MBA degrees, as we observe in Table 7.5.

While the large groups increased expansion overseas in the late 1990s, the proportion of top managers with overseas working experience did not seem to increase in a parallel way. This is probably related to the fact that most of the foreign affiliates were located in China and hence foreign working experience may not necessarily have helped or facilitated work and decision-making in the Chinese context.

7.7 INNOVATION CAPABILITIES OF THE GROUP

As regards the competitive capabilities of Taiwanese business groups, we focus on technological innovation, which is the core competence of many second-generation Taiwanese groups in global markets.

While the early industrialization of Taiwan was driven mainly by labor-intensive sectors such as textile and toys, the later stage of development turned to more technology-intensive industries such as electronics by using the OEM model. Over time, Taiwan became one of the most innovative countries in the world, ranking fourth globally in terms of the number of US patents in 2003, surpassed only by the USA, Japan, and Germany. Business groups became the main engine for innovation in Taiwan (Hobday 1995). Fig. 7.3 shows the number of US patents applied for by the 500 largest Taiwanese and Korean firms during 1992–2000. While independent Taiwanese firms appear to have been more innovative than their Korean counterparts, business group affiliated firms in both countries generated more patents than did independent firms.

Between 1990 and 1999 about 40 percent of the US patents from Taiwan-based recipients were granted to business group affiliates. Seven of the top ten recipients from Taiwan to receive US patents between 1970 and 1999 were business group affiliates (Mahmood et al. 2006). It is thus important to explore the form and

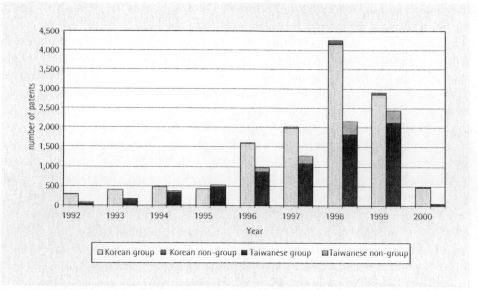

Figure 7.3 Patenting over time by the 500 largest firms in Korea and Taiwan, 1992–2000

Source: Compiled from the directory Business Groups in Taiwan, see the data section of the text for details.

functioning of the innovation capabilities in Taiwanese groups, and particularly the reason why certain groups are more innovative than others.

Table 7.6 provides a list of the top thirty most innovative groups in terms of successful domestic patent application in Taiwan in 2005. It shows that innovation in Taiwanese groups was driven mainly by the younger high-tech groups operating in semi-conductor, computing, and electronics sectors. While the vibrant venture capitals helped the overall atmosphere for innovation in Taiwan, foreign technological linkages such as OEM, licensing, joint ventures, and so on also played a critical role in enhancing Taiwanese groups' innovative capabilities (Amsden and Chu 2003). Mahmood and Zheng (2009) find that the Taiwanese groups that received the most innovative benefits from foreign ties were the ones that combined a large number of external ties with an internal structure marked by a high degree of intra-group connectivity (such as operation ties) among affiliates. They argue that such structures provide the optimal combination of search and integration necessary for innovative success.

As discussed earlier, the inter-firm ties among group firms serve as an important coordination mechanism within Taiwanese business groups. Moreover, these ties have been shown to have impacted strongly on the innovative activity of group affiliates (Mahmood et al. 2006). In the Hon Hai group, for instance, Mahmood, Mitchell, and Chung (2006) note that each subsidiary has a particular mission, such as making specific components for system assembly. Although the primary focus of a subsidiary is on achieving its mission, rather than on contributing to innovation at

Table 7.6 Top thirty most innovative Taiwanese groups based on domestic patent applications, 2005

Rank	Group name	Year of establishment	Main products	Patents
1	TSMC	1987	Semiconductor	3,981
2	Hon Hai	1974	Electronics	3,346
3	Benq	1984	Computing, electronics	1,712
4	Inventec	1975	Computing, Mobile communications	1,479
5	Liteon	1989	Optical drive	1,091
6	Acer	1979	Computing	1,058
7	Advanced Semiconductor	1984	Semiconductor	868
8	Kinpo	1973	Electronics	861
9	Walsin Lihua	1966	Wire and cable	674
10	Via Technologies	1992	Computing	657
11	Teco Electric & Machinery	1956	Electric machinery	636
12	Shin Kong	1952	Chemical materials	526
13	UMC	1980	Semiconductor	495
14	Media Tek	1997	Semiconductor	422
15	Wistron	2001	Computing, communications	406
16	Lien Hwa Mitac	1955	Computing	399
17	Chi Mei	1960	Petro-chemical	381
18	Delta Electronics	1975	Electronics	359
19	Tatung	1950	Machinery	338
20	Asustek	1990	Computing	328
21	Formosa Plastics	1954	Plastic products	321
22	Macronix	1989	Semiconductor	278
23	Spil	1984	Electronics	248
24	Quanta Computer	1988	Computing	224
25	WPG Holdings	1981	Electronics	162
26	Ritek	1988	Storage media	157
27	Powerchip Semiconductor	1994	Electronics	126
28	D-Link	1987	Computing, communications	110
29	Wintek	1990	Electronics	100
30	First International Computer	1979	Computing	90

Source: Compiled from the directory Business Groups in Taiwan, see the data section of the text for details.

other affiliates, operating and managerial links between affiliates can indirectly facilitate innovation by providing component knowledge that helps a partner's systemic innovation.

As another example, one of the reasons why United Microelectronics and Taiwan Semiconductor Manufacturing have been more innovative than other firms within the same industry, such as Nanya Technology Corporation, may have something to do with their access to downstream customers within their groups that offer relevant component knowledge. United Microelectronics Inc. has both buyer–supplier ties and equity ties with Faraday Technology, a sister affiliate of the United Microelectronics Corporation (UMC) group that specializes in integrated circuit (IC) design services. Similar ties exist between the Taiwan Semiconductor Manufacturing Corporation (TSMC) and the Global UniChip Corporation, an affiliate within the TSMC group that specializes in chip design. In comparison, Nanya Technology had no operating ties and only two investment ties with the other nineteen members of the Formosa Plastics Group. To the extent that links within groups facilitate or constrain resource sharing, differences in affiliates' access to other members of the group may contribute to differences in their innovative activities.

To reinforce this point with another example, consider two firms—the United Microelectronics Corporation (UMC group) and Vanguard International Semiconductor (TSMC group)—that are in a similar set of businesses but have different patenting performance. UMC received 2,680 domestic patents from 1991 to 1999. Vanguard International received 531 patents during the same period. Based on 1998 data, UMC had 15 investment ties, 9 director ties, and 5 buyer–supplier ties with the 15 other firms in the UMC group, as can be seen in Fig. 7.4A. By contrast, Vanguard had only 1 investment tie, 4 director ties, and no buyer–supplier ties with the 13 other firms in the TSMC group, as can be seen in Fig. 7.4B. Overall, then, UMC had far more ties than Vanguard. To the extent that intra-group ties help firms gain access resources and information necessary for innovative activities, the difference in number of ties offers a key explanation behind the heterogeneity in patenting performance across firms within the same industry.

As the preceding discussion suggests, some Taiwanese groups have been able to develop strong innovative capabilities of their own. While many Taiwanese groups have become more innovative over time, the relatively small size of Taiwanese groups as compared to their Japanese and Korean counterparts, however, might make it more difficult for them to develop substantial marketing capability. Very few Taiwanese groups, barring Acer, have been able to develop a global brand name. This is corroborated by the trend in Fig. 7.5, which shows a decreasing trend for average advertising intensity (advertising expenditure divided by net sales) for group-affiliated as well as independent-listed firms. To the extent that a strong marketing capability is necessary for sustaining a strong innovative capability, a weak marketing capability signals a potential problem for business groups in Taiwan as they try to compete with the likes of Samsung, Sony, Panasonic, Lucky-Goldstar (LG), and so on while fending off threats from lower-cost players from China.

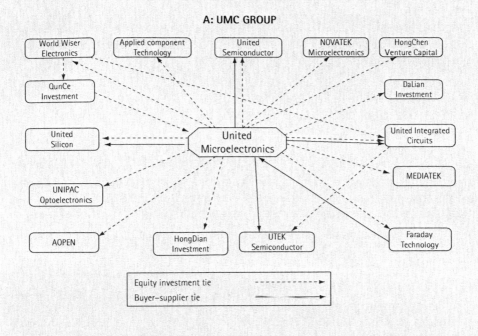

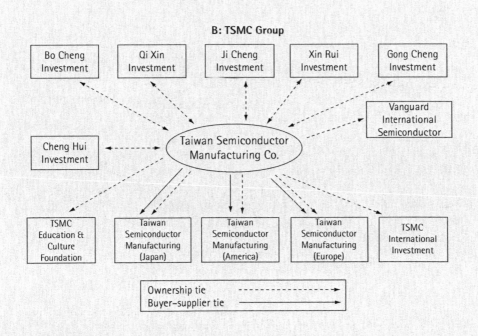

Figure 7.4 Investment and operating (buyer-supplier) ties among UMC group and TSMC group affiliates, 1998

Source: Compiled from the directory Business Groups in Taiwan, see the data section of the text for details.

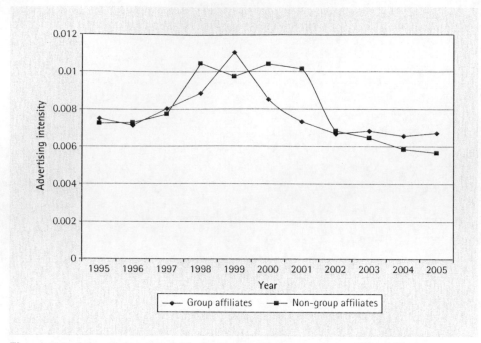

Figure 7.5 Advertising intensity for listed firms over time, 1995–2005

Source: Compiled from the directory Business Groups in Taiwan, see the data section of the text for details.

Many Taiwanese groups responded to rising domestic wages in the 1990s by shifting their production facilities to China rather than investing heavily in manufacturing productivity. As Table 7.7 indicates, between the years 1992 and 1998 Taiwanese groups increased their innovative capability by 30 percent. The rise in productivity was significantly modest, however, for marketing and manufacturing capabilities (4 percent and 1 percent respectively). While easy access to cheap labor allowed some Taiwanese groups to stay competitive in the short run, poor manufacturing capability might have become the weakest link in Taiwanese business groups' move toward improving their competitive capabilities.[8]

---

[8] We estimate firm capabilities using the stochastic frontier estimation (SFE) methodology. This approach views capabilities as an "intermediate transformation ability" that allows a firm to convert inputs available to the firm (i.e., its resources) into desired outputs (i.e., its objectives). We expect that firms that are efficient in deploying their resources will have superior capabilities, and will thus exhibit better performance than their less-efficient competitors. SFE enables us to estimate empirically the efficient frontier (i.e., the desired goal) and thus the level of productive efficiency (i.e., the firm's capability) achieved by each firm. Interested readers can also refer to Mahmood, Zhu, and Zajac (2009) for more discussion.

Table 7.7 Input, output, and capability of forty-eight listed group affiliates in Taiwan, 1990–8 (%)

Year	Innovation capability	Marketing capability	Manufacturing capability
1990	0.71	0.71	0.89
1992	0.79	0.74	0.91
1994	0.86	0.76	0.92
1996	0.87	0.79	0.92
1998	0.93	0.81	0.93

Note: The group affiliates belong to forty business groups in the top 100 list of Taiwanese business groups.

7.8 THE FUTURE OF TAIWANESE BUSINESS GROUPS

As the world economies, especially those in emerging markets, keep growing in the long term, we expect Taiwanese business groups will be able to maintain their momentum of expansion in the coming decades. We also foresee that groups specializing in electronics and finance sectors will dominate the top thirty lists, while groups in "traditional" industries will gradually fade away if they cannot increase their economics of scale and maintain competitive advantages in their current sectors.

Since 2000 we have also seen a new direction for the growth of business groups: mergers and acquisitions. Because of insufficient infrastructure in capital markets in the past, M&A activities were not dynamic in Taiwan. Most of the business groups grew by establishing subsidiaries themselves. However, with the improvement of regulatory institutions and the globalized capital markets (such as private equity), we have seen more and more M&A by Taiwanese business groups since 2000. For example, in 2006 the Hon-Hai group spent US$929.6 million to purchase Premier, the leading digital camera original equipment manufacturer in the world. Analysts predict that Premier's capabilities in manufacturing digital camera, camera lens, overhead projector, and other optics products will bring significant synthesis to the group (*Taipei Times* 2006). Some M&A activities involve foreign companies and become cross-border M&A. For instance, Lite-On group paid 277 million euros for Finnish Perlos Corporation, the world's largest handset casing maker. Not only will Taiwanese groups conduct more purchases; many other firms (domestic and foreign) will also try to acquire and/or merge with group affiliates. As the M&A markets advance, we expect the industrial restructuring of business groups to accelerate in the future, particularly in terms of exiting current industries.

In terms of product and geographical diversification, we expect to see an increasing trend. In 2006 overseas facilities contributed 42.3 percent of total production of Taiwanese firms; the rate rose to 45.9 per cent in 2007 (*BGT* 2008). It seems that globalization of manufacturing activities by business groups will become significantly faster than it was in the previous decade. The groups specializing in finance will follow the footsteps of groups in manufacturing and expand overseas in order to provide services. As far as location choice is concerned, we think that the revisions of labor laws in China will mean that more and more Taiwanese business groups will move out of China and look for other emerging markets as their production base. Vietnam seems to be the next hot spot for Taiwanese groups, as demonstrated by the case of the steel mill project by Formosa Plastics group.

In regard to family domination in ownership and control, we foresee that the founding family will maintain its superior ownership rights in group affiliates. The family may build more and more layers in the ownership pyramid in the future and use private investment and holding companies to be the ultimate shareholders. We have, nevertheless, a different view for family management. Since most of the groups were established during the period of 1950–70, leadership transition to the second- or even third-generation successors has become prevalent. With US-education background and a different mindset, the next generation (or third-generation) group leaders may not prefer family members in the inner circle. Hence we project a gradual decline of family executives in the top management by the end of the 2000s. In other words, there may be a certain extent of separation of ownership and control in Taiwanese business groups. However, the speed of decline will be slow, owing to the increasing number of family members as the family grows in generations.

From the pattern of evolution of Taiwanese business groups since the 1970s, we see a clear influence of global markets, local institutions, and existing social structure. As the groups become bigger in terms of both scale and scope, we expect to see business groups increasingly influencing both markets and society. We think that the impact of the group form on policies and laws, entrepreneurship and innovation, capital markets and investment, social income and distribution, as well as community and environment, will be a promising agenda for studies of Taiwanese business groups in the 2000s.

REFERENCES

AMSDEN, A. H. (1985). "The State and Taiwan's Economic Development," in P. B. Evans, D. Rueschemeyer, and T. Skocpol (eds.), *Bringing the State Back In*. Cambridge: Cambridge University Press, 78–106.

AMSDEN, A. H., and HIKINO, T. (1994). "Project Execution Capability, Organizational Know-How and Conglomerate Corporate Growth in Late Industrialization," *Industrial and Corporate Change*, 3/1: 111–47.

AMSDEN, A. H., and CHU, W.-W. (2003). *Beyond Late Development: Taiwan's Upgrading Policies*. Cambridge, MA: MIT Press.

BGT (various years). *Business Groups in Taiwan*. Tapei: China Credit Information Service.

Business Week (2005). "Why Taiwan Matters: The Global Economy Couldn't Function Without It," May 16.

Business Weekly (2008). "Formosa's Steel Firm in Vietnam," July 14.

CHANG, S.-J. (2006) (ed.). *Business Groups in East Asia: Financial Crisis, Restructuring, and New Growth*. Oxford: Oxford University Press.

CHANG, S.-J., and HONG, J. (2000). "Economic Performance of Group-Affiliated Companies in Korea: Intragroup Resource Sharing and Internal Business Transactions," *Academy of Management Journal*, 43/3: 429–48.

CHANG, S.-J., CHUNG, C.-N., and MAHMOOD, I. P. (2006). "When and How Does Group Affiliation Promote Firm Innovation? A Tale of Two Emerging Economies," *Organization Science*, 17/5: 637–56.

CHENG, T.-J. (2001). "Transformation of Taiwan's Economic Structure in the 20th Century," *China Quarterly*, 165: 19–36.

CHU, Y.-P. (2001). "Liberalization Policies since the 1980s," in C.-C. Mai and C.-S. Shih (eds.), in *Taiwan's Economic Success since 1980*. Northampton, MA: Edward Elgar, 89–119.

CHUNG, C.-N. (2001). "Markets, Culture and Institutions: The Emergence of Large Business Groups in Taiwan, 1950s–1970s," *Journal of Management Studies*, 38/5: 719–45.

CHUNG, C.-N. (2004). "Institutional Transition and Cultural Inheritance: Network Ownership and Corporate Control of Business Groups in Taiwan, 1970s–1990s," *International Sociology*, 19/1: 25–50.

CHUNG, C.-N. (2006). "Beyond Guanxi: Network Contingencies in Taiwanese Business Groups," *Organization Studies*, 27/4: 461–89.

CHUNG, C.-N., and LUO, X. (2008a). "Human Agents, Contexts, and Institutional Change: The Decline of Family in the Leadership of Business Groups," *Organization Science*, 19/1:124–42.

CHUNG, C.-N., and LUO, X. (2008b). "Enter or Exit: An Institutional Perspective on Corporate Restructuring of Business Groups in Emerging Economies," *Organization Science*, 19/5: 766–84.

CHUNG, C.-N., and MAHMOOD, I. P. (2006). "Taiwanese Business Groups: Steady Growth in Institutional Transition," in S.-J. Chang (ed.), *Business Groups in East Asia: Financial Crisis, Restructuring, and New Growth*. Oxford: Oxford University, 70–93.

CHUNG, C.-N., MAHMOOD, I. P., and MITCHELL, W. (2006). "A Contingency Theory of Political Connections: Business Group Diversification In Emerging Economies." Paper presented at Academy of Management Best Paper Proceedings, Atlanta, GA.

CLAESSENS, S., DJANKOV, S. and LANG, L. H. P. (2000). "The Separation of Ownership and Control in East Asian Corporations," *Journal of Financial Economics*, 52/1–2: 81–112.

Council for Economic Planning and Development (2007). *Taiwan Statistical Data Book*. Taipei: Council for Economic Planning and Development.

DAVIS, G. F., DIEKMANN, K. A., and TINSLEY, C. H. (1994). "The Decline and Fall of the Conglomerate Firm in the 1980s: The Deinstitutionalization of an Organizational Form," *American Sociological Review*, 59/4: 547–70.

The Economist (1998). "Taiwan: The Survivor's Tale," Nov. 7.

Far Eastern Economic Review (2000). "Crisis? What Crisis," Dec. 21.

Far Eastern Economic Review (2001). "Banking on a New Regime," May 17.

FEENSTRA, R. C., and HAMILTON, G. G. (2006). *Emergent Economies, Divergent Paths: Economic Organization and International Trade in South Korea and Taiwan*. New York: Cambridge University Press.

GERLACH, M. (1992). *Alliance Capitalism: The Social Organization of Japanese Business*. Berkeley and Los Angeles: University of California Press.

GHEMAWAT, P., and KHANNA, T. (1998). "The Nature of Diversified Business Groups: A Research Design and Two Case Studies," *Journal of Industrial Economics*, 46/1: 35–61.

GOLD, T. B. (1985). *State and Society in the Taiwan Miracle*. Armonk, NY: M. E. Sharpe.

GRANOVETTER, M. (1995). "Coase Revisited: Business Groups in the Modern Economy," *Industrial and Corporate Change*, 4/1: 93–140.

GRANOVETTER, M. (2005). "Business Groups and Social Organization," in N. Smelser and R. Swedberg (eds.), *Handbook of Economic Sociology*. Princeton: Princeton University Press, 429–50.

HAMILTON, G. G. (1997). "Organization and Market Processes in Taiwan's Capitalist Economy," in M. Orrù, N. W. Biggart, and G. G. Hamilton (eds.), *The Economic Organization of East Asian Capitalism*. Thousand Oaks, CA: Sage, 237–93.

HAMILTON, G. G., and BIGGART, N. W. (1988). "Market, Culture, and Authority: A Comparative Analysis of Management and Organization in the Far East," *American Journal of Sociology*, 94 (supplement): S52–S94.

HAMILTON, G. G., and KAO, C.-S. (1990). "The Institutional Foundation of Chinese Business: The Family Firm in Taiwan," in Craig Calhoun (ed.), *Comparative Social Research*. Greenwich, CT: JAI Press, 135–51.

HOBDAY, M. (1995). *Innovation in East Asia: The Challenge to Japan*. Aldershot and Brookfield, VT: Edward Elgar.

KHANNA, T., and PALEPU, K. (2000). "The Future of Business Groups in Emerging Markets: Long-Run Evidence From Chile," *Academy of Management Journal*, 43/3: 268–85.

KHANNA, T., and RIVKIN, J. W. (2001). "Estimating the Performance Effects of Business Groups in Emerging Markets," *Strategic Management Journal*, 22/1: 45–74.

KHANNA, T., and YAFEH, Y. (2007). "Business Groups in Emerging Markets: Paragons or Parasites?" *Journal of Economic Literature*, 45/2: 331–72.

KOCK, C. J., and GUILLÉN, M. F. (2001). "Strategy and Structure in Developing Countries: Business Groups as an Evolutionary Response to Opportunities for Unrelated Diversification," *Industrial and Corporate Change*, 10/1: 77–1113.

LA PORTA, R., LOPEZ-DE-SILANES, F., and SHLEIFER, A. (1999). "Corporate Ownership around the World," *Journal of Finance*, 54/2: 471–517.

LI, K.-T. (1988). *Economic Transformation of Taiwan, ROC*. London: Shepheard-Walwyn.

LUO, X., and CHUNG, C.-N. (2005). "Keeping It All in the Family: the Role of Particularistic Relationships in Business Group Performance during Institutional Transition," *Administrative Science Quarterly*, 50/3: 404–39.

MAHMOOD, I. P., and MITCHELL, W. (2004). "Two Faces: Effects of Business Group Market Share on Innovation in Emerging Economies," *Management Science*, 50/10: 1348–65.

MAHMOOD, I. P., and ZHENG, W. (2008). "Whether and How: Effects of International Joint Ventures on Local Innovation?" *Research Policy*, 389.

MAHMOOD, I. P., MITCHELL, W., and CHUNG, C. N. (2006). "The Structure of Intra-Group Ties: Innovation in Taiwan Business Groups." Duke Fuqua Working Paper.

MAHMOOD, I. P., ZHU, H., and ZAJAC, E. (2009). "Where Can Capabilities Come From? How Different Types of Network Ties Affect Capability Acquisition." NUS/ IER Hitotsubashi Working Paper.

MORCK, R., WOLFENZON, D., and YEUNG, B. (2005). "Corporate Governance, Economic Entrenchment, and Growth," *Journal of Economic Literature*, 43/3: 655–720.

NUMAZAKI, I. (1993). "The Tainanbang: The Rise and Growth of a Banana-Bunch-Shaped Business Group in Taiwan," *Developing Economies*, 31/4: 485–510.

PALEPU, K. (1985). "Diversification Strategy, Profit Performance and the Entropy Measure," *Strategic Management Journal*, 6/3: 239–55.

POWELL, W. W., and SMITH-DOERR, L. (1994). "Networks and Economic Life," in N. J. Smelser and R. Swedberg (eds.), *Handbook of Economic Sociology*. Princeton: Princeton University Press, 368–402.

SAHLIN-ANDERSON, K., and ENGWALL, L. (2002) (eds.), *The Expansion of Management Knowledge: Carriers, Flows, and Sources*, Stanford: Stanford University Press.

TAKAO, T. (1989). "Management in Taiwan: The Case of the Formosa Plastics Group," *East Asian Cultural Studies*, 28: 63–90.

Taipei Times (2006). "Hon Hai to Gobble up Camera Maker," June 21.

THOMPSON, J. D. (1967). *Organizations in Action: Social Science Bases of Administrative Theory*. New York: McGraw-Hill.

TIEN, H.-M. (1989). *The Great Transition: Political and Social Change in the Republic of China*. Stanford, CA: Hoover Institution Press, Stanford University.

UZZI, B. (1997). "Social Structure and Competition in Interfirm Networks: The Paradox of Embeddedness," *Administrative Science Quarterly*, 42/1: 35–67.

WADE, R. (1990). *Governing the Market: Economic Theory and the Role of Government in East Asian Industrialization*. Princeton: Princeton University Press.

WASSERMAN, S., and FAUST, K. (1994). *Social Network Analysis: Methods and Applications*. New York: Cambridge University Press.

YEH, Y.-H., and WOIDTKE, T. (2005). "Commitment or Entrenchment? Controlling Shareholders and Board Composition," *Journal of Banking & Finance*, 29/7: 18–57.

YEH, Y.-H., KO, C.-E., and SU, Y.-H. (2003). "Ultimate Control and Expropriation of Minority Shareholders: New Evidence from Taiwan," *Academia Economic Papers*, 31/3: 263–99.

ZHU, H.-J., and CHUNG, C.-N. (2008). "How the Content of Political Connections Affects Industrial Restructuring: Evidence from Taiwan." Paper presented at the Academy of Management Conference, Anaheim, CA.

CHAPTER 8

··

BUSINESS GROUPS IN CHINA

··

KEUN LEE
YOUNG-SAM KANG

8.1 INTRODUCTION

··

APART from some incidence in the early twentieth century, modern-style business groups emerged in China in the mid-1980s as a consequence of the reform and restructuring of state-owned enterprises (SOEs), which aimed at increasing economies of scale and specialization (Keister 2000; Lee and Jin 2009). Since their early emergence, a substantial number of Chinese business groups have succeeded in becoming major players in the world economy, and the Chinese government, at both central and local level, has played an important role in the formation and development of business groups (Hahn and Lee 2006; Lee and Jin 2009). China has its own specific definition of business groups, used in official statistics and government policies. In terms of ownership, the state still holds the dominant position as the controller of the business groups in China. However, non-government ownership has grown more quickly since the early 2000s. Business groups with private and other ownership accounted for about 45 percent of a total of 2,856 business groups in 2007, although their share in terms of sales was still less than 20 percent. Business groups in China have their own unique characteristics, reflecting the socio-economic context of the country, but they still share some characteristics with the groups in other countries. They are also diversified, but seem to be less so than their counterparts in other countries, and a tendency to refocus has even been reported in some recent studies (see, e.g., Seo et al. 2006).

This chapter provides a descriptive analysis of the business groups in China, extending and updating the recent literature, such as Hahn and Lee (2006). Section 8.2 discusses a basic profile of business groups in China. Section 8.3 outlines the history of business groups in China, and Section 8.4 focuses on the role of the state in the emergence of the business groups. Section 8.5 discusses the problems of ownership structure and agency costs in the Chinese business groups, and Section 8.6 deals with their business structure and diversification. Section 8.7 examines the competitiveness of business groups in China.

8.2 BASIC PROFILE OF THE BUSINESS GROUPS IN CHINA

China has its own specific definition of business groups, which is used in official statistics and government policies. The National Statistics Bureau of China (NSBC) defines a business group as a collection of legally independent entities that are partly or wholly owned by a parent firm and registered as affiliated firms of that parent firm. They also have to be approved by the relevant government bureau and registered with the State Administration for Industry and Commerce.

Of course, only large business groups, *qiye jituan*, not small and private business groups, can be registered. According to the State Administration for Industry and Commerce (SAIC), the core company of a business group in China, *qiye jituan*, should have a registered capital of over 50 million yuan plus at least five affiliated companies, and the business group should have a total registered capital (including the core and other affiliated companies) of over 100 million yuan. One of the most important characteristics of large business groups in China, which distinguishes them from their counterparts in Korea or Japan, is that most business groups are multi-industry entities owned by the state but not by particular families, while small business groups are family owned.

The weight of business groups in the Chinese economy can be seen in Part A of Table 8.1. First, the number of business groups registered increased from 2,472 to 2,926 during the period 1998–2007, a 18.4 percent increase. In terms of the number of total workers employed in the groups, the growth was much faster, namely 55 percent, with the figure increasing from 20.9 million to 32.4 million over the same period. The sales revenues of all the registered business groups, calculated as a ratio to GDP, were substantial, reaching 93.2 percent by 2007, which is comparable to other countries. The ratio grew rapidly during the nine-year period, from 41.6 percent in 1998 to 93.2 percent in 2007, reflecting the fast growth of business groups in the economy.

Part B of Table 8.1 compares shares of total revenues by ownership types of business groups. It shows that the share of state ownership was almost 90 percent

Table 8.1 Basic statistics of business groups in China, 1998–2007

Part A: Shares in the economy

Variables	1998	1999	2000	2001	2002	2003	2004	2005	2006	2007
Numbers	2,472	2,757	2,655	2,710	2,627	2,692	2,764	2,845	2,856	2,926
Total assets (yuan bn.)	6,699	8,732	10,698	12,805	14,254	17,017	19,472	23,076	27,121	34,355
Percentage of GDP	79.4	97.4	107.8	116.8	118.5	125.3	121.8	126.0	128.0	137.7
Total revenue (yuan bn.)	3,508	4,377	5,326	6,562	7,712	10,010	12,639	15,551	18,964	23,257
Percentage of GDP	41.6	48.8	53.7	59.8	64.1	73.7	79.1	84.9	89.5	93.2
No. employees (000)	20,900	23,420	22,820	25,240	25,180	25,850	26,712	28,359	30,104	32,393
Percentage of urban workers	9.67	10.45	9.86	10.54	10.16	10.08	10.09	10.38	10.63	11.04

Source: Calculated from the data in National Bureau of Statistics, China (2008, 2009).

Part B: Sales revenues by ownership types of business groups

Ownership types	2000	2001	2002	2003	2004	2005	2006	2007
State ownership (yuan bn.)	4,749	5,806	6,709	8,485	10,365	12,396	14,965	18,127
(%)	89.2	88.5	87.0	84.8	82.0	79.6	78.9	77.9
Collective ownership (yuan bn.)	316	344	409.3	463.5	570.7	616	1128.3	1,331
(%)	5.9	5.2	5.3	4.6	4.5	4.0	5.9	5.7
Private ownership and others (yuan bn.)	261	413	594	1,061	1,703	2,559	2,870	3,799
(%)	4.9	6.3	7.7	10.6	13.5	16.4	15.1	16.3
Total (yuan bn.)	5,326	6,562	7,712	10,010	12,639	15,571	18,964	23,257

Notes:

1. Enterprises owned by town and village, so-called township and village enterprises (TEVs), are classified under collective ownership.
2. 'Others' includes foreign firms and Sino-foreign joint ventures.

Source: Calculated from the data in National Bureau of Statistics, China, (2006, 2008).

in 2000 but had decreased to less than 80 percent by 2007. In contrast, the share of private ownership and others increased, with its share of 4.9 percent in 2000 increasing to 16.3 percent in 2007. The share of total revenues of the collectively owned business groups was around 4–6 percent. Although these figures show dominance of state ownership in the size of revenues, the shares in terms of the number of companies are quite different. Fig. 8.1 shows that the share of business groups with private ownership and others was substantial at 44 percent in 2007, a rapid increase from 19 percent in 2000. In other words, almost half of the business groups in China were private. In contrast, the share of business groups owned by the state decreased rapidly, from 65 percent in 2000 to 45 percent in 2007, when it accounted for less than half. The share of business groups under collective ownership hovered around 10 percent, showing not much change.

The number of Chinese firms included in *Fortune*'s "Global 500" also reflects the growth of big business groups in China. As shown in Table 8.2, the number of Chinese firms on the list in 2006 was 24, including two Hong Kong firms. Among those, Sinopec, the largest firm in China, was ranked 17th with revenue of US$131.6 billion. China National Petroleum and State Grid Corporation were ranked 24th and 29th. Table 8.3 lists the top thirty business groups in China, selected in terms of the size of sales in 2006. They are enormous in size and have a selected strategic

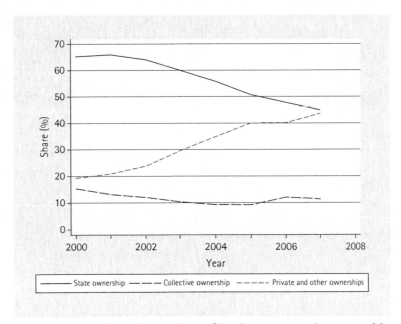

Figure 8.1 Trend in the number of business groups by ownership types (% in total) in China, 2000–8

Source: Calculated from the data in National Bureau of Statistics, China (2006a/2008).

Table 8.2 Chinese firms in *Fortune's* Global 500, 2006

Ranking	Name	Headquarters	Revenue (US $ m.)	Profit (US $ m.)
17	Sinopec	Beijing	131,636	3,703
24	China National Petroleum	Beijing	110,520	13,265
29	State Grid Corporation	Beijing	107,186	2,238
170	Industrial & Commercial Bank of China	Beijing	36,833	6,179
180	China Mobile Limited	Beijing	35,914	6,260
192	China Life Insurance	Beijing	33,712	174
215	Bank of China	Beijing	30,751	5,372
230	China Construction Bank	Beijing	28,532	5,810
237	China Southern Power Grid	Guangzhou	27,966	1,074
275	China Telecom	Beijing	24,791	2,280
277	Agricultural Bank of China	Beijing	24,476	728
290	Hutchison Whampoa	Hong Kong	23,661	2,578
299	Sinochem Corporation	Beijing	23,109	345
307	Baosteel	Shanghai	22,663	1,622
342	China Railway Engineering	Beijing	20,520	143
384	China Railway Construction	Beijing	18,736	70
385	First Automotive Works	Changchun	18,711	70
396	China State Construction	Beijing	18,163	281
402	Shanghai Automotive	Shanghai	18,010	90
405	COFCO Limited	Beijing	17,953	281
435	China Minmetals	Beijing	16,902	154
457	Jardine Matheson	Hong Kong/ Hamilton	16,281	1,348
469	China National Offshore Oil	Beijing	16,039	3,007
488	China Ocean Shipping	Beijing	15,414	1,093

Source: http://money.cnn.com/magazines/fortune/

sector. It is easy to see that, in terms of the listed strategic sectors, manufacturing was not dominant, unlike the situation in Korea or Japan; instead there are more examples of firms in energy, utilities, and trading. Moreover, most were state-owned enterprises, with twenty-seven out of the thirty being state-owned.

If we look at the top 500 Chinese business groups, rather than the top 30, the industrial distribution changes, with more dominance on manufacturing. Using data for the top 500 business groups in 2006, Table 8.4 shows that the manufacturing sector had the biggest share, with around 70 percent in all criteria, ranging from the number of firms, shareholders' equity, sales revenue, profit, tax, and the number of employees. The service sector took the second largest share of the indicators, accounting for 20–35 percent, depending upon the indicators.

Table 8.3 Largest business groups in China, 2006

Name of group	Revenue (yuan bn.)	Employee (000)	Ownership	Major business lines
China Petrochemical Co.	1,097.5	649.7	State	Oil refining and petrochemicals
China National Petroleum Co.	923.2	1,012.8	State	Oil (fuels, lubricants), natural gas, petrochemical, oil exploration services, oil exploration equipments
State Grid Co. of China	855.3	794.5	State	Builds and operates power grids and provides power supply
China Mobile Communications Co.	286.3	371.0	State	Telecommunications, mobile communications
China Southern Power Grid	223.5	173.2	State	Power generation
China Telecom	198.7	400.3	State	Fixed service telecommunications provider
Sinochem Group	184.5	17.8	State	Chemical fertilizer
Baosteel Group Co.	183.4	91.3	State	Steel, finance, coal processing, engineering
China Railway Engineering Co.	163.8	268.0	State	Railways
China FAW Group Co.	158.6	117.6	State	Automobiles
China Railway Construction Co.	150.7	218.3	State	Railways
Dongfeng Motor Co.	147.2	134.2	State	Automobiles
China State Construction Engineering Co.	144.8	404.1	State	Property and real-estate construction
Shanghai Automotive Industry Co.	144.1	82.0	State	Passenger cars, commercial vehicles and components
Legend Holdings	138.9	30.3	Privately owned company	IT, equity investment and real estate development
China Minmetals Co.	135.0	36.3	State	Production and trading of metals and minerals; finance, real-estate and logistics
China National Offshore Oil Co.	132.4	48.0	State	Oil and gas
China Ocean Shipping (Group) Company	127.6	64.0	State	Freight forwarding, shipbuilding, ship-repairing, terminal operations

(continued)

Table 8.3 Continued

Name of group	Revenue (yuan bn.)	Employee (000)	Ownership	Major business lines
China Communications Construction Company	115.1	77.0	State	Construction and design of transportation infrastructure dredging and port machinery manufacturing
Haier Group	108.0	54.0	Collective, TVEs	Electronics, white goods, financial services
Aluminum Corporation of China	106.1	188.2	State	Aluminum products
China Resources (Holding) Company Limited	100.4	171.5	State	Retail, power, breweries, real estate, food, medicine, textiles, chemical products, gas, compressor
China Netcom Group	97.0	248.7	State	Fixed-line telephone services, telecommunications, data services
China Metallurgical Group Co.	90.7	113.3	State	EPC business (engineering, procurement and construction), natural resources exploitation, papermaking business, equipment fabrication
China Unicom Group	87.9	145.9	State	Mobile communication service, Unicom Horizon CDMA Service, mobile value-added service
China Huaneng Group	84.2	66.7	State	Power generation, IT, transportation, renewable energy, environment protection
Shenhua Group Co. Limited	83.6	141.2	State	Coal production, transportation, Electricity generation
Ping An Insurance (Group)	81.7	48.8	Privately held	Insurance, financial services
China International Trust and Investment Company (CITIC Group)	81.3	77.6	State	Financial services: banking, securities business, insurance, trusts business, funds, futures
Zhongguo Xianjian Group	78.4	664.9		
COFCO Group	75.4	82.5	State	Producer and supplier of processed agricultural products (including oilseed, wheat, and rice)

Sources: The list of business groups and the data of employees and revenues come from Enterprise Research Institute in Development Research Center of the State Council (2007). Other information is collected from related websites.

Table 8.4 China's top 500 business groups by sector, 2006

Sectors	Number of units	Total assets (yuan bn.)	Total share-holders' equity (yuan bn.)	Revenue (yuan bn.)	Employees (million)	Profit tax (yuan bn.)
Total	500	20,432	7,837	14,724	19.01	1,789
The primary sector	5	228.3	46.6	145	1.41	5.9
The manufacturing sector	363	12,917	5,435	10,942	13.81	1,411
The service sector	132	7,287	2,355	3,637	3.78	372.7
Share (%)						
The primary sector	1.00	1.12	0.59	0.98	7.42	0.33
The manufacturing sector	72.6	63.2	69.4	74.3	72.7	78.9
The service sector	26.4	35.7	30.1	24.7	19.9	20.8

Source: Enterprise Research Institute in Development Research Center of the State Council (2007: 7).

8.3 HISTORY OF BUSINESS GROUPS IN CHINA

Most of the largest business groups in China emerged around the mid-1980s, and more specifically in conjunction with some policy experiments in 1985 and 1986 (Keister 2000). The concept of a "business group" appeared in the State Council's official documents for the first time in 1986. However, even before the SOE reform and experiment, there had been various attempts for enterprises to expand their scope of integration since economic reform had begun in the late 1970s. For instance, firms in the same business sector formed a horizontal association to share brands, marketing channels, and production facilities to fill the gaps in underdeveloped markets (Hahn and Lee 2006). These attempts eventually led to the recognition of the many limitations of a loose horizontal association without centralized ownership and control. An attempt to solve these problems was the transition of horizontal associations into business groups with a clear power structure (Hahn and Lee 2006).

From the year 1987, when the regulation "Several Suggestions on Forming and Developing Business Groups" was enacted, business groups came out at a quite rapid rate, both voluntarily and with the state's assistance, predominantly in the state-owned sector (Keister 2000). The Chinese government encouraged the restructuring of SOEs into business groups in order to provide them with economy of scale and increasing specialization. The government also thought that they could implement industrial policies more effectively with business groups. Learning from the experience of Korea and Japan, Chinese government believed that it would be less costly and more efficient to implement industrial policies in an economy led by a few big business groups.

The concept of business group was articulated by the government, and accordingly the state-owned firms were given incentives to encourage them to form business groups. Preferential policies for business groups, such as the right to set up finance companies that could play the role of intra-group banks, were granted. The State Council also selected the first batch of fifty-seven large business groups as the national trial group in 1991.[1] The national trial group was extended to a group of 120 business groups after the second batch of national trial group was chosen in 1997. The national trial business groups were granted various privileges, including investment decision-making, financing, foreign trade, debt–equity swap, and capital injection (Hahn and Lee 2006).

Business groups in China were formed and evolved through three paths (Hahn and Lee 2006; Lee and Hahn 2007). The most common way of setting up a business group was establishing subsidiaries through spin-offs. Firms separated core parts of their production, established subsidiaries that would be profitable businesses, and transformed themselves into holding companies.[2] Spin-offs sometimes involved the

---

[1] According to Ma and Lu (2005), there were two reasons why the government chose the national trial groups: to make groups in particular sectors become international players and to solve the matter of SOEs that were performing poorly by incorporating them into business groups led by SOEs that were performing well.

[2] Establishing business groups through spin-offs often involved irregular diversion of the parent firms' resources for the benefit of subsidiaries. Expropriation of state property in the form of asset-stripping, tax evasion, debt reduction, and dividend manipulation was reported.

establishment of new firms with investment from parent firms and other firms: this represents the second path—joint ventures with other companies. In this situation, the joint venture could often take advantage of pooling capital, equity, or brand names. The last path through which business groups were formed involved mergers and acquistions (M&As). Intense market competition led firms to be involved in M&As through which firms hoped to increase market share, achieve scale economies, enhance brand names, and capitalize on superior managerial talent (Lee and Hahn 2007). Hair Groups, the biggest in household electric appliances industry, and China International Marine Container Group, a globally dominating producer of marine shipping containers, are good examples of groups whose growth have been propelled by M&As.

Lee and Jin (2009) discuss three alternative theories to explain the emergence of business groups in China: specifically, the market-based view, the state-activism view, and the resource-based view. Using firm-level data and variables representing different theories, they verify that the joint-venture path should be the most dynamic and privately motivated way toward forming a business group and is consistent with the market-based and resource-based views; that the M&A path seems to be consistent with the state-activism view, implying top-down manner restructuring; and that the spin-off path seems to be close to the resource-based view. They also find that the greater autonomy given together with or after changing into a shareholding corporation is one of the most consistent and significant factors leading to a business group, regardless of whether it was through an M&A, a spin-off, or a joint-venture path. This implies that the SOEs have gone from being traditional SOEs to shareholding corporations, and then finally to business groups.

With the decision of the Communist Party to establish a socialist market economy in 1993, private ownership began to be regarded officially in China. As a result, many non-state firms emerged, and many of them built their own business groups to show up their size and reputation (Ma and Lu 2005). From the year 1998, the state made efforts to create "highly competitive large business groups" in the key pillar industries in the national economy. In 1998, the fifteen industrial ministries were closed and the State Council began directly to control state-owned groups at the central level. In 2003, the Chinese government established the State-Owned Assets Supervision and Administration Commission of the State Council (SASAC), which played a crucial role in the reform of state-owned business groups. Charged with exercising the rights and authority of ownership on behalf of the government, SASAC took over the supervisory role that all the former industrial ministries previously had and clearly demarcated authority among different levels of the government.

The central SASAC owns several hundreds firms that are controlled at many layers, with individual enterprise at the bottom level, an investment or holding company in the middle, and the SASAC at the top. In 2006, the central SASAC was the controlling shareholder of the 168 largest companies listed on the Chinese exchange in Shanghai and Shenzhen, which accounted for 33.8 percent of domestic market value (Naughton 2008).

8.4 THE ROLE OF THE STATE IN THE
GROWTH OF BUSINESS GROUPS

··

The role of the state in the emergence and development of business groups could be said to have been more important in China than in its neighbors in East Asia such as Japan and Korea, because Chinese business groups emerged through a gradual transition, guided and controlled by the Communist Party, from a planned to a market economy. In fact, the government was actively involved in the establishment and development of Chinese business groups, at the central and the provincial level.

The central government as a developmental state promoted big business groups because it considered they were a useful "device for economic catch-up" (Lee 2006), as was the case for Korea and Japan. The State Council designated and made relevant benefits and privileges available to a certain business groups. Also, the local government and their ministries tried to promote their own business groups through various schemes that included transformation of the former government units in charge of state-owned companies into holding companies.

Table 8.5 shows the importance of the 131 business groups directly controlled by the central government or the State Council. These 131 (4.5 percent) out of a total of 2,926 business groups accounted for 48.3 percent of total assets and 41.8 percent of total revenues of all business groups in China in 2007. The state gave them a variety of grants and favorable treatments to make them grow. Relevant Ministries of the State Council also had a similar role to boost big business groups: 141 business groups (4.8 percent) registered with relevant Ministries of the State Council, representing 10.9 and 9.9 percent, respectively, of the assets size and the sales revenue of all the registered business groups in China.

Plenty of strategic considerations were also involved in building business groups. Starting in the early 1990s, the Chinese government began to encourage the creation of big business groups with the intention of strengthening international competitiveness of Chinese firms. For the formation of big business groups, the Chinese government promoted M&A among big firms with a policy initiative called a "strong-strong combination" (qiangqiang lianhe in Chinese). Administrative means were often used in this process. For example, the Shanghai Baosteel Group, the biggest business group in the Chinese iron and steel industry, was founded in 1998 through mergers and restructuring of the Shanghai Metallurgical Holding Group and the Shanghai Meishan Group by the former Shanghai Baoshan Iron and Steel Corporation, which became the core company of this new group. The biggest difficulty in building this group was the different affiliations of the involved firms. The Shanghai city government controlled some companies, whereas the central government controlled others. Extensive negotiations took place before the Shanghai city government finally agreed on the merger of the firms (Hahn and Lee 2006).

In provinces, the formation of some business groups was initiated by the local governments with the aim of improving enterprise performance by sharing existing

Table 8.5 Distribution by the levels of state units in charge, 2007

Levels of State Units	Groups		Assets			Revenue		
	Number	Share (%)	Amount (yuan bn.)	Share (%)	Average (yuan bn.)	Amount (yuan bn.)	Share (%)	Average (yuan bn.)
The State Council	131	4.5	16,607	48.3	126.77	9,718	41.8	74.18
Relevant Ministries of the State Council	141	4.8	3,738	10.9	26.51	2,296	9.9	16.28
Provincial Governments	777	26.6	6,585	19.2	8.48	5,321	22.9	6.85
Bureau of Provincial Governments	670	22.9	3,106	9.0	4.64	2,136	9.2	3.19
Others	1,207	41.3	4,319	12.6	3.58	3,787	16.3	3.14
Total	2,926	100.0	34,355	100.0	11.74	23,257	100.0	7.95

Source: Calculated from the data in National Bureau of Statistics, China (2008).

managerial resources across a wider array of businesses in order to respond to the increasing market competition. The supply of skillful managerial talent was very limited in many localities in China. Some local governments restructured all the SOEs under their supervision into several business groups. In 1993, Siping county in Liaocheng city of the Shandong province restructured the twenty-nine SOEs under its supervision into five business groups, based on these groups' industrial categories, in order to share both established brands and managerial talent (Hahn and Lee 2006).

In some cases, business groups were built under public policy considerations. Regarding the SOEs under their control, local governments had conflicting objectives: the promotion of profitable enterprises and social stability. As market competition increased, the profitability of many SOEs decreased. At that point, local governments were often more concerned about the social tension that might be caused by massive lay-offs. Accordingly, local governments tended to favor their responsibility to maintain social stability. Faced with unprofitable enterprises, they often merged these enterprises with better-performing enterprises—"forced marriages" (*lalangpei* in Chinese)—rather than having them go bankrupt; this led to the emergence of new business groups or the expansion of existing ones.

8.5 Corporate ownership, governance and agency costs

In China, there are several types of enterprises by firm types: state-owned enterprises (SOE), wholly state-owned enterprises (WSOEs), limited liability companies, and limited companies. State-owned enterprises are firms owned by the central or a provincial government. Both SOEs and WSOEs are owned by the state; however, the latter group firms, which are 100 percent owned by the government, are granted special autonomy and privileges. The limited liability company (*youxian zeren gongsi* in Chinese) is a legal form of business company offering limited liability to its owners. A limited company (*gufen youxian gongsi* in Chinese) is a shareholding corporation in which liability of each shareholder is limited by shares, which is most close to a typical corporation issuing stocks in capitalist economies.

Depending on whether they are jointly owned by foreigners and Chinese or wholly owned by foreigners, enterprises are classified into Sino–foreign joint entures, joint ventures with Hong Kong, Macao, and Taiwan, foreign-invested limited companies, and Hong Kong, Macao, and Taiwan-invested limited companies.[3] Table 8.6 shows

---

[3] In Tables 8.6, 8.7, 8.8, and 8.10, the data of two types of business groups, the foreign invested limited companies as well as the Hong Kong, Macao, and Taiwan invested limited companies are merged in "Others."

Table 8.6 Distribution by types of parent companies, 2007

Ownership types of parent companies	Business groups		Assets			Revenues		
	Number	Share (%)	Amount (yuan bn.)	Share (%)	Average (yuan bn.)	Amount (yuan bn.)	Share (%)	Average (yuan bn.)
SOEs	300	10.3	15,840	46.1	52.80	9,522	40.9	31.74
WSOEs	662	22.6	10,284	29.9	15.53	6,339	27.3	9.57
SOEs + WSOEs	962	32.9	26,124	76.0	27.16	15,861	68.2	16.49
Limited Liability Companies	1,331	45.5	4,882	14.2	3.67	4,746	20.4	3.57
Limited Companies	397	13.6	2533	7.4	6.38	1,743	7.5	4.39
Sino-foreign Joint Ventures	38	1.3	170	0.5	4.47	189	0.8	4.98
Joint ventures with Hong Kong, Macao and Taiwan	33	1.1	70	0.2	2.12	60	0.3	1.82
Others	165	5.6	575	1.7	3.49	658	2.8	3.99
Total	2,926	100	34,354	100	11.74	23,257	100	7.95

Source: Calculated from the data in National Bureau of Statistics, China (2008).

that the state-owned economy (including SOEs and WSOEs) kept the leading position among the ownership types of parent companies in China in 2007. Although the share of both SOEs and WSOEs in terms of number was relatively small at 32.9 percent, they accounted for 76.0 percent of total assets and 68.2 percent of total sales revenue. However, it is interesting to see that the limited liability companies, which accounted for only 20.4 percent of sales revenue, had the leading position in terms of number among all types of owners. SOEs and WSOEs were also dominant in terms of the average size of assets of the parent company of a business group. In particular, the average size of the parent companies of SOEs was as much as 4.5 times the average size of all the business groups in terms of assets.

The dominance of state ownership is more pronounced when we focus on the top 500 business groups. Table 8.7 shows several basic statistics for the top 500 business groups in 2005 by ownership types. There were 101 state-owned enterprises ranked in the top 500 groups, accounting for 20.2 percent, and 177 wholly state-owned enterprises, accounting for 35.4 percent; thus the number of corporations in the state-owned economy (both SOEs and WSOEs) comprised 55.6 percent of the 500 business groups. When these statistics are compared to those shown in Table 8.6, it can be seen that a bigger portion of state-owned business groups was included in the top 500 business groups, indicating that the state owned bigger business groups.

Among the top 500 business groups, SOEs and WSOEs constitute 51.6 percent and 31.0 percent respectively in terms of assets, 58.8 percent and 27.1 percent in terms of shareholders' equity, 49.9 percent and 26.6 percent in terms of revenue, 27.7 percent and 37.9 percent in terms of exports, 61.0 percent and 24.9 percent in terms of profit and tax, and 44.3 percent and 32.1 percent in terms of the number of employees. If the two groups are totaled (SOEs + SWOEs), the state-owned economy represented 82.6 percent, 85.8, 76.5, 65.6, 86.0, and 76.4 percent in terms of total assets, shareholders' equity, revenue, exports, total amount of profit and tax, and the number of employees, respectively. From a comparison with the statistics in Table 8.6, it is evident that bigger business groups are owned by the state, although the time difference between the data in the two tables should be considered.

For the rest of the groups, in terms of the number of units, the limited liability companies accounted for 28.6 percent, and the limited companies for 9.0 percent.[4] The other remaining groups accounts for negligible portion. In terms of total assets, the limited liability companies comprised 9.9 percent and the limited companies accounted for 5.7 percent. In terms of the revenue, the limited liability companies accounted for 14.6 percent and the limited companies for 5.6 percent; and so on.

When we look at the average size of the top 500 business groups by firm types in 2006, as shown in Table 8.8, the state-owned ones are seen to have been bigger than the others. In terms of the assets, state-owned enterprises (SOE) were the biggest among the top 500. In 2006, the average assets of the SOE group was 104.5 billion yuan. Thus the assets of the SOEs were 2.56 times bigger than the average asset size of

---

[4] The limited companies consist of two types of firms, the private company limited by shares and the "public limited company." In limited liability companies (LLCs), a member's liability to repay the LLC's obligations is limited to its "capital contribution"

Table 8.7 Main economic indicators of top 500 groups by types of parent companies, 2005

Ownership types of parent companies	Number of units	Assets (yuan bn.)	Shareholders' equity (yuan bn.)	Revenue (yuan bn.)	Exports (yuan bn.)	Profit and tax (yuan bn.)	Employees (000)
SOEs	101	10,550.25	4,605.04	7,348.19	276.77	1,091.72	8,423.8
WSOEs	177	6,329.58	2,119.62	3,911.32	379.39	446.20	6,103.4
Limited Liability Companies	143	2,020.15	724.46	2,147.64	226.74	163.75	3,067.8
Limited Companies	45	1,156.02	235.06	821.28	66.35	54.56	1,010.5
Sino-foreign joint ventures	10	67.09	30.19	98.20	9.87	8.80	127.3
Joint ventures with Hong Kong, Macao and Taiwan	3	40.69	21.47	29.78	1.93	4.31	43.4
The others	21	268.41	101.20	367.06	40.09	19.61	228.7
Total	500	20,432.19	7,837.03	14,723.48	1,001.15	1,788.95	19,005

Shares (%)

Ownership types of parent companies	Number of units	Assets	Shareholders' equity	Revenue	Exports	Profit and tax	Employees
SOEs	20.2	51.6	58.8	49.9	27.7	61.0	44.3
WSOEs	35.4	31.0	27.1	26.6	37.9	24.9	32.1
(SOEs+WSOEs)	55.6	82.6	85.8	76.5	65.6	86.0	76.4
Limited Liability Companies	28.6	9.9	9.2	14.6	22.7	9.2	16.1
Limited Companies	9.0	5.7	3.0	5.6	6.6	3.1	5.3
Sino-foreign joint ventures	2.0	0.3	0.4	0.7	1.0	0.5	0.7
Joint ventures with Hong Kong, Macao, and Taiwan	0.6	0.2	0.3	0.2	0.2	0.2	0.2
The others	4.2	1.3	1.3	2.5	4.0	1.1	1.2

Source: Enterprise Research Institute in Development Research Center of the State Council (2007:18).

Table 8.8 Average size of top 500 groups by the ownership types, 2006

Ownership types	Assets (yuan bn.)	Revenue (yuan bn.)	Employees (000) (yuan bn.)
SOEs	104.5	72.8	83.4
WSOEs	35.8	22.1	34.5
Limited Liability Companies	14.1	15.0	21.5
Limited Companies	25.7	18.3	22.5
Sino-foreign Joint Ventures	6.7	9.8	12.7
JVs with Hong Kong, Macao and Taiwan	13.6	9.9	14.5
Others	12.8	17.5	10.9
Total Average	40.9	29.4	38.0

Source: Enterprise Research Institute in Development Research Center of the State Council (2007: 13).

the top 500 groups, while the asset size of business groups with other ownership types were all below the average. The other groups can be ranked as follows in terms of the average asset size: wholly state-owned enterprises (35.8 billion yuan), limited companies (25.7 billion yuan), limited liability companies (14.1 billion yuan), and joint ventures with Hong Kong, Macao, and Taiwan (13.6 billion yuan).

In terms of size by average revenue, SOEs were also bigger, with an average revenue of 72.8 billion yuan, 2.47 times bigger than the top 500 average. They were followed by wholly state-owned enterprises (22.1 billion yuan), limited companies (18.3 billion yuan), limited liability companies (15.0 billion yuan), joint ventures with Hong Kong, Macao, and Taiwan (9.9 billion yuan), and the Sino–foreign joint ventures (9.8 billion yuan). Similar results are drawn from the analysis of the average number of employees.

As seen in the previous discussion, the dominance of the state in ownership is still an important characteristic of the business groups in China. Such ownership structure should have some implications for corporate governance and agency costs. In the listed business groups in China, a large portion of shares are non-tradable shares owned by state-related agencies, and the role played by minority shareholders, including holders of tradable shares, is negligible (Tenev et al. 2002). Such weak legal and market mechanisms for exercising control over the managers provide a good ground for managerial entrenchment and often lead to severe agency problems (La Porta et al. 1999).

Given this situation, formation of business groups may lead to more private benefits for managers and the controlling shareholders, because the potential agency costs are aggravated in group-type firms with more serious asymmetric information. Under the pyramidal structure of business groups, controlling shareholders easily transfer profits across firms, often from firms that have low cash-flow rights to ones that have high cash-flow rights—so-called tunneling.

In China, the irregular diversion of parent companies' resource to subsidiaries was often reported (Fan 1996). Such a diversion took various forms of expropriation of state property in the form of tax evasion, debt reduction, and dividend manipulation. Lee and Hahn (2004) investigated these phenomena in the context of the history of economic reform and explained how the control power over firms had changed over time since economic reform had taken place in China. According to them, the outsiders, the supervisory state and party organs, had strong power in controlling firms until the 1980s. However, from the end of the 1990s managers started to have de facto and de jure control over firms.

A series of empirical studies have reported agency problems related to the state-dominant ownership as well as to the weak legal and market mechanisms for exercising control over managers. Xu and Wang (1999) reported a positive correlation between ownership concentration and profitability using the data of Chinese listed companies during the period 1993–5. They found that a firm's profitability is positively correlated to the fraction of shares held by legal persons, whereas it is either negatively correlated or uncorrelated to the fraction of shares held by the state. Their findings indicate that ownership concentration, especially by legal persons, alleviates the agency problem by strengthening the shareholders' control over managers.

Tian (2001) uses data of listed firms in China during the period 1994–8 and finds that firms having a non-government majority shareholder outperform those having the government as a majority shareholder. Moreover, he also finds that there is a U-shaped relationship between the size of government equity holding and corporate value. According to him, the U-shaped relationship indicates interest-maximization behavior by the state. The grabbing hand by the state decreases corporate value under a certain threshold, but the government also decreases corporate value by providing a helping hand when its financial interests become sufficiently large.

Wang et al. (2004), using public company data for the period from 1994 to 2000, find that the degree of ownership concentration is positively correlated with operating performance. They also report that legal person ownership shows no difference from state ownership in terms of its impact on performance.

8.6 BUSINESS STRUCTURE AND DIVERSIFICATION

Typical business groups in China have a core company at the first tier, closely related companies at the second tier, semi-closely related companies at the third ties, and loosely related companies at the bottom. The core firms are also called the parent company or group company because they have majority rights to the assets of their subsidiaries and unite the business group into a single controlled structure. They are generally a large industrial or commercial enterprise, with their business defining the primary business area of the group. They have their business and thus they can survive independently of their member firms. It is possible for core companies to exist as a pure holding company, but this is not the common case (Keister 2000; Lee and Hahn 2007).

The core firms also directly control and manage several specialized affiliate companies such as finance companies (*caiwugongsi* in Chinese) and research and development companies. The finance company is an independent non-bank financial firm responsible for a business group's financing activity. The main role of a finance company in a business group is to raise funds from banks as well as from member firms and to lend them to member firms in need of financing. In early stage of economic reforms, the capital market in China was underdeveloped, and thus firms had difficulties in accessing capital that they needed. The finance company emerged to overcome this situation. Business groups have been given by the government rights to set up finance companies. The first finance company in China was set up in 1987. In 2007, there were 81 finance companies that were registered with China National Association of Finance Companies.

Many business groups also have research and development companies to fulfill the demand for research and development. Table 8.9 shows the aggregate amount of R&D investments by Chinese business groups which was hovering around 1 percent of sale revenue during the period 2001–5.

In addition to the relationship between a core firm and its member firms in a business group, member firms have diverse types of inter-firm relations. It is typical for firms in a business group to be connected to each other through cross-shareholdings, interlocking directorates, loan dependence, transaction of intermediate goods, and joint subsidiaries (Goto 1982). Cross-shareholding developed in China so that member firms could share their interests with other firms in the same group, rather than being competitors. Cross-shareholding enabled member firms to be involved in joint projects together and to increase overall investment in research and development that would otherwise have been too risky (Keister 2000). Interlocking directorates occurred when several firms in a business groups shared a manager on the boards of directors. According to Li (1995), interlocking directorates were the consequence of the practice of the state appointing key positions in the SOEs. However, it should be recognized that they developed so that insufficient managerial resources in a business group could be utilized. Firms in Chinese business

Table 8.9 Research and development expenditure of business groups, 2001–5

Year	Sales revenue (yuan bn.)	R&D expenditure (yuan bn.)	R&D ratio (%)
2001	6,562	66.9	1.02
2002	7,712	80.7	1.05
2003	10,009	90.5	0.90
2004	12,639	120.1	0.95
2005	15,551	150.7	0.97

Source: Calculated from the data in National Bureau of Statistics, China (2006b).

groups were also linked among themselves through cross-lending as well as through cross debt guarantees toward the commercial banks. Production relations can often be seen among member firms, because many firms in a business group do business in the same industry. Joint-venture-based subsidiaries with foreign firms in other Asian countries or in Western countries (*zhongwai hezi gonsi* in Chinese) were often built to access high technology as well as foreign markets. However, empirical evidence shows that they had a limited impact on technology transfer (Kang and Lee 2008).

Regarding diversification, it seems certain that business groups in China also pursued diversification. Part A of Table 8.10 shows that they had on average 9.9 subsidiaries in 2007, which cannot be taken as small. While Part A, based on the whole sample, cannot show the exact number of segments that were doing business, Part B, based on the listed business groups, shows that on average they had 7.62 subsidiaries and were doing business in 2.2 segments out of a total of 19 business segments. In Part C, when we divide the sample (about 220 business groups as of 2000) into those that have two or less segments of business, and those that are diversified and thus have more than two segments of business, we can see that roughly half of the listed sample can be classified as diversified. As shown in Part C, some of them (more than 70) were doing business in more than 4 business segments as of 1999. But this number dropped rapidly toward 2003, which indicates some refocusing in the 2000s (Seo et al. 2006).

However, this refocusing tendency cannot be verified by the data of the whole sample shown in Part A of Table 8.10. It is shown that the average number of subsidiaries was still increasing in the 2000s, from 8.3 in 2000, to 9.7 in 2005 and to 9.9 in 2007. This might indicate that the listed business groups are more exposed to market competition or sensitive to profitability and thus have conducted some refocusing. The story is that business groups in China pursued diversification in the early 1990s, but that fierce market competition forced them to withdraw to their traditional core line of business, as argued in Lee and Woo (2002). However, Chinese business groups that have diversified business have tended to diversify into related rather than unrelated fields. Huang (2000) also reports that the great majority of M&As in China involves horizontal, vertical, and related diversification. In general, listed business group are relatively less diversified than are Korean *chaebol* (Lee and Woo 2002).

Less diversification among the Chinese business group meas that they cannot expect the diverse benefits enjoyed by the Korean *chaebol*, such as the diversification of risks, related cross-subsidization of temporary loss-making, but potentially promising business (Lee and Woo 2002). Most of the new businesses among Korean *chaebol*, including the memory business of Samsung, were making huge losses during their early days. Affiliate companies in Chinese business groups would have more difficulties in finding such help from other member companies. In this respect, they would be more vulnerable to firm-specific or sector-specific risks than Korean *chaebol* firms.

Table 8.10 Trends and degree of diversification

Part A. Number of subsidiaries by firm types

Ownership types	2000			2005			2007		
	No. of parent companies	No. of subsidiaries	Average number of subsidiaries	No. of parent companies	No. of subsidiaries	Average number of subsidiaries	No. of parent companies	No. of subsidiaries	Average number of subsidiaries
SOEs	538	6,805	12.6	349	5,603	16.1	301	5002	16.6
WSOEs	696	2,067	3.0	676	2,446	3.6	661	2576	3.9
Limited liability companies	665	6,392	9.6	1,202	13,033	10.8	1331	15509	11.7
Limited companies	438	1,562	3.6	390	1,805	4.6	397	1793	4.5
Sino-foreign Joint ventures	43	1,747	40.6	29	1,663	57.3	38	1615	42.5
Joint ventures with Hong Kong, Macao, and Taiwan	28	597	21.3	33	794	24.1	33	831	25.2
Others	247	2,778	11.2	166	2,135	12.9	165	1775	10.8
Total	2,655	21,948	8.3	2,845	27,479	9.7	2,926	29,101	9.9

Sources: Calculated from the data in National Bureau of Statistics, China (2001, 2006a, 2008).

Year	Observation	No. of business groups	Average number of subsidiaries	Average number of segments	No. of segments per subsidiary
1994	270	162	6.29	2.22	0.35
1995	270	162	6.29	2.24	0.36
1996	270	162	6.29	2.25	0.36
1997	270	164	6.78	2.30	0.34
1998	270	165	7.28	2.36	0.32
1999	270	170	7.77	2.47	0.32
2000	270	184	8.26	2.50	0.30
2001	270	191	8.76	2.31	0.26
2002	270	189	9.27	2.09	0.23
2003	270	189	9.27	2.09	0.23
Average		173.8	7.62	2.28	0.30

Notes: 1. A firm is defined as a business group when the firm has at least four subsidiaries.
2. One of twenty-two industries (segments), which comprise twelve industries based on one-digit standard industry classification (SIC) system plus ten manufacturing industries based on two-digit, are assigned to each firm.

Source: Manually collected from annual reports of public companies listed on the Shanghai Stock Exchange or the Shenzhen Stock Exchange.

Part C. Distribution of business groups by number of business segments

	1994	1995	1996	1997	1998	1999	2000'	2001	2002	2003
SEGMENT	2.6	2.63	2.6	2.61	2.7	2.7	2.8	2.5	2.3	2.3
1	38	38	38	47	46	44	44	60	59	56
2	63	61	60	67	63	74	73	74	88	88
DIVER 0	101	99	98	114	109	118	117	134	147	144
3	62	63	63	55	59	58	60	51	65	66
4	38	38	38	42	33	30	24	31	19	18
5	8	9	10	11	20	20	21	16	4	4
6	1	1	1	3	4	9	11	4	1	1
7	0	0	0	0	0	0	2	1	0	0
DIVER 1	109	111	112	111	116	117	118	103	89	89

Notes: DIVER 0 counts the number of business groups with one or two segments, and DIVER one counts those with three or more. This table shows distribution of listed firms with more than two subsidiaries.

Source: Seo et al. (2006).

8.7 EFFICIENCY AND COMPETITIVENESS

Now let us turn to the issue of competitiveness. Statistics of the top 500 business groups provide some evidence of the competitiveness of big business groups in China. Table 8.11 indicates the strong growth orientation of big business groups. According to the table, aggregate total assets of the top 500 grew annually by between 9.32 percent and 20.29 percent, profit and tax grew by between 18.47 percent and 38.70 percent, and revenue grew by between 18.59 percent and 29.98 percent during the period 2002–6.

Table 8.12 confirms the overall tendency to improve efficiency of China's top 500 business groups. The total factor productivity increased between 2002 and 2006, from 4.49 percent in 2002 to 7.30 percent in 2006. The output per worker also increased from 357.6 thousand yuan in 2002 to 756.7 thousand yuan in 2006. The profit and tax ratio increased from 8.00 percent in 2002 to 11.59 percent in 2006. The ratio of profit to stockholders' equity increased from 7.59 percent in 2002 to 13.83 percent in 2006. The profit and tax per worker

Table 8.11 Growth performance of top 500 business groups (yearly growth in %), 2002–6

Variables	2002	2003	2004	2005	2006
Total assets	11.32	20.29	9.32	18.74	17.55
Number of employees	−0.17	1.14	−4.74	6.45	5.67
Export sales	18.57	16.93	29.31	13.74	25.37
Profit and tax	33.70	18.47	38.70	22.41	23.72
Net profit	29.90	32.79	49.75	23.90	22.58
Revenue	18.59	29.98	21.79	22.03	21.50
Total stockholders' equity	11.27	13.00	8.99	16.60	15.43

Source: Enterprise Research Institute in Development Research Center of the State Council (2007: 2).

Table 8.12 Economic efficiency of China's top 500 business groups, 2002–6

Variables	2002	2003	2004	2005	2006
Total factor productivity (%)	4.49	5.29	6.31	6.85	7.30
Output ratio per worker (000 *yuan*/worker)	357.6	459.6	587.6	673.6	756.7
Profit and tax ratio (%)	8.00	8.26	10.44	11.28	11.59
Profit ratio of stockholders' equity (%)	7.59	8.92	12.26	13.02	13.83
Profit and tax per worker (000 *yuan*/worker)	41.0	48.0	69.9	80.4	94.1
R&D ratio (%)	1.05	0.91	0.79	0.78	0.89

Source: Enterprise Research Institute in Development Research Center of the State Council (2007: 3).

increased from 41.0 thousand yuan to 94.1 thousand yuan in 2006. However, the R&D to sales ratio showed some stagnating tendency.

To examine further the competitiveness of the business group in China, in comparison with stand-alone firms, we ran simple OLS regressions with the data of the firms listed on the Shanghai or Shenzhen Stock Exchange during the period 1995–2006. We used the China Stock Market and Accounting Research Database (CSMAR), designed by the China Accounting and Finance Research Centre of the Hong Kong Polytechnic University (the Centre) and developed by the Shenzhen GTA Information Technology Corporation Limited (GTA IT Co. Ltd.).

We classified the listed firms into business group firms and stand-alone firms and we also divided the period into two subperiods (1995–2000 and 2001–6). For the first period, 1995–2000, we defined a firm as a business group if it had at least four subsidiaries in 1998. For the second period, 2001–6, we defined a firm as business group if it had at least four subsidiaries in 2002. Then, with reference to each variable to be compared, we ran simple OLS regressions with both a dummy for business group firms and dummies for industrial sectors. Table 8.13 shows the results of

Table 8.13 Comparison of business groups with non-business groups

Part A: Size

Dependent variable	Control variable	1995–2000	2001–2006
Log (asset)	Sector dummies	Larger than non-BG	Larger than non-BG
Log (revenue)	Sector dummies	Larger than non-BG	Larger than non-BG

Part B: Performance

Dependent variable	Control variable	1995–2000	2001–2006
ROA	Size, sector dummies	Lower than non-BGs	Lower than non-BGs
ROIC	Size, sector dummies	Lower than non-BGs	Lower than non-BGs
NI/Sales	Size, sector dummies	Slightly lower than non-BGs	Indifferent
EBIT/Sales	Size, sector dummies	Lower than non-BGs	Indifferent
$(Sales_t - Sales_{t-1}) /$ $Sales_{t-1}$	Size, sector dummies	Slightly lower than non-BGs	Indifferent

Notes:
1. Non-BGs non-business group firms. A firm is defined as a business group when it has at least four subsidiaries. So one is assigned as group dummy for firms with at least four subsidiaries, zero otherwise. Size is measured by sales.
2. ROA (return on assets) = Net Income / Total Assets; ROIC (return on invested capital) = EBIT / Total Assets; EBIT = earnings before interest and tax; NI: net income $Sales_t$ Sales at time t $Sales_{t-1}$: sales at time t−1.

comparing the size, accounting performance, and growth propensity of these two types of firms.

First, Part A of Table 8.13 shows that business groups are definitely larger than non-business group firms in terms of both assets and sales. Accounting performance and growth of business groups compared to non-business group firms can be seen in Part B of Table 8.13. Business groups are apparently outperformed by non-business groups in terms of return on assets in both periods. However, they are not very different from non-business groups when return on sales revenue is used as a comparison. Given that return on assets is composed of two components, sales to assets and return to sales, we can conclude that the poor performance of the business group stems mainly from poor turnover rate (sales to asset), not from profit margin.[5]

In terms of firm growth, business groups appear to have grown slightly more slowly than non-business group firms did during the period 1995–2000. But in the period 2001–6, business groups were not different from non-business group firms in terms of firm growth. Overall, business groups grew at almost the same rate as non-business groups.

8.8 SUMMARY AND CONCLUDING REMARKS

The Chinese government has an explicit definition for business groups, which have to be registered at the SAIC. With at least five affiliated companies, the business group as a total should have a registered capital of over 100 million yuan. From this definition, the number of business groups registered increased from 2,472 in 1998 to 2,926 in 2007, a 18.4 percent increase. Two of the most important characteristics of large business groups in China, distinct from their counterparts in Korea or Japan, are that they are less diversified, and that they used to be owned by the state rather than by particular families. The government had controlling power over 45 percent of business groups in 2007. The dominance of the state is most evident in terms of total revenue, the state-controlled firms accounting for 78 percent of total revenue. However, non-government ownership is growing fast, with business groups with private and other ownership accounting for about 45 percent of a total of 2,856 business groups in 2007, although their share in terms of sales was still less than 20 percent. In terms of sectors, firms in the top thirty tend to be in energy, utilities and services, whereas the share of manufacturing increases in the top 500.

Chinese business groups typically maintain a vertical structure, with a core company at the first tier, closely related companies at the second tier, semi-closely related companies at the third tier, and loosely related companies at the bottom. The core firm is also called the parent company or group company, because it has majority rights to subsidiaries and unites the business group into a single controlled structure. The core firm is generally a large industrial or commercial enterprise, with

---

[5] Return/Assets = Return/Sales * Sales/Assets.

its business defining the primary business area of the group. Some large business groups have finance companies and R&D companies as affiliated companies.

While the performance of business groups seems to have improved over time, they are showing some inferior or comparable performance relative to stand-alone firms. In this comparison, it is interesting to confirm in the business groups in China, as in those in other countries, both the strength (high growth) and the weakness (lower profitability) of business groups.[6] That is understandable, as business groups in China are also known to have a multi-tier structure, leading to asset-stripping and agency costs, as in their counterparts in other countries. Our regression results confirming low asset turnover seem to be compatible with this argument. It remains to be seen what the long-term growth path of the Chinese groups will be.

REFERENCES

AOKI, M., KIM, H. K., and OKUNO-FUJIWARA, M. (2000). *The Role of Government in East Asian Economic Development: Comparative Institutional Analysis.* Oxford and New York: Oxford University Press.

CHOO, K., LEE, K., RYU, K., and YOON, J. (2009). "Performance Change of the Business Groups in Korea over Two Decades: Investment Inefficiency and Technological Capabilities," *Economic Development and Cultural Change,* 57/2: 359–86.

Enterprise Research Institute in Development Research Center of the State Council (2007). *Annual Report on the Development of China's Large Enterprise Groups.* Beijing: Zhongguo fazhan chubanshe.

FAN, G. (1996). "Lun Zichan Chongzu" (Studies on the Reorganization of Assets), in M. HONG (ed.), *Qiye Gaigezhongde Zichanchongzu: Anli Yanjiu yu Lilun Fenxi* (The Reorganization of Assets in the Reform of Enterprises: Case Studies and Theoretical Analysis). Beijing: Jingji Guanli Chubanshe (Economic Management Publishing House), 125–32.

FEENSTRA, R. C., YANG, M., and HAMILTON, G. G. (1997). "Business Groups and Trade in East Asia: Part 2, Product Variety." NBER working paper.

GOTO, A. (1982). "Business Groups in Market Economy". *European Economic Review,* 19: 53–70.

HAHN, D., and LEE, K. (2006). "Chinese Business Groups: Their Origins and Development," in S. J. Chang (ed.), *Business Groups in East Asia: Financial Crisis, Restructuring, and New Growth.* Oxford: Oxford University Press.

HUANG, J. S. (2000). "1997 nian shangshi gongsi jianbing feishangshi giye anli fenxi" (Analysis of the M&A of Non-Listed Firms by Listed Firms in 1997). www.mergers-china.com/redianjujiao/bzsddetail.asp?id=169 (in Chinese).

KANG, Y. S., and LEE, K. (2008). "Performance and Growth of Large Firms in China," *Seoul Journal of Economics,* 21/1: 229–59.

---

[6] Korean *chaebol* have also grown, showing both strength and weakness. As has been analyzed well in Choo et al. (2009), those that promoted strength (investment in R&D), while minimizing weakness, survived the financial crisis and showed long-term viability.

KEISTER, L. A. (2000). *Chinese Business Groups: The Structure and Impact of Interfirm Relations during Economic Development.* Oxford and New York: Oxford University Press.

LA PORTA, R., FLORENCIO, L. S., and SHLEIFER. A. (1999). "Corporate Ownership around the World," *Journal of Finance,* 54: 471–517.

LEE, K. (2006). "Business Groups as an Organizational Device for Catch-up," in J. Nakagawa (ed.), *Managing Development: Globalization, Economic Restructuring and Social Policy.* London and New York: Routledge.

LEE, K., and HAHN, D. (2004). "From Insider–Outside Collusion to Insider Control in China's SOEs," *Issue and Studies,* 40/2: 1–45.

LEE, K., and HAHN, D. (2007). "Market Competition, Plan Constraints, and the Hybrid Business Groups: Explaining the Business Groups in China," *Seoul Journal of Economics,* 20/4: 481–504.

LEE, K., and JIN, X. (2009). "The Origins of the Business Groups in China: Testing of the Three Paths and the Three Theories," *Business History,* 51/1: 77–99.

LEE, K., and WOO, W. T. (2002). "Business Groups in China Compared with Korean Chaebols," in R. Hooley and J. H. Yoo (eds.), *Post-Crisis Challenges for Asian Industrialization.* Amsterdam: JAI Press.

LI, Z. (1995). *Modern Chinese Business Groups (Zhongguo Xiandai Qiye Jituan).* Beijing: Zhongguo Shangye Ban.

MA, X., and LU, J. W. (2005). "The Critical Role of Business Groups in China," *Ivey Business Journal,* 69/5: 1–12.

MEYER, M. W., and LU, X. (2004). "Managing Indefinite Boundaries: The Strategy and Structure of a Chinese Business Firm," *Management and Organization Review,* 1/1: 57–86.

National Bureau of Statistics, China (2001). *2000 Zhongguo daqiyejituan (2000 Chinese Big Business Groups).* Beijing: China Statistics Press.

National Bureau of Statistics, China (2006a). *2005 Zhongguo daqiyejituan (2005 Chinese Big Business Groups).* Beijing: China Statistics Press.

National Bureau of Statistics, China (2006b). *China Statistical Yearbook 2005.* Beijing: China Statistics Press.

National Bureau of Statistics, China (2008). *2007 Zhongguo daqiyejituan (2007 Chinese Big Business Groups).* Beijing: China Statistics Press.

National Bureau of Statistics, China (2009). *China Statistical Yearbook 2008.* Beijing: China Statistics Press.

NAUGHTON, B. (2008). "China's Institutional Catch-Up: Achievement and Challenges." Paper delivered at "China's Economic Catch-Up: Assessment and Prospects," 2008 SNU-NEAR International Conference.

NOLAN, P. (2001). *China and the Global Economy.* Basingstoke and New York: Palgrave.

SEO, B. K., LEE, K., and WANG, X. (2006). "Explaining Performance Changes in the Business Groups: Three Hypotheses in the Case of China." Paper presented at the 2006 Convention of the East Asian Economic Association (EAEA), held in Beijing, Nov.

TENEV, S., ZHANG, C., and BREFORT, L. (2002). *Corporate Governance and Enterprise Reform in China.* Washington: World Bank and the International Finance Corporation.

TIAN, L. (2001). "Government Shareholding and the Value of China's Modern Firms." William Davidson working paper number 395.

WANG, X., XU, L. C., and ZHU, T. (2004). "State-Owned Enterprises Going Public: The Case of China," *Economics of Transition,* 12/3: 467–87.

XU, X., and WANG, Y. (1999). "Ownership Structure and Corporate Governance in Chinese Stock Companies," *Chinese Economic Review,* 10: 75–98.

CHAPTER 9

....

BUSINESS GROUPS IN THAILAND

....

NATENAPHA WAILERDSAK

AKIRA SUEHIRO

9.1 INTRODUCTION

....

THE present chapter aims to examine the development of business groups in Thailand, one of the fastest-growing economies in the world during 1985–95 from the perspective of "catch-up industrialization" (Lee 2006; Suehiro 2008). It considers business groups, not just as a response to market failure or institutional voids in emerging markets (Leff 1978; Khanna and Palepu 1997), but as vehicles for economic catch-up with more industrialized nations.

This chapter consists of seven parts. Section 9.2 reviews the key characteristics of large enterprises in Thailand. Section 9.3 briefly describes the development of business groups in Thailand, with an emphasis on family-run groups, and their survival despite changes in economic and political environments until the 2000s. Section 9.4 then sketches the structure of ownership and management of family business groups. Section 9.5 examines the business diversification and internationalization strategies of major business groups before and after the 1997 Asian

The authors would like to thank the editors for their enthusiastic encouragement and valuable comments, and all participants who took part in the discussions at Kyoto International Conference on the Evolutionary Dynamics of Business Groups in Emerging Economies, where the authors presented their paper on November 26, 2007. We gratefully acknowledge the Asian Development Bank Institute (Tokyo), the Institute of Developing Economies (Chiba), and the Thailand Research Fund for their financial support of the research.

financial crisis. Section 9.6 looks at the impacts of the crisis, and at corporate governance reform, focusing on the banking sector and listed companies. Finally, Section 9.7 concludes the chapter by looking at the competitive capabilities of leading Thai business groups, and considers their future challenges. Our database, which has been accumulated for a period of three decades, is used for this analysis.

9.2 Principal characteristics of large enterprises in Thailand

Five principal characteristics of large enterprises in Thailand stand out. First, the pattern of enterprise ownership commonly seen in Thailand and Asian latecomers to industrialization resembles a *tripod structure*, with the three agents consisting of state enterprises, domestic private enterprises (mostly family business), and foreign or multinational enterprises (Suehiro 1989, 2008).

Table 9.1 summarizes the top 100 companies in Thailand defined in terms of total sales from 1979 to 2004 and shows the distribution of these companies in accordance with type of capital ownership. It reveals that, of the top 100 companies, there were 68 domestic private enterprises (including family business and non-family business) in 1979, and these accounted for 49 percent of total sales that year. The prominent role and high concentration of domestic enterprises continued up to the Asian financial crisis of 1997. However, after the crisis, state enterprises and foreign or multinational enterprises, in turn, increased their proportions. In 2004, in terms of numbers, there were 14 state enterprises, 31 domestic private companies, and 55 foreign or multinational enterprises; in terms of total sales, 33 percent belonged to state enterprises, 19 percent to domestic private enterprises, and 48 percent to foreign or multinational enterprises. The reasons behind these dramatical changes are discussed in Section 9.3.5.

Secondly, almost all families in domestic private enterprises are *descendants of immigrant Chinese*.[1] Their business usually emerged from small, private companies that were founded by Chinese who emigrated from the provinces of China or by their descendants. In 1997 non-ethnic Chinese or "indigenous" groups represented only 11 of the 220 largest business groups, such as the Siam Cement Group (SCG) owned by the Crown Property Bureau, Boon Rawd Brewery of the Bhirom Bhakdi family, and the Srivikorn family. Other domestic private enterprises are limited to state

---

[1] In 2000 ethnic Chinese were a demographic minority (10% of the population) in Thailand. The Tiochew people formed the largest Chinese dialect group in Thailand, followed by the Hainanese and Hakka people. The Hokkien and Cantonese people, who settled in significant numbers in other South East Asian countries, were in a minority. (Brooker Group 2003). In 1911 a Nationality Act was passed to allow anyone born in Thailand to take Thai nationality.

Table 9.1 Top 100 companies in Thailand by total sales and capital ownership, 1979–2004

Ownership type	1979	1989	1997	2004
Number of company	100	100	100	100
State enterprises	2	5	9	14
Domestic private enterprises	68	62	61	31
Family business	*55*	*57*	*56*	*26*
Non-family business	*13*	*5*	*5*	*5*
Foreign or multinational enterprise	30	33	30	55
Total sales (Baht m.)	207,418	719,085	2,426,527	4,979,761
Percentage	100.0	100.0	100.0	100.0
State enterprises	7.6	14.9	15.7	32.7
Domestic private enterprises	49.2	53.0	55.0	19.2
Family business	*41.9*	*50.1*	*52.9*	*16.4*
Non-family business	*7.3*	*3.0*	*2.1*	*2.8*
Foreign or multinational enterprise	43.2	32.0	29.2	48.1

Notes: The amount of annual sales of a financial institution is calculated by its gross revenue. Family business includes firms owned by the Crown Property Bureau. Foreign or multinational enterprise indicates a firm in which foreigners own 30% or more of its shares.

Source: Suehiro (2006: 61, 287).

enterprises or government-owned companies such as the Petroleum Authority of Thailand (PTT), Thai Airways, Krungthai Bank, and the Electricity Generating Authority of Thailand (EGAT) (Suehiro 2006: 304–11; see also Table 9.3).

Thirdly, large enterprises usually develop into massive *diversified business groups* (*klum thurakit* in Thai), rather than a unitary organization. These groups operate businesses across a range of industries or sectors, and enjoy a position of oligopolistic domination over one or more sectors. The family business groups are organized under a *kongsi* (from the Tiochew dialect) structure of management; this is the system where a family gathers all its business (and property) under one umbrella controlled by the founder. Strategically, such groups often pursue unrelated diversification rather than related diversification or vertical integration, and resemble a web structure, with a number of affiliated companies being created, and then taken over by the founder's sons/daughters and successive generations. This is especially relevant in an extended family environment (Wailerdsak 2008c).

Fourthly, nearly all large enterprises are dominated by *a small number of major shareholders*—that is, government agencies for state enterprises, owner families or Thai corporations for domestic private enterprises, and parent companies for foreign firms (Phiphatseritham 1982; Suehiro and Wailerdsak 2002). This is the case not only for private limited companies but also for public companies listed on the Stock Exchange of Thailand. Widely held corporations, whose shares are held by a large number of shareholders who do not have significant controlling rights, are rare (Suehiro 2001b: 32).

Lastly, the core or affiliated firms of most domestic private enterprises have been listed on the stock exchange for fundraising. The stock market has actively developed since the end of the 1980s, when Thailand enjoyed an unprecedented economic boom. In particular, the Thai government policy of enhancing information disclosure and corporate governance after the 1997 crisis has intentionally targeted listed companies through the stock market. Very few of the foreign or multinational enterprises, on the contrary, have listed their firms on the Stock Exchange of Thailand.

9.3 DEVELOPMENT OF BUSINESS GROUPS IN THAILAND

We have divided the development of business groups in Thailand into five periods according to their emergence, core business, and changes in economic and political environments.[2]

9.3.1 The rise of European and Chinese capitalists, 1855–1932

To trace the development of Thai capitalist groups, it is necessary to go back to the year 1855, when Thailand signed a commercial pact with Britain—between Sir John Bowring and King Rama IV (Mongkut 1850–68)—known as the Bowring Treaty and was thus integrated into the worldwide capitalist economy. After the conclusion of the treaty, Thai trade grew rapidly with the characteristics of a typical colonial-era economy, exporting primary produce of rice, teakwood, and tin and importing manufactured goods. Siam became the rice granary of colonized Asia. By the end of the nineteenth century, three major capitalist groups had emerged.

The first and most influential capitalist groups were the European trading houses, colonial commercial banks, and mining companies, which advanced into Siam shortly after the conclusion of the treaty (Suehiro 1989: 42). A second source of capitalist group was the indigenous, or *sakdina*, group, consisting of the king, members of the royal family, and high-class bureaucrats (the *khun-nang* class). Their central institution was the Privy Purse Bureau (which later became the

---

[2] We define business group as a business organization that owns and operates two or more firms under single ownership (particular family, corporate, or state-sponsored company). The fact that a listed company is included in a group is not essential to this definition, since that would lead to the omission of a large number of business groups in Thailand during the 1970s and 1980s.

Crown Property Bureau). The bureau served as a kind of royal investment company, placing funds in real estate, housing, the construction of tramways and railways, commercial banking, and manufacturing. For example, it established the Siam Commercial Bank Co. Ltd in 1906 and Siam Cement Co. Ltd in 1913.

Meanwhile, between the early nineteenth century and 1950, some seven million Chinese boarded ships leaving the ports of southern China bound for Bangkok. Over a million of them stayed on in Siam. The typical migrant arrived with no more than "one pillow and one mat" and made his fortune. They worked as coolies to earn some capital, and as soon as possible set up a shop or small trading business (Skinner 1957; Phongpaichit and Baker 1998).

Thus emerged the third and most important source of entrepreneurship, consisting of three groups of successful Chinese merchants. They were called *Chae Sua* (in the Hokkien dialect) or *Chao Sua* (in Thai), which means wealthy Chinese merchant or tycoon. The first and largest group began by tax farming, which for much of the nineteenth century was the Siamese government's principal source of revenue. They included the Bisalputra, Bisolputra, and Jotikabukhana families in the reign of King Rama IV, and the Sophanodon and Laohasetti families in the reign of King Rama V (Suehiro 1989: 72–83). A second group of Chinese capitalists began as compradors (*Nai Na* in Thai), mediating between local customers/suppliers, and the European trading houses and commercial banks, and later set up their own businesses (Suehiro 1989: 87–90).

These two Chinese capitalist groups were overshadowed after the First World War by a third group, which established business empires, mainly in the rice business. They were the "Big Five" of Wanglee (sae Tan, Poon Phol), Boolsuk (sae Loh, Serm Suk/Mc Thai), Bulakul (sae Mah, Mah Boonkrong/Chokchai), Iamsuri (sae Iam, Kamol Kij), and Lamsam (sae Ung, Thai Farmers Bank/Kasikornbank). Throughout the 1930s and 1940s, these five families not only dominated the rice industry but also built authority and prestige in the Chinese community. They founded the Chinese Chamber of Commerce of Thailand in 1910 (Suehiro 1989: 110–22). They have continued to maintain their influence more or less even in the postwar Thai economy.

9.3.2 State-led industrialization and the rise of bureaucrat capitalists, 1932–57

Until the late 1930s, Thailand's business was almost entirely small scale. A few families had done well in the rice trade but such families were very rare. Openings for manufacture were limited, because the lowest import duties in Asia had been levied on a variety of manufactured goods imported from Europe, Japan, and mainland China to Thailand up to the year 1927. There was no essential government support to promote local manufacturers (Suehiro 1989: 100–2). Entering the 1920s, in many other Asian countries, nationalists flung out the colonial rules and then flung out the Chinese (or Indian) migrant merchant communities for collaborating in colonial exploitation.

For a time, Thailand appeared to move in the same direction. In June 1932 the People's Party (*Khana Rasadorn*) carried out a military coup to open an era of constitutional monarchy. The military government became the successor to the old royalist rule. Prime Minister Phibun Songkhram (1938–44) promoted the nationalist idea "a Thai economy for the Thai people," which meant Thai peasants selling rice to, and buying manufactured goods from, organizations run on the people's behalf by the Thai government to the exclusion of the Chinese (Suehiro 1989: ch. 4; Phong-paichit and Baker 2002). They set up over 100 state enterprises to dislodge Chinese merchants from their dominant position in commerce and manufacturing.

Piriyarangsan (1983) defined the capitalist development of Thailand from 1932 to 1960 as "bureaucratic capitalism" (*thun-niyom khun-nang*). Bureaucratic capitalists meant political or military leaders and politico-bureaucrats (not technocrats) who acted as directors and shareholders in a variety of firms. These bureaucratic capital-ists had taken part openly in business activities in two ways: the politicians had set up state enterprises in which they were board members, but had then invited leading Chinese businessmen to run them and make them profitable; or existing Chinese-owned businesses had stacked their boards with Thai politicians and generals.

A good example may be seen in the progress of collaboration between Chinese businessmen and political leaders between the 1947 military coup and the 1958 military coup. These groups, or "Chinese business blocs" in Skinner's research during this period (Skinner 1958), included the Asia Trust (including Bangkok Bank), Thai-Hua, Lamsam-Wanglee, Ayudhya, and Mahaguna (including the Union Bank of Bangkok). For instance, in 1952 the Asia Trust Group led by Chin Sophonpanich, the epitome of the *Chao Sua*, invited Police Director-General Phao Sriyanon, son-in-law of Field Marshal Phin, to be chairman of the Asia Trust Co. The next year he asked Brigadier-General Siri Siriyothin to be chairman of the Bangkok Bank (Suehiro 1989: 171). He maintained a close relationship with military leaders until the 1970s. The Bangkok Bank Group thus became the nation's largest bank.

9.3.3 Private capital-led industrialization and the rise of multinational enterprises and domestic business groups, 1960s–70s

After the military coup in 1957 led by Field Marshal Sarit Thanarat (prime minister 1958–63), the government touted *phatthana* (development) as part of the nationalist mission to protect Thailand against communism in the cold-war era, and embarked on a policy of promoting industrialization through private capital from both do-mestic and foreign sources. Around 1960, the World Bank helped Thailand to set up infrastructure for modern economic management: a Board of Investment (BOI), which offered incentives to local and foreign entrepreneurs; the National Economic Development Board (NEDB, later NESDB), which wrote five-year plans; a Budget Bureau to manage the government accounts. During this period (the 1960s to the

1970s), three types of business groups emerged: financial groups, industrial groups, and agribusiness groups.

Financial groups are defined here as any group of companies that a commercial bank serves as the core of corporate structure, establishing subsidiaries and affiliated companies to engage in finance, securities, and insurance, as well as diversifying into unrelated sectors in commerce or industry. These, and in particular a big four, had developed from former commercial banking groups in the Chinese business bloc during the 1950s—namely, the Bangkok Bank of the Sophonpanich family, the Thai Farmers Bank (later Kasikornbank) of the Lamsam family, the Bangkok Metropolitan Bank of the Tejapaibul family, and the Bank of Ayudhya of the Ratanarak family (Suehiro 1989: 245–65; see also Hewison 1989). By 1979 the four major banks had founded a total of 295 companies spread across finance, trade, and manufacture. Even though the level of group shareholdings in the financial sector was reduced after the 1997 crisis, all groups (except Tejapaibul family) were still perceived to have significant influence over the functioning of Thailand's financial system in 2005 (Wailerdsak 2006b).

The development of *industrial groups* was closely connected with import substitution industrialization (ISI). Importantly, all these groups extended into new ventures with foreign partners, mainly Japanese, in the form of joint venture (Suehiro 2006: 189–92). For example, Sukree Bodiratnangkura set up a cloth import business and then became Thailand's textile magnate (Sukree/TBI). Thaworn Phornprapha set up a scrap-metal dealership and an auto repair shop, which later turned into a Nissan importer and assembler, and went on to dominate the automotive industry (Siam Motors). Thiem Chokwatana also started a grocery business. He later moved into manufacture with the help of Japanese firms (Lion Corp., Wacoal Co., and so on) and built the Sahapat (Saha/SPI) consumer goods group.

The *agribusiness group* emerged in the late 1970s when the government switched to a strategy of export-oriented industrialization (EOI), following the pattern of the Four Asian Tigers—Hong Kong, South Korea, Singapore, and Taiwan (World Bank 1993: 1). This group rapidly expanded by integrating agricultural exports with industrial activity, not only in such traditional products as rice, sugar, and natural rubber, but also in new commercial agricultural and fishery products such as broiler chicken, hatchery shrimp, and canned tuna. They include the Charoen Pokphand (CP) of the Chearavanont family, Soon Hua Seng of the Dumnernchanvanit family, TIPCO of the Supsakorn family, and Metro of the Laohathai family.

Table 9.2 presents the largest forty business groups in Thailand in 1979, 1989, 1997, and 2000. The rankings were created by the authors based on total sales of group-affiliated companies that appeared among the top 1,000 companies in Thailand each year. Looking at the largest forty groups in 1979, we can find these easily prominent position of three major types of business groups—namely, four financial groups, fifteen industrial groups, and twelve agribusiness groups. Apart from these groups, commercial bankers, a modern retailer (the CDS group), and a construction contractor (the Italthai group) are also included into the largest forty groups in 1979.

Table 9.2 Largest forty business groups in Thailand, 1979–2000

Rank	1979 Group name	1979 Total sales (Baht m.)	1989 Group name	1989 Total sales (Baht m.)	1997 Group name	1997 Total sales (Baht m.)	2000 Group name	2000 Total sales (Baht m.)
1	Siam Cement	14,483	Siam Cement	70,908	Siam Cement	366,716	Siam Cement	285,221
2	Bangkok Bank	13,716	Bangkok Bank	49,506	Bangkok Bank	194,999	PTT*	210,654
3	Chawkwanyu	9,843	Thai Airways*	44,942	CP	141,145	CP	192,540
4	Siam Motors	7,041	CP	39,956	Thai Farmers Bank	139,279	TCC	171,772
5	CP	6,266	Krungthai Bank*	33,961	Krungthai Bank*	127,291	Thai Airways*	124,145
6	Krungthai Bank*	6,103	Thai Farmers Bank	33,306	TCC	117,942	Bangkok Bank	107,662
7	BMB	5,129	PTT*	27,612	PTT*	110,825	Krungthai Bank*	103,376
8	Thai Farmers Bank	4,865	Chawkwanyu	26,797	Bank of Ayudhya	91,741	Thai Farmers Bank	74,183
9	Metro	4,814	TCC	22,323	Thai Airways*	88,307	Shin	70,383
10	Boon Rawd Brewery	3,457	Metro	18,708	Boon Rawd Brewery	78,763	CDS	53,793
11	Chaiyaporn Rice	3,286	Bank of Ayudhya	18,429	Hong Yiah Seng/ TPI	67,816	Saha/SPI	53,175
12	Saha/SPI	3,151	Saha/SPI	17,238	Thai Military Bank	52,175	Soon Hua Seng	46,346
13	Sukree/TBI	2,418	Saha-Union	16,586	CDS	48,676	Siam Motors	43,817
14	Laemthong Sahakarn	2,309	Siam Motors	14,092	Shin	48,584	Boon Rawd Brewery	43,212
15	Hong Yiah Seng	2,221	Hong Yiah Seng/ TPI	12,943	Saha/SPI	46,458	UCOM	42,986
16	Bank of Ayudhya	2,193	Soon Hua Seng	12,828	Italthai	40,821	Bank of Ayudhya	38,573
17	Kamol Sukosol	2,188	MMC Sittipol	11,304	MMC Sittipol	38,555	Thai Union Frozen	32,584
18	Thai Roon Ruang	2,056	Boon Rawd Brewery	10,698	UCOM	37,510	Saha-Union	32,177
19	MMC Sittipol	1,919	Osothsapha	10,609	Siam Motors	35,851	Mitr-Phol/Banpu	25,853
20	U Chu Liang	1,807	Srifuengfung	10,303	Metro	35,325	Osothsapha/Premier	25,825
21	Kwang Soon Lee	1,763	Sukree/TBI	9,352	Soon Hua Seng	34,859	Italthai	25,061
22	Soon Hua Seng	1,697	Thai Military Bank	8,464	C.Thong/COSMO	33,856	Sahaviriya	23,074
23	Italthai	1,686	Laemthong Sahakarn	7,714	BMB	32,971	Betagro	22,680
24	Saha-Union	1,685	CDS	7,558	Osothsapha/ Premier	32,227	Metro	22,528
25	CDS	1,637	Thonburi Panich	7,143	Phatraprasit	29,458	Krating Daeng	18,172
26	Srifuengfung	1,573	Siew	7,007	Saha-Union	26,166	Thai Military Bank	18,035
27	Siew	1,543	BMB	6,741	Mitr Phol/Banpu	25,821	Thai Life Insurance	17,104

Rank	1979		1989		1997		2000	
	Group name	Total sales (Baht m.)	Group name	Total sales (Baht m.)	Group name	Total sales (Baht m.)	Group name	Total sales (Baht m.)
28	PSA	1,417	KPN	6,523	Siam City/Limsong	25,713	The Mall	16,171
29	Wanglee	1,407	Ocean Insurance	6,059	Thai Union Frozen	24,816	Serm Suk	16,037
30	Bangkok Rice	1,339	Thai Union Frozen	5,546	Srifuengfurg	23,630	Hua Kee	15,961
31	Osothsapha	1,321	Italthai	5,098	Sahaviriya	23,282	EGAT*	14,722
32	Sahaviriya	1,236	C.Thong/COSMO	4,971	Siam Steel Pipe	21,537	Sarasin	13,645
33	Puey Heng Long	1,197	Capital Rice	4,677	Thai Life Insurance	18,887	Jasmine	13,599
34	Seng Thong Rice	1,185	Siam Rice	4,624	Land and House	18,311	Thai Summit	13,401
35	Kend Seng Chuan	1,180	SP International	4,513	Asia/Uachukiat	18,118	P Charoenphan	13,167
36	Mitr Phol	1,122	Thai Life Insurance	4,451	Ch Karnchang	17,106	Laemthong	13,018
37	Pattanakit Rubber	1,101	Unicord	4,230	Betagro	17,096	Ngow Hock	12,846
38	Asia Trust Bank	1,096	Sarasin	4,154	Krating Daeng	15,447	SP International	12,704
39	Metro Machinery	1,058	Thai Roong Ruang	4,151	Serm Suk	13,647	Capital Rice/STC	12,698
40	Bangkok Bank of Commerce	1,031	Sahaviriya	4,104	Wanglee/Phoon Phol	13,155	Ch Karnchang	11,957
Number of new entrants				18		12		11
Number continuing in top forty (compared to previous selected year)				22		2		29

Notes: Business groups comprise only state enterprises and domestic private enterprises. The data for 1979 contain only domestic private enterprises. Siam Cement Group includes the Siam Commercial Bank and firms owned by the Crown Property Bureau. BMB = Bangkok Metropolitan Bank; CDS = Central Department Store; CP = Charoen Pokphand; EGAT = Electricity Generating Authority of Thailand; PTT = Petroleum Authority of Thailand; TCC = Thai Charoen Corporation. Chawkwanyu family had been the largest shareholder of the Thai Oil Company before the government took over its business.

Source: Compiled by the authors, using Suehiro's database on enterprises in Thailand in 1979–2000.

9.3.4 Economic boom and the rise of new business groups, 1980s–97

From the mid-1980s, the *new capitalists* grew rapidly, owing to a very rapid sequence of policy changes. These included conversion to export of manufactured goods, deregulation of heavy and chemical industries, increased openness to foreign investment, and a financial liberalization, which led to the boom of the stock market and real estate—the bubble economy, particularly between 1991 and 1994 under the liberal technocrat governments of Anand Panyarachun and Chuan Leekpai. Thailand grew by 10 percent per annum in the decade 1985–95—one of the fastest-growing economies in the world, according to the World Bank (1993). By the early 1990s, the country was being touted as Asia's "fifth tiger" (Muscat 1994).

Several existing Thai groups expanded and diversified into heavy industries— petrochemicals, cement, and steel such as the Siam Cement group (SCG), the Thai Petrochemical Industry (TPI) of the Leophairatana family, Sahaviriya of the Viriyaprapaikit family, Siam Steel Pipe of the Leeswadtrakul family. Moreover, the government opened up new telecommunications projects to privatization. New groups took advantage of these contracts to gain expertise in the new growth area. The expansion of the urban population and especially of the new middle class also boosted the domestic demand for new businesses in service industries (modern retail, finance, hotels, and media/entertainment) and infrastructure (power generation, and land/ property development) (Phongpaichit and Baker 2002: 170–1).

Among the huge number of *new* players, a handful of business groups expanded their operations, as evidenced in the largest forty groups in 1989 and 1997 (see Table 9.2). These included Shin of the Shinawatra family, Jasmine of the Bodharamik family, UCOM of the Bencharongkul family, TelecomAsia (Later True) of the CP group in telecoms, BEC World of the Maleenont family in TV broadcasting, GMM Grammy of the Damrongchaitam family in the music business, Italthai of the Karnasuta family, Ch. Karnchang of the Trivisvavet family, and Land and Houses of the Asavabhokhin family in construction and property development.

The successes of new capitalists were founded on three conditions: political connections to win government concessions or to convince the government to protect them from increased competition; a spiralling stock market and the Bangkok International Banking Facilities (BIBF) offshore banks (established in 1993); and off-the-shelf technology. Despite of the economic boom, entry into the banking industry was still regulated by licenses. Investors in petrochemicals and steel were able to persuade government to extend the life of protective tariff regimes. The booming telecoms sector was cartelized by a system of government concessions (Niyomsilpa 2003). The property market was still partially protected by restrictions on foreign ownership of land.

9.3.5 Aftermath of the crisis and the surviving business groups, 1997 and thereafter

The 1997 crisis was a major turning point for the Thai economy. Significant parts of several major sectors were shifted under government and foreign ownership (see Table 9.1). Around a quarter of Thailand's major family business groups were completely damaged. Some disappeared, while others were reduced to a tiny fraction of their former scale. The losers included several of the great dynastic surnames of the postwar business community. Table 9.3 shows the situation after the crisis, by presenting the largest forty business groups in 2000 and their lines of business.

They seem to have been fated by two factors—sector and structure. Several had prospered as joint-venture partners of multinational enterprises, mainly Japanese, in the export-oriented sectors of manufacturing spearheaded by automotive, electronics, and other technology-based sectors, and were now discarded. Some were in other sectors targeted by foreign capital such as finance and modern retail businesses. The most vulnerable were families that had expanded into a variety of new industries without modifying the *kongsi* structure of family management. These families were even more at risk if they were simultaneously negotiating the difficult transition from the second to third generation (Phongpaichit and Baker 2008: 269).

Domestic capital in manufacturing industry was now, for the most part, confined to agribusiness and some other subsectors based on locally available resources or cheap labor. Many domestic firms that survived the crisis were in sectors that still enjoyed some government protection, such as real estate, media/entertainment, liquor, healthcare, telecomunications, and some segments of tourism (Phongpaichit and Baker 2008: 270).

On the other hand, the wave of corporate debt restructuring of collapsed banks and companies, and the privatization process of several state enterprises proposed by the IMF and World Bank after the crisis, had increased the weight of state enterprise or government-sponsored companies in the structure of capital ownership (see Table 9.1). In early 1998, four small and medium banks were put under the control of the Bank of Thailand. TPI PLC, the largest petrochemical company, became the largest defaulting debtor (US$3.5 billion) and the first victim of the new bankruptcy law under the Corporate Debt Restructuring Advisory Committee (CDRAC), which was set up in June 1998 to oversee and facilitate voluntary debt-restructuring negotiations. They became the state-controlled banks and companies. Also, though some state enterprises sold shares to the public, the government was still the major shareholder. For this reason, we categorize them as state enterprises in Table 9.1.

In sum, we can say that the 1997 crisis brought change to the *tripod structure* of dominant capital in Thailand. It boosted the control of government through state enterprises, enhanced the fortunes of multinational enterprises, and triggered a reorganization of local business groups.

Table 9.3 Largest forty business groups in Thailand and their business lines, 2000

Rank	Group name	No. of firms	Type	Family name (Chinese name, dialect)	Major business lines
1	Siam Cement/ Siam Commercial Bank	54	T	Crown Property Bureau	Construction materials, petrochemicals, pulp and paper, distribution, banking, finance, insurance, real-estate
2	PTT	8	S	PTT	Oil and natural gas, petrochemicals, international trading
3	CP	25	C	Chearavanont (Chia, Tiochew)	Agro-industry, aquaculture, retail, petrochemicals, telecommunications, chemicals, international trading, real-estate, insurance
4	TCC	21	C	Sirivadhanabhakdi (Tia, Tiochew)	Breweries, liquor, property development, hotels, insurance, consumer products
5	Thai Airways	2	S	Thai Airways	Airline services, aircraft-related businesses
6	Bangkok Bank	11	C	Sophonpanich (Tan, Tiochew)	Banking, finance, insurance, real-estate, warehousing, healthcare, petrochemicals
7	Krungthai Bank	4	S	Krungthai Bank	Banking, finance, leasing
8	Kasikornbank/ Loxley	13	C	Lamsam (Ung, Hakka)	Banking, finance, life insurance, telecommunications, computer, IT, chemicals, hotels, real-estate
9	Shin	10	C	Shinawatra (Khu, Hakka), Damapong	Telecommunications, satellite, IT, e-business services, media, advertising, international business, real-estate
10	Central Department Store	13	C	Chirathivat (Tae, Hainanese)	Retail/ wholesale, hotels, manufacturing, distribution, real-estate, food outlets, trading

Rank	Group name	No. of firms	Type	Family name (Chinese name, dialect)	Major business lines
11	Saha/SPI (Sahapathanapibul)	23	C	Chokwatana (Lee, Tiochew)	Consumer products, textiles/ garments, cosmetics, footwear, food/ beverages, office equipment, machinery and electrical equipment, plastics
12	Soon Hua Seng/ Kaset Rung Ruang	10	C	Dumnernchanvanit (Tia, Tiochew)	Agricultural products, pulp and paper, cold storage and warehousing, power generation, real-estate, insurance, leasing, transportation
13	Siam Motors	8	C	Phornprapha (Tan, Tiochew)	Automobile and motorcycle, parts, industrial machinery and equipment, recreation, transport, real-estate, construction, natural resources
14	Boon Rawd Brewery	4	T	Bhirom Bhakdi	Liquor, non-alcoholic beverages, trading, consumer products, real-estate
15	UCOM	4	C	Bencharongkul (Kow, Tiochew)	Telecommunications, insurance, airline services
16	Bank of Ayudhya	11	C	Ratanarak (Lee, Tiochew)	Banking, finance, insurance, construction materials, lignite mining, media, TV Channel 7
17	Thai Union Frozen	4	C	Chansiri (Tan, Tiochew), Niruttinanond	Food products, agro-industry (canned/ frozen seafood), trading, packaging, property development, transportation
18	Saha-Union	13	C	Darakananda (Tan, Tiochew)	Textiles, footwear, plastics, rubber, metal, trading, electronics, computers, power generation, services
19	Mitr Phol/ Banpu	10	C	Wongkusolkit (Wong, Tiochew)	Energy, mining, sugar production, power

(continued)

Table 9.3 Continued

Rank	Group name	No. of firms	Type	Family name (Chinese name, dialect)	Major business lines
					generation, insurance, finance, port, real-estate
20	Osothsapha/ Premier	7	C	Osathanugrah (Lim)	Pharmaceuticals, consumer/ healthcare products, finance, insurance, real-estate, energy drink, hotels, construction, trading, advertising
21	Italthai	5	C	Karnasuta (Tan, Hokkien)	Construction, civil engineering, energy, real-estate, infrastructure, trading, manufacturing, hotels
22	Sahaviriya	5	C	Viriyaprapaikit (Ngow, Tiochew)	Steel, port, IT equipment, construction, real-estate, agriculture, finance
23	Betagro	7	C	Taepaisitphongse (Tae, Tiochew)	Agro-industry, animal feed, veterinary products, food, farm equipment, real-estate, construction
24	Metro	12	C	Laohathai (Lao, Taiwanese), Tangtrongsakdi	Agro-chemicals, industrial chemicals, metal, plastics, petrochemicals, food, real-estate, telecommunications, warehousing
25	Krating Daeng	4	C	Yoovidhaya (Hainanese)	Pharmaceuticals, beverages, real-estate
26	Thai Military	1	S	Armed Forces	Banking, finance, leasing
27	Thai Life Insurance	1	C	Chaiyawan (Wo, Tiochew)	Finance, insurance, brewing and distribution, hospital, industrial, real-estate
28	The Mall	2	C	Umpujh (Yu, Tiochew)	Department stores, real-estate, entertainment, garments/ textiles, retail, industrial estate
29	Serm Suk/ McThai	2	C	Bulsook (Loh, Tiochew)	Beverages, fast food restaurants
30	Hua Kee	6	C	Nithivasin (Lao, Tiochew)	Paper, steel bars, petrochemicals, chemicals, hotel,

Rank	Group name	No. of firms	Type	Family name (Chinese name, dialect)	Major business lines
					property development, food, restaurants
31	EGAT	2	S	EGAT	Power plants, dams, hydro power construction, transmission business
32	Sarasin	2	C	Sarasin (Huang)	Automobile, beverages, home furnishing
33	Jasmine	4	T	Bodharamik	Telecom operator and service provider, systems integration and distribution, IT
34	Thai Summit	6	C	Jungrungruangkit (Chung, Tiochew)	Automotive parts, hotels, real-estate, finance
35	P Charoen Phan/ GFPT	7	C	Sirimongkolkasem (Tan, Tiochew)	Agro-industry, animal feed, veterinary products, poultry meat, livestock and shrimp farming
36	Laemthong	8	C	Kanathanavanich (Chia, Tiochew)	Agricultural products, animal feed, food, dairy products, real-estate
37	Ngow Hock	1	C	Tanthuwanit (Tan, Tiochew)	Shipping and terminal, real estate, palm oil
38	SP International	4	C	Phornprapha (Tan, Tiochew)	Motorcycles, financing, real estate
39	Capital Rice/ STC	3	C	Pichetpongsa (Huang), Vanichjakvong	Agricultural commodities, animal feed, frozen seafood, container terminals, real-estate, transport, aquaculture, food
40	Ch Karnchang	3	C	Trivisvavet (Tia, Tiochew)	Construction, expressways, mass transit, property development, utilities, insurance

Notes: The ranking is taken from Table 9.2, based on total sales of group affiliates that appeared among the top 1000 companies in 2000. Therefore, it may not include all the groups' affiliates. Ethnicity of the group: C=Chinese-Thai; S=State/public enterprises; T=Thai. Chinese names and dialects refer to Suehiro (2006: 304–311).
Sources: Major business lines compiled from Brooker Group (2003) and company websites.

9.4 OWNERSHIP AND MANAGEMENT

From the evidence of several empirical studies conducted by the authors, it is clear that very few family business groups in Thailand separated ownership and management (Suehiro 2001b; Suehiro and Wailerdsak 2004). They maintain family control through direct and indirect ownership, occupying top management positions, and grooming sons/daughters to succeed the founding patriarchs (Suehiro 2006; Wailerdsak 2008b). For a classic example of how a founding family adheres to exclusive control over the group ownership and management, let us consider the case of the Chirathivat family, which runs the Central Department Store Group (Central), Thailand's biggest chain of department stores (Sappaiboon 2000; Saengthongkham et al. 2003).

The Central Group was founded by Tiang Chirathivat or Jeng (Tae) Nee Tiang, who arrived in Thailand from Hainan Island in 1925. In 1951 he opened a small shop selling imported clothes, cosmetics, books, and other periodicals in a back street near the Oriental Hotel in Bangkok and named it the Hang Sentan Trading (Central Trading Registered Ordinary Partnership), a landmark step in the Chirathivat family business. In 1956 Tiang opened a modern-type department store called the Central Department Store in the Wang Burapa district, the first store of this kind in Thailand. By introducing fixed price tags to consumers who were traditionally accustomed to bargaining over every purchase, the store essentially revolutionized the whole concept of retailing. The store also subcontracted the manufacture and sale of internationally famous brands (of sport shirts, tableware, and so on) from their foreign owners (Saengthongkham et al. 2003).

Over the years, additional Central Department stores were established in the Silom, Chidlom, Lad Phrao, and other areas of Bangkok. Within a year of the Silom branch being completed, Tiang died, and, according to the Hainanese business culture, his eldest son or Samrit took over the business with the help of his siblings. The group has since expanded its network of stores, and entered into an extensive range of activities, including retail and wholesale, real estate and property development, hotels, fast-food franchises, manufacturing, and distribution. By 2009 the group had became the largest department store chain in South East Asia, comprised of approximately 230 identifiable companies. Department-store operations were controlled by the Central Retail Corp. Ltd (CRC), which was 82.5 percent owned by the Chirathivat family alone in 2009.

As Table 9.4 shows, the flagship Central Department Store Co. Ltd (CDS), and its major subsidiaries, were exclusively controlled by Tiang's sons, daughters, and grandsons, particularly from his eldest son (Samrit) and his second son (Wanchai). Since its foundation, CDS has never made a public offering of its stock, which is entirely owned by members of the Chirathivat family or family-owned investment companies.

Tiang himself passed away in 1968 in his early 60s. But he had married three times and had had twenty-six children—fourteen boys and twelve girls. In just three generations, members of the Chirathivat family who could trace their ancestry directly to the founder already exceeded 160. For some time there was no problem at all in recruiting competent personnel from within the ranks of the family (including those who had married in). In 2004 about fifty family members were actively involved in the business. In 1992, when Samrit passed away, also of illness, leaving two wives and ten children, Tiang's second son, Wanchai, was promoted to group chairman. Wanchai and the next four eldest sons—the "Five Tigers" or *ha-sua*—formed themselves into a "family council," which met regularly and functioned much like the board of directors of an orthodox company (Suehiro 2002: 281–300; Saengthongkham et al. 2003).

To be fair, the Central may be a somewhat extreme case of family business, whereby the *kongsi* management system is executed, in which family members help to take care of group companies. Not many families can maintain such thorough control of their business once it has expanded and diversified to such a degree. However, when they need to raise funds from outside, the owner family occasionally seeks to control the public-listed companies through family-owned investment companies[3] or holding companies. Companies within a group are interlocked in complex formal and informal relationships including stock pyramid, cross-share-holdings, interlocking directorates, and personal transfer (Suehiro 2006: 88–97; Wailerdsak 2008c).

Typically, the stock pyramidal structure consists of an owner family at its top tier. The owner family then exerts its control over a large number of affiliated companies through multilateral instruments. The authors discovered *three* types of stock pyramids of business groups based on holding companies in Thailand: from family-owned holding companies through a non-listed core company to a great number of listed and non-listed companies (such as Central, Soon Hua Seng, NTS); or from family-owned holding companies through a core listed company to a great number of listed and non-listed companies (such as CP, Saha/SPI, Shin, Saha-Union); or the case that the core firm itself is a listed company in the banking sector (such as Kasikornbank, Bangkok Bank), which further invests in a number of listed and non-listed companies. For in-depth information and samples of the stock pyramid of major Thai business groups, see the authors' research (Suehiro and Wailerdsak 2002; Suehiro 2006; Wailerdsak 2008c).

[3] A family-owned "investment company" is defined here as a company financed totally by members of a particular family with the aim of investing in both its group companies and outside corporations. This aim is different from the "holding company," which aims systematically to keep control over ownership and management within the group. Rather, the aim of the former is to reduce the individual income-tax burden on family members. The investment companies first appeared in family business groups, which controlled commercial banks, and then spread to the manufacturing groups during the late 1960s. Many of them were named after a family name, the founder's name, or the founder's children's names.

Table 9.4 Directorship of the Chirathivat family in the Central Department Store group, 2003

Chirathivat family	Relationship	Age in 2003	Family council	Central Department Store Co. Ltd	Central group of companies	Central Retail Corp.	Central Patana PLC	Central Plaza Hotel PLC
Tiang	Founder	Passed away						
Samrit	S1 Tiang	Passed away						
Kriangsak*	S1 Samrit			EXD				
Suchada*	W Kriangsak			EX-VPR				
Prin*	S2 Samrit	41	DR	EXD		DR	EXD	DR
Tos*	S3 Samrit	38	DR		CEO, retail business	CEO		
Yuwadi*	D3 Samrit			PR	DR			
Nitsini*	D5 Samrit			EXD				
Siriket*	D6 Samrit			EXD				
Wanchai	S2 Tiang	76	CH	CH	CH	DR	CH	CH, EXD
Vat*	S1 Wanchai			EXD		DR		
Kobchai*	S2 Wanchai	48	DR		CEO, property business	DR	CEO, PR	
Sakchai*	S3 Wanchai							
Surangrat*	W Sakchai							
Pichai*	S4 Wanchai			DR	CEO, mfg & wholesales			
Suthiporn	S3 Tiang	73	DR	EXD	VCH	DR		EXD
Narongrit*	S Suthiporn			EX-VPR		DR		
Wanthanee*	W Narongrit			EX-VPR				
Suchitra	D1 Tiang	68	DR		VCH			DR
Suthikiati	S4 Tiang	61	DR	EXD	VCH, hotel, food, and franchising	DR	EX-VCH	PR, CEO

Chirathivat family	Relationship	Age in 2003	Family council	Central Department Store Co. Ltd	Central group of companies	Central Retail Corp.	Central Patana PLC	Central Plaza Hotel PLC
Thiradej*	S1 Suthikiati	39						DR
Thirayuth*	S2 Suthikiati	38						DR
Suthichart	S5 Tiang	58	DR			DR	EXD	DR
Suthichai	S6 Tiang	62	DR	EXD	EX-CH	DR	EX-CH	EXD
Suthisak	S7 Tiang	58	DR		DR	DR	EXD	DR
Sudhitham	S8 Tiang	56	DR		DR, general affairs	DR	EXD	DR
Suthidej	S9 Tiang	53					EX-VPR	
Suthiphand	S10 Tiang	51	Secretary					
Sutthilak	S11 Tiang	52	DR	DR	DR	DR		
Suthipak	S13 Tiang	42					Senior VPR	
Mukda	D2 Tiang					DR		
Sukulya	D5 Tiang		DR					
Supatra	D6 Tiang	46	DR	EX-VPR	DR, marketing			DR
Bussaba	D9 Tiang		DR		DR			
Wanlaya	D10 Tiang		Assist. Secretary			EXD		

Notes: CH=Chairman; VCH=Vice Chairman; CEO=Chief Executive Office; EX-CH=Executive Chairman; EXD=Executive Director; DR=Director; PR=President; VPR=Vice President.

*third generation; S1=eldest son; S2=second son, etc.; D1=eldest daughter; D2=second daughter, etc.; W=wife.

Sources: Family council members, family relationships, and generations from Saengthongkhan et al. (2003: 95–7). Executive positions from Brooker Group (2003: 168–172) and Tangsriwong (2004). For the directorship of the Central Department Store Group, see Suehiro (2003).

9.5 STRATEGIES OF DIVERSIFICATION
AND INTERNATIONALIZATION

9.5.1 Diversification

As mentioned earlier, one principal characteristic of a Thai business group is an active diversification of its business into unrelated fields. Three factors explain why Thai business groups have diversified their operations and how their success has become possible.

First, the limited scale and size of domestic markets and the product market failure forced business groups to diversify. Meanwhile, the government also attempted to back this strategy through its industrialization promotion policy, which involved granting privileges, including tax incentives (for example, exemption from corporation income tax for three to seven years from the starting year of operation), and other measures designed to protect domestic industries from foreign competition. The government has positively assisted import substitution industries, especially for consumer goods, since the 1960s, and from the mid-1980s it has been promoted export-oriented and heavy and chemical industries, and from the 1990s the service sectors, including telecommunications industry.

Secondly, at the same time, the government granted privileges to foreign firms and made it possible for domestic companies to secure the capital, production technology, and managerial know-how that are so essential to diversification through joint-venture projects with foreign firms. Particularly since the 1980s, many existing business groups have entered into new growth industries unrelated to their main business lines. For example, SCG's move into tyres (with Michelin of France), petrochemicals (with Japanese Mitsui Chemical), steel (with Japanese Yamato Steel), and electronics (with Japanese Mitsubishi Electrical and NEC), and the CP group's advance from agribusiness into petrochemicals (tied up with Solvay Ltd of Belgium), telecommunications (with NYNEX Corp., a subsidiary of American Bell Atlantic), and modern retail business (with Dutch Makro). The interests of multinationals, particularly from Japan and the Four Asian Tigers, looking for suitable investments to help them move into Thailand happened to dovetail perfectly with those of family-run business groups looking for new sources of capital to fuel their own expansion drives.

Thirdly, generational transition within these business groups tended to promote business diversification. It is not unusual to find Thai business groups that have stayed intact for three generations since their foundation (Suehiro and Wailerdsak 2004; Suehiro 2006). We have seen the rise of a new generation of skilled family managers (the offspring of the owners) with high levels of education, including studies in North America, Europe, or Japan, experience from abroad, and close relationships with overseas corporations (Wailerdsak 2005). These young generations have often acquired modern concepts of business administration, new technologies, and know-how, thus providing themselves with opportunities to advance into newly growing industries,. They are completely different from the founder's generation, in line with the government's new promotion policies, the upgrading of the industrial sectors, and the progress of information technology in Thailand.

9.5.2 Internationalization

Prior to 1989, virtually no firms ventured overseas. A small trickle of outward investment was created by banks and trading companies setting up overseas branches, mainly in Hong Kong, Singapore, and the USA. This attitude was a response to the Thai government's strict control over foreign-exchange transactions and capital movement. After 1989, however, the outflow increased gradually up to a peak in the mid-1990s of around twenty billion baht a year, equivalent to 0.45 percent of GDP, or a third of the inflow of foreign investment (Pananond 2008: 236).

Financial liberalization, especially the shift of membership from the IMF's Article 14 to Article 8—no restriction on foreign-exchange transactions for current accounts in 1990 and the creation of the BIBF in 1993—significantly eased the financial difficulties for ambitious Thai firms venturing abroad. Against the background of the West's prolonged recession, foreign firms were increasingly ready to sell their technology off the shelf or to enter into non-equity joint ventures (Phongpaichit and Baker 1998: 55).

In the boom decade (1988–96), the pioneers of outward investment included several of the largest Thai business groups such as CP and SCG. CP founded its first agribusiness in China in 1979 as the country's economy opened up. By the mid-1980s, the Chia Tai Group (CP's name in China) had diversified into new areas, including assembling motorcycles, brewing beer, developing industrial estates, electronics, power plants, running hypermarkets, and building petrochemical complexes. It had become the largest single foreign investor in China. By 1997, CP had over 200 subsidiaries operating in 20 countries, was listed on 7 stock markets, and employed over 100,000 people. SCG was the second largest overseas investor. It had first ventured overseas in the early 1990s with a project in the USA. Over 1993–7, it had launched twenty-seven projects in plastics and construction materials in China, Indonesia, the Philippines, and Vietnam, and in petrochemicals in India, among others (Siam Cement PLC 1999).

During this period, the outward investment from Thailand shifted from investment in financial institutions to basic manufacturing industries, particularly food processing (CP, Saha/SPI, Mitr-Phol, Betagro), manufacture of parts for the automotive or electrical sectors (Thai Summit, Sammitr), and textiles (Saha-Union), more technologically intensive industries such as chemical and petrochemicals (TPI, TOA, Srithai Superware), telecommunications (Shin, Jasmine), and services such as hotel (Dusit Thani), property development, and construction (Board of Investment 2007). Similarly, the geographical diversity also deepened. Thai investors increasingly concentrated their activities in the opening markets of neighboring countries such as Laos, Cambodia, Myanmar, and Vietnam (CLMV), together with ASEAN and China.

Also, some investments flowed to Hong Kong, the USA, and European Union (EU) in order to bypass trade barriers of economic blocs.

Although the financial crisis forced considerable divestment of overseas ventures (for example, Thai President Foods (TF), the country's largest noodle producer known for its Mama brand), the momentum to expand overseas activities was not seriously damaged. Indeed, according to the Bank of Thailand's economic report, a total amount of outward investment in the five years 2003– 7 amounted to 92 billion baht, exceeding the 69 billion baht in 1993–7, the five years before the financial crisis.

The emergence of a more region-wide market within South East Asia under the impact of the ASEAN Free Trade Area (AFTA) tariff-reduction scheme, and the spectacular rise of China, created opportunities for Thai firms. After the 1997 financial crisis, the government became aware that outward investment needed to be a part of national economic strategy. Even in 2003, the BOI launched a scheme that targeted three types of industries: those in which Thailand might become a regional center, including petrochemicals, auto parts, and agribusiness; those where local firms needed to move outward because of poor prospects for expansion at home, such as garments, fisheries, and jewelry; and those where Thailand might have global potential, including animal feeds, sugar, leather products, and tourism (Pananond 2008: 244–5).

9.6 Financial crisis and corporate governance

The business environment for Thai business groups changed dramatically with the Asian financial crisis of 1997. The rapid depreciation of baht was a body blow to groups that had been working to expand their businesses by taking out loans based on the US dollar, saddling them with massive exchange losses. The bursting of stock-market and property bubbles also brought down the prices of stock and real estates, which combined with a widespread credit crunch to make it considerably harder to borrow from banks. Faced with this sudden dilemma, Thai business groups responded broadly in three patterns: bankruptcy or closure of operation, selection and concentration, and tie-up with foreign capital.

9.6.1 Three patterns of corporate response

9.6.1.1 *Bankruptcy or closure of operation*

One of the most spectacular failures was the Bangkok Metropolitan Bank (BMB) group led by Udane Tejapaibul, a great *Chao Sua* and the most respected figure in

Thai–Chinese business community. From the 1950s, the BMB group had developed their business lines—from banking and finance to insurance, the liquor business (Mekong-brand whisky), and the construction of industrial estates, town houses, and big shopping centers such as the World Trade Center (later changed to Central World)—into a giant business group, embracing 108 firms just before the crisis. However, after the 1997 crisis BMB suffered heavy losses and a huge volume of bad loans as group companies failed to repay borrowing.

The Bank of Thailand (BOT) stepped in to dismiss the bank's directors, including the president (Wichian, Udane's eldest son), and then ordered the bank to decrease capital and arrange a debt-to-equity swap with the BOT. Consequently, in January 1998, BMB came under the direct control of the government. By 2002 the BMB group had been forced to close four finance companies and to sell off its stakes in the beer industry and the World Trade Center. After seventy years of prosperity, the Tejapaibul family business had come to an end (Brooker Group 2003: 689–91). For more details on the collapse of Thai financial business groups including commercial banks and finance companies, see Suehiro (2002: ch.4) and Wailerdsak (2006a).

9.6.1.2 *Selection and concentration*

A second group of enterprises managed to see out the crisis by dint of downsizing and following a strategy of selection and concentration. Overcoming increased corporate debt in the process of diversification programs during the boom years and economic difficulties after the crisis, they had to concentrate their management resources into a few core sectors where they could identify a competitive advantage in an ever-intensifying domestic and international market.

CP, for instance, had found the distribution and retail trade a handy money-spinner during the boom years but now saw no option but to sell off most of its shares in Siam Makro, Lotus Distribution International, and Sunny Supermarket to foreign partners. CP also decided to withdraw from the petrochemical industry. Still trimming its sails, in January 1999 CP started to consolidate thirteen agro-industrial companies into a single firm, Charoen Pokphand Foods PLC (CPF). The group considered its priorities and defined two areas—agro-industry and telecommunications—as "core businesses." Other spheres of activity, including automobiles, petrochemicals, real estate, and modern retail business (excepting the profitable CP Seven-Eleven, which had later become CP All PLC), were designed as "non-core businesses" and accordingly given a lower priority (Suehiro 2006: ch. 6).

A similar trend could be observed at another major Thai family-run business group discussed earlier, the Central. In the early 1990s, Central jointly set up a strategic holding company, Central Retail Corporation (CRC), with the Robinson Department Store Group, triggering an intense struggle between the Central/Robinson group and the CP group for supremacy in the modern retail sector. Through CRC, the Central Group opened a series of gigantic shopping malls called Big C Supercenter and Carrefour (the latter were run by CenCar Co. Ltd), along with mini-marts called Tops on the outskirts of Bangkok and a large number of provincial cities.

The 1997 crisis swiftly prompted the Central/Robinson group to sell most of its stake in these three major companies to foreign partners or new foreign participants: in 1999 Casino of France took a 68 percent stake in Big C Supercenter PLC, Carrefour took a 99.99 percent stake in CenCar Co. Ltd, and Royal Ahold of Holland acquired 49 percent of the stock in Tops. In turn, Central decided to disband the strategic alliance with Robinson and concentrate investment in more traditional fields such as department stores, hotel service, and real estate.

9.6.1.3 *Tie-up with foreign capital*

A third pattern of responses to the crisis was to defend existing enterprises through tie-ups with foreign capital or new shareholders. Many business groups faced with gigantic foreign-exchange losses and snowballing dollar-based foreign debt took this approach. In Thailand, one legacy of the 1997 crisis had been a tug of war between domestic business groups and foreign capital over boardroom control, notably in the major commercial banks, domestic steel and auto-part industries, telecommunications, modern retail, and real estate. Almost overnight, the relationship between Thai business groups and their foreign/multinational partners went through a 180-degree change, from a friendly and reciprocal relationship to a more hostile and competitive one (Suehiro 2008: 196). The Alien Business Law, which was adjusted in 1999, shifting thirty-three industries into classifications that allowed foreign majority participation, supported this process (Phongpaichit and Baker 2004; Wailerdsak 2006a).

9.6.2 Corporate governance reform: Financial sector

As well as colossal debts and a sudden drastic business downturn, the 1997 crisis also brought a new kind of challenge to Thai business groups—the need to conform to *global standards* of management, as defined by the IMF and the World Bank. The program of financial institutional reform prescribed by the global lenders after the crisis included new principles of accounting and auditing for Thai companies—principles that would bring local companies into line with the Anglo-American concept of good corporate governance (Wailerdsak 2006b: 270–304).

For a start, this meant that commercial banks and finance companies had to learn to conform to new international standards of capital adequacy and loan-loss provisioning, as laid down by the Bank for International Settlements (BIS). They were saddled with a huge burden from non-performing loans and faced the need to recapitalize. If they failed to meet the new standards, they were put under the direct control of the government, as we saw in the case of Bangkok Metropolitan Bank, or were forced to sell off their shareholdings and transfer management control to foreign bankers, as in the case of four small and medium banks (owned by either a single family or a group of families). The five largest banks survived but experienced a dramatic change of ownership and capital structure. In the three that were controlled by a dominant family, the family share was scythed down from more than 30 percent before the crisis to below 5 percent for the Bangkok Bank and the

Kasikornthai Bank, and 10 percent for the Bank of Ayudhya in 2009. Foreign share-holders acquired major stakes, yet the family retained management control (Wai-lerdsak 2008a: 27–8). Some foreign investors and minority shareholders tended to hold shares of these banks through Thailand Securities Depository (TSD) and Non-Voting Depository Receipts (NDVR). Table 9.5 presents the name of commercial banks, their ultimate owners, or their largest shareholders in 2008.

Then after 2000, the mergers and acquisitions among banks had continued. Thai Military Bank merged with DBS Thai Dhanu Bank and Industrial Finance Corpora-tion of Thailand (IFCT) in September 2004. Bank of Asia/ABM Amro was resold to Singaporean UOB in 2004 and subsequently merged into UOB Radanasin in 2005, and changed its name to United Overseas Bank (Thai). Thanachart Bank was newly established in April 2002.

In addition, of the 91 finance companies operating before the crisis, 56 were closed down by government order in December 1997. Others lapsed over following months. In early 2004, the BOT announced the first Financial Sector Master Plan, which intensified an explosion of mergers, reorganization, re-licensing, and acquisitions among financial institutions. The remaining 31 finance companies were offered the options of elevating themselves into a universal bank, or a retail bank,[4] or a specialized non-bank institution. Twenty firms or groups submitted applications. Four were granted licenses to become universal banks, including TISCO Bank, Kiatnakin Bank, ACL Bank, and MEGA International Commercial Bank. Another four became retail banks, including Land and Houses Retail Bank, AIG Retail Bank, Thai Credit Retail Bank, and GE Money Retail Bank (Wongwuttiwat 2007).

All of the remaining banks understood that in the context of the Basel Standards, increased foreign share ownership, and closer scrutiny, especially of credit practices, they could no longer primarily act as merchant banks providing loans to affiliated entrepreneurs, and taking capital stakes in outside ventures (Wailerdsak 2008a: 28). The banking business groups, which have the commercial banks at core, have been forced continuously to reorganize. Their economic power fell greatly, so we can say that the age of the Thai financial groups had come to the end.

9.6.3 Corporate governance reform: Listed companies

The post-crisis reforms also had a significant impact on listed companies. In January 1998 the Stock Exchange of Thailand and Ministry of Finance issued a joint directive obliging companies listed on the exchange to meet a series of new requirements (Suehiro 2001a: 68–76). Among other things, companies were called upon to appoint

---

[4] Universal banks are qualified and well-capitalized financial institutions requiring a minimum of five billion baht of tier-one capital. These banks may provide most financial services to all groups of customers, but are not permitted to engage in trading, insurance underwriting and brokering, or underwriting equity securities. Retail banks, with smaller capital requirement (250 million baht of tier-one capital), may offer financial services to retail customers and SMEs within the same limitations as universal banks, but they cannot conduct business related to foreign-exchange and derivatives products.

Table 9.5 Ownership of commercial banks, 2008

Bank name	Year of opening	Ultimate owners	Total asset (US$ bn)	Number of full branches	Shares held by	
					Thai owner (%)	Foreign (%)
Private Banks						
1 Bangkok	1944	Sophonpanich	47.5	127	<5.0	22.0
2 The Siam Commercial	1906	Crown Property Bureau	34.3	168	23.7	34.7
3 Kasikornthai (Thai Farmers)	1945	Lamsam	30.8	141	<5.0	42.1
4 TMB (Thai Military)	1957	Ministry of Finance, Army Force	25.7	135	34.1	29.0
5 Ayudhya	1945	GE Capital and Ratanarak	21.2	137	25.1	32.9 (GE)
6 United Overseas (Thai)	2005	United Overseas Bank Singapore	5.9	86	–	98.5
7 Thanachart	2002	Tanachart Capital, Bank of Nova Scotia (Canada)	8.4	33	74.5	24.98 (BNS)
8 Standard Chartered (Thai)	2005	Standard Chartered Bank (British)	6.1	24	–	99.8
9 TISCO	2005	CDIB&Partners Investment	3.4	3	–	34.5
10 Kiatnakin	2005	Thepkanchana, Wattanavekin	18.1	4	17.2	25.1
11 ACL	2005	Bangkok Bank	2.1	5	19.3	20.1
12 MEGA International Commercial	2005	Subsidiary of Mega International (Taiwan)	0.4	2	–	100.0
State-Owned Banks						
13 Krungthai	1966	FIDF	38.1	138	55.5	16.3
14 Siam City	1941	FIDF	13.5	104	47.6	19.6
15 Bank Thai	1998	FIDF	8.2	43	32.9	39.4
Retail Banks						
16 Land and Houses Retail	2005	Land and Houses, Harnpanich, Asavabhokin	0.69	4	90.5	–
17 AIG Retail	2005	American International Group Inc. (sold to Ayudhya in 2009)	0.82	1	–	99.5
18 Thai Credit Retail	2006	Thai Life Insurance, Chaiyawan	0.81	2	100.0	–
19 GE Money Retail	2006	Sold to Ayudhya in 2007	–	–	–	–

Notes: Thai owner means only the ultimate owners; foreign owner means total combined foreign institutional shareholders that appeared in the top ten shareholders. Kasikornthai Bank, TMB Bank, and Standard Chartered (Thai) Bank changed names in 2005. FIDF = Financial Institute Development Fund.

Sources: Bank name, total asset, and number of full branches from Bank of Thailand, as of December 2008. Ultimate owners and percentage of shares compiled by Wailerdsak based on data collected from *56–1 Annual Report* (in Thai, March 2008) and websites of each bank. For the ownership changes in 1996 and 2000, see Phongpaichit and Baker (2000: 222); Suehiro (2002: 167); and Wailerdsak (2008a: 26–7).

at least two independent directors; to establish an audit committee composed of experts from outside the company; to demonstrate transparency in management for investors, especially by drawing up a prospectus (a document formally called *Form 56/1*), including detailed information on the background of each director and his or her personal connection to the owner of the company, and to publish annual reports in both Thai and English. In short, Thailand's listed companies, including family-run ones, were called upon to introduce a style of management that paid due attention to the interests of international investors and minority shareholders, and that emphasized transparency and disclosure of information vis-à-vis shareholders and investors in general rather than being tightly focused on the family that owned the business.

The new trends—toward prioritizing the interests of shareholders outside the family owning the company, toward lending greater weight to the opinions of external directors relative to those of the owner and his family or friends, and toward introducing accounting and auditing systems strict enough to meet the requirements of the International Accounting Standards Committee (IASC) or the American Financial Accounting Standards Board (FASB)—reflect the fact that Thai business groups are being forced into a fundamental rethink of the way they do business in line with the movement of globalization and liberalization. Since they sought salvation through partnerships with foreign capital and fresh infusions of foreign investment capital, Thai companies have had no choice but to move in the direction of global standards after the crisis.

9.7 CONCLUSION

Business groups in Thailand, particular the family-run ones, have been the driving force of the country's economic development. The dynamism came from the entrepreneurship of Chinese immigrants, beginning in the late nineteenth century. Some expanded into sprawling business groups by riding the rapid trends of change under the government's catch-up industrialization policy after the 1960s. They seized available investment opportunities, some of them in the domestic market, and some in competitive world markets as exporters and investors. But the ownership and control of these business groups were still highly concentrated. In the years following the 1997 crisis, multinational capital acquired a much greater role in some key sectors of the economy. On the other hand, the domestic business groups that survived and even prospered in the shake-out were concentrated in sectors oriented to the domestic market and often sheltered by government provisions.

Four major "competitive capabilities" can explain the survival rates and the continuing development of business groups in Thailand. They include (1) *the capability to adapt themselves to new environment*—changing government policies, which provided incentives to promote industries or to undertake liberalization in the financial sector and industrial investment; (2) *organizational/managerial capability*—continuous management reforms in terms of ownership structure and organization/management styles, which enabled them to become more transparent in their operation and corporate governance; (3) *human resource capability*—well-educated family managers, and non-family professional managers and skilled labor; and (4) *technological and marketing capability*—strategic alliances with foreign capital by means of joint ventures, which enabled local firms to advance into newly growing industries and markets.

Nevertheless, despite high growth rates, Thailand was unable to develop the industrial and technological infrastructure needed to bring its economic development to a newer stage. Up to 1997, Thailand had been moving successfully from the factor-driven stage of development (depending on the input of low-cost labor, natural resources, and imported technology) to the investment-driven stage (improving efficiencies by extensive joint venturing and heavy investment in trade-related infra-structure). After 1997 Thailand was at a critical juncture of progressing to the innovation-driven stage (the ability to innovate and produce products and services at the frontier of global technology). In his policy proposal for Thai government in 2003, Porter (2003: 12) made the very relevant point that "competitiveness ultimately depends on improving the microeconomic capability of the economy and the sophistication of local companies and local competition . . . Without an improvement in microeconomic fundamentals, current growth will be short-lived."

His observation is even more crucial in post-crisis Thailand. In order to be able either to compete at home or to venture out in the future, Thai business groups, being the leading agents of growth, and the government now have to make the necessary investments in technology, innovation, and human resources, particularly in "non-family" professional managers and skilled labor such as engineers and technicians. In the long run, these investments will assist further in the improvement of other competitive capabilities, and finally lead to a sustainable growth.

REFERENCES

Board of Investment (ed.) (2007). "Thai Overseas Investment," *Investment Promotion Journal*, 18/2 (Feb.), 13–52.

Brooker Group (2003) (ed.). *Thai Business Groups: A Unique Guide to Who Owns What*. 5th edn. Bangkok: Brooker Group.

HEWISON, K. (1989). *Bankers and Bureaucrats: Capital and State in Thailand*. New Haven: Yale University Southeast Asian Monograph No. 34.

KHANNA, T., and PALEPU, K. (1997). "Why Focused Strategies May Be Wrong for Emerging Markets," *Harvard Business Review*, 75/4: 41–51.

LEE, K. (2006). "Business Groups as an Organizational Device for Economic Catch-Up," in J. Nakagawa (ed.), *Managing Development: Globalization, Economic Restructuring and Social Policy*. London and New York: Routledge, 217–33.

LEFF, N. (1978). "Industrial Organization and Entrepreneurship in the Developing Countries: The Economic Groups," *Economic Development and Cultural Changes*, 26/4: 611–75.

MUSCAT, R. J. (1994). *The Fifth Tiger: A Study of Thai Development Policy.* Helsinki: United Nations University Press.

NIYOMSILPA, S. (2003). "Telecommunications, Rents and the Growth of Liberalization Coalition in Thailand," in K. S. Jomo and F. C. Brian (eds.), *Ethnic Business: Chinese Capitalism in Southeast Asia.* London: Routledge Curzon.

PANANOND, P. (2008). "Finding Some Space in the World: Thai Firms Overseas," in P. Phongpaichit and C. Baker (eds.), *Thai Capital after the 1997 Crisis.* Chiangmai: Silkworm Books, 235–47.

PHIPHATSERITHAM, K. (1982). *Analysis of Large-Scale Business Ownership in Thailand.* Bangkok: Thammasat University Press (in Thai).

PHONGPAICHIT, P. (2006) (ed.). *The Struggle of Thai Capitals 1: Adaptation and Dynamics.* Bangkok: Matichon (in Thai).

PHONGPAICHIT, P., and BAKER, C. (1998). *Thailand Boom and Bust.* Chiangmai: Silkworm Books.

PHONGPAICHIT, P., and BAKER, C. (2002). *Thailand Economy and Politics.* 2nd edn. New York: Oxford University Press.

PHONGPAICHIT, P., and BAKER, C. (2004). "Aftermath: Structural Change and Policy Innovation after the Thai Crisis," in K. S. Jomo (ed.), *After the Storm: Crisis, Recovery and Sustaining Development in Four Asian Economies.* Singapore: National University of Singapore Press, 150–72.

PHONGPAICHIT, P., and BAKER, C. (2008) (eds.). *Thai Capital after the 1997 Crisis.* Chiangmai: Silkworm Books.

PIRIYARANGSAN, S. (1983). *Thai Bureaucratic Capitalism, 1932–1960.* Bangkok: CUSRI.

PORTER, M. E. (2003). *Thailand's Competitiveness: Creating the Foundations for Higher Productivity.* Bangkok: NESDB.

SAENGTHONGKHAM, W., TANGSRIWONG, P., and DAMRONGSUNTHORNCHAI, S. (2003). *70 Years Chirathivat Central: Further Struggle and Further Growth.* Bangkok: Manager Magazine (in Thai).

SAPPAIBOON, T. (2000, 2001). *The 55 Most Famous Wealthy Families*, 2 vols. Bangkok: Nation Multimedia Group (in Thai).

Siam Cement PLC (1999). *The Siam Cement Public Company Limited Annual Report 1998.* Bangkok: Siam Cement PLC.

SKINNER, W. G. (1957). *Chinese Society in Thailand: An Analytical History.* Ithaca, NY: Cornell University Press.

SKINNER, W. G. (1958). *Leadership and Power in the Chinese Community of Thailand.* Ithaca NY: Cornell University Press.

SUEHIRO, A. (1989). *Capital Accumulation in Thailand 1855–1985.* Tokyo: UNESCO and the Centre for East Asian Cultural Studies.

SUEHIRO, A. (1993). "Family Business Reassessed: Corporate Structure and Late-Starting Industrialization in Thailand," *Developing Economies*, 31/4: 378–407.

SUEHIRO, A. (2001a). "Asian Corporate Governance: Disclosure-Based Screening System and Family Business Restructuring in Thailand," *Shakai Kagaku Kenkyu*, 52/5: 55–98.

SUEHIRO, A. (2001b). "Family Business Gone Wrong? Ownership Patterns and Corporate Performance in Thailand." ADB Institute Working Paper, no. 19. Tokyo: ADB Institute.

SUEHIRO, A. (2002) (ed.). *Institutional Reform and Corporate Restructuring in Thailand: From Crisis to Recovery*. Chiba: Institute of Developing Economies (in Japanese).

SUEHIRO, A. (2006). *A Study of Family Business: Agents of Late Industrialization*. Nagoya: Nagoya University Press (in Japanese).

SUEHIRO, A. (2008). *Catch-up Industrialization: The Trajectory and Prospects of East Asian Economies*. Singapore: National University of Singapore Press.

SUEHIRO, A., and WAILERDSAK, N. (2002). "Ownership Changes and the Actual Management of Listed Companies: Ultimate Owners and Top Management," in A. Suehiro (ed.), *Institutional Reform and Corporate Restructuring in Thailand: From Crisis to Recovery*. Chiba: Institute of Developing Economies, 312–69 (in Japanese).

SUEHIRO, A., and WAILERDSAK, N. (2004). "Family Business in Thailand: Its Management, Governance and Future Challenges," *ASEAN Economic Bulletin*, 21/1: 81–93.

TANGSRIWONG, P. (2004). "Chirathivat in Retail Business Sectors," *Phu Chatkan Magazine* (Jan.) (in Thai).

WAILERDSAK, N. (2005). *Managerial Careers in Thailand and Japan*. Chiangmai: Silkworm Books.

WAILERDSAK, N. (2006a). *Business Groups and Family Business in Thailand before and after the 1997 Crisis*. Bangkok: BrandAge Books (in Thai).

WAILERDSAK, N. (2006b). "Thai Family Business in the Globalization Blizzard," in P. Phongpaichit (ed.), *The Struggle of Thai Capitals 1: Adaptation and Dynamics*. Bangkok: Matichon, 41–99 (in Thai).

WAILERDSAK, N. (2008a). "Companies in Crisis", in P. Phongpaichit and C. Baker (eds.), *Thai Capital after the 1997 Crisis*. Chiangmai: Silkworm Books, 17–57.

WAILERDSAK, N. (2008b). "Women Executives in Thai Family Businesses," in V. Gupta et al. (eds.), *Culturally Sensitive Models of Gender in Family Business*. Hyderabad: ICFAI University Press, 19–39.

WAILERDSAK, N. (2008c). "Family Business in Thailand: Ownership Structure and Stock Market," in V. Gupta et al. (eds.), *Culturally Sensitive Models of Family Business in Southern Asia*. Hyderabad: ICFAI University Press, 108–33.

WONGWUTTIWAT, P. (2007) (ed.). *Commercial Bank in Thailand 2007*. Bangkok: Research Department, Bangkok Bank PLC.

World Bank (1993). *The East Asian Miracle: Economic Growth and Public Policy*. New York: Oxford University Press.

CHAPTER 10

BUSINESS GROUPS IN SINGAPORE

LAI SI TSUI-AUCH
TORU YOSHIKAWA

10.1 INTRODUCTION

LIKE many other economies, the Singaporean economy is dominated by business groups. As in a number of other East and South East Asian economies, family-controlled business groups control a high stake of the economy in Singapore. However, unlike many others, the Singaporean economy has a predominance of government-linked business groups rather than family-controlled ones. The creation and development of these government-linked groups reflect the active role of the Singaporean government in the economy. These groups are constituted by unusual hybrids of state and private enterprises. Their group firms compete with their family-controlled counterparts and multinational corporations, and sometimes with each other.

The Asian economic crisis of 1997 caused an upheaval in Singaporean business practices. The government quickly restructured the financial sector and strengthened corporate laws and accounting practices. It encouraged both government-linked groups and private-sector banking groups to divest their non-core assets and to professionalize their corporate governance. The government also prompted them to diversify their businesses beyond Asia. More than a decade after the crisis, it is timely

The authors sincerely thank Alan Chua, Jia Yi Chow, and Kay Heng Phang for their research assistance.

to take stock of the development and change of the business groups and assess their competitive capabilities.

The remainder of this chapter is divided into four sections. In Section 10.2 we describe the characteristics of the largest business groups. Section 10.3 outlines the political and economic contexts of Singapore. Section 10.4 summarizes the emergence and growth of the business groups as well as their change in the historical contexts of Singapore and the region, with a specific focus on the extent of the changes in these groups by 2006 as compared to 1997 when the Asian economic crisis occurred. We examine the competitive capabilities of these groups in Section 10.5.

10.2 SINGAPOREAN BUSINESS GROUPS: PROFILES AND CHARACTERISTICS

Table 10.1 shows the largest business groups, arranged in descending order according to the total assets of the group in 2006.[1] It gives an indication of the group size in terms of both the total assets and the number of subsidiaries and associated companies. A subsidiary is a company in which the group, directly or indirectly, holds more than half of the issued share capital, or controls more than half of the voting power, or controls the composition of the board of directors. An associated company is an entity in which the group has between 20 percent and 50 percent of the voting rights, and over which the group has significant influence, but the group does not control these companies' financial and operating policy decisions. Out of the thirty business groups, the top three are banking groups in Singapore.

Out of the thirty groups, there are altogether twenty Singaporean groups, nine Hong Kong-based groups (reflecting the importance of foreign investments especially from Hong Kong), and one Indonesian group. Out of the twenty domestic groups, eight are government-linked groups and twelve are private sector groups. Out of the twelve private-sector groups, eleven groups are controlled by ethnic Chinese families. One of them, UOB-Kay Hian, was not listed in 1997, and hence the annual report for that year is unavailable for our comparison between 1997 and 2006. Therefore, in this chapter we analyze the ten largest ethnic Chinese family-controlled groups together with the eight government-linked groups.

All the government-linked groups belong to the stable of the Temasek Holdings Ltd, the largest government holding company, which was founded in 1974 as a limited holding company to manage the state's investments in government-linked

---

[1] In this chapter, we adopt the definition of a business group from Granovetter (2005) as a set of legally separate firms linked together in formal and/or informal ways, which dominate most emerging economies (Hamilton 1997; Chung 2001).

Table 10.1 Basic information on the largest business groups in Singapore, 2006

Ranks by total assets of the groups	Names of the groups (abbreviations)	Countries of origin	Total assets (S$ m.)	No. of subsidiaries	No. of associated companies
1	Development Bank of Singapore (DBS)	Singapore	197,372	88	17
2	United Overseas Bank (UOB)	Singapore	161,312	95	21
3	Oversea-Chinese Banking Corporation (OCBC)	Singapore	151,220	43	16
4	Singapore Telecom (SingTel)	Singapore	33,606	139	36
5	Jardine Matheson Holdings (JMH)	Hong Kong	31,256	8	3
6	Jardine Strategic Holdings (JSH)	Hong Kong	28,205	4	3
7	Singapore Airlines (SIA)	Singapore	23,369	24	32
8	Hongkong Land (HKL)	Hong Kong	22,969	37	15
9	Keppel Corporation (Keppel Corp.)	Singapore	13,816	144	39
10	City Developments (CDL)	Singapore	11,004	223	84
11	Fraser and Neave (F&N)	Singapore	9,672	166	52
12	Hong Leong Finance (HLF)	Singapore	7,504	2	0
13	Neptune Orient Lines (NOL)	Singapore	6,550	123	45
14	Noble Group (NG)	Hong Hong	5,864	34	0
15	Keppel Land (Keppel Land)	Singapore	5,261	102	30
16	UOL	Singapore	4,651	48	6
17	United Industrial Corporation (UIC)	Singapore	4,620	48	10
18	Singapore Land (SG Land)	Singapore	3,748	27	8

(continued)

Table 10.1 Continued

Ranks by total assets of the groups	Names of the groups (abbreviations)	Countries of origin	Total assets (S$ m.)	No. of subsidiaries	No. of associated companies
19	Asia Food & Properties (AF&P)	Indonesia	3,634	156	43
20	SembCorp Marine (SembMarine)	Singapore	3,429	33	12
21	Dairy Farm International (DFI)	Hong Kong	3,261	15	4
22	Singapore Petroleum (SPC)	Singapore	3,140	12	10
23	Wing Tai (Wing Tai)	Singapore	2,745	33	18
24	Mandarin Oriental International (MOI)	Hong Kong	2,722	12	7
25	UOB-Kay Hian (UOB-KH)	Singapore	2,710	12	1
26	GuocoLand (GL)	Singapore	2,700	63	8
27	Wheelock Properties (WP)	Hong Kong	2,467	22	4
28	Pacific Century Regional Developments (PCRD)	Hong Kong	2,407	18	12
29	Hotel Properties (HP)	Singapore	2,190	73	4
30	Jardine Cycle & Carriage (JCC)	Hong Kong	1,993	10	12

Source: Compiled from annual reports of companies.

corporations. According to the Singapore Department of Statistics (2001), the government-linked corporations are entities in which a holding company wholly owned by the Singaporean government (through the Ministry of Finance Inc.) has an equity interest of 20 percent or more. Temasek Holdings, a private limited company that is not publicly listed, is the largest shareholder of many government-linked corporations. It does not conduct trade or business but instead holds investments, thus deriving income from dividends, interest, and rentals. Its sole shareholder, the Ministry of Finance Inc., can veto its decisions. Temasek Holdings owns more than 200 government-linked corporations that cover a wide spectrum of industries including transportation and logistics, ship repair and engineering, power and gas, telecommunications, media, financial services, manufacturing, and properties.[2] Temasek Holdings alone accounted for one-third of stock-market capitalization of SGX in 2006 (Goldstein and Pananond 2008). Yet Temasek often claims that it does not control its subsidiaries (*Straits Times* 2007b), which, however, contrasts with the prevailing perceptions (US Embassy of Singapore 2001; Worthington 2003).

The ten ethnic Chinese family-controlled groups ultimately belong to four families. These may be regarded as mega-groups. Some business groups under these mega-groups are controlled by other business groups under the same family, as shown in the chain of control over UOB, UOL, UIC, and SG Land within the Wee family in Fig. 10.1. Each group consists of independent firms that are linked to a core company. Both the core company and its independent firms often pursue unrelated diversification rather than related diversification and vertical integration, and resemble a web structure rather than a unitary organization. The ethnic Chinese firms diversify substantially in order to maximize revenues, reduce risks, and penetrate new markets and sectors. The networking between different firms is unavoidably fluid and loose.

To facilitate the coordination of such a diverse group and to balance conflicting interests, a business family tends to rely on one or several holding companies, which integrate separate product and regional divisions. The holding company is a pragmatic device to direct the operations of various companies. Unlike the Western business groups, which allow their companies to operate with considerable autonomy, ethnic Chinese enterprises within a business group have interlocking ownership and management ties. The founder's authority pervades the entire group and its subsidiaries through the control over decisions on finance, investment, market expansion, personnel, and so on. Through cross-ownership and interlocking directorate, the founding families are able to control and coordinate the strategies of its subsidiaries and affiliates (Hamilton 1997; Tong and Yong 1998; Brown 2000).

The unwieldy holding structure of large family-controlled business groups can be explained in terms of history, strategy, and social organization. Historically, the groups have developed tremendously diversified business lines that are unrelated to each other, and hence grouping them together under a single holding company is impractical (Yeung 2003b). Strategically, consolidation into a single holding company does not add value. For instance, there is no single holding company (except the family-owned, privately held shareholding company) in the Hong Leong group, because its business in both its listed and non-listed subsidiaries is immensely diversified (hotel, property, industrial, manufacturing, finance, and so on), and each requires highly specialized knowledge and competence to run. Lastly, family organization may change over time with the demise of the founding patriarch, which

---

[2] Although government-linked corporations are clearly vital to Singapore's economy, there is no precise measure of their centrality. The Ministry of Finance (1993) estimated that the public-sector and government-linked corporations accounted for 60% of Singapore's GDP as of 1993. However, the Singapore Department of Statistics (2001) estimated that government-linked corporations contributed only 12.9% of GDP in 1998, and that the non-government-linked public-sector corporations (such as the statutory boards) accounted for another 8.9%, for a total public-sector share of 21.8%. This estimate is low relative to the contribution of multinational corporations (i.e., 42%) (Low 2001b). Nevertheless, this latter estimate includes only government-linked corporations in which the government holds equity of at least 20%.

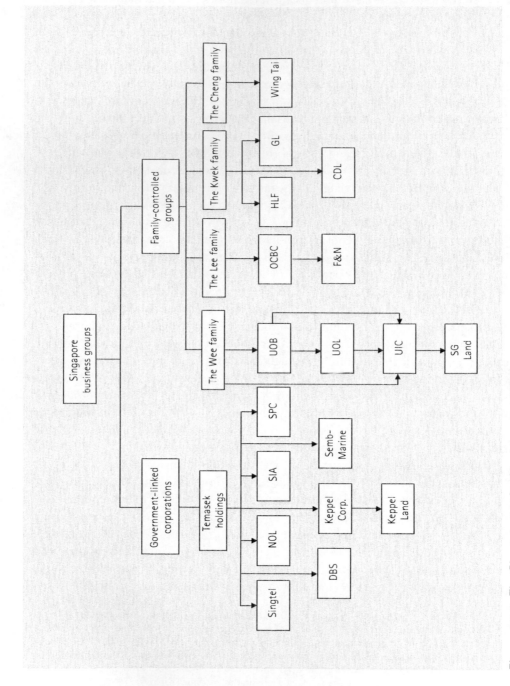

Figure 10.1 The Singaporean business groups, 2006

Source: Based on annual reports of companies.

Table 10.2 Principal activities of the Singaporean business groups, 2006

Business groups	Banking & finance	Hotels & restaurants	Investment & stockbrokers	Property	Telecom & post	Transportation	Retailing & trading	Building & construction	Engineering	Food & beverage	Others	Total no. of sectors involved
DBS	✓		✓								✓	3
SingTel					✓		✓		✓		✓	4
SIA		✓				✓	✓		✓			4
NOL			✓			✓	✓					3
SPC						✓	✓		✓			3
Keppel Corp.	✓	✓	✓	✓			✓	✓	✓		✓	8
Keppel Land		✓	✓	✓			✓					4
SembMarine						✓	✓	✓	✓			4
UOB	✓	✓	✓	✓								4
UOL		✓	✓	✓						✓	✓	5
UIC		✓	✓	✓			✓			✓		5
SG Land		✓	✓	✓			✓			✓		5
OCBC	✓		✓	✓								3
F & N		✓	✓	✓			✓			✓	✓	6
CDL		✓	✓	✓				✓			✓	5
HLF	✓			✓							✓	3
GL				✓							✓	2
Wing Tai		✓	✓	✓			✓	✓			✓	6

Sources: Annual reports of companies.

often leads to the rise of several family lines. Each inherits different business lines and may develop them further (Tong and Yong 1998; Yeung 2003b). We will, however, not be going into a detailed analysis of this mega-group level, as there is insufficient data because of the inadequate disclosure of the business groups.

Table 10.2 summarizes the identified groups' principal activities and degree of diversification. The government-linked groups compete directly with private business groups in all activities except food and beverage. They apparently dominate activities in telecommunications and post and in transportation and engineering. Among the government-linked groups, all except NOL engage in three or more activities. Keppel Corporation is the most diversified group, being involved in eight sectors. Among the family-controlled business groups, all except GL engage in three or more activities. Both F&N and Wing Tai are the most diversified, each being involved in six sectors.

Several business groups have made it to international ranking. For example, five firms were on the Global 1,000 Listings (*Business Week* 2004) of the world's top companies by market value. They include SingTel (ranked 208), DBS (ranked 444), UOB (ranked 456), OCBC (ranked 599), and SIA (ranked 740). SIA, in particular, has been the "only Asian company outside of Japan to make *Fortune*'s 50 company 'All-Star' list' from 2002 to 2004" (Tsui-Auch 2005a). In the *Industry Week* 1000, which ranks manufacturing companies around the globe (*Industry Week* 2005), SPC, Keppel Corp., and F&N made it to the list in 2005.

10.3 THE SINGAPORE CONTEXT

10.3.1 Developmental state-led economic development till 1997

Prior to the self-government of Singapore in 1959, the ethnic Chinese business community had become an important economic and political force. However, the government attempted to forge a multi-ethnic and multicultural society after 1959, de-emphasizing the "Chineseness" of Singapore in response to the "internal ethnic imperatives as well as the regional geographical compulsions" (Vasil 1995: 34). The Western-educated ruling elites were wary of the ethnic business community, regarding the Chinese traders as rentiers who did not engage in real production (Low 2001a). Because of this distrust, and the lack of indigenous capital for industrial development as well as the small domestic economy, the government sought to rely on foreign capital for economic development and was not interested in assisting Chinese businesses for its industrialization effort.

Following the separation of Singapore from Malaysia in 1963, the government adopted a "two-legged" policy that relied on multinational corporations and government-linked corporations for industrialization (Rodan 1989). On the one hand, it used tax incentives to entice multinational corporations to establish manufacturing operations and hire local personnel. On the other, having been inspired by the Japanese horizontal corporate groups and Korean *chaebol,* the government created large government-linked corporate groups and statutory boards both for national-security objectives and to spearhead development in other sectors such as finance, air travel, and telecommunications. The state continued to stage mergers and acquisitions among government-linked corporations to form "national champions" to compete in the global economy (Yeung 2000). In early 1997, before the Asian currency crisis, for example, NOL, the national shipping line, obtained a fund of S$824 million from Temasek Holdings and Government of Singapore Investment Corporation, two major investment arms of the state, to support its acquisition of American President Lines (USA), which turned out to be the largest foreign acquisition by the Singaporean firm. The acquisition was also waived by SGX to obtain shareholders' approval.

Although the state was generally not attentive to the interests of ethnic Chinese firms, it did pay some heed to the family-controlled banks, because these enterprises facilitated the import/export trade, and their owners had close working and personal relationships with political leaders (Hamilton-Hart 2000; Low 2001a). Several former and current ministers and top civil servants in fact have served as chairmen and directors in local banks (Loh et al. 2000; Yeung 2003a). The local banks were protected by the Monetary Authority of Singapore (MAS), as no new licenses for full and restricted banks had been granted since 1970 and 1983 respectively (Yeung 2003b).

While the Singaporean state has consistently used inward FDI as a key policy instrument to develop its economy, its policy toward outward FDI has changed over time. Till the late 1970s, it encouraged the relocation of labor-intensive production to nearby lower-wage countries that benefited from quota-free entry into major Western markets under the Multi-Fibre Agreement. After the 1980s, the state identified outward FDI and the development of offshore opportunities as a long-term solution to the nation's small domestic economy. Hence, it devised a regionalization strategy to develop industrial estates in Indonesia, Vietnam, China, and India, and steered the regional expansion especially through the government-linked corporations (Pereira 2005).

10.3.2 Re-regulation by the Singaporean state after 1997

Singapore survived the Asian currency crisis in remarkably good shape. However, the business groups were negatively affected by the devastated property sector, economic slowdown, and the political and economic changes in the South East Asian countries, as many of them were involved in webs of regional business networks.

The crisis activated the institutional capacities of the developmental state to re-regulate the economy (Yeung 2000). It urged domestic firms to undertake global rather than regional expansion strategies, thus moving beyond the crisis-ridden South East Asian region to the USA, Europe, and Middle East for overseas investment (Yeung 2003a). In addition, it announced the first corporate governance code in 2001 and offered the revised version in 2005, which recommended, among others, an inclusion of independent directors for at least one-third of the board and the separation of the roles of chairperson and CEO.

The state continued to exert pressure on domestic firms to restructure. On the one hand, it encouraged more mergers and acquisitions to form "national champions" in order to strengthen their organizational capabilities and competitive advantages (Yeung 2000). On the other hand, it attempted to divest the non-core assets of government-linked groups in light of the financial debacles of the Japanese horizontal corporate groups and Korean *chaebol*, and the need to raise funds for further foreign acquisitions and to create new investment opportunities for the domestic private sector (Low 2001b; US Embassy of Singapore 2001).

The economic restructuring policy was sector specific. In the liberalization program for the banking sector in 1999, the government removed the foreign shareholding limit of 40 percent for local banks to allow foreign banks to compete freely with local banks (Low 2001a) and announced plans to issue six full bank licenses to foreign banks by 2001. The long-term impact of the liberalization was to foster mergers and acquisitions, a consolidation process to achieve economies of scale for the survival and growth of the sector. To reduce the risk of a bubble economy built on speculation and to avoid a bank-induced crisis, the MAS began a close monitoring of the banks' performance, and demanded that banks divest non-financial activities by July 17, 2004, although it eventually postponed the deadline to three years thereafter. To discourage controlling families' rule over local banks, the MAS imposed the Banking Corporate Governance Regulations in 2005, which are more stringent than the corporate governance codes.

10.4 BUSINESS GROUPS: EMERGENCE, GROWTH, AND CHANGE

10.4.1 Government-linked groups

10.4.1.1 *Emergence and growth prior to 1997*

Temasek Holdings was founded in 1974 to manage the state's investments in government-linked corporations. For sectoral- or national-security reasons, the Ministry of Finance holds special shares in Temasek Holdings' subsidiaries, including SIA and SingTel. In these first-tier subsidiaries, Temasek Holdings not only proposed broad strategies but also appointed former politicians, civil servants, and high-ranking military officials to positions of chairmen, directors, and senior management (Low

2001b). For example, the DBS was perceived as "an institution run along civil service lines" before the Asian currency crisis (*Business Times* 2005). Nevertheless, these appointed managers and directors were appraised and compensated based on the standards of the private-sector organizations. The state's strategy to entice multinational corporations led to the presence of a critical mass of professionally managed corporations that enhanced organizational imitation of the managerial enterprise, including the professionalization of management.

In line with the economic policy of the state for regional diversification, the Temasek Holdings and the Keppel group took advantage of the incentives offered by various state agencies to spearhead the process of penetrating the South East Asian markets and the newly opened China market in the early 1980s (Pereira 2005). What was particularly ambitious was that Keppel led a consortium of nineteen Singaporean firms to establish a joint venture with the local government in China to develop the Suzhou industrial park in 1994. However, the high level of government involvement (through equity ownership and policy-making, involving twenty statutory boards) seems to have hampered the development. In contrast, the Wuxi-Singapore Industrial Park, which was established in the same period of time and which involved a low level of government involvement, succeeded as a commercial venture (Yeung 2000).

The government-linked corporations' contribution to economic development was a subject of debate. They certainly catalyzed Singapore's economic success and created employment. Temasek-affiliated firms enjoyed some of the best credit ratings in Asia because of their strong cash flow generated from their dominance in the local market and conservative financial policies (Goldstein and Pananond 2008). However, critics asserted that (1) these corporations tended to be risk averse; (2) they received special privileges because of their links to the government; (3) they used capital less efficiently than did private firms; (4) they crowded out private investment and usurped entrepreneurial activity; and (5) their unrelated diversification made them "jacks of all trades, but masters of none" (US Embassy of Singapore 2001; Worthington 2003). For example, Keppel Corp. grew from a modest establishment of Keppel Shipyard Pte Ltd in 1968 into one of the most widely diversified industrial conglomerates in Singapore, which included 9 public-listed companies and over 140 active subsidiaries by the early 1990s (Dicken and Yeung 1999). The government began to encourage the highly diversified groups to divest their non-core holdings only after it became clear that they provided less potential long-term shareholder value than did the less diversified groups.

10.4.1.2 *Merger, divestment, and international diversification*

In line with the government's policy, the government-linked groups prompted the pace of mergers and acquisitions. For example, the DBS and the Post Office of Singapore Bank (POSB) announced a merger in 1998. Being able to tap into deposit-rich POSB, the DBS aimed to become a regional bank with a global presence. The acquisitions that the DBS subsequently made in Indonesia, Thailand, and Hong Kong were seen as the state's wish to create an HSBC (Hong Kong-based global player) in Singapore (Yeung 2003b).

In the Temasek Charter (2002), the government announced that it would divest its holdings in government-linked corporations if these businesses were "no longer strategic to Singapore or when viable market alternatives or regulatory frameworks are in place." However, some divestments appeared to be internal shuffling among the government-linked groups. For instance, the DBS group sold its stake in equity investments and some properties, notably, the DBS Land. However, the DBS Land was acquired by Pidemco, a subsidiary of the Singapore Technologies group, another government-owned holding company, and was later renamed Capital Land (US Embassy of Singapore 2001). Another example is that DBS Bank sold its subsidiary, DBS (China) Investment, to Temasek's Edgefield Investments (*Straits Times* 2008).

Temasek Holdings aimed to help develop its first-tier subsidiaries such as DBS, SIA, SingTel, and NOL into leading international businesses. The Temasek group's 2004 report, the first ever, revealed that it had spent S$3.3 billion on acquisitions in thirty-five countries over the previous two years. Out of the seven groups that disclosed the information on the locations of their subsidiaries, five had increased their penetration beyond Asia and two had decreased their presence beyond the region. In particular, three of them (NOL, SingTel, and SPC) had a majority of subsidiaries located outside Asia as of 2006 (see Table 10.3).

Table 10.3 Percentage of subsidiaries of business groups that operated outside Asia out of the total number of subsidiaries, 1997 and 2006

Types of business groups	Names of business groups	1997 (%)	2006 (%)
Government-linked corporations	DBS	2.94	28.89
	SingTel	20.41	54.55
	SIA	10.53	9.09
	NOL	46.73	66.67
	SPC	N.A	50.00
	Keppel Corp.	11.02	11.98
	Keppel Land	6.67	3.57
	SembMarine	0.00	12.82
Family-controlled corporations	UOB	10.14	13.04
	UOL	37.14	13.04
	UIC	2.08	0
	SG Land	N.A	0
	OCBC	5.97	5.13*
	F&N	2.08	21.65
	CDL	5.26	42.67
	HLF	0	N.A
	GL	4.35	7.87
	Wing Tai	1.96	0

The figure is calculated based on OCBC's annual report of 2005 because there was insufficient information in that of 2006.

Note: N.A. = Not available, because of a lack of information stated in the annual reports.

In some cases, however, acquisitions proved to be costly, reflecting the limited knowledge of new markets among the managers in the government-linked groups. Under pressure for rapid acquisitions, some government-linked corporations purchased foreign assets at a considerable premium—for example, in the case of SingTel's acquisitions of Optus, Australia's second largest telecom operator. Air New Zealand, in which SIA bought a 25 percent stake in order to penetrate the Australian market via Ansett, its Australian subsidiary, is another example. Ansett went bankrupt in 2001, leaving Temasek Holdings to write off the investment (Goldstein and Pananond 2008).

At worst, Temasek Holdings and its government-linked corporations' acquisitions drew resistance from various countries because of its ownership structure. For instance, SingTel's failure to acquire Cable & Wireless of Hong Kong Telecom was attributed primarily to China's reluctance to permit a Singaporean entity to control its telecom assets (see Jayasankaran 2001; Mauzy and Milne 2002), given the ownership and management links between SingTel, the government, and the political (Lee) family in Singapore (Yeung 2003b). In 2005, the Indian authority rejected a joint bid by a Temasek unit, Singapore Technologies Telemesia, and Telekom Malaysia for a stake of 48 percent of a mobile phone operator. The reason given was that SingTel, a subsidiary of Temasek, already held a stake in another telecommunications venture, and Indian laws forbid the same group to hold two mobile licenses in the same region (Straits Times 2006a).

In particular, Temasek Holdings' purchase of a controlling stake in Thailand's Shin Corp., which was owned by the family of the country's then Prime Minister, provoked a deep political crisis that subsequently gave rise to the military coup of September 2006. That Thailand's strategic industry was sold to a firm that was wholly owned by a foreign government incensed the opposition. The events that unfolded after the coup led to many setbacks for Temasek's presence in Thailand. The Shin's share price fell significantly, reportedly resulting in paper losses for Temasek of almost US$680 million as of November 2006 (Arnold 2006). Further, Temasek's 2007 financial report showed a 31 percent fall in net profit that was "due partly to the 'impairment charge' to reduce its investment value in Shin Corp" (Goldstein and Pananond 2008). Hence, Temasek paid heavy prices for its attempt to acquire Shin Corp.

In another incident, Temasek Holding was accused by an Indonesian competition watchdog in 2007 for violating anti-monopoly laws because of its indirect stakes in two top telecommunications companies in the country. Indonesian law forbids a business group from owning majority stakes in multiple companies within a sector that will have a combined market share of over 50 percent. Although Temasek's subsidiaries, SingTel and ST Telemedia, owned less than 50 percent of each of the two companies, Temasek, through its control of the two subsidiaries, was seen as effectively owning the majority stake in these two companies in the same sector. Essentially, the watchdog viewed Temasek and its subsidiaries as constituting a "Temasek Business Group", which is a single entity (Straits Times 2007a). A member of the parliamentary commission on foreign affairs described its control over the two top Indonesian telecommunications companies as the "onslaught of capitalist alliances," reflecting an attempt to monopolize strategic sectors of the Indonesian economy. The vice president of the country urged Temasek to admit to violation of the country's anti-monopoly laws (*Straits Times* 2007c).

Government-linked corporations had an advantage when they attempted to enter foreign markets especially through acquisitions, because they could expect financial assistance from the government. However, at times they were hampered by the relative lack of experience in operating in foreign countries and by the ownership structure. Evidently, they were at a relatively early stage of overseas expansion and were yet to acquire sufficient knowledge and experience to succeed in foreign business. This also happened with firms from other countries; for example, Japanese electronics and automotive firms faced local political resistance in the USA during the 1970s and 1980s with their substantial increase in exports to that market. They eventually overcame the resistance by shifting their manufacturing facilities to the USA and by being more politically sensitive. Managers of government-linked corporations were able to learn from such experiences and thus improve their skills when operating in foreign countries. However, the Singaporean political culture, which is shaped by a one-party state without credible opposition parties (Worthington 2003; Gourevitch and Shinn 2005), tends to make managers of government-linked corporations less sensitive toward political resistance in host countries. In addition, as compared to the Japanese private-sector companies, Singaporean government-linked corporations were hampered by the government ownership, which often aroused suspicion from foreign government and their nationals.

Table 10.4 Equity holding in the business group's core company by the largest block shareholder, 1997 and 2006

Types of business groups	Core companies	1997 (%)	2006 (%)
Government-linked corporations	DBS	40.45	28.08
	SingTel	82.17	56.50
	SIA	54.32	56.67
	NOL	33.35	68.21
	SPC	61.75	44.97
	Keppel Corp.	33.03	21.92
	Keppel Land	58.34	53.33
	SembMarine	59.82	62.04
Family-controlled corporations	UOB	31.65	21.82
	UOL	40.02	28.31
	UIC	26.85	26.91
	SG Land	56.47	72.42
	OCBC	40.47	19.29
	F&N	25.64	22.06
	CDL	48.44	48.62
	HLF	54.65	47.04
	GL	57.49	72.78
	Wing Tai	42.20	39.69

Source: Compiled from annual reports of companies.

10.4.1.3 *Changes in ownership and corporate governance reform*

The state had attempted to reduce its role in government-linked corporations even before the Asian economic crisis began. The results of this effort, however, were mixed. As shown in Table 10.4, the government's stake in five out of the eight government-linked corporations decreased (especially in the DBS and SingTel). However, its stake in three of them increased, especially in NOL.

Government-linked corporation groups have modified the corporate governance structures. As the government-linked corporations are increasingly commercially driven and involved in joint ventures with private-sector firms, they have reduced their recruitment of directors of the board and top management personnel from the civil-service sector and increased that from the corporate sector. As shown in Table 10.5, there was an increase in the proportion of independent, outside directors in five out of seven government-linked corporations (which disclosed a sufficient clarity on the backgrounds of directors in their annual reports for our analysis). Two companies, SingTel and Keppel Corp., made drastic changes in board structure. The board of SingTel in 1997 had no outside director at all; it was composed of internally

Table 10.5 Percentage of outside directors on the board of the core companies of the business groups, 1997 and 2006

Types of business groups	Core companies	1997 (%)	2006 (%)
Government-linked corporations	DBS	10	8
	SingTel	0	45
	SIA	10	30
	NOL	38	54
	SPC	13	33
	Keppel Corp.	0	27
	Keppel Land	20	8
	SembMarine	N.A.	44
Family-controlled corporations	UOB	22	30
	UOL	0	0
	UIC	25	N.A.
	SG Land	14	7
	OCBC	11	21
	F&N	25	40
	CDL	18	0
	HLF	8	40
	GuocoLand	50	29
	Wing Tai	33	18

Notes: In the case of NOL, information on the backgrounds of three out of ten directors was insufficiently stated and hence we take into account only eight directors. For the same reason, we take into account only eight out of eleven directors in the case of SPC. N.A. = Not available, because of a lack of information on the majority of directors (five out of nine directors are unknown).

Source: Based on annual reports of companies and media reports.

Table 10.6 Identities of board chair/president, CEOs/managing directors in government-linked corporations, 1997 and 2006

Core companies	Board chair/president		CEO/MD	
	1997	2006	1997	2006
DBS	G	G	G	P
SingTel	G	P	G	G
SIA	G	G	G	G
NOL	G	G	G	P
SPC	N.A.	G	N.A.	G
Keppel Corp.	G	G	G	G
Keppel Land	G	G	G	G
SembMarine	G	G	G	G

Notes: G = government-linked (serving in government-linked corporations, statutory boards, civil service, army, or as members of the parliament and ministers. P = Private sector. N.A. = Not available, because of insufficient data to determine the backgrounds of the personnel.

Source: Based on annual reports of companies and media reports.

groomed insiders who constituted 80 percent of the board, one member of the parliament, one ex-military personnel, and a director of Temasek Holdings. As of 2006, however, outside directors accounted for 45 percent of the board of directors of SingTel. Keppel Corp. had no outside director on board in 1997 but increased the representation of outside directors to 27 percent in 2006. Out of the six government-linked corporations that increased the outsider representation, however, only NOL reached the Anglo-American standard of having the majority of the board members as independent outside directors. Nevertheless, the control by the government of the company remained substantial, given that its ownership increased to over 68 percent.

While the ratio of outside directors had increased in many government-linked corporations, a high level of state control can be seen in the government representation in the leadership echelon. As shown in Table 10.6, few board chairs, presidents, CEOs, and managing directors came from the private sector. Nevertheless, one significant change that can be detected is that the government-linked corporations that had not made a separation of the roles of chair and CEO in 1997 (such as DBS, SingTel, SPC, and Keppel Land) eventually did so in 2006, which is in line with the recommendation in the Singapore corporate governance codes.

10.4.2 Family-controlled business groups

10.4.2.1 *Emergence and growth till 1997*

Family-controlled business groups emerged from smaller, private companies that were founded by immigrants and run by their family members across generations. For example, the UOB, the largest family-controlled group by total assets in the country in 2006, was founded in 1935 as the United Chinese Bank (which it was called until 1965) by Wee Kheng Chiang and a group of fellow Chinese businessmen. In 1974 Wee Kheng Chiang's son Wee Cho Yaw took over the baton and still continued to serve as the bank's Chairman and CEO in 2006. The bank expanded through the acquisition of other banks and non-financial assets. The OCBC, which was the second largest family-controlled group by total assets in 2006, was incorporated as a limited company in 1932 as a result of the merger of three local Hokkien family banks. Lee Kong Chian, the largest shareholder (and chairman from 1938 to 1965), later passed the baton to his son Lee Seng Wee, who served as chairman from 1995 to 2003. The OCBC acquired numerous commercial and industrial concerns in Singapore and the region to form a highly diversified conglomerate that resembles the Japanese horizontal corporate group with cross-ownership among its associated companies and subsidiaries.

The family-controlled business groups had a long history of regionalizing their operations even before the state's regionalization drive. Economically, they engaged in sectors that promised relatively quick returns on investment such as property development, finance, and trading. Culturally, they found it advantageous to tap into the existing ethnic business (or "bamboo") networks in the region (Tsui-Auch 2005b). CDL, which has diversified beyond Asia, represents an exception. The celebrated Singaporean entrepreneur Kwek Leng Beng, the owner of the Hong Leong group, bought his first London hotel, The Gloucester, in 1992, and the CDL group under his stable invested in Britain's Copthorne chain of seventeen hotels in 1995 (Yeung 2003b).

The family-controlled business groups have increased their reliance on stock markets for financing their expansion since the 1960s. The founding family sought to control the public-listed companies through an associated bank, financial company, or holding company, and consequently the layers of ownership structure obscure the family's control of the company. Raising capital in (international) financial markets, however, requires them to be more transparent in the governance and financial control systems (Brown 2000). This prompted the professionalization of management. Further, because of their distanced relationship from the state capital, Chinese businesses (except the banks) were left to fend for themselves, which averted the tradition of cronyism and patronage politics in government–business relations (Low 2001a). Often, because of their distanced relationship from the state, they needed to gain legitimacy in the eyes of the regulatory authorities and the public, and hence tended to take the state imperative for professionalism seriously.

Nevertheless, the business families maintained family control through direct and indirect ownership, occupying top management positions, and grooming sons to succeed the founding patriarchs. This strategy of maintaining family control and corporate rule over generations while co-opting outside management talent resembles that of government-linked corporations. Government-linked corporations also recruited outside management talent, but maintained corporate control and rule in the hands of the closely knit political elite (Tsui-Auch and Lee 2003).

Companies within a family-controlled business group are interlocked in complex formal and informal relationships, including cross-holdings and interlocking directorates (see Figs. 10.2 and 10.3), and conduct intra-group trade, capital, technology,

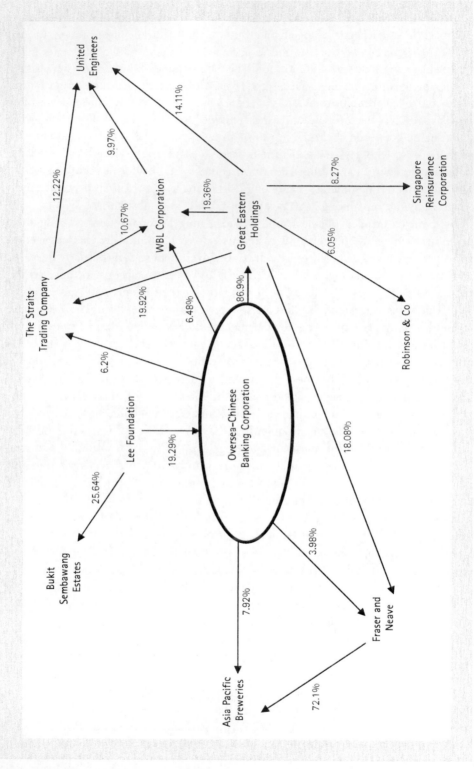

Figure 10.2 Cross-ownership within the OCBC group, 2006

Source: Compiled from annual reports of companies.

	OCBC	F&N	WBL	The Straits Trading Company	Asia Pacific Breweries	United Engineers	Singapore Reinsurance Corporation	Robinson And Co.	Bukit Sembawang Estates	Great Eastern Holding (Listed only in the year 2000)
OCBC	■	-	-	-	-	-	-	-	-	-
F&N	1	■	-	-	-	-	-	-	-	-
WBL	2	0	■	-	-	-	-	-	-	-
The Straits Trading Company	0	0	1	■	-	-	-	-	-	-
Asia Pacific Breweries	0	1	0	0	■	-	-	-	-	-
United Engineers	0	0	1	1	0	■	-	-	-	-
Singapore Reinsurance Corporation	0	0	0	0	0	0	■	-	-	-
Robinson and Co.	1	0	2	1	0	0	0	■	-	-
Bukit Sembawang Estates	1	0	1	1	0	0	1	0	■	-
Great Eastern Holding (Listed only in the year 2000)	5	1	1	2	0	0	1	1	2	■

Figure 10.3 Interlocking directorates within a family-controlled business group: OCBC, 2006

Source: Compiled from annual reports of companies.

and personnel transfers (Loh et al. 2000). Interlocking directorates, which manifest a modern form of maintaining personal relationships, have replaced traditional information networks and performed the function of coordination and control in the market place (Zang 1999).

10.4.2.2 *Merger, divestment, and international diversification*

The local banking groups experienced the greatest organizational change as a result of the liberalization policy that brought about stiff foreign competition in the domestic market. The other large family-controlled banks swiftly modeled after DBS (which merged with the state-owned Post Office of Singapore Bank) engaging in mergers and acquisitions to achieve economies of scale for further growth and expansion. The OCBC acquired Keppel–TatLee Bank (previously owned by the government-linked Keppel Group), and United Overseas Bank made a friendly takeover of the Overseas Union Bank.

In addition, the tightly state-regulated banks were subjected to government pressure to divest their non-core activities not related to banking. The overcapitalized UOB group and OCBC group untangled cross-shareholdings with affiliated non-banking companies by meeting the limit of 10 percent of the equity holding in these companies by July 17 2007. They claimed to have completed the divestment.

However, the banks and other private-sector business groups have made only limited forays outside Asia. As seen in Table 10.3, four out of the eight groups that disclosed sufficient data on diversification in both years increased their geographical diversification beyond Asia, and another four actually reduced their international reach. Although the government urged its domestic firms to move away from the crisis-ridden South East Asian region, the crisis opened windows of opportunities for them to strengthen their regional business networks and alliances with local and foreign firms. Clearly, Asia remains the most important region for their cross-border investments. Even within the group controlled by the Kwek family, a large proportion of its investments (with the exception of CDL) was located in Singapore and Malaysia because of the historical legacy of the founders' families and the accompanying cultural advantages (Yeung 2003b).

10.4.2.3 *Changes in ownership and corporate governance reform*

Family ownership decreased in six main firms of the private business groups, but such ownership increased in the four others (see Table 10.4). Nevertheless, as of 2006, only four out of nine companies that reported sufficient background information of directors increased the outsider representation on the board, but four reduced such representation and one remained unchanged (Table 10.5). Two companies had no outsider on board and none of the family-controlled firms had a majority of outside directors. In addition, only a few of the most senior posts came from the external labor market (see Table 10.7). Especially in the business groups controlled by the Wee family and the Kwek family, the family members occupied the most senior posts and represented the family interests on the board. In 1997 five main companies (UOB,

Table 10.7 Relationships of board chair/president, CEOs/managing directors to the controlling families of the private business groups, 1997 and 2006

Core companies	Chairman		CEO/MD	
	1997	2006	1997	2006
UOB	F	F	F	F
UOL	F	F	L	L
UIC	F	F	L	L
SG Land	F	F	L	L
OCBC	F	L	F	E
F&N	L	L	N.A.	E
CDL	F	F	F	F
HLF	F	F	F	F
GuocoLand	L	L	F	F
Wing Tai	F	F	F	F

Notes: F=family members; E=recruited from external labour market; L=long-time associate; N.A.=Not available, because of insufficient data about the backgrounds of personnel.

CDL, HLF, Wing Tai, and OCBC) did not have a separation of roles between CEO and president. In 2006 only OCBC separated the roles, with both roles taken over by professional managers.

The chairperson cum CEO of the UOB, Wee Cho Yaw, advocated his ideal model: "family control with professional management, where the former provides the direction and the latter, the expertise." He said: "To be honest, to leave a company totally to professional management, I have my reservations" (*Straits Times* 2006b).

The infusion of professional managers into the family-controlled groups has not always proceeded smoothly. At OCBC, the elderly directors of the board who voted with the founding family stepped down in 2000. OCBC hired Alex Au, a former Hong Kong banker, as CEO in 1999. Yet Au appeared to lack the board of directors' support on strategic issues and resigned abruptly in 2002. Several banking analysts suspected that Au resigned because Lee Seng Wee (the chairperson and the largest shareholder) took a hands-on approach in strategic issues.

The insistence on family control, however, ultimately depends on the availability of family members to succeed the business. For example, the OCBC, unlike the UOB, has no successor from the family. After the resignation of Alex Au, the Lee family relinquished the post of CEO to another expatriate manager. Further, Lee Seng Wee stepped down as the chairman of OCBC and shifted from executive to non-executive director in 2003. The chairperson's post was then handed over to an outsider. Hence, without competent successors from the family, even the family-controlled groups have had to rely on talents from the external labor market.

10.5 CONCLUSIONS

A comparison of the government-linked and family-controlled groups paves the way for an analysis of the competitive capabilities and constraints of these business groups in this section.

As compared to many state-owned enterprises elsewhere, the government-linked corporations in Singapore have generally been recognized to be well managed because they are run like private-sector businesses, with a focus on bottom-line performance (Singh and Ang 1998; US Embassy of Singapore 2001). Their performance is much debated, however, as some argue that it is comparable to that of their counterparts in the private sector (Sun 2002), while others assert it is below that of their counterparts (Webb and Saywell 2002). Few companies, with the exception of SIA, have rewarded its shareholders well. From 1997 to 2006, for example, Temasek's had average shareholder returns of 8 percent a year, against 9.3 percent for the Straits Times Index (*Financial Times* 2007).

The state serves as both an enabling mechanism and a constraint to the growth of government-linked groups (Dicken and Yeung 1999). On the one hand, strong relationships with the government brought financial privileges and useful information on policy directions. On the other, the government-linked label and experience also hampered their growth. Government-linked corporations, which used to operate in the highly regulated sectors of industries with national strategic concerns, naturally ventured into similar industries through their international expansion. Thus, they inevitably induced hostility from host-country governments and nationals (for example, in China, Australia, Thailand, and Indonesia), as those government were concerned that their strategic industries might fall into the hands of a foreign government, the ultimate owner of the government-linked corporations.

Because of the persistently high level of state ownership in the government-linked companies and the relatively low proportion of outside directors on their boards, the Singaporean government's claim that it had relinquished its control over the government-linked corporations did not necessarily convince foreign governments and nationals. Although the government-linked corporations claimed that they are run on business principles, they were ultimately accountable to their major shareholder, the Temasek Holdings, which was in turn owned by the Ministry of Finance. Further, because of its status as a private limited company, the Temasek Holdings was not required to make its accounts of operations public. The insufficient degree of transparency on decisions and operations further reinforced the suspicions of local partners, government, and nationals in host countries (Yeung 2003b).

In addition, managers of Temasek Holdings and its subsidiaries did not seem to be properly trained to navigate the political economy of emerging markets, although many of them were as well qualified in terms of their formal education (for example, with an MBA) as the managers in the private-sector firms. The failure of the Suzhou industrial park in China in the 1990s demonstrates that Temasek companies that had done remarkably well in Singapore were incapable of managing their Chinese investments. These government-linked corporations, which were so used to a contractual business culture in Singapore, proved to be excessively formalistic in China's emerging business community (Kumar et al. 2005) and failed to navigate the complex system in which interpersonal *guanxi* played an important role. However, the family-controlled businesses in Singapore used to rely on interpersonal *guanxi* for commercial transactions and could handle *guanxi* better than the government-linked corporations (Yeung 2003b). In the controversial 2007 deals in Thailand and Indonesia, the managers of Temasek Holdings failed to detect the hostility of the nationals in a country where political democratization reforms were advancing in parallel with growing affluence. Learning from the blunder in Indonesia, Temasek Holdings announced the adoption of a "three-pronged strategy to meet the challenge posed by the rising tide of nationalism," which included avoiding investment in "iconic" companies, tying up with local partners, and seeking minority stakes (*Straits Times* 2007c). Whether they will enact these strategies remains to be seen. It is likely that future investments of government-linked corporations in Thailand and Indonesia will be subjected to tight scrutiny and that the search for local partners will be challenging.

Even though government-linked corporations such as NOL and SingTel have expanded in terms of size and geographical extent, it is questionable whether their operations are functionally integrated, because they run their foreign operations as independent entities. This may reflect their choice of expansion strategy—namely, unrelated diversification, which does not require high degrees of functional integration or transfer of core competencies between business units, as the strategy of related diversification requires, but manages independent units through financial control (Hoskisson and Hitt 1988). This strategic choice might be reasonable, given the relative lack of operating experience in overseas markets of these corporations at the early stage of overseas expansion. Although investors who seek financial returns do not usually favor unrelated diversification, because theory says that such a strategy is often value destroying (Amihud and Lev 1981; Berger and Ofek 1995), government-linked corporations can afford to do so because of their dominant positions in the domestic market. The management of government-linked corporations can be less accountable to other shareholders, which allows them to pursue unrelated diversification. Further, they may be pursuing unrelated diversification overseas in order to expand markets for their various businesses because of the limited growth opportunities in the domestic market. In fact, some commentators have pointed out that government-linked corporations would be tempted to expand overseas so as to avoid divestment (Goldstein and Pananond 2008), which eventually defeats one of the state policies.

The fundamental belief that government-linked corporations are instruments for nation-building and safeguards of national security is likely to inhibit their full divestment (Webb and Saywell 2002). This belief is reinforced by the continued recruitment of ex-civil servants into board and senior management positions, though to a lesser extent. These personnel, who tend to be risk adverse, are likely to resist divestment and greater competition from the private sector (US Embassy of Singapore 2001; Saywell and Plott 2002). Further, the government, as the largest shareholder, has relative autonomy to ignore market pressures from institutional investors to divest its equity in these corporations. Even among those that shed non-core assets, such divestment may not be genuine, as the asset could be sold to another government-linked corporation that was under the state's ownership control, as shown in the DBS's sale of DBS Land to a subsidiary of Singapore Technologies (US Embassy of Singapore 2001).

Unlike the government-linked corporations, which received financial privileges from the state, many private-sector groups started off as small- and medium-sized enterprises. Despite the visible hand of the Singaporean state, the private sector has maintained much of its entrepreneurial drive. In fact, the early move of Kwek Leng Beng to acquire British hotels was followed by a wave of Singaporean acquisitions of European hotels both by private-sector firms and by government-linked corporations. Nevertheless, the high degree of international diversification of CDL was an exception even within the business group controlled by the Kwek family. Indeed, regionalization strategy is still preferred because of geographical proximity and cultural advantages. Their capabilities in network formation and exploitation in Asia endowed them with a competitive advantage over Western firms in the region and hence it does not make economic sense to give up privileged access to markets and information in Asia. Moreover, the challenges to build and maintain a direct presence outside Asia are tremendous, and the difficulty to transplant their business networks is immense, as shown in the initial difficulties of Japanese firms in the West (Hu 1995). As compared to the government-linked corporations, the private-sectors groups have had lower pressure and less support for diversification beyond Asia.

To finance the expansion, family-controlled firms listed their companies in the stock exchanges in Singapore or elsewhere. They adapted to the listing requirements including governance and auditing. They adopted professional management even before the Asian currency crisis, with outside managers providing the expertise and the controlling families providing the strategic directions. To facilitate the coordination of the loosely connected business empires and to balance the conflicting interests, the controlling families relied on the holding company structure and maintained control through cross-ownership and interlocking directorate. As compared to the government-linked groups, private-sector business groups (and banks, to a lesser extent) are freer to disregard government pressure, both in theory and in practice, for recruiting a higher proportion of independent directors. This freedom is perhaps reflected in a lower percentage of private-sector firms showing an increase in outsider representation than the government-linked corporations.

Despite the normative pressures for the professionalization of corporate governance and management, both family-controlled groups and government-linked groups have maintained significant ownership of and control over their enterprises. This reflects embeddedness in the norms of trusting insiders and cultural preferences for control (Tsui-Auch 2004; Tsui-Auch 2005a). Nevertheless, with the rise of mainland China as both a competitor and a new market, ethnic Chinese family-controlled groups have increasingly expanded their operations to China. Externally, they have increasingly turned to international financial markets to secure access to capital to fund their internationalization efforts. Internally, they are undergoing organizational transformations through professionalization of management and governance (Yeung 2006). Brown (2000: 27) succinctly commented: "Effectively combining centralized decision-making with functional divisions and geographical dispersal was a key problem. Chinese companies needed greater power-sharing..." To sustain the organizational and strategic changes, the business groups will need fresh perspectives and resources beyond those offered by trusted insiders, regional network ties, and traditional business activities. They have few alternatives but to loosen their control, though this is likely to be at an incremental pace.

REFERENCES

AMIHUD, Y., and LEV, B. (1981). "Risk Reduction as a Managerial Motive for Conglomerate Mergers," *Bell Journal of Economics*, 12/2: 605–17.

ARNOLD, W. (2006). "Bangkok Insists Phone Deal Broke Law," *International Herald Tribune*, Nov. 16.

BERGER, P. G., and OFEK, E. (1995). "Diversification's Effect on Firm Value," *Journal of Financial Economics*, 37/1: 39–65.

BIGGART, N. W. (1991). "Explaining Asian Economic Organization: Toward a Weberian Institutional Perspective," *Theory and Society*, 20: 199–232.

BROWN, R. A. (2000). *Chinese Big Business and the Wealth of Asian Nations*. New York: Palgrave.

Business Times (2005). "Fock Siew Wah to Step Down from DBS Board," Apr. 1.

Business Week (2004). www.businessweek.com/magazine/content/04_30/b3893138.htm

CHUNG, C. N. (2001). "Markets, Culture, and Institutions: The Emergence of Large Business Groups in Taiwan, 1950s–1970s," *Journal of Management Studies*, 38: 719–45.

DICKEN, P., and YEUNG, H. W.-C. (1999). "Investing in the Future: East and Southeast Asian Firms in the Global Economy," in K. Olds et al. (eds.), *Globalization and the Asia-Pacific*. London: Routledge, 107–28.

Financial Times (2007). "Temasek Warns of Tougher Future," Aug. 3.

GOLDSTEIN, A., and PANANOND, P. (2008). "Singapore Inc. Goes Shopping Abroad: Profits and Pitfalls," *Journal of Contemporary Asia*, 38/3: 417–38.

GOUREVITCH, P., and SHINN, J. J. (2005). *Political Power and Corporate Control: The New Global Politics of Corporate Governance*. Princeton: Princeton University Press.

GRANOVETTER, M. (2005). "Business Groups and Social Organization," in N. Smelser and R. Swedberg (eds.), *Handbook of Economic Sociology*. Princeton: Princeton University Press, 429–50.

HAMILTON, G. G. (1997). "Organization and Market Processes in Taiwan's Capitalist Econmy," in M. Orrú, N. W. Biggart, and C. C. Hamilton (eds.), *The Economic Organization of East Asian Capitalism*. Thousand Oaks, CA, London, and New Delhi: Sage, 237–96.

HAMILTON-HART, N. (2000). "The Singapore State Revisited," *Pacific Review*, 13/2: 195–216.

HOSKISSON, R. E., and HITT, M. A. (1988). "Strategic Control Systems and Relative R&D Investment in Large Multiproduct Firms," *Strategic Management Journal*, 9: 605–21.

HU, Y.-S. (1995). "The International Transferability of the Firm's Advantages," *California Management Review*, 37/4: 73–88.

Industry Week (2005). www.industryweek.com

JAYASANKARAN, S. (2001). "Blueprint for an Asian Superbank," *Far Eastern Economic Review*, Mar. 29, 48–51.

KUMAR, S., SIDDIQUE, S., and WONG, Y. H. (2005). *Mind the Gaps: Singapore Business in China*. Singapore: Institute of Southeast Asian Studies.

LOH, G., GOH, C. B., and TAN, T. L. (2000). *Building Bridges, Carving Niches: An Enduring Legacy*. Singapore: Oxford University Press.

LOW, L. (2001a). *The Political Economy of Chinese Banking in Singapore*. Research Paper Series, No. 2001–015, Faculty of Business Administration, National University of Singapore.

LOW, L. (2001b). "The Singapore Developmental State in the New Economy and Polity," *Pacific Review*, 14/3: 411–41.

MAUZY, D. K., and MILNE, R. S. (2002). *Singapore Politics under the People's Action Party*. London and New York: Routledge.

Ministry of Finance (1993). *Interim Report of the Committee to Promote Enterprise Overseas*. Singapore: Singapore Government.

PEREIRA, A. (2005). "Singapore's Regionalization Strategy," *Journal of the Asia Pacific Economy*, 10/3: 380–96.

RODAN, G. (1989). *The Political Economy of Singapore's Industrialization: National State and International Capital*. Basingstoke: Macmillan.

SAYWELL, T., and PLOTT, D. (2002). "Re-Imaging Singapore," *Far Eastern Economic Review*, July 11, 44–7.

Singapore Department of Statistics (2001). *Contribution of Government-Linked Companies to Gross Domestic Product*. March. Singapore: Ministry of Trade and Industry.

SINGH, K., and ANG, S. H. (1998). "The Strategies and Success of Government-Linked Corporations in Singapore." Research Paper Series No. 98-06. National University of Singapore, Faculty of Business Administration.

Straits Times (2006a). "Perceived Govt Links don't Hinder Business: Temasek," Sept. 7, H22.

Straits Times (2006b). "UOB's Wee Cho Yaw Makes Case for Family-Run Businesses," Oct. 23, H19.

Straits Times (2007a). "Watchdog Needs to Explain Shift in Stance, Says Temasek," Nov. 21, H26.

Straits Times (2007b). "Temasek Must Follow Indonesian Laws, Says V-P Jusuf," Nov. 22, 25.

Straits Times (2007c). "Temasek's Strategy to Counter Nationalism," Nov. 23, 3.

Straits Times (2008). "DBS sells China Unit to Temasek for $44.5m," Mar. 6, H33.

SUN, Q. (2002). "The Performance of Singapore Government-Linked Companies," *Pulses*, Oct. 27–9. Singapore: Singapore Exchange.

Temasek Holdings Limited (2002). The Temasek Charter. www.temasekholdings.com.sg

TONG, C. K., and YONG, P. K. (1998). "*Guanxi, xinyong* and Chinese Business Networks," *British Journal of Sociology*, 49/1: 75–96.

Tsui-Auch, L. S. (2004). "The Professionally Managed Family-Ruled Business: Ethnic Chinese Business in Singapore," *Journal of Management Studies*, 41/4: 693–723.

Tsui-Auch, L. S. (2005a). "Singapore Business Group: The Role of the State and Capital in Singapore Inc.7," in S.-J. Chang (ed.), *Business Group in East Asia: Financial Crisis, Restructuring, and New Growth.* Oxford: Oxford University Press, 94–115.

Tsui-Auch, L. S. (2005b). "Unpacking Regional Ethnicity and the Strength of Ties in Shaping Ethnic Entrepreneurship," *Organization Studies*, 26/8: 1189–216.

Tsui-Auch, L. S. and Lee, Y.-J. (2003). "The State Matters: Management Models of Singaporean Chinese and Korean Business Groups," *Organizational Studies*, 24/4: 507–34.

US Embassy of Singapore (2001). "*Government-Linked Corporations Face the Future*," Mar. http://singapore.usembassy.gov/ep/2001/government-linkedcorporation2000.html

Vasil, R. (1995). *Asianising Singapore: The PAP's Management of Ethnicity.* Singapore: Heinemann Asia.

Webb, S., and Saywell, T. (2002). "Untangling Temasek," *Far Eastern Economic Review*, Nov. 7, 42–6.

Worthington, R. (2003). *Governance in Singapore.* New York: RoutledgeCurzon.

Yeung, H. W.-C. (2000). "State Intervention and Neoliberalism in the Globalizing World Economy: Lessons from Singapore's Regionalisation Programme," *Pacific Review*, 13/1: 133–62.

Yeung, H. W.-C. (2003a). "Managing Economic (In)security in the Global Economy: Institutional Capacity and Singapore's Developmental State." A revised paper presented at the conference on "Globalization and Economic Security in East Asia: Governance and Institutions," Sept. 11–12, Institution of Defence and Strategic Studies, Nanyang Technological University, Singapore.

Yeung, H. W.-C. (2003b). *Chinese Capitalism in a Global Era.* London: Routledge.

Yeung, H. W.-C. (2006). "Change and Continuity in Southeast Asian Ethnic Chinese Business," *Asia Pacific Journal of Management*, 23: 229–54.

Zang, X. (1999). "Personalism and Corporate Networks in Singapore," *Organization Studies*, 20/5: 861–77.

CHAPTER 11

....

BUSINESS GROUPS
IN INDIA

....

JAYATI SARKAR

11.1 INTRODUCTION

....

THE objective of the present chapter is to examine the evolution of family business groups in India, one of the fastest-growing emerging economics in recent times and a country where business groups have been an integral part of the economy ever since formal industrial activity took its roots in the country around the latter half of the nineteenth century. Going back in history, one finds that Indian business groups have originated and expanded under strikingly different institutional environments, during the colonial period dominated by British rule, the post-independence years when private-sector economic activity was regulated with an inbuilt bias against business groups, and finally during the increasingly liberalized and globalized policy environment since the 1990s. The chapter seeks to provide a historical overview of this process of evolution of Indian business groups in economic activity, focusing specifically on the dynamics underlying its persistence and resilience as a dominant organizational form despite significant changes in the institutional environment from time to time. In doing so, the chapter seeks to highlight, in light of the existing theoretical and empirical literature on business groups, important elements of their

I would like to thank the editors of this volume, Asli M. Colpan, Takashi Hikino, and James R. Lincoln, participants of the International Conference on Evolutionary Dynamics of Business Groups in Emerging Economies organized by Kyoto University and Doshisha University in November 2007 at Kyoto, and Subrata Sarkar for their helpful suggestions and comments. The usual disclaimer applies.

organizational structure, diversification strategies, their governance and performance, and finally on changes in their competitive capabilities, if any, over time.

The chapter is organized as follows. Section 11.2 examines the origins and early development of family business groups in India. Section 11.3 traces the evolution of the policy and institutional environment in which family groups have operated since the independence of India from British rule in 1947. Different elements of structure and strategy of business groups are discussed in a historical perspective in Sections 11.4, 11.5, and 11.6. The performance of group-affiliated firms vis-à-vis stand-alone firms is analyzed in Section 11.7 and Section 11.8 concludes the chapter.

11.2 INDIAN BUSINESS GROUPS: ORIGINS AND EARLY DEVELOPMENT

On the basis of several well-cited historical accounts on Indian business,[1] one can trace the beginnings of family-owned business groups in industrial activity to the second half of the nineteenth century.[2] Prior to this period, industrial activity was monopolized by European business houses, and the participation of Indians in business activities was confined essentially to trading and money-lending enterprises delineated by family, caste, and ethnicity. However, with increased British investment in industrial ventures in India, there was an unintended demonstration effect on Indian entrepreneurs, who were drawn by the opportunities created by a favorable business climate put in place essentially to serve British interests (Tripathi 2004).

The involvement of Indians in domestic industrial activity started in the textile industry with the setting-up of the Bombay Spinning and Weaving Company in July 1854 by Cowasji Nanabhai Davar, which was followed by the entry of a large number of textile mills promoted by other entrepreneurs. The beginnings of the first business group in India in the pre-independence era, the Tata group, can be traced to these textile mills. A few years later, the foundations of other major business groups such as the Khataus, Birlas, and Mafatlals were laid.

The genesis of family business groups in India lies in a combination of individual initiatives and entrepreneurial zeal in the Schumpeterian sense, the direct and indirect exposure of entrepreneurs to ideas and business developments in countries in the West, and changes in institutional conditions following the consolidation of

---

[1] For comprehensive historical accounts of Indian business groups, see, among others, Mehta (1955), Piramal and Herdeck (1986), Dutta (1997), and Tripathi (2004). The account in this section draws significantly from these sources.

[2] For a definition of Indian business groups, see Section 11.4.

British rule in India (Tripathi and Mehta 1990).[3] The motivation of business leaders to float new ventures, to expand and diversify, coupled with the role that family finance came to play in funding new projects, led to the evolution of the group structure over time. With an underdeveloped stock market and banking system, and the difficulty for Indian entrepreneurs to access other sources of cheap industrial finance purportedly because of obstacles set up by the British, most new industrial ventures during this time were floated and financed by individuals engaged in trade and commerce. The first round of industrial projects set off a chain reaction where surplus funds generated in these projects were reinvested to promote other industrial and finance activities. With a major source of finance originating within the family, the need to acquire formal ownership and control of the promoted companies logically followed. This was often accomplished through the incorporation of many of these ventures as joint stock companies where family members and acquaintances were issued shares. Thus, a group of companies, each with a distinct legal entity, became associated with a family that had either direct equity control (the "inner circle") or indirect control through companies that were under its direct control (the "outer circle") (Hazari 1966). This spawning process thereby led to the formation of the business group as an institution in India.

The consolidation of group firms under a single umbrella was further facilitated through the managing agency system. A family that promoted a company or group of companies also set up a managing agency firm, usually a proprietorship or a partnership comprising several family members, and entrusted it with managing the affairs of the companies under the family's control. In addition, a managing agency promoted other group companies by reinvesting the profits of existing concerns. This form of expansion set off a process of vertical and horizontal integration within a group that bypassed the hazards of market transactions and generated scale and scope economies (Mehta 1955). Finally, having a managing agency as part of a business group enabled the group to cope with a deficient managerial market in the early years of industrialization while ensuring family control over group affiliates.

The preceding account of the origins of family business groups in India conforms broadly to several of the formal definitions of business groups that exist in the literature. With family businesses in India being deeply rooted in the joint family structure and bound by relational contracts within the community with high degrees of trust and reciprocity (Encarnation 1989; Dutta 1997), these groups conform to the sociological perspective, which views business groups as a network of firms bound together through formal and informal ties identifiable along geographical, political, ethnic, kinship, and religious lines (Granovetter 1994, 1995). At the same time, Indian business groups can be understood from an economic perspective, which highlights groups as diversified structures with legally independent firms under common

---

[3] One such instance of "aggressive, rational and creative" dynamism is the foray of Indians in the cotton textile industry despite the absence of tariff protection from cheaper British imports (Morris 1967).

administrative and financial control, which often rests with a family (Chang and Hong 2002; Fisman and Khanna 2004). Finally, the dynamics of evolution of business groups in India can be understood from an institutionalist perspective, which sees a group as a diversified hybrid organizational structure that comes up in response to missing markets and weak institutions, combining the functions of both firms and markets (Leff 1978; Khanna and Palepu 2000a).

The forces that led to the emergence of business groups in India were also instrumental in charting its growth in the pre-independence period. It was a combination of entrepreneurial initiative, the growing self-identity among Indians and their need to achieve economic autonomy or *swadeshi*,[4] the expertise gained from managing existing industrial ventures, as well as exposure to modern ideas and education that became critical factors in the decision of business groups to expand and diversify during this period. While entrepreneurial capabilities as well as market opportunities generated the first push to invest in new ventures, the revenues generated and the experiences gained in managing such enterprises helped in the growth and sustenance of internal capital and labor markets, which, by enabling groups to overcome existing market imperfections, further fed into the growth process. Thus, it was an open-ended mutually enforcing mechanism that enabled Indian family groups to proliferate and dominate the industrial scene in the pre-independence period, to the extent that, during 1918–39, the share of Indian groups in capital employed more than doubled from 13 per cent to 34 per cent (Tripathi 2004), with three among the top four groups controlled by Indians (Hazari 1966).

11.3 EVOLUTION OF INSTITUTIONAL ENVIRONMENT: 1947–2006

The extensive literature on business groups has linked their relevance and functioning inextricably to the institutional environment in which these organizations operate. In India, the evolution of groups has taken place in the backdrop of significant changes in institutional environment from time to time. Three structural breaks can be identified in this respect. First is the evolution of groups since their inception in the late nineteenth century to 1947, when India gained independence from the British (Section 11.2 above); second is the post-independence period up to 1991, when the environment in which groups operated was extensively regulated by the government; and, finally, the post-1991 period, when structural reforms were initiated

---

[4] For further details, see, among others, Tripathi and Mehta (1990) and Tripathi (2004).

in 1991, ushering in a period of liberalization and globalization of the Indian economy.

The regulated regime was the outcome of the industrial policy framework adopted in the years following independence that accorded "commanding heights" to the public sector and only a residual role to the private sector in the country's developmental process. Consequently, private-sector activity was subjected to extensive state regulation that included a host of restrictions such as industrial and import licensing, locational restrictions, and regulations to curb the concentration of economic power. The government followed a policy of import substitution with infant industry protection, the underlying rationale being that domestic industrial capabilities can be effectively built up under protected markets.

As the private corporate sector including business groups strived to find their footing in an increasingly regulated environment, evidence accumulated on the ineffectiveness of the licensing regime in achieving the policy objective of growth with social justice (Marathe 1989). The first attempts at liberalization were made in the mid-1980s, but the momentum faltered in the late 1980s, with growing political resistance and the looming parliamentary elections in 1989. The economy began to slow down, and this state of affairs continued until June 1991, when India faced a severe foreign-exchange crisis. As a result, the Government of India turned to the International Monetary Fund (IMF) and the World Bank for financial assistance, and ensuing circumstances compelled the government to commit in July 1991 to a comprehensive and sustained structural reforms program that had as its core the liberalization of the industrial and trade policy regime.

Formalized in the detailed Statement on Industrial Policy of 1991, the new set of reforms involved both internal and external liberalization. Among the drastic changes that had implications for the private sector was the abolition of licensing for almost all industries in a phased manner and the removal of curbs placed on the expansion of large business houses under the Monopolies and Restrictive Trade Practices (MRTP) Act of 1969. As a result, business houses were now free to invest, expand and diversify, consistent with their capabilities. Simultaneously, initiatives were taken to encourage international competition through a more liberalized policy toward both inward- and outward-bound foreign direct investment, and by reducing trade barriers to shift away more decisively from the policy of import substitution. Comprehensive financial sector reforms initiated in 1992 deregulated the banking sector and financial institutions in a phased manner, and ensured the free pricing of primary issues and transparency in the functioning of the stock market, bringing it under the purview of a stock-market regulatory authority, the Securities and Exchange Board of India. Among the various measures instituted to provide low-cost finance to corporates were allowing entry of foreign institutional investors and permitting Indian companies to raise capital abroad. Entrepreneurship and financing of start-ups were encouraged through explicit regulations for venture capital funds. Finally, corporate governance reforms were initiated in the late 1990s in line with international best practices.

11.4 CHARACTERISTICS OF INDIAN
BUSINESS GROUPS

From a host of definitions used over the years to characterize Indian business groups, a business group in the Indian context can be defined as an agglomeration of privately held and publicly traded firms operating in different lines of business, each of which is incorporated as a separate legal entity, *but* which are collectively under the entrepreneurial, financial, and strategic control of a common authority, typically a family, and are interlinked by trust-based relationships forged around a similar persona, ethnicity, or community.[5] In short, the defining characteristic of an Indian business group is the *control* exercised on a group of firms by an apex body, typically a family, through equity channels (equity ownership) as well as non-equity channels (administrative control through board of directors, interlocking director-ships, and related-party transactions).[6] As elucidated in Bertrand and Mullainathan (2003), such control is different from that usually exercised by stand-alone firms owning other firms as subsidiaries as is typical in the USA, where formal control rights equal cash-flow rights. In contrast, in a group, the ultimate owner (apex body) can use *indirect* ownership chains via pyramiding of affiliates to create a divergence between ownership and control so as informally to exercise control even over affiliates in which it has minority equity stakes.

The following sections trace the evolution of business groups since independence, with special reference to the post-reforms period beginning in 1991, highlighting important elements of its structure, strategy, and performance. Reliable and detailed firm/group level information on structural characteristics and financial performance were sparse before the early 1990s, and hence the pre-reform data relevant to the present analysis are primarily sourced from those reported in published books and articles. The post-reform analysis up to 2006[7] is, however, largely based on the data sourced from Prowess, a computerized database containing detailed time series information (from 1990 onwards) published in annual reports, along with stock-marker data, ownership information, and corporate governance characteristics on a large number of Indian companies (over 10,000). Several published empirical studies on the Indian corporate sector have been based on the Prowess database.

As of 2006, the Prowess database identified 2,922 firms affiliated with a total of 560 Indian owned business groups, a predominant majority of these identified with specific families. Although business groups as a collective entity are not formally defined under Indian law, the boundaries of a group as identified in the database are

---

[5] See Hazari (1966); Leff (1978); and Khanna and Palepu (2000a).
[6] Encarnation (1989: 45), for instance, emphasizes multiple forms of ties among group members in the context of Indian business groups.
[7] 2006 was the latest year for which data were available at the time of writing the chapter.

determined by the set of firms that, while being independently incorporated, are interconnected through various formal and informal linkages, as discussed above. Thus, in the Prowess database, a group is any entity with control over at least two firms, with the affiliation of a firm to a group identified on the basis of available information in the public domain suggesting that the ultimate owner(s) of the group has either management control, equity control, and/or other forms of formal and informal business ties with the firm.[8]

11.4.1 The importance of business groups in corporate-sector activity

Business groups in India, since their inception, have dominated corporate-sector activity despite significant changes in institutional environment. Coexisting with a large number of non-affiliated stand-alone firms are group-affiliated firms. Their dominance in total corporate-sector activity is evident from the fact that group affiliates accounted for 88 percent of total assets of the top fifty corporate-sector

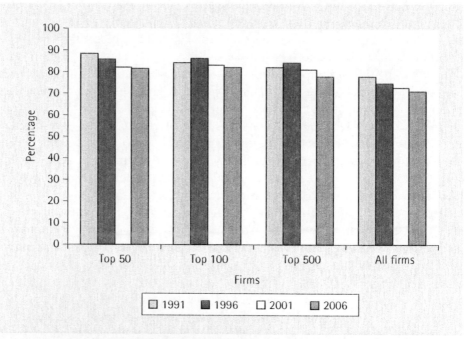

Figure 11.1 Share of group-affiliated firms in total assets, 1991–2006

Source: Computed from Prowess.

[8] Prowess associates a company to a group based on: prospectus/letter of offer, annual reports, disclosure on related party transactions, company website, house journals, equity shareholding details of listed companies, and the MRTP list.

firms (ranked by assets) in 1991, and remained at a significantly high level of around 80 per cent in 2006 (Fig. 11.1). Such dominance in terms of asset share is also evident in the top 100 and top 500 firms, as well as for the corporate sector as a whole, where the share was around 70 percent in 2006.

An analysis of asset share by major industry groups reveals that not only are business groups dominant in industries that require significant capital investment, such as petroleum extraction and refining, motor vehicles, electricity, and so on, but that groups have significant presence even in industries such as software services, where the relative advantage of family-business groups over stand-alone firms in terms of capital requirements is likely to be minimal at best (Khanna and Palepu 2005).

Table 11.1 lists the top ten business groups in India as of 2006, along with year of foundation, total assets, and major lines of business.

11.4.2 The persistence of economic concentration among business groups

A key feature of the concentration of corporate-sector activity among business groups is that, while as of 2006 there were 500-odd distinct family groups, historically only a few large groups have accounted for a disproportionate proportion of total business group assets. This is evident from Fig. 11.2, which presents the group-level concentration ratios from the late 1930s to 2006, computed as a share of the largest two groups (2-group), the largest three groups (3-group), and the largest four groups (4-group) in the total assets of the top twenty business groups at different points of time. As evident from the figure, the 2-group, 3-group, and 4-group ratios were rather high and stable over the sixty-three years, a time period spanning the pre-independence years, the post-independence regulated regime, as well as the liberalized regime. While there was some decline in the share in the post-liberalized period, no discernible trend is evident from the estimates presented in Fig. 11.2. Lorenz curve estimates of the inequality of asset distribution across business groups computed for 1996 and 2006 further reveal an increased skewness in favor of the top few groups.

A more in-depth insight into the growing skewness among business groups can be obtained by analyzing the relative ranking of the top twenty groups since the 1960s. A persistence of the ranking among the top twenty groups can be indicative of the fact that, despite the development of markets, larger groups continue to enjoy disproportionate advantages relative to others. On the other hand, evidence of churning in the ranks could signify differences across various family groups in terms of their entrepreneurial responses and abilities to exploit/adjust to emerging opportunities under changing market conditions. Recent analysis by Khanna and Palepu (2005) that tracks the relative ranking of the top fifty business groups during two thirty-year periods, 1939–69 and 1969–99, concludes that, while there has been significant persistence of concentrated family ownership, there was a relative lack of persistence

Table 11.1 Top ten business groups in India, 2006

Group name	Year of foundation	Total assets (Rs Crore)	Controlling ownership	Major business lines
Reliance group (Mukesh Ambani)	1966	108510.95	Mukesh Ambani family	Exploration and production of oil and gas, petroleum refining and marketing, petrochemicals, textiles, retail
Tata group	1875	97969.39	Ratan Tata family	Information systems and communications, engineering, materials, services, energy, consumer products, chemicals
Anil Dhirubhai Ambani group	1966	46666.86	Anil Ambani family	Communications, financial services, generation, transmission and distribution of power, infrastructure, entertainment
Aditya Birla group	1918	45513.94	Kumaramangalam Birla family	Aluminium and copper production, carbon black, cement, viscose staple fiber, insulators
Essar (Ruia) group	1956	35538.01	Ruia family	Manufacturing and services of steel, energy, power, telecommunications, shipping ports and logistics, construction, mining minerals
Om Prakash Jindal group	1952	26040.34	Om Prakash Jindal family	Hot-rolled coils and other flat-rolled products, power generation
Bharti Telecom group	1986	21334.34	Sunil B. Mittal family	Telecom, agri business, insurance, retail
Vedanta Resources group	1975	19239.43	Anil Agarwal family	Metals and mining
Larsen & Toubro group	1946	17891.05	Non-family	Engineering and construction projects, heavy engineering and electrical and electronics, information technology
Mahindra & Mahindra group	1954	14998.47	Keshub Mahindra family	Automotive, farm equipment, financial services, infrastructure, infotech, speciality businesses

Note: Reliance Group and ADA Group split from the parent group, Reliance Group in 2005. Exchange Rate of US$ to Rupee in 2006: $1= R5.45. 100 crore = 1 billion.

Source: Year of foundation and total asset estimates from Prowess; major business lines compiled from relevant company websites.

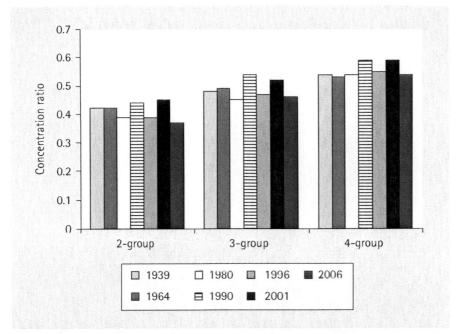

Figure 11.2 Group-level concentration ratios in top twenty groups, 1939–2006

Source: Computed from Prowess.

of the identity of the top business groups over time; thirty-two of the top fifty groups in 1969 were not in the list in 1939, and forty-three of the top groups in 1999 were not in the top fifty in 1969. The present analysis considers the top twenty business groups over much narrower windows of ten years that coincide with distinct policy environments, with 1969–80 capturing the height of the regulated regime, 1980–90 the period of gradual liberalization, and beyond 1990 the period of progressive liberalization (Table 11.2).

Apart from the period 1990–2000, when, as might be expected, there was a significant turnover of rankings among the top twenty, with only nine managing to remain in the list while eleven new groups made their entry, in the remaining periods, more than 50 per cent of the groups continued to remain in the list. While there have been changes in the relative rankings of those that continued during the ten-year periods, some with ranks up, some with ranks down, and some maintaining their positions, there have seldom been dramatic changes in ranking, where ranks have changed by more then five places (up or down) among them.[9] Even when groups have split, such as the Birlas, Goenkas, or Reliance, at least some faction of these groups has continued to find a place in the top twenty list. Of those groups that

---

[9] Among the notable exceptions in this regard are Reliance moving from a rank of eighteen in 1980 to the third rank in 1990, and Essar Ruia moving from the twentieth position in 1990 to the third position in 2000.

Table 11.2 Evolution of top twenty business groups, 1969–2006

Rank	1969 Group	1969 Assets (in Rs crore)	1980 Group	1980 Assets (in Rs crore)	1990 Group	1990 Assets (in Rs crore)	2000 Group	2000 Assets (in crore)	2006 Group	2006 Assets (in crore)
1	Tata	505.36	Tata	1,538.97	Tata	7,546	Reliance	65,914.12	Reliance (Mukesh)	108,510.95
2	Birla	456.4	Birla	1,431.99	Birla	7,235	Tata	58,987.05	Tata	97,969.39
3	Martin Burn	153.06	Mafatlal	427.54	Reliance	3,241	Essar Ruia	23,384.37	Reliance (Anil)	46,666.86
4	Bangur	104.31	J. K. Singhania	412	J. K. Singhania	1,829	Aditya Birla	19,409.55	Aditya Birla	45,513.94
5	Thapar	98.8	Thapar	348.06	Thapar	1,763	Larsen & Toubro	19,395.65	Essar Ruia	35,538.01
6	S. Nagarmull	95.61	ICI	343.01	Mafatlal	1,297	Om Prakash Jindal	17,102.82	Om Prakash Jindal	26,040.34
7	Mafatlal	92.7	Sarabhai	317.94	Bajaj	1,228	RPG Enterprises	12,906.22	Bharti Telecom	21,334.34
8	ACC	89.8	ACC	274.51	Modi	1,192	Bajaj	10,947.07	Vedanta Resources	19,239.43
9	Walchand	81.11	Bangur	264.33	M A Chidambaram	1,032	Thapar	7,635.5	Larsen and Toubro	17,891.05
10	Shriram	74.13	Shriram	241	TVS	909	Mahindra & Mahindra	7,222.19	Mahindra & Mahindra	14,998.47
11	Bird Heilgers	68.62	Kirloskar	220.37	Shriram	800	Vedanta Resources	7,055.17	Bajaj	14,805.32
12	J. K. Singhania	66.84	Hindustan Lever	219.3	UB	716	Jaiprakash	6,649.65	TVS	13,737.13
13	Goenka	65.34	Larsen and Toubro	216.03	Bangur	674	Birla K. K.	6,606.15	Krishna	12,849.59
14	Sahu Jain	58.75	Modi	198.82	Kirloskar	633	TVS	6,588.2	Jaiprakash	12,067.57
15	Macneill & Barry	57.28	TVS	188.64	Walchand	626	M. A. Chidambaram	6,409.52	RPG Enterprises	10,707.58
16	Sarabhai	56.72	Mahindra & Mahindra	186.03	Mahindra & Mahindra	620	Krishna	6,173.44	Videocon	10,293.36
17	Scindia	55.99	Bajaj	179.26	Goenka	570	Birla B. K.	5,281.42	Wipro	9,120.87

Rank	1969		Window 1		Window 2		Window 3		Window 4	
18	Lalbhai	51.2	Reliance	166.33	Nanda (Escorts)	537	Lalbhai	4,804.35	I L & F S Group	9,040.5
19	Killick	51.08	ITC	156.29	Lalbhai	479	Zee Telefilms	4,256.86	Birla K. K.	8,934.86
20	ICI	50.06	Walchand	150.36	Essar Ruia	437	Murgappa Chettiar	4,220.50	Thapar	7,901.48
			Number of new entrants	9	Number of new entrants	6	Number of new entrants[1]	11	Number of new entrants[1]	4
			Number continuing in top 20 (1969–1980)	11	Number continuing in top 20 (1980–1990)	14	Number continuing in top 20 (1990–2000)	9	Number continuing in top 20 (2000–2006)	16
			No rank change	5	No rank change	5	No rank change	0	No rank change	5
			Number rank up	3	Number rank up	5	Number rank up	4	Number rank up	4
			Number rank down	3	Number rank down	4	Number rank down	5	Number rank down	6
			No. rank up 5–10[2]	1	No. rank up 5–10	2	No. rank up 5–10	1	No. rank up 5–10	1
			No. rank up > 10[3]	1	No. rank up > 10	1	No. rank up > 10	1	No. rank up > 10	0
			No. rank down 5–10	2	No. rank down 5–10	1	No. rank down 5–10	1	No. rank down 5–10	1
			No. rank down > 10	1	No. rank down > 10	0	No. rank down > 10	0	No. rank down > 10	1

Notes: [1] refers to the number of groups that entered the Top 20 list in a given time window/and have not appeared in previous windows. [2] refers to the number of groups whose respective ranks have increased by more than ten places. Rank down is analogously defined. [3] refers to the number of groups whose respective ranks have moved up by five to ten places.

Sources: Data for 1969 sourced from Khanna and Palepu (2005); data for 1980 and 1990 sourced from Piramal (2003); data for 2000 and 2006 sourced from Prowess.

entered at different points in time, five of the nine that entered in 1969–80 survived until 2006, but only one of the six that entered in 1980–90 remained among the top twenty in 2006. The extent of attrition was significantly lower among the eleven entrants during 1990–2000, with eight of these continuing in the list in 2006. Overall, the picture that emerges is that of substantial *persistence* of the identity of business groups in the top twenty if one goes back twenty-six years; more significantly, if one goes by the vintage of groups that are in the top twenty in terms of the year of first venture, six of the groups, including the oldest group, Tata, belong to the pre-independence period, nine belong to the regulated period of the 1950s–70s, and the remaining are the post-liberalization entrants (Table 11.1).

11.5 FAMILY OWNERSHIP AND CONTROL

A key feature of business groups, particularly in emerging economies, is the prevalence of concentrated ownership and control. As in their counterparts in East Asia, Japan, and several European countries, concentrated ownership and control structures of Indian business groups are the norm rather than the exception. Family ownership and control of group affiliates in India have devolved through holding company structures, either through a single holding company (for example, the Tata group) or multiple ones (for example, the Anil Dhirubhai Ambani (ADA) group). In some cases (for example, the Reliance group), promoter control is built without any identifiable holding company, but around a flagship company via a complex network of subsidiaries, private companies, and trusts in which family members have major ownership stakes. With a holding company/flagship company at the helm, where the ultimate owner or promoter of a group has enough shares to have absolute control, other group affiliates are typically organized as pyramids, through which the promoter can exert "informal" control over affiliates lower in the pyramid without holding substantial equity in them (Bertrand et al. 2002). Such a group structure in India is further complicated by a web of cross-holdings among group affiliates formed through circular chains of intra-group equity investments.

Estimates of equity ownership of promoters in Indian business groups reveal that during 2001–6, on an average, the direct stake of promoters in group affiliates was 41 percent, whereas the extent of indirect ownership as reflected in the data on "Persons Acting in Concert" (PACs) was 5.35 percent.[10] In several cases (for example, Reliance

---

[10] Persons Acting in Concert (PACs), as defined by the Securities Exchange Board of India, are individuals/companies or any other legal entities through which controlling shareholders can exert indirect control on the affiliate.

Industries), indirect holdings through PACs exceeded direct cash-flow rights.[11] Further examination of the shareholding pattern in flagship companies of the top four groups (Table 11.3) reveals that, among the promoters, direct ownership by family members is relatively low, ranging from as low as zero in the case of Tata Steel to a maximum of 0.75 percent in Reliance Industries. Instead, family instead is exerted indirectly either through closely held group holding companies (Tata Steel and Reliance Communications) or through other privately owned companies (Reliance Industries and Hindalco Industries) that are owned by the promoters.

In the literature, the existence of pyramidal structures has been associated with the phenomenon of tunneling, under which incentives are created for the controlling shareholder(s) at the top of the pyramid to use unfairly priced transactions to expropriate resources from affiliated companies lower down the pyramid to those higher up the pyramid where cash-flow rights of the shareholder(s) are higher (Johnson et al. 2000). Tunneling by nature is clandestine, as promoters employ covert ways to conceal the diversion of funds. In the Indian case, this is likely to be further aggravated by the *opaqueness* of ownership structure caused by the fragmentation of holdings across a number of closely held entities that can make it difficult to track chains of control and thereby the flow of diverted funds, should such diversion occur (Sarkar and Sarkar 2008). Notwithstanding such measurement problems, Bertrand et al. (2002) found evidence of tunneling in Indian groups by tracking the propagation of exogenous shocks received by one group affiliate, to the other affiliates in a pyramid. More recent evidence shows that ownership complexity through pyramiding and cross-holdings reduces the informativeness of earnings to minority shareholders (Marisetty and Chalmers 2005), leads to expropriation of minority shareholders in group affiliates through the issuance of debt (Sarkar and Sarkar 2008), and, in general, goes against the interests of minority shareholders in group affiliates (Kakani and Joshi 2006).

Concomitant with financial control of promoters in group affiliates through a complex ownership structure is promoter control of the management of group affiliates accomplished through setting the strategic vision, the philosophy, and the management practices of a group at the group headquarters, and through the inclusion of family members in the boards of affiliates. In the case of the Tata group, for instance, Tata Sons, the promoter of all key group companies, serves as the group headquarters with two decision-making bodies, the Group Executive Office and the Group Corporate Centre, defining and reviewing the business portfolios of the group, ensuring synergy among the group affiliates, implementing corporate governance programs, managing human resources, and so on, and in general dealing with strategic issues facing affiliates.[12] In other cases, as with the ADA group, group holding companies primarily control the affiliates through the

---

[11] As of 2006, this was the case for 106 affiliates across 86 groups and accounting for approximately 11% of affiliates.

[12] Similarly, Aditya Birla Management Corporation of the Aditya Birla Group, and Reliance Industries of the Reliance Group, serve as group headquarters, respectively.

Table 11.3 Promoter ownership by type in major group affiliates, March 2007

Type of promoters	Reliance Industries (Reliance group)		Tata Steel (Tata group)		Reliance Communications (ADA group)		Hindalco Industries (Aditya Birla group)	
	Number	Share (%)	Number	Share (%)	Number	Share (%)	Number	Share (%)
Family members	5	0.75	0	0	3	0.49	5	0.12
Trusts	2	7.60	2	0.18	0	0	0	0
Holding companies	0	0	1	24.08	0	63.98	0	0
Privately held companies	15	38.76	0	0	1	0.15	6	13.18
Publicly listed companies	1	0.01	7	5.88	2	1.57	6	8.51
Others	0	0	0	0	0	0	0	0
Total	23	47.12	19	30.14	7	66.19	17	21.81

Source: Computed from Prowess.

competitive allocation of financial resources, while granting them more autonomy in strategic decision-making within the ambit of an overall group philosophy and governance practices. Thus, following Hoskisson et al. (1993), while the management of the Tata group and of many others organized along similar lines is akin to the M-form with strategic control (the cooperative M-Form), others, such as the ADA group, mimic the M-form with budgetary control (the competitive M-form).

A major avenue of family control and governance in all business groups is through family representation on the boards of affiliates. This takes the form of having controlling shareholder(s) from the founding family on the boards in the capacity of chairman and/or the chief executive or as non-executive (gray) directors. Executive (inside) directors of an affiliate belonging to the founding family also sit on the boards of other group affiliates. A study (Sarkar and Sarkar 2009) analyzing the board characteristics of 500 large Indian companies, 378 of which are group affiliates, reports that, in the year 2003, as much as one-fifth of the board of affilates consisted of gray directors, the corresponding figure being one-quarter for stand-alone companies.

Table 11.4 also presents two specific characteristics of group affiliates in terms of managerial control and ties that have prevailed over the years—namely, the presence of promoter directors on company boards and the incidence of multiple directorships among company directors. As is evident from the table, the percentage both of companies in which a promoter is present as a director (promoter director), and of companies where the promoter serves as a chairman or managing director is distinctly higher for group affiliates. That this can have governance implications is borne out by evidence from a study of Indian firms for the years 2003 and 2004 indicating that controlling shareholders on the board increase the extent of opportunistic earnings management (Sarkar et al. 2008). With respect to multiple directorships, the percentage of busy directors (those with three or more directorships) has continued to remain high, estimated at around 56 percent for 500 large firms as of 2003. Comparable estimates with regard to the USA show that only 6 percent of directors are busy (Ferris et al. 2003). Splitting by director types and ownership groups (Table 11.4), the percentage of busy insider directors is significantly higher at 65 percent for group affiliates compared to 45 percent for stand-alones. This is true for independent directors as well, although the differentials are lower, 65 percent for group affiliates and 60 per cent for stand-alones. Evidence as of 2003 revealed that, while the market perceives multiple directorships in stand-alones as a signal of better directorial quality, it discounts the same in the case of group affiliates (Sarkar and Sarkar 2009).

Finally, Table 11.4 highlights the existence of substantial managerial integration or an "inner circle"[13] among group affiliates; around 84 percent of directorial positions for inside directors originates *within* group affiliates, with around 75 percent of these positions originating within a *single group*. In direct contrast to this, relatively few inside directors of non-affiliates occupy a directorial position as an outside director in group affiliates (12.21 percent), and even fewer (8.87 percent) of the directorships

---

[13] Useem (1984) used the term to characterize interlocking of managerial positions among a small group of American executives.

Table 11.4 Board characteristics of 500 large Indian companies, 2003

Board characteristics (number or percentage)	Group-affiliated companies N=332	Non-affiliated companies N=168	All companies N=500
Total number of directors (board size)	9.78	8.80	9.46
Percentage of (executive) inside directors	23.73	28.80	25.38
Percentage of (non-executive) outside directors	76.27	71.20	74.62
Percentage of gray directors	19.56	22.34	20.46
Percentage of independent directors	56.71	48.86	54.16
Has promoter director (% of sample companies)	43	37	41
Has promoter as chairman or managing director (% of sample companies)	29	25	28
Percentage of busy inside directors (3 or more directorships)	64.65	44.71	58.17
Percentage of busy independent directors (3 or more directorships)	64.56	59.64	62.97
Mean percentage of directorships in group-affiliates			
Inside directors	84.11	12.21	N.A.
Independent directors	66.93	38.12	
Mean percentage of directorships within one group			
Inside directors	75.01	8.87	N.A.
Independent directors	43.44	23.64	
Mean percentage of directorships within non-affiliates			
Inside directors	15.89	87.79	N.A.
Independent directors	33.07	61.88	

Notes: N.A.=not applicable. N=number of observations.
Sources: Sarkar and Sarkar (2009); Prowess.

are concentrated within a single group. Instead, around 88 percent of (multiple) directorial positions of inside directors in non-affiliates are, on an average, concentrated in non-affiliates themselves.

The picture of within-group concentration of directorial positions for inside directors surprisingly extends to independent directors with about 67 percent of their directorships in group affiliates being located within other group affiliates, and notably 43 percent of directorships concentrated within a *single* group. These estimates appear to be rather high relative to the corresponding estimates for independent directors of non-affiliated firms.

11.6 BUSINESS GROUP STRATEGIES

11.6.1 Diversification

In India, the growth of diversified business groups has been due to multiple factors that changed with shifts in the institutional environment. During the colonial period, business group diversification was determined not only by the urge for financial, managerial, and product market integration (Mehta 1955; Hazari 1966), but also by the entrepreneurial responses of different groups to emerging market opportunities and the huge profits reaped during the war periods (Tripathi 2004). By the 1950s, groups were characterized by extensive diversification, with some like the Birlas diversifying into almost every industry except steel, power, and transport, and the Tatas, while focusing on their core competencies in steel, engineering, and power, branching across many other non-related industries and services.

The strategy of unrelated diversification continued to be pursued during the regulated regime, but with a changed rationale, driven now more by the obstacles imposed by the "license raj" and monopoly regulations on the organic growth of firms via capacity expansion. Most of the big business groups, eager to grow, worked around these obstacles to their scale by increasing their scope through pursuing unrelated diversification. Once the capacity constraint was hit in a particular line of activity, a group sought to expand its operations by applying for licenses in other industrial activities irrespective of whether these were related.[14] As a result, non-market forms of entrepreneurship and associated rent-seeking behavior emerged, with the success of obtaining licenses reportedly depending significantly on the ability of big groups to seek state patronage. According to the Industrial Licensing Policy Enquiry Committee in 1967, larger business houses were found to "maneuver" the government to obtain a disproportionately large share of industrial licenses. Some groups, however, continued to flourish despite not being wholly successful in acquiring licenses.[15]

The onset of economic liberalization and the associated deregulation of private-sector industrial activity and development of the markets raised questions as to whether unrelated diversification would continue to be an optimal strategy for business group diversification. One of the major implications of the institutionalist view is that, while diversified business groups with their internal factor and capital markets may be optimal organizational solutions in the absence of well-functioning markets, their relative advantage in this respect is likely to decline as external markets develop (Hoskisson et al. 2000; Khanna and Palepu 2000b). The importance of internal markets

[14] For example, the Birla Group operated in as diverse industries as jute, textiles, automobiles and tea, and the Goenka Group diversified into apparently unrelated businesses such as carbon black, agribusinesses and typewriters (Ghemawat and Khanna 1998; Kedia et al. 2006).

[15] Khanna and Palepu (2005) cite the case of the Tata group, for which all 119 new proposals for expansions in businesses between 1960 and 1989 were rejected.

may also decline in a globalized environment as business groups move to high-end product markets where competitive success against foreign firms is likely to be determined more by industry-specific, technological, and marketing capabilities than by their ability to share intra-group "generic resources" (Guillen 2000; Kim et al. 2004). While unrelated diversification may be an optimal growth response in a regulated regime, deregulation of markets can enable groups to choose their lines of business based purely on market opportunities and their core competencies.

Select evidence with respect to conglomerate diversification in the USA shows that the institutional environment can matter in the choice of diversification strategy. For instance, it is argued that antitrust laws during the 1950s–70s inhibited intra-industry growth and forced firms to grow through unrelated diversification, while the relaxation of such laws in the 1980s enabled firms to refocus on core competencies.[16] With respect to whether diversification creates or destroys value, while some studies conclude that unrelated diversification by conglomerates may have added value in the USA, the overall evidence is inconclusive.[17] Comparable evidence on group diversification from emerging economies is also ambiguous (Peng and Delios 2006; Khanna and Yafeh 2007). While one strand of evidence suggests that groups in emerging markets such as India and Chile can add value through diversified rather than focused strategies because of the ability of groups to fill up "institutional voids" (Khanna and Palepu 2000a, b), several other studies do not find such evidence (Chacar and Vissa 2005; Petitt et al. 2005).

A scanning of existing academic literature as well as coverage by the business press on the strategic responses of Indian business groups to the changes in policy environment post-reforms reveals a wide range of responses. There are some groups that have refocused on core competencies and streamlined group operations toward increased product relatedness, some others that have maintained their diversified bases but with an increased focus on select activities, some that have reported no change, and, at the other extreme, some that have pursued extensive diversification (Khanna and Palepu 1999; Khandwalla 2002; Kedia et al. 2006). An analysis of the trends in diversification of Indian groups for the top ten groups as of 2006 is presented in Table 11.5 for four points in time, 1991, 1996, 2001, and 2006. The measure computed to capture the extent to which groups have pursued diversification is the share of a group's core industry—the 2-digit industry that accounted for the highest proportion of a group's assets in 1991—in a group's total assets. A decline in the proportion would capture broadly a focus away from a group's core business to other areas of activity. Notably, across all the four time points, with the exception of the ADA group, where energy/electricity gave way to telecommunications, the core industry of the groups remained the same. Consistent with the preceding discussion, data in Table 11.5 reveal that, while some groups like the Tatas, ADA, Bharti Telecom,

---

[16] Similarly, the deregulation and subsequent improvement of capital markets in the 1980s is considered to have increased its relative benefits vis-à-vis internal capital markets, making diversification less attractive (see Davis et al. 1994; Akbulut and Matsusaka 2005; and the references therein).

[17] See, e.g., Berger and Ofek (1995); Akbulut and Matsusaka (2005); and Peng and Delios (2006).

Table 11.5 Share of the industry accounting for the largest proportion of group assets in the top ten business groups, 1991–2006 (%)

Business group	Type of industry	1991	1996	2001	2006
Reliance (Mukesh Ambani)	Petroleum products (refineries)	50.74	69.07	71.27	83.76
Tata	Finished steel (including saleable steel)	33.84	28.55	19.98	20.62
Anil Dhirubhai Ambani	Energy/electricity	99.82	68.08	57.03	34.65
Aditya Birla	Aluminium, ferro alloys	46.33	40.43	47.78	41.61
Essar Ruia	Hot-rolled coils and other flat-rolled products	45.33	54.99	35.00	41.27
Om Prakash Jindal	Hot-rolled coils and other flat-rolled products	90.24	96.26	88.85	92.13
Bharti Telecom	Telephones/ telecommunications	N.A.	N.A.	18.18	6.74
Vedanta Resources	Basic metals, copper	99.99	100.00	87.48	94.39
Larsen and Toubro	Industrial contracts and turnkey projects	96.06	96.00	81.92	75.67
Mahindra & Mahindra	Utility Vehicles including jeeps	69.55	68.60	49.23	39.15

Note: N.A. = Not applicable
Source: Computed from Prowess.

L&T, and Mahindra and Mahindra gave increased importance to other lines of activity relative to their core industry, other groups—namely Aditya Birla, Reliance (Mukesh Ambani), Essar Ruia, the Jindal group, and Vedanta Resources—chose to stick to or expand their core businesses in a significant way.

Finally, unrelated diversification pursued by Indian business groups across the different policy environments has gone hand in hand with diversification along vertical lines (Hazari 1966; Patibandla 2006). Proponents of transaction-cost theory argue that business groups can bypass high transaction costs in market exchange through a variety of vertical strategies (Williamson 1971; Hennart 2001). As Li et al. (2006) highlight in the context of examining the strategic responses of business groups to market failures, vertical strategies may be as relevant as horizontal expansion, especially with respect to product markets. A case in point is the Reliance group in India, which started in the 1960s with trading in textiles and yarn and moved on to in-house production of rayon, since local manufacturers were unable to maintain quality and adequate supply. Subsequently, the group integrated forward to retail outlets, and integrated backward to petrochemicals, oil, and gas. At later stages, by leveraging on the experiences gained in vertical integration in terms of tackling regulated markets and managing highly capital-intensive projects, the group forayed into unrelated industries such as cement and telecommunications (Li et al. 2006).

11.6.2 Internationalization

A striking phenomenon in the post-reforms period has been the growing internationalization of group companies through outward direct foreign investment (ODFI). Internationalization has its roots in the regulated regime when group companies as well as stand-alones, faced with restricted capacities and markets at home, were forced to venture abroad in order to grow. This, despite the fact that government policies regulating ODFI were themselves restrictive (Pradhan 2007).[18] One of the forerunners of the strategy of growing through international diversification during the regulated regime was the Birla group, followed by the Tatas, Thapars, and Kirloskars among others (Ranganathan 1984). While such international forays accounted, on an average, for only 0.01 percent of total world ODFI between 1974 and 1984,[19] these were nonetheless valuable to the extent of helping to sow the seeds of many global acquisitions by business groups later on in the post-reforms period.

Since the reforms, Indian ODFI has undergone considerable change in terms of its magnitude, geographical focus, and sectoral composition because of the reorientation of ODFI policies toward promoting global competitiveness of Indian enterprises (Kumar 2004; Pradhan 2007). Dubbed as the "Second Wave," Indian ODFI during the post-reforms period has overwhelmingly concentrated in developed countries, accounting for around 60 percent of total ODFI, with the sectoral composition moving away from manufacturing to services (Kumar 2006). With regard to the motives for ODFI, while market-seeking was the over-riding motive for internationalization during the regulated regime (the "First Wave"), this expanded post-liberalization to include improving global competitiveness, acquiring strategic assets, completing the value chain through backward and forward linkages so as to become top international producers. Notably, group-affiliated firms continued to take the lead in global acquisitions.

Data compiled on 360 international acquisitions by Indian firms between January 2001 and December 2006[20] show that, of the 267 acquisitions for which the ownership of the companies could be conclusively established, 65.92 percent had group affiliates as the acquirer, 21.35 percent had stand-alones, and the rest had foreign firms. Overall, group acquisitions had become more broad-based, with seventy-one Indian groups involved. On the one hand were groups like the Tatas and Birlas that had been active in ODFI during the regulated regime and were in a position to leverage the experiences they had gained in terms of integrating diverse management teams, communicating

---

[18] The existing ODFI regulations involved prior permission, cumbersome approval systems, limits on the extent of Indian ownership, and restrictions on product ranges.

[19] UNCTAD (2006); Pradhan (2007).

[20] Compiled from monthly volumes of "Mergers and Acquisitions" published by the CMIE.

across borders and time zones, and integrating compensation practices, and existing marketing and distribution capabilities. On the other hand were groups that, though not active earlier, developed acquisition capabilities in the post-liberalized period and expanded through cross-border acquisitions in the software, pharmaceuticals, and auto-component sectors (Khanna 2007). Further, several groups went for high-valued acquisitions, resulting in some of their affiliates being catapulted into the ranks of top international producers.[21] The driving force in all the major deals ranged from building forward and backward linkages[22] to building front-end sales capabilities in international markets with low-cost back-end production capabilities at home.[23]

11.7 BUSINESS GROUP PERFORMANCE

Theoretically, economic liberalization can have conflicting performance impacts on business groups. Groups that pursued unrelated diversification in the regulated regime can in a liberalized regime benefit from restructuring their businesses in line with their core competencies. Even as market institutions develop, groups may continue to enjoy comparative advantages vis-à-vis the stand-alones with respect to internal capital and labor markets, other non-marketable inputs like entrepreneurship, implicit trust-based contracting, and group reputation built over the years that they can leverage to explore emerging market opportunities in a liberalized environment (Maurer and Sharma 2001; Khanna and Yafeh 2007).

On the negative side, the complex structures of business groups can create organizational rigidities that can make it difficult for them to adapt themselves to a fast-changing environment relative to stand-alones. Also, the unique and valuable capability of business groups to forge and utilize contacts in a protected and regulated regime (Kock and Guillen 2001) is likely to become less useful in a liberalized environment, notwithstanding the possibility that such capabilities may be successfully redirected to get privileged access to new opportunities, even in the liberalized environment (Ghemawat and Khanna 1998). Finally, if group affiliation did confer benefits in the regulated regime to the extent that affiliated firms outperformed stand-alones, increased competition among firms following liberalization can potentially wipe out such performance differentials.

---

[21] Tata Tea of the Tata group became the second largest global manufacturer and distributor of tea after acquiring Tetley Tea; and Hindalco of the Aditya Birla Group, after the acquisition of Novelis Inc., became the largest global manufacturer of aluminum rolling products.

[22] Hindalco's acquisition of Novelis Inc. is an example of an upstream producer acquiring a leading downstream player in Western markets.

[23] Examples are the acquisitions of Tetley and Corus by the Tata group, and acquistions in auto components, pharmaceuticals, and software (Khanna 2007).

A comparison of Indian group-affiliated and stand-alone firms with respect to key variables for 2006 shows that group affiliates were on an average six times larger than their stand-alone counterparts in terms of sales and four times as large in terms of assets. Also, affiliated firms were on an average significantly older and more leveraged. Finally, affiliated firms as of 2006 had significantly higher profitability and market value.

Fig. 11.3 depicts the trend in profitability, as measured by return on assets (ROA) and trends in market to book value ratio (MBVR) of group-affiliated and stand-alone firms for the period 1991–2006. As is evident from the figure, ROA, after declining for the first ten years, recovered for both ownership groups after 2001, with their fortunes over the years fluctuating largely in tandem. As for performance differentials between affiliated and stand-alone firms, the year-wise means tests that were conducted reveal that, other than for a few years in the early and late 1990s, there was no significant difference between the performance of affiliated and stand-alone firms. In particular, in later years, as liberalization gathered momentum, there is no evidence that group affiliates outperformed stand-alone firms in a statistical sense. With regard to trends in market values of group-affiliated and stand-alone firms, except for a couple of years in the mid-1990s, the market values of both stand-alones and affiliated firms moved closely together, with the latter outperforming the former in a statistical sense only in the last two years of the period considered—that is, 2005 and 2006.

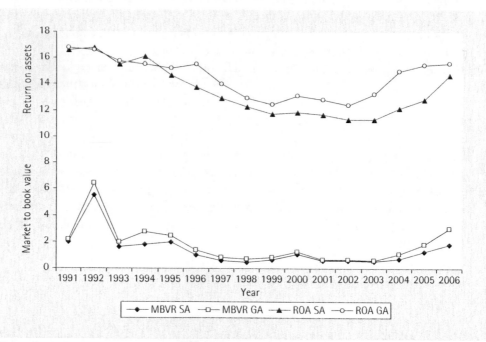

Figure 11.3 Return on assets and market to book value ratio for Indian stand–alone firms and group affiliates, 1991–2006

Note: ROA SA: return on assets (ROA) of standalones; ROA GA: ROA of group affiliates; MBVR SA: market to book value ratio (MBVR) of standalones; MBVR GA: MBVR of group affiliates.

Source: Computed from Prowess.

11.8 CONCLUDING OBSERVATIONS

This chapter analyzes the evolution of business groups in India and attempts to understand the structure and strategies of these groups through the lens of history. Specifically, the evolution of groups in India as in many other countries is a path-dependent process, where the functioning of the groups at any time is a reflection of their past strategies and structure. The basic conclusion that can be derived from this study is that the evolution of business groups has elements of both continuity and change. The continuity, despite structural shifts in the policy and institutional environment from time to time, has been preserved in terms of their dominance in corporate-sector activity. Several of the groups, such as Tata and Birla, that were established in the pre-independence era have continued to remain in leadership positions over time, although the economic and institutional environments in which they have operated have changed from being under colonial rule, to being excessively regulated, to finally becoming increasingly market oriented. Continuity is also apparent in the continued spirit of entrepreneurship, the persistence of concentrated ownership and control structures, the extent of managerial integration, and by and large the continued diversified structures of groups. While the number of groups multiplied post-independence and new groups formed to increase the total number of groups to over 500 by the year 2006, the bulk of group activity has continuously remained in the hands of the top four or five groups, leading to a persistence of inter-group inequality over time.

Elements of change in the evolution of Indian groups are apparent from the turnover among groups in terms of their relative importance in the group hierarchy. The present analysis reveals that there can be considerable heterogeneity in group responses in a dynamic environment; not all groups, or group-affiliated firms, can thrive when the rules of the game change. While some leadership positions remained undisputed, the analysis reveals that there was also considerable churning at the medium and lower end, even among those in the top twenty, with groups new in the block growing aggressively at the expense of the older business groups. Elements of change were also found in the growth strategies pursued by groups over time, and bring to the fore their adaptive capabilities in the face of changing conditions. These include the ability to tailor strategies in tune with irreversible changes in the institutional environment and the ability to leverage comparative advantages to access resources and markets in order to expand. Thus, during the regulated regime, despite the implicit mistrust of big business groups and obstacles placed to stifle their growth in all respects, a large number of new groups emerged, and most of the major business houses that dominated corporate-sector activity in the colonial period continued to expand and consolidate.

The shift in the 1990s to a deregulated environment led to considerable restructuring of strategies across groups, although it is not possible to decipher any dominant strategy. While some groups continued to diversify, some moved toward core competencies. By leveraging the financial strength and managerial expertise accumulated over time across diverse industries during the regulated regime, groups of colonial vintage were able to foresee emerging opportunities and enter activities away from their traditional base, such as software and pharmaceuticals.

The value of analyzing the evolution of business groups in India particularly lies in the insights it can throw on the different theoretical perspectives on business groups, and especially how their role changes with institutional development. Indian groups fit into the prototype of the sociological conception of groups, yet serve the economic function of filling up institutional voids as the institutional approach predicts. However, contrary to received wisdom underlying these theoretical approaches, the theory that the move toward greater market orientation and the reduction of transaction cost is likely to weaken the role of groups as a hybrid organizational form between the firm and the market is defied in the Indian case. In the years since liberalization and market development, family business groups in India have continued to thrive as a dominant organizational form with neither the extent of their intermediation in the product market, labor market, and capital market, nor the extent of social ties as manifested in the existence of an "inner circle" showing any marked signs of decline, and with group affiliates continuing to perform at par with stand-alone companies. This, notwithstanding the evidence that group diversification may cease to have a beneficial effect on affiliates, that board structures may not be effective in governance, and that minority investors can be expropriated through tunneling activities by controlling shareholders.

References

AKBULUT, M. E., and MATSUSAKA, J. (2005). "The Waning of Corporate Diversification." Working Paper, University of Southern California.

BERGER, P. G., and OFEK, E. (1995). "Diversification's Effect on Firm Value," *Journal of Financial Economics*, 37: 39–65.

BERTRAND, M., and MULLAINATHAN, S. (2003). "Pyramids," *Journal of the European Economic Association*, 1/2–3: 478–483.

BERTRAND, M., MEHTA, P., and MULLAINATHAN, S. (2002). "Ferreting out Tunneling: An Application to Indian Business Groups," *Quarterly Journal of Economics*, 117/1: 121–48.

CHACAR, A., and VISSA, B. (2005). "Are Emerging Economies Less Efficient? Performance Persistence and the Impact of Business Group Affiliation," *Strategic Management Journal*, 26: 933–46.

CHANG, S.-J., and HONG, J. (2002). "How Much Does the Business Group Matter in Korea?" *Strategic Management Journal*, 23/3: 265–74.

DAVIS, G. F., DIEKMANN, K. A., and TINSLEY, C. H. (1994). "The Decline and Fall of the Conglomerate Firm in the 1980s: The Deinstitutionalization of an Organizational Form," *American Sociological Review*, 59/4: 547–70.

DUTTA, S. (1997). *Family Business in India*. New Delhi: Response Books.

ENCARNATION, D. (1989). *Dislodging Multinationals: India's Comparative Perspective*. Ithaca, NY: Cornell University Press.

FERRIS, S., JAGANNATHAN, M., and PRITCHARD, A. C. (2003). "Too Busy to Mind Business? Monitoring by Directors with Multiple Board Appointments," *Journal of Finance*, 58/3: 1087–111.

FISMAN, R., and KHANNA, T. (2004). "Facilitating Development: The Role of Business Groups," *World Development*, 32/4: 609–28.

GHEMAWAT, P., and KHANNA, T. (1998). "The Nature of Diversified Business Groups: A Research Design and Two Case Studies," *Journal of Industrial Economics*, 46/1: 35–61.

GRANOVETTER, M. (1994). "Business Groups," in J. N. Smelser and R. Swedberg (eds.), *The Handbook of Economic Sociology*. Princeton: Princeton University Press, 453–75.

GRANOVETTER, M. (1995). "Coase Revisited: Business Groups in the Modern Economy," *Industrial and Corporate Change*, 4/1: 93–130.

GUILLEN, M. F. (2000). "Business Groups in Emerging Economies: A Resource Based View," *Academy of Management Journal*, 43: 362–80.

HAZARI, R. K. (1966). *The Corporate Private Sector: Concentration Ownership and Control*. Bombay: Asia Publishing House.

HENNART, J. F. (2001). "Theories of the Multinational Enterprise," in A. M. Rugman and T. L. Brewer. (eds.), *Oxford Handbook of International Business*. New York: Oxford University Press, 127–49.

HOSKISSON, R. E., HILL, C. W., and KIM, H. (1993). "The Multidivisional Structure: Organizational Fossil or Source of Value?" *Journal of Management*, 19: 269–98.

HOSKISSON, R. E., EDEN, L., LAU, C., and WRIGHT, M. (2000). "Strategy in Emerging Economies," *Academy of Management Journal*, 43: 249–67.

JOHNSON, S., LA PORTA, R., LOPEZ-DE-SILANES, F., and SHLEIFER, A. (2000). "Tunneling," *American Economic Review* (Papers and Proceedings), 90/2: 22–7.

KAKANI, R. K., and JOSHI, T. (2006). "Cross Holding Strategy to Increase Control: Case of the Tata Group." Working Paper: 06–03, XLRI School of Management, Jamshedpur.

KEDIA, B. L., MUKHERJEE, D., and LAHIRI, S. (2006). "Indian Business Groups: Evolution and Transformation," *Asia Pacific Journal of Management*, 23: 559–77.

KHANDWALLA, P. N. (2002). "Effective Organisational Response by Corporates to India's Liberalisation and Globalistion," *Asia Pacific Journal of Management*, 19: 423–48.

KHANNA, T. (2007). "Tata-Corus: India's New Steel Giant," *Economic Times*, Feb. 14.

KHANNA, T., and PALEPU, K. (1999). "Policy Shocks, Market Intermediaries and Corporate Strategy: The Evolution of Business Groups in Chile and India," *Journal of Economics and Management Strategy*, 8/2: 271–310.

KHANNA, T., and. PALEPU, K. (2000a). "Is Group Affiliation Profitable in Emerging Markets? An Analysis of Diversified Indian Business Groups," *Journal of Finance*, 55/2: 867–91.

KHANNA, T., and PALEPU, K. (2000b). "The Future of Business Groups in Emerging Markets: Long-Run Evidence from Chile," *Academy of Management Journal*, 43/3: 268–85.

KHANNA, T., and PALEPU, K. (2005). "The Evolution of Concentrated Ownership in India: Broad Patterns and a History of the Indian Software Industry," in R. Morck (ed.), *A History of Corporate Governance around the World: Family Business Groups to Professional Managers*. Chicago and London: University of Chicago Press.

KHANNA, T., and YAFEH, Y. (2007). "Business Groups in Emerging Markets: Paragons or Parasites," *Journal of Economic Literature*, 45: 331–72.

KIM, H., HOSKISSON, L. TIHANYI, R., and HONG, J. (2004). "The Evolution and Restructuring of Diversified Business Groups in Emerging Markets: The Lessons from Chaebols in Korea," *Asia Pacific Journal of Management*, 21: 25–48.

KOCK, C. J., and GUILLEN, M. F. (2001). "Strategy and Structure in Developing Countries: Business Groups as an Evolutionary Response to Opportunities for Unrelated Diversification," *Industrial and Corporate Change*, 10/1: 77–101.

KUMAR, N. (2004). "India," in D. H. Brooks and H. Hill (eds.), *Managing FDI in a Globalizing Economy: Asian Experiences*. New York: Palgrave Macmillan for ADB.

KUMAR, N. (2006). "Emerging Multinationals: Trends, Patterns and Determinants of Outward Investment by Indian Enterprises." RIS Working Paper, New Delhi.

LEFF, N. (1978). "Industrial Organization and Entrepreneurship in the Developing Countries: The Economic Groups," *Economic Development and Cultural Change*, 26/4: 661–75.

LI, M., RAMASWAMY, K., and PETIT, P. B. (2006). "Business Groups, Market Failures, and Corporate Strategy: An Integrative Framework," *Asia Pacific Journal of Management*, 23/4: 559–77.

MARATHE, S. S. (1989). *Regulation and Development: India's Policy Experience of Controls over Industry*. 2nd edn. New Delhi: Sage Publications.

MARISETTY, V. B., and CHALMERS, K. (2005). "Corporate Ownership Structure and Earnings Informativeness of Indian Firms," *Proceedings of the International Conference, 2005: Emerging Securities Market—Challenges and Prospects—Vol. I*. Hyderabad: ICFAI University Press.

MAURER, N., and SHARMA, T. (2001). "Enforcing Property Rights through Reputation: Mexico's Early Industrialisation, 1878–1913," *Journal of Economic History*, 61/4: 950–73.

MEHTA, M. M. (1955). *Structure of Indian Industries*. Bombay: Popular Book Depot.

MORRIS, D. M. (1967). "Values as an Obstacle to Economic Growth in South Asia: Historical Survey," *Journal of Economic History*, 27/4: 588–607.

PATIBANDLA, M. (2006). *Evolution of Markets and Institutions: A Study of an Emerging Economy*. London and New York: Routledge

PENG, M. W., and DELIOS, A. (2006). "What Determines the Scope of the Firm over Time and around the World? An Asia Pacific Perspective," *Asia Pacific Journal of Management*, 23: 385–405.

PETITT, P. B., RAMASWAMY, K., and LI, M. (2005). "A Temporal Study of Diversification, Group Affiliation and Performance among Indian Manufacturers," *Academy of Management Proceedings*, E1–E6.

PIRAMAL, G. (2003). "Big Business and Entrepreneurship," www.india-seminar.com/2003/528/528%20gita%20piramal.htm

PIRAMAL, G., and HERDECK, M. (1986). *India's Industrialists*, vol. i. Washington: Three Continents Press.

PRADHAN, J. P. (2007). "Growth of Indian Multinationals in the World Economy: Implications for Development." ISID Working Paper, No. 2007/04, Institute for Studies in Industrial Development, New Delhi.

RANGANATHAN, K. V. K. (1984). "Indian Joint Ventures Abroad: With Special Reference to Islamic Countries," *Economic and Political Weekly, Review of Management*, M69–M77.

SARKAR J., and SARKAR, S. (2008). "Debt and Corporate Governance in Emerging Economies: Evidence from India," *Economics of Transition*, 16/2: 292–334.

SARKAR, J., and SARKAR, S. (2009). "Multiple Board Appointments and Firm Performance in Emerging Economies: Evidence from India," *Pacific Basin Finance Journal*, 17/2: 271–93.

SARKAR, J., SARKAR, S., and SEN, K. (2008). "Board of Directors and Opportunistic Earnings Management: Evidence from India," *Journal of Accounting Auditing and Finance*, 23/4: 189–208.

TRIPATHI, D. (2004). *The Oxford History of Indian Business*. New Delhi: Oxford University Press.

TRIPATHI, D., and MEHTA, M. J. (1990). *Business Houses in Western India, 1950–1956*. New Delhi: Manohar.

UNCTAD (2006). United Nations Conference on Trade and Development, *World Investment Report, 2006: FDI from Developing and Transition Economies: Implications for Development*. New York: UNCTAD.

USEEM, M. (1984). *The Inner Circle: Large Corporations and the Rise of Business Political Activity in the US and UK*. New York: Oxford University Press.

WILLIAMSON, O. E. (1971). "The Vertical Integration of Production: Market Failure Considerations," *American Economic Review*, 61: 112–23.

Group 2. Latin America

CHAPTER 12

....

BUSINESS GROUPS IN ARGENTINA

....

EDUARDO FRACCHIA

LUIZ MESQUITA

JUAN QUIROGA

12.1 INTRODUCTION

....

THIS chapter presents the origins, main profile, and recent evolution of Argentine business groups. It is intended to further the study of the dynamics of business groups in Argentina. For that, we will review the origins and evolution of business groups, addressing in particular the way they have responded to recent transformations in the business environment. In short, the chapter is intended to offer research on an exploratory basis on the experience of business groups in emerging countries, in an attempt to enrich the understanding of their strategic decisions and behaviors, especially when facing major environmental transformations.

Carrera et al. (2000) have described the convenience of studying the origins and evolution of Argentinian business groups, and particularly their strategic responses to recent transformations in the business environment. Starting in 1991, Argentina launched a broad program of reform, resulting in what Ghemawat and Kennedy (1999) defined as a "Competitive Shock" (Carrera et al. 2003). This is a sudden, significant, and permanent alteration in the way of doing business, which is due to changes in the rules of the economic game, increasing the relevance of competitive forces in a company's economic

As part of this chapter builds on previous research with Alejandro Carrera, Pankaj Ghemawat, Héctor Rocha, Guillermo Perkins, Roberto Vassolo, and Álvaro Vilaseca, we would like to thank all of them.

results. The main drivers behind the reforms were: economic stabilization (with the convergence of inflation to international value), the organization of the Mercosur as a trading and economic block, the commercial and financial liberalization of the economy, a broad privatization process, and deregulation/re-regulation of sectors of the economy, mainly the ones linked to public services and privatized companies. After December 2001, Argentina went through the worst crisis it had ever experienced (Gerchunoff and Llach 2003)—financially, economically, politically, and socially.

One interesting feature of the present study is that it combines qualitative and quantitative data, collected both through in-depth interviews and from public information sources on Argentine business groups.

The chapter is organized as follows. The next section focuses on previous studies on business groups in Argentina. Then Section 12.3 presents the origins of Argentinian business groups. Section 12.4 briefly addresses a basic profile of business groups in Argentina in terms of size, ownership, governance, and structure. After that, we deal with the analysis of the recent evolution of business groups in Argentina. Finally, Section 12.6 presents some concluding remarks.

12.2 BUSINESS GROUPS IN ARGENTINA

As Argentina can be considered a medium-sized economy, with a low number of business groups, we analyzed the entire population of Argentine business groups; instead of only the public ones (thus avoiding the problem of selection that could have been encountered, as indicated by Khanna and Yafeh 2007).[1] For that, we first identified business groups that were in existence in 2007, based on public information. That list is presented in Table 12.1, which gives the year each business group was founded, the main economic sectors in which it was mainly involved, and sales figures.

According to Table 12.1, Argentine business groups are large companies in terms of relative size for the local market. Nevertheless, the variety within the set of business groups is very broad in terms of size, sectors, and foundation year. The groups were, generally, more than thirty years old and belonged to different sectors of the productive system. According to size, the sample can be divided into two broad categories. In the first, we find those groups that are considered large in Argentina, though of medium size in international terms. These business groups had sales of over US$1 billion in 2007. The second category comprises groups with average sales

---

[1] The fact that a business group has two or more listed companies is, therefore, not essential for defining Argentinian business groups in this chapter.

Table 12.1 Business groups in Argentina: Preliminary profile

Business groups	Year founded	Main sectors	Sales in $ 000 *	
			1997	2004/5
Techint	1952	Steel. oil and gas; construction	7,000.0	19,800.0
Bunge & Born	1884	Agribusiness; chemicals	1,340.0	4,634.0
AGD[†]	1948	Agribusiness; transport	840.6	3,809.0
P. Companc	1946	Food; agribusiness	1,621.0	2,949.0
Arcor	1951	Food; agribusiness	1,070.0	2,790.0
Bulgheroni[‡]	1928	Oil and gas	N.A.	2,586.0
Coto	1960	Food; retail; transport;	N.A.	2,224.0
Clarín	1945	Media; entertainment; publishing	1,651.0	2,237.5
Aluar/Fate	1940	Aluminum; rubber	654.7	2,076.0
Sancor	1936	Food; financial and health services	720.1	1,204.0
SocMa	1954	Construction; food	2,170.0	1,181.4
Werthein	1904	Telecommunications; financial services; food; beverages; agribusiness;	N.A.	945.0
Ledesma	1914	Sugar; paper	250.0	851.0
Cartellone	1918	Construction; beverages; food; electricity	560.0	705.0
Pescarmona	1907	Construction; electronics and iT	658.0	556.0
Eurnekian	c.1970	Transport services; real-estate	n/a	483.0
Román	1961	Logistic; transportation services	120.0	472.0
Bagó	1934	Pharmaceutical	400.0	437.0
Sidus	1938	Pharmaceutical; biotechnology	200.0	395.0
Roggio	1908	Construction; road services; garbage disposal	508.2	358.0
L; nación	1870	Media; publishing;	179.0	351.0
Alpargatas	1883	Textile; shoe; retail	422.0	311.0
IRSA	1990	Real-estate; retail	N.A.	261.0
Sava/Gancia	1946	Beverages; food;	200.0	248.0
SCP	1927	Entertainment; oil and gas	360.0	130.0
Banco Velox / Disco	c.1970	Financial services; retail	2,118.3	N.App
Bemberg	1888	Food; beverages; agribusiness	892.0	N.App
Acindar	c.1940	Steel; electricity	600.8	N.App
Fortabat	1926	Cement; transport; entertainment	383.8	N.App
G&Z	c.1880	Domestic goods; food	204.0	N.App

Notes:

* Exchange rate in 2004/5: US$ 1=$3.1; Sales in $m. (Argentine peso). 1997: US$ 1= $ 1.

‡ Sales of Pan American Energy (PAE), the main firm in which Bulgheroni has 40% participation. N.A=not available; N.App.=not applicable (as those business groups have disappeared).

† ADG is considered as "related diversified" because its transport companies provides services to its agricultural companies.

Sources: Compiled by the authors, based on *Mercado, Apertura, América Economía*; and companies' financial reports.

of $300 million. Although there are some exceptions, the groups in the second category act predominantly in the domestic market and, generally, are more likely to have a tradition of family management.

Business groups in Argentina have usually been studied from a historical perspective. Because of this, the main studies tend to relate the collective behavior of business groups (and companies' decisions) to the different stages of evolution in the industrialization process of the country (Kosacoff et al. 1992; Kosacoff 1993). Rooted in microeconomics, such studies deal mainly with market configuration, political links, and the concentration and power of big organizations (among them, business groups) as part of the development process of the national economy (Azpiazu 1989; Basualdo 2000; Kosacoff and Ramos 2001; Azpiazu et al. 2004; Rougier and Schvarzer 2006).

However, there has been a lack of studies focusing on the strategy of Argentine companies facing the challenge of sustained growth in a more global context or, even, a regional one. There are a few works that have taken this kind of approach—the most important being Bisang (1998a, b, 2000), Kosacoff et al. (1999), and Kosacoff (2000), although these were still rooted mainly in industrial organization.

More recently, from a business and managerial perspective, a new research stream concerned with the strategic behavior of business groups has emerged. From a case-study perspective (Fracchia 2002; Carrera et al. 2003), with formal tests of specific hypothesis (Carrera et al. 2000), and anchored in quantitative and qualitative data (Carrera et al. 2000; Fracchia and Mesquita 2007), these address the strategic responses given by business groups to main environmental changes. The present study is intended to bring insight to this new line of research into the recent evolution of business groups in Argentina.

Business groups in Argentina—as, for example, in Belgium (Kurgan-van Hentenryk 1997)—do not tend to trade their capital publicly. In 2007, the shares of only one business group were traded as a holding, and less than 40 percent of business groups publicly traded any of the stock of the firms belonging to them.[2] So, there is not a great deal of public information about business groups, and accessing it is not easy.

Access to economic and financial data for these groups was limited because of the specific circumstances of each business group. Many of these business groups manage their companies in a very autonomous fashion. In other words, they grant a wide latitude in management to each individual company. Additionally, access was restricted to companies in which groups participate without exercising full control.

To counterbalance this, we worked with two additional sources of data and information. First, we surveyed top executives from twenty-one business groups.[3] For that, we

---

[2] Previously, some business groups (such as G&Z, Acindar, Alpargatas) transformed themselves, as holdings, into joint-stock companies with access to the capital market (see Carrera et al. 2000).

[3] The survey was designed by Professor Pankaj Ghemawat, who coordinated a larger project at the Harvard Business School to study the behavior of business groups in emerging countries undergoing Competitive Shocks. The survey had sixty-eight questions covering the reality of business groups according to eight topics, namely: ownership, corporate strategy, internationalization processes, strategic alliances, capital markets, top management labor market, coordination mechanisms among group companies, and family business nature. The questionnaire emphasized aspects related to corporate

conducted a personal interview with a member of each business group—in most cases, the actual owners, CEOs, or top managers.[4] This meant that the information from local business groups was based not only on a series of systematic data obtained through this survey, but also on public information and on direct contact with top managers. Secondly, part of the information pertaining to the remaining groups was compiled from public sources.

12.3 BUSINESS GROUPS IN ARGENTINA: ORIGINS

Grupos economicos (business groups) have always existed in Argentina. Despite that, they originated at different times, and followed different development paths, resulting in some very diverse business portfolios and strategic profiles. In this section we provide an analysis of the genesis of business groups in Argentine history. As a further illustration, Table 12.2, based on Khanna and Yafeh (2007), summarizes the main aspects related to the process of the origination of business groups in Argentina.

In addition, Fig. 12.1 summarizes this process by listing the main business groups that emerged and disappeared within each major historical period. A first set of Argentine business groups originated at the end of nineteenth century and early in the twentieth century, within Argentina's agricultural exports model. Up to 1930, Argentina consolidated an open economy model supported by its natural comparative advantages and the development of its agribusiness sector. Aligned with this, initial business groups operated in the agricultural sector through land acquisition, and also in manufacturing or service activities related to that sector.

From the 1940s, in an environment where economic policy supported the substitution of imports within the framework of a closed economy, new companies arose that became the basis of future business groups. Through regulations, protectionism, and state-owned firms, some Argentine firms benefited from supply contracts or a closed and protected domestic market. Although this meant there were frequent market and policy distortions, many of those firms grew into larger business groups, thanks to the stabilized cash flows they achieved, even in unrelated businesses (Carrera et al. 2003).

From the mid-1960s to the end of the 1980s, a second set of business groups started to develop. This was due either to the actions of some businessmen, who thought diversifying their businesses was the only logical way to grow in a closed and stagnant market, or

strategy and internationalization processes. In the first category, it sought to study the evolution in the degree of diversification and the degree of vertical and/or horizontal integration.

[4] In general, these interviews, following the questions in the survey, were especially valuable in terms of the informal discussion carried out with group representatives. Each meeting lasted an average of two hours. They were prepared according to a preliminary in-depth study of each business group, which allowed for additional information to be covered. There was a clear attempt not to sort that information on the basis of prior knowledge, but, rather, to be very objective as regards the answers provided by group representatives.

Table 12.2 Business groups in Argentina: Origins

Main business groups	State backing		Privatization-related			Family ties
	Promoted	Contracting/sourcing	Opportunity	Strategic	New business	
Business groups originating before 1930						
Bemberg	X					X
Bulgheroni	X	X		X		X
Cartellone	X	X			X	X
Pescarmona	X	X			X	X
Werthein	X		X			X
Business groups originating during 1930–75						
AGD				X		X
Aluar/Fate	X	X	X	X		X
P Companc		X	X	X		Managed by the first generation
SocMa	X	X	X		X	Managed by the first generation
Techint	X	X	X			
Business groups originating after 1990						
Avila						Managed by the first generation
IRSA						Managed by the first generation

Source: Compiled by the authors, based on Khanna and Yafeh (2007).

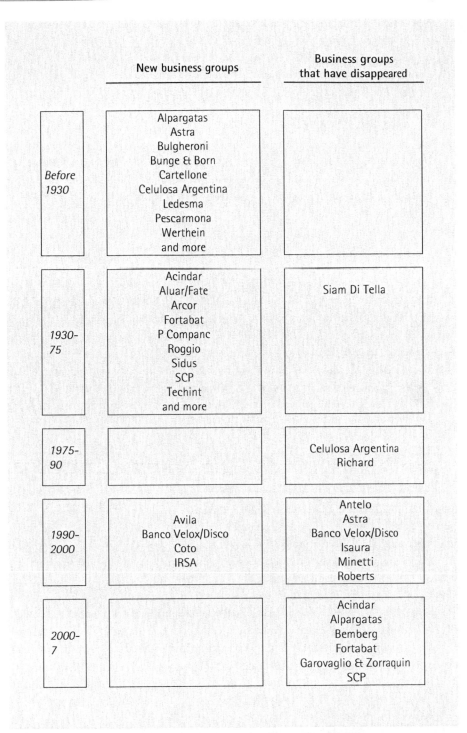

	New business groups	Business groups that have disappeared
Before 1930	Alpargatas Astra Bulgheroni Bunge & Born Cartellone Celulosa Argentina Ledesma Pescarmona Werthein and more	
1930–75	Acindar Aluar/Fate Arcor Fortabat P Companc Roggio Sidus SCP Techint and more	Siam Di Tella
1975–90		Celulosa Argentina Richard
1990–2000	Avila Banco Velox/Disco Coto IRSA	Antelo Astra Banco Velox/Disco Isaura Minetti Roberts
2000–7		Acindar Alpargatas Bemberg Fortabat Garovaglio & Zorraquin SCP

Figure 12.1 Business groups in Argentina: Origins and evolution

Source: Compiled by the authors.

to the growth certain companies attained as a result of becoming state suppliers and basking in extremely favorable protectionist environments (Bisang 1998a, b).

From the mid-1970s on, some movement toward liberalization began taking place in Argentina (first as a financial liberalization, then as a trade one). This was neither very successful nor sustained for any length of time. Consequently, by the end of the 1980s, Argentina was displaying a growing macroeconomic instability. The general impairment of economic performance was worsened by a loss of efficiency in regulating institutions. Finally, the deterioration of the judicial system further contributed to the extreme uncertainty engulfing the country at the end of this decade. In this environment, the hyperinflation phenomenon of mid-1989 and early 1990 became a turning point. This situation brought about the reform process that would yield a new economic order.

Throughout the 1990s, Argentina underwent a broad transformation process. The achievement of economic stability, the renewed acces to trade, the leading role played by external funds, and the backtracking of the state as a business player were the main traits of this transformation. Through the *Convertibilidad* (Convertibility) Law—which was passed in 1991 and which enabled the country to eliminate hyperinflation in the same year, opened product and capital markets, and deregulated several sectors of the economy—the Argentine government was able to guarantee economic stability. At the same time, the administration proceeded to privatize state companies (including utilities, as well as other firms with businesses such as airports, air transport, steel, and media), restructure external debt, eliminate promoted activities, deregulate several economic sectors (including oil and mining), and introduce tax and labor reforms. Throughout this period, the public sector incurred in an increasing level of expense and a significant rise in sector indebtedness. Moreover, emphasizing the regional approach, this decade saw the launching of MERCOSUR.[5] This reform process was introduced in the context of a dynamic international environment that was continuously exposed to globalization, technological breakthroughs, and recurrent currency crises in emerging economies.

In short, as a consequence of the process described, there was, during the 1990s, a harsh change of rules. Modern and market-driven reforms resulted in sudden, significant, and permanent alterations in the ways of doing business. In other words, it is possible to say that the country went through a profound Competitive Shock.

The market for tradable goods and some services were the most affected at the beginning. The deregulation and privatization plans produced dramatic changes in the rules governing those sectors. Increasing external competition and the arrival of new multinational corporations forced Argentine companies to meet the challenge of achieving high productivity and competitiveness levels to survive in business. As for the financial sector, the impact of the Competitive Shock was not felt until after 1995

---

[5] The MERCOSUR (Mercado Común del Sur) is a regional agreement that works as a Customs Union. It was created in 1991 when Argentina, Brazil, Paraguay, and Uruguay signed the Asunción Treaty. In 1997 the block had a population of 220 million people and a GDP of US$1.3 billion. During 1990–7, the trade exchange between the countries in the Treaty increased by more than 400%.

and the Tequila Effect.[6] A different situation was found in the automotive sector, which, in the reform program, was one of the few sectors favored by industrial protectionist policies.

The consolidated business groups were already being forced to perform in this context of strong competition and extensive change in the legal framework and regulations. In addition, there were great opportunities, mainly related to the privatization process, for Argentine business groups. Only a few new agents from the business group organizations took part in the value creation process. Few new business groups emerged during this period.

From 1998 on, the Argentine economy underwent a major slowdown. In December 2001, after a bank crisis, the Argentine government derogated the *Convertibilidad* Law and devalued the local currency. At the same time, it declared a sovereign debt default.

In a very short period of time Argentine faced what can be called an Anticompetitive Shock (Carrera et al. 2003). The country underwent the worst crisis of the last hundred years (Gerchunoff and Llach 2003). Main economic variables suffered a major collapse. As foreign debt was extremely high relative to Argentine's capacity to generate foreign cash (by the end of 2000, total public debt was more than five times its exports, according to Gerchunoff and Llach 2003),[7] the country ended up declaring the biggest ever sovereign default in history.

After that, a political and social crisis took place in Argentina. An interim government took control of the situation, until mid-2003, when a new president was elected. Throughout 2003–7 Argentina embarked on a period of governability recovery, economic growth, and debt renegotiation (together with credit access). Its main political orientation was, according to the elected President's words, "to reconstruct a local capitalism that allows for the promotion of social ascending mobility." Assisted by a favorable international environment, and by a tight orthodox fiscal policy, Argentina experienced a sustained economic recovery (with GDP growing at an average yearly rate of 8 percent for the period 2003–7).

Throughout this period, no new business groups emerged.[8] Some new local business agents did appear, but so far they do not seem to have responded to the business group way of organization. They mainly emerged as focused businesses (or with tightly related diversification). Most of them are related to the acquisition of assets belonging to foreign firms that decided to leave the country,[9] mainly

[6] "Tequila Effect" is the name given to the impact of the 1994 Mexican economic crisis on the South American economy. The Tequila Effect occurred because of a sudden devaluation in the Mexican peso, which then caused other currencies in the region (the Southern Cone and Brazil) to decline.

[7] Brazil and Turkey were the two countries that followed Argentina in that ranking. By that time both had suffered a financial crisis.

[8] As was already explained, we are not considering Private Equity Investment Funds, which appear to have main participation in the new ways of organization.

[9] The post-devaluation environment is obviously vital for an understanding of these strategies. Changes in the relative price structure and foreign nominated debts resulted in heavy burdens for agents who had previously acted in Argentina.

in business sectors related to government interests and regulation, such as energy, banking, and health services. In addition, these new actors do not provide financial backing for their own operations (something understandable after the default).

In parallel, some dynamism has also been observed in the agribusiness sector, which has expanded particularly under the recent soy boom (Adeco, El Tejar and Los Grobo). Although these are family businesses and have shown continued and sustained growth, they still remain as single businesses (and, thus, they do not correspond to a business group way of organization).

Finally, it can be seen that since the late nineteenth century and up to the 1970s, business groups tended to generate, form, and consolidate in Argentina. Founded by family entrepreneurs, they all seem to have emerged aligned to the different economic policies that Argentina pledged (although following different consolidation paths), many of them with some state backing. During the 1990s, only a few business groups emerged. As opposed to what had happened previously, their origins were not closely linked to any state backing role. None of the business groups that emerged in this period has turned either into a large business group[10] or into an unrelated diversified one. Finally, we have to say that from 2002 no business groups have emerged at all. We will come back to this issue in the last section of the chapter.

12.4 BASIC PROFILE OF ARGENTINE BUSINESS GROUPS

12.4.1 Size

Table 12.1 above summarizes business groups according to their sales level. Seen from a greater perspective, Argentine business groups do not seem to be large. In the 1990s, the largest business groups in Argentina represented 10 per cent of Argentina's private-sector activity (Carrera et al. 2003), and since then this percentage has progressively diminished. Local firms' participation among the biggest 500 firms in Argentina has been decreasing continually since 1993 (Encuesta Nacional de Grandes Empresas 2006, 2007). In terms of Latin America, only 13 firms belonging to Argentine business groups made it into the 500 América Economía in 2006 (that is, the biggest 500 firms in Latin America). In fact, Argentinian firms in general (business groups, MNCs, subsidiaries, etc.) showed a low participation: 40 out of 500 firms.

---

[10] With the exception of Coto, a business group where size is related to the nature of its main business (retail).

12.4.2 Ownership

In Argentina most business groups follow a classic pattern of organization: privately held, family owned (Fisman and Khanna 2004). Founding families generally own the conglomerate through shareholdings in a hierarchy of holdings and subsidiaries. More than 75 per cent of the families owning business groups declared that they possess more than 50 per cent of the group's equity (see Table 12.3).

Only some business groups publicly trade part of the capital of the firms within the group. In fact, 42 percent of business groups have no firms at all that have opened any of their capital to the stock market. At the same time, 26 per cent of business groups publicly trade stocks of all the firms that are part of the group (see Table 12.4).

Argentina has never had a developed stock market. In such an imperfect financial market environment, not only are firms unlikely publicly to trade their stocks, but business groups are in a position to find better and quicker ways for their firms to access cash, thus enjoying a competitive advantage over their stand-alone competitors (Carrera et al. 2003).

An additional feature of business groups in developing countries is the scant separation between ownership and management, since these are, in general, family businesses. In the Argentinian case, 94 percent of business groups showed actual

Table 12.3 Business groups in Argentina: Ownership

Family-owned capital (as % of total equity)	Business groups (as % of all business groups surveyed)
0	0
1–49.99	21
50–99.99	63
100	16

Source: Compiled by the authors.

Table 12.4 Business groups in Argentina: Publicly traded companies

Publicly traded capital (asset value of companies publicly traded as a % of total business-group asset value)	Business groups (as % of all business groups surveyed)
0	42
1–49.99	11
50–99.99	21
100	26

Source: Compiled from a survey conducted by the authors.

Table 12.5 Business groups in Argentina: Active family involvement

Youngest family generation already actively running the business group	Business groups (as % of all business groups surveyed)
First generation	0
Second generation	28
Third generation	33
Fourth generation or more	33
No family involvement	6

Source: Compiled from a survey conducted by the authors.

Table 12.6 Business groups in Argentina: Overlapping generations in family businesses

No. of family generations co-running the business group	Business groups (as % of all business groups surveyed)
Only one generation	31
Two generations	63
Three generations	6
Four generations	0

Source: Compiled from a survey conducted by the authors.

active involvement of family members. In fact, in 66 per cent at least the third generation was already working in the business group (see Table 12.5).

This pattern usually emerges from the coexistence of several generations co-managing business groups. At least two generations coexisted in 69 percent of the business groups under study (see Table 12.6).

12.4.3 Governance, structure, and control

The board composition of business groups shows that family involvement is very high. On average, more than 60 percent of the positions on the Boards of Directors of the business groups surveyed were occupied by family members (see Table 12.7).

Another typical feature of business groups is related to interlocking directorates. While in Argentina interlocking directorates is not a common practice *between* business groups, it is a usual practice *within* business groups (that is, between firms belonging to the same business group) (see Table 12.8).

As can be seen from this section, Argentinian business groups do not use complex structures to achieve control over all their members. Rather, they tend to follow traditional and simple mechanisms. Lack of both financial market development and institutional stability are among the main reasons for such behaviors. Control is

Table 12.7 Business groups in Argentina: Governance—board composition

Type of director	Average percentage of board members
Family member among top management	43
Family member not involved in business group management	18
Internal professional (non-family) director	19
External director	14
Other	6

Source: Compiled from a survey conducted by the authors.

Table 12.8 Business groups in Argentina: Governance—interlocking directorates

Directors shared by different firms (%)	Business groups (as % of all business groups surveyed)
<10	10
10–24.99	14
25–50	19
>50	57

Source: Compiled from a survey conducted by the authors.

Table 12.9 Business groups in Argentina: Organizational structure

Organizational structure type	Business groups (as % of all business groups surveyed)
Functional	0
Hierarchical (classical)	39
Hierarchical (complex)	56
Other	6

Source: Compiled from a survey conducted by the authors.

achieved by possessing a majority of shares, active family involvement, and a certain degree of interlocking directorates within business groups (but not between them). Consequently, almost all Argentinian business groups are organized under a hierarchical structure, with a holding unit coordinating all the rest (see Table 12.9).

To illustrate this, Fig. 12.2 presents the organization structure of two business groups (one of a related-diversified business group—vertically integrated—and one of an unrelated diversified business group).

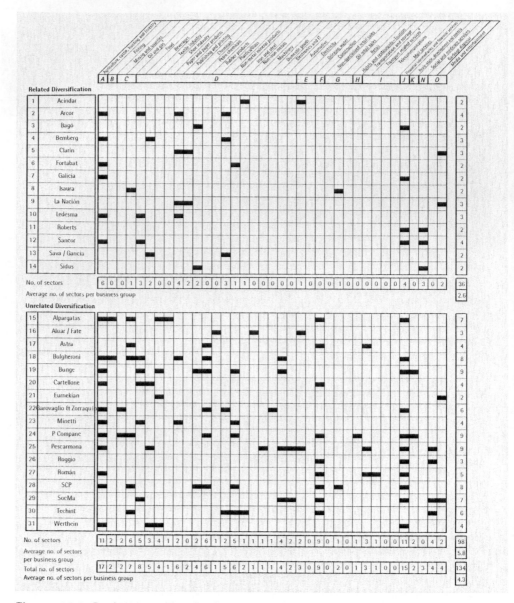

Figure 12.2 Business groups in Argentina: Diversification, main business sectors, 1990

Notes: * Includes all extraction, transportation, refinery and distribution processes. † Includes, among others, paint, pharmaceutical, and plague-control products. ‡ Includes, among others, services such as toll collecting and port administration. Letters A–O correspond to the SIC-code system (at a 2-digit level). Bunge & Born was omitted from this figure because its headquarters are not currently in Argentina. In recent years Bunge & Born has been operating in the international commodities markets as a multinational business group.

From the information we have gathered in Sections 12.3 and 12.4 on the profile of Argentinian business groups, we can summarize three main characteristics. They are (1) family owned, in that a family (or a group of families) has the power to make strategic decisions; (2) large, in that they have revenues above US$100 million (as per the exchange rate of 2007);[11] and (3) diversified, as the firms integrating each business group are either involved in more than one industry or have a predominant role in a business to which activities belonging to different links in a single value chain are associated. With reference to this last point, firms such as state-owned firms, private-equity investment funds, large focused family-owned firms, or small family-owned diversified sets of firms do not constitute the object of study of the present research.

12.5 BUSINESS GROUP DYNAMICS: EVOLUTION SINCE THE 1990S

While, on the one hand, business groups can gradually redefine their objectives in the different stages of development in their national economies (Paredes and Sánchez 1994; Kock and Guillén 2001), on the other hand, since they are institutions in a permanent state of flux that need to adjust to environmental needs, when a major environmental transformation takes place, they can either seize new opportunities, or perish.

As Argentina has gone through major transformations, both economic and political, since the start of the 1990s, this section analyzes the recent evolution of business groups. We will consider two main factors. First, we will analyze the way in which business groups have responded strategically in terms of degree and type of diversification during the relevant period. Secondly, we will take a deeper look at the dynamic of dissolution of business groups.

12.5.1 Strategic response: Business diversification

Despite the fact that business groups manifested non-uniform development paths throughout the 1990s, a general trend was observed in the diversification level of business groups. On average, business group diversification grew from 4.3 business lines in 1990 to 4.6 in 1997/2000 (see Table 12.10 and Figs. 12.3 and 12.4). In addition,

---

[11] For previous years that figure has been adjusted according to PPP.

Table 12.10 Business groups in Argentina: Dynamics of business diversification

Related diversification		No. of sectors*			Unrelated diversification		No. of sectors*		
Rank	Business groups	1990	1997/2000	2007	Rank	Business groups	1990	1997/2000	2007
1	Acindar	2	2	N.A.	22	Alpargatas	7	4	N.A.
2	AGD	N.A.	4	4	23	Aluar/Fate	3	3	3
3	Arcor	4	5	5	24	Astra	4	N.A.	N.A.
4	Avila	N.A.	3	3	25	Banco Velox/Disco	N.A.	3	N.A.
5	Bagó	2	2	2	26	Bulgheroni	8	3	N.A.
6	Bemberg	3	3	N.A.	27	Bunge	9	N.A.	N.A.
7	Bulgheroni	N.A.	N.A.	1	28	Cartellone	4	6	5
8	Clarín	3	5	5	29	Eurnekian	2	2	4
9	Coto	N.A.	3	3	30	Garovaglio & Zorraquin	6	5	N.A.
10	Fortabat	2	4	N.A.	31	Minetti	4	N.A.	N.A.
11	Galicia	2	2	2	32	P. Companc	9	10	N.A.
12	IRSA	N.A.	4	4	33	Pescarmona	9	9	7
13	Isaura	2	N.A.	N.A.	34	Roggio	3	9	8
14	La Nación	3	3	3	35	Román	5	N.A.	N.A.
15	Ledesma	3	5	5	36	SCP	8	12	N.A.
16	P. Companc	N.A.	N.A.	3	37	SocMa	7	10	7
17	Roberts	2	N.A.	N.A.	38	Techint	6	8	5
18	Román	N.A.	2	2	39	Werthein	4	4	6
19	Sancor	4	4	4					

Related diversification

Rank	Business groups	No. of sectors *		
		1990	1997/2000	2007
20	Sava/Gancia	2	3	3
21	Sidus	2	2	2
	Business groups with related diversification	14	17	16
	Average no. sectors/per business group	2,6	3,3	3,2

Unrelated diversification

Rank	Business groups	No. of sectors *		
		1990	1997/2000	2007
	Business groups with unrelated diversification	17	14	8
	Average no. sectors/per business group	5,8	6,3	5,6
	Total no. business groups	31	31	24
	Average no. sectors/per business group	4,3	4,6	4,0

Notes: * Number of sectors in which each business group was involved. N.A. = not applicable. (some business groups did not work as a group during some period of time, so the number of business sectors in which such a group is involved is not an applicable qualification).

Source: Elaborated by the authors.

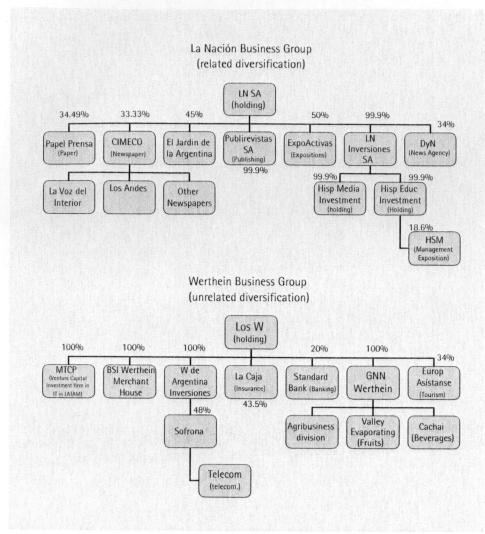

Figure 12.3. Business groups hierarchical structure: Two cases

Source: Compiled by the authors, based on Apertura and Vassolo and Perkins (2005); and companies' financial info.

this pattern was observed in business groups with both related- and unrelated-diversification strategies.[12]

---

[12] Business or industry diversification presents some methodological difficulties when it comes down to measuring it (Iacobucci and Rosa 2005). To counterbalance these drawbacks, we address diversification measuring through both quantitative and qualitative means. As described by Khanna and Yafeh (2005), we measure the number of different sectors in which each business group operates (at a 2-digit SIC code level). At the same time, we classify the type of diversification of each business group. For that, using the categorization presented by Rumelt (1974), we classify each business group as having either *related diversification* (Dominant Business or Related Business according to Rumelt's categories, which will include Vertical Integration) or *unrelated diversification*. Geographic diversification was measured as the number of countries in which the business groups declared they were present.

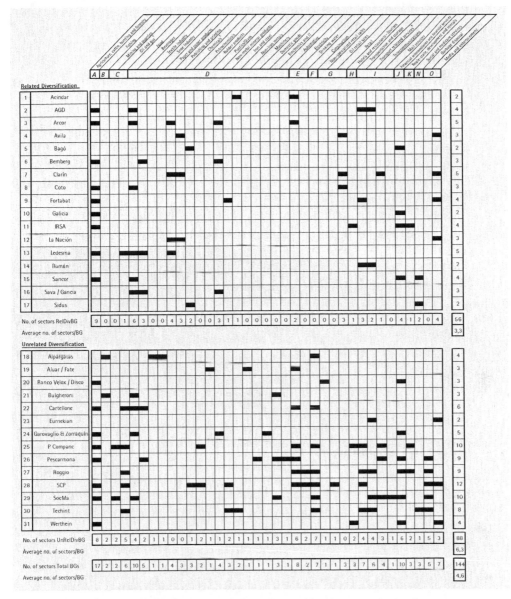

Figure 12.4 Business groups in Argentina: Diversification, main business sectors, 1997–2000

Notes: * Includes all extraction, transportation, refinery and distribution processes. † Includes, among others, paint, pharmaceutical and plague control products. ‡ Includes among others services such as toll collecting and port administration. Letters A–O correspond to the SIC-code system (at a 2-digit level).

Source: Compiled from a survey conducted by the authors.

Although inverse behaviors were expected in the light of market-driven reforms and trade liberalization (Carrera et al. 2003; Fracchia and Mesquita 2007), abundant business opportunities and the privatization process were the main inductors of such behaviors (Carrera et al. 2003; Fracchia and Mesquita 2007). In the situation that followed the Competitive Shock, privatizations emerged as a significant platform for some business groups to gain access to new businesses (something that has already been stated by Achi et al. 1998). This opportunity embodied a natural and realistic alternative to reallocating resources for those business groups with a previous and historical strong background of dealing with the state (the so-called contractors) (Carrera et al. 2003).

After the main reform of the 1990s, a different behavior was observed. From 2000 on, the trend toward diversification growth reversed. On average, business group diversification diminished from 4.6 in 1997–2000 to 4.0 in 2007 (see Table 12.10, Figs. 12.3, 12.4, and 12.5). While this pattern of behavior could be observed mainly in business groups pursuing unrelated-diversification strategies, the ones pursuing related-diversification strategies sustained their diversification level, although this was in part due to the fact that during this period some business groups turned from unrelated-diversified strategies to more focused ones.

Since Argentina's financial crisis, there has not been a unique strategic behavior of business groups.[13] Four main trends can be identified. First, some business groups focused mainly in the domestic market and, burdened with financial problems, had to concentrate resources (including top management) on debt renegotiation (Coto, La Nación, Sancor).

Secondly, other business groups sold part of their assets as a way to cancel debts, thus focusing their strategies (Bunge & Born, Román, P. Companc). This partly reflects what would be expected, according to the literature that analyzes privatization processes in emerging countries and the intervention of local business groups. After 1997–2000, those business groups that had participated in privatizations in an opportunistic way actually ceased some of the activities deployed during privatizations.[14]

A third set of business groups consolidated their business positions (Arcor, Bagó, Sidus). Despite the crisis affecting Argentina, they maintained the same strategic behavior they had already been implementing, focusing on an internationally driven business orientation. In fact, these business groups are among the firms that have recently begun to be called *Multilatinas*.[15] Because they were already focused internationally before the crisis took place, they were better prepared to cope with the financial

---

[13] It should also be stated that, although business groups often originate from a strong financial company (as the case of many Korean and Mexican business groups), in Argentina only one business group originated in that way. In 2007, 30% of the business groups participated in some way in a financial sector.

[14] This also reflected, in some way, the internal financial market function that is traditionally attributed to business groups (Shin and Stulz 1998), especially in markets with institutional imperfections, as is the case of the emerging economies (Leff 1976; Ghemawat and Khanna 1998; Khanna and Yafeh 2007).

[15] Multinationals from Latin America (Goldstein and Toulan 2007).

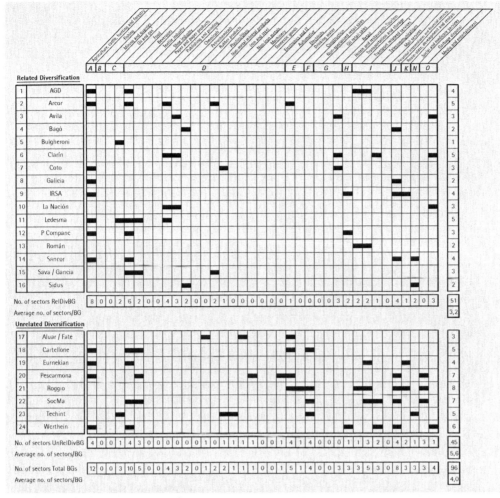

Figure 12.5 Business groups in Argentina: Diversification, main business sectors, 2007

Notes: * Includes all extraction, transportation, refinery and distribution processes. † Includes, among others, paint, pharmaceutical and plague control products. ‡ Includes among others services such as toll collecting and port administration. Letters A–O correspond to the SIC-code system (at a 2-digit level).

Source: Compiled from a survey conducted by the authors.

distress that resulted from devaluation. Their size also helped them to avoid being easy targets for any foreign agent acquisitions' strategy (Fracchia and Mesquita 2007).

And, fourthly, in complete contrast to the trend observed during the previous decade, business groups ceased to consider increasing unrelated diversification. After 2002, only two business groups deployed additional business line expansion, taking advantage of foreign firms leaving their activities in Argentina (Werthein in telecommunications, and Eurnekian in airport services).

Many "unrelated diversified business groups" have managed to survive in the changing economic and institutional environment of Argentina. That is why it is interesting to analyze the competitive capabilities of those groups. We would point out first that business groups in underdeveloped countries—such as Argentina—tend to provide substitutes for institutions that are lacking. As a consequence, many business groups are in a position to survive environmental changes. Another key point to consider is that the "unrelated-diversification" strategy may be a good one to deal with the problem of the scale of the internal market. As the internal market in Argentina is not large, many business groups tend to grow by developing economic activities in several economic sectors at the same time. This strategy is determined by the infrastructure and financial capital of the business groups concerned. And the strategy becomes easier as the group becomes more diversified.

Moreover, the "unrelated-diversification" strategy makes it easier for business groups to take advantage of the economic opportunities that institutional changes generate. Most business groups of this kind are strongly linked to the public sector, which makes it easier for them to take up the new opportunities. As a consequence, the "unrelated-diversification" strategy seems to work well in changing environments, as in the case of Argentina.

12.5.2 Strategic response: Internationalization

Historically, Argentinian business groups' development was focused mainly on the domestic market (the few exceptions being those whose businesses were naturally oriented to international markets—for example, AGD or Bunge & Born).

Although some business groups began activities in foreign markets in the 1980s, it was during the 1990s that the process of internationalization took off in a big way among the Argentinian business groups. As analyzed in Carrera et al. (2000), during this period business groups greatly boosted their business internationalization processes. Such processes featured exports, strategic alliances with foreign-market partners, and even direct foreign investment.

Business groups that took a more active involvement in developing international activities, such as Techint, Arcor, and Sidus, have shown a higher sustainable performance (Carrera et al. 2003). This was due, on the one hand, to the effects of the changes that those business groups underwent as they had to raise their domestic standards in order to meet the international ones (in terms of competition, quality, and regulation compliance). On the other hand, internationalization lowered the effect that Argentine's cycle volatility had on these business groups (something that became clear in 2002). Firms like Bagó and Aluar are examples of this.

From the early 2000s on, Argentinian business groups have shown an increasing concentration on their internationalization (Fracchia and Mesquita 2007). Lately, there has been a second phase of expansion for those business groups that participated in Argentina's privatization process. After some years of experience and learning, these business groups are now participating in other countries' privatization processes as a way of internationalizing their utilities businesses (Cartellone and Roggio are the main examples).

12.5.3 Dissolution of business groups

The first thing that should be highlighted is the fact that, as can be observed in Fig. 12.1, the dissolution of business groups in Argentina is a recent phenomenon, one that has been seen since 1990. Before then, only a few business groups disappeared—all of them as a consequence of a financial crisis that was due to overexpansion (Rougier and Schvarzer 2006).

During the 1990s some business groups ceased to exist. A basic uniform pattern was observed. In the context of increasing foreign competition, these business groups disappeared because of the opportunities for mergers and acquisitions (M&A) that appeared. Owner families sold their companies to foreign specialized competitors that wanted to launch their businesses in Argentina—or even in a local region.

After 2001, another set of business groups dissolved. But the pattern was somewhat different from the one observed during the previous decade. The Argentinian crisis represented a difficult test for local firms: a depressed domestic market, a very high level of debt nominated in foreign currencies, and no credit access. Argentinian business groups were no exception.

Three main patterns for the dissolution of business groups were observed. Some of them disappeared as a consequence of financial distress—actually generated even before 2001 (examples are Alpargatas, Garovaglio y Zorraquin, and SCP). Another set of business groups, with activities mainly focused in the domestic market and confronted with big debts nominated in dollars, decided to sell their firms as the best way to find a solution to their problems (for example, Acindar, Bemberg, and Fortabat). A final set of business groups is represented by those that decided to sell part of their assets, as a way to generate cash to alleviate their debts. Although these groups did not disappear, they reduced their size considerably and transformed themselves from unrelated-diversified business groups into related-diversified ones (P. Companc, which sold its traditional energy business, was the most typical example).

12.6 FINAL REMARKS

According to the present study, business groups have been an important economic actor throughout the development of modern Argentina. Having somewhat uniform characteristics (family owned, hierarchical structure, diversified), Argentine business groups were active during every phase of the development of the country.

Since the 1990s, the strategic behavior of existing Argentine business groups has been characterized by two main trends. First, most business groups have been mainly directed toward reducing the scope of their business and even toward specialization (after an initial brief period in which they broadened their scope). This was partly in order to reduce financial distress, but was also a way to compete with foreign corporations—seen not only in market competition but also in the firms' acquisition strategies. The second trend has been the drive of business groups toward the internationalization of their activities.

Apart from this common behavior, a few business groups can also be mentioned as pursuing unrelated diversification strategies. For instance, Eduardo Eurnekian has recently declared that the Eurnekian business group's core business is always going to be "the one that has the largest income figure" (*Apertura* 2007). But such an attitude is not widespread, so we can say that the entrepreneurial capability that it is alleged is being exploited by business groups (see Guillén 2000) does not seem to be enough to generate this kind of behavior in the recent conditions in Argentina.

It can be observed that, since the 1990s in Argentina, while some business groups have dissolved, new ones have not tended to emerge. The selling opportunities of the 1990s, and the heavy financial distress encountered after the crisis of 2002, are among the main reasons explaining the dissolution of business groups in Argentina.

In addition, there are other factors, not analyzed in the present study, that could have contributed to those events. We cannot avoid mentioning the fact that business groups are also family firms. Business groups such as Fortabat, Perez Companc, and SocMa, to mention some examples, have encountered serious problems of succession, and these cannot be ignored when considering the behavior observed recently in these groups.

One salient aspect of this dissolution process that needs further analysis is the fact that many of the foreign acquisitions of Argentinian business groups came not only from big MNCs but from business groups from other emerging economies (especially from Brazil and Chile, thus showing very different trends in other Latin American business groups). This might emphasize something that has already been pinpointed in this chapter—that not all business groups are alike, and that a more profound study of the recent Argentinian case might shed light over this subject area.

Interesting, also, is the fact that no new business groups have emerged in Argentina recently. Two types of actors have emerged. The first are new entrepreneurial agents (as already stated in Section 12.3). But they cannot be considered as proper business groups, as they do not fully address the three main characteristics that we considered in our profile of Argentinian business groups profile—that they are (1) family owned; (2) large; and (3) diversified.

This is an issue that to be studied further in the years to come, particularly because it raises another important characteristic of business groups in emerging economies: the role of political links. After the 2002 crisis, the Argentine government did not pursue an active involvement with local business groups. The new business entrepreneurs that have emerged lately are in some way related to the political power. But how this is going to evolve remains to be seen.

The second type of actors that seems to be emerging represents the appearance of a new way of organization: the so-called private equity investment funds (PEIFs). These have already been addressed in the literature on business groups in emerging economies (see Khanna and Yafeh 2007). PEIFs constitute a way of organization that is different from business groups: they generally operate via professional management, usually participate through stock holding, and in most cases their permanence commitment is low (as they buy to sell after some time).

In Argentina, PEIFs constitute the main local agent taking an active role in capturing some of the emerging opportunities. Most interesting is the fact that some traditional families that were former owners of business groups in Argentina have reinvested part of their fortunes in these kinds of organizations—for example, Miguens (former owner of Bemberg), Grüneisen (Astra), and Soldati (SCP). Even some families that are still owners of business groups are participating in some PEIFs (for example, Macri (SocMa) and Escassany (Galicia)).

As a further illustrations of these recent trends, Fig. 12.6 shows how these two types of new business actors that emerged in Argentina after 2002 (the PEIFs and the entrepreneurial agents) relate to the main characteristics of business groups.

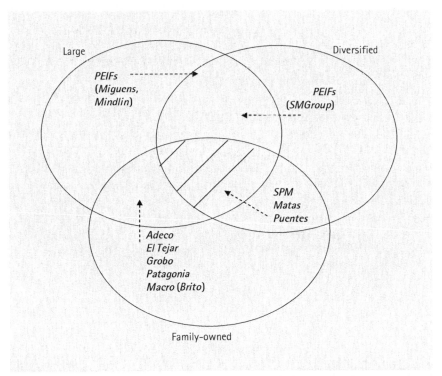

Figure 12.6 New development of organizations: Business groups, 2002–7.

Source: Elaborated by the authors.

Looking ahead, business groups still represent a main economic agent in emerging economies. And the present study highlights that Argentina is no exception. In this sense, although the classical question about *why business groups exist* is still relevant (an interest that can be traced even to Coase's seminal work), a not insignificant number of questions regarding *the how* of these organizations is still unanswered (Granovetter 1994). As Granovetter (1994) highlighted, these questions are of vital importance because they might even precede *the why* question. This study intends to shed some light on them, by presenting the Argentinian case.

This research has concentrated on the recent strategic behavior and adaptive capabilities of Argentine business groups. Its historical perspective, together with its focus on the recent strategic behavior of business groups, has raised interesting aspects that need further analyses. We agree with Professor Ghemawat in that the window for observation in this study is not long enough. The process that is being studied has not stopped: it is still showing signs of activity. A future study with a longer timeframe should be undertaken.[16] No single development path (much less, a desired one) seems to lie ahead for business groups in Argentina. The future of business groups is still open, and further research should concentrate on their study.

REFERENCES

ACHI, Z., BOULAS, C., BUCHANAN, I., FORTEZA, J., and ZAPPEI, L. (1998). "Conglomerates in Emerging Markets: Tigers or Dinosaurs?" *Strategy & Business*, 11: 59–69.

AHARONI, Y. (1966). *The Foreign Investment Decision Process*. Boston: Harvard Business School Press.

AMATORY, A. (1997). "Growth via Politics: Business Groups Italian-Style," in T. Shiba and M. Shimotani (eds.), *Beyond the Firm: Business Groups in International and Historical Perspective*. Oxford: Oxford University Press.

AMSDEN, A., and HIKINO, T. (1994). "Project Execution Capability, Organizational Know-How and Conglomerate Growth in Late Industrialization," *Industrial and Corporate Change*, 3: 111–47.

AZPIAZU, D. (1989). *Cara y contracara de los grupos económicos: Estado y promoción industrial en la Argentina*. Buenos Aires: Cántaro.

AZPIAZU, D., BASUALDO, E., and KHAVISSE, M. (2004). *El nuevo poder económico en la Argentina de los años 80*. Buenos Aires: Siglo XXI Editores Argentinos.

BASUALDO, E. (2000). *Concentración y centralización del capital en la Argentina durante la década del noventa*. Buenos Aires: Universidad Nacional de Quilmes Ediciones.

BISANG, R. (1998a). "Apertura, reestructuración industrial y los conglomerados empresarios", *Desarrollo rconómico*, 38 (special no.), 143–76.

BISANG, R. (1998b). "La estructura y dinámica de los conglomerados económicos en Argentina," in W. Peres (ed), *Grandes empresas y grupos industriales Latinoamericanos*. Madrid: Siglo XXI Editores.

---

[16] The research team is planning to conduct a new set of interviews among business groups, with a similar survey as the one used in this study, before 2010.

BISANG, R. (2000). "The Responses of National Holding Companies," in B. Kosacoff (ed.), *Corporate Strategies under Structural Adjustment in Argentina*. Basingstoke: Palgrave Macmillan.

CARRERA, A., FRACCHIA, E., ROCHA, H., and VILASECA, A. (2000). "The Strategic Response from Argentine Economic Groups to the Competitive Shock of the 90s." Paper presented at the 20th Annual International Conference of Strategic Management Society, Vancouver, Canada.

CARRERA, A., MESQUITA, L., PERKINS, G., and VASSOLO, R. (2003). "Business Groups and their Corporate Strategies in the Argentinean Roller Coaster of Competitive Shocks and Anti-Competitive Shocks," *Academy of Management Review Executive*, 17/3: 32–44.

Encuesta Nacional de Grandes Empresas (2006). INDEC.

Encuesta Nacional de Grandes Empresas (2007). INDEC.

FELDENKIRCHEN, W. (1997). "Business Groups in the German Electrical Industry," in T. Shiba and M. Shimotani (eds.), *Beyond the Firm: Business Groups in International and Historical Perspective*. Oxford: Oxford University Press.

FISMAN, R., and KHANNA, T. (2004). "Facilitating Development: The Role of Business Groups," *World Development*, 32/4: 609–28.

FRACCHIA, E. (2002). "Grupos económicos en la convertibilidad: Análisis de su comportamiento a partir de un estudio de casos." Presented at the annual meeting of the Asociación Argentina de Economía Política, Tucuman, Argentina.

FRACCHIA, E. and MESQUITA, L. (2007). "Corporate Strategies of Business Groups in the Wake of Competitive Shocks: Lessons from Argentina," in R. Grosse and L. Mesquita (eds.), *Can Latin American Firms Compete?* Oxford: Oxford University Press.

GERCHUNOFF, P., and LLACH, L. (2003). *El ciclo de la ilusión y el desencanto: Un siglo de políticas económicas argentinas*. Buenos Aires: Ariel.

GHEMAWAT, P., and KENNEDY, R. (1999). "Competitive Shocks and Industrial Structure: The Case of Polish Manufacturing," *International Journal of Industrial Organization*, 17/6: 847–67.

GHEMAWAT, P., and KHANNA, T. (1998). "The Nature of Diversified Business Groups: A Research Design and Two Case Studies," *Journal of Industrial Economics*, 46/1: 35–61.

GOLDSTEIN, A., and TOULAN, O. (2007). "'Multilatinas' Go to China: Two Case Studies," in R. Grosse and L. Mesquita (eds.), *Can Latin American Firms Compete?* Oxford: Oxford University Press.

GRANOVETTER, M. (1994). "Business Groups," in N. Smelser and R. Swedberg (eds.), *Handbook of Economic Sociology*. Princeton: Princeton University Press; New York: Russell Sage Foundation.

GUILLÉN, M. (2000). "Business Groups in Emerging Economies: A Resource-Based View," *Academy of Management Journal*, 43/3: 362–80.

IACOBUCCI, D., and ROSA, P. (2005). "Growth, Diversification, and Business Group Formation in Entrepreneurial Firms," *Small Business Economics*, 25/1: 65–82.

KHANNA, T., and PALEPU, K. (1997). "Why Focused Strategies may be Wrong for Emerging Markets," *Harvard Business Review*, 75: 41–51.

KHANNA, T., and PALEPU, K. (2000a). "The Future of Business Groups in Emerging Markets: Long Run Evidence from Chile," *Academy of Management Journal*, 43/3: 268–85.

KHANNA, T., and PALEPU, K. (2000b). "Is Group Membership Profitable in Emerging Markets? An Analysis of Diversified Indian Business Groups," *Journal of Finance*, 55/2: 867–91.

KHANNA, T., and RIVKIN, J. (2001). "Estimating the Performance Effects of Business Groups in Emerging Markets," *Strategic Management Journal*, 22/1: 45–74.

KHANNA, T., and YAFEH, Y. (2005). "Business Groups and Risk Sharing around the World," *Journal of Business*, 78/1: 301–40.

KHANNA, T., and YAFEH, Y. (2007). "Business Groups in Emerging Markets: Paragons or Parasites?" *Journal of Economic Literature*, 45: 331–72.

KOCK, C., and GUILLÉN, M. (2001). "Strategy and Structure in Developing Countries: Business Groups as an Evolutionary Response to Opportunities for Unrelated Diversification," *Industrial and Corporate Change*, 10/1: 77–113.

KOSACOFF, B. (1993). "La industria Argentina: Un proceso de reestructuración desarticulada," in CEPAL, *El desafío de la competitividad: La industria Argentina en transformación*. Buenos Aires: Alianza Editorial.

KOSACOFF, B. (2000). "Business Strategies under Stabilization and Trade Openness in the 1990s," in B. Kosacoff (ed), *Corporate Strategies under Structural Adjustment in Argentina*. Basingstoke: Palgrave Macmillan.

KOSACOFF, B., and RAMOS, A. (2001). *Cambios contemporáneos en la estructura Industrial Argentina (1975–2000)*. Buenos Aires: Universidad Nacional de Quilmes Ediciones.

KOSACOFF, B., FUCHS, M., and BISANG, R. (1992). "Internacionalización y desarrollo industrial: Inversiones externas directas de empresas industriales Argentinas." Working paper No. 43, ECLAC, Buenos Aires.

KOSACOFF, B., CHUDNOVSKY, D., and LÓPEZ, A. (1999). *Las multinacionales Latinoamericanas: Sus estrategias en un mundo globalizado*. Buenos Aires: Fondo de Cultura Económica.

KURGAN-VAN HENTENRYK, G. (1997). "Structure and Strategy of Belgian Business Groups," in T. Shiba and M. Shimotani (eds.), *Beyond the Firm: Business Groups in International and Historical Perspective*. Oxford: Oxford University Press.

LEFF, N. (1976). "Capital Markets in the Less Developed Countries: The Group Principle," in R. McKinnon (ed.), *Money and Finance in Economic Growth and Development*. New York: Marcel Decker.

MORIKAWA, H. (1992). *Zaibatsu: The Rise and Fall of Family Enterprise Groups in Japan*. Tokyo: University of Tokyo Press.

PAREDES, R., and SÁNCHEZ, J. (1994). "Grupos económicos y desarrollo: El caso de Chile." Working paper, CEPAL.

ROUGIER, M., and SCHVARZER, J. (2006). *Las grandes empresas no Mueren de Pie. El (o)Caso de Siam*. Buenos Aires: Grupo Editorial Norma.

RUMELT, R. (1974). *Strategy, Structure, and Economic Performance*. Cambridge, MA: Harvard University Press.

SHIMOTANI, M., and SHIBA, T. (1997). "The History and Structure of Business Groups in Japan," in T. Shiba and M. Shimotani (eds.), *Beyond the Firm: Business Groups in International and Historical Perspective*. Oxford: Oxford University Press.

SHIN, H., and STULZ, R. (1998). "Are Internal Capital Markets Efficient?" *Quarterly Journal of Economics*, 113: 531–52.

SUZUKI, K. (1997). "From Zaibatsu to Corporate Complexes," in T. Shiba and M. Shimotani (eds.), *Beyond the Firm: Business Groups in International and Historical Perspective*. Oxford: Oxford University Press.

VASSOLO, R., and PERKINS, G. (2005). "La Nación." Case Study, PE-C-115-IA-1-s. IAE Business School, Buenos Aires.

CHAPTER 13

....

BUSINESS GROUPS IN BRAZIL

....

DANTE M. ALDRIGHI

FERNANDO A. S. POSTALI

13.1 INTRODUCTION

....

AS in many other countries, business groups in Brazil are typically owned by families and owe much of their evolution and weight in the national economy to government policies. Nonetheless, their structures and strategies seem to present some idiosyncrasies. Overall, they are much less diversified than their counterparts in other countries, such as in Turkey and South Korea. Moreover, the government-related entities either control a significant number of business groups or hold a decisive stake in the controlling coalition or in the capital structure of those enterprises privatized in the 1990s. And, in contrast with some other countries, foreign entities in Brazil have been among the leading protagonists in the corporate scene. Their investments were wooed by successive national administrations from the 1950s to the 1970s with a view to supporting the state-led strategy of industrialization and thereafter to help privatization or to mitigate foreign-currency shortage.

Focusing on the context wherein business groups in Brazil emerged and have evolved, this chapter endeavors to shed some light on why their structures and strategies exhibit some peculiarities. As a rule, the current main Brazilian business groups typically originated before 1960; were either founded or strongly supported, through various types of subsidies, by the state; have one ultimate controlling shareholder (a family or governmental entities) owning a great number of firms through pyramidal schemes; started to target more systematically export markets only in the 1970s and 1980s; and only after 1990 have pursued a strategy of direct investment abroad.

The chapter is structured as follows. The next section provides a brief, stylized account of the origins and development of Brazilian business groups, emphasizing economic policies and institutions that have shaped the structure of incentives and constraints they have faced. Section 13.3 dwells on the structures and strategies of Brazilian business groups, especially on their ownership and control structures, the level of business diversification, and the extent of internationalization in their trading and investment activities. Based on a large sample of public companies operating in Brazil over the period 1997–2002, it also presents descriptive statistics about the relevance of pyramidal ownership arrangements, controlling shareholders' identities, and the divergence between controlling shareholders' voting rights and cash-flow rights. Finally, the last section concludes.

13.2 THE EMERGENCE AND DEVELOPMENT OF BUSINESS GROUPS IN BRAZIL

13.2.1 Brazilian business groups during the state-led industrialization phase

The origins of the current leading Brazilian business groups can be traced back predominantly to before 1960: among the twenty-nine largest Brazilian business groups in 2007, eighteen were founded before 1950 and four in the 1950s (see Table 13.1). The pioneering groups began operating in light industries, retail trade, banking, electrical energy, and civil construction. Given the financial constraints of the private sector and its unwillingness to bear the risk of huge investments in capital-intensive industries, President Vargas's administration took the lead to diversify the industrial base in the 1940s and 1950s into those "strategic" sectors, setting up an iron-mining company in 1941 (Companhia Vale do Rio Doce, now Vale), a steelmaker in the following year (Companhia Siderúrgica Nacional), and a company operating in the oil and gas upstream sector in 1953 (Petrobras). Originally founded as single firms, they would gradually multiply the number of plants and extend their activities to other industries. In the subsequent two decades, further large state-owned enterprises were founded, such as Eletrobrás (1962) and Telebrás (1972), functioning as holdings of local concessionaires of public services in, respectively, electric energy and telecommunication. It is no wonder that fourteen out of the current twenty-nine largest Brazilian business groups were born as state-controlled companies. Five of them still remain under government control and nine were privatized in the 1990s (Table 13.1).

Table 13.1 The largest economic units in Brazil, 2007

Rank	Economic unit	Year of foundation*	Year of privatization	Type of business group†	Capital origin‡	Gross revenue (R$ m.)	Net worth (R$ m.)	Business areas
1	Petrobras	1953	-	LBG & DBG	BRS	218,254.20	120,160.20	Exploration, production, and distribution of oil and gas, petrochemicals, energy, and transportation
2	Bradesco	1943	-	LBG & DBG	BRP	74,533.80	35,665.40	Banking and finance, holding, electrical energy, mining, information technology, and cable TV services
3	Vale	1942	1997	LBG & DBG	BRP	66,384.40	61,712.80	Minerals and metals, logistics, railways, steel, and energy
4	Itaúsa	1945	-	LBG & DBG	BRP	56,413.60	33,933.20	Banking and finance, real estate, information technology, computers, wood paneling, ceramic, metallurgy sanitary goods, and chemicals
5	Banco do Brasil	1803	-	LBG	BRS	55,416.60	24,262.10	Banking and finance, and information technology
6	Telefonica	-	1998	Foreign	SP	41,101.40	18,524.60	Telecommunications, and information technology

(continued)

Table 13.1 Continued

Rank	Economic unit	Year of foundation*	Year of privatization	Type of business group[+]	Capital origin[‡]	Gross revenue (R$ m.)	Net worth (R$ m.)	Business areas
7	AmBev	-	-	Foreign	BEL	37,016.20	17,607.30	Beverages and food
8	Votorantim	1918	-	LBG & DBG	BRP	35,356.90	27,168.70	Cement, metals, pulp and paper, energy, agribusiness, chemicals, mining/metals, finance, biotechnology, and information technology
9	Gerdau	1901	-	LBG & DBG	BRP	34,184.30	20,571.70	Steel, iron mining, banking, and electricity
10	Fiat	-	-	Foreign	IT	33,279.50	4,179.20	Car manufacturing
11	Odebrecht	1944	-	LBG & DBG	BRP	31,406.20	6,634.10	Engineering, heavy construction, infrastructure, chemical/petrochemicals, public services concession, mining, sugar/ethanol, and insurance
12	Volkswagen	-	-	Foreign	GER	28,205.00	N.A.	Car manufacturing
13	Unibanco	1924	-	LBG	BRP	27,259.20	13,771.00	Banking and finance
14	Bunge	-	-	Foreign	NE	25,426.50	6,226.20	Food, chemicals and petrochemicals
15	Oi	1972[(a)]	1998	LBG	BRP	25,153.20	13,154.90	Telecommunications
16	ABN AMRO	-	-	Foreign	NE	24,971.70	12,258.70	Banking and finance
17	Eletrobrás	1962	-	LBG	BRS	24,861.70	80,348.90	Electrical energy holding

Rank	Economic unit	Year of foundation*	Year of privatization	Type of business group†	Capital origin‡	Gross revenue (R$ m.)	Net worth (R$ m.)	Business areas
18	Ultra	1937	–	LBG & DBG	BRP	20,841.10	4,635.60	Chemicals, petrochemicals, transportation and logistics, and fuel distribution
19	ArcelorMittal Br	–	–	Foreign	LX	19,335.20	15,141.60	Steel and metals
20	Shell Brasil	–	–	Foreign	NE/GB	19,327.70	3,120.10	Petroleum and gas, fuel and lubricant distribution, and energy
21	Santander	–	–	Foreign	SP	19,270.80	9,600.10	Banking and finance
22	Carrefour	–	–	Foreign	FR	19,257.30	4,586.00	Hypermarket chain
23	Usiminas	1956	1991	LBG & DBG	BRP	18,513.20	12,588.40	Flat steel, steel goods, metals, mechanics, logistics and transportation
24	Pão de Açúcar	1948	–	LBG	BRP/FR	17,642.60	5,149.80	Hypermarket chain, food retailer, finance
25	TIM Brasil	–	–	Foreign	IT	17,214.70	7,750.50	Telecommunications
26	HSBC	–	–	Foreign	GB	16,108.10	5,102.90	Banking and finance
27	Brasil Telecom	1972[a]	1998	LBG	BRP	15,997.40	7,072.30	Telecommunications
28	Cemig	1952	–	LBG	BRS	15,789.50	8,708.70	Electric energy
29	Wal-Mart	–	–	Foreign	US	15,002.40	N.A.	Retail trade
30	JBS–Friboi	1962	–	LBG	BRP	14,727.10	3,050.40	Beef processing and transportation
31	CSN	1941	1993	LBG & DBG	BRP	14,423.20[c]	7,542.30	

(continued)

Table 13.1 Continued

Rank	Economic unit	Year of foundation*	Year of privatization	Type of business group†	Capital origin‡	Gross revenue (R$ m.)	Net worth (R$ m.)	Business areas
32	CPFL Energia	1912	1997	LBG	BRP	14,207.40	5,043.00	Electric energy generation and distribution
33	Cargill	-	-	Foreign	US	13,586.20	282.20	Agribusiness and food
34	Chevron	-	-	Foreign	US	13,114.30	1,416.00	Oil distribution, chemicals and petrochemicals
35	Claro	-	-	Foreign	MX	13,083.00	8,692.00	Telecommunications
36	Camargo Corrêa	1939	-	LBG & DBG	BRP	12,421.20	7,939.40	Engineering, cement, footwear, textiles, electric energy, highway concessions, steel and metal, and banking
37	Nestlé	-	-	Foreign	SW	12,402.90	1,679.30	Food and pharmaceutical
38	Embratel	-	1998	Foreign	MX	11,765.20	8,182.10	Telecommunications
39	AES Eletropaulo	-	2001	Foreign	US	11,292.00	3,321.80	Electric energy
40	Embraer	1969	1994	LBG	BRP	10,295.10	5,401.60	Aircraft manufacturing
41	Souza Cruz	-	-	Foreign	GB	9,958.00	1,575.70	Tobacco
42	Sadia	1944	-	LBG	BRP	9,844.00	2,945.10	Chilled and frozen foods
43	Unilever Brasil	-	-	Foreign	GB/NE	9,700.00	N.A.	Food, hygiene and cleaning products

Rank	Economic unit	Year of foundation*	Year of privatization	Type of business group†	Capital origin‡	Gross revenue (R$ m.)	Net worth (R$ m.)	Business areas
44	Neoenergia	1960[b]	1997	LBG	BRP	9,025.30	7,579.70	Electric energy generation, transmission, distribution and trading
45	TAM	1961	-	LBG	BRP	8,474.00	1,494.30	Civil aviation
46	Light	1899	1996	LBG	ERP	8,138.40	2,668.30	Electric power services
47	Copel	1954	-	LBG	BRS	7,920.10	7,467.70	Electric energy and telecommunications
48	Andrade Gutierrez	1948	-	LBG & DBG	BRP	7,891.30	4,917.70	Engineering/construction, electric energy, public concessions, real-estate, and telecommunication
49	Perdigão	1934	-	LBG	BRP	7,788.60	3,226.00	Chilled and frozen foods
50	Lojas Americanas	1929	-	LBG	BRP	7,722.40	436.70	Retail trade and e-trade

*Foundation year only for Brazilian economic groups.

†Business group is here understood as a group of firms strictly controlled by the same entity and that either involves at least one listed firm or is diversified into at least three industries.

ªTelebras, the state-owned telecommunication holding that was privatized in 1998, was founded in 1972.

ᵇNeoenergia is a holding group founded in 1997 to acquire stakes in privatized companies in the electric sector. Its first acquisition was Coelba, founded in 1960.

ᶜGross revenue and net worth refer solely to CSN and do not include Vicunha's.

Note: LBG = listed-firm business group (business group that is composed of at least one listed affiliated firm); DBG = diversified business group (a business group diversified into at least three industries); LBG&DBG = a listed-firm and diversified business group (a business group that is composed of at least one listed affiliated firm and at the same time is diversified into at least three industries).

‡BRS = Brazilian state-controlled group; BRP = Brazilian privately controlled group; BEL = Belgian; FR = French; GB = British; GER = German; IT = Italian; LX = Luxembourg; MX = Mexican; NE = Dutch; PT = Portuguese; SP = Spanish; SS = Swiss; US = American; N.A. = not available.

Sources: Valor Grandes Grupos (2008); business groups' websites.

Until the 1970s, the state-led strategy of industrialization relied on a complex array of incentives and subsidies—such as protectionist trade policies, below-market interest rate loans, and tax exemptions—to strengthen certain industries, benefiting not only Brazilian firms and business groups but also subsidiaries of multinational enterprises (Fishlow 1972). Throughout this period, Banco Nacional de Desenvolvimento Econômico (BNDE), the development bank wholly owned by the federal government, was pivotal in directing private investment towards the policy-targeted sectors.

"Plano de Metas" (Targets Plan) and the "II Plano Nacional de Desenvolvimento" (Second National Development Plan, henceforth, II PND)—covering, respectively, the periods 1956–61 and 1975–9—are two remarkable instances of how those industrial policies fostered the growth of business groups. Plano de Metas, implemented under President Kubitscheck's administration, had the purpose of boosting investment in infrastructure, car manufacturing, and some segments in the intermediate and capital goods industries, such as oil production, steel, and cement. Even though state-owned enterprises and foreign firms were at the forefront of this "Big Push," some industries were left to Brazilian private business groups, which also benefited from demand spillovers derived from leading firms.

The II PND, implemented under the military regime, aimed at overcoming the structural and external constraints then obstructing the Brazilian economic growth. It targeted infrastructure (railways, telecommunications, and energy—petrol, ethanol, and electricity) and those segments in the producer-goods sector needed to achieve a comprehensive domestic industrial matrix (Hermann 2005). The government provided strong incentives to induce Brazilian business groups to embark on that strategy of catching up, ranging from abundant subsidized credit to tax exemption for investments in targeted industries, to protection from foreign competition, and even to capital grants.

The external shocks that battered highly indebted developing economies from 1979 to 1983 culminated in the debt crisis, bringing to an end the Brazilian state-guided development strategy. Inasmuch as its financing inflated the external debt, the II PND is partly to blame for the gestation and severity of the debt crisis. Nonetheless, it also turned out to be a vehicle by which the dramatic dollar shortage was attenuated after 1983 (De Castro and de Souza 1985). Indeed, insofar as its large-scale projects began to mature, increasing exports and decreasing imports of intermediate and capital goods significantly improved Brazil's current account.

Yet, the federal government got entangled in dire fiscal straits, in part because it imposed two sharp currency devaluations (in 1979 and 1983), after having "nationalized" most of the external debt owed by the private sector. Being forced to bear the heavy burden of the external debt service throughout the 1980s and 1990s, the government had to relinquish the leadership in the economic development strategy. This fiscal crisis translated into high and growing inflation and interest rates as well as low and volatile rates of economic growth, spurring in turn most of business groups to adopt defensive strategies. Exploiting the mix of high interest rates and liquidity afforded by the inflation-indexed government bonds, the business groups invested at best in marginal plant enlargements and too little in innovation. Some of the financially distressed business groups only managed to survive thanks to government bailouts, carried out through the BNDES's subsidized loans and capital injections.[1] The end result was meaningfully epitomized as "the lost decade:" chronic stagnation, high inflation, and severe fiscal crisis.

On the political front, after two decades under military rule, Brazil resumed in 1984 its path toward democracy and, four years later, the Congress enacted a new Constitution. For some, its populist bias, added to some equivocal subsequent legislative and jurisdictional measures, worsened the quality of the general economic regulation framework, magnifying contractual uncertainties (Bacha and Bonelli 2005: 179–80).

13.2.2 Structural changes in the Brazilian economy since the 1990s

"Plano Real," the economic stabilization plan launched in 1994, was a turning point in Brazil's recent economic history, managing to cut down the annual inflation rate from 2,708 percent in 1993 to just 15 percent in 1995. It created a new currency ("real"), whose peg to the dollar was reached by high interest rates. Contributing to reduce macroeconomic uncertainty and volatility, currency stabilization improved the general business environment, which, together with trade liberalization put pressure on firms to heighten productivity. Brazil's pegged exchange-rate regime combined with domestic inflation rates persistently above the average of its main trade partners resulted in an overvalued real exchange rate, compelling firms and business groups to revise their strategies. For instance, some of them were induced to make direct investment abroad. Banks were also affected by the dramatic plunge in the inflationary tax revenues, which brought to light inefficiencies, mismanagement, and even wrongdoing, as in the cases of Banco Nacional, Bamerindus, and Banco Econômico.

Another watershed in the Brazilian corporate environment was privatization. Beginning in the middle of the 1980s, it gathered momentum mainly during President Fernando Henrique Cardoso's administration. Over the period 1990–4, 68 companies were sold, primarily from the steel, fertilizer, and petrochemical sectors, generating US$11.8 billion worth in revenues and debt transfers (see BNDES 2002). So far as foreign investors were concerned, the then macroeconomic instability and absence of a clear regulatory framework made their participation in the privatization auctions negligible.

The success of Plano Real and the important institutional changes that removed long-standing state monopolies in key sectors (notably in energy, mining, telecommunications, and oil and gas upstream) paved the way to speed up the privatization process during Cardoso's two administrations (1995–2002) as well as to enlarge its

---

[1] In the 1980s, this bank changed its name to Banco Nacional de Desenvolvimento Econômico e Social (National Bank for Economic and Social Development), BNDES.

scope to include infrastructure sectors.[2] With a view to disciplining businesses in those naturally limited competition sectors, a new regulatory framework, involving the creation of several industry-specific regulatory authorities, was established.

Landmarks in Brazilian privatizations in the 1990s were the selling of Usiminas in 1991, Companhia Siderúrgica Nacional (CSN) in 1993, Embraer and Copesul in 1994, Companhia Vale do Rio Doce (Vale) in 1997, and Telebras in 1998. Telebras, the former Brazilian telecommunications holding, was then split into twelve companies, most of which transferred to Telefonica (an Spanish group), Brasil Telecom, and Telemar. Later on, Usiminas, Embraer, Vale, Brasil Telecom, and Telemar became leading Brazilian private business groups, while the acquisition of Copesul and CSN allowed, respectively, Odebrecht and Vicunha to skyrocket.

Trade liberalization also had remarkable effects on market structures and business groups' strategies. Starting in 1988, it was intensified in the following years, notably under President Collor's administration (1990–2). Average tariffs plummeted from 42.6 percent in 1988 to 13.4 percent in 1995, and non-tariff barriers were replaced by tariffs (Menezes Filho et al. 2006). Moreover, MERCOSUR, the allegedly customs union constituted in 1991 by Brazil, Argentina, Uruguay, and Paraguay, stimulated intra-bloc trade flows and intra- and across-bloc direct investment flows (Bonelli 1998). Except for minor setbacks prompted by overvalued exchange rate, increasing trade deficits and the 1998–9 currency crisis, Brazilian trade liberalization has been preserved.

Fierce global competition, stemming from privatization, trade openness, and financial liberalization, triggered major restructurings and a wave of mergers and acquisitions in various Brazilian sectors in the 1990s. There were around 2,300 such deals over the period 1994–2000, 61 percent of which involved foreign capital. Most were concentrated in food and beverage industries, followed by financial institutions, and telecommunications. Noteworthy among such deals was the merger of the two largest Brazilian breweries (Brahma and Antarctica) into AmBev, the largest Latin American beverage group, which some years later merged with Interbrew into InBev, a Belgian-controlled business group.

13.2.3 Institutional changes related to corporate governance

Since the end of the 1990s, material shifts have taken place in the institutional setting shaping corporate governance in Brazil. First, in 1997 the Federal Government managed to put through a law abolishing equal treatment to minority shareholders in the case of transfer of control, guaranteed until then by the 1976 Corporate Law. The rationale for that legal change lay in the government's aim to maximize revenues to be collected from the then imminent privatization of some important state-owned enterprises. Secondly, the approval of the new Corporate Law in 2001 represented a

---

[2] The US$78.6 billion worth in privatization revenues raised over that period resulted predominantly from deals in the sectors of infrastructure and services (85%). Foreign investors were responsible for 53% of that amount, followed by domestic firms (26%). See BNDES (2002).

step forward in strengthening minority shareholders' rights vis-à-vis the former law, even though the new law is still far from providing a legal framework effectively curbing expropriation from controlling shareholders.

Thirdly, the São Paulo Stock Exchange (Bovespa) launched in December 2000 new listing segments ("Special Corporate Governance Levels" and "Novo Mercado"), wherein firms, voluntarily and by contract, commit themselves to higher governance standards. This private-led institutional innovation provides a mechanism of governance certification, allowing firms' self-selection regarding their respective governance quality. To be listed on Bovespa's Level 1, companies must, amidst other requirements, provide better disclosure as compared with that which is legally mandatory and maintain a minimum free-float of 25 percent of the firm's capital. Level 2 requires, in addition, that companies comply with tougher rules regarding financial reports, disclosure, board composition, and minority shareholders' rights. Finally, firms listed on the Novo Mercado, on top of Level 2's obligations, are allowed to issue only voting shares (see BM&FBOVESPA).

Leading Brazilian business groups typically have their main firms listed on Level 1 (e.g. Vale, Votorantim, Gerdau, Sadia, Odebrecht, Camargo Corrêa, Ultra, Brasil Telecom, the largest banks (Itaúsa, Bradesco, and Unibanco), Pão de Açúcar, Usiminas, and Eletrobrás (see Table 13.2)). This is probably due either to their deliberate avoidance to migrate to higher governance standards or to specific industry-level regulation or legislation. Thus, the average market value of firms listed on Level 1 is well above that for the other listing segments: R$12.77 billion against R$2.18 billion for the traditional segment, R$2.48 billion for the Novo Mercado, and R$1.87 billion for Level 2 (data as of February 2009; see BM&FBOVESPA 2009).

Considering the sample of the 29 largest Brazilian business groups in 2007, only Andrade Gutierrez did not have a controlling stake in at least one publicly traded company, though it took part in the controlling coalition of Light SA, CCR, and Oi-Telemar. Out of the 43 publicly traded companies controlled by the sample groups, 13 were listed on the Bovespa's conventional segment, 21 on Level 1, 1 on Level 2, and 8 on the Novo Mercado. The major business groups with at least one company listed on the Novo Mercado were the following: CPFL Energia, Vale (a logistic subsidiary), Perdigão, Embraer, Camargo Corrêa, Light, JBS-Friboi, and the state-controlled Banco do Brasil.

13.2.4 Equity stakes of government-related institutions on private groups

Since the 1990s BNDES and pension funds of currently or formerly state-owned companies have played a critical role in the Brazilian corporate sector restructuring. The Brazilian private banking system, notwithstanding its robustness, has recurrently been loath to provide long-term financing, not least because acquiring bonds issued by the Brazilian government has long delivered high returns and liquidity. As the

Table 13.2 Brazilian business groups' companies listed on Bovespa, 2007

Business group	Companies listed on Bovespa	Bovespa governance level	Listed on NYSE? (a)	Outside directors (%) (a)	Type of largest ultimate shareholder	Cash flow rights	Voting rights	Largest ultimate shareholder
1. Petrobras	Petróleo Brasileiro S.A.	T	Yes	89	Government	39.83	57.57	Federal Government
2. Bradesco	Banco Bradesco S.A.	N1	Yes	88	Family	24.55	42.42	Fundação Bradesco/ Aguiar family
	Bradespar	N1	–		Family	27.44	76.19	
3. Vale	Cia. Vale do Rio Doce	N1	Yes	100	Pension fund	18.31	26.41	Previ
	Log-In Logística Intermodal S.A.	NM	–		Pension fund	5.72	8.26	
4. Itaúsa	Itaúsa Investimentos Itaú S.A.	N1	Yes	80	Family	19.09	30.79	Villela and Setúbal families
	Banco Itaú Holding Financeira S.A.	N1	–		Family	8.49	26.65	
	Itautec S.A. – Grupo Itautec	T	–		Family	17.95	28.94	
	Duratex S.A.	N1	–	–	Family	7.88	27.25	
	Elekeiroz S.A.	T	–	–	Family	17.69	29.05	
5. Banco do Brasil	Banco do Brasil S.A.	NM	No	83	Government	65.30	65.30	National Treasury
8. Votorantim	Votorantim Celulose e Papel S.A.	N1	Yes	67	Family	51.78	100.00	Ermírio de Moraes family
9. Gerdau	Gerdau S.A.	N1	Yes	100	Family	8.59	67.74	Gerdau family
	Metalúrgica Gerdau S.A.	N1	–		Family	19.16	60.70	
11. Odebrecht	Braskem S.A.	N1	Yes	100	Family	66.64	90.34	Odebrecht family
13. Unibanco	Unibanco	N1	Yes	67	Family	31.99	62.89	Moreira Salles family
	Unibanco União de Bancos Brasileiros	N1	–		Family	18.50	78.58	

Business group	Companies listed on Bovespa	Bovespa governance level	Listed on NYSE?	Outside directors (%) (a)	Type of largest ultimate shareholder	Cash flow rights	Voting rights	Largest ultimate shareholder
15. Oi	Telemar Norte Leste S.A.	T	Yes	40	Shareholders' coalition	18.32	97.23	Andrade Gutierrez, La Fonte Group, BNDESPar, Asseca, Lexpart Part., Previ and other pension funds, and Fundação Atlântico
	Contax Participações S.A.	T	-	-	Shareholders' coalition	19.81	58.80	
17. Eletrobrás	Centrais Elétricas Brasileiras S.A.	N1	No	100	Government	58.22	68.77	Federal Government
18. Ultra	Ultrapar Participações S.A.	N1	Yes	100	Family	23.99	66.05	Andrade family
23. Usiminas	Usinas Siderúrgicas de Minas Gerais S.A	N1	No	92	Shareholders' coalition	28.72	57.08	Camargo Corrêa, Ermirio de Moraes Family, CVRD, Nippon Steel, and Usiminas' pension fund
24. Pão de Açúcar	Cia Brasileira de Distribuição	N1	Yes	100	Family/foreign investor	51.08	99.94	Diniz family and Casino
27. Brasil Telecom	Brasil Telecom Participações S.A.	N1	Yes	100	Shareholders' coalition	5.96	16.18	Investment funds (BNDESPar and some pension funds) and CVC fund
	Brasil Telecom S.A.	N1	-	-	Shareholders' coalition	3.91	16.04	
28. Cemig	Cia. Energética de Minas Gerais	N1	Yes	93	Government	22.27	50.96	State of Minas Gerais

(continued)

Table 13.2 Continued

Business group	Companies listed on Bovespa	Bovespa governance level	Listed on NYSE?	Outside directors (%) (a)	Type of largest ultimate shareholder	Cash flow rights	Voting rights	Largest ultimate shareholder
30. JBS-Friboi	JBS S.A	NM	No	80	Shareholders' coalition	-	-	Batista family
31. CSN	Cia. Siderúrgica Nacional	T	Yes	78	Family	43.38	43.38	Steinbruch family
32. CPFL Energia	CPFL Energia S.A.	NM	Yes	100	Shareholders' coalition	72.16	72.16	Votorantim Group, Bradespar, and Camargo Corrêa Group, Previ, and other state-related pension funds
36. Camargo Corrêa	Camargo Corrêa Cimentos S.A.	NM	No	-	Family	65.66	65.66	Camargo family
	São Paulo Alpargatas S.A.	N1		-	Family	44.12	66.99	
40. Embraer	Empresa Brasileira de Aeronáutica	NM	Yes	100	Disperse	13.92	13.92	Previ
43. Sadia	Sadia S.A.	N1	Yes	100	Shareholders' coalition	27.98	66.57	Fontana family and other families
44. Neonergia	Afluente Ger. e Transm. Energ. Eletr.	T	No	-	Pension fund	41.01	92.80	Previ
	Cia. Eletricidade Estadual da Bahia	T		-		41.02	92.81	
	Cia. Energética de Pernambuco	T		-	Pension fund	39.53	99.58	
	Cia. Energética do R. Grande do Norte	T		-	Pension fund	37.23	85.38	
45. TAM	Tam S.A.	N2	Yes	100	Family	51.5	99.97	Amaro Family

Business group	Companies listed on Bovespa	Bovespa governance level	Listed on NYSE?	Outside directors (%) (a)	Type of largest ultimate shareholder	Cash flow rights	Voting rights	Largest ultimate shareholder
46. Light	Light Participações S.A.–Lightpar	T	No	100	Shareholders' coalition	53.11	81.61	CEMIG, Andrage Gutierrez Group,
	Light S.A.	NM	-	-	Shareholders' coalition	52.24	52.24	Pactual Part., and Luce Fundo de Investimento
47. Copel	Cia. Paranaense de Energia–COPEL	T	Yes	80	Government	55.04	85.04	State of Parana
48. Andrade Gutierrez	Andrade Gutierrez Participações S.A.	Not listed	No	-	Family	100.00	100.00	Andrade and Gutierrez families
	Andrade Gutierrez Concessões S.A.	Not listed		-	Family	77.13	77.13	
49. Perdigão	Perdigão S.A.	NM	Yes	75	Shareholders' coalition	37.80	37.80	Previ, Petros, Sistel, Valia and other pension funds
50. Lojas Americanas	Lojas Americanas S.A.	T	No	91	Family	-	-	Velame Adm. (Lehmann, Telles and Sicupira families)

Notes: Bovespa's levels of governance: T = Traditional; N1 = Level 1; N2 = Level 2; NM = Ncvo Mercado.(a) Percentage of outside directors (non-executive directors) in the board's composition (data refer to 2006).

Sources: Valor Grandes Grupos (2008); Bovespa; business groups' websites; and CVM.

contribution from Brazilian capital markets was unimportant until the beginning of the 2000s, long-term financing was provided almost exclusively by BNDES and foreign loans.

Since its inception in the 1950s, BNDES has been a powerful policy vehicle. Up to the end of the 1970s, it was the financial lever of industrial policies, guiding capital allocation to targeted industries through low-cost, long-term financing either to state- or privately owned companies and business groups. During the stagnant 1980s, BNDES and its wholly owned subsidiary BNDES Participações SA (BNDE-SPar) mainly supported financially stressed firms, bailing them out through lending, debt–equity swap, and recapitalization. In the following decade, both were actively engaged in privatization and firms' restructuring (including those that were newly privatized), turning out to be critical in making some consortia viable and some bids successful. At the end of 2008, BNDESPar's portfolio in corporate equity reached R$52.7 billion (estimated market value), concentrated at both the sectoral and firm levels.[3] In 2007, BNDESPar held representatives in 11 fiscal committees and in 26 boards of directors. It was also a member of shareholders' agreement in 64 of the 142 firms wherein it had an equity stake (see BNDESPar 2008).

Also decisive in the 1990s privatizations in Brazil were pension funds of erstwhile or ongoing state-controlled firms, such as Previ, Petros, Funcef, Valia, and Sistel.[4] Previ held an asset portfolio worth R$137.42 billion at the end of 2007, of which more than two-thirds were in equity capital, either directly or through exclusive investment funds that owned holding companies that, in turn, held stakes in almost all firms affiliated to business groups. For example, Previ is a leading shareholder in CPFL Energia, Neonergia, and Itapebi through an investment fund it wholly owns, "521 Participações S. A.," a special purpose entity set up with the sole objective of taking part in the privatization of the electrical energy sector.

13.2.5 Resilience

As far as longevity is concerned, the 29 Brazilian business groups that stood among the top 50 business groups in Brazil in 2007 emerged before 1970 (for groups born from privatization, the date was considered to be the corresponding state-owned company's foundation date). A rough, though conventional, indicator of resilience to changing economic and political environment is the percentage of the top largest firms in a certain year that still remain among the top largest ones some years later. Reckoning this "survival rate" for the top twenty and top ten Brazilian private groups (ranked by net worth) for three periods, the following results were

---

[3] Its equity portfolio was concentrated in the following industries: oil and gas, electrical energy, mining, steel, paper and cellulose, and telecommunications.

[4] The first three are the pension funds of, respectively, Banco do Brasil, Petrobras, and Caixa Econômica Federal, all of which are controlled by the Federal Government. The latter two are the pension funds of Vale and Telebrás/Embratel, all privatized in the 1990s.

found: (1) from among the twenty largest Brazilian private groups in 1978, ten (50%) remained among the top twenty in 1988 (for the ten largest, the percentage is the same); (2) from the top twenty in 1988, eleven (55%) persisted among the top twenty in 1998 (40% for the ten largest); (3) from the top twenty in 1998, fifteen (75%) stayed in the top twenty list in 2005 (90% for the ten largest); and (4) from the top twenty in 1978, six (30%) were in the top twenty list in 2005 (40% for the top ten) (see Table 13.3).[5]

Notwithstanding the considerable influence of private business groups on politics and government policies, those failing economically also seem to have failed politically to eschew bankruptcy, at least after the return to democracy. Traditional and economically powerful business groups in the 1970s, such as Bonfiglioli, Matarazzo, and Comind, respectively, the third, sixth, and eighteenth largest business groups in terms of net worth in 1978, went bust in the following decade. Analogously, Bamerindus (the sixth largest in 1988), Econômico (the twenty-fourth in 1988), and Nacional (the thirty-second in 1978) did not survive the economic turbulences in the 1990s, despite the intimate relations of their controlling shareholders with politicians.

As regards the status in 2005 of the twenty largest Brazilian private business groups in 1978, ten still existed as such (six of which were among the top twenty), two had been acquired by other Brazilian business groups and three by foreign groups, three had gone bankrupt, one had undergone governmental intervention owing to financial frauds, and information was not available for one of them. Among the six groups that were in the top twenty in both 1978 and 2005, three were primarily engaged in finance, two had started in the engineering and heavy construction industry but subsequently diversified their activities, and one had also diversified, notably into capital-intensive industries, such as paper and pulp, mining, metals, cement, and chemical products.

Amidst the largest Brazilian business groups in 2007, none operated at a significant scale in electronics, nor in car making. Those undertaking businesses in knowledge- or skilled-labor-intensive industries were the following: Embraer (aircraft manufacturer), Petrobras (oil exploration and production in deepwater environments), Odebrecht (engineering and heavy construction), and Oi and Brasil Telecom (telecommunications). Most were engaged in at least one of the following core businesses: banking, chemical and petrochemical, mining, steel, electric energy, pulp and paper, retail trade, food, and agribusiness (see Table 13.1). With respect to the sectoral composition of the top ten Brazilian groups, banks stood out (Bradesco, Banco do Brasil, Itaúsa, and Unibanco), followed by oil and gas production and distribution (Petrobras), iron mining (Vale), steel and iron (Gerdau), telecommunications (Oi), and the diversified groups Votorantim and Odebrecht.

---

[5] These figures were calculated using data drawn from *Balanço Anual: Gazeta Mercantil*, the only available source with longitudinal ranking for business groups since 1978. Its major shortcoming is that the ranking refers just to Brazilian private business groups. Therefore, the turnover rate is overestimated when comparing figures before and after the 1990s, decade in which a wave of privatization took place.

Table 13.3 Top twenty largest private business groups, 1978, 1988, 1998, and 2005

Business group	1978	1988	1998	2005	Status in 2005
Safra	-	-	-	20	Still operating
Andrade Gutierrez	20	6	13	19	Still operating
Nemofeffer/ Suzano	-	11	20	18	Suzano Group
Aracruz	-	-	15	17	Still operating
Pão de Açúcar	-	-	-	16	Still operating
CPFL Energia	-	-	-	15	Privatized in 1997 and under Brazilian control
Embraer	-	-	-	14	Privatized in 1994 and under Brazilian control
Neoenergia	-	-	-	13	A holding company set up in 1997 engaged in the electric energy sector
Odebrecht	-	9	14	12	Still operating
CSN	-	-	7	11	Privatized in 1993 and under Brazilian control
Camargo Corrêa	4	3	9	10	Still operating
Brasil Telecom/ Tele Centro Sul	-	-	4	9	Resulted from the privatization of Telebrás in 1998 and under Brazilian control
Usiminas	-	-	8	8	Privatized in 1991 and under Brazilian control
Unibanco	11	19	10	7	Still operating
Gerdau	-	15	18	6	Still operating
Tele Norte Leste/ Telemar	-	-	1	5	Resulted from the privatization of Telebrás in 1998 and under Brazilian control
Itaú/Itaúsa	5	4	6	4	Still operating
Bradesco	1	1	3	3	Still operating
Votorantim	2	2	5	2	Still operating
Vale	-	-	2	1	Privatized in 1997 and under Brazilian control
Denerge	-	-	19	-	Controlled by Rede Group
Antarctica	-	-	17	-	Merged with Bhrama into AmBev
Norquisa/Copene	-	-	16	-	Acquired by Braskem (Odebrecht Group)
Sul América	8	18	12	-	Still operating
C. R. Almeida	-	14	11	-	Still operating
Vicunha	-	20	-	-	Still operating and CSN's controlling shareholder
Itamarati	-	17	-	-	Still operating
Matarazzo	6	16	-	-	Bankrupted in 1983
Klabin	19	13	-	-	Still operating
Mendes Júnior	-	12	-	-	Still operating
Santista	-	10	-	-	Acquired by Bunge Born
Real	10	8	-	-	Acquired by ABN AMRO in 1998

Business group	1978	1988	1998	2005	Status in 2005
Belgo-Mineira	-	7	-	-	Acquired by ArcelorMittal
Bamerindus	-	5	-	-	Bankrupted and the good assets acquired by HSBC
Comind	18	-	-	-	Liquidated by the government in 1985 owing to frauds
Varig	17	-	-	-	Bankrupted and part of it sold to Gol group
Alpargatas	16	-	-	-	Acquired by Camargo Corrêa
Econômico	15	-	-	-	Under the intervention of the Federal Government since 1994
Dedini	14	-	-	-	Still operating
Unipar	13	-	-	-	Still operating
Paulo Ferraz	12	-	-	-	No information available
Brahma	9	-	-	-	Merged with Antarctca into Ambev
Villares	7	-	-	-	Acquired by a Spanish Group
Bonfiglioli	3	-	-	-	Banco Auxiliar liquidated in 1987 and CICA acquired by Grupo Ferruzzi

Source: Gazeta Mercantil, Balanço Anual (various issues).

13.3 OWNERSHIP, CONTROL, AND STRATEGIES OF BRAZILIAN BUSINESS GROUPS

This section focuses on the structures of ownership and control of the largest Brazilian business groups, their business diversification, and the extent of internationalization in their operations, through either trade or direct investments.

Firstly, it is necessary to clarify the meaning of the term "business groups" as employed in this chapter. We base our analysis on *Valor Grandes Grupos*, henceforth *VGG*, because this report, published yearly by the business-specialized newspaper *Valor Econômico*, provides an in-depth empirical survey on business groups in Brazil. *VGG*'s definition of "business group," however, is not rigorous, since it considers as such any group of firms under the control of the same entity, regardless of the scope of their businesses and the existence of at least one public company amidst them. As used herein, business group means a group of firms that, in addition to being strictly controlled by the same entity, either embraces at least one listed firm (what we call a "listed-firm business group") or is diversified into at least three industries (what we dub a "diversified business group"). Caixa Econômica Federal and Safra apart, the ranking of the top fifty economic units running businesses in Brazil shown in

Table 13.1 is that elaborated by *VGG*. These two groups were excluded, as they are neither diversified nor comprise listed firms. Although several of the economic units that *VGG* classifies as foreign business groups are clearly organized as business groups, others are not, for which reason we refer to them simply as foreign economic units.

13.3.1 Ownership and control

From among the fifty largest economic units operating in Brazil in 2007, twenty-three were controlled by Brazilian private entities (such as families, privately owned firms, pension funds, or mutual funds), five by federal or state governments, twenty-one by foreign firms, and one was jointly controlled by a Brazilian family and a foreign group (see Table 13.1). Privatization of formerly state-owned firms and public-service concessions greatly contributed to this profile: nine from those twenty-three Brazilian business groups and seven from the twenty-one foreign economic units resulted from privatization.[6]

Worth mentioning is that families controlled fifteen from among those twenty-four Brazilian private business groups (including Pão de Açúcar) ranked as the fifty largest business groups operating in Brazil (see Table 13.2). Five of the remaining nine groups (Vale, Oi, Usiminas, CPFL, and Light) were originally state-owned and, since their respective privatizations, have been controlled by those same or other family-controlled groups jointly, as a rule, with pension funds of state-controlled business groups (predominantly Previ). These pension funds together with state-owned groups or agencies (such as Petrobras, BNDESPar, or Banco do Brasil) are also important, or even controlling, sharcholders in the other four private business groups—Brasil Telecom, Embraer, Neoenergia, and Perdigão.

Overall, the ownership of Brazilian business groups is structured through pyramidal schemes, involving just a few, if any, publicly traded companies.[7] Moreover, the largest ultimate shareholders in these companies usually hold more than 50 percent of their voting capital—Embraer and Perdigão being notable exceptions—and own, as a consequence of the recurring use of pyramids and non-voting preferred shares, voting rights far exceeding their cash-flow rights (Table 13.2). If there are two or more large-block shareholders, they are typically connected through a formal voting agreement.

In the light of the intricate coalitions formed among some Brazilian business groups, pension funds, governmental agencies, and foreign investors to partake in the privatization bids as well as in the ownership and control arrangements that

---

[6] Former state-owned business groups whose control was taken over by Brazilian entities are the following: Vale, Usiminas, CSN, CPFL Energia, Embraer, Neoenergia, and Light. Oi-Telemar and Brasil Telecom emerged from the break-up and privatization of Telebras. Economic units that were privatized in the 1990s and since then have been controlled by foreigners are: ArcelorMittal Brasil, Santander, AES Eletropaulo, Telefonica, Tim Brasil, Claro, and Embratel. HSBC was allowed to enter the Brazilian banking industry after buying the "good" assets of Bamerindus, a privately owned bank whose control was transferred to the federal government on the grounds of its appalling financial distress.

[7] Among the more than seventy companies composing the group Votorantim, only one has shares traded on Bovespa. Andrade Gutierrez has none (see Table 13.2).

afterward prevailed for the winning bidders, some cases of business groups privatized in the 1990s are examined below.

13.3.1.1 *Newly privatized business groups' ownership structures*

The complex arrays that have led BNDESPar, Banco do Brasil, Petrobras, and pension funds of companies currently or formerly controlled by the government to hold large equity stakes or even to take part in the controlling coalitions in some business groups stem primarily from their participation in the privatization process. Given its intent to maximize revenues from the privatization auctions, the Federal Government urged BNDES and pension funds to act as financiers for the bidders, notably Brazilian private groups.

Privatized in 1997, Vale was initially acquired by a consortium that later transferred its control to Valepar SA, a private company jointly owned by Previ and other government-related pension funds, three private Brazilian groups (Bradesco, Opportunity, and Vicunha), and BNDESPar. After a number of ownership restructurings, the distribution of Valepar's voting capital ended up being the following (as of June 2008): Litel (a private company wherein Previ has a 80.6% stake and the remaining shares are held by the pension funds Funcef, Petros, and Funcesp): 49.00 percent; Bradespar (Bradesco Group): 21.21 percent; Mitsui: 18.24 percent; and BNDESPar: 11.52 percent. Government-related entities therefore control more than 60 percent of Valepar's voting capital, which in turn owns 53.9 percent of Vale's voting capital (and 33.3% of its total capital). Furthermore, BNDESPar owns a 6.9 percent direct stake in Vale's voting capital and the Federal Government holds special class preferred ("golden") shares entitling it to veto "strategic" issues proposals.

Oi, a telecommunications group formerly called Telemar, is structured along a complicated pyramidal ownership arrangement. Telemar Participações SA has a 52.45 percent stake in Tele Norte Leste Participações SA's common shares (and just a 17.48% one in its total capital); Tele Norte Leste Participações SA in turn holds a 97.35 percent stake in Telemar Norte Leste SA's voting capital. As of August 2008, Telemar Participações SA's voting capital was distributed among Andrade Gutierrez Group (19.3%), La Fonte Group (19.3%), BNDESPar SA (31.3%), Fiago Participações SA (24.9%),[8] and Fundação Atlântico de Seguridade Social (5.0%). This ownership composition resulted from the restructuring undertaken in June 2008 with a view to accomplishing Brasil Telecom Participações SA's takeover, which effectively happened in January 2009. Telemar Participações SA's prior control embraced some Brazilian private business groups, governmental institutions (BNDESPar and Banco do Brasil), pension funds, and a foreign investment fund.[9]

---

[8] Fiago is a holding company owned by Previ, Petros, Funcef, and the pension fund of Telemar's employees, Fundação Atlântico de Seguridade Social.

[9] AG Telecom Participações SA, Asseca Participações SA (owned by Grupo GP Investimentos), L. F. Tel SA, and Lexpart Participações SA (owned jointly by Opportunity, Citigroup, and state-owned firms' pension funds) each held 10.275% of its voting capital; Alutrens Participações SA (owned by Banco do Brasil and private-sector insurance firms) owned 10%; Fundação Atlântico de Seguridade Social, 4%; BNDESPar SA, 25%; and Fiago Participações SA, 19.9%.

As Telemar, Brasil Telecom SA also had BNDESPar, Citigroup, Opportunity, and pension funds among its largest ultimate shareholders. Its common shares were almost entirely owned (99.07%) by Brasil Telecom Participações SA, whose control was in the hands of Solpart Participações SA, a holding company owning 51.00 percent of its common shares and 18.78 percent of its total capital. Solpart, in turn, was controlled by Techold Participações SA, a company entirely owned by Invitel SA, a holding company controlled by Zain Participações SA and that had as minority shareholders Previ, Fundação 14 BrT (the pension fund of Brasil Telecom SA's employees), and the pension funds of Petrobras, Caixa Econômica Federal, and Embratel. Finally, Zain Participações SA's owners were Investidores Institucionais FIA (an investment fund comprising BNDESPar and some pension funds), with 45.85 percent of its voting capital, the foreign investment fund Citigroup Venture Capital International Brazil LP (42.47%), and Opportunity Fund (9.00%). The acquisition of Brasil Telecom by Oi in 2008 gave rise to a pyramidal ownership structure involving seven intermediate companies between the controlling shareholders (La Fonte, Andrade Gutierrez e Fundação Atlântico) and Brasil Telecom SA. Federal Government's support was decisive in making the takeover possible: on top of providing credit via BNDES, it changed the Brazilian National Plan of Concessions in order to remove regulatory impediments to the deal.

The voting coalition controlling Usiminas groups the Japanese company Nippon (holding a 21.57% stake in the total voting capital in November 2008), Votorantim Participações SA (11.56%), the pension fund of Usiminas's employees (10.13%), Camargo Corrêa Cimentos SA (7.93%), and Vale (5.89%). Although not taking part in this agreement, Previ has a 10.44 percent interest in Usiminas's voting capital.

Until 2009, CPFL Energia was controlled by an agreement of shareholders gathering VBC Energia (holding 28.02% of the voting capital), 521 Participações SA (an investment entity owned by Previ, owning 31.10%), and Bonaire Participações SA, a holding controlled by four pension funds (Funcesp, Petros, Sistel and Sabesprev), with a 12.65 percent interest. Three family-controlled groups (Votorantim, Bradesco, and Camargo Corrêa) wholly owned indirectly VBC Energia, but both Bradespar and Votorantim Participações sold their stakes, in 2007 and 2009 respectively, allowing Camargo Corrêa SA to become the sole owner of VBC.

Neoenergia is a holding company jointly controlled, through a formal agreement, by Previ, Banco do Brasil-Banco de Investimento SA, and the Spanish group Iberdrola. Besides holding directly and indirectly a 45.70 percent stake in Neoenergia's voting capital, Previ owns 51 percent of the shares of a mutual fund that holds 6.49 percent of that capital. This fund's remaining shares are owned by Banco do Brasil-Banco de Investimento SA, which also owns directly and indirectly an 8.81 percent stake in Neoenergia. Iberdrola's interest in this company is 39.00 percent.

Finally, Embraer, a leading aircraft manufacturer privatized in 1994, presents a very uncommon ownership structure among Brazilian business groups, inasmuch as its capital is relatively widely held. Nonetheless, seven of its shareholders have individual stakes exceeding 5 percent, two of which are government-related institutions—Previ (14.2%) and BNDESPar (5.2%). More than 50 percent of Embraer's common shares are owned by foreign institutional investors or traded on the NYSE, although the group's by-laws restrain the total votes cast by foreign shareholders.[10]

13.3.1.2 *Pyramidal ownership structures in Brazil*

This subsection presents empirical evidence, produced by Aldrighi and Mazzer Neto (2007), on the relevance of pyramidal arrangements of ownership amidst public companies in Brazil. The sample covers public companies that in at least one year within the period 1997–2002 complied with the legal requirement of filing reports on ownership structures with the Comissão de Valores Imobiliários (CVM), the Brazilian securities market regulator. The number of firms that submitted these reports ranged from 666 in 2002 to 836 in 1998.

The first step was identifying the "largest ultimate shareholder" for every sample company, defined as the shareholder holding, directly and indirectly, the largest voting stake. Indirect ownership or pyramidal ownership means that there is at least one firm between the firm under scrutiny and its corresponding ultimate shareholder. A company is said to have an ultimate controlling shareholder if it has a shareholder owning directly and indirectly at least 50 percent of its total voting rights. Then the largest ultimate shareholders were classified into the following categories: (1) an individual or a family; (2) the state or governmental agencies; (3) a foreign firm; (4) a mutual fund; (5) a pension fund; (6) a foundation or a cooperative; or (7) a privately held company.

The data analysis revealed that, on average, 52.4 percent of the sample firms were involved in pyramidal arrangements. Despite the shrinking number of firms under pyramidal ownership over the period, they still represented 49.3 percent of the sample in 2002. The frequency of pyramids was higher in paper and cellulose (78.8%) and telecommunications (72.6%). For the sample firms with pyramidal ownership structures, the number of intermediate companies between the company analyzed and the largest ultimate shareholder averaged 2.06. In 2002, this number was one for 50.0 percent of the firms organized as pyramids, two for 22.4 percent, three for 13.4 percent, eight for two firms, and nine for one of them.

For pyramidal firms, families represented, on average, 63.8 percent of the largest ultimate shareholders, against 54.9 percent for the whole sample, indicating that the frequency of pyramids was higher for family shareholders. Foreign investors (averaging 19.0%), governments (8.2%), and mutual funds (3.7%) followed in importance (see Table 13.4).

Regarding the existence of a controlling shareholder, differences between pyramidal and non-pyramidal firms seem irrelevant: 78.6 percent of the sample firms had a shareholder owning more than 50 percent of the firm's voting capital, against 74.6 percent of the pyramidal firms. Firms with an ultimate shareholder holding more than 90 percent of the voting capital represented 39 percent of the whole sample and

---

[10] The Brazilian Government owns a "golden share," entitling it to veto a number of corporate issues. Moreover, keeping Embraer under the control of Brazilians was a condition imposed on its privatization.

Table 13.4 Identity of the largest ultimate shareholders, 1997–2002 (%)

Category	Non-pyramidal firms	Pyramidal firms	All firms
Government	12.86	4.09	8.27
Foreign investors	22.06	16.35	19.07
Families	45.23	63.77	54.94
Foundations	0.55	3.03	1.85
Mutual funds	4.60	2.98	3.75
Pension funds	3.43	1.21	2.27
Privately-held firms	5.92	1.72	3.72
Others	5.32	6.86	6.13
Total	100.00	100.00	100.00

Note: Figures are the average percentage over the period 1997–2002.
Source: Aldrighi and Mazzer Neto (2007).

37.4 percent of the firms organized as pyramids. Discrepancies between cash-flow rights and voting rights for the largest ultimate shareholders were meaningful, notably for pyramidal groups. The average cash-flow right and voting right were, respectively, 51.0 percent and 73.3 percent, implying an average wedge of 22.3 percentage points (see Table 13.5). Families showed the highest average gap (27.1 percentage points), especially those involved in pyramidal ownership (32.4). Listed companies presented a slightly higher average wedge of rights vis-à-vis the average public company.

13.3.1.3 Boards of directors

The controlling shareholders of Brazilian business groups are predominantly families. Although they are usually members of their affiliated publicly traded companies' board of directors, they are not their chairmen, CEOs or executive (see Table 13.6).

Table 13.5 Cash–flow rights, voting rights, and discrepancies between rights, public companies, and listed firms, 1997–2002

Variable	Type	Overall mean	Pyramids mean
Voting rights	All public firms	73.3	71.4
	listed	70.4	68.7
Cash-flow rights	All public firms	51.0	40.8
	listed	46.1	37.2
Divergence	All public firms	22.3	30.6
	listed	24.3	31.4

Note: Figures are the average percentage over the period 1997–2002.
Source: Aldrighi and Mazzer Neto (2007).

Table 13.6 Controlling shareholders' participation in the management and boards of directors of business groups' publicly traded companies, 2007

Group	Companies traded on Bovespa	Is the largest ultimate shareholder			
		One of the directors?	The chairman?	One of the executives?	The CEO?
4. Itaúsa	Itaúsa Investimentos Itaú S.A.	Yes	No	No	No
	Banco Itaú Holding Financeira S.A.	Yes	No	No	No
	Itautec S.A.–Grupo Itautec	Yes	No	No	No
	Duratex S.A.	Yes	No	No	No
	BFB Leasing S.A.–Arrendamento Mercantil	Yes	No	No	No
	Elekeiroz S.A.	Yes	No	No	No
8. Votorantim	Votorantim Celulose e Papel S.A.	Yes	Yes	No	No
9. Gerdau	Gerdau	Yes	Yes	Yes	Yes
	Metalúrgica Gerdau	Yes	Yes	Yes	Yes
11. Odebrecht	Braskem	Yes	Yes	No	No
13. Unibanco	Unibanco Holdings	Yes	No	Yes	Yes
	Unibanco União de Bancos Brasileiros	Yes	No	Yes	Yes
	Dibens Leasing S.A. Arrendamento Mercantil	No	No	No	No
15. Oi	Telemar Norte Leste	Yes	No	No	No
	Telemar Participações	Yes	No	No	No
	Amazônia Celular	No	No	No	No
	Coari Participações	No	No	No	No
	Contax Participações	Yes	No	No	No
18. Ultra	Ultrapar Participações	Yes	No	No	No
23. Usiminas	Usinas Siderúrgicas de Minas Gerais	No	No	No	No
31. CSN	Cia. Siderúrgica Nacional	Yes	Yes	Yes	Yes

(continued)

Table 13.6 Continued

Group	Companies traded on Bovespa	Is the largest ultimate shareholder			
		One of the directors?	The chairman?	One of the executives?	The CEO?
32. CPFL Energia	CPFL Energia	Yes	Yes	No	No
	Cia. Piratininga de Força e Luz	Yes	Yes	No	No
	CPFL Geração de Energia	No	No	No	No
	Cia. Paulista de Força e Luz	No	No	No	No
	Rio Grande Energia	No	No	No	No
36. Camargo Corrêa	Camargo Corrêa Desenv. Imobiliário	No	No	No	No
	São Paulo Alpargatas	No	No	No	No
43. Sadia	Sadia	Yes	Yes	No	No
45. TAM	Tam	Yes	Yes	No	No

Source: Data drawn from each company's IAN (a mandatory report that public companies should file with the CVM, the Brazilian Securities and Exchange Commission).

As of 2007, Gerdau and CSN were major exceptions, inasmuch as a member of the controlling family was simultaneously the CEO and the chairman of their listed companies. In that same year, there were business groups whose controlling shareholder was the board's chairman but not the CEO, as in the cases of Votorantim Celulose e Papel, Braskem (Odebrecht), CPFL Energia and Companhia Piratininga, Sadia, and TAM. Unibanco's controlling shareholder was a director and CEO of two publicly traded companies belonging to the group. Amidst the sample groups' listed companies, only Telemar Norte Leste had a more than 50 percent overlap between board and management.

13.3.2 Business diversification

The extent of business diversification varies significantly across the largest Brazilian privately controlled business groups (see Table 13.1). Some are focused on a single business, such as Oi and Brasil Telecom (telecommunications), Unibanco (banking and finance), Embraer (aircraft manufacturing), Neoenergia, CPFL Energia and Light (electrical energy), Sadia and Perdigão (chilled and frozen foods), TAM (airline), and Pão de Açúcar (retail trade). Others have their own core business but also subsidiaries and affiliates operating in ancillary and vertically related industries,[11] as are the cases of Vale (specialized in mining but controlling firms engaged in logistics, railways, steel, and energy), Ultra (fuel distribution, chemicals, petrochemicals, and logistics), Gerdau (steel, iron mining, energy, and banking), and Usiminas (steel, metal goods, mechanics, and logistics). Finally, there are reasonably diversified economic groups conducting business in unrelated industries, such as Odebrecht, Votorantim, Vicunha/CSN, Camargo Corrêa, and the bank-centered Bradesco and Itaúsa. As for the largest state-owned business groups, excluding Petrobras, they concentrate their businesses on single activities (Eletrobrás, Cemig, and Copel on electrical energy, and Banco do Brasil on banking and finance). Petrobras has undertakings in energy and gas exploration, production, and distribution, petrochemicals, and transportation. As a rule, the largest Brazilian business groups are composed of leading firms in the respective markets wherein they have core businesses (De Siqueira 2000).

To a greater or lesser degree, government policies have influenced the development and diversification of most Brazilian business groups. This influence took different forms through time: trade protection favored light industries before the Second World War, state-led import substitution industrialization focused on intermediate and capital-good sectors from the 1940s to the 1970s, and thereafter government procurement and state funds supported corporate restructuring, modernization, internationalization, and privatization bids.

Overall, policy incentives and privatization have tended to foster Brazilian business groups' diversification, whereas trade liberalization, deregulation, and global competition have probably spurred them to strengthen their position in a few markets or to diversify primarily into technologically related industries, as a way to prevent take-overs from rivals or market share shrinking. The account below tries to cast some light on the main aspects driving the evolution of some leading Brazilian business groups, emphasizing the importance of policy incentives to shape their strategies.

Votorantim, Odebrecht, and Camargo Corrêa have clearly pursued business diversification, even though sometimes relinquishing operations in one or more industries. Founded in 1918 as a textile mill, Votorantim soon after began to engage in other activities: cement (a business then stimulated by import substitution policies), rayon and chemicals (the machines for the plant were exempted from import duties), and steelmaking in the 1930s; refractory artefacts, metallurgy and metalworking, paper, aluminum (a plant set up in the following decade would be financed by the BNDE), non-metallic mining, and hydro-electrical energy (for the group's self-consumption) in the 1940s; agribusiness (sugar cane), zinc, and nickel in the 1950s; ceramics and alcohol in the 1960s; transport services, and trade in textiles and machines in the 1970s; paper and cellulose, heavy equipments, and concentrated orange juice in the 1980s; banking and finance and electrical energy in the 1990s; and biotechnology and information technology in the 2000s. This group also disposed of businesses in some of these industries, such as textile, biotechnology (its two affiliates

---

[11] This may be associated with strategic reaction to uncertainties and contract imperfections (Khanna and Yafeh 2007).

were acquired by Monsanto in 2008), and electrical energy (selling to Camargo Corrêa in 2009 its interest in VBC, one of CPFL Energia's controlling shareholders), on top of transferring a 49.9 percent stake in Banco Votorantim to Banco do Brasil in 2009—these last three deals probably being related to the financial crisis at the time. On the other hand, VCP, the group's arm in paper and pulp, acquired 56 percent of Aracruz's voting capital in 2009—28 percent from the families Lorentzen, Almeida Braga, and Moreira Salles (Unibanco Group) and 28 percent from Safra Group, for which BNDES's financial support was crucial. In September 2009, VCP and Aracruz merged into Fibria. Until then, VCP and BNDESPar held, respectively, 28 percent and 12.49 percent of Aracruz's voting capital. After the merger, BNDESPar and Votorantim became the largest shareholders of Fibria, with stakes of, respectively, 34.9 percent and 29.3 percent.

In the same vein, public-sector construction procurement allowed Camargo Corrêa and Odebrecht—founded as civil construction companies, respectively, in 1939 and 1944—to gain strength and broaden their range of activities to more technologically sophisticated heavy-construction projects. State-led restructuring industrial policies and privatization boosted their business scope. Odebrecht diversified into chemicals and petrochemicals in the 1980s, and thereafter into concessions in highways and basic sanitation services. Privatization catapulted this group, together with Petrobras, into the leadership in the Brazilian petrochemical market. Camargo Corrêa significantly enlarged its range of activities in the 1970s, entering the businesses of real estate, agribusiness, cement, metals, mining, textiles, and finance. Later, it extended its interests to shipbuilding, environmental engineering, footwear, highway concessions, electrical energy, and steelmaking—in the last three industries, by taking part, through privatization bids, of the controlling block in CCR (a leading operator in highway concessions), CPFL Energia, and Usiminas. Along the way, some formerly secondary businesses (such as those in energy, textile, cement, and footwear) turned into the group's main activities.

Privatization also accelerated the expansion of Vicunha, a group whose origin traces back to a weaving mill in 1946. After turning into the largest Brazilian textile group (Vicunha Têxtil), it has, since the 1980s, branched out its interests into several industries, such as mining, cement, energy, railway, logistics, trading, and banking and financial services (by setting up Banco Fibra in 1989). After acquiring a relevant stake in CSN, the former state-owned steelmaker privatized in 1993, the group's two controlling families became its largest ultimate shareholder. In 2001 the cross-shareholdings interests between Vale and CSN were eliminated. Bradespar and Previ, which together with CSN were the controlling shareholders of Valepar SA, agreed to sell their stakes in CSN to Vicunha Siderurgia SA in exchange for the block of voting shares CSN held in Valepar SA. The progressive control of CSN by those two families was reached by means of increasing indebtedness, financed primarily by BNDES.

Vale and Gerdau have followed the strategy of vertical diversification around their core businesses. Even though steelmaking has persisted as its main activity, Gerdau Group extended its businesses to banking (to finance its suppliers and customers), iron mining and manufacturing (in 1986) and, more recently, to electrical energy. Analogously, Vale has maintained its focus on the exploration and production of iron ore and pellets while owning several companies engaged in closely related industries, such as steel, railways, logistics, and energy, besides assets in copper and nickel mining companies. The acute global competition in the mining sector has led Vale to search for gains in scale and scope, compelling it to make several acquisitions since 2000, out of which the US$18.243 billion purchase of Inco in 2006 stands out. Conversely, Vale sold its stakes in several steelmakers (Açominas, CSN, CST, Usiminas, Gerdau, and Siderar) and disposed of businesses in pulp and paper, fertilizers, ships, and wood.

Rather than diversification, Brazilian business groups' domestic and foreign acquisitions and disposals in the 2000s seem to point primarily to cost reduction, ownership streamlining, and synergy and scale gains. Recent moves in the petrochemical market are a case in point. Producing paper and pulp since the 1920s, Suzano Group diversified into petrochemicals in 1974. After strengthening its petrochemical branch, notably through privatization bids in the 1990s, Suzano Petroquímica was acquired by Petrobras, in a friendly takeover, in August 2007. Ipiranga Group, in turn, started operating in oil production, petrochemicals, and fuel distribution, but in the 1970s its businesses also included hotels, agribusiness, fishing, and transportation. Sharp competition in the 1990s, brought about by trade liberalization, led Ipiranga to dispose of its peripheral activities and refocus on its original activities. In 2007, Ipiranga's controlling shareholders sold its control to Braskem, Petrobras, and Ultrapar, implying a greater concentration in that sector. As a result, Grupo Ultra, an important player in the production of chemicals and petrochemicals (Oxiteno SA) and in integrated logistics for bulk cargo (Ultracargo), gained a significant share in the market for fuel distribution (through Ipiranga and Ultragaz), ascending to the eighteenth position in the ranking of business groups in Brazil in 2007.

These recent moves seem to be illustrative of the implications unleashed by the changing competition context. To avoid being an easy prey, Suzano Petroquímica and Ipiranga had either to gain market share (notably via acquisitions) or to jettison their assets to other major players. Consolidation in that industry being inexorable, it was indeed advanced by both private and state-controlled business groups, sometimes through alliances. Takeovers were reached either through privatization bids or through acquisitions of private groups, in which BNDESPar and Petrobras had a significant role.

Besides seeking cost curtailment and economies of scale, the takeover of Brasil Telecom by Oi, now Brazil's largest telephone operator, was partly motivated by Brazilian government's firm intent to create a national champion, thus preventing foreign players from dominating the domestic market for telecommunications services. As regards the merger in November 2008 of Itaú and Unibanco, respectively the third and fourth largest Brazilian banks in terms of net worth, the rationale appears to be the sharp competition among the large banks to take on the leadership in the domestic market.

Concerning banking activities, out of the twenty-four largest Brazilian private groups in 2007, three had banking as their core business, three had banks among their affiliates (Vicunha, Gerdau, and Votorantim), one had a bank, Bradesco, taking part in the controlling coalition (Vale), two had banks among their non-controlling shareholders (Neoenergia and Embraer), and one, Camargo Corrêa, had a substantial, but apparently passive, stake in a large bank (Itaú).

13.3.3 Internationalization: Trade and foreign direct investment

Although some Brazilian business groups operating in tradable sectors had already started their export drive in the 1970s, it was notably with the maturation in the 1980s of investments undertaken under the aegis of the II PND that a larger number of privately and state-controlled business groups in Brazil took export markets seriously. The achievement of productive capacity in scale-economy, capital-intensive industries contributed to mitigate the balance-of-payments crisis Brazil underwent at the beginning of the 1980s (De Castro and de Souza 1985). Lower trade barriers put pressure on Brazilian business groups and firms to develop new strategies, shifting their attitude toward foreign competition away from a merely defensive reaction to a more aggressive behavior with respect to their rivals' domestic markets.

Foreign sales from the ten Brazilian business groups with the highest exports in 2006 amounted to almost US$35 billion, accounting for 26 percent of the country's export value. The leading exporters were Petrobras Group (US$11.9 billion, tantamount to an 8.7 percent share of overall Brazilian exports), Vale (8.43%), Embraer (2.38%), Votorantim (1.1%), and Usiminas (1.2%) (Análise Comércio Exterior 2007). Export values as a fraction of total sales vary sharply from group to group, ranging from high ratios (more than 40% in the cases of Vale, Embraer, Sadia, and Perdigão) to low ones (for example, exports were responsible for just 13% of Votorantim's total sales in 2007). Factor endowment (Brazil's abundance in minerals, land, and petroleum) combined with economies of scale account for some of the international competitiveness of many Brazilian business groups. For other groups, the leading factors seem to be specific technological and organizational competence, as in the cases of Embraer, Odebrecht, Camargo Corrêa, Sadia and Perdigão.[12]

Some Brazilian business groups also achieved internationalization through foreign direct investment (FDI) abroad. Their outward FDI flows grew significantly in the 1990s but gained momentum over the period 2004–7. The main motivations behind this expansion were protectionism (FDI functioning as a substitute for exports, as in Gerdau's steelworks in the USA), access to raw materials and new markets (as in the

---

[12] In May 2009, Sadia merged with Perdigão. However, the deal had not yet been approved by the Brazilian antitrust authorities in November 2009.

cases of Petrobras's and Vale's foreign subsidiaries), and incentives coming from free trade areas (MERCOSUR and NAFTA, the latter making Mexico attractive to Brazilian groups).

Vale and Gerdau are the Brazilian groups that advanced the most on this front. Vale started to invest abroad only in 2000, but since then has set up joint ventures, subsidiaries, and affiliates with operating plants in all continents. Assets held abroad accounted for 46 percent of Vale's total assets in 2006.[13] Gerdau's direct investment abroad started earlier, in 1980, and was expanded by the purchase of several steelworks in Canada, Chile, Argentina, and the United States (the AmeriSteel). In 2003 Gerdau and the Canadian firm Co-Steel merged their steel businesses in North America, and Gerdau took on the control of the new firm. Until 2007, this group had acquired a number of other steelmakers in the USA, including Chaparral Steel Company. Clearly this foray into the American market paralleled protectionism against steel imports, disguised as anti-dumping measures. In 2005 Gerdau Group extended its operations into Spain, wherein it acquired, jointly with Santander, Corporación Sidenor SA, and in 2007, taking its first step into Asia, it established a joint venture with Kalyani. In 2007, Gerdau's assets abroad matched its domestic assets in terms of value. Embraer too has a large share of its assets abroad (45% in 2006).

Camargo Corrêa (with foreign assets representing 26% of its total assets), Votorantim (5%), Odebrecht (15%), and Ultrapar Participações SA (2%) appear as emerging foreign direct investors. Votorantim Group began to extend production facilities overseas only after 2000, in the cement, metals, paper and pulp, and agribusiness sectors. Ultrapar has three units producing chemical specialties in Mexico (since 2003), one chemical plant in Venezuela (acquired in 2007), besides other units in Argentina and the United States. The first direct investment Camargo Corrêa made abroad was the acquisition of a cement manufacturer in Argentina in 2005 (Loma Negra), and in the following year its textile arm, Santista Têxtil, merged with the Spanish Tavex Algodonera. Odebrecht acquired a Portuguese firm in the heavy construction sector in 1988 and incorporated in 1992 the British firm SLP Engineering, a firm specialized in providing components for offshore platforms. The remaining groups have a limited amount of FDI, most of which are represented by trading and commercial offices. Specifically, the three largest Brazilian banks have a modest international standing as compared either with their domestic operations or with foreign banks of similar scale.

Petrobras is the sole state-controlled business group holding a significant share of its overall assets abroad (around 12% in 2006). It owns exploration businesses in various Asian and African countries, a refining plant in Japan, and exploration and production operations in the United States and in several Latin American countries. In Argentina its operations are significantly diversified, ranging from oil exploration and production to gas and energy, petrochemicals, and electrical energy.

---

[13] These percentages were drawn from FDC-CPII (2007).

Conversely, foreign investors have significant stakes in some Brazilian groups. The Portuguese Banco Espírito Santo had 4.88 percent of Banco Bradesco's voting capital in 2007. In the mining and steel sectors, Mitsui had 18.2 percent of the voting capital of Valepar, while Nippon Group had 21.6 percent of Usiminas's voting capital. Casino Group co-controlled Pão de Açúcar together with the Diniz family. Also in 2007 Iberdrola Energia SA (wholly controlled by Iberdrola) held a direct 39.00 per cent stake in Neoenergia.

Closing this section, it should be mentioned that, among the twenty-nine largest Brazilian business groups, twenty had companies whose shares were traded as American depositary receipts (ADRs) on the New York Stock Exchange (NYSE) in 2008 (see Table 13.2).

13.4 CONCLUDING REMARKS

The Brazilian economy has undergone remarkable changes since the 1980s. The state stopped ruling the economic development strategy, leaving ample latitude for firms and business groups to make decisions about allocation of their capital (De Castro 2003). Trade liberalization, privatization of most of the largest state-controlled firms, and monetary stabilization have redefined the environment shaping firms' incentives and constraints, bringing about an outstanding corporate restructuring by means of mergers and acquisitions.

As regards the structures and strategies of Brazilian business groups, some characteristic features stand out. First, families control most of them. Secondly, state-controlled entities (such as Petrobras, BNDES, and Banco do Brasil) and pension funds of state-owned companies have significant stakes in the largest private business groups. This ownership structure is, to a great extent, accounted for by the privatization design, conceived primarily to maximize government's revenues. Thirdly, state-controlled groups have dramatically shrunk their share among the largest groups operating in Brazil. Fourthly, diversification strategies vary widely among the sample business groups. Whereas some of them are focused on specific sectors, others engage in a rather diversified range of businesses, probably on the grounds of risk-sharing or economies of scope.[14] There are also groups that, despite focusing on core businesses, have subsidiaries or affiliates operating in vertically related industries, perhaps for strategic motives, contractual shortcomings, or also scope economies. Fifthly, most of the largest Brazilian groups have attempted to internationalize their operations. In some of them, export markets have represented a significant share in their total revenue. On top of trade, foreign direct investment has been another vehicle of Brazilian business groups' internationalization, being forwarded mainly by

---

[14] See Schneider (2009) for a typology of business groups.

Petrobras, Gerdau and Vale. Sixthly, Brazilian business groups present a considerable longevity. The majority of them were created before 1950, and state support was critical to ensure their development.

Finally, the examination of a dataset built out of reports from hundreds of firms over the period 1997–2002 showed that pyramidal ownership structures were common among the sample companies. It is likely that these ownership arrangements serve different purposes. Some controlling shareholders probably use them as an "internal capital market" for financing new enterprises, as argued by Almeida and Wolfenzon (2006). For others, pyramids may operate as a device for expropriating minority shareholders. They may still serve as a mechanism for ensuring the family's control over the firm, preventing other holders of block of shares from contesting it. Finally, tax avoidance should not be neglected as a motive lying behind pyramids.

REFERENCES

ALDRIGHI, D. M., and MAZZER NETO, R. (2007). "Evidências sobre as estruturas de propriedade de capital e de voto das empresas de capital aberto no Brasil," *Revista Brasileira de Economia*, 61/2: 129–52.

ALMEIDA, H. and WOLFENZON, D. (2006). "A Theory of Pyramidal Ownership and Family Business Groups," *Journal of Finance*, 61/6: 2637–80.

Análise Comércio Exterior (2007). www.analisecomercioexterior.com.br

BACHA, E. L., and BONELLI, R. (2005). "Uma interpretação das causas da desaceleração econômica do Brasil," *Revista de Economia Política*, 25/3: 163–89.

BM&FBOVESPA (2009). *Boletim Informativo*, 8/14 (Feb.).

BM&FBOVESPA www.bovespa.com.br/indexi.asp

BNDES (2002). "Privatização no Brasil."

BNDESPAR (2008). BNDES Participações. Relatório de Administração.

BONELLI, R. (1998). "As estratégias dos grandes grupos industriais brasileiros nos anos 90." Discussion Paper, IPEA, Rio de Janeiro.

DE CASTRO, A. B. (2003). "El Segundo Catch-Up Brasileño: Caracteríticas y Limitaciones," *Revista de la Cepal*, 80: 73–83.

DE CASTRO, A. B. and DE SOUZA, F. E. P. (1985). *A Economia brasileira em Marcha Forçada*. Rio de Janeiro: Paz e Terra.

DE SIQUEIRA, T. (2000). "Os Grandes Grupos Brasileiros: Desempenho e Estratégias na Primeira Metade dos Anos 90," *Revista do BNDES*, 7/13: 3–32.

FDC-CPII (2007). Fundação Dom Cabral and the Columbia Program on International Investment, "Brazil's Multinationals Take Off." Release of the FDC-CPII 2007 Ranking of Brazilian Multinational Enterprises, Nova Lima and New York.

FISHLOW, A. (1972). "Origins and Consequences of Import Substitution in Brazil," in L. de Marco (ed.), *International Economics and Development*. New York: Academic Press.

Gazeta Mercantil, *Balanço Anual*, various issues.

HERMANN, J. (2005). "Auge e declínio do modelo de crescimento com endividamento: o II PND e a crise da dívida externa (1974–1984)," in F. Giambiagi, A. Villela, L. de Castro, and J. Hermann, *Economia Brasileira Contemporânea (1945–2004)*. Rio de Janeiro: Elsevier.

KHANNA, T., and YAFEH, Y. (2007). "Business Groups in Emerging Markets: Paragons or Parasites?" *Journal of Economic Literature*, 45: 331–72.

MENEZES FILHO, N. A., GONZAGA, G., and TERRA, M. C. (2006). "Trade Liberalization and the Evolution of Skill Earnings Differentials in Brazil," *Journal of International Economics*, 68/2: 345–67.

SCHNEIDER, B. R. (2009). "How States Organize Capitalism: A Comparative Political Economy of Diversified Business Groups," *Review of International Political Economy*, 16/1.

Valor Grandes Grupos (2008). Supplement of *Valor Econômico*.

CHAPTER 14

....

BUSINESS GROUPS IN CHILE

....

FERNANDO LEFORT

14.1 INTRODUCTION

....

ECONOMIC activity in Chile is dominated by several business groups that operate in most sectors of the economy. In general terms, Chilean business groups tend to be structured as a collection of listed and non-listed companies presenting highly concentrated ownership and hanging under a listed holding company. These characteristic pyramidal structures are used to obtain funding from minority shareholders without losing control. Many of the large companies affiliated to Chilean business groups have traded in a relatively developed capital market with a considerable participation of institutional investors since 1986 (when Chilean pension funds where authorized to invest in companies' shares).

Most Chilean business groups are relatively young and are successfully run by the second or third generation of the founding families. However, in some cases control has passed to teams of executives and to foreign companies.

In this chapter I look at the main features of Chilean business groups and try to find some stylized factors that help in an understanding of their dynamic evolution. Business groups have been the traditional business structure in Chile for a long time.

Mansaku Maeda and Ignacio Galvez provided outstanding research assistance. This research has been partially funded by the Bicentennial Program of Science and Technology through a Social Science Ring, SOC-04. The author acknowledges the excellent comments of the editors of the book and participants at the Kyoto conference.

Their origins and evolution have responded to several key political and economic events. As in many other countries in Latin America, a large number of today's most important Chilean companies were founded by the Chilean state. Two large-scale waves of privatizations ended up with a massive transfer of large companies to the private sector and the emergence of several of the actual business groups.

On the other hand, the 1982 debt crisis meant that most bank-based conglomerates became bankrupt. However, as some traditional business groups disappeared, others that were financially more robust emerged by acquiring controlling stakes from the government or the bankrupt groups.

There are two main areas of activity covered by the Chilean business groups. On the one hand, large, more diversified family-controlled groups tend to exploit and export natural resources. On the other hand, a few successful family-owned retail chains have evolved into business groups with operations in several countries of Latin America.

The Chilean economy enjoyed macroeconomic stability and economic growth during the late 1980s and 1990s fostered by policies aimed to encourage the growth of Chilean exports. Hence most business groups flourished and expanded especially in the export and utility sectors. As the per capita income level of the Chilean population increased, old family-owned retail firms started to become large companies with a widespread presence in the country and in Latin America. Although some unrelated diversification occurred early in the 1970s and 1980s, most large Chilean groups have chosen to grow by expanding their main business activities elsewhere in Latin America.

Chilean business groups show high ownership concentration, tightly controlled pyramid structures, and friendly board of directors. This situation has changed very little since 1990. Although management has become increasingly professional, strategic decisions tend to be made by the leaders of the controlling families.

Section 14.2 describes the evolution of business groups in Chile. Section 14.3 gives a detailed account of corporate and control structures of Chilean business groups. Section 14.4 describes the main strategies and capabilities of Chilean business groups, presenting some stylized facts. Section 14.5 concludes.

14.2 EMERGENCE AND LONG-TERM EVOLUTION OF BUSINESS GROUPS IN CHILE

14.2.1 General background

A business group is a collection of separate firms that are tied by ownership relations and that, in spite of their legal autonomy, tend to respond to a common "group" strategy. As it turns out, most firms in Latin America are linked in some way or another to a business group that exercises tight control over the firm and owns a large proportion of its shares. Lefort (2005a) presents evidence regarding the identity of controllers in large listed Latin American companies, the degree of affiliation to business groups, and the extent of the separation of cash flow and control rights. His results show several interesting features. First, family-owned firms in most Latin American economies are the predominant form of corporation, even among large listed firms. Secondly, on average, almost 80 percent of large listed firms are affiliated to a business group. Although these groups use very different forms to exercise control, they all tend to hold a large proportion of the cash-flow rights of the controlled companies. Thirdly, although business groups may be structured in different ways, they tend to be used effectively to separate cash from control rights. That is, the controlling shareholders of a business group usually achieve disproportionate voting power through pyramids, dual class shares, and cross-holdings, retaining control of the affiliated companies but leveraging their cash investments in those companies. Finally, business groups in Chile and Latin America are characterized by the lack of separation between ownership and managerial activity. That is, it is generally the case that affiliated firms are not only controlled but also effectively managed by the group owners.

14.2.2 Historical background

Business groups have been the predominant form of corporate structure in Chile for a long time. Their origins and evolution importantly respond to several key political and economic events. As in many other countries in Latin America, a large proportion of the most important Chilean companies as of 2008 were founded by the Chilean state. In particular, during the first half of the twentieth century a number of large state-owned companies were created in the context of a national plan of industrialization under the supervision of a public entity (CORFO).

CORFO was created in 1939 with the objective of fostering national economic activity. Hence, since its beginning, CORFO has created key companies that constituted the basis for Chile's industrialization—among many others, the National Electricity Company (ENDESA), the National Oil Company (ENAP), the Pacific Steel Company (CAP), and the National Sugar Industry (IANSA). In addition, CORFO put in place several development plans, including financial credits and mixed ownership in key areas related to the exploitation of natural resources—for example, mining, agriculture, and fishery. Starting in 1960, CORFO led an investment plan in basic services including telecommunications (ENTEL).

With few exceptions, the companies founded by the Chilean state became, during the following years, the basis for many of the business groups currently operating in Chile. In addition, during the socialist government of 1970–3, a large-scale plan of nationalization of private companies meant that the number of state-owned companies controlled by CORFO reached over 500 in 1973. After the military coup that took place that year, many companies were given back to their original owners, and two large-scale waves of privatizations ended up with a massive transfer of large companies to the private sector and the emergence of several business groups.

However, not all companies started as a direct consequence of a government initiative. A few emblematic private Chilean companies were founded by Chilean entrepreneurs during the nineteenth century and the first half of the twentieth century, and others emerged during the 1950s despite the difficult economic conditions, the tremendous financial repression, and the utter lack of capital markets. For example, until 1958 there were quantitative and qualitative restrictions on bank credit as well as ceilings on the nominal interest rate that could be charged. In this period, inflation rates were high and volatile, ranging between 20 and 80 percent per year, generating negative real interest rates, which naturally led to more intense credit rationing. In addition, direct access to bond markets by firms did not seem possible either, partly because of the upper limits on interest rates and the prohibition to index financial instruments to inflation that existed until 1958. Moreover, high taxes on dividends, an oppressing regulatory environment, and a poor economic background made equity investment very unattractive.

In spite of these unfavorable conditions, companies such as CMPC of the Matte group (pulp production), COPEC (oil distribution), which was acquired by the Angelini group in the early 1980s, Fallabella of the Solari–Fallabella group (retail), among others, were created by Chilean entrepreneurs and in 2008 were still the basis of successful, long-lasting business groups. Moreover, the basis for two of the largest and most well-known Chilean groups, Angelini and Luksic, were established in the 1950s as their founders entered the mining and fishing business.

However, financial repression and credit rationing during a large part of the twentieth appearance of bank-centered groups. Large companies belonging to social networks had access to cheap financing through related banks. Lagos (1961) identifies eleven large groups, all related to banks operating in Chile by 1958. Garretón and Cisternas (1970) identify nineteen additional groups by 1966, most of them small family groups.

The socialist period of 1970–3 imposed severe conditions on the development and continuity of groups. However, for 1978 Dahse (1979) and González (1978) identify more or less the same groups as those listed in previous studies, although some important changes in property and some new associations had taken place.

In the mid-1970s the first round of privatization took place at relatively attractive prices, in the context of a recently liberalized economy, a naive legal environment, and primitive capital markets. This gave the incentive for the creation of significantly indebted groups or conglomerates mostly around banks. Hachette and Lüders (1992) indicate that the most important groups that appeared in that period were Cruzat-Larraín, BHC, and Claro.

Following this period came the 1982 debt crisis, which is perhaps one of the most important events to have shaped the way in which Chilean corporations are organized even in the late 2000s. The crisis meant that most bank-based conglomerates became bankrupt. In addition, very restrictive regulations affecting the banking industry and the relationship between banks and companies were adopted as a consequence of the crisis. The debt crisis also brought it a large shock for groups. Bank failures and state intervention caused several conglomerates, such as Vial and BHC, to disappear; others, like Cruzat-Larraín, were reduced. However, while some traditional business groups disappeared as a consequence of the debt crisis, other financially more robust groups emerged by acquiring controlling stakes from the government or the bankrupt groups. That was the case, for instance, of the Angelini and Luksic groups.

The second round of privatization, which took place during the second half of the 1980s, produced a significant boost to the upsurge of new and more active groups. The privatization process was implemented partly with the purpose of achieving dispersed firm ownership. Pension funds were allowed to buy equity for the first time, but eligible firms had to adopt important statutory restrictions, particularly in terms of ownership concentration. Yet business groups rapidly took control over most newly privatized firms. In some cases, however, the large size of the firms being privatized required associations between Chilean and foreign companies.[1]

The Chilean economy enjoyed macroeconomic stability and economic growth during the late 1980s, fostered by policies aimed to encourage the growth of Chilean exports. Traditional business groups invested in exportable natural resources, including forestry, mining, fruit, and fisheries.

By the end of the 1980s, new groups arose in the utilities sectors. For instance, the privatization of the state-owned electric companies gave rise to the Enersis group, run by the team of executives that had privatized the company. In some cases, emblematic state-owned companies were acquired by foreign companies, as in the case of the telephone company CTC, acquired by Telefonica of Spain in 1990. Likewise, water supply and sanitary services company Aguas Andina ended up controlled by Spaish AGBAR during the 1990s.

In the financial sector, the pension reform and the growing importance of insurance companies meant the appearance of few groups built around financial businesses. In many cases, the banks and other financial services were acquired by multinational conglomerates that tended to adopt a business group structure in Chile. Examples are Santander, BBVA, and ING, among others. In addition, some Chilean businessmen organized financial services groups during the 1990s, starting from traditional brokerage firms and regional banks that were in trouble during the debt crises of the 1980s. With very few exceptions, because of the legal reforms that occurred after the 1982 debt crisis, there is a clear separation between industrial and financial business groups.

Economic success was the rule during most of the 1990s. Hence most business groups flourished and expanded, especially in the export and utility sectors. The natural resource-based, export-oriented business groups profited from the outward orientation and macroeconomic stability of the Chilean economy. The business groups based on utility services benefited from their natural monopolist position

---

[1] Like Carter-Holt in the case of the Angelini group.

and the growing income level of the country. However, a new phenomenon was arising, as the per capita income level of the Chilean population increased. Old family-owned retail firms started to become large companies with a widespread presence in the country. Three of them are noteworthy: Jumbo, Falabella, and Almacenes Paris. As they become larger and their operations were more sophisticated, these companies started to operate as business groups, operating through simple pyramidal structures in several sectors related to retail, such as malls, real estate, and consumer financial services.

After the Asian crisis, economic growth regained strength in Chile. Historical high international prices for most commodities produced in Chile meant increased profits for most business groups, and even more influence over the Chilean economy. As large profits accumulated over several years, Chilean business groups had to look for alternative ways to expand their operations. Although some unrelated diversification has happened, most large Chilean groups have chosen to expand their main business activities elsewhere in Latin America. This has happened in the energy, retail, mining, and forestry sectors.

Interestingly, only three groups have been operating without interruptions since the 1960s: the Matte, Angelini, and Luksic groups. Paredes and Sánchez (1995) interpret this evidence as an indication of significant mobility and the absence of barriers to entry or exit of groups. In any case, although business groups have been the predominant form of corporate structure in the Chilean economy, they have not had an easy ride over the pronounced political and economical cycles that have affected the Chilean economy. The corporate structures set in place by Chilean businessmen since 1950 may have been useful for dealing with financially repressed markets and business opportunities arising from government intervention. However, they have not been able to assure long-running stability in the face of the profound shocks affecting the Chilean economy. This is also an indication that, in spite of some cases of liaisons between economic and political power that enabled the creation or solidification of a particular business group during the intense privatization periods, in general terms, there has been a lack of strong and durable networks between the business community and the political authorities of the country. As a consequence, Chilean business groups are, in general, younger than comparable groups in Asian and other Latin American countries. As yet, family businesses have rarely passed the second generation.

14.2.3 The main Chilean business groups in 2008

The Chilean Superintendence of Securities (SVS) pragmatically defines a business group as two or more listed companies that are controlled by the same shareholder (or group of shareholders), even when one of the companies is just an investment company holding shares of a single operating firm. Under that definition, the number of business groups operating in Chile has increased dramatically since the late 1980s.

Table 14.1 Main features of the twenty-five largest business groups in Chile, 2007

	Business group/ family	Consolidated sales volume (US$ m.)	Year of foundation	Controller identity	% of control	Listed holding company
1	Angelini	12,289	1934	Angelini family 2nd generation	61.9	Antarchile
2	ENDESA	9,387		ENDESA Spain, since 1997	60.0	ENERSIS
3	Luksic	9,280	1957	Luksic family 2nd generation	80.3	Quiñenco
4	Paulmann	7,570	1978	Paulmann family 1st generation	63.7	Cencosud
5	Solari-Cuneo-Del Rio	5,679	1937	Solari, Cuneo, Del Rio families 2nd generation	87.7	
6	Claro	4,810	1872	Claro Family 1st generation	49.7	Marinsa
7	Matte	4,476	1920	Matte family 2nd generation	80.1	PASUR, Minera V.
8	Santander Chile	4,115	1977	Banco Santander S. A., 1977	76.9	
9	Ibáñez	3,817	1957	Ibañez family 2nd generation	50.0	
10	Marin-Del Real	2,575	1905	Marin-Del Real families	61.7	INDIVER
11	Sigdo Koppers	1,916	1960	6 business-men	76.0	Sigdo Koppers
12	Calderón	1,894	1956	Calderón family	80.6	
13	CAP	1,583	1946	Disperse ownership		Invercap S.A.
14	Said	1,367	1946	Said family / BBVA	24.4	
15	Penta	1,342	1986	C. Delano/ C. Lavin	96.6	
16	CTC	1,267	1990	Telefonica S. A. (Spain), 1990	44.9	

(continued)

Table 14.1 Continued

	Business group/ family	Consolidated sales volume (US$ m.)	Year of foundation	Controller identity	% of control	Listed holding company
17	SQM	1,187	1968	Julio Ponce and Potash Co.	27.0	Norte Grande
18	Urenda	1,044	1983	Urenda family	24.6	Empresas Navieras
19	Saieh	850		Saieh family 1st generation	49.0	Corp Group Banking
20	Femández León	793		Femandez Leon family	29.0	Almendral S.A.
21	Larrain– Vial	553	1964	Larrain, Vial families	49.6	
22	Aguas Andinas	508		AGBAR, Spain	56.6	Inverisiones Aguas Metropolitanas S.A.
23	Yarur	461	1957	Yarur Family	63.4	
24	Hurtado Vicuña	302	1978	Hurtado, Vicuña families		Pacifico V Region
25	IANSA	211		E,D&F Man, England	62.1	Campos Chilenos
26	Chilean SEOs	29,885		Chilean government	100.0	

Source: SVS, El Mercurio and company statements.

The twenty-year period starting in 1988 corresponds to one of the longest and most stable periods in terms of high economic growth in the Chilean economic history. Hence, this period of economic growth and political stability encouraged the appearance of new business groups and contributed to the consolidation of others. In fact, eleven of the twelve groups that were present in 1988 were still present in 2007. The important increase in their number in the mid-1990s is due, in part, to the increase in the number of listed companies during those years, since the SVS definition requires at least one company to be listed. Since 1996 an increasing number of foreign corporations have acquired domestic firms traditionally controlled by Chilean family business groups. This wave of acquisitions and the 1999 slowdown in the aftermath of the Asian crisis generated a stabilization of the number of business groups in Chile. After 2000 the number of business groups increased again, particularly in the financial and public-works sectors.

In 2008 Chilean business groups constituted a heterogeneous set in terms of size, structure, ownership identity, industrial sector, and diversification. Although the SVS identified 138 different groups in 2007, no more than twenty-five had a relevant size in terms of annual sales and presented a corporate structure that, because of its diversification and utilization of holding companies, qualified as a business group. Table 14.1 summarizes key features of the twenty-five main private business groups (plus one group of state-owned companies) operating in Chile in 2007 with two or more companies listed on the local stock exchange. Some large family groups that operated through non-listed companies are not considered in this sample, since there is no public information available for them. Table 14.1 shows that, of the twenty-five largest business groups in Chile, fifteen are classic family-run business groups. In all fifteen, there are members of the family sitting on the companies' boards and/or acting as executives. Leadership of the groups falls, generally, to the second-generation male members.

Five of the twenty-five largest groups are controlled by multinational companies operating in utilities, financial services, and sugar industries. Although they do not constitute proper groups and present no diversification in their activities, they have adopted Chilean-type pyramids structured from an investment holding company. In a couple of cases, local businessmen and international companies share control over a few companies. For example, the Said family and BBVA from Spain jointly control a set of financial-services companies originally owned by the Chilean family. In the case of the fertilizer company SQM, a local businessman who took control of the company after privatization competes for control of the company with the Canadian Potash Co. The last set of business groups were formed by the association of several local businessmen and do not classify as a typical family group. They are Sigdo-Koppers and Penta; Sigdo-Koppers became a listed company in 2005.

Another interesting feature of Chilean business groups is that, regardless of the identity of the controller, they all use investment holding companies as a means to exercise control. Moreover, in all but eight cases, the holding company is listed on the stock exchange. Table 14.1 also shows some measures of the concentration of ownership, indicating the percentage of shares controlled by the controlling shareholder in the holding company or in the main productive company of the group. In the next section, I explain in more detail the ownership and control structures of Chilean business groups.

14.3 GOVERNANCE AND CONTROL STRUCTURES OF CHILEAN BUSINESS GROUPS

Unlike the situation in the USA and the UK, corporate ownership in Chile is characterized by a high degree of ownership concentration. Furthermore, as in most emerging economies, the identifying feature of corporate structure in Chile is

Table 14.2 Importance of Chilean conglomerates, 1990–2002

Conglomerates	1990		1994		1998		2002	
	Assets (US$ m.)	Relative size (%)	Assets (US$ m.)	Relative size (%)	Assets (US$ m.)	Relative size (%)	Assets (US$ m.)	Relative size (%)
Largest	4,617	22.0	9,454	14.0	16,220	23.0	11,306	20.5
5 largest	9,264	44.0	34,018	51.0	37,704	54.0	26,304	47.6
10 largest	16,784	79.0	46,316	69.0	49,357	70.0	37,008	67.0
20 largest	18,784	88.0	54,259	81.0	57,570	82.0	46,655	84.5
All conglomerates	19,422	91.0	57,973	87.0	63,957	91.0	49,729	90.0
Non-affiliated	1,841	9.0	8,879	13.0	6,059	9.0	5,511	10.0
Total	21,263	100.0	66,852	100.0	70,017	100.0	55,241	100.0

Sources: Lefort and Walker (2000c) and author calculations.

the generalized presence of business groups. In this subsection, I describe the main features of the control and capital structures of Chilean business groups and relate them, when possible, to some of the events discussed previously.

The importance of business groups in the Chilean economy can be seen from the percentage of the total assets of listed companies in the Chilean stock exchange controlled directly and indirectly by business groups. Table 14.2 shows that Chilean business groups controlled over 90 percent of the assets of the largest companies operating in Chile in 2002. This proportion has remained very stable since 1990. Furthermore, an indication of the concentration of wealth in the country is that the five largest business groups have controlled almost 50 percent of the total assets of listed companies in the local stock exchange.

However, not all business groups have the same characteristics. In the Chilean economy, as well as in most Latin American economies, many multinational companies operate using a structure mimicking that of a traditional family-owned business group. Consider, for instance, that at any point in time an individual firm might be classified as any of four possible combinations of categories: (1) family owned and affiliated to a business group;[2] (2) family owned and non-affiliated to a business group; (3) non-family owned and affiliated to a business group; and (4) non-family owned and non-affiliated to a business group. Fig. 14.1 summarizes the distribution of data, as of 2006, in these four categories along the two dimensions. For instance, the figure shows that in 2006, of the 198 listed, non-financial Chilean firms, a total of 158 (80%) were family businesses, while a total of 129 (65%) belonged to an economic group. Now, 105 (53% of the total) firms were both family business and belonged to a group (family group), while only 16 (8% of the total) were neither family nor affiliated to a group. The figure also shows that a majority (66%) of family businesses were also affiliated to a business group, and that most firms affiliated to a business group (80%) were family controlled.

As Lefort and Walker (2000c) showed, pyramidal schemes are the most common way of achieving control in Chilean business groups, since cross-holdings are forbidden by law and dual class shares are relatively rare. In order to understand the control and capital structures of Chilean business groups it is necessary to consolidate their holdings in the different companies they control. Here, I analyze data sources from Lefort and Walker (2007a), which referred to the minority and controlling shareholders' investments in subsidiary and parent companies.

14.3.1 Control mechanisms

An interesting feature of business groups in Chile is that they tend to be constructed through similar pyramid structures, regardless of the identity of the controller.

---

[2] Here, affiliation refers to the condition of being controlled by a business group.

	Group affiliated	Non-group affiliated	Total
Family business	105 (53%)	53 (27%)	158 (80%)
Non-family business	24 (12%)	16 (8%)	40 (20%)
Total	129 (65%)	69 (35%)	198 (100%)

Figure 14.1 Family business and group affiliation of Chilean listed companies, 2006

Source: Lefort (2005a).

14.3.1.1 *Pyramids*

Chilean business groups mostly use simple pyramid structures to separate control from cash-flow rights. Chilean Corporations Law prohibits cross-holdings, and, although they are allowed, dual class shares are relatively rare in Chilean companies. As of December 2006, only 10 out of 165 non-financial companies, including investment and holding companies, had more than one class of shares. In all cases, the preferred shares had limited voting powers to elect members of the board of directors.

Table 14.3 indicates that Chilean groups use relatively simple pyramidal structures; it is relatively rare to find more than four layers of listed companies consolidated. However, the table clearly indicates that the number of layers used by groups has increased in the twenty-first century. By 1990, only 13 percent of public corporations affiliated to groups were second or higher level. This figure increased to almost 33 percent by 1998, reaching more than 45 percent by the year 2004. It is important to keep in mind that, although Chilean business groups are formed through relatively simple pyramid schemes of listed companies, it is not always easy to ascertain the way the pyramid structures are controlled. The reason is that there are very few people among the largest shareholders. Controllers of these structures hold shares through private investment companies with fantasy names that participate at all levels of the pyramidal structure, making it very difficult to identify the identity of the ultimate owners by investors and regulators.[3]

---

[3] The large difference between personal income and corporate tax rates explains the wide use of private holding companies. A legal reform passed in 2000 requires listed companies to disclose the identity of the ultimate controlling shareholder.

Table 14.3 Pyramid schemes, 1990–2004

Year	Corporations Level 1	Corporations Level 2	Corporations Level 3	Corporations Level 4	Corporations Level 5	Corporations Level 6
1990	93	13	0	0	0	0
	87.7%	12.2%				
1994	124	45	2	1	0	0
	72.0%	26.6%	1.1%	0.5%		
1998	96	40	5	2	0	0
	67.1%	27.9%	3.5%	1.4%		
2004	59	27	16	3	3	1
	54.1%	24.8%	14.7%	2.8%	2.8%	0.9%

Source: Lefort and Walker (2000c) and author calculations.

Table 14.4 Ownership and control structure of Chilean conglomerates, 2002

Conglomerates	Total Assets		Debt		Equity Minority Shareholders		Controlling Shareholders		Separation of cash and control rights	
	US$ m.	Relative size (%)	US$ m.	% of assets	US$ m.	% of assets	US$ m.	% of assets	% of equity rights	% of total rights
Largest	11,306	20	6,568	58	2,410	21	2,329	21	49	26
5 largest	26,304	48	13,905	53	5,323	20	7,076	27	57	37
10 largest	37,008	67	20,406	55	6,616	18	9,987	27	60	37
20 largest	46,655	84	25,561	55	8,649	19	12,445	27	59	36
All conglomerates	49,729	90	27,207	55	9,288	19	13,234	27	59	36
Non-afiliated	5,511	10	2,390	43	1,160	21	1,961	36	63	55
Total	55,241	100	29,597	54	10,448	19	15,196	28	59	38

Sources: Lefort and Walker (2000c) and author calculations.

In spite of these problems, Chilean business groups are relatively simple. An interesting hypothesis is that the simplicity of these structures is due to legislation put in place in order to protect pension funds from expropriation. Moreover, since tax laws in Chile allow tax credits on dividend payments, pyramid structures are not penalized by tax considerations. Another consideration regarding the control structures of Chilean business groups is that, because Chilean banks are forbidden to hold company shares, groups are structured around holding companies instead of banks. That norm is a direct consequence of the debt crisis of 1982.

Table 14.4 summarizes the most salient features of the consolidated structures of Chilean business groups as a consequence of the widespread use of pyramids. It is especially interesting to notice the extent of separation between cash and control rights. In 2002 Chilean business groups directly or indirectly owned 59 percent of the consolidated equity of the listed firms controlled by the group, usually retaining over two-thirds of shares in each layer of the pyramid and thus retaining total control of each company.

14.3.1.2 *Boards*

Because of the high degree of ownership concentration in Chilean companies, control is exercised, in practice, through board members elected directly or indirectly by the controlling groups. A survey of board practices at large listed Chilean companies indicates that less than 50 percent of all board members are not directly related by family to the controlling shareholders or are not executives in the company or in another company owned by the same controlling shareholder.[4] Moreover, on average, in 2003 each board member of a company affiliated to a business group sat on 1.3 boards of the same group. Table 14.5 shows that the largest groups tend to centralize board positions around fewer people, as compared to smaller groups, and that few people sit on boards of companies belonging to different groups. The table also shows, however, that the practice of trusting few people outside the group is slowly diminishing.

This evidence suggests that even board members elected with minority shareholder votes rarely sit in companies controlled by other groups. Exceptions are board members elected by pension funds in large corporations. Iglesias (2000) shows that, in those companies where the pension funds own shares, 10 percent of board members are elected with their votes. Despite this, the evidence provided in Table 14.6 shows that controlling shareholders of Chilean business groups are increasingly favoring independent directors to sit on the boards of their companies, indicating a trend toward the professionalization of Chilean boards.

External mechanisms of control and corporate governance are rarely important in Chile. For instance, in the vast majority of companies, high ownership concentration eliminates the possibility of hostile takeovers. However, since 1998 a large number of acquisitions have taken place in Chile. Lefort and Walker (2001) analyze twelve major acquisitions involving transfer of control between 1996 and 1999. They found that the average excess price for these twelve acquisitions was 70 percent, while the average

---

[4] Spencer Stuart and the Business School of the Pontificia Universidad Católica de Chile prepared the 2006 Board Index Report based on board practices used by sixty-seven large listed Chilean companies.

Table 14.5 Board composition, 1994–2003

	Number of seats in board			Number of different directors			Ratio		
	1994	1998	2003	1994	1998	2003	1994	1998	2003
Largest	63	79	65	33	35	45	1.9	2.3	1.4
5 largest	268	281	272	173	155	190	1.5	1.8	1.4
10 largest	405	368	419	276	228	285	1.5	1.6	1.5
Rest	693	802	369	453	533	319	1.5	1.5	1.2
Total	1429	1530	788	935	951	604	1.5	1.6	1.3

	Directors in at least in 2 groups			Directors in at least in 3 groups			Directors in at least in 4 groups		
	1994	1998	2003	1994	1998	2003	1994	1998	2003
All groups	114	72	106	15	8	46	0	0	12

Source: Lefort and Walker (2000c) and author calculations.

Table 14.6 Independent board members, 2000–3 (%)

Directors	2000	2001	2002	2003
Elected by minority shareholders				
1 Smallest companies	14.59	18.10	16.23	15.48
2 Second quintile	17.72	16.94	15.83	15.67
3 Third quintile	24.30	22.59	21.67	22.71
4 Fourth quintile	27.06	26.50	27.87	28.23
5 Largest quintile	32.25	36.13	35.47	29.70
Average	22.33	23.09	21.98	21.79
Independent: elected by controlling shareholders				
1 Smallest companies	4.34	3.25	3.45	4.57
2 Second quintile	11.94	8.27	14.06	11.15
3 Third quintile	5.60	8.78	9.36	8.00
4 Fourth quintitle	8.94	7.95	9.63	10.89
5 Largest quintile	5.90	5.42	7.15	8.17
Average	8.07	7.67	9.07	8.52

Source: Lefort and Urzua (2008).

control block purchased amounted to 40 percent of shares. On average, the cumulative abnormal return was approximately 5 percent, indicating that the average acquisition was perceived as value enhancing by the market.

14.3.1.3 Strategic decisions

Among family-controlled Chilean business groups, strategic decisions are still made by family leaders and instructions are passed to teams of professional managers to be executed. Chilean legislation forbids executives of a company to be members of the board of the same company. Hence, family leaders tend to sit in the board as chairman or vice-chairman and nominate other family members and/or professional outsiders in key executive positions. During the 1990s, an increase in the number of professional managers in family-owned business groups occurred. As previously discussed, after the year 2000, there was also an increase in the number of outsiders sitting in the boards of companies. However, this professionalization of family-owned groups has not meant a decreased leadership of the families in the strategic decision-making. In fact, executive committees have been used to discuss strategic decision in the trusted circle of the family.

On the other hand, Chilean business groups are very jealous of the strategic information they have. This can be seen in the reluctance of groups to share ownership, boards, and information with members of other families or groups. Since 2007, several infractions to the inside information regulations have shown that some families tend to consider the companies they run as though they were closed companies despite the presence of minority shareholders.

14.3.2 Capital and ownership structures

Lefort and Walker (2007a) constructed consolidated balance sheets at the business group level, for all non-financial listed companies, in order to describe ownership and capital structure of Chilean economic groups. Some of the results are summarized in Tables 14.7 and 14.8. As was indicated above, companies affiliated to groups hold 90 percent of total non-financial, listed assets in Chile. Table 14.8 also shows that business groups have increased their use of debt, reaching almost 55 percent in 2002. The evidence presented in Table 14.7 also shows that, in general, controlling shareholders hold more equity than, in principle, is needed for control. The average controlling shareholder held 59 percent of the consolidated equity capital of the business groups in 2002. When interpreting this concentration figure, it is important to keep in mind that a four-layers pyramid structure can be controlled with less than 10 percent of consolidated equity.

Some other interesting facts about capital structure in Chilean business groups are the following. Minority shareholders own around 40 percent of the equity controlled by Chilean groups, with pension-funds managers and ADRs representing 25 percent each of minority shareholders interest. Regarding debt composition, Lefort and Walker (2000c) showed that firms affiliated to business groups are able to get significantly more long-term and bond debt financing than non-affiliated firms.

14.3.3 Impact of control structures on company valuation

We now have a better understanding about the ownership and control structure of business groups in Chile, and we have several competing conceptual frameworks in order to explain the costs and benefits of business groups in emerging markets. Khanna and Palepu (1999a, b) find that group affiliation improves firm economic performance in India and Chile. They also find that the degree of diversification of the conglomerate increases performance only after it has reached a certain threshold. Khanna and Palepu (1999c) found that in Chile and India the performance of groups increased after economic reform was performed, indicating that part of the benefits of affiliation is not related to a poor economic environment.

More recently, Lefort and Walker (2007b) have show that in most Chilean companies the traditional agency conflict between owners and managers is better characterized by the horizontal agency problem between controlling and minority shareholders. Hence, they performed a regression analysis of measures of firm market valuation and performance on agency conflict indicators at the firm level, including a series of control variables. In summary, they found that firms whose controlling shareholders have higher coincidence between cash flow and control rights tend to have consistently higher market values. This result is interpreted as an indication that potential conflicts of interest between controlling and minority shareholders are penalized by the Chilean capital market. When controlling adequately for endogeneity and omitting variable biases, they found that an increase in the degree of coincidence

Table 14.7 Control structure of Chilean conglomerates, 1990–2002

Conglomerates	1990		1994		1998		2002	
	Equity controlled by shareholders (%)	Ratio (debt & controlling equity) / controlling equity	Equity controlled by shareholders (%)	Ratio (debt & controlling equity) / controlling equity	Equity controlled by shareholders (%)	Ratio (debt & controlling equity) / controlling equity	Equity controlled by shareholders (%)	Ratio (debt & controlling equity) / controlling equity
Largest	55.4	1.5	63.7	0.8	18.4	10.6	49.1	3.9
5 largest	52.5	1.6	52.4	1.2	53.0	2.5	57.1	2.7
10 largest	52.9	1.6	53.2	1.3	56.0	2.2	60.2	2.7
20 largest	52.1	1.6	52.8	1.3	56.1	2.3	59.0	2.7
All conglomerates	52.3	1.6	53.6	1.3	57.0	2.3	58.8	2.8
Non-affiliated	85.3	0.5	98.0	0.1	93.5	0.9	-	-
Total	55.2	1.4	60.0	1.0	60.4	2.1	-	-

Sources: Lefort and Walker (2000c) and author calculations.

Table 14.8 Capital structure of Chilean conglomerates, 1990–2002

Conglomerates	1990		1994		1998		2002	
	Debt/ assets (%)	Equity/ assets (%)	Debt/ assets (%)	Equity/ assets (%)	Debt/ assets (%)	Equity/ assets (%)	Debt/ assets (%)	Equity/ assets (%)
Largest	27.3	72.7	14.0	86.0	53.2	46.8	58.1	41.9
5 largest	26.6	73.4	14.7	85.3	46.0	54.0	52.9	47.1
10 largest	26.6	73.4	17.9	82.1	44.9	55.1	55.1	44.9
20 largest	25.4	74.6	18.2	81.8	45.7	54.3	54.8	45.2
All conglomerates	25.9	74.1	18.5	81.5	46.7	53.3	54.7	45.3
Non-affiliated	22.5	77.5	11.1	88.9	42.7	57.3	43.4	56.6
Total	25.6	74.4	17.6	82.4	46.4	53.6	53.6	46.4

Source: Lefort and Walker (2000c) and author calculations.

between cash and control rights of one standard deviation (0.21) increased share prices by 10 percent.

On the other hand, Lefort and Walker (2007a) found no significant evidence of a group effect on companies' market valuation. This result might be interpreted as supporting the idea that the economic benefits of the efficiency gained by the actions of the business group are being captured by the controlling shareholders.

Lefort (2005b) shows that, in the Chilean case, the shares of family-managed companies are traded in the market at a discount. The findings of the paper are interpreted as evidence that family business in Chile present worse corporate governance practices than non-family businesses, mainly related to the lack of professionalization of management practices. Hence, although Chilean families might have successfully decreased the agency costs imposed to them, they might still be imposing a larger agency cost than non-family businesses to minority shareholders, and the market is penalizing them for that.

14.4 STRATEGY AND STRUCTURE OF MAIN CHILEAN BUSINESS GROUPS

14.4.1 Main areas of economic activity

Even though it is difficult to characterize a general strategy for Chilean business groups, some patterns emerge after careful examination. Table 14.9 presents a list of the main companies affiliated to each one of the twenty-five main business groups that operate in Chile. The table also shows the main companies that are still state owned. For each company, the table indicates the type of economic activity that better characterizes it.

At first glance, the information provided in the table shows an important degree of unrelated diversification. Large family-controlled groups like the Angelini, Luksic, Matte, and Claro groups have important interests in very diverse activities. For instance, the economic activities of the Angelini group include the production of cellulose, the commercialization of oil derivates, and electricity generation. In the case of the Luksic group, the activities include important interests in the mining industry through Antofagasta Minerals, beverages, telecommunications, and banking services. The Matte group produces cellulose and electricity and provides financial and harbor services. Finally, the Claro group is involved in maritime transportation, glass products, harbor services, and wine.

However, other types of business groups emerge as we look carefully at Table 14.9. On the one hand, there are several multinational controlled groups of companies very focused on their main line of activities. They are mainly in utilities, energy, and financial services. On the other hand, family-controlled business groups that started in the retail sector, like Paulmann, Solari, Calderon, and Ibanez, have remained very

Table 14.9 Sectors of economic activity of main Chilean business groups

Business group Individual firms	Economic sector
Angelini group	Industrial holding
Celulosa Arauco	Forestal sector: Production and commercialization of cellulose and wood
Copec	Commercialization of gasoline and diesel for industrial, automobile and residential consumption
Forestal Cholgúan S.A.	Forestal activity
Igemar; Eperva	Activities in fishing industry through Igemar and Eperva, fishmeal production
Cía. de Seguros de Vida Cruz del Sur S.A.	Insurance company
Abastible	Commercialization and distribution of gas
Minority Interest	
Metrogas	Commercialization and distribution of natural gas
Colbún; Guacolda	Electricity generation
Endesa España	
Endesa	Electricity generation
Pehuenche	Electricity generation
Chilectra	Electricity distribution
Enersis S.A.	Electricity generation and distribution
Luksic group	
Banco de Chile	Banking activity
Banchile Corredores de Bolsa S.A.	Stock brokerage
Banchile Corredores de Seguros Ltda.	Insurances brokerage
Madeco S.A.	Production and commercialization of cables, pipes, plastic containers
Telsur	Telecommunications activities
Antofagasta Minerals	Copper production and exploration, mainly in Chile Owns a rail network servicing the mining region in northern Chile
CCU	Beverages production
Viña San Pedro Tarapacá S.A.	Production and commercialization of wine
Paulmann group.	
Cencosud S.A.	Supermarkets in Chile, Argentina, Colombia and Brazil
Almacenes Paris	Activities in supermarkets, department stores, homecenters, financial services, shopping centers and real-estate
Banco Paris	Banking activity
Paris Corredores de Seguros Ltda.	Insurances brokerage
Solari-Cuneo-Del Rio group	
S.A.C.I.Falabella	Department store company
Banco Falabella	Financial services
Megacenter	Real-estate activities
Sodimac	Home improvement and construction materials distribution

Claro group	Holding with activities in industrial, transportation, communications and harbor sectors.
Sudamericana de Vapores	National and international maritime transportation, harbor activities
Elecmetal	Production of steel replacements for mining, construction and industrial consumption
Cristalerias de Chile	Production of glass and crystals for many purposes
Viña Santa Rita	Wine production
Matte group	
Bicecorp	Bank and financial services
CMPC	Cellulose, forest and paper sector
Puerto Lirquén	Harbor services
Colbún	Electric generation
BICE Corredores de Bolsa S.A.	Stock brokerage
Bice Corredores de Seguros Limitada	Insurances brokerage
Santander Chile	
Banco Santander	Commercial and investment bank
Santander Investment S.A. Corredores de Bolsa	Stock brokerage
Santander Corredora de Seguros S.A.	Insurances brokerage
Santander Asset Management S.A. Administradora General de Fondos	Funds administration
Ibáñez group	
D&S	Food distribution
Saitec	Inmobiliary activity
Presto	Financial services to customers
Marin–Del Real	
CGE	Electricity generation and distribution in Chile and Argentina (1995)
Essa	Electricity generation and distribution in Argentina
Gasco	Gas distribution
Metrogas S.A.	Natural gas distribution
Tusan	Industrial sector
Sigdo Koppers	
Ing. Y Construccion SK S.A; Enaex	Industrial, transportation and logistic services Industrial construction
SKC	Machinery sale and lease and comercialization of automobile intakes and services
Sigdopack	High-tech plastic containers production
Somela	Kitchen appliances
CTI, Frimetal	Electrodometic lines
Calderón	
Ripley	Department store. Real-estate investments in commercial centers
Banco Ripley	Financial services
Banripley Corredora de Seguros Ltda.	Insurances brokerage

(continued)

Table 14.9 Continued

CAP	
Cía. Siderúrgica Huachipato	Steel production in Chile
Cía.Minera del Pacifico	Production and sale of Iron ore
Masa	Handling of manganese mining and iron alloy production. Iron pellets production
Cintac; Intasa	Steel products manufacturing and sales
Said group	
Embotelladora Andina	Participation in banking and pension fund administration
Parque Arauco	Production and distribution of beverages, juices, and mineral water through Embotelladora Andina
AFP Provida	Real-estate business in retail and entertainment sector through Parque Arauco
BBVA	Banking activity
Penta group	
Banco Penta	Bank and insurance sector
Compañía de Seguros Generales Penta – Security S.A.	Insurances brokerage
Penta Corredores de Bolsa S.A.	Stock brokerage
Administradora de Fondos de Pensiones CUPRUM S.A.	Pension funds administration
Las Americas AFI	Investment funds
Minority interest	
Banmedica	Health sector
Co. de Telefonos de Chile S.A.	
CTC	Telecommunications sector
Telefónica Móviles Chile S.A.	Mobile phones
Telefónica Larga Distancia S.A.	Long distance carrier
Ponce group	
Sociedad Química y minera de Chile	Production and commercialization of vegetable nutrients, iodine, and lithium
Urenda group	
Empresas Navieras S.A.	Maritime transportation services
Agencias Universales S.A.	Maritime transportation services
Compañia Chilena de Navegación Interoceánica S.A.	Maritime transportation services
Portuaria Cabo Froward S.A.	Investments in harbor and airport Infrastructure
Minority interest	
Antofagasta Terminal Int; Soc. Term Puerto Arica	Owns harbor terminals through Antofagasta Terminal Internacional and Sociedad Terminal Puerto Arica S.A.
Saieh group	
Corpbanca	Bank holding and financial services
CORPCapital Corredores de Bolsa S.A.	Stock brokerage
Corpbanca Corredores de Seguros S.A.	Insurances brokerage
Fernández León group	
Almendral and Entel	Telecommunications sector
Consorcio AGF	Mutual funds and financial services

Minority interest

Pucobre	Copper deposits exploitation
Banmedica	Health sector

Larraín group. Watt's S.A., Cic S.A.   Stock-broker, investment banking

Watt's S.A.; Viña Sta. Carolina   Massive consumption products, linked to food and wine industry. Activities in retail industry

CIC S.A., Larrain-Vial   Home furniture production, commercialization, and distribution

Agbar group

Aguas Andinas S.A.   Production and distribution of drinkable water.
Empresa de Servicios Sanitarios de Los Lagos S.A.   Sanitation activities: collection, treatment and final disposage of sewage

Yarur group

Bci (Banco Crédito e Inversiones)	Financial services, Insurance and banking activity
BCI Corredor de Bolsa S.A.	Stock brokerage
BCI Corredores de Seguros S.A.	Insurances brokerage
BCI Administradora General de Fondos S.A.	Funds administration

Sociedad de Inversiones Campos Chilenos S.A.

Iansa S.A.   AgroIndustrial holding, mainly sugar production and food and services for the agricultural sector

Hurtado Vicuña group

Almendral and Entel	Telecommunications sector
Consorcio AGF	Mutual funds administration and financial services

Minority interest

Pucobre   Copper deposits exploitation

Chilean government entreprises

Banco del Estado de Chile (1953)   Banking, insurance and financial services activities.
Empresas de Ferrocarriles del Estado (1884)   Railroads entreprise, passengers and shipments transportation
Empresa Nacional de Petróleo (ENAP) (1950)   Hydrocarbons exploration, production and commercialization (natural gas, petroleum and its derivatives)
Corporación Nacional del Cobre de Chile (1976)   Exploration and exploitation of mining resources of copper and its byproducts.
Empresas Portuarias (1998, through n°19.542 law)   Harbor services
Empresa Nacional del Carbón (1971)   Exploitation of carboniferous deposits in VIIIth region in Chile
Metro S.A. (1968)   Subway transportation in Santiago

Source: Company statements.

focused in spite of the high growth of their operations. Only in the twenty-first century have these groups entered the financial services sector as a complement to their retail operations. Finally, younger groups that started their operations in the financial sector like Penta and Saieh have also remained very focused.

14.4.2 Competitive capabilities of Chilean business groups

By looking at the information provided by Table 14.9, it is possible to visualize a general picture regarding the competitive capabilities of Chilean business groups. In simple terms there are two areas in which local family-controlled business groups have flourished and been able to compete successfully internationally: natural resource exploitation and retail/commercial products distribution.

14.4.2.1 *Exploiting natural resources*

The first area of development is quickly explained by the fact that Chile is a country rich in natural resources, especially minerals, fishery, and forestry. In addition, liberal economic policies and free access to private entrepreneurs for the exploitation of natural resources explain the important presence of private local capital in these sectors.

The development of industries based on the exploitation of Chilean natural resources started early in the nineteenth century. Foreign investors exploited nitrates ('Chilean salitre') until the First World War. The Sociedad Química y Minera de Chile SA is the heir of the old nitrate producers of the Chilean northern area. SQM was privatized starting in 1983 and remained under the control of Julio Ponce, former executive of the company. The SQM group is focused on non-metallic mining activities like the extraction of iodine and lithium.

The development of the forestry sector began in 1920, when Luis Matte Larrain, together with forty-three other shareholders, created the paper and cardboard factory Compania Manufacturera de Papeles y Cartones (CMPC). In 1924 CMPC acquired its only meaningful rival, the Santa Victoria factory, and the Matte group started its own saga. Soon afterwards, the company built a new cellulose (wood pulp) plant, a hydroelectric power plant, planted 25,000 pine trees, and purchased, in 1931, an industrial plant in Argentina capable of producing 20,000 pounds a day of wood pulp. After more acquisitions of land, in the 1950s CMPC built a new pulp mill and a newsprint plant, consolidating one of the most significant Chilean companies based on the exploitation of renewable natural resources without state support.

Another example is provided by the Angelini group. In 1948 the Italian immigrant Anacleto Angelini arrived in Chile. He founded Pinturas Tajamar, a small paint factory, with US$100,000 in capital. In collaboration with some Chilean associates, he acquired, in 1957, a fishery, Pesquera Eperva SA, and entered the forestry-products business in 1958 through an investment in the company Sociedad Maderas Prensadas Cholguán SA. Because of the well-conducted business and the financially prudent policies, both lines of businesses flourished. Between 1975 and 1977, Eperva bought the state's controlling interests in Pesquera Indo SA and Pesquera Iquique. The fishing operation of Angelini grew sevenfold between 1977 and 1987, becoming the largest in the country.

Following the military coup that overthrew the left-wing socialist government of 1970–3, the nation's largest holding company of this period, run by the Cruzat and Larraín families, seized the opportunity offered by the aggressive privatization program and took control of Compañía de Petróleos de Chile SA (Copec). A period of unrelated diversification followed. Copec got into the forestry business by purchasing government-owned Empresa Forestal Arauco Ltda., Industrias de Celulosa Arauco SA, and Celulosa Constitución SA, becoming the largest privately owned enterprise in the nation. However, the 1982 debt crisis found Copec struggling, because of the high amount of dollar-denominated debt in the wake of the virtual collapse of the Chilean peso. The Cruzat–Larraín group could not pay its debts and had to surrender the enterprise. Angelini had been financially prudent and was thus in a position to acquire the interests of the debt-ridden conglomerates such as Cruzat-Larraín, which has emerged during the privatizations of the 1970s but had failed in the 1980s. Angelini went into partnership with Carter Holt Harvey Holdings Ltd, a New Zealand conglomerate, and jointly held 60 percent of Copec. With twenty-six affiliated companies, Copec was the major holding company in Chile at the end of 1989, and Angelini was chosen as the entrepreneur of the decade by the business magazine *Gestion*. Under the rule of Angelini, Copec concentrated on export growth in the forestry and fishing sectors, consolidating both operations by opening the most modern cellulose plant in Chile in 1991 and fusing the largest fishing companies in Chile.

The beginning of another large Chilean family business group is associated with the exploitation of copper. In the early 1950s, Luksic was approached by one member of a three-way partnership of Frenchmen who had been developing a nearby copper mine. Luksic agreed to buy out the mine, negotiating an agreement to pay over a twenty-five-year period. By 1954, lacking the resources to operate the copper mine, Luksic sought a buyer for the holding. As the legend has it, Luksic approached Nippon Steel, offering to sell the mine for CLP 500,000, worth about US$45,000 at the time. The Japanese are said to have misunderstood Luksic, and agreed to pay him US$500,000 instead.

In short, it can be argued that the success of several large family-controlled Chilean business groups is due mainly to the exploitation of rich natural resources in an outward-oriented economy that provided a stable macroeconomic framework and a competitive exchange rate.[5] In some cases, the exploitation of natural resources was a long-standing private initiative, while in others it began as a public initiative that was later privatized. In those cases, economic groups and families that were connected to the privatization process and/or had a liquidity advantage above competitors were able to acquire large state-owned assets.

---

[5] See Eyzaguirre and Lefort (2002).

14.4.2.2 *Retail and distribution of commercial products*

The other set of successful Chilean family-owned business groups can be found operating in the retail and distribution sectors. In this case, the most likely explanation for the growth and success of these groups is related to the fact that the small size of the Chilean market precluded the competition in this sector from large multinational retail companies.

The business groups belonging to this category share several distinctive features. First, they were established more than a hundred years ago by entrepreneurs who opened small shops in a particular city of Chile. Secondly, they grew at a relatively slow pace until the 1970s. Thirdly, they initiated an aggressive expansion in the 1980s, opening new stores in several geographic locations. A key aspect of this expansion process was the acquisition of strategically located land properties where they could build new stores and develop commercial areas. Fourthly, they all developed financial platforms to provide consumer credit to their costumers. Providing funds to credit-rationed customers at high interest rates has become the more profitable part of their business.

Regarding the structure of these business groups, they all show a relatively narrow diversification strategy compared to the other types of business groups. The core business for these groups has remained the retail operation, but we also see them entering into financial services in a move that was to support the growth of the core retail business.

An indication of the nature of the competitive capabilities can be seen in the wake of the international competition that started during the 1990s. Several retail chains, such as Carrefour, JC Penny, and Home Depot, among others, tried to enter the Chilean market unsuccessfully. They all ended up selling their stores to local business groups. The competitive advantages of the local families are related to several factors. On the one hand, by the time multinational companies considered that the Chilean market was attractive enough to enter, local retail companies had already acquired the best locations in the most populated cities. On the other hand, Chilean retail companies had competed fiercely among themselves and, hence, had developed very efficient logistics and business practices. Finally, the knowledge of the local market built after decades of operation, especially regarding the use of credit to high-risk customers, proved to be key in the competition with multinational companies.

Falabella provides a good example. Salvatore Falabella opened the first tailor shop in Chile in 1889. With the arrival of Alberto Solari in the company, the group began operations in 1937 as a small retail chain. After 1993 Falabella SA dramatically increased its market share in Chile and successfully explored investing in other countries, such as Peru, Colombia, and Argentina. In 2001 it bought out the operation of Home Depot in Chile. In 2003 it merged with Sodimac (home improvement retail) belonging to the Del Rio family and in 2004 it opened the Falabella Bank. In 2008 the Solary–Del Rio group had consolidated sales over US$5,600 million.

Another example is the Ibanez family, which controls the D&S group. D&S is a group of companies whose core business is food retail through the different retail formats. The core business includes the supermarkets and hypermarkets called LIDER. Also, the financial services company grants credit to consumers through the PRESTO card. The beginnings of D&S go back to 1893, when the Import and Wholesale Distribution Company Gratenau y Cia. was founded in Valparaíso by German businessmen who came from Hanover. In 1987 the first Ekono Hypermarket opened its doors. The basic concept was the original economical supermarket format, but its larger sales room allowed for the inclusion of non-food products. In 1993 the first Ekono Supermarket in Argentina was opened. In October 1997, as a result of a capital increase, the company entered the international financial markets through its first ADR issue in the New York Stock Exchange.

The importance of the distribution business in local groups is not exclusive to the retail sector. The Angelini group, with consolidated sales of over US$12 billion in 2008, was built around COPEC. The Compañía de Petróleos de Chile SA (COPEC) was founded in 1934 by a team of Chilean entrepreneurs with the goal of importing and distributing fuel nationally. Although faced by competition from the major world oil companies, Copec was able to establish a national distribution network, with service stations and storage tanks, and to make itself the national leader in its field.

In the first decade of the twenty-first century, the retail business in Chile has witnessed a wave of mergers and acquisitions that have consolidated the market position of a few large actors operating in Chile and Latin America. The acquisition of Almacenes Paris by Paulmann's CENCOSUD in 2005 and the merger between Solari's Falabella and Del Rio's SODIMAC in 2003, left the retail market in Chile as a market with three large players: Falabella/SODIMAC, CENCOSUD, and D&S. In 2007 Falabella and D&S tried to merge, but the operation was prohibited by the antitrust commission.

14.4.2.3 *Multinational companies*

In the case of the Chilean utilities sectors, the presence of local family groups has been steadily decreasing. After the privatization of the state-owned utilities companies, many of them were acquired by multinational corporations. That was the case in the electricity, water supply, and telecommunications sectors, where ENDESA Spain, Telefonica Spain, and AGBAR have a predominant position. Thus the evidence supports the idea that in these sectors local groups have been unable to compete with large, geographically diversified multinationals.

In the financial sector, family-controlled business groups compete with international banks. Since the debt crises of 1982, business groups in Chile have been unable to rely on lending from their own banks. Hence, local banks like BCI, Banco de Chile, BICE, and Security are managed by business groups independently from their other operations. In fact, for the groups owning BCI, Security, and Penta, these banks are their core business. In the case of the Matte group, this entered the banking business in 1979 in association with Rothschild, creating the BICE Bank, but Eleodoro Matte already had vast experience in the financial sector. Another example comes from the Luksic group. By the end of the 1990s, the Luksic group had entered the banking business. In 1998 it acquired a controlling stake in Banco Edwards, and in 1999 it began buying Banco de Chile stock, thus setting off a bidding war with Penta, the financial group formed by five former executives of the Cruzat–Larrain group. Banco de Chile and Banco de A. Edwards were merged at the beginning of 2002 to form, at the time, Chile's largest bank. It retained the Banco de Chile name. In 2006 Banco de Chile and CITIBANK Chile merged under Banco de Chile's umbrella.

In spite of the presence of local business groups in the financial sector, commercial banking in Chile is dominated by foreign banks such as Santander, BBVA, Scotiabank, and ITAU, probably because of technological advantages from their worldwide operation.

Although it can be argued that groups such as Santander Chile, ENDESA, CTC, and Aguas Andinas are not proper business groups but mere subsidiaries of multinational companies, they have engaged in practices that are homologous to those of local business groups. On the one hand, in most cases, the multinational companies acquired Chilean business groups and maintained the holding–pyramid type of structure of the original group. On the other hand, they have elected for their boards Chilean personalities coming from the political, business, and academic arenas, and have engaged in the Chilean business group dynamics.

14.4.3 International expansion strategies of Chilean business groups

The Chilean economy has enjoyed almost twenty-five years in a row of economic bonanza. In consequence, most business groups that were in good shape after the debt crises of 1982 have grown and expanded their operations. In addition, many new groups, local and foreign, have been formed during this period, and have also expanded. However, although the size of the Chilean economy has also increased, successful Chilean business groups have experienced a much higher rate of growth than the economy. Hence, their expansion strategies have had an international component.

In simple terms, business groups based on the exploitation of natural resources have been able to expand their production, increasing their exports many times over, and helped, in addition, but by the important increase in the international prices of commodities. In some cases, new industries like wine have been exploited, as a consequence of the outward-looking/export-oriented strategies set in place by local businesses. To give one an idea of this expansion: Chilean exports increased from US$17 billion in 1997 to US$66.6 billion in 2007.

As for business groups focused in the retail sector, as already mentioned, their initial expansion was carried out in Chile, serving increasing sectors of the domestic market.

However, recent expansion of the operations of these business groups has occurred through large investments in other countries in Latin America. The success achieved by companies like Falabella, Jumbo, Homecenter, and others in several countries in Latin America indicates that the period of fierce domestic competition has allowed them to build some strong competitive capabilities. The extent of this expansion in Latin America can be seen by considering that accumulated direct investment of Chilean companies abroad went from US$5 in 1997 to US$32.5 billion in 2007.

In some cases, the expansion has occurred in terms of both exports and investment abroad. For example, in 1996 Copec embarked on a new stage of investments outside Chile. A noteworthy acquisition made toward this effort by the Copec subsidiary Celulosa Arauco y Constitución was that of the Argentinian market pulp producer Alto Paraná, which had strategically located assets, offered a significant business growth potential, and represented a major step forward in the diversification of the company's forestry and industrial holdings.

14.4.4 Reorganization through holding companies

As already mentioned, most Chilean business groups are structured around a listed holding company that owns shares in a set of listed and non-listed operating companies. Chilean business groups exercise tight control of all companies from the holding companies, electing board members and executives and making strategic decisions.

An example of such a structure can be seen in the case of the Angelini group. As an outcome of Copec's long history, the company accomplished the grouping-together of more than 100 different companies, which forced a restructuring of the organization in 2003. Under the new structure, the liquid fuels and lubricants assets were grouped together under a new subsidiary, Compañía de Petróleos de Chile COPEC SA. This marks one of the milestones in the company's history, because "greater autonomy was thus given to the fuels area," according to former chairman Mr Lamarca. Likewise, all subsidiaries were brought under the umbrella of the new parent company: Empresas Copec SA, a financial holding company that groups together all Copec's different operating activities. The control of Empresas Copec is done from a holding listed company, Antarchile. The Angelini family owns 61.9 percent of Antarchile. Fig. 14.2 shows the Angelini group structure.

In 1996 the Luksic group ownership structure was also reorganized. All financial and industrial investments were placed under the control of Quiñenco, and mining and railway investments remained part of Antofagasta plc. This new structure simplified control within the Luksic group and opened the doors to the capital markets for Quiñenco. In June 1997, Quiñenco succeeded in raising US$280 million on the New York and Chilean stock exchanges. At roughly the same time, the Luksic group pushed ahead with the Los Pelambres mining project, today one of the world's largest copper mines. Fig. 14.3 shows the group structure.

Angelini Group

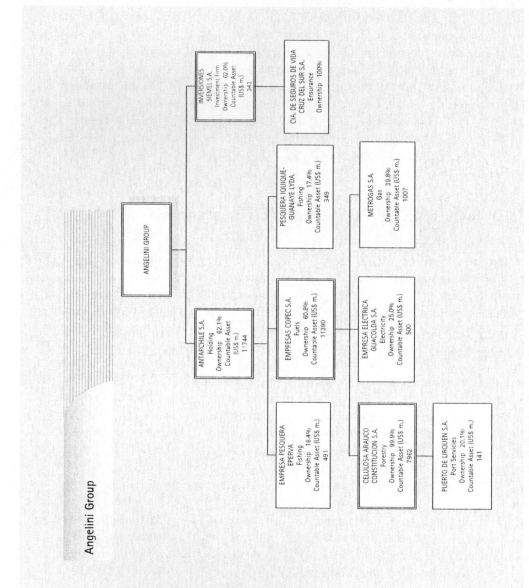

ANGELINI GROUP

INVERSIONES SIEMEL S.A.
Investment Firm
Ownership 62.0%
Countable Asset
(US$ m.)
343

CIA. DE SEGUROS DE VIDA
CRUZ DEL SUR S.A.
Ensurance
Ownership 100%

ANTARCHILE S.A.
Holding
Ownership 62.1%
Countable Asset
(US$ m.)
1'744

EMPRESAS COPEC S.A.
Fuels
Ownership 60.8%
Countable Asset (US$ m.)
11390

PESQUERA IQUIQUE-
GUANAYE LYDA.
Fishing
Ownership 17.4% (US$ m.)
349

EMPRESA PESQUERA
EPERVA
Fishing
Ownership 18.4%
Countable Asset (US$ m.)
491

EMPRESA ELECTRICA
GUACOLDA S.A.
Electricity
Ownership 25.0%
Countable Asset (US$ m.)
500

METROGAS S.A.
Gas
Ownership 39.8%
Countable Asset (US$ m.)
1007

CELULOSA ARAUCO
CONSTITUCION S.A.
Forestry
Ownership 99.9%
Countable Asset (US$ m.)
7962

PUERTO DE URIQUEN S.A.
Port Services
Ownership 20.1%
Countable Asset (US$ m.)
141

Figure 14.2 The Angelini group, 2007

Source: Company reports.

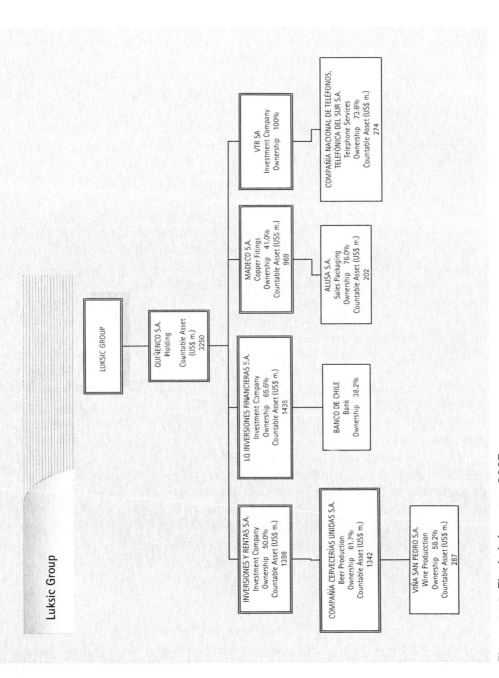

Figure 14.3 The Luksic group, 2007

Source: Company reports.

14.5 CONCLUSIONS

While it is difficult to characterize a general strategy and structure for "the" Chilean business group, it is possible to lay down some stylized facts. This chapter has argued that many of the largest, most successful Chilean business groups started and/or received a major push as a consequence of the privatization of state-owned companies, and that a solid financial position at the time of the privatizations seems to have been a key to success.

The largest domestic Chilean business groups in general represent unrelated diversification. A significant category is the pattern of unrelated diversification via exploitation of the natural resources of the country. Further unrelated diversification of these groups resulted from the investment opportunities arising from the privatization plans and the failure of highly indebted groups during the 1982 debt crises. A second category is the groups mainly in the retail sector that also have an interest in financial services. Then, finally, we see the presence of multinationals in Chile that are formed as "pyramidal" groups, and are focused in their business portfolios. The financial services industry especially is dominated by foreign banks that also participate in the pension fund and insurance businesses, while multinational companies are also dominant in the utilities sectors.

Expansion in the mid-1990s of the operations of Chilean business groups traditionally serving the domestic market occurred through large investments in other countries in Latin America. This happened in the retail sector, with significant investments in Peru, Argentina, and Colombia, and indicates that fierce domestic competition has allowed Chilean retail companies to build strong competitive capabilities. On the other hand, business groups focused on the exploitation of natural resources have dramatically increased their exports and widened their operational basis, exploiting resources in other countries.

Finally, large Chilean business groups are organized around holding companies. These companies trade at a 30 percent discount of their net asset value. Controlling shareholders hold large amounts of equity and firmly control decisions at shareholders' meetings. Chilean family groups are tightly controlled by the founding families. Although management has become increasingly professional, strategic decisions are made by the owners.

REFERENCES

BEARLE, A., and MEANS, G. (1932). *The Modern Corporation and Private Property.* New York: Macmillan.

BEBCHUK, L. (1999). "Separation of Ownership and Control." Working paper Harvard Law School.

CASELLI, F. and GENNAIOLI, N. (2002). "Dynastic Management." Harvard University, unpublished paper.

CLAESSENS, S., DJANKOV, S., FAN, J., and LANG, L. (1999a). "Expropriation of Minority Shareholders in East Asia" *Journal of Financial Economics*, 58: 81–112.

CLAESSENS, S., DJANKOV, S. and KLAPPER, L. (1999b). "The Role and Functioning of Business groups in East Asia and Chile," *ABANTE*, 3/1: 91–107.

CLAESSENS, S., DJANKOV, S., FAN, J., and LANG, L. (2000). "The Cost of Group Affiliation: Evidence from East Asia." Mimeograph.

CHAMI, R. (2001), "What's Different about Family Business?" IMF Working Paper.

DAHSE, F. (1979). "Mapa de la extrema riqueza." Editorial, Aconcagua, Santiago, Chile.

DIETL, H. (1998). *Capital Markets and Corporate Governance in Japan, Germany and the United States.* London: Routledge.

EYZAGUIRRE, N., and LEFORT, F. (2002). "Capital Markets in Chile, 1985–97: A Case of Successful International Financial Integration," in G. Perry and D. M. Leipziger (eds.), *Chile Recent Policy Lessons and Emerging Challenges.* WBI Development Studies. Washington: World Bank.

FISMAN, R., and KHANNA, T. (1998). "Facilitating Development: The Role of Business Groups." Harvard Business School, Working Paper No. 98-076.

GARRETÓN, O. G., and CISTERNAS, J. (1970). "Algunas características del proceso de toma de decisiones en la gran empresa: La dinámica de la concentración." Working paper, Sercotec-Odeplan, Santiago, Chile.

GHEMAWAT, P., and KHANNA, T. (1998). "The Nature of Diversified Business Groups: A Research Design and Two Case Studies," *Journal of Industrial Economics* (Mar.).

GONZÁLEZ, J. (1981). "Evaluación social de la acción los grupos económicos en Chile." Unpublished manuscript. Escuela de Negocios de Valparaíso.

HACHETTE, D., and LÜDERS, R. (1992). "La Privatización en Chile." Working Paper IE-PUC, 147.

IGLESIAS, A. (2000)."Pension Reform and Corporate Governance: Impact in Chile," *ABANTE*, 3/1 (Oct.–Apr.), 109–41.

KHANNA, T., and PALEPU, K. (1997). "Why Focused Strategies May be Wrong for Emerging Markets," *Harvard Business Review* (July–Aug.), 3–10.

KHANNA, T., and PALEPU, K. (1999a). "The Right Way to Restructure Conglomerates in Emerging Markets," *Harvard Business Review* (July–Aug.), 125–34.

KHANNA, T., and PALEPU, K. (1999b). "Policy Shocks, Market Intermediaries, and Corporate Strategy: Evidence from Chile and India," *Journal of Economics and Management Strategy*, 8/2 (June), 271–310.

KHANNA, T., and PALEPU, K. (1999c). "The Future of Business Groups in Emerging Markets: Long Run Evidence from Chile." Harvard Business School, Working Paper No. 99-077.

KHANNA, T., and PALEPU, K. (2000). "Is Group Affiliation Profitable in Emerging Markets: An Analysis of Diversified Indian Business Groups," *Journal of Finance*, 55/2: 867–91; formerly titled "Corporate Strategy and Institutional Context: An Empirical Analysis of Diversified Indian Business Groups." Harvard Business School, Working Paper No. 96-051.

KHANNA, T., and RIVKIN, J. (2000). "Estimating the Performance Effects of Business Groups in Emerging Markets," *Strategic Management Journal*, 22/1: 45–74.

LAGOS, R. (1961). "La Concentración del poder económico," *Editorial del Pacífico.*

La Porta, R., López-de-Silanes, F., Shleifer, A., and Vishny, R. (1996). "Law and Finance." NBER WP 5661.

La Porta, R., López-de-Silanes, F., Shleifer, A., and Vishny, R. (1997). "Legal Determinants of External Finance," *Journal of Finance*, 52/3: 1131–50.

La Porta, R., López-de-Silanes, F., and Shleifer, A. (1999). "Corporate Ownership Around the World," *Journal of Finance*, 54/2: 471–517.

Lefort, F. (2003). "Gobierno Corporativo: ¿Qué es? Y ¿Cómo andamos por casa?" *Cuadernos de Economía*, 40/120: 207–37.

Lefort, F. (2005a). "Ownership Structure and Market Valuation of Family Businesses in Chile," *Corporate Ownership & Control*, 3/2: 90–105.

Lefort, F. (2005b). "Ownerhsip Structure and Corporate Governance in Latin America," *ABANTE*, 8/1: 55–84.

Lefort, F. (2007). "The Effect of Agency Conflicts on Payout Policies: The Case of Chile," *El Trimestre Económico*, 75/299: 597–639.

Lefort, F., and Urzua, F. (2008). "Board Independence, Firm Performance and Ownership Concentration: Evidence From Chile," *Journal of Business Research*, 61: 615–22.

Lefort, F., and Walker, E. (2000a). "Corporate Governance: Challenges for Latin America," *ABANTE*, 2/2: 99–111.

Lefort, F., and Walker, E. (2000b). "The Effects of Economic and Political Shocks on Corporate Governance Systems in Chile," *ABANTE*, 2/2: 183–206.

Lefort, F., and Walker, E. (2000c). "Ownership and Capital Structure of Chilean Conglomerates: Facts and Hypothesis in Chile," *ABANTE*, 3/1: 3–27.

Lefort, F., and Walker, E. (2001). "Gobierno corporativo, protección a accionistas minoritarios y tomas de control." Discussion Paper 1, SVS, Chile.

Lefort, F., and Walker E. (2007a). "Do Markets Penalize Agency Conflicts between Controlling and Minority Shareholders? Evidence from Chile," *Developing Economies*, 45/3: 283–314.

Lefort, F., and Walker E. (2007b). "The Effect of Corporate Governance Practices on Company Market Valuation and Dividend Policy in Chile," in A. Chong and F. Lopez-de-Silanes (eds.), *Investor Protection in Latin America*. Stanford: Stanford University Press.

Majluf, N., Abarca, N., Rodriguez, D., and Fuentes, L. A. (1998). "Governance and Ownership Structure in Chilean Economic Groups," *ABANTE*, 1/1: 111–39.

Paredes, R., and Sánchez, J. M. (1995). "Organización industrial y grupos económicos: El caso de Chile." Mimeo, Programa de Postgrado en Economía Ilades-Georgetown University, Santiago.

Rajan, R., Servaes, H., and Zingales, L. (2000). "The Cost of Diversity: The Diversification Discount and Inefficient Investment," *Journal of Finance*, 55/1: 35–80.

Scharfstein, D. (1998). "The Dark Side of Internal Capital Markets II: Evidence from Diversified Conglomerates." Working paper. MIT Sloan School of Managment.

Scharfstein, D., and Stein, J. (1997). "The Dark Side of Internal Capital Markets: Divisional Rent Seeking and Inefficient Investment." NBER working paper, No. 5969.

Shleifer, A., and Johnson, S. (1998). "Coase and Corporate Governance in Latin America," *ABANTE*, 2/2: 113–31.

Shleifer, A. and Vishny, R. W. (1997). "A Survey of Corporate Governance," *Journal of Finance*, 52/2: 737–83.

Stein, J. (1997). "Internal Capital Markets and the Competition for Corporate Resources," *Journal of Finance*, 52/1: 111–33.

THOMSEN, S., and PEDERSEN, T. (2000). "Ownership Structure and Economic Performance in the Largest European Companies," *Strategic Management Journal*, 21/6: 689–705.

WALKER, E., and LEFORT, F. (2001). "Pension Reform and Capital Market Development: Are there any (Hard) Links?" Pension Reform Primer, World Bank.

WOLFENZON, D. (1999). "A Theory of Pyramidal Structures." Unpublished working paper. Harvard University, Cambridge, MA.

CHAPTER 15

BUSINESS GROUPS
IN MEXICO

TAEKO HOSHINO

15.1 INTRODUCTION

THE purpose of this chapter is to reveal the reasons behind the growth of large Mexican business groups and the changes in their characteristics under the neo-liberal economic reforms and intensified competition that have occurred since the second half of the 1980s.

Mexico experienced the emergence and growth of business groups during the process of import substitution industrialization (ISI). They are generally called *grupos económicos,* or economic groups, and have played important roles as actors of economic development.[1] These groups have common characteristics such as a structure consisting of an apex holding company and multi-tiered subsidiaries, diversified businesses, and control by an owner family. In the literature on Mexican business groups that focused on their growth in the period of ISI, as in the standard arguments for the emergence of business groups (Leff 1974; Granovetter 2005; Khanna and Yafeh 2007), their emergence was explained as a response by Mexican capitalists to conditions imposed by economic underdevelopment, such as insufficient development of market institutions, shortage of capital and human resources,

---

[1] In this chapter, therefore, business group refers to a large-scale business entity—called *grupo industrial* or *grupo* in Spanish in Mexico—that consists of a group of large companies that are under the common control of an owner family. Group companies form a hierarchical shareholding structure with a holding company at its apex that is generally listed on stock exchanges.

and lack of a trustworthy legal system. Business groups also benefited from protection from international competition because of the government policies on trade and foreign direct investment (Cordero and Santín 1977; Derossi 1977; Hoshino 1990).

The external debt crisis of 1982 decisively put an end to the ISI policy that had been pursued for almost forty years. As part of the neo-liberal economic reforms that followed, trade liberalization and deregulation of foreign investment were implemented, developments that exposed business groups to fierce competition from imports and foreign multinationals. One curious phenomenon in this process was that, apart from a shuffle in their rankings, business groups continued to grow and still maintained many of the characteristics mentioned above. Why have business groups continued to grow and why do they still maintain their principal characteristics, in spite of changes in the conditions that favored their emergence? These are the principal inquiries dealt with in this chapter.

This chapter's basic conclusion is as follows. Although some favorable conditions for growth were lost, others have still been maintained or have newly appeared. Business groups that grow are those that excel in their ability to adapt. They have grown by exploiting these favorable conditions and have been flexible enough to modify their structure. This chapter arrives at this conclusion by exploring the conditions that favored the growth of leading business groups and the changes observed in their strategy, structure, ownership, and management from the mid-1980s to the late 2000s.

The remainder of the chapter is divided into five sections. Section 15.2 provides basic information on the twenty largest Mexican business groups—the targets of analysis of this chapter—and a brief history of their emergence and evolution. Section 15.3 deals with changes in the economic environment since 1982 and the corresponding restructuring of large business groups. In Sections 15.4 and 15.5, changes in strategy, structure, ownership, and management from the mid-1980s to the late 2000s are examined. Finally, the concluding remarks of this chapter are presented.

15.2 MEXICAN BUSINESS GROUPS AND THEIR HISTORICAL BACKGROUND

15.2.1 The twenty largest business groups in Mexico

Large business groups occupy a predominant position in the Mexican economy. One indicator is their position in the ranking of the largest 500 companies in Mexico. Mexico has a highly concentrated economic structure and the share of aggregate sales of the largest 50 companies amounted to 76 percent of the total sales of the largest ranking 500 companies in 2006 (*Expansión* 2007),[2] with a high concentration among the largest 50. Business groups are one of three pillars that constitute the largest 50 companies. They are 25 in number and 40 percent in aggregate sales, and there are no Mexican private stand-alone companies in the largest 50. The other two pillars are foreign multinationals and state-owned companies, which account for 19 and 6 in number, and 29 percent and 31 percent in aggregate sales respectively. In a previous study, this author estimated similar figures for the year 1986. Important changes in the intervening twenty years were an increase of the share of foreign multinationals by 11 percent and a corresponding decrease of state-owned companies by 12 percent. The share of Mexican business groups has hardly changed. They maintain their position as leading actors in the Mexican economy (Hoshino 2001b: 11–12).

This chapter focuses on the first twenty of the largest twenty-five business groups. Table 15.1 contains their basic information.[3] According to the table, sales are highly concentrated in the upper groups of the list. The sales of Carso, the first in the list, amount to 32 percent of the aggregated sales of these twenty groups. When the following two groups, Cemex and Femsa, are added, the share increases to 51 percent.

Table 15.2 shows the activities of twenty business groups indicated by ISIC codes at the 2-digit level. The majority of groups operate in more than two activities. The largest group, Carso, is the most widely diversified into unrelated industries. Another widely diversified group is Bal, with eight activities. Five groups—namely, Bimbo, Televisa, Mabe, Lala, and Coppel—specialize in just one activity each. The rest of the thirteen groups are involved in between two and four activities. The two activities that are the most popular with these business groups are the manufacture of food, beverages and tobacco, and the retail trade.

Business groups have a large number of subsidiaries. As the annual reports of the listed companies, which are sources of the data for Table 15.1, refer only to principal subsidiaries, the number of subsidiaries indicated in that table is not exhaustive. An exhaustive count would give far larger figures. Group companies form a multi-tiered structure, with holding companies at the apex and subsidiaries below. In most cases, holding companies are listed, and, in the case of larger business groups, some subsidiaries also, which means that the latter are pyramidal with respect to the control structure.[4] Shareholdings of apex holding companies are concentrated with

---

[2] The ranking of *Expansión* frequently includes both consolidated data for business groups and data of their subsidiaries. In order to avoid double counting, it is necessary to drop the data of subsidiaries from the ranking. After this procedure, the number of groups and stand-alone companies covered by the ranking for the year 2006 is reduced from 500 to 362.

[3] Concerning the name of these groups, the name of the holding company is used when it is identified. When it is not identified, a commonly used name in the media or the name of the owner family is used as the name of the group.

[4] We use the term 'pyramidal' for those hierarchical groups that have two or more listed subsidiaries, following Morck (Chapter 21, this volume). For other groups organized in a hierarchical structure with one or no listed subsidiaries, we employ the term 'hierarchical' only.

Table 15.1 The twenty largest business groups in Mexico, 2006

Ranks by total sales	Group name	Total sales[1] (pesos bn.)	Principal listed companies (abbreviation in stock exchanges)	No. of principal subsidiaries	No. of employees	Controlling family	Main industries involved
1	Carso	555	América Móvil (AMX) Teléfonos de México (TELMEX) Carso Global Telecom (TELECOM) Grupo Carso (GCARSO) Carso Infraestructura y Construcción (CICSA) Grupo Financiero Inbursa (GFINBUR)	82	209,562	Slim family	Telecommunications, tabacco, porcelain, construction materials, metal products and equipment, financial services, retailing, restaurant, real estate, construction,
2	Cemex	197	Cemex (CEMEX)	27	54,635	Zambrano family	Cement
3	Femsa	126	Fomento Económico Mexicano (FEMSA) Coca Cola FEMSA (KOF)	8	97,770	Garza Lagüera family	Beverages, retailing
4	Bal	77	Industrias Peñoles (PEÑOLES) Grupo Nacional Provincial (GNP) Grupo Palacio de Hierro (GPH)	47	21,255	Bailleres family	Non-ferrous metal mining, insurance, retailing
5	Alfa	77	Alfa (ALFA)	26	38,818	Garza Medina family	Chemicals, autoparts, foods, telecommunications

(continued)

Table 15.1 Continued

Ranks by total sales	Group name	Total sales[1] (pesos bn.)	Principal listed companies (abbreviation in stock exchanges)	No. of principal subsidiaries	No. of employees	Controlling family	Main industries involved
6	Gruma	76	Grupo Financiero Banorte (GFNORTE) Gruma (GRUMA) Grupo Industrial Maseca (MASECA)	31	34,064	González Barrera family	Foods, financial services
7	Grupo México	71	Grupo México (GMEXICO)	15	18,865	Larrea family	Non-ferrous metal mining, railroad transportation
8	Bimbo	64	Grupo Bimbo (BIMBO)	6	85,494	Servitje family	Foods
9	Soriana	58	Organización Soriana (SORIANA)	2	60,322	Martin family	wholesale, retailing
10	Modelo	57	Grupo Modelo (MODELO)	32	36,911	Fernández family	Beverages
11	Salinas	50	Grupo Elektra (ELEKTRA) Grupo Iusacell (CEL) TV Azteca (TVAZTCA) Grupo Movil Access (MOVILA)	63	47,355	Salinas family	Retailing, financial services, telecommunications, TV
12	Comercial Mexicana	46	Controladora Comercial Mexicana (COMERCI)	5	38,437	González Nova family	Retailing, restaurant
13	Liverpool	38	El Puerto de Liverpool (LIVEPOL)	4	30,000	(data noth available)	Retailing
14	Televisa	38	Grupo Televisa (TLEVISA)	21	16,205	Azcárraga family	TV

Ranks by total sales	Group name	Total sales[1] (pesos bn.)	Principal listed companies (abbreviation in stock exchanges)	No. of principal subsidiaries	No. of employees	Controlling family	Main industries involved
			Empresas Cablevisión (CABLE)				
15	Mabe	34	(non-listed)	n.a.	21,402[2]	Berrondo family	Consumer electronics
16	Gigante	32	Grupo Gigante (GIGANTE)	23	35,427	Losada family	Retailing
17	Xignux	32	(non-listed)	27	33,573	Garza Herrera and Garza Garza family	Autoparts, wire & cable, foods
18	Lala	28	(non-listed)	n.a.	27,859[2]	Non (Cooperative)	Beverages, foods
19	Coppel	27	Coppel (ALMACO)	3	34,557	Coppel family	Retailing
20	Vitro	27	Vitro (VITRO)	28	22,294	Sada family	Glass

Notes: The table was made by the following procedure. Groups are ranked by total sales. When the consolidated sales of a group holding company appear in the ranking of Expansión, they are taken as total sales of the group. In the cases of No.1 Carso, No.4 Bal, No.3 Gruma, and No. 11 Salinas, the group consists of various listed holding companies connected by common shareholdings of the same block shareholders. In these cases, the aggregate sales of the listed holding companies in the ranking of Expansión are taken as total sales of the group. The number of principal subsidiaries and the number of employees are taken from the annual reports of the listed holding companies, except when indicated otherwise. When a group consists of various listed holding companies, their numbers are aggregated. [2] Data taken from Expansión [2007]

Sources: Annual reports of principal listed companies of the groups and Expansión 2007.

Table 15.2 Principal activities of the twenty largest Mexican business groups, 2006*

Group name	Activities 23	31	35	36	37	38	50	61	62	63	71	72	81	82	83	Total
Carso	✓	✓		✓		✓	✓		✓	✓		✓	✓	✓	✓	11
Cemex			✓	✓												2
Femsa		✓		✓				✓	✓							4
Bal	✓				✓	✓			✓		✓		✓	✓	✓	8
Alfa		✓	✓			✓						✓				4
Gruma		✓				✓								✓	✓	4
Grupo Mexico	✓				✓						✓					3
Bimbo		✓														1
Soriana								✓	✓						✓	3
Modelo		✓	✓			✓										3
Salinas									✓			✓	✓	✓		4
Comercial Mexicana									✓	✓						2
Liverpool									✓				✓			2
Televisa												✓				1
Mabe						✓										1
Gigante									✓	✓						2
Xignux		✓				✓										2
Lala		✓														1
Coppel									✓							1
Vitro				✓		✓										2
	3	8	3	4	2	8	1	2	9	3	2	4	4	4	4	61

Notes: Codes are as follows:
23 Metal ore mining, 31 manufacture of food, beverages and tobacco
35 Manufacture of chemicals and chemical, petroleum, coal, rubber and plastic
36 Manufacture of non-metallic mineral products, except products of petroleum and coal
37 Basic metal industries, 38 manufacture of fabricated metal products, machinery and equipment
50 Construction, 61 wholesale trade, 62 retail trade
63 Restaurants and hotels, 71 transport and storage, 72 communication
81 Financial institutions, 82 insurance, 83 real-estate and business services

Source: Based on annual reports of principal listed companies of the group and organized by the International Standard of Industrial Classification codes (ISIC Rev.2).

the families indicated in Table 15.1, except in the case of Lala, which is a business group based on a cooperative of dairy products producers.

How did these characteristics come about? We will see by tracing the history of the emergence and evolution of the large business groups.

15.2.2 The emergence and evolution of Mexican business groups

S. H. Haber (1989: 3) defined the period from the 1890s to the 1930s as the first wave of Mexican industrialization. In this period, production of a wide range of industrial products came to be dominated by large, modern companies that used mass-production techniques to satisfy the mass market. These companies form the origins of a proportion of today's business groups. F. Brandenburg (1964: 98) called those that emerged in this period the first generation of Mexican capitalists. Within the twenty largest groups, Alfa, Femsa, Liverpool, Cemex, Vitro, Modelo, and Bal originated in this period.

Conditions that favored the emergence and growth of these first industrial endeavors were Mexico's underdeveloped economy and market growth. The founders of these nascent industries were merchants, immigrants, or their descendants, and/or dwellers of the border cities with the United States (Derossi 1977: 181; Camp 1989: 63–4; Hoshino 2001a: 45). They could exploit these conditions for implanting modern industries that were missing in Mexico by making use of easy access to information, knowledge, and financial and human resources. They undertook large-scale investment in production and distribution, and became the first movers in their respective industries, thereby assuring themselves dominant positions in the industries thereafter. The Mexican markets to obtain materials and to sell products were imperfect and unstable, so, in order to guarantee stable supplies of materials, reduce transaction costs, and secure outlets for products, these companies expanded vertically and ultimately into technologically unrelated businesses. A typical example is that of Cervecería Cuauhtémoc, a beer company established in 1890 and the origin of Femsa, Alfa, and Vitro. This company diversified into the production of beer bottles, bottle caps, and labels and packaging; later these developed into spin-off businesses producing, respectively, glass, steel, and paper, to form Vitro (glass) and Alfa (steel and paper). The original beer company actually belongs to Femsa (Hoshino 1993: 516–17).

ISI, which had progressed at a slow pace, gained momentum from the Second World War as a result of the government's industrialization policy thereafter, and continued until 1982. The rapid progress of industrialization was a condition that favored the growth of business groups, because of the increasing business opportunities it engendered. An additional condition that emerged in this period was the introduction of government policies that also favored their growth. Restriction on imports by tariff and import license and regulation of foreign direct investment protected business groups from competition from imports and foreign companies.

Policies such as the *Mexicanization* of the mining industry and the national contents regulation of the automobile industry, which required the multinational assemblers to use auto-parts produced in Mexico, encouraged business groups to engage in lucrative businesses promoted by the government (Hoshino 2001a: 117–18). In response to these opportunities, business groups that had emerged in the first wave of industrialization further diversified their businesses. and, at the same time, new business groups emerged and grew. Within the twenty groups studied, new groups that appeared in this period were Gruma, Grupo México, Bimbo, Soriana, Comercial Mexicana, Televisa, Mabe, Gigante, Lala, and Coppel. According to studies by Cordero and Santín (1977) and Derossi (1977), by the early 1970s business groups had evolved into a group of companies with diversified businesses held under the managerial control of an owner family. Their competitive edges resided in financial and human resources, as well as the technological, marketing, and managerial capabilities that were nurtured in the process of growth, and then were mobilized when the groups diversified into new businesses.

15.2.3 Consolidation of business groups

The period from the early 1970s to 1982 deserves a special mention. It is important, because business groups experienced a rapid expansion in scale and opened up their ownership by listing on the stock market in this period. Government policy played an important role in these events. By the presidential decree issued in 1973, holding companies owned by Mexicans were given the fiscal incentives of consolidation of the account settlement of majority-owned subsidiaries or of tax exemption on capital gains from stock-market transactions of shares of minority-owned companies. Applicants for the incentives were required to fulfill at least five of ten conditions, such as the *Mexicanization* of foreign companies, the listing of holding company shares, import substitution, the foundation of firms in industry or tourism, and investment in Mexico's underdeveloped regions. It was a decree proposed by leading figures of the Mexican private sector to the government in order to institutionalize business groups that had already developed and to strengthen the function of the holding company as the headquarters for business groups' activity (DESC 1998: 66–79). Another important legislation promulgated in 1973 was the Foreign Investment Law. The law stipulated that the approval of the Foreign Investment Committee was necessary for foreign direct investment to occur, and foreign capital participation was limited to 49 percent as a rule and to a much lower percentage in specified areas. The law effectively contained the activity of foreign multinationals and gave greater room for Mexican companies to grow.

Responding to this government encouragement, large business groups began to list their holding companies, forming them when they were missing, and to contract joint ventures with foreign multinationals at the subsidiary level. The process was fostered by the economic boom that had started in the second half of the 1970s as a result of soaring petroleum exports (Jacobos 1981; Hoshino 1990). Some large business groups had already formed holding companies within their groups, so that the hierarchical control structure of business groups may well have been in existence already. However, it was during this period that the hierarchical or, in the case of groups with listed subsidiaries, the pyramidal structure became apparent, because of the listing of holding companies; and these became widespread because of the fiscal incentives.

Active investment by business groups was possible, however, only on the basis of the availability of funds for investment, and one important source of funds was borrowing from international commercial banks. Mexican private firms in the past had suffered from a poor credit standing with the international finance community, but the situation changed when the country became an oil producer, which immediately enhanced its international prestige and credit rating. The result was an unprecedented amount of loans flowing into large business groups.

15.3 NEOLIBERAL ECONOMIC REFORM AND RESTRUCTURING OF MEXICAN BUSINESS GROUPS

15.3.1 Change of economic environment

The external debt problem of 1982 and the subsequent economic crisis forced the Mexican government to abandon ISI and to adopt a neoliberal strategy that attached importance to macroeconomic equilibrium, an improved control on government expenditure, and export-oriented growth. Of the neoliberal reforms implemented, those that had the most significant impact on business groups were trade liberalization, the deregulation of foreign direct investment, and the privatization of state-owned companies.

Radical trade liberalization was initiated in 1985. Because of an increase of imports, competition in the internal market intensified by the early 1990s, and competitiveness became necessary, not only for exports but also for sales in the internal market. The Foreign Investment Law was reformed, first in 1989, when regulation supporting the existing law was issued, and finally in 1993, when the new Foreign Investment Law was promulgated. Under the reformed law, 100 percent participation of foreign capital was admitted, except for some specified areas, and the approval of the Foreign Investment Committee was no longer required, provided a project met certain criteria (Aspe 1993: 166–8). This meant that foreign multinationals could now invest more freely in Mexico without complicated negotiation with the Foreign Investment Committee and without looking for partners for joint ventures. The privatization of state-owned companies began in the middle of the 1980s on a small scale and acquired momentum in the years around 1990. In contrast to the first two reforms, which affected business groups negatively because they brought intensified competition, privatization had a positive effect, in the sense that it offered groups an opportunity to buy out state-owned companies as a useful means by which they could restructure their own businesses.

In 1982 the external debt taken on by business groups amounted to about $20 billion. By successive devaluations, its value in pesos rapidly increased, and the majority of indebted companies were driven to suspend service of their debts. Those heavily indebted business groups had to tackle the difficult task of rescheduling repayment of these debts, while responding to intensified competition.

15.3.2 The rise and fall of business groups

Intensified competition and huge external debts were two difficult problems large business groups faced in the 1980s. Some groups overcame them successfully, but others failed. While existing business groups were striving to adapt to the changing economic environment, new business groups emerged by grasping the opportunities presented by radical economic reforms. As a result of these processes, there was a shuffle in the composition of dominant business groups.

According to a previous study by this author on large business groups in mining and manufacturing sectors, there were 47 business groups positioned within the largest 100 companies and groups in Mexico 1986 and 45 groups in 1998. Of the 47 groups in the 1986 list, only 20 also appeared in the 1998 list. Thus, 27 groups had disappeared and 25 new groups appeared on the list. Of the 27 groups that had fallen from the list, no fewer than 15 had been acquired by other business groups or by foreign multinationals. Of the 25 newcomers, at least 6 groups were newly formed; 10 were old groups that had just made the list with the disclosure of information upon listing on the stock market (Hoshino 2001b: 6–8).

How did existing business groups adapt to the changing economic environment, and how did newly formed business groups grasp business opportunities? To answer these questions, let us consider the cases of Alfa and Carso.

15.3.2.1 The case of Alfa

Alfa is typical of those business groups that were heavily indebted and cut off some of their businesses in order to improve their financial condition and face the intensified competition.

Alfa was the largest and most indebted business group in Mexico in the early 1980s. In 1982 Alfa declared a moratorium to its foreign creditor banks. Thereafter, until 1988 negotiations took place between them. The problem was principally settled by combining two resolutions. One was repayment with Mexican government bonds issued specifically for the repayment of external debts. Another was a debt–capital swap. A large portion of shares, which were transferred to creditor banks, were repurchased later by the group on the secondary market at discounted prices.

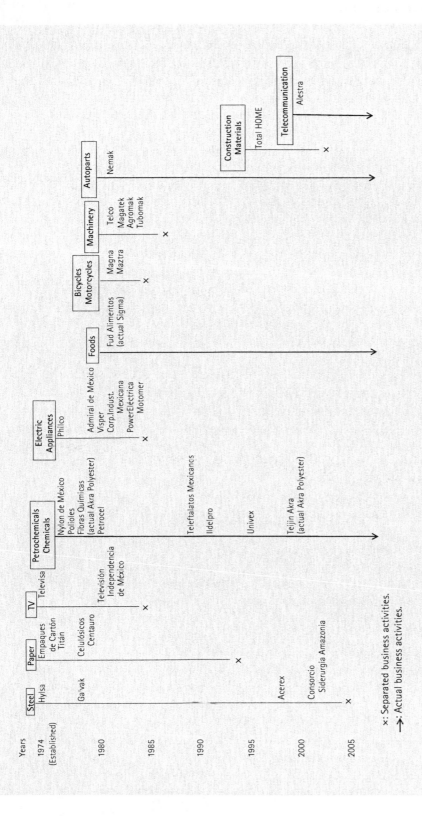

Figure 15.1 Changes in Alfa's business activities and principal subsidiaries

Sources: Hoshino (1993) and Annual Report (2007).

It is interesting to note how the Mexican government assisted in restructuring the external debts of large business groups. In 1983, to help the heavily indebted private companies, the government established a fiduciary named FICORCA, which assumed the exchange risk brought on by the devaluation of the Mexican currency (Vidal 2000: 135–8). The government also assisted heavily indebted business groups in contracting loans from nationalized banks, referred to later, when the groups purchased Mexican government bonds to use for repayment of external debts. Alfa made use of these programs. In addition, the Mexican government provided unprecedented assistance to Alfa. In 1981, one year before the moratorium, the government development bank BANOBRAS provided Alfa with a large amount of finance at exceptionally favorable terms (Hoshino 1993).

Another formidable task Alfa faced was restructuring its businesses better to confront intensified competition. Alfa did so by eliminating non-competitive businesses and concentrating resources on a few selected companies. Fig. 15.1 indicates changes in Alfa's business activities and principal subsidiaries. The figure shows that its activities have changed drastically and that the range of diversification has been narrowed since 1982. During the restructuring, even those businesses that were considered to be the origin and pride of Alfa, such as steel and paper, were cut off.

15.3.2.2 *The case of Carso*

Carso is a representative of those business groups that arose during the 1980s and used the privatization of state-owned companies as an opportunity further to enhance their position. Fig. 15.2 indicates the pyramidal control structure of Carso in 2006. The group consists of four apex holding companies and their respective subsidiaries. They are Grupo Financiero Inbursa (GFINBUR) in finance, Grupo Carso (GCARSO) in commerce, industry, and infrastructure, Carso Global Telecom (TELECOM) in telecommunications, and America Movil (AMX) in mobile telecommunications. Below the four apex holding companies, the second-tier subholding companies are allocated. This massive pyramidal structure was formed in little more than two decades.

The growth of Carso can be divided into three stages. The first stage is from 1966 to 1980. In 1966 Carlos Slim Helu, the founder of Carso, entered the securities brokerage business by establishing a brokerage company, which exists as a core company of GFINBUR in the late 2000s. At this stage, neither he nor his business had a high profile.

The second stage is from 1980 to 1990. In 1980 a holding company, precursor of GCARSO, was established, and began to grow by buying up large companies one after another. Many of the principal subsidiaries of GCARSO were acquired in this period. Growth of the group took place against the background of the restructuring of the Mexican financial sector in the 1980s. In 1982 the government nationalized private banks in an effort to prevent the capital flight provoked by the external debt crisis. Soon after the nationalization, large compensations were paid to shareholders of nationalized banks, and many of them, with compensation payments, shifted their business over to the Mexican Securities Exchange (BMV), which the government had

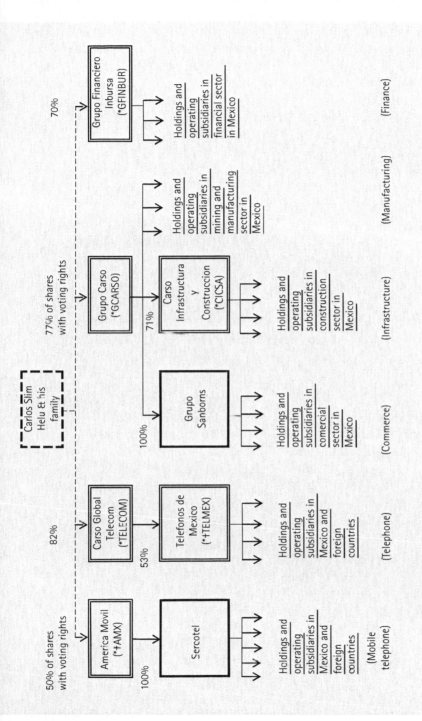

Figure 15.2 Hierarchical structure of Carso, 2006

Notes: Principal activities in parentheses; → indicates shareholdings between companies and its direction; dotted line indicates direct or indirect shareholding by family. ☐ Companies listed on the Stock Exchange; * in Mexico; *+ in New York and/or other international market.

Sources: Compiled by author from annual reports.

been seeking to nurture and strengthen. Carlos Slim found business partners in these people. In addition, nationalized banks held shares of a variety of large private companies, which were later put up for sale. A proportion of the companies taken over by GCARSO were those that were put on sale. Thus Carso partially inherited the investors and businesses of these nationalized banks (Hoshino 1996: 52–3).

The third period runs from 1990. A great leap for the group was the acquisition by GCARSO of Teléfonos de México (TELMEX) in 1990, the sole, state-owned, telephone company in Mexico, in alliance with South Western Bell of the USA and France's Cable and Radio, during its privatization. In 1996 the shares of TELMEX were separated from GCARSO and transferred to TELECOM, a newly established holding company. In 2000 the mobile-phone business, which had developed within TELMEX, was separated from TELMEX to form AMX. In 1999 AMX began overseas expansion to Latin American countries by acquiring local companies in telecommunications. Later on, in 2004, TELMEX also advanced to Latin American countries by acquiring local companies. In 2006 almost 80 percent of sales of the group were achieved by TELMEX and AMX.

15.3.3 Factors in the successful adaptation and emergence of the twenty largest business groups

The twenty business groups analyzed in this chapter are those that were able to adapt to or emerge in Mexico's changing economic environment. Were there any common factors that can explain their success?

One of the important factors that affected business groups' ability to adapt was whether they had significant debts when the neoliberal economic reform started. Cemex, Bimbo, and Grupo Mexico were free from debt—in the cases of Cemex and Bimbo, thanks to their cautious attitudes toward taking on debt, and in the case of Grupo Mexico, thanks to earnings in dollars from export. This factor is important, because non-indebted business groups could swiftly reorient their business strategy and exploit business opportunities brought by the changing economic environment. Most important was the acquisition of companies being put up for sale because of circumstances such as privatization, restructuring of business groups, and the separation of shares of companies held by the nationalized banks. Business groups with severe external debt could not reorient their strategy swiftly and could not fully exploit these opportunities while they were negotiating debt rescheduling and were in a tight financial condition—a scenario that partly explains the fall in ranking of Alfa.

Another important factor was whether business groups could successfully exploit the opportunities of acquisition referred to above. The most important opportunity for acquisition was the privatization of state-owned companies, as the case of Carso shows. Other examples of privatization were the case of Grupo Mexico, which acquired two copper-mining companies and railway companies; the case of Gruma, which acquired a reprivatized bank nationalized in 1982; and the case of Salinas, which acquired the government TV broadcasting station (Hoshino 1996: 40, 48). A further opportunity was the acquisition of subsidiaries from restructuring or bankrupt business groups. Cemex, Femsa, Bimbo, and Mabe acquired former rival companies in the industries in which they were involved. As a result, their dominant position in their respective industries was reinforced (Hoshino 1997: 34–7; 2001b: 18–23).

Whether business groups owned a prosperous venture was also an important determinant of their capacity to adapt. One of the few prosperous Mexican businesses in the latter half of the 1980s was the securities brokerage in the stock market, which experienced an unprecedented boom from the mid-1980s to the early 1990s. This boom was caused in part by the enormous quantity of bonds issued by the government to finance its swelling deficit. It was also fueled by the huge amount of capital that flowed into the BMV. This was money that flowed back into Mexico after fleeing abroad during the first half of the 1980s, or that had been deposited in banks until their nationalization, or surplus capital held by companies that saw no other attractive investment opportunities because of the depressed economy (Peñolosa Webb 1989: 514). As referred to earlier, many ex-shareholders of banks moved on to the security brokerage business. These newcomers and pre-existing brokers, including Carlos Slim, made up an important part of the players in privatization. Slim differed from other brokers in that he betted on TELMEX, while others put their money on the reprivatized banks. Shortly after reprivatization, the majority of banks went into bankruptcy, and were bought out by foreign banks, because of non-performing loans caused by the Mexican peso crisis in 1994. Another prosperous sector in Mexico after the 1980s was the *maquiladoras*, in-bond industries that consist mainly of the automobile industry and the electric and electronic industries. Those business groups that had investments in activities related to these industries, such as auto-parts in the cases of Alfa and Xignux and electrical appliances in the case of Mabe, received relatively good results.

15.4 CHANGING STRATEGY AND PERSISTENT STRUCTURE

15.4.1 Globalization as new orientation of business strategy

After the mid-1980s, as internal market competition intensified, the strategy of business groups underwent significant changes. The principal change that can be observed was in the orientation of business activity, which became more global with respect to market, location, fund raising, and partnership; some business groups have grown to become multinationals (Salas-Porras 1998; Garrido 1999; Hoshino 2001b; Basave Kunhardt 2006). Table 15.3 shows the overseas activities of nineteen of the

Table 15.3 Overseas activities of principal subsidiaries of business groups, 2006

Ranking	group name	Listed companies on Mexican stock exchange	Overseas revenues (% of total)	Overseas investment						Listed on foreign stock exchanges		Debt in dollar	
				North America	Central America & Carribean	South America	Europe	Asia	Others	NYSE*	LATIBEX†	Bank loan	Corporate bond
1	Carso	AMX	53	✓	✓	✓				✓	✓	✓	✓
		TELMEX	27		✓	✓				✓	✓	✓	✓
		GCARSO	11		✓							✓	
		CICSA	–									✓	
		GFINBUR	–										
2	Cemex	CEMEX	82	✓	✓	✓	✓	✓	✓	✓		✓	✓
3	Femsa	FEMSA	24		✓	✓				✓		✓	✓
		KOF	46		✓	✓				✓		✓	✓
4	Bal	PENOLES	75						✓			✓	✓
		GNP	–										
		GPH	–										
5	Alfa	ALFA	56	✓	✓	✓	✓	✓		✓	✓	✓	✓
6	Gruma	GRUMA	69	✓	✓	✓	✓	✓	✓		✓	✓	✓
		MASECA	–										
		GFNORTE	–										
7	Grupo México	GMEXICO	71	✓	✓	✓	✓	✓				✓	✓
8	Bimbo	BIMBO	31‡	✓	✓	✓	✓	✓				✓	✓
9	Soriana	SORIANA	–										
10	Modelo	GMODELO	29		✓	✓					✓	✓	
11	Salinas	ELEKTRA	10		✓						✓	✓	
		CELL	–										
		TVAZTCA	–								✓		
		MOVILA	–								✓		✓

| Ranking | group name | Listed companies on Mexican stock exchange | Overseas revenues (% of total) | Overseas investment | | | | | | Listed on foreign stock exchanges | | Debt in dollar | |
				North America	Central America & Carribean	South America	Europe	Asia	Others	NYSEC*	LATIBEX†	Bank loan	Corporate bond
12	Comercial Mexicana	COMERCI	–										✓
13	Liverpool	LIVEPOL	–										
14	Televisa	TELEVISA	12							✓			✓
		CABLE	–										
15	Mabe	–	N.A.	✓		✓							
16	Gigante	GIGANTE	N.A.	✓		✓						✓	✓
17	Xignux	XIGNUX§	59		✓	✓						✓	✓
19	Coppel	ALMACO	–										
20	Vitro	VITRO	56	✓	✓	✓	✓				✓	✓	✓

Notes: *– there is neither export nor overseas investment. † New York Stock Exchange; ‡ The international market for Latin American Securities, which is created in 1999 by the Spanish government and regulated by the Sapanish Security Market Law; §The figure does not include revunue from Europe and Asia; Xignux does not list stocks, but issues bonds in BMV.

Sources: Annual reports.

largest business groups in 2006; Lala is excluded, as its data were unavailable. According to the table, more than half of the groups had overseas revenues, and in seven cases more than half the revenenues came from overseas activities.

15.4.1.1 *Competitive advantages of Mexican business groups*

Competitive advantages would be a necessary condition for any business group to advance to the global market. Principal products or services that are exported or produced overseas by Mexican business groups are varied, but include: telecommunications services (AMX, TELMEX), retail commerce (GCARSO, SORIANA, ELEKTRA, GIGANTE), cement (CEMEX), beer and soft drinks (FEMSA, KOF, GMODELO), non-ferrous metal (PENOLES, GMEXICO), auto parts (ALFA, XIGNUX), petrochemical products (ALFA), ham and sausage (ALFA), *tortilla* or Mexican corn bread (GRUMA), bakery products (BIMBO), TV broadcasting (TLEVISA), and glass (VITRO). Business groups have a long history of producing these products and services, so the necessary technological and marketing capabilities were nurtured during their growth.

With respect to overseas direct investment, principal destinations are the United States and other Latin American countries. Geographical concentration to the American continent is explained by the geographical proximity and similarities in language, culture, and the economic level of consumers, including the United States, which has a huge Hispanic population. Mexican business groups have a competitive advantage there compared with non-Latin American companies, because they can make use of the skills that they have nurtured while conducting their business in a similar environment like Mexico, skills such as providing products suited to local conditions and building distribution channels in a less-developed market. They also have the advantage of the comparative ease of communication with which they can negotiate with governments and labor unions, develop distribution networks, and manage employees. This is often referred to as the 'Latin American' advantage (Tavares 2007: 57). However, these advantages may lose their effectiveness outside Latin America, or in competition with business groups from host countries or with other multinationals that originated in Latin America.

A predominant position in the Mexican market may be an additional advantage, because it provides them with monopoly rents, which make it possible for groups to compete in markets with less favorable conditions. One of this evidence is a fact that the percentages of overseas profit in the total profit were far less than percentages of overseas revenues indicated in Table 15.3 in the case of AMX, TELMEX, CEMEX, GRUMA, and BIMBO.[5]

Some business groups, such as Cemex, Alfa, Gruma, Bimbo, and Vitro, extended their investment outside the American continent. Until 2000, Cemex invested primarily in Latin America and Asia, where the group had a competitive advantage over Holcim and Lafarge, two multinational rivals that originated in Europe. However,

---

[5] The percentages of overseas profit in the total profit of AMX, TELMEX, CEMEX, GRUMA, and BIMBO were 37%, 1%, 62%, 59%, and 10% in 2006 respectively. Figures are calculated by the author, based on data from the annual reports for the year 2006 of the five holding companies.

from 2000 onward, the group changed its principal destination to developed countries by means of large-scale M&As in the USA, Great Britain, and Australia. A counter-move by the two European rivals was a large-scale investment in developing countries, especially in India and China. It seems that the marketing capabilities of the three multinationals are converging as they compete for a larger share in the global market.[6] Overseas production of auto parts by Alfa is another example of a company improving its marketing capability, while globalizing its business activities. Its strategy is to be a global provider of specified auto parts (aluminum heads and monoblocks for an automobile engine). It acquired OEM, which made the same parts in Europe and the USA, and thus acquired a leading position as a provider of these parts for principal automobile assemblers globally. The examples of Cemex and Alfa suggest that the competitiveness of business groups that have advanced outside the American continent lies in their marketing capability, which continues to evolve during the globalization process.

15.4.1.2 *Fund raising*

The international financial market became more important in Mexican business groups' fund raising after the early 1990s. The background to this move was a global investment boom in emerging markets and a development in the reform of the Mexican security market. In this reform, in order to enhance the listing of business groups on the BMV and the investment by foreigners in their shares, an instrument called the Neutral Investment Mechanism was introduced. In this mechanism, a trust fund is set up in a bank for foreigners who would like to invest in a Mexican company. This trust fund purchases shares of the company with money provided by the foreigner, and keeps these shares. In exchange for shares kept in the trust, certificates called Certificados de Praticipación Ordinarias (CPOs) are issued to foreigners. It is called neutral, because investment by means of CPOs is not counted as foreign investment, so that foreigners can invest in restricted areas and acquire shares that have a restriction on shareholders. For the principal shareholders in business groups, this has the merit of being able to obtain funds without worrying about the risk of losing control of votes, because CPOs confer the right to dividends but not the right to vote. Active listing of business groups took place in the 1990s. Of the thirty listed companies in the BMV presented in Table 15.3, nineteen listed their shares after the year 1990. In addition to listing on the BMV, eight companies included in Table 15.3 listed on the New York Stock Exchange and eight companies on the LATIBEX in Spain.

---

[6] In the cement industry, the market in developing countries differs from the developed countries' market in that the market for self-builders of houses is very large. In this market, cement is sold packaged as consumer goods. In developed countries, cement is mainly sold in bulk as an intermediary good in the construction market. The marketing skills needed differ accordingly. Where cement is packaged, skills are needed to build a distribution network of retailers and to propagate a trademark. In the bulk market, the ability to deliver concrete to construction sites is important, which requires an integrated chain consisting of cement plants, grinding plants, and ready-mix concrete plants.

It seems that companies were listed because of the large premium proceeds that were expected from initial public offerings and the greater access to debt finance denominated in foreign currency. In an analysis of listings of Mexican companies on the New York Stock Exchange in the mid-1990s, G. Babatz Torres (1997: 90, 103–05) pointed out that, after making an equity issue, these companies liquidated peso-denominated liabilities and replaced them with dollar-denominated ones by contracting bank loans and/or placing corporate bonds. He considered that listing on the New York Stock Exchange was a first step for access to the international financial market. However, Table 15.3 shows that in 2006 there were many companies that had debts in dollars without being listed abroad. It seems that the entry barrier to the international financial market has been lowered. The principal merit of foreign fund raising is the financial cost, which has been much cheaper than in the domestic market. The large-scale M&As that were implemented after the 1990s were generally financed by the proceeds of listings and/or loans from international commercial banks, and a large sum of debt in dollars thus accrued were replaced by bonds, which have more favorable conditions for repayment. By lowering the financial cost in this way, business groups were able to finance overseas expansion.

15.4.1.3 *Strategic alliance*

Strategic alliance between business groups and other companies, mostly foreign multinationals, has been formed principally by transferring shares to allied companies, jointly setting up subsidiaries to promote new ventures, or contracting agreements in areas such as technological assistance, the use of distribution networks, and the use of patents and trademarks. In the case of KOF, a soft-drink division of FEMSA, Coca-Cola Company of the United States has a 30 percent share. In the case of GRUMA, a holding company of the international foodstuffs division of Gruma, Archer Daniels Midland of the United States has a 27 percent share. Anheuser-Bush of the United States acquired a 35 percent share of the holding company of Modelo. In the case of Mabe, General Electric of the United States has had about 40 percent share of the holding company since 1987.

The main advantages of all these alliances can be summed up as follows. First, through such an alliance business groups can gain access to resources that multinationals possess. In an unknown foreign market, such an alliance provides the benefit of access to existing distribution networks, market information, and the established brand names of partners. In a new venture, an alliance also offers access to technology and finance. Secondly, through an alliance business groups can avoid overwhelming competition by converting potential competitors into allies.

At times, however, alliances intensify competition, because rivals can follow the example of others. An example of this can be seen in the supermarket business. In this sector, the former largest business group Aurrera formed a strategic alliance with Walmart of the United States in 1991 by offering capital participation and investing in a new type of retail stores. Because of intensified competition, other business groups in this sector followed Aurrera's strategy. They invested in the same type of retail stores and formed similar strategic alliances: Comercial Mexicana with Costco of the

United States, and Gigante with Price Smart and Office Depot of the United States. Aurrera was finally bought out by Walmart in 1997—a development that demonstrates the risk for principal owners of business groups of losing control of their business to their ally.

15.4.2 Persistent control structure

The hierarchical or pyramidal control structure of business groups, which was consolidated during the second half of the 1970s, has remained basically unchanged since then.

Fig. 15.3 shows the structure of Bimbo, which has a typical hierarchical control structure. Its apex holding company is Grupo Bimbo, which has been listed in BMV since 1980. The group does not list its subsidiaries. The principal roles of the apex holding company is to raise funds in the financial market, to allocate them among subsidiaries, and to form business strategy and plans. Below Grupo Bimbo, subholdings are formed according to their products and to the geographical location of business activities, and below them come operating subsidiaries. Although new subholdings and operating subsidiaries have been added and subgroups have been frequently reorganized since the mid-1980s, Bimbo's hierarchical structure itself has not changed.

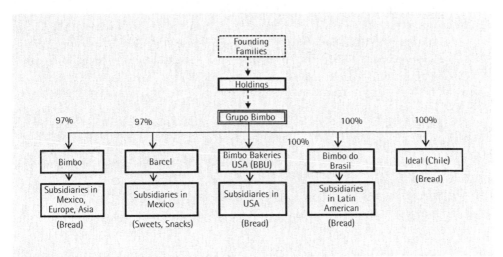

Figure 15.3 Hierarchical structure of Grupo Bimbo, 2006

Notes: ☐ Company listed on the Mexican Stock Exchange; Principal products in parenthesis; → Indicates shareholdings between companies and its direction; dotted line indicates direct or indirect shareholding by founding family members. *Source*: Compiled by author from Annual Report.

An interesting phenomenon is that newly formed business groups have also employed similar control structures. This suggests that these structures are consistent with growth. Let us consider the case of Carso of Fig. 15.2. One of the peculiarities of Carso is that it consists of four apex holding companies. These companies were formed as spin-offs of previously established holding companies. Although subsidiaries of four apex holding companies carry out transactions among themselves, it is unknown whether there exists a headquarters that coordinates the activities of all four holding companies. At any rate, they are under the common ownership and control of Carlos Slim and his family. The spin-offs from holding companies can perhaps be explained by the rapid growth of newly entered industries, which made it possible for newly formed holding companies to raise funds by themselves. At the same time, the growth of new business sectors made it difficult for pre-existing holding companies to achieve managerial control of increasingly complicated business activities.

Control structures, however, have modified to some degree. One important modification has been the location of partnership with multinationals in the group structure. In the 1970s, when business groups began to diversify their business, the participation of foreign capital in groups' operating companies increased for technological and financial reasons. Actual foreign capital participation is also found in holding companies, which are located on the upper tier of the control structure. In the case of Carso, 21 percent of the shares with voting rights of TELMEX, a holding company in the second tier, are held by AT&T of the United States. All alliances with multinationals referred to above are contracted by the apex or holding companies of the second tier. This presents a risk for the controlling families of business groups, from the increased influence of allied multinationals in higher levels of management and the increased chance of being taken over when the business group's shares are listed on the stock market. We will see how the owner families of business groups deal with these problems by examining the ownership structure and the methods of management control by families.

15.5 OWNERSHIP AND CONTROL BY FAMILIES

15.5.1 Ownership structure of largest business groups

Table 15.4 shows the shareholding breakdown in the listed companies of eighteen business groups for which information is available. The table indicates that company shares are concentrated in the hands of the largest block shareholders, mainly families, with very high percentages. Of the thirty-one companies in this table, in twenty the shares held by the largest block shareholders are more than the majority of total shares issued. In cases in which shareholdings are far below the majority share, one way to secure control of the votes in the general assembly of shareholders is to issue shares with limited voting rights. In eight companies this type of shares is

Table 15.4 Shareholding in principal listed companies of business groups by the largest block shareholder, 2006

Group name	Main subsidiaries	Largest block shareholder	% of Shareholding in total shares	in shares with voting right
Carso	AMX	Family	19.4	50.0
	TELMEX	TELECOM	53.1	71.2
	TELECOM	Family	82.0	82.0
	GCARSO	Family	76.8	76.8
	CICSA	GCARSO	71.2	71.2
	GFINBUR	Family	70.0	70.0
Cemex	CEMEX	n.a.	n.a.	n.a.
Femsa	FEMSA	Family	37.1	71.8
	KOF	FEMSA	53.7	63.0
Bal	PEÑOLES	⎫	79.3	79.3
	GNP	⎬ Family	70.4	70.4
	GPH	⎭	77.9	77.9
Alfa	ALFA	Family	45.0	45.0
Gruma	GFNORTE	⎫	16.7	16.7
	GRUMA	⎬ Family	46.0	46.0
Grupo México	GMEXICO	Family	46.5	46.5
Bimbo	BIMBO	Family	69.9	69.9
Soriana	SORIANA	Family	86.2	86.2
Modelo	GMODELO	Family	44.9	56.1
Salinas	ELEKTRA	⎫	72.9	72.9
	CEL	⎪	76.7	76.7
	TVAZTCA	⎬ Family	62.2	75.8
	MOVILA	⎭	83.9	83.9
Comercial Mexicana	COMERCI	Family	67.2	73.2
Liverpool	LIVEPOL	n.a.	n.a.	n.a.
Televisa	TLEVISA	Family	15.1	43.7
	CABLE	TLVISA	51.0	51.0
Gigante	GIGANTE	Family	65.1	65.1
Xignux	XIGNUX*	Family	97.0	97.0
Coppel	ALMACO	Family	99.9	99.9
Vitro	VITRO	Family	27.5	27.5

Notes: *Full name is Grupo Xignux. The company issues the company's bond on the Mexican Stock Exchange.
Source: Annual reports.

issued, and in three cases their issuance ensures that owner families hold the majority of the votes. Another method through which owner families control votes is by restricting shareholding of foreigners by means of issuing shares that can be acquired only by Mexicans, providing the minimum percentage of 51 percent shareholding by Mexicans in the statute of company. AMEX, TELMEX, FEMSA, GMEXICO, CEL,

TVAZTCA, CABLE, and ALMCO, among others, issued these kinds of shares in 2006.

Packaging of shares with voting rights and of those with limited voting rights is another instrument to restrain participation of minority shareholders in votes and to permit owner families to decrease the cost of controlling votes. By making a package, shareholders who represent the packaged shares are obliged to pay higher prices in order to acquire equal voting rights with those who have non-packaged shares with voting rights. This mechanism is observed, for example, in CEMEX, TVAZTCA, COMERCI, TLEVISA, and CABLE.

The CPO Neutral Investment Mechanism is another instrument for owner families to assure control on votes. CPOs are issued, for example, in CEMEX, ALFA, TELE-VISA, TVAZTCA, and VITRO.

By combining these mechanisms, it is possible to control votes with reduced shares. CEMEX is the most prominent case in this respect. The company issues two kinds of shares, A shares, which only Mexicans can acquire and which constitute 64 percent of total shares issued, and B shares, which have no restriction on shareholders and which make up the rest of shares. CEMEX issues 97 percent of shares in packages of CPO composed of two A shares and one B share. Holders of CPOs do not have the voting rights of A shares in their package. In the contract of the trust fund, there is a clause that provides that the votes of A shares in CPOs are counted as having the same results as the majority of votes of A shares in the hands of Mexicans (Cemex 2007: 1, 145). Although CEMEX reported that no shareholder individually held more than 5 percent of total shares in 2006, with these mechanisms, it is possible to control votes with quite a reduced percentage, much less than 5 percent, of total A shares.

15.5.2 Unification of votes and prevention of dispersion of family-held shares

In the case of a company owned and managed by a family, after numerous rounds of succession, the ownership of shares might be split between members of new generations and might lead to a situation in which unification of votes becomes increasingly difficult, and could increase the chance that some members of the family sell their shares to an outsider. Because of these reasons, in order to maintain family control, a mechanism is needed both that allows the family to unify votes from shares whose ownership has been subdivided because of succession, and that avoids the dispersal of shares that become increasingly easy to sell because of the company's listing on the Stock Exchange.

Holding companies and trusts, which keep shares owned by family members, are used to serve this function. According to annual reports of listed companies, in PEÑOLES, GNP, GPH, GMEXICO, BIMBO, CEL, TVAZTCA, and MOVILA, shares owned by family members are held by holding companies owned by owner families.

In AMX, FEMSA, GMODELO, and TLEVISA, shares owned by family members are deposited in trusts set up in banks.

In the case of trusts, the whole or a significant part of shares owned by family members and their corresponding voting rights are deposited in a bank as a trusted property. According to the descriptions of annual reports, such trusts have the following two functions. One is to unify the vote of family members and another is to fix the order of purchasing priority when a member of the family wants to sell his shares. The condition of the trust is determined by its participants and is documented in a contract (Hoshino 2006: 168–9).

Differences between a holding company and a trust are the payments of a dividend and the right to dispose of the entrusted shares. Holding companies seem to have more coercive power over family members than do trusts. Supposedly, which one of these two instruments is chosen depends on the convenience for the controlling family of the business group and the strength of their cohesion (Hoshino 2006: 170).

15.5.3 Top management of the largest business groups

The preceding analysis shows that owner families, by tacitly making use of various instruments, maintain tight control over the votes of the general assembly of shareholders, and consequently over the board of directors. If their control of votes is solid, how is their control of management?

Table 15.5 shows the number of family members in the positions of chairman of the board and chief executive officer (CEO) in thirty listed companies of the largest business groups. According to the table, in almost all companies, owner families preside over the board of directors. In eleven cases, the CEO is same person as the chairman of the board. In eight cases, the CEO is a close relative of the chairman. In eleven cases the CEO is not a member of the owner family but is a salaried manager. Considering an owner family's concern with controlling votes, this proportion of salaried CEOs seems unexpectedly high. According to a previous study by this author, the involvement of owner families in top management posts, including the subordinate senior managers, was also scarce, and the study concluded that the assumption of executive management posts by owner families is actually quite limited (Hoshino 2004: 16–18). It seems that family members of business groups tend to retreat from the executive posts.

Bimbo is a case in which we can see how roles in management are divided between the board and executive managers. Executive top managers of Bimbo constitute two internal committees. One is the Executive Committee, which is composed of fifteen top executive managers, including the CEO of the apex holding company, Grupo Bimbo (Fig. 15.4).

The role of the Executive Committee is to draw up the year's business strategy, and, for that purpose, a long and intensive meeting is organized once a year. The result must be reported to the Board of Directors in order to acquire approval for implementation. Apart from the Executive Committee, there is another committee

Table 15.5 Chairman and CEO of principal listed companies of business groups, 2006

Group name	Listed company	Chairman of the board	CEO's kinship with chairman
Carso	AMX	Family	Brother-in-law
	TELMEX	Salaried manager (co–chairman)]	Cousin
		Family (co–chairman)	
	GCARSO	Family	
	USCOM	Family	
	GFINBUR	Family	Same as chairman
Cemex	CEMEX	Family	Same as chairman
Femsa	FEMSA	Family	Son-in-law
	KOF	Family	
Bal	PEÑOLES	Family	
	GNP	Family	Son
	GPH	Family	
Alfa	ALFA	Family	Same as chairman
Gruma	GFNORTE	Family	
	GRUMA	Family	
Grupo México	GMEXICO	Family	Same as chairman
Bimo	BIMBO	Family	Nephew
Soriana	SORIANA	Family	Son
Modelo	GMODELO	Family	Same as chairman
Salinas	ELEKTRA	Family	
	CEL	Family	
	TVAZICA	Family	
	MOVILA	Family	Same as chairman
Comercial Mexicana	COMERCI	Family	Son
Leverpool	LIVEPOL	Family	Same as chairman
Televisa	TLEVISA	Family	Same as chairman
	CABLE	Family	
Gigante	GIGANTE	Family	Same as chairman
Xignux		Family	Same as chairman
Coppel	ALMACO	Family	Same as chairman
Vitro	VITRO	Family	Son

Note: Blank cell indicates that the CEO is a salaried manager.

Source: Annual reports of main listed companies of the groups.

known as the Directive Committee, which is composed of the nine top managers indicated in Fig. 15.4 with a doubled-lined frame. Its role is to command the operation of business, and it meets regularly and frequently. The CEO of Grupo Bimbo is the sole family member in the two committees (Hoshino 2005a: 192–4).

One of the facts that suggests the importance of salaried executive managers in top management is that the rewards paid to executive managers are significantly higher

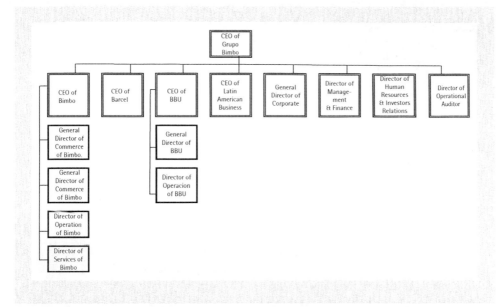

Figure 15.4 The executive committee of Grupo Bimbo, 2006

Note: ☐ Indicates members of Directive Committee.
Sources: Compiled by the author from annual report and interview.

than the honorary fees paid to directors of the board, according to the annual reports of companies submitted to the BMV (Hoshino 2005b: 22–3). This difference in rewards reflects a difference in participation in management in terms of both time and intensity, a situation that may produce an information gap between board members and executives. Although the board of directors has the final say in decision-making, top managers hold countervailing influence based on this information gap.

Another fact that suggests the increasing importance of salaried executive managers is that their withdrawal is considered as a risk for business. Comments to this effect are included in the risk factors for investors revealed in the annual reports of GCARSO, ALFA, GMEXICO, TVAZTCA, and GIGANTE in 2006.

According to Lomnitz and Pérez-Lizaur (1987), in family businesses, family issues and management issues are often mixed up. In this system, the head of a firm is a patron, and it is considered the patron's obligation to offer employment to his relatives. Although this might be a widely diffused image of family businesses in Mexico, it seems inapplicable to the top management of today's largest business groups. According to Derossi (1977: 128, 137), who conducted a survey on 336 Mexican entrepreneurs at the end of 1960s, there was a decrease in family member participation and an increase in importance given to salaried managers in firms that had been more recently established and were bigger in scale and more modern in their activities. The trend to which Derossi referred has intensified since the 1980s, especially during the 1990s.

The increased participation of salaried executives in top management posts can be explained by two reasons. One is a limitation of human resources within the owner family. Relative to the scale of a business group, the human resource pool of an owner family is too small (Hoshino 2004: 23–4). Another reason is that highly qualified managers have become necessary. Groups tried hard to improve the quality of top management by training and promoting existing salaried employees and by recruiting managers in the labor market. At the same time, CEOs from owner families have also improved in quality through education and training. This was necessary not only in order to adapt to the competitive environment, but also to control the subordinate executive managers, who have been increasingly been recruited from qualified personnel (Hoshino 2005b: 32–5).

From this perspective, the control of the owner family is not as solid as it might otherwise seem. This conclusion makes us appreciate the importance for owner families of making their family members participate in their business as a CEO. The presence of a family CEO helps to close the information gap between top managers and the board of directors and to facilitate communication between the two parties (Hoshino 2005b: 20–4, 35).

15.6 CONCLUDING REMARKS

For large Mexican business groups, the years since the mid-1980s have been among the most troublesome and challenging years in their history. Liberalization of imports and deregulation of foreign direct investment, which were implemented as part of a neoliberal economic reform, had a severe impact on business because of intensified competition. Notwithstanding, large Mexican business groups continued to grow and to be predominant actors in the Mexican economy. How did they manage to grow in spite of this difficult economic environment?

The analysis in this chapter shows that there are two types of business groups that occupy predominant positions. One type comprises the business groups that had existed before: those that had developed in the period of ISI. They had to restructure their business drastically in order to adapt to the new economic environment. The other type is the newly emerged business group; such groups rose by exploiting business opportunities presented by this new environment. A common characteristic of these two types of business groups is their capacity to adapt.

However, this new environment also had some characteristics that were favorable for the restructuring and growth of business groups. One such element was an increased opportunity to acquire existing companies that were put up for sale because of privatization, the restructuring of business groups, or the separation of shares held by nationalized banks. Another favorable element was the increased access to funds raised on the international financial market because of the reform of the Mexican security market and an investment boom in emerging markets on a global scale. An additional favorable factor was the role of the Mexican government in paving the way for resolving the external debt problem and for restructuring business groups by means of FICORCA, bank loans, the implementation of the Neutral Investment Mechanism, and so on.

A common approach for adapting to the new economic environment was to globalize business activities. By export and direct investment, business groups extended their activities abroad. Such activity was supported by technological and marketing capabilities nurtured in the process of growth, capabilities that continued to evolve while the groups were competing in the global market. In order to boost competitiveness, groups contracted strategic alliances with foreign multinationals. To finance business restructuring and overseas expansion, they increased access to international financial markets, where they could raise funds at a reduced financial cost by combining various debt instruments.

Drastic restructuring notwithstanding, business groups maintain the principal characteristics consolidated in the 1970s, such as diversified business activities, hierarchical or pyramidal structure, and control by owner families although with some modifications.

In those business groups that implemented drastic restructuring because of the external debt problem in the early 1980s, businesses have been reduced and resources have been concentrated in selected sectors. However, the newly emerged business groups as well as some of the pre-existing business groups with sound financial conditions diversified their businesses by acquisitions of existing companies. In the period of ISI, business groups that had gained a monopolistic position in one business had the option of diversifying to another business for further growth. After the 1990s there was the further option of overseas expansion. Some business groups opted for geographical diversification instead of business diversification.

The control structure of business groups remains basically unchanged in the late 2000s. This can possibly be explained by the fact that such structures are not incompatible with growth. Businesses can be restructured by adding new companies to the lower tiers or by separating non-preferential subsidiaries from the group. If the growth of a subsidiary is very rapid, it is possible to spin off another subsidiary. Holding companies at the apex can function as fund-raisers and allocators, and also as coordinators of diversified businesses. The control structure, however, has been modified, in that foreign capital can now participate in the upper tiers of the structure after contracting the strategic alliance.

Business group ownership is still highly concentrated in the families of founders in the late 2000s. They continue to hold shares of the apex holding company. In order to secure a majority of votes, various instruments are used, instruments such as issuing shares with limited voting rights and/or restrictions on holders, making packages of shares, and issuing CPOs. Families also make use of holding companies and/or trusts for unifying votes from shares held by family members and for avoiding the dispersal of those shares. Nevertheless, some modifications in management practice can be observed. Salaried managers have begun to hold top positions in great numbers.

There is a division of roles between family members and salaried managers, in that the former directs and the latter executes. The control structure helps this division of roles. The human resource pool of the family tends to be small, relative to the scale of a group. By placing owner family members in key executive positions and salaried managers in subordinate positions, business groups aim to make an efficient use of the family's limited human resources and to improve management capacity. Whether owner families can maintain effective control over their business groups will largely depend on whether they can provide qualified managers from the family and whether they can maintain family cohesion, which tends to dissipate as time goes by.

References

Aspe, P. (1993). *Economic Transformation, the Mexican Way.* Cambridge, MA: MIT Press.

Babatz Torres, G. (1997). "Ownership Structure, Capital Structure, and Investment in Emerging Markets: The Case of Mexico." PhD dissertation presented to the Department of Economics of Harvard University.

Basave Kunhardt, J. (2006). "Desempeño exportador empresarial e impacto económico," in María de los Angeles Pozas (ed), *Estructura y dinámica de la gran empresa en México: cinco estudios sobre su realidad reciente.* Mexico: El Colegio de México, 111–46.

Brandenburg, F. (1964). *The Making of Modern Mexico.* Englewood Cliffs, NJ: Prentice-Hall.

Camp, R. A. (1989). *Entrepreneurs and Politics in Twentieth-Century Mexico.* New York: Oxford University Press.

Cemex (2007). *Reporte anual que se presenta de acuerdo con las disposiciones de caracter general aplicables a las emisoras de valores y a otros participantes del mercado de valores por el año terminado el 31 de diciembre de 2006.* Mexico: Cemex.

Cordero, S., and Santín, R. (1977). "Los grupos industrials: una nueva organización económica en México," *Cuadernos del CES*, 23. Mexico: El Colegio de México.

Derossi, F. (1977). *El empresario mexicano.* México: Universidad Nacional Autónoma de México (originally published as *The Mexican Entrepreneur*, Paris: OECD, 1971).

DESC (1998). *DESC 25 años de historia.* Mexico: DESC.

Expansión (2007). "500 empresas más importantes de México" (June 25 – July 9: 176–95.

Garrido, C. (1999). "El caso mexicano," in D. Chudnovsky et al. (eds.), *Las multinacionales latinoamericanas: sus estratégias en un mundo globalizado.* Buenos Aires: Fondo de Cultura Económica de Argentina, 165–258.

Granovetter, M. (2005). "Business Groups and Social Organization", in J. N. Smelser and R. Swedberg (eds.), *The Handbook of Economic Sociology.* Princeton: Princeton University Press, 429–50.

Haber, S. H. (1989). *Industry and Underdevelopment: The Industrialization of Mexico, 1890–1940.* Stanford: Stanford University Press.

Hoshino, T. (1990). "Corporate Groups in Mexico: High Growth and Qualitative Change in the 1970s to the Early 1980s," *Developing Economies*, 28/3: 302–28.

Hoshino, T. (1993). "The Alfa Group: The Decline and Resurgence of a Large-Scale Indigenous Business Group in Mexico," *Developing Economies*, 31/4: 511–34.

Hoshino, T. (1996). "Privatization of Mexico's Public Enterprises and the Restructuring of the Private Sector," *Developing Economies*, 34/1: 34–60.

Hoshino, T. (1997). "Adaptation of Mexican Companies to the New Economic Environment," *Transformation of the Business Sector under Economic and Political Reforms: The Case of Mexico*, Joint Research Program Series, 121 (mimeo). Tokyo: Institute of Developing Economies, 17–48.

Hoshino, T. (2001a). *Industrialization and Private Enterprises in Mexico*. Chiba: Institute of Developing Economies-Japan External Trade Organization.

Hoshino, T. (2001b). "Keizai gurobaruka to mekisiko minkan bumon no saihen (Structural Changes of Mexican Private Sector in the Era of Globalization)," *Azia keizai*, 42/5: 2–36.

Hoshino, T. (2004). "Family Business in Mexico: Responses to Human Resource Limitations and Management Succession." Discussion Paper, 12, Chiba: Institute of Developing Economies–Japan External Trade Organization.

Hoshino, T. (2005a). "Mekisiko ni okeru familii Bijinesu no keieisha, purofiru no henka to sono haikei" (Executive Managers of Family Business in Mexico: Changing Profile and its Background), in H. Taeko (ed.), *Familii Bijinesu no Top Management, Ajia to Raten America ni okeru Kigyou Keiei* (Top Management of Family Business: Business Administration in Asia and Latin America). Tokyo: Iwanami Shoten, 157–204.

Hoshino, T. (2005b). "Executive Managers in Large Mexican Family Businesses." Discussion Paper, 40. Institute of Developing Economies–Japan External Trade Organization, Chiba.

Hoshino, T. (2006). "Estructura de la propiedad y mecanismos de control de las grandes empresas familiars en México," in María de los Angeles Pozas (ed.), *Estructura y dinámica de la gran empresa en México: Cinco estudios sobre su realidad reciente*. Mexico: El Colegio de México, 112–76.

Jacobos, E. (1981). "La evolución reciente de los grupos de capital privado nacional," *Economía mexicana*, 3: 23–44.

Khanna, T., and Yafeh, Y. (2007). "Business Groups in Emerging Markets: Paragons or Parasites?" *Journal of Economic Literature*, 45: 331–93.

Leff, N. H. (1974). "El espíritu de empresas y la organización industrial en los paises menos desarrollados: Los grupos," *El Trimestre Económico*, 41 (July–Sept.), 521–41.

Lomnitz, L., and Pérez-Lizaur, M. (1987). *A Mexican Elite Family, 1820–1980: Kinship, Class and Culture*. Princeton: Princeton University Press.

Peñolosa Webb, T. (1989). "La banca mexicana: Situación actual y perspectivas frente a la apertura de los servicios financieros," *Comercio exterior*, 39/6: 512–34.

Salas-Porras, A. (1998). "Estratégias de las empresas mexicanas en sus procesos de internacionalización," *Revista de la Cepal*, 65: 133–53.

Tavares, M. (2007). "Outward FDI and the Competitiveness of Latin American Firms," in R. Grosse and L. F. Mesquita (eds.), *Can Latin American Firms Compete?* Oxford: Oxford University Press.

Vidal, G. (2000). *Grandes empresas, economía y poder en México*. Mexico: Plaza y Valdes and Universidad Autónoma Metropolitana.

Group 3. The Middle East, Eastern Europe, and Africa

CHAPTER 16

BUSINESS GROUPS IN ISRAEL

KONSTANTIN KOSENKO
YISHAY YAFEH

16.1 INTRODUCTION

BUSINESS groups of various forms and types have existed in Israel nearly since its independence. This chapter, which is based on a newly constructed and unique database, examines their emergence, ownership structure, diversification, and historical evolution. Israel differs from most countries in which business groups are present and constitutes a rare and intriguing case for academic research on this organizational form for several reasons. First, the traditional view that groups make up for missing institutions (for example, underdeveloped financial markets or incomplete labor market institutions, and so on) cannot easily explain the presence of groups in contemporary Israel, a high-income country that also ranks highly in most of the commonly used measures of rule of law and institutional quality. Nevertheless, despite its developed institutional structure, the Israeli economy is home to a number of large and diversified business groups (primarily family controlled), which are often pyramidal in structure, where an ultimate (individual) owner maintains control over a large number of both public and private companies.

A second reason for studying Israeli business groups is that Israel offers an unusual example of a very high turnover rate of economic and business elites—unlike most business groups in other countries, the most powerful groups in Israel of the early twenty-first century did not exist at all in the early 1990s. By contrast, 'old' groups (dating back to the early phases of the state) have mostly disintegrated.

Yet another reason to study business groups in Israel is the existence of certain features that may have affected the formation and evolution of groups: governments in Israel have a history of aggressive involvement in the economy and ties to the business elites, on the one hand, and an agenda of liberalization and privatization, on the other. In addition, the economic environment in Israel combines fast and recent economic growth, based especially on the high-technology sectors, with mass migration (primarily from the former Soviet Union) and a high degree of integration into the global economy. The extent to which these factors affect the prevalence and performance of groups has never been explored.

If standard arguments on the emergence of business groups against the background of underdeveloped market institutions seem inadequate for the Israeli case, what can account for the presence and growth of groups and what is their economic role? In this chapter we hope to offer preliminary answers to this puzzle. The study begins with a brief summary of the relevant institutional and economic characteristics of Israel, and proceeds to provide a broad historical overview of Israel's business groups, focusing primarily on forces that facilitated their growth, and on the evolution of privately owned business groups in parallel to the demise of government-controlled ones. We also discuss in this section the privatization and ownership changes since 1990 and the evolution of Israel's business elite. Following the historical overview, we present a detailed picture of the major business groups in Israel, their economic activity, ownership and control structure, and performance using panel data on 650 public companies from 1995 to 2005. We define a business group as a group where at least three public companies are controlled by the same (ultimate) shareholder. In doing so, we identify some 20 business groups controlling about 160 listed companies and close to a half of the total stock-market capitalization. These groups are family controlled, highly diversified, and often pyramidal in structure. We also find that group affiliation has no significant impact on accounting profitability, but that it is associated with lower market valuation. In part, this seems to be due to conflicts between controlling and minority shareholders; and, in part, this may reflect the fact that, in a developed economy, where external (financial and other) markets are developed, business groups have no advantage in allocating resources internally. We discuss these issues, as well as the possible reasons for the continued existence of groups in Israel in the last section, which concludes the chapter.

16.2 INSTITUTIONAL AND HISTORICAL BACKGROUND

16.2.1 Israel: An institutional and economic overview

An important theme in the literature on business groups is that their presence often reflects institutional deficiencies in the environment in which they operate (Khanna and Yafeh 2007). Thus, business groups may make up for missing economic institutions, which could range from financial markets to labor training institutions and contract enforcement. Groups may also take advantage of underdeveloped institutions in order to hurt minority shareholders—a phenomenon often referred to as "tunneling" (see Johnson et al. 2000). In addition, underdeveloped institutions may enable groups to influence the government and become "entrenched" (Morck et al. 2005). Therefore, before proceeding to the discussion of business groups in Israel, it is important to describe the institutional features of the Israeli economy—the purpose of this brief discussion is both to serve as a comparison between Israel and other institutional environments in which groups operate, and to argue that contemporary Israel is highly developed institutionally, so that common explanations for the ubiquity of business groups against the background of institutional voids cannot be easily applied in this context.

The Israeli economy in the early twenty-first century is an integral part of the developed world. The country's per capita GDP (on a purchasing power parity basis, according to the International Monetary Fund) is ranked 34th out of over 180 countries, lower than that of wealthy West European economies, but significantly higher than that of East European countries, all emerging economies, and even some of the old members of the European Union.[1] The Israeli economy's performance is especially impressive in the rapidly growing high-tech sectors—by some measures Israel has one of the world's highest concentrations of venture capital activity and investment (Mayer et al. 2005). In addition to being a high-income country with a developed high-tech sector, Israel has a well-developed financial system, both in terms of the size of the banking system and the stock market and in terms of high-quality regulation (La Porta et al. 2006). Israel's financial system in the 2000s is far more advanced than it was even in the early 1990s: globalization and the massive influx of foreign investors, as well as dramatic structural reforms in the financial system, have helped change the system beyond recognition to the extent that, in some respects (for example, disclosure requirements), Israel's financial market institutions are on par with those of some of the leading common-law countries. Israel also ranks highly in business openness, political freedom, and indices of "Doing Business." Against this backdrop, the ownership structure of Israeli firms seems puzzling: listed Israeli firms are characterized by very high ownership concentration—about 60 percent of the shares are typically held by a controlling block, a figure that is high in comparison with that of most (large) economies in Europe and North America. As will become evident later in the chapter, many of these tightly controlled firms are affiliated with pyramidal business groups.

---

[1] See www.imf.org/external/pubs/ft/weo/2008/01/weodata/index.aspx Figures refer to 2007.

The preceding facts suggest that missing or underdeveloped market institutions cannot easily account for the concentration of ownership and for the persistence of business groups in Israel in the first decade of the twenty-first century. Is this phenomenon driven by cultural factors, political economy considerations, or economic factors other than poor institutions? We will argue that none of these arguments provides an easy answer. The following historical review is designed to serve as a starting point in addressing these issues.

16.2.2 The historical evolution of business groups in Israel since 1950[2]

The history and development of business groups in Israel (often referred to as "ownership groups") is comprised of several distinct time periods (see Fig. 16.1), when the nature of the groups, the extent of their activities, and their economic power were affected by extensive government involvement in the economy, by the intended policies and actions of state organizations, and the unintended consequences of these policies (especially in the early decades after independence and in

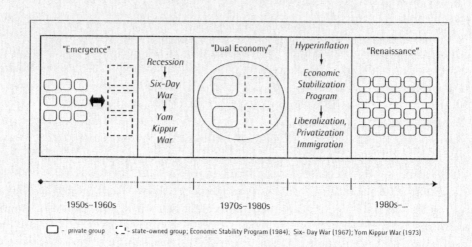

Figure 16.1 Evolution of business groups in Israel, 1950–90s: Historical milestones

---

[2] This section draws on a number of sources, in particular Aharoni (1976, 2006); and Kosenko (2008).

the mid-1980s), by extremely unusual changes in the business elite (in the 1960s and 1990s), by a financial crisis and far-reaching economic reforms (the Economic Stabilization Program of the mid-1980s), and by demographic changes (the heavy influx of immigrants in the 1990s). This section focuses on the main historical milestones of business groups in Israel.

16.2.2.1 *The early years*

The early years after the establishment of the State of Israel—when the first generation of the Israeli groups emerged—may be described as a period of overlapping spheres of influence associated with the ruling Labor Party and its political affiliates, the government, and state institutions. The lack of separation between the "State" as a concept and its leadership, as well as the agenda of nationalization of natural resources, water, land, and services on which the security of the state was dependent, created a situation in which heavy government involvement took place in almost all areas of economic activity, leading immediately to a high level of economic concentration. The fact that local capital markets were de facto under full government control made it almost impossible for small entrepreneurs to raise money from public sources and to establish their own businesses. Therefore most of the companies and business plants in that period were founded and controlled by three major ownership groups in the public sector: the government, the Jewish Agency, and the Histadrut (the association of labor unions).

With regard to the government's policy toward investment and the control of economic enterprises, various distinct periods can be identified: until the mid-1950s the government invested mainly in the establishment of utility and infrastructure companies. In the early 1960s the government's economic activity expanded, as it established construction and housing companies, banks, an insurance company, and many others. The Israeli government tried to promote economic growth through direct and indirect subsidization of firms in what were deemed to be "strategic industries," while privately owned companies, which could not meet their liabilities, were simply transferred to full government ownership. Thus the government's influence kept growing, and the range of its activities covered all the principal industries.

The policy of the Jewish Agency, the executive arm of the World Zionist Federation, in the first few years after its establishment was determined by its role as a "government in the making." At that time, the Jewish Agency performed extensive financial functions via the main financial institution of the Zionist Federation—Bank Leumi (the former Anglo Palestine Bank)—and, together with the government, invested in the country's infrastructure, agriculture, transport, and construction. With the establishment of the State of Israel, the resources of the Jewish Agency were directed toward the absorption of waves of immigrants. This reduced the sources of capital available to the Agency, and it had to diminish its holdings in most of the establishments under its control. During the next three decades most of the Jewish Agency's companies were transferred in various ways to the hands of the government or of the Histadrut.

The Histadrut (the main association of labor unions), using its economic arm, Hevrat ha-Ovdim, started setting up independent economically oriented enterprises soon after its establishment. In 1921, long before the establishment of the State of Israel, Bank Hapoalim (one of the two largest banks in present-day Israel) was established, followed two years later by the Solel Boneh construction company, which acted as an embryonic Ministry of Public Works. With Zionism and Socialism as its main objectives, profitability was helpful but not a goal in and of itself (Aharoni 1976)—the Histadrut undertook investments that were intended to "increase the welfare of Jewish workers" and to provide them with jobs, and, at the same time, serve the interests of the Zionist movement. This policy led to very close cooperation between the Histadrut and the Jewish Agency in infrastructure projects with economic, security, and political importance. It is important to note that the managerial staff of government, Jewish Agency, and Histadrut-affiliated companies in the first two decades after the State's establishment consisted primarily of politically promoted cadres or former military officers; there was no place for professional managers or market forces, and the assignment of managers was based primarily on political loyalty and affiliation with the ruling Labor Party. Indeed, according to Aharoni (2006), job rotation of managers was widely practiced in the public sector as a deliberate attempt to prevent the emergence of "managers" as a separate "class."

In addition to the three groups of economic enterprises associated with the government, the Jewish Agency, and the Histadrut, nine other privately owned business groups operated in the early decades of the State of Israel. These groups consisted mainly of small enterprises owned by a single family or by a few families in partnership. In contrast with "national interests" such as rapid economic development and mass job creation, which allegedly guided the public groups, privately owned businesses sought to make a profit. Most of their founders (who were also their managers) came from Europe and brought with them capital and professional experience they had accumulated abroad. Their activities covered most industries (see Table 16.1): banking and insurance, manufacturing and commerce, tourism, and more. Much like the government and the Jewish Agency, these family-controlled groups relied on sources of finance outside Israel and had diversified business interests. Vertical (pyramidal) control was not a common characteristic of the privately owned groups at the time, perhaps because of the symbiotic nature of the relationship between the government and the business sector, which led to a preference for a cross-shareholding pattern of ownership. Generally the interests of the state and of privately owned groups coincided, and this became evident when they jointly established large economic enterprises (for example, Klal, the Industrial Development Bank, the Eilat Pipeline Company, Delek, and the Israel Corporation), which, through their investments in a range of companies, constituted the "gravity centers" of Israel's economic activity (Aharoni 1976). Financial investment in these enterprises was very attractive, as their "joint" nature constituted an implied guaranteed profit and insurance to privately owned business groups. The government,

Table 16.1 Distribution of business groups affiliated firms by industry, 1966

Industry		Government	Jewish Agency	Histadrut	Elran group	Discount Bank	Central Company	Williams group	Africa-Israel Investments	Meir group	Miami group	Saharov group	P.A.C
Agriculture	Field crops	*	***	***	*						*		*
	Livestock	***	*	**									
Manufacturing	Food	*	**	***	*	*		*	*	*		*	
	Textiles	*	**	*		*	*	*		*			
	Clothing		*	*	*			*				*	
	Furniture			*									
	Paper			*									
	Printing and publishing			**									
	Leather products		*										
	Rubber products	*	*	**	*								*
	Industrial chemicals	**											
	Mineral non-metallic products	*	**	**		*				*			*
	Diamonds	*	*			*							
	Basic metal	*	*	*	*	*	*	*					
	Metal products	*	*	***		*							
	Machinery		*	*		**							
	Electronic components	*	**	**			*						
	Transportation	*		*			*			*			*
	Others	*	*	****			**	*	*				
Other	Real-estate	****	**	***		*	**	*	*	*		**	**
	Mining	**	*	**									

(continued)

Table 16.1 Continued

Industry		Government	Jewish Agency	Histadrut	Elran group	Discount Bank	Central Company	Williams group	Africa-Israel Investments	Meir group	Miami group	Saharov group	P.A.C
Banking	Trade	***	***	****	*	*	*	*		*	*	*	**
	Banks	***	**	**	*	*	**	*		*			
	Investment Companies	***	***	***	**	*	**	*	*	*	*	*	
	Non-bank loan providers	*	**	***			*	*		*			*
	Insurance	*			***	*		*	*			*	*
	Underwriters		*			*							
	Holding companies	**	*	****		*	*	*					

Source: Aharoni (1976): *1–4 companies; **5–9 companies; ***10–15 companies; ****more than 15 companies.

which dictated the business course of these joint formations by providing direct support, licenses, and favored contracts, was not interested in economic profits and viewed the private groups as a tool to spur economic growth. At the same time, privately owned business groups, while cooperating with the government in these ventures, diversified their business portfolios, relying on the government's implicit support. In contrast with the prevalent cooperation with the government, cooperation among the privately owned groups themselves in the 1950s and 1960s was not common,[3] and there was little evidence of the existence of broad networks or social ties among the controlling families. Nevertheless the fact that the boards of the "gravity centers" consisted of the representatives from all the existing business groups may suggest that these centers played a major role in the exchange of information and the creation of business ties among early privately owned groups.

16.2.2.2 *The 1960s and 1970s*

The devaluation at the beginning of the 1960s and the recession that started in 1966 had a profound effect on the ownership of the Israeli groups. Against the background of the inter-generational transition that took place in the management of the private companies, old disputes both within controlling families and between business partners resurfaced and even intensified. In those years many companies were sold, and the ownership map in Israel changed—as early as the mid-1960s the private sector was left with only two of the nine initial groups. Private-sector companies were sold mainly to those who had the financial resources to acquire them—either foreign investors or Histadrut-related companies. This wave of mergers and takeovers created a certain duality in the economy, with many small businesses existing side by side with several large companies controlled by the public sector. According to previous studies (e.g. Bichler and Nitzan 1996), during these years the Israeli dual economy was characterized by a "big economy" of about fifty firms, surrounded by a perimeter of a "small economy" comprising the rest of the private sector. As a result of these processes, new business groups began to emerge and to strengthen their influence and presence on the local stage.

In the late 1960s, business groups maintained their position and increased their economic strength against the background of the widespread construction activity of the defense industry following the 1967 war. Most of the defense-related companies were closely related to state-owned business or to other groups: for example, the IDB group (controlled at the time by the Recanati and Carasso families) had a stake in Elbit—one of the major providers of avionics military technology; the Histadrut-controlled Koor conglomerate owned Tadiran, Soltam, and Telrad—major suppliers of military and defense-related products. Hence, Israel's economic growth, much of which was due to defense-related industries in the late 1960s and early 1970s, boosted the rapid expansion of these groups (Maman 1999). The role of business groups in the economy became even more pivotal during the "the lost decade" and the hyperinflation period of 1974–84. This

---

[3] An exception is the (small) Elran group, which owned about half of its companies jointly with other privately owned groups.

period generated conditions for growth and increased the profitability and power of the big business groups. Direct incentives and capital subsidies, cost-plus procurement contracts, and windfall profits from the government's preferential lending practices—all contributed to an impressive increase in the size of the largest business enterprises, despite the negative effects of economic stagnation on profitability of the business sector as a whole (Bruno and Meridor 1991; Shalev 1996). Indeed, the defense and financial sectors, which constituted the core of most of the groups, were the only two economic sectors that continued to expand during this period.

As a result of these processes, three types of business groups emerged as dominant in the Israeli economy, starting in the late 1970s: the manufacturing-centered Koor group (Histadrut controlled), the bank-based Hapoalim (Histadrut controlled) and Leumi groups (initially Jewish Agency controlled, later government controlled), and the diversified family-controlled IDB and Eisenberg groups. Most of them consisted of many firms, which had an independent legal status and separate management and boards of directors, and were owned directly by holding companies, which, in turn, were owned by the parent firm in each group. This pattern of vertical-pyramidal control became a distinctive feature of all Israeli groups around this time period (Maman 1999). Starting in the late 1970s these business groups became increasingly intertwined through a web of business, political, and kinship ties. The government, on the other hand, gradually started to loosen its central role in the economy, moving from direct economic involvement to policies of indirect support and subsidization. Group-affiliated companies expanded quickly during the economically difficult 1970s and 1980s (Bichler and Nitzan 1996), so that by the mid-1980s much of Israel's economy was in the hands of a few group-affiliated companies, which accounted for a significant share of GDP, employed a large share of the labor force, and controlled most of the capital (Aharoni 1976, 2006; Maman 1999).

16.2.2.3 *The crisis of the 1980s and the transformation of the 1990s*

Israel's business groups faced a "dark" period in the mid-1980s and most of them encountered a severe crisis for two main reasons: first, the banking crisis (1983), which led to a de facto nationalization of the banks; and, second, the Economic Stabilization Program of 1985, which was designed primarily to curb inflation and led to deep cuts in the defense budget. The end of "related lending" and the adverse effects of defense cuts on business group profitability were early signs of the demise of the "old" business groups in Israel a decade later.

In the years following the Economic Stabilization Program there was a consensus regarding the need for a drastic change in economic policy-making in Israel (see Ben Bassat 2002): direct government ownership in the business sector, following the declared policy of privatization, declined from around 27 percent in 1985 to a mere 10 percent in 1993. Most government-owned companies were quickly transferred to the control of business groups: Israel Chemicals, which controlled most of Israel's mineral resources, was sold to the Eisenberg family; Shikun U-Pituach, the leading construction company, was split between the Klal conglomerate, the Eisenberg family, and Bank Hapoalim. Klal itself became a partnership jointly owned by the IDB (Recanati family) business group and the government-controlled Bank Hapoalim.

The privatization and the liberalization of the late 1980s were soon followed by a very large influx of immigrants, which, together with the change in government attitudes and new opportunities for expansion in the construction and infrastructure sectors, precipitated a profound transformation in the ownership and structure of the existing business groups. By the end of the 1990s not a single existing group managed to maintain its 1960s and 1970s size and structure; in fact, most of the old groups ceased to exist, at least under the same ownership (Aharoni 2006).

The most dramatic transformation took place in the Histadrut-controlled group of companies, which virtually disappeared in the 1990s: a combination of a decline in labor union membership, a profound change in social values and attitudes, and economic constraints forced the Histadrut to sell most of the companies under its control (including Koor, its flagship holding company) to private hands. The Jewish Agency group was also forced to forgo its control of large businesses (for example, Africa-Israel and Rasko construction companies), which were sold to private, family-controlled groups or transferred to Bank Leumi, which, at the time, was government controlled.

A central feature in the economic transformation in the 1990s was the privatization of the banking sector. Of the largest five banks—Hapoalim, Leumi, Discount, Mizrahi, and First International—only the latter was family controlled (by the Safra family), while the other four were controlled by the state following the banking crisis of 1983. As part of the government's efforts to privatize its holdings in the banking system, the controlling stakes in Bank Mizrahi were sold to the Ofer and Wertheim families, and control of Bank Hapoalim was sold to the Arison family (a few other families acquired smaller stakes). The large holding companies such as IDB and the Israel Corporation were also sold to new owners, all of whom represented "new wealth"—families that had not been part of the old economic establishment. At around the same time period, the government imposed restrictions on the economic activities of banks, which were forced to sell some of their equity stakes in major non-financial companies. Many of these shares were sold to the same families, so that the privatization policy tended to increase economic concentration in the Israeli economy, at least in the non-high-tech sectors. In addition to the declining economic importance of the government, the Jewish Agency and the Histadrut, all the privately owned family groups of the 1960–70s disappeared during the 1990s and early 2000s, in part because of their inability to adjust to new market conditions, and in part because of natural succession factors and the inability or unwillingness of the descendants to maintain the family business. Their main holdings were sold to new, much wealthier, family groups, whose business expansion was helped by generous bank credit. An interesting illustration of these changes was the acquisition of IDB, a holding company, which was a central part of the Recanati family business group, by Mr Nohi Dankner, one of the rising new tycoons, in 2003. Using bank finance provided by Bank Leumi (controlled by the government) and Mivtachim (a pension fund), Mr Dankner managed to take over IDB from the Recanati family, which was in decline, and established it as a central company in his new and expanding business empire.

Another dramatic economic and social change in Israel starting in the early 1990s was the rapid rise of the high-tech industries, which created a new generation of wealthy entrepreneurs, among whom only very few had any relations to family-owned pyrami-dal groups. The business interests of high-tech entrepreneurs were generally narrowly focused in comparison with those of non-high-tech business groups, and mostly concentrated on stand-alone innovative companies, rather than on creating diversified business empires. Perhaps the availability of venture capital funding, together with ultimate access to foreign (mostly US) stock markets, as well as the unique character-istics and business skills of the advanced technology sectors, may explain the relatively minor presence of business groups in the booming Israeli high-tech sector—clearly, the competitive advantage of groups was primarily elsewhere.

As a result of the changes of the 1980s and 1990s, a new, third generation, of business groups emerged. Business groups with pyramidal structures remained common throughout the 1990s and the first decade of the twenty-first century, but, in contrast with earlier business groups, most of the new ultimate owners today are entrepreneurs rather than government-related institutions and "old" families. This new generation of entrepreneurs emerged in the 1980s and 1990s and enjoyed considerable business knowledge, as well as experience and wealth, often created or inherited abroad. The new controlling families accumulated power during the 1990s, taking over a variety of business interests and gaining control of newspapers and TV channels as well (Djan-kov et al. 2003; Aharoni 2006). New tycoons have become household names. Lev Levayev, for example, an immigrant from the former Soviet Union, who had amassed his wealth in the diamond trade, took over one of the largest construction companies, Africa–Israel, which had previously been under government (Bank Leumi) control. The Arison family is associated with the biggest Israeli bank—Hapoalim. Other families—Dankner, Tshuva, Ofer, and others—now control Israel's largest holding company (IDB, part of the Dankner group), the largest oil company (Delek, con-trolled by Mr Tshuva), and the largest shipping company (Zim, part of the Ofer group). By the end of the 1990s, the old business elites had been replaced by new ones, and a new era for business groups in Israel was ushered in. Table 16.2 presents a graphical summary of the evolution of business groups in Israel.

16.3 STRUCTURE, STRATEGY, AND PERFORMANCE OF BUSINESS GROUPS

The analysis in this section is based on a newly constructed dataset consisting of quarterly data for the 650 companies traded on the Tel Aviv Stock Exchange (TASE)

Table 16.2 History of the Israeli business groups

Period	Groups	Sector	Affiliated firms	Principal activities	Management	Major companies	Origins
The 1950s and the early 1960s	GOVERNMENT	State	145	All industries	Labor party members	El-Al, Israel Railways, Bezeq, Israel Electric Corp	1948
	JEWISH AGENCY FOR ISRAEL	State	122	All industries	Jewish Agency officials	Bank Leumi, Rasko, Zim, Mekorot	1920
	THE HISTADRUT	State	305	All industries	Histadrut officials	Koor, Bank Hapoalim, Solel Bone, Tnuva, Mashbir	1920
	ELRAN GROUP	Private	15	Banking and finance	Family members	Bank Elran	1934, immigrants from Germany.
	DISCOUNT BANK	Private	35	Banking and finance	Professional + family members	Bank Discount, Bank Mercantil, Discount Investment, Barclays (Discount) Bank.	1935, immigrants from Greece.
	THE CENTRAL ISRAEL COMPANY	Private	40	Manufacturing/ trading/banking and finance/construction	Professional	Ordan, Swiss–Israel Bank	1944, partnership
	AFRICA – ISRAEL INVESTMENTS	Private	16	Construction/ insurance/ manufacturing	Professional	Migdal	1934, South African Jews
	WILLIAMS GROUP	Private	12	Finance/ manufacturing	Family + professional	Bank Israel–Britannia	1937, immigrants from England

(continued)

Table 16.2 Continued

Period	Groups	Sector	Affiliated firms	Principal activities	Management	Major companies	Origins
	MIAMI GROUP	Private	20	Hotels/oil/ manufacturing/ trading	Professionals	King David Hotel, Continental Pipelines	1949, partnership
	MEIR GROUP	Private	8	Investment	Family	Meir Holding Company, Migdal Shalom	1921, immigrants
	SAHAROV GROUP	Private	15	Manufacturing/ construction	Family	Saar, Plywood Israel	1904
	P.A.C	Private	20	Construction/ manufacturing/ trading	Professional	Gav-Yam, Israel Corporation of America	1921, USA Jews
The late 1960s–mid 1980s	GOVERNMENT	State	~1000	All industries	Labor Party members	Jewish Agency for Israel group holdings	1948
	THE HISTADRUT	State	~2000	All industries	High rank members	Koor, Bank Hapoalim	1920
	IDB (former Discount)	Private	~30	Diversified	Family, professional	P.A.C. group holdings, discount bank, Elbit	1970
	EIZENBERG GROUP	Private	~10	Investment/real–estate/shipping	Family	Israeli/Zim/Israel Chemicals	1968
The 90s	IDB (Dankner Group)	Private	20	Diversified	Family, professional	Klal, Discount Investment, Selcom, Koor	2003
	LEVAEV GROUP	Private	7	Real estate/ Investment	Family, professional	Africa–Israel	1996
	OFER GROUP	Private	4	Banking/ manufacturing/ shipping	Family, professional	Israeli Zim/Israel Chemicals	1999
	DELEK GROUP (TSHUVA)	Private	11	Real-estate/oil/high-tech	Family, professional	Delek Israel	1991–4

Period	Groups	Sector	Affiliated firms	Principal activities	Management	Major companies	Origins
	FISHMAN GROUP	Private	3	Real-estate/telecommunications	Family, professional	Jerusalem Economy Ltd, Industrial Buildings	1989
	ARISON GROUP	Private	3	Banking and finance/real-estate	Professional	Bank Hapoalim, Housing and Construction	1991–99
	BRONFMAN-ALON GROUP	Private	3	Banking/food and retail chains	Family, professional	Bank Discount, Blue Square	1989
	BINO GROUP	Private	3	Oil and gas/real estate/banking	Professional	Paz Oil, FIBI	1999
	NIMRODI GROUP	Private	7	Real-estate/media/hotels	Family, professional	ILDC, Maariv	1989–1992
	AKIROV GROUP	Private	3	Real-estate/telecommunications	Family, professional	Alrov	1983
	GOLDSTEIN GROUP	Private	8	Computers	Professional	Formula	1982
	BOROWITZ GROUP	Private	3	Air industry	Professional	Knafaim	1989
	FEDERMAN GROUP	Private	3	Electronics	Professional	Elbit	1989
	ZELIKAND GROUP	Private	4	Electronics/real-estate	Family, professional	Elco, Electra	1992

Other Groups: Oren, Bar, Shahar-Kaz, Wertheim, Eyal, Saban, Habmurger. – All are diversified, vertically controlled private groups.

Note: The number of affiliated companies in the 1990s – includes only listed firms.

Source: Aharoni (1976); authors' calculations, see Kosenko (2008); www.nfc.co.il

during the eleven-year period 1995–2005 (an unbalanced panel of about 27,000 observations; see Kosenko 2008 for a more detailed description). Using reports to the TASE and the Israel Securities Authority (ISA), we collect, for each firm, financial data from its financial statements, as well as data on ownership structure (ownership concentration and the equity stakes of controlling shareholders and managers). Using data from the Company Registrar, we also collect ownership data for private companies that hold stakes in publicly traded firms; this information is used to construct equity ties within business groups where some companies are listed while others are privately held. Finally, we use mandatory reports to the ISA to derive information on family ties between shareholders in public companies. These data are supplemented by various media sources, so that we are able to trace ownership stakes of related parties.

16.3.1 Ownership and control

We define a controlling shareholder as a shareholder whose equity stake satisfies the following two conditions: (1) it is at least 25 percent; and (2) it is higher than the combined holdings of the second and third largest shareholders. This definition is more stringent than the definitions commonly used in the literature, where a 20 percent equity stake (by a family or another entity) is often regarded as sufficient to guarantee control. The reason for using a stricter definition is the extreme concentration of ownership in Israel, where controlling and other large shareholders typically hold at least 60 percent of the equity. Therefore, the figures reported in this study are probably an underestimate of the extent of family and group control in Israel in comparison with other countries.

Using data on individual marital ties and on privately held companies, we identify the ultimate (direct or indirect) owners of each public company in the sample and classify them, following La Porta et al. (1999), into five categories: (1) an individual or a family; (2) a private corporation; (3) the government; (4) joint ownership (trusts, partnerships, etc.); and (5) foreign ownership. A sixth category consists of companies for which no shareholder satisfies the two criteria, so that ultimate ownership and control cannot be established (this does not necessarily imply that they are widely held). A business group is defined as a group where at least three public companies are controlled by the same (ultimate) shareholder.

Three-quarters of the firms for which an ultimate owner can be identified (or about one half of the entire sample) are controlled by an individual or a family, a figure that has remained stable over time. About one-sixth of all publicly traded companies in Israel are affiliated with one of twenty-one business groups; close to half of the 100 larger Tel Aviv companies are group affiliated, and an even larger fraction of the 25 largest Tel Aviv companies—as in other countries, group-affiliated companies tend to be relatively large (Khanna and Yafeh 2007).

Fig. 16.2 describes the market share of business groups from 1996 to 2006. Note that the pharmaceutical giant Teva (which is not group-affiliated) accounted, at

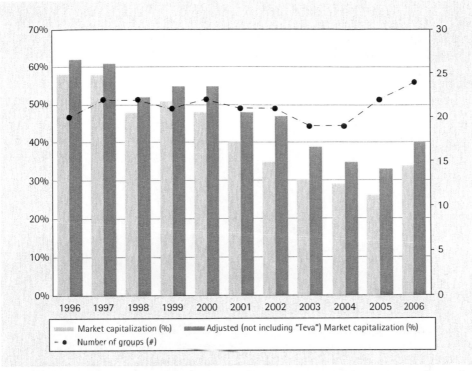

Figure 16.2 Number of groups (right axis) and their share in total stock-market capitalization (left axis), 1996–2006

Source: Authors' calculations, see Kosenko (2008).

times, for up to 20 percent of total stock-market value. Examining the market share of business groups out of total market value, excluding Teva (denoted as 'adjusted market capitalization'), suggests that, as of 2006, group firms, which have remained roughly constant in number, accounted for about 40 percent of total stock-market value. The corresponding figure for the 1990s was even higher, but in recent years, there is a declining trend. The ten largest groups—all of which are family owned—account for nearly a third of total market value, placing ownership concentration in Israel among the highest in the Western world, as described in Fig. 16.3 (see also Claessens et al. 2000; Faccio and Lang 2002).

As for group structure, Fig. 16.4 displays the pyramidal organization of the largest (in terms of number of affiliated companies) Israeli group, IDB. This structure is common: about 80 percent of all group-affiliated companies in Israel are part of pyramidal structures similar to that of IDB. Pyramids vary substantially in size, with the largest pyramids containing as many as seven levels. Pyramids vary considerably in structure as well: some have the core (largest) group companies located at the top, others at the lowest levels, and some in between. This suggests that different group owners may have different preferences regarding risk and possibly also the treatment of minority shareholders, although an in-depth examination of the determinants of

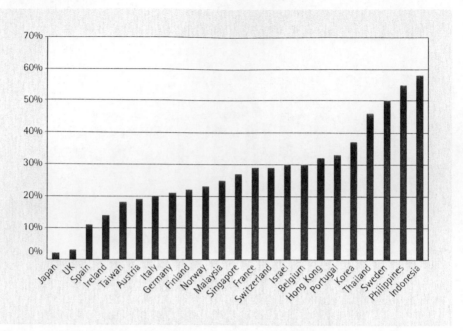

Figure 16.3 The market share of the ten largest families, 1990s

Source: Faccio and Lang (2002) for European countries; Claessens et al. (2000) for Asian countries.

the location of firms within a pyramid is beyond the scope of the present chapter. Finally, pyramids vary also in the extent of the gap between control and cash-flow rights: in the most extreme cases (in firms located in low levels of group pyramids), full control rights are accompanied by a mere 3 percent stake of the cash-flow rights.

A final organizational characteristic of business groups is diversification and the spread of their economic activity: Israel's contemporary business groups are present in all the main sectors in the economy, with relatively smaller group representation in the high-technology industries (Fig. 16.5). The market share of group-affiliated companies in the financial sectors (banking, mortgage banking, insurance, and so on) is roughly twice as high as in manufacturing, suggesting the centrality of finance in group activity. The largest Israeli groups (for example, IDB, Africa–Israel, and Delek) are highly diversified, with a presence in financial services, manufacturing, telecommunications, real estate, energy, construction, tourism, and other sectors. Even relatively small groups have well-diversified holdings (see Table 16.2). In general, a common feature of all the large groups is significant involvement in real-estate and construction activities both in Israel and abroad.

16.3.2 Corporate governance

Within the groups, changes have taken place in corporate governance, so that groups in the twenty-first century rely primarily on professional (rather than family)

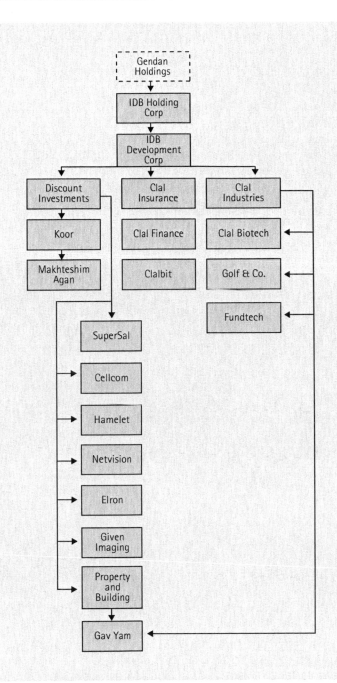

Figure 16.4 The IDB pyramid, 2006 (publicly traded companies only)

Source: Author's calculations—see Kosenko (2008).

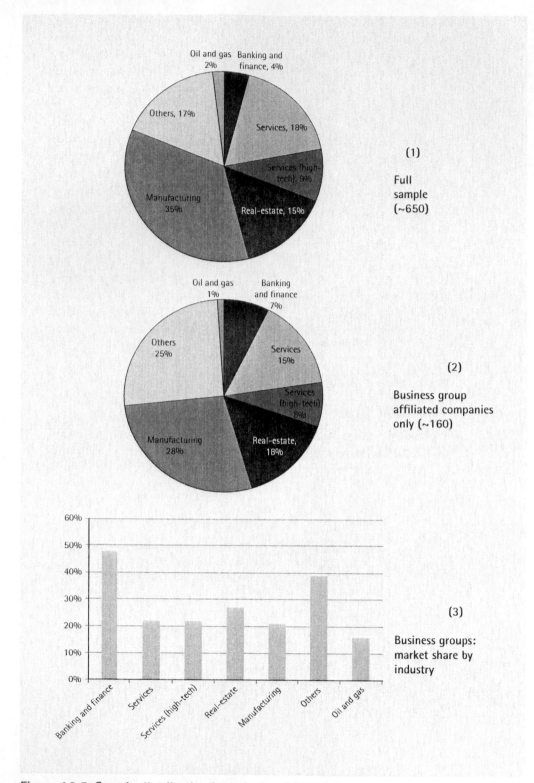

Figure 16.5 Sample distribution by industry, 1995–2005

Source: Author's calculations—see Kosenko (2008).

management to run group companies. The boards of the largest groups (for example, IDB, Delek, or Africa–Israel) and their management teams consist of highly trained and generally well-respected professionals, with an occasional representative of the controlling family on the board (for example, Ms. Zviya Levayev, the founder's daughter, in the Africa–Israel group), a feature that usually entails an uproar in the economic press. The group chairman is typically the controlling shareholder (for example, Mr Dankner in the IDB group, or Mr Levayev in the Africa–Israel group), and it is quite evident from the economic press that the overall strategy of the group is formulated by the controlling shareholder (for example, Mr Levayev's strategic decision on major investments in Russia by the Africa–Israel group) even though the execution of these strategic plans is carried out by professional managers.

Given this division of labor between the controlling shareholders and their appointed professional managers, and in view of the highly concentrated ownership of Israeli public companies, shareholder–manager conflicts are rare and typically resolved by tight monitoring of management—as predicted in the literature (see Shleifer and Vishny 1997), and by close cooperation between the ultimate owners and the managers of affiliated companies. Nevertheless, while some professional managers have worked in some of the groups for a long time, there have been occasional public conflicts between a few of them and the controlling families (for example, between Ms Arison, whose family controls Bank Hapoalim, and the chief professional manager of the group, Mr Nehama, who was forced to resign).

In contrast with the relatively "harmonious" relations between controlling families and professional managers in most groups, conflicts have occasionally arisen between the controlling shareholders and minority shareholders, whose interests have allegedly been compromised by related party transactions and conspicuous consumption of "perks" by group insiders. We return to this issue when we evaluate the performance of group-affiliated companies.

16.3.2 International expansion, high leverage, and other group strategies

The third generation of Israeli business groups has adopted a strategy of rapid diversification using internal capital markets and, more importantly, has levered the close relationships between groups and the banking sector to increase the competitiveness and market power of affiliated firms in different fields of economic activity. Business groups and their controlling tycoons have also managed to raise large amounts of money on the nascent corporate bond market, where a sequence of pension-related reforms has increased dramatically the demand for corporate debt by institutional investors.

The cheap finance raised by groups, largely on the basis of the personal reputation of the controlling parties, has often been used to support a strategy of internationalization and during the 1990s and early 2000s many groups expanded aggressively beyond Israel's borders. Foreign interests of Israeli business groups today typically involve very large-scale operations in real estate and construction throughout most of Eastern Europe, where, in some countries, they dominate much of the commercial real-estate and construction scene. Apparently, many of Israel's business groups possess some sort of comparative advantage in "getting things done" in mega-real estate projects in poorly regulated emerging markets (especially in Eastern Europe).

International diversification by Israel's business groups has not been limited to real estate and construction in the newly opened economies of Eastern Europe. Some groups have been involved in operations in oil, insurance, real estate, and other industries in Western Europe, South America, Asia, and the USA. As an illustration of this trend, the internationalization of the Delek group (one of the largest business groups) has been primarily driven by its construction/real-estate and energy companies, which are present in the USA, Canada, the UK, Germany, and Switzerland among the developed economies as well as, more recently, in India. According to press reports, the group is exploring entry possibilities into China and Vietnam. Nevertheless, the overwhelming reliance of many of Israel's groups on debt finance from domestic banks and institutional investors (through the bond market) and on real-estate-related global investments has exposed the vulnerability of some of the largest groups (for example, Africa–Israel), whose continued existence is now in jeopardy, both because of the difficulty it faces in paying off its enormous debts and because its real-estate investments appear less promising today than they did some years ago.

It is interesting to note that the changing economic scene, starting in the the 1990s, has also changed the interaction between business groups: unlike their predecessors, Israel's new tycoons have expanded inter-group business ties and social relations, which are reflected, for example, in direct and indirect interlocking ties between boards of directors. These ties have allegedly been used as a mechanism to increase their economic influence and market power, and occasionally to foster inter-group cooperation. For example, the Delek and IDB groups are jointly involved in a large-scale investment project in real-estate development in Las Vegas.

16.3.3 Performance of Israeli groups

Table 16.3, which presents sample statistics for group and non-group firms, suggests that average accounting profitability (ROA) is relatively high among group-affiliated companies, but that their market valuation (market to book ratios) is low in comparison with that of unaffiliated firms. Group-affiliated companies are, on average, older and (much) larger, and more leveraged, and their growth rate is lower in comparison with non-group companies (these differences are all statistically significant). Not surprisingly, because of their pyramidal structure, the gap between control and cash-flow rights is higher in group firms than in other companies (for unaffiliated firms, the difference between control and cash-flow rights is calculated when a controlling block holds above 50 percent of the equity and thus has full (100 percent) control).

Table 16.3 Sample statistics: Group-affiliated vs. unaffiliated firms, 1995–2005

Measures	Affiliated (~160)	Unaffiliated (~490)	Statistically significant difference?
ROA (return on assets, %)	2.13	1.5	Yes
TQ (market to book ratio)	1.15	1.24	Yes
Age (years since IPO)	14	10	Yes
Size (total assets in thousands NIS)	6,478,491	816,894	Yes
Leverage (debt to assets)	0.54	0.48	Yes
Average annual sales growth (1995–2005, %)	4	5.7	Yes
R&D to sales (%)	3	6	Yes
Dividend to sales (%)	0.1	0.05	Yes
Ownership (% of equity held by the controlling shareholder)	41.23	59.96	Yes
Wedge (control rights minus cash-flow rights)	60	40	Yes
TA100 (% of companies in the Tel-Aviv 100 Index)	53	47	–

Turning to multivariate regressions, we examine several specifications where the dependent variable is an accounting measure of performance, ROA (the results are similar when using other accounting profitability measures such as return on equity), and a stock-market-based performance measure, the ratio of market to book value. We include the following firm-specific control variables: firm size (log assets), firm age (number of years since the IPO), leverage (debt to assets), sales growth, dividend to sales ratio, R&D to sales, and a dummy variable denoting companies included in the Tel Aviv 100 index. We also control for ownership structure and include a group affiliation dummy, which is the main variable of interest, the percent of equity held by the controlling shareholders, the gap between control and cash-flow rights, the combined market value of all other group firms, and a Herfindahl–Hirschman index (HHI) for the extent of group diversification.

Table 16.4 presents the results. In columns (1) and (2) the dependent variable is ROA and columns (3) and (4) display similar regressions where the dependent variable is the market to book ratio. The main conclusion from these regressions is that, in comparison with unaffiliated companies, group-affiliated companies are not associated with significantly higher accounting profit rates; they are, however, associated with lower market valuations. Both accounting profitability and market value are positively associated with the ownership stake of the controlling shareholders. In line with the literature (see, e.g., Claessens et al. 2002), market value is negatively associated with the gap between control and cash-flow rights (although this pattern

Table 16.4 Group affiliation and performance regressions, quarterly data, 1995–2005

	ROA (1)	ROA (2)	Market to Book (3)	Market to Book (4)
Intercept	+	+	+	+
Group affiliation	−0.07	0.6	−0.28**	−0.37***
Ownership	0.008**	0.007**	0.001***	0.001***
Log (age)	0.12**	0.15**	−0.05***	−0.06***
Log (size)	0.33***	0.36***	−0.36***	−0.28***
Sales growth	0.19***	0.29***	0.014	0.02**
Leverage	−0.06	−0.001	0.001**	0.0007*
Dividend to sales (*1000)	−0.0043*	−0.002*	−0.004**	−0.004**
TA100 dummy	−0.14*	−0.2*	0.27***	0.4**
R&D intensity	−0.02	−0.06**	0.4**	0.7**
Group*Wedge		0.08**		−0.001***
Group*HHI		−0.19		−0.04
Period dummies	Yes	Yes	Yes	Yes
Industry dummies	Yes	Yes	Yes	Yes
R-adjusted	0.28	0.29	0.52	0.61

Notes: *** denotes statistical significance at the 1 % level, ** at 5%, * at 10%; for definitions of variables, see Table 16.3

is not observed in the ROA regressions). This may suggest that group firms are traded at a discount because of potential agency problems, which are perhaps due to their pyramidal structure, discussed above. An alternative interpretation for the group discount is that, in a developed economy like Israel, there is little economic justification for the existence of diversified business groups; this interpretation is not fully supported by the results, as the coefficient on group diversification is negative but not statistically significant. Finally, it is possible that the group discount is due to concerns about the stability of family ties within the groups and about the possibility that family control might increase the likelihood that management would not be chosen solely on the basis of merit; we do not have data to test this hypothesis.

16.4 DISCUSSION AND CONCLUDING REMARKS

This study has uncovered the following stylized facts: some 20 business groups control a large number of public companies in Israel (about 160 firms), valued at about 40 percent of the total stock-market capitalization. These business groups span all major industries, with a particularly strong presence in finance and real estate.

Group-affiliated companies tend to be larger, older, and more leveraged than other firms. Controlling for other firm attributes, group firms are not more profitable than other companies, but are traded at lower values.

Unlike the appearance of business groups in the early decades after the establishment of the State of Israel against the background of institutional and economic underdevelopment, the rise of the new business groups in the 1990s took place in an economically and institutionally developed economy, and their continued importance in a high-income country is puzzling. It is difficult to explain the rise and predominance of new diversified business groups by invoking cultural or political arguments: Israel (including the controlling shareholders of the new groups) is culturally diverse, and it is hard to point to a particular common set of values that could affect the formation of business groups. Politically, government favors and crony capitalism exist, of course, but it is difficult to imagine that these would be the dominant factors in the formation of business groups in a vibrant and open democratic society. The competitive capabilities of business groups are also unclear, and the financial crisis of 2007–8 has exposed the weakness of many of them. Their growth strategy, which has often been based on high leverage and risky real-estate investments abroad, portrays them as vulnerable, and the reputation and 'magic touch' of some of the controlling shareholders have not prevented a precipitous decline in the prices of both stocks and bonds of major business groups. This, in conjunction with their less than stellar performance since 2000, suggests that, so far, diversified business groups have "refused" to disappear from the landscape of the modern economy of contemporary Israel for reasons that are as yet poorly understood and could include family considerations, prestige, and the personal ego of the ultimate owners. There is little to suggest that they possess any clear capabilities and that economic motives propel their growth.

In terms of economic policy, the efficiency of the existing economic structure, where a large number of business groups are spread over some of the main (albeit mostly traditional) sectors, raises questions about the efficiency of resource allocation in the Israeli economy and about its exposure to shocks, some of which could arise because of micro-mismanagement of one of the large groups, which could have macroeconomic implications. In view of the current global crisis, these issues and, in particular, whether some of the groups are "too big to fail" and should be bailed out by the government, are discussed daily in the economic press.

We conclude with a brief comparison between the history of groups in Israel and in many other countries. The emergence of business groups in Israel, as well as their subsequent development, was the result of intertwined political and economic factors. The state itself, like other late-industrializing countries, was deeply involved in economic development and became a crucial factor in the emergence of early business groups. In this sense, Israel resembled many other emerging markets described in Khanna and Yafeh (2007). As in other countries, Israeli business groups typically enjoyed a mutually beneficial relationship with the government and often functioned as an implementation mechanism for developmental policies. As in other countries, this cooperation may have been, in part, politically motivated—in the context of Israel, a natural outcome of the government's attempt to guarantee the survival of Israel (Sadan 1985). However, in contrast with other countries, even in the 1950s and 1960s, when Israel's business groups emerged and economic institutions were weak and underdeveloped, Israel's business groups never directly replaced missing labor or capital-market institutions as is often argued (Khanna and Palepu 2000)—the training of labor and the allocation of capital were carried out directly by the government, although group diversification may have reflected some product market imperfections.

A second, more striking, difference between Israel and other countries where business groups exist is that Israel has experienced an unusually high rate of turnover of controlling shareholders—ownership of the largest groups has changed three times since Israel's independence. One possible (sociological) explanation for this unusually high turnover rate could be that, unlike many societies in Asia and Europe, Israel does not have a tradition of hierarchical long-term family dynasties or a family code of ethics. This may account for the relatively short life of early family groups in Israel and the inability or unwillingness of the second generation to maintain the family business. More generally, the high death rate of business groups in Israel, combined with the difficulty in pointing out their competitive strength and their vulnerability to the 2007–8 financial crisis, suggest that, in contrast with other countries, it is quite possible that business groups, or at least some of them, will not survive in the long run.

REFERENCES

AHARONI, Y. (1976). *Structure and Conduct in Israeli Industry.* Tel-Aviv: The Israel Institute of Business Research (in Hebrew).

AHARONI, Y. (2006). "The New Economic Elites," in E. Ben Raphael and Y. Sternberg (eds.), *New Elites in Israel.* Jerusalem: Bialik Institute (in Hebrew).

BEN BASSET, A. (2002) (ed.). *The Israeli Economy, 1985–1998: From Government Intervention to Market Economics.* Cambridge, MA: MIT Press.

BICHLER, S., and NITZAN, J. (1996). "From War Profits to Peace Dividends: The New Political Economy of Israel," *Capital and Class,* 60/3: 61–94.

BRUNO, M., and MERIDOR, L. (1991). "The Costly Transition from Stabilization to Sustainable Growth: Israel's Case," in M. Bruno, S. Fischer, E. Helpman, N. Liviatan, and L. Meridor (eds.), *Lessons of Economic Stabilization and its Aftermath.* Cambridge, MA: MIT Press: 241–75.

CLAESSENS, S., DJANKOV, S., and LANG, L. (2000). "The Separation of Ownership and Control in East Asian Corporations," *Journal of Financial Economics,* 58/1–2: 81–112.

CLAESSENS, S., DJANKOV, S., FAN, J., and LANG, L. (2002). "Disentangling the Incentive and Entrenchment Effects of Large Shareholdings," *Journal of Finance,* 57/6: 2741–71.

DJANKOV, S., McLEISH, C., NENOVA, T., and SHLEIFER, A. (2003). "Who Owns the Media?" *Journal of Law and Economics,* 46/2: 341–81.

FACCIO, M., and LANG, L. (2002). "The Ultimate Ownership of Western European Corporations," *Journal of Financial Economics*, 65/3: 365–95.

JOHNSON, S., LA PORTA, R., LOPEZ DE SILANES, F., and SHLEIFER, A. (2000). "Tunneling," *American Economic Review*, 90/2: 22–7.

KHANNA, T., and PALEPU, K. (2000). "Is Group Membership Profitable in Emerging Markets? An Analysis of Diversified Indian Business Groups," *Journal of Finance*, 55/2: 867–91.

KHANNA, T., and YAFEH, Y. (2007). "Business Groups in Emerging Markets: Paragons or Parasites?" *Journal of Economic Literature*, 45/2: 331–73.

KOSENKO, K. (2008). "Evolution of Business Groups in Israel: Their Impact at the Level of the Firm and the Economy," *Israel Economic Review*, 5/2: 55–93.

LA PORTA, R., LOPEZ-DE-SILANES, F., and SHLEIFER, A. (1999). "Corporate Ownership around the World," *Journal of Finance*, 54/2: 471–517.

LA PORTA, R., LOPEZ-DE-SILANES, F., and SHLEIFER, A. (2006). "What Works in Securities Laws," *Journal of Finance*, 61/1: 1–32.

MAMAN, D. (1999). "The Social Organization of the Israeli Economy: A Comparative Analysis," *Israel Affairs*, 5/2–3: 86–101.

MAYER, C., SCHOORS, K., and YAFEH, Y. (2005). "Sources of Funds and Investment Strategies of Venture Capital Funds: Evidence from Germany, Israel, Japan and the UK," *Journal of Corporate Finance*, 11/3: 586–608.

MORCK, R., D. WOLFENZON, and B. YEUNG (2005). "Corporate Governance, Economic Entrenchment, and Growth." *Journal of Economic Literature*, 43/3: 657–722.

SADAN, E. (1985). "National Security and National Economy," in Z. LANIR (ed.), *Israeli Security Planning in the 1980s: Its Politics and Economics.* Tel-Aviv: Tel Aviv University Press, 119–29 (in Hebrew).

SHALEV, M. (1996). "The Labor Movement in Israel: Ideology and Political Economy," in E. Goldberg (ed.), *The Social History of Labor in the Middle East.* Boulder, CO: West View Press, 131–63.

SHLEIFER, A., and VISHNY, R. (1997). "A Survey of Corporate Governance," *Journal of Fnance*, 52/2: 737–83.

CHAPTER 17

....

BUSINESS GROUPS
IN TURKEY

....

ASLI M. COLPAN

17.1 INTRODUCTION

....

THE present chapter aims to examine the evolution of the Turkish large-enterprise economy focusing on the family-owned diversified business groups. Turkey presents a still-unexplored yet fascinating national instance of the primacy of business groups, because that nation exemplifies an environment that differs both from East Asia, which is usually taken as the region of dynamic business groups, and from Latin America, often cited as the continent of politically connected business groups crowding out budding independent enterprises. By concentrating on the different geographical environment of Turkey, the present research provides a fresh look at the development of business groups.

In doing so, this study, utilizing the data in various primary and secondary sources, first comes up with a comprehensive list of the largest economic players in Turkey such as business groups, independent companies, state-owned enterprises,

I am grateful for many insightful suggestions and comments to Melih Colpan, Takashi Hikino, Jim Lincoln, Behlül Üsdiken, and participants at the "Evolutionary Dynamics of Business Groups in Emerging Economies" conference in Kyoto, November 26–28, 2007. I would also like to thank Barış Tan and Koç University's Graduate School of Business for all the support they provided in collecting corporate data and making arrangements with several business groups during my visit to the university in 2006. Finally, I would like to express my deep gratitude to all the executives and directors at the several business groups, and particularly at Alarko Holding, Doğan Holding, Koç Holding, Sabancı Holding, Şahinler Holding, Yaşar Holding and Zorlu Holding, who cooperated extensively with this research project.

and multinational subsidiaries. That list reveals that business groups remain the core element of the large-enterprise economy of Turkey. The chapter then focuses on the overall growth strategies of Turkish business groups. These discussions lead to structure and governance concerns.

To investigate these issues, a series of interviews was conducted with senior corporate executives of the largest groups. Some interviewees were members of the founding families while others were salaried professional managers, so the way in which groups function is thoroughly revealed. The interviews were supplemented by a questionnaire survey in which most of the largest family-owned business groups were included.[1] The overall picture that emerged from interviews and the questionnaire is enriched by an individual study of the history of the Koç group—the largest, one of the oldest and the one that other groups have often emulated. Ultimately, this chapter provides a systematic study of the historical evolution of the large-enterprise economy in Turkey, and its core actor, family-owned diversified business groups, which have driven the modern Turkish economic development, especially since the Second World War.

17.2 DEVELOPMENTAL BACKGROUNDS OF 'BIG BUSINESS' IN TURKEY

The large-enterprise economy in Turkey has developed with two major characteristic players: business groups that grew slowly after the establishment of the Turkish Republic; and the state-owned enterprises, many of which were founded within the activist policy frameworks, from the Etatist policy of the 1930s to the import substitution regime of the 1960s.[2] The family-owned group enterprises basically exhibit a similar pattern of long-term evolution to the one that has been observed in other emerging nations, although the pace and viability of the long-term development of Turkish groups have historically been less than impressive, especially in the light of the dynamism exhibited by their counterparts in South Korea and some other East Asian nations (Amsden 2001). Except for the cases in infrastructure-related entities such as postal service, railroads, and electricity generation and distribution, many of the state-owned enterprises were originally formed as a political response to unique circumstances, in that the indigenous Turkish population did not adequately develop their own enterprises, especially those in the capital-intensive sector (Buğra 1994; Karluk 1999).

---

[1] A questionnaire was sent to the chairman/CEO of 67 business groups in Turkey in May 2007, of which 20 provided usable responses; 11 of these are among the large business groups listed in Table 17.1; their answers are examined in this chapter.

[2] This section draws on Colpan and Hikino (2008).

Large private-sector businesses began to play a significant and extensive role in the Turkish economy only after the Second World War. Given the economic size and developmental level of the nation by the 1950s, with a GDP per capita similar to that of Japan and more than double that of South Korea at that time, large enterprises should have energized Turkish economy long before that decade (Maddison 2001). While a few of the large business groups of Turkey can trace their origins as far back as the 1920s, the delayed arrival of the large-enterprise economy, especially that centered around private businesses, stands as a symptom of the nation's developmental struggle in the twentieth century. Japan, which had a level of development roughly equal to that of Turkey in the first half of the twentieth century, had committed to large enterprises that resemble the family-owned diversified business groups of Turkey as a vitally critical instrument of rapid catch-up since the late nineteenth century (Morikawa 1992). As for South Korea, even though it started with a much lower level of economic development, it succeeded in diffusing the "East Asian Miracle" after the 1960s through its extensive reliance on large business groups (Steers et al. 1989; Amsden and Hikino 1994; Kang 1996).

Large firms were in fact active even before the establishment of the Turkish Republic in 1923. Some enterprises of considerable size emerged in the Ottoman Empire period, especially those in agriculture, food-processing, banking, trading, mining, and railroads. Most of these belonged either to non-Muslim minorities or to European entrepreneurs and commercial houses as well as the state. The relative absence of the Turkish Muslim majority in private business was partially explained by the capitulary regime that eventually favored non-Muslim entrepreneurs through the exclusion of the Turkish population from foreign-trade privileges. The other factor worth mentioning is the social change in the Tanzimat (Reform) Period from 1839 to 1876, which provided attractive jobs in the modernized public bureaucracy to Muslim Turks, while recognizing business and trade as a secondary status (Buğra 1994; Kepenek and Yentürk 2000; Şahin 2002). The Ottoman government still established several major state-owned enterprises, such as TEKEL in 1862, which dealt with tobacco, salt, and alcoholic beverages mainly for securing tax revenues through the monopolistic supply of those key commodities, and Ziraat Bankası in 1888, which started providing modern banking services as a much-needed government-backed institution (Kepenek and Yentürk 2000).

The initial organized efforts to create a national business class became an objective in the early days of the Republican Period, although a similar drive had actually started as early as 1908, when the Committee of Union and Progress commonly designated as the Young Turks came to power. The new government gave several tax allowances and exemptions; awarded customs exemptions for importing industrial machinery and apparatus; granted land parcels to those who would build factories; provided various types of financial incentives; assigned profitable sectors to private businesses; and established joint businesses with private entrepreneurs. Even the statesmen themselves sometimes became directly involved in establishing private industries in the early years of the Republic (Yerasimos 1977; Buğra 1994). Landowners scarcely got involved in industrial activities, by contrast, as their wealth accumulation had remained inadequate to commit to new businesses and also because the government did not want the landowners, the traditional sources of power, to take up an active role in the modern nation (Buğra 1994; Karademir et al. 2005). Among the prominent business families active in the early twenty-first century, only groups such as Çukurova, Koç, and Sabancı had their business origins in the 1920s and the early 1930s.

After the Great Depression, state policy moved toward more direct interventions, adopted within the Etatist policies in which the state extensively established public enterprises while employing selective policies to dispossess non-Muslim businesses. As long as the indigenous private investment remained stagnant and was insufficient to replace non-Muslim minorities as a business class, the government itself had to act extensively as an enterprise proprietor as well as as an operator (Yerasimos 1977; Buğra 1994; Karademir et al. 2005). Theoretically, then, these enterprises were pilot factories that were expected to be given eventually to the private sector, although the plan did not actually materialize until after the 1980s. Two interesting cases among the state-owned enterprises were Sümerbank and Etibank, which were founded in 1933 and 1935, respectively. These were actually holding companies, establishing and managing diverse industrial enterprises, Sümerbank in weaving, mining, cellulose, ceramics, and chemistry, and Etibank in energy and mining. In the 1950s some of the industrial subsidiaries these banks owned and controlled became independent operating companies or integrated with other state enterprises in similar product domains. In the end, most of these financial institutions and their remaining operating enterprises would be privatized in the 1990s (Karluk 1999).

Industrial policies favoring private businesses were reinstated, especially in the Democratic Party period of the 1950s, which explains the concentration of the foundation of today's large private businesses in this period. Eventually, then, private enterprises, especially large family-owned business groups, belatedly came to have a significant role in Turkey's economic scene in that decade. Although established business groups such as Eczacıbaşı, Borusan, Yaşar, and Anadolu had originated earlier, they gradually increased their economic presence through product diversification from the 1950s. The years of planned economic development with policies for import substitution and market protectionism from 1960 to the end of 1970s certainly assisted the growth of businesses in several industries in this period. Some other groups, however, such as Zorlu, Sanko, Ciner, and Fiba, were formed after the 1980s. Despite the shift of policies gradually to liberalize domestic markets to international competition since that decade, these new groups would challenge the established ones in a very different macroeconomic and polity environment.

In spite of the rise of the private businesses, several key state-owned businesses were still established after the 1950s for the purpose of developing the industrial economy: Türkiye Petrolleri Anonim Ortaklığı in 1954, to secure a supply of crude oil from foreign nations; Petkim, which eventually started a large-scale petrochemical industry in Turkey in 1965; and still more in the 1980s (Buğra 1994; Karluk 1999; Yaprak et al. 2007).

17.3 BUSINESS GROUPS IN THE TWO-PILLAR LARGE-ENTERPRISE ECONOMY OF TURKEY

The comprehensive picture of the large-enterprise economy of contemporary Turkey is represented in Table 17.1.[3] By ranking the fifty largest economic players by the number of employees in 2005, the table also illustrates the relative significance of individual economic players such as diversified business groups and state-owned enterprises. Naturally, the choice of employee count as the size indicator results in the over-representation of labor-intensive sectors and possibly state-owned enterprises, although other figures, such as sales and assets, which are customarily used in industrial economies for that purpose, have their own problems of double counting in terms of consolidated assets and sales and/or missing data at the business group level. This is because, as is regrettably the case for most groups of enterprises controlled by the family, Turkish groups feature all the complexities of closed and cross-owner-ship, pyramidal structure, and inter-company sales within a group. On the other hand, a few private business groups could have well been missed, as they do not publish the data on the number of employees, while state-owned enterprises should be well represented, as they customarily do provide that information. For all of its incomplete-ness and shortcomings, Table 17.1 is the most comprehensive representation of the large business units of Turkey, because it includes private-sector businesses and groups and state-owned enterprises in non-manufacturing sectors such as agriculture, mining, and services as well as in industry.

Table 17.1 highlights the major characteristics of the large-enterprise economy in Turkey: the two-pillar regime with a strong presence of diversified business groups and the remaining legacy of state-owned enterprises. In terms of these two features, Turkey shares the same basic characteristics that distinguish the industry structure of emerging economies from that of mature industrial nations (Hikino and Amsden 1994; Chandler et al. 1997). The prominence of such diversified business groups in many emerging economies has attracted much attention, partly because this partic-ular economic player has acted as the prime engine for industrial growth in dynamic markets such as South Korea and Malaysia, while family dynasties have also been criticized for their strong influence on the political as well as the economic agendas of relevant nations (Morck et al. 2005; Chang 2006; Khanna and Yafeh 2007). In many of the emerging economies, then, market failure has forced the government to establish and operate large production facilities, especially in infra-structure-related sectors such as transportation services, power generation and transmission, and scale-intensive manufacturing industries in intermediate goods such as iron and steel and petroleum refining, which supply inexpensive raw materials and feedstock to downstream users. Even in Taiwan, which is often cited as a representative economy of private small-scale firms, such upstream

---

[3] This section draws on Colpan and Hikino (2008).

Table 17.1 The fifty largest economic players in Turkey, 2005

Rank	Group/enterprise name	Year of foundation*	Employees	Type[†]	Controlling ownership	Business lines	Listed companies[‡]
1	Koç Group	1926	81,926	Family BG	Koç family	Diversified	21[§]
2	Türk Telekom	1995 (1840)	51,737	Foreign	Saudi Oger (Saudi Arabia) and Telecom Italia (Italy)	Telecommunications	0
3	Sabancı Group	1932	45,000	Family BG	Sabancı family	Diversified	12[§]
4	TCDD[¶]	1856	39,000	State	State	Railways	0
5	Zorlu Group	1953	31,509	Family BG	Zorlu family	Diversified	4
6	TEDAŞ	1993 (1935)	31,256	State	State	Electricity distribution	0
7	PTT	1840	30,088	State	State	Postal and financial services	0
8	Oyak Group	1961	30,000	Military BG	Armed forces pension fund	Diversified	7
9	Çukurova Group	1923	26,500	Family BG	Karamehmet family	Diversified	1
10	Ülker Group	1944	23,500	Family BG	Ülker family	Diversified	3
11	T.C. Ziraat Bankası	1863	20,373	State	State	Universal banking services, insurance	0
12	TEKEL A.Ş.	1862	17,728	State	State	Tobacco, tobacco products, alcoholic and non-alcoholic beverages, salt, matches, tea, coffee	0
13	İş Bankası Group	1924	17,111	Employee and political party BG	T.İş Bankası A.Ş. employees fund, CHP (Republican People's Party)	Diversified	11[§]
14	Doğuş Group	1951	16,450	Family BG	Şahenk family	Diversified	5
15	Türkiye Şeker Fabrikaları A.Ş.	1925	16,445	State	State	Sugar processing, industrial machinery, industrial alcohol	0

(continued)

Table 17.1 Continued

Rank	Group/enterprise name	Year of foundation*	Employees	Type[†]	Controlling ownership	Business lines	Listed companies[‡]
16	Anadolu Group	1949	14,841	Family BG	Yazıcı and Özilhan families	Diversified	5
17	Sanko Group	1966	14,000	Family BG	Konukoğlu family	Diversified	1
18	Ciner Group	1978	13,600	Family BG	Ciner family	Diversified	4
19	Türkiye Taşkömürü Kurumu	1848	13,347	State	State	Coal mining	0
20	Tekfen Group	1956	12,500	Family BG	Akçağılar, Berker and Gökyiğit families	Diversified	1
21	Türkiye Kömür İşletmeleri Kurumu	1957 (1937)	12,268	State	State	Coal mining, mining machinery, port management, laboratory services	0
22	Şahinler Group	1982	12,000	Family BG	Şahin family	Diversified	0
23	Doğan Group	1950	11,666	Family BG	Doğan family	Diversified	9[§]
24	THY	1933	11,121	State	State	Aviation, technical services	0[§]
25	Boydak Group	1957	11,100	Family BG	Boydak family	Diversified	0
26	T.Halk Bankası	1933	10,509	State	State	Universal banking services, insurance	0
27	EUAS Elektrik Üretim A.Ş.	2001 (1935)	10,324	State	State	Electricity generation	0
28	Çay İşletmeleri	1971 (1938)	9,586	State	State	Tea processing, food	0
29	Fiba Group	1987	8,599	Family BG	Özyeğin family	Diversified	3
30	Eczacıbaşı Group	1942	8,300	Family BG	Eczacıbaşı family	Diversified	5
31	TRT	1964	8,000	State	State	Television, radio	0

Rank	Group/enterprise name	Year of foundation*	Employees	Type[+]	Controlling ownership	Business lines	Listed companies[‡]
32	T. Vakıflar Bankası‖	1954	7,164	State	State	Universal banking services, insurance	5[§]
33	Yaşar Group	1945	7,000	Family BG	Yaşar family	Diversified	6
34	Devlet Hava Meydanları İşletmesi	1933	6,884	State	State	Airport services	0
35	Alarko Group	1954	6,400	Family BG	Alaton and Garih families	Diversified	2[§]
36	Makina ve Kimya Endüstrisi	1923	6,508	State	State	Military weapons and systems	0
37	BIM Birleşik Mağazalar A.Ş.	1995	6,383	Family	Topbaş and Khereji families	Chain store	0[§]
38	Profilo Group	1954	6,000	Family BG	Kamhi family	Diversified	0
39	Enka Group**	1957	5,000	Family BG	Tara and Gülçelik families	Diversified	3
40	Güriş Group	1958	5,000	Family BG	Yarrantürk family	Diversified	1
41	Kale Group	1957	5,000	Family BG	Bodur family	Diversified	0
42	Metro Group Türkiye	1990	5,000	Foreign	Metro A.G. (Germany)	Chain store, real-estate	0
43	Nergis Group[††]	1967	4,997	Family BG	Çağlar and Şankaya families	Diversified	1[§]
44	STFA Group[‡‡]	1938	4,736	Family BG	Türkeş and Akkaya families	Diversified	0
45	Türkiye Petrolleri Anonim Ortaklığı	1954	4,746	State	State	Hydrocarbon exploration, drilling, well completion and production, natural gas storage, oil trade and transportation	0

(continued)

Table 17.1 Continued

Rank	Group/enterprise name	Year of foundation*	Employees	Type[†]	Controlling ownership	Business lines	Listed companies[‡]
46	Tarım İşletmeleri Genel Müdürlüğü	1937	4,744	State	State	Crop and animal production and related activities	0
47	Borusan Group	1944	4,500	Family BG	Kocabıyık family	Diversified	2
48	Çelebi Group	1958	4,500	Family BG	Çelebioğlu family	Diversified	1
49	Sodexho Toplu Yemek ve Servis A.Ş	1992	4,500	Foreign	Sodexho (France)	Food and business services	0
50	Kibar Group	1972	4,500	Family BG	Kibar family	Diversified	0

*In the case of enterprises formed through spin-offs and split-offs, the year of foundation of the original organization is indicated within parentheses.

[†]BG = business group.

[‡]Companies listed on the Istanbul stock exchange under a common controlling shareholder.

[§]Indicates that a top organization of the group/enterprise itself is also listed.

[¶]Employee count is as of 2004.

[‖]Vakıf Bank is a unique case in that it is controlled by over 40,000 charitable foundations managed by the Turkish Prime Ministry's General Directorate of Foundations (the GDF).

**Employee count is as of 2001.

[††]Employee count of the two largest group companies, Sifaş and Yeşim, is shown, since no information on the entire group is available.

[‡‡]Employee count of the largest group company, Sofra, is shown, since no information on the entire group is available.

Source: Compiled by Aslı M. Colpan, with the assistance of Melih Colpan, Takashi Hikino, Yılmaz Karakas, and Barış Tan. Business groups/enterprises considered in this study were selected in the following way: business groups that had at least two firms listed on the Istanbul Stock Exchange; all companies, whether independent or affiliates of business groups, in the top 100 list of the Istanbul Chamber of Industry's annual list of largest industrial companies in terms of sales, assets or employees (for a company that is the affiliate of a business group, the name of the business group is indicated); all companies listed in the non-manufacturing-sector section of *Capital 500*; business groups/enterprises whose owner has more than US$500 million in *The Economist's* list of the fifty richest people in Turkey in 2005; all large state-owned enterprises, except for those in public services; all banks listed in the Banks Association of Turkey.

Table 17.2 Significance levels of Turkish economic players, 2005

Economic players	Employees	
	Total number	Ratio %
Largest player	81,926	10.72
5 largest players	249,172	32.62
10 largest players	367,016	48.04
Family business groups	389,124	50.94
All business groups	436,235	57.10
State-owned enterprise	260,091	34.05
Foreign-owned enterprise	61,237	8.02
Total 50 players	763,946	100.00

Source: Calculated from Table 17.1.

industries are dominated by state-owned monopolies, with iron and steel, petroleum refining, and petrochemicals as their major examples (Hsueh et al. 2001).

Foremost of all, according to Table 17.1, diversified groups play a significant economic role as the largest businesses of Turkey.[4] Out of the 50 economic players on the list, 28 are such diversified business groups, with 3 out of the top 5 places occupied by business groups. Of the remaining 22, 18 are state-owned enterprises.[5] Among the private-sector large businesses owned by Turkish families, only BIM has a focused operation, while 26 others are all diversified groups. Oyak, which belongs to the armed forces pension fund, and İş Bankası, which is owned by its employees' fund and a political party, also take the form of business groups. Table 17.2 illustrates that diversified business groups in total account for around 57 percent of all fifty economic players in terms of employment generation. State-owned enterprises still have a major role in the economy with their 34 percent share in terms of employee count, although their presence has been declining, because of the privatization drive since the 1980s. Foreign-owned enterprises, incidentally, play a marginal role, accounting for only 8 percent in terms of employees of the largest fifty players.

[4] Within this chapter Turkish business groups are defined as groups consisting of legally independent, privately held and publicly owned, companies operating in multiple industries, which are controlled through a top holding company with various equity and non-equity arrangements (Khanna and Yafeh 2007; Colpan and Hikino 2008).

[5] Interestingly, a unique case is that of Vakıflar Bankası, controlled by over 40,000 charitable foundations managed by the Turkish Prime Ministry's General Directorate of Foundations, as it has five listed subsidiaries in banking services and insurance, and may be considered a pyramidal business group. Nevertheless, given the focus here on diversified groups and in order to avoid a categorical confusion, we classify this bank under the state-owned enterprise category in our analyses.

17.4 Mechanism to warrant the overall growth strategies of business groups

17.4.1 Diversification strategy into unrelated products

Exhibiting the characteristic pattern of extensive diversification into unrelated product markets, business groups have remained a core and dynamic element of the large-enterprise economy in Turkey. Within the contemporary Turkish economy, this growth model marks a sharp contrast to the product-focused growth that another pillar, state-owned enterprises, has adopted. While those public firms were often legally bound to concentrate on their inherent domains or eventually restricted to limited industry spheres under populist political pressure after the early 1980s, the distinctive model of entry into products and industries by business groups surely deserves a careful and systematic examination.

17.4.1.1 *Economic rationales and competitive capabilities*

Imperfect markets in terms of product, capital, labor, and information, combined with incentives resulting from industrial policies institutionalized by the government, have functioned as the foremost rationales for Turkish business groups to invest in diverse industry spheres, as has been the case in many other emerging nations. In Turkey, it should be added, uncertainty induced by the arbitrary changes of state intervention, thanks to inconsistent and ambiguous economic policies among different governments, or even within the same administration, further encouraged the adaptation of unrelated diversified-type operations for the purpose of risk reduction (Buğra 1994; Buğra and Üsdiken 1995; Özen 2003). Further, as concrete economic policy formation and execution on the part of the administrative branch were often motivated by political reasons, personal contact with politicians and bureaucrats remained important, and also personal access to insider information regarding political and policy agendas became a critical factor in maximizing business opportunities and minimizing financial losses (Buğra 1994: 150–6; Karademir et al. 2005: 15).[6]

These explanations, however, should not imply the weakness of viable competitive resources within the groups. Certainly Turkish business groups accumulated competitive capabilities that can be applied specifically to their own economic settings. The business groups in our survey indicated, as illustrated in Table 17.3, that the strength of their groups lay in financial capabilities, the quality of the people they employed in the group, as well as organizational form, design, and functioning of the group. Interestingly, R&D and advertising and marketing capabilities were

---

[6] Even within the export promotion schemes in the liberal market-friendly period of the 1980s, for instance, different governmental executive offices exploited their own power to favor or harm individual entrepreneurs and business groups that were targeted for political reasons (Buğra 1994: 150–6).

Table 17.3 Competitive capabilities of the largest business groups, 2007

Characteristics of capabilities	Strongly disagree	Somewhat disagree	Neutral	Somewhat agree	Strongly agree
	1	2	3	4	5
The strength of our group lies in internal R&D capabilities			$X^{3.18}$		
The strength of our group lies in advertising and marketing capabilities			$X^{3.45}$		
The strength of our group lies in financial capabilities				$X^{4.10}$	
The strength of our group lies in the quality of people we employ in the group					$X^{4.45}$
The strength of our group lies in the organizational form, design, and functioning of the group				$X^{4.27}$	

Note: The numbers in the table show the average figures of the answers given to our questionnaire by the 11 business groups.
Source: Based on the questionnaire answers of the 11 business groups, all of which are included in Table 17.1.

generally seen as relatively less significant regarding the overall capabilities and competitiveness of the business groups. Relationships between the individual operating companies, according to the questionnaire responses, were thus aiming to achieve synergies or cooperation mostly in the utilization of financial resources and human and managerial resources, followed by information resources.

As the case of Koç in Section 17.4.3 shows, contact capabilities in sourcing of technology and information, and project execution capabilities, especially that of imported technology and knowledge, can be cited as the other key capabilities of Turkish business groups. Once individual groups had nurtured and accumulated competitive resources in such functions, they could then apply those assets to their advantages, thus further enhancing those resources and capabilities. This mechanism of increasing return in various strategic and operational functions certainly constitutes a key element of the resilience and dynamism of the business groups.

17.4.1.2 Product diversification and business portfolios

Whatever the origins of individual business groups, they eventually ended up with a widely stretched product portfolio, as shown by Fig. 17.1. These groups thus evolved into broad economic activities in manufacturing, finance, and services that were far

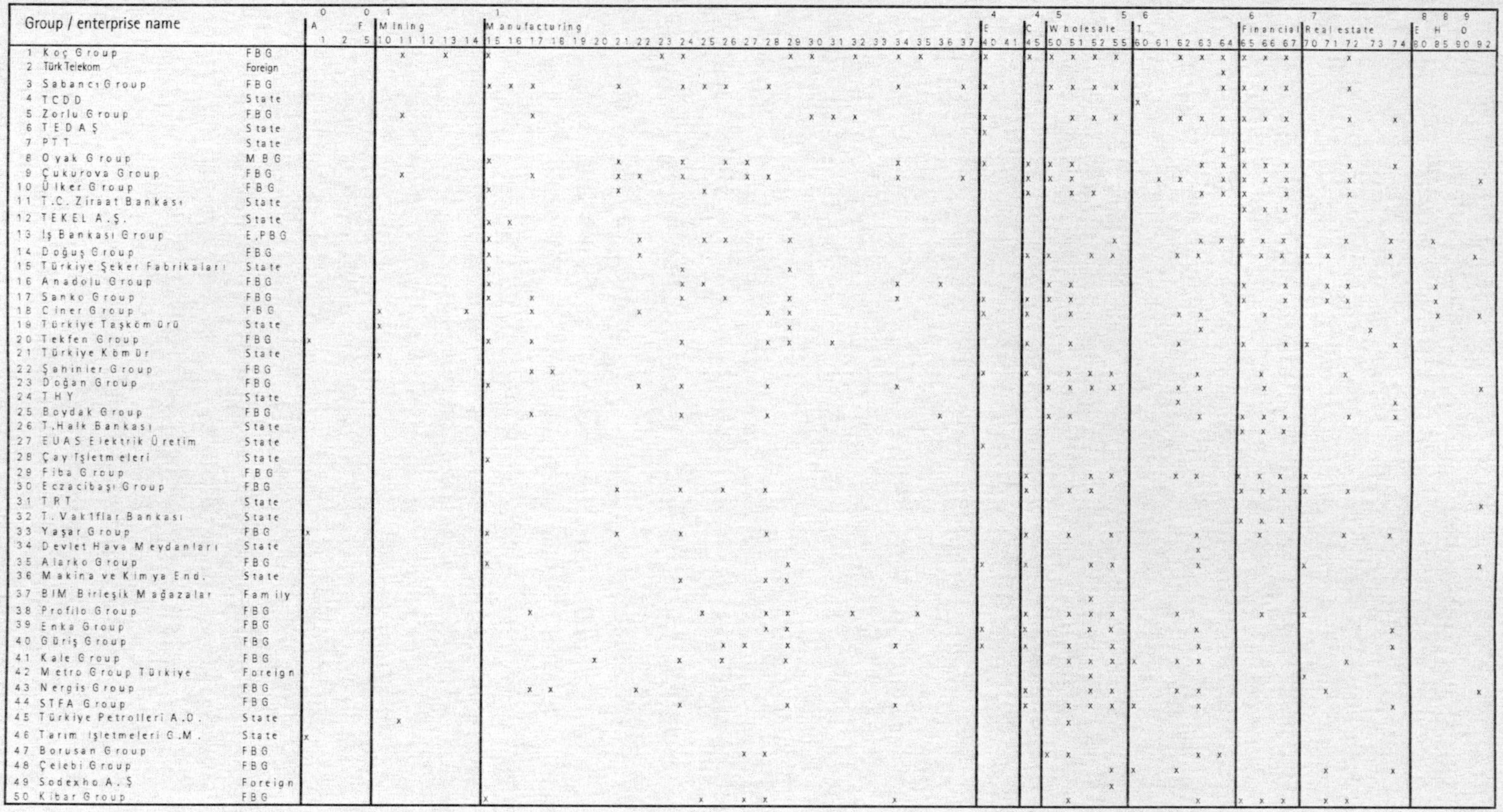

Figure 17.1 Concentration and diversification of the fifty largest economic players in Turkey, 2005

Note: Category 0, Division 1: Agriculture, hunting and forestry, Division 5, Fishing; Category 1, Division 10: Mining and quarrying, Division 15: Manufacturing; Category 4, Division 40: Electricity, gas and water supply Division 45: Construction; Category 5, Division 50: Wholesale and retail trade, Division 55: Hotels and restaurants; Category 6, Division 60: Transport, storage and communications, Division 65: Financial intermediation; Category 7, Division 70: Real estate, renting and business activities; Category 8, Division 80: Education, Division 85: Health and social work; Category 9, Division 90: Other community-related.

Source: Based on Table 17.1 organized by International Standard Industry Classification codes (Colpan and Hikino 2008).

beyond their original businesses and activities. Originally established as a pharmaceutical company, the Eczacibasi group represents a telling illustration. In sharp contrast to the industry-focused and R&D-oriented model that all the major pharmaceutical firms in mature economies have customarily implemented, Eczacıbaşı has followed a developmental trail that closely resembles that of unrelated diversification, which the Koç group spearheaded in Turkey. Establishing the first modern pharmaceutical factory in 1952, the company then pursued a dual path, during which Eczacıbaşı, in addition to pharmaceuticals, extended its industry portfolio into paper products, building materials, investment banking, insurance, fabricated metal products, cosmetics, real estate, and IT services.

Fig. 17.2 amply illustrates the extent of product diversification of the fifty largest economic players in Turkey. As the figure shows, business groups are in general highly diversified, with a peak in twelve 2-digit ISIC industries.

Table 17.4 then illustrates the direction of diversification of business groups. The table specifies the industries with the highest number of involvement by business groups:

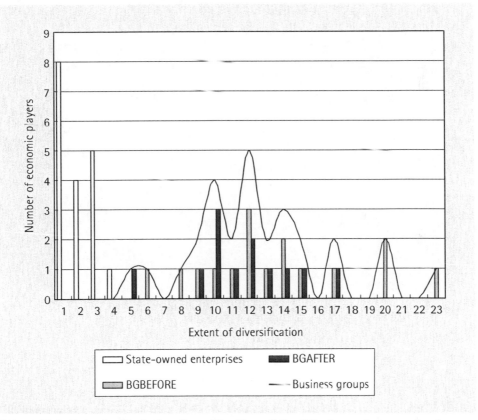

Figure 17.2 Extent of industry diversification of the fifty largest economic players, 2005

Source: Calculated from Figure 17.1 (Colpan and Hikino 2008).

Table 17.4 Direction of industry diversification of the fifty largest economic players, 2005

Industries	All 50 economic players	Business groups			State-owned enterprises (N=18)
		All (N=28)	BGBEFORE (N=16)	BGAFTER (N=12)	
I. Agriculture, hunting, forestry and fishing (ISIC 1~2, 5)	3	2	2	0	1
II. Mining and quarrying (ISIC 10~14)	9	6	3	3	3
III. Manufacturing (ISIC 15~37)	125	117	77	40	8
15. Food	16	13	9	4	3
17. Manufacture of textiles	10	10	4	6	0
24. Chemicals and chemical products	15	13	10	3	2
28. Manufacture of fabricated metal products	13	12	8	4	1
29. Manufacture of machinery and equipment	14	11	8	3	3
34. Manufacture of motor vehicles, trailers, and semi-trailers	10	10	6	4	0
IV. Electricity, gas, and water supply (ISIC 40~41)	12	10	5	5	2
V. Construction (ISIC 45)	18	18	11	7	0
VI. Wholesale and retail trade (ISIC 50~52)	49	46	28	18	1
50. Motor vehicle sales and related activities	10	10	7	3	0
51. Wholesale trade and commission trade	22	21	12	9	0
52. Retail trade	17	15	9	6	0
VII. Hotels and restaurants (ISIC 55)	18	17	10	7	0
VIII. Transport, storage, and communications (ISIC 60~64)	50	44	25	19	5

Industries	All 50 economic players	Business groups			State-owned enterprises (N=18)
		All (N=28)	BGBEFORE (N=16)	BGAFTER (N=12)	
62. Air transport and related services	13	12	6	6	1
63. Supporting and auxiliary transport activities	22	20	10	10	2
IX. Financial intermediation (ISIC 65~67)	56	46	27	19	10
65. Financial intermediation	19	15	9	6	4
66. Insurance and pension funding	19	16	9	7	3
67. Activities auxiliary to financial intermediation	18	15	9	6	3
X. Real estate, renting and business activities (ISIC 70~74)	41	38	23	15	2
72. Computer and related services	15	15	9	6	0

Note: Individual numbers represent the total count of groups and/or enterprises within specific industry categories.
All operating activities for business groups and state-owned enterprises with more than 10 and 3 entries, respectively, are shown. Results for broad industry categories are shown in bold letters. Industry No. 74 is not shown because of diverse yet miscellaneous activities under that category.

Source: Calculated from Figure 17.1 (Colpan and Hikino 2008).

construction, wholesaling (including international trade) and retailing, hotels and restaurants, transportation activities, IT-related services, and all types of financial intermediation.[7] The diversification patterns of business groups formed before and after market liberalization in Turkey, represented by BGBEFORE and BGAFTER respectively, are discussed below.

17.4.1.3 Two categories of business groups

A closer look at the business groups in Turkey identifies two strategic categories or subgroups in terms of their diversification strategies. The first category comprises the leading players founded between the 1920s and the 1950s that diversified into unrelated fields rather early. Even before the Turkish efforts of economic liberalization since the early 1980s, these business groups had been operating in four or more 2-digit ISIC industries (categorized as BGBEFORE to represent the pre-1980 group formation).[8] Examples of such cases include Koç, Sabancı, Çukurova, and Yaşar. Most of the established business groups in this category have their origins in construction, retail, and the wholesale trade, often with government contracts, or in low-tech industries, particularly textiles. Their early growth came mainly via internal growth within low-tech industries, or licensing agreements and occasionally joint ventures with international firms in modern industries where local knowledge was limited. Continuous state contracts and procurements usually helped.

After the market liberalization of the 1980s, these established business groups embarked upon expansion into new and diverse business domains, mostly through three routes: organic growth through internal investment; joint ventures, licensing agreements, and partnerships with international firms; and the acquisition of Turkish companies, especially the buyout of privatized state-owned enterprises. An example of an alliance with foreign firms can be seen in the Anadolu group's entry into foods and electronics through partnerships with McDonalds and Samsung, respectively. The acquisition of Tüpraş, the giant petroleum refining company, by Koç is an illustration of entering a new industry by buying out a public enterprise in the process of privatization.

The second strategic subcategory of business groups represents those that originated mostly in the 1950s and afterwards, that had no or limited diversification (in less than four 2-digit ISIC industries) before the 1980s, but that embarked upon wide-ranging diversification activities after that decade (categorized as BGAFTER). Coming from textiles, metal-processing, banking, and several other industries, these groups diversified expansively into several businesses, following similar routes to the forerunning groups after the 1980s. A representative example of these growth strategies is the Zorlu group, which was originally in textiles but which diversified

---

[7] Yurtoglu (2000) argues that banks serve as the "main bank" of the Turkish business groups, although the extent and importance of their role are not directly comparable to the Japanese or German cases.

[8] The criteria of four industries is chosen, because up to three categories can represent related diversification—e.g. financial intermediation (ISIC 65), insurance and pension funding (ISIC 66), and auxiliary to financial intermediation (ISIC 67), or machinery and equipment (ISIC 29), electrical machinery and apparatus (ISIC 31), and radio, television and communication equipment and apparatus (ISIC 32).

into a high-technology domain by the acquisition of a Turkish electronics company and also into financial services when the group bought out a state-owned bank in the privatization process in the 1990s. Another example is the Ciner group, which diversified into energy, mining, and tourism through the acquisition of state-owned enterprises, while the Fiba group entered into clothing retailing by buying the franchising rights in Turkey from Marks & Spencer, and the Kibar group entered into the automotive sector, becoming the distributor of Hyundai automobiles of South Korea, all in the 1990s.

17.4.1.4 *Diversification conduct before and after market liberalization*

The liberalization policy gradually to open domestic markets to international competition that started in 1980 denotes a critical change in the Turkish economy. Especially for the latecomer groups that started diversifying after the liberalization drive of the 1980s, this should have meant entering a more hostile economic environment, which was not quite conducive to begin a commitment to broad industry diversification. As the examples of several groups mentioned above illustrate, however, the growth strategy adopted by individual groups in liberalized markets has, in fact, remained expansive.

Besides the general economic opportunities of industries and sectors with their rapid growth and high profitability especially in services and finance, the deregulation and privatization drive initiated by the government created many new open domains for economic activities. After all, the privatization of state-owned enterprises provided the best opportunity for individual companies and business groups to attempt a new entry into different product and industry markets. Liberalization of regulations in certain sectors such as banking meant an extensive move toward those areas. Industrial policy agendas that designated specified industries for strategic purposes also induced many enterprises and business groups to commit themselves to those targeted industries. For instance, several groups entered into tourism and overseas trade thanks to systematic government incentives to these businesses in the 1980s. The gradual shift of policies to liberalize domestic markets to international competition after the early 1980s created yet another opportunity for profit-making (Öniş 1992; Şahin 2002). By becoming a local agent for international companies that were targeting the enlarged Turkish markets or, more strategically, by forming a joint venture with a global player, the large domestic groups were certainly able to take advantage of the policy change and economic opportunity.

A series of econometric tests conducted in Colpan and Hikino (2008) have actually illustrated the catch-up behavior in terms of the extent of diversification committed by several energetic latecomer groups (Fig. 17.2 points to the similar extent of diversification carried out by the two types of business groups).[9] An intriguing

---

[9] The only visible difference in terms of product diversification among Turkish business groups seems to come from firm size measured by employee count, which has a significant and positive effect on product diversification. The larger the size of groups, therefore, the more product diversification the groups commit to.

question to be asked here is how the latecomer business groups could actually get close to the forerunning ones in terms of the extent of their product portfolios. Certainly, with the exogenously given market opportunities, the latecomers sought to secure their positions in the multi-industry oligopolistic game with extensive investments. Entry into the newly burgeoning service industry by an established group should also have brought in "bandwagon effects" (Knickerbocker 1973). Given the relatively abundant accumulation of competitive resources on the part of established business groups, however, this way of entering into various economic activities should have put extra burdens on latecomers. While this question warrants a more systematic examination, one critical factor that functioned favorably for the groups that started diversifying growth in the 1980s was the loose credit allocation by commercial banks in the second half of that decade and the early 1990s, which eventually assisted many groups that did not have an abundant pool of internal cash reserve to take a growth path to develop into a member of Turkey's elite business groups.

The ultimate trajectory of diversifying growth for both of the two subcategories of business groups should, however, be understood in a dynamic context. While business groups have certainly all been divesting themselves of their unprofitable businesses, they seem to have invested simultaneously into diverse products and industries, mostly growing ones such as financial services, energy, and information-technology domains, as mentioned earlier. A closer look at the distribution of sales of the two largest groups, Koç and Sabancı, at the 2-digit industry level actually reveals that the extent of the groups' product diversity remained relatively stable from the mid-1990s to the mid-2000s. On the other hand, a few groups, like Yaşar, have had to narrow their product scope, as they faced significant financial troubles with the onset of the 1994 and 2001 economic crises. Even so, most latecomer groups, such as Sanko, Şahinler, Ciner, and Zorlu, have chosen to increase their product portfolios since the 1990s (Colpan and Hikino 2008).

This dynamic behavior exhibited by the vibrant emerging groups does not, however, imply that the behavioral domains occupied by the forerunning groups and the latecomer ones have become close or even identical. Reflecting the historical timing of their emergence as a business group, the relative difference in terms of their strong domains still remains, while the different directions of industry diversification can be seen in Table 17.4 (see Colpan and Hikino 2008 for the econometric tests). Because of the government-induced opportunities in import-substitution regimes up to the late 1970s, the established groups invested extensively in large-scale manufacturing facilities, which created a huge entry barrier for the latecomer groups. Faced both with this crowd-out effect in manufacturing and with growing economic opportunities in the burgeoning services and finance, where more profit opportunities were created after the 1980s for all economic players, the emerging business groups looked particularly to such non-manufacturing sectors for profit-making opportunities. Because established groups also found investment outlets in the burgeoning service and finance industries, rivalry within and between the two subcategories of business groups became fierce. Hence, compared to the forerunning groups, the latecomers' manufacturing commitment remained low overall, while in services and finance few differences can be detected between the two categories.

17.4.2 Belated international expansion

This diversity in terms of products, industries, and sectors should be complemented by another form of diversification: geographical or international expansion. In terms of geographical diversity, however, most groups' international presence in terms of both foreign direct investment and merchandise export has escalated only since the early 1990s. The delayed internationalization stems partially from the import substitution regime, which did not quite value the outward flow of merchandise and capital. It is also the symptom of the inadequate competitiveness of Turkish products and businesses in international markets. For instance, the Sabancı group was active in only four countries with six subsidiaries as late as 1990. The group became active in eleven countries with nineteen subsidiaries by 2005. The Zorlu group is another extreme case, as its international presence increased from five foreign subsidiaries in 1995 to twenty-eight in 2005. The Koç group is the most internationally diverse, with forty-five affiliated companies operating in twenty-three countries by 2004 (data from respective business groups). The larger the business group, then, the more foreign direct investment it tends to have, as Table 17.5 illustrates. This difference in terms of the overall size of the groups is most visible for wholly owned overseas manufacturing operations, while wholly owned non-manufacturing facilities, which include sales and services, is the most committed type of international activity in general. Furthermore, thanks to the outward-oriented growth policies since the 1980s, there is some indication that older and newer business groups have equally exploited the opportunities in international markets. As for export commitment, groups in general have become export-oriented, as Table 17.5 illustrates, and there do not seem to be any systematic differences between groups' export commitment depending on the size or the diversification timing of the business groups. Our limited sample for international activities, however, deserves some caution.

Arçelik, a key Koç group company in consumer electronics, is a telling example of the rapid and successful internationalization of a Turkish business group since the late 1980s. Arçelik basically followed a two-pronged strategy in its international expansion: organic growth through exports and targeted acquisitions of new companies. Arçelik originally began exporting on an opportunistic basis to utilize its production surplus in neighboring countries, especially in the Middle East and North Africa. As the country abandoned the import substitution regime and turned toward an export-led growth model in the 1980s, however, exporting started to gain in importance. In this context, first an original equipment manufacturing (OEM) contract was secured with Sears Roebuck in the USA in 1988 to supply refrigerators. That was followed by a similar, but much larger, European deal with Whirlpool for dishwashers nine years later (Root and Quelch 1997). By the late 1990s, however, the

Table 17.5 Internationalization of Turkish business groups, 2007

Business group	Export sales in total sales (%)	International scope (number of countries)				Total number of countries
		100%-owned manufacturing	Joint-venture manufacturing	100%-owned non-manufacturing	Joint-venture non-manufacturing	
Group A	25–50	2–3	2–3	7–10	7–10	23
Group B	11–24	7–10	2–3	10+	1	14
Group C	50+	2–3	2–3	10+	10+	15
Group D	25–50	7–10	7–10	7–10	0	10
Group E	50+	2–3	2–3	10+	2–3	11
Group F	25–50	4–6	0	7–10	0	13
Group G	11–24	4–6	4–6	7–10	0	16
Group H	1–10	2–3	0	4–6	2–3	6
Group I	25–50	1	1	7–10	7–10	8
Group J	25–50	1	0	7–10	0	8
Group K	11–24	1	2–3	4–6	0	7

Note: 1 means only domestic operations. Business groups are ranked by the number of employees for the entire group.

Source: Based on the questionnaire answers, annual reports, and data provided by the 11 business groups.

company had set up sales offices in France, Germany, and the UK and had identified specific strategies to enter each market not only through OEM but through its own brand, thanks to its heavy investments in R&D (Bonaglia et al. 2008).

The other pillar of Arçelik's internationalization strategy consisted of targeted acquisitions of foreign competitors to penetrate new markets and reinforce technological and productive capabilities. The first experiences with direct investment took place in developing countries (Tunisia and Uzbekistan), but did not live up to expectations. Following the 2001 macroeconomic crisis in Turkey, causing the demand for consumer durables to contract substantially, the need to internationalize became more pressing. After a failure in its first bid in Europe, Arçelik acquired three foreign companies—Blomberg in Germany, Elektra Bregenz in Austria, and Arctic in Romania—and the Leisure (cookers) and Flavel (appliances and TV sets) brands in Britain in 2002. Arçelik then launched the construction of a refrigerator and washing machine greenfield plant in Russia in 2005, followed by entry into the Chinese market through a partnership agreement with a leading white-good producer in 2007. In the same year it also bought Shanghai-based Changzhou Casa Shinco Electrical Appliances and started operating a washing-machine factory in China. Arçelik thus established itself as one of the leading international producers, rapidly expanding into neighboring geographical markets and, more recently, venturing into distant ones such as China and the USA (Bonaglia et al. 2008).

In its successful internationalization, leveraging on business group resources has been a key factor for Arçelik. Not only does group membership allow Arçelik to tap into intra-group capital markets and nurtured management skills; the accumulated technological know-how and established overseas networks within the group have also been instrumental in the company's internationalization efforts. The Koç name by itself functions as a critical competitive asset insofar as it enjoys international recognition, especially among overseas manufacturers and distributors. Thanks to these resources, Arçelik has had a competitive advantage in its internationalization trajectory.

17.4.3 Strategic evolution of the Koç group as a leading case

The Koç group is one of the oldest groups among the influential businesses and stands as the largest established group in Turkey. As such, a brief look at the example of Koç clearly exemplifies the evolution of one of the most successful business groups in Turkey. Table 17.6 illustrates the Koç group's growth strategy from 1920s to 2007.

The founder of the Koç group, Vehbi Koç, originally started his enterprise as a retail merchant in Ankara, in which business transactions with the government constituted the first step toward the long-term growth of his enterprise. In the 1920s and thereafter, Koç became a franchisee and representative of such US companies as Standard Oil (New Jersey), General Electric, and Ford Motor, which subsequently functioned as the major source for business expansion. The

Table 17.6 The Koç group's growth strategy from the 1920s to 2007

	1923	1930	1946	1960	1980
Economic and social background as a dividing line	Establishment of Turkish Republic.	Great Depression.	Liberal policy declaration by RPP in 1946 and the DP coming to power in 1950.	Military intervention. Change in Constitution in 1961.	Military intervention. Change in Constitution in 1982.
Major policy background	Initial organized efforts to create a national business class. Systematic incentives to Turkish private business, joint business establishment by state and private entrepreneurs.	Etatism. Extensive establishment of public enterprises in several industries and employment of selective policies to replace and dispossess non-Muslim businesses.	Liberalism and support of private enterprise. Incentives to move into industrial sector, foreign exchange allocations to importers and government contracts. Liberalization of trade regime short lived. Protectionist trade measures dominated.	Planned economy with import substitution and market protectionism policies. Systematic incentives to move into industrial sector.	Gradual liberalization of domestic markets to international competition in terms of merchandise and capital. Export promotion incentives. Customs union with the EU in 1996. Extensive privatization of state enterprises.
Product diversification strategy	Original establishment of enterprise that will later form the group. Initial business in retail merchandise followed by contracting especially for public businesses.	Franchisee and representative of US companies including GE and Ford Motor. Unsuccessful experiments in initial manufacturing activity (iron pipe).	Extensive diversification into manufacturing industry to replace imported goods. Light bulb, radiator, matches, washing machines,	Diversification continues into manufacturing sector, including tractor, passenger car, tomato paste, fiber glass. Entry in mass retailing by acquisition of	Entry into banking sector by acquiring a majority share of American Express Bank. Joint venture with Kingfisher of UK in home improvement retailing. Attempts to

	1923	1930	1946	1960	1980
			refrigerators and others. Entry into tourism by establishment of hotel and related areas.	majority shares of Migros Türk.	increase IT-related services, e.g. agency of Apple products in Turkey. Diversification into petroleum refining via acquisition of a state enterprise.
Internationalization strategy	Agency agreement with Standard Oil.	Establishment of first Turkish company in the USA; Ram Commercial Corporation.	First joint venture with a foreign company, GE, to produce light bulbs. Initial OEM exports for GE to Middle Eastern countries.	Establishment of foreign trade companies and beginning of export efforts in the 1970s.	Extensive export commitment and escalating foreign direct investment.
Technology acquisition			Technology licensing agreements with Arcor of Israel, GE, and others for manufactured goods.	Joint venture and licensing agreements with foreign companies, including Siemens, Ford, and others. Establishment of the first R&D division in the private sector in 1975.	Continued licensing agreements and joint ventures with international companies while investing in in-house R&D.

Note: Major strategies are shown. RPP = Republican People's Party, DP = Democrat Party.

cooperation of business people in Turkey with minority backgrounds, with their foreign-language knowledge, international relations, and business experience, became the critical means by which Koç formed several contacts with foreign enterprises. In the early 1950s and afterwards, as the shortage of foreign exchanges forced the government to introduce several import substitution measures such as import restrictions, tariff barriers, and quotas, and to institute several incentives for the establishment of local industries, the company's interest turned toward domestic production. Then came the successful production of the first locally manufactured automobiles, tractors, trucks, light bulbs, refrigerators, and washing machines, among other products. As Turkish society became modernized and people's income rose, demand for these goods naturally expanded, especially after the 1950s, whereas local supply remained limited to expensive imports coming from industrial nations that did not necessarily fit into the domestic conditions for usage, a symptom of market imperfection in emerging economies. While the original international manufacturer was often not interested in product customization, as the marginal gain in total sales volume and net profits did not warrant the high costs of modification, domestic businesses in Turkey had enough incentives for commitment to localized and relatively less expensive products. These pioneering ventures became possible mostly through joint ventures and licensing agreements with foreign companies, because local know-how had not yet reached a high enough level to achieve independent production (İdil 1999; Dündar 2006; Subaşı 2006). Once Koç had learned to import technology, start production, and customize products, the group would accumulate "project execution capabilities," as coined by some economists (Westphal 1990; Hikino and Amsden 1994), which subsequently functioned as a competitive advantage as the group routinely used that procedure. While continuing licensing agreements and joint ventures, Koç also established the first R&D division in the private sector in 1975. As has been shown in the typical case of Koç's subsidiary Arçelik, some businesses then began accumulating enough skills in technology and design to develop their own competitive products and to expand into international markets.

Koç's advancement in overseas expansion came with the liberalization policy that started in 1980 to open up the Turkish market to international transactions. The customs union that promoted Turkey's economic integration into the EU in 1996, and the next waves of internationalization of the economy in general, then, resulted in the acceleration of the group's globalization. With increasing inward investment by foreign companies, and imports increasing in both quantity and value, however, the group began to face an intensifying competition in its home market. Yet the group did not really focus its activities. Thanks to the new profit-making opportunities that came with liberalization (see Section 17.4.1.4), the group continued to enter into new profitable fields while it got out of others (İdil 1999; Subaşı 2006; Colpan and Hikino 2008). Using internal growth, joint ventures, and acquisitions, Koç was eventually operating in a diverse range of industries, including automotive, consumer electronics, food, retailing, petrochemicals, banking and insurance, tourism, construction, and IT services, and was active in twenty-three countries through direct investment by 2007.

17.5 FAMILY OWNERSHIP, HOLDING COMPANY, AND GOVERNANCE MECHANISMS

17.5.1 Family control and the holding company

The founding family members of the representative business groups in Turkey essentially control the entire business group through a holding company with various institutional arrangements. Equity holdings such as pyramidal and/or complex web of intercorporate shareholding structures are typical instruments used for that purpose by the groups (Yurtoglu 2000; Orbay and Yurtoglu 2006).[10] As an example, Fig. 17.3 illustrates the ownership structure in 2007 of Beko Elektronik (later named Grundig Elektronik), which represents part of a pyramidal structure of the Koç group. As the figure shows, the Koç family controls the majority stake of Beko Elektronik by owning more than 50 percent in Arçelik (through Temel Ticaret ve Yatırım AŞ, Koç Holding, and individual family member stakes), which in return holds 72.46 percent of shares in Beko Elektronik.

Besides those equity ties, interlocking directorates are also used to gain effective control over a large number of companies within groups. Beko Elektronik, for instance, shares three board members with Arçelik and Koç Holding (see Table 17.7). Notably, Rahmi M. Koç, who is the chairman in Beko Elektronik and Arçelik, is also the honorary chairman and a board member of Koç Holding. The CEO and vice chairman of Koç Holding are also on the boards of Arçelik and Beko Elektronik.

As far as the entire structure of the business groups is concerned, the holding company plays the central role for family control, as is depicted in Fig. 17.4, which illustrates the organizational structure of the Koç group. As the figure shows, the Koç group is controlled by the pure holding company at the top of the entire organization. The founding family established a pure holding company as a legally independent entity in which two major roles were assigned: owning and controlling operating units as subsidiaries, which would simultaneously or subsequently become publicly listed companies with their controlling shares held by the parent holding company; and coordinating and managing the activities of those subsidiaries for maximizing operational efficiency. The holding company organization thus functions both as the control mechanism adopted by the founding family and as an eventual headquarters for the entire group. Understandably, as the size of business groups gets larger, the separation between the strategic decision-making based on a majority shareholding by the founding family and the more operational execution of individual subsidiaries becomes clearer (Gökşen and Üsdiken 2001).

---

[10] It should be noted that, although the majority of the groups have converted some of their operating companies into publicly held corporations, the remaining few groups have still kept the whole group closely held (see Table 17.1 for the numbers of listed firms in each group).

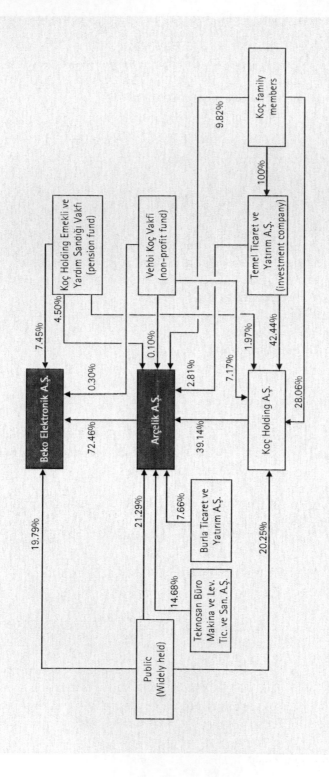

Figure 17.3 Part of a pyramidal ownership structure of the Koç group, 2007

Note: Operating companies of the Koç group are shaded. Burla Ticaret ve Yatırım and Teknosan belong to the Burla family, who is a long-term business partner of the Koç family.

Source: Drawn based on the information in the Year Book of Companies; Istanbul Stock Exchange.

Table 17.7 Interlocking directorates at Beko Elektronik, Arçelik, and Koç Holding, 2007

Beko Elektronik A.Ş.	Arçelik A.Ş.	Koç Holding A.Ş.
Rahmi M. Koç* (Chairman)	Rahmi M. Koç* (Chairman)	Rahmi M. Koç* (Honorary Chairman)
Dr. Bülent Bulgurlu (Vice Chairman)	Dr. Bülent Bulgurlu (Vice Chairman)	Dr. Bülent Bulgurlu (CEO)
Temel K. Atay	Temel K. Atay	Temel K. Atay (Vice Chairman)
A. Gündüz Özdemir	A. Gündüz Özdemir (General Manager)	Suna Kıraç* (Vice Chairman)
Aydın İ. Çubukçu	Mustafa V. Koç*	Mustafa V. Koç* (Chairman)
İ. Tamer Haşimoğlu	Semahat S. Arsel*	Semahat S. Arsel*
Fatih K. Ebiçlioğlu	M. Ömer Koç*	M. Ömer Koç*
C.Ş.Oğuzhan Öztürk (General Manager)	Robert Sonman	İnan Kıraç*
	F. Bülend Özaydınlı	Hasan Subaşı
		H. Yavuz Alangoya
		Helmut Oswald Maucher
		John H. Mc Arthur
		Dieter Christoph Urban

Note: Interlocking directorates between companies are shaded. * represents family members.

Source: Compiled from Year Book of Companies, 2007, Istanbul Stock Exchange.

Tax saving is another reason why business groups adopted the holding company organization. In the first half of the 1960s the Turkish government provided an exemption from corporate tax for the income that a parent holding company earned from its participations in affiliated companies, which eliminated the concern about double taxation (Buğra 1994: 184; Tax Guide 2009).

Koç thus initiated the establishment of such a holding company in 1963, after which most major groups followed suit. As Koç faced the "expanding scope of activities and the advancing age of the founder," the enterprise adopted the institution of a holding company as "an appropriate form of organization which would centralize decision making in a way to assure the continuity of the enterprise without compromising the family control over the business" (Buğra 1994: 79). In the case of two notable groups listed in Fig. 17.1, Zorlu and Doğan, the entire group is deliberately or unintentionally divided into two subgroups, each of which is controlled by a separate holding company. For both groups, however, the founding families still direct the entire businesses through the majority ownership of the holding companies and the influential presence of family members on the board of those companies. Answers to our questionnaire show that, on the unconsolidated basis (holding company only), the personal ownership by family members was 21–40 percent and the institutional ownership by the family through a collective organization amounted to 41–60 percent on average.

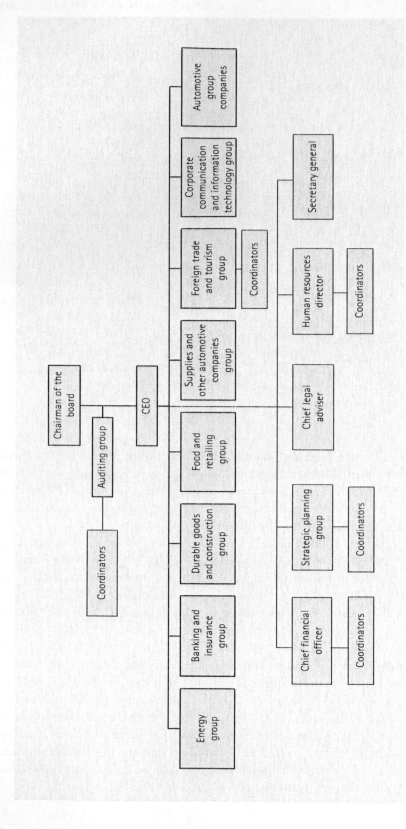

Figure 17.4 Organizational structure of the Koç group, 2007

Source: Adapted with some simplification from the organization chart provided by Koç group.

A few largest groups, such as Koç in 1982 and Sabancı in 1997, then converted their holding companies into publicly listed entities. Alarko, Nergis, Doğan, and İş Bankası are other notable cases. For groups whose holding company is traded publicly, the most frequently cited answer to the question on our questionnaire as to why the company was converted to public ownership is that external investment is beneficial to the group and to the family. Other reasons quoted were that public listing helps improve the group image in society and that they consider that the Turkish stock exchanges function efficiently to raise capital. The majority of groups, however, have kept the top organization of the group closely held. Those business groups cited reasons such as the Turkish stock exchanges not functioning effectively, the founding family's preference to maintain the dominant control of the group, and tax advantages expected for a closely held company.

Naturally, even when the top holding company was traded publicly, the founding families continued to own the majority of shares of the holding company, so that they kept the ultimate control of the entire group in their own hands. This persistent ascendancy of family influence on business groups, however, has faced challenges, thanks to corporate governance "reforms" since the late 1990s. These are discussed in detail in the next two sections.

17.5.2 "Institutionalization" of corporate governance

The term "institutionalization" has become the buzzword in the governance of family-owned groups particularly since the late 1990s. The word has been employed to mean "the presence of a system dependent on rules and principles given the informal aspect of family relations" in Turkey (Ararat 2005). But it has been popularly used in most cases to imply the separation of control from management, in which family members give up their managerial positions and concentrate on their supervisory functions as directors of the board. This implies the increasing presence of professional non-family managers in the top management positions, including the CEO position, of the holding companies of business groups, while such professionals have long occupied the executive positions in the affiliated companies of groups. In the top organizations of established groups, replies to our questionnaire show that the presence of professional non-family CEOs has become widespread. On the contrary, for younger groups, where the first generation is still in power, this change is less evident. The Şahinler group, where the founder, Kemal Şahin, rules as the chairman and CEO of the holding company, is a good example of the conventional integration of direction and execution.

Another aspect of the so-called institutionalization has then been the increase of the outside and independent directors on the boards of the top holding companies as well as affiliated companies. This "reform" comes from the global move toward a more balanced composition of boards of directors. It is thought that the dominance of inside directors, whether family or not, can create an agency problem in which the insiders align with the managing executives and eventually ignore the basic interests of outside shareholders, especially minority ones. One way to minimize this conflict is to recruit outsiders who independently represent the right of external shareholders. Certainly, the boards of the holding companies of some established groups and their operating affiliates now embrace famous academics, prominent business executives, and other celebrities invited from outside. Even when companies are not publicly traded, knowledge, experience, and discipline are the other important factors that groups name as the benefits brought by outside directors (*Capital* 1993: 98). Table 17.8 lists the notable number of outside directors in the holding companies of the largest business groups in Turkey. As the table shows, Turkish business executives both from within and from outside the groups are often sitting on the board alongside family members.[11]

Tables 17.9 and 17.10 show the historical changes in the particular case of the Koç group from 1981 to 2005. The number of family members on the board of the holding company seemed to stay stable with around six people, while the number of outside independent board members increased, especially after 1999, to include foreign individuals (such as John McArthur, the former dean of Harvard Business School, who joined the board in 1999). As Table 17.9 shows, insider business executives from within the group and outside prominent academics or business executives were represented on the board of this group, even in the 1980s. Of the top management positions of the holding company, the CEO is always on the board. Table 17.10 shows the shift of the position of CEO from a family member to a salaried professional manager after 2000. The number of family members in senior executive management positions also seem to have declined. As the tables show, there is the possibility for top salaried managers (other than the CEO) eventually to become a member of the board. A notable example is Hasan Subaşı, who has worked in the Koç group since 1969 in different executive capacities, in this regard.

17.5.3 Family control and global standards in governance

Theoretically, then, the corporate governance apparatus of established Turkish business groups seems to follow the global or American standard as far as two critical mechanisms are concerned. First, the board of directors concentrates on strategic planning, supervision, and monitoring, while the managing executives, represented by the CEO, implement the strategic decisions made by the board. Secondly, any self-serving behavior by inside directors is supposed to be checked and regulated by the monitoring of outside independent directors on the board. Although this professionalization of top management ranks, including the position of CEO, means that the founding family no longer carries out the executive functions, interestingly, one board member of the holding company of a business group we interviewed designated the role of the CEO as the "eventual representative of the family."

---

[11] Üsdiken and Yıldırım-Öktem (2009) argue that the number of real "independent directors" is actually less, as retired professional executives from group companies, board members of international or Turkish firms with which the group has partnerships, and executives of consulting firms with which the group has business relations are often also included in these numbers of "outside directors."

Table 17.8 Composition of the board of directors in the largest holding companies in Turkey, 2007

Board members	Group A	Group B	Group C	Group D	Group E	Group F	Group G	Group H	Group I	Group J
Family members	6	6	6	6	1	2	2	5	4	3
Prominent Turkish business executives within group	2	1	–	6	2	3	–	1	–	2
Prominent Turkish business executives outside group	3	2	5	–	3	–	5	2	–	1
Prominent Turkish academics	–	–	–	–	–	3	–	–	–	–
Prominent international business executives	3	–	–	–	–	–	–	–	–	1
Prominent international academics	1	–	–	–	–	–	–	–	–	–
Prominent international politicians and government officials	–	–	–	–	–	–	–	–	–	–
Total members on the board	15	9	11	12	6	8	7	7	4	7

Note: Groups are ranked by the number of employees for the entire group.

Source: Based on the questionnaire answers of 10 of the 11 business groups.

Table 17.9 Board composition at Koç Holding, 1981–2005

Board of directors	1981	1991	1995	2000	2005
Vehbi Koç*	Chairman				
Rahmi M. Koç*	x	Chairman	Chairman	Chairman	Hon. Chairman
Mustafa V. Koç*					Chairman
Suna Kıraç*	x	x	x	x	x
Sevgi Gönül*	x	x	x	x	
Semahat S. Arsel*	x	x	x	x	x
Erdogan Gönül*			x	x	
İnan Kıraç*		x	x		x
Can Kıraç*	x	x	x		
Ömer Koç*					x
Temel Atay				x	x
Hasan Subaşı			x	x	x
Alpay Bağrıaçık				x	
Fazlı Ayverdi		x	x		
W. Wayne Booker				x	x
Helmut Oswald Maucher				x	x
John H. Mc Arthur				x	x
Dieter Cristoph Urban					x
H. Yavuz Alangoya					x
Bülend Özaydınlı					x
Evren Artam				x	
Nevzat Tüfekçioğlu					x
Uğur Ekşioğlu			x		
Tevfik Altınok			x		
Bernar Nahum	x				
Ziya Bengü	x				
Isak De Eskinazis	x				
M. Fahir İlkel	x	x			
Kemal Oguzhan	x				
Hasan F. Yazici	x				
Emre Gönansay	x				

Note: * represents family members.

Source: Adapted from company annual report of 1981 and data provided by Koç group.

In reality, then, the distinction and separation of functional roles have not been clearly defined, or implemented, particularly on the part of family members. Our interviews show that the members of the family of a large group, who held the non-executive board membership, still went to the headquarters of their group as often as every single day. Some board members of the founding family of yet another group, who had previously occupied executive positions, even visited operating companies

Table 17.10 Top management composition at Koç Holding, 1981–2005

Top management (executive management)	1981	1991	1995	2000	2005
CEO	Rahmi M. Koç*	Can Kıraç*	Inan Kıraç*	Temel Atay	Bülend Özaydınlı
Executive board	Suna Kıraç*	İnan Kıraç*	Uğur Ekşioğlu	Rahmi M. Koç*	
	Fahir İkel	Uğur Ekşioğlu		Suna Kıraç*	
	Can Kıraç*			Temel Atay	
Presidents & VPs	Fahir İkel	Erdoğan Gönül*	Çelik Arsel*	Mustafa V. Koç*	Ali Y. Koç*
	Can Kıraç*	Çelik Arsel*	Tevfik Altınok	Ömer Koç*	Dr. Bülent Bulgurlu
	Tunç Uluğ	Gökçe Bayındır	Hasan Subaşı	Cengiz Solakoğlu	Hasan Bengü
	Erdoğan Karakoyunlu	Ural Belgin	Necati Arıkan	Hasan Subaşı	Rüşdü Saraçoğlu
	Samim Şeren	Selçuk Gezdur	Temel Atay	Dr. Bülent Bulgurlu	Tamer Haşimoğlu
	Ahmet Binbir	Iezcan Yaramancı	Alpay Bağrıaçık	Kutsan Çelebican	Ali Tarık Uzun
	İnan Kıraç*	Kaya Kotanı	Gökçe Bayındır	Selçuk Gezdur	Ömer Bozer
	Yüksel Polat	Hasan Subaşı	Kaya Kotan	Tuğrul Kutadgobilik	Erol Memioğlu
	Metin İplikçi	Cengiz Solakoğlu	Cengiz Solakoğlu	Nevzat Tüfekçioğlu	Kudret Önen
	Uğur Ekşioğlu	Davut Ötükçü	Tunç Uluğ	Hasan Bengü	
	Berti Kahmi	Erdoğan Karakoyunlu		Nedim Esgin	
		Necati Arıkan			
		Tunç Uluğ		Bülend Özaydınlı	
				Nadir Özşahin	
		Tevfik Altınok		Mehmet Ali Berkman	
		Alpay Bağrıaçık		Aydın Çubukçu	
				A. Gündüz Özdemir	

Note: * represents family members. Exact names of positions may differ from one year to another.

Source: Adapted from company annual report of 1981 and data provided by Koç group.

on a regular basis, for instance, once a week. Interestingly, then, some of the senior managers interviewed identified the non-executive chairman of the board as the "invisible CEO" of the entire group, which implied the eventual dominance of the board chair in strategic execution as well as decision-making, regardless of his nominal role within the group.

The functioning of the board of the group holding company in most cases still predominantly followed the voice of the founding family, according to the executives whom we interviewed, not only because non-family board members were still fewer in number and as outsiders did not have adequate and concrete information to influence decision-making, but because the family collectively owned the majority of shares of the holding company anyway. It was also because in several cases a family working group actually functioned beside the formal institutionalized board, and it was that unofficial family committee that made ultimate planning decisions for the entire group. After all, it was the majority-owning founding family that screened and selected outside directors, while minority shareholders, if any, still did not have effective voice in that process, or any other aspects of governance mechanism, for that matter.

These concerns regarding governance practice illustrate that in many cases the reality of the board's and its chairman's functioning still differed in significant ways from the neat and appealing picture portrayed on paper. What is legitimate in terms of contemporary governance standard is another question. If family directors' involvement, such as visits to company headquarters or factories or their informal meetings with managing executives, is limited to gathering information to give them better knowledge for long-term planning and a more effective voice in board meetings, then the directors' behavior would be acceptable and even recommendable. However, if these involvements go beyond these aims and turn toward eventual interference in executive functions, then that intervention is likely to be problematic, or at least against the designated roles. For the publicly listed holding companies, then, family control always faces a criticism of minority shareholder exploitation, as long as the board functions in a way to favor only family interests, rather than company interests.

17.5.4 Organizational design and control styles

The characteristics of Turkish business groups in terms of ownership, governance, and strategy will all be integrated into the group organizational design, an example of which, for the Koç group, was given in Fig. 17.4. That diversified group structure, with operating units or subsidiaries organized along product and industry categories, at first glance resembles the structure of the classical Chandlerian large enterprises with multidivisional structure, adopted by most large enterprises in industrialized economies, especially since the Second World War (Chandler 1977; Fligstein 1990).

The diversified group form, as well as the above-mentioned multidivisional structure, differs from the centralized design of the functional organization that large businesses originally adopted in industrial and emerging economies, including Turkey. That is because both the group form and multidivisional structure exhibit multi-unit, divisionalized, and decentralized designs. Both thus illustrate the clear division of labor between the planning and formulation of strategic resource allocation at the top, and the implementation and execution of those strategic plans at the operating levels. For both, functionally organized units, such as finance, personnel, legal, marketing and distribution, supplement the top management as "staff" functions, while "line" operating units are actually responsible for the production and distribution of goods and services (Chandler 1977). Roughly speaking, however, the similarities between those dominant organizational structures in different developmental settings end here.

Critical differences in the organizational design and control styles between the Chandlerian multidivisional enterprise in mature industrial nations and the diversified business group form in emerging economies lie in two managerial and operational principles. The first concerns the relationships among the operating units that are product-centered in the multidivisional form, but product-unrelated in the diversified group form, as explained earlier. The second difference, which we would like to stress here, lies in the way the top management organization controls those individual operating units. The central headquarters of the multidivisional enterprises usually directs significant operating divisions through strategic planning and decision-making, supplemented by budget allocation. As designated by some management scholars, it is the "style" of strategic control as categorized by Goold and Campbell (1987).

By comparison, the control principle based on which the holding company, as the top managerial body of business groups, administers operating subsidiaries, has a strong element of financial or budgetary control. The financial control in its pure operation implies that the top management organization does not get involved in strategy formulation or operating decisions. Put another way, individual operating units receive a certain amount of budget from the top managerial organization and then take charge of the basic decision-making regarding the strategic allocation of financial, human, material, and information resources (Goold and Campbell 1987).

The operational characteristics of Turkish business groups, especially those of large established groups such as Koç and Sabancı, stand somewhere between strategic control and financial control, as can be concluded from the descriptions above. Our questionnaire survey, as well as interviews, confirmed that this combination or integration of the two control mechanisms was common understanding on the part of the top management itself of many groups, although the relative weight of strategic and financial control varied across groups. Interestingly enough, a few top management said explicitly in their interviews that the relationships were financial in theory, but the holding company was still influential anyway in the major strategic and operating decision-making of affiliates. Given the wide and diverse product and industry portfolios, the groups cannot rely solely on strategic control. But their commitment to strategic control remains strong, as symbolized by the huge headquarters of the two largest groups in Istanbul. This aspiration toward strategic involvement in actual operations and the reluctant institutionalization of the financial control mechanism naturally collide to create the basic organizational conflict that will need to be solved strategically or operationally in a creative manner in the future.

17.6 CONCLUSION

The two pillars of the Turkish large-enterprise economy, business groups and state-owned enterprises, have faced drastic changes in their business environments since the 1980s. The liberalization of the Turkish economy after the early 1980s, followed by the formation of a customs union with the EU in 1996, resulted in increasing competition in the domestic market. The financial crises of 1994 and 2000–1 created macroeconomic instability that hindered the stable long-term growth of enterprises. Certainly, the free-market ideology and resulting policy of privatization seriously restrained the economic viability of state-owned enterprises. The diversified business groups, by contrast, have exhibited an amazing resilience and adaptability.

All these elements of liberalization and an increasingly competitive market, coupled with consecutive financial crises, should theoretically have created an environment for the dissolution of diversified business groups, or at least accelerated strategic reform for a more focused business portfolio, where each group possessed competitive resources and capabilities. The growth strategy on the part of individual groups since the 1980s, however, remained expansive, as opportunities exogenously created by policy changes and market forces dictated the direction of investment. As soon as business groups recognized potential market prospects, they internalized those profit opportunities through the mobilization of their accumulated capabilities in such functions as finance, human resources, contact, and project execution. All these complicated modifications of strategy employed by business groups in Turkey imply that they exist because of their adoptive capabilities, in which the business groups invested extensively. The form and functioning of those capabilities may well be different from the product-specific resources and capabilities that are customarily observed in mature industrial economies. But accumulated adaptive capabilities within the Turkish business groups have functioned reasonably well in changing macroeconomic and microeconomic as well as political settings.

The historic shift of market environment ultimately highlighted the viability of these business groups, in comparison to other large economic agents such as state-owned enterprises, domestic enterprises with concentrated product and industry portfolios, and international firms operating in Turkey. Turkey is no exception to the international rule in this regard, as the liberalization of domestic economy and the big bang of financial crises in Latin American and East Asia did not undermine the collective economic standing of business groups, even when individual ones struggled and even disappeared. Ironically, as has been typically observed in South Korea since the Asian financial crisis of 1997, the largest and most powerful groups actually increased their economic power.

A potential dilemma faced by business groups in Turkey, however, comes from a different source: a conflict between the economic prominence of the business groups that their adaptive capabilities have yielded and the private preference of the founding families that still control the basic strategic directions of corporate growth. For the sake of continuous viability and social legitimacy of their own groups, the families have adopted the management and governance model of global standards. More salaried professional managers have started playing the decision-making roles by occupying the senior executive positions, even at the board level of the commanding holding company. Outside and independent directors have also begun to sit on the boards of the holding as well as the affiliated companies. This drive toward professionalization is likely to lead to a collision course as long as families continue to hold onto a closed control. How the business groups in Turkey could or should resolve this conflict will determine their future course.

REFERENCES

AMSDEN, A. H. (2001). *The Rise of "The Rest": Challenges to the West from Late-Industrialization Economies*. New York: Oxford University Press.

AMSDEN, A. H., and HIKINO, T. (1994). "Project Execution Capability, Organizational Know-how and Conglomerate Corporate Growth in Late Industrialization," *Industrial and Corporate Change*, 3: 111–148.

ARARAT, M. (2005). "2004 yılı Istanbul sanayi odası III. Sanayi kongresi oturum sonuçları," in *Aile Şirketlerinde Kurumsallaşma*. Istanbul: Istanbul Sanayi Odası Yayınları.

BAKER, G. P., and SMITH, G. D. (1995). *The New Financial Capitalists: Kohlberg Kravis Roberts and the Creation of Corporate Value*. New York and Cambridge: Cambridge University Press.

BONAGLIA, F., COLPAN, A. M., and GOLDSTEIN, A. (2008). "Innovation and Internationalization in the White Goods GVC: The Case of Arçelik," *International Journal of Technological Learning, Innovation and Development*, Special Issue on "Global Value Chains & Innovation Networks: Prospects for Industrial Upgrading in Developing Countries," 1/4: 520–535.

BUĞRA, A. (1994). *State and Business in Modern Turkey: A Comparative Study*. New York: State University of New York Press.

BUĞRA, A. (1998). "Class, Culture and State: An Analysis of Interest Representation by Two Turkish Business Associations," *International Journal of Middle East Studies*, 30/4: 521–539.

BUĞRA, A., and ÜSDIKEN, B. (1995). "Societal Variations in State-Dependent Organizational Forms: The South-Korean Chaebol and the Turkish Holding," Research Paper SBE/AD 95-01, Boğaziçi Üniversitesi, Istanbul.

Capital (1993). "Öncülerin Başarı Öyküleri" (Nov.), 98.

CHANDLER, A. D., JR. (1977). *The Visible Hand: The Managerial Revolution in American Business*. Cambridge, MA: Harvard University Press.

CHANDLER, A. D., JR. (1990). *Scale and Scope: The Dynamics of Industrial Capitalism*. Cambridge, MA: Harvard University Press.

CHANDLER, A. D., JR., AMATORI, F., and HIKINO, T. (1997). *Big Business and the Wealth of Nations*. Cambridge: Cambridge University Press, 1997.

CHANG, S. J. (2006). "Introduction: Business Groups in Asia," in S. J. Chang (ed.), *Business Groups in East Asia: Financial Crisis, Restructuring, and New Growth*. Oxford: Oxford University Press.

COLPAN, A. M., and HIKINO, T. (2008). "Türkiye'nin büyük şirketler kesiminde işletme gruplarının yeri ve çeşitlendirme stratejileri" (Diversifying to be the Leading Developmental Agent: Business Groups in Turkey's Large-Enterprise Economy), *Yönetim Araştırmaları Dergisi* (Management Research Journal), 8/1–2: 23–58.

DÜNDAR, C. (2006). *Özel Arşivinden Belge ve Anılarıyla Vehbi Koç*. Istanbul: Doğan Kitapcılık AŞ.

ERTUNA, Ö. (2005). *Türkiye'nin 500 Büyük Sanayi Kuruluşu'nun Yirmi Yılı (1983–2004)*. Istanbul: Istanbul Sanayi Odası Yayınları.

FLIGSTEIN, N. (1990). *The Transformation of Corporate Control*. Cambridge, MA: Harvard University Press.

GOOLD, M., and CAMPBELL, A. (1987). *Strategies and Styles: The Role of the Centre in Managing Diversified Corporations*. Oxford: Basil Blackwell.

GÖKŞEN, N. S., and ÜSDIKEN, B. (2001). "Uniformity and Diversity in Turkish Business Groups: Effects of Scale and Time of Founding," *British Journal of Management*, 12: 325–340.

GUILLÉN, M. F. (2000). "Business Groups in Emerging Economies: A Resource-Based View," *Academy of Management Journal*, 43: 362–380.

HIKINO, T., and AMSDEN, A. H. (1994). "Staying Behind, Stumbling Back, Sneaking Up, Soaring Ahead: Late Industrialization in Historical Perspective," in W. J. Baumol, R. R. Nelson, and E. N. Wolff (eds.), *Convergence in Productivity: Cross-Country Studies and Historical Evidence*. New York: Oxford University Press.

HSUEH, L., HSU, C., and PERKINS, D. H. (2001). *Industrialization and the State: The Changing Role of the Taiwan Government in the Economy, 1945–1998*. Cambridge, MA: Harvard Institute for International Development.

İDIL, E. (1999). "İlk ve hep en büyüklerden Vehbi Koç ve ailesi," in *75 Yılda Çarkları Döndürenler*. Istanbul: Tarih Vakfı Yayınları.

JENSEN, M. C. (1993). "The Modern Industrial Revolution, Exit, and Failure of Internal Control Systems," *Journal of Finance*, 48: 831–880.

KANG, M. H. (1996). *The Korean Business Conglomerate: Chaebol Then and Now*. Berkeley, CA: Institute of East Asian Studies.

KARADEMIR, B., ÖZGEN, H., OSBORN, R. N., and YAPRAK, A. (2005). "The Co-evolution of Institutional Environments, Markets, Organizational Capabilities, and Organizational Strategies: A Comparative Case Study of Turkish Family Holdings." Paper presented at 21st Colloquium of European Group for Organizational Studies, Berlin, June 30 – July 2.

KARLUK, S. R. (1999). *Türkiye Ekonomisi: Tarihsel Gelişim, Yapısal ve Sosyal Değişim*, Istanbul: Beta Basım Yayım Dağıtım AŞ.

KEPENEK, Y., and YENTÜRK, N. (2000). *Türkiye Ekonomisi*. Istanbul: Remzi Kitabevi.

KHANNA, T., and PALEPU, K. (2000). "The Future of Business Groups in Emerging Markets: Long-Run Evidence from Chile," *Academy of Management Journal*, 43: 268–285.

KHANNA, T., and YAFEH, Y. (2007). "Business Groups in Emerging Markets: Paragons or Parasites?" *Journal of Economic Literature*, 45/2: 331–372.

KNICKERBOCKER, F. T. (1973). *Oligopolistic Reaction and the Multinational Enterprise*. Cambridge, MA: Harvard University Press.

KOCK, C., and GUILLEN, M. F. (2001). "Strategy and Structure in Developing Countries: Business Groups as an Evolutionary Response to Opportunities for Unrelated Diversification," *Industrial and Corporate Change*, 10: 77–113.

MADDISON, A. (2001). *The World Economy: A Millennium Perspective*. Paris: OECD Development Centre.

MORIKAWA, H. (1992). *Zaibatsu: The Rise and Fall of Family Enterprise Groups in Japan*. Tokyo: University of Tokyo Press.

MORCK, R., WOLFENZON, D., and YEUNG, B. (2005). "Corporate Governance, Economic Entrenchment, and Growth," *Journal of Economic Literature*, 43/3: 655–720.

ÖNİŞ, Z. (1991). "The Evolution of Privatization in Turkey: The Institutional Context of Public-Enterprise Reform," *International Journal of Middle East Studies*, 23/2: 163–176.

ÖNİŞ, Z. (1992). "Redemocratization and Economic Liberation in Turkey: The Limits of State Economy," *Studies in Comparative International Development*, 27: 3–23.

ORBAY, H., and YURTOGLU, B. B. (2006). "The Impact of Corporate Governance Structures on the Corporate Investment Performance in Turkey," *Corporate Governance: An International Review*, 14: 349.

ÖZEN, S. (2003). "Türk holdinglerinin ilgisiz çeşitlenmesinin nedenleri üzerine bir tartışma," *Ulusal Yönetim ve Organizasyon Kongresi Bildiri Kitabı*, Afyon Kocatepe Universitesi, Afyon, 669–671.

ROOT, R., and QUELCH, J. (1997). "Koç Holding: Arcelik White Goods." Harvard Business School Case 598–633.

ŞAHİN, H. (2002). *Türkiye Ekonomisi*, Ezgi Kitabevi Yayinlari, Bursa, Turkey.

STEERS, R. M., SHIN, Y. K., and UNGSON, G. R. (1989). *The Chaebol: Korea's New Industrial Might*. New York and Tokyo: Harper & Row, Ballinger Division.

SUBAŞI, H. (2006). Board Member, Koç Holding, Interview on July 24, Istanbul.

Tax Guide (Vergi Rehberi) (2009). *Capital*, Special supplement, prepared by Ernst & Young (Jan).

ÜSDIKEN, B., and YILDIRIM-ÖKTEM, Ö. (2008). "Changes in the Institutional Environment and 'Non-Executive' and Independent Members of the Boards of Directors of Firms Affiliated with Large Family Business Groups," *Amme İdaresi Dergisi*, 41/1: 43–71.

WESTPHAL, L. E. (1990). "Industrial Policy in an Export-Propelled Economy: Lessons from South Korea's Experience," *Journal of Economic Perspectives*, 4: 41–60.

YAMAK, S., and ÜSDIKEN, B. (2006). "Economic Liberalization and Antecedents of Top Management Teams: Evidence from Turkish 'Big' Business," *British Journal of Management*, 17: 177–94.

YAPRAK, A., KARADEMIR, B., and OSBORN, R. N. (2007). "How Do Business Groups Function and Evolve in Emerging Markets? The Case of Turkish Business Groups," in A. Rialp and J. Rialp (eds.), *Advances in International Marketing*. Amsterdam: Elsevier, 275–94.

YERASIMOS, S. (1977). *Azgelişmişlik Sürecinde Türkiye*. Istanbul: Gözlem Yayınları.

YURTOGLU, B. B. (2000). "Ownership, Control and Performance of Turkish Listed Firms," *Journal of Applied Economics and Economic Policy*, 27/2: 193–222.

YURTOGLU, B. B. (2003). "Corporate Governance and Implications for Minority Shareholders in Turkey," *Corporate Ownership & Control*, 1/1: 72–86.

CHAPTER 18

··

BUSINESS GROUPS
IN RUSSIA

··

SERGEI GURIEV

18.1 INTRODUCTION

··

BUSINESS groups play a critically important role in Russian economy. In a famous
interview to the *Financial Times* in 1996, Boris Berezovsky (both an entrepreneur
and a high-ranking bureaucrat at that point) suggested that seven groups controlled about 50 percent of Russian economy. In a more systematic study, Boone
and Rodionov (2002) went through the ownership of the top sixty-four listed
Russian corporations in 2002. They analyzed the shares in the total revenue of
these firms controlled by the government, private owners, foreign owners, and so
on. While the government controlled 43 percent of the output in these firms, the
eight largest groups (including five diversified and three specialized) controlled
another 49 percent. In the summer of 2003, the World Bank carried out a broader-
based study of Russian firms trying to include non-listed companies as well. This
study showed that twenty-two leading business groups accounted for about 40
percent of both revenues and employment in the Russian industry (World Bank
2005; see also Guriev and Rachinsky 2005). The same study estimated the government ownership at about 30 percent and foreign ownership below 10 percent.
Therefore the large private business groups—at least in 2002–3—were the major
players in the Russian economy. While their influence has somewhat decreased
since than, they still dominate the Russian business landscape. Both the Boone–
Rodionov and the World Bank studies have shown that Russia is one of the world
"leaders" if not the leader in terms of the widely used measure of nationwide

ownership concentration—the share of top ten families in the stock-market capi-talization. This share (60 percent) is not only ahead of continental Europe, but also ahead of the East Asian countries prior to the 1997 crisis—even ahead of Suharto's Indonesia and Marcos's Phillipines (Guriev and Rachinsky 2005). What is even more striking is that most of these groups emerged from scratch in the course of between ten and fifteen years—unlike their counterparts in the continental Europe, Asia, and other emerging markets, where building the largest business groups has taken generations.

This chapter tracks the evolution of Russian business groups since their emergence during privatization in the 1990s and the restructuring and consolidation that followed. As in other economies, the growth of business groups in Russia has been a natural response to multiple market and government failures that gave rise to "institutional economies of scale." We argue that some of the business groups will grow into major multinational companies while others will be acquired by foreign multinationals (either unit by unit or wholesale). Few are likely to remain diversified conglomerates. We also discuss the phenomenon of government-owned business groups and so-called state corporations. While the focus of the chapter is on private business groups, understanding their evolution would be virtually impossible with-out reference to state-owned groups, or the large state-owned firms (which may be bigger than many business groups but essentially have one business unit).

18.2 Emergence and evolution
of business groups

18.2.1 Russian privatization and the emergence of business groups

How did large Russian business groups emerge?[1] In the late 1980s all industrial assets in Russia were in state ownership and were inalienable elements of the command economy. Each plant was a part of the respective ministry's hierarchy. Gorbachev's reforms of the late 1980s did decentralize control over the firms, partially shifting authority into the hands of managers and workers (Boyko et al. 1995). So, when the Russian government started to discuss the privatization of these firms, it had to take into account these insiders' interests. The first stage of privatization, so-called voucher privatization, gave substantial privileges to the workers and especially to

---

[1] A business group is defined here as a group of legally independent firms linked together in formal and informal ties (Khanna and Yafeh 2007). Whether a listed company is included in a group or not is not essential in the definition taken in this chapter.

the managers of the firms. The designers of privatization understood all the limitations of the approach but also argued that the window of opportunity was narrow
and therefore decided to proceed with this bargain (Shleifer and Treisman 2000). For
these reasons they also had to opt for the fast mass privatization rather than case-
by-case privatization to establish as many private owners as possible before the
window for privatization was closed. Their major goal was to entrench private
property and to provide political support for further reforms. The reformers believed
that the secondary market would eventually reallocate the assets to the most efficient
owners (Boycko et al. 1995)

Thus, most of the enterprises were initially privatized by their insiders (see the
comparison of Russian privatizations to privatization in other countries in Megginson 2005 and Guriev and Megginson 2006). Only in the later stages were outsiders
(mostly bankers) able to purchase industrial assets from the insiders in the secondary
market; later on these outsiders built the business groups as we know them now. Out
of this list of Russian business groups (see Table 18.1), only a few are owned and run
by their Soviet-time managers. Yet, another implication of the mass privatization was
the disintegration of the Soviet-time state-owned business groups. Most assets were
privatized at the level of individual plants. Only very few Soviet ministries or sub-
ministries or large integrated business groups were privatized jointly (the most
notable examples include Lukoil and Avtovaz).

Thus the newly emerged business groups did not necessarily reproduce firm
boundaries that had existed before transition. On the one hand, it was a positive
development, as the process of reassembling the plants and business units into the
new groups followed profit-maximizing rationale and therefore should have been
more effective. Liberalization of prices and of foreign trade drastically changed
relative prices and created new business opportunities. On the other hand, the
emerging M&A market was not efficient and therefore some of the new business
group boundaries were far from optimal. In particular, holdup and disorganization
of vertical production links were claimed to be important factors in the subsequent
output decline (Blanchard and Kremer 1997).

Once the voucher privatization was over, the government also privatized some
assets case by case in open auctions, including the notorious loans-for-shares deals.
Freeland (2000) describes the lack of transparency in loans-for-shares auctions and
argues that the new buyers of these assets paid a fraction of the fair market price. In
the late 1990s and the early 2000s the secondary M&A market finally started to
function. A repeated survey of ownership of Russian industrial firms showed that
insider ownership had been slowly but steadily crowded out by the outsider ownership (Guriev et al. 2004; Lazareva et al. 2007).

Many of these outsiders were the large business groups. Once these business
groups had been formed, the new owners set to establish majority control and
restructure. Boone and Rodionov (2002) present an archetypical story. New owners
diluted the other shareholders (including the government) to attain a majority
ownership stake (in many cases in the range of 60–90 percent). Once they had the
majority of equity, they had very strong incentives to increase the market value of

Table 18.1 Russian oligarchs, 2003

Senior partner(s)	Holding company / firm (major sector(s))	Employment		Sales		Other rankings*	Events 2003–8	Substantial assets abroad
		000	(% sample)	Rbn	(% sample)			
Oleg Deripaska	Base Element / RusAl (aluminum, auto)	169	(3.9)	65	(1.3)	P, BR, DS, K, F	Has also purchased many unrelated assets, including construction	+
Roman Abramovich	Millhouse / Sibneft (oil)	169	(3.9)	203	(3.9)	S, BR, DS, K, H**, F	Sold oil to government, purchased many other assets including a large stake in Evraze	+
Vladimir Kadannikov	AutoVAZ (automotive)	167	(3.9)	112	(2.2)	BR, K	Sold to government	
Sergei Popov, Andrei Melnichenko, Dmitry Pumpiansky	MDM (coal, pipes, chemical)	143	(3.3)	70	(1.4)	F	Split the group into banking (Popov), chemicals (Melnichenko), coal (Melnichenko-Popov), and pipes (Pumpiansky)	
Vagit Alekperov	Lukoil (oil)	137	(3.2)	475	(9.2)	S, P, BR, DS, K, F		+
Alexei Mordashov	Severstal (steel, auto)	122	(2.8)	78	(1.5)	BR, DS, F	Spun off automotive assets to management, unsuccessfully bid for Arcelor	+
Vladimir Potanin, Mikhail Prokhorov	Interros / Norilsk Nickel (non-ferrous metals)	112	(2.6)	137	(2.6)	B, S, P, BR, DS, K, F	In the process of dividing assets between Potanin and Prokhorov	
Alexandr Abrarrov	Evrazholding (steel)	101	(2.3)	52	(1.0)	F	Sold a large stake to Abramovich	+
Len Blavatnik, Victor Vekselberg	Access-Renova/TNK-BP (oil, aluminum)	94	(2.2)	121	(2.3)	DS, F	Bought many unrelated assets including in utilities, growing share of assets owned separately by Blavatnik and Vekselberg	+

(continued)

Table 18.1 Continued

Senior partner(s)	Holding company / firm (major sector(s))	Employment		Sales		Other rankings*	Events 2003–8	Substantial assets abroad
		000	(% sample)	Rbn	(% sample)			
Mikhail Khodorkovsky	Menatep/Yukos (oil)	93	(2.2)	149	(2.9)	B, S, P, BR, DS, K, H, F	Imprisoned, company bankrupt, assets nationalized	
Iskander Makhmudov	UGMK (non-ferrous metals)	75	(1.7)	33	(0.6)	K		
Vladimir Bogdanov	Surgutneftegaz (oil)	65	(1.5)	163	(3.1)	P, BR, DS, K, F		+
Victor Rashnikov	Magnitogorsk Steel (steel)	57	(1.3)	57	(1.1)			
Igor Zyuzin	Mechel (steel, coal)	54	(1.3)	31	(0.6)		Suffered from critical comments by Vladimir Putin on antitrust grounds	
Vladimir Lisin	Novolipetsk Steel (steel)	47	(1.1)	39	(0.8)	F		
Zakhar Smushkin, Boris Zingarevich, Mikhail Zingarevich	IlimPulpEnterprises (pulp)	42	(1.0)	20	(0.4)		sold a 50% stake to international paper	
Shafagat Tahaudinov	Tatneft (oil)	41	(1.0)	41	(0.8)			
Mikhail Fridman	Alfa/TNK-BP (oil)	38	(0.9)	107	(2.1)	B, S, P, BR, DS, K, F	Bought many unrelated assets, including telecoms, financial, retail, media	+
Boris Ivanishvili	Metalloinvest (ore)	36	(0.8)	15	(0.3)	P*	Sold to Vasilly Anissimov and Alisher Usmanov, **, left Russia	The group continue to grow in metals and ore
Kakha Bendukidze	United Machinery (engineering)	35	(0.8)	10	(0.2)	BR, K	Sold to government, left Russia, worked in Georgian government	

Senior partner(s)	Holding company / firm (major sector(s))	Employment		Sales		Other rankings*	Events 2003–8	Substantial assets abroad
		000	(% sample)	Rbn	(% sample)			
Vladimir Yevtushenkov	Sistema/MTS (telecoms)	20	(0.5)	27	(0.5)	S, P, BR, DS, K, F	Acquired many unrelated assets including real estate	
David Yakobashvili, Mikhail Dubinin, Sergei Plastinin	WimmBillDann (dairy/juice)	13	(0.3)	20	(0.4)		Acquired many upstream and downstream assets	
Total		1,831	(42.4)	2,026	(39.1)			

Notes: Each entry lists the leading shareholder(s) in a respective business group, the name of the holding company or the flagship asset, and one or two major sectors. We report several individual per group only when there is equal or near equal partnership.

Ranking is based on employment in the sample and may therefore be different from actual, as the sample disproportionally covers assets of different oligarchs. Employment and sales are based on official firm-level data for 2001. The exchange rate was $1=29 rubles.

*Other oligarch rankings:

B – Berezovsky's Group of Seven (Financial Times, 1996)

S – Classified as oligarchs in the "Sale of the Century" (Freeland, 2000, p. xv–xvii)

P – Pappe (2000)

BR – Boone and Rodionov (2002)

DS – Dynkin and Sokolov (2002)

K – Kommersart (2003)

H – Hoffman (2003)

F – Forbes (2004)

**Anisimov and Usmanov

Source: Gurler and Rachinsky (2005).

their companies.[2] Thus it was not surprising that many of these groups became the leaders of restructuring. The restructuring has taken place both at the plant level and at the group level. In many cases, restructuring did involve specialization and the breakup of diversified groups into specialized companies or holdings with the subsequent sale or separation of ownership.

18.2.2 Political risk and evolution of Russian business groups

Analysis of the incentives to restructure should take into account the high political risk (of an outright expropriation by the state) faced by all private Russian groups in Russia. Even though business group owners have large majority stakes in the groups, their incentives to maximize the long-run shareholder value are undermined by weak protection of their property rights. This issue is specific to Russia and other transition countries. Private property rights in these countries are vulnerable to predation from the government, which in turn relies on the public perception of the property rights' illegitimacy. The study of representative samples in twenty-eight transition countries (Denisova et al. 2009) showed that the majority of voters believe that privatization was carried out in an unfair way, and that the assets should be nationalized. Thus the current owners face a substantial political risk—any politician in office can appeal to the median voter's preference for forced nationalization. This political risk creates the crucial tradeoff for the controlling shareholders: they can focus on restructuring or they can opt for an initial public offering (IPO) or a block sale to a strategic blockholder. The longer the sale is delayed, the greater the return—strong incentives result in a deeper restructuring and hence a greater stock price increase. On the other hand, delaying the sale also raises a probability of expropriation by the government. The immediate equity sale sacrifices the returns to restructuring but resolves the problem of political risk. Different business groups—and different divisions of the business groups—addressed this tradeoff in very different ways. The oil companies (supposedly most vulnerable to expropriation) wanted to sell right away to foreign investors. Some managed to sell (like TNK, which sold 50 percent to BP, and Lukoil, which sold 8 percent to Conoco, which then increased its stake to 20 percent); some were too late (like Yukos). Russian steelmakers—another major industry of choice for Russian business groups—have always been less vulnerable to expropriation, so they still do not have foreign blockholders.

---

[2] Most Russian corporations have no dual class shares. Some companies have preferred (non-voting) stock inherited from the voucher privatization in 1992–4. In one of the three privatization options, the insiders would get 25% non-voting preferred shares (which remain non-voting as long as at least 10% of corporate profits are distributed to preferred stockholders as dividends). Many companies have diluted or bought out these preferred shares since then, but as of 2009 a few companies still have the preferred stock.

This tradeoff hinges on the assumption that strategic foreign investors are less vulnerable to expropriation than the large Russian entrepreneurs. The reason is that, in order to expropriate rich Russians, the government can appeal to the median voter's feeling of injustice of privatization. Whenever the expropriation targets a stake that has been purchased at a high price by a law-abiding foreign company, this case loses the popular appeal. Also, expropriation of a large multinational corporation is costlier, as foreign governments and other foreign investors are likely to punish the expropriating government. Indeed, even though we have seen quite a few outright expropriations of domestic owners, there has never been a complete expropriation of a major foreign investor.

Political risk also affects the groups' evolution in yet another way. To hedge against the poor protection of property rights within Russia, in the second half of the 2000s Russian business groups have been very active in purchasing assets outside Russia. Skolkovo (2008) tracks the foreign investment of the largest Russian companies (many of them business groups or leading group members). This study estimates that by 2007 the top twenty-five Russian multinational companies and business groups had invested abroad about US$90 billion (this was close to 10 percent of Russian GDP). Consistent with the political risk conjecture, it was the private business groups that expanded abroad rather than the state companies (which by definition do not face nationalization risk). While *all* private companies increased their UNCTAD's Transnationality Index substantially in 2004–7, most state-owned companies had a decrease in the Index or raised it by a small margin. For the top ten internationalized private companies/groups, the Transnationality Index was in the range of 30–40 percent. (The Index is calculated by averaging the relative shares of foreign assets, foreign employees, and foreign sales in the respective totals of the company.)

Table 18.1 (taken from Guriev and Rachinsky 2005) describes major private business groups in the Russian economy around 2003.[3] This table is based on the above-mentioned World Bank survey that was carried out in the summer of 2003. This snapshot of ownership structure in Russia was taken at exactly the peak of the influence of the large private business groups. Their (relative) eclipse started in 2003 when the two major shareholders of Yukos Oil Company were arrested and the so-called Yukos affair began. The Yukos affair —expropriation of the largest Russian oil companies by the government and imprisonment/exile of its major shareholders—signaled the new stage in the development of business groups in Russia, renationalization of their assets, and the new rise of state companies and state corporations. Since the Yukos affair, the government has nationalized quite a few companies—including parts of the business groups in Table 18.1 as well as whole business groups. Just to illustrate the scale of renationalization, it is instructive to consider Table 18.1. Roman Abramovich has kept his holding company, Millhouse Capital, but sold its most important asset, Sibneft, to the state-owned natural gas monopoly, Gazprom. Avtovaz was also nationalized. All Mikhail Khodorkovsky's and Kakha Bendukidze's Russian assets were nationalized.

---

[3] Table 18.2 presents a more recent picture, that of 2008 (before the acute phase of the global financial crisis). This snapshot is incomplete and covers only the four major groups.

Other business groups sold only their less important units to the state. Moreover, the state no longer controls just a few companies in the energy sector, as was the case in 2003. As shown in the data from Boone and Rodionov, and Guriev and Rachinsky, in 2002–3 the state dominated only natural gas, electric energy, and fixed-line telecommunications—these were the firms designated for privatization, but in gas and telecoms the privatization never happened. As of 2009, the government also controls a major market share in the oil, automotive, machinery, banking, and some other industries. In terms of Table 18.1, out of the 40 percent of the economy controlled by the private business groups in 2003, about 10 percent had been nationalized in the next five years; if one assumes a similar share of nationalization from the other private owners, as of 2009 the government ownership should be around 50 percent of the economy.

18.2.3 The rise of the state-owned companies

Some of this expansion has occurred through the state or state companies making the business groups M&A offers that they could not refuse (especially after the Yukos affair). In other cases, the establishment and growth of the state business groups were financed through the taxpayers' money (and there has been a lot of tax money due to the high oil price and high oil tax rates—again, hiked after the Yukos affair). While the government has tried to make sure these state companies are specialized, many of them did diversify into unrelated industries. For example, until 2008 the natural gas company Gazprom owned one of the largest banks, Gazprombank, a huge insurance company, a large asset management company, a leading media company, and so on. The state company Russian Technologies (formerly known as Rosoboronexport) was initially created to export Russian weapons but eventually evolved into a conglomerate with hundreds of companies in all industries. An analysis of the structure of state-owned business groups goes beyond the focus of the chapter. It is, however, important that in modern Russia state-owned companies—mostly non-listed—tend to build large business groups rather than to focus on their core business. This implies that the market imperfections that produce large gains for the private business groups also affect the state ones.

18.3 OWNERSHIP AND GOVERNANCE
OF BUSINESS GROUPS

Unlike pyramids and family firms in other non-Anglo-Saxon countries, Russian groups do not face the issue of separation of ownership and control. According to Bertrand and

Mullainathan (2003) and Aganin and Volpin (2005), such separation may arise because of (1) controlling shareholders holding only small cash-flow ownership stakes and (2) several levels of the "pyramids," or business group hierarchies, being listed. Neither of these is the case in Russia. Most leading groups have majority shareholders; only one group (Sistema) lists both the holding company and the subsidiaries.

While the groups' shareholders initially acquired relatively small stakes, they subsequently turned them into majority equity stakes via buyout, dilution, and expropriation of other shareholders, including foreigners and government (Boone and Rodionov 2002). As discussed above, this resulted in an unprecedented consolidation of ownership—the main shareholders controlled 60–90 per cent of both control and cash-flow rights. At this level of equity participation, the owners have very strong incentives to maximize the value of the company.

Virtually all Russian groups list at only one level and therefore avoid the problems of pyramidal ownership. Most prefer listing the lowest level, keeping 100 percent control at the top and sectoral segment level. Some list the sectoral units (but in this case its subsidiaries are usually 100 percent owned by the segment company). The only exception is the Sistema group, which has listed both the individual group members and the group's holding company itself. Quite in line with the "pyramids" argument, Sistema has a substantial "conglomerate discount." The market capitalization of Sistema is often below the market value of its stake in its major telecommunications company MTS (which accounts for about a half of Sistema's assets, according to Sistema's own estimates of the value of its non-listed assets). Clearly, investors expect expropriation of MTS in favor of other group members.

Therefore it is not surprising that the groups' controlling shareholders want to improve corporate governance at all levels within the groups. The groups' owners understand that better corporate governance raises the stock price—either in a potential IPO or in an equity sale to a potential blockholder.[4] Hence, apart from restructuring the company to raise productivity, they also improve corporate governance to create commitment devices that would limit expropriation of minority shareholders. This is why the largest business groups and their units now have independent directors. It is very common to have foreign independent directors— to send a strong signal that companies want to implement the best practice of corporate governance. This is crucial, as most business groups still have a controlling owner—not even the founder's family but the founding entrepreneur himself.[5] These entrepreneurs are still very active in running their businesses.

While the process of delegating control to professional managers has certainly started by the 2000s, it is being slowed by the lack of investor protection. As outlined in Burkart et al. 2003, family firms delay hiring professional managers in countries with a low level of investor protection. This is still an important problem in Russia.

---

[4] Black et al. (2006) do show that Russian companies with better corporate governance do have a higher market capitalization (even controlling for company fixed effects).

[5] According to *Forbes* (2008), out of eighty-seven Russian billionaires, only one is female: Elena Baturina, the wife of the Mayor of Moscow.

Yet, as the institutional environment is improving, more delegation from owners to managers is to be expected, as well as the dilution of the consolidated ownership through management's equity options.

18.4 STRATEGY AND STRUCTURE
OF BUSINESS GROUPS

How are Russian business groups structured? Table 8.3 presents an example: the structure of Basic Element, the business group controlled by Oleg Deripaska, allegedly Russia's richest businessman in 2008 (*Forbes* 2008).

A typical business group structure has three major tiers—a holding company, industry-level divisions, and individual plants. The holding company has a majority owner—either a founding entrepreneur or a group of entrepreneurs who started the business.[6] The holding company owns sectoral segment divisions. Each second-level division owns assets in a specific industry. Table 18.2 describes the structure for the four largest diversified business groups (Alfa, Basic Element, Renova, and Sistema). Usually, the top-level holding company has a majority stake (in many cases, a supermajority stake or even 100 percent) in the mid-level divisions' equity. This structure allows different skills to be concentrated at each level. The lower-level units (single plant) focus on production and operations issues. The middle level coordinates investment (in human and physical capital) and marketing in a particular industry. The top level's job is to create and exploit synergies at the level of the whole group—in terms of managing political and economic risks, and raising finance. Understanding the functioning of this level is critical for understanding Russian business groups.

What do the owners and the top managers of Russian business groups actually do? Do they create value and how? Why do diversified groups compete successfully with other, more specialized businesses? A consistent explanation seems to be provided by the main argument in Khanna and Yafeh (2007): in an economy with imperfect political and economic institutions and underdeveloped markets, size matters. Large business groups may be an optimal response to the multiple market failures and government failures. Larger groups have lower financial costs, are more effective in lobbying, in access to courts, and in resisting predatory bureaucracy,[7] take advantage

---

[6] Notice that as of 2009 most large Russian business groups are still run by their founders. This is explained by two factors. First, the founding entrepreneurs are still young (a median owner is still in his late forties). Secondly, the quality of corporate governance in Russia is still quite low, so—according to the logic of Burkart et al. (2003)—it may be too risky for the founders to delegate control to professional managers.

[7] In principle, predation by the government officials may have the opposite effect: fearing predation, firms may hide in the informal sector. Hence, predation may create a disincentive to increase a firm's size,

Table 18.2. Sectoral structure of selected Russian business groups, 2008

Group (major beneficiary)	Sector segments (self-defined)	Number of major firms in each segment
Alfa (Mikhail Fridman)	Oil and gas	1
	Financial	5
	Telecom	4
	Technology	1
	Media	1
	Retail trade	3
Basic Element (Oleg Deripaska)	Energy	5
	Resources	4
	Manufacturing	5
	Financial	7
	Construction	6
	Aviation	5
Renova (Victor Vekselberg)	Metallurgy	6
	Oil and chemicals	3
	Energy, housing and utilities	5
	Machine engineering	1
	Development and construction	1
	Infrastructure	1
	Telecom	4
	Financial	2
Sistema (Vladimir Evtushenkov)	Telecommunications assets	Telecommunications (50), media (1), cinema (1)
	Consumer assets	6 (real-estate, financial services, travel, trade, healthcare, retail)
	Technology and industry	Technology, radar and space, pharmaceuticals, innovation, and venture capital
	Others	Petrochemicals

Note: Different groups use different classifications for sectors. We use the groups' own definitions.
Source: Groups' websites.

of internal capital and labor markets, and resolve hold-up problems via vertical integration. For the sake of brevity, we will label this effect "institutional economies of scale." In the presence of such "institutional economies of scale," size may be more important than specialization and focus. Large business groups therefore have a

as larger firms are more likely to be visible to the predators. However, this argument can apply only to the small business. In this chapter we discuss large business groups where the issue of hiding in the shadow sector is not relevant.

Table 18.3. Sectoral structure of the Basic Element business group

Sector	Companies
Energy	DOZAKL, CEAC Holding, United Oil Company, EuroSibEnergo, UC RUSAL
Resources	Batu Mining, Janu Jyldyz Gold Limited, LPK Continantal Management, SMR
Manufacturing	GAZ Group, RM Systems, Military Industrial Company, Aviacor, JSC Russian Corporation of Transportation Manufacturing
Financial services	Ingosstrakh, Soyuz Bank, Element Leasing, NPF Socium, IngosstrakhInvestments, Be Healthy, NPF Stroycomplex
Construction	Glavstroy, BaselCement, Altius Development, Transstroy
Aviation	JSC Kuban Airlines, Gelendzhik Airport, Anapa Airport, Krasnodar Airport, Sochi Airport

Source: Compiled based on information on Basic Element's website (www.basel.ru/en/).

serious advantage in buying under-valued assets in emerging markets, and especially in Russia where institutional economies of scale include both missing markets and corrupt and predatory government.[8]

Yet some groups decide to take advantage of benefits of specialization and spin off the sectoral segments. Even given the institutional economies of scale, speciali-zation does pay off; it is especially true for groups with a relatively low expropria-tion risk. In some cases the specialization decisions go as far as an ultimate dissolution of the diversified business group itself. A good example of splitting a large business group into specialized segments or firms is the story of the MDM group. The three managers-entrepreneurs who built the group divided their assets into pipe production (taken over by one of the owners), banking (by another owner), fertilizers (by the third owner), and coal (still jointly owned by two initial owners).

In other cases, the spin-offs were sold to the management of the business units (Severstal steel company sold its large automotive division SeverstalAvto, now re-named Sollers, to the management) or to foreign investors (Basic Element's alumi-num company Russian Aluminum sold two plants to ALCOA).

---

[8] It is illustrative that investment strategy of one of the largest business groups, Alfa Group, states this in no uncertain terms: "We are opportunistic investors. Simply stated, we are value-oriented investors. In evaluating any investment opportunity, our investment philosophy is driven by the opportunity to purchase assets that, due to perceived risk, low liquidity, disinterest or a lack of understanding on the part of market participants, are undervalued. We believe the most attractive opportunities are in world emerging markets . . ." (Alfa Group 2008).

Therefore, while some diversified conglomerates continue to prosper in modern Russia, the overall level of diversification of business groups is decreasing. While initial allocation of ownership was rather spontaneous, the secondary M&A market has been redistributing industrial assets in favor of groups that specialize in particular sectors.

It is also important that—as in many other countries with weak contract enforcement—vertical integration is more likely than vertical separation and outsourcing. As shown in Guriev and Rachinsky (2005), most business groups are vertically integrated. In the major Russian exporting industries such as oil and metals, there are virtually no non-integrated producers. The remaining non-vertically integrated supply chains often generate substantial controversies. One of the most famous recent examples is the "Mechel Affair" (*New York Times* 2008). Mechel is a coal mining and steel company. Mechel produces more coal than needed for its own steel factories, so it sells coal to other Russian steel makers. Allegedly, in 2008, it held up its customers (charging them double the world price), which led to criticism by Prime Minister Putin, resulting in an instantaneous fall in stock price by 38 percent. Mr Putin's suggestion was to encourage Mechel to move to long-term contracts (fully in line with the hold-up theory of vertical integration, Williamson 1979; Grossman and Hart 1986).

18.5 COMPETITIVE CAPABILITIES AND PERFORMANCE OF BUSINESS GROUPS IN RUSSIA

Do business groups outperform stand-alone firms in Russia? While many groups are now specialized or vertically integrated, quite a few have remained diversified and hold unrelated assets. Why are there large diversified business groups?

One of the most important institutional economies of scale is political influence (Grossman and Helpman 1994). One of the examples of successful lobbying by large business groups is the political economy of Russia's possible accession to the World Trade Organization (WTO) (for a discussion, see Guriev and Rachinsky 2005). In 2000 the newly elected President Vladimir Putin announced the WTO accession as one of the priorities of Russia's economic policy. At that point the large business groups had a stake in the steelmaking industry and therefore were interested in the WTO accession, as the latter would protect their export markets. The automotive sector (which would be hurt by WTO accession, because of the lower import tariffs) was then controlled by stand-alone companies. However, shortly afterwards the expansion of the leading business groups resulted in acquisitions of the automotive assets, which quickly changed their interest in the WTO accession. Not surprisingly, as of 2009 Russia has not joined WTO.

The business groups' lobbying efforts are often aligned to social welfare. For example, Guriev, Yakovlev, and Zhuravskaya (2008) have studied the effect of the composition of lobbies in Russian subnational units on the internal trade barriers. They show that, if the local governments are captured by local lobbyists, the firms in neighboring jurisdictions are likely to suffer. On the other hand, the national business groups lobby for a lowering of internal trade barriers—very much like multinational companies that bring down international trade barriers.

The institutional economies of scale above should imply that large business groups should be more efficient—in raising finance, protecting their property rights, getting the best talent. Whenever markets are not developing and the government is inefficient and corrupt, size matters. Large business groups outperform others through creating an internal capital and labor market, in overcoming fixed costs of maintaining government relations, and so on.

This is precisely the prevailing view in the private sector: for example, Boone and Rodionov (2002)—as well as Shleifer and Treisman (2005)—argue that, after initial asset stripping and dilution of other shareholders, the owners of the business groups restructured their assets, improved corporate governance, and undertook substantial investment.

The view that business groups outperform stand-alone firms is mostly based on anecdotal evidence comparing similar companies that are and are not members of large business groups. However, systematic evidence on the superior performance of business groups is scarce. It is virtually impossible to calculate the conglomerate discount, as most holding companies are not listed (except for the Sistema group, which is discussed above). The other approach is to compare the market value of group members with stand-alone companies. Judging by the growth of the owners' personal wealth, this is certainly the case. Fig. 18.1 tracks the evolution of the wealth of Russia's billionaires (the vast majority of whom are the owners of business groups). Their personal wealth growth, both total and per capita, outperforms the growth of Russian stock-market capitalization.

Forbes estimates their personal wealth based on stock-market prices; therefore it takes into account the improvements in corporate governance and the sharing of some of the shareholder value with minority shareholders. An econometric analysis of market values of Russian companies is carried out in Maury and Liljeblom (2007), who do show that, while "oligarch-owned" (that is, group member) firms were initially undervalued when compared to firms controlled by other domestic owners, the situation changed in later years. In the 2000s, business groups outperformed stand-alone firms in terms of market capitalization. Maury and Lilljeblom control for industry-fixed effects and other variables; yet their approach is certainly subject to the criticism of endogeneity of ownership (Himmelberg et al. 1999).

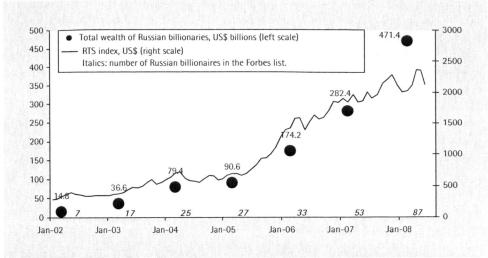

Figure 18.1 Russians on the Forbes list and Russia's stock market, 2002–8

Notes: Russian billionaires have either diversified groups or large firms. Out of the top 10, 7 owned diversified groups. Their wealth/GDP went up from 5% in 2002 to 37% in 2008 (US had about 400 billionaires whose total wealth had never exceeded 10% of GDP).

Source: Forbes; Russion Trading System.

On the other hand, even larger benefits to minority shareholders do not imply that large business groups are socially efficient. As the market for capital control, financial, and labor markets in Russia is imperfect, the resulting distribution of ownership and control may be suboptimal. Therefore comparing shareholder value in business groups and stand-alone companies may be misleading. This is why it may be a better idea to check technical productivity measures (as in Schoar 2002). While this approach is also problematic (the emergence of groups may have externalities on others[9]), at least it takes into account the redistribution between owners and providers of labor and capital. Such an exercise was carried out by Guriev and Rachinsky (2005), who show that, controlling for industry and regional dummies, the total factor productivity growth of large business groups was higher than in other private firms and state-owned firms. While Guriev and Rachinsky's results can be treated only as indicative, they are consistent with the anecdotal evidence and point to the benefits of group membership at least for the firm-level efficiency. Why are Russian groups different from the ones studied by Bertrand and Mullainathan and by Aganin

[9] There is a whole tradition in transition economics to link the economies of size to rent-seeking blaming the business groups, for insecure property rights (see, e.g,. Sonin 2003; Polischuk and Savvateev 2004; Hoff and Stiglitz 2004; Braguinsky and Myerson 2007; Guriev and Sonin 2009).

and Volpin? The answer goes back to the particular history of ownership concentration in Russia (discussed above) that has created a legacy of aligned ownership and control. The controlling owners have very strong incentives to raise market value—both through restructuring and via protecting outside investors. The higher the market value, the more there is to cash in and the lower the cost of capital for further expansion.

Yet another question is whether private business groups outperform state business groups and whether the nationalization of assets of private business groups in the second half of 2000s was efficient. This issue is a subject of further research. We can report only the comparisons of performance of private and state firms in Russia. Brown et al. (2006) show that, controlling for firm-level fixed effects, privatization in Russia worsens (at least initially) rather than improves firm performance. This finding—the opposite to the large empirical literature on privatization around the world (Megginson 2005)—may be explained by two effects. First, the inferior performance takes place only immediately after the privatization and then starts to improve—so Brown et al.'s analysis should be repeated for later years too. They do find that the privatized firms' performance is initially low, but then increases relative to that of the state firms; after five years, privatized firms outperform the state firms. Secondly, the state firms may receive unfair preferential treatment from the state, which improves their performance.

18.6 CONCLUDING REMARKS

The Russian economy is dominated by a score of business groups. The size and structure of these groups are driven by specific features of Russia's institutional environment: underdeveloped financial markets, imperfect contract enforcement, and high political risk. Fully in line with the argument in Khanna and Yafeh (2007), Russian business groups are a response to these inefficiencies, so it is not surprising that they outperform rather than underperform stand-alone firms.

As of 2009, most of these groups are still controlled by their founding entrepreneurs. There are two processes, however, that may eventually reduce their ownership and control. First, as the corporate governance is improving, the controlling owners are more likely to hire professional managers and dilute their majority stakes for the sake of the management's compensation. Secondly, in order to hedge the political risk, the initial owners may cash in via IPO/SEO or via a block sale to a strategic investor; they will also diversify the political risk via international expansion. As this ownership dilution takes place, the groups will also spin off unrelated business divisions to increase specialization and focus. While there are still many large diversified business groups, these are less common than before. And those diversified groups that still exist provide a substantial autonomy to its sectoral segments.

It is, however, far from certain that the diversified groups will dissolve themselves into specialized firms or single-sector segments. As the large business groups outperform the stand-alone firms whenever institutions are imperfect, the exodus of business groups will happen only when there is a substantial progress in the quality of institutions. On the other hand, this may be a question of "if" rather than of "when." The recent literature on oligarchic economies shows that institutional development (and the lack thereof) may itself be endogenous to the concentration of ownership structure in the economy. The domination of large business groups may slow down the development of political and market institutions—see Rajan and Zingales (2003), Sonin (2003), and Guriev and Sonin (2009) for arguments about how the domination of large business groups may be a stable equilibrium in a setting with endogenous institutions.

The 2008–9 financial crisis may also have a substantial impact on these groups. Many of them have used their assets as collateral for further expansion; hence the collapse of asset prices will force a bailout by the government or divestment in favor of foreign owners or government. In the latter case, the question remains as to what the government will do with the assets. They may contribute to further expansion of the state-owned business groups. It is also likely that these assets will eventually be privatized, but whether they will go back to their former owners is not clear. It may well be the case that new boundaries of business groups will emerge. What is clear, however, is that, as long as there are multiple market failures and government failures in the Russian economy, business groups will remain an optimal response to the institutional weaknesses and are therefore likely to prevail in Russia.

REFERENCES

AGANIN, A., and VOLPIN, P. (2005). "History of Corporate Ownership in Italy," in R. K. Morck (Ed.), *The History of Corporate Governance around the World*. Chicago: University of Chicago Press, 325–61.

Alfa group (2008). Aug. 30. www.alfagroup.ru

BARCA, F., and BECHT, M. (2001) (ed.). *The Control of Corporate Europe*. New York: Oxford University Press.

Basic Element (2008). www.basel.ru

BERGLÖF, E., and PEROTTI, E. (1996). "Corporate Governance Structure of the Japanese Financial Keiretsu," *Journal of Financial Economics*, 36: 259–84.

BERTRAND, M., and MULLAINATHAN, S. (2003). "Pyramids," *Journal of the European Economic Association*, 1/2–3 (Apr.–May), 478–83.

BLACK, B., LOVE, I., and RACHINSKY, A. (2006). "Corporate Governance Indices and Firms' Market Values: Time Series Evidence from Russia," *Emerging Markets Review*, 7/4: 361–79.

BLANCHARD, O., and KREMER, M. (1997). "Disorganization," *Quarterly Journal of Economics*, 112/4: 1091–126.

BOONE, P., and RODIONOV, D. (2002). "Rent seeking in Russia and the CIS." Brunswick UBS Warburg, Moscow.

BOYCKO, M., SHLEIFER, A., and VISHNY, R. (1995). *Privatizing Russia*. Cambridge, MA: MIT Press.

BRAGUINSKY, S., and MYERSON, R. (2007). "A Macroeconomic Model of Russian Transition: The Role of Oligarchic Property Rights," *Economics of Transition*, 15/1: 77–107.

BROWN, D., EARLE, J., and TELEGDY, A. (2006). "The Productivity Effects of Privatization: Longitudinal Estimates from Hungary, Romania, Russia, and Ukraine," *Journal of Political Economy*, 114: 61–99.

BURKART, M., PANUNZI, F., and SHLEIFER, A. (2003). "Family Firms," *Journal of Finance*, 58: 2173–207.

CLAESSENS, S., DJANKOV, S. D., and LANG, L. H. P. (2000). "The Separation of Ownership and Control in East Asian Corporations," *Journal of Financial Economics*, 58/1–2: 81–112.

DE LONG, J. BRADFORD (1998). "Robber Barons," in A. Aslund (ed.), *Perspectives on Russian Economic Development*. Moscow: Carnegie Endowment for International Peace.

DENISOVA, I., ELLER, M., FRYE, T., and ZHURAVSKAYA, E. (2009). "Who Wants to Revise Privatization? The Complementarity of Market Skills and Institutions," *American Political Science Review*, 103/2: 284–304.

DYNKIN, A. and SOKOLOV, A. (2002). "Integrated Business Groups in Russian Economy," *Voprosy Ekonomiki*, 4: 78–95 (in Russian).

EKELUND, R., and TOLLISON, R. (1980). "Mercantilist Origins of the Corporation," *Bell Journal of Economics*, 11/2: 715–20.

FACCIO, M., and LANG, L. H. P. (2002). "The Ultimate Ownership of Western European Corporations," *Journal of Financial Economics*, 65: 365–95.

Financial Times (1996). "Moscow's Group of Seven," Nov. 1, p. 17.

Financial Times (2002a). "Putin's Bid to Join WTO Splits Business—Russia's Oligarchs Seek to Protect their Interests from Foreign Encroachment," Mar. 27.

Financial Times (2002b). "Sale of Russian Oil Group Leaves Questions over Fairness," Dec. 19, p. 6.

Forbes (2004). "The World's Richest People," Feb. 26.

Forbes (2008). "The World's Billionaires," May 3.

Forbes Russia (2004). "Russia's 100 Richest People," May 13 (in Russian).

FREELAND, C. (2000). *Sale of the Century: Russia's Wild Ride from Communism to Capitalism*. New York: Crown Business.

GRAHAM, E. (2003). *Reforming Korea's Industrial Conglomerates*. Washington: Institute for International Economics.

GROSSMAN, G., and HELPMAN, E. (1994). "Protection for Sale," *American Economic Review*, 84: 833–50.

GROSSMAN, SANFORD J., and HART, OLIVER D. (1986). "The Costs and Benefits of Ownership: A Theory of Vertical and Lateral Integration," *Journal of Political Economy*, 94/4 (Aug.), 691–719.

GURIEV, S., and MEGGINSON, W. (2006). "Privatization: What Have We Learned?" in F. Bourguignon and B. Pleskovic (eds). *Beyond Transition. Proceedings of the 18th ABCDE*. Washington: World Bank.

GURIEV, S., and RACHINSKY, A. (2005). "The Role of Oligarchs in Russian Capitalism," *Journal of Economic Perspectives*, 19/1 (Winter), 131–50.

GURIEV, S., and SONIN, K. (2009). "Dictators and Oligarchs: A Dynamic Theory of Contested Property Rights," *Journal of Public Economics*, 93: 1–13.

GURIEV, S., LAZAREVA, O., RACHINSKY, A., and TSUKHLO, S. (2004). "Concentrated Ownership, Market for Corporate Control, and Corporate Vovernance," *Problems of Economic
Transition,* 47/3: 6–83.

GURIEV, S., YAKOVLEV, E., and ZHURAVSKAYA, E. V. (2008). "Interest Group Politics in a
Federation," Jan. 17. SSRN: http://ssrn.com/abstract=983883

HIMMELBERG, C., HUBBARD, G., and PALIA, D. (1999). "Understanding the Determinants of
Managerial Ownership and the Link between Ownership and Performance," *Journal of
Financial Economics,* 53/3: 353–84.

HOFF, K., and STIGLITZ, J. (2004). "After the Big Bang? Obstacles to the Emergence of the
Rule of Law in Post-Communist Societies," *American Economic Review,* 94/3 75–63.

HOFFMAN, D. E. (2003). *The Oligarchs.* New York: Public Affairs.

HOGFELDT, P. (2004). "The History and Politics of Corporate Ownership in Sweden."
Mimeo, Stockholm School of Economics.

KHANNA, T., and YAFEH, Y. (2007). "Business Groups in Emerging Markets: Paragons or
Parasites?" *Journal of Economic Literature,* 45/2: 331–72.

Kommersant (2003). *Who Owns Russia?* Moscow: Vagrius (in Russian).

KUMAR, K., RAJAN, R., and ZINGALES, L. (2003). "What Determines Firm Size?" Mimeo,
GSB, University of Chicago.

LAPORTA, R., LOPEZ-DE-SILANES, F., SHLEIFER, A., and VISHNY, R. W. (1998). "Law and
Finance," *Journal of Political Economy,* 106: 1113–55.

LAPORTA, R., LOPEZ-DE-SILANES, F., SHLEIFER, A., and VISHNY, R. W. (1999). "Corporate
Ownership around the World," *Journal of Finance,* 54: 471–517.

LAZAREVA, O., RACHINSKY, A., and STEPANOV, S. (2007). "A Survey of Corporate Governance in Russia." CEFIR/ NES Working Paper No. 103. SSRN: http://ssrn.com/
abstract=997965

MAURY, B., and LILJEBLOM, E. (2007). "Oligarchs, Institutional Change, and Firm Valuation: Russian Evidence." SSRN: http://ssrn.com/abstract=959369

MEGGINSON, W. L. (2005). *The Financial Economics of Privatization,* 1st edn. New York:
Oxford University Press.

MIWA, Y., and RAMSEYER, J. M. (2003). "Does Ownership Matter? Evidence from
the Zaibatsu Dissolution Program," *Journal of Economics and Management Strategy,* 12:
67–90.

MORIKAWA, H. (1992). *Zaibatsu: The Rise and Fall of Family Enterprise Groups in Japan.*
Tokyo: University of Tokyo Press.

Moscow Times (2003a). "Tycoons Talk Corruption in Kremlin," Feb. 20.

Moscow Times (2003b). "Foreign Used Car Prices May Rise Again," Apr. 22.

New York Times (2008). "Putin's Criticism Puts a $6 Billion Hole in a Company," July 26.

OLSON, M. (1971). *The Logic of Collective Action: Public Goods and the Theory of Groups.*
Cambridge, MA: Harvard University Press.

PAPPE, Y. (2000). *The Oligarchs.* Moscow: Higher School of Economics (in Russian).

POLISCHUK, L., and SAVVATEEV, A. (2004). "Spontaneous (Non-)Emergence of Property
Rights," *Economics of Transition,* 12/1: 103–27.

PSI Foundation (2003). *Large Russian Business: A Digest of Corporate Statistics.* Moscow: PSI
Foundation. (in Russian).

RAJAN, R. G., and ZINGALES, L. (2003). *Saving Capitalism from the Capitalists: Unleashing
the Power of Financial Markets to Create Wealth and Spread Opportunity.* New York:
Crown Business.

SCHARFSTEIN, D., and STEIN, J. (2000). "The Dark Side of Internal Capital Markets: Divisional Rent-Seeking and Inefficient Investment," *Journal of Finance*, 55: 2537–64.

SHLEIFER, A., and TREISMAN, D. S. (2005). "A Normal Country: Russia after Communism," *Journal of Economic Perspectives*, 19/1: 151–74.

SCHOAR, A. (2002). "The Effect of Diversification on Firm Productivity," *Journal of Finance*, 62/6 (Dec.), 2379–403.

SHLEIFER, A., and TREISMAN, D. (2000). *Without a Map: Political Tactics and Economic Reform in Russia.* Cambridge, MA: MIT Press.

Skolkovo (2008). "Emerging Russian Multinationals: Achievements and Challenges." Research Report, Skolkovo Business School, Moscow.

SONIN, K. (2003). "Why the Rich May Favor Poor Protection of Property Rights?" *Journal of Comparative Economics*, 31: 715–31.

STIGLER, G. (1971). "The Theory of Economic Regulation," *Bell Journal of Economics and Management Science*, 2/1: 3–21.

Vedomosti (2003a). "Khodorkovsky Confessed: Yukos Shareholders will Support Union of Right Wing Forces, Yabloko, and the Communist Party," Apr. 8 (in Russian).

Vedomosti (2003b). "Take Away and Divide: People's Aspirations have not Changed in 86 Years," July 18 (in Russian).

WILLIAMSON, O. E. (1979). "Transaction-Cost Economics: The Governance of Contractual Relations," *Journal of Law and Economics*, 22 (Oct.), 233–61.

World Bank (2005). *From Transition To Development: A Country Economic Memorandum for the Russian Federation.* Moscow: World Bank.

YAKOVLEV, E., and ZHURAVSKAYA, E. (2003). "State Capture and Controlling Owners of Firms." Russia CEM 2003 background paper, CEFIR, Moscow.

CHAPTER 19

BUSINESS GROUPS IN SOUTH AFRICA

ANDREA GOLDSTEIN

19.1 INTRODUCTION

AS a result of both natural and policy factors—the importance of mining in the economy, market imperfections, and apartheid and post-apartheid policies—business groups have played an important role in South African economic development.[1] This in turn has been reflected in a high degree of concentration, in terms of both ownership and business activities. Whether the overall implications have been positive or mixed is unclear. Groups have undoubtedly played an important role in making major investments to realize economies of scale and scope, and in adopting and exploiting new technologies. However, at times a small number of large business groups may have lobbied for "wrong" policies not necessarily in the interest of the country's population (see, e.g., Malan and Leaver 2003 on tobacco controls).

The relationship between strategy and structure has evolved since the end of apartheid in 1994, as the South African economy has opened to international competition and liberalization. Large groups have reduced their exposure to mining,

Londiwe Xulu at Business Leadership SA, as well as Ernst & Young SA and *Who Owns Whom*, kindly provided background data. For most incisive and helpful comments and suggestions on earlier drafts, I thank Aslı Colpan, Takashi Hikino, Merle Lipton, and Grietjie Verhoef, as well as two anonymous referees and Kyoto Conference participants. The chapter builds on previous research with Neo Chabane, Will Prichard, and Simon Roberts but does not commit any of them, nor does it represent the views of the OECD and/or its Members.

[1] A business group is defined as a group where two or more listed companies are controlled by the same ultimate shareholder.

decreased product diversification, engaged in overseas expansion, and evolved toward governance structures more similar to OECD norms. Some of them have listed overseas, and all have seen the weight of institutional investors increase. This has translated into the appointment of non-family professional executives (including of a non-South African woman as CEO of the largest business group in 2006).

In a changing economic and technological environment, the centrality of traditional family-centered diversified business groups has diminished. Other forces, however, have acted to support black-owned business groups. Affirmative action policies have focused on corporate ownership, and the persistence of market imperfections has shepherded the emergence of diversified groups controlled by politically well-connected black tycoons. In fact, the business history of South Africa must consider the role played by ethnic mobilization in determining the boundaries of business groups, including in the emergence of black-owned economic groups since 1994.

This chapter updates a previous analysis of the changing face and strategies of South African big business (Chabane et al. 2006). In particular, I examine whether the group structure that characterized the country's business system under apartheid is now being used in the context of black economic empowerment. The next section presents an historical overview of the development of South African business groups. I then sketch the main policy developments since 1994 and their influence on groups. Section 19.5 analyzes the case of Anglo-American and Rembrandt, by far South Africa's largest groups, to show how changes in their strategies have simplified their corporate structures in the sense of lower business diversification. The following section analyzes the recent rise of black groups in the broader framework of changing state–business relations. I conclude by framing the discussion in the broader pictures of the discussion on the transformation of corporate ownership in emerging economies and of the dynamics of economic growth and job generation in South Africa.

19.2 SOUTH AFRICAN BUSINESS GROUPS IN HISTORICAL PERSPECTIVE

Business history in Southern Africa is inevitably and closely tied with the discovery of precious metals and diamonds (Thompson 1995; Feinstein 2005). The technical and financial pressures for amalgamation were inexorable, and about two dozen adventurers, promoters, and financiers were soon in control—the so-called Randlords, who established the monopolistic De Beers Consolidated Mines (DBCM) (Wheatcroft 1985). Cecil Rhodes and other magnates participated in politics, introduced the brutally racist Master and Servant Bill, and some of them became art collectors, philanthropists, and country gentlemen in Britain (Stevenson 2002). By the end of the nineteenth century fewer than ten British, French, and German groups controlled the 124 companies that accounted for more than a quarter of the world's total gold output.

Ernest Oppenheimer founded the quintessential South African corporation—Anglo American (hitherto Anglo)—in 1917 with capital from Britain, the USA, and South Africa to exploit the Orange Free State field potential.[2] Knighted in 1921, Sir Ernest made Anglo the largest single shareholder in De Beers in 1924 and formally established the cross-holdings linking the two companies in 1929.[3] One year later, the London-based Central Selling Organization was formed to bear the costs of keeping large stocks of diamonds off the sales market, facilitate more orderly marketing, and stabilize the industry (Knight and Stevenson 1986). By 1939 the Central Selling Organization controlled 97 percent of the world's diamond trade.

The group system started in response to the practical necessities of risky mining investment, but it soon became more than a financial arrangement (Gregory 1962). In the 1890s De Beers was already investing in ancillary activities like frozen meat to supply the miners, coal-mining, explosives, and land (Turrell and Van-Helten 1987: 269). Shareholders saw the advantage of this strategy in reducing costs of production for minerals and prices of supply of important indirect and indirect inputs—such as food staples for miners (Phimister 1978), as well as in insuring against new discoveries of diamond mines. In the face of market imperfections, the centralization of technical, managerial, and administrative services was an additional feature to the South African group system.

Apartheid was instituted after the National Party victory in the 1948 elections. Direct government investment underpinned national firms in steel, petro-chemicals, fertilizers, and the utilities, although the only state-owned business group—the Industrial Development Corporation—never gained the same prominence as IRI in Italy. Following the divestment of foreign firms and sanctions in the 1960s, traditional private-owned groups started diversifying into a range of consumer goods and food products (including beer, farms, and vineyards). Sanlam, for instance, "acquire[d] large quantities of shares at bargain-basement prices in companies operating in vehicles, computers, and electronics" (Feinstein 2005: 179).

By and large, the contours of big South African business remained unchanged until 1994 and the birth of multi-racial democracy. Six main multi-layered diversified corporate groupings controlled the majority of economic activity as represented by market capitalization on the Johannesburg Stock Exchange (JSE), Africa's largest (see Table 19.3). Each group had a primary business activity and diversified in a number of others (Table 19.1). The use of pyramids allowed ownership to be diffused in the groups' operating companies and subsidiaries, while control was maintained firmly

---

[2] One of six sons of a German Jewish cigar merchant, Ernest Oppenheimer was born in 1880 and went to South Africa in 1902 as a diamond buyer for a London firm. Oppenheimer named the new company Anglo American to disguise his German roots during the First World War. In 1919 he bid for diamond mines in Namibia, and created Consolidated Diamonds Mines as a rival to De Beers.

[3] De Beers held 38% of the stock of Anglo American, and Anglo American held 34% of De Beers. Oppenheimer was chairman of both De Beers and the Diamond Corporation. The association with N. M. Rothschild & Sons dated from 1887, when a former adviser of the merchant bank (American engineer Gardner Williams) had been appointed DBCM general manager (Newbury 1987: 29).

Table 19.1 South Africa's largest business groups in the 1980s

Major features	Anglo American	Sanlam	Old Mutual	Rembrandt	Liberty Life	Anglovaal
				Business groups		
Controlling shareholder	Oppenheimer family	Policy-holders	Policy-holders	Rupert family	Gordon family	Mennel and Hersov families
Core business	Mining (De Beers, Minorco)	Insurance	Insurance	Tobacco (Rothmans)	Insurance	Mining
Other major interests:						
Consumer durables	Toyota SA		Caterpillar*			Grinaker, Contred
Other consumer goods	South Africa Breweries and affiliated companies		CG Smith*	Malbak, Stellenbosch Farmers' Winery	South Africa Breweries and affiliated companies	Avtex, Irvin & Johnson, National Brands
Industrial commodities	AECI, Highveld Steel, Mondi					Alpha
Mining	See above	Engen (oil)	Rand Mines*	Federale Mynbou, Gencor, Goldfields, Total SA (oil)		Anglovaal Mining, Rand Mines
Financial services	First National	ABSA	Nedbank	Volkskas	Stanbic	
Number of subsidiaries and associated companies[†]						
1986	180[‡]	56	173	21	139	102
2006	56		58	38	16	n.a.[§]

Notes: *Owned by Barlows, in which Old Mutual held a 29 percent controlling stake.
[†] As reported by *Who Owns Whom in South Africa.*
[‡] Including 47 non-South Africa incorporated companies.
[§] In 1995–96, Anglovaal concentrated its activities into two listed entities covering mining and industrial interests. Anglovaal Industries was named AVI in 2003 and was renamed African Rainbow Minerals in 2005.

Sources: McGregors (various years) and other corporate information.

in the hands of the founding family—Oppenheimer in AA, Rupert in Rembrandt, Gordon in Liberty, and Menell and Hersov in Anglovaal.[4,5] The exceptions were Sanlam and Old Mutual, which were owned by the holders of their insurance policies. On average, the three largest shareholders owned 52 percent of the ten largest non-financial domestic firms (the fourth highest share among eighteen English-origin legal systems) (La Porta et al. 1998: 1147, table 7).

In South Africa, the groups' diversification did not correspond to the development of strong organizational capabilities that could be applied to adopt and adapt imported technologies across different industries (Amsden 2001). With the exception of some mining companies and SASOL (which pioneered the production of oil and petrol from coal on the basis of the Fischer–Tropsch process), the rest of the South African economy was characterized by low levels of technological development. Corporate structures were similar to Chandler's "personal capitalism"—managerial structures were relatively unsophisticated, and relationships between the groups were characterized by cooperation and some contestation for position, but only a relatively low level of competition (Chandler et al. 1997). The formation of diversified business groups facilitated investments in marketing (but with the limits of a relatively small domestic market, especially in view of the fact that the majority of the black population could not access it) and to some extent in manufacturing, and not in managerial and organizational capabilities. Individual owner-managers continued to control business firms. It was this legacy that the African National Congress (ANC) found on gaining power in 1994.

19.3 MAIN FORCES ACTING ON STRATEGY AND STRUCTURE SINCE 1994

The South African business environment has changed rather dramatically since 1994, providing new incentives and introducing new constraints. The initial reference of the ANC was the kind of government intervention that has been identified as crucial to the so-called East Asian miracle (Amsden 1989, 2001). While this initial attitude did not depend on state ownership, it certainly did not contemplate privatization either. This soon changed, and the government's 1996 macroeconomic strategy document included privatization as one of the main goals. Nonetheless, only two deals of some global significance—the sale of minority stakes to foreign partners in

---

[4] In South Africa the dilution of voting powers has traditionally been obtained through the pyramidal structure, since the issuance of non- and low-voting shares, a common device in continental Europe, was prohibited until 1995 (Bebchuck et al. 2000). As regards the functioning of the courts, South Africa performs rather worse than the mean for the English legal origin grouping in terms of tenant eviction (3.68 versus 3.02) and rather better for check collection (1.68 versus 2.76) (Djankov et al. 2003).

[5] In 1998 the Anglovaal shareholding was split equally between the Hersov and Menell families.

Telkom in 1997 and South African Airways in 1999—were completed by the Mandela government. Although the first Mbeki government made privatization a higher policy priority at first and the sale of government's controlling stake in Telkom and its floatation went ahead in 2003, other deals were slowed down or put on hold. This low priority given to state divestiture is important because it closed a possible avenue for group diversification.

Although a Regulation of Monopolistic Conditions Act was enacted as early as in 1955, high levels of concentration were the norm under apartheid (Fourie et al. 1995). The creation of national champions was often sanctioned by the state—as in the case of the beer and wines and spirits markets, where a market-sharing agreement was allowed. Moreover, at the end of the 1980s, South Africa had the most dispersed tariff system in the world, with many tariffs being effectively firm specific, since the number of producers in any one product market was limited (Belli et al. 1993). Against this backdrop, the issue of the concentration of economy-wide power in the hands of a few groups, much more than the debate about competition policy *per se*, took center stage immediately after the end of apartheid (Gerson 1993). The new system promised to use competition policy to correct the faults of the old system and promote policy goals of employment and empowerment.

If the new government did not touch the ownership structure of the economy via privatization, it tried to do it through black economic empowerment (BEE). The ANC Freedom Charter of 1955 stated, first, that "the people shall share in the country's wealth" and that "the land shall be shared among all those who work it." In 1994 the Reconstruction and Development Program (RDP) restated these fundamental goals with the objective of creating a "democratic, non-racial, non-sexist and prosperous society." Additionally, the restructuring program of state-owned enterprises (SOEs) was couched in terms of promoting the economic empowerment of historically disadvantaged communities. Almost a decade elapsed between the first formal steps toward a formal BEE policy and the June 2002 Mining Charter, which requires ownership of minerals to be transferred to the state in order to facilitate black ownership and participation in the mining industry. To bring clarity to the new dispensation and reassure investors, the government also unveiled specific scorecards with clearly identifiable BEE benchmarks against which to measure their progress. This method of scoring seems to provide some leeway for companies that are not keen to give over an ownership stake in their company, providing them with the opportunity to score heavily on other aspects of the Charter and make up for the poor ownership scoring.

Business has vigorously promoted exchange control liberalization and overseas listings, arguing that this would allow South African firms to be valued in a hard currency, reducing the risk premium for changes in the value of the rand, and improving their expansion capability as well as the ability to increase investment in South Africa. Since the late 1990s, several major companies have moved their primary listings overseas. In the process they have also modified their corporate structure to clear up cross-holdings. The first important issue was by Billiton, which was listed by Gencor on the London Stock Exchange (LSE) in 1997. South African Breweries (SAB) followed in early 1999 and in May 1999 Anglo American joined Billiton and SAB in the FTSE 100 index.[6] South African companies have generally found relationships with investors, analysts, and financial and accounting regulators more demanding than in their home country, where companies such as Anglo or SAB were used to dictating the terms of engagement (*Financial Times* 2000b).

Rather than London listings enabling groups to raise capital to fund investments in South Africa, there was a much more striking pattern of outward acquisition and investments (Goldstein 2007; Goldstein and Pritchard 2009). Under apartheid, sanctions and currency controls did not prevent South African groups from building substantial international operations. The total stock of outward FDI grew from US$8.7 billion in 1995 to US$28.8 billion in 2004; Anglo's extensive international investments in mining and paper are detailed below.

Finally, South Africa took an early lead in corporate governance reforms in emerging markets with the 1994 King Report on Corporate Governance, which advised companies to consider the interests of a variety of stakeholders. In 1995 the JSE made it compulsory for listed companies to disclose the extent of their compliance with the Report (Malherbe and Segal 2001). The 1998 Insider Trading Act, for its part, enabled the Financial Services Board to take more forceful action against illegal transactions. A second, more comprehensive Report (King II) was issued in 2002. In 2003 the JSE listing rules were again updated to require listed companies to comply with the recommendations contained in King II or to explain their lack of compliance.

19.4 THE CONTOURS AND CHARACTERISTICS OF BIG BUSINESS GROUPS

The forces examined in the previous section have all tended to discourage the expansion of business groups. For instance, established groups have had few opportunities to diversify into new sectors such as telecoms via the acquisition of SOEs. Similarly, both greater attention to corporate governance and tighter competition policies have made investors and public authorities alike more suspicious of diversification and 'empire-building' by business groups. BEE, on the other hand, has played in the opposite direction, for reasons that are better explained below.

The ranking of the top twenty listed companies in 2007 includes only six companies from the 1989 listing and twelve from the 1999 one. Although these restructuring patterns are reflected in the declining significance of the major groups (Table 19.2), their significance remains more than marginal. In 1994, 83 of the top 100 companies

---

[6] In October 1998 Anglo American Corporation of South Africa absorbed Minorco to create Anglo American plc.

Table 19.2 Summary of control of JSE market capitalization (% of total), 1986–2006[1]

	1986	1990	1991–5	1996–2000	2001–3	2004	2005	2006
Anglo American	54.1	44.2	38.9	22.7	23.3	18.7	17.3	21.0
Sanlam	11.3	13.2	12.7	11.2	6.1	2.7	1.6	2.3
Stanbic/Liberty Life	2.3	2.6	5.8	9.0	5.2	4.7	4.3	3.5
Rembrandt/Remgro	4.4	13.6	13.2	10.2	9.2	7.9	7.8	7.8
SA Mutual/Old Mutual	10.9	10.2	11.2	10.4	9.9	4.5	4.5	5.5
Anglovaal	2.1	2.5	3.1	1.2	0	0	0	0
Top 5 groups collectively	85.1	83.9	85.9	70.6	53.6	38.5	35.5	40.1
Black-owned groups	–	–	–	7.4	4.2	6.3	5.8	5.1
Foreign	6.1	2.1	–	–	–	18.5	14.2	20.8
Institutions	0.7	4.9	–	–	–	10.3	13.7	9.1
Directors	8.1	6.7	–	–	–	5.8	8.2	6.7

Note: Control is assessed by taking into account the various cross-holdings of shares that exist and may be associated with a relatively small direct shareholding in any given company.

Source: McGregors (various years).

were owned or controlled by the top six groups at the time. By 2004, the number of companies controlled by these groups had dropped to 47. Of the top twenty companies in 2004, thirteen were part of a major business grouping.[7] Three of them (Anglo American, Amplats, and AngloGold) were still effectively part of the Anglo group. The other big players are mostly private and partly privatized South African firms. Nonetheless, this broad generalization should not obscure the fact that market imperfections and policy actions still exist that justify diversification. Besides the case of black groups, one of the new JSE darlings is Bidvest—a diversified industrial and services group, composed of more than 2,500 business units from food and food services to vehicle retailing, freight, and terminal business—that was founded in 1988. The group explains its horizontal diversification in terms of the ability to control "well-established and effective distribution networks which . . . afford a key competitive advantage in the markets we serve" (Bidvest 1997: 6). This statement testifies to the relevance of the incomplete markets argument in explaining business groups in South Africa.

The main drivers of unbundling and de-concentration have been financial. Complex cross-holdings and pyramid ownership structures, despite reinforcing family control, failed to promote effective management and maximize profit. In general, groups were trading significantly below their net asset value (*The Economist* 1995). Mergers and acquisitions (M&As) increased dramatically from 1994 to a peak of 1,019 deals in 1998 (Ernst & Young SA, various years). As shown in Table 19.1, in 2006 the four large business groups for which comparable figures are available have a third the number of subsidiaries and associated companies they had in 1986. SAB, for instance, bought back 10 percent of its stock from Liberty Life and Anglo in 1999 to acquire the flexibility needed to make acquisitions. BEE has been another forceful driver of M&A activity, with the combined value of BEE deals, mostly in unrelated businesses, growing almost fivefold between 2002 and 2006. According to Ponte et al. (2007), "most of the ownership changes made in the 1990s turned out to be deals more favorable to white conglomerates than to new black businesses."

South African companies' ownership has become more global and more institutional. As domestic and foreign institutions have become important shareholders in most South African blue chips, hostile takeover bids have also become more frequent.[8] A further example of dynamism is faster directors' turnover. No fewer than twenty-four CEOs of companies listed on the JSE left their posts in the first eight months of 2006, an unprecedented occurrence (*Financial Week* 2006).

---

[7] This includes some that are identified by McGregors as jointly controlled by one of the major conglomerates together with another entity.

[8] The first large-scale such attempt in the history of market for corporate control in South Africa involved an attempt in November 1999 by Nedcor banking group to acquire at least 50.1% of Stanbic (Goldstein 2000).

19.5 CONTINUITY AND CHANGE AT TWO GROUPS

Anglo and Rembrandt dominated the South African business landscape in the twentieth century, and a comparison of their strategic approaches to changing world and domestic economic circumstances is particularly interesting.

19.5.1 Anglo American

It is difficult to overestimate the significance of the Oppenheimer family to the South African economy, and Anglo American was so synonymous with its homeland that it earned the moniker South Africa Inc. Harry Oppenheimer served as a United Party MP in 1948, bankrolled the Progressive Party during apartheid, and facilitated the democracy negotiations in the 1980s. In 1982, when black miners formed a labor union, Anglo became the first company to recognize it. While the National Party government targeted AA when it launched a Commission of Inquiry into its activities in 1964, Anglo benefited enormously from at least three key pillars of apartheid: the migrant labor system, the pass system, and the compound system (Innes 1984). Nonetheless, at the same time as they set up a wide range of national champions in South Africa, the Oppenheimers maintained a very close relationship with the United Kingdom. As the *Financial Times* (2000a) wrote in Harry's obituary: "Anglo's top executives were seen as smooth Rhodes scholars educated at Oxford (Cambridge men, it was said, somehow did not fit in), who belonged to a discreet inner circle."

In 1994 major Anglo-related companies had a strong presence in car, media, paper, retail, beer, sugar, match, banking, and chemical industries. The reasons for unrelated diversification ranged from the opportunity to establish joint ventures with foreign multinationals (for example, the automotive industry) to state policies favoring the creation of national champions. The market power that Anglo enjoyed in gold and other mining business created the surplus capital to invest in other sectors, some related (for instance, the production of chemicals such as calcium cyanide), others completely unrelated. In addition, Anglo "could afford to initiate projects which would take many years to come to fruition" (Feinstein 2005: 174). Anglo activities collectively accounted for 43.3 percent of the JSE's market capitalization in 1994. The Oppenheimer family directly owned only 8.1 percent but had ultimate control because of the structure of ownership.[9] The linkages were reinforced by the overlapping of Directors and Chief Executives. In 1997 Julian Ogilvie Thompson was chairman of Minorco, Anglo, and AAIT, while Nicky Oppenheimer was an

---

[9] For example, De Beers Consolidated owned 38.6% of Anglo and 10% of the Anglo American Investment Trust (AAIT), but De Beers was in turn controlled by Anglo through Anglo's 29.4% stake in De Beers Centenary, while AAIT (52% owned by Anglo) owned a further 25.8% directly of De Beers Consolidated and 23.4% of De Beers Centenary. Further down the pyramid, 30% of Mondi Paper was owned by Anglo, together with a further 17% owned by De Beers and 53% by AMIC (itself 49.9% owned by Anglo and 26.7% by De Beers).

executive deputy chairman of Anglo and a director of AAIT and Minorco (and was later appointed as head of De Beers). AAIC Deputy Chair Leslie Boyd once held a record twenty-nine board positions. A narrow focus on ownership would therefore miss the control and coordination structures.

Simply because of its size, the restructuring of Anglo American has been the most significant process of change in the corporate structure of South Africa. Anglo's urbane, liberal, intellectual, and consensual corporate culture, reinforced by individual membership in some of the high places of the British establishment, clearly helped Anglo in its move to London. Milestones included the unbundling of JCI in 1995, the merging of gold interests under AngloGold and the restructuring of platinum holdings under Amplats in 1997, the creation of FirstRand through the merger of FNB and Southern Life with RMB in 1998, and LSE listing in 1999. In 2002 Anglo sold its remaining holding in SAB, Boart Longyear and Samancor Chrome were sold in mid-2005, and Highveld Steel was sold in 2006–7. In 2007 Anglo demerged Mondi and established Mondi as a dual-listed company structure. In 2007 the Tongaat-Hulett, of which Anglo American South Africa owned 50.34 percent, also spun off Hulamin (Hulett Aluminium) to focus on the agri-processing business. The group's structure in 2006 is depicted in Fig. 19.1.

Anglo has long been international in reach, and has at times been the world's biggest gold, platinum, and diamond producer. The Central Selling Organization has also been the world's most successful global cartel.[10] In 1990 De Beers moved its international headquarters to Switzerland and Luxemburg. The new companies control all De Beers business outside South Africa. In the 2000s AA has grown by acquisition to become a global mining house with interests mainly in gold, platinum, and coal, but also in forestry, paper, and pulp. Nonetheless, since Australia's BHP Billiton knocked Anglo off its perch as the world's biggest mining company in June 2001, shares have trailed the FTSE index of the top thirteen miners by 33 percent

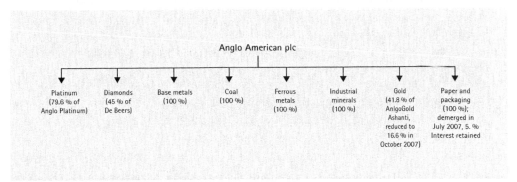

Figure 19.1 Anglo American after restructuring, 2006

Source: Based on the information provided on the group's website.

---

[10] Oppenheimer successfully fought off a US government antitrust suit in 1945 on the ground that it was American dealers who cooperated with him, not he who told them what to do.

(*Business Report* 2007). In fact, while AA remained the world largest mining company by turnover in 2006 (US$33.1 billion, versus US$32.8 billion for BHP Billiton), its growth over 2005 was much lower than for the industry's top forty (13% versus 37%) (PwC 2007). A US$6.2 billion plan to increase mining of base metals, coal, and diamonds was announced in October 2005.

This strategic reorientation is intimately connected with the relationship between Anglo, on the one hand, and both the Oppenheimers and South Africa, on the other. Nicky Oppenheimer, son of Harry Oppenheimer, resigned as Deputy Chairman in 2001 but has remained a non-executive director. Through a highly complex transaction in 2001, Anglo, as part of a consortium also including the Oppenheimer family and the Government of Botswana, purchased and delisted De Beers. De Beers' holding in Anglo was distributed to its shareholders, and Anglo increased its share in De Beers to 45 percent. The Oppenheimer family holds a contract for the management of De Beers, although there are recurrent rumors that Anglo may eventually acquire full control over the diamond business. E. Oppenheimer & Son Holdings Limited reduced its Anglo holdings from 3.49 percent to 2.35 percent on November 10, 2006 when it sold 17 million shares to China Vision Resources (led by Citic Pacific chairperson Larry Yung).

Partly to shed its clubby South African culture and improve its standing in the City, Anglo appointed a British chairman in 2002, Royal Dutch/Shell's former chairman Sir Mark Moody-Stuart. It went a step further by appointing a black executive, Lazarus Zim, as CEO of Anglo SA in 2004. The personification of this international strategy (and 'de-Oppenheimerization') was the arrival of Cynthia Carroll, an American woman, as chief executive in March 2007 (*The Economist* 2007). Anglo broke with tradition even to consider Carroll as a top executive, insofar as former chief executives Gavin Relly and Ogilvie Thompson both started as personal assistants to Harry Oppenheimer.[11]

Anglo inevitably has to massage its message depending on the audience. Global investors and fund managers want to hear what the company is doing about reducing the earnings' dependency on South Africa, home to 61 percent of employees and 50 percent of assets. Tshwane, on the other hand, is concerned that AA remains committed to the country, despite the often difficult relationship that the company has maintained *vis-à-vis* the ANC in recent years. In September 2004, President Mbeki tongue-lashed Trahar over his comments on the political risk of doing business in South Africa. In May 2005, Deputy Minerals and Energy minister Lulu Xingwana slammed Anglo American for appointing 'a CEO for whites and a CEO for blacks' and criticized De Beers for having a "lily-white and male dominated" board. The companies were also criticized for not doing enough to meet transformation targets set out in their respective empowerment charters.

---

[11] Under Clifford Elphick, the last of Harry's personal assistants, E. Oppenheimer & Son was transformed in 2006 from a family holding structure to quite a sizeable business with about ninety people operating in offices all around the world.

19.5.2 Rembrandt

In 1928–9 the Carnegie Corporation launched the Commission on the Poor White Problem in South Africa, which convinced the government to allocate more funds for improving the position of rural Afrikaner whites. Afrikaner business, however, remained underdeveloped.[12] In the post-1948 period, the restructuring of white business composition gave a prominent role to SOEs in order to create jobs for Afrikaner workers and also included direct assistance to private Afrikaner companies (Bunting 1964). Interlocking directorships with state corporations gave many Afrikaner undertakings a crucial inside edge. Government contracts and subsidies benefited particularly Federale Volksbeleggings, the industrial investment subsidiary of Sanlam.[13] By 1962, the Afrikaner share of the financial sector had grown from 6 percent in 1948/9 to 13 percent, to 9 percent of industrial production (from 6% in 1948/9) and to 28 percent of commerce (from 25% in 1948/9) (Clark 1994).

In this setting a business group rose to the status of undisputed champion of Afrikaner capitalism. Anton Rupert started the Voorbrand Tobacco Company in 1940 and soon after bought the wine-making company, Distillers Corporation. Voorbrandt was taken up by Rembrandt in 1946, when Rupert also founded a second investment company jointly with the Herzog family, Tegkor. The latter, Rembrandt, and the Rembrandt Trust were interconnected by capital and directorship ties, giving rise to a pyramidal structure with interests in a variety of new industries, including wool and coal (Dommisse 2005: 80). The overall group's diversification in South Africa, taking advantage of market power and ample liquidity, was mirrored by the quick internationalization of the tobacco business. By 1968 Rembrandt had thirty-four factories in twenty countries, and four years later it was the world's sixth-largest tobacco manufacturer (Dommisse 2005: 199), a global position that no company outside the Triad could claim at the time.

Rupert had a complex relationship with the apartheid government. On the one hand, he introduced minimum wages in his company in 1961 at much higher levels than the average wage at the time and held views on racial issues that placed him in occasional confrontation with Prime Minister Verwoerd (Gilliomee 2003). On the other hand, the help of the Nationalist government proved crucial. In 1948 Rembrandt received one of the first Federale Volksbeleggins loans. Competitors' entry into the tobacco business remained difficult, and all calls to advocate tobacco control were blocked (Malan and Leaver 2003). The other major business of the group, alcohol beverages, was similarly protected.

---

[12] At the beginning of the Second World War, Afrikaner undertakings accounted for only 5% of the total turnover in the urban economy (and only 1% in the mining sector and 3% in manufacturing). And in 1945, of the 117 undertakings with a capitalization of more than £1 million, only one (Sanlam) was considered an Afrikaner company.

[13] FVB, established in 1940 on the mandate of the Ekonomiese Volkskongres of 1939, operated as a people's institution (*volksinrigting*). The FVB would operate as an industrial management company for Afrikaners, without conducting any business directly.

Beginning in the 1970s Rembrandt expanded in various other economic sectors in South Africa, acting on many occasions as the white knight of Afrikaans business when disputes arose that could be detrimental to the long-term interests of this community (Dommisse 2005: 275). In addition, Rembrandt was embroiled in a long dispute with Sanlam, the insurance company, which eventually let to its taking over Volkskas. Rupert also spearheaded the Small Business Development Corporation (SBDC), a non-profit company lending to small and medium-sized businesses, and created one of world's largest luxury goods empires.[14]

Since 1994 Rembrandt has gone through a complex restructuring that has involved rebalancing between domestic and international operations, clarifying the control structure, and managing the socio-economic transformation of South Africa. In 1995 Rembrandt and Richemont consolidated their respective tobacco interests in Rothmans International, at the time the world's fourth largest cigarette manufacturer, which was then delisted. Then in 1999 these interests were merged with those of British American Tobacco (BAT), to create the world's second-largest cigarette producer.[15] As at March 31, 2008, Compagnie Financière Rupert, a Swiss limited partnership, held 9.1 percent of the Richemont equity and controlled 50 percent of the voting rights. Johann, who had joined the family business in 1985, and Jan Rupert were on the Board of Directors of Compagnie Financière Richemont, the parent company—the only South Africans along with thirteen other members of eight different nationalities. Jointly with two additional South Africans, they were also among the thirteen directors of Richemont in 2007.

In South Africa, the group business in 2000 consisted of four listed companies—namely, TIB, Tegkor, RBB, and Rembrandt (Fig. 19.2). In order to unlock shareholder value, in September 2000 the four-tier pyramidal structure was eliminated and the underlying investments were reorganized into two groups of companies (Fig. 19.3). One group, which remained in Rembrandt (renamed VenFin), consisted of the technology-oriented interests; Rembrandt Trust held all Venfin's unlisted B ordinary shares and was entitled to 47 percent of the total votes exercisable by shareholders. The other, rechristened Remgro, consisted of mining, financial, and industrial investments and was most probably the biggest group in South Africa. Remgro controlled companies as diverse as Distell, Dorbyl, Rainbow Chickens, Total SA, Medi-Clinic, and Transvaal Sugar, while also having interests in ABSA, Nampak, FirstRand, and Gencor, on top of its BAT stake.

While Johann Rupert chaired Remgro and VenFin, and created the only interlock, both companies were run by non-family CEOs. The Afrikaner nature of both

---

[14] In 1972 the overseas tobacco interests of Rembrandt were consolidated in Rothmans International. In 1988 the Rupert family separated local and overseas interests with the founding of Compagnie Financière Richemont (Richemont)—a Swiss-listed luxury-goods group that also acquired the shares in Rothmans International. In 1993 Richemont's tobacco and luxury goods operations were separated into Rothmans International and Vendôme.

[15] In August 2008 Richemont's luxury-goods business was separated from its other interests, and 90% of the group's shareholding in British American Tobacco were distributed to unit-holders.

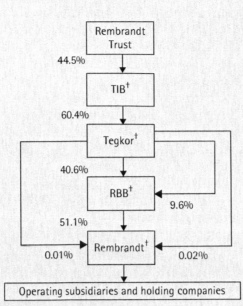

Figure 19.2 Rembrandt's structure before 2000

Note: Figures refer to ownership stakes.
Source: Based on the information provided in the group's website.

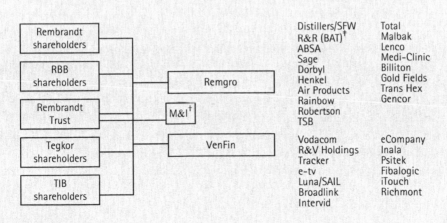

* In June 2009, Remgro acquired the entire issued ordinary share capital of VenFin, on a basis that excludes VenFin's interest in DiData. The Competition Tribunal approved the transaction in November 2009, subject to minor conditions.

† M&I performs management service for Remgro and VenFin.

‡ Remgro unbundled its investment in British American Tobacco in November 2008 by way of an interim divient to its shareholders.

Figure 19.3 Rembrandt's structure after 2000*

Source: Based on the information provided on the group's website.

companies is striking—all five members of Remgro's executive committee and three-quarters of VenFin's management committee. Consistent with the different nature of their investment portfolios, VenFin had a much younger management—40 years versus 55—and also a female CEO.

The Ruperts' engagement with major BEE players was earlier and more integrated than the Oppenheimers'. In fact, the Ruperts also maintained very strong civil engagements in South Africa, despite their traditionally low public profile (*Financial Times* 2007). After handing over control of the empire, Anton became involved in conservation and took a lead in the creation of trans-frontier conservation areas or "peace parks." Johann sat on an investment council of senior business leaders that was regularly consulted by President Mbeki.

In sum, the Ruperts seemed ready to adapt their positions to suit the evolving policy dispensation. During the 1970s and 1980s, their relationship with the government became much friendlier (Van Walbeek 2004). Similarly, Johann's approach to the ANC was less confrontational than Anglo's and his approach to BEE favored individual initiative, combined with the development of alliances with key black business groups, rather than a collective effort (*Sunday Times* 2002).

19.6 BLACK OLIGARCHS?

The process of BEE can be split into two distinct timeframes. During the first phase, transfers of ownership were facilitated by the introduction of special purpose vehicles whereby financial institutions provided funding to black entrepreneurs, who in turn offered as collateral preference equity capital in the companies acquired. From the groups' side, it was important to conclude highly visible and large-scale deals, especially to the extent that they concerned assets that they wanted to dispose of in any case. In the first phase, empowerment groups tended to follow a diversified and acquisitive approach to expansion. The results were initially impressive, but this highly leveraged strategy could not be sustained in the face of worsening conditions on global financial markets.

Since the late 1990s, BEE deals have been mainly concluded through the private equity model and have been strongly supported by the Industrial Development Corporation (IDC), the state-owned development finance body. More transparent business groups—such as Mvelaphanda Holdings (Mvela), Pamodzi, Royal Bafokeng, Safika, Shanduka, and Thebe—have emerged, with the capabilities required to build a base in a particular sector, and the dominant mining companies have concluded a flurry of deals with them. Although their holdings are largely investment positions, not controlling, the major black groups show a straddling of industries similar to that of the big six in the past. Nonetheless, the black elite remains dominated by a few people with strong political credentials, such as stints in prison or in exile, who may sometimes have supplemented these personal assets with foreign

Table 19.3 The main "black oligarchs", 2007

Name	Former political roles	Funding vehicle	Holdings	Directorships[1]
Cyril Ramaphosa	NUM general secretary (1982–91), MP and Chair Constitutional Assembly (1994–6), ANC SG (1991–4)	Shanduka Ramaphosa (established in November 2000)	Alexander Forbes (18%, bought April 2003), Bidvest (14.4%, July 2003), Standard Bank (1.2%, July 2004), Mondi Shanduka Newsprint (42%, August 2004), Mondi Packaging (40%, August 2004), Assore (11.74%, November 2005), Liberty Life (1.5%, November 2005), Downing, Reynard and Associates (unlisted, 25%, May 2006) Kangra Coal (unlisted 40%, July 2006)	Alexander Forbes, Bidvest (ch), MTN Group (ch), SABMiller, Standard Bank
Tokyo Sexwale	Robben Island inmate. Gauteng premier	Mvelaphanda Investment Holdings (established in 1999, merged with Rebserve in 2004)	Northam and Transhex from Remgro, ABSA (10% bought by a consortium led by Tokyo Sexwale), 70% stake of East Daggafontein	Absa, Gold Fields, Mvelaphanda Group (ch), Mvelaphanda Resources (ch), Northam Platinum (ch), Trans Hex (ch)
Cheryl Carolus	UDF activist. ANC deputy SG, high commissioner in London, CEO of SA Tourism	Peotona Group Holdings (also includes former First Rand Retail CEO Wendy Lucas-Bull)	De Beers (2%, November 2005), IQ Business Group (10%, January 2006), Fenner SA (25%, May 2006), Lafarge Mining (4.4%, July 2006), Lafarge Industries (1.5%, July 2006)	
Popo Molefe	Robben Island inmate. Premier of North West province and NEC member	Lereko	Sun International (7%), Sappi's plantation land portfolio (25%)	Imperial Holdings, PetroSA (ch), Armscor (ch)

(continued)

Table 19.3 Continued

Name	Former political roles	Funding vehicle	Holdings	Directorships[1]
Manne Dipico	Northern Cape premier, 1994–2004, and President Thabo Mbeki's parliamentary adviser, 2004–5	Pamodzi Holdings (with ANC SG Kgalema Motlanthe through Pambi Trust)	Ponahalo, BEE company which bought a 26% stake in De Beers Consolidated Mines (18%)	
Patrice Motsepe	None	ARM group	ARM (42.7%), Ubuntu-Botho empowerment grouping in Sanlam (9.4%), Teal Resources established a JSE secondary after initially listing in Toronto	ARM (non-executive since 2004), Harmony Gold, Teal, ABSA, Sanlam
Nthatho Motlana	12 years on Robben Island			NAIL and Metlife (ch)
Mzi Khumalo	Nelson Mandela's personal physician		Metallon (Zimbabwe's largest gold producer)	
Sakumzi Macozoma	Robben Island inmate. Member of Parliament (1994–6) and Member, ANC National Elections Committee (1991–2008)			Liberty Group, Liberty Hold, Murray & Roberts, Standard Bank, Stocks Hotels, VW SA
Marcel Golding	Former trade unionist	Hosken Consolidated Investments (HCI), established in 1997 through a reverse listing of assets put together under the SA Clothing & Textile Workers Union (Sactwu) investment arm		e.tv (CEO)
Mamphela Ramphele	Internally banished to the town of Tzaneen from 1977 to 1984	Circle Capital Venture		Anglo American, MTN Group, MediClinic, Business Partners, Mellon, Nelson Mandela and Rockefeller Foundations; resigned from Standard Bank board because of a potential conflict of interest

Note: [1] ch = chairmanship.

education but have no experience in business (Table 19.3). The main criticism levied at BEE is in fact that black capitalists basically bring political capital, rather than managerial skills, and are very often sidelined in business structures and confined to non-operational, public-relations positions (Andreasson 2007). Hence the term "black oligarchs," which is often used to define businessmen with ANC connections who have been at the receiving end of the juiciest deals.

How much truth is there in this view? There is no doubt that many successful black capitalists have maintained a very visible political profile and campaigned in this sense—thus devoting less time to business. The largest BEE groups are built to take advantage of opportunities and, "absent a market need and the managerial means to integrate business, group performance is inconsistent" (Fruin 2008: 248). Nonetheless, in South Africa ownership concentration levels do not seem unprecedented in historical perspective (Morck 2005). Moreover, while the number of black directors in major firms remains low, it is increasing rapidly, which is somehow at odds with the idea that the corporate elite is restricted to a few individuals. In 1980 there were no black directors on the boards of JSE-listed companies, increasing to 15 in 1993, to 98 in 1997, and 207 in 2003 (*Mail & Guardian* 2006). In 2007 almost two-thirds of JSE-listed companies had at least one black director, although out of 558 positions about 83 percent were non-executive. While it was not uncommon a few years previously to see a few BEE kingpins sitting on nine to twelve boards each, Mlambo-Ngcuka (2006) estimated that the fifteen most active directors sat on an average of four boards each. Although there is no discernible evidence that changing the composition of South African boards influences corporate strategies, BEE transactions have not, on average, exploited black empowerment groups to the benefit of white corporate South Africa (Jackson III et al. 2005).

In fact, the crucial point is the risk that BEE elites may develop into a "plutocracy." In South Africa an entrepreneurial bourgeoisie can be seen as a state of nation-building—or, as Iheduru (2004: 2) put it, "the vanguard of black integration into the economic mainstream." In this sense, nurturing a small cohort of black businesspeople that control a diversified set of corporate assets is a faster strategy than waiting for the development of a rich landscape of black small and medium-sized enterprises. However, economies of this kind can be vulnerable to crises from a generational change in business leadership or from inherent inflexibility. More so when the black capitalist class is interlinked with the ANC and government (Southall 2006, 2007). In such settings, popular and political uneasiness with the structure of economic power is to be expected, especially if the rent-seeking proclivities of this elite fail to produce new wealth and jobs.

19.7 CONCLUSIONS

Business groups played a towering role in the economic history of South Africa in the twentieth century, as economic, institutional, and political factors combined to make it viable to put a wide range of production activities under common ownership and management. In particular, it is difficult to overestimate the role of Anglo American at the core of the South African economy, as the largest group in both the export-oriented mining complex and the import-substituting manufacturing industry. While younger and smaller, the Rembrandt group assumed a similar role in the second half of the century, acquiring considerable international exposure in the tobacco industry.

The country's economy has gone through a remarkable transformation since the late 1980s under the dual pressure of political democratization and economic globalization. Viewed against the background of the skepticism that prevailed in 1994, South Africa has achieved a remarkable transition from an authoritarian and race-base regime to a multi-party and multi-ethnic democracy. Despite the pressures that the new authorities faced to accommodate pent-up social demands through relaxed fiscal policies, the macroeconomic framework remained prudent, public finances were stabilized, inflation was brought down, foreign capital was attracted in growing amounts, and economic growth, after lagging for a time, improved. Big business, and groups in particular, exerted continuous domination over the South African system of innovation, with a heavy concentration in the cluster of industries associated with the resource-based segment of the economy and in parts of the services sector (OECD 2007).

It can be argued that the country is now closer to the 'norm' that at any other period in its modern history, with all races equally franchised and no productive sector accounting for an inordinate share of the economy. In this setting, family-controlled business groups such as Anglo and Rembrandt do not dominate the South African economy to the same extent as in the past, but they still play a very important role at the pinnacle of capitalism. There are two basic reasons for this. First, while transformation has the benefit of stimulating business activity by prying loose entrenched capital (such as family or founder stakes in private companies), in South Africa many institutional and physical infrastructures remain underdeveloped. As long as investors hold most companies in deep mistrust,[16] the governance of large corporations will remain in the hands of a few reputable business groups. Moreover, South African groups enhance economic welfare insofar as they partly offset the nation's above-mentioned problems. Respected business families can leverage their reputation to raise savings, control many listed companies, transfer skills, and create a larger and more buoyant consumer market. In addition, South African large firms and groups have played a critically important role in creating, accumulating, and dispersing knowledge; they have tended to patent inventions not only in the technological fields that are associated to their own industries but also, by virtue of their innate diversification, outside such core technological fields, therefore acting as vehicles for building up knowledge capital for innovation across wide areas of the economy (OECD 2007).

---

[16] Haile et al. (2008) employ trust games to investigate the effect of heterogeneity in income and race on cooperation in South Africa. An intriguing finding is that the low-income subjects from both racial groups invest significantly less in partnerships with the high-income subjects of the other racial group than in any other partnership. This severely limits the investment opportunities of black savers.

Secondly, in an environment of rapid change business groups operate at an advantage in identifying good business opportunities and entering into new lines of operations. The two business dynasties analyzed in the chapter, now in the third and second generation respectively, have progressively delegated executive functions to professional managers while maintaining, especially in the case of the Ruperts, the power and responsibility of providing strategic orientation. The experience of the Oppenheimers and the Ruperts is more than vaguely reminiscent of that of the Tatas in India (Khanna and Palepu 2004), although their social engagement is arguably of a different scale. In this setting, they have also acquired the capacity to act as venture capitalists and explore new opportunities for diversification, in particular in the New Economy in the case of Ruperts.

The relationship with the state and the role of public policies are other big issues in the contemporary debate on business groups (see Schneider, Chapter 23, this volume). Past South African governments emphasized the links between racial mobilization, corporate ownership, and "national champions," and business groups flourished in this environment. It is now generally agreed that it is essential to the country's long-term development and future stability that previously disadvantaged groups, black people in particular, share in its wealth. The policy of affirmative action is seen as useful in this regard, with a focus on empowerment transactions, ownership patterns, and the formation of black "national champions." The risk, however, is that this emphasis leads to a worsening in distribution coefficients, without necessarily leading to faster economic growth. In addition, there seems to be a disconnection between a strategy of favoring the development of business groups to build a high-tech, high-wage, capital-intensive economy, and the combination of surplus labor and shortage of capital that characterizes the country (Lipton 2007). Given the poor state of disciplining forces—on the part of the state or resulting from rivalry and domestic competition—it is not surprising that corporate investment has remained low and that growth has picked up only modestly.

To conclude, the prospects for South African business groups after fifteen years of progressive adaptation to a new global and domestic dispensation are not necessarily bad. The traditional ones have become more international and may thrive, although by becoming progressively detached from South Africa (Anglo possibly more than Remgro). New ones may keep exploiting political connections and imperfections in the functioning of various markets. At any rate, at this stage the black oligarchs do not seem to be excessively large by the standards of the global economy where most of them are operating. Still, there are risks in the long run. On the one hand, over time growing share of the population may question the legitimacy of their property rights. On the other hand, BEE groups may find it increasingly difficult to fund the investments needed to nurture competitive capabilities.

REFERENCES

AGHION, P., BRAUN, M., and FEDDERKE, J. (2006). "Competition and Productivity Growth in South Africa." CID Working Paper, 132.

AMSDEN, A. (1989). *Asia's Next Giant.* Oxford: Oxford University Press.

AMSDEN, A. (2001). *The Rise of the Rest.* Oxford: Oxford University Press.

ANC (1985). *The Nature of the South African Ruling Class.* National Preparatory Committee Document for the National Consultative Conference.

ANC (1992). *Ready to Govern.* Pretoria: African National Congress.

ANC (1997). "The Core Values of the RDP." Discussion Document for the 50th National Conference.

ANDREASSON, S. (2007). "The Resilience of Comprador Capitalism: 'New' Economic Groups in Southern Africa," in A. E. F. Jilberto and B. Hogenboom (eds.), *Big Business on the Rise: Conglomerates and Economic Groups in Developing Countries and Transition Economies under Globalization.* London: Routledge.

BARR, G., GERSON, J., and KANTOR, B. (1995). "Shareholders as Agents and Principals: The Case for South Africa's Corporate Governance System," *Journal of Applied Corporate Finance,* 8/1: 1–32.

BEBCHUK, L., KRAAKMAN, R., and TRIANTIS, G. (2000). "Stock Pyramids, Cross-Owner-ship, and Dual Class Equity: The Creation and Agency Costs of Separating Control from Cash-Flow Rights," in R. Morck (ed.), *Concentrated Corporate Ownership.* Chicago: NBER and University of Chicago Press.

BELLI, P., FINGER, M., and BALLIVIAN, A. (1993). "South Africa: Review of Trade Policy Issues," World Bank, Southern Africa Department, *Informal Discussion Papers on Aspects of the South African Economy,* 4.

BIDVEST (1997). *Annual Report.* Johannesburg: Bidvest.

BEEC (2001). Black Economic Empowerment Commission, *Black Economic Empowerment Commission.* Johannesburg: Skotaville Press.

BUNTING, B. (1964). *The Rise of the South African Reich.* Johannesburg: Penguin Africa Library.

Business Report (2007a). "Anglo's Challenge is to Determine how to Take South Africa Inc into the Future," Jan. 31.

Business Report (2007b). "Rich Get Richer," Mar. 11.

CARGILL, J., ET AL. (2000). *Empowerment 2000: New Directions.* Johannesburg: Business Map Foundation.

CHABANE, N., GOLDSTEIN, A., and ROBERTS, S. (2006). "The Changing Face of Big Business in South Africa: Ten Years of Political Democracy," *Industrial and Corporate Change,* 15/3: 549–77.

CHANDLER, A., JR. (1990). *Scale and Scope: The Dynamics of Industrial Capitalism.* Cambridge, MA: Harvard University Press.

CHANDLER, A., JR., AMATORI, F., and HIKINO, T. (eds.) (1997). *Big Business and the Wealth of Nations.* Cambridge: Cambridge University Press.

CLARK, N. (1994). *Manufacturing Apartheid: State Corporations in South Africa.* New Haven: Yale University Press.

CROSS, T. (1994). "Afrikaner Nationalism, Anglo American and Iscor: The Formation of the Highveld Steel & Vanadium Corporation, 1960–70," *Business History,* 36/3: 81–99.

Department of Trade and Industry (DTI) (2003). *South Africa's Economic Transformation: A Strategy for Broad-Based Black Empowerment.* Pretoria: DTI.

DJANKOV, S., LA PORTA, R., LOPEZ-DE-SILANES, F., and SHLEIFER, A. (2003). "Courts: The Lex Mundi Project," *Quarterly Journal of Economics,* 118/2: 453–517.

DOMMISSE, E. (in cooperation with W. Esterhuyse) (2005). *Anton Rupert: A Biography.* Cape Town: Taffelberg.

The Economist (1995). "Not a Golden Titan, More a Pig in a Poke," Oct. 7.

The Economist (2007). "A New Broom," June 30.

Empowerdex (2004). Economic Empowerment Rating Agency, "Pioneers, Powers and Pundits." Research document.

Empowerdex (2007). *Trailblazers: South Africa's Champions of Change.* Cape Town: Double Storey Books.

Ernst & Young SA (various years). *Mergers & Acquisitions: A Review of Activity for the Year.* Johannesburg: Ernst & Young SA.

FEINSTEIN, C. (2005). *An Economic History of South Africa: Conquest, Discrimination, and Development.* Cambridge: Cambridge University Press.

Financial Times (2000a). "Randlord who Opposed the System," Aug. 21.

Financial Times (2000b). "A Whole Day away from Johannesburg," Nov. 23.

Financial Times (2007). "A Luxury Leader Goes Incognito," July 1.

Financial Week (2006). "CEOs Leaving in Droves," Sept. 13.

FINE, B., and RUSTOMJEE, Z. (1996). *South Africa's Political Economy: From Minerals-Energy Complex to Industrialization?* London: Hurst.

FOURIE, F. C. v. N., LEWIS, D., and PRETORIUS, W. J. (1995). "Towards Competition Policy Reform in South Africa: Background Working Paper." Mimeo.

FRUIN, M. (2008). "Business Groups and Interfirm Networks," in G. Jones and J. Zeitlin (eds.), *The Oxford Handbook of Business History.* Oxford and New York: Oxford University Press.

GERSON, J. (1993). "Should the State Attempt to Reshape South Africa's Corporate and Financial Structures?" in M. Lipton and C. Simkins (eds.), *State and Market in Post Apartheid South Africa.* Johannesburg: Witwatersrand University Press.

GERSON, J., and BARR, G. (1996). "The Structure of Corporate Control and Ownership in a Regulatory Environment Unbiased toward One-Share-One-Vote," *Corporate Governance: An International Review,* 4/2: 78–97.

GILLIOMEE, H. (2003). *The Afrikaners.* Cape Town: Tafelberg.

GOLDSTEIN, A. (2000). "Big Business and the Wealth of South Africa: Policy Issues in the Transition from Apartheid." University of Pennsylvania, Christopher H. Browne Center for International Politics, Working Paper, 00–02.

GOLDSTEIN, A. (2007). *Emerging Multinationals in the Global Economy.* Houndmills: Palgrave Macmillan.

GOLDSTEIN, A., and PRITCHARD, W. (2009). "South African Multinationals," in R. Ramamurti and J. V. Singh (eds.), *Emerging Multinationals from Emerging Markets.* Cambridge: Cambridge University Press.

GREGORY, T. (1962). *Ernest Oppenheimer and the Development of Southern Africa.* Oxford: Oxford University Press.

GURIEV, S., and RACHINSKY, A. (2005). "The Role of Oligarchs in Russian Capitalism," *Journal of Economic Perspectives,* 19/1: 131–50.

HAILE, D., SADRIEH, A., and VERBON, H. (2008). "Cross-Racial Envy and Underinvestment in South African Partnerships," *Cambridge Journal of Economics,* 32/5: 703–24.

HANDLEY, A. (2005). "Business, Government and Economic Policymaking in the New South Africa, 1990–2000," *Journal of Modern African Studies,* 43/2: 211–39.

HIGGINSON, J. (2007a). "Privileging the Machines: American Engineers, Indentured Chinese and White Workers in South Africa's Deep-Level Gold Mines, 1902–1907," *IRSH,* 52: 1–34.

HIGGINSON, J. (2007b). "A World Briefly Upended: An Examination of Jeremy Krikler's White Rising: The 1922 Insurrection and Racial Killing in South Africa," *Journal of the Historical Society*, 7/1: 1–34.

HIRSCH, A. (2005). *Season of Hope: Economic Reform under Mandela and Mbeki*. Pietermaritzburg: University of KwaZulu-Natal Press.

IHEDURU, O. (2004). "Black Economic Power and Nation-Building in Post-Apartheid South Africa." *Journal of Modern African Studies*, 42/1: 1–30.

INNES, D. (1984). *Anglo American and the Rise of Modern South Africa*. London: Heinemann.

JACKSON III, W., ALESSANDRI, T., and BLACK, S. (2005). "The Price of Corporate Social Responsibility: The Case of Black Economic Empowerment Transactions in South Africa," Federal Reserve Bank of Atlanta, Working Paper Series, 2005–29.

JONES, S. (1996). "Business Imperialism and Business History," *South African Journal of Economic History*, 11/2.

KANTOR, B. (1998). "Ownership and Control in South Africa under Black Rule," *Journal of Applied Corporate Finance*, 10/4: 69–78.

KHANNA, T., and PALEPU, K. (2004). "The Evolution of Concentrated Ownership in India: Broad Patterns and a History of the Indian Software Industry." NBER Working Paper No. 10613.

KHANNA, T., and YAFEH, Y. (2007). "Business Groups in Emerging Markets: Paragons or Parasites?" *Journal of Economic Literature*, 45/2: 331–72.

KNIGHT, J., and STEVENSON, H. (1986). "The Williamson Diamond Mine, De Beers, and the Colonial Office: A Case-Study of the Quest for Control," *Journal of Modern African Studies*, 24/3: 423–46.

LANDES, D. (2006). *Dynasties: Fortunes and Misfortunes of the World's Great Family Businesses*. New York: Viking.

LA PORTA, R., LOPEZ-DE-SILANES, F., SHLEIFER, A., and VISHNY, R. (1998). "Law and Finance," *Journal of Political Economy*, 106/6: 1113–55.

LIPTON, M. (1986). *Capitalism and Apartheid*. Cape Town: David Philip.

LIPTON, M. (2007). *Liberals, Marxists & Nationalists: Competing Interpretations of South African History*. Houndmills: Palgrave MacMillan.

LUMBY, A. (1995). "Industrial History in South Africa: Past Trends and Future Needs," *South African Journal of Economic History*, 10/1.

McGregors (various years). *Who Owns Whom in SA*. Johannesburg: McGregors.

Mail & Guardian (2006a). "Anatomy of Fast Money," Aug. 11.

Mail & Guardian (2006b). "Black Power Still Limited in Boardrooms," Sept. 23.

MALAN, M., and LEAVER, R. (2003). "Political Change in South Africa: New Tobacco Control and Public Health Policies," in J. de Beyer and L. Waverley (eds.), *Tobacco Control Policy: Strategies, Successes and Setbacks*. Washington: RITC and the World Bank.

MALHERBE, S., and SEGAL, N. (2001). "Corporate Governance in South Africa." Presented at the OECD–EBRD Meeting on Corporate Governance in Developing Countries and Emerging Economies, Paris, Apr. 23–24.

MLAMBO-NGCUKA, P. (2006). "Address Delivered at the Empowerdex Book Launch of Trailblazers." Johannesburg, Sept. 22.

MORCK, R. (ed.) (2005). *A History of Corporate Governance around the World. Family Business Groups to Professional Managers*. Chicago: NBER and University of Chicago Press.

NEWBURY, C. (1987). "Technology, Capital, and Consolidation: The Performance of De Beers Mining Company Limited, 1880–1889," *Business History Review*, 61/1: 1–42.

New York Times (2006). "Tradition-Breaking Choice to be Chief of Mining Giant," Oct. 25.

OECD (2007). *OECD Reviews of Innovation Policy: South Africa*. Paris: OECD.

PHIMISTER, I. R. (1978). "Meat and Monopolies: Beef Cattle in Southern Rhodesia, 1890–1938," *Journal of African History*, 19/3: 391–414.

PONTE, S., ROBERTS, S., and VAN SITTERT, L. (2007). "'Black Economic Empowerment,' Business and the State in South Africa," *Development and Change*, 38/5: 933–55.

PwC (PricewaterhouseCoopers) (2007). *Mine: Annual Review of Global Trends in the Mining Industry*. London: PwC.

SHAIN, M. (1994). *The Roots of Antisemitism in South Africa*. Johannesburg: Witwatersrand University Press.

SOUTHALL, R. (2006). "Black Empowerment and Present Limits to a More Democratic Capitalism in South Africa," in S. Buhlungu, J. Daniel, R. Southall, and J. Lutchman (eds.), *State of the Nation: South Africa 2005–2006*. Pretoria: HSRC Press.

SOUTHALL, R. (2007). "The ANC, Black Economic Empowerment and State-Owned Enterprises: A Recycling of History?" in S. Buhlungu, J. Daniel, R. Southall, and J. Lutchman (eds.), *State of the Nation: South Africa 2007*. Pretoria: HSRC Press.

STEVENSON, M. (2002). *Art and Aspirations: The Randlords of South Africa and their Collections*. Cape Town: Ferwood Press.

Sunday Times (2002). "Afrikaner Path to Wealth Stinks, Rupert Warns Nafcoc," Sept. 29.

TERREBLANCHE, S. (2002). *History of Inequality in South Africa 1652–2002*. Durban: Natal University Press.

THOMPSON, L. (1995). *A History of South Africa*. New Haven: Yale University Press.

TURRELL, R. and VAN HELTEN, J. J. (1987). "The Investment Group: The Missing Link in British Overseas Economic Expansion before 1914?" *Economic History Review*, 40/2: 267–74.

VAN WALBEEK, C. (2004). "Tobacco Control in South Africa in the 1990s: A Mix of Advocacy, Academic Research and Policy," *South African Journal of Economic History*, 19/1–2.

VAUGHN, M., and VERSTEGEN RYAN, L. (2006). "Corporate Governance in South Africa: A Bellwether for the Continent?" *Corporate Governance*, 14/5: 504–12.

VERHOEF, G. (1999). "The Development of Diversified Conglomerates: Federale Volksbeleggings," *Journal for Contemporary History*, 24/2: 55–78.

VERHOEF, G. (2003). "Afrikaner Nationalism in Business: United White Front?" Presented at the conference South Africa in the 1940s: Worlds of Possibilities, Queen's University, Kingston, Sept. 2–4.

VICAT TURRELL, R., and VAN-HELTEN, J.-J. (1987). "The Investment Group: The Missing Link in British Overseas Expansion before 1914?" *Economic History Review*, 40/2: 267–74.

WEST, A. (2006). "Theorising South Africa's Corporate Governance," *Journal of Business Ethics*, 68/4: 433–48.

WHEATCROFT, G. (1985). *The Randlords*. New York: Atheneum.

PART III

ECONOMIC, SOCIOPOLITICAL, AND MANAGERIAL UNDERPINNINGS OF BUSINESS GROUPS

CHAPTER 20

BUSINESS GROUPS IN EMERGING MARKETS: PARAGONS OR PARASITES?

TARUN KHANNA

YISHAY YAFEH

20.1 INTRODUCTION

DIVERSIFIED business (or corporate) groups are ubiquitous in emerging markets (for example, Brazil, Chile, China, India, Indonesia, South Korea, Mexico, Pakistan, Thailand, and many more) and even in some developed economies (for example, Italy and Sweden). These groups typically consist of legally independent firms, operating in multiple (often unrelated) industries, which are bound together by

This chapter is an abbreviated and slightly modified (to suit this volume) version of "Business Groups in Emerging Markets: Paragons or Parasites?" *Journal of Economic Literature*, 45 (June 2007), 331–72; of which some parts have been omitted for brevity. Note that no footnotes present in the original version of the article are included in this chapter. The interested reader is encouraged to refer to the original and complete version. We thank Sui Lin Yap for excellent assistance in reorienting the article to be included in this volume.

persistent formal (for example, equity) and informal (for example, family) ties. Varying degrees of participation by outside investors characterize many business groups around the world. Table 20.1 suggests that, in all countries for which data are available, the fraction of firms classified by domestic sources as group affiliated is substantial, ranging from about a fifth in Chile to about two-thirds in Indonesia. The table also indicates that, in virtually all emerging markets, group-affiliated firms tend to be relatively large and economically important.

But groups around the world vary considerably in form: some are extremely diversified whereas others are more focused. In some groups there is considerable vertical integration and intra-group trade; in others, less. Some groups are deeply involved in banking and financial services, whereas others are not. Some of this diversity is illustrated in Table 20.2, which displays partial data on the extent of group diversification, vertical integration, and involvement in financial services in nine emerging markets. Groups in Chile, for example, are far more diversified than groups in South Korea, which, in turn, are more diversified than groups in Taiwan; groups in the Philippines are far more vertically integrated than groups in India and far more involved in financial services than groups in Thailand. Moving from structure to ownership and control, some business groups are vertically controlled ("pyramids"), whereas others are horizontally linked through cross-shareholdings. The extent of family involvement also varies considerably across groups. Finally, in certain countries, business groups are a politically important force, enjoying close relations with the government; in others the relations between groups and governments tend to be more turbulent.

The ubiquity and diversity of business groups make the study of this institution fascinating. Conceptually, this hybrid organizational form between firm and market can shed new light on the theory of the firm and its boundaries. Empirically, the ubiquity of business groups outside the United States and the United Kingdom makes them relevant to a variety of fields within economics, including industrial organization, corporate finance, development and growth, and even open-economy macro to the extent that it deals with financial crises. In addition, the comparative study of business groups in emerging markets may shed new light on some economic phenomena in developed economies. For example, although many business groups are highly diversified, unlike American conglomerates each group firm is an independent entity, and the equity stake of outside investors can vary across group firms. Why are diversified entities in the United States organized as conglomerates rather than business groups? Is the answer related to economic and financial development? Or is it perhaps due to differences in the rule of law, social structure, or political economy? Is it due to unique historical developments in the United States? The study of business groups in emerging markets in this volume is significant, as it offers some answers.

The present chapter attempts to make three contributions to the literature on business groups. The first is motivated by the view that the diversity of business groups around the world is due to the diversity of the underlying conditions leading to their formation. This approach is at the basis of a novel taxonomy of business groups along three dimensions:

Table 20.1 Group affiliation around the world

Country	Years of data	Number of firms	Number of group affiliated firms	(Median size of group affiliated firms)/ (Median size of unaffiliated firms)	Median ROA of affiliated firms %	Median ROA of unaffiliated firms %	Median standard deviation of ROA, group affiliated firms %	Median standard deviation of ROA, unaffiliated firms %
Argentina	1990–97	25	11	5.5	3.9	7.8**	3.7	4.9**
Brazil	1990–97	105	51	2.5	3.3	1.8**	4.1	5.1
Chile	1989–96	225	50	18.7	5.9	2.2*	4.4	4.1
India	1990–97	5446	1821	4.4	11.7	9.6*	4.6	4.4*
Indonesia	1993–95	236	153	2.8	7.3	7.8	1.9	2.5*
South Korea	1991–95	427	218	3.9	4.8	5.1	1.9	2.6*
Mexico	1988–97	55	19	2.3	8.2	6.1	3.1	2.6
Philippines	1992–97	145	37	3.4	7.3	4.0	2.5	2.9
Taiwan	1990–97	178	79	2.0	5.1	6.2	1.7	2.3**
Thailand	1992–97	415	258	2.3	2.9	4.4*	4.3	4.9**
Turkey	1988–97	40	21	1.0	24.6	26.3	6.2	9.1
Prewar Japan	1932–43	58	17	6.8	5.5	6.4	4.4	7.1

Notes: The table shows summary statistics on group risk and operating performance for eleven emerging markets as well as for prewar Japan. Firm numbers, as well as statistics on firm size (total assets) and median return on assets (ROA), are all based on the year for which we have maximal coverage for the country in question. In prewar Japan, group affiliation refers to affiliation in the largest three zaibatsu only. Significance levels for the comparisons of medians are based on Wilcoxon signed-rank tests. Firms with profit rates above 100 percent or below −100 % are excluded from the analysts.

* and ** denote a difference between group-affiliated and other firms that is significant at the 5 % and 10 % levels, respectively. See Khanna and Yafeh (2005) for data sources and for more information on the sample and variable definitions.

Table 20.2 Group heterogeneity around the world

Country	Group diversification	Group vertical integration	Group assets in financial firms
Brazil	1.4	0.04	N/A
Chile	5.1	0.05	0.24
India	4.2	0.04	0.05
Indonesia	2.1	0.04	0.45
South Korea	1.7	0.04	N/A
Mexico	2.7	0.02	0.05
Philippines	3.1	0.06	0.60
Taiwan	1.6	0.02	0.01
Thailand	3.5	0.04	0.35

Notes: Group diversification is measured as the number of two-digit industries in which the group operates. Group vertical integration is the average input–output coefficient across all pairs of firms within the group, and involvement in financial services is measured as the fraction of all group assets in group financial firms. See Khanna and Yafeh (2005) for data sources and for more information on the sample and variable definitions.

1. Group structure: the extent of horizontal diversification; the extent of vertical integration; and the extent of involvement in the financial sector.
2. Group ownership and control: the extent to which the group is pyramidal in structure; the extent to which it is family controlled.
3. Group interaction with society: the nature of the interaction between business groups and the state; the extent of monopoly power wielded by groups.

This taxonomy is used to derive six testable hypotheses about the reasons for the formation of business groups, their prevalence in different economic environments, and the welfare implications associated with their presence. In general, the framework in which economic agents form business groups in response to the economic and institutional environment within which they operate is in the spirit of work by Aoki (2001) or Greif (2006), who emphasize that institutions should be analyzed within a particular economic context. Because groups arise for different reasons and in different environments, we argue that their impact on social welfare is ambiguous, even though much of the existing literature suggests that they are uniformly welfare reducing: groups may sometimes play a positive role by making up for underdeveloped economic institutions, but they can also be detrimental to social welfare because of rent-seeking or monopoly power. There is, therefore, no clear verdict on the extent to which groups should be viewed as "paragons" or "parasites," and the answer is likely to vary across countries, groups, and possibly time periods.

The second contribution of the (original) study is the presentation of new stylized data and evidence on several facets of business groups that go beyond the existing literature. (That presentation, however, has been removed from this chapter because the national chapters in this volume collect historical data on the origin of business groups in specific nations. Interested readers are referred to table 4 in the original

JEL article.) In that article we present comparable data on the origins and emergence of business groups around the world. This is key, because group membership should generally be viewed as endogenous. Another example of novel data in this chapter is preliminary evidence supporting the view that groups do not only respond to their environment but also shape and influence it. Although econometric evidence on this point is almost entirely absent, historical evidence in several countries is supportive of this view. This dynamic effect of groups on their economic environment is sometimes socially welfare-enhancing, and sometimes not.

The third contribution of the present study is to question some of the conventional wisdom in the literature. For example, groups, we argue, are not purely rent-seeking organizations, as some of the literature has portrayed them. Nor should groups be equated with pyramids, and pyramids are not always the, or even a, way of disenfranchising minority shareholders.

The rest of the chapter is organized around the taxonomy of business groups around the world: Section 20.2 focuses on dimensions related to the structure of business groups; in Section 20.3 we examine dimensions related to ownership and control; Section 20.4 focuses on two dimensions of the interaction between business groups and society; and the concluding section, Section 20.5, delineates a future research agenda.

20.2 STRUCTURE AND FORM OF BUSINESS GROUPS

20.2.1 Structure of business groups: Diversification

Prevailing managerial theories advocate that companies should discover their source of competitive advantage and remain true to it. This "conventional wisdom" is not based on unambiguous theoretical predictions: corporate diversification can be beneficial to shareholders if a firm has certain resources that can be profitably deployed outside the industry in which it operates, such as entrepreneurial skills, technology, and so on. In addition, when equity markets function poorly, it may be possible to lower risk through diversification across industries. In contrast with these positive arguments for diversification, there are also theoretical foundations for the view that diversification can be harmful if it is driven by managerial objectives such as "empire-building" or risk aversion, or if it leads to agency problems among division managers (see, e.g., Rajan et al. 2000; Scharfstein and Stein 2000). Empirically, the common view in the United States, that diversification "destroys shareholder value," has been supported by evidence on the relative performance of firms focused on a small number of industries in comparison with diversified firms—which suggests that, in the United States, the costs associated with diversification typically exceed the benefits.

The ubiquity of diversified (and often fairly successful) business groups in many countries outside the United States is, therefore, in sharp contrast with the prevailing conventional wisdom. Why, then, is diversification in the form of business groups so common in emerging markets? Leaving aside (for now) the question why the typical institutional mechanism for diversification is conglomerates in the United States and business groups in emerging markets, the following hypothesis offers one possible explanation:

> Hypothesis 1. Diversified business groups should be more common in economies with less-developed market institutions.

Hypothesis 1 is based on the conjecture that corporate focus need not necessarily be a good strategy in environments less economically developed than the United States, where the benefits of diversification may exceed the costs. The main reason is that some of the institutions that make diversification unnecessary or even harmful in developed economies do not exist or are underdeveloped in poorer countries. Capital markets are incomplete and may be plagued with informational and other problems, making risk reduction through diversification and the use of internal capital markets relatively efficient in comparison with poorly regulated external markets. Labor markets may also lack institutions training skilled labor and management, making diversified business groups, where trained personnel can be used for a variety of tasks across many group firms, a possible substitute for these institutions.

20.2.1.1 *Evidence on groups and the diversification discount in emerging markets*

A starting point in the discussion of the validity of Hypothesis 1 is the question whether or not a diversification discount exists in emerging markets. The general answer seems to be that the diversification discount tends to be lower in environments where markets, including, but not limited to, financial markets, are less developed, in line with Hypothesis 1. In some cases, diversified entities are even traded at a premium rather than a discount. For example, Fauver, Houston, and Naranjo (2003), who, following US studies, rely on stock-market data, find that the diversification discount is a feature of high-income countries, with developed (financial) markets and institutions. By contrast, in low-income countries, there is no market discount—and sometimes there is even a premium—for corporate diversification. Qualitatively similar results are reported by Claessens et al. (2003), who use both stock-market and accounting variables to measure the value of diversification. They find a diversification premium in the relatively poor countries in East Asia (Indonesia, the Philippines, or Thailand) and a diversification discount in the richer countries in the region (for example, Hong Kong or Taiwan). Although both Fauver, Houston, and Naranjo (2003) and Claessens et al. (2003) refer to multi-segment firms in general, not specifically to corporate groups, there is some time-series evidence on business groups indicating that the relative advantage of groups declines as market institutions develop. For example, Khanna and Palepu (2000b) document the declining (stock-market and accounting profitability-based) group premium over a decade associated with economic reform and development of market institutions in Chile. Lee, Peng, and Lee (2001) observe that companies affiliated with the South Korean business groups, the *chaebol*, used to be traded at a premium until the early 1990s—but the premium turned into a discount starting around 1994 (see also Ferris et al. 2003). A number of other studies discussed below concur and claim that since the late 1990s the relative performance of group-affiliated companies in South Korea has not been very good, although this aggregate statistic masks considerable variation between some groups that have done very well (for example, Samsung) and some groups that have done very poorly (for example, Daewoo).

Table 20.1, where unconditional risk and returns characteristics of diversified business groups around the world are displayed, suggests a more nuanced picture, which casts some doubt on the view that the benefits of diversification are higher in institutionally underdeveloped emerging markets. Although firms within certain diversified groups—for example, in Brazil and the Philippines—outperform their non-group-affiliated peers, the relative performance of firms affiliated with diversified groups cannot be easily related to economic development, to the often cited differences in legal origins across countries (La Porta et al. 1997, 1998), or to measures of financial development. Indeed, country-specific institutional characteristics, especially those associated with financial markets, suggest that it is hard to find common institutional features among the countries where group firms seem to do relatively well: for example, among the countries where group firms are characterized by low risk and low return, South Korea ranks relatively high in contract enforcement and Argentina relatively low. We conclude that diversified business groups are sometimes associated with good performance of affiliated firms, but the relation between the costs and benefits of diversification, on the one hand, and economic and institutional development, on the other, is probably more complex than what Hypothesis 1 suggests. The ambiguity of the results implies that, in emerging markets too, there are certainly cases of diversified groups that destroy shareholder value in line with the evidence on the United States.

Ignoring the ambiguity of the evidence in Table 20.1, leaving aside sample selection issues, and assuming that a causal interpretation can be assigned to the correlation between diversification and performance, the particular reason(s) why diversification may be optimal in (at least some) environments with relatively underdeveloped institutions is not clear. We examine several possible explanations.

20.2.1.2 *Evidence on groups, diversification, and internal capital markets*

Historical observations on the US economy suggest that capital markets may be the underdeveloped institution driving the empirical correlation between diversification and shareholder value in different environments. There is evidence suggesting that the "diversification discount" may have been smaller in the United States in earlier periods when financial markets (more than other institutions?) were less developed. This might suggest that, in such an environment, raising capital in an internal capital market of a diversified entity might have been more efficient than communicating with external potential providers of capital, primarily because of information problems.

But are internal capital markets the main reason why diversified business groups are formed in underdeveloped countries? And, if so, are information problems in financial markets the crucial factor? Direct evidence on these questions is scarce. A series of studies on business groups in South Korea is indirectly supportive of the underdeveloped financial markets version of Hypothesis 1: Chang and Choi (1988), one of the earliest studies of diversified groups in South Korea, find that group-affiliated firms were more profitable than other South Korean companies in the 1980s, but several more recent studies on the South Korean *chaebol* report relatively poor performance of group-affiliated companies in the 1990s (although some groups have continued to do very well). One interpretation of this pattern is that, as the South Korean economy became more mature and financial markets more liberalized in the 1990s, the advantage of business groups in accessing capital was gradually eroded. Nevertheless, other explanations for this pattern, not related to underdeveloped institutions (capital or other), are certainly possible: For example, South Korea faced a severe crisis in 1997–8, for which some observers blamed business groups. In the aftermath of the crisis, the government's approach toward the big business groups underwent deep changes, and this may have affected the ability of group-affiliated firms to generate profits. In addition, the fact that the founding generation of owners-managers had to turn over the keys to the second generation, typically within the family, may also have had adverse effects. It is very difficult to disentangle the impact of these different forces; the focus on one economic force or another in the existing literature seems to be somewhat arbitrary.

More evidence on the conjecture that the performance of diversified business groups is related to internal capital markets (and imperfections in external capital markets) can be found in studies estimating investment–cash-flow sensitivities for group and non-group firms (in the spirit of Fazzari et al. 1988; Hoshi et al. 1991; and Shin and Stulz 1998). Shin and Park (1999) apply this methodology to South Korean business groups, and Perotti and Gelfer (2001) to Russian financial–industrial groups (FIG), and find that individual group firms are not very sensitive to their own cash flows when making investment decisions; they are, however, sensitive to the cash flows of the rest of the group, suggesting the existence of an internal capital market that transfers resources across firms. The welfare implications of this internal capital market are, however, ambiguous: on the positive side, a group can include a main bank (or a cash cow) and provide funding to affiliated firms too small or opaque to have easy access to outside financial markets. This should be particularly valuable when the protection of creditors and accounting standards are weak, so that arm's-length lending will be limited. The very limited evidence in the literature is insufficient to evaluate this conjecture: Shin and Park (1999) argue that internal capital markets within the South Korean *chaebol* are actually inefficient (supporting too much investment by group firms with weak investment opportunities), whereas Perotti and Gelfer (2001) do not take a stand on the efficiency of such transfers in Russia. Overall, these studies provide mixed evidence on the validity of Hypothesis 1.

Another approach to evaluate whether diversified groups emerge in response to capital market imperfections is that of Khanna and Yafeh (2005), who test the extent to which diversified groups make up for underdeveloped financial markets by providing mutual insurance or risk-sharing among group firms. They find that risk-sharing is a characteristic of business groups only in a small number of emerging markets, most notably South Korea, and to a lesser extent Thailand and Taiwan. They do not find a clear relation between the extent of group diversification and the prevalence of within-group risk-sharing, and neither do they find any evidence that risk-sharing is more common where external financial markets are less developed. This study is therefore inconsistent with Hypothesis 1 with respect to the provision of insurance in environments where the availability of state-contingent claims is very limited.

20.2.1.3 *Evidence on group diversification for reasons unrelated to capital markets*

There is some evidence supporting a version of Hypothesis 1 in which diversification is beneficial in emerging markets for reasons unrelated to financial markets. Imperfections in labor markets (both for skilled employees and for executives), limited enforcement of contracts, inadequate rule of law, and other institutional deficiencies may give rise to business groups that generate these public goods for the benefit of group members. In line with this argument, Hyundai, for example, established a training center for technical personnel to be used by the entire group, as well as an applied research institute.

Diversified groups may be efficient if they make up for missing institutions related to the process of entrepreneurship: new ventures initiated by business groups rely not only on capital infusion from the group, but often also on the group brand name and implicitly on its reputation, providing a guarantee that is scarce in emerging markets (Maurer and Sharma 2001). There is also an internal (within-group) market for talent. In this sense, some business groups are perhaps closer to private equity firms than to conglomerates. Jones (2000: 50–1) makes this point in relation to British trading houses in the early twentieth century: one of the primary functions of these early groups (which, like many modern venture capital funds, were often organized as partnerships) was "identifying opportunities and placing potential British investors in touch with them." It may be possible to argue that, in present-day India, Tata Industries comes close to this view of a business group as a quasi-venture capitalist, albeit with longer investment horizons than typical American private equity funds (Khanna and Palepu 2005). Another Indian group, Birla, helped found and finance new firms, which were later spun off using the entrepreneurial talent of its employees. The process of "spawning" new companies by established business groups may potentially be important in emerging markets, where it is probably difficult to start *de novo*.

Khanna and Palepu (1999a) use survey data in order to try and identify sources of benefits from affiliation with a diversified group. Their analysis, which is based on intra-group confidential information, indicates that in both Chile and India group activity increased during periods following extensive liberalization and pro-market reforms, and in a way that apparently enhanced profitability. Their survey evidence suggests that this was primarily due to group advantages in product and labor (rather than capital) markets.

At present, the precise identification of the sources of group advantage remains an empirical challenge. Studies such as Khanna and Palepu (2000a, b), who find that in India and in Chile the relation between diversification and profitability among business groups is non-linear (beyond a certain level diversification is associated with higher profits), can be interpreted in many ways. One way forward is perhaps to exploit variations in the nature of market imperfections across different countries. This is difficult if types of market imperfections are positively correlated (for example, where capital markets are underdeveloped, labor markets may also be so), but some interesting examples can nevertheless be found. For example, diversification in Chile, where financial markets are fairly developed and the rule of law is relatively good, is unlikely to be due to the same mix of reasons that led to the emergence of diversified groups in Suharto's Indonesia. Another related possibility is to try and disentangle various reasons for the existence of diversified groups by looking at changes in their activities and scope in response to shocks (Ghemawat and Khanna 1998). For example, a business group whose primary function is to form an internal capital market is likely to shrink or disappear in response to financial market development, whereas other groups would not. Not much research has been carried out along these lines.

Despite the ambiguity of the results in this section, our impression is that there is some tentative evidence suggesting that, at least under some circumstances, groups can make up for underdeveloped institutions in both capital and labor markets (Khanna and Palepu 1997; Khanna 2000). Although it is difficult to draw firm conclusions from this, one possible implication might be that the profit-maximizing level of diversification (and perhaps also the level of diversification that maximizes social welfare) may be higher for companies (or groups) operating in emerging markets than it is for American firms. It is not clear, however, why the business group form (rather than a fully owned conglomerate) is the most popular way to attain this level of diversification in many less-developed economies. One possibility is that, from the point of view of controlling shareholders, the group structure is preferable, and only a unique historical event prevents the existence of business groups in the United States as well—diversified American groups were common through the mid-1930s until tax policies introduced by President Roosevelt induced either the integration of groups into conglomerates or the spin-off of controlled subsidiaries (Morck 2005). A possible rationale for the superiority and predominance of the group form in emerging markets is that the group structure insulates the controlling shareholder from institutional investor pressure and takeovers, and bestows undisputed control and economic influence with limited capital investment. The group form may be preferred also because of legal considerations, especially in relation to corporate liability and the ability of the controlling shareholder to choose not to bail out ailing group firms (Nicodano 2003). By contrast, the conglomerate form may be more appropriate than a business group for the purpose of tax-reducing income-smoothing across divisions.

20.2.2 Structure of business groups: The extent of vertical integration

Limited contract enforcement, weak rule of law, corruption, and an inefficient judicial system should all lead to high transaction costs between unrelated parties. Under such circumstances, intra-group trade, within the context of long-run relationships supported by family and other social ties, may be relatively cheap and efficient. This argument is summarized in the following hypothesis:

> *Hypothesis 2.* The presence of business groups, the extent of their vertical integration, and the volume of intra-group trade should all be higher in environments with underdeveloped legal and judicial institutions, where contracting is costly.

20.2.2.1 *Evidence on groups, vertical integration, and contracting costs*

Surprisingly, we are not aware of any direct evidence testing this prediction—which is similar to the Coase–Williamson arguments on the boundaries of the firm—in the context of business group structure. Data on the volume of intra-group trade are not readily available, and the rudimentary data on vertical integration in Table 20.2 are ambiguous (probably in part because of the dubious quality of the available data). On the one hand, vertical integration among groups in the Philippines is high, in line with the poor institutional infrastructure in that country. But the extent of vertical integration in relatively uncorrupt Chile is higher than in Indonesia, suggesting that there may be other explanations besides contracting costs that may account for this variation. One possibility is that vertical integration serves primarily as a means to obtain monopoly power or alleviate the double monopoly problem, rather than as a tool to overcome contracting difficulties (although the existence of contracting difficulties and opportunities to exercise monopoly power may be correlated). This view is corroborated by the CEO of the Indonesian group Astra International, who described in a private interview the motivation for the vertical-integration strategy of his group as driven by the pursuit of monopoly power rather than by the inadequacy of contracting institutions. The food production within the Thai CP Group has been considerably vertically integrated, but, again, the stated purpose was not contracting difficulties. In addition, there seems to be considerable variation in the extent of vertical integration across groups within the same country, suggesting that group and industry-specific factors play a role that is sometimes more important than country-specific institutional factors. The more systematic evidence on vertical integration provided by Chang (2003) is consistent with this view: he constructs group and industry-specific measures of vertical integration for South Korea and finds it to be considerable in the largest groups and in certain industries (for example, automobiles). He argues that vertical integration may have been an efficient strategy in the past (in line with Hypothesis 2), but it involves considerable difficulties in the twenty-first century.

20.2.3 Structure of business groups: Involvement in the financial sector

Group involvement in banking, insurance and other aspects of the financial system may be related to transaction-costs considerations similar to those driving vertical integration. A variation of Hypothesis 2 may apply to financial services as well: contracting costs, institutional quality, and financial development should explain business group involvement in financial services, in addition to country-specific government regulations.

20.2.3.1 *Evidence on group involvement in financial services*

Historically, British multinational business groups in the early twentieth century were heavily involved in financial services overseas, in line with Hypothesis 2 on high financial contracting costs in these environments (Jones 2000). Chilean business groups were also involved in finance prior to the liberalization and financial development of the 1980s (a number of other examples are mentioned in the unabbreviated version of this article).

The existing evidence on the performance of group-affiliated financial institutions is, to some extent, consistent with the view that group involvement in this sector makes up for its underdevelopment. Maurer (1999) and Maurer and Haber (2007) emphasize the positive roles of related lending within Mexican business groups in the period 1888–1913, when contracting institutions were in their infancy. By contrast, La Porta, Lopez-de-Silanes, and Zamarripa (2003) document the negative sides of "related lending" in contemporary Mexican groups. A conceptual difficulty in the discussion of this issue is the endogeneity of financial underdevelopment, which may actually be due to group influence; this makes the relation between business group involvement in financial services and the development of these services complex.

20.3 OWNERSHIP AND CONTROL
OF BUSINESS GROUPS

20.3.1 Pyramidal versus other groups

We now turn to variation in ownership and control characteristics in business groups around the world. Perhaps the most important distinction in this category is between pyramidal and other organizational structures. This is because of the strong link in the literature, dating back to Berle and Means (1932: bk. 1, ch. 5), between pyramids and the expropriation of minority shareholders: in pyramidal groups there is typically a large divergence between the large shareholder's "control rights," which are often very high, and "cash-flow rights," which are typically much smaller (see, e.g., Bebchuk et al. 2000; Bianchi et al. 2001). This, in combination with the inadequacy of some of the regulatory institutions in many emerging markets, generates an environment in which "tunneling" (the expropriation of minority shareholders) can become a common feature of the economy:

> *Hypothesis 3.* (*a*) Pyramidal groups should be particularly common in countries with poor investor protection and inadequate rule of law. (*b*) These countries should have under-developed equity markets because investors will demand a discount when buying shares of companies affiliated with a pyramidal group.

20.3.1.1 *Evidence on pyramids, tunneling, and financial development*

The literature on pyramidal groups and conflicts of interest between majority and minority shareholders is discussed in great detail in Morck, Wolfenzon, and Yeung (2005). Their reading of the evidence is consistent with Hypothesis 3: family-controlled pyramidal business groups in countries where minority shareholders are not well protected are associated with the expropriation of small shareholders, and this adversely affects financial development. In line with Hypothesis 3, tunneling has become the main focus of much of the recent literature on business groups. In what follows we raise a number of conceptual issues related to the literature on pyramidal groups and tunneling.

First, how many of the business groups around the world are actually vertically controlled pyramids and where are they located? Despite the centrality of this question, the answer is less clear cut than it should be. La Porta, Lopez-de-Silanes, and Shleifer (1999), who do not focus specifically on business groups, find that widely held firms are rare outside the United States and the United Kingdom. By contrast, concentrated family ownership, often exercised through pyramids and other mechanisms that enable control in excess of cash-flow rights, are quite common around the world. This view is supported by Barca and Becht's description (2001) of ownership and control of European firms (see also Faccio and Lang 2002), and by the evidence in Claessens, Djankov, and Lang (2000) and Claessens, Djankov, Fan, and Lang (2002) on the ownership and control of Asian firms. But, even within this general framework, there seems to be considerable cross-sectional variation. Khanna and Thomas (2009) study business groups in Chile, where, they argue, pyramidal equity ties characterize less than half of all group firms. According to Barontini and Caprio (2005), unlike Claessens et al.'s description (2002) of Asian firms, a wedge between cash flow and control rights in family-dominated firms in continental Europe is far more commonly associated with dual shares than with pyramidal structures. By contrast, Chang (2003a) argues that in South Korea pyramidal structures are common, Polsiri and Wiwattanakantang (2006) estimate (without providing precise data) that about half of the business groups in Thailand are pyramidal, and Yurtoglu (2000) discusses the prevalence of pyramids in Turkey. Some pyramidal groups can also be found in other countries such as Indonesia, Malaysia, and Mexico. Part of the difficulty in mapping pyramidal groups stems from the fact that business group structures are often more complex than textbook pyramids, making a dichotomous classification of groups into pyramids and non-pyramids difficult. The Samsung group, for example, involves both vertical pyramidal control and horizontal cross-shareholding, making the decision whether or not it should be considered a pyramid difficult (Kang 1997).

Secondly, in much of the literature, the link between pyramidal groups and the expropriation of minority shareholders is an unquestioned axiom. This is unwarranted: the empirical evidence on the prevalence and severity of profit tunneling from minority shareholders within pyramidal groups is far from clear cut, although there is certainly anecdotal evidence on incidents of tunneling in Europe (Johnson et al. 2000), and more systematic evidence from pyramidal Indian business groups (Bertrand et al. 2002) and South Korean business groups (Bae et al. 2002; Joh 2003; Baek et al. 2006). But even these convincing studies of tunneling raise a number of unanswered questions. For example, Bertrand, Mehta, and Mullainathan (2002) find that Indian firms located lower within pyramidal groups are less sensitive to industry-specific shocks to their profitability than are firms located in upper levels. They interpret this result as evidence that positive shocks to firms in lower levels of the pyramid are siphoned off to firms in upper levels of the group pyramid, an activity that serves the interests of controlling shareholders, but not of minority shareholders holding an equity stake in the tunneled firms only. This interpretation is plausible for positive shocks (additional profits are taken away by the controlling shareholders), but it is less self-evident why tunneling would make firms located in low levels of the group pyramid less sensitive to negative shocks. Bae, Kang, and Kim (2002) examine acquisitions of often ailing companies by other group firms within the South Korean *chaebol* groups and find that within-group takeovers rarely raise the value of the bidder, but do raise the value of other group members. They also provide some examples (from the Lucky-Goldstar (LG) group, for instance) showing how such takeovers benefited controlling shareholders at the expense of minority shareholders. Very closely related methodologically is a study by Baek, Kang, and Lee (2006), whose focus is on private securities offerings within South Korean groups, rather than on takeovers. They find that some of these securities are offered to other group members at prices that are very far off from their true values, and document negative stock-price responses to such deals. But the tunneling interpretation favored in these studies is not the only one possible; some intra-group takeovers and securities placements may also constitute efficient mutual insurance or risk-sharing, as Khanna and Yafeh (2005) document for South Korea. Furthermore, Buysschaert, Deloof, and Jegers (2004) report a positive price response to within-group equity sales in a small sample of pyramidal Belgian groups, suggesting that these transactions are not always interpreted as harmful to minority shareholders.

Beside the caveat that not all groups are pyramids and the fact that some of the empirical results on tunneling are open to more than one interpretation, even where groups are pyramidal in structure, reputation and other safeguards might preclude minority shareholder exploitation. Holmen and Högfeldt (2005), for example, dispute the equation of pyramids and tunneling in present-day Sweden, where there is adequate investor protection. Historically, in the early twentieth century tunneling did not seem to be a major concern for British investors, who were eager to invest money in multinational trading groups with certain pyramidal characteristics; affiliation with one of the family-controlled British merchant houses was apparently viewed as a stamp of certification, rather than as a reason for fear of expropriation (Jones 2000: ch. 6).

Finally, much of the literature pays only scant attention to the participation constraints of investors in these pyramidal schemes. Why, on a routine basis, do investors continue to invest in situations where their investment is likely to be expropriated? It is, perhaps, possible to argue that naive investors in emerging markets invest in business groups prone to tunneling because of inexperience or inadequate human capital; we find this implausible. Another possibility is that the feasible alternatives available to investors are extremely limited, although this claim probably did not apply historically to British investors in merchant houses. An explanation that we find more plausible is that group reputation for fair treatment of minority shareholders is an important consideration (see Gomes 2000 for a related theoretical model). This could be group reputation for risk-sharing (or assistance to poorly performing companies), which reduces the default risk of group-affiliated companies, a feature that investors may find attractive even if they know that they are exposed to a certain risk of expropriation by controlling shareholders. A more formal mechanism is proposed by Faccio, Lang, and Young (2001), who find that some groups, especially in Europe, are known to pay higher dividends and thus compensate investors for the risk of expropriation. Finally, it is possible that at least some part of the alleged tunneling may in fact represent returns to some core asset, with the investing public's participation constraints being satisfied. This asset can be a socially productive one, such as some core entrepreneurial ability, or a socially detrimental lobbying capability (see, e.g., Faccio 2006). The literature provides very few answers to these questions.

20.3.2 Family versus non-family groups

Another dimension related to ownership and control in the taxonomy of business groups around the world has to do with the role of family considerations in the presence, evolution, and performance of groups:

> *Hypothesis 4.* (*a*) Family-controlled groups are likely to be more common in countries with inadequate rule of law, where transactions with outsiders are costly. (*b*) Family considerations influence the formation, structure, and performance of family-controlled groups; in some cases, groups may continue to exist for family-related societal reasons, even when they no longer enhance economic efficiency.

20.3.2.1 *Evidence on groups and families*

Evidence on the relation between families and the prevalence of business groups and economic institutions is provided by La Porta, Lopez-de-Silanes, and Shleifer (1999), who document higher presence of family firms (not necessarily groups) in environments where contracting is difficult. Fogel (2006), using data on the largest business groups and individual companies in over forty countries, also suggests that family ownership is more common in economies with poor institutions. One reading of these findings is that kinship and other social ties facilitate economic transactions (Granovetter 2005) and, more generally, that business groups are networks whose prevalence facilitate the creation of "trust," which makes up for incomplete contracts and imperfect rule of law. Fogel (2006), by contrast, claims that family ownership and control are the cause of economic and institutional underdevelopment. In addition to these two international comparisons, the present volume includes evidence of the prevalence of family-controlled business groups in a number of countries.

We regard the family-firms line of research on groups as highly promising, both with respect to the prevalence of family-controlled groups in different environments, and with respect to the interaction between family considerations and group performance and efficiency. Contrasts between business groups that are single-family controlled and those that are either government controlled (in Singapore or in China) or controlled by multiple families (for example, LG in South Korea for at least part of its history or some joint ventures between the Koc and Sabanci groups in Turkey) would be particularly interesting.

Analyzing groups from this perspective is, however, difficult for two main reasons. First, while most prior studies have focused on the link between families and firm performance, performance might also affect the stability of the familial contract and thereby the structure of families. Bertrand et al. (2008) take a first step in addressing this issue when they treat the number of male offsprings as an endogenous outcome. Secondly, in many cultures it is not at all clear that "what one sees is what one gets" with regard to the family assets. In other words, the best assets of the family might not be the publicly listed parts (Bertrand et al. 2008 and Khanna and Palepu 1999a attempt to address this issue). Furthermore, the equity contracts that are visible to the public observer and the social scientist might not be the most meaningful contracts in systems where relationship contracting predominates (Khanna and Thomas 2009).

20.4 INTERACTIONS BETWEEN BUSINESS GROUPS AND SOCIETY

20.4.1 Business groups, politics, and governments

This part of the taxonomy focuses on the nature of the interaction between business groups, governments, and politics. Because business groups have enjoyed close ties to their governments in many countries, it is not surprising that the political economy literature on groups has often viewed government-supported business groups as rent-seeking "parasites." Influential papers such as Krueger (1974) or Bhagwati (1982) while not directly studying groups, have been used in support of arguments on rent-seeking through the power exercised by incumbent businesses, typically family-based business groups. Indeed, the interaction between groups and the state has received much attention since the 1970s, to the extent that an impression that all groups are deeply politically involved has been generated:

> *Hypothesis 5.* Business groups are formed with government support, expand and diversify with government nurturing, and their performance is a function of their rent-seeking ability and opportunities.

In general, there is substantial evidence supporting the first part of the hypothesis—business groups in emerging markets are very often, though not always, formed with government support. But, as the groups evolve and (some of) the countries develop, the relations between groups and governments become far more complex, so that there is considerable variation in this dimension across groups and countries.

20.4.1.1 *Evidence on the origins of groups: The role of governments*

In many countries, the very appearance of the business group phenomenon was strongly influenced by government policies. The Japanese prewar *zaibatsu* groups emerged as a result of a government privatization program in the early 1880s, and expanded and diversified their activities in response to government contracts awarded under preferential terms (Hadley 1970). The South Korean business groups, the *chaebol*, enjoyed close ties to the government of General Park; the government controlled the allocation of credit and foreign currency, and the *chaebol* enjoyed preferential access to these and other resources (see, e.g., Clifford 1994; Kim 1997; Chang 2003). The privatization policies of Prime Minister Mahathir's government in Malaysia enriched certain ethnic Malay-owned business groups dramatically (Gomez and Jomo 1999). The Salim group in Indonesia had family ties with President Suharto and expanded, as did other Indonesian groups, with the assistance of government-granted monopolies and licenses. Keister (1998, 2004) describes how the government actively encouraged the formation of business groups in China and protected them from foreign competition. In Israel, family-owned groups emerged as an outcome of certain government economic policies (Maman 2002), and the rise of the "oligarchs" in Russia is yet another recent (and very extreme) example of the emergence of groups under the auspices of the government (Guriev and Rachinsky 2005).

20.4.1.2 *Evidence on the relations between mature groups and governments*

While in most countries groups emerged with at least some degree of government support, often in the context of development-oriented mercantilist policies, the relations between mature groups and the state can vary considerably. In some circumstances, groups continue to enjoy close ties with the authorities. Fisman (2001) provides convincing econometric estimates of the value of political connections enjoyed by business groups in Indonesia during the Suharto regime (see also Leuz and Oberholzer-Gee 2006).

But governments and business groups do not always operate symbiotically. First, there are a number of historical examples when governments harmed, rather than assisted, business groups. This has happened both in times of wrenching societal transformation—for example, when the Chinese Communist Party took power in 1949—and in an ongoing sense when groups struggled in the face of an inimical state—for example, India's socialist government in the few decades following Indian independence; indeed, Khanna and Palepu (2005) point out that the turnover in leading Indian groups since independence is far too high to be consistent with entrenchment and close group–government ties.

Even where governments were not hostile toward business groups, the relationship between them often changed over time, as groups became stronger and more independent. This seems to have been the case in Japan in the 1930s (Franks et al. 2006) and in South Korea starting in the 1980s (Amsden 1989; Clifford 1994; Kim 1997; Lee et al. 2002; Chang 2003), where the expression the "Republic of Samsung" is sometimes used.

20.4.1.3 *The welfare implications of close ties between groups and governments*

The prevailing assumption in much of the literature is that government support of groups is socially harmful. Despite the negative implications of government favors of the type described above, there may also be a bright side: business groups may have helped governments orchestrate a "Big Push" in several sectors simultaneously—arguably in prewar Japan (see, e.g., Ohkawa and Rosovsky 1973). In other cases, governmental favoritism towards business groups controlled by an ethnic minority may have helped preserve social equilibrium, as in Malaysia. The appropriate counterfactual against which this government policy should be judged may well be race riots and chaos.

Social welfare might be enhanced by group–government liaisons if, for instance, the relation between groups and governments supports tax collection and fiscal policy. Do governments favor groups because it is easy to collect taxes from them? If so, this would be reminiscent of medieval rulers who partitioned their territories into fiefdoms controlled by quasi-independent lords who could rule them as they saw fit as long as they paid their taxes to the government. This issue has rarely been addressed in the literature.

Analytically, it might not always be sensible to study just the interaction between the private sector and the government, without considering additional constituencies. For example, Musacchio (2004) argues that the rise of business groups (and concentrated ownership) in Brazil coincided with the rising power of organized labor, with the government playing only a background role.

20.4.1.4 *Evidence on the political ability of groups to shape their environment*

Can business groups use their political clout to shape their business environment? This central question has no systematic answer in the existing literature. Historically, groups have often invested in market-supporting infrastructure and launched new industries—the Japanese *zaibatsu* are a good example. There are also claims that business groups in Mexico exerted influence in favor of free trade with the United States, from which the groups were hoping to benefit. Kim (1997) argues that the South Korean groups lobbied for liberalization in the 1980s, and Chari and Gupta (2008) show that in India industries with a high presence of group-affiliated firms were more likely to be associated with liberalization of foreign entry in the early 1990s than industries dominated by state-owned firms. By contrast, groups may resist certain political reforms, improvements in minority shareholder protection, or antitrust legislation—this seems to have been the case in South Korea since the Asian financial crisis (Chang 2003).

Two conclusions emerge from this discussion. First, political economy explanations for the formation and effectiveness of groups, beyond the traditional focus on government favors, should receive more attention. Secondly, it might be fruitful to view the relations between groups and the state as the equilibrium outcome of a game, in the spirit of work by Aoki (2001) and Greif (2006). These games are typically complex, and their application to a particular context is not always straightforward. Nevertheless, conceptually, the result of such a government–business group game might well be rent-seeking and cohabitation, but it might also be an uneasy coexistence, quite distinct from the outcome of groups currying favor with the state.

20.4.2 Business groups and monopoly power

There are good theoretical reasons to suspect that business groups may wield considerable market power. They may, under some circumstances, drive their rivals out of markets, or prevent entry, because of their "deep pockets," "first mover advantage," and ties to the government. "Multimarket contact" (Bernheim and Whinston 1990) between diversified business groups competing with each other repeatedly in many sectors may facilitate collusion. And business groups may bundle together different group products in order to extract more rents from distributors and ultimate buyers. It is not clear, however, if these considerations are the rationale behind the formation of business groups.

> *Hypothesis 6.* (*a*) Business group formation should involve horizontal mergers, vertical foreclosure, entry deterrence, and other mechanisms designed to increase market power. (*b*) Monopoly power should be reflected in high profit rates. (c) Group presence should be especially pronounced in environments where monopoly rents can be extracted such as industries and countries with trade barriers and weak antitrust enforcement.

20.4.2.1 *Evidence on business groups and monopoly power*

The theoretical conjectures associating business groups with monopoly power enjoyed popular support in the past, albeit without rigorous empirical tests. The view that business groups harm competition dates back to the Great Depression in the United States. Morck (2005) argues that President Roosevelt sought to dissolve America's groups (by taxing intercorporate dividends) partly on these grounds. One of the primary objectives of the postwar American occupation reforms in Japan was the dissolution of the prewar *zaibatsu*, which was driven by strong views on their anticompetitive effects and the resulting social tension that may have contributed to the rise of militarism in Japan (Hadley 1970; Yafeh 1995).

Nevertheless, despite the plausibility of arguments on groups and monopoly power, the literature on the industrial organization effects of business groups has not developed much. Empirical evidence on the hypothesis that business groups restrict competition is also surprisingly scarce. Casual observation suggests that not all groups enjoy high profit rates and monopoly rents (Table 20.1). Weinstein and Yafeh (1995) argue that (in the 1980s) Japan's bank-centered groups competed aggressively against each other rather than colluded. Although there are no similar studies for emerging markets, there are occasional descriptions of the intense rivalry between the South Korean *chaebol*. These are not formally substantiated, and, even if true, do not necessarily preclude anticompetitive entry deterrence. There is also fairly systematic evidence on changes in the relative size and rankings of business groups over time, which could be interpreted as evidence of competition or erosion of monopoly power—the list of top ten business groups has changed dramatically since the 1970s in India and Taiwan, but has remained very stable in South Korea and Thailand. It is not clear, however, why groups in some countries wield less power to restrict entry than groups in other countries. Overall it is surprising that no attempts have been made to use modern New Empirical Industrial Organization (NEIO) techniques to assess the market power of business groups in emerging markets.

20.5 DIRECTIONS FOR FUTURE RESEARCH

The country-specific chapters in this *Handbook* provide an insightful cross-country comparison of the formation and developments of business groups. Yet they still leave questions in our proposed research agenda to be explored. Future projects could include a more thorough investigation of business groups' decisions to integrate vertically, or an enquiry into whether countries with more business groups are more prone to macroeconomic crises than those with more stand-alone firms. These should be important directions for both empirical as well as theoretical future research. In addition to these questions, this final section outlines a few general directions for future research about business groups in emerging markets.

20.5.1 Origin and formation of business groups

The general assumption of group membership exogeneity is a limitation that scholars should endeavor to get around. We view this as an important direction for both theoretical and empirical future research. The existing theoretical literature on the formation of business groups remains no more than a handful of models. Kali (1999) studies the endogenous formation of business networks in response to limited contract enforcement by the legal system; Maurer and Sharma (2001) also focus on imperfect property rights. Ghatak and Kali (2001) and Kali (2003) emphasize imperfect information in capital markets as another possible motive. Almeida and Wolfenzon (2006b) offer a theoretical explanation for the formation of pyramidal groups that is based on the ability of controlling shareholders to access the cash flows of all group firms so as not to rely on underdeveloped external financial markets. A particularly intriguing theoretical direction (also related to underdeveloped financial markets) would relate the formation of groups to risk attitudes: are groups a mutual insurance arrangement attracting risk-averse economic agents? Kim (2004) is the only existing model along these lines.

Existing empirical studies of the formation of groups often employ empirical techniques that are not fully convincing. For example, Chung (2001, 2006) examines the origin and evolution of groups in Taiwan, distinguishing between reasons related to market forces, culture, and societal institutions, but the relative empirical importance of these factors is hard to disentangle. Tsui-Auch (2005) documents a tendency among ethnic Chinese entrepreneurs in Singapore to form diversified business organizations (in comparison with ethnic Indian entrepreneurs), and attributes this interesting observation to the cultural heterogeneity of the Chinese community. The empirical support for this claim, however, is suspect, because of other systematic differences in the background of Chinese and Indian entrepreneurs in Singapore. More sophisticated empirical analyses of the differential origins of business groups are likely to be valuable.

20.5.2 Evolution and dynamics of business groups

Historical and dynamic (over a long period of time) perspectives of business groups can enrich our understanding of this institution in several ways. It would be interesting to compare the validity of cross-sectional explanations for the ubiquity and performance of business groups with time-series-based perspectives (Jones and Khanna 2006): do groups evolve in a fashion that is consistent with missing institutions, risk-sharing, tunneling, use of a scarce resource, and so on? Many more historical studies with explicit hypotheses in mind, especially with competing hypotheses whose testable implications can be contrasted in time-series data, could shed further light on the evolution of groups, on path dependence (ways in which "history matters"), and on the *raison d'être* of group formation and development.

20.5.3 Longevity of business groups

Although there is no systematic evidence on the question whether or not the longevity of group affiliates exceeds that of otherwise comparable, unaffiliated firms, in many countries very long-lived groups can be found. In some cases, groups have survived, without a substantial change in structure, over a long period, starting in an era when the country was poor, all the way to prosperity (as, for example, in Sweden). This is related to the impression that, if groups ever dissolve, this tends to conincide with dramatic changes in government policy. Can groups ever die peacefully? We are not sure. One of the few examples of such a process is provided by Jones (2000), who describes the demise (or refocus) of British trading houses starting in the 1970s in response to a changing environment (the rise of diversified institutional investors in London, decolonization abroad, a decline in trade in raw materials, and so on).

Are there cultural or societal reasons that would prevent corporate structure in emerging markets from self-evolving into a more focused structure as the country develops? What is the role of government in this process? Is it advisable, or even possible, for the state to forcibly dismantle groups, as has been attempted in South Korea? Even if groups have run their course, is it clear that the desired policy is to try and dissolve them (Khanna and Palepu 1999b)? Is a policy of benign neglect more desirable (as in India)? Is it clear that, when the social costs of corporate groups exceed their social benefits, private costs to group owners will also exceed private benefits? Can groups involving substantial inefficiencies persist for a long time? If so, is it because of a weak corporate control environment? Or is it because of social reasons (for example, families who diversify to accommodate disparate interests of the next generation)?

20.5.4 Counterfactuals to business groups

When considering the welfare consequences of groups, it is unclear what the appropriate counterfactual should be: against what alternative should groups be evaluated? The ideal is a well-functioning market economy, but in reality the world consists of distant second bests. In the absence of groups, would there be other forms of networks? Would market-supporting institutions emerge spontaneously? Is there a way to infer the appropriate counterfactual from policy interventions in the 1990s and the early twenty-first century (for example, in South Korea or China)? Almeida and Wolfenzon (2006a), who evaluate the welfare implications of business groups as a function of measures of efficiency of external financial markets, provide an interesting starting point for addressing this issue. Also relevant is the model of Maksimovic and Phillips (2002), who suggest that conglomerates are an efficient equilibrium outcome to certain business opportunities, whereas for others stand-alone firms are better suited. The equivalent for business groups would be that groups are an efficient outcome for certain situations in which the appropriate counterfactual is not necessarily stand-alone firms but some other, not well-specified, outcome. Also related is the observation in Maurer and Haber (2007) that, when restrictions were imposed on related lending within Mexican business groups in 1997, the result was a large decline in the size of the credit market, not the emergence of a competitive equilibrium in which all firms could access loans on equal footing.

Conceivably, the relevant counterfactual to business groups may change with economic development—in early stages, in the absence of groups, the plausible feasible alternative may well be underdevelopment and limited market institutions. In more advanced economies, in the absence of business groups, perhaps superior capital, labor, and other market institutions would develop; this conjecture has never been tested.

To conclude, we believe that any blanket characterization of business groups as either paragons or parasites would be unwarranted, both because of the nature of the existing evidence and because of the continued existence of unanswered puzzles. Part of the difficulty stems from the vast differences across countries, groups, and time periods, and part from the multiple effects that groups tend to have. Progress is likely to result from casting a broader net for relevant data; this includes paying attention to historical data and evidence, using group origin as a relevant variable, and exploiting time-series variation. To us, business groups continue to be a fascinating topic for research, still posing many interesting questions with implications for a variety of important issues in economics and finance.

References

ALMEIDA, H., and WOLFENZON, D. (2006a). "Should Business Groups Be Dismantled? The Equilibrium Costs of Efficient Internal Capital Markets," *Journal of Financial Economics*, 79/1: 99–144.

ALMEIDA, H., and WOLFENZON, D. (2006b). "A Theory of Pyramidal Ownership and Family Business Groups," *Journal of Finance*, 61/6: 2637–80.

AMSDEN, A. H. (1989). *Asia's Next Giant: South Korea and Late Industrialization*. New York and Oxford: Oxford University Press.

AOKI, M. (2001). *Toward a Comparative Institutional Analysis*. Comparative Institutional Analysis Series. Cambridge and London: MIT Press.

BAE, K. H., KANG, J. K., and KIM, J. M. (2002). "Tunneling or Value Added? Evidence from Mergers by Korean Business Groups," *Journal of Finance*, 57/6: 2695–740.

BAEK, J. S., KANG, J. K., and LEE, I. (2006). "Business Groups and Tunneling: Evidence from Private Securities Offerings by Korean Chaebols," *Journal of Finance*, 61/5: 2415–49.

BARCA, F., and BECHT, M. (eds.) (2001). *The Control of Corporate Europe*. Oxford: Oxford University Press.

BARONTINI, R., and CAPRIO, L. (2005). "The Effect of Family Control on Firm Value and Performance: Evidence from Continental Europe." ECGI Finance Working Paper, no. 88/2005.

BEBCHUK, L. A., KRAAKMAN, R., and TRIANTIS, G. G. (2000). "Stock Pyramids, Cross-Ownership, and Dual Class Equity: The Mechanisms and Agency Costs of Separating Control from Cash-Flow Rights," in R. K. Morck (ed.), *Concentrated Corporate Ownership*. NBER Conference Report series. Chicago and London: University of Chicago Press, 295–315.

BERLE, A., and MEANS, G. (1932). *The Modern Corporation and Private Property.* New York: MacMillan.

BERNHEIM, B. D., and WHINSTON, M. D. (1990). "Multimarket Contact and Collusive Behavior," *RAND Journal of Economics*, 21/1: 1–26.

BERTRAND, M., MEHTA, P., and MULLAINATHAN, S. (2002). "Ferreting out Tunneling: An Application to Indian Business Groups," *Quarterly Journal of Economics*, 117/1: 121–48.

BERTRAND, M., JOHNSON, S., SAMPHANTHARAK, K., and SCHOAR, A. (2008). "Mixing Family with Business: A Study of Thai Business Groups and the Families behind Them," *Journal of Financial Economics*, 88/3: 466–98.

BHAGWATI, J. N. (1982). "Directly Unproductive Profit-Seeking (DUP) Activities," *Journal of Political Economy*, 90/5: 988–1002.

BIANCHI, M., BIANCO, M., and ENRIQUES, L. (2001). "Pyramidal Groups and the Separation between Ownership and Control in Italy," in F. Barca and M. Becht (eds.), *The Control of Corporate Europe.* Oxford: Oxford University Press, 154–87.

BUYSSCHAERT, A., DELOOF, M., and JEGERS, M. (2004). "Equity Sales in Belgian Corporate Groups: Expropriation of Minority Shareholders? A Clinical Study," *Journal of Corporate Finance*, 10/1: 81–103.

CHANG, S. J. (2003). *Financial Crisis and Transformation of Korean Business Groups: The Rise and Fall of Chaebols.* Cambridge, New York, and Melbourne: Cambridge University Press.

CHANG, S. J., and CHOI, U. (1988). "Strategy, Structure and Performance of Korean Business Groups: A Transactions Cost Approach," *Journal of Industrial Economics*, 37/2: 141–58.

CHARI, A., and GUPTA, N. (2008). "Incumbents and Protectionism: The Political Economy of Foreign Entry Liberalization," *Journal of Financial Economics*, 88/3: 633–56.

CHUNG, C. N. (2001). "Markets, Culture and Institutions: The Emergence of Large Business Groups in Taiwan, 1950s–1970s," *Journal of Management Studies*, 38/5: 719–45.

CHUNG, C. N. (2006). "Beyond Guanxi: Network Contingencies in Taiwanese Business Groups," *Organization Studies*, 27/4: 461–89.

CLAESSENS, S., DJANKOV, S., and LANG, L. H. P. (2000). "The Separation of Ownership and Control in East Asian Corporations," *Journal of Financial Economics*, 58/1–2: 81–112.

CLAESSENS, S., DJANKOV, S., FAN, J. P. H., and LANG, L. H. P. (2002). "Disentangling the Incentive and Entrenchment Effects of Large Shareholdings," *Journal of Finance*, 57/6: 2741–71.

CLAESSENS, S., DJANKOV, S., FAN, J. P. H., and LANG, L. H. P. (2003). "When Does Corporate Diversification Matter to Productivity and Performance? Evidence from East Asia," *Pacific-Basin Finance Journal*, 11/3: 365–92.

CLIFFORD, M. L. (1994). *Troubled Tiger: Businessmen, Bureaucrats, and Generals in South Korea.* New York: Sharpe.

FACCIO, M. (2006). "Politically Connected Firms," *American Economic Review*, 96/1: 369–86.

FACCIO, M., and LANG, L. H. P. (2002). "The Ultimate Ownership of Western European Corporations," *Journal of Financial Economics*, 65/3: 365–95.

FACCIO, M., LANG, L. H. P., and YOUNG, L. (2001). "Dividends and Expropriation," *American Economic Review*, 91/1: 54–78.

FAUVER, L., HOUSTON, J., and NARANJO, A. (2003). "Capital Market Development, International Integration, Legal Systems, and the Value of Corporate Diversification: A Cross-Country Analysis," *Journal of Financial and Quantitative Analysis*, 38/1: 135–57.

FAZZARI, S. M., HUBBARD, R. G., and PETERSEN, B. C. (1988). "Financing Constraints and Corporate Investment," *Brookings Papers on Economic Activity*, 1: 141–95.

FERRIS, S. P., KIM, K. A., and KITSABUNNARAT, P. (2003). "The Costs (and Benefits?) of Diversified Business Groups: The Case of Korean Chaebols," *Journal of Banking and Finance*, 27/2: 251–73.

FISMAN, R. (2001). "Estimating the Value of Political Connections," *American Economic Review*, 91/4: 1095–102.

FOGEL, K. (2006). "Oligarchic Family Control, Social Economic Outcomes, and the Quality of Government," *Journal of International Business Studies*, 37/5: 603–22.

FRANKS, J., MAYER, C., and MIYAJIMA, H. (2006). "Evolution of Ownership: The Curious Case of Japan." Unpublished.

GHATAK, M., and KALI, R. (2001). "Financially Interlinked Business Groups," *Journal of Economics and Management Strategy*, 10/4: 591–619.

GHEMAWAT, P., and KHANNA, T. (1998). "The Nature of Diversified Business Groups: A Research Design and Two Case Studies," *Journal of Industrial Economics*, 46/1: 35–61.

GOMES, A. (2000). "Going Public without Governance: Managerial Reputation Effects," *Journal of Finance*, 55/2: 615–46.

GOMEZ, E. T., and JOMO, K. S. (1999). *Malaysia's Political Economy: Politics, Patronage and Profits.* 2nd edn. Cambridge: Cambridge University Press.

GRANOVETTER, M. (2005). "Business Groups and Social Organization," in N. Smelser and R. Swedberg (eds.), *The Handbook of Economic Sociology.* 2nd edn. Princeton: Princeton University Press, 429–50.

GREIF, A. (2006). *Institutions and the Path to the Modern Economy: Lessons from Medieval Trade.* Cambridge: Cambridge University Press.

GURIEV, S., and RACHINSKY, A. (2005). "The Role of Oligarchs in Russian Capitalism," *Journal of Economic Perspectives*, 19/1: 131–50.

HADLEY, E. M. (1970). *Antitrust in Japan.* Princeton: Princeton University Press.

HOLMEN, M., and HÖGFELDT, P. (2005). "Pyramidal Discounts: Tunneling or Agency Costs?" Unpublished.

HOSHI, T., KASHYAP, A., and SCHARFSTEIN, D. S. (1991). "Corporate Structure, Liquidity, and Investment: Evidence from Japanese Industrial Groups," *Quarterly Journal of Economics*, 106/1: 33–60.

JOH, S. W. (2003). "Corporate Governance and Firm Profitability: Evidence from Korea before the Economic Crisis," *Journal of Financial Economics*, 68/2: 287–322.

JOHNSON, S., BOONE, P., BREACH, A., and FRIEDMAN, E. (2000). "Corporate Governance in the Asian Financial Crisis," *Journal of Financial Economics*, 58/1–2: 141–86.

JONES, G. (2000). *Merchants to Multinationals British Trading Companies in the Nineteenth and Twentieth Centuries.* Oxford and New York: Oxford University Press.

JONES, G., and KHANNA, T. (2006). "Bringing History (Back) into International Business," *Journal of International Business Studies*, 37/4: 453–68.

KALI, R. (1999). "Endogenous Business Networks," *Journal of Law, Economics, and Organization*, 15/3: 615–36.

KALI, R. (2003). "Business Groups, the Financial Market and Modernization," *Economics of Transition*, 11/4: 671–96.

KANG, C. K. (1997). "Diversification Process and the Ownership Structure of Samsung Chaebol," in T. Shiba and M. Shimotani (ed.), *Beyond the Firm: Business Groups in International and Historical Perspective.* Oxford: Oxford University Press, 31–58.

KEISTER, L. A. (1998). "Engineering Growth: Business Group Structure and Firm Performance in China's Transition Economy," *American Journal of Sociology*, 104/2: 404–40.

KEISTER, L. A. (2004). *Chinese Business Groups: The Structure and Impact of Interfirm Relations during Economic Development*. Oxford: Oxford University Press.

KHANNA, T. (2000). "Business Groups and Social Welfare in Emerging Markets: Existing Evidence and Unanswered Questions," *European Economic Review*, 44/4–6: 748–61.

KHANNA, T., and PALEPU, K. (1997). "Why Focused Strategies May Be Wrong for Emerging Markets," *Harvard Business Review*, 75/4: 41–51.

KHANNA, T., and PALEPU, K. (1999a). "Policy Shocks, Market Intermediaries, and Corporate Strategy: The Evolution of Business Groups in Chile and India," *Journal of Economics and Management Strategy*, 8/2: 271–310.

KHANNA, T., and PALEPU, K. (1999b). "The Right Way to Restructure Conglomerates in Emerging Markets," *Harvard Business Review*, 77/4: 125–34.

KHANNA, T., and PALEPU, K. (2000a). "Is Group Affiliation Profitable in Emerging Markets? An Analysis of Diversified Indian Business Groups," *Journal of Finance*, 55/2: 867–91.

KHANNA, T., and PALEPU, K. (2000b). "The Future of Business Groups in Emerging Markets: Long-Run Evidence from Chile," *Academy of Management Journal*, 43/3: 268–85.

KHANNA, T., and PALEPU, K. (2005). "The Evolution of Concentrated Ownership in India: Broad Patterns and a History of the Indian Software Industry," in R. Morck (ed.), *A History of Corporate Governance around the World: Family Business Groups to Professional Managers*. Chicago: University of Chicago Press, 283–320.

KHANNA, T., and THOMAS, C. (2009). "Synchronicity and Firm Interlocks in an Emerging Market," *Journal of Financial Economics*, 92/2: 182–204.

KHANNA, T., and YAFEH, Y. (2005). "Business Groups and Risk Sharing around the World," *Journal of Business*, 78/1: 301–40.

KIM, E. M. (1997). *Big Business, Strong State: Collusion and Conflict in South Korean Development, 1960–1990*. Albany, NY: SUNY Press.

KIM, S. J. (2004). "Bailout and Conglomeration," *Journal of Financial Economics*, 71/2: 315–47.

KRUEGER, A. O. (1974). "The Political Economy of the Rent-Seeking Society," *American Economic Review*, 64/3: 291–303.

LA PORTA, R., LOPEZ-DE-SILANES, F., SHLEIFER, A. and VISHNY, R. W. (1997). "Legal Determinants of External Finance," *Journal of Finance*, 52/3: 1131–50.

LA PORTA, R., LOPEZ-DE-SILANES, F., SHLEIFER, A. and VISHNY, R. W. (1998). "Law and Finance," *Journal of Political Economy*, 106/6: 1113–55.

LA PORTA, R., LOPEZ-DE-SILANES, F., and SHLEIFER, A. (1999). "Corporate Ownership around the World," *Journal of Finance*, 54/2: 471–517.

LA PORTA, R., LOPEZ-DE-SILANES, F., and ZAMARRIPA, G. (2003). "Related Lending," *Quarterly Journal of Economics*, 118/1: 231–68.

LEE, K., PENG, M., and LEE, K. (2001). "Institutions and Changing Performance of Corporate Groups: The Case of the Chaebols in Korea." Unpublished.

LEE, C. H., LEE, K., and LEE., K. (2002). "Chaebols, Financial Liberalization and Economic Crisis: Transformation of Quasi-Internal Organization in Korea," *Asian Economic Journal*, 16/1: 17–35.

LEUZ, C., and OBERHOLZER-GEE, F. (2006). "Political Relationships, Global Financing, and Corporate Transparency: Evidence from Indonesia," *Journal of Financial Economics*, 81/2: 411–39.

MAKSIMOVIC, V., and PHILLIPS, G. (2002). "Do Conglomerate Firms Allocate Resources Inefficiently across Industries? Theory and Evidence," *Journal of Finance*, 57/2: 721–67.

MAMAN, D. (2002). "The Emergence of Business Groups: Israel and South Korea Compared," *Organization Studies*, 23/5: 737–58.

MAURER, N. (1999). "Banks and Entrepreneurs in Porfirian Mexico: Inside Exploitation or Sound Business Strategy?" *Journal of Latin American Studies*, 31/2: 331–61.

MAURER, N., and HABER, S. (2007). "Related Lending and Economic Performance: Evidence from Mexico," *Journal of Economic History*, 67/3: 551–81.

MAURER, N., and SHARMA, T. (2001). "Enforcing Property Rights through Reputation: Mexico's Early Industrialization, 1878–1913," *Journal of Economic History*, 61/4: 950–73.

MORCK, R. (2005). "How to Eliminate Pyramidal Business Groups: The Double Taxation of Intercorporate Dividends and other Incisive Uses of Tax Policy," in J. Poterba (ed.), *Tax Policy and the Economy*, vol. 19. Cambridge, MA, and London: MIT Press, 135–79.

MORCK, R., WOLFENZON, D., and YEUNG, B. (2005). "Corporate Governance, Economic Entrenchment, and Growth," *Journal of Economic Literature*, 43/3: 655–720.

MUSACCHIO, A. (2004). "Law and Finance in Historical Perspective: Politics, Bankruptcy Law and Corporate Governance in Brazil, 1850–2002." Unpublished.

NICODANO, G. (2003). "Bankruptcy Risk: Are Business Groups More Efficient than Conglomerates and Stand-Alone Units?" Unpublished.

OHKAWA, K., and ROSOVSKY, H. (1973). *Japanese Economic Growth: Trend Acceleration in the Twentieth Century*. Stanford: Stanford University Press.

PEROTTI, E. C., and GELFER, S. (2001). "Red Barons or Robber Barons? Governance and Investment in Russian Financial–Industrial Groups," *European Economic Review*, 45/9: 1601–17.

POLSIRI, P., and WIWATTANAKANTANG, Y. (2006). "Thai Business Groups: Crisis and Restructuring," in S. Chang (ed.), *Business Groups in East Asia: Financial Crisis, Restructuring, and New Growth*. Oxford: Oxford University Press, 147–78.

RAJAN, R., SERVAES, H., and ZINGALES, L. (2000). "The Cost of Diversity: The Diversification Discount and Inefficient Investment," *Journal of Finance*, 55/1: 35–80.

ROBERTS, J. G. (1973). *Mitsui, Three Centuries of Japanese Business*. New York: Weatherhill.

SAMPHANTHARAK, K. (2003). "Internal Capital Markets in Business Groups." Unpublished.

SCHARFSTEIN, D. S., and STEIN, J. C. (2000). "The Dark Side of Internal Capital Markets: Divisional Rent-Seeking and Inefficient Investment," *Journal of Finance*, 55/6: 2537–64.

SHIN, H. H., and PARK, Y. S. (1999). "Financing Constraints and Internal Capital Markets: Evidence from Korean Chaebols," *Journal of Corporate Finance*, 5/2: 169–91.

SHIN, H. H., and STULZ, R. M. (1998). "Are Internal Capital Markets Efficient?" *Quarterly Journal of Economics*, 113/2: 531–52.

TSUI-AUCH, L. S. (2005). "Unpacking Regional Ethnicity and the Strength of Ties in Shaping Ethnic Entrepreneurship," *Organization Studies*, 26/8: 1189–216.

WEINSTEIN, D. E., and YAFEH, Y. (1995). "Japan's Corporate Groups: Collusive or Competitive? An Empirical Investigation of Keiretsu Behavior," *Journal of Industrial Economics*, 43/4: 359–76.

YAFEH, Y. (1995). "Corporate Ownership, Profitability, and Bank–Firm Ties: Evidence from the American Occupation Reforms in Japan," *Journal of the Japanese and International Economies*, 9/2: 154–73.

YURTOGLU, B. B. (2000). "Ownership, Control and Performance of Turkish Listed Firms," *Empirica*, 27/2: 193–222.

CHAPTER 21

THE RIDDLE OF THE GREAT PYRAMIDS

RANDALL MORCK

21.1 A RIDDLE

BUSINESS groups inspire much confusion. One of my fondest academic recollections is of a conference of distinguished economists discussing capitalism. To the Americans and British, capitalism forced brisk competition—maximizing efficiency or tearing away civility, depending on the political leanings of the speaker. To everyone else, capitalism turned the economy over to a handful of old moneyed families. Neither side accorded the other much leeway: the Americans and Brits marveled at the conspiracy theories circulating in less enlightened parts of the world; the others marveled at the naivety of the Anglo-Saxons.

Only recently has either side taken the other seriously. It turns out both are right, and capitalism is different in different countries. Remarkably, this stems largely—primarily, I argue—from differences in corporate governance regarding pyramidal groups.

Economics assumes the business sector consists of corporations. The corporate governance literature assumes these are controlled by officers and directors. The

I am grateful for numerous helpful suggestions from participants at the "Evolutionary Dynamics of Business Groups in Emerging Economies" conference hosted by Kyoto University and Doshisha University, Nov. 26–28, 2007. Special thanks are due to Asli Colpan, Takashi Hikino, and Jim Lincoln.

management and business strategy literatures analyze how these top decision-makers guide their corporations through different economic conditions.

For large listed firms in America and Britain, this roughly reflects reality (Morck et al. 1988; Franks et al. 2005; Villalonga and Amit 2008). But elsewhere in the world these assumptions are implausible. In most countries, large businesses come in groups (Granovetter 1994; La Porta et al. 1999; Bebchuk et al. 2000; Morck et al. 2000). Since the term "business group" is used in different ways by different authors (Khanna and Yafeh 2007), we must pause to clarify this.

Countries in which business groups are important often have articulated bodies of Business Group Law (Bermann and Pistor 2004), which law students learn alongside other subjects. These give precise definitions of business groups, the duties of group firms' officers and directors to the group versus their firms, the duties of one group firm to another, the duties of controlling shareholders to public shareholders, and so on.

Problems arise because these definitions, duties, and so on differ across countries. For example, Canadian governments define a group as two or more listed firms with a common controlling shareholder holding at least a 20 percent voting block, or exercising control via dedicated board positions and the like.[1] A threshold below 51 percent makes sense, because most small shareholders seldom vote and most institutions vote routinely as management recommends. Korean law uses a similar definition, as do the legal systems of many European countries (Barca and Becht 2001). In contrast, China defines a business group as any set of legally distinct corporations, listed or not, under common control (Lee and Kang, Chapter 8, this volume). Japanese bureaucrats, scholars, and businesses use conflicting and inconsistent definitions, causing some to despair that the term has no real meaning (Miwa and Ramseyer 2006). This permits a lively debate as to what constitutes a group, where group boundaries lie, and even whether definite boundaries exist (Khanna and Yafeh 2007). These issues of taxonomy lie beyond the scope of this study.

Further confusion arises because many countries lack formal Business Group Law altogether, leaving definitions to the definer. Since firms in many large business groups populate many different industries, some British and American authors mislabel business groups as conglomerates.

Following most of the finance literature (La Porta et al. 1999), we define a group as two or more listed firms under a common controlling shareholder, presumed to be the largest blockholder voting at least 20 percent or, alternatively, 10 percent. We say the group is pyramidal if one listed group firm is a controlled subsidiary of another.

Such a bright line rule, despite obvious costs, permits broader comparisons, which reveal the startling importance of a remarkably few very large business groups in many countries. It also neatly distinguishes business groups from conglomerates— single corporations with divisions in multiple industries—and from holding companies—parent corporations with subsidiaries. Thus Singer, a conglomerate with renowned sewing-machine and missile-guidance-systems divisions, is not a business

---

[1] See Statistics Canada, *Directory of Intercorporate Ownership* (various years).

group, because it is a single listed corporation. Likewise, American apartment-building businesses, often structured as a holding company fully owning separately incorporated properties, are not business groups, because their subsidiaries are unlisted. For our purposes, more nebulous groupings of businesses tied together by product chains, common directors, or historical ties are also not business groups. Other definitions are better for other purposes; and no exclusive right is claimed.

21.2 GREAT PYRAMIDS

At first glance, American and British economists are apt to think of a business group as an odd, but innocuous structure. What, after all, is especially interesting about two or more listed firms being controlled by a single person? This misapprehends the actual scope of business groups where they are most important.

The sheer scale of these groups often startles Anglo-American observers. Högfeldt (2005) shows that the largest single business group in Sweden, controlled by the Wallenberg family, comprises dozens of large firms organized into tiers of listed firms controlled by other listed firms controlled by yet other listed firms, but ultimately controlled by the Wallenberg family firm, a closed-end fund called Investor. Remarkably, the market capitalizations of this group's member firms add up to over half the total value of the country's entire stock market.

Sweden is extreme—usually it takes three, four, or even a dozen business groups to account for the bulk of a country's large business sector. But it is hardly unique. The Hees–Edper Group, controlled by a branch of the Bronfman family, was Canada's largest business group in the 1990s. It comprised several hundred firms, some listed and some unlisted, organized into sixteen tiers of firms with control blocks in other firms (Morck et al. 2000). Twelve such business groups included about 40 percent of the assets of the country's top 100 private-sector domestically controlled corporations at the time (Morck et al. 2005a). An even more extreme example is the business group of the Naboa family, whose member firms roughly correspond to Ecuador's big business sector and provided the incomes of about 3 in 11 Ecuadorians in the 1990s (De Cordoba 1995). The Hong Kong billionaire Li Kashing sits atop a huge group spanning virtually every sector of the region's economy. Handfuls of wealthy families dominate the economies of India (Sarkar, Chapter 11, this volume), Korea (Hwang and Seo 2000; Bae et al. 2002; Kim, Chapter 6, this volume), Spain (Sacristán-Navarro and Gómez-Ansón 2007), Turkey (Orbay and Yurtoglu 2006; Colpan, Chapter 17, this volume), other major European economies (Faccio and Lang 2002), and elsewhere. One, twelve, or twenty wealthy families, each controlling an empire of dozens—sometimes hundreds—of listed and unlisted corporations, are still remarkably askew the Anglo-American vision of capitalism.

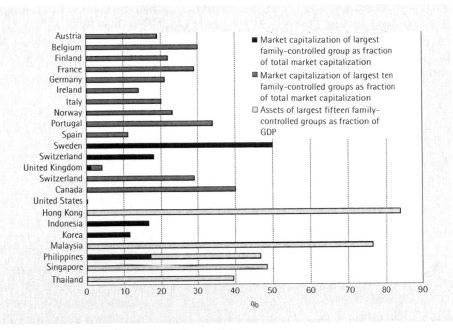

Figure 21.1. Great pyramids of the world

Source: Morck et al. (2005c).

Fig. 21.1 compares the assets or market capitalizations of the largest one, ten, or fifteen businesses or business groups in each country to the size of the country's economy. Since the data come from various studies, all three figures are not available for all countries. Despite this incompleteness, the figure should give pause to American or British economists attributing the views of people in other countries to conspiracy theories. Appreciable chunks of many countries' large business sectors really are controlled by tiny handfuls of wealthy families.

21.3 PYRAMID POWER

The proximate cause of this remarkable difference in the meaning of capitalism across countries is differences in corporate governance.

In the United States and United Kingdom, a corporation is a singular thing, as illustrated in Fig. 21.2. Large corporations in those countries are almost always *free-standing*—that is, they neither control, nor are controlled by, other listed corporations. If they have subsidiaries, these are virtually always unlisted and, except for joint ventures, fully owned. Large corporations in these countries are also usually *widely held*—that is, they have no controlling shareholders, and are owned almost entirely by small investors, referred to by investment managers as "widows and orphans"—that is, public shareholders who bought their shares on the open stock market, either in their own investment accounts or via mutual funds, pension funds, and the like. These free-standing, widely held companies are also usually professionally managed—key decisions are in the hands of a CEO and top executives, selected for their expertise and talent in a competitive job market.

Elsewhere, this governance model is displaced to varying extents by another, the pyramidal group depicted in Fig. 21.3. A business family's firm (the apex firm in Fig. 21.3) controls a first tier of listed firms (here, A1 and A2), each of which controls yet more listed firms (B1, B2, and so on), each of which controls still other listed firms—in a broadening cascade of control. In each case, one firm controls the other with a large block of shares, and the controlled firm's remaining shares are sold to public shareholders. Obviously, a 51 percent block bestows control, but in practice small shareholders often do not vote, so much smaller blocks—20, 10, or even 5 percent—suffice to let the executives of the upper-tier firm appoint the directors and officers of the lower-tier firm.

The most immediate importance of pyramidal business groups is their remarkable power to magnify merely large family fortunes into control over corporate assets worth vastly more, and in some cases adding up to substantial fractions of a national economy. To see how this works, assume the family firm in Fig. 21.3 is worth $1 billion, and that this firm is all the family owns. Though $1 billion constitutes a substantial fortune, it is miniscule compared to the total gross domestic products of even relatively small nations. However, pyramiding can magnify this paltry billion

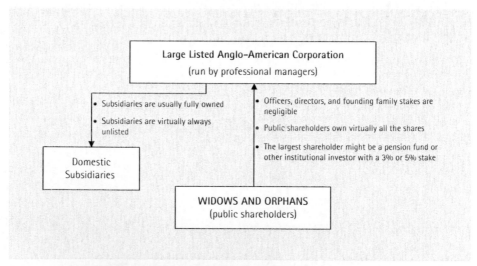

Figure 21.2. A stylized Anglo–American corporation

Large listed corporations in America and Britain are almost always freestanding (they neither control, nor are controlled by, other listed corporations) and are usually widely held (they have no controlling shareholders, and are owned almost entirely by small investors, called "widows and orphans" by investment managers. This ownership can be either direct or indirect, via mutual funds, pension funds, and the like. Subsidiaries are virtually always unlisted and are usually fully owned. Source: SEC filings

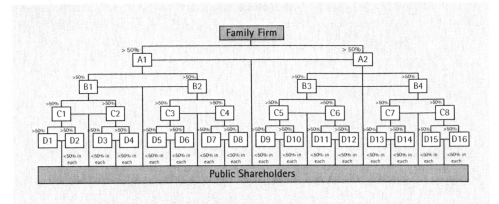

Figure 21.3. A stylized pyramidal business group

Large listed corporations in many countries are organized into pyramidal groups. In these structures, a family firm controls a first tier of listed firms (here, firms A1 and A2), each of which controls other listed firms (for example, A1 controls B1 and B2). Each of these controls yet more listed firms, and so on. A control block of every firm's shares is held by the firm above it, with remaining shares sold to public investors. At the apex, the family controls the family firm, and hence all the firms spreading out beneath it.

into control over a noticeable swathe of a national economy. Suppose the family firm controls B1 and B2, firms that are also worth $1 billion each, by owning a 50 percent block plus one share in each. This puts $2 billion worth of corporate assets under the family's control. The next tier multiplies control over these two corporations into control over $4 billion corporations, and the next tiers multiply this into control over $8 billion, then $16 billion, and then $32 billion corporations. By adding addition tiers, the family can lever its billion dollar fortune into control over the assets of an arbitrarily large group of operating companies in the lowest tier.

Structures like Fig. 21.3—sometimes augmented by supervoting shares, special director appointment rights, and cross-holdings—let one family control half the Swedish economy by market capitalization (Högfeldt 2005); let two families control close to half of Indian big businesses by assets (Sarkar, Chapter 11, this volume); and so on.

Pyramidal business groups like these let mere handfuls of wealthy families control national economies. They are why capitalism looks so different in different countries. Capitalism truly does entrust the governance of large swathes of a nation's economy to handfuls of elite families in many countries. And it truly does induce fierce competition between rival corporations in others. It all depends on whether corporations are free-standing and run by profit-motivated professionals, or family-controlled pyramidal groups.

Misgovernance risk in independent firms is probably firm-specific, and therefore diversifiable; but too much pyramiding by too few families can make misgovernance risk undiversifiable, and therefore raise capital costs. Also, the intelligence to run a great business group is probably no more hereditary than general intelligence

(Herrnstein and Murray 1994; Kincheloe et al. 1996), motivating the American tycoon Warren Buffett to remark:

if we were to pick our United States Olympic team based on the eldest son and the eldest daughter of those who represented us in all the events 24 years ago, we would think that was asinine; but to hand the resources of society, and the resources to command the labor of society and the materials of society, to a bunch of people simply because they happen to have the right last name strikes me as just as foolish. (Whyte 2007)

The American robber baron Andrew Carnegie famously argued it was worse than foolish, positing that growing up rich virtually disqualifies one as an effective CEO (Carnegie 1891) This so-called Carnegie Conjecture (Carnegie 1891: 56) is that "the parent who leaves his son enormous wealth generally deadens the talents and energies of the son, and tempts him to lead a less useful and less worthy life than he otherwise would." This conjecture has support in studies of estate taxes and heirs' subsequent careers (Holtz-Eakin et al. 1993).

Even if there is a competent heir, family feuds can seriously undermine a business (Bertrand et al. 2008). If such disputes destabilize one firm, this is no great matter. But if they destabilize the governance of a huge group of firms constituting an appreciable portion of a country's economy, such disputes can attain macroeconomic importance (Morck et al. 2005c).

All of this is consistent with findings that inherited corporate control bodes ill for firm performance in America (Villalonga and Amit 2006), Canada (Morck et al. 2000; Smith and Amoako-Adu 2005), Denmark (Bennedsen et al. 2007), and other developed economies (Morck and Yeung 2004; Bertrand and Schoar 2006).

21.4 A BALM FOR ALL ILLS

Large pyramidal business groups are not clearly bad for a developing nation's economy, though. Numerous studies, many on specific developing countries such as India or Chile, others across many developing economies, find business group member firms outperforming free-standing firms (Khanna 2000; Khanna and Palepu 2000a, b, c, 2005; Khanna and Rivkin 2001; Khanna and Yafeh 2005, 2007).

This literature, as a whole, suggests that business group firms have an advantage in emerging economies, which they lose in developed countries. The precise economics underlying these findings are unclear. However, most of these studies postulate business groups circumventing market failures.

Certainly, many developing economies' capital, labor, and product markets malfunction. Corrupt or sclerotic courts that render arm's-length contracts unenforceable magnify costs of doing business by, for example, rendering loans or bills effectively uncollectable. Corruption in schools and universities can render

well-trained graduates effectively indistinguishable from those who bribe or intimi-
date their way to certification.

Business groups can sidestep these problems. If one group firm owes money
to another, the family controlling both simply tells the debtor to pay. A family-
controlled firm gains little from cheating another firm run by the same family. This
nicely bypasses clogged or unreliable courts. In a country with inadequate business
schools, the best training may be apprenticeship. Business groups let talented people
rise and move from firm to firm without relying on an arm's-length job market rife
with fraudulent certifications. The best business school in such a country might well
be the dinner table of a powerful business family.

These considerations help explain some of the features of business groups.

First, business groups are usually highly diversified, containing firms from numerous seemingly unrelated industries. This is observed in India (Sarkar, Chapter 11, this
volume), Mexico (Hoshino, Chapter 15, this volume), Taiwan (Chung and Mahmood, Chapter 7, this volume), Thailand (Suehiro and Wailerdsak, Chapter 9, this
volume) and other developing economies (Khanna and Yafeh 2005, 2007). Wide
diversification makes sense if a group must contain most firms that might need to do
business with each other, borrow or lend to each other, or hire each other's employees. A broader spectrum of firms permits a fuller intra-group simulation of developed economies' arm's-length markets.

In borrowing and lending especially, default is important. If each group firms
lends to other group firms in a wider range of industries, its overall default risk is
better diversified and therefore mitigated (Heaney and Holmen 2008). Firms with
excess retained earnings can also subsidize firms encountering bad luck, or capitalize
new controlled subsidiaries (Almeida and Wolfenzon 2006a), adding additional
layers to the pyramid. Of course, the highest value use of those retained earnings
might well be investments outside the group, so this is clearly a second-best capital
allocation (Almeida and Wolfenzon 2006b). Nonetheless, it might dominate in
countries with deeply dysfunctional arm's-length markets.

This default risk mitigation might endow group firms with higher debt capacities
than otherwise similar free-standing peers—a substantial tax advantage in some
countries. Group firms' leverage is elevated in Canada (Daniels et al. 1995), Italy
(Bianco and Nicodano 2006), and perhaps elsewhere. However, evidence that risk-
spreading across business groups mitigates the effects of financial crises is remarkably
scant. Such an effect is disputed in Japan (Hoshi et al. 1990, 1991; Hayashi 2000), not
evident in Thailand (Chutatong et al. 2006), and goes the wrong way in Korea and
other East Asian economies, where low-tier pyramidal group firms fared worst
around the 1997 crisis (Lemmon and Lins 2003; Baek et al. 2004).

Secondly, business groups are usually pyramids of listed firms under a family-
controlled apex firm. Perhaps amid ambient corruption and mistrust, the controlling
family ensures good behavior, making sure all group firms honor contracts, debts,
and bills; and treat employees, managers, customers, and suppliers fairly (Khanna
and Palepu 2000a, b; Khanna and Rivkin 2001; Khanna and Yafeh 2005, 2007).

A pyramidal structure lets the family wield control over all the firms in the group—a necessary condition for enforcing such norms.

Thirdly, business group member firms are relatively strong performers in developing economies—Chile (Khanna and Palepu 2000a), India (Khanna and Palepu 2000b), Russia (Guriev and Rachinsky 2005), and others—but mediocre-to-weak performers in developed economies like Canada (Morck et al. 2000), Israel (Kosenko and Yafeh, Chapter 16, this volume), and Sweden (Högfeldt 2005). This pattern, also evident in cross-country studies (Khanna and Rivkin 2001), also makes sense; for if pyramidal groups' primary advantage lies in circumventing weak institutions, that advantage should evaporate in economies with sound institutions that enforce contracts, educate employees, and provide capital. Thus, Sarkar (Chapter 11, this volume) finds that the superior performance of Indian group member firms, reported in earlier studies (Khanna and Palepu 1999, 2000b, c), faded as liberalization strengthened market institutions.

21.5 MAY PHARAOH REST IN PEACE

Developing economies often have both weak markets and weak governments. Another possibility is that large family pyramidal groups might also substitute for dysfunctional governments. This thesis unites into one theory all the various ways business groups substitute for dysfunctional markets and institutions, discussed above. This is thus a synthesis of these other proposals, not an alternative hypothesis.

In the mid-twentieth century, state-led development became fashionable. Its strongest proponents was perhaps Paul Rosenstein-Rodan (1943), who describes how every firm in a developed economy depends critically on scores of other firms for inputs and complementary outputs; for building, maintaining, and operating transportation and communications systems; for employing the firm's consumers; and for innumerable other services that fit together like a jigsaw puzzle. A steel mill in a primeval jungle—without suppliers, customers, transportation, or communications—is essentially valueless. Each firm needs not just one firm filling each such niche; it needs many competing firms. A steelmaker dependant on one mine for ore, or one railroad for market access, can be "held up." The mine could hike its ore price, or the railroad its freight rates, to bleed the steelmaker—keeping it barely alive, as any rational parasite treats its host. Or the mine might provide low-grade ores and the railroad shoddy service, each knowing the steelmaker had no alternative.

By merely existing, competing mines, railroads, phone companies, and shipping firms make the steelmaker financially viable. If enough pieces of this jigsaw puzzle are missing, the steel mill is unviable and is not built. Entrepreneurs founding mines, railroads, phone companies, and shipping firms confront similar problems; for each relies on the existence of countless other firms scattered throughout the economy.

Rosenstein-Rodan saw this logjam blocking initial development: no rational entre-preneur dares build and then wait for the rest of the economy to form in its own good time, paying exorbitant prices to monopolistic suppliers until competition develops.

Rosenstein-Rodan therefore prescribed centrally planned development, a "big push," to break this logjam. State planners, financed with foreign aid, could coordi-nate the development of firms across sectors, so that steelmakers, mines, phone companies, and railroads all appeared and grew as needed. State control would prevent hold-ups and ensure all provided quality goods and services. The state could use one firm's profits to finance another's expansion, provide or train workers or managers for other firms, or build infrastructure for all—hospitals, roads, bridges, telecom systems, and even schools and universities.

Rosenstein-Rodan saw a state-directed big push as the only option, because economics describes stock markets and private-sector banks as financing individual firms, not the industrializations of whole countries. Financing tailored to individual firms was, he rightly concluded, unable to account for externalities and unable to provide the needed coordination. Thus, he concludes: "There has never been a [private sector] scheme of planned industrialisation comprising a simultaneous planning of several complementary industries" (Rosenstein-Rodan 1943: 204).

He was right about the problem, but wrong about the solution. Many countries mounted massively expensive aid-financed state-run big-push programs, and none brought successful development.

Meiji Japan is illustrative (Morck and Nakamura 2007). The country established state-owned enterprises (SOEs) in every modern sector in the 1870s, seeking to replicate the whole ensemble of a state-of-the-art industrial economy. Lacking hard budget constraints, the SOEs hemorrhaged money; lacking competitors, they pro-duced expensive shoddy products; and run by political appointees, they were ill managed. A decade later, the government was mired in foreign and domestic debt, the currency was evaporating in an accelerating near-hyperinflation, and the econo-my had grown little. In the 1880s a liberal government organized the world's first mass privatization, auctioning off scores of SOEs to private buyers. Most SOEs ended up in coalescing pyramidal groups resembling Fig. 21.3. These groups, called *zaibatsu*, each spanned all major sectors. Each was run by either a great business family—Mitsui, Sumitomo, Suzuki, Iwasaki (Mitsubishi)—or a tycoon like Nissan's Yoshisuke Ayukawa. By the 1920s, Japan was pulling abreast continental Europe in both industrial composition and per capita gross national product.

Postwar South Korea is another striking example (Lim and Morck 2009). After the Korean War, the dictator Syngman Rhee used American foreign aid to establish a constellation of SOEs. Learning from Rosenstein-Rodan, rather than Japanese histo-ry, Rhee entrusted these to political appointees and charged government planners with coordinating their expansion. The result was a lost decade. After Rhee's demise, a mass privatization, and a government fiscal crisis, President Park Chunghee increasingly distanced government from business, though he continued subsidizing exporters. Under Park, and especially after him when Korea attained democracy, huge family-controlled pyramidal groups (*chaebol*) arose, acquiring failed SOEs and establishing scores of new businesses across all major sectors.

In both Korea and Japan, rapid development occured after governments abandoned state-run big-push plans. Rapid development corresponds to business groups expanding across industries, with profitable firms tunneling money to nascent firms or to individually unprofitable firms necessary to the group's prosperity.

These historical narratives prove Rosenstein-Rodan right about the need for a big push, but wrong about the need for state control. A large pyramidal business group is precisely a private-sector "scheme of planned industrialisation comprising a simultaneous planning of several complementary industries."

That such groups privatized big-push coordination is evident in biographies and *zaibatsu* archives (Morck and Nakamura 2007). Even more direct evidence comes in the recollection of Koo Cha-kyung, Chair of Korea's Lucky-Goldstar (LG) *chaebol*:

My father and I started a cosmetic cream factory in the late 1940s. At the time, no company could supply us with plastic cups of adequate quality for cream jars, so we had to start a plastics business. Plastic caps alone were not sufficient to run the plastic molding plant, so we added combs, toothbrushes, and soap boxes. This plastics business also led us to manufacture electric fan blades and telephone cases, which in turn led us to manufacture electrical and electronic products and telecommunications equipment. The plastics business also took us into oil refining, which needed a tanker shipping company. The oil refining company alone was paying an insurance premium amounting to more than half the total revenue of the then largest insurance company in Korea. Thus, an insurance company was started. This natural step-by-step evolution through related businesses resulted in the Lucky-Goldstar group as we see it today. (Chapter 22, this volume)

Further work to see if family business groups ran big-push efforts in other countries, now and historically, is needed. The thesis is plausible for several reasons.

First, although group firms might subsidize each other, the group as a whole has a hard budget constraint. Mismanagement cannot be tolerated long by a profit-maximizing business family. In contrast, SOEs abide remarkable mismanagement (Shleifer and Vishny 1992, 1994; Boycko et al. 1996; Dyck 1997; Lopez-de-Silanes et al. 1997; Shleifer 1998; Claessens and Djankov 1999, 2002; Morten 2000; Cragg and Dyck 2003).

Secondly, both Meiji Japan and postwar Korea hosted numerous business groups, each spanning most sectors. These, in theory at least, competed to develop new ventures faster and more efficiently than each other—and thus than a monopoly group or central planner would have done. For example, had LG not found additional profitable uses for its plastic, other business groups that achieved optimal economies of scale faster would have outpaced it. In contrast, state-led big-push efforts typically capitalize one SOE per sector, as in 1870s Japan and Syngman Rhee's Korea, with competition between SOEs dismissed as wasteful duplication (Krueger 1978, 1998; Ranis 1995).

Thirdly, Meiji Japan and, to a lesser extent, postwar Korea were open economies with economically liberal governments, their guiding hands badly burned by fiscal crises. Openness let imports replace missing jigsaw pieces, at least for easily transported goods. Trade openness let firms with excess capacity, like LG's plastics factory, achieve economies of scale exporting. Their earlier state-led big-push efforts, and analogs elsewhere, entailed massive state subsidy and import substitution programs (Prebisch 1979). Soft SEO budget constraints undermined competition and tariffs left gaps in industrial jigsaw puzzles gaping. Trade barriers may be inevitable in state-led big-push programs because they reduce performance pressure on the bureaucrats running the SOEs.

A notable exception is Singapore, whose initial state-led big-push was successful (Tsui-Auch and Yoshikawa, Chapter 10, this volume). Perhaps openness to global competition and multiple business groups competing can neutralize the downside of state involvement. Or perhaps Singapore had uniquely sound public-sector governance, a lucky chance other countries cannot hope to replicate. The extent to which state firms accelerated Singapore's big-push remains disputed, and its government foresees withdrawal from the economy as its big-push growth phase ends (Tsui-Auch and Yoshikawa, Chapter 10, this volume).

21.6 DIVERGING TUNNELS

Section 21.4 explains large pyramidal business groups in developing economies; Section 21.5 explains how they might even substitute for governments coordinating big-push growth. But large pyramidal groups persist in highly developed economies, such as Canada, continental Europe, and parts of East Asia. Why do they not die out as economies develop?

One possibility, called *tunneling* in the finance literature (Johnson et al. 2000), occurs where the controlling family, instead of acting impartially, favors one group firm over another. Orchestrating a big push necessarily involves tunneling resources between group firms, so profitable firms can subsidize individually unprofitable firms whose existence is nonetheless necessary to the group as a whole. Sidestepping weak markets can also involve transferring resources between group firms that buy, sell, finance, or hire from each other.

However, tunneling can also enrich the controlling shareholder. To see this, recall Fig. 21.3, where each firm is controlled by the firm above it via an equity stake of 50 percent plus one share. Suppose firm D_1 pays out $1 million in dividends. Half of this, or $500,000, goes to firm C_1 and the rest goes to widows and orphans. Suppose C_1 passes its receipts along to its shareholders: half of $500,000, or $250,000, goes to B_1 and the rest goes to widows and orphans. If B_1 forwards half of its receipts to its shareholders, A_1 gets $125,000 and the family firm gets $62,500. Of the $1 million paid out by D_1, a paltry $62,500 goes to the controlling family; while $937,500 goes to the widows and orphans who own stock in the chain of firms leading upwards through the pyramid from D_1 to the family firm.

The family gets only 6.25 percent of firm D_1's cash flows, despite wielding over 50 percent of the votes in its shareholders meetings. Early writers on corporate governance understood how pyramiding induces extreme separations of ownership from control (Berle and Means 1932; Bonbright and Means 1932). To illustrate, consider a chain of control through the Bronfman family's Hees–Edper pyramid in the mid-1990s. The family owned Broncorp Inc., which controlled HIL Corporation with a 19.6% equity stake. HIL owned 97% of Edper Resources, which owned 60% of Brascan Holdings, which owned 5.1% of Brascan, which owned 49.9% of Braspower Holdings, which owned 49.3% of Great Lakes Power Inc, which owned 100% of First Toronto Investments, which owned 25% of Trilon Holdings, which owned 64.5% of Trilon Financial, which owned 41.4% of Gentra, which owned 31.9% of Imperial Windsor Group (Directory of Intercorporate Ownership, 1998). Multiplying these out reveals the family's ownership of Imperial Windsor's cash flows to be 0.03%. That is, $1 million of extra dividends paid by Imperial Windsor increases the family's wealth by $300. Despite this minuscule ownership, the family held full control of Imperial Windsor by controlling the firms above it in a chain leading to the pyramid's apex—either through equity blocks or through more subtle mechanisms like super-voting shares or special rules for appointing directors.

This separation of ownership from control is extreme in the business groups of some countries—as in Canada (Morck et al. 2000) and Sweden (Högfeldt 2000), where intercorporate control blocks can be 20 percent or less, though often fortified with super-voting shares—and relatively minor elsewhere—as in Argentina (Fracchia, Mesquita and Quiroga, Chapter 12, this volume) and Russia (Guriev, Chapter 18, this volume), where control blocks are typically two-thirds or more and many group firms are unlisted.

Where the separation of ownership from control is large, a controlling family might be tempted to organize a business transaction between the family firm and, say, firm D1 in which the latter would lose $1 million. That way, the whole amount goes to the family, with widows and orphans hopefully unaware that the money ever existed. This can be done by instructing D1 not to collect on debts or bills owed it by the family firm. More likely, D1 and the family firm can contract to transfer goods or services from one to the other at artificial transfer prices, set to leave D1 $1 million poorer and the family firm $1 million wealthier.

Transfer pricing by multinational firms is well known, where it transfers taxable income out of high-tax countries and into low-tax countries, lowering the multinational's overall taxes (Hines 1996; Desai et al. 2001). Objectionable transfer pricing in multinationals hides money from tax authorities; in pyramidal groups it hides money from widows and orphans. This aside, the two are identical.[2]

Tunneling is denounced by corporate governance advocates as "expropriation" of public shareholders' wealth. But where tunneling is commonplace, shareholders rationally anticipate it and pay lower prices for affected stocks—both at initial public offerings (IPOs) and subsequently. If widows and orphans pay depressed prices, dividends depressed by tunneling are a fair return. Nothing is expropriated.

---

[2] As noted above, tunneling need not be socially undesirable if it shifts risk (Lincoln and Gerlach 2004) or coordinates big-push development (Morck and Nakamura 2007).

However, even without expropriation, tunneling can retard an economy's growth. This is because, *ceteris paribus*, expected tunneling cuts entrepreneurs' proceeds from share issues. Even if the company is impeccably governed at its IPO, shareholders rightly worry it might someday end up low in a pyramidal group and its shares fetch a depressed price. Possible tunneling thus makes capital costlier to start-ups, curbing competition and leaving existing businesses in sedate peace. This perhaps explains why thoughtful observers in many countries find scant connection between local versions of capitalism and intense competition.

Might pyramidal groups persist in developed economies because the controlling families value the fruits of tunneling too much to dismantle their pyramidal groups, even after their economic justification is passed? The empirical evidence is oddly inconsistent with this. Tunneling is most evident in developing economies (Johnson et al. 2000; Bae et al. 2002; Bertrand et al. 2002, 2008; Friedman et al. 2003; Joh 2003; Lang 2005; Baek et al. 2006; Cheung et al. 2006; Claessens and Laeven 2006). Although specific cases of tunneling occasionally occur in developed economies (Johnson et al. 2000), evidence on systematic tunneling is mixed. For example, some studies find tunneling in Canada (Gadhoum 2006; Bozec and Laurin 2008), but others dissent (Tian 2006; Walid and Paul 2006). Tunneling seems limited in Sweden (Holmen and Knopf 2004), and other developed European economies (Faccio et al. 2001).

21.7 ETERNAL LIFE

Why do business groups persist in developed economies without profitable tunneling? Two answers suggest themselves.

First, the tunneling examined in the empirical studies referred to above is the siphoning of money from lower-tier firms to the apex or firms near it. But tunneling need not involve money. Business families might gain important non-pecuniary benefits from controlling a vast business group—political influence, social status, power, or even a degree of impunity from the rule of law—often on scales dwarfing American managerial perks (Nenova 2003; Dyck and Zingales 2004). These are benefits that rational individuals might value, but that standard economic theories have difficulty incorporating. Algebraic intractability is, of course, no excuse, and the literature might benefit greatly from work along these lines.

Secondly, business groups might persist because tunneling is not the only pecuniary benefit their controlling shareholders glean. The most powerful politicians in many countries tend to come from their greatest business families—especially where corruption is worse (Faccio 2006). Instances of political connections delivering business families major pecuniary benefits are documented in Argentina (Masami 2006), Indonesia (Fisman 2001), Israel (Kosenko and Yafeh, Chapter 16, this volume), Malaysia (Johnson and Mitton 2003), Mexico (Hoshino, Chapter 15, this volume),

Russia (Guriev, Chapter 18, this volume), Taiwan (Chung and Mahmood, Chapter 7, this volume), and Thailand (Suehiro and Wailerdsak, Chapter 9, this volume).

These benefits include subsidies, tax favors, cheap foreign exchange, preference acquiring privatized SOEs, and the like. These are often the work of nationalist politicians, who see large business groups as national monuments and national-building tools. This may reflect genuine respect, or camouflage lucrative political rent-seeking (Morck et al. 2005b).

Such ties matter: more politically connected firms get more generous state bailouts during crises (Faccio 2006). Perhaps ruling a pyramidal business group matters, because it gives a business family political influence far greater than its wealth alone would merit (Krueger 2002; Morck and Yeung 2004; Fogel 2006). Little debate exists about the high returns businesses can earn from capturing and manipulating governments (Krueger 1974). Recall how pyramiding can magnify modest family fortunes into control over corporate assets worth orders of magnitude more. It seems plausible that an analogous magnification of political influence arises (Morck and Yeung 2004). And non-pecuniary benefits from political influence might be more important than pecuniary benefits. High social status, especially elevation above the rule of law, might matter more even than state bailouts in financial crises.

Despite not knowing precisely what these benefits are, financial economists dub them private benefits of control and measure them from the difference between ordinary investors' valuations of shares and controlling shareholders' valuations. Ordinary investors buy shares to receive future dividends, takeover bids, and other pecuniary returns. Controlling shareholders get these plus pecuniary and non-pecuniary benefits of tunneling or influencing governments. When one controlling shareholder sells a control block to another controlling shareholder, the price paid often far exceeds the price ordinary shareholders pay for shares at the same time. However, this control premium is again large for developing economies, but very small in most developed economies—with certain exceptions, like Italy (Dyck and Zingales 2004). Similar findings ensue from firms with multiple classes of stock with different voting rights (Nenova 2003). The persistence of large family-controlled pyramidal business groups thus remains something of a mystery.

21.8 THE UNDEAD

The large pyramidal business groups that persist in developed economies tend to be very old. Canada's Bronfmans grew wealthy exporting beverages to America in the 1920s (Morck et al. 2005a). Italy's Agnelli family's group remained prominent throughout the twentieth century (Aganin and Volpin 2005). Sweden's Wallenberg empire arose in the 1930s, and Högfeldt (2005) reports no major listed Swedish firm less than thirty years old. East Asia's great families retain their business groups, despite impressive growth rates (Claessens et al. 2000).

Long-lived family-controlled pyramidal groups are efficient if they optimally allocate capital, labor, and other resources. But entrusting large swathes of an economy to a few powerful families induces great inequality. Economics entails tradeoffs between efficiency and equality (Okun 1975), but this may not apply here. Such tradeoffs are evident in countries whose wealthiest citizens are self-made, but not where they inherited their wealth (Morck et al. 2000). Greater inequality associated with inherited wealth actually correlates with worse inefficiency, not greater efficiency. Moreover, countries whose great businesses and business groups die more quickly, making way for new giants, grow faster (Fogel et al. 2008).

Thus, whether we seek efficiency or equality, old-moneyed wealth can be too great and old businesses and business groups can live too long. Recall the above arguments: Inherited corporate control restricts top management positions to a suboptimally small pool of candidates. Pyramidal business groups can induce extreme separation of ownership from control, permit tunneling, and entrench insiders. Very large pyramidal groups tightly concentrate economic power, which cannot but have undemocratic political effects. Pyramidal business groups large enough to constitute an important slice of a national economy, but entrusting corporate governance to few people, render the risk of misgovernance systematic, rather than firm-specific, and so contribute to macroeconomic instability.

These findings and arguments suggest a final explanation for the persistence of business groups: they are undesirable for the economy as a whole, but persist because the families controlling them have disproportionate political influence, which they use to lock in a status quo that is advantageous to them.[3] Substantial economic evidence is also consistent with this hypothesis (Morck et al. 2005c). However, some suggest that family-controlled business groups are important to social solidarity in parts of Europe (Högfeldt 2005).

Such elite entrenchment may not be solely, or even primarily, a problem in developed economies; and might explain the persistence of family-controlled pyramidal groups in developing countries that have been developing the longest. Mexico, Argentina, and many other Latin American countries seemed poised for industrialization a century ago, and still do (Haber 1989, 1997; Bortz and Haber 2002; Haber et al. 2003, 2008). None of Argentina's largest business groups is controlled by a founder; but founders' children, grandchildren, and great-grandchildren control about a third each (Fracchia, Mesquita, and Quiroga, Chapter 12, this volume). Mexico's greatest business groups are over a century old (Hoshino, Chapter 15, this volume). Although India's lesser groups rise and fall, its greatest ones have persisted since the mid-nineteenth century (Khanna and Palepu 2005; Sarkar, Chapter 11, this volume).

Do these countries' business elites fear for their privileged positions should their countries development succeed? Developing economies need great business families

---

[3] Here the sociology literature is instructive—see Hamilton and Biggart (1988), Guillén (2001), Schneider (Chapter 23, this volume), and others.

for all the reasons enumerated above; developed economies do not. Might perpetually unsuccessful development be a symptom of excessively powerful, old, entrenched elites (Rajan and Zingales 2003, 2004; Rajan 2004)? If so, can such powerful and deeply entrenched special interests be weakened, and economic development brought to completion, by dismantling their pyramids?

21.9 ICONOCLASTS

Large pyramidal groups are virtually unknown in the USA and UK; and large business groups do not involve business families in Japan and Germany. That these are also the largest developed economies is at least an interesting coincidence.

Pyramidal business groups existed in the USA until the 1930s, when President Roosevelt's New Deal took deliberate aim at them. The Internal Revenue Service worried about tax evasion via transfer pricing between group firms subject to different tax rules. The Federal Trade Commission worried about hidden monopolies, with apparently competing firms controlled by a single family or tycoon. Progressive reformers, such as Adolf Berle and Gardiner Means, sought to democratize corporate America by remaking businesses as democratic republics governed by shareholder democracy, and had little use for pyramidal groups run by "robber barons" or their progeny. Though Roosevelt's populist credentials seem genuine, voters' fury at big business after the Crash of 1929 and the Great Depression no doubt made the pyramidal groups' controlling shareholders tempting targets for his political strategists.

The New Dealers launched a multi-pronged attack on pyramiding in the mid-1930s (Morck 2005). New tax laws subjected intercorporate dividends to double taxation. If we return to Fig. 21.3, Firm D_1's income is taxed, as are dividends it pays to C_1, and dividends C_1 pays to B_1, and so on. A dividend by Imperial Windsor, the bottom-tier firm in the Hees–Edper pyramid described above, would thus be taxed seventeen times as it percolated up to the controlling family. Intercorporate dividends in the USA are still taxed at 7 percent in the recipient's corporate income taxes unless the recipient owns over 80 percent of the paying firm. In Canada, intercorporate dividends are entirely exempt if the recipient owns 20 percent or more of the paying firm. The Canadian approach is near universal: only Korea applies a minimal intercorporate dividend tax; and French and Belgian attempts at such taxes were terminated by the European Commission's Parent-Subsidiary Directive, forbidding any taxation of intercorporate dividends.

Augmenting this tax penalty, the USA established capital-gains-tax holidays for divesting or taking private listed subsidiaries. This mix of carrots and sticks created tremendous pressure on pyramidal groups to restructure into one or more free-standing companies.

Further augmenting these tax penalties and incentives, the USA adopted a Public Utilities Holding Companies Act, banning pyramids over two tiers high in industries designated public utilities. The logic here was that pyramids might tunnel money from public utilities, whose regulated rates of return and cost-plus bases render them plump cash cows, to subsidize unfairly group firms in competitive industries.

These reforms apparently triggered a massive restructuring of US industry into large free-standing firms, most of which were widely held. By 1937, big American businesses were roughly as widely held and freestanding as at the end of the twentieth century (Holderness et al. 1999). Repeal of the intercorporate tax was considered by the George W. Bush administration on the ground that it collects no revenue; but ultimately rejected. Obviously, if the tax were perfectly successful in preventing pyramiding, it would generate zero revenue.

UK business groups persisted until the 1970s. Their demise seems due to the London Stock Exchange's 1968 Takeover Rule requiring any one acquiring 30 percent of a listed firm to buy 100 percent. This meant that a raider could readily force a pyramidal group's controlling shareholder either to accede to a takeover or to take the target private. Pyramidal groups apparently disappeared quickly under this onslaught (Franks et al. 2005).

Several other countries enacted analogous mandatory takeover laws, but they are largely dead letters without intense hostile takeover activity, and so should have no appreciable impact in most countries.

A postwar US military government, staffed by New Dealers charged with remaking Japan as a democracy, ruled from 1945 to 1952. To this end, it dismantled Japan's largest pyramidal groups, or *zaibatsu* (Morck and Nakamura 2005), seizing the families' apex firms and the intercorporate control blocks connecting the lower tiers, and either bestowing these on employees or selling them into the stock market. By 1952, Japanese big businesses were largely widely held and free-standing, as in post-New Deal USA. Hostile takeovers, greenmail, and other aspects of Anglo-American capitalism distressed Japanese managers in the 1950s and 1960s, until an effective anti-takeover defense was devised. This entailed forming new business groups called horizontal *keiretsu*, whose members each bought very small equity stakes in many other member firms. A typical member firm's stock might thus be two-thirds owned by several dozen other member firms, each holding only 1 or 2 percent. This terminated takeovers for several decades. These structures appear to be fading, as financially strained firms occasionally sell their intercorporate blocks (Lincoln and Shimotani, Chapter 5, this volume). This again raises the specter of takeovers, and Japanese firms are now adopting poison pills (Morse and Moffet 2008).

Pyramidal groups never disappeared entirely from Japan. Some smaller *zaibatsu* eluded the New Dealers; and after the Americans had departed, new pyramidal groups formed, though these were called vertical *keiretsu*, rather than *zaibatsu*, perhaps because they were smaller—containing relatively few listed firms and spanning relatively few sectors.

Family-run pyramidal groups are less prominent in Germany than in most other continental European economies, but never disappeared entirely (Franks and Mayer 2001). Major National Socialist reforms during the Great Depression permanently changed the country's big-business sector (Fohlin 2005). Adolf Hitler sought Party control over the entire economy, but balked at socialist policies like mass nationalizations. Instead, the government transferred small shareholders' voting rights to their depository banks. Thus, putting Nazis in charge of the big banks gave the Party dominant voting blocks in most listed firms. Essentially, the National Socialist Party appropriated all widows' and orphans' voting rights.

Augmenting this, corporate directors' duties were reformed. Rather than acting narrowly for shareholders or employees, directors would act for all stakeholders—most importantly, for their Reich and Führer. A further reform, the *Führerprinzip*, gave Party representatives on corporate boards absolute power over their companies and an absolute duty to Hitler (Fohlin 2005).

Remarkably, these laws remained until recently.[4] German supervisory board directors still have a divided loyalty to shareholders and German workers, and the default remains that banks, rather than public shareholders, vote public shareholders' shares. The result is large diffuse business groups loosely controlled by major banks voting small investors shares. Thus, Germany—like the USA, the UK, and Japan—entrusts big businesses to professional managers (Franks and Mayer 2001). However, family-controlled groups persist in the background, especially for a so-called *Mittelstand* of medium-sized firms (Fohlin 2005).

All these systems evolve continually. For example, reforms in the 1990s and 2000s might change the German governance. One reform requires banks to advise shareholders annually that they may vote their shares if they wish. Another proposal would let non-German employees vote for labor representatives on supervisory boards (von Rosen 2007). Yet another change is nascent institutional investors.

That family-controlled pyramidal business groups faded from all four of these major capitalist economies perhaps explains the commonplace association of industrialization with the rise of professional managers and the eclipse of family control (Chandler 1977; Chandler and Hikino 1990). This generalization is unjustified, for family-controlled pyramidal business groups remain predominant virtually everywhere else (Morck and Steier 2005).

21.10 DARING THE GODS

The empirical evidence is generally consistent with large family-controlled pyramidal groups aiding early stage industrialization by substituting for weak market institutions in a largely free market economy, and for central planners during big-push growth. This study does not presume to dictate such policies to governments. Rather, it highlights pros and cons of permitting large pyramidal groups to predominate

---

[4] For details, see Fohlin (2007: 299–313).

under various circumstances, and outlines how such groups have been dismantled in the past by governments choosing that option.

These advantages are offset by a set of burdens such groups can impose. One plausible cost is that capital is made more expensive for the innovative upstart firms that are critical to sustained growth. While individual cases of family pyramids bankrolling upstarts exist (Khanna and Palepu 2005), it seems plausible that self-interest would preclude families whose wealth rests on existing business empires from financing disruptive technologies that might undermine those empires (Morck et al. 2000, 2005c; Rajan and Zingales 2003, 2004).

Even new entrepreneurial firms, not initially belonging to pyramidal groups, are likely to be valued as if tunneling were possible, for little in most countries prevents them from coming under the control of a pyramidal group subsequently. Thus, firm-level governance provisions—commitments to certain board structures, and so on—appear markedly less important empirically than the institutional protections offered by law and regulation (Durnev and Kim 2005; Krishnamurti et al. 2005). Strategies such as high leverage, which might lock in commitments to disgorge profits and discourage takeovers by group member firms, may be somewhat more effective (Harvey et al. 2004).

Standard Anglo-American approaches to improving corporate governance—independent directors, chairs, or board committees and the like—are unlikely to be effective in family-controlled pyramidal groups. It would take a very brave independent director indeed to oppose a family that controlled not just the firm on whose board she sits, but a major fraction of her country's economy, and perhaps its government too. The most critical corporate governance laws and regulations in most countries are thus not about board structures, but about the rights public shareholders have against controlling shareholders (Djankov et al. 2008).

Citing the lack of evidence of shareholder wealth expropriation in many continental European countries (Holmen and Knopf 2004), some European policy advocates argue that pyramiding is innocuous if legal institutions are strong (Belcredi and Caprio 2004). However, this logic is not entirely clear, because expropriation of shareholders' wealth is not really the issue. If shareholders rationally expect controlling shareholders to divert firms' cash flows to fund private benefits, the firms' share prices should be discounted at the IPO and subsequently (Jensen and Meckling 1976). The real public-policy issue is whether or not extensive pyramiding and private benefits accruing to controlling shareholders raise the cost of capital in general, and especially for innovative new firms. While some work begins to address this issue (Orbay and Yurtoglu 2006), much more remains undone.

Though economists are uncomfortable speaking of power, such a discussion is unavoidable here. Pyramiding greatly concentrates economic power, and to an extent that may not be clear to even the sharpest outside observers. For example, large pyramidal groups are rife in Russia, but the ultimate controlling shareholders are shadowy anonymous entities that probably hide powerful political leaders and their associates (Chernykh 2008). That precisely such hidden pyramidal control can disguise market power, frustrate tax authorities, and manipulate government clearly motivated the New Dealer's Depression Era attack on US pyramidal groups (Morck 2005).

Of course, influence can also run the other way. Mussolini's Fascists, and subsequent Italian governments, used large pyramidal groups of listed firms with SOEs, rather than family firms, at their apexes to lock in de facto state control over what superficially seemed a free-market economy (Mussolini 1933; Amatori 1997; Aganin and Volpin 2005); and this may be the Russian government's objective too. Pyramidal business groups also appear to be forming in China (Lu and Yao 2006)— perhaps to the same end. Large pyramidal business groups controlled by state or party organs might give pause to liberal democratic reformers, for these are tried and true methods of projecting state power through an economy painted superficially with liberal free-market colors. These considerations make developing an economic theory of power all the more urgent.

References

Aganin, A., and Volpin, P. (2005). "The History of Corporate Ownership in Italy," in R. Morck (ed.), *A History of Corporate Governance around the World*. Chicago: University of Chicago Press, 325–61.

Almeida, H., and Wolfenzon, D. (2006a). "A Theory of Pyramidal Ownership and Family Business Groups," *Journal of Finance*, 61: 2637–80.

Almeida, H., and Wolfenzon, D. (2006b). "Should Business Groups Be Dismantled? The Equilibrium Costs of Efficient Internal Capital Markets," *Journal of Financial Economics*, 79/1: 99–144.

Amatori, F. (1997). "Growth via Politics: Business Groups Italian Style," in T. Shiba and M. Shimotani (eds.), *Beyond the Firm: Business Groups in International and Historical Perspective*. Oxford: Oxford University Press.

Bae, K. H., Kang, J. K., and Kim, J. M. (2002). "Tunneling or Value Added? Evidence from Mergers by Korean Business Groups," *Journal of Finance*, 57/6: 2695–740.

Baek, J. S., Kang, J. K., and Park, K. S. (2004). "Corporate Governance and Firm Value: Evidence from the Korean Financial Crisis," *Journal of Financial Economics*, 71/2: 265–313.

Baek, J. S., Kang, J. K., and Lee, I. (2006). "Business Groups and Tunneling: Evidence from Private Securities Offerings by Korean Chaebols," *Journal of Finance*, 61/5: 2415–49.

Barca, F., and Becht, M. (2001). *The Control of Corporate Europe*. Oxford: Oxford University Press.

Bebchuk, L. A., Kraakman, R., and Triantis, G. (2000). "Stock Pyramids, Cross-Ownership, and Dual Class Equity: The Mechanisms and Agency Costs of Separating Control from Cash-Flow Rights," in R. Morck (ed.), *Concentrated Corporate Ownership*. Chicago: University of Chicago Press, 295–315.

Belcredi, M., and Caprio, L. (2004). "Separation of Cash-Flow and Control Rights: Should it be Prohibited?" *International Journal of Disclosure and Governance*, 1: 171–85.

Bennedsen, M., Nielsen, K., Pérez-González, F., and Wolfenzon, D. (2007). "Inside the Family Firm," *Quarterly Journal of Economics*, 122: 647–91.

Berle, A., and Means, G. (1932). *Modern Corporation and Private Property*. New York: Commerce Clearing House.

BERMANN, G., and PISTOR, K. (2004). *Law and Governance in an Enlarged European Union.* Oxford: Hart Publishing.

BERTRAND, M., and SCHOAR, A. (2006). "The Role of Family in Family Firms," *Journal of Economic Perspectives*, 20: 73–96.

BERTRAND, M., MEHTO, P., and MULLAINATHAN, S. (2002). "Ferreting out Tunneling: An Application to Indian Business Groups," *Quarterly Journal of Economics*, 117/1: 121–48.

BERTRAND, M., JOHNSON, S., SAMPHANTHARAK, K., and SCHOAR, A. (2008). "Mixing Family with Business: A Study of Thai Business Groups and the Families behind Them," *Journal of Financial Economics*, 88: 466–98.

BIANCO, M., and NICODANO, G. (2006). "Pyramidal Groups and Debt," *European Economic Review*, 50: 937–61.

BONBRIGHT, J., and MEANS, G. (1932). *The Holding Company: Its Public Significance and its Regulation.* New York: McGraw-Hill.

BORTZ, J., and HABER, S. (2002). *The Mexican Economy, 1870–1930.* Stanford: Stanford University Press.

BOYCKO, M., SHLEIFER, A., and VISHNY, R. (1996). "A Theory of Privatisation," *Economic Journal*, 106/435: 309–19.

BOZEC, Y., and LAURIN, C. (2008). "Large Shareholder Entrenchment and Performance: Empirical Evidence from Canada," *Journal of Business Finance & Accounting*, 35: 25–49.

CARNEGIE, A. (1891). "The Advantages of Poverty," in E. Kirkland (ed.), *The Gospel of Wealth and Other Timely Essays.* Cambridge, MA: Harvard University Press.

CHANDLER, A. (1977). *The Visible Hand: The Managerial Revolution in American Business.* Cambridge, MA: Belknap Press.

CHANDLER, A., and HIKINO, T. (1990). *Scale and Scope: The Dynamics of Industrial Capitalism.* Cambridge, MA: Belknap Press.

CHERNYKH, L. (2008). "Ultimate Ownership and Control in Russia," *Journal of Financial Economics*, 88: 169–92.

CHEUNG, Y. L., RAU, R., and STOURAITIS, A. (2006). "Tunneling, Propping, and Expropriation: Evidence from Connected Party Transactions in Hong Kong," *Journal of Financial Economics*, 82/2: 343–86.

CHUTATONG, C., RAJA, K., and WIWATTANAKANTANG, Y. (2006). "Connected Lending: Thailand before the Financial Crisis," *Journal of Business*, 79: 181–218.

CLAESSENS, S., and DJANKOV, S. (1999). "Politicians & Firms in Seven Central & Eastern European Countries," World Bank working paper.

CLAESSENS, S., and DJANKOV, S. (2002). "Privatization Benefits in Eastern Europe," *Journal of Public Economics*, 83/3: 307–24.

CLAESSENS, S., and LAEVEN, L. (eds.) (2006). *A Reader in International Corporate Finance.* Washington: World Bank.

CLAESSENS, S., DJANKOV, S., and LANG, L. (2000). "The Separation of Ownership and Control in East Asian Corporations," *Journal of Financial Economics*, 58: 81.

CRAGG, M., and DYCK, A. (2003). "Privatization and Management Incentives: Evidence from the UK," *Journal of Law, Economics & Organization*, 19/1: 176–217.

DANIELS, R., MORCK, R., and STANGELAND, D. (1995). "In High Gear: A Case Study of the Hees–Edper Corporate Group," in R. Daniels and R. Morck (eds.), *Corporate Decision-Making in Canada.* Calgary: University of Calgary Press, 223–40.

DE CORDOBA, J. (1995). "Heirs Battle over Empire in Ecuador," *Wall Street Journal* (electronic edn.), Dec. 20.

DESAI, M., FOLEY, F., and HINES, J. (2001). "Repatriation Taxes and Dividend Distortions," *National Tax Journal*, 54: 829.

DJANKOV, S., LA PORTA, R., LOPEZ-DE-SILANES, F., and SHLEIFER, A. (2008). "The Law and Economics of Self-Dealing," *Journal of Financial Economics*, 88: 430–65.

DURNEV, A., and KIM, E. H. (2005). "To Steal or Not to Steal: Firm Attributes, Legal Environment, and Valuation," *Journal of Finance*, 60/3: 1461–93.

DYCK, A. (1997). "Privatization in Eastern Germany: Management Selection and Economic Transition," *American Economic Review*, 87/4: 565–97.

DYCK, A., and ZINGALES, L. (2004). "Private Benefits of Control: An International Comparison," *Journal of Finance*, 59/2: 537–600.

FACCIO, M. (2006). "Politically Connected Firms," *American Economic Review*, 96/1: 369–86.

FACCIO, M., and LANG, L. (2002). "The Ultimate Ownership of Western European Corporations," *Journal of Financial Economics*, 65/3: 365–95.

FACCIO, M., LANG, L., and YOUNG, L. (2001). "Dividends and Expropriation," *American Economic Review*, 91/1: 54–78.

FOGEL, K. (2006). "Oligarchic Family Control, Social and Economic Outcomes, and the Quality of Government," *Journal of International Business Studies*, 37/5: 603–22.

FISMAN, R. (2001). "Estimating the Value of Political Connections," *American Economic Review*, 91: 1095–1102.

FOHLIN, C. (2005). "The History of Corporate Ownership and Control in Germany," in R. Morck (ed.), *A History of Corporate Governance around the World*. Chicago: University of Chicago Press, 223–77.

FOHLIN, C. (2007). *Finance Capitalism and Germany's Rise to Industrial Power*. Cambridge: Cambridge University Press.

FRANKS, J., and MAYER, C. (2001). "Ownership and Control of German Corporations," *Review of Financial Studies*, 14: 943–77.

FRANKS, J., MAYER, C., and ROSSI, S. (2005). "Spending Less Time with the Family: The Decline of Family Ownership in the United Kingdom," in R. Morck (ed.), *A History of Corporate Governance around the World*. University of Chicago Press, 581–607.

FRIEDMAN, E., JOHNSON, S., and MITTON, T. (2003). "Propping and Tunneling," *Journal of Comparative Economics*, 31/4: 732–50.

GADHOUM, Y. (2006). "Power of Ultimate Controlling Owners: A Survey of Canadian Landscape," *Journal of Management & Governance*, 10: 179–204.

GRANOVETTER, M. (1994). "Business Groups," in N. Smelser and R. Swedberg (eds.), *Handbook of Economic Sociology*. Princeton: Princeton University Press.

GUILLÉN, M. F. (2001). *The Limits of Convergence: Globalization and Organizational Change in Argentina, South Korea, and Spain*. Princeton: Princeton University Press.

GURIEV, S., and RACHINSKY, A. (2005). "The Role of Oligarchs in Russian Capitalism," *Journal of Economic Perspectives*, 19: 131–50.

HABER, S. (1989). *Industry and Underdevelopment: The Industrialization of Mexico, 1890–1940*. Stanford: Stanford University Press.

HABER, S. (1997). *How Latin America Fell Behind: Essays on the Economic Histories of Brazil and Mexico, 1800–1914*. Stanford: Stanford University Press.

HABER, S., MAURER, N., and RAZO, A. (2003). *The Politics of Property Rights: Political Instability, Credible Commitments, and Economic Growth in Mexico, 1876–1929*. Cambridge: Cambridge University Press.

HABER, S., NORTH, D., and WEINGAST, B. (2008). *Political Institutions and Financial Development*. Stanford: Stanford University Press.

HAMILTON, G., and BIGGART, N. (1988). "Market, Culture, and Authority: A Comparative Analysis of Management and Organization in the Far East," *American Journal of Sociology*, 94 (supplement): S52–S94.

HARVEY, C. R., LINS, K., and ROPER, A. (2004). "The Effect of Capital Structure when Expected Agency Costs are Extreme," *Journal of Financial Economics*, 74/1: 3–30.

HAYASHI, F. (2000). "The Main Bank System and Corporate Investment: An Empirical Reassessment," in M. Aoki and G. Saxonhouse (eds.), *Finance, Governance, and Competitiveness in Japan*. Oxford: Oxford University Press, 81–97.

HEANEY, R., and HOLMEN, M. (2008). "Family Ownership and the Cost of Under-Diversification," *Applied Financial Economics*, 18: 1721–37.

HERRNSTEIN, R., and MURRAY, C. (1994). *The Bell Curve: Intelligence and Class Structure in American Life*. New York: Free Press.

HINES, J. (1996). "Altered States: Taxes and the Location of Foreign Direct Investment in America," *American Economic Review*, 86: 1076–94.

HÖGFELDT, P. (2005). "The History and Politics of Corporate Ownership in Sweden," in R. Morck (ed.), *A History of Corporate Governance around the World*. Chicago: University of Chicago Press, 62: 517–79.

HOLDERNESS, C., KROSZNER, R., and SHEEHAN, D. (1999). "Were the Good Old Days that Good? Changes in Managerial Stock Ownership since the Great Depression," *Journal of Finance*, 5/2: 435–69.

HOLMEN, M., and KNOPF, J. (2004). "Minority Shareholder Protections and the Private Benefits of Control for Swedish Mergers," *Journal of Financial and Quantitative Analysis*, 39: 167.

HOLTZ-EAKIN, D., JOULFAIAN, D., and ROSEN, H. S. (1993). "The Carnegie Conjecture: Some Empirical Evidence," *Quarterly Journal of Economics*, 108: 413–35.

HOSHI, T., KASHYAP, A., and SCHARFSTEIN, D. (1990). "The Role of Banks in Reducing the Costs of Financial Distress in Japan," *Journal of Financial Economics*, 27: 67–88.

HOSHI, T., KASHYAP, A., and SCHARFSTEIN, D. (1991). "Corporate Structure, Liquidity, and Investment: Evidence from Japanese Industrial Groups," *Quarterly Journal of Economics*, 106: 33.

HWANG, I., and SEO, J. (2000). "Corporate Governance and Chaebol Reform in Korea," *Seoul Journal of Economics*, 13/3: 361–89.

JENSEN, M., and MECKLING, W. (1976). "Theory of the Firm: Managerial Behavior, Agency Costs and Ownership Structure," *Journal of Financial Economics*, 3/4: 305–60.

JOH, S. W. (2003). "Corporate Governance and Firm Profitability: Evidence from Korea before the Economic Crisis," *Journal of Financial Economics*, 68/2: 287–322.

JOHNSON, S., LA PORTA, R., LOPEZ-DE-SILANES, F., and SHLEIFER, A. (2000). "Tunneling," *American Economic Review*, 90/2: 22–7.

JOHNSON, S., and MITTON, T. (2003). "Cronyism and Capital Controls: Evidence from Malaysia," *Journal of Financial Economics*, 67/2: 351–82.

KHANNA, T. (2000). "Business Groups and Social Welfare in Emerging Markets: Existing Evidence and Unanswered Questions," *European Economic Review*, 44/4–6: 748–61.

KHANNA, T., and PALEPU, K. (1999). "The Right Way to Restructure Conglomerates in Emerging Markets," *Harvard Business Review*, 77: 125–34.

Khanna, T., and Palepu, K. (2000a). "Emerging Market Business Groups, Foreign Inter-mediaries, and Corporate Governance," in R. Morck (ed.), *Concentrated Corporate Ownership*. Chicago: University of Chicago Press, 265–92.

Khanna, T., and Palepu, K. (2000b). "Is Group Affiliation Profitable in Emerging Markets? An Analysis of Diversified Indian Business Groups," *Journal of Finance*, 55/2: 867–91.

Khanna, T., and Palepu, K. (2000c). "Why Focused Strategies May Be Wrong for Emerging Markets," in J. Garten (ed.), *World View: Global Strategies for the New Economy*. Cambridge, MA: Harvard Business School Press, 21–36.

Khanna, T., and Palepu, K. (2005). "The Evolution of Concentrated Ownership in India: Broad Patterns and a History of the Indian Software Industry," in R. Morck (ed.), *A History of Corporate Governance around the World*. Chicago: University of Chicago Press, 283–320.

Khanna, T., and Rivkin, J. (2001). "Estimating the Performance Effects of Business Groups in Emerging Markets," *Strategic Management Journal*, 22: 45–74.

Khanna, T., and Yafeh, Y. (2005). "Business Groups and Risk Sharing around the World," *Journal of Business*, 78/1: 301–40.

Khanna, T., and Yafeh, Y. (2007). "Business Groups in Emerging Markets: Paragons or Parasites?" *Journal of Economic Literature*, 45/2: 331–72.

Kincheloe, J., Steinberg, S., and Gresson, A. (1996). *Measured Lies: The Bell Curve Examined*. New York: St Martin's Press.

Krishnamurti, C., Sevic, A., and Sevic, Z. (2005). "Legal Environment, Firm-Level Corporate Governance and Expropriation of Minority Shareholders in Asia," *Economics of Planning*, 38: 85.

Krueger, A. (1974). "The Political Economy of the Rent-Seeking Society," *American Economic Review*, 64/3: 291–303.

Krueger, A. (1978). "Alternative Trade Strategies and Employment in LDCs," *American Economic Review*, 68: 270–4.

Krueger, A. (1998). "Why Trade Liberalisation is Good for Growth," *Economic Journal*, 108: 1513–22.

Krueger, A. (2002). "Why Crony Capitalism is Bad for Economic Growth," in S. H. Haber (ed.), *Crony Capitalism and Economic Growth in Latin America: Theory and Evidence*. Stanford, CA: Hoover Institution Press, 1–23.

La Porta, R., Lopez-de-Silanes, F., and Shleifer, A. (1999). "Corporate Ownership around the World," *Journal of Finance*, 54/2: 471–517.

Lang, L. (2005) (ed.). *Governance and Expropriatio: Corporate Governance in the New Global Economy*. Cheltenham: Edward Elgar.

Lemmon, M. L., and Lins, K. (2003). "Ownership Structure, Corporate Governance, and Firm Value: Evidence from the East Asian Financial Crisis," *Journal of Finance*, 58/4: 1445–68.

Lim, W., and Morck, R. (2009). "Harvard–Korea Development Institute Research Project on the History of Chaebols." Unpublished typescript, Korea Development Institute, Seoul.

Lincoln, J. R., and Gerlach, M. L. (2004). *Japan's Network Economy: Structure, Persistence, and Change*. New York: Cambridge University Press.

Lopez-de-Silanes, F., Shleifer, A., and Vishny, R. (1997). "Privatization in the United States," *RAND Journal of Economics*, 28/3: 447–71.

Lu, Y., and Yao, J. (2006). "Impact of State Ownership and Control Mechanisms on the Performance of Group Affiliated Companies in China," *Asia Pacific Journal of Management*, 23: 485.

MASAMI, I. (2006). "Mixing Family Business with Politics in Thailand," *Asian Economic Journal*, 20: 241–56.

MIWA, Y., and RAMSEYER, M. (2006). *The Fable of the Keiretsu*. Chicago: University of Chicago Press.

MORCK, R. (2005). "How to Eliminate Pyramidal Business Groups: The Double Taxation of Intercorporate Dividends and Other Incisive Uses of Tax Policy," *Tax Policy and the Economy*, 19: 135–79.

MORCK, R., and NAKAMURA, M. (2005). "A Frog in a Well Knows Nothing of the Ocean: A History of Corporate Ownership in Japan," in R. Morck (ed.), *A History of Corporate Governance around the World*. Chicago: University of Chicago Press, 367–459.

MORCK, R., and NAKAMURA, M. (2007). "Business Groups and the Big Push: Meiji Japan's Mass Privatization and Subsequent Growth," *Enterprise and Society*, 8/3: 543–601.

MORCK, R., and STEIER, L. (2005). "The Global History of Corporate Governance: An Introduction," in R. Morck (ed.), *A History of Corporate Governance around the World*. Chicago: University of Chicago Press, 1–64.

MORCK, R., and YEUNG, B. (2004). "Family Control and the Rent-Seeking Society," *Entrepreneurship: Theory and Practice*, 28: 391–409.

MORCK, R., SHLEIFER, A., and VISHNY, R. (1988). "Management Ownership and Market Valuation: An Empirical Analysis," *Journal of Financial Economics*, 20/1–2: 293–315.

MORCK, R., STANGELAND, D., and YEUNG, B. (2000). "Inherited Wealth, Corporate Control, and Economic Growth: The Canadian Disease?" in R. Morck (ed.), *Concentrated Corporate Ownership*. Chicago: University of Chicago Press, 319–69.

MORCK, R., PERCY, M., TIAN, G., and YEUNG, B. (2005a). "The Rise and Fall of the Widely Held Firm: A History of Corporate Ownership in Canada," in R. Morck (ed.), *A History of Corporate Governance around the World*. Chicago: University of Chicago Press, 65–140.

MORCK, R., TIAN, G., and YEUNG, B. (2005b). "Who Owns Whom? Economic Nationalism and Family Controlled Pyramidal Groups in Canada," in E. Eden and W. Dobson (eds.), *Governance, Multinationals and Growth*. Cheltenham: Edward Elgar, 44–67.

MORCK, R., WOLFENZON, D., and YEUNG, B. (2005c). "Corporate Governance, Economic Entrenchment, and Growth," *Journal of Economic Literature*, 43/3: 655–720.

MORSE, A., and MOFFETT, S. (2008). "Japan's Companies Gird for Attack; Fearing Takeovers, They Rebuild Walls; Rise of Poison Pills," *Wall Street Journal*, Apr. 30 p. A.1.

MORTEN, B. (2000). "Political Ownership," *Journal of Public Economics*, 76: 559.

MUSSOLINI, B. (1933). *Political and Social Doctrine of Fascism*. London: Hogarth Press.

NENOVA, T. (2003). "The Value of Corporate Voting Rights and Control: A Cross-Country Analysis," *Journal of Financial Economics*, 68/3: 325–51.

OKUN, A. (1975). *Equality and Efficiency: The Big Tradeoff*. Washington: Brookings Institution.

ORBAY, H., and YURTOGLU, B. (2006). "The Impact of Corporate Governance Structures on the Corporate Investment Performance in Turkey," *Corporate Governance: An International Review*, 14: 349.

PREBISCH, R. (1979). "Introduccion al estudio de la crisis del capitalismo periferico," *El trimestre economico*, 46/183: 547–67.

RAJAN, R. (2004). "Why Are Structural Reforms So Difficult? The Benefits of Structural Reforms Aren't Always as Obvious as the Smaller, Short-Term Costs," *Finance and Development*, 41/2: 56–7.

RAJAN, R., and ZINGALES, L. (2003). "The Great Reversals: The Politics of Financial Development in the Twentieth Century," *Journal of Financial Economics*, 69/1: 5–50.

RAJAN, R., and ZINGALES, L. (2004). *Saving Capitalism from the Capitalists: Unleashing the Power of Financial Markets to Create Wealth and Spread Opportunity.* Princeton: Princeton University Press.

RANIS, G. (1995). "Another Look at the East Asian Miracle," *World Bank Economic Review,* 9/3: 509–34.

ROSENSTEIN-RODAN, P. (1943). "Problems of Industrialisation of Eastern and South-Eastern Europe," *Economic Journal,* 53: 202–11.

SACRISTÁN-NAVARRO, M., and GÓMEZ-ANSÓN, S. (2007). "Family Ownership and Pyramids in the Spanish Market," *Family Business Review,* 20/3: 247–65.

SHLEIFER, A. (1998). "State versus Private Ownership," *Journal of Economic Perspectives,* 12/4: 133–50.

SHLEIFER, A., and VISHNY, R. (1992). "Pervasive Shortages under Socialism," *RAND Journal of Economics,* 23/2: 237–46.

SHLEIFER, A., and VISHNY, R. (1994). "Politicians and Firms," *Quarterly Journal of Economics,* 109/4: 995–1025.

SMITH, B., and AMOAKO-ADU, B. (2005). "Management Succession and Financial Performance in Family Controlled Firms," in R. Watson, (ed.), *Governance and Ownership.* Cheltenham: Edward Elgar, 27 ff.

TIAN, G. (2006). "Pyramidal Groups and Firm Performance: Empirical Evidence from Canadian Corporations." UNSW Working Paper. Sydney: University of New South Wales.

VAN ROSEN, R. (2007). "Corporate Governance in Germany," *Journal of Financial Regulation and Compliance,* 15/1: 30–41.

VILLALONGA, B., and AMIT, R. (2006). "How Do Family Ownership, Control and Management Affect Firm Value?" *Journal of Financial Economics,* 80/2: 385–417.

VILLALONGA, B., and AMIT, R. (2008). "How Are US Family Firms Controlled?" *Review of Financial Studies,* 22/8: 3047–91.

WALID, B. A., and PAUL, A. (2006). "Separation of Ownership from Control and Acquiring Firm Performance: The Case of Family Ownership in Canada," *Journal of Business Finance & Accounting,* 33: 517–43.

WHYTE, K. (2007). "An Interview with Warren Buffett: Talking about the Joys of Making Billions and Giving it away—and why the Kids shouldn't Get it," *Maclean's Magazine,* electronic edn., Oct. 15.

CHAPTER 22

....

ECONOMIC INSTITUTIONS AND THE BOUNDARIES OF BUSINESS GROUPS

....

RICHARD N. LANGLOIS

22.1 INTRODUCTION

....

THE theory of the boundaries of the firm, or the economics of organization more broadly, is at the core of what Oliver Williamson (1975) long ago branded "the New Institutional Economics" (Langlois 1986; Klein 2000). Williamson's own work has focused largely on the boundaries question and related issues.[1] By most accounts, Ronald Coase's famous 1937 paper "The Nature of the Firm," which ultimately set in

The author is grateful for helpful comments from Asli Colpan and Takashi Hikino as well as from participants at the Kyoto International Conference "Evolutionary Dynamics of Business Groups in Emerging Economies," November 26–28, 2007, Kyoto University and Doshisha University.

[1] "Transaction cost economics is part of the New Institutional Economics research tradition. Although transaction cost economics (and, more generally, the New Institutional Economics) applies to the study of economic organization of all kinds, this book focuses primarily on the economic institutions of capitalism, with special reference to firms, markets, and relational contracting. That focus runs the gamut from discrete market exchange at the one extreme to centralized hierarchical organization at the other, with myriad mixed or intermediate modes filling the range in between" (Williamson 1985: 16).

motion modern thinking about the boundaries of the firm, was among the founding documents of the New Institutional Economics. It may thus seem odd to claim, as I wish to do here, that the modern-day economics of organization actually pays far too little attention to institutions. What I mean, of course, is that, although its subject is itself an institution—the firm and its various alternatives—the economics of organization does not make much analytical use of institutions in the wider senses of F. A. Hayek (1967), Douglass North (1990), Avner Greif (2006), and others. This observation is related to the much more common claim that the economics of organization does not make adequate use of history (Langlois 2004).[2]

By contrast, the literature on business groups around the world is thick with both institutional and historical detail. I take it as my charge in this volume to discuss the economics of organization, and the economics of institutions more broadly, and to suggest the ways in which those theoretical strands can help to organize the institutional and organizational facts about business groups. But I also want to examine the ways in which the facts about business groups can influence how we think theoretically about the boundaries of the firm.

22.2 INSTITUTIONAL ANALYSIS: COMPARATIVE AND HISTORICAL

Although economists from the classicals through Marshall and his followers had a lot to say about issues of economic organization, it was Coase's 1937 paper that touched off the modern literature on the subject, albeit with a lag of a quarter century or so. In that paper Coase asked the fundamental question "why are there firms?" and responded with the famous answer: firms can exist only if there is a "cost to using the price mechanism" (Coase 1937: 390). Broadly speaking, the economics of organization consists in theorizing about the nature and sources of these costs, now called transaction costs.

The set-up here is an instance of what Coase in his later writings (Coase 1964) would call *comparative-institutional analysis*. Rather than comparing the world we observe against an abstract theoretical model (a practice Coase derided as "blackboard economics"), we should set two real-world institutions side by side and compare their respective costs and benefits. From the point of view of prescription or policy analysis, Coase's plea amounted to a salutary attack on the doctrine of "market failure." It is meaningless to compare real-world institutions against a blackboard standard of perfection, and dangerous to imply (often tacitly) that government intervention is in order without specifying the precise institutional

---

[2] Jones and Khanna (2006) make the case for history in the more directly relevant context of international business studies.

form of that intervention and scanning it thoroughly for "government failure" (Coase 1964; Demsetz 1969). But the doctrine of comparative-institutional analysis also operates at the level of explanation. Implicitly in Coase, and explicitly in Williamson, one explains an observed organizational form by comparing that form with hypothetical discrete alternatives in order to show that the observed form minimizes transaction costs.[3] The thought experiment is to compare "the market" as an organizational structure with "the firm" as an organizational structure.

But, to an extent not often appreciated, the imperfect "market" in the economics of organization is actually a relatively well-functioning market as real-world markets go. The underlying assumption, normally unspoken, is that relevant background institutions—things like respect for private property, contract law, courts—are all in place. Whatever transaction costs then arise are thus the result of properties inherent in "the market" itself, not of inadequacies in background institutions.[4] There is generally a tacit factual or historical assumption as well: that the relevant markets exist thickly or would come into existence instantaneously if called upon.[5] In the economics of organization, then, firms arise because, under certain circumstance, they are inherently superior to markets—even when those markets exist thickly and are well supported (albeit in ways normally unspecified) by background institutions.

In this respect, the economics of organization shares an outlook with another relevant body of literature, that of the late Alfred Chandler (1977, 1990) on the managerial corporation. Chandler certainly cannot be accused of ignoring history. To a far greater extent than the economics of organization, he understood that markets take time to develop and that, in part at least, real-world firms often integrated vertically because markets were initially thin and underdeveloped.[6] Yet, and also to a far greater

---

[3] "The underlying viewpoint that informs the comparative study of issues of economic organization is this: Transaction costs are economized by assigning transactions (which differ in their attributes) to governance structures (the adaptive capacities and associated costs of which differ) in a discriminating way" (Williamson 1985: 18).

[4] As I will argue in due course, the imperfections that the economics of organization tends to discover in "markets" are not in fact inherent but are the result of the historical state of the market (market thickness or extent) or of institutions, especially those intermediate-level institutions I will describe as market-supporting institutions.

[5] Williamson (1975: 20) is fond of assuming that "in the beginning there were markets." He means this as a heuristic dictum not a historical claim: let's assume that markets and firms are both equally capable—that both (and other forms, too, perhaps) exist and have at their disposal the same productive capabilities. This makes it easy to conduct a (static) comparative-institutional analysis. We can compare firms and markets as discrete institutional choices and then explain observed forms strictly on the basis of differences in transaction costs (and perhaps also production costs as understood in neoclassical terms).

[6] "[I]ntegration . . . should be seen in terms of the enterprise's specific capabilities and needs at the time of the transaction. For example, Williamson (1985: 119) notes that: 'Manufacturers appear sometimes to have operated on the mistaken premise that more integration is always preferable to less.' He considers backward integration at Pabst Brewing, Singer Sewing Machine, McCormack [sic] Harvester, and Ford 'from a transaction cost point of view would appear to be mistakes.' But when those companies actually made this investment, the supply network was unable to provide the steady flow of a wide variety of new highly specialized goods essential to assure the cost advantages of scale. As their industries grew and especially as the demand for replacement parts and accessories expanded, so too did the number of suppliers who had acquired the necessary capabilities . . . the point is that an understanding

extent than the economics of organization, Chandler believed in the inherent superiority of the firm—that is, of the large managerial corporation—over markets (and over other kinds of firms) at their real-world best. Steeped in Max Weber via Talcott Parsons, he saw the modern corporation much as Weber saw bureaucracy: as a modern and efficient attractor toward which developed economies were naturally tending (Langlois 2007). And, whereas Chandler is most attentive to history, background institutions are conspicuous by their absence from his explanatory framework (if not always from his narrative). In his account, the rise of the large multi-unit enterprise in the United States was driven by impersonal economic forces: the lowering of transportation and communications costs attendant on the railroad and telegraph, along with increases in *per capita* income, that made it economical to produce or package goods centrally and in volume. This imperative required careful professional management to assure high throughput and thus lower costs (Chandler 1977). As the managerial firm matured, its (Weberian) advantage began to show, and the large multi-unit enterprise was able to adapt existing capabilities and develop new ones in a manner superior to older networks of owner-managed firms (Chandler 1990). Although the adoption of the managerial corporation took different paths in Europe and Japan, those differences seem more a matter of historical accident, managerial decisions, or even national culture.[7] Antitrust policies, corporate law, or the state of development of financial markets seem to matter little.

All this stands in sharp contrast to the literature on business groups, especially business groups outside the developed world, and to the related literature on the multinational corporation. Although much in these literatures draws upon both transaction-cost economics and the work of Alfred Chandler, the central explanatory focus lies not on a comparison of existing institutions with ideal or "optimal" ones in the abstract but rather on the roles of history and institutions in shaping organizational structure.

22.3 COMPLEMENTARITY AND SIMILARITY

As Harvey Leibenstein (1968) long ago pointed out, economic growth is always a process of "gap-filling"—that is, of supplying the missing links in the evolving chain of complementary inputs to production. Especially in a developed and well-functioning economy, one with what I like to call market-supporting institutions (Langlois 2003), such gap-filling can often proceed in important part through the

---

of the changing boundaries of the firm required an awareness of the specific capabilities of the firm and the characteristics of the industry and market in which it operates *at the time* the changes were made" (Chandler 1992: 88–9).

[7] Culture is, of course, a kind of background institution, albeit a somewhat controversial one among social theorists. On this see E. L. Jones (2006).

"spontaneous" action of more-or-less anonymous markets. In other times and places, notably in less-developed economies or in sectors of developed economies undergoing systemic change, gap-filling requires other forms of organization—more internalized and centrally coordinated forms.

Gap-filling is necessary because information about some inputs are unmarketable; and because private information about markets cannot always be proven and made public information. Of course, gap-filling will also be necessary where universalistic markets have not been developed, or where the inputs are, in principle, marketable but for some reason such markets have not arisen. For any given economic activity there is a minimum quantum of various inputs that must be marshaled. If less than this minimum variety is universalistically available, the entrepreneur has the job of stepping into the breech [*sic*] to fill the lack of marketable inputs; i.e., he must be an input-completer. (Leibenstein 1968: 5)

By the 1970s, economists focusing on economic history or developing countries began to suggest that one could explain organizational forms like the multinational corporation (Hymer 1970) and business groups (Leff 1978) as institutional mechanisms for gap-filling. As Leff (1978: 667) put it, the "institution of the group is thus an intrafirm mechanism for dealing with deficiencies in the markets for primary factors, risk, and intermediate products in the developing countries."[8]

Let us take a closer look at the nature of the "gaps" involved. Adam Smith (1976: I. i. 1) tells us in the first sentence of *The Wealth of Nations* that what accounts for "the greatest improvement in the productive power of labour" is the continual subdivision of that labor. Growth in the extent of the market makes it economical to specialize labor to tasks and tools, which increases productivity—and productivity is the real wealth of nations. As the benefits of the resulting increases in per capita output find their way into the pockets of consumers, the extent of the market expands further, leading to additional division of labor—and so on in a self-reinforcing process of organizational change and learning (Young 1928; Richardson 1975).

Although it may not have been obvious in the eighteenth century, the division of labor actually increases, or at least changes, the problem of economic coordination. In a world of undivided labor, what we may think of as crafts production, each worker undertakes multiple stages of production. In principle, a gunsmith, for example, would make all parts of a rifle: lock, stock, and barrel. From the standpoint of transaction costs, coordination is cheap in this world, since each worker can easily make adjustments between stages that are all under his or her control. With greater extent of the market, it begins to pay to assign workers full-time to smaller subsets of tasks. This yields efficiencies, many of which Smith noted. As a pure organizational innovation (that is, holding technology constant), the division of labor is actually capital saving as well as labor saving (Leijonhufvud 1986). But coordination between stages of production has now become more difficult (Becker and Murphy 1992)—and, arguably, more urgent, since workers under the division of labor are no longer substitutes for one another but

---

[8] I should note that Leff defines business groups as excluding family-owned pyramids, but clearly his arguments apply a fortiori to groups under a broader definition.

complements: if one artisanal gunsmith stops working, fewer rifles get made; but if an operative responsible for an entire stage of production stops working, *no* rifles get made (Leijonhufvud 1986).

It is difficult to imagine the division of labor without also imagining a coextensive *division of knowledge* (Hayek 1937). This implies that, in contrast to the implicit and often explicit assumptions of comparative-institutional analysis, knowledge about how to operate within the chain of production—how to fill gaps—must necessarily be bounded and local (Langlois and Foss 1999). The capabilities of economic actors must necessarily be limited. As George Richardson (1972) observed, what determines the limits of the "knowledge, experience, and skills" of economic actors is the degree to which the activities they undertake are *similar*. Shaping a wooden gunstock and rifling a gun barrel are complementary activities in the production of firearms, but they require quite different sets of tools and techniques. It is quite natural, then, that economic actors would find it less costly to take on activities similar to those they already undertake. A woodworker might make a variety of unrelated products from wood, a metalworker a variety of unrelated metal goods. Edith Penrose (1959) makes a version of this idea the centerpiece of her theory of the growth of the firm. In her account, production requires *resources* of various kinds, and these invariably come in lumpy bundles. Firms take advantage of the non-convexities involved by integrating into new activities to which their resources are applicable, thus spreading fixed costs over more units. For example, at the turn of the twentieth century, meatpackers Armour and Swift moved into production of by-products like fertilizer, leather, soap, and glue (Chandler 1990: 168), thus taking advantage of the resources they had built up in the processing of animals for meat.

But, whereas similarity can generate excess resources, complementarity can create resource bottlenecks. In order to take advantage of capabilities and resources in excess capacity, the entrepreneur must typically invest in *new* complementary resources (Teece 1986), and only by accident would these resources also be similar. In other words, in order to take advantage of excess resources, the entrepreneur may be required to fill gaps. If necessary complementary resources (or the products of those resources) are not cheaply available on markets—for any of a variety of reasons we will consider presently—the entrepreneur may be forced into integrating vertically even though his or her capabilities are ill adapted to the new activities (Silver 1984).

In Penrose's theory, the processes of similarity and complementarity co-evolve: integration into similar activities creates the need for dissimilar complementary activities; the filling of those needs in turn creates new capabilities and resources, which also come in lumpy bundles; and the process continues. For example, the American meatpackers had to invest in new distribution facilities and various kinds of new and unrelated production facilities in order to take proper advantage of the by-products of meatpacking and the capabilities they had acquired in the distribution of refrigerated foodstuffs.[9] Not surprisingly, the same dynamic is arguably at

---

[9] "To market the by-products of the packing plants, they built large, separate distributing organizations for fertilizer and leather, and they formed smaller organizations to distribute glue,

work in business groups, especially those in developing countries. Kim (Chapter 6, this volume) cites Koo Cha-Kyung, a former chairman of the LG Group.

My father and I started a cosmetic cream factory in the late 1940s. At the time, no company could supply us with plastic caps of adequate quality for cream jars, so we had to start a plastics business. Plastic caps alone were not sufficient to run the plastic molding plant, so we added combs, toothbrushes, and soap boxes. This plastics business also led us to manufacture electric fan blades and telephone cases, which in turn led us to manufacture electrical and electronic products and telecommunications equipment. The plastics business also took us into oil refining, which needed a tanker shipping company. The oil refining company alone was paying an insurance premium amounting to more than half the total revenue of the then largest insurance company in Korea. Thus, an insurance company was started. This natural step-by-step evolution through related businesses resulted in the Lucky-Goldstar group as we see it today. (Aguilar and Cho 1985: 3)

Notice that the "natural step-by-step evolution through related businesses" involved both spreading excess resources over similar activities and calling forth dissimilar complementary activities.

22.4 FIRMS, MARKETS, AND INSTITUTIONS

Penrose provides us with a theory of the growth of the firm. But the dynamic of similarity and complementarity she depicts is more than that: it is arguably a theory of economic development more generally. Economic historians, especially those of what we might call the Stanford School (David 1975, 1990; Rosenberg 1976), have long stressed the importance of such complementarities for the pace and direction of technological change and economic growth. Even earlier, the Swedish economist Erik Dahmén (1970, 1988) wrote about complementarities and gap-filling in the context of what he called *development blocks*.[10] And, as Morck (Morck and Nakamura 2007; Morck, Chapter 21, this volume) reminds us, the Austrian economist Rosenstein-Rodan (1943) saw the coordination of economic development across sectors as the key to economic growth, arguing for a "Big Push" in which governments would orchestrate investment in and coordination among sectors.[11] It is certainly correct to

---

materials derived from animal fat (including soap, oleo oil, and stearin), and chemical and medicinal products. Indeed, by 1900 Armour and Swift had become two of the 'Big Five' in the American fertilizer industry, as well as the two largest American leather producers; Armour, too, was one of the major makers of glue and abrasives. And just as important, these companies used their refrigerated transportation, storage, and branch office facilities to distribute butter, eggs, poultry, and fruit, while Armour soon became the country's largest marketer of butter. To obtain such produce the company invested in a large buying organization that had its own traffic division and its own sales force and delivery networks" (Chandler 1990: 168).

[10] Dahmén (1970) was first published in Swedish in 1950.
[11] See also Murphy et al. (1989).

say that firms—and specifically business groups—exist (in part at least) in order to solve the problems of coordinating complementarities in a growing economy. But that does not explain why and when other institutional structures like markets or multidivisional firms arise to solve the same kinds of problems.[12]

A satisfying explanation, I argue, will have to be a contingent one, an explanation that takes into account the facts on the ground of markets and institutions. With only a little oversimplification, we can think of these contingent facts as falling on three levels.

- *The level of markets.* How extensive are markets for complementary resources? How easy is it to marshal the necessary complementary capabilities (or their outputs)?
- *The level of market-supporting institutions.* How well developed are the institutional structures that help markets function well—that reduce the costs of coordinating complementary activities through relatively anonymous exchange among legally separate entities rather than through internal coordination within an organization? Such institutions would run the gamut from technological standards (Langlois and Robertson 1992) to legal and organizational innovations like double-entry book-keeping (Rosenberg and Birdzell 1986) or the anonymous limited-liability corporation (Hansmann and Kraakman 2000).
- *The level of political institutions.* What is the character of the state, the organization with a territorial monopoly on the use of force? How well protected are property rights? In what ways does the government intervene in the economy? What is the nature and degree of corruption?

Quite obviously, these three levels are interrelated and blur into one another.[13] Markets can be small because of political barriers to trade as well as because of geographical or technological ones. Market-supporting institutions like the Law Merchant (Milgrom et al. 1990) are also about the protection of property rights, and many of them serve or have served functions sometimes assumed by territorial governments (Greif 2006). Nonetheless, this taxonomy will be useful in organizing the explanations for business groups and their alternatives.

Paul Robertson and I (Langlois and Robertson 1995) have proposed a conceptual framework for thinking about vertical integration at the first of these levels. Begin with the initial conditions: how are economic capabilities in the relevant economy organized at time zero? Do those capabilities reside within the boundaries of vertically integrated entities (of whatever sort) or are they spread among distinct specialized organizations? Secondly, think about the effect of economic change on the nature of the complementarities in the economy and on the problems of coordination among those complementarities. For example, are the changes *systemic*, in

---

[12] As for governments: Morck (Chapter 21, this volume) argues persuasively that, contra Rosenstein-Rodan, governments have had a miserable track record in attempting to orchestrate Big Push development. (This is so for reasons that a different Austrian economist, F. A. Hayek (1945), might have appreciated.) For example, Japan's Big Push did not take place until the government ceded ownership and control to the *zaibatsu* business groups (Morck and Nakamura 2007).

[13] This is arguably so because the institutions at all three levels—even the level of market capabilities—are made of the same stuff, namely rules of behavior (Langlois and Robertson 1995).

that they entail simultaneous change in multiple stages of production? Or can change proceed in *autonomous* fashion without destabilizing existing task boundaries?[14]

Using this framework, we can explain, for example, the rise of the large multi-unit enterprise in the United States in the late nineteenth century. In the ante-bellum period, economic capabilities in the American economy were small scale and localized, with much of economic activity coordinated through non-specialized wholesalers (Porter and Livesay 1971). After the Civil War, per capita income rose despite a flood of immigration; and the railroad, the inland waterways, and the telegraph lowered transportation and communications costs. As Chandler (1977) tells us, these forces expanded the extent of the market dramatically, and it began to pay to centralize certain stages of production that partook of economies of scale. The resulting change was systemic: in many instances the entire chain of production needed to be reorganized. Refrigerated meatpacking needed not only refrigerated rail cars but also a whole new network of refrigerated warehouses, ice stations, and retail outlets; petroleum required consolidation of refining into larger plants and the transportation of refined products by rail; branded consumer goods such as soap and cigarettes called for new high-throughput packaging and distribution facilities; and so on. These requirements typically resulted in large vertically integrated firms—multi-unit enterprises, as Chandler calls them—not because of the inherent superiority of managers in coordinating complementary activities but rather because of the (often short-run) deficiencies of markets in achieving this kind of systemic innovation and in coordinating high-throughput production. Entrepreneurs such as Swift, Rockefeller, and Duke resorted to vertical integration, not because of static transaction costs but because of what I like to call *dynamic transaction costs* (Langlois 1992)— the costs of *changing* the pattern of coordination among complementary stages.

Again, this kind of gap-filling explanation for vertical integration may not seem surprising to those familiar with the literature on multinationals and business groups in the developing world; but it is arguably more original (or more controversial) in the context of (American) business history, where the tools of comparative-institutional analysis have held sway.[15] Of course, in the late nineteenth century, the USA *was* a developing economy. By world-historical standards, property rights there were secure, and government-induced barriers to entrepreneurial activity were modest. But, relative to today's American economy, the nineteenth-century economy obviously lacked not only markets for a variety of newly needed complementary inputs but also the market-supporting institutions that might have encouraged the supply of those inputs in a less-integrated fashion. Indeed, my argument is that the Chandlerian corporation arose because the pace of systemic change in the structure of complementary activities was sufficiently rapid that appropriate innovation in market-supporting institutions could not keep up, making vertical integration a smoother and speedier alternative (Langlois 2003). In other times and places,

---

[14] The terms *systemic* and *autonomous* are from Teece (1986).

[15] In the work not only of Williamson (1985) himself but also of such top-notch economic historians as Lamoreaux, Raff and Temin (2003, 2008).

however, market-supporting institutions have arisen as a way of coordinating complementary activities.

In the American Midwest before the coming of the railroad, as indeed throughout much of agricultural history, wheat was stored, shipped, and traded by the sack (Cronon 1991). Each sack of wheat was the product of a specific identifiable farmer, which meant that repeated trades could generate reputation effects that assured the quality of the grain in the market. At the same time, however, this mode of storage meant large transaction and transportation costs, as the sacks moved by wagon and river to St Louis or Chicago. With the coming of the railroad in the mid-nineteenth century, it became economical to store and ship wheat in bulk, using the newly invented mechanical grain elevator. This reduced transportation costs dramatically.[16] But, as it necessitated mixing together the grain of many different farmers, it destroyed the system of quality control that had relied on the ability to associate wheat with particular farmers. To solve this problem, the Chicago Mercantile Exchange paid the costs of creating standardized categories for wheat and of persuading farmers and buyers to adopt those standards (Cronon 1991). Coupled with a system of inspection, standardization solved the quality-control problem and allowed wheat to continue to be traded on the market. Vertical integration between farming and grain elevators would also have solved the quality problem, but that solution would have generated even greater costs. Farming and grain transportation are dissimilar activities requiring different capabilities; more importantly, integration would have damaged the high-powered incentives (Williamson 1985) that individual ownership placed on farmers. Although vertical integration between farming and transportation (and maybe milling) would have buffered some of the many risks of agricultural production, well-developed commodities markets—which permit greater asset diversification—are arguably even better able to buffer such risks.[17]

So when would we expect the problems of coordinating complementary activities to be solved by the emergence of market-supporting institutions (and thus by markets, broadly understood) and when by vertical integration? This is a crucial—and, in my view, under-researched—question. Clearly, issues of cost matter, as in the grain example. Such issues include neoclassical economies of scale; Williamson-style transaction costs; the costs of diversifying into activities requiring capabilities dissimilar from those one already possesses; and the costs of setting up and maintaining market-supporting institutions (Langlois 2006). Once again, these costs are contingent: they depend on the nature and level of capabilities and of market-supporting institutions already in place. And this suggests two related hypotheses (holding other things constant, of course).

The first is that the processes involved are likely to be path dependent and linked to the passage of time. I have already suggested that, as in the case of the multi-unit

---

[16] A typical large elevator of the era could simultaneously empty twelve railroad cars and load two ships at the rate of 24,000 bushels per hour (Cronon 1991: 113).

[17] Even today, farming in the USA is highly vertically disintegrated and non-corporate. In 1997, 86% of all farms were family owned and farming corporations accounted for only 5.3% of receipts (Allen and Lueck 2004).

enterprise in the USA in the late nineteenth century, vertically integrated organization may be able to respond to systemic change more rapidly than more-decentralized alternatives in a world where markets are thin and relevant market-supporting institutions underdeveloped. But the reverse may be true in a world with thick markets and effective market-supporting institutions (Langlois 2003; Rajan and Zingales 2003). Moreover, we would expect that, as time passes, market-supporting institutions would eventually arise. But the nature and timing of those institutions would be affected by the earlier choice of vertically integrated structure. For example, the rise of the large multi-unit enterprise arguably biased technological change (at least initially) in directions that made internal coordination cheaper and thus reinforced the vertically integrated structure (Langlois 2003). Think about filing cabinets, carbon paper, and punched-card tabulators (Yates 2000).

The second hypothesis, which has resonances at least as far back as Gerschenkron's famous "backwardness" thesis (1962), is that the way an economy responds to the problems of coordinating economic development depends not only on its own institutions and capabilities but also on institutions and capabilities elsewhere. It depends not only on an economy's own history but on the history of other economies as well. The force of this observation is that an economy at the frontier of economic development (however we care to define that) is likely to respond to the coordination problem differently from an economy lagging behind that frontier. Specifically, an economy at the frontier is arguably more likely to rely on decentralized modes of coordination. This is so because uncertainty is greater at the frontier—uncertainty about technology, organizational form, market direction. As a result, selection pressures are high, making decentralized search a more successful strategy (Nelson and Winter 1977; Acemoglu et al. 2006). By contrast, economies further away from the frontier not only possess a less-developed array of market-supporting institutions but also suffer less uncertainty about what the frontier looks like. Follower economies need only look to leading economies for guidance.[18] Away from the frontier, selection pressure is less severe and cutting-edge learning less of an issue. So a more-centralized structure will have fewer disadvantages, and, indeed, many organizational alternatives may survive successfully (Langlois 1984).

Consider two examples, one from recent history and one from more distant history. The personal-computer industry developed in the United States beginning in the late 1970s (Langlois and Robertson 1992). After a period of competition among designs, the industry adopted a dominant standard, now called the Wintel (Windows-Intel) architecture.[19] This architecture encouraged extreme vertical disintegration of production. Stages of production with economies of scale, like the making of microprocessors or operating-system software, became the province of large firms, but the likes of Intel and Microsoft are far less vertically integrated than the IBM of the 1950s and 1960s. And Dell Computer, the most successful assembler of the late twentieth century, gained its

---

[18] As Marx says in the preface to the first German edition of *Capital*, the "country that is more developed industrially only shows, to the less developed, the image of its own future."

[19] Putting aside the Apple Macintosh niche standard.

advantage by explicitly employing a strategy of vertical disintegration (Baldwin and Clark 2006). As the power of microprocessors increased in the 1980s and 1990s, the personal computer came to displace the older mainframe and minicomputer firms, completely transforming the industry from a vertical model to a horizontal model (Grove 1996). Notice that this is the opposite of the Chandler story: here technological standards enabled even radical change to take place in autonomous fashion and, coupled with a high level of other market-supporting institutions, creatively destroyed a pre-existing structure of multi-unit enterprises.

Similarly, the cotton industry of Lancashire was the cutting edge of the first Industrial Revolution. That industry grew out of the highly decentralized putting-out system, which had made Britain a world leader in woolens during the early modern period, and which had creatively destroyed the older system of guild production in cities. The mechanization of the Industrial Revolution, using first water and then steam power, did not destroy the decentralized structure of the industry: even though hand-powered spinning and weaving gave way to factory production, those factories were by and large specialized units (Lyons 1985).

The industry remained readily accessible to the small capitalist because of its geographical concentration within the Lancashire area, the absence of any restrictions upon entry, the increasing separation of the spinning and weaving processes, the extension of the range of products manufactured by the industry, and the growth of a wide range of external economies offered by the auxiliary industries of the region, especially through the development of specialized markets for cotton, yarn, cloth, cotton waste, machinery, and mill stores. Employers could rent land and warehouses, obtain advances from agents, brokers, and banks, and secure long credit terms from machine-makers. Above all, they could rent room, power, and even machinery through a system which long remained the palladium of the small master, first in spinning and then in weaving. (Farnie 1979: 210)

This contrasts sharply with the situation in follower economies, like the USA and Germany, where markets were thinner and "external economies" largely absent, and thus where vertical integration prevailed to a much greater extent (Temin 1988; Brown 1992).

22.5 INTERMEDIATE TIES, PYRAMIDS, AND NATURAL STATES

So far I have talked generally about vertical integration and disintegration, not specifically about business groups. And I have yet to engage the third level of contingent facts, political institutions. I now propose to argue that business groups and political institutions are closely related; indeed, in some of their forms, they are the same thing.

Scholars generally distinguish business groups from more loosely arranged structures like business networks. "When ownership and control are more centralized and organizational subunits enjoy limited autonomy, the commonly used term is business groups. When subunits enjoy more autonomy with respect to ownership, control, and operations, interfirm network is the correct term. In other words, business groups are more centralized and closely held, while interfirm networks are more decentralized and loosely held" (Fruin 2008). Indeed, in some eyes, the "groupness" of a business group is orthogonal to its structure of corporate governance. Mark Granovetter (1995: 95) considers business groups to be "collections of firms bound together in some formal and/or informal ways, characterized by an 'intermediate' level of binding." Purely anonymous market relations do not qualify in Granovetter's definition; but neither do American-style conglomerates, whose wholly owned divisions have little connection with one another and are but modular pieces on the financial chessboard. But a variety of governance structures, from hierarchical and structured *chaebol*, on the one hand, to Marshallian industrial districts (Marshall 1920: IV. x. 3), on the other, would qualify as business groups in Granovetter's sense. As in the personal-computer industry in the twentieth century and the Lancashire textile industry in the nineteenth, industrial districts are inter-firm networks that involve shared information and culture more than ties of ownership.[20] In other cases, however, an industrial district might also involve patterns of overlapping ownership. The Naugatuck Valley brass industry in Western Connecticut was an industrial district in which there was significant overlapping ownership of enterprises, and this identifiable group of owners was also responsible for bringing into existence various market-supporting institutions and complementary resources such as banks and a rail link to New Haven (Everett 1997). And there can also be links among firms not geographically clustered—with or without cross-ownership—as in the much-disputed case of the Japanese *keiretsu* (Lincoln and Shimotani, Chapter 5, this volume).

Explaining the existence of business groups in Granovetter's sense is arguably easier than explaining the mantle of ownership and governance those groups take on. "Intermediate" linkages are essential to the process of gap-filling. Links among entrepreneurs, whether formal or informal, permit the sharing of information about gaps and encourage the coordination of necessary complements (Kock and Guillén 2001). For example, British merchant houses in the nineteenth century took good advantage of well-developed capital markets in Britain by floating specialized "free-standing" companies to pursue opportunities abroad; yet the success of those merchants rested fundamentally on "intermediate ties" of various sorts, both within the trading houses and with the local economy (Jones and Colpan, Chapter 3, this volume). "These companies were not merely perceiving opportunities for trade intermediation, but in some instances creating the trade itself. Once established in a country, they acquired and utilized local knowledge and information which

---

[20] The personal-computer industry is not as localized as was the Lancashire textile industry, but Silicon Valley is clearly a hub, with nodes at places like Austin, Seattle, and Taipei.

reduced the costs of diversification into other activities. Knowledge and information emerge at the heart of the capabilities of these firms" (Jones and Wale 1998: 382).

Even though business groups in the sense of "intermediate ties" can be organized in a variety of ways, there seems to be one dominant form of ownership and governance. Most often, business groups are organized as pyramids of listed and unlisted firms, generally but not always under family control.[21] This stands in contrast to the model more typical in the United States and some other Western countries, where firms tend to be free-standing and widely held, with subsidiaries that are generally unlisted and wholly owned. The multi-unit (Chandler 1977) and multidivisional (Chandler 1990) forms that Chandler chronicles are of this latter type. But those managerial forms are in fact a relative oddity throughout the world, where the pyramidal form dominates (La Porta et al. 1999). The business groups of Korea and Taiwan are starkly different along a number of dimensions: the former are hierarchically organized, vertically integrated, and focused on exporting complete systems (such as cars, white goods, or consumer electronics), whereas the latter are more permeable, less integrated, and more focused on intermediate products (Hamilton and Feenstra 1995). Yet, from the perspective of ownership, business groups in both countries fit the definition of pyramids. So do the nineteenth-century British merchant houses.

In a sense, it would seem, there is something "natural" about pyramidal groups: they seem to crop up whenever governments do not take active measures to beat them down (Morck, Chapter 21, this volume). Meir Kohn (2009) argues that, throughout most of history, the family firm has been the "natural" form of business organization. The family bond lowers monitoring costs, helps align incentives, and provides enforcement mechanisms, all of which help explain this form's resiliency.[22] Most business groups are controlled by families, so one might think of the pyramidal group as just an extension of the natural family firm. Yes, but there is more to the story.

North, Wallis, and Weingast (2009) have recently put forward a theory of what they call the *natural state*. This form of state is "natural" in the same sense as is the pyramidal group: it is the default form of organization. Apart from the hunter-gatherer lifestyle before the Neolithic Revolution and a few present-day open-access orders (more on which presently), the natural state has been the *only* form of territorial government throughout history. North et al. (2009) model the natural state not as a single-person natural monopolist in the use of force (North 1981; Olson 1993) but as a relatively stable coalition of elites who limit access to the resources of society in order to "create credible incentives to cooperate rather than fight among themselves" (North et al. 2009: 18).

Prominent among the resources that elites seek to limit is the ability to form productive organizations.

---

[21] Morck (Chapter 21, this volume) defines a group as "two or more listed firms under a common controlling shareholder, with control presumed to lie with the largest blockholder voting at least 10 per cent or 20 per cent."

[22] Cf. our earlier discussion of farming (Allen and Lueck 2004).

By devising ways to support contractual organizations and then extending the privilege of forming those organizations to their members, the dominant coalition creates a way to generate and distribute rents within the coalition as well as a credible way to discipline elites because elite organizations depend on the third-party support of the coalition. The ability of elites to organize cooperative behavior under the aegis of the state enhances the elite return from society's productive resources—land, labor, capital, and organizations. (North et al. 2009: 20)

Clearly, this fits the picture of business groups in many times and places in history.[23]

The coalitional function of business groups is not, of course, incompatible with their gap-filling function. Although the former speaks to governance issues whereas the latter speaks more directly to issues of vertical integration, the governance dimension and the gap-filling dimension are linked, for one crucial kind of gap is the absence of transactional rules and procedures. As North et al. (2009: 16) note, "most organizations have their own internal institutional structure: the rules, norms, and shared beliefs that influence the way people behave within the organization." For example, in pre-Meiji Japan, Mitsui and Sumitomo—favored business partners of the Shogunate—were forced to create their own institutional rules.

Both families managed without money and modern economic institutions, like corporation or contract law. Consequently, both families developed *house rules*—constitutions dictating how business should be done; profits calculated, allocated, and disbursed; and power passed from generation to generation. House rules assigned key decisions to *family councils*—parliaments representing clans according to precise voting formulae. Thus, in an environment without ambient business law, merchant houses formulated their own laws and, as far as we can tell, adhered to them rigidly. Private legal systems served both merchant houses well, making their behavior predictable and their promises credible. (Morck and Nakamura 2007: 10)

Natural states or limited-access orders stand in contrast to *open-access orders*. In the latter, which characterize the polities today in places like North America, much of Europe, and Japan, the allocation of resources is not restricted to elites but is open to the majority of the population. The key defining dimension of an open-access order is anonymity or impersonality. Whereas in a natural state the allocation of resources depends on status and identity—which family group you belong to, for example—in an open-access order all who meet specified abstract criteria participate in resource allocation and are permitted to form organizations. This creates an incentive for the formation of more complex contractual organizations, which do not rely (solely) on coalitional dynamics for enforcement but also have recourse to abstract third-party rules and procedures (North et al. 2009: 22–3). Open-access orders thus have greater scope for the introduction of market-supporting institutions, and we would expect

---

[23] Khanna and Yafeh (2007: 352) argue that, in general, "there is substantial evidence [that] business groups in emerging markets are very often, though not always, formed with government support. But as the groups evolve and (some of) the countries develop, the relations between groups and governments become far more complex so that there is considerable variation in this dimension across groups and countries." However, all their examples of cases in which governments have tried to harm or discourage business groups involve dramatic changes in the coalition of elites or open-access orders like the USA.

to see greater use of such institutions to coordinate complementary activities in such societies.

Nonetheless, the pyramidal governance structure of the business group continues to manifest itself even in modern open-access societies like Canada, Israel, or Sweden. Indeed, Morck (2005) argues that, but for the taxation of intercorporate dividends and other government policies, pyramidal business groups would be important in the USA as well. Why do pyramids persist in open-access societies?

One much-discussed possibility is that they are a vehicle for unproductive rent-seeking. Majority stakeholders can transfer resources among units of the group in ways that benefit themselves at the expense of minority stockholders, a process called *tunneling* (Johnson et al. 2000). The problem is that empirical evidence of the phenomenon is at best mixed (Khanna and Yafeh 2007). Moreover, Morck (Chapter 21, this volume) insists that, even if tunneling does take place, potential minority investors are aware of the possibility and pay a discounted price for the stock as a result. Now, such a discount does not by itself imply that there is no inefficiency: it could represent an inefficient equilibrium.[24] In such a case, however, we would expect to see poorer performance among units of business groups than among free-standing firms; and the empirical evidence of this is at best mixed, ambiguous, and beset by problems of endogeneity (Khanna and Yafeh 2007; Masulis et al. 2009). This has led some authors to wonder whether the explanation for pyramids in open-access societies might actually lie outside the economic (Morck, Chapter 21, this volume). Writing in the context of Israel, for example, Kosenko and Yafeh (Chapter 16, this volume) argue that, "in a developed economy, where external (financial and other) markets are developed, business groups have no advantage in allocating resources internally." The reasons for their existence appear to have more to do with prestige, political ties, family considerations and factors other than economic efficiency.

There may yet be another explanation. Even in developed open-access societies, pyramidal business groups may exist because they play a gap-filling role. In this case, the issue is not vertical integration but governance. In developed economies—which increasingly means one integrated global economy—markets are relatively thick and market-supporting institutions relatively abundant, making it possible to coordinate complementary activities in a decentralized way. But there are still gaps: new products, new processes, new ways of organizing, new profit opportunities to seize.

There is a durable thread in the literature of organization, running at least from Frank Knight (1921) through Oliver Hart (1989), that associates residual rights of control with innovation and uncertainty. In a world of uncertainty and new opportunities, it is impossible to specify all future contingencies in a contract. Residual rights of control accord their holders the ability to decide and act within the gaps of inevitable contract incompleteness—the ability, in Knight's terms, to exercise

---

[24] Analogous, for example, to the case of workers in Alchian-and-Demsetz's theory of joint production (1972), who find themselves in a high-shirking low-compensation equilibrium (we pretend to work and they pretend to pay us, as the old Soviet saying goes) but would prefer to be in a high-effort high-compensation equilibrium.

entrepreneurial *judgment* (Langlois and Cosgel 1993). Thus by retaining significant control in enterprises at lower stages of the pyramid, the owners of a business group can exercise this kind of judgment. This is a function entirely analogous to that of venture capitalists (Gompers and Lerner 2004).[25] Significantly, venture capitalism as an institution flourishes in those economies like the USA where pyramids have been suppressed or are otherwise not the norm. It is an interesting question whether the American system (suppressed pyramids + venture capital) is a superior institutional structure to that of the pyramids found abundantly elsewhere in the world, especially along the dimension of innovation.

22.6 CONCLUSIONS

All growing economies are "developing" economies: they all face the problem of coordinating an array of complementary activities in a world in which knowledge is limited and local. Such coordination is a matter of "gap-filling." In economies where markets are relatively thick and institutions (both political institutions and what I call market-supporting institutions) are firmly in place, coordination can take place through relatively anonymous markets and relatively autonomous firms. In "less-developed" economies, where markets are relatively thinner and institutions weak, coordination is often more cheaply undertaken within the boundaries of business groups organized as financial pyramids, often under family control. These organizations are intimately linked to the coalition of territorial rulers that North and his co-authors (2009) call a natural state; and, indeed, such business groups are typically themselves *examples* of a natural state, in that they represent a self-enforcing coalition with its own rules, norms, and mechanisms of enforcement.

But even in "developed" economies, novelty and change create the sorts of gaps that call for business groups, including less-formal sets of "intermediate" relationships, as, for example, in geographic (or, increasingly, "virtual") industrial districts. In this sense, the economics of organization generally can learn from the literature on business groups outside the developed world. The problem of gap-filling in highly developed economies differs from that in less-developed economies because the path ahead is cloudier, which suggests that more-decentralized organizational structures may be more successful at the cutting edge of technology. But pyramidal business groups persist in highly developed economies with strong institutions of third-party enforcement and investor protection. The reasons for this, I suggest, have to do with

---

[25] The parent firms in a pyramid "hold significant control rights in the junior firm so as to offset the potentially large moral hazard problem associated with being an outside investor with limited minority shareholder protections. This is the same rationale for giving superior control rights to venture capitalists" (Masulis et al. 2009: 5–6).

the function of residual rights of control in governance, which permit adaptation to new possibilities and the exercise of entrepreneurial judgment.

REFERENCES

ACEMOGLU, D., AGHION, P., and ZILIBOTTI, F. (2006). "Distance to Frontier, Selection, and Economic Growth," *Journal of the European Economic Association*, 4/1: 37–74.

AGUILAR, F. J., and CHO, D. S. (1985). "Gold Star Co. Ltd," *Case no. 9-385-264*. Boston: Harvard Business School Press.

ALCHIAN, A., and DEMSETZ, H. (1972). "Production, Information Costs, and Economic Organization," *American Economic Review*, 62/5: 772–95.

ALLEN, D. W., and LUECK, D. (2004). *The Nature of the Farm: Contracts, Risk, and Organization in Agriculture*. Cambridge, MA: MIT Press.

BALDWIN, C. Y., and CLARK, K. B. (2006). "Architectural Innovation and Dynamic Competition: The Smaller 'Footprint' Strategy." Harvard Business School Working Paper, No. 07-014.

BECKER, G. S., and MURPHY, K. M. (1992). "The Division of Labor, Coordination Costs, and Knowledge," *Quarterly Journal of Economics*, 107/4: 1137–60.

BROWN, J. C. (1992). "Market Organization, Protection, and Vertical Integration: German Cotton Textiles before 1914," *Journal of Economic History*, 52/2: 339–51.

CHANDLER, A. D., JR. (1977). *The Visible Hand: The Managerial Revolution in American Business*. Cambridge, MA: Belknap Press.

CHANDLER, A. D., JR. (1990). *Scale and Scope: The Dynamics of Industrial Capitalism* Cambridge, MA: Belknap Press.

CHANDLER, A. D., JR. (1992). "Organizational Capabilities and the Economic History of the Industrial Enterprise," *Journal of Economic Perspectives*, 6/3: 79–100.

COASE, R. H. (1937). "The Nature of the Firm," *Economica*, NS 4: 386–405.

COASE, R. H. (1964). "The Regulated Industries: Discussion," *American Economic Review*, 54/3: 194–97.

CRONON, W. (1991). *Nature"s Metropolis: Chicago and the Great West*. New York: W. W. Norton.

DAHMÉN, E. (1970). *Entrepreneurial Activity and the Development of Swedish Industry, 1919–1939*. Trans. Axel Leijonhufvud. Homewood, IL: Richard D. Irwin.

DAHMÉN, E. (1988). "'Development Blocks' in Industrial Economics," *Scandinavian Economic History Review*, 36/1: 3–14.

DAVID, P. A. (1975). *Technical Choice Innovation and Economic Growth: Essays on American and British Experience in the Nineteenth Century*. New York: Cambridge University Press.

DAVID, P. A. (1990). "The Dynamo and the Computer: An Historical Perspective on the Modern Productivity Paradox," *American Economic Review*, 80/2: 355–61.

DEMSETZ, H. (1969). "Information and Efficiency: Another Viewpoint," *Journal of Law and Economics*, 12/1: 1–22.

EVERETT, M. J. (1997). "External Economies and Inertia: The Rise and Decline of the Naugatuck Valley Brass Industry." PhD Dissertation, University of Connecticut.

FARNIE, D. A. (1979). *The English Cotton Industry and the World Market, 1815–1896*. Oxford: Clarendon Press.

FRUIN, W. M. (2008). "Business Groups and Interfirm Networks," in G. Jones and J. Zeitlin (eds.), *The Oxford Handbook of Business History*. Oxford: Oxford University Press.

GERSCHENKRON, A. (1962). *Economic Backwardness in Historical Perspective: A Book of Essays*. Cambridge, MA: Belknap Press of Harvard University Press.

GOMPERS, P., and LERNER, J. (2004). *The Venture Capital Cycle*. 2nd edn. Cambridge, MA: MIT Press.

GRANOVETTER, M. (1995). "Coase Revisited: Business Groups in the Modern Economy," *Industrial and Corporate Change*, 4/1: 93–130.

GREIF, A. (2006). *Institutions and the Path to the Modern Economy: Lessons from Medieval Trade*. New York: Cambridge University Press.

GROVE, A. S. (1996). *Only the Paranoid Survive*. New York: Currency Doubleday.

HAMILTON, G. G., and FEENSTRA, R. C. (1995). "Varieties of Hierarchies and Markets: An Introduction," *Industrial and Corporate Change*, 4/1: 55–91.

HANSMANN, H., and KRAAKMAN, R. H. (2000). "Organization Law as Asset Partitioning," *European Economic Review*, 44/4–6: 807–17.

HART, O. (1989). "An Economist"s Perspective on the Theory of the Firm," *Columbia Law Review*, 89/7: 1757–74.

HAYEK, F. A. (1937). "Economics and Knowledge," *Economica*, 4/13: 33–54.

HAYEK, F. A. (1945). "The Use of Knowledge in Society," *American Economic Review*, 35/4: 519–30.

HAYEK, F. A. (1967). *Studies in Philosophy, Politics and Economics*. Chicago: University of Chicago Press.

HYMER, S. (1970). "The Efficiency (Contradictions) of Multinational Corporations," *American Economic Review*, 60/2: 441–8.

JOHNSON, S. R., ET AL. (2000). "Tunneling," *American Economic Review*, 90/2: 22–27.

JONES, E. L. (2006). *Cultures Merging: A Historical and Economic Critique of Culture*. Princeton: Princeton University Press.

JONES, G., and WALE, J. (1998). "Merchants as Business Groups: British Trading Companies in Asia before 1945," *Business History Review*, 72/3: 367–408.

JONES, G., and KHANNA, T. (2006). "Bringing History (back) into International Business," *Journal of International Business Studies*, 37/4: 453–68.

KHANNA, T., and YAFEH, Y. (2007). "Business Groups in Emerging Markets: Paragons or Parasites?" *Journal of Economic Literature*, 45/2: 331–72.

KLEIN, P. G. (2000). "New Institutional Economics," in B. Bouckeart and G. De Geest (eds.), *Encyclopedia of Law and Economics*. Cheltenham: Edward Elgar, 456–89.

KNIGHT, F. H. (1921). *Risk, Uncertainty, and Profit*. Boston: Houghton-Mifflin.

KOCK, C. and GUILLÉN, M. F. (2001). "Strategy and Structure in Developing Countries: Business Groups as an Evolutionary Response to Opportunities for Unrelated Diversification," *Industrial and Corporate Change*, 10/1: 77–113.

KOHN, M. (2009). "The Origins of Western Economic Success: Commerce, Finance, and Government in Pre-Industrial Europe." Dartmouth College, Hanover, unpublished manuscript. http://www.dartmouth.edu/~mkohn

LA PORTA, R., LOPEZ DE-SILANES, F., and SHLEIFER, A. (1999). "Corporate Ownership around the World," *Journal of Finance*, 54/2: 471–517.

LAMOREAUX, N. R., RAFF, D. M. G., and TEMIN, P. (2003). "Beyond Markets and Hierarchies: Toward a New Synthesis of American Business History," *American Historical Review*, 108/2: 404–33.

LAMOREAUX, N. R., RAFF, D. M. G., and TEMIN, P. (2008). "Business History and Economic Theory," in G. Jones and J. Zeitlin (eds.), *Oxford Handbook of Business History* (Oxford: Oxford University Press.

LANGLOIS, R. N. (1984). "Internal Organization in a Dynamic Context: Some Theoretical Considerations," in M. Jussawalla and H. Ebenfield (eds.), *Communication and Information Economics: New Perspectives.* Amsterdam: North-Holland, 23–49.

LANGLOIS, R. N. (1986). "The New Institutional Economics: An Introductory Essay," in R. N. Langlois (ed.), *Economics as a Process: Essays in the New Institutional Economics.* New York: Cambridge University Press, 1–25.

LANGLOIS, R. N. (1992). "Transaction Cost Economics in Real Time," *Industrial and Corporate Change,* 1/1: 99–127.

LANGLOIS, R. N. (2003). "The Vanishing Hand: The Changing Dynamics of Industrial Capitalism," *Industrial and Corporate Change,* 12/2: 351–85.

LANGLOIS, R. N. (2004). "Chandler in a Larger Frame: Markets, Transaction Costs, and Organizational Form in History," *Enterprise & Society,* 5/3: 355–75.

LANGLOIS, R. N. (2006). "The Secret Life of Mundane Transaction Costs," *Organization Studies,* 27/9: 1389–410.

LANGLOIS, R. N. (2007). *The Dynamics of Industrial Capitalism: Schumpeter, Chandler, and the New Economy.* The Graz Schumpeter Lectures. London: Routledge.

LANGLOIS, R. N. and COSGEL, M. M. (1993). "Frank Knight on Risk, Uncertainty, and the Firm: A New Interpretation," *Economic Inquiry,* 31: 456–65.

LANGLOIS, R. N., and FOSS, N. J. (1999). "Capabilities and Governance: The Rebirth of Production in the Theory of Economic Organization," *Kyklos,* 52/2: 201–18.

LANGLOIS, R. N., and ROBERTSON, P. L. (1992). "Networks and Innovation in a Modular System: Lessons from the Microcomputer and Stereo Component Industries," *Research Policy,* 21/4: 297–313.

LANGLOIS, R. N. and ROBERTSON, P. L. (1995). *Firms, Markets, and Economic Change: A Dynamic Theory of Business Institutions.* London: Routledge.

LEFF, N. H. (1978). "Industrial Organization and Entrepreneurship in the Developing Countries: The Economic Groups," *Economic Development and Cultural Change,* 26/4: 661–75.

LEIBENSTEIN, H. (1968). "Entrepreneurship and Development," *American Economic Review,* 58/2: 72–83.

LEIJONHUFVUD, A. (1986). "Capitalism and the Factory System," in Richard N. Langlois (ed.), *Economics as a Process: Essays in the New Institutional Economics* (New York: Cambridge University Press), 203–23.

LYONS, J. S. (1985). "Vertical Integration in the British Cotton Industry, 1825–1850: A Revision," *Journal of Economic History,* 45/2: 419–25.

MARSHALL, A. (1920). *Principles of Economics.* 8th edn. London: Macmillan and Co.

MASULIS, R. W., PHAM, P. K., and ZEIN, J. (2009). "Pyramids: Empirical Evidence on the Costs and Benefits of Family Business Groups around the World." Working Paper. http://ssrn.com/paper=1284499 accessed July 11, 2009.

MILGROM, P., NORTH, D. C., and WEINGAST, B. R. (1990). "The Role of Institutions in the Revival of Trade: The Law Merchant, Private Judges, and the Champagne Fairs," *Economics and Politics,* 2: 1–23.

MORCK, R. (2005). "How to Eliminate Pyramidal Business Groups: The Double Taxation of Intercorporate Dividends and Other Incisive Uses of Tax Policy," in J. M. Poterba (ed.), *Tax Policy and the Economy* (Cambridge, MA: MIT Press), 135–79.

MORCK, R., and NAKAMURA, M. (2007). "Business Groups and the Big Push: Meiji Japan"s Mass Privatization and Subsequent Growth," *National Bureau of Economic Research Working Paper Series*, No. 13171.

MURPHY, K. M., SHLEIFER, A., and VISHNY, R. W. (1989). "Industrialization and the Big Push," *Journal of Political Economy*, 97/5: 1003–26.

NELSON, R. R., and WINTER, S. G. (1977). "In Search of Useful Theory of Innovation," *Research Policy*, 5: 36–76.

NORTH, D. C. (1981). *Structure and Change in Economic History*. New York: Norton.

NORTH, D. C. (1990). *Institutions, Institutional Change and Economic Performance*. New York: Cambridge University Press.

NORTH, D. C., WALLIS, J. J., and WEINGAST, B. R. (2009). *Violence and Social Orders: A Conceptual Framework for Interpreting Recorded Human History*. New York: Cambridge University Press.

OLSON, M. (1993). "Dictatorship, Democracy, and Development," *American Political Science Review*, 87/3: 567–76.

PENROSE, E. T. (1959). *The Theory of the Growth of the Firm*. Oxford: Basil Blackwell.

PORTER, G., and LIVESAY, H. C. (1971). *Merchants and Manufacturers: Studies in the Changing Structure of Nineteenth-Century Marketing*. Baltimore: Johns Hopkins University Press.

RAJAN, R., and ZINGALES, L. (2003). *Saving Capitalism from the Capitalists: Unleashing the Power of Financial Markets to Create Wealth and Spread Opportunity*. New York: Crown Business.

RICHARDSON, G. B. (1972). "The Organisation of Industry," *Economic Journal*, 82/327: 883–96.

RICHARDSON, G. B. (1975). "Adam Smith on Competition and Increasing Returns," in A. S. Skinner and T. Wilson (eds.), *Essays on Adam Smith*. Oxford: Clarendon Press, 350–60.

ROSENBERG, N. (1976). *Perspectives on Technology*. New York: Cambridge University Press.

ROSENBERG, N., and BIRDZELL, L. E., JR. (1986). *How the West Grew Rich*. New York: Basic Books.

ROSENSTEIN-RODAN, P. N. (1943). "Problems of Industrialisation of Eastern and South-Eastern Europe," *Economic Journal*, 53/210–11: 202–11.

SILVER, M. (1984). *Enterprise and the Scope of the Firm*. London: Martin Robertson.

SMITH, A. (1976). *An Enquiry into the Nature and Causes of the Wealth of Nations*. The Glasgow Edition. Oxford: Clarendon Press.

TEECE, D. J. (1986). "Profiting from Technological Innovation: Implications for Integration, Collaboration, Licensing, and Public Policy," *Research Policy*, 15/6: 285–305.

TEMIN, P. (1988). "Product Quality and Vertical Integration in the Early Cotton Textile Industry," *Journal of Economic History*, 48/4: 891–907.

WILLIAMSON, O. E. (1975). *Markets and Hierarchies: Analysis and Antitrust Implications*. New York: Free Press.

WILLIAMSON, O. E. (1985). *The Economic Institutions of Capitalism*. New York: Free Press.

YATES, J. (2000). "Business Use of Information and Technology during the Industrial Age," in A. D. Chandler, Jr., and J. W. Cortada (eds.), *A Nation Transformed by Information: How Information Has Shaped the United States from Colonial Times to the Present*. New York: Oxford University Press), 107–35.

YOUNG, A. A. (1928). "Increasing Returns and Economic Progress," *Economic Journal*, 38/152: 527–42.

CHAPTER 23

....

BUSINESS GROUPS AND THE STATE: THE POLITICS OF EXPANSION, RESTRUCTURING, AND COLLAPSE

....

BEN ROSS SCHNEIDER

23.1 INTRODUCTION

....

BUSINESS groups combine empirically a variety of features that have fascinated researchers from a range of disciplines (see Colpan and Hikino, Chapter 2, this volume, for a full review). However, debate and theorizing, both generally and in relation to politics, are unlikely to progress unless we distinguish clearly the features of interest to different disciplines and construct definitions accordingly. At a minimum, distinctions are necessary among three types of business groups—informal, pyramidal, and diversified—and the theoretical approaches associated with each. Unfortunately, most definitions of business groups lump together all three

I am grateful to the conference participants, Asli Colpan, Takashi Hikino, James Lincoln, Randall Morck, and David Soskice for feedback and suggestions.

dimensions and usually add in family ownership as well. My view is that we should think of these features not as dimensions of the same core phenomenon but rather as defining characteristics of three separate phenomena that have different origins and consequences and that may or may not coincide empirically.

Informal business groups are a first subtype, though it turns out to be an extremely rare one. Regardless of other features of ownership and diversification, the central theoretical focus of some scholars is on the voluntary, non-economic, social networks that hold some business groups together. The Japanese *keiretsu* are the most famous and well-studied informal groups (though Lincoln and Shimotani (Chapter 5, this volume), question whether the label of business group is appropriate). The research and theoretical debate on these rare informal groups will probably revolve around core issues in economic sociology and network analysis, and shade into discussions of clusters, other kinds of economic networks, and social capital generally (Granovetter 2005), which for most other scholars of business groups are separate entities.

For scholars of ownership patterns and corporate finance, informal ties are not central concerns. Rather, the key issue in this financial approach is *pyramidal* control, where a group controls many firms through partial and often quite small ownership shares in a chain or hierarchy of firms where each is partially owned and fully controlled by the one above it. Such pyramids are common in developing countries, are formal rather than informal, and may also characterize groups that are not diversified (Morck 2005a). The core theoretical, and sometimes normative, concerns in this view of business groups are tunneling, expropriation of minority shareholders, and the generally discouraging effects these practices can have on the healthy growth of local equity markets and, by extension, overall economic development (Morck et al. 2005).

In a third theoretical approach, *diversified* business groups are usually pyramids but rarely informal, though neither ownership nor type of coordination matters for the key issue of explaining diversification into multiple sectors of the economy. The theoretical puzzle here is explaining why diversified business groups would deviate from the contemporary norm of specialization in US firms and from the conventional managerial prescription to concentrate on "core competence." The answers vary but generally focus on elements of the institutional and economic environments in which business groups operate that would make diversification rational and efficient. In various formulations, diversified business groups are a logical response to technology borrowing and economies of scope, capital and managerial scarcity, and several kinds of informational and institutional "failure" (see, respectively, Leff 1978; Khanna and Palepu 1997; Amsden 2001).

Informal networks, pyramids, and diversification may all be present simultaneously in many business groups, but there is no a priori, theoretical reason to think they arose from the same causes.[1] In fact, different concepts and theories are likely to be useful in

---

[1] Family management and control would comprise a fourth set of distinct questions and theoretical issues. Family control may, though, be more causally connected to pyramidal ownership and diversification, in that information asymmetries created by these corporate structures increase the returns to trust and kinship bonds (see Schneider 2008).

explaining the origins, functioning, and impact of each facet. These distinctions are also crucial for political analysis as politics differ along each dimension. The informal *keiretsu*, for instance, evolved in postwar Japan in the wake of the break-up by US occupation forces of the prewar *zaibatsu*. In other words, formal policy prohibition of business group governance arrangements (holding companies) encouraged informality. Although rarely so directly encouraged, pyramids thrive in permissive institutional environments (for example, where the issuance of non-voting shares is common) where regulators do not or cannot impede ownership structures that provide greater control than cash-flow rights. Lastly, politics and policy generally have a more direct and visible impact on diversification strategies, both intended and unintended. Unintended incentives come from political volatility and uncertainty, while intended promotion is inspired by a variety of different policy goals.

Much of this chapter, especially the analysis of business groups as objects of policy, focuses on the diversification dimension (Section 23.2). The growth of diversified business groups has been associated with a wide range of policies: from import substitution industrialization (ISI) in Latin America (Guillén 2001), to export-oriented growth in East Asia (Amsden 2001), to social democracy in Scandinavia (Högfeldt 2005), to defense contracting in Israel (Maman 2002). Diversified business groups manifest a kaleidoscopic and ever-changing array of activities and subsidiaries, some that have connections and synergies but others that have no apparent relation to one another. However, a comparative analysis of how states promote diversification helps identify three ideal typical patterns of diversification—organic, portfolio, and policy induced—which in turn highlight inter-regional differences, especially between Latin America and Asia.

Understanding why business groups dominate the economies of so many developing countries requires an examination of what advantages business groups have over potential rivals such as specialized domestic firms and MNCs (Section 23.3). Much of the political advantage of business groups derives from their towering size in their domestic economies, and this size advantage results in large part from diversification and a pyramidal structure (which allows owners to use smaller amounts of their own capital to control vast assets and significant shares of economic activity). Other political advantages may also accrue to family control and management, mostly because families can make longer-term political commitments than can hired managers. Business groups also have better capacity to get and use economic and political information, especially through privileged access to the policy-making process. This access does not mean that business groups can always dictate or even veto policies, but it does at least give them a big insider advantage.

Yet, not all groups pursue equally politicized strategies. Business groups vary over time, across countries, and within countries in terms of what could be called degrees of political intimacy (Section 23.4). This intimacy is not just based on clientelist or crony exchanges of rents for support but is also a function of business groups' commitment to the policies and development strategy of the government. Although precise thresholds are hard to set in the middle range, it is easier to identify firms on the far ends of the continuum of intimacy, either incestuous or arm's length. Yet, contrary to views of path dependence and entrenchment, many firms that adopt strategies of high political intimacy end up, after a brief politically induced boom, in dire straits.

23.2 THE STATE AND DIVERSIFICATION

I compare economic and political logics to construct a typology of different kinds of business groups elsewhere.[2] The discussion here focuses exclusively on the political factors, though it starts with a summary of the typology of organic, portfolio, and policy-induced groups to highlight the differences among strategies. The analysis turns then to the government-imposed, external limits on group diversification, especially in policies toward state enterprises, MNCs, and banking.

Beyond a range of economic incentives to diversify, policy-makers sometimes directly push, or entice, groups into new sectors. For example, for Turkish groups, "the decision to enter into a new area of activity is often taken via suggestions and recommendations of government authorities rather than through an evaluation of market signals" (Bugra 1994: 187). When in the 1970s the Park regime in Korea embarked on the plan to promote heavy and chemical industries (HCI), planners called on existing *chaebol* to take the lead in developing new sectors. The government "chose Hyundai and Daewoo to develop power plant facilities and Hyundai, Samsung, and Daewoo to build ships" (Chang 2003: 4). In Latin America, when governments decided in the 1990s to privatize huge state enterprises, the only buyers with sufficient resources were local business groups or MNCs, and governments often preferred domestic buyers (Manzetti 1999).[3] In more diffuse fashion, new tax incentives in Taiwan in the 1960s encouraged firms to establish new firms rather than expand existing ones, and these new firms had lasting effects on the structure and diversity of Taiwanese groups for decades afterwards (Chung 2001). Other policies provided more indirect incentives for diversification. Under ISI, for example, firms rarely exported, so, once domestic markets were saturated in particular product lines, firms had nowhere to invest other than in new sectors.

These kinds of policy-induced groups can be conceptually distinguished from others based on other stronger economic motivations, organic and portfolio (see Fig. 23.1). *Organic groups* develop largely according to the logics of economies of scope and vertical integration, and their subsidiaries are thus likely to have stronger synergies in organization, personnel, and expertise. New investments are more likely

---

[2] This section summarizes parts of Schneider (2009b). For discussions of other economic incentives, see Leff (1978); Khanna and Palepu (1997); Amsden (2001); Khanna and Yafeh (2007).

[3] In one sample in Latin America, over 80% of the largest business groups participated in the privatization process, and over two-thirds leveraged privatization into greater diversification (Schneider 2008).

	Organic	Portfolio	Policy induced
Core motivations	Economies of scope (and vertical integration)	Risk management	Government incentives
Scope of diversification	Narrower	Broadest	Broader
Integration of management	High	Variable	Variable
Group ties to subsidiary	Longer term	Shorter term	Shorter term

Figure 23.1 Three types of diversified business groups

to be greenfield plants, especially as firms extend their economies of scope.[4] Forays into new sectors through greenfield investment require long lead times and tend to occur incrementally and sequentially, and the resulting subsidiaries are likely to remain in the groups for long periods or forever. Management connections across member firms tend to be denser and closer, especially in instances of economies of scope that rely on the transfer of personnel among subsidiaries.

Portfolio groups diversify to manage risk and maximize returns in the market for corporate governance (buying and selling firms). Managing risk tends to preoccupy owners of groups in more volatile sectors or countries, while opportunistic acquisitions are likely to inform portfolio strategies in more stable environments. Portfolio groups are more likely to buy firms rather than build them from the ground up and to spin off firms if they run into trouble. Bank-centered groups naturally tend to develop as portfolio groups. Because portfolio groups often expressly buy subsidiaries in sectors completely unrelated to core group firms, the technological incentives to integrate management are lower, and group owners, especially in developed countries, often allow subsidiary managers considerable autonomy. However, broad diversification raises problems of agency and information asymmetries, especially in less competitive markets and in developing countries, that can encourage greater management integration (often through kinship networks).

Lastly, *policy-induced groups* diversify in response to government incentives or directives. As noted above, these policies can range from industrial promotion, to privatizations, to tariff and other protections. This category would also include a subset of patrimonial business groups that arise in cases of purer political or crony capitalism under personal dictators such as Suharto, Marcos, Somoza, or Putin,

---

[4] For example, from 1938 to 1993, Samsung created sixty-two new firms, nearly double the number it acquired; most of the acquisitions came in the early decades and the establishment of new firms in the later decades. Moreover, many of the acquisitions were horizontal, while the creation of firms was in new sectors (Kang 1997: 37).

where governments determine the structure of groups more directly by distributing concessions to family, friends, and supporters.[5] Patrimonial groups may coexist with other groups; in Indonesia, in 1996, the sales of "Suharto-linked groups" were nearly double those of "independent groups" (Hanani 2006: 188). In patrimonial groups, the pattern of diversification depends less on any economic logic than on government-created rents (the fortunes of these groups are examined further in Section 23.4).

As ideal types, organic, portfolio, and policy-induced groups can be analytically distinguished, and countries or periods identified with the predominance of a particular type. In practice, however, some groups may mix these strategies by combining, for example, a core set of organic subsidiaries with another set of risk-balancing portfolio investments. In other cases, organic or portfolio groups may be induced by particular policies to enter new sectors, especially during periods of rapid policy change. Over time, individual groups may shift their predominant diversification strategy and structure. Samsung started out in the 1940s and 1950s under ISI as a bank-centered portfolio group, then shifted after the military government took away its banks to a policy-induced group, but along the way developed economies of scope in project execution that helped it shift by the 1980s and 1990s to an organic group focused more on electronics technologies (Kang 1997: 37–45).

Despite this empirical complexity, the typology is still useful in identifying broad trends or clustering across countries and periods. Khanna and Yafeh (2007: 334) calculate a diversification index that is nearly twice as high in Latin America and South East Asia as it is in Taiwan and Korea. Business groups in South East Asia and Latin America were also much more likely to have financial subsidiaries. These data fit with the view that groups in East Asia, especially Japan, Taiwan, and Korea, have tended to be more organic and clustered in manufacturing sectors with greater economies of scope (Amsden 2001). In contrast, countries with long-standing personal dictatorships (as in some countries in South East Asia and Central America) tend to generate more policy-induced, patrimonial groups, as do politicized processes of sweeping privatization (as in Chile (in the 1970s), Argentina, and many countries of Eastern Europe). And portfolio groups tend to predominate where groups grow out of banks or raw-material commodities or in countries where volatility and uncertainty have been greater, as has been common in South East Asia and Latin America (Schneider 2008).

The discussion so far, like most existing scholarship, has focused on factors that push or pull business groups into new sectors. What is missing is an examination of barriers to entering new sectors, crucial external constraints or parameters that decisively shape group structure. Government policies established significant external boundaries for group expansion by setting the terms of group interaction with

---

[5] See, e.g., Rivera (2003) on the Philippines; King and Szelényi (2005: 213) on "parasitic financial-industrial groups" in Russia, Ukraine, and Rumania; and Ganev (2001) on the rise of a patrimonial group in Bulgaria, the dominant Multigroup conglomerate.

MNCs, state enterprises, and banks.[6] That is, where governments reserved certain sectors for state enterprises or MNCs, or put banks off limits, then groups had to find other areas into which they could expand.

Countries vary a great deal in terms of the sectoral distribution and proportion of the production accounted for by MNCs. Among developed countries, MNCs are rare in Japan, where they account for only 2 percent of total sales, but more common in the United States and large countries of Europe. where their sales range from 11 percent in Germany to 32 percent in France (Barba Navaretti and Venables 2004: 5). For most of the twentieth century, Swedish governments of varying ideological persuasions imposed severe restrictions on foreign ownership to protect national groups from being taken over (Högfeldt 2004: 15). Among developing countries, governments excluded MNCs from many sectors in Korea and India but welcomed them in Latin America and South East Asia. In all these cases, government policy heavily conditioned, if not directly regulated, the presence of MNCs. For business groups, the most important impact of MNCs comes in terms of the opportunities they close off or leave open (Amsden 2001; Guillén 2001). In the formative decades of the 1960s and 1970s, the heavy presence of MNCs in Latin American manufacturing closed off opportunities and pushed business groups into services and commodities, while the relative absence of MNCs in Korea left open more possibilities for *chaebol* expansion in manufacturing (Maman 2002). Of course, there is nothing automatic about groups taking advantage of opportunities; however, once MNCs are established in particular sectors, domestic firms tend to avoid direct competition.

State enterprises also closed off some opportunities for groups and expanded others. Cross-regional variations were similar to MNC presence, with state enterprises typically occupying a larger slice of the economy in Europe and Latin America than in Asia. State enterprises in most countries were concentrated in public utilities, mining, oil, and other capital-intensive manufacturing sectors like steel. Also, as was sometimes the case with MNCs, some governments directed state enterprises to invest together with domestic firms or buy inputs from local suppliers, which also drew business groups into new sectors (Evans 1979). Lastly, the eventual privatization of many state enterprises after the 1980s opened up previously closed options for group diversification.

Banking regulations also had profound impacts on group evolution. Where banks faced few regulatory restrictions, they were usually core group enterprises. For example, the two largest groups in Sweden, the Wallenberg and Handelsbank groups, grew in the early twentieth century out of their respective banks (Collin 1998: 726). In Latin America, through much of the twentieth century, banks were pivotal in the

---

[6] In one extreme example of setting parameters, Russian legislation in the 1990s stipulated that "banks could participate in only one financial-industrial group; banks could own no more than 10 percent of the stock of any company in the FIG; there could be no more than 20 firms in each FIG; there could be no more than 25,000 workers at each firm; and there could be no more than 100,000 workers overall" (Johnson 1997: 335). Although less specific, Tunisian legislation before 1988 essentially banned business groups by prohibiting the formation of holding companies with subsidiaries in different sectors (Cammett 2007: 77).

formation and evolution of business groups, as they were in the Philippines, South Africa, Russia, Chile (before the 1980s), Indonesia, Turkey, Taiwan (after the 1980s), and Thailand (Schneider 2009b). Business groups without banks are more common in countries with legal and regulatory restrictions on groups owning banks and on banks owning non-financial firms or lending to firms that are part of the same group, as in the United States, Korea, India, Taiwan (pre-1980s), and Chile (post-1980s). Also, most governments around the world regulate foreign ownership of banks, so MNC purchases of domestic banks that once belonged to groups are usually the result of government reforms to open up the financial sector, as was common in Latin America in the 1990s and 2000s (Martinez-Diaz 2009).

The importance of government regulation in shaping the structure of business groups is perhaps most visible in the response, usually very rapid, by business groups to changes in banking rules. For example, in the 1980s the Korean government relaxed restrictions on *chaebol* investment in financial firms and permitted *chaebol* to own limited shares in banks and controlling shares in non-bank financial firms (insurance, brokerage, and so on). By the late 1990s the top thirty *chaebol* owned seventy-six non-bank financial firms (Chang 2003: 60–1). In Mexico, several dramatic changes in banking regulations after 1980 restructured the largest groups several times in the space of a few decades. Unrestrictive regulations prior to 1980s meant that most banks were parts of business groups (Camp 1989). Then, in 1982, the government nationalized banks, stripping groups of their banking subsidiaries. By the 1990s, the government decided to re-privatize the banks, though with restrictions on foreign ownership, so that most banks ended up again in business groups (though different ones). By the late 1990s, the government had relaxed restrictions on foreign ownership; MNCs bought up many banks, and by the 2000s few Mexican business groups had large banking subsidiaries.

In sum, government policies on these three kinds of ownership—MNCs, state enterprises, and banks (of or by other non-financial firms)—set clear limits on the range of diversification possible and hence explain a great deal of cross-national variation in group structure. Business groups may devise diversification strategies based on economies of scope or risk reduction, but they are ultimately constrained by the boundaries established by government policies. These three policy boundaries, though, differ in their effects over time. Banking regulations and state ownership (nationalization or privatization) can change quickly, sometimes overnight, and business groups can adjust just as quickly by buying up (or relinquishing) banks and state enterprises. In contrast, MNC entry, especially in manufacturing, establishes a path-dependent boundary that is subject to much less change in the short run and has a decisive long-term impact on group strategy.

A full analysis of these external restrictions on business group expansion would also examine the varying motives that political leaders have to intervene. The most common motives are inspired by various kinds of nationalism, state-led development, as well as more pragmatic or panicked reactions to short-term crises. However, even pro-labor governments like the Social Democrats in Sweden had reasons to support business groups (Högfeldt 2005). It is hard to establish clear patterns of cross-national variation in these motivations; however, in broad brush strokes, nationalism in Latin America tended to be more permissive with regard to the entry of MNCs and more expansive with state enterprises than states in East Asia (see Gereffi and Wyman 1990), which left more space for business groups to expand in Asia.

23.3 POLITICAL ADVANTAGES
OF BUSINESS GROUPS

Another way to approach the issue of business groups and politics is to consider the advantages they have over smaller specialized firms or MNCs.[7] Business groups have several market advantages, including access to low-cost capital, but it is in politics that they most outdistance their rivals. As is common for big firms everywhere, there are numerous cases where business groups lobby successfully for individual benefits, and Section 23.4 examines more examples of crony capitalism and patrimonial groups. The focus here is more on generic political advantages, especially access and information. Although substantial, these advantages should not be overstated and are no guarantee to longevity, as the high turnover among business groups in some countries attests.

A first advantage is that business groups benefit disproportionately from measures designed to favor "national capital" or the "national bourgeoisie," as with restrictions on foreign ownership, discrimination in public contracts, sympathetic regulations, or subsidized credit. Preferential policies have continued through a series of changing development strategies. So, for example, business groups benefited under ISI from protection, licensing, and subsidized credit (Guillén 2001), then later during privatization from favorable regulation (Manzetti 1999: 83–4). Privatized firms also sometimes retained special protections. In Brazil, for example, the government retained a "golden share" (veto power) in part to fend off MNC suitors in privatized firms (Aldrighi and Postali, Chapter 13, this volume). Overall, though the origins of business groups cannot be tied to any single development strategy, government commitment to a "national bourgeoisie," using the policies *du jour*, gives business groups a leg up.

Moreover, business groups simplify coordination and communication for governments. When policy-makers need information or cooperation, they regularly call together, formally or informally, the heads of the largest business groups (Schneider 2004a). In Mexico, for example, all major business group owners belonged to the Consejo Mexicano de Hombres de Negocios (CMHN or Mexican Council of Businessmen). The CMHN had forty or so members, by invitation only, and CMHN explicitly excluded MNCs and smaller firms. The CMHN met every month for lunch

---

[7] This section draws on Schneider (2008).

with a government minister and usually annually with the President of Mexico. This sort of access was repeated throughout Latin America, though usually more informally, and if anything with smaller numbers of the very largest business groups. This privileged access gave owners of business groups ample opportunity to present their views, as well as gain important advantages in information on policy-making.

This access was part of a broader informational edge that business groups had, based also on internal research departments and formal access to information on policy-making, either directly or through business associations. Beyond the extreme case of CMHN, governments around the world regularly set up myriad public–private or business–government councils and forums, usually inviting representatives of business associations to participate (Campos and Root 1996; Schneider 2009a). Within associations, business groups tend to wield more influence than smaller firms, and MNC members are fairly passive and discreet (Schneider 2004a). Moreover, business groups sometimes paid employees to be presidents and directors of business associations.[8] In other cases, larger members make voluntary contributions to associations, which helps amplify their voices.

Beyond formal relations, business groups also have informal means of increasing access, and adjust their "political investments" according to their returns in their evolving political systems (for a full analysis of this portfolio approach to politics, see Schneider, forthcoming). Among other things, business groups contribute to electoral campaigns and parties, and cultivate ties with high-level bureaucrats. Especially in appointive bureaucracies, as in the Americas, top officials tend to circulate through high-level positions in the executive branch, think tanks, consulting firms, and management positions in private firms. Along the way, they are likely to have a lot of contact with major business groups. Overall, all forms of privileged access increased the potential returns from politically sensitive assets (for example, subject to government promotion, regulation, or intervention, as in public utilities and media) for business groups relative to other foreign or national investors.[9]

This view of political advantages is less restrictive than several formulations that emphasize path dependence or economic entrenchment (North 1990; Bebchuk and Roe 1999; La Porta et al. 2000: 21; Morck et al. 2005). In their strongest form these arguments posit a closed loop or vicious reinforcing cycle where business groups have great power in the political system and wield that power for economic gain that in turn increases their political power (and the intensity of their interests in maintaining government protection for their firms). The main flaw with this strong

---

[8] Interview with Agustín Legorreta, ex-president of Banamex, the largest business group in Mexico before 1982, July 28, 1998.

[9] The fact that nearly all business groups are family owned and managed in most countries provides some additional political advantages (at the same time it may detract from managerial performance) largely because of their ability to make long-term commitments and political investments. Managers of MNCs, for example, come and go, but owners of business groups stay on. Group owners can cultivate long-term relations with elected politicians and technocrats who are likely to rise in executive positions, and they can be expected to work against the career ambitions of those who cross them.

entrenchment argument is that it cannot account for high turnover among major business groups.[10]

It is remarkable that some business groups have survived for generations, but what is more relevant analytically is that many seemingly invincible economic empires have collapsed and similar-looking new ones have emerged to replace them. The incumbents change, but the business group form lives on. In Brazil, less than one-quarter of the 500 largest firms in 1973 were still among the top 500 by 2006 (*Valor Online* 2006). By another calculation, of the forty largest business groups in Brazil in 1978, only nineteen were still among the forty largest in 2005. Of the twenty-one that had disappeared, six had been acquired by other Brazilian groups, five had been bought out by MNCs, and ten had gone bankrupt (Aldrighi and Postali, Chapter 13, this volume). In Mexico from 1986 to 1998, a period that began with economic crisis and rapid market reform, twenty-seven business groups disappeared from the ranks of the largest and twenty-five new groups emerged. Of the twenty-seven that disappeared, fifteen were acquired by other groups or MNCs (Hoshino, Chapter 15, this volume). The point theoretically is that a high level of turnover among business groups is not consistent with interest group formulations of path dependence and entrenchment (the next section takes up the question of why rates of turnover vary cross-nationally).[11]

Self-seeking entrenchment may, though, be a better way to understand continuity in the financial view of business groups and the resilience of pyramids. Most countries have enacted reforms for stock markets and corporate governance over the 1990s and 2000s, in many cases with a view to strengthening protections for minority shareholders (see Oman 2003). However, what is revealing in these various reform efforts is what they have left out; most lack significant challenges to pyramidal corporate structures. The standard Machiavellian reform calculus seems especially strong here: the potential beneficiaries (future minority shareholders) of reform are weak (because they are dispersed, stand each to gain little, and may be unaware they are potential beneficiaries), while the losers (owners of pyramidal groups) are strong, well organized, and stand to lose a great deal. With the cards stacked this way, the absence of reform is not surprising.

The experience of one country that did eliminate pyramids, the United States, is illuminating (Morck 2005b). Business groups were the dominant corporate form in the United States prior to the reforms in corporate taxation enacted in 1935 by the Roosevelt administration that essentially outlawed business groups by making their dividends subject to double taxation. The key item in these reforms was to raise intercorporate taxation of dividends (which is quite low in most countries), which meant that the profits of lower-tier firms would be taxed again and again as they passed up the multiple tiers in large pyramidal business groups. Business groups in the United States responded

[10] Another problem is that major policies affecting business groups, especially market reforms in the 1990s, changed dramatically in ways that hurt many pre-existing business groups, sometimes mortally, without much evidence that business groups had a direct hand in designing these reforms. For a review, see Schneider (2004b).

[11] Similarly, Khanna and Yafeh (2007: 357–8) find that "the turnover in leading Indian groups across the past sixty years is far too high to be consistent with entrenchment and close group–government ties".

by selling off subsidiaries or buying them outright, and pyramids were quickly extinct.[12] This case of reform is revealing on two counts. First, the elimination of pyramids was fairly simple in terms of legal and regulatory instruments. The Roosevelt reformers knew what tax changes they wanted and got Congress to enact new regulations, and pyramidal business groups rapidly disappeared.[13]

Secondly, the reform happened under extreme political circumstances that empowered government reformers and discredited business elites. The collapse of several highly indebted business groups in the wake of the 1929 crash contributed to the popular view that business groups shared a large measure of responsibility for the depression. Writing in the *American Economic Review* in 1935, Blakey and Blakey captured vividly some of the outrage directed at pyramidal business groups: "There can be no denying that the President's message was an attack upon wealth; he and his followers would say, not upon innocent wealth, but upon concentrated, monopolistic, taxevading, unsocial wealth, and particularly upon that taken from the masses by the vicious, pyramided, consciousless holding companies" (Blakey and Blakey 1935, cited in Morck 2005b: 156). A plausible working hypothesis is that anti-pyramid reforms are unlikely without similarly extreme political conditions.

Overall, though, arguments that emphasize rent seeking, interest groups, and path dependence or a general bias to continuity need to avoid two pitfalls. The first is the assumption of fairly direct translation of economic into political power. Resources always help in politics, but they are rarely the only factors. The second is methodological—namely, selection bias. If the analysis focuses exclusively on the evaluation of existing groups, it is usually possible to find significant rents somewhere in their histories, and conclude that rents, and the political pressure deployed to get them, were essential to their success. However, adding to the sample the other business groups that disappeared, despite their rents, greatly weakens the correlation.

23.4 Degrees of political intimacy

Beyond generic political advantages, the degree of political intimacy varies significantly across business groups. A well-known example is the distinction between Suharto and non-Suharto groups in Indonesia (Hanani 2006). While such distinctions are less black

---

[12] Diversified conglomerates (with wholly owned subsidiaries in multiple sectors) of course lived on and thrived in the postwar period until the 1980s, when they succumbed to regulatory reform, hostile takeovers, and institutional investors (Zorn et al. 2006). That diversified conglomerates had such different political and institutional dynamics from pyramidal groups underscores the argument in the introduction that we need clearly to differentiate business groups on these multiple dimensions.

[13] The only other country with a similar minimal presence of business groups is the United Kingdom. Reforms there came later and relied on a different, but equally straightforward, takeover regulation (Morck 2005b: 7–8).

and white in other regions, most countries manifest clear cases on each end of the continuum of intimacy. The concept of political intimacy is not restricted narrowly to crony capitalism, as found under Suharto, Marcos, or Yeltsin, but also comprises business groups that most thoroughly "buy into" the government's major policies, be they developmentalist, as in Brazil or Korea in the 1970s, or neo-liberal, as in Argentina or India in the 1990s. A major external indicator of a group's level of intimacy would be periods of rapid expansion in group activities that cannot be explained by normal economic factors, as in the expansion of the *chaebol* in Korea in the 1970s, the meteoric rise of the Cruzat–Larrain grupo in Chile in the same period, or the rapid growth of many business groups through privatization in the 1990s. Cronyism characterized relations in many cases, but it was also combined with official industrial policies or market reforms that granted business groups preferential access to subsidies, protection, or state assets.

Business groups on the more intimate end of the spectrum generally have more volatile fortunes, rising quickly when they are close to political patrons and falling dramatically, Icarus like, once the incumbents or policies change or the business group falls out of favor. However, some adept groups use their close connections, like a gravitational slingshot, to launch them into longer-term expansion even after their government patrons have decamped. However, on the end of greater political intimacy, Icarus groups seem to outnumber slingshot groups. These differences are best illustrated by contrasting the longer-term trajectories of groups in particular countries.

In Mexico, business groups in the northern city of Monterrey historically stood apart from those in Mexico City in cultural, familial, and political terms (Camp 1989). Monterrey groups were largely independent (at least through the 1980s), generally opposed central governments in the twentieth century, and sometimes counter-mobilized through new parties and associations. The Banamex and Carso groups represent the other end of the spectrum, though with very different endings. Banamex was the largest bank and the core of one of the largest business groups throughout much of the twentieth century. Banamex retained close, harmonious relations with a series of presidents and developed a dense network of ties through major business associations. In addition, Banamex responded enthusiastically to a series of development policies in the second half of the twentieth century designed to promote particular sectors and regulate the entry of MNCs (Hoshino, Chapter 15, this volume). In particular, MNCs in many sectors could enter Mexico only in joint ventures, and Banamex offered itself as a well-connected partner. Even before the government dismantled these policies, it nationalized Banamex in 1982, and, though compensated, the owners were unable to reconfigure a major new group. Carlos Slim, owner of the Grupo Carso, in contrast, cultivated close ties to President Carlos Salinas (1988–94), bought into privatization in a big way, and went on, after Salinas had gone into exile in 1994, to construct the largest business group in Latin America. Slim may have benefited from the fact that his closest political intimacy was relatively short, which may have helped him leverage this brief gravitational boost onto a less dependent trajectory (though Carso's flagship telephone monopoly, Telmex, continued to benefit from favorable government regulation long after 1994).

Chile in the 1970s and 1980s offers one of the most spectacular examples of Icarus groups. In the mid-1970s the Pinochet dictatorship embarked on radical neo-liberal reform that included a fire sale of government-owned firms as well as overnight opening of product and capital markets. Two business groups, Cruzat–Larraín and BHC, had especially close relations with the Pinochet government, maintained in part by a handful of economists who circulated through top positions in government as well as top jobs in these groups. Both business groups leapt at new opportunities and used international loans to buy up dozens of firms the government was auctioning off, to become, in the span of a few years, the dominant companies in Chile. Cruzat–Larraín grew from eleven companies in 1974 to eighty-five companies just three years later, while BHC grew from eighteen to sixty-two companies in the same period. By 1978, these two groups controlled more than 37 percent of the assets of the 250 largest firms in Chile and 40 percent of private-sector bank assets (Silva 1997: 160–1). The next two largest groups, Matte and Luksic, controlled only 12 percent of the assets of the 250 largest firms. But, when the debt crisis hit Chile with devastating impact in 1982, Cruzat–Larraín and BHC collapsed, and the government took over most of their assets. The Matte and Luksic groups survived to become two of the largest groups in the 2000s.[14]

In other countries the reversals of fortune have been less extreme. In Brazil, as noted above, turnover on the list of largest groups has been high, though how much of the turnover is due to changing political fortunes is unclear. Two business groups, Votorantim and Villares, illustrate well the range of political strategies over the late twentieth century. Votorantim earned a reputation in the 1970s for refusing to follow government direction, and subsidy, into new sectors, preferring instead to stick with its own more gradual and focused strategy of growth and diversification.[15] Villares, in contrast, grew very rapidly in the 1970s, and responded to several government initiatives to expand into sectors such as capital goods, metals, and even computing. In one instance, Paulo Villares planned, with government support, to invest in capital goods. By coincidence he met then president Ernesto Geisel, who asked him how much Villares was planning to invest. When Villares responded, Geisel immediately said: "double it, and we'll make sure it works out." Villares doubled the investment, but by 1982 the government was in the middle of an economic crisis, and Geisel was no longer in office (interview, August 2, 2006). By the late 1980s Villares was selling off subsidiaries, and by the 1990s, in part because of a debilitating family crisis, the group was a marginal operation compared to its standing in the 1970s. Votorantim, in contrast, entered the 1990s in much stronger shape and continued to thrive into the 2000s.

In Argentina, several Icarus groups soared in the early 1990s only to plummet by the 2000s. Among the groups that endorsed Menem's stabilization polices and

---

[14] In a longer-term calculation of high turnover in Chile, only three of the largest groups in the 2000s were among the large groups in the 1960s (Lefort, Chapter 14, this volume).

[15] Evans (1979) provides an early comparison of these two groups and highlights the fact that Votorantim was the only business group in Brazil that resisted policy and other inducements to enter into joint ventures with MNCs in the 1960s and 1970s. For a complete history of both groups, see Reiss (1980).

participated in broad privatization policies were Macri, Fortabat (Loma Negra), Perez Companc, Soldati, and Techint. Most of these groups went into debt to buy up privatized firms in new sectors, and most of them came out poorly (see Fracchia, Mesquita, and Quiroga, Chapter 12, this volume). Fortabat and Perez Companc ended up selling out to Brazilian firms, while Macri and Soldati sold off many subsidiaries and came through the decade in much leaner form (Finchelstein 2004) (interview with Santiago Soldati, September 18, 2007). More of a slingshot case, Techint was, among the intimate groups, one that came through well, in part because its acquisitions were more closely related to its core steel business and because it relied more on exports than other business groups. One of the groups that chose to maintain its distance was Arcor, a group with core activities in candies and diversified subsidiaries in related industries (sugar, packaging, and other food products).

In sum, business groups differ in their propensity to invest in politics, to seek rents, to follow government policies, and to prosper through politics. The consequences also differ. Some politicized groups rise and fall quickly, often through acquisitions and then spin-offs, in an Icarus syndrome. Other initially politicized business groups leverage their political gains into long-term growth, in a sort of gravitational slingshot. The non-politicized firms experience neither the policy induced booms, nor the subsequent busts, but grow more slowly, usually through greenfield investments rather than large-scale, leapfrogging acquisitions.

The collapse of politically connected firms raises two further, related questions: why do governments withdraw support for previously favored firms, and why, more generally, do turnover rates among top business groups vary cross-nationally? On the first question, Khanna and Yafeh (2007: 359) propose a possible life cycle of relations: "from government protégés to a strong lobby with often captured regulators . . . Or to a sector that loses favor with the authorities because of its excessive influence." Although systematic data are lacking, some prominent cases seem to fit this life-cycle hypothesis. For example, excessive influence seems a plausible motive in the intervention by the Russian government in Yukos; however, it would be important to add "anti-government" to characterize the perceived quality of Yukos's influence (see Guriev and Rachinsky 2005). Similarly, firms that do not show active enough enthusiasm for government patrons may fall out of favor, as was reportedly part of the reason for the government's withdrawal of support for the Kukje *chaebol* in the 1980s (Kang 2002).

Government turnover, especially from one end of the political spectrum to the other (for example, from left to right or from democratic to authoritarian), can turn previously cozy relations into liabilities. What look like normal, close relations between business groups and one government may seem like "excessive influence" to the next. So, when he took office in 1998, Kim Dae Jung presumably had few incentives (beyond avoiding the collapse of the financial system) to come to the rescue of *chaebol* he had so long publicly reviled. Similarly, the de la Rua government in Argentina might not have worried overly about the business groups that had strongly supported, and at least initially benefited from, the previous Peronist government of Carlos Menem. More generally, incoming governments with strong commitments to new development strategies may view existing business groups as part of the discredited old order. This disdain may have informed some of the actions, or rather inactions, in favor of existing business groups on the part of radical neo-liberal reformers such as Salinas and Fernando Collor in Brazil in the early 1990s. Collor in fact openly castigated what he considered retrograde, rent-seeking businesses. His government did not last long enough to do more than initiate a process of trade liberalization, but the opening did in the end have mortal consequences for several large business groups.

Presumably some of these factors help explain cross-national variation in levels of turnover among the largest business groups. For example, Khanna and Yafeh (2007: 362) find that "the list of the top ten business groups has changed dramatically over the past three decades in India and Taiwan, but has remained very stable in South Korea and Thailand." In Latin America, high rates of turnover characterize Brazil, Mexico, Chile, Argentina, and Peru, in contrast to greater stability in Colombia and possibly Venezuela. Turnover in Russia from the 1990s to 2000s was very high: "out of the seven or eight business groups that dominated Yeltsin's Russia," two succumbed to the 1998 crisis and the leaders of three others are in exile or prison (Guriev and Rachinsky 2005: 135). Other countries in Asia, Europe, and elsewhere with lower levels of turnover in the late twentieth century included Italy, Sweden, Japan, Singapore, South Africa, and Turkey.

Although we lack systematic cross-national data, these lists suggest several hypotheses.[16] First, the clustering of the largest countries (save Japan) in the high-turnover camp might mean that there are fewer barriers to entry for new, emerging business groups in larger countries with multiple regional economic poles. Secondly, the clustering of developed countries in the low-turnover group probably means that rates of turnover decline once countries have gone through initial industrialization and specialization in world markets. In addition, lower political volatility and democratic stability may also allow groups to forge more durable protections. Lastly, and relatedly, the concentration in the high-turnover group of countries that have gone through crisis and reform (along the lines of the processes traced in Chile and Mexico in this section) suggests that radical reform is a strong candidate for a decisive short-term explanatory variable.

23.5 CONCLUSION

This chapter has sought to bring political relations and policy into the comparative analysis of the strategies and structures of business groups. Previous explanations for the emergence and survival of diversified groups have emphasized economic factors

---

[16] More precise measures of turnover will have to take care over the selection of the time period for comparison, because some countries are characterized by "punctuated equilibrium," with long periods of stability interrupted by brief moments of turbulence and turnover. Picking periods of either stasis or turmoil would give misleading rankings.

such as shallow capital markets and capital pooling, weak institutional environments and transaction costs, and imperfect markets and missing intermediary institutions such as venture capital and consulting firms. This chapter has emphasized instead political factors such as government and policy volatility, and development strategies, as well as specific policies designed to support business groups or regulate their entry into particular sectors. In addition, the deeper historical roots of weak economic institutions and market imperfections often lie in politics.

Business groups also have significant political advantages over potential rivals, especially privileged access to political leaders and policy-makers that provides crucial insider information as well as opportunities to seek specific rents. However, despite these advantages, business groups often fail, which suggests important limits to theories of entrenchment and path-dependent rent seeking. And, while governments differ in their degree of openness to influence by business groups, so too do firms in their willingness to exploit their opportunities for close connections to political leaders. Understanding these differences in political strategies helps identify business groups that pursue full-contact relations with government, often to their subsequent regret when political conditions and leaders change, versus business groups that opt for more arm's length relations.

This chapter demonstrates that business groups have flourished under all sorts of institutional and policy regimes. This would be even clearer if we included more business groups from developed countries. The implication of this broad spectrum of nurturing environments is that it makes less sense for researchers to attempt to tie the emergence of business groups with any one set of policies, institutions (or missing institutions), or development strategies. Rather, a better point of departure is the assumption that business groups are likely to emerge in any context that does not directly threaten them. Put in ecological terms, business groups, especially diversified business groups, are likely to thrive anywhere natural predators are lacking. Where takeovers are easier, as in the United States in the 1980s or Argentina in the 2000s, diversified groups or conglomerates succumb. What is striking though is how rare such episodes are.

This chapter also advanced several general conceptual and methodological arguments. The first was a suggestion for a greater conceptual and theoretical division of labor, by distinguishing informal groups, pyramids, and diversified groups into separate phenomena to be explained, rather than lumping them all together in a single entity. The hope is that some prior disaggregation and division of research tasks will aid later cumulation and synthesis. The second methodological point was a recommendation for adding an archaeological or postmortem component to the study of business groups. Nearly all empirical studies focus on existing business groups, and seek in their characteristics or environments the sources of their structure and success. However, the many cases, some notorious, of failures of large groups can potentially, as in any good study of morbidity, tell us a lot about the healthy. Expanding our universe of cases to include ex-business groups and the examination of the reasons for their collapse leads to a third, broader, implicit methodological suggestion that researchers get closer to the objects of their inquiry through longer-term historical analysis of individual cases using qualitative sources such as company archives, periodicals, and interviews. Even with greater disciplinary division, most researchers are still interested in core elements of strategy and behavior, and following individual companies over time, as business groups confront shifting contexts and opportunities, can often be the best way to reveal those strategies.

REFERENCES

AMSDEN, A. (2001). *The Rise of "the Rest": Challenges to the West from Late-Industrializing Economies.* Oxford: Oxford University Press.

BARBA NAVARETTI, G., and VENABLES, A. (2004). *Multinational Firms in the World Economy.* Princeton: Princeton University Press.

BEBCHUK, L., and ROE, M. (1999). "A Theory of Path Dependence in Corporate Ownership and Governance," *Stanford Law Review,* 52 (Nov.), 127–70.

BLAKEY, R., and BLAKEY, G. (1935). "The Revenue Act of 1935," *American Economic Review,* 25/4: 673–90.

BUĞRA, A. (1994). *State and Business in Modern Turkey.* Albany, NY: State University of New York Press.

CAMMETT, M. (2007). *Globalization and Business Politics in Arab North Africa: A Comparative Perspective.* New York: Cambridge.

CAMP, R. (1989). *Entrepreneurs and Politics in Twentieth-Century Mexico.* New York: Oxford University Press.

CAMPOS, J., and ROOT, H. (1996). *The Key to the Asian Miracle: Making Shared Growth Credible.* Washington: Brookings Institution.

CHANG, S. J. (2003). *Financial Crisis and Transformation Korean Business Groups: The Rise and Fall of Chaebols.* New York: Cambridge University Press.

CHUNG, C. N. (2001). "Markets, Culture, and Institutions: The Emergence of Large Business Groups in Taiwan, 1950s–1970s," *Journal of Management Studies,* 38/5 (July), 719–45.

COLLIN, S. O. (1998). "Why Are These Islands of Conscious Power Found in the Ocean of Ownership? Institutional and Governance Hypotheses Explaining the Existence of Business Groups in Sweden," *Journal of Management Studies,* 35/6 (Nov.), 719–46.

EVANS, P. (1979). *Dependent Development.* Princeton: Princeton University Press.

FINCHELSTEIN, D. (2004). "El Comportamiento Empresario Durante la Década de los Noventa: El Grupo Macri," *Realidad Económica,* 203 (Apr.), 26–49.

GANEV, V. (2001). "The Dorian Grey Effect: Winners as State Breakers in Postcommunism," *Communist and Post-Communist Studies,* 34: 1–25.

GEREFFI, G., and WYMAN, D. (1990) (eds.). *Manufacturing Miracles.* Princeton: Princeton University Press.

GRANOVETTER, M. (2005). "Business Groups and Social Organization," in N. Smelser and R. Swedberg (eds.), *Handbook of Economic Sociology.* 2nd edn. Princeton: Princeton University Press.

GUILLÉN, M. (2001). *The Limits of Convergence: Globalization and Organizational Change in Argentina, South Korea, and Spain.* Princeton: Princeton University Press.

GURIEV, S., and RACHINSKY, A. (2005). "The Role of Oligarchs in Russian Capitalism," *Journal of Economic Perspectives*, 19/1 (Winter), 131–50.

HANANI, A. (2006). "Indonesian Business Groups: The Crisis in Progress," in S. J. Chang, *Business Groups in East Asia*. New York: Oxford University Press.

HÖGFELDT, P. (2004). "The History and Politics of Corporate Ownership in Sweden". NBER Working Paper 10641, Cambridge, MA.

HÖGFELDT, P. (2005). "The History and Politics of Corporate Ownership in Sweden," in R. Morck (ed.), *A History of Corporate Governance around the World*. Chicago: University of Chicago Press.

JOHNSON, J. (1997). "Russia's Emerging Financial Industrial Groups," *Post-Soviet Affairs*, 13/4: 333–65.

KANG, C. K. (1997). "Diversification Process and the Ownership Structure of Samsung Chaebol," in T. Shiba and M. Shimotani (eds.), *Beyond the Firm*. New York: Oxford University Press.

KANG, D. (2002). *Crony Capitalism: Corruption and Development in South Korea and the Philippines*. New York: Cambridge University Press.

KHANNA, T., and PALEPU, K. (1997). "Why Focused Strategies May be Wrong for Emerging Markets," *Harvard Business Review*, 75/4 (July–Aug.), 41–51.

KHANNA, T., and YAFEH, Y. (2007). "Business Groups in Emerging Markets: Paragons or Parasites?" *Journal of Economic Literature*, 45 (June), 331–72.

KING, L., and SZELÉNYI, I. (2005). "Post-Communist Economic Systems," in N. Smelser and R. Swedberg (eds.), *Handbook of Economic Sociolog*. 2nd edn. Princeton: Princeton University Press.

LA PORTA, R., LÓPEZ-DE-SILANES, F., SHLEIFER, A., and VISHNY, R. (2000). "Investor Protection and Corporate Governance," *Journal of Financial Economics*, 58/1: 3–27.

LEFF, N. (1978). "Industrial Organization and Entrepreneurship in the Developing Countries: The Economic Groups," *Economic Development and Cultural Change*, 26/4 (July), 661–75.

MAMAN, D. (2002). "The Emergence of Business Groups: Israel and South Korea Compared," *Organization Studies*, 23: 737–58.

MANZETTI, L. (1999). *Privatization South American Style*. New York: Oxford University Press.

MARTINEZ-DIAZ, L. (2009). *Globalizing in Hard Times: The Politics of Banking-Sector Opening in the Emerging World*. Ithaca, NY: Cornell University Press.

MORCK, R. (2005a) (ed.), *A History of Corporate Governance around the World: Family Business Groups to Professional Managers*. Chicago: University of Chicago Press.

MORCK, R. (2005b). "How to Eliminate Pyramidal Business Groups: The Double Taxation of Inter-Corporate Dividends and Other Incisive Uses of Tax Policy," *Tax Policy and the Economy*, 19/1: 135–79.

MORCK, R., WOLFENZON, D., and YEUNG, B. (2005). "Corporate Governance, Economic Entrenchment, and Growth," *Journal of Economic Literature*, 43/3 (Sept.), 655–720.

NORTH, D. (1990). *Institutions, Institutional Change and Economic Performance*. New York: Cambridge University Press.

OMAN, C. (2003) (ed.). *Corporate Governance in Development: The Experiences of Brazil, Chile, India, and South Africa*. Paris: OECD and CIPE.

REISS, G. (1980). "Development of Brazilian Industrial Enterprise: A Historical Perspective." PhD dissertation, University of California, Berkeley.

RIVERA, T. (2003). "The Leading Chinese–Filipino Business Families in Post-Marcos Philippines," in K. S. Jomo and B. Folk (eds.), *Ethnic Business*. London: RoutledgeCurzon.

SCHNEIDER, B. R. (2004a). *Business Politics and the State in 20th Century Latin America*. New York: Cambridge University Press.

SCHNEIDER, B. R. (2004b). "Organizing Interests and Coalitions in the Politics of Market Reform in Latin America," *World Politics*, 56 (Apr.).

SCHNEIDER, B. R. (2008). "Economic Liberalization and Corporate Governance: The Resilience of Business Groups in Latin America," *Comparative Politics*, 40/4 (July), 379–98.

SCHNEIDER, B. R. (2009a). "Business–Government Interaction in Policy Councils in Latin America: Cheap Talk, Expensive Exchanges, or Collaborative Learning?" Background paper prepared for the IDB, Washington.

SCHNEIDER, B. R. (2009b). "A Comparative Political Economy of Diversified Business Groups, or How States Organize Capitalism," *Review of International Political Economy*.

SCHNEIDER, B. R. (forthcoming). "Business Politics in Latin America: Sources of Convergence and Divergence," in D. Coen, W. Grant, and G. Wilson (eds.), *Oxford Handbook of Business and Government*. Oxford: Oxford University Press.

SILVA, E. (1997). "Business Elites, the State, and Economic Change in Chile," in S. Maxfield and B. R. Schneider (eds.), *Business and the State in Developing Countries*. Ithaca, NY: Cornell University Press.

Valor Online (2006). Sept. 25.

ZORN, D., DOBBIN, F., DIERKES, J., and KWOK, M. S. (2006). "Managing Investors: How Financial Markets Reshaped the American Firm," in K. Cetina and A. Preda (eds.), *The Sociology of Financial Markets*. New York: Oxford University Press.

CHAPTER 24

CORPORATE GOVERNANCE OF BUSINESS GROUPS

BRIAN K. BOYD

ROBERT E. HOSKISSON

24.1 INTRODUCTION

PRIOR commentaries of research on business groups have highlighted two characteristics of work to date. First, business groups are a relatively underserved research topic, given their prominence in the global economy, especially in emerging economies. Secondly, independent of the volume of research, studies of business groups have covered a limited range of topics (Granovetter 1995; Yiu et al. 2007). Both of these limitations apply equally, if not more so, to the more focused domain of the corporate governance of business groups. While governance is a prominent topic in many disciplines, including management, finance, sociology, and other areas, there have been only a handful of articles that have addressed the intersection of governance and business groups.

The goal of this chapter is to offer an integrative framework for studying the governance of business groups. We begin with a brief summary of the studies focused on the governance of business groups. Next, we review key theoretical perspectives, including agency, resource dependence, institutional theory, and the rubber-stamp model. This section will also examine how board roles may vary across groups in different nations. Next, we examine factors that affect how groups are organized, using the framework of horizontal and vertical connections proposed by Yiu and colleagues (2007). Finally, we integrate these sections to lay out an agenda for future studies. We develop a series of promising research questions across levels of analysis including the governance of business group types as well as member firms within the business group and institution differences and associated governance requirements.

24.2 GOVERNANCE AND BUSINESS GROUPS

What is corporate governance, and how does it relate to the effective management of business groups? While there are many definitions of corporate governance, most center around the role of boards of directors. Lorsch and MacIver (1989) characterized governance as the board's duty to govern the firm, with its primary role exercising power over the top management team and employees. Stating the case more broadly and succinctly, Demb and Neubauer (1992) framed corporate governance as the accountability for firm performance. Charkham (1994) compared corporate governance to the set of checks and balances associated with different branches of government. As such, governance is the system that both directs and controls corporations. Typically, as noted, the focus of corporate governance is on boards of directors: the Cadbury governance code for UK firms, for example, addressed the structure and responsibilities of corporate boards. While most definitions of corporate governance focus on boards of directors, other definitions are more broad, and include the firm's ownership structure as well (see, e.g., Useem 1996; Denis and McConnell 2003). Reporting and disclosure requirements—such as the Sarbanes Oxley Act in the United States—can also fall under the umbrella of corporate governance. For purposes of this chapter, we will focus primarily on the role of the board of directors as a governance mechanism.

By virtue of their complexity, and differences from nation to nation, business groups have been described as being almost invisible to academic researchers (Granovetter 2005). Given the paucity of research on groups (Granovetter 1995; Yiu et al. 2007), it is not surprising that there is limited attention paid to governance issues among groups. Some studies that do address governance of groups focus on ownership issues versus the board of directors (see, e.g., Volpin 2002). Other studies may collect samples in regions where business groups are pervasive, but not distinguish group and non-group firms in their analyses (see, e.g., Zona and Zattoni 2007). Business groups in Chile represent an exception to this omission, with studies treating board characteristics as both a predictor and an outcome variable.

Some business groups are characterized by formal and explicit ties, which makes it relatively easy to identify group members. However, other groups, such as the Japanese *keiretsu*, have far more cloudy definitions of group membership. Khanna and Rivkin (2006) studied a variety of metrics to identify group membership in a sample of Chilean firms. Board interlocks were a prominent predictor of group membership, as were patterns of ownership and indirect equity ties. In contrast, family ties and direct equity links were less effective predictors of group membership. The authors concluded that the study of board ties is an important avenue for business group research.

A second Chilean study examined the performance implications of network connections. Silva, Majluf, and Paredes (2006) examined contingency effects of both family ties and board interlocks on performance. An important finding of their study was that family linkages were more consistently associated with performance than board ties. The latter finding is due to the potential for business groups to destroy, as well as enhance, firm value (Chang 2003). As shown by this review, little is known about the role of boards of directors in business groups. In the following section, we will explore different theories of governance, and how they may relate to the management of groups.

24.3 THEORETICAL PERSPECTIVES ON GOVERNANCE

To begin our review of theoretical perspectives that can be applied to the corporate governance of business groups, we begin with agency theory and resource dependence theory, which offer very different views on the primary function of boards of directors. Next, we examine institutional theory, which focuses on the role of social influences in shaping the board and its actions. Finally, we consider the rubber-stamp perspective on corporate boards. While this is not a theoretical perspective *per se*, this label has been used to describe boards that are relatively inert. We will identify key aspects of each perspective, as well as their particular relevance to business groups.

24.3.1 Agency model of corporate boards

Of the different theoretical perspectives used to study corporate governance, agency theory is the most prevalent. A content analysis of studies published between 1982 and 2008 reported that the bulk of governance studies published in management journals were framed using agency theory (Boyd et al. 2008). The central focus of agency theory lies in a separation of ownership from control, so that the firm's top executives have minimal or no equity in the companies they manage (Berle and Means 1932; Fama and Jensen 1983). An agency problem develops when managers and owners have divergent interests, such as competing preferences for risk. These competing interests become more problematic when there are information asymmetries between owners and agents, or when owners have limited means of disciplining top managers. Consequently, the firm's board of directors is charged with monitoring management on behalf of the owners. While there is a wealth of studies linking governance characteristics to a variety of strategic and tactical outcomes (e.g., Hoskisson et al. 2002; Boyd et al. 2005; Deutsch 2005;), there are also a number of null and mixed findings regarding governance characteristics and firm performance (Dalton et al. 1998).

One limitation of agency research is that the bulk of studies are based on US firms, or firms in other Anglo economies such as the UK. Since the norms for separation of ownership from control differ broadly outside the USA and the UK, the relevance of a traditional agency view for many business groups is arguable (Morck et al. 2005). In fact, one review concluded that the likelihood of managerial agency problems is minimal in many world economies, given the presence of controlling shareholders who have both the incentive and the ability to discipline top executives (LaPorta et al. 1999). However, these same conditions also give rise to a different type of agency problem, where dominant shareholders use their control to abuse minority investors. This is known in the management literature as principal–principal agency theory (Dharwadkar et al. 2000). For example, Bae and colleagues (2002) describe examples of two Korean business groups—LG Group and Samsung—that conducted acquisitions or other deals that provided uneven benefits to majority versus minority investors. Exploitation of minority investors has been linked with a variety of governance conditions, including legal protection, board composition, and other monitoring factors (Bae et al. 2002; Volpin 2002). In family-run business groups, there is also the potential for some family members to exploit other family owners (Morck and Yeung 2003). Overall, it has been argued that the potential for agency problems is more severe in family-based business groups than in free-standing firms (Chang 2003: Morck et al. 2005). However, there is still very limited empirical analysis of the board's role and potential agency problems in business groups. It is also important to note that, while pyramidal group structures are often cited as being prime candidates for the abuse of minority investors, empirical evidence to date is inconclusive on this topic (Khanna 2000).

24.3.2 Resource dependence model of corporate boards

Research on corporate governance has been dominated by agency theory. This emphasis has overshadowed a longer running stream of research on boards as a mechanism to manage challenges and opportunities that emerge beyond the firm's boundaries. Influenced by general systems theory (Bertalanffy 1968), management scholars began to develop theories to explain how firms interact with, and are affected by, their external environments. Resource dependence proposed that executives would respond to, and even proactively manage, their environments (Pfeffer and Salancik 1978; Hillman and Dalziel 2003). Boards of directors figure prominently in the firm's efforts to navigate its environment.

There is a sizable research stream on the role of personal networks as a firm's conduit to crucial information and resources that are not available internally

(Granovetter 1985). One of the most important conduits is the web of external ties that are provided by the board of directors (Mizruchi 1996). Board members are predominantly CEOs and executives of other firms, and typically serve on the boards of one or two other firms (Davis 1996). These board seats bring executives into contact with other executives with comparable ties, thus creating a broad, and complex, set of linkages to other firms. These patterns of board ties have been linked with many aspects of strategic change and adaptation (see, e.g., Useem 1984; Boyd 1990; Haunschild 1993; Carpenter and Westphal 2001). By recruiting prominent executives, the board of directors also helps to secure access to resources by bolstering the firm's legitimacy (Selznick 1949). Finally, a board comprised of experienced directors can also offer valuable insight regarding both the framing and the execution of a company's strategy (Lorsch and MacIver 1989).

The resource dependence model has great relevance for business groups. In a recent review, Khanna and Yafeh (2007: 334) commented that "groups do not only respond to their environment, but also shape and influence it." If business groups do not shape it, they may be reshaped by other power players who are entering the market, such as foreign institutional investors (Ahmadjian and Robbins 2005). Historically, most business groups are created in response to inefficient markets, characterized by poor access to capital, resources, and market information. Groups attempt to overcome these constraints through varying combinations of diversification, vertical integration, and acquisition of financial institutions (Khanna and Yafeh 2007). The boards of business groups have a potentially important role to play in managing group uncertainty, by serving as a connection to other members of the same group, entirely different business groups, and third-party organizations (Kim et al. 2004). Incidentally, Khanna and Yafeh (2007: 334) note that statistical analysis of business groups and their environments "is almost absent." Consequently, there are many opportunities for research on how boards help business groups meet these external demands, which we will address in a subsequent section.

24.3.3 Boards as an institutional phenomenon

Both agency and resource dependence perspectives could be described as being performance oriented: agency hypotheses typically address the prevention of adverse outcomes, while resource dependence looks for ways optimally to respond to external threats. Institutional theory takes a very different perspective on governance, as the focus is not on organizational efficiency. Instead, this perspective examines how organizational decisions are influenced by the social setting in which the firm operates.

Institutional theory proposes that firms in a given setting will gradually become more homogeneous with the passage of time. Firms adopt increasingly common processes and structures, not necessarily because these attributes are competitively desirable, but because there are political and social pressures to conform to institutional norms (DiMaggio and Powell 1983; Meyer and Rowan 1983). Isomorphism is the process of increasing similarity, and can be normative, coercive, or mimetic. Normative isomorphism is associated with increasing professionalism. Trade groups, educators, socialization, and other sources can lead to diffusion of a set of standard practices. For instance, a director might take a positive experience with a CEO assessment practice on one board to the other boards on which he or she serves. As an example, interlocks among Chinese business group members are routinely used to share expertise (Lee and Kang, Chapter 8, this volume). Coercive isomorphism exists when rules—ranging from legislation to voluntary guidelines—are imposed on organizations. Coercive isomorphism explains why many countries develop agency-oriented regulations and governance codes, despite pressing evidence of agency abuses. As Granovetter (2005: 435) commented, the framing of many laws is rooted in agency theory. There is a widespread implicit assumption that such framing is inherently desirable, such that, "as countries advance, they will increasingly adopt similar legislation." A common example of this phenomenon is the widespread adoption of governance codes, such as Singapore, that emphasize board independence and CEO duality (Tsui-Auch and Yoshikawa, Chapter 10, this volume). In general, these codes are based more on similar provisions made in foreign governance codes, rather than on specific incidents regarding CEO duality or board composition. Similarly, Brazil has adopted multiple tiers of voluntary governance practices (Aldrighi and Postali, Chapter 13, this volume). Wholesale adoption of governance practices from other regions can be problematic, for two reasons. First, there is scant empirical evidence supporting many of the governance guidelines. Secondly, some practices may not be equally desirable from country to country (Norburn et al. 2000; Finkelstein and Mooney 2003; Finegold et al. 2007). Turkey, for instance, is one of many countries that have followed global standards to improve governance by adding unaffiliated outside board members. However, faced with powerful family members who also serve on the board, and the relatively smaller amount of knowledge held by these outsiders, these unaffiliated directors carry little influence regarding key decisions (Colpan, Chapter 17, this volume).

A third type of imitation, mimetic isomorphism, occurs when firms adopt behaviors or processes solely through imitation of others. Mimetic behavior is usually based on high-status firm—market leaders, high performers, or other highly prominent companies (Di Maggio and Powell 1983). As an example of this process, in Germany, the adoption of stock options was originally contested, but, as key Germany firms had "exposure to high-status institutional environments" in which this pay practice was legitimate, they began to change, and over time this practice became widely accepted (Sanders and Tuschke 2007). Foreign firms are often prime candidates for imitation. Mimetic behavior is particularly relevant to the governance of business groups, for two reasons. First, mimetic behavior is more common in environments characterized by high uncertainty (Oliver 1991). For instance, business groups in both China and Russia, for example, were established using horizontal *keiretsu* and *chaebol* groups as templates (Johnson 2000; Keister 2000). Therefore, the same market inefficiencies that gave rise to many business groups also create prime conditions for imitation. Secondly, imitation can be costly to the firm, because the process or behavior is not appropriate to the setting, or because the adopter does not have the absorptive capacity to implement it effectively. Consequently, adopted behaviors and methods might be inefficient, or even counterproductive, in the new setting (Newman 2000).

24.3.4 Boards as a rubber stamp

The rubber-stamp perspective, also labeled as managerial control, asserts that boards are powerless figureheads. The boards of many firms have been characterized as the organizational equivalent of an appendix—an organ that serves no useful purpose. Such boards provide little or no contribution in the way of oversight or strategy support, and perhaps minimal or no contribution to the firm's prestige as well (Mace 1971; Drucker 1981). With a rubber-stamp board, the power for all strategic decisions resides with the firm's top executives. While the board may provide some legitimacy, the simplest explanation for its presence is that most firms are legally required to create a board of directors. Rubber-stamp boards can exist in a variety of settings, with varying implications. For instance, consider a smaller firm that is managed by its founder. Having created the firm and holding a majority ownership stake, the CEO might see little need for monitoring, and might possibly require only limited advice regarding strategic direction. Consequently, the CEO might create a board populated by friends and family simply to conform to regulatory requirements. An inactive board in this setting might lead to lost opportunities, but the consequences may not be fatal to the organization. A more problematic case is the board of a large firm that is comprised of many fragmented owners. In this environment, top executives might create a weak board as a means to evade monitoring and pursue their own agendas. A third scenario is that of a firm that is legally an independent entity, but is essentially just a division of another firm. Kriger (1988), for instance, noted that the boards of many subsidiary companies are often characterized as "dummy" or "captive" boards. This could happen in many joint venture firms, which are dominated by two powerful owners, one of which may dominate with slightly more ownership.

The rubber-stamp scenario has several implications for business groups. While it may be difficult to envision a situation where an inert board is actually desirable, the negative implications might vary substantially across settings. For example, some groups have very strong ownership of their subsidiaries, while others might hold only the minimal levels needed to establish control. The monitoring and control needs differ substantially in these two settings. Similarly, the potential for principal–principal conflicts, where dominant owners take advantage of minority shareholders, will also vary depending on the ownership structure. Therefore, rubber-stamp boards may be more problematic in settings that have greater potential for the abuse of minority investors. Cultural differences suggest that the potential for agency problems will vary substantially for business groups in different regions. Self-maximization is a core assumption of agency theory. However, the likelihood of self-serving behavior can vary across nations. Hofstede (2001) found that the United States scored much higher on the "individualism" value index than other nations. Italy also reported a high ranking on individualism, particularly in regard to neighboring European nations. A strong proclivity to individualism creates greater temptation to maximize one's own benefit at the expense of the company. A second cultural characteristic related to agency problems is time orientation. Agency problems can arise when a manager has the opportunity to create an immediate personal benefit by sacrificing the firm's long-term interests. When a manager's mindset is oriented toward long-term outcomes, there is less potential for divergence between personal and company goals. Hofstede's data reveal systematic differences in time orientation across regions: both the US and many European nations have fairly short time orientations. Brazil has a longer term outlook than the USA, but an appreciably shorter one than much of Asia. Also, it is important to note that regions are not monolithic in their values: Thailand, for example, reported a much shorter time orientation than either Hong Kong or Taiwan. As the needs for oversight will differ based on national characteristics, so will the implication of different governance structures. For example, CEO duality has a small, negative relationship with firm performance in the USA (Boyd 1995), and a modest, positive correlation with firm performance in many European firms, a finding attributed to cultural differences (Boyd et al. 1997). Additionally, the effect differed by country in the study of European duality: the use of CEO–chairmen was positively linked with return on investment in the UK sample, but non-significant for the Italian and Swiss samples. Consequently, board monitoring may be more critical in business groups characterized by high levels of individualism (for example, in Italy), versus levels that are moderate (for example, in Brazil) or low (for example, in Thailand or Taiwan).

Generally, most studies of governance topics are framed using a single theoretical perspective. However, as shown in this section, there are multiple perspectives on the role of the board of directors. Integrative frameworks offer the potential to improve our understanding of organizations, as they can test for both contradictions and points of overlap between different governance predictions (e.g., Boyd 1995; Hillman and Dalziel 2003). In the next section, we examine how Yiu and colleagues (2007) integrated agency and resource roles to deal with coordination challenges associated with business groups.

24.4 Coordination processes within business groups

Business groups are far from monolithic. Not only are there differences in the structure of business groups across countries; there can also be substantial variation in the manner that groups are configured within a single nation. For example, large business groups in China tend to be state owned, while smaller groups are typically owned by families (Lee and Kang, Chapter 8, this volume). In Taiwan, the degree of group diversification seems to be related to the extent of political ties among group members (Chung and Mahmoud, Chapter 7, this volume). And, in Thailand, family-owned groups can be family managed, professionally managed, or use a combination of both approaches (Suehiro and Wailerdsak, Chapter 9, this volume). In order to make prescriptions regarding the governance of business groups, it is necessary to understand the different ways that groups can be configured.

We focused on a framework offered by Yiu and colleagues (2007) because it offers four different types of groups that might require different governance arrangement and thereby allows us to suggest how these different types of groups might require different governance mechanisms for illustrative purposes. Although Yiu and colleagues (2007) describe only four ideal types or organizational forms, in practice it may be useful to think of these as four archetypes with many potential intermediate configurations. The first part of their model examines how four factors combine to shape business groups: market conditions, social setting, political and economic factors, and agency factors. As shown in Fig. 24.1, these four elements will shape the need for different types of connectivity within a group. The first component, *external market conditions*, is rooted in transaction-cost economics. Here, business groups emerge in response to underdeveloped market institutions. Mexico is an ideal example of these conditions, which include poor legal protection, lack of both

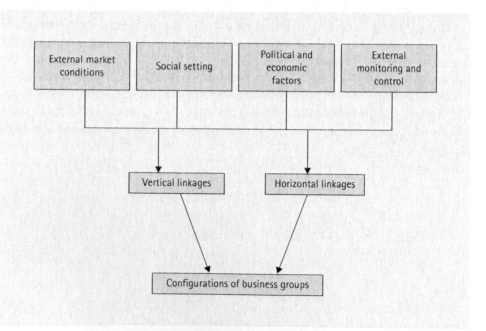

Figure 24.1 Determinants of business group configuration

Source: Adapted from Yiu et al (2007).

human and financial capital, and a weak economy. Many of the groups in Chile were formed under similar conditions, as are the groups in many emerging economies. It is important to note that not all groups are affected by imperfect market conditions. In Thailand, for instance, many groups have been launched following the creation of the Thai Stock Exchange, which should presumably have eased access to capital through an improved market for equity capital. Similarly, many of the most powerful Israeli groups have formed as recently as the 1990s, despite having fairly sophisticated market conditions. The *social setting* is another factor that can shape business groups. The rationale for this component is that organizational survival is rooted in alignment to the local social context. Consequently, the structure of groups will be influenced by local conditions. In India, for instance, there is a norm of social solidarity, which leads to high degrees of trust and reciprocity. In contrast, Chilean groups have a reputation for being very guarded with strategic information (Lefort, Chapter 14, this volume). Consequently, among Chilean groups, it is common to keep ownership, board members, and even company information private within a group. The third component, *political and economic factors*, is related to efforts by host governments to advance national economic development (Keister 1998). For instance, initial business groups in both China and Israel were state supported. Governments often take special initiatives to protect domestic groups, such as policies in Mexico to protect groups from foreign competition. As seen in Argentina, there can be considerable upheaval when a state decides to reduce its support for groups. Finally, *external monitoring and control* represents the potential for agency conflicts. Pyramidal holdings are common in many groups, including those in Argentina, Chile, Italy, Mexico, Taiwan, Thailand, and others. Different pyramids vary widely in the strength of their ownership chains, with corresponding variability in the potential for the abuse of minority investors.

Faced with these four sources of constraint, business groups respond with two types of internal coordination mechanisms: horizontal and vertical connections. Horizontal ties refer to connections among individual group firms, and can take many forms. Each member firm in a group usually has its own board of directors. Anecdotally, shared board ties, or interlocks, are common within member firms of a group—a point raised by many of the country chapters in this volume. While these interlocks can serve many purposes, including both resource provision and oversight, little research has been done empirically to assess the role of interlocks among group members. Social ties among the board members are another type of horizontal connection, and can be considered a less formal counterpart to official board connections. Cross-shareholdings are a third type of horizontal connection, where group members hold reciprocal shares of other member firms. These equity links can serve as a monitoring mechanism, and also help to protect members from outsiders, such as takeover threats. A final type of horizontal connection is resource exchange between member firms. Groups that are vertically integrated or pursue related diversification will have higher levels of cross-firm transactions than groups that pursue unrelated diversification. Russian groups, as an example, rely heavily on vertical integration and scale economies as a source of competitive advantage.

In contrast, South Africa'a and Japan's post-war bank-centered groups have loose ties between members; for example, they have unobtrusive interaction to coordinate activities through integrative mechanisms such as a president's council.

Vertical ties are a chain of command that runs through a group hierarchically, often described as a pyramid. Equity connections are the foundation of this command structure, and are often supplemented by placing loyal personnel, such as family members, in key positions as members of subordinate groups (Yiu et al. 2007). Some groups have virtually no vertical connectivity, such as groups with only lateral cross-holdings, such as bank-centered business groups in Japan (Granovetter 1995). Other groups, in comparison, are characterized by strong one-way ownership ties. These vertical ties exist when there is a dominant owner, usually a family or a government. For groups with vertical connections, some will have very strong equity links (for example, near total ownership of subordinate member firms), while others will maintain only the minimum ownership level needed to maintain control, possibly through voting rights. These chains can include a mix of public and private firms as well. Both Zattoni (1999) and Volpin (2002) show simplified examples of Italian pyramids, while Morck and Yeung (2003) show the interplay of public and private equity in Canada's Brofman family group. While some nations may allow a combination of cross-holdings and pyramids (for example, Thailand), other nations prohibit cross-holdings among pyramid members (for example, Chile and Italy).

Owner involvement can take various forms in these vertical chains. Israel, for instance, has a very tight ownership chain accompanied by strict monitoring. Strategy development is often managed in these groups as a collaboration between owners and subordinate management (Kosenko and Yafeh, Chapter 16, this volume). Korea, in comparison, exerts very strong control over the strategies of group members (Kim, Chapter 6, this volume). Owner elites in pyramids can often enhance their control through mechanisms such as disproportionate voting rights or non-voting stock. Maman (1999) describes how Israeli groups enhance control through placement of managers in a variety of governance roles in subordinate firms, including board seats, executive committee, and chairman positions.

Yiu et al. (2007) suggest that the combination of horizontal and vertical connections yields four possible configurations of business groups, as shown in Fig. 24.2: network (N-form), club (C-form), holding (H-form), and multidivisional (M-form) forms. The first, N-form groups, have strong horizontal connections but weak owner control. Such groups are essentially networks, with potentially strong business transactions, social ties, and interlocks among member firms. These groups are often structured around a focal product, with group members comprising an analogue of a vertically integrated firm. A typical example of this type of business group is the *guanxi qiye* in Taiwan, such as the Lin Yuan Group, where numerous enterprises are organized around a large corporation in high-tech industries or industries focused on exporting their goods.

The second type, C-form, has relatively weak horizontal and vertical connections. As with the N-form, group members are not controlled by a dominant owner. Additionally, while group members coordinate with each other, the degree of

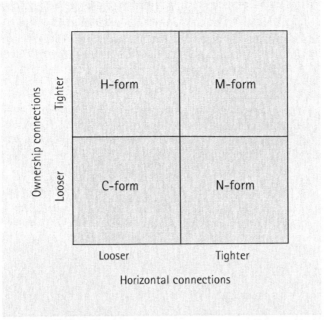

Figure 24.2 Horizontal and vertical dimensions of business groups

Source: Adapted from Yiu et al (2007).

exchange is weaker than for network groups. A typical example is the Japanese horizontal *keiretsu*. The third type are H-form groups; these have weak horizontal connections, but also have a dominant owner. These H-form groups are organized like a holding company with a portfolio of diversified subsidiaries. Examples of this type of business group can be seen among business groups in India, China, and Singapore. Finally, the M-form business group is characterized by high levels of both horizontal and vertical connection. These M-form groups have a dominant owner that shapes the strategies of member firms. Additionally, group members will operate in either related industries or vertically integrated businesses, and are likely to have other forms of connection, such as board interlocks or social ties. Large Korean *chaebol*, family business groups in Central Europe including Germany and Italy, and Belgian industrial business groups, for instance, fall into this category.

Both the role and the degree of involvement of the board of directors are likely to vary widely across each of these four group forms. Agency and resource provision roles will vary widely: some groups will need primarily one role, while other group types will require that the board attend to both areas. Further, the intensity of the board's participation in a given role will vary as well. Given these complexities, board roles in business groups will not be a straightforward topic to analyze. In the next section, we develop a research agenda to help advance future studies on boards and business groups based on different levels of analysis.

24.5 STRUCTURAL CONFIGURATIONS AND GOVERNANCE ATTRIBUTES OF BUSINESS GROUPS

....

While there has been a shortage of studies on the governance of business groups, the reverse is true for future research opportunities. In this section, we identify a number of topic areas that could advance our understanding of how business groups are governed, as well as opportunities to help groups operate more efficiently. To discuss these opportunities we organize the rest of this chapter at different levels of complexity and evaluation.

Given their complex nature, governance issues in groups can be studied at multiple levels, as shown in Fig. 24.3. The first level is the board of individual business group member firms. This level is comparable to the bulk of governance studies that examine samples of individual firms. These types of studies would treat governance characteristics of individual firms as either a predictor or an outcome variable. For example, tunneling and other value-destroying tactics have been observed in many business groups (see, e.g., Chang 2003). Agency theory could be used to determine what governance structures facilitate expropriation, and which other structures could prevent such problems. Similarly, many aspects of board composition and process have been linked with firm performance. Consequently, are there board characteristics that explain why some members of a business group are more successful than others? Also, rubber-stamp boards have been reported in many nations. Are rubber-stamp boards more common in different types of groups, or at different vertical levels in a business group? And, do the performance implications of inert boards differ across settings as well? Given the complexity of these issues and the fact that this level is covered in standard governance research approaches, our focus emphasizes the group and institutional levels.

The next level of analysis is to study the entire governance network of a business group. Fig. 24.3 shows two simplified business groups, each with very different structures: Group A is decentralized, with extensive lateral ties among members, possibly an N-form group. In contrast, Group B depicts a traditional hub-and-spoke configuration, with multiple hierarchical levels, possibly a C-form or an M-form group, depending on the salience of the vertical ownership ties. Questions raised at this level could include the causes and consequences of different aspects of network structure, as well as the flow of information and resources across the network. For example, the framework developed by Yiu and colleagues (2007) would argue that network density would differ, on average, for N- versus C- or M-form organizations. Similarly, the resource dependence perspective would argue that the need for connections would differ depending on environmental conditions. Consequently, one would expect that network characteristics would change in response to increased uncertainty or competition. There are also opportunities for multi-theoretic studies, such as assessing the relative importance of agency and resource dependence factors in shaping ties within a network. For instance, does the pattern of board ties among members of a group mirror ownership patterns, within

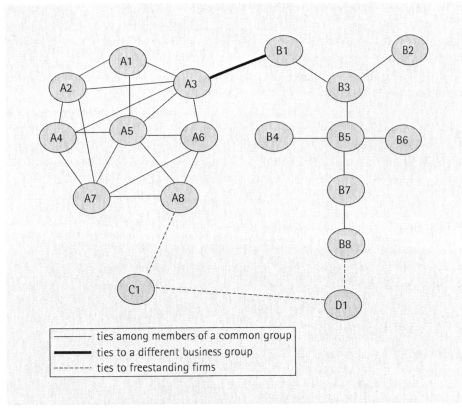

Figure 24.3 Possible patterns of board ties for groups with other entities

group transactions, both, or neither? Finally, studies should examine how information and resources flow through a group network. Some business groups, for instance, use their board networks as a tool to identify and develop promising managers. Future studies could examine how high performing groups utilize their networks as human capital tools.

A third level of analysis concerns ties outside the business group network. As seen in Fig. 24.3, these third-party ties could include links to other business groups (for example, the single point of contact between A and B) as well as links to non-group entities (for example, group A is connected to firm C, and group B is connected to firm D). Additionally, groups A and B also share an indirect connection via firms C and D. Anecdotally, cross-group ties are observed in some regions, while business groups in other areas might shun this type of connection. These connections will often be examined through the lens of institutional influences. For example, one promising research question is to assess how cultural and social factors shape the use, or avoidance, or cross-group ties. A second research question examines how third-party ties are used to procure external resources, and how these resources are subsequently disseminated throughout a group. Belderbos and Sleuwagen (1996), for instance, noted that groups can benefit from sharing the expertise of member firms regarding foreign markets. As described elsewhere in this volume, Mexican groups leverage their regional expertise to facilitate expansion into other Latin American markets (Hoshino, Chapter 15, this volume). A related opportunity is to examine the factors that shape the balance of within-group and third-party ties. While business groups often maintain strong networks of internal ties, this process is far from monolithic, even within a geographic region. One study of Israeli business groups (Maman 1999) reported marked differences in the composition of interlocks. From research using a fifteen-year window, one group was found to rely almost exclusively on within-group ties. In contrast, two other groups reported a roughly even balance between within-group and external ties. Additionally, the balance of ties varied for each group over time. Therefore, more attention is needed on explaining why groups choose certain types of interlocks. To examine these levels of analysis in more depth, we examine first the business group level using the framework by Yiu et al. (2007) illustrated above and follow in the next subsection with suggestions for research at the institutional level. Table 24.1 provides a summary of research opportunities regarding the boards of business groups.

24.5.1 Extending the structural configurations framework to governance differences

Given the variety of business groups suggested by the Yiu et al. (2007) archetypes, a significant opportunity that we take up in this section is to explore how the boards of different group types might vary, given the various organizing mechanisms used to classify them and the potential roles boards might play. Drawing on Fig. 24.2, we might expect systematic differences in board roles across the four archetypes. C-form groups are likely to have the weakest requirement for an active board: there is little interdependence between group members regarding strategy, and ownership influences are limited. As such, rubber-stamp boards could be more prevalent among C-form groups. These boards need some coordinating mechanism to manage the social ties. In C-form groups in Japan, such as the bank-centered horizontal *keiretsu*, a president's council might perform this role (Kim et al. 2004). In comparison, the N-form and H-form groups will have greater needs of their boards of directors, albeit in different ways: N-form boards should emphasize resource exchange over monitoring, with the opposite balance for H-form groups.

N-form boards may lack an overall strategic focus, given the lack of vertical relationships through ownership that could lead to a break-up through in-fighting and resource appropriation problems. Lorenzoni and Baden-Fuller (1995) identify the need for a "strategic center" in such business groups in order to manage the web of relationships. There may be either a super board such as a president's council or the board of a dominant firm that connects the firms through a critical set of

Table 24.1 Research questions on the governance of business groups

Topic	Potential research questions
Boards of individual members of a business group	• How do different needs for oversight and coordination affect aspects of board composition? • What governance structures facilitate/hinder tunneling, expropriation, and other value-diluting activities? • Are rubber stamp boards more or less prevalent in certain types of groups, or at different levels of a pyramid? • How do the roles for inside and outside directors differ from group versus non-group firms?
Overall network of a business group	• Are interlocks, cross shareholdings, and informal ties substitutable? • How does network density vary across different business group organizational forms? • How do network characteristics change in response to new environmental conditions? • What is the relative importance of agency and resource dependence factors in shaping the level of ties among members of a group? • How can boards of a business group be used as a human capital assessment and development tool?
Ties outside of a business group	• Are there cultural or social factors that drive the use, or avoidance, or ties with other groups? • How does knowledge and expertise acquired from third-party ties diffuse to other parts of a business group? • What drives the balance of within-group versus external ties?
Adoption of governance practices	• How do horizontal and vertical connections affect adoption of practices? • What is the relative importance of internal and external connections? • How influential are practices of foreign alliances and joint venture partners?
Performance	• How does adherence to governance guidelines affect group valuation? • What is the relative importance of de jure and de facto adoption? • Is conforming to local or global norms more relevant to performance? • Do high and low performing groups differ in the gap between formal rules and actual practice? • How can signaling theory be applied to the boards of business groups? Do investors respond to governance stimuli in the same manner as for US firms?
Director characteristics	• What role does director demography play in the execution of group strategies? • How much emphasis is placed on director social capital when recruiting new business group member firm board members? • Does director social capital affect the performance of business groups? • Are mimetic processes driven more by director experiences based on within-group ties among member firms, or by those based on external ties? • What role does director characteristics play in acquisition and divestiture decisions?
Diversification and divestment	• What strategic outcomes do business group directors associate with diversification at the group and affiliate firm levels? • How do business group member firm boards engage in mimetic activity? • What is the relative influence of internal versus external board ties in business groups? • Is the diffusion process faster for some group types than for others? • What modifications do business group member firms make to their boards of directors following restructuring?

centralized information links to facilitate efficient resource exchange and distribution as well as equitable distribution of rent generation. It may be that informal network cultural controls and the threat of being ostracized will prevent problems normally associated with the lack of traditional monitoring.

Alternatively, H-form boards are likely to have strong resource distribution mechanisms, but monitoring may be inefficient. The may be two problems with such firms. Dominant firm boards may be in control overall, leading to inefficient leadership and management of members. In this case, boards of member firms may be rubber stamps of the headquarter firm, which would be inefficient for the member firms' needs. This could lead to tunneling, as specified in previous research (Chang 2003). As such, future research could examine under what type of business group archetype and associated governance arrangements tunneling is more or less likely to occur. Another type of problem would be too much decentralization among member firms, with independent firms' boards managing their own firms without a centralized board to coordinate members firms. This could create chaotic management approaches that would lead to possible cross purposes among controlling boards and thereby inefficiencies in monitoring. Of course, this may be less of a problem if the firms have little in common in regard to resource coordination, as in an unrelated diversification strategy among member firms.

Finally, M-form groups will need both monitoring and resource provision. Usually an M-form group would be more appropriate for firms where resource coordination between member firms would be more salient, such as in groups where vertical integration or more tightly related product diversification is pursued among member firms. Several types of problems might be studied among M-form groups. Usually, vertical integration and related diversification require more centralization (Hill and Hoskisson 1987). Because each member firm has its own board of directors, the coordination among boards may be difficult without a mechanism to align the activities of all boards in the group. In other words, the subsidiary boards may create unnecessary bureaucracy, which will hinder required centralization, given the strategy being implemented among member firms. Similarly, such a redundant board might hinder resource distribution among member firms, complicating resource transfer horizontally between member firms.

To study these issues, we suggest two types of studies that might be relevant for examining the question of differing roles across groups. First, comparative analyses could be used to test whether there are in fact differences in board roles across the four forms. These analyses could be based on surveys and interviews with directors (see, e.g., Ravasi and Zattoni 2006; Zona and Zattoni 2007). A second avenue for future study is to examine the performance implications of these governance roles. This approach would argue that there is a contingency effect—that is, some "matching" between the emphasis of different roles, specific organizational strategies and forms, and overall group and individual member-firm performance.

A related research opportunity is to take a closer look at the characteristics of boards and individual directors, and how these factors relate to group structure and performance. A recent study of business group resources offers some insight on this question. A study of Chinese groups found that older groups and those whose executives came from government service suffered from lower performance, while groups that cultivated the development of internal capabilities and international exposure had a higher performance (Yiu et al. 2005). In a similar vein, local market knowledge was identified as an important element in the survival of Argentinean groups (Carrera et al. 2003). Extending these findings to business group boards, not all directors have the same access to resources and capabilities, and some skill sets will be more useful than others. A social capital perspective could help explain how groups acquire strategic resources that lay beyond the group's borders. Diversified groups, for instance, have broader and more complex decision environments. Correspondingly, a broad network of board ties is desirable in these settings (Geletkanycz et al. 2001). Thus, one opportunity would be to examine how direct and indirect board ties, as well as other connections, affect the effectiveness of acquisitions and diversification strategies. Chung (2006), for instance, examined how one form of social capital, personal ties, was used by groups to gain access to new market opportunities.

A similar research opportunity examines the board's role in shaping the type of diversification strategy pursued by a group. For Western economy firms, the pursuit of unrelated diversification is often seen as the sign of a governance failure (Amihud and Lev 1981). However, there are mixed findings whether a "diversification discount" exists for business groups as well. Some evidence suggests that group diversification is a sign of hedging, such as the emphasis on more stable profits versus higher profits. Alternately, though, unrelated diversification is also seen as an appropriate response to inefficient market conditions. Regardless of the performance effects, there is also evidence that many groups are engaged in substantial restructuring (see, e.g., Carrera et al. 2003; Hoskisson et al. 2005; Choi et al. 2007). How do group boards fit into the shifting emphasis on the type of diversification? For instance, are the changes in group diversification posture based on director experiences with other firms, as with acquisition activity in the United States (Haunschild 1993)? If so, how might imitation patterns differ between groups? Given the differences in owner control, one might expect a more rapid change in diversification posture among H- and M-form groups than either C- or N-form groups.

Another set of studies could look at how restructuring affects governance of boards. If restructuring is triggered by excessive diversification and poor performance because of weak governance, are such oversights corrected after restructuring? As such, it would be important to heed the call of Hoskisson and Turk (1990) and Johnson (1996) to pay more attention to post-restructuring governance and to how boards of business groups change over time. Similarly, it would be important to ask how issues such as currency shocks trigger the need for restructuring of business groups as they did in Korea; for example, how do boards change to accommodate policy changes associated with such shocks?

A final recommendation for future research in this area concerns the basic strategic orientation of the firm. Strategic orientation is a construct developed by Shortell and Zajac (1990) that subsumes the Miles and Snow strategy typology into a continuum:

prospectors and defenders as anchors, and analyzers as the midpoint. Does owner-ship structure cause some business groups boards to take a more conservative posture than others? Morck and Yeung (2003) suggest that family-based groups might try to block innovation, both within their own group and by competitors. Innovation leads to the potential loss of control for family owners and thus such control risk is pertinent for such owners (Gomez-Mejia et al., in press). While creative destruction has the potential to enhance firm value in the long run, suppres-sing innovation may be in the financial interest of group owners. Also, second- and third-generation family members have the potential to be less skilled than founders, and the lack of turnover could cause group governance to become rigid and insulated from outside events. In Israel, older family groups have been eclipsed by a wave of technology entrepreneurs (Kosenko and Yafeh, Chapter 16, this volume), and might be considered as evidence for Morck and Yeung's argument. One opportunity for study would be to assess whether the boards of H- and M-form groups have appreciably different strategic and thereby different governance orientations than the directors of C- and N-form groups. Next, we example institutional level issues.

24.5.2 Institutional processes

As noted earlier, an expectation of institutional theory is that organizations in a common setting will become increasingly similar over time. There is an open debate whether governance practices are converging worldwide, and whether this is a positive or negative development. Thus, one major opportunity for research on business groups centers on the potential for increasingly standardized governance, and the performance implications of this process.

There are several arguments favoring the notion of growing convergence in governance practices. Organizations such as the World Bank and the OECD advocate global governance practices. And many of the country-specific guidelines emphasize similar issues, such as the need for more independent or non-executive directors, transparency, and the separation of CEO and chairman positions (Norburn et al. 2000). Additionally, evidence presented in several of this volume's chapters speaks to both proactive and reactive governance changes in the pursuit of legitimacy. In Russia, the increased use of independent directors was intended to "send a strong signal that companies want to implement the best practices of corporate governance" (Guriev, Chapter 18, this volume), in the hopes of boosting stock performance. Similarly, Korea instituted rules requiring a minimum number of outsiders following their economic crisis (Kim, Chapter 6, this volume), and Turkey has been character-ized as following pressure of global standards to create more balanced boards (Colpan, Chapter 17, this volume). However, there are challenges to the notion of common governance systems, including incompatibilities and resistance in local areas (Coffee 1999). A recent paper reviewed studies conducted at both the firm and the country level, and concluded that convergence is less prevalent than widely believed (Yoshikawa and Rasheed 2009). Separately, there is limited evidence regarding the effectiveness of many governance recommendations. For example, there are few empirical data to support the arguments that aspects of board composition or the separation of CEO and chairman positions are inherently desirable. Further, not only is the evidence inconclusive, but virtually none of these analyses has been done in countries in which most business groups operate.

There is also some support for the argument that boards are changing their governance practices solely as window dressing. In Brazil, for instance, the boards of business groups have chosen to follow new governance guidelines. The São Paolo stock exchange is relatively unusual, in that there are multiple tiers of voluntary governance compliance. The leading business groups on that exchange have chosen to follow the least stringent level of compliance (Aldrighi and Postali, Chapter 13, this volume). As a second example, Korean firms began adding more outside directors to their boards in the aftermath of the Asian economic crisis. While both *chaebol* and non-*chaebol* firms added more outsiders, closer scrutiny revealed that many of the *chaebol* outsiders came from affiliated firms, or had other ties to the group. Consequently, a *chaebol* could project an aura of board independence while still thwarting "the government's policy objective of improved monitoring of management" (Choi et al. 2007: 955).

More broadly, a recent study characterized two types of compliance in governance practices: de jure and de facto (Khanna et al. 2006). De jure convergence exists when a region adopts a set of rules without accepting the underlying principles of those rules. De facto convergence occurs when firm behavior and attitudes adhere to the intent of those rules. Khanna and colleagues argued that there are three factors underlying potential discrepancies between rules and actual practice: a lack of understanding of the implications of good governance, the absence of complementary institutions, and poor enforcement. In an empirical analysis, they found that there was greater convergence in governance rules for countries that were in geographic proximity or had strong trading partners. Interestingly, they also found that US guidelines had no measurable influence on their own. Also, they found "virtually no evidence of de facto similarity" (Khanna et al. 2006: 71). Stated differently, there are major gaps between the adoption of governance rules and the actual practices used in different nations.

There are multiple opportunities to examine the intersection of institutional processes, governance codes, and business groups. While the role of mimetic behavior has been well documented among traditional boards (Haunschild 1993), how does this translate to the boards of business groups? For example, what types of ties are the most influential: ties within the group, or external ties? Institutional theory would also argue that groups in developing economies are influenced by practices in Western countries (Newman 2000). Groups such as those found in Mexico have extensive alliances with foreign multinationals (Hoshino, Chapter 15, this volume); do these connections carry special weight in shaping governance practices? Sanders and Tuschke (2007) provide evidence among developed economies that there is diffusion among some governance devices. But do these influences happen between developed and less-developed economies where business groups with stronger social ties might resist or support such institutional influences. Also, how would such influences transfer between governance mechanisms in different emerging economies, both with business groups? Also, how might adoption influences vary for groups with differing levels of horizontal and vertical connectivity (Yiu et al. 2007)?

There are also questions relating to governance adoption and firm performance. Many firms adopt governance practices solely for the legitimacy they infer to investors (Westphal and Zajac 2001). Signaling theory offers a number of promising research questions. First, groups vary widely across regions in the strength of equity ties across members. Is there a lesser need for market signals among groups with tight ownership connectivity? Secondly, many groups are often undervalued, reflecting the potential for agency abuse of minority investors. Does de jure acceptance of governance practices help to offset the group discount? If so, does de facto acceptance offer any additional benefit to the firm's performance? Thirdly, it would be informative to compare whether high- and low-performing business groups differ in the gap between de facto and de jure use of leading governance practices. It may be that better performing business groups are those that adopt governance procedures that are more in accord with their own country's or region's institutional pressures (Hoskisson et al. 2004). Finally, it would be useful to examine whether signaling benefits extend to operational performance and efficiency. In Korea, for example, the inclusion of outside directors is associated with better market valuation (Choi et al. 2007), while in Scandanavia the presence of foreign directors has a comparable effect (Oxelheim and Randoy 2003). For both studies, the presence of these directors is believed to be a signal of superior governance that is translated into a higher Tobins q score. What is not addressed, however, is whether these board characteristics translate into other metrics of firm performance, such as profitability, market share, growth rates, and so on. In the specific context of Korea, outside directors have been strongly criticized: because of "a lack of monitoring skills and incentive to monitor CEOs actively, outside directors appear to be ineffective in disciplining poorly performing CEOs" (Chang and Shin 2006: 86). While these directors may provide some symbolic utility, the perception among Korean firms is that they provide little tangible value to the operation of the firm.

24.6 CONCLUSION

In summary, governance of business groups presents an important, but underresearched area for future study. Although some research has been accomplished on this topic, there are many areas that need attention. In particular, we first need to understand the variation among business groups, both at the archetype level and at the institutional level. Different functional forms of business groups, such as those introduced by Yiu et al. (2007), are likely to require different monitoring and resource provisions of their boards. Although there is a large body of research examining governance of independent firms, very little of this research is focused on firms within a business group. The business group itself is likely to affect member firms' boards of directors and their governance procedures as well as be influenced by such member firms' governance procedures. As such, business groups represent an important moderating or mediating effect of governance procedure among member firms. The nature of institutional country effects in which business groups are embedded is another important factor that shapes the governance of business groups and their member firms. Examining how such influences within countries as well as across countries facilitate change or inertia among governance procedures will provide an important agenda for future research.

References

AHMADJIAN, C., and ROBBINS, G. (2005). "A Clash of Capitalisms: Foreign Shareholders and Corporate Restructuring in 1990s Japan," *American Sociological Review*, 70: 451–71.

AMIHUD, Y., and LEV, B. (1981). "Risk Reduction as a Managerial Motive for Conglomerate Mergers," *Bell Journal of Economics*, 12: 605–17.

BAE, K. H., KANG, J. K., and KIM, J. M. (2002). "Tunneling or Value Added? Evidence from Mergers by Korean Business Groups," *Journal of Finance*, 57: 2695–740.

BELDERBOS, R., and SLEUWAGEN, L. (1996). "Japanese Firms and the Decision to Invest Abroad: Business Groups and Regional Core Networks," *Review of Economics and Statistics*, 78: 214–20.

BERLE, A., and MEANS, G. (1932). *The Modern Corporation and Private Property*. New York: Macmillan.

BERTALANFFY, L. (1968). *General Systems Theory*. New York: George Braziller.

BOYD, B. (1990). "Corporate Linkages and Organizational Environment: A Test of the Resource Dependence Model," *Strategic Management Journal*, 11: 419–30.

BOYD, B. K. (1995). "CEO Duality and Firm Performance: A Contingency Model," *Strategic Management Journal*, 16: 301–12.

BOYD, B. K., HOWARD, M., and CARROLL, W.O. (1997). "CEO Duality and Firm Performance: An International Comparison," in H. Thomas, D. O'Neal, and M. Ghertman (eds.), *Strategy, Structure and Style*. Chichester: John Wiley & Sons, 23–39.

BOYD, B. K., GOVE, S., and HITT, M. A. (2005). "Consequences of Construct Measurement Problems in Strategic Management Research: The Case of Amihud and Lev," *Strategic Management Journal*, 26: 367–75.

BOYD, B. K., HAYNES, K., and ZONA, F. (2008). "Dimensions of CEO–Board Relations." Working Paper.

CARPENTER, M. A., and WESTPHAL, J. D. (2001). "The Strategic Context of External Network Ties: Examining the Impact of Director Appointments on Board Involvement in Strategic Decision Making," *Academy of Management Journal*, 44: 639–60.

CARRERA, A., MESQUITA, L., PERKINS, G., and VASSOLO, R. (2003). "Business Groups and their Corporate Strategies in the Argentine Roller Coaster of Competitive and Anti-Competitive Shocks," *Academy of Management Executive*, 17/3: 32–44.

CHANG, J. J., and SHIN, H. H. (2006). "Governance System Effectiveness following the Crisis: The Case of Korean Business Group Headquarters," *Corporate Governance: An International Review*, 14: 85–97.

CHANG, S. J. (2003). "Ownership Structure, Expropriation, and Performance of Group-Affiliated Companies in Korea," *Academy of Management Journal*, 46: 238–53.

CHARKHAM, J. (1994). *Keeping Good Company: A Study of Corporate Governance in Five Countries*. New York: Oxford University Press.

CHOI, J. J., PARK, S. W., and YOO, S. S. (2007). "The Value of Outside Directors: Evidence from Corporate Governance Reform in Korea," *Journal of Financial and Quantitative Analysis*, 42: 941–62.

CHUNG, H. M. (2006). "Managerial Ties, Control and Deregulation: An Investigation of Business Groups Entering the Deregulated Banking Industry in Taiwan," *Asia Pacific Journal of Management*, 23: 505–20.

COFFEE, J. (1999). "The Future as History: The Prospects for Global Convergence in Corporate Governance and its Implications," *Northwestern University Law Review*, 93: 641–707.

DALTON, D. R., DAILY, C. M., ELLSTRAND, A. E., and JOHNSON, J. L. (1998). "Meta-Analytic Reviews of Board Composition, Leadership Structure, and Financial Performance," *Strategic Management Journal*, 19: 269–90.

DAVIS, G. F. (1996). "The Significance of Board Interlocks for Corporate Governance," *Corporate Governance*, 4: 154–9.

DEMB, A., and NEUBAUER, F. F. (1992). *The Corporate Board: Confronting the Paradoxes*. New York: Oxford University Press.

DENIS, D. K., and MCCONNELL, J. J. (2003). "International Corporate Governance," *Journal of Financial and Quantitative Analysis*, 38: 1–36.

DEUTSCH, Y. (2005). "The Impact of Board Composition on Firms' Critical Decisions: A Meta-Analytic Review," *Journal of Management Studies*, 31: 424–44.

DHARWADKAR, R., GEORGE, G., and BRANDES, P. (2000). "Privatization in Emerging Economies: An Agency Theory Perspective," *Academy of Management Review*, 25: 650–69.

DIMAGGIO, P. J., and POWELL, W. W. (1983). "The Iron Cage Revisited: Institutional Isomorphism and Collective Rationality in Organizational Fields," *American Sociological Review*, 48: 147–60.

DRUCKER, P. F. (1981). *Toward the Next Economics, and Other Essays*. New York: Harper & Row.

FAMA, E. F., and JENSEN, M. (1983). "Separation of Ownership and Control," *Journal of Law and Economics*, 26: 301–25.

FINEGOLD, D., BENSON, G. S., and HECHT, D. (2007). "Corporate Boards and Company Performance: Review of Research in Light of Recent Reforms," *Corporate Governance: An International Review*, 15: 865–78.

FINKELSTEIN, S., and MOONEY, A. C. (2003). "Not the Usual Suspects: How to Use the Board Process to Make Boards Better," *Academy of Management Executive*, 17/2: 101–13.

GELETKANYCZ, M. A., BOYD, B. K., and FINKELSTEIN, S. (2001). "The Strategic Value of CEO External Directorate Networks: Implications for CEO Compensation," *Strategic Management Journal*, 22: 889–98.

GOMEZ-MEJIA, L., HAYNES, K., NUNEZ-NICKEL, M., JACOBSON, K., and MOYANO-FUENTES, J. (in press). "Family-Owned Firms: Risk Loving Or Risk Averse?" *Administrative Science Quarterly*.

GRANOVETTER, M. (1985). "Economic Action and Social Structure: The Problem of Embeddedness," *American Journal of Sociology*, 91: 481–510.

GRANOVETTER, M. (1995). "Coase Revisited: Business Groups in the Modern Economy," *Industrial and Corporate Change*, 4/1: 93–130.

GRANOVETTER, M. (2005). "Business Groups and Other Social Organizations," in N. J. Smelser and R. Swedberg (eds.), *The Handbook of Economic Sociology*. 2nd edn. Princeton: Princeton University Press, 429–50.

HAUNSCHILD, P. R. (1993). "Interorganizational Imitation: The Impact of Interlocks on Corporate Acquisition Activity," *Administrative Science Quarterly*, 38: 564–92.

HILL, C. W. L., and HOSKISSON, R. E. (1987). "Strategy and Structure in the Multiproduct Firm," *Academy of Management Review*, 12: 331–41.

HILLMAN, A. J., and DALZIEL, T. (2003). "Boards of Directors and Firm Performance: Integrating Agency and Resource Dependence Perspectives," *Academy of Management Review*, 28: 383–96.

HOFSTEDE, G. (2001). *Culture's Consequences*. 2nd edn. Thousand Oaks, CA: Sage.

HOSKISSON, R. E., and TURK, T. A. (1990). "Corporate Restructuring: Governance and Control Limits of the Internal Capital Market," *Academy of Management Review*, 15: 459–77.

HOSKISSON, R. E., HITT, M. A., JOHNSON, R. A., and GROSSMAN, W. (2002). "Conflicting Voices: The Effects of Institutional Ownership Heterogeneity and Internal Governance on Corporate Innovation Strategies," *Academy of Management Journal*, 45: 697–716.

HOSKISSON, R. E., YIU, D., and KIM, H. (2004). "Corporate Governance Systems: Effects of Capital and Labor Market Congruency on Corporate Innovation and Global Competitiveness," *Journal of High Technology Management*, 15: 293–315.

HOSKISSON, R. E., JOHNSON, R. A., TIHANYI, L., and WHITE, R. E. (2005). "Diversified Business Groups and Corporate Refocusing in Emerging Economies," *Journal of Management*, 31: 941–65.

JOHNSON, J. (2000). *A Fistful of Rubles*. Ithaca, NY: Cornell University Press.

JOHNSON, R. A. (1996). "Antecedents and Outcomes of Corporate Refocusing," *Journal of Management*, 22/3: 439–83.

KEISTER, L. A. (1998). "Engineering Growth: Business Group Structure and Firm Performance in China's Transition Economy," *American Journal of Sociology*, 104: 404–40.

KEISTER, L. (2000). *Chinese Business Groups: The Structure and Impact of Interfirm Relations during Economic Development*. Oxford: Oxford University Press.

KHANNA, T. (2000). "Business Groups and Social Welfare in Emerging Markets: Existing Evidence and Unanswered Questions," *European Economic Review*, 44: 748–61.

KHANNA, T., and RIVKIN, J. W. (2006). "Interorganizational Ties and Business Group Boundaries: Evidence from an Emerging Economy," *Organization Science*, 17: 333–52.

KHANNA, T., and YAFEH, Y. (2007). "Business Groups in Emerging Markets: Paragons or Parasites?" *Journal of Economic Literature*, 45: 331–72.

KHANNA, T., KOGA, J., and PALEPU, K. (2006). "Globalization and Similarities in Corporate Governance: A Cross-Country Analysis," *Review of Economics and Statistics*, 88: 69–90.

KIM, H., HOSKISSON, R. E., and WAN, W. P. (2004). "Power Dependence, Diversification Strategy and Performance in Keiretsu Member Firms," *Strategic Management Journal*, 25: 613–36.

KRIGER, M. P. (1988). The Increasing Role of Subsidiary Boards in MNCs: An Empirical Study," *Strategic Management Journal*, 9: 347–60.

LaPorta, R., Lopez-De-Silanes, F., and Shleifer, A. (1999). "Corporate Ownership around the World," *Journal of Finance*, 54: 471–517.

Lorenzoni, G., and Baden-Fuller, C. (1995). "Creating a Strategic Center to Manage a Web of Partners," *California Management Review*, 37/3: 146–63.

Lorsch, J. W., and MacIver, E. (1989). *Pawns or Potentates: The Reality of America's Corporate Boards*. Boston: Harvard Business School Press.

Mace, M. L. (1971). *Directors: Myth and Reality*. Boston: Harvard Business School Press.

Mace, M. (1986). *Directors: Myth and Reality*. 2nd edn. Boston: Harvard Business School Press.

Maman, D. (1999). "Interlocking Ties within Business Groups in Israel: A Longitudinal Analysis, 1974–1987," *Organization Studies*, 20: 323–39.

Meyer, J. W., and Rowan, B. (1983). "Institutionalized Organizations: Formal Structure as Myth and Ceremony," in W. Meyer, B. Rowan, and T. E. Deal (eds.), *Organizational Environments Ritual and Rationality*. Beverly Hills, CA: Sage Publications, 21–44.

Mizruchi, M. S. (1996). "What Do Interlocks Do? An Analysis, Critique, and Assessment of Research on Interlocking Directorates," *Annual Review of Sociology*, 22: 271–98.

Morck, R., and Yeung, B. (2003). "Agency Problems in Large Family Business Groups," *Entrepreneurship Theory and Practice*, 27: 367–82.

Morck, R., Wolfenzon, D., and Yeung, B. (2005). "Corporate Governance, Economic Entrenchment, and Growth," *Journal of Economic Literature*, 43: 655–720.

Newman, K. L. (2000). "Organizational Transformation during Institutional Upheaval," *Academy of Management Review*, 25: 602–19.

Norburn, D., Boyd, B. K., Fox, M. A., and Muth, M. M. (2000). "International Corporate Governance Reform," *European Business Journal*, 12/3: 116–33.

Oliver, C. (1991). "Strategic Responses to Organizational Processes," *Academy of Management Review*, 16: 145–79.

Oxelheim, L., and Randoy, T. (2003). "The Impact of Foreign Board Membership on Firm Value," *Journal of Banking and Finance*, 27: 2369–92.

Pfeffer, J., and Salancik, G. R. (1978). *The External Control of Organizations: A Resource Dependence Perspective*. New York: Harper & Row.

Ravasi, D., and Zattoni, A. (2006). "Exploring the Political Side of Board Involvement in Strategy: A Study of Mixed-Ownership Institutions," *Journal of Management Studies*, 43: 1671–702.

Sanders, W. G., and Tuschke, A. C. (2007). "The Adoption of the Institutionally Contested Organizational Practices: The Emergence of Stock Option Pay in Germany," *Academy of Management Journal*, 57: 33–56.

Selznick, P. (1949). *TVA and the Grass Roots: A Study of Politics and Organization*. Berkeley and Los Angeles: University of California Press.

Shortell, S. M., and Zajac, E. J. (1990). "Perceptual and Archival Measures of Miles and Snow's Strategic Types: A Comprehensive Review of Reliability and Validity," *Academy of Management Journal*, 33: 817–32.

Silva, F., Majluf, N., and Paredes, R. D. (2006). "Family Ties, Interlocking Directors and Performance of Business Groups in Emerging Countries: The Case of Chile," *Journal of Business Research*, 59: 315–21.

Useem, M. (1984). *The Inner Circle: Large Corporations and Business Politics in the US and UK*. New York: Oxford University Press.

USEEM, M. (1996). *Investor Capitalism: How Money Managers are Changing the Face of Corporate America*. New York: Basic Books/HarperCollins.

VOLPIN, P. F. (2002). "Governance with Poor Investor Protection: Evidence from Top Executive Turnover in Italy," *Journal of Financial Economics* 64: 61–90.

WESTPHAL, J. D., and ZAJAC, E. J. (2001). "Decoupling Policy from Practice: The Case of Stock Repurchase Programs," *Administrative Science Quarterly*, 46/2: 202–28.

YIU, D. W., LU, Y., BRUTON, G. D., and HOSKISSON, R. E. (2007). "Business Groups: An Integrated Model to Focus Future Research," *Journal of Management Studies*, 44: 1551–79.

YOSHIKAWA, T., and RASHEED, A. (2009). "Convergence of Corporate Governance: Critical Review and Future Directions," *Corporate Governance: An International Review*, 17: 388–404.

ZATTONI, A. (1999). "The Structure of Corporate Groups: The Italian Case," *Corporate Governance: An International Review*, 7: 38–48.

ZONA, F., and ZATTONI, A. (2007). "Beyond the Black Box of Demography: Board Processes and Task Effectiveness within Italian Firms," *Corporate Governance: An International Review*, 15: 852–64.

CHAPTER 25

THE KIN AND THE PROFESSIONAL: TOP LEADERSHIP IN FAMILY BUSINESS GROUPS

BEHLÜL ÜSDIKEN

25.1 INTRODUCTION

MUCH of the growing research interest in business groups has been driven by concerns with their emergence, evolution, and persistence within late-industrializing economies (e.g., Khanna and Yafeh 2007). This has, in turn, stimulated nationally based or internationally comparative empirical studies on the performance of group-affiliated and independent firms (e.g., Guillén 2000; Khanna and Rivkin 2001; Chang 2003). More recently, attention has also begun to turn toward the strategic responses and the fate of business groups in view of changes in their economic and institutional environments (e.g., Chung 2004; Kim et al. 2004; Hoskisson et al. 2005; Aulakh and Kotabe 2008).

That business groups are often family based has long been recognized in these streams of literature (see, for early examples, Hamilton and Biggart 1988; Amsden 1989; Biggart 1990; Whitley 1990). Yet, accounts on the implications of this central feature of business groups for their top leadership have been largely confined to theoretical conjectures or highly general observations. Only a few studies have appeared, typically on the South Korean *chaebol*, that have provided some more systematic evidence (e.g., Shin and Chin 1989).

There does, however, seem to have been a renewed interest more recently, as empirical investigations have begun to emerge on the leadership of family business groups. Very much like those focusing on strategic changes, these studies have been motivated by economic and institutional shifts that have been taking place in countries where business groups have been prevalent. Indeed, although they have manifested variations in timing, scale, and pace, most of these countries have been moving toward a more liberalized and open economy (see, e.g., Hoskisson et al. 2000 and various contributions to this volume, such as Fracchia, Mesquita, and Quiroga, Chapter 12; Chung and Mahmood, Chapter 7; Sarkar, Chapter 11). Moreover, during or prior to the introduction of economic policy and institutional changes in this direction, many of these countries have encountered what were perhaps the most acute economic crises in their histories. Though again in varying degrees, these macro-level events have sparked not only the demise of some business groups and concomitant attempts on the part of others to reshape their strategies and structures, but also a shift in attitude in the ways they have come to be seen by governmental authorities as well as international bodies and academic researchers (Luo and Chung 2005; Khanna and Yafeh 2007; Kim, Chapter 6, this volume). Primary targets of attention have, therefore, become, on the one hand, the often highly diversified strategic postures of business groups and, on the other, the dominant role of owner families in their leadership (Kim et al. 2004; Tsui-Auch 2004).

The present chapter addresses the latter issue by taking stock of the available literature with a view to assessing whether and to what degree changes have been forthcoming in who runs family business groups. To this end, the chapter begins by pointing to distinctions made between control, rule, and management (e.g., Scott 1990; Tsui-Auch 2004) to be employed as a guiding framework in examining continuity and change in leadership. This is accompanied by a review of the earlier literature that has had something to say on the way family business groups were run. The chapter then turns to identifying and discussing the different perspectives that have informed more recent studies, followed by an assessment of the scant empirical evidence that is available. The penultimate section considers the benefits of bringing in a power perspective, largely neglected in the present literature, as an additional approach for addressing change and continuity in the top leadership of family business groups. The concluding section explores the issues that require further research attention and the methods that need to be pursued.

25.2 CONTROL, RULE, AND MANAGEMENT

To a large degree, Chandler's description (1977) of the "managerial enterprise," presumed to typify the large firm with widely dispersed ownership and professional management, has served as a frame of reference, both in earlier (e.g., Hamilton and Biggart 1988; Whitley 1990; Morikawa 2001) and more recent (e.g., Carney 1998; Chung and Luo 2008; Suehiro and Wailerdsak, Chapter 9, this volume) assessments of the way family business groups are run. For Chandler (1977), the managerial enterprise was characterized by a separation of ownership and management whereby strategic and operational decision-making in the firm rested with a hierarchy of salaried managers. They were governed by a board largely made up of full-time professional executives with minimal or no ownership and, possibly, representatives of shareholders, though the latter did not partake in any significant way in key decisions. According to Chandler (1977, 1990), the managerial or "modern business enterprise" constituted a later stage in firm development relative to the "personal" or "family-controlled" enterprise. Of the latter two, the personal enterprise was run by its owners, possibly together with a small number of salaried managers. The family-owned form, on the other hand, included more extensive managerial hierarchies, though owning families remained influential often by holding senior executive positions. The move to the modern enterprise therefore signified a shift of "control" from owners to salaried managers who had little or no ownership involvement.

Going beyond Chandler's broad notion of control, Scott (1990) suggested that it is useful to distinguish between those who control firms because of their ownership rights and those who can exercise strategic decision-making powers and thus "rule" businesses. In Scott's words (1990: 352), rulers "are the active leadership group in the enterprise, the 'dominant coalition'... of business leaders who formulate corporate strategy and exercise the powers of strategic management." Those in control and those who rule need not necessarily be the same, though "rulers," according to Scott (1990), may include owners or their agents as well as salaried managers and representatives of other outside parties with interests in the firm. So control and rule may and do become disassociated in varying degrees, and the extent to which those in control can constrain the rulers is likely to depend on the relative shares held by the former and the legal frameworks surrounding the relationships between the two groups.

Extending Scott (1990), Tsui-Auch (2004) proposed that ruling the firm, in turn, needs to be distinguished from its management, which involves implementation of strategy and the monitoring of day-to-day operational matters, typically carried out by senior as well as middle-level managers. Such a bifurcation is likely to prove useful for a more pointed comparative assessment of the variations in and the extent of changes that may have been occurring in the top leadership of family business groups. Specifically, it permits an appraisal of the reach of professionalization and the varying roles of salaried managers. Thus, it becomes possible to distinguish, as Tsui-Auch (2004) does, between business groups where owner families not only rule but also manage and those in which family members act only as rulers. Beyond this categorical division, variation may be identified in the extent to which the family actively partakes in strategy implementation and operational decision-making. Conversely, non-family managers may possibly penetrate into the ruling group, again in varying degrees.

25.3 EARLY DEPICTIONS OF LEADERSHIP IN FAMILY BUSINESS GROUPS

Early literature on business groups, in noting the typically family-based nature of this form of organization, implied that they were not only owned but also run by the founding families (see, e.g., Biggart 1990). Attention was drawn to the role of cultural heritage and the prevalent tendencies to retain family rule and management, together with the ways that were employed to that effect, such as adoption and marriage (Morikawa 2001), polygamy (Suehiro 1993), holding multiple key positions (Shin and Chin 1989; Hamilton 1997), and the professionalization of later generations through better education (Lee and Yoo 1987; Suehiro 1993; Buğra 1994; Kim 1996). Reference has also been made to the short organizational histories of business groups in many countries, which allowed founders to remain in charge (e.g., Yoo and Lee 1987 and, for a more recent example, Guriev, Chapter 18, this volume).

With the Chandlerian (1977) managerial enterprise serving as a reference, the early literature tended to treat professionalization largely as a question of societal and organizational "modernization." Shin and Chin (1989), for example, pointed to theoretical claims that industrialization and ensuing social change will lead to recruitment practices based on universalistic criteria of expertise and educational qualifications. Along these lines, they argued that the education level of owners could be positively associated with openness to employing non-family managers. Shin and Chin (1989) also hypothesized (but failed to obtain empirical support) that younger owners were more likely to recruit managers with no kinship or social ties (see also Shin 1998). Drawing upon anecdotal examples, other agent-based interpretations were offered by suggesting that the "philosophy" of the top leader had an important role to play in the extent of professionalization (Yoo and Lee 1987; Biggart 1990). In organizational terms, growth, diversification, and the use of more capital-intensive technologies were considered as leading to the development of managerial hierarchies, given the limits to family capacity (e.g., Biggart 1990; Whitley 1990; Koike 1993; Chung et al. 1997; Ungson et al. 1997; Morikawa 2001).

Thus, Biggart (1990) posited that the South Korean *chaebol*, for example, constituted a blend that combined personalistic rule by a patriarch with professionalized management, in the sense of both employing salaried executives and using sophisticated managerial techniques. Although the very top positions were often reserved for sons and other members of the family, salaried managers could also climb to higher levels, though how much this happened was likely to vary significantly across business groups (Yoo and Lee 1987; Biggart 1990). Shin and Chin (1989: 6), basing their comments on an examination of "top managerial executives" in 100 leading *chaebol* in the late 1970s, reported that close to 80 percent of these positions were occupied by non-family managers (see also Lee and Yoo 1987). Other commentaries that followed have also been at one in claiming that *chaebol* management was becoming increasingly professionalized (e.g., Kim 1996; Chung et al. 1997; Ungson et al. 1997).

Likewise, for the horizontally structured and smaller Taiwanese business groups, Hamilton (1997) noted that affiliated firms often had a non-family manager as the top executive. This, he argued, served to separate day-to-day management from the ruling of the group, which was carried out not by salaried managers but by an "inner circle" of owners, their families, and possibly a few trusted associates. In fact, Chung (2003) found in a study of 100 top Taiwanese groups that, even before the institutional reforms in this country, these "inner circles" were not completely dominated by family members. With respect to operational management levels, Wailerdsak and Suehiro (2004) claimed that by the mid-1980s professional managers were already employed by owner-families in Thailand to help them in running their businesses. Likewise, Tsui-Auch (2004) concluded in a qualitative study on business groups in Singapore that by the early 1980s salaried managers had to a large degree taken on day-to-day management in a majority of cases. Notably though, as Carney (1998) has suggested, the salaried management teams in these overseas Chinese family business groups were likely to have been smaller than those in, for example, the South Korean *chaebol*.

Altogether, then, this early literature, albeit limited in its empirical base, does suggest a notable, though possibly internationally variable, degree of professionalization, even in earlier stages in the development of business groups. Yet, two caveats are in order. First, it appears that greater incorporation of salaried managers over time has happened within the bounds of persistent and strong familial rule. Biggart (1998: 316), for example, maintained in a later article that, although more professional managers were to be found in higher ranks, "patrimonial control continued to characterize Korean businesses." Professional managers appeared to be employed for the technical expertise they possessed and had little influence on the way the groups were ruled (Carney 1998). Moreover, various authors suggested that founders or their heirs remained actively involved in the operational matters even of affiliated firms, implying that in practical terms the distinction between control, rule, and management in family business groups may not have been distinct either (Whitley 1990; Koike 1993; Ungson et al. 1997; Shin 1998).

Secondly, entry of salaried managers into higher echelons seems to have been constrained to a considerable degree by pre-existing social ties or, at least, by trust and loyalty relations developed through long service (Lee and Yoo 1987; Biggart 1990; Chung et al. 1997; Carney 1998). This led Shin and Chin (1989: 16), for example, to refer to an "extended family" and Tsui-Auch (2004: 698) to introduce a novel category of "family-related managers," which includes not only family members and relatives but also friends and loyal employees considered as being part of the family. In an early and rare empirical study on the *chaebol*, Shin and Chin (1989) found that common regional and high-school ties with the owner played a significant role in being employed as a high-ranking executive. Basing their comments on findings indicating the predominance of family members, Shin and Chin (1989: 19) concluded that trust and loyalty served as the most important criteria for recruitment to top positions in the *chaebol*. Priority was therefore given to the strongest ties; then, when these were used up, weaker ties were utilized. In addition, Lee and Yoo (1987) claimed that, in South Korea, quite a high proportion of executives from outside these close circles were not really "professional managers," as they were likely to have been recruited because of their political links.

In sum, the broad picture to emerge from the early literature is that business groups constituted a mixture of family rule and subordinated professional managerial hierarchies. There was limited entry on the part of non-kin into ruling circles, and this was often confined to those who had some kind of quasi-family links. Operational management appeared to be carried out by salaried managers, though quite often under close control and intervention by those who ruled. It is against this background that theoretical views and more recent empirical work on professionalization of top leadership in business groups needs to be assessed.

25.4 CHANGING CONTEXTS AND BUSINESS GROUP LEADERSHIP

Given the changes that have been occurring since the 1990s in and around the so-called emerging economies, more recent literature has continued drawing upon the Chandlerian account about the evolution of the managerial enterprise. Internationalization of business groups and changes in domestic markets as well as organizational growth have been considered as potential drivers of professionalization in their leadership. Taking into account the alterations occuring in regulatory frameworks of business activity in those countries, these techno-economic views have often been framed within a broad theme of market-oriented institutional change. Companion institutionalist ideas have been employed either jointly or separately in suggesting additional sources of pressure toward greater professionalization. Standing in opposition to these universalistic and change-oriented theoretical claims have been approaches ascribing strong influence to cultural traditions and nationally based social institutions as sources of continuity in family rule and management (cf. Whittington and Mayer 2000).

25.4.1 Techno-economic views

The central tenet of the Chandlerian argument (1977, 1990) has been that increasing organizational size, coupled with expanding markets, more advanced technologies, and greater competition, will drive firms toward managerial enterprise. This argument rests on the reasoning that such market and technological conditions, together with larger scale, will make planning, resource allocation, and control in business organizations more complex. Greater complexity of the management task will, in turn, require executives with professional expertise and skills.

Underlying these techno-economic arguments is a selection premise that organizational forms (in this particular instance, business groups) that possess characteristics better aligned with market and technological conditions are more likely to prevail and survive (Chung 2003; Suehiro and Wailerdsak 2004; Chittoor and Das 2007). They are therefore essentially universalistic and propose evolution toward the managerial enterprise, though possibly with time lags, as the pace of developments that foster this particular form are likely to vary internationally.

That the kind of external conditions described by Chandler (1977) are becoming increasingly relevant for business groups has been justified further by reference to changes taking place within many late-industrializing countries. Globalization and the concomitant relaxation of restrictions on foreign capital and goods, it has been argued, have resulted in more competitive market environments because of increased flows of foreign direct investment and imports (Suehiro and Wailerdsak 2004; Luo and Chung 2005; Chittoor and Das 2007; Kim, Chapter 6, this volume). This has been accompanied in many instances by the internationalization of business groups themselves, as they too have increasingly turned toward foreign markets through exports and/or direct investments (Wailerdsak and Suehiro 2004; Yeung 2006; see also Tsui-Auch and Yoshikawa, Chapter 10; Sarkar, Chapter 11; Hoshino, Chapter 15; all in this volume). New opportunities for diversification have also emerged, as governments in many of these countries have attempted to promote privatization of state-owned enterprises, often in sectors alien to business groups (Chung 2003). Contributing to greater uncertainty in external environments have been the conditions generated by the economic crises that many of the late-industrializing countries have gone through.

Along Chandlerian lines, altogether these changes have been interpreted in the more recent literature as accentuating the need for professional managerial expertise (e.g., Wailerdsak and Suehiro 2004; Chittoor and Das 2007). Top-level planning, decision-making, and monitoring of performance are believed to have become more complex, especially when linked with increasing diversification (Chung 2003; Tsui-Auch 2004; Yeung 2006; Chung and Luo 2008). Diversity of viewpoints, knowledge, and experience in higher echelons has become more critical, therefore, for being competitive and innovative (Carney and Gedajlovic 2003; Chung and Luo 2008). So have strategy implementation and the employment of more sophisticated management systems (Gedajlovic et al. 2004). These functional needs have, in turn, been considered as necessitating the retreat of the family and the expansion of professionalization in the top leadership of business groups. As in Chandler (1977), the expectation to that effect has been based on the core premise that professional managers are likely to be better than the family and their kin in dealing with and producing desired outcomes efficiently under novel conditions (e.g., Shin 1998; Young et al. 2001; Chang 2006a). The case made is that the superior education and talents of professional managers recruited on the basis of merit will outweigh, especially beyond a "threshold," the benefits typically attributed to family rule and management, such as lower agency costs, better coordination, and long-term commitment (Chung and Mahmood, Chapter 7; Suehiro and Wailerdsak, Chapter 9; both this volume).

25.4.2 Institutionalist views

An alternative set of views, often subsumed under the label "institutionalist," have also been evoked in accounting for the expectation that greater professionalization of top leadership is likely in business groups in the face of contextual changes that have been occurring. Fundamentally different from the techno-economic position, the essence of this perspective is that the impetus for change comes from the "institutional environment," typically conceived as comprising rules, norms, and models surrounding firms (see, e.g., Scott 2008). Within this broad thrust, however, institutional ideas have been employed in at least three different ways, at times jointly, with emphases on (*a*) alterations in regulatory frameworks; (*b*) normative influences; and (*c*) the effects of exemplars considered as best practice.

One way in which institutional ideas have been brought into studies of professionalization in business groups has been by pointing to the effects of legal and regulatory changes in many late-industrializing countries, which have involved reductions in state intervention in the economy, deregulation of financial markets, and the encouragement of foreign direct investments. These changes have often been mediated or imposed by international agencies such as the International Monetary Fund (IMF) and the World Bank, which have turned out to be powerful actors in shaping economic policies and institutions in the aftermath of economic crises (Tsui-Auch 2004; Luo and Chung 2005; Yeung 2006; see also Kim, Chapter 6; Suehiro and Wailerdsak, Chapter 9; both this volume). Governments have responded to pressures from such international bodies, as well as foreign creditors and institutional investors, by attempting to reform institutional structures with the aim of attracting foreign investments and facilitating economic recovery (Carney 2004; Wailerdsak and Suehiro 2004; Luo and Chung 2005; Üsdiken and Yildirim-Öktem 2008; see also Kim, Chapter 6, this volume, Tsui-Auch and Yoshikawa, Chapter 10, this volume). Geared, as they have been, toward greater liberalization and internationalization, these institutional changes have, in turn, served to reshape the economic environments of business groups. Thus, primacy in this version of institutionalist views is attached to alterations in the institutional landscape (see, e.g., Chung 2003). However, given a shift toward market-oriented institutions, the explanations that are offered for forthcoming professionalization have relied, very much along the lines discussed above, on the necessity to adapt to economic imperatives brought about by the new conditions.

Used as a complement to these views, or as a separate argument, has been a second institutional theme, which suggests that in particular time periods certain organizational models may come to be seen as the most contemporary and appropriate and therefore gain the character of a transnational standard. The diffusion of such models will stem from their prevalence in countries that are powerful and serve as reference societies, such as the United States. The most recent wave of such international expansion has involved models of "good" corporate governance. Framed largely by agency theoretic premises, the focus in these models has been on making company boards more active mainly by the incorporation of outside independent directors. Professionalization of management has been an undertone, not least because the origins of such models have been in a context (notably, the USA) where family managers (and even family rulers) have largely been in retreat (Anderson and Reeb 2004). Nevertheless, the expansion of corporate governance models to late-industrializing countries has not only brought governance practices considered as "good" in the USA, such as a higher proportion of outside directors, but also led to formal and non-formal pressures toward greater professionalization at top levels (Chang and Shin 2006; see also Kim, Chapter 6; Tsui-Auch and Yoshikawa, Chapter 10; both this volume). This has been due to the emergence of a broader normative climate endorsing professionalization of governance and management, promoted, in addition to international agencies and the state, by the business press, business schools, and foreign consultancies (Young et al. 2001; Tsui-Auch 2004; Luo and Chung 2005; Chang 2006b). Moreover, greater professionalization, it has been argued, has increasingly come to serve as a positive signal not only to state authorities but also to foreign investors, creditors, and customers (Chung 2003; Tsui-Auch 2004; Chang 2006a).

A third institutionalist idea employed in recent literature has been at one with the preceding theme in pointing to the influence of external models but with an accent on mimetic effects. So, Tsui-Auch and Lee (2003), for example, pointed to the modeling effects of state enterprises on family business groups in the professionalization of top level leadership. Likewise, Tsui-Auch and Yoshikawa (Chapter 10, this volume) and Boyd and Hoskisson (Chapter 24, this volume) suggested that multinational firms are likely to be a source of imitation too. In a somewhat different vein, education abroad has been considered as a vehicle for transporting foreign models of management. Young et al. (2001), for example, posited that younger-generation family members educated in business schools in the USA and the United Kingdom were likely to be more open to adopt US-based models of corporate governance and grant more say to outsider directors. Similarly, Chung and Luo (2008) hypothesized that owners with an MBA education in US business schools were likely to have fewer family members among those ruling their business groups. This, they argued, would be due to cognitive change brought about by exposure to the US model, transforming these owners into change agents pushing professionalization forward within their own contexts.

25.4.3 Culturist accounts and the national business systems perspective

Standing in contrast to the two sets of ideas discussed above are cultural and national business system perspectives that are at one in their skepticism about family business groups moving toward professional top leadership in view of recent economic and institutional changes. These two perspectives do differ, however, with respect to the claims they make as to why such a shift may not readily take place.

25.4.3.1 Culturist views

In broad terms, the culturist position has stressed the values, beliefs, and mental frames that characterize different societies and how they are brought to bear on work settings.

However, literature addressing cultural influences on the predominance of family rule and management has been largely confined to overseas Chinese business groups in East Asia. This particular literature has attributed family domination in business groups to the unique role of the family within Chinese culture and the lack of trust to non-kin (Suehiro 1993; Tsui-Auch and Lee 2003; Yeung 2006). Young et al. (2001), for example, concluded in their qualitative study on firms in Hong Kong and Taiwan that, in East Asia generally, the effects of more recently introduced corporate governance regulations have turned out to be limited because of this family-based culture. Although culturist views need to account for the prevalence of family rule and involvement in management in business groups in many other parts of the world (Khanna and Yafeh 2007), they represent, at least for East Asia, the strongest position with respect to barriers to a swift transition toward the managerial and externally governed enterprise (Carney 1998; Tsui-Auch and Yoshikawa, Chapter 10, this volume).

25.4.3.2 *The national business system perspective*

The major companion to the culturist position in arguing for the persistence of extant forms of business organization as well as variations among countries has been the national business system perspective. The central claim of this perspective has been that nationally specific social institutions mold the dominant form of business organization in a country and the distinctive features it possesses (see, e.g., Whitley 1999). There is some degree of affinity with culturist views in that the national business system perspective also takes into account the influence of pre-industrial values and beliefs on forms of economic organization. However, this is accompanied by a consideration of the legacy of political traditions in shaping state structures as well as financial, educational, and labor-relations systems framing the industrialization process (Whitley 1999). So, family rule and centralization of decision-making in the South Korean *chaebol*, for example, have been attributed, on the one hand, to lack of trust in non-kin and the personal nature of authority relationships. They have also been associated, however, with dependence on state support, which not only was often fraught with uncertainty but also relied on personal ties of the owners with political and bureaucratic authorities (Whitley 1999).

According to national business system theorists, fundamental changes in dominant organizational forms in different societies will require radical alterations in economic and institutional contexts (Whitley 1999). So, as Carney (2004) has also suggested, fundamental organizational change is most likely in the aftermath of a major political discontinuity, as in the well-known case of intervention by the US military government following the Second World War to disband the *zaibatsu* in Japan (Morikawa 1992). Though not perhaps equally dramatic, an instance of strong regulative pressure with radical consequences is also provided by Morck (Chapter 21, this volume) with reference to state action aimed at pyramidal groups in the USA in the mid-1930s. For the proponents of the national business systems perspective, on the other hand, recent regulatory changes in East and South Asia, for example, have not been on a scale to radically transform the external context of family business groups (Whitley 1999). This has been primarily due to the deep-rooted and interconnected nature of pre-existing institutions (Young et al. 2001). When alterations in the institutional environment remain limited, change in established forms of organization can only be incremental and slow (Carney 2004). So as Whitley (1999: 201) put it some time ago in referring to the South Korean *chaebol* and in a way that exemplifies the national business systems position, there seemed to be "little indication that family managers are willing to hand over the reins of power to 'professional' managers."

25.5 CHANGE OR CONTINUITY? THE
EMPIRICAL EVIDENCE

Although not very extensive, available empirical research provides some evidence concerning the professionalization of leadership in family business groups following the changes in the 1990s and 2000s in economic and institutional conditions. For the most part, this research has involved the horizontally structured overseas Chinese groups in East Asia, though a number of studies, mostly in this volume, are also available on the vertically structured business groups in some other parts of the world.

25.5.1 Rule and management in horizontally structured business groups

In one of the early studies specifically addressing the issue of top leadership, Chung (2003) examined whether any changes had occurred in the way Taiwanese business groups were ruled after political and regulatory alterations and the ensuing shift to a more marketized economy. His findings indicated that the structural pattern by which an "inner circle" served as "rulers" of these groups persisted throughout the period from mid-1970s to the mid-1990s covered by the study. Chung (2003) also reported that the proportion of salaried managers within these "inner circles" had increased in the post-transition period at the expense of family members and the owners' business associates. However, akin to Tsui-Auch's notion (2004) of "family-related managers," these salaried executives were most likely to be loyal and committed employees with long tenures and were therefore more like quasi-kin than professional managers (see also Carney and Gedajlovic 2003). Moreover, family and relatives still constituted more than half the inner circle, and the drop in the proportion of family members was around 10 percent (see also Chung and Mahmood, Chapter 7, this volume). Moreover, as indicated in a further study on Taiwanese business groups, there was not even a single case where the key leader was not a family member (Chung and Luo 2008), and this leader, as Chung and Mahmood (Chapter 7, this volume) have indicated, is the most powerful person in the entire business group. In fact, Chung and Luo (2008), using a larger data set and more rigorous analyses than previous studies, showed that changes in market conditions had no effects on the extent of family presence within inner circles. They did, however, find support for the hypothesis that second-generation group leaders were likely to have fewer family members in the period following the introduction of political and market reforms. Chung and Luo (2008) also obtained findings in line with the view that leaders with management education in the USA were likely to have a lower proportion of members with family ties, though this was the case in both the pre- and the post-transition periods.

Tsui-Auch (2004), in a qualitative study, again drawing upon a mixture of institutionalist and economistic ideas, compared Singaporean business groups before and after the Asian currency crisis. She concluded that the crisis had not essentially altered the "family-ruled, professionally managed" form that these groups had taken long before (see also Tsui-Auch and Yoshikawa, Chapter 10, this volume). There were cases, she argued, in which family rule appeared to weaken, though these also happened to be instances where there were no descendants readily available to take over. In a companion study comparing pre- and post-crisis top leadership in fourteen firms affiliated with ten different business groups in Singapore, Tsui-Auch (2006: 113) showed that in only one of these firms was there a shift to a chairperson who was not from the family. Notably, however, in this particular case the top executive position remained in the hands of a family member. Moreover, there was no difference between the two periods in the ratio of salaried managers in this position either, as this stayed around 20 percent both before and after the currency crisis.

In their contribution to this volume on Thai business groups, Suehiro and Wailerdsak (Chapter 9) also showed that owner families were likely to be heavily represented in both boards and executive management. With 1997 data on the core firms of the ninety-one largest business groups, they reported that, irrespective of being listed or not, there were very few cases where a family member did not hold either a chairperson or a top executive position or both at the same time. Even in the few exceptional cases where this was not the case, there would be at least one family member as a director. In a companion study of board members and top executives of listed firms in the aftermath of the Asian crisis, Wailerdsak and Suehiro (2004) concluded that the presence of families on company boards and their dominant role persisted. Their findings also indicated that family members were present among top executive ranks too, though at a level that was significantly less than that of boards. Nevertheless, they conjectured that employing a greater proportion of professional managers did not necessarily mean a shift in their influence, as the split between families ruling the group and the salaried managers undertaking operational management, as Suehiro and Wailerdsak (Chapter 9, this volume) believed, was not altered.

25.5.2 Rule and management in vertically structured business groups

There is also similar evidence from contexts where business groups are larger and vertically structured, often with some kind of an overarching body at the apex, such as a holding company, a parent company, or a central office. There, too, despite changes in economic and institutional environments, founding families seem to have maintained a dominant role as rulers, together with a mixture of family and professional management within executive ranks at the group and affiliate-firm level. Empirical evidence to support this contention is provided in the various contributions to this volume, as well as in a few additional studies that are available. Basing their work on a survey of twenty-one Argentine business groups, Fracchia, Mesquita, and Quiroga (Chapter 12, this volume), for example, concluded that one of the main characteristics of these groups was still the influence that the owner families had over strategic decisions. Their survey showed that family presence in boards was on average above 60 percent, while salaried managers from within the group constituted around 20 percent of the directors. In almost all the groups that were surveyed, there was what Fracchia et al. referred to as "active family involvement," descending in two-thirds of the cases to the third or later generations. Lefort (Chapter 14, this volume) also observed that three-fifths of the largest twenty-five business groups in Chile were "classic family-run groups" where family members sit on boards and/or assume executive roles. He also claimed that, although professionalization of management had been expanding, it was still the leaders of the owner families who made the strategic decisions.

Colpan (Chapter 17, this volume), using a survey of eleven large Turkish business groups, contended that, after more than two decades' experience with market-oriented reforms, the founding families still had a dominant presence in the boards of the apex holding company, which maintained a tight control not only on the strategies of affiliate firms but also on their major operational decisions. Supporting this contention, Gökşen and Üsdiken (2001) showed that, in the largest twenty Turkish business groups in the late 1990s, family members constituted on average around 40 percent of the board of the holding company. In a more recent study, Yildirim-Öktem and Üsdiken (2010) noted that in the ten large business groups that they studied, as in the example provided by Colpan (Chapter 17, this volume), the chairperson of the holding board was invariably from the founding family. Colpan's interviews also suggested that, despite what recently appeared to be a shift to a salaried chief executive officer (CEO) for the entire group, the chairperson from the family still served as the "real" CEO (see also Chang and Shin 2006 for a similar conclusion for the chairpersons of South Korean business groups). Note should also be made, however, that Gökşen and Üsdiken's study (2001) showed that there was considerable professionalization within the apex holding company as family members constituted, on average, only around 9 percent of the managers in this top-level organization.

Turning to affiliated firms, Hoshino (Chapter 15, this volume) reported that almost all the thirty listed affiliates of the largest groups in Mexico had a family member as the chairperson. Aldrighi and Postali (Chapter 13, this volume) claimed that large Brazilian business groups usually had a family member in the boards of main affiliate firms. Sarkar (Chapter 11, this volume) also noted that a major mechanism for control over affiliates of business groups in India was to place family members in executive or non-executive roles in boards of directors. However, figures that she reported, based on a study of 500 listed affiliate firms some ten years or so after the introduction of market reforms, were significantly lower than those for Mexican business groups. In the Indian case, less than half the affiliate firms had a founding family member on their boards. Similarly, Silva et al.'s findings (2006) showed that the proportion of family members in boards and CEO positions of listed affiliates in Chilean business groups was 22 percent. Gökşen and Üsdiken (2001) also found that family representation in the boards of listed firms affiliated to large Turkish business groups was on average slightly above 20 percent. In a more recent study on ten of the largest Turkish groups, Üsdiken and Yildirim-Öktem (2008) found a very similar average figure for both listed and non-listed affiliate firms. A companion study by Yildirim-Öktem and Üsdiken (2010) showed that group firms that were larger, older, and had higher direct ownership of founding family members tended to have a smaller proportion of salaried managers in their boards.

Hoshino's results for Mexican business groups (Chapter 15, this volume) also indicated considerable family involvement in the executive management of affiliated firms. In the thirty groups that she examined, in only about a third was the CEO a non-family salaried manager. In the rest a family member was either the CEO or held both the chairperson and the top executive positions. Sarkar (Chapter 11, this volume) again found that this was less likely to be the case in Indian business groups, as only close to 30 percent had a chairperson or a managing director who was a family member. Sarkar's findings may be capturing a size effect, as Chang and Shin (2006) also found that, among listed firms in South Korea, those that were affiliated to one of the largest thirty *chaebol* were less likely to have a family member as the top executive person compared to standalone firms or those linked to smaller groups.

Along similar lines, Aldrighi and Postali (Chapter 13, this volume) claimed that, in Brazilian business groups, despite a presence in the boards of affiliated firms, family members were unlikely to hold positions as board chairperson, CEO, or a top executive. Goldstein (Chapter 19, this volume) made a similar claim about business groups in South Africa. What the discussion by these authors implies is that this may be due to listing abroad and thus to the pressure of institutional investors. Nevertheless, Aldrighi and Postali (Chapter 13, this volume) also indicated that there were cases where family members were CEOs of main affiliates, together with seats on the board, sometimes as the chairperson. Likewise, Goldstein (Chapter 19, this volume) posited that, despite professionalization at executive levels, the controlling families, now in the second or third generations, maintained their influence on strategy-making. Implying a greater move toward professionalization, Kosenko and Yafeh (Chapter 16, this volume) claimed that, although tight monitoring by owners continued, strategies for affiliate firms were jointly developed with salaried managers.

Taken altogether, the evidence reviewed above does not point to a panorama that is radically different from the observations and the evidence provided by the early literature on business groups reviewed in the third section of this chapter. It may also well be that family rule may still be extending beyond strategy-making to interventions in operational decisions, due not least to continuing presence of owners in boards and at times in executive positions within affiliate firms (see also recent assessments by, e.g., Kim et al. 2004; Chang and Shin 2006; Aulakh and Kotabe 2008). There does perhaps seem to be some indication that there is greater professionalization of executive management in group firms, though possibly more so in those that are larger and listed abroad. Much less known however is whether and to what degree this is accompanied by greater decision-making influence on the part of managers who are not from the owning families.

25.6 BRINGING IN A POWER PERSPECTIVE

The perspectives considered above, despite occasional references, tend to neglect the role that interests and power may play in providing additional explanatory potential in accounting for whether and why change may or may not come about in top leadership (see Carney 2004 as an exception). Differently from others, a power-based approach to leadership in family business groups would begin with the central premise that owners have what Mayer and Whittington (2004) have called a "political unwillingness" to share group rule, and even management, with non-family managers or outsiders. Given this unwillingness, family owners are likely to resist relinquishing their power to rule and manage as much as they can. This is perhaps best illustrated by Tsui-Auch and Yoshikawa (Chapter 10, this volume) when they quote the leader of a business group in Singapore as saying: "to be honest, to leave a company totally to professional management, I have my reservations." Bertrand et al. (2008), in a rare empirical study, also showed that family size was positively associated with the number of positions held by family members in Thai business groups. Arguably then, turning top leadership to professionals can be seen as essentially a political issue, particularly when it involves a shift in who rules the organization. The desire to retain leadership within the family therefore goes beyond considerations suggested in standard economistic accounts, such as reduction of agency costs or problems associated with enforcement of contracts regarded as typical in late-industrializing countries (e.g., Bertrand et al. 2008; Guriev, Chapter 18, this volume). Neither does it have to do necessarily with claims akin to those of stewardship theory in the management literature, which emphasizes advantages of retaining family rule and management, like stronger commitment, a longer-term orientation, and speed in decision-making (see, e.g., Tsui-Auch 2006). It probably has more to do with having overall power in running one's own (or one's family's) enterprise and thus preserving the capacity to exercise authority and shape strategy (Gedajlovic et al. 2004; Mayer and Whittington 2004). Moreover, as Morck (Chapter 21, this volume) also argues, actually ruling and managing large business groups may provide greater status and potential influence over political and bureaucratic circles (see also Buğra 1994). Not only may this open up avenues for access to critical resources; it may also serve as a guarantor of long-term survival (Morck, Chapter 21, this volume).

Moreover, to the extent that business success depends on such ties, the reluctance to have non-kin involvement at higher echelons can be associated with concerns about secrecy (Buğra, 1994; Hamilton 1997; Chung and Luo 2008).

Shifts toward professional rule and management can then come about because of alterations in power and dependence relations with environmental actors and the ways these affect internal power distribution (Pfeffer and Salancik 1978). Power vis-à-vis the environment is associated with dependencies arising from the need to access valued resources. As resource needs become altered, so does the degree of organizational autonomy and power relations with external actors. So, as Carney (2004) has pointed out, reduced dependence on the state for finance, for example, has enabled the South Korean *chaebol* to influence and resist institutional reforms (see also Young et al. 2001; Chang 2006; Chang and Shin 2006). On the other hand, at a more general level, Koike (1993) has suggested that increasing need for outside finance, technological know-how, or marketing knowledge may lead to the generation of new external dependencies. Very much along these lines, Aldrighi and Postali (Chapter 13, this volume) and Goldstein (Chapter 19, this volume) noted that listing abroad, for example, resulted in becoming subject to greater influence by institutional investors.

Notable from a power perspective are also the effects of altered environmental dependencies and the actions of external actors on internal power distribution and the ways that the former can be employed as resources by groups within organizations for advancing their claims and interests (Fligstein 1987). With respect to rule and management in business groups, this relates to how changes in the external environment may serve to tilt the balance from owner families to salaried managers. Although not referring explicitly to the role played out by power, some of the literature reviewed in previous sections has in fact implied that moves toward greater professionalization originated from alterations in external dependencies and the outside pressures that these generated. As mentioned above, Aldrighi and Postali (Chapter 13, this volume) and Goldstein (Chapter 19, this volume), for example, claimed that the appointment of salaried executives to very top positions in Brazilian and South African group firms listed abroad had to do with the greater influence of institutional investors. Likewise, Tsui-Auch and Yoshikawa (Chapter 10, this volume) suggested that the need for foreign finance led Singaporean groups to turn more toward professional managers (see also Tsui-Auch 2004). So did Chung and Luo (2008) when they reasoned that including more professionals within the inner circles of Taiwanese business groups had to do with the need to attract foreign capital.

Again without explicit association with power, extant literature has also made occasional reference to conditions that may serve to enhance the significance of professional expertise and, thus, the power of salaried managers. Tsui-Auch (2006), for example, claimed that the early turn to salaried managers in Singaporean business groups came when listing of some of the affiliate firms generated a need for employing outsiders with necessary training to carry out the novel administrative requirements. Even more explicitly, Chang (2006b) voiced the expectation that the post-crisis corporate governance reforms in South Korea would result in limiting the power of *chaebol* chairmen and help salaried managers to acquire a more active role in strategy-making. Similarly, Chung and Luo (2008: 130) reasoned that economic conditions created by institutional transition in Taiwan would make non-family executives more "valuable and powerful."

As a power-based approach has not been brought into discussions and studies of top leadership in business groups, none of the conjectures mentioned above has been put to a direct empirical test. Nevertheless, they do provide examples of the kinds of antecedents that need to be considered in taking a power perspective. They also show, together with the preceding discussion, how the premises of and the reasoning employed in power-based views differ from the currently more popular economistic and institutional perspectives in examining change and continuity in business group leadership.

25.7 CONCLUDING DISCUSSION

Top leadership has been one of the least-researched areas within the recent expanding interest in business groups. As reviewed above, available scant evidence suggests that change has been limited, despite economic and institutional alterations as well as major economic crises that have unfolded within a broader context of expanding globalization. Most notably, the way the business groups are ruled has persisted, still remaining very much in the hands of the controlling families. The mixture of family rule with professionalized operational management that Biggart (1990), amongst others, identified some two decades ago also appears to persist. The available evidence also indicates that the continuity observed in these patterns has been largely similar across a broad range of the so-called emerging economies, though some further expansion of professionalism may be taking place in some contexts.

That the way business groups are ruled and their mixed character have remained essentially the same may appear puzzling when looked at from a purely techno-economic perspective or from the view that assigns a paramount role to the intro-duction of market-based institutional reforms. It may appear less so if one takes a national business systems or a power perspective, as reviewed above, recognizing the path-dependent nature of organizational evolution. Adding to the "puzzle" for the former perspectives are research findings that are contrary to widely held beliefs that professionalization in business groups is likely to lead to superior outcomes, espe-cially in more marketized and internationalized settings. Luo and Chung's study (2005) on Taiwanese business groups, for example, showed that over the period 1973–96 there was no relationship between the extent of particularistic ties within the inner circle and the likelihood of exit from the top 100 list. In fact, they found that after institutional reforms greater family presence had positive effects on performance, though up to a threshold level, which was also lower for the larger and more diversified groups. Their results also showed, very much in line with a power perspective, that family presence within inner circles was not affected by business group performance (see also Chung and Luo 2008). Again notably, Silva et al. (2006) found a positive relationship between the extent of family ties (among board members and the CEOs) and performance of listed firms affiliated to Chilean business groups.

Whether this is seen as a puzzle or not, more research is needed to decipher what is happening, why, and with what consequences. More specifically, at least three sets of possible research avenues may be identified. One of these is the need for comparative research especially across business groups from different regions of the world. So far there has been almost none of this kind of research, at least with respect to the way business groups are ruled and managed. This kind of inquiry is likely to require large-scale quantitative data to describe, understand, and explain the similarities and differences in who rules and manages business groups in different countries and how this may or may not be changing.

Secondly, there is the need for a better description and understanding of what exactly is happening and what it is that may be changing. Judging from the chapters included in this volume and the recent studies that have been reviewed, it seems that in many settings there is some kind of a move toward greater incorporation of salaried managers into higher echelons of business groups, though within a context of persistent family rule. The question of what these changes amount to exactly still remains. Indeed, going beyond what numbers may indicate, there is the need to examine what changes may be occurring in the relationships between rulers and the salaried managers. As Colpan (Chapter 17, this volume) has shown, softer and richer data obtained through interviews may suggest a different picture, indeed one of even more constrained change, relative to those that may be indicated by figures (see also Tsui-Auch 2004). Therefore, more qualitative studies are required to obtain a better sense of what has been happening between the rulers and their executives.

Finally, there is a need to accumulate knowledge with respect to the relative merits of different theoretical perspectives that have had something to say about the ways in which business groups are ruled and managed. The limited available evidence that has been reviewed above lends little support to techno-economic and institutional reform-based perspectives. This would suggest the incorporation of alternative theoretical lenses in a comparative or complementary manner. Systematic empirical studies emanating from different theoretical positions, however, are almost non-existent. They are, on the other hand, likely to be useful in informing future theory-based work on various facets of business groups.

References

Amsden, A. H. (1989). *Asia's Next Giant: South Korea and Late Industrialization.* New York: Oxford University Press.

Anderson, R. C., and Reeb, D. M. (2004). "Board Composition: Balancing Family Influence in S&P 500 Firms," *Administrative Science Quarterly,* 49: 209–37.

AULAKH, P. S., and KOTABE, M. (2008). "Institutional Changes and Organizational Trans-formation in Developing Economies," *Journal of International Management*, 14: 209–16.

BERTRAND, M., JOHNSON, S., SAMPHANTHARAK, K., and SCHOAR, A. (2008). "Mixing Family with Business: A Study of Thai Business Groups and the Families Behind Them," *Journal of Financial Economics*, 88: 466–98.

BIGGART, N. W. (1990). "Institutionalized Patrimonialism in Korean Business," *Comparative Social Research*, 12: 113–33.

BIGGART, N. W. (1998). "Deep Finance: The Organizational Bases of South Korea's Financial Collapse," *Journal of Management Inquiry*, 7: 311–20.

BUĞRA, A. (1994). *State and Business in Modern Turkey: A Comparative Study*. New York: State University of New York Press.

CARNEY, M. (1998). "A Management Capacity Constraint? Obstacles to the Development of the Chinese Family Business," *Asia Pacific Journal of Management*, 15: 137–62.

CARNEY, M. (2004). "The Institutions of Industrial Restructuring in Southeast Asia," *Asia Pacific Journal of Management*, 21: 171–88.

CARNEY, M., and GEDAJLOVIC, E. (2003). "Strategic Innovation and the Administrative Heritage of East Asian Family Business Groups," *Asia Pacific Journal of Management*, 20: 5–26.

CHANDLER, A. D. (1977). *The Visible Hand: The Managerial Revolution in American Busi-ness*. Cambridge, MA: Belknap Press.

CHANDLER, A. D. (1990). *Scale and Scope: The Dynamics of Industrial Capitalism*. Cambridge, MA: Belknap Press.

CHANG, J. J., and SHIN, H.-H. (2006). "Governance System Effectiveness Following the Crisis: Korean Business Group Headquarters," *Corporate Governance*, 14/2: 85–97.

CHANG, S.-J. (2003). "Ownership Structure, Expropriation and Performance of Group Affiliated Companies in Korea," *Academy of Management Journal*, 46: 238–54.

CHANG, S.-J. (2006a). "Business Groups in East Asia: Post-Crisis Restructuring and New Growth," *Asia Pacific Journal of Management*, 23: 407–17.

CHANG, S.-J. (2006b). "Korean Business Groups: The Financial Crisis and the Restructuring of Chaebols," in S.-J. Chang (ed.), *Business Groups in East Asia: Financial Crisis, Restructuring and New Growth*. Oxford: Oxford University Press, 52–69.

CHITTOOR, R. and DAS, R. (2007). "Professionalization of Management and Succession Performance: A Vital Link," *Family Business Review*, 20: 65–79.

CHUNG, C.-N. (2003). "Managerial Structure of Business Groups in Taiwan: The Inner Circle System and its Social Organization," *Developing Economies*, 41: 37–64.

CHUNG, C.-N. (2004). "Institutional Transition and Cultural Inheritance: Network Owner-ship and Corporate Control of Business Groups in Taiwan, 1970s–1990s," *International Sociology*, 19: 25–50.

CHUNG, C.-N., and LUO, X. (2008). "Human Agents, Contexts, and Institutional Change: The Decline of Family in the Leadership of Business Groups," *Organization Science*, 19: 124–42.

CHUNG, C.-N., and MAHMOOD, I. P. (2006). "Taiwanese Business Groups: Steady Growth in Institutional Transition," in S.-J. Chang (ed.), *Business Groups in East Asia: Financial Crisis, Restructuring and New Growth*. Oxford: Oxford University Press, 70–93.

CHUNG, K. H., LEE, H. C., and JUNG, K. H. (1997). *Korean Management: Global Strategy and Cultural Transformation*. Berlin: Walter de Gruyter.

FLIGSTEIN, N. (1987). "The Intraorganizational Power Struggle: Rise of Finance Personnel to Top Leadership in Large Corporations, 1919–1979," *American Sociological Review*, 52: 44–58.

GEDAJLOVIC, E., LUBATKIN, M. H., and SCHULZE, W. S. (2004). "Crossing the Threshold from Founder Management to Professional Management: A Governance Perspective," *Journal of Management Studies*, 41: 899–912.

GÖKŞEN, N. S., and ÜSDIKEN, B. (2001). "Uniformity and Diversity in Turkish Business Groups: Effects of Scale and Time of Founding," *British Journal of Management*, 12: 325–49.

GUILLÉN, M. F. (2000). "Business Groups in Emerging Economies: A Resource-Based View," *Academy of Management Journal*, 43: 362–80.

HAMILTON, G. G. (1997). "Organization and Market Processes in Taiwan's Capitalist Economy," in M. Orru, N. W. Biggart, and G. G. Hamilton (eds.), *The Economic Organization of East Asian Capitalism*. Thousand Oaks, CA: Sage, 237–93.

HAMILTON, G. G., and BIGGART, N. W. (1988). "Market, Culture and Authority: A Comparative Analysis of Management and Organization in the Far East," *American Journal of Sociology*, 94 supplement, 52–94.

HOSKISSON, R. E., EDEN, L., LAU, C. M., and WRIGHT, M. (2000). "Strategy in Emerging Economies," *Academy of Management Journal*, 43: 249–67.

HOSKISSON, R. E., JOHNSON, R. A., TIHANYI, L., and WHITE, R. E. (2005). "Diversified Business Groups and Corporate Refocusing in Emerging Economies," *Journal of Management*, 31: 941–65.

KHANNA, T., and RIVKIN, J. W. (2001). "Estimating the Performance Effects of Business Groups in Emerging Markets," *Strategic Management Journal*, 22: 45–74.

KHANNA, T., and YAFEH, Y. (2007). "Business Groups in Emerging Markets: Paragons or Parasites?" *Journal of Economic Literature*, 45: 331–72.

KIM, E. M. (1996). "The Industrial Organization and Growth of the Korean Chaebol: Integrating Development and Organizational Theories," in G. G. Hamilton (ed.), *Asian Business Networks*. New York: Walter de Gruyter, 231–51.

KIM, H., HOSKISSON, R. E., TIHANYI, L., and HONG, J. (2004). "The Evolution and Restructuring of Diversified Business Groups in Emerging Markets: The Lessons from Chaebols in Korea," *Asia Pacific Journal of Management*, 21: 25–48.

KOIKE, K. (1993). "Introduction," *Developing Economies*, 31: 363–77.

LEE, S. M., and YOO, S. (1987). "The K-Type Management: A Driving Force of Korean Prosperity," *Management International Review*, 27/4: 68–76.

LUO, X., and CHUNG, C.-N. (2005). "Keeping it All in the Family: The Role of Particularistic Relationships in Business Group Performance during Institutional Transition," *Administrative Science Quarterly*, 50: 404–39.

MAYER, M., and WHITTINGTON, R. (2004). "Economics, Politics and Nations: Resistance to the Multidivisional Form in France, Germany and the United Kingdom, 1883–1993," *Journal of Management Studies*, 41: 1057–82.

MORIKAWA, H. (1992). *Zaibatsu: The Rise and Fall of Family Enterprise Groups in Japan*. Tokyo: University of Tokyo Press.

MORIKAWA, H. (2001). *A History of Top Management in Japan*. Oxford: Oxford University Press.

PFEFFER, J., and SALANCIK, G. R. (1978). *The External Control of Organizations*. New York: Harper and Row.

SCOTT, J. (1990). "Corporate Control and Corporate Rule: Britain in an International Perspective," *British Journal of Sociology*, 41: 351–73.

SCOTT, W. R. (2008). *Institutions and Organizations: Ideas and Interests*. 3rd edn. London: Sage.

SHIN, Y. K. (1998). "The Traits and Leadership Styles of CEOs in Korean Companies," *International Studies of Management and Organization*, 28/4: 40–8.

SHIN, E. H., and CHIN, S. K. (1989). "Social Affinity among Top Managerial Executives of Large Corporations in Korea," *Sociological Forum*, 4: 3–26.

SILVA, F., MAJLUF, N., and PAREDES, R. D. (2006). "Family Ties, Interlocking Directors and Performance of Business Groups in Emerging Countries: The Case of Chile," *Journal of Business Research*, 59: 315–21.

SUEHIRO, A. (1993). "Family Business Reassessed: Corporate Structure and Late-Starting Industrialization in Thailand," *Developing Economies*, 31: 378–407.

SUEHIRO, A., and WAILERDSAK, N. (2004). "Family Business in Thailand: Its Management, Governance and Future Challenges", *ASEAN Economic Bulletin*, 21: 81–93.

TSUI-AUCH, L. S. (2004). "The Professionally Managed Family-Ruled Enterprise: Ethnic Chinese Business in Singapore," *Journal of Management Studies*, 41: 693–723.

TSUI-AUCH, L. S. (2006). "Singaporean Business Groups: The Role of the State and Capital in Singapore Inc.," in S.-J. Chang (ed.), *Business Groups in East Asia: Financial Crisis, Restructuring and New Growth*. Oxford: Oxford University Press, 94–115.

TSUI-AUCH, L. S., and LEE, Y.-J. (2003). "The State Matters: Management Models of Singaporean Chinese and Korean Business Groups," *Organization Studies*, 24: 507–34.

UNGSON, G. R., STEERS, R. M., and PARK, S.-H. (1997). *Korean Enterprise: The Quest for Globalization*. Boston: Harvard Business School Press.

ÜSDIKEN, B., and YILDIRIM-ÖKTEM, Ö. (2008). "Changes in the Institutional Environment and 'Non-Executive' and 'Independent' Members of the Boards of Directors of Firms Affiliated with Large Family Business Groups," *Amme İdaresi Dergisi*, 41/1: 43–71.

WAILERDSAK, N., and SUEHIRO, A. (2004). "Top Executive Origins: Comparative Study between Japan and Thailand," *Asian Business and Management*, 3: 85–104.

WHITLEY, R. (1990). "East Asian Enterprise Structures and the Comparative Analysis of Forms of Business Organization," *Organization Studies*, 11: 47–74.

WHITLEY, R. (1999). *Divergent Capitalisms: The Social Structuring and Change of Business Systems*. Oxford: Oxford University Press.

WHITTINGTON, R., and MAYER, M. (2000). *The European Corporation*. Oxford: Oxford University Press.

YEUNG, H. W. C. (2006). "Change and Continuity in Southeast Asian Ethnic Chinese Business," *Asia Pacific Journal of Management*, 23: 229–54.

YILDIRIM-ÖKTEM, Ö., and ÜSDIKEN, B. (2010). "Contingencies versus External Pressure: Professionalization in Boards of Firms Affiliated to Family Business Groups in Late Industrializing Countries," *British Journal of Management*, 21: 115–30.

YOO, S. and LEE, S. M. (1987). "Management Style and Practice of Korean Chaebols." *California Management Review*, 29/4: 95–110.

YOUNG, M. N., AHLSTORM, D., BRUTON, G. D., and CHAN, E. S. (2001). "The Resource Dependence, Service and Control Functions of Boards of Directors in Hong Kong and Taiwanese Firms," *Asia Pacific Journal of Management*, 18: 223–44.

CHAPTER 26

DIVERSIFICATION STRATEGY AND BUSINESS GROUPS

ANDREW DELIOS

XUFEI MA

26.1 INTRODUCTION

THE aim of this chapter is to examine recent developments in the strategies of diversified business groups. We assess the business group strategy by focusing on two prominent areas of growth: product diversification and geographic diversification. This chapter thus attempts to identify the ways in which these strategies have been developed by business groups in the last decade of the twentieth century and the first decade of the twenty-first. From this we hope to develop an insight into the future competitiveness of business groups, as coupled to the nature of their competitive advantages as impetuses to their strategies in both their domestic and their international markets.

The main focus of the chapter is diversification, rather than other strategic issues, although these are clearly interrelated elements. Also, as we are dealing with business groups at the turn of the century, these groups are often operating in business environments where liberalization and privatization are part of the main goals of policy-makers (Hoskisson et al. 2000), which contrasts to developed-country markets, where the institutional underlay of competitive markets has been a feature of these economies for a much longer period.

The rest of this chapter is organized as follows. First, Section 26.2 begins with a brief review of the contextual elements in the environments in which most of the business groups operated through the 1990s and 2000s. Then, in Section 26.3, we review theoretical perspectives on business groups in brief, given that these conceptual underpinnings are the specific focus of other chapters in this *Handbook*. We follow this discussion with a review of the progression of business group research strategies. Next, in Section 26.4, we discuss how business groups have evolved in their approaches to product and geographic diversification. Although a concise summary is untenable, given that we are looking at trends in sixteen countries each with a large number of groups, we do attempt to draw broad conclusions. We link these conclusions to developments in the theory chapters to highlight how such descriptive country analyses can begin to address the theoretical issues that are central to our understanding of strategic issues for business groups as they enter the 2010s. Finally, we conclude with Section 26.5, in which we discuss future research on business group strategy as related to research design and research questions. This final section is driven by the overarching issue that naturally falls out of the analyses presented in this *Handbook*; namely, "What are the consequent research opportunities for scholars concerned with understanding strategy, competition and business groups?"

26.2 BUSINESS ENVIRONMENTS

As is clearly evident in this *Handbook*, business groups can be found in a large number of countries that are truly diverse in a variety of characteristics at both national and subnational levels: institutions, the role of governments, and governance systems (Singh 2004). But although differences exist across the various countries in which business groups are common, within this group of countries we can also find common characteristics, as compared to countries in which business groups are less common (Delios et al. 2007). In taking such a broad brush to the depiction of these environments, there will necessarily be exceptions. It is interesting to note, however, that there are areas in which a number of countries are in similar stages in transition, which can potentially influence the viability, strategy, and performance of business groups in their domestic markets.

26.2.1 Institutional environments

Emerging and developed economies in which a large proportion of the business groups are situated are characterized by varying degrees of development in government, business, legal, and other types of institutions (Peng 2000). These differences in national institutional environments can differentiate the strategies and structures commonly found in these different environments (Whitley 1992). For example, institutions in many Asian countries are less developed than those in the countries of the European Union or North America (see the chapters in Part II of this volume). Underdeveloped financial markets, inadequate financial intermediaries, poor corporate governance, and underdeveloped banks characterized many of these economies, if not in the late 2000s, then earlier in the decade or even in the 1990s. Coupled with poorly developed communications infrastructures and lax corporate reporting requirements, these institutional features restrict information flows and impede market efficiency. Other institutional characteristics include inadequately trained, inflexible, and relatively unproductive labor; scarce management talent; unreliable property-rights protection; weak consumer protection regulations; inefficient governments and judicial systems, and a weak legal environment (Khanna and Palepu 1997; La Porta et al. 1999; Johnson et al. 2000; World Bank 2002).

While obviously a simplification of institutional environments, this brief description brings us to the point that national institutions are a critical factor in shaping economic activity and firm behavior (North 1990). Weaknesses in a country's political and legal institutions can lead to market failure. Together these weaknesses can lead to high transaction costs for firms engaging in market-based exchange for inputs and outputs (Williamson 1975; Wan and Hoskisson 2003). Under such circumstances, corporate-level product diversification can be a strategic action by a firm to create substitutes for absent factors and institutions (Wan and Hoskisson 2003). Business groups are thought to be an organizational response to institutional weaknesses, in which product diversity levels can be increased by developing connections between multiple-affiliated firms (Khanna and Palepu 2000; Khanna and Rivkin 2001). The resultant product diversity across the affiliated firms in a single business group can help these affiliated firms develop internal markets to compensate for institutional voids (Khanna and Palepu 1997).

26.2.2 Governments

A second important feature of the business environment is the role played by governments and their affiliated agencies and corporations. Governments can adopt a mix of direction and regulation, alongside the pursuit of free-market orientations (Hamilton and Biggart 1988; Wade 1990; World Bank 1993; Lasserre and Schutte 1995; Aoki et al. 1996). A number of governments in countries where business groups are common have combined intervention with free-market support, if not in the late 1990s than at least in the recent past. Many participate directly in business when necessary or profitable; they often do so with a great frequency, under the idea that there can be efficiency or other gains related to government participation in an economy. Hence, governments have been promoters, partners, regulators, and actors in business in ways that can assist firms in many areas, but they also compete against them, or stage conditions under which competition is heightened. This means that firms operating in many economies in which business groups are common often have to engage in more complex relationships with regulators and governments than they would in developed markets. Scholars have also noted that, in emerging markets, governments can provide various forms of support and subsidies for rapid business growth (Chang and Hong 2000; Guillén 2000), which leads to the next two theoretical perspectives on the emergence of business groups. The government underlay has fed into the theoretical perspectives on business groups, such as the political perspective Schneider (Chapter 23, this volume) or the leverage and resource-based perspective Guillén (Chapter 27, this volume).

26.2.3 Governance systems

A combination of cultural, firm, and institutional characteristics differentiate corporate governance systems in countries in which business groups are common from those in other countries, such as the USA and the United Kingdom (Boyd and Hoskisson, Chapter 24, this volume). Family-based corporate governance systems differ significantly from the equity market or bank-led governance systems that dominate in North America and Western Europe respectively and that exist to lesser degrees in some economies in Asia. The different composition, characteristics, and interests of major owners in many emerging economies, and the underlying differences in legal systems and other traditions that support such governance, challenge existing frameworks and analyses that are used to understand the efficiencies and effectiveness of these alternative governance systems.

26.2.4 Environments and change

For most of the last two decades of the twentieth century and the first decade of the twenty-first, a large number of emerging economies have enjoyed rapid economic growth and less rapid, but progressive, development in supporting institutions (Hoskisson et al. 2000). These developments have not been uniform across these countries, which has led to differing trajectories in the evolution of social, legal, regulatory, language, governance, and business systems. These differing trajectories have been compounded by the variance in histories, geographies, cultures, economies, and colonial experiences within which these supporting institutions are embedded.

The consequence is that economic systems vary widely—with some emerging economies having relatively large and free markets that offer firms considerable strategic flexibility, while others are restrictive and highly regulated. Countries in which business groups are common also differ temporally in respects that are unrelated to their stages of economic and political development, with great variations in sociocultural, political, and technological sophistication.

Such points are hardly contentious, yet the exact nature of each environment and its specific trajectory requires detailed analysis at the country level, as can be found in the various national chapters in this *Handbook*. As is clear in these chapters, institutions, government, and governance systems shared commonalities that helped foster the development of business groups, but in each nation these features also underwent change, and in some cases dramatic change, that influenced the strategy, structure, and performance of business groups. It is as a consequence of this change in the domestic environment that scholars have become concerned with the viability of business groups, alongside concerns about how their common and well-noted predilection for extensive product diversification, but narrow geographic diversification, will advance.

26.2.5 Product and geographic diversification

Research on product and geographic diversification is a central and important theme in research on firms situated in emerging markets (Leung and White 2004). These two diversification phenomena emerged as prominent strategies for firms during the 1970s to 1990s, a period of rapid development in many emerging economies in Asia and Latin America. As domestic markets continue to grow and mature, firms will continue to face these diversification issues.

Research on product diversification in emerging economies is a subset of research on product diversification that has long been a central focus of academic and practitioner interest in strategy (Rumelt et al. 1994; Palich et al. 2000). Strategy research on product diversification asks the following important questions: What should be the product scope of a firm? Why do firms diversify their product lines? What types of firms diversify their products? How do firms diversify their product portfolio? What are the outcomes of product diversification?

In early approaches to these questions, researchers such as Williamson (1975) and Gort (1984) argued that product diversification was fundamentally a risk-spreading practice that firms adopt to reduce unpredictable changes in profitability in different industrial sectors. From this starting point, a tremendous range of research has been brought to the product-diversification question. Related approaches include research that has focused on the context-specific nature of product diversification and the impact of organizational ownership on product-diversification strategy. For example, Ramaswamy et al. (2002) explored how the different objectives and monitoring predispositions of distinct ownership groups in firms in India can influence their product-diversification strategy. Strategy research has also evaluated managerial motives as a force for product diversification (Besanko et al. 2000). Agency theorists note that, instead of pursuing economic efficiency and/or enhancing shareholder wealth, executives are motivated to pursue a product diversification strategy in attempts to increase their private benefits (Jensen 1986; Hoskisson and Hitt 1990).

Aside from motives and incentives for product diversification, the relationship between product diversification and performance has also been a central issue in strategy research (Hoskisson and Hitt 1990; Datta et al. 1991; Montgomery 1994; Palich et al. 2000). A general conclusion in this literature is that increasing product diversification can impact positively on performance, because of economies of scope and scale, greater exploitation of internally generated resources, increased market power, risk reduction, and learning. At the same time, the costs of product diversification—primarily the costs of managerial and organizational complexity—increase with greater product diversification, particularly unrelated product diversification.

This leads to the observation that the benefits of product diversification will decline if expansion exceeds beyond an optimal point for a firm.

Despite extensive research, empirical analyses of the effects of product diversification on performance have yielded mixed results (Markides and Williamson 1994; Palich et al. 2000). If there is any consistency in results, it emerges in the general finding that related product diversifiers tend to have better corporate performance than unrelated product diversifiers. Meanwhile, for geographic diversification, Grant et al. (1988), Datta et al. (1991), and Hitt et al. (1997) provided some support of a positive relationship. Ultimately, the relationship between geographic diversification and performance might be somewhat more complicated, invoking a sigmoid shape in which performance declines during early stages of internationalization, then elevates at modest levels of geographic diversification, and declines again at high levels of geographic diversification (Lu and Beamish 2004).

Without going too extensively into these debates and this literature, the central point to emerge for the discussion of these strategies for business groups is whether the widespread product diversification seen in many of these groups can be sustained in markets that are developing, and often rapidly, in their institutional environment. As part of this development, governments are shifting priorities to privatization, liberalization, and openness to competition, and governance systems rooted in families in the state are also undergoing reforms. Will business groups be able to sustain their competitive positions in such evolving environments? Further, will business groups be able to secure the benefits that other nations' firms have been able to obtain in their processes of geographic diversification? Part of the answers to these questions rests in the nation chapters in this *Handbook*. Further, in investigating these issues, researchers should also be able better to understand core theoretical explanations for the strategy and performance of business groups.

26.3 STRATEGY AND PERSPECTIVES ON BUSINESS GROUPS

In the different theoretical approaches to business groups, the starting point has been the definition of a business group, which also varies quite widely. Some definitions, such as that found in Guillén (Chapter 27, this volume), follow the work of Granovetter (1995), who defined business groups as collections of firms that are linked together by both formal and informal means. This definition tends to capture most forms of business groups in a variety of countries worldwide, but often does not include financially centered collections of firms, or at times network collections of firms such as those found in mainland China, Taiwan, and Japan (horizontal *keiretsu* or *kigyou shudan*) (Guillén, Chapter 27, this volume).

Even though definitions do vary, the thrust of much of the research on business groups has been largely consistent across scholars concerned with business groups. Strategy and management-oriented researchers focusing on business groups have been concerned with the rationales for the existence of diversified business groups, with the identification of the underlying sources of competitiveness of business groups, and with the strategies that business groups have used to grow and compete in their domestic markets. At the risk of creating a somewhat overly gross categorization of prior research, these approaches can be identified as: (1) an economics perspective; (2) a political perspective; and (3) a leverage and resource-based perspective.

26.3.1 An economics perspective

The economic perspective on business groups is perhaps the perspective that has had the most widespread and strongest influence on the development of management-oriented research on business groups. The economics perspective is grounded in the same fundamental premise of research on transaction-cost economics—namely, that it emerges from a consideration of the comparative efficiency of markets and firms. This perspective conceives of business groups as emerging as rationale responses to market failures and the associated transaction costs. This perspective argues that business group affiliated firms use internal transactions, made efficient by the size and scope of the business group, to fill institutional voids caused by poorly performing or nonexistent institutions in emerging economies (Leff 1978; Khanna and Palepu 1997).

The economic perspective hence focuses on the economic efficiency of business groups, which comes from their internalization of transactions given a weak institutional environment. As weak institutional environments tend to be most pronounced in emerging economies, a consistent feature of the organizational environment in these markets is the prominent role played by business groups (Khanna and Palepu 1997; Guillén 2000; Khanna and Rivkin 2001). Theorists argue that, as a relatively efficient way of organizing business transactions in emerging economies, business groups have been regarded as functional substitutes to fill institutional voids in these markets (Khanna and Palepu 1997).

26.3.2 A political perspective

The political perspective focuses on the proactive role played by major political institutions, such as governments, in an emerging economy, as an influence on the formation and strategy of business groups (Schneider, Chapter 23, this volume). Scholars grounding their research in a political perspective view business groups as the product of favorable government policies that encouraged the formation and development of business groups as a way for an emerging economy to close the GDP gap between it and developed economies (Evans 1979; Amsden 1989).

The political perspective places an emphasis on a business group's political capital as derived from its political connections with different levels of governments in an emerging economy (Lu and Ma 2008). Governments in all markets, but particularly activist governments in emerging economies, can affect the size and structure of markets and ultimately influence the competitiveness of firms (Hillman and Keim 1995). Government involvement has been a particularly pronounced factor in the initial formation and development of business groups in emerging economies (Mahmood and Rufin 2005).

This point can be well illustrated by the experience of business groups in many emerging economies. Business groups in South Korea (Chang and Choi 1988; Guillén 2000), China (Keister 2000), Indonesia and Latin America (Granovetter 1995) were the products of government policies. Business groups, such as these ones, were formed to function, at least in part, as a government tool to achieve political or economic objectives (Ghemawat and Khanna 1998; Guillén 2000). Close political connections with governments provided business groups with political capital and other scarce politically oriented resources that were unavailable to independent and unaffiliated local firms (Evans 1979; Amsden 1989; Peng et al. 2005).

This point of preferential access to political capital is important in emerging economies. Research in the political perspective has pushed forward this idea to focus on the source of business groups' political connections to identify the origins and extent of their political capital. Political connections with governments are an important precondition for business groups to develop and sustain their project execution capability (Guillén 2000), which is a consideration for the third theoretical perspective on business groups. Political capital can hence lead to favorable economic treatment and provide access to critical resources controlled by various levels of governments, which will ultimately help improve a business group affiliate's competiveness and its performance (Hillman and Keim 1995; Fisman 2001). These political resources can also be transferable, making politically tied business groups appealing to firms entering a business group's domestic market.

26.3.3 A leverage and resource-based perspective

The third perspective places an importance on leverage and resources. Indeed, the idea of leveraging political connections to gain resources and overcome institutional voids, as stated in our conclusion to the previous section, is largely consistent with this emerging third theoretical perspective on business groups (Amsden and Hikino 1994; Guillén 2000; Kock and Guillén 2001). For example, in many business groups, the development of project execution capability can be traced back to the possession of powerful political contacts. This point creates a degree of similarity between the political perspective and the leverage and resource-based perspective, as both place a high value on political contacts. Notably, however, the leverage and resource-based perspective places a high value on government protectionism as an important precondition for the rise and development of business groups (Guillén 2000), which, in turn, suggests that the value of resources is contingent on institutional conditions.

Building from these points, the leverage and resource-based perspective is a theoretical view that contends that business groups have arisen and prospered in late-developing economies because they could leverage local and foreign contacts to take advantage of asymmetric foreign trade and investment flows (Kock and Guillén 2001). In economies such as Taiwan and South Korea, many diversified business groups emerged because an entrepreneur could enter new industries by leveraging political connections and then establishing connections for resources with foreign firms (Amsden and Hikino 1994). In this process, a mutually reinforcing dynamic relationship emerges between the experience of business groups in terms of forging relationships with foreign firms, and the arrival of foreign firms seeking such capable and accessible local firms as local partners in the emerging economy (Amsden and Hikino 1994; Guillén 2000; Kock and Guillén 2001). Over time, business groups emerge as a set of firms collectively internalizing the capabilities required to execute such projects and develop what can be called project execution capabilities (Amsden and Hikino 1994). These capabilities can confer benefits to groups and their affiliates in these emerging economies, as discussed in greater detail in Guillén (Chapter 27, this volume).

26.3.4 Research strategies

A variety of approaches have been utilized to investigate the growth, strategy, and competitiveness of business groups. These strategies have yielded insights into the three core theories we briefly reviewed. Although there have been multiple approaches, in general, research on business groups has commonly utilized a comparison research strategy (see Fig. 26.1).

The first such comparison strategy that gained traction in the management and strategy literatures emerged from the need to acquaint management and strategy scholars with the features of business groups and the types of advantages business groups possessed. This comparison was made primarily between business group affiliated firms and non-business groups affiliated firms. The conclusion of the bulk of these comparison studies was that group affiliation had a positive effect on the economic performance of group-affiliated members in emerging economies (Peng and Delios 2006). For example, Khanna and Rivkin (2001) found that the profitability of group affiliates was higher than otherwise comparable unaffiliated firms in six out of fourteen emerging economies. Similar comparison-oriented studies between group-affiliated and non-group-affiliated firms found positive effects to group affiliation in the contexts of China (Keister 2000; Ma et al. 2006), South Korea (Chang and Choi 1988; Chang and Hong 2000), India, and Chile (Ghemawat and Khanna 1998; Khanna and Palepu 2000).

A second set of comparison approaches explores how the institutional environment in which a firm or group of firms is situated influences their strategy and performance. This comparison was oriented to the identification and examination of

Business group affiliated firms	versus	Non-business group affiliated firms
Institutions where business groups are common	versus	Institutions where business groups are not common
Institutions in the past	versus	Institutions in the present and future
Business groups in their home countries	versus	Business groups in their host countries
Multinational firms in their home countries	versus	Multinational firms in countries where business groups are common
Multinational firms	versus	Business groups

Figure 26.1 Research approaches on business groups

institutional environments in which business groups were common, and those in which business groups were not common. These studies could be cross-sectional in nature, comparing two or more countries at the same point in time, or longitudinal in nature, comparing two points in time for a single country, such as South Korea (Lee et al. 2008).

The third set of comparison studies has evolved from the latter point of the second set of comparison studies. Scholars have become increasingly interested in exploring institutional effects in the present day (defined as the time at which a study was executed), to cast future projections about the development of institutions and the future of business groups. The opposite time sequence to this approach has been to take the present day again as an anchoring point, but move back in time, often by multiple decades to observe the existence of business groups in countries in which they are largely absent in the present day. The research by Morck (Chapter 21, this volume) is fully reflective of this third comparison study approach.

The fourth comparison study leverages the phenomenon of the internationalization of business groups and their affiliated firms. In some nations, such as South Korea and Japan, firms affiliated respectively with *chaebol* and *keiretsu* have been internationalizing for decades. But in other nations, notably, India and China, the internationalization process is a comparatively recent phenomenon for the firms from these nations. As the internationalization and global competition process is a current and strengthening phenomenon, researchers can explore how the growth, competitiveness, and strategy of business groups and their affiliates share similarities or exhibit differences in their domestic markets and in their foreign markets. Such studies have been extensive for the case of Japan, for example (Beamish et al. 1997).

The fifth comparison continues from the theme of leveraging the internationalization process. In this case, however, the comparison can involve multinational firms as they move from an institutional setting in which business groups are largely absent to an institutional setting in which business groups are common. This research strategy can provide insight into the adaptive processes and strategies multinational firms invoke to compete against business groups in their home environments. Plausibly, such a comparison can also help extend theory on business groups by connecting existing explanations on business groups' growth, competitiveness, and strategy to the emerging experiences of developed country multinational firms in their entries in institutionally weak markets (Delios et al. 2008; Ma and Delios forthcoming).

The sixth comparison is separated from the fourth and fifth comparisons by its own approach. As the internationalization processes continue for emerging economies in terms both of maturing as recipients and of sources of foreign direct investment, the opportunity emerges to compare the growth and strategies of business group affiliated firms and developed-country multinational firms as they compete in similar sets of markets. Will these two sets of firms leverage the same sets of capabilities? Will there be a convergence in strategic stances of these firms? Although the phenomenon is still recent, these are just two of the many relevant and timely questions that can be explored not only to provide insight into the underlying theoretical framing of business groups, but also to develop an improved understanding of the phenomenon in general.

26.4 DEVELOPMENTS IN BUSINESS GROUPS' STRATEGIES

The nation chapters in this *Handbook* detail the types and extent of business groups in each nation, the specifics of the historical development of business groups, the strategies of product diversification and geographic diversification, the governance structure of the business groups, and the strategic challenges facing the groups at the end of the first decade of the twenty-first century. In this section, we focus on understanding cross-national trends in strategies and strategic challenges.

We initiate this comparison by summarizing the reported trends in each nation chapter, as captured in Table 26.1. In the table, we list the business groups by country and by world region. We present several examples of the large groups, followed by columns depicting current strategic issues, product diversification strategies and geographic diversification strategies.

Table 26.1 Strategy and diversification in business groups

Country of the business groups	Representative groups	Strategic issues	Product diversification strategy	Geographic diversification strategy
Asia				
Japan (Lincoln and Shimotani, Chapter 5, this volume)	Horizontal groups: Mitsui, Mitsubishi, Sumitomo, Fuyo, Sanwa, DKB. Vertical groups: Hitachi, Toyota. Matsushita Electric, Fujitsu, Denso	Softening of inter-firm linkages such as intra-group trading and cross-shareholdings. Weakening of group structure in 1990s and 2000s.	Group diversification shifting to corporate diversification in a hierarchically organized firm.	Aggressive FDI-related internationalization within the group through the 1980s, more independent internationalization from the 1990s.
South Korea (Kim, Chapter 6, this volume)	Samsung, Hyundai Motor, SK, LG, Lotte, Posco, GS, Hamjin, Hyundai Heavy Industries, Hanwha, Hynix	Emerged from import substitution policies, substantial changes in policies and governance since 1997. Development of resource pooling strategies in the late 1990s.	Policy initiatives directed at reducing product scope, but product diversification levels essentially unchanged among top 30 groups, since the 1990s.	Heavy internationalization efforts since the 1990s, focus on China, the US and risky emerging markets.
Taiwan (Chung and Mahmood, Chapter 7, this volume)	Formosa Plastics, Hon Hai, Asustek, Kinpo, Quanta Computer, Lien-Hwa-Mitac, Benq, Acer, Inventec, TSMC	Push to adapt to rapidly declining environment for manufacturing, to develop capabilities, such as innovation, suited for international expansion and competition with leading multinational firms.	Steadily increasing rates of product diversification, with a combination of entry and exit from 2-digit industries from the 1980s and 1990s. Somewhat of a plateau reached in the mid-2000s.	Substantial internationalization of top 100 groups through the 1990s and 2000s, pace likely to be maintained or accelerate in the 2010s.
China (Lee and Kang, Chapter 8, this volume)	China Petrochemical, China National Petroleum, China Mobile Communications, China Telecom, Sinochem	Dominance of state-owned companies among leading business groups. Legacy of competition in protected	Modest diversification levels that have been consistent over time, either through stable industry holdings, as	Recent internationalization efforts particularly in resource-related industries, at times face opposition from

Country of the business groups	Representative groups	Strategic issues	Product diversification strategy	Geographic diversification strategy
	Group, Baosteel Group, China Railway, Legend Holdings, Haier Group	industries, low levels of investments in capability generating resources.	part of limited entry and exit in industry and product segments.	overseas regulators. Private groups active in international growth.
Thailand (Wailerdsak and Suehiro, Chapter 9, this volume)	Siam Cement, PTT, CP, Thai Charoen, Thai Airways, Bangkok Bank, Krungthai Bank, Kasikorn Bank, Shin Corp, Central Department Store	Facing need to transition to more open, competitive environment leading to investments in product specific competencies, such as innovative capabilities, brands and technology.	Substantive levels of product diversification via strong growth up to the 1997-crisis. Growth slower post-crisis, with a concomitant increase in foreign ownership.	Financial market liberalization in the early 1990s spurred international growth via FDI, which continued even after the onset of the 1997 financial crisis.
Singapore (Tsui-Auch and Yoshikawa, Chapter 10, this volume)	Government-linked groups such as DBS, Singtel, SIA, NOL, Keppel Corp., SembMarine. Private groups such as UOB, UOL, SG Land, Dairy Farm International	Separation of state interest and private interest in government-linked groups, development of independent directors and senior managers (non-state and non-family) in all groups.	Stable set of modest to highly diversified industries for government linked groups. Private owned groups undertook industry consolidation domestically in response to regulatory changes.	Substantial internationalization effort for government-linked groups but face domestic opposition in host countries in South East Asia given state links. Modest internationalization for private groups.
India (Sarkar, Chapter 11, this volume)	Reliance, Tata, Anil Dhirubhai Ambani, Aditya Birla, Essar, Om Prakash Jindal, Bharti Telecom, Vedanta Resources, Larsen and Toubro, Mahindra and Mahindra	Substantial changes in regulatory environment leading to greater competition and emergence of focus and diversification strategies in groups in their move to a market orientation.	Both highly diversified and narrowly focused groups, with very high levels of diversification among the most widely diversified groups.	Relatively nascent stage of international expansion for group affiliates, although recent acceleration in latter half of 2000s, with many high profile international acquisitions.

(continued)

Table 26.1 Continued

Country of the business groups	Representative groups	Strategic issues	Product diversification strategy	Geographic diversification strategy
Latin America				
Argentina (Fracchia, Mesquita, and Quiroga, Chapter 12, this volume)	Techint, Bunge and Born, AGD, P. Companc, Arcor, Bulgheroni, Coto, Clarin, Aluar/Fate, Sancor	Substantial entry and exit of groups since the 1950s, including the emergence of private, non-state backed groups following liberalization and privatization in the 1990s.	Groups pursue related and unrelated diversification. Broad level of diversification seen in 1990, still in evidence at end of 2000s.	Internationalization via alliances, exports and to a lesser extent FDI, occurred from the 1990s, with the consequence being an increased focus on capability development.
Brazil (Aldrighi and Postali, Chapter 13, this volume)	Petrobras, Bradesco, Vale Itaúsa, Banco do Brasil, Safra, Andrade Gutierrez, Nemofeffer/Suzano, Aracruz, Pão de Açucar	Significant family and state ownership in public groups, and private groups. Ownership transitions are an important precursor to strategic transitions to capability development.	Low to high levels of product diversification as often accompanied by vertical integration. Defensive and technology-related diversifications more common in the 2000s.	Internationalization followed liberalization initiatives with some groups taking international leadership positions in their industries, most others have regional export activities.
Chile (Lefort, Chapter 14, this volume)	Angelini, Luksic, Paulmann, Solari-Cuneo-Del Rio, Claro, Matte, Ibáñez, Marin-Del Real, Sigdo Koppers	Emergence of groups from remnants of state-owned firms, and also as off-shoots of multinational firms in Chile. Capabilities tend to be domestically rooted.	Substantial levels of unrelated product diversification, often structured under a pyramidal, holding company structure.	Historical focus has been on growth domestically, but international growth has exploited natural resource advantages or brand recognition regionally in Latin America.
Mexico (Hoshino, Chapter 15, this volume)	Carso, Cemex, Femsa, Bal, Alfa, Gruma, Grupo Mexico, Bimbo, Soriana, Modelo	High levels of debt in existing groups. Substantial number of new entrants, exit and entry by business groups across businesses.	Growth and restructuring in business areas, by acquisitions and the use of strategic alliances, no clear contraction in product scope.	Growth in globalization initiatives in response to intensified domestic competition, modest levels of internationalization.

Country of the business groups	Representative groups	Strategic issues	Product diversification strategy	Geographic diversification strategy
Middle East, Eastern Europe and Africa				
Israel (Kosenko and Yafeh, Chapter 16, this volume)	IDB, Levaev, Ofer, Fishman, Arison, Bino, Nimrodi, Akirov, Goldstein, Borowitz, Federman, Zelikand	Growth from state to family and professionally managed firms, as emerged from mid-1980s policy reforms.	Modest levels of horizontal diversification, focus on a core business area, broadly defined. Vertical integration prominent.	Substantial internationalization efforts supported by cheap financing from mid-1990s. Focus on capital intensive, Ricardian rent, related investments.
Turkey (Colpan, Chapter 17, this volume)	Koc Group, Sabanci Group, Zorlu Group, Oyak Group, Cukurova Group, Ulker Group, Is Bankasi Group, Dogus Group	Group-level resources fostered rapid growth, with a low reliance on product-specific capabilities for competitiveness. Challenges exist in the succession and meritocratization of management.	Early and late groups both widely diversified, although the latter only after market liberalization initiatives undertaken in the 1980s. Alliances and acquisitions common for diversification.	Comparatively low levels of internationalization given focus of product expansion domestically. Extensive FDI and exporting remain the exception, not the norm.
Russia (Guriev, Chapter 18, this volume)	Alfa, Basic Element, Renova, Systema, UGMK, Menatep/Yukos, Severstal, Lukoil	Emerged during the big bang privatization phase, heavy concentration of industrial activity.	Growth by diversification for industry consolidation and exploitation of group resources such as political influence and lobbying capabilities.	High levels of internationalization as a political risk mitigation strategy.
South Africa (Goldstein, Chapter 19, this volume)	Anglo, Sanlam, Old Mutual, Rembrandt, Liberty Life, Anglovaal, and Black Oligarchs including Cyril Ramaphosa, Tokyo Sexwale, Cheryl Carolus	Shift in capital from entrenched interests, to a wider pool of firms and entrepreneurs. Greater level of diversification in the economy as a whole.	Older groups concentrated in traditional product areas such as mining, insurance, and tobacco. Newer groups have wider levels of product diversification.	Internationalization primarily the domain of older groups, although not extensive. Newer groups have comparatively nascent levels of exploration in new geographic markets.

As can be seen in the table, groups persist in all the countries represented in the economy, with the exception of Japan, where the group structure has become substantially weaker in the 2000s. Indeed, and as mentioned before, a subset of scholars on business groups does not conceptualize the horizontal and vertical groups in Japan as being a business group. Aside from Japan, business groups continue to prevail in each of the other fourteen nations, albeit with some evident changes. In South Korea, for example, the largest groups have continued to dominate in the economy, even if smaller groups became weaker following the policy reforms implemented in response to the 1997 Asian economic crisis.

In other economies, such as India, groups persist, but their formation rates or the rate of new entrants have declined substantially, following the market liberalization initiatives instituted in response to the 1991 foreign-exchange-precipitated crisis. In economies such as Israel and Argentina, there has been a substantial entry and exit of business groups, with different forms of groups emerging over time. Overall, however, groups remain ubiquitous in the economy.

In some countries, such as Chile, China, and South Africa, we can see an emergence of a new group type, to accompany existing incumbents. In Chile, it is the strong growth of foreign-owned groups that now accompany the formerly state-owned groups that previously dominated. In China, it is the strong growth of privately owned groups that now accompany the state-owned groups that previously dominated. In South Africa, it is the strong growth of the black oligarchs that now accompany the mining and banking-centered groups that dominated the economy.

Aside from these entry and exit patterns in business groups, we can see that, in most economies, with the exception of South Korea and Japan, business groups are at worst struggling with internationalization, and at best progressing past the nascent stage of the internationalization process by exporting and foreign direct investment. Until a large number of economies experienced changes in the institutional environment that strengthened the external transactional environment and experienced changes in government policy that reduced protectionism and economic isolation, business groups remained centered strongly on domestic competition and domestic growth. With the creation of a more open, competitive, and internationalized business environment, business groups not only had to contend with increased rates of foreign entry and the growth of new entrants, but also had increased opportunities and motives to move abroad.

Interestingly, the opportunity has seemed to outweigh the competitive challenges for groups. Although the aforementioned research on strategy and product diversification suggests that product focus and related diversification are the organizational outcomes of markets that are maturing in terms of their level of institutional development and openness of competition, the nations depicted in Table 26.1, with the possible exception of Japan, continue to have groups that compete in a wide variety of unrelated product areas. Even in countries such as South Korea, which have instituted policy reforms aimed at the structure and governance of groups, extensive diversification among the eminent groups in the economy remains the rule without notable exceptions.

These trends, while not necessarily extraordinary, are noteworthy from the perspective that there is no sign that the dominance of the domestic product market of groups is in decline. At the same time, the extent, and for that matter the level of success, of the nascent internationalization process of the groups remains a question.

There are a related number of relevant issues that emerge from these trends. For example, each of the three theoretical perspectives on business groups grounds its discussions of the value of business groups in the economic, political, and other institutional characteristics in the home country of the business group. Each of these explanations for the existence and growth of business groups can be pushed forward if one examines their activities in foreign markets. Extending the example, a tenet of the economic perspective is that business groups emerged as an organizational form to diversify widely to overcome weak institutions and become more efficient than a standalone firm. If this is the case, and the performance advantages of a business group are rooted in its home market, what are the performance consequences for business groups when they have gone abroad? Do the competitive advantages of business group affiliation translate to advantages in overseas markets? The answers to simple questions such as these have implications for our understanding of the conceptual underpinnings of business groups, particularly if researchers can identify whether advantages stem from efficiencies of internal governance or from another factor such as size that yields economies of scope.

This latter point brings us to the issues of competition, resources, and capabilities in business groups. Almost by definition, the emergence of a more competitive, open, and institutionally strong market necessitates success on the basis of the development and growth of competitive capabilities. Typically, such capabilities are thought to reside either in upstream areas of the firm, such as technology and innovation, or in downstream areas of the firm, such as brands and distribution. Within each national chapter, there are statements to the effect that groups have either begun to develop, or have become stronger in certain capabilities, but the evidence remains somewhat ephemeral. Certainly, it is not only an expected outcome, but a desired outcome, to see competition emerge on the basis of the strength of value creation of a firm, as tied to meeting consumers' needs more effectively than competitors (Singh and Delios 2005), yet it is not a foregone conclusion that this will occur within groups, nor is it an unavoidable destination in their path of development. As can be seen in the experience of Samsung (Chang 2008), the organizational and leadership challenges to a substantial alteration in the strategic stance and competitiveness of a company are anything but trivial.

This point brings us to the issue of where business groups are positioned in terms of their fundamental nature (Schneider, Chapter 23, this volume) and capability development (Guillén, Chapter 27, this volume). Table 26.2 uses the categorizations developed by Schneider and Guillén to reflect on how far the groups have progressed in various nations, all of which have been undergoing institutional development, and experiencing changes in the regulatory environment, as a consequence of the shifts in government preferences and policies.

Table 26.2 Capability development in business groups

Capability (see Guillén, Chapter 27, this volume)			Type of Group (see Schneider, Chapter 23, this volume)		
Contact (Stage I)	Generic (Stage II)	Organizational Technological (Stage III)	Organic	Portfolio	Policy-induced
China	India	Japan	Japan	India	China
Russia	Turkey	South Korea	South Korea	Turkey	Russia
	South Africa	Taiwan	Taiwan	South Africa	Singapore
	Israel			Israel	
	Chile			Chile	
	Mexico			Mexico	
	Brazil			Brazil	
	Argentina			Argentina	
	Thailand			Thailand	
	Singapore				

Note: The exact placement of specific nations within this typology necessarily creates questions of categorization. Groups within a nation will vary in their capabilities, and the types of capabilities will vary within a group. Further, as Schneider acknowledges, the three major group types and their underlying core motivations are not necessarily mutually exclusive and at times are concurrent or sequential; hence a nation's groups could reasonably be placed in more than one group type.

The expected consequence of these developments in the domestic environments would be for groups to arrive at Stage III level of capability development, and at an organic organizational form, as perhaps a precursor to an eventual shift to a corporate, hierarchical organizational structure. Yet, as our categorization by country depicts, most groups remain as primarily reliant on generic capabilities, and they are structured as a portfolio of business entities. These paths of development suggest some progression towards Stage III, but this progression is slowed by the substantial inertia of the groups.

Without a doubt, changing domestic environments have impelled groups to change their organizations and their strategies, but these changes have yet to result in profound changes in their competitive positioning. Turning back to the history of groups (Morck, Chapter 21, this volume), we can see that, if there have been real, deep, and enduring changes to group organizational structure and strategy, these changes have come from explicit qualitative changes in domestic policies and regulations aimed specifically and effectively at business groups, such as in the United States in the early years of the twentieth century. Gradual, even if relentless, changes in the development of institutions, in structural reforms, in privatization, and in levels of domestic and foreign competition exert pressure on business groups, but groups adapt to such pressure by a combination of pliability and resilience. The pliability emerges in their modest internationalization efforts. The resilience comes from their maintenance of an unrelated product diversification strategy.

Ultimately, this resilience raises the question of whether substantive organizational change can be expected in environments in which dominant economic entities are firmly enmeshed in the policy-making and social environment of business. Business groups often have the contact and generic non-market management capabilities to direct the nature of change in their business environments. This point raises the question of whether business groups are reacting to the institutions in their home business environments or whether institutions are being actively shaped by the business groups themselves. In this sense, instead of envisioning the strategy of business groups as being exogenous to environmental forces such as institutional environments, governments, and governance systems, we can instead picture each of these elements as being co-determined, or endogenous to one another.

26.5 Research design and research questions

The research reported in the various chapters in this *Handbook* represents substantial extensions and encapsulations of our understanding of business groups. The purpose of this chapter has been to capture some of these developments with reference to how business group researchers can help inform strategy, and how research on strategy can benefit from an extension of the agenda on research groups. Building from the three theoretical perspectives that we have identified, alongside a coupling to the research strategies that business group researchers have explored, we have suggested three new comparisons that can be made to advance business group research.

Fundamentally, before research on business group strategy and performance can proceed, it needs to move beyond conjecture about capabilities to studies that are specifically designed to identify the nature of group or affiliate capabilities, and their consequent relationship to strategy and performance. The literature on business group strategy and performance has become well populated with the types of comparison studies we have identified earlier, particularly of the form where the performance of business group affiliates and non-group affiliates have been compared to develop inferences about the types, nature, and values of group-specific capabilities. Two opposing views on this point can be found in Guriev (Chapter 18, this volume) and Estrin et al. (2009).

Recent studies have pushed the sophistication of the empirical work, providing us with greater confidence in the robustness of the findings (Carney et al. 2009; Estrin et al. 2009). Even so, these studies do not necessarily provide findings beyond what we observed earlier in the short history of business group research. Instead, recent research continues to substantiate, or at least to help to develop, a lasting contention of business group scholars—namely, that the business group structure was not necessarily an economically efficient one.

Recent studies continue to push the comparison approaches focused on performance and then make attributions to the core theories (economic, political, leverage and resource-based) that we identified earlier. This is interesting to a point, but the findings are inconclusive, with a consequent lack of substantive insight into the question of where the competitive advantages, if at all, of business groups reside. We make this point fully cognizant of the fact that much strategy research on performance operates at a high level of inference; but, at the same time, such a high level of inference at this particular juncture of business group research is exactly what business group research *does not* require. Instead, we need to identify more solid evidence that business groups are developing capabilities that can foster good performance in environments characterized by low levels of protectionism and regulation, by increased levels of foreign competition, and by consumers who make choices based upon the superior quality or price advantages of a firm's products and services. These are inevitable, although not completely inexorable, features of many of the environments in which business groups operate.

Although the current trajectory of business group research, especially as reported in this volume, points to the development of technological, marketing, and other innovative capabilities that can foster the growth and competitiveness of business groups in open and competitive environments (Colpan, Hikino, and Lincoln, Chapter 1, this volume), it is still not immediately clear that all, or even most, of the business groups have moved in that direction. The reason for the lack of clarity is simply that the evidence remains at a highly descriptive level. This statement is not meant to cast aspersions on the quality of the research; indeed, if anything, the research reported in this volume has a deep and expansive coverage of business groups, yet to be seen in any other set of collected works. That said, the research is aimed at description, but not investigation, of the specific capabilities that are fostering the growth and competitiveness of business groups in the 2010s and beyond. To that end, business group researchers need to adopt and expand the techniques and research designs found in contemporary strategy research on capabilities fully to exploit the tremendous opportunity that the changes in the environment of business groups offer (e.g. Mahmood et al. 2009). In so doing, however, researchers also need to operate with the cognizance of the endogeneity of the institutional environment to the strategy and actions of firms. Firms can actively shape their institutional environments through their strategic actions (Oliver 1991). In essence, both firms and institutions are endogenous to an environment. In this sense, instead of assuming a linearity and temporal contiguousness to business group strategy and environmental change, research should move beyond this presumption that business groups are primarily in a reactive behavior mode to institutional development (Bluedorn et al. 1994). This approach is especially necessary, given the prioritization of economic development among many emerging and developing economy governments, their focus on nurturing domestic firms, their extensive use of government-linked corporations, and their extensive economic intervention (Delios et al. 2007).

Aside from these basic yet essential issues related to the research design for business group research, we believe that future research directions are captured by five research questions that we consider important for business groups researchers to start, or to continue, to explore.

- How does the process of institutional transition in a business group's home market affect its strategy and its competitiveness?
- How can our understanding about the rationales for the growth and competitiveness of business groups be augmented by deep, cross-national comparisons of business groups?
- What is the nature of a business group affiliate's competitive advantages? What unique capabilities does business group membership confer on affiliated firms?
- What capabilities does a business group have to facilitate the internationalization process for affiliated firms, and their competitiveness in global markets?
- How does the ownership structure of a business group influence its strategy and its competitiveness?

Scholars concerned with business groups might use these five research questions to extend our understanding of the business group phenomenon, of the theoretical and conceptual issues related to business groups, and of the strategy-related implications of business group research. We discuss each of these research questions in turn.

26.5.1 Institutional transition

- How does the process of institutional transition in a business group's home market affect its strategy and its competitiveness?

This question concerns the process of institutional transition and the evolution of business groups and their strategies. This question has already gained currency in the research community, given the substantial transitions that have been made in a number of emerging economies since the 1990s. In the most extreme case, as discussed in Lincoln and Shimotani (Chapter 5, this volume), transition has led to the imminent demise of business groups. In other instances, it has led to substantial changes in the strategy and structure of business groups (Kim, Chapter 6, this volume). Researchers need to continue to explore these questions to identify the adaptive responses business groups are making to institutional transition, particularly as much of the rationale for their existence is connected to idiosyncratic features of the institutional environments in which they were founded.

26.5.2 Cross-national comparisons

- How can our understanding about the rationales for the growth and competitiveness of business groups be augmented by deep, cross-national comparisons of business groups?

This research question is strongly related to the illustration we have provided on the directions that research on business groups can take. By invoking cross-national comparisons, we can identify whether there is an institutional substitution or replacement effect. We can identify whether firms or business groups can arbitrage institutional advantages from their home to their host countries, or perhaps in the opposite direction. Further, we can identify whether business group structures emerge for reasons not connected to an economic or political perspective on the rise and growth of business groups.

26.5.3 Capabilities and competitive advantages

• What is the nature of a business group affiliate's competitive advantages? What unique capabilities does business group membership confer on affiliated firms?

This research question is very much self-evident in its intent and in the design. It is also an enduring question in business group research. The phenomenological trend that facilitates the investigation of this research question is the ongoing intensification of outward foreign direct investment by the affiliates of business groups. As these affiliates move abroad, we can gain more acute insight into whether a business group's advantages are simply related to an institutional substitution effect, or whether there are other sources of unique capabilities that a business group can confer on affiliated firms. To the extent that other forms of unique capabilities can be identified, we can also reflect back on the first question concerning the proposed longevity of business groups, given institutional transition.

26.5.4 Capabilities and international expansion

• What capabilities does a business group have to facilitate the internationalization process for affiliated firms, and their competitiveness in global markets?

This question is clearly related to the previous question, as it involves utilizing the internationalization setting to identify how the business group structure facilities the international expansion process, and an affiliate's competitiveness in global markets. The question is more refined than the preceding one in the sense that researchers can seek to pinpoint whether business groups convey advantages related to size, such as economies of scope and access to financial resources, or whether their advantages are rooted in what are regarded as intangible assets, such as unique and strong brands and a good corporate reputation.

26.5.5 Ownership structure

• How does the ownership structure of a business group influence its strategy and its competitiveness?

This final question links research on ownership structure issues to business group research, much as exhibited in Boyd and Hoskisson (Chapter 24, this volume). The ownership structure issue has become a strong area of research for scholars concerned with firms in emerging economies, yet there has been little consideration of how business groups vary in their ownership structure, be it by identity of main owner or even concentration in ownership, and how this variance influences the strategy and performance of a business group and its affiliates. For example, do we see differences in diversification and performance in the group or its affiliates depending on the type of ownership (bank, private, state) that predominates in the group? Researchers can also explore whether there are principal–agent or principal–principal issues in the ownership and governance of business groups, with an identification, for example, of whether expropriation issues are more or less pronounced in state-owned business groups than in privately owned business groups.

Although we suggest and argue for a deepened focus on these five research questions, we would be remiss if we failed to state that clearly there are a number of other issues that business group researchers could explore. That said, our core premise remains the same. Business groups are an intriguing and enduring phenomenon that has yet to penetrate strategy research to the extent that they could as an organization for study. Strategy research and our understanding of core strategy issues related to performance, diversification, ownership, governance, and internationalization, to name a few, can only benefit by a well-structured, comparative set of investigations into business groups, much as we have advocated herein in our statements of the research opportunities for scholars concerned with understanding strategy, competition, and business groups.

References

AMSDEN, A. H. (1989). *Asia's Next Giant: South Korea and Late Industrialization.* New York: Oxford University Press.

AMSDEN, A. H., and HIKINO, T. (1994). "Project Execution Capability, Organizational Know-How and Conglomerate Corporate Growth in Late Industrialization," *Industrial and Corporate Change*, 3/1: 111–47.

AOKI, M., KIM, H. K., and OKUNO-FUJIWARA, M. (1996). *The Role of Government in East Asian Economic Development.* Oxford: Clarendon Press.

BEAMISH, P. W., DELIOS, A., and LECRAW, D. J. (1997). *Japanese Multinationals in the Global Economy.* Cheltenham: Edward Elgar.

BESANKO, D., DRANOVE, D., and SHANLEY, M. (2000). *Economics of Strategy.* New York: John Wiley.

BLUEDORN, A. C., JOHNSON, R. A., CARTWRIGHT, D. K., and BARRINGER, B. R. (1994). "The Interface and Convergence of the Strategic Management and Organizational Environment Domains," *Journal of Management*, 20: 201–62.

CARNEY, M., SHAPIRO, D., and TANG, Y. (2009). "Business Group Performance in China: Ownership and Temporal Considerations," *Management and Organization Review*, 5/2: 167–93.

CHANG, S. (2008). *Sony versus Samsung: The Inside Story of Electronics Giants' Battle for Global Supremacy.* Singapore: Wiley.

CHANG, S., and CHOI, U. (1988). "Strategy, Structure and Performance of Korean Business Groups: A Transactions Cost Approach," *Journal of Industrial Economics*, 37/2: 141–58.

CHANG, S., and HONG, J. (2000). "Economic Performance of Group-Affiliated Companies in Korea: Intra-Group Resource Sharing and Internal Business Transactions," *Academy of Management Journal*, 43/3: 429–48.

DATTA, D. K., RAJAGOPALAN, N., and RASHEED, A. (1991). "Diversification and Performance: Critical Review and Future Directions," *Journal of Management Studies*, 28: 529–58.

DELIOS, A., SINGH, K., and XU, W. (2007). "Strategy Research in Asia," in H. Yeung (ed.), *Handbook of Research on Asia Business.* Cheltenham: Edward Elgar, 19–45.

DELIOS, A., XU, D., and BEAMISH, P. W. (2008). "Within-Country Product Diversification and Foreign Subsidiary Performance," *Journal of International Business Studies*, 39/4: 706–24.

ESTRIN, S., POUKLIAKOVA, S., and SHAPIRO, D. (2009). "The Performance Effects of Business Groups in Russia," *Journal of Management Studies*, 46/3: 393–420.

EVANS, P. (1979). *Dependent Development.* Princeton: Princeton University Press.

FISMAN, R. (2001). "Estimating the Value of Political Connections," *American Economic Review*, 91/4: 1095–102.

GHEMAWAT, P., and KHANNA, T. (1998). "The Nature of Diversified Business Groups: A Research Design and Two Case Studies," *Journal of Industrial Economics*, 46/1: 35–61.

GORT, M. (1984). *Diversification and Integration in American Industry.* Westport, CT: Greenwood.

GRANOVETTER, MARK (1995). "Coase Revisited: Business Groups in the Modern Economy," *Industrial and Corporate Change*, 4/1: 93–130.

GRANT, R. M., JAMMINE, A.P., and THOMAS, H. (1988). "Diversity, Diversification, and Profitability among British Manufacturing Companies, 1972–1984," *Academy of Management Journal*, 31: 771–801.

GUILLÉN, M. F. (2000). "Business Groups in Emerging Economies: A Resource-Based View," *Academy of Management Journal*, 43/3 (June 2000), 362–80.

HAMILTON, G. G., and BIGGART, N.W. (1988). "Market, Culture and Authority: A Comparative Analysis of Management and Organization in the Far East," *American Journal of Sociology*, 94: S52–S94.

HILLMAN, A. J., and KEIM, G. D. (1995). "International Variation in the Business–Government Interface: Institutional and Organizational Considerations," *Academy of Management Review*, 20: 193–214.

HITT, M. A., HOSKISSON, R. E., and KIM, H. (1997). "International Diversification: Effects on Innovation and Firm Performance in Product-Diversified Firms," *Academy of Management Journal*, 40: 767–98.

HOSKISSON, R. E., and HITT, M. A. (1990). "Antecedents and Performance Outcomes of Diversification: A Review and Critique of Theoretical Perspectives," *Journal of Management*, 16/2: 461–509.

HOSKISSON, R. E., EDEN, L., LAU, C., and WRIGHT, M. (2000). "Strategy in Emerging Economies," *Academy of Management Journal*, 43/3: 249–67.

JENSEN, M. C. (1986). "Agency Costs of Free Cash Flow, Corporate Finance, and Takeovers," *American Economic Review*, 76: 323–9.

JOHNSON, S., BOONE, S., BREACH, A., and FRIEDMAN, E. (2000). "Corporate Governance in the Asian Financial Crisis," *Journal of Financial Economics*, 3/4: 305–60.

KEISTER, L. A. (2000). *Chinese Business Groups: The Structure and Impact of Interfirm Relations during Economic Development*. New York: Oxford University Press.

KHANNA, T., and PALEPU, K. (1997). "Why Focused Strategies May Be Wrong for Emerging Markets," *Harvard Business Review*, 75/4: 41–51.

KHANNA, T., and PALEPU, K. (2000). "Is Group Affiliation Profitable in Emerging Markets? An Analysis of Diversified Indian Business Groups," *Journal of Finance*, 55: 867–91.

KHANNA, T., and RIVKIN, J. W. (2001). "Estimating the Performance of Business Groups in Emerging Markets," *Strategic Management Journal*, 22: 45–74.

KOCK, C., and GUILLÉN, M. F. (2001). "Strategy and Structure in Developing Countries: Business Groups as an Evolutionary Response to Opportunities for Unrelated Diversification," *Industrial & Corporate Change*, 10/1:1–37.

LA PORTA, R., LOPEZ-DE-SALINES, F., and SHLEIFER, A. (1999). "Corporate Ownership around the World," *Journal of Finance*, 54/2: 471–517.

LASSERRE, P., and SCHUTTE, H. (1995). *Strategies for Asia Pacific*. London: Macmillan.

LEE, K., PENG, M. W., and LEE, K. (2008). "From Diversification Premium to Diversification Discount during Institutional Transitions," *Journal of World Business*, 43/1: 47–65.

LEFF, N. (1978). "Industrial Organization and Entrepreneurship in Developing Countries: The Economic Groups," *Economic Development and Cultural Change*, 26: 661–75.

LEUNG, K., and WHITE, S. (2004). "Taking Stock and Charting a Path for Asian Management Research," in K. Leung and S. White (eds.), *Handbook of Asian Management*. London: Kluwer Academic Publishers.

LU, J. W., and BEAMISH, P. W. (2004). "International Diversification and Firm Performance: The S-Curve Hypothesis," *Academy of Management Journal*, 47/4: 598–609.

LU, J. W., and MA, X. (2008). "The Contingent Value of Local Partners' Business Group Affiliation," *Academy of Management Journal*, 51/2: 295–314.

MA, X., and DELIOS, A. (forthcoming). "Host Country Headquarters and an MNE's Subsequent Within-Country Diversifications," *Journal of International Business Studies*.

MA, X., YAO, X., and XI, Y. (2006). "Business Group Affiliation and Firm Performance in a Transition Economy: A Focus on Ownership Voids," *Asia Pacific Journal of Management*, 23/4: 467–83.

MAHMOOD, I. P., and RUFIN, C. (2005). "Government's Dilemma: The Institutional Framework for Imitation and Innovation," *Academy of Management Review*, 30/2: 338–60.

MAHMOOD, I. P., ZHU, H., and ZAJAC, E. (2009). "Where Can Capabilities Come From? How Different Types of Network Ties Affect Capability Acquisition," NUS/ IER Hitotsubashi Working Paper.

MARKIDES, C., and WILLIAMSON, P. J. (1994). "Related Diversification, Core Competencies and Corporate Performance," *Strategic Management Journal*, 15: 149–65.

MONTGOMERY, C. (1994). "Corporate Diversification," *Journal of Economic Perspectives*, 8: 163–78.

NORTH, D. C. (1990). *Institutions, Institutional Change, and Economic Performance*. New York: Norton.

OLIVER, C. (1991). "Strategic Responses to Institutional Process," *Academy of Management Review*, 16: 145–79.

PALICH, L.E., CARDINAL, L.B., and MILLER, C.C. (2000). "Curvilinearity in the Diversification–Performance Linkage: An Examination of over Three Decades of Research," *Strategic Management Journal*, 21: 155–74.

PENG, M. W. (2000). *Business Strategies in Transition Economies*. Thousand Oaks, CA: Sage.

PENG, M. W., and DELIOS, A. (2006). "What Determines the Scope of the Firm over Time and around the World? An Asia Pacific Perspective," *Asia Pacific Journal of Management*, 23/4: 385–405.

PENG, M. W., LEE, S., and WANG, D. (2005). "What Determines the Scope of the Firm over Time? A Focus on Institutional Relatedness," *Academy of Management Review*, 30: 622–33.

RAMASWAMY, K., LI, M., and VELIYATH, R. (2002). "Variations in Ownership Behavior and Propensity to Diversify: A Study of the Indian Corporate Context," *Strategic Management Journal*, 23: 345–58.

RUMELT, R. P., SCHENDEL, D., and TEECE, D. J. (1994). *Fundamental Issues in Strategy: A Research Agenda*. Boston: Harvard Business School Press.

SINGH, K. (2004). "Towards the Development of Strategy Theory: Contributions from Asian Research," in K. Leung and S. White (ed.), *Handbook of Asian Management*. London: Kluwer Academic Publishers.

SINGH, K., and DELIOS, A. (2005). *Strategy for Success in Asia*. Singapore: Wiley.

WADE, R. (1990). *Governing the Market*. Princeton: Princeton University Press.

WAN, W. P., and HOSKISSON, R. E. (2003). "Home Country Environments, Corporate Diversification Strategies, and Firm Performance," *Academy of Management Journal*, 46/1: 27–45.

WHITLEY, R. (1992). *European Business Systems: Firms and Markets in their National Contexts*. London: Sage.

WILLIAMSON, O. E. (1975). *Markets and Hierarchies: Analysis and Antitrust Implications*. New York: Free Press.

World Bank (1993). *The East Asian Miracle: Economic Growth and Public Policy*. New York: Oxford University Press.

World Bank (2002). "Building Institutions for Markets," *World Development Report. 2002*. Washington: World Bank.

CHAPTER 27

....

CAPABILITY BUILDING IN BUSINESS GROUPS

....

MAURO F. GUILLÉN

27.1 INTRODUCTION

....

THE rise of large, diversified business groups in developing and newly industrialized countries has captured the imagination of academics, journalists, and policy-makers. In this chapter I argue that the rise of business groups is best approached from a resource-based perspective—that is, by looking at the distinctive capabilities, strengths, and weaknesses of this form of organization compared to other types of firms—such as product-focused firms, small and medium enterprises, and foreign multinationals—under different development circumstances. The main argument is that business groups appear in developing and newly industrialized countries because entrepreneurs and firms learn the capability to combine the necessary domestic and foreign resources for repeated industry entry. Combining domestic and foreign resources requires entrepreneurs to establish networks of relationships with relevant actors. Such a capability, however, can be developed and maintained as a valuable and rare skill only under asymmetric foreign trade and investment conditions with the rest of the world—that is, when the development path is either open to exports and outward foreign investment but not to imports and inward investment, or vice versa. Thus, development symmetries allow diversified business groups to thrive at the expense of foreign multinationals and local small and medium firms.

Firms and organizational forms are phenomenological accomplishments that differ from each other because they accumulate distinctive capabilities over time

(Biggart and Guillén 1999). The so-called resource-based view of the firm in the field of business strategy provides an understanding of the sources and consequences of such heterogeneity across firms (Barney 1986, 1991; Peteraf 1993). Like development theorists, students of business strategy have long been fascinated by why firms find it attractive to diversify into related and unrelated product lines (Ramanujam and Varadarajan 1989; Hoskisson and Hitt 1990). The large modern corporation in the United States and Western Europe grew within a core technology family and, subsequently, through related diversification (Chandler 1990). By contrast, large business groups operating in a wide range of unrelated manufacturing and service industries are characteristic of many capitalist countries that industrialized after the Second World War (Amsden and Hikino 1994; Granovetter 1995; Khanna and Palepu 1997). Business groups are more diversified than the Chandlerian modern industrial enterprise, but less coordinated (Amsden 1989: 125).

For the purposes of this chapter, a business group is defined as a "collection of firms bound together in some formal and/or informal ways" (Granovetter 1995: 95). Diversified business groups have three main features: they are active in a wide variety of industries, operate under the general guidance of a single entrepreneur, and fall short of constituting a fully integrated organizational structure. The Korean *chaebol*, the Indian business houses, the Pakistani and Turkish family holdings, or the Latin American and Spanish *grupos*, among others, come to mind as examples of such business groups. By contrast, the Japanese *keiretsu*, the Chinese *guanxiqiye* networks in Taiwan and among the overseas Chinese throughout South East Asia, or the Italian small-firm industrial districts are mere interorganizational alliances lacking the entrepreneurial coordination proposed in the above definition. Diversified business groups in developing and newly industrialized economies are also different from the conglomerates of the advanced countries in that they grew not in search of financial diversification but as a result of their ability to set up new business ventures across a variety of industries quickly and at low cost.

27.2 RESOURCES, CAPABILITIES, AND BUSINESS GROUPS

The existence of diversified business groups long after the conglomerate form fell from grace in the most advanced countries has generated a considerable theoretical and empirical literature (for reviews, see Granovetter 1995; Hoskisson et al. 2005; Khanna and Yafeh 2007). Economists, economic sociologists, and development scholars have proposed three main ways to study business groups in emerging economies. They have made different assumptions and predictions as to the conditions under which business groups become an important actor in the economy. Each of the theories emphasizes a different domestic factor to account for the importance of business groups: market failure, social structure, or state activity. Thus, they do not consider international influences or how the domestic economy relates to the global economy (Guillén 2000).

These previous theories, while observing the importance of capabilities, emphasized other aspects. First, economics assumes that diversified business groups can exist only in the absence of a well-functioning market. Thus, it regards business groups as functional substitutes for allocation failures in the markets for production inputs or outputs (Leff 1978). Business groups are but the internalization of market failure by entrepreneurs seeking to overcome the difficulties of obtaining capital, labor, raw materials, components, and technology in emerging economies. Groups step in where the market does not work or is not allowed to work by institutionalizing an alternative allocation mechanism so that production can take place (Khanna and Palepu 1997; Khanna and Yafeh 2007). Secondly, economic sociology underlines how social and cultural patterns spawn different types of organizations. This perspective assumes that firms are isomorphic with the social structure surrounding them, and seeks to identify how vertical, horizontal, and reciprocal authority patterns affect organization at the firm and inter-firm levels. Economic sociologists have intensively analyzed East Asian countries, finding that business groups guided by a single entrepreneur proliferate in countries with vertical social relationships (Korea), though not when reciprocal (Japan) or horizontal (Taiwan) ones are the norm (Orrù et al. 1997).Thirdly, scholars of late economic development observed that "autonomous" states with the ability to allocate capital and other resources at will encourage a few entrepreneurs to enter new industries, thus facilitating capability building and the proliferation of business groups (Evans 1979; Amsden 1989).

The point of departure from previous theorizing on business groups is the lead by Granovetter (1995: 122) that "the general orientation of the state toward economic development and business may shape the structure of business groups." The central argument is that asymmetric development paths at the national level provide some entrepreneurs with opportunities for diversification and business group formation (Guillén 2000; Kock and Guillén 2001).

Entrepreneurs and firms need to gain access to three types of resources when entering an industry: inputs (labor, capital, raw materials), technology, and market access in the forms of distribution channels and contracts with foreign and domestic customers or with the state (Markides and Williamson 1996). Entrepreneurs and firms that learn how to combine such resources quickly and effectively will be best able to create a business group by repeatedly entering a variety of industries. This capability for repeated industry entry consists of a bundle of complementary skills that facilitate conducting feasibility studies, obtaining licenses from the state, arranging financial packages, securing technology and know-how, building plants, hiring and training the workforce, and establishing supply and distribution channels.

While economists and economic sociologists have generally remained silent on the issue of firm-level resources and capabilities, dependency and late-industrialization theorists have in fact referred to the skills required for new industry entry as "integrative abilities" (Evans 1979: 281) or "project-execution capabilities" (Amsden and Hikino 1994) or "capabilities to diversify" (Amsden 1989: 151, 174). In fact, both dependency and late-industrialization scholars note that business groups emerge at the center of dense networks of contacts with the state and with foreign multi-nationals (Frank 1967: 210–11; Evans 1979: 154–58, 280–2; Amsden 1989: 139–55, 231–5).

Implicit in dependency and late-industrialization analyses is the fact that the capability to combine resources for industry entry is generic in nature and difficult to trade because it is embodied in the organization's founder, owners, managers, and routines. It is also assumed to be in excess supply immediately after the entrepreneur or firm has consummated entry into a new industry. Once the new plant has been set up and is in production, the capability to enter new industries becomes idle. Therefore, it is a capability that, as predicted by the resource-based view (Peteraf 1993), encourages those who possess it to diversify across industries rather than become specialists in one industry or product line.

While dependency and late-industrialization theories identify a generic and non-tradable capability as the key to business group formation, they fail to specify the conditions that enable entrepreneurs to maintain that capability as an inimitable and valuable asset against the interests and competition of other organizational forms, including non-diversified firms and foreign multinationals. This theoretical problem is most apparent in Amsden and Hikino's analysis (1994). A generic and non-tradable capability to combine the resources necessary for industry entry is not sufficient for a business group to sustain its advantages in a variety of industries over time. According to the resource-based view, it is imperative that certain limits to competition exist so that the capability can be accumulated through a process of learning-by-doing, and maintained over time as inimitable and hence valuable (Peteraf 1993; Markides and Williamson 1996; Peng 2001). Such limits may result from a variety of "barriers," ranging from causal ambiguity and time lags to size advantages and preferential access to resources. For reasons of superior foresight or even sheer luck, entrepreneurs and firms may be heterogeneous in their ability to enter new industries, because access to the required resources is, or has been, unevenly distributed (Barney 1986).

27.3 DEVELOPMENT STRATEGIES AND LIMITS TO RESOURCE ACCESS

Until recently, scholarship on business groups has not paid enough attention to the fact that access to resources by entrepreneurs and firms in developing and newly industrialized countries is very sensitive to the development path followed by each country. In particular, foreign trade and direct investment patterns tend to have a momentous impact on resource accessibility by entrepreneurs and firms. In developing and newly industrialized countries—unlike in the more advanced ones—some of the resources for new industry entry are domestic (labor, access to home market), while others, at least in part, are situated beyond the country's boundaries (raw materials, capital, technology, know-how, access to foreign markets). If foreign trade and investment policies are such that only local entrepreneurs and firms can combine the required domestic and foreign resources, they may be in a position to accumulate a valuable and inimitable capability that enables them to enter a variety of industries quickly. Business groups will result, as entrepreneurs and firms with that capability enter one industry after another.

Research on the political economy of development suggests that it is crucial to distinguish between outward and inward foreign trade and investment flows, because they need not be correlated with each other (Guillén 2001). When flows are asymmetric, they create the potential for heterogeneity in resource access and capability building by entrepreneurs. Inward and outward flows appear cross-classified in Fig. 27.1. The impact of different development paths on the proliferation of business groups and other organizational forms can be directly derived from the characteristics of each of the four cells in the figure. Subsidiaries of foreign multinational enterprises (MNEs) are more likely to proliferate in the two upper cells characterized by permissive policies toward inward investment, while state-owned enterprises should be more likely in the two lower cells with restricted inward flows resulting from nationalist policies such as protectionism and a preference for domestic ownership.

Predicting which cells are more munificent to business groups (or to firms affiliated to business groups) is a more complicated question that requires additional analysis. The circumstances associated with the two symmetric cells on the diagonal of Fig. 27.1 (cells 2 and 4) do not produce heterogeneity in resource access across entrepreneurs and firms. By contrast, the cells off the diagonal (cells 1 and 3) describe asymmetric situations in which only some (local) entrepreneurs and firms have access to domestic and foreign resources simultaneously. Business groups will appear when such asymmetries persist long enough to allow entrepreneurs and firms to develop a combinative capability that encourages them to enter multiple industries. Let us examine each cell noting the implications of foreign trade and investment flows for business group formation, and the limitations of previous theories of development in predicting the rise of various organizational forms.

27.4 BUSINESS GROUPS UNDER
ASYMMETRIC CONDITIONS

The two off-diagonal cells in Fig. 27.1 describe situations with asymmetric foreign trade and investment flows. First, the low–high configuration or the nationalist–modernizing

Level of inward flows:	Level of outward flows:	
	High (modernizing)	Low (populist)
High (pragmatic)	HIGH: Allow Imports and inward investment HIGH: Export-led growth and outward investment *Context conducive to:* Foreign MNEs and SMEs 4	HIGH: Allow imports and inward investment LOW: Import substitution and local investment *Context conducive to:* Foreign MNEs and **business Groups** 1
Low (nationalist)	3 LOW: Protectionism and local ownership HIGH: Export-led growth and outward investment *Context conducive to:* State firms and **business groups**	2 LOW: Protectionism and local ownership LOW: Import substitution and local investment *Context conducive to:* State firms and SMEs

Figure 27.1 Foreign trade, foreign investment, and business groups in newly industrialized countries

Note: MNEs stands for Multinational Enterprises, and SMEs for Small and Medium Enterprises.

Source: Guillén (2001).

development path offers the well-connected entrepreneur or firm the possibility of contributing to export-led development by combining domestic and foreign resources under such restrictive inward policies as protection against imports and limited inward foreign investment. As resource-based researchers have argued (Peteraf 1993; Markides and Williamson 1996), preferential access to resources constitutes a competitive capability only if it enables diversification that is beyond the means of other actors. Under nationalist–modernizing development such inputs as local labor or physical resources will be available only to domestic entrepreneurs and firms and not to foreign MNEs as long as their access is restricted by nationalist policies. In its drive to increase exports, the state is likely to channel preferential investment or export loans to certain entrepreneurs and firms. Process-related knowledge will be available only to the few entrepreneurs with connections to foreign multinationals or who can be trusted by them. Given that the ability to set up and run manufacturing plants or service operations is subject to a steep learning curve, entrepreneurs and firms who manage repeatedly to obtain operating permits from the government and technology licenses from a foreign MNE will be in a position to reduce the cost of entering new industries (Amsden and Hikino 1994). This experience effect will advantage diversified business groups over non-diversified firms when it comes to enter a new industry. Finally, access to markets can be allocated in discriminating ways by the government (domestic market entry permissions, contracts with the state, certification of general trading companies for export) or by foreign MNEs (original equipment manufacturing contracts for export).

Late-industrialization theorists prescribe policies conducive to nationalist–modernizing development. However, they predict the rise of business groups because the autonomous state prefers to deal with only a few entrepreneurs for control and accountability reasons (Amsden 1989). The continued growth of business groups, however, is likely to undermine the presumed reason for their own existence—state autonomy. The resource-based view adopted here improves late-industrialization analysis because it can account for the continued growth of business groups even when the government starts worrying about their increasing power and leverage. The capability to combine resources for industry entry will remain inimitable as long as low–high foreign trade and investment flows persist, encouraging those who possess the capability to enter multiple industries so as fully to utilize it. It is important to realize that, in restricting imports and inward foreign investment, countries make it possible for business groups to grow at the expense of foreign firms and, indirectly, small and medium firms. Thus, business groups are seen here neither as a substitute for poorly developed markets nor as the result of state autonomy but as substitutes for foreign MNEs and small and medium firms.

The second off-diagonal cell in Fig. 27.1 (cell 1) represents the high–low or pragmatic–populist development path. Entrepreneurs and firms who manage to establish ties to the state, foreign MNEs, and moneylenders will benefit in a way that mirrors the low–high configuration. Typical of countries in the pragmatic–populist cell are a relaxation or even liberalization of regulations concerning foreign equity investment, especially when import-substitution efforts escalate from consumer non-durable goods to intermediate, durable, and capital goods (Evans 1979; Haggard 1990). This is an asymmetric development path insofar as exports and outward foreign investment remain low. MNE involvement in an import-substitution environment is more likely if the state introduces incentives and limits entry to only a few, non-competing players (Evans 1979: 163–4). Moreover, states invoke "nationalistic" ideologies to support policies encouraging foreign multinationals to add value locally (Evans 1979: 49). In the pragmatic–populist environment, foreign MNEs will tend to manufacture or distribute their products in collaboration with local entrepreneurs who know how to navigate the treacherous conditions created by economic and political populism, including powerful labor unions, import-competing interests among the local businesses, idiosyncratic credit allocation practices, and attempts by the state to force MNEs to contribute to "local accumulation" through control sharing (Evans 1979: 44, 163–212). MNEs may also choose to sell manufacturing licenses to local entrepreneurs either because attaining minimally efficient plant scales is difficult inside the country or because access to personnel, natural resources, and distribution channels is important but hard for a foreigner to obtain. A similar argument applies in the case of privatizations of state-owned enterprises, a typical policy initiative in pragmatic–populist countries that tends to attract coalitions of foreign MNEs and local entrepreneurs with complementary skills.

Dependency theorists predict the rise of business groups under pragmatic–populist development as part of the triple alliance among the leading local entrepreneurs, foreign MNEs, and the state. Moreover, they argue that the "vast majority of the local bourgeoisie"—the small and medium-sized firms—will be marginalized (Evans 1979: 282–3). The resource-based view, however, clarifies that state and multinational activity in an economy undergoing import-substitution growth is not enough to sustain the advantages of diversified business groups over time. Trade and foreign investment flows need to be asymmetric for entrepreneurs and firms to be able to enter a variety of new industries, forming a business group in the process. Their cumulative experience in repeated industry entry will advantage them over non-diversified entrepreneurs or firms and MNEs as long as conditions do not shift. Most importantly, the resource-based view presents business groups as brokers between domestic and foreign actors, while dependency theorists argue that the state is the broker (Evans 1979: 277–9). Finally, the resource-based view sees business groups as substitutes for foreign MNEs, while dependency sees them as complementary organizational forms.

27.5 THE DISADVANTAGES OF BUSINESS GROUPS UNDER SYMMETRIC CONDITIONS

Symmetric foreign trade and investment flows reduce or even delete the value of the generic capability to enter a variety of industries. When both inward and outward trade and investment flows are simultaneously at high or at low levels, domestic entrepreneurs have no exclusive claim to resources. Under high–high conditions, foreign MNEs, for example, can operate freely inside the country and across its borders in either direction, and they will locate activities in the country that are export competitive. Local knowledge about inputs might still be important, but freedom to operate will facilitate international sourcing and other integration strategies that are likely to lie beyond the reach of local business groups. Knowledge about the domestic market will lose value as the MNE uses its operations in the country to sell in foreign markets where it is already established. Moreover, a local firm not affiliated to a business group will also be at an advantage over those affiliated to one as long as it develops product-focused expertise and avoids the liabilities that membership in a group entails: resource sharing, mutual loan guarantees, cross-subsidization, and so on. Hence, one would expect the capability to combine domestic and foreign resources to lose its inimitability, rarity, and value as inward and outward trade and investment become more symmetric.

The market-failure approach to the existence of business groups—espoused by modernization and neoclassical theories of development—cannot explain why it is local business groups and not foreign MNEs that internalize inefficient input market transactions by bringing them within the boundaries of the firm. The resource-based view, by contrast, offers an explanation based on limits to resource access. The capability to enter new industries is valuable and inimitable only when foreign trade and investment flows are asymmetric. When development policies cause inward and outward flows to be simultaneously high—as prescribed by both modernization and neoclassical theories—foreign MNEs can tackle whatever market failures persist much more readily than local business groups. Thus, market failure could be conceptualized as a necessary condition for the appearance business groups, but never as a sufficient condition because, in the absence of asymmetries, foreign MNEs are generally better prepared to fill in for market failures.

The low–low cell in Fig. 27.1 is not conducive to business groups either, for two reasons. First, import-substitution processes that exclude direct foreign activity typically result in a variety of bottlenecks that slow down the growth of new industries because of the lack of appropriate technology and capital, in the form of either loans or direct investment. Opportunities for diversification will be reduced if the requisite technology and capital are not available. Thus, low–low conditions are likely to result in market saturation and sluggish economic growth, problems that tend to inhibit business concentration in the long run, for they make it difficult for firms to obtain the foreign resources necessary to grow and diversify. As Evans (1979: 315) has pointed out, "strategies that put autarky ahead of accumulation are not permitted to countries in which the triple alliance [among business groups, multinationals, and the state] dominates the political and economic scene." The second reason is that maintaining a "low profile" is politically more advantageous in a nationalist–populist context because private businesses, whether domestic or foreign, come under the threat of expropriation (Haggard 1990; Kaufman and Stallings 1991). It should be noted that nationalist–populist conditions usually lead to widespread market failure. Contrary to modernization and neoclassical theories of development, however, the resource-based view (or dependency theory for that matter) does not predict the rise, growth, or proliferation of business groups under such circumstances.

Based on the analysis summarized in Fig. 27.1, the resource-based view of business groups predicts that this form of organization will appear and thrive in newly industrialized countries when asymmetric trade and investment conditions enable a few entrepreneurs and firms to develop the capability of combining foreign and domestic resources for repeated industry entry. These entrepreneurs or firms prosper because they are in a position to act as brokers in a political–economic structure of competition characterized by restricted cross-border access to resources. Such asymmetries—akin to what Burt (1992) calls "structural holes"—enable actors who can bridge them to diversify into a variety of industries. The advantages associated with the capability to act as a cross-border resource broker can be sustained only to the extent that asymmetries in foreign trade and investment persist over time.

27.6 AN EVOLUTIONARY MODEL
OF BUSINESS GROUPS

The resource-based view of business groups articulated above can be cast in terms of an evolutionary model (Kock and Guillén 2001). In Fig. 27.2 we refer to "Stage I" business groups as those that use their "contact" capabilities to engage in a variety of economic activities at the beginning of a country's industrial development. After setting up a business based on contacts and imported effectiveness and efficiency, local firms are expected to attempt to develop some organizational and technological capabilities of their own, based on the experience they gain through actual participation in a business, which then allow them to succeed in the country's internal selection environment. Amsden and Hikino (1994) suggest that the most likely candidates for such "Stage II" capabilities are the "generic skills" of project execution and mass production. If we assume that foreign firms with large organizational and technological capabilities are also likely to command the abilities to execute projects and ramp up to mass production to a certain extent themselves, we can argue that selection among locals in Stage I centers more on the actually scarce capability—that is, contacts—rather than on the locals commanding such "generic skills" themselves. However, in Stage II, with an increasing number of locals competing for further business, the scarcity of contact capabilities will slowly diminish and efficiency concerns come to dominate. Thus, it is in this stage that a local firm with a mix of contact and superior "generic capabilities" may out-compete others. We also argued that Stage II capabilities require a greater degree of relatedness for sustainable diversification than Stage I capabilities. Furthermore, compared to contact capabilities, Stage II capabilities apparently reside at a deeper level in the firm or group. While contacts are essentially carried and used at the very top level—that is, the entrepreneur or entrepreneurial group itself—project execution and mass production skills are rather a type of organizational knowledge residing at the level of team members, employees, and shopfloor managers who actually execute the set-up of a new firm.

Business groups may evolve into Stage III when the increasing exposure of these diversifying business groups to a variety of markets and a large number of foreign (standardized) technologies raises the overall skill level of the entrepreneur or firm.

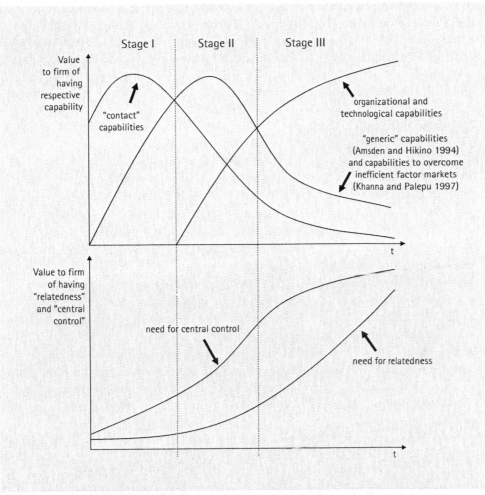

Figure 27.2 Evolution of capabilities and "efficient" organizational characteristics

Source: Kock and Guillén (2001).

Benefiting from the shelter of protectionism and other asymmetries, firms have time to accumulate knowledge about markets (customers and competitors) and the relative profitability and prospects of different lines of business, as well as gain a deeper understanding of the organizational and technological capabilities that underlie their acquired production technologies. This improved capability base implies that the individual firm may now be better able to cope with more advanced innovative challenges. As a consequence, some firms may be able to utilize their emergent operational and technological capabilities to create their first rudimentary product or process innovations. As the operational and technological capabilities resulted from using basically mature foreign technologies, we cannot expect that such innovations result in world-standard new goods or processes. Rather, under the assumption of path dependence, we would expect these firms to create products or processes that simply constitute significant improvements over the mature technologies used before. These inventions may allow the firm to move away from completely mature and standardized technologies and products towards technologies that incorporate more idiosyncratic know-how. Thus, we argue that the selection environment in late-developing countries may change from emphasizing Stage I and II capabilities to organizational and technological capabilities related to advanced product and process innovation—that is, Stage III.

This would imply a focus on creating more relatedness within the businesses operated by a business group in Stage III, compelling the firm to implement a centralized M-form organization to capitalize on economies of scope (Hill 1988). This could take the form of the existing units being trimmed to create a business core—that is, to create one large, centralized M-form structure by divesting the most unrelated units—or individual firms within a group or cluster of already related firms could create their own related diversified subfirm within the umbrella of a large business group. The resulting structure could then look like a number of centralized M-forms held together by an M-form or holding company (Cable and Yasuki 1985). The rationale for the continued existence of such an umbrella superstructure could be found in (i) the prevailing importance of contact capabilities and (ii) inefficient capital markets, allowing the overall group to economize on these underdeveloped markets (Kock and Guillén 2001).

Overall, we suggest that the changes in the selection environment from Stage I to Stage III are partially based on a reduction in the protectionist and corruption-based property-rights asymmetries and are partially a cause of these developments (Kock and Guillén 2001).

27.7 EMPIRICAL ILLUSTRATIONS

The underlying logic of business group formation in an asymmetric nationalist–modernizing context is well illustrated by the case of the Korean *chaebol*. Previous research has noted that establishing and nurturing ties to the government has been essential to the *chaebol*'s growth (Fields 1995; Kim, Chapter 6, this volume). A few studies have pointed out that ties to foreign MNEs have also been important (Kim 1997; Ungson et al. 1997: 140–51). The overwhelming presence of the business groups in the Korean economy has its roots in the early importance of political connections when awarding permits to enter new industries, government contracts, subsidized loans, export incentives, import licenses to acquire equipment and raw materials, and permissions to hire workers. The state policy-making apparatus created by General Park in the 1960s preferred to deal only with a handful of entrepreneurs, for the obvious control reasons, and persuaded the favored ones to enter risky undertakings by expanding their licenses in already established and profitable industries, protecting them from foreign imports, and lending them money at subsidized rates. In addition to favoring a few entrepreneurs, the Korean state exhibited an early bias against foreign-owned enterprises, making it possible for the privileged domestic entrepreneurs to increase their exports and outward foreign investment without having to face significant imports and inward foreign investment (Kim 1997: 125–32). Thus, business groups (in manufacturing and trading) and state-owned enterprises—in steel, electricity, gas, railroads, and highways (Amsden 1989: 90–2)—grew in importance, as predicted in cell 3 of Fig. 27.1.

The Korean entrepreneurs privileged by the state to enter new industries learned how to produce at low cost massive amounts of different types of goods. They neither designed nor marketed the products, because rapid economic development could not wait for research or marketing capabilities to be created from scratch (Amsden 1989). Rather, they focused on manufacturing—often merely assembling—products to specification for Japanese, American, and European MNEs and retailers. This pattern of "original equipment manufacturing" (OEM) was first used in textiles, shoes, toys, and electrical appliances, and later extended to more technologically advanced industries in intermediate, capital, and durable consumer goods. In the typical OEM contract, the foreign MNE provides the technology and markets the product while the local firm secures permits from the state, hires and manages the workforce, and undertakes the manufacturing activities. Until the early 1990s, more than 80 percent of Korea's exports were accounted for by OEM contracts (Park 1994). Until the late 1990s, even Samsung Electronics—Korea's largest exporter—derived about two-thirds of its sales from OEM contracts with such companies as Tandy, Unisys, Hewlett-Packard, Apple, IBM, Dell, and Tektronix. Thus, the *chaebol* established ties to the state to secure critical resources inside the country (labor, capital, domestic market access) and to foreign MNEs in order to access technology and export markets. By the 1980s, the *chaebol* were increasingly manufacturing products with their own brands, but they wee still relying heavily on foreign technology: by the 1990s around 60 percent of total Korean payments for royalties and fees were accounted for by the seven largest *chaebol*.

The Korean *chaebol* developed the capability to access domestic and foreign resources for repeated industry entry by creating group-level staff offices to coordinate not only financial allocation but also planning, technology acquisition, plant construction and equipping, human resource management, and export–import activities (Amsden 1989: 167; Fields 1995: 183–208; Kim 1997: 54–7; Ungson et al. 1997). When a *chaebol* targeted a new industry for entry—frequently in response to government incentives or guidance—the group-level office would conduct feasibility studies and facilitate access to resources and expertise from group companies, the state, and foreign MNEs. Over time, repeated industry entry following the same blueprint has allowed the *chaebol* to reduce the costs and time of setting up new ventures (Amsden 1989; Amsden and Hikino 1994). While this internalized capability has allowed the largest groups to grow much more quickly than smaller groups and non-diversified local firms, it represents an advantage over MNEs only insofar as the state restricts imports and inward foreign investment.

The *chaebol* have been very active in politics and policy-making. The "symbiotic" relationship between government and business groups in Korea has deep roots in the country's social and political traditions (Biggart 1990; Kim 1997). Surveys show that they share with bureaucratic, political, and military elites a common regional origin and educational background. Tellingly, about 20 percent of the Korean entrepreneurial and managerial elite had previously worked for the government. An additional 6 percent of them served as officers in the army, an institution that provided up to half of President Park's and 20 percent of President Chun's political appointees (Jones and Sakong 1980: 210–47; Chul 1994). By the early 1990s, about one-third of fathers-in-law of *chaebol* owners were high-ranking government officials (Cumings 1997: 329). In addition, presidential campaigns have routinely been funded by contributions from the largest *chaebol*. But the importance of political connections should not obscure the equally critical relevance of ties to foreign providers of capital, process-related knowledge, and access to markets, which all Korean business groups have had to establish and maintain if they were to diversify into a panoply of new industries. Those ties have become a valuable and rare capability only insofar as the state has restricted access by foreigners.

It was not long before the organizational dynamics of Korea's nationalist–modernizing development path acquired a momentum of its own. Since the late 1970s the combined sales of the ten largest business groups in Korea have represented more than 40 percent of GDP. Those proportions, of course, are inflated because of the patterns of intense intra-group shipments. A better indicator is value added. The top six *chaebol* accounted in 1990 for 15 percent of Korea's value added, easily the world's highest concentration of economic power (Amsden 1989: 116; Woo 1991: 171–3; Lee 1994, exhibits 4 and 8). Starting in the mid-1970s, the state began to see its authority, autonomy, and freedom of action erode as a result of growing *chaebol* power (Kim 1997). Not surprisingly, every single South Korean president since Syngman Rhee attempted at least once to curb *chaebol* growth. The most important episodes occurred under General Park in 1974, Chun in 1980, Roh in 1990, Kim Young Sam in 1993, and Kim Dae Jung in 1998. The government attempted to slow down the growth of the *chaebol* and reassert state authority by asking or requiring them to shed subsidiaries, focus on core industries, list companies on the stock market, sell real estate, eliminate cross-company subsidies, and reduce debt–equity ratios.

Late-industrialization theory's emphasis on state autonomy (Amsden 1989) is inconsistent with the *chaebol*'s continued growth, even after the state realized its own autonomy was being compromised and took measures to arrest the trend. It is simply not possible to observe how the *chaebol* grew vigorously during the 1980s and 1990s (Kim 1997) and argue that it was because an autonomous state continued to allocate resources at will and to control the privileged entrepreneurs' every move. The answer to this puzzle is provided by the resource-based view: foreign trade and investment asymmetries persisted during the 1980s and 1990s (Guillén 2001), thus making it possible for the *chaebol* to continue expanding. Indeed, the *chaebol* have opposed attempts by the state to reduce asymmetries in foreign trade and investment, knowing that their pattern of diversification and growth owes much to them.

For example, President Chun introduced a series of neo-liberal reforms during the early 1980s—monetary stabilization, privatization of banks, partial deregulation of credit, selected trade liberalization, and a somewhat less restrictive policy toward MNEs. The attempt to increase imports and inward foreign investment represented a shift from nationalist to pragmatic policies, and the *chaebol* responded by mobilizing politically to water down the reforms (Lee 1997: 74–7). Contrary to the government's expectation, the biggest *chaebol* ended up benefiting from the reforms to a greater extent than the smaller groups and the independent firms. They managed to access new sources of relatively cheap credit, acquire stakes in the privatized banks, set up financial management companies, and enter into new joint venture agreements with MNEs (Kim 1997: 181–200).

The continued, although somewhat reduced, asymmetries in trade and foreign investment in Korea since 1997 have made the *chaebol* resilient to changes in the global economy. As a result of the 1997 Asian financial crisis, twelve of the top thirty *chaebols* collapsed or went through major restructuring (Guillén 2001). However, their degrees of cross-industry diversification dropped only slightly (Kim, Chapter 6, this volume). As Chang (2003) has documented, the *chaebol* continue to reign supreme in the Korean economy. Their international expansion has reached new levels, while foreign multinationals continue to have only a timid and sparse presence in the local economy.

The rise of business groups under the pragmatist–populist conditions of cell 1 in Fig. 27.1 can be illustrated by the case of Argentina. With only a couple of exceptions, the growth to prominence of the Argentine *grupos económicos* began in the early 1950s—that is, toward the end of the populist presidency of General Juan Domingo Perón. Acute economic problems brought about by staunchly nationalist–populist policies forced him to "retreat" from economic nationalism by stabilizing the economy, seeking foreign investment, and allowing the business groups to conduct some of the activities previously allotted to the state. The groups diversified into new industries with the cash flows generated in profitable and protected domestic markets subject to import-substitution conditions. They did so by gaining concessions and permits from the state and borrowing technology from foreign MNEs (Lewis 1992: 195–210, 349–59).

The Argentine groups have always been ideal local partners for many of the manufacturing and service MNEs venturing into the country, in spite of the frequent zigzags in policies regarding foreign investment. The government privileged the groups when short-run economic instability or financial crises afflicted the country. As Lewis (1992) documents, macroeconomic, credit, trade, and foreign-investment policies oscillated between nationalism and pragmatism several times between the 1950s and the 1990s. Previous research on Argentina supports the prediction that business groups expand more rapidly during periods of asymmetric pragmatic–populism than during periods of symmetric nationalist–populism (Bisang 1994: 20–4). For example, the first military junta of 1976–81 pursued a neo-liberal line away from the nationalist policies of the 1970–6 period—that is, imports and inward foreign investment were allowed to increase. At the same time, however, firms and state-owned enterprises continued in an import-substitution mode, resulting in acutely asymmetric pragmatic–populist conditions (Lewis 1992: 448–75; Waisman 1987). The dictatorship showered the business groups with contracts to provide public services or improve the performance of state-owned enterprises, better conditions for export, and freer access to domestic and international credit. After the groups' expansive strategies failed in 1982, the state nationalized their accumulated foreign debt. The groups also grew rapidly when the first democratic presidency attempted asymmetric policies of the pragmatic–populist kind in 1985–6. The groups, however, retrenched swiftly, as more symmetric nationalist–populist conditions set in during the late 1980s after the failure of pragmatism in foreign trade and investment (Lewis 1992: 478–93).

The first years of the Menem presidency after 1989 entailed a rapid increase in imports and inward foreign investment accompanied by a lagging increase in exports and outward foreign investment—that is, an asymmetric pragmatic–populist strategy was followed. Under Menem, the business groups were exposed to increased competition because of tariff cuts. They benefited, however, from the crackdown on the unions' power, renewed technical, licensing, and marketing ties with foreign multinationals, and Latin America's most ambitious privatization program, affecting over sixty state-owned manufacturing and service firms valued at US$26 billion. Of the fifty-four companies privatized until February 1993, one or more of the top ten Argentine business groups participated in thirty-two of them. In twenty-five of those thirty-two instances business groups were joined by at least one foreign MNE, which typically provided capital and technology (Kosacoff and Bezchinsky 1994: 135–9). Successful bidding for privatized public services or state-owned manufacturing enterprises has frequently been based on political connections as well as on the ability to meet requirements as to minimum assets and technological know-how. Accordingly, entrepreneurs and firms with connections to the state and foreign MNEs and lenders have benefited the most from privatization. Thus, entrepreneurs with access to both domestic and foreign resources have thrived when Argentina pursued an asymmetric pragmatic–populist development strategy (Bisang 1994: 50–3). In so doing, they created business groups across a wide variety of manufacturing and service industries. While some of the business groups succumbed during the 2001–2 crisis, others thrived under the continuing asymmetrical conditions of Argentine development during the early years of the twenty-first century (Fracchia et al., Chapter 12, this volume).

While the Argentine *grupos* have not accumulated group-level capabilities to the same extent as the Korean *chaebol*, they too have developed the ability to set up new ventures or to take over privatized companies quickly and in a cost-effective manner. The groups' central offices provide functions such as human resource management, planning, legal advice, cash-flow coordination, and targeting of new business opportunities (Bisang 1994: 32). As in Korea, the business groups have loomed large in Argentine politics and economic policy-making. Cabinet ministers and other top political appointees have frequently been recruited among the managerial ranks of the largest groups, especially when an asymmetric pragmatic–populist strategy, as opposed to a symmetric one, was to be pursued (Lewis 1992). The Argentine business groups, though, have not always succeeded at influencing policy-making in their favor.

Finally, the case of Spain illustrates that a pragmatic–modernizing development strategy is not conducive to business groups, as the resource-based view predicts. The country initially pursued an asymmetric nationalist–modernizing development strategy until the late 1970s, combining relatively low imports and inward investment with increasing exports. As a result, several diversified business groups formed around banks (Central, Bilbao, Vizcaya, Urquijo, Banesto), large chemical or steel companies (Unión Explosivos Río Tinto, Cros, Altos Hornos de Vizcaya), as well as whenever entrepreneurs diversified out of traditional light industries such as food and beverages (Rumasa). With the one exception of Rumasa—which was more of a freelance player—the other groups grew on the basis of connections with the state and foreign partners, as several meticulously researched case studies of these groups indicate (Muñoz 1969; Tamames 1977; Muñoz et al. 1978).

While the industrial crisis of the 1970s hit Spanish industry hard, it was the subsequent process of market liberalization and integration with Europe that caused the definitive decline of many of the groups. Protectionist trade barriers and restrictions against foreign MNEs were lifted during the 1980s. As a result of the reduction in trade and investment asymmetries, some of the business groups collapsed under international competitive pressure, while others succeeded in refocusing on one core activity or were acquired by foreign MNEs. While they had previously developed a capability to take advantage of asymmetric conditions, the sudden and lasting reduction of such imbalances rendered the capability obsolete. By the mid-1990s only the industrial groups organized around such banks as BCH and BBV or large retailers (El Corte Inglés) had survived, while virtually all others disappeared either gradually or as the result of bankruptcy procedures and takeovers. As foreign MNEs found themselves free to operate in the country, business groups built on the assumption of asymmetric foreign trade and investment suffered. Moreover, foreign companies and investors were allowed to take over many privatized public services and state-owned manufacturing companies without the collaboration of a local partner. Although some of the groups and the banks resisted pragmatic–modernizing policies, especially in their core industries, they were unable to derail the considerable political and social momentum created in favor of membership in the European Union, which required the abandonment of nationalist policies toward imports and inward foreign investment.

Consider the example of the Unión Explosivos Río Tinto (UERT), which was originally founded as a mining company with the participation of British capital. The firm grew via diversification during the 1960s when Spain implemented asymmetric policies similar to those of Korea. Given its contacts with the government, local banks, and foreign MNEs (Rhône-Poulenc, Hoechst, Shell, Toyo, Tioxide International, Gulf, Texaco), UERT diversified into fertilizers, chemicals, oil, plastics, engineering, pharmaceuticals, cosmetics, real estate, and consulting services. By the mid-1970s it was the largest diversified conglomerate in the country, but barely 14 percent of total sales were exports (Muñoz et al. 1978: 428–33). The economic crisis of the 1970s forced many of its companies into bankruptcy. Subsequently, Spain's bid to become a member of the European Union meant that trade and investment protectionism had to be abandoned. Like many of the other Spanish groups, UERT collapsed as a business group during the 1980s, with its various companies falling into the hands of several foreign MNEs.

27.8 IMPLICATIONS AND CONCLUSION

This chapter has approached the rise and fall of diversified business groups in developing and newly industrialized countries from a resource-based perspective, which offers an alternative explanation to others emphasizing market imperfections, hierarchical social patterns, or state autonomy. The core argument posits that business groups grow and thrive only under certain conditions that enable them to accumulate distinctive capabilities with which they diversify into different industries. It was noted that entrepreneurs and firms in developing and newly industrialized countries need to combine domestic and foreign resources in order to enter industries, and asymmetries in foreign trade and investment were proposed as allowing for business group formation. Entrepreneurs and firms with the internalized capability to access resources enter one industry after another, creating business groups and not integrated companies, because their diversification follows a logic of repeated access to foreign and domestic resources under asymmetric foreign trade and investment rather than one of technological, marketing, or financial strength—that is, the usual logic of business growth based on intangible assets. Future research could design empirical studies to ascertain the extent to which the resource-based view offers a more complete and successful explanation of business groups than other existing alternatives.

REFERENCES

AMSDEN, A. H. (1989). *Asia's Next Giant: South Korea and Late Industrialization*. New York: Oxford University Press.

AMSDEN, A. H., and HIKINO, T. (1994). "Project Execution Capability, Organizational Know-How and Conglomerate Corporate Growth in Late Industrialization," *Industrial and Corporate Change*, 3/1: 111–47.

BARNEY, J. (1986). "Strategic Factor Markets: Expectations, Luck, and Business Strategy," *Management Science*, 32/10: 1231–41.

BARNEY, J. (1991). "Firm Resources and Sustained Competitive Advantage," *Journal of Management*, 17: 99–120.

BIGGART, N. W. (1990). "Institutionalized Patrimonialism in Korean Business," *Comparative Social Research*, 12: 113–33.

BIGGART, N. W., and GUILLÉN, M. F. (1999). "Developing Difference: Social Organization and the Rise of the Auto Industries of South Korea, Taiwan, Spain, and Argentina," *American Sociological Review*, 64/5 (Oct.), 722–47.

BISANG, R. (1994). "Perfil tecno-productivo de los grupos económicos en la industria argentina." Working Paper No. 94-12-1671, CEPAL, Santiago, Chile.

BURT, R. S. (1992). *Structural Holes: The Social Structure of Competition*. Cambridge, MA: Harvard University Press.

CABLE, J., and YASUKI, H. (1985). "Internal Organization, Business Groups and Corporate Performance: An Empirical Test of the Multidivisional Hypothesis in Japan," *International Journal of Industrial Organization*, 3: 401–20.

CHANDLER, A. D., JR. (1990). *Scale and Scope*. Cambridge, MA: Harvard University Press.

CHANG, S. J. (2003). *Rise and Fall of Chaebols: The Financial Crisis and Transformation of Korean Business Groups*. Cambridge: Cambridge University Press.

CHUL, Y. S. (1994). "South Korea's Top Bureaucratic Elites, 1948–1993," *Korea Journal*, 34/3: 5–19.

CUMINGS, B. (1997). *Korea's Place in the Sun: A Modern History*. New York: Norton.

EVANS, P. (1979). *Dependent Development*. Princeton: Princeton University Press.

FIELDS, K. J. (1995). *Enterprise and the State in Korea and Taiwan*. Ithaca, NY: Cornell University Press.

FRANK, A. G. (1967). *Capitalism and Underdevelopment in Latin America*. New York: Monthly Review Press.

GRANOVETTER, M. (1995). "Coase Revisited: Business Groups in the Modern Economy," *Industrial and Corporate Change*, 4/1: 93–130.

GUILLÉN, M. F. (2000). "Business Groups in Emerging Economies: A Resource-Based View," *Academy of Management Journal*, 43/3 (June), 362–80.

GUILLÉN, M. F. (2001). *The Limits of Convergence: Globalization and Organizational Change in Argentina, South Korea, and Spain*. Princeton, NJ: Princeton University Press.

HAGGARD, S. (1990). *Pathways from the Periphery: The Politics of Growth in the Newly Industrializing Countries*. Ithaca, NY: Cornell University Press.

HILL, C. W. L. (1988). "Internal Capital Market Controls and Financial Performance in Multidivisional Firms," *Journal of Industrial Economics*, 37: 67–83.

HOSKISSON, R. E., and HITT, M. A. (1990). "Antecedents and Performance Outcomes of Diversification: A Review and Critique of Theoretical Perspectives," *Journal of Management*, 16/2: 461–509.

HOSKISSON, R. E., JOHNSON, R. A., TIHANYI, L., and WHITE, R. E. (2005). "Diversified Business Groups and Corporate Refocusing in Emerging Economies," *Journal of Management*, 31/6: 941–65.

JONES, L. P., and SAKONG, I. (1980). *Government, Business, and Entrepreneurship in Economic Development: The Korean Case*. Cambridge, MA: Council on East Asian Studies, Harvard University.

KAUFMAN, R. R., and STALLINGS, B. (1991). "The Political Economy of Latin American Populism," in R. Dornbusch and S. Edwards (eds.), *The Macroeconomics of Populism in Latin America*. Chicago: University of Chicago Press, 15–43.

KHANNA, T., and PALEPU, K. (1997). "Why Focused Strategies May be Wrong for Emerging Markets," *Harvard Business Review* (July–Aug.), 41–50.

KHANNA, T., and YAFEH, Y. (2007). "Business Groups in Emerging Markets: Paragons or Parasites?" *Journal of Economic Literature*, 45/2: 331–72.

KIM, E. M. (1997). *Big Business, Strong State*. Albany, NY: State University of New York Press.

KOCK, C., and GUILLÉN, M. F. (2001). "Strategy and Structure in Developing Countries: Business Groups as an Evolutionary Response to Opportunities for Unrelated Diversification," *Industrial & Corporate Change*, 10/1: 1–37.

KOSACOFF, B., and BEZCHINSKY, G. (1994). "New Strategies of Transnational Corporations in Argentina," *CEPAL Review*, 52 (Apr.), 129–53.

LEE, B. K. (1994). "Stimulating the Will to Innovate in Private and Public Enterprises: Korean Technology Policy." mimeo. Cambridge, MA: MIT Sloan School of Management.

LEE, Y. H. (1997). *The State, Society and Big Business in South Korea*. New York: Routledge.

LEFF, N. (1978). "Industrial Organization and Entrepreneurship in Developing Countries: The Economic Groups," *Economic Development and Cultural Change*, 26: 661–75.

LEWIS, P. H. (1992). *The Crisis of Argentine Capitalism*. Chapel Hill, NC: University of North Carolina Press.

MARKIDES, C. C., and WILLIAMSON, P. J. (1996). "Corporate Diversification and Organizational Structure: A Resource-Based View," *Academy of Management Journal*, 39/2 (Apr.), 340–67.

MUÑOZ, J. (1969). *El poder de la banca en España*. Madrid: ZYX.

MUÑOZ, J., ROLDÁN, S., and SERRANO, A. (1978). *La internacionalización del capital en España, 1959–1977*. Madrid: Edicusa.

ORRÙ, M., BIGGART, N. W., and HAMILTON, G. G. (1997). *The Economic Organization of East Asian Capitalism*. Thousand Oaks, CA: Sage Publications.

PARK, J. C. (1994). "Korean Exports: Their Development," *Ki-Eop Kyung-Young* (Journal of Management), 435 (July), 36–9 (in Korean).

PENG, M. W. (2001). "The Resource-Based View and International Business," *Journal of Management*, 27: 803–29.

PETERAF, M. A. (1993). "The Cornerstones of Competitive Advantage: A Resource-Based View," *Strategic Management Journal*, 14/3 (Mar.), 179–91.

RAMANUJAM, V., and VARADARAJAN, P. (1989). "Research on Corporate Diversification: A Synthesis," *Strategic Management Journal*, 10/6 (Nov.–Dec.), 523–51.

TAMAMES, R. (1977). *La oligarquía financiera en España*. Barcelona: Planeta.

UNGSON, G., STEERS, R. M., and PARK, S. H. (1997). *Korean Enterprise: The Quest for Globalization*. Boston: Harvard Business School Press.

WAISMAN, C. H. (1987). *Reversal of Development in Argentina: Postwar Counterrevolutionary Policies and their Structural Consequences*. Princeton: Princeton University Press.

WOO, J. E. (1991). *Race to the Swift: State and Finance in Korean Industrialization*. New York: Columbia University Press.

CHAPTER 28

....

TECHNOLOGICAL INNOVATION AND BUSINESS GROUPS

....

MIKE HOBDAY

ASLI M. COLPAN

28.1 INTRODUCTION

....

THE aim of this chapter is to examine the challenges facing diversified business groups in late-industrializing economies, as they acquire technology and learn to innovate.[1] In particular, we assess the role business groups play in technological innovation processes. The chapter thus attempts to identify the internal business strategies as well as external conditions that lead business groups to take a positive and developmental role in those economies. From this we hope to develop policy- and business-oriented conclusions and suggestions.

The main focus of the chapter is technological innovation, rather than organizational or institutional innovation, although the latter often accompany the former. Also, as we are dealing with business groups in the late-industrializing economies of the twentieth century, the core activity is usually incremental 'catch-up' innovation and technological acquisition, which involves significant technology transfer from

---

[1] This chapter focuses on business groups in late-industrializing economies, which have been challenged by limited access to leading-edge technology and science and their distance from advanced-country markets and clusters.

developed and industrialized countries. This is to be contrasted with the R&D and new product-based 'leadership innovation' of leading corporations operating in the most advanced economies.

Section 28.2 begins an analytical discussion of business groups and their capabilities in the catch-up context, touching on recent debates over negative versus positive features of technologically unrelated diversification. Section 28.3 turns to the experience of the technology development of some successful business groups in Asia. Since Asia embodies the most successful cases of technology development within late industrialization, we specifically take on the case of Asia and Asian business groups in this chapter to pinpoint technological progress clearly. Focusing on electronics, the largest export sector in the region, we identify various technology learning stages and strategies that enabled business groups to overcome their difficulties and begin to catch up with the West and Japan. This is followed by a discussion on the role of business groups in technological innovation. The section then turns towards identifying alternative models of technology development in electronics, pointing to considerable variety in industrial structure, organizational form, patterns of ownership, and government policies across Asia. It then identifies the common "principles of success" in the electronics industry across different models of Asian technological progress, and hints at the role of the developmental state in "disciplining" business groups by demanding reciprocity for subsidies and other advantages provided to them. Despite the fact that there can be no Asian model for directly imitating and, as Gerschenkron (1962) stressed, latecomers need to follow their own paths to development by building on their own capabilities, institutions, and opportunities, our conclusion shows that there are some important learning points from the Asian case with respect to technology development.

28.2 DEBATES ON THE CAPABILITIES
OF BUSINESS GROUPS

A business group in a late-industrializing economy can be described as a group that typically has activities covering several sectors and industries and that has considerable market power as a monopolist or oligopolist in many or most of these sectors. A single family may well have considerable control over its ownership and management, but there may also be management from outside the family. Despite the diversified interests, the family may provide stability and coherence and there are often personal and operational ties, besides formal equity ties, among the affiliates of the group (Intarakumnerd 2000). Khanna and Palepu (1997) argue that some diversified business groups operate as holding companies with full ownership in many enterprises, while others are collections of publicly traded companies, with some degree of central control.

A strong argument made by their proponents is that business groups can overcome and compensate for institutional deficiencies in developing countries by internalizing external functions (e.g. Khanna and Palepu 1997). For example, there may be a lack of venture capital, because the capital market is underdeveloped, or there may be an insufficient skilled labor force and the business groups can overcome these barriers to development. Khanna and Palepu (1997) argue that the developing-country context drives the strategy of business groups, and they often imitate the functions of institutions present in developed market economies and are, therefore, suited to the institutional contexts in most emerging economies. Besides certain drawbacks of business groups, such as rent-seeking within protected markets and the cozy political connections of many groups, business groups therefore have several benefits.

From the product market side, Amsden and Hikino (1994) argue that business groups in late-industrializing economies typically pursue unrelated diversification in the absence of competitive propietary technology, and that these strategies are influenced by external investment opportunities supported by project execution capabilities that are applicable to a wide range of industries.[2] In their view, the resource-based theory, which stresses the benefits of focus and specialization, under-values the importance of generic project execution capabilities, which they contend underpin the widely observed unrelated diversification paths of business groups in emerging economies.[3]

Yet, as those emerging markets get more liberalized and become subject to international competition, the arguments suggesting the move towards related diversified portfolio is strong. Guillén argues as the environment shifts, firms will have to move from emphasizing generic capabilities of contact and project execution to stressing technological and organizational capabilities (Guillén, Chapter 27, this volume). Guillén suggests that this could be possible by divesting most unrelated businesses and therefore by creating a business core under a centralized M-form structure. Or it may be possible that a number of such related firms under the M-form structures can be held together by a holding company or another M-form "umbrella-superstructure." The continuing significance of contact capabilities and the withstanding inefficient capital markets, according to Guillén, may explain the persistence of such distinctive structures.

On the other hand, Khanna and Palepu (1997) contend that the commonly held view that business groups are backward forms and that, as developing countries evolve, they will in time adopt Western-style institutional structures and focused corporations is flawed. Instead, they argue that there is no one institutional context and that anyway these contexts can take a very long time to evolve. Therefore, business groups and their advantages can persist for long periods of time and that governments and business leaders should not blindly apply the logic of the Western thinking: that, to be competitive, firms should scale back the scope of their activities.

---

[2] The same could probably be said about general management capabilities and generic manufacturing assembly process capabilities, which are also applicable across industries.

[3] Research by Intarakumnerd (2000) on Thailand and Vargas (2004) on Mexico shows that project execution capabilities are also important for related diversification.

Taking a different view, business groups may maintain their diversified product portfolios under holding or other "umbrella-superstructure" forms, because their accumulated resources and capabilities in different industries may support several product units that are controlled by the group-level headquarters. As technology is advanced at the product and industry level by the affiliated companies, accumulation of resources and capabilities, including those in administration, finance, human resources, and marketing at the group level, can explain the persistence of such structures of diversified business groups (Colpan and Hikino, Chapter 2, this volume). Interestingly, there is also little evidence of groups' dismantling or even focusing in many of the nations covered in this volume, despite the emergence of liberalizing and more competitive environments in those economies.

While the arguments briefly summarized above by several authors frame the business group debate in an appealing way, they do not particularly focus on technology acquisition and innovation. Moreover, they do not look at technological performance or processes, the issues to which we now turn based on the experiences of Asian business groups.

28.3 Technology development
in business groups

28.3.1 Technological learning processes in Asian business groups

Asian business groups such as Samsung, Hyundai, Daewoo, and Lucky Goldstar in South Korea and Tatung, Sampo and Teco in Taiwan in the 1950s and 1960s faced two sets of significant latecomer challenges. First, they needed to surmount their dislocation from the main international sources of innovation, technology, and research— the technology disadvantage. Secondly, they needed to overcome the small size of local markets and their distance (geographical, brand, and otherwise) from the advanced markets they needed to export to, to earn foreign exchange (the market disadvantage). Only by overcoming these latecomer difficulties could these business groups succeed in export markets.

Focusing on electronics, the largest export sector in East Asia, we can identify various technology learning strategies that enabled business groups to overcome their difficulties and begin to catch up with the West and Japan.[4] In fact, the business groups passed through various historical stages of technological development (see Table 28.1). The initial entry stage began in the 1960s, with firms producing

---

[4] Unless otherwise stated, evidence for this section is from Hobday (1995).

Table 28.1 Transition in electronics: From OEM to ODM to OBM

Phases	Technological transition	Market transition
1960s/1970s OEM	Local firm learns assembly process for standard, simple goods	Foreign transnational corporation/buyer designs, brands and distributes
1980s ODM	Local firm designs* and learns product innovation skills	Transnational corporation buys, brands and distributes and gains PPVA
1990s OBM	Local firm designs and conducts R&D for new products	Local firm organizes distribution, develops own-brand name and captures PPVA

Notes: OEM = original equipment manufacture; ODM = own design and manufacture; OBM = own brand manufacture; PPVA = post-production value-added.
*or contributes to the design, alone or in partnership with the foreign company.

Source: Hobday (1995).

labor-intensive products under joint ventures or subcontracting arrangements (called original equipment manufacture (OEM)) with Japanese, American, and European firms. Transnational corporations (TNCs) and foreign buyers were initially attracted by low labor costs. Foreign firms supplied the business groups with training, advice on manufacturing processes, and also the capital goods needed for production. Local technicians, engineers, managers, and factory workers benefited from the larger foreign buyers and TNCs through formal training courses. The TNC motivation was to ensure that quality and delivery were adequate.

Through the 1960s and 1970s business groups learned by manufacturing simple consumer electronics and by assembling and testing semiconductors. Firms used their assembly experiences from other sectors such as electrical goods, bicycles, and clothing. Gradually these firms upgraded their production processes and improved the quality and speed of manufacturing. This long initial period, through the 1960s and 1970s, can be called "learning the art of assembly."

During the early 1980s the electronics sector took off worldwide, overtaking clothing and other sectors as the main export industry in East Asia. To meet export demands, business groups were forced to acquire additional technological know-how and skills. Some learned to design products independently of the foreign buyers, although most continued to manufacture for the TNCs under OEM arrangements, which was the most important channel for export marketing during the 1980s. The firms also benefited from the improving technological infrastructures and the supply of well-educated human resources developed within the business groups (discussed in detail in the next section).

The first business groups to enter electronics (for example, Samsung of South Korea) tended to graduate from simple to advanced learning over a period of two decades or so. Later entrants began at the more advanced stages, missing out early phases. The OEM system became a training school as firms entered new sectors, secured a market channel, and acquired technology.

During the late 1980s and early 1990s firms began learning how to develop their own product designs and compete, at least in some areas, at the technological frontier (where research and development (R&D) becomes essential to competitive advantage). Nevertheless, business groups also continued to produce a large proportion of their exports under OEM arrangements, depending on foreign companies for access to markets, key components, and capital goods. Investing in skills enabled the business groups to increase their export earnings by broadening their customer base and expanding their product ranges. Learning how to design new products enabled them to capture a larger share of the value-added. During the latter half of the 1980s, business groups in Taiwan and South Korea made the transition from consumer electronics and simple assembly activities to complex products, including computers, industrial electronics, telecommunications devices, semiconductors, and peripherals.

By the late 1980s, firms had gained impressive entrepreneurial and managerial skills, sufficient to exploit foreign technology and market channels to their advantage. Gradually, the leading firms (such as Samsung and Hyundai of South Korea) narrowed the technology gap with the market leaders and were able to negotiate more equal technology partnerships with Japanese, European, and American TNCs.

Business groups pursued tenacious and bold strategies toward technological acquisition and international marketing. Through training, hiring, and learning, firms transformed their initial low-cost labor advantages into highly competitive low-cost precision engineering capabilities. Samsung acquired foreign firms in Silicon Valley to gain technological skills and access to markets. Others formed long-term R&D partnerships with foreign market leaders. In some cases, experimental design and R&D began fairly early on. However, there was a general tendency for firms to begin with simple tasks and accumulate capabilities gradually and systematically in a path-dependent, cumulative manner, with skills and knowledge gradually building on each other. Government learning progressed in tandem with business group learning. The South Korean government, for example, encouraged the business groups to expand their electronics activities by improving the educational and technological infrastructure.

As Table 28.1 indicates, learning extended beyond technology to markets and marketing. Firms learned to package, distribute, and market their goods. Some established marketing departments at home and then in the advanced countries. Marketing know-how enabled firms to diversify their customer base and to increase their growth opportunities. Like technology, export marketing involved substantial investments in skills and organization. The major business groups (for example, Hyundai) succeeded in establishing their own brand names abroad, organizing their own distribution outlets and advertising directly to customers in the West.

There were many connections between the stages of technology and market development. Firms learned to improve both their technology and their marketing skills simultaneously in order to increase profit and market share. The channels for learning technological and marketing capabilities were combined together in the

OEM/ODM (own design and manufacture) system. To increase sales of production capacity to key customers, joint engineering projects were carried out, enabling the business groups to share the costs of learning with their customers. Later on, to bring innovative new products to the market, the larger firms made heavy, long-term investments in R&D.

By using exports as a discipline to lead technological development, companies overcame the deficiencies of local markets. Exports provided the missing demand–pull mechanism to allow manufacturers to narrow the innovation gap. Local competition stimulated innovation, and successful exporters were imitated by others. Export demand provided the focusing device for learning and forced the pace of progress.

During the 1980s, the OEM system not only expanded but also transformed. With advances in design capabilities, by the late 1980s, foreign buyers and TNCs began purchasing goods under the so-called ODM, allowing local companies to exploit their own design talents. Sometimes, the latecomers designed goods independently, using their own knowledge of the international market. In other cases, they worked closely with foreign buyers and TNCs. The emergence of ODM signified a new phase of technological progress, indicating that business groups had internalized much of the ability to understand foreign-market needs, then to design and develop new electronic products for these overseas markets.

As with OEM, the ODM system allows the foreign buyer or TNC to brand and distribute the goods manufactured locally, allowing the latecomer to circumvent the need for heavy marketing investments. In the Taiwanese computer industry, ODM was encouraged by large international trade shows, which attracted US firms such as IBM, Apple, Dell, Intel, and AT&T, and Japanese firms such as Fujitsu and Hitachi. Taiwanese PCs and notebook computers were purchased in large volumes and sold in discount stores and other outlets in Japan and the USA, usually bearing the brand of the TNC buyer.

In contrast with the Western Schumpeterian focus on radical invention, R&D, and advanced product designs, East Asian innovation grew out of the need to compete from behind the technology frontier, fuelled by the firms' ambition to catch up. The comparison with standard Western business models is striking. Business groups began by learning mature, standardized manufacturing processes. Once manufacturing capabilities were in place, companies moved onto advanced process engineering, product–process interfacing, and product design. Only since the mid-1990s, and only selectively, have the leading business groups exploited R&D for new product development and moved towards OBM (own brand manufacture) (Hobday et al. 2004). In this sense, they reversed the normal Schumpeterian cycle of innovation, passing from mature to early stages, from standard to experimental manufacturing processes, and from incremental production improvements to R&D.

Although not the focus of this chapter, some of the most important supports to technological innovation were on the organizational fronts. The most important of these were the new forms of vertical inter-company partnerships formed under OEM and ODM. These enabled business groups to exploit foreign export channels, to overcome barriers to entry, and systematically to acquire technology. OEM allowed the business groups to couple the technology pull of Western markets with local technological efforts. The expansion and sophistication of OEM provided the route for technology transfer from buyers in the West and Japan, and enabled the business groups systematically to climb up the technology ladder.

28.3.2 The role of business groups in technological innovation

So what has actually been the specific role of business groups in technological innovation? While the above section identified the processes of technological learning starting from OEM to OBM manufacturing, we now turn to identify the factors to explain the positive and negative effects of business groups on innovation in the late-industrializing context.

We argue that business groups facilitate innovation by providing what Mahmood and Mitchell (2004) term "innovation infrastructure," which covers the set of competitive assets including financial and human resources, knowledge sourcing, and vertical intermediation. A group name connoting credibility and reputation as well as ties with the government are the other assets that are critical in acquiring and/ or nurturing resources vital for innovation. Leveraging such business group resources is, therefore, a key benefit used for the successful innovation of group members.

Let us begin first with financial resources. Group membership allows firms easily to tap into intra-group capital markets, which firms in less-developed economies critically lack. While in developed countries venture capital firms or other external funding organizations provide the necessary capital to firms, the shortage of such sources in emerging economies can allow business groups to perform as venture capitalists. As such, business groups can work more effectively to allocate resources to new innovative prospects compared to outside capital markets. Further, successful group firms can acquire bank credits, as well as domestic and foreign investment, much more easily than independent non-group firms, thanks to the reputation and credibility of large business groups in emerging economies (Servaes 1996; Mahmood and Mitchell 2004).

Scientific labor markets within the group also provide critical advantages, as technology-oriented human resources are difficult to obtain from external markets in emerging economies. Business groups can thus nurture scientific personnel performing the functions of research facilities and educational organizations simultaneously. They can relocate such researchers from intra-group companies to new businesses when necessary (Mahmood and Mitchell 2004; Chang et al. 2006). Such transfer and sharing can then result in the rapid diffusion of technological capability across the affiliates of the business group (Kim 1997). Moreover, business groups can attract the most-qualified people from the best universities to start with, thanks to the opportunities they provide, so placing business groups in an advantageous standing.

Outward-looking group-affiliated firms will then be in an advantageous position to source the necessary knowledge for innovation, once the best available human talent is pooled collectively within the groups. As we discussed in the above section, contacts and partnerships with international firms is indispensable for emerging country firms' technological acquisition. Thanks to the established overseas relationships and networks that leading groups have nurtured, their constituent firms have easier access to the information and knowledge that foreign firms possess. Further, those international firms may be skeptical about licensing technology or partnering with a firm in an emerging economy because of inadequate property rights and difficulties in formulating enforceable contracts (Hobday 1995; Mahmood and Mitchell 2004). In such cases, the group name by itself can sometimes function as a critical competitive asset insofar as it enjoys international recognition, especially among overseas manufacturers (Bonaglia et al. 2008). Government ties that the business groups possess may also function positively in such instances, as groups will be better positioned to protect property rights and enforce contracts compared to the unaffiliated firms (Mahmood and Mitchell 2004).

Lastly, internal vertical intermediaries such as suppliers and distributors that provide access to skills, equipment, and customers create a competitive advantage for some group-affiliated firms, since those complementary sectors of the economy are likely to be weak in emerging economies. By having the internal vertical intermediation activities readily available within the group, with the correct strategy group-affiliated firms can be in a superior position compared to independent firms to exploit that innovation infrastructure (Mahmood and Mitchell 2004).

Nonetheless, business groups may also hinder innovation, as the groups may erect entry barriers that prevent independent companies from entering an industry. Mahmood and Mitchell (2004) argue that resources such as capital, labor, and information that bring economic rents to business groups in the presence of market imperfections may also assist business groups to build entry barriers. Business groups may, for instance, make a particular industry unprofitable for potential newcomers by driving them out with predatory price cutting, thanks to their abundant internal resources. Business groups may also moderate competition with other groups, thanks to their interdependence in multiple markets, which may ultimately deter new entrants. Further, diversified business groups can close out markets to start-up firms, as they may set up preferential arrangements between groups firms that are concurrently buyers and sellers. As a result, because new independent firms will be deterred from entry into those markets where business group firms are dominant players, a lack of access to new and diverse ideas would eventually inhibit technological innovation in the industry.

Morck and Yeung (2003) argue that family business groups may subvert new and independent innovative firms that compete with their own firms. They suggest that one way to do this is by starving innovative upstarts of capital. The business groups may utilize their political influence to subvert the financial institutions, which they have employed to become prosperous, to lock in their positions (Rajan and Zingales 2001; Morck and Yeung 2003). Morck and Yeung then go one step further to propose that business groups may also block "creative destruction," even among their own firms. When an innovation by a firm within a business group is harmful to the business of another firm within the group, causing an overall negative financial interest to the total group, then it is more likely that such innovation will not take place. While such blocking of "creative self-destruction" may be optimal for the business group, it will impede the overall economic growth of the economy in which business groups are located (Morck and Yeung 2003).

The Korean *chaebol* represents the most notable dilemma in terms of the innovation enhancement and hindrance by the business groups. The *chaebol* certainly played a significant role in establishing the technological infrastructure in South Korea. Kim (1997: 196–8), for instance, shows that the *chaebols* were in the most favorable position to attract the best entrants to the workforce. This in return assisted the rapid accumulation of technological skills within business groups. The *chaebols* exploited their capabilities in acquiring knowledge from the international community to identify, negotiate, and finance technology transfer. Their political ties then helped them to acquire licenses for new businesses and to receive preferential financing from the government (Kim 1997).

Nevertheless, because *chaebol* eventually internalized so many market activities, the small and medium-sized sector in South Korea has been underdeveloped. The Korean business groups—with their extreme vertical integration with inflexible and inefficient supply chains—eventually inhibited the formation and growth of small entrepreneurial firms and specialized SMEs, and the services and technology they could have provided. This absence of a SME network, for instance, caused *chaebols* in automobiles and electronics to rely heavily on the Japanese firms for component supplies (Hobday 1995; Kim 1997; Kim, Chapter 6, this volume).

Furthermore, Kim (1997: 34) argues that the *chaebols'* escalating power caused monopolistic abuses, including scarcity creation, price gouging, and predatory behavior in the South Korean market. The political ties that supported the growth of *chaebols* also led to economic inefficiency at the macroeconomy level. The huge size, bureaucratic structures, rigid hierarchies, and unwieldy conglomeration of *chaebols* were the other critical drawbacks. While early strategies and structures have enabled several business groups to mobilize large resources and to cross-subsidize risky operations, the old approach has often become a liability, preventing firms from competing at the innovation frontier. The scale-intensive formula, for instance, restricted corporate flexibility of the Korean *chaebol* and slowed responses to market changes. Bureaucracy and centralized communications along vertical hierarchies may then have stifled the innovation capacity of some young South Korean engineers and researchers (Hobday 1995; Chang 2003).

Kim (1997: 197–8), however, suggests that *chaebols* are still more of an asset than a liability in South Korea's technological progress. Thanks to their competitive resources, including those in technology, human, organization, and finance, they continue to play the most important role in developing South Korea's technological capabilities that push the globalization drive of Korean businesses. Then again, competition policies as introduced in the 1980s in enhancing the inter-*chaebol* rivalry have helped to stimulate strategic efficiency and innovative capabilities among the business groups. Meanwhile, policies geared toward the promotion of SMEs, especially the technology-oriented ones, are helping to build an efficient subcontracting network between large and small firms (Kim 1997). This division of labor between large diversified business groups and specialized technology-oriented SMEs in South Korea is, however, too embryonic yet to present an opportunity for a systematic examination.

28.3.3 Alternative models of technological progress in Asian development

While the above section has focused primarily on business groups, it would be wrong to suggest this particular organizational structure was the only provider of innovation and successful exporting form. Indeed, across the so-called four dragons (see Fig. 28.1) there was considerable variety in industrial structure, organizational form, patterns of ownership, and government policies.

The Japanese *zaibatsu* and *keiretsu* models influenced the aggressive business group style of the South Korean *chaebol* in their efforts to catch up. The South

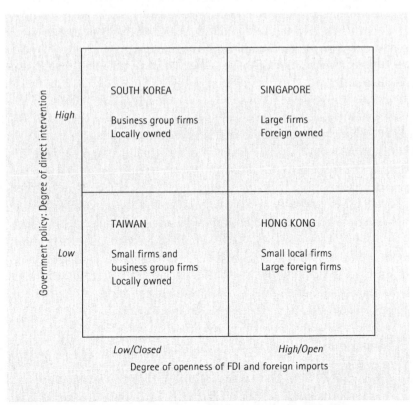

Figure 28.1 Diversity of catch–up models: The four dragons

Korean government patronized the business groups, and its policies resulted in highly concentrated industrial structures, with the *chaebol* dominating electronics and many other industries. However, Taiwan and Hong Kong depended to a large extent on small Chinese family-owned businesses, some of which grew large, but most of which remained focused on particular product groups. In the case of Taiwan there was a mixed industrial structure, but small firms played a major role in leading electronics exports. In both Hong Kong and Taiwan small firms proliferated, resulting in a highly dispersed industrial structure in electronics. An interesting lesson from those two economies is that small scale need not necessarily be a hindrance to export growth in sectors such as electronics. This is an important point, as many observers look to South Korea for economic policy lessons. However, in electronics and other sectors such as clothing, footwear, sewing machines, and bicycles Taiwanese firms matched or exceeded the performance of the *chaebol* in export value (Hobday 1995).

Small-scale overseas Chinese firms relied on speed and flexibility, while the South Korean business groups took a high-volume, process-intensive route to electronics. Many Taiwanese and Hong Kong firms specialized in fast-changing market niches. Taiwan's approach drew from a variety of cultural sources. Local firms combined their traditional overseas Chinese business acumen with modern management training received in leading US corporations, universities, and business schools. Many of Taiwan's high-technology exporting firms owe more to the American management influence than to the Japanese *keiretsu* model.

While Taiwan and South Korea relied mostly on locally owned firms, Singapore (then Malaysia, Thailand, Vietnam, and increasingly, China[5]) depended more on foreign TNCs for exports. In Singapore, TNC investments were encouraged because the government believed, rightly or wrongly, that the local entrepreneurial base was too weak to lead industrialization. Yuan and Low (1990) discuss the balance between private and state entrepreneurship and explain the historical choices of the government. Successive policies encouraged TNCs to transfer technology to the subsidiaries and to build up Singapore as the leading South East Asian headquarters for electronics manufacturing.

As Fig. 28.1 shows, there were also striking contrasts in the degree of government intervention in electronics. During the 1960s and 1970s, both South Korea and Singapore followed highly interventionist policies. However, Singapore intervened mainly indirectly through subsidies and other inducements to TNCs, supporting them with infrastructural and educational policies, often for the benefit of specific foreign firms. South Korea intervened both indirectly and directly in the strategic affairs of the *chaebol*, offering cheap finance, setting export targets, preventing some diversifications and allowing others. During the 1980s the government intervened much less directly, as the *chaebol* grew in size and competence.

---

[5] China entered in the 1970s and 1980s with a mix of FDI (TNCs represented around 80% of electronics exports) and OEM, compressing the cycle of technological catch-up.

In stark contrast to South Korea and Singapore, Hong Kong pursued a non-interventionist, *laissez-faire* approach to electronics and economic development in general, relying on capitalists that had fled from Shanghai during the communist revolution. In the case of Taiwan, the government intervened selectively in scale-intensive areas such as semiconductors, but left most electronics export activity to the strategies of private companies in the market place.

The figure also illustrates important differences in orientation of industrial policy. While Hong Kong and Singapore pursued conventional export-led policies, South Korea and Taiwan combined these policies with import protection, restrictions on foreign direct investment (FDI), and the controlling or banning of imports, to reserve local markets and protect local firms from external competition. South Korea was the most restrictive toward FDI, receiving much less than the other three, despite its greater size. Taiwan often negotiated the terms of FDI and tied TNCs to local content rules and export targets. In sharp contrast, Singapore and Hong Kong encouraged FDI with low taxation, special incentives, and welcoming policies and schemes, allowing a degree of freedom seldom witnessed in South Korea and Taiwan. While import protection was followed in South Korea, the practice took place within an overall framework of export-led industrialization. This coupling of export-led growth with import restriction, which had occurred earlier in Japan, contrasts sharply with the Latin American and Indian approaches, where the local market has traditionally been the primary focus of policy, rather than the export market.

The histories show striking contrasts among the non-Japanese models of East Asian development. Policy diversity led to plurality in industrial concentration, corporate ownership and strategy, patterns of innovation and paths of industrial development. Despite these differences, each of the Asian newly industrializing economies achieved unprecedented technological progress.

At least four important similarities in macroeconomic policy, industrial orientation, and technological development explain how each country succeeded in electronics and overcame latecomer disadvantages. First, firms undoubtedly benefited from low rates of interest, relatively low inflation, and high savings. There can be little doubt that achieving macroeconomic stability was a key factor in East Asian development. Stability, coupled with the commitment of each government to industrial development, provided firms with an environment for long-term planning and investment.

Secondly, the latecomers responded to the outward-looking, export-led industrial policies of each country. Export-led growth provided the framework to enable firms to overcome their dislocation from the centers of innovation and demanding international markets, providing the demand-pull for innovation. Where import substitution was evident, as in the case of South Korea and Taiwan, import restrictions were conducted within an overall policy of export-led growth. Exports acted as a focusing device for technology investments and encouraged the growth of a variety of institutions to enable exports to flourish. Arrangements such as OEM, joint ventures, licensing, and subcontracting were encouraged by government policies, allowing firms to acquire and adapt foreign technologies.

Thirdly, each economy developed a thriving educational and technological infrastructure. In the early stages removing illiteracy and supplying a sound general education was the priority. Once literate, children then went on to receive vocational education in the crafts and engineering. By developing, adapting, and improving training and education policies, each country supplied a sufficient number of technicians and engineers for firms to develop. Each country set up institutes for engineering training and support for industry; many firms benefited from their services and supplies of well-trained engineers and technicians. Vocational courses, often directed toward company needs, were carried out in local universities and polytechnics.

Fourthly, where there were weaknesses in firm capability, governments intervened to ensure that the entrepreneurial base was strong enough to lead industrialization. "Entrepreneurial failure," a particular form of market failure, occurs when firms are insufficient in numbers or dynamism, or both, to lead industrialization. Without a sufficiently talented cadre of firms, no industrial strategy can be successful, almost by definition. Policies to overcome entrepreneurial (or corporate) failure took various forms. In Singapore the government set about attracting TNCs to develop the electronics industry, and took control of other industries itself. In South Korea market mechanisms appeared inadequate, so the government built up the business groups to overcome the problem of corporate failure. In Taiwan, in many scale-intensive sectors, state-owned firms were established to organize industrial development.

28.3.4 The role of government in technological catch-up and business group–government relations

As noted above, the role of government in the development of the business groups is an important feature in explaining their success. Amsden (1995) argues that the nature and style of government intervention, and government business relations, were critical in disciplining the business groups and gaining reciprocity for advantages (for example, subsidies, investments support, and protection) especially in terms of exports and productive investment.

As Amsden (1989: 14) points out for the case of Korea, General Park Chung Hee (President from 1961 to 1979) allowed the "millionaires" who promoted his reforms into the heart of state decision making. Park wanted these so-called tycoons to create large plants to realize economies of scale and to promote national capitalism. According to Park's philosophy, the role of government was to oversee the millionaires to prevent any abuse of power. Competition policies were introduced, not always successfully, to curb the abuse of market power by the *chaebol*, to stimulate efficiency, and to prevent monopolistic practices. Despite conflicts with government, as Amsden (1989: 130–6) argues, local firms shared many of the development aims and philosophies of the state. Productivity and competition were enhanced by inter-*chaebol* rivalry, led by powerful business leaders. Since the 1960s this rivalry is entrenched in the structures of oligopoly in South Korea. The origin of the competitiveness of the domestic industry was, therefore, the direct outcome of successive government's policies.

Amsden (1995) contends that East Asia's business groups performed successfully because governments used exports as a performance standard for subsidies, even among groups with protected internal markets. Governments looked to the Japanese model of business group success, where the role of exports was very important in shaping the direction of Japanese business groups. In South Korea subsidies to business groups in the 1960s were tied to export targets, which were overseen by government agencies and administered through trade associations. Rewards were given to successful exporters, and there were penalties for failures (Amsden 1995, citing Haggard 1990). Credit from government-owned banks was linked to export targets, while exports became the "subsidy allocation principle." In Taiwan, similar industrial shaping was structured by economic leaders; indeed, ten out of the first fourteen Ministers of Finance were engineers rather than economists, and believed in government making things happen, rather than leaving them to the market; they were also familiar with Japan (Vogel 1991: 26–7). Directors of Taiwan state-owned banks were held personally responsible for loans and investment decisions they made, in terms of their promotion and salary (Amsden 1995), which again linked business groups to national development performance.

From Vogel's and Amsden's views, business groups can be seen as instruments of state-engineered industrialization, playing a critical role in achieving export growth, human resource progress, investment, and resource mobilization. Under the guidance of the developmental state, business groups helped to develop a managerial and entrepreneurial class, at a time when, otherwise, this class might have been too weak or small to lead industrialization. Consistent with Gerschenkron (1962), government intervention was especially important at the early stage of late industrialization, when initial capability building and resources mobilization are essential, as capital and other markets are not yet developed.

Regarding technology, Amsden argues that Asia's latecomers could not industrialize with new technology, products, and processes and were limited in natural resource endowments. In the absence of access to new technologies, there was a need for government involvement to ensure technology transfer and in South Korea and other countries business groups became instruments of this policy. As a result, technological and industrial strategy was based on unrelated diversification, supported by a growth in manufacturing skills, project execution capabilities, and the upgrading of technician and engineering skills. The government acted to subsidize and stimulate these processes to ensure the acquisition of technology. Business groups emerged to reflect the nature of industrial growth across the economy and the particular stage of development.

28.4 CONCLUSIONS AND IMPLICATIONS

Each emerging economy has its own history and its own set of opportunities and difficulties. Therefore, there can be no model for imitation from the Asian case or "one best way" to develop firm level organizational structures. However, the Asian examples provide some insights into the key features that shaped the nature of business groups and led some business groups to play a positive role in technological development. The experiences also hint at potential weaknesses of the business group form and the existence of other business structures that are also suitable for leading technological development. There are perhaps five main policy and business conclusions arising from the Asian case.

First, the overall economic strategy and orientation of the particular developing countries appear central to the business group performance. In Asia, export-led growth and outward-looking strategies encouraged business groups to become integrated into global markets and helped them acquire foreign technology through their external partners (especially large TNC buyers). Even where there was government subsidy, internal business group cross-subsidy, and local market privileges, business groups needed to acquire technology to compete. By contrast, if business groups in emerging markets are protected from competition under an import substitution regime and guaranteed access to local markets, on the face of it, there will be fewer incentives and opportunities to acquire foreign technology and less incentive and need to compete technologically. In South Korea and Taiwan, export-led growth and internal rivalry favored technology seeking and innovation on the part of business groups.

Secondly, the economic stage of development, the level of "backwardness," and the corresponding domestic entrepreneurial capacity appear to be critical in an understanding of the role of business groups in national economic development. In the case of late entry, on the basis of a few well-developed industrial capabilities, the business group can compensate for an inadequate infrastructure, poorly developed markets, and the lack of investment finance, skilled labor, and other resources. In some Asian cases, business groups proved to be a highly effective instrument in overcoming the late-entry problem by mobilizing these resources. It may not be the only organizational form suited for this, but, by internalizing the functions of markets in more developed economies, business groups helped to mobilize investments in technology and facilitated technological innovation.

In the early latecomer context, a distinctive technological capability cannot be the core of business strategy or broader economic development, almost by definition. The capabilities to develop new products and technologies based on R&D cannot be the driver of business competitiveness, as it is in the case of developed-country firms, which benefit from rare, distinctive, and hard-to-imitate technological advantages (Barney 1991). Therefore, a technology-focused strategy is also wrong for business groups in emerging economies at early stages of development. Instead, generic, low-cost technological and managerial capabilities will tend to be more important. In the case of business groups in South Korea and Taiwan, the OEM subcontracting system provided not only a channel of technology, but also economies of scale and access to international markets. Generic project execution capabilities were important (Amsden and Hikino 1994), as were low-cost mass-production process capabilities and progressive incremental improvements to standard process technologies. By contrast, in the case of business groups making the transition to own-brand/own-product leadership status focused, distinctive innovation capabilities are required as the business groups start to compete as leaders. Therefore, as business groups reach the technology frontier in particular product markets, they may wish to question the business group structure if it proves slow, costly, or cumbersome. More investment is needed on the technology upgrading, and this might require a new effective organization model. However, in many cases in the abovementioned nations, this upgrading advanced stage has not yet been reached, and business groups operate as hybrid latecomers, followers, and leaders depending on the product in question (Hobday et al. 2004).

Thirdly, the existence of role models to learn from, and the viability of possible organizational alternatives, appear to be a key factor in the developments of Asia's exporting success. In the case of South Korea and Taiwan, Japan and the Japanese business groups provided a successful role model to learn from. However, in the case of Singapore, Malaysia, Thailand and, later, China, exports were led by the subsidiaries of foreign TNCs, which provided a route into international markets. In the case of Taiwan, while business groups were important, small focused entrepreneurial firms were perhaps even more important for leading exports and acquiring technology. In some cases the formation of diversified business groups may be the only or best option, or it may be one organizational form among several.

Fourthly, the internal technological and managerial capability and culture of the business group is an important factor in understanding the role of the business group in development. Business groups are not all the same. Some are led by visionaries with a commitment to national economic development. Others may be motivated by generating huge personal wealth for themselves and family members. In the former case, the business group may well prove a strong and valuable instrument for national economic development. In the latter case, the business group may be a negative, obstructing, rent-seeking organization. However, firms do not exist in isolation from the wider context. Therefore, the embeddedness of the business group in a particular context (Granovetter 1985) and the political economy of business-group–state relations may well play a central role in shaping the culture of the business group.

Fifthly, the political economy of the business group–government relations and the competence of government clearly play a part in shaping the progress and performance of business groups. Even in the successful Asian cases, business groups revealed episodes of rent seeking and "non-rational" diversification. However, there is also evidence to show the importance of a strong and relatively competent developmental state in disciplining the business groups to perform a positive developmental role and, in particular, to seek the technology required for exporting. In some countries, this healthy relationship does not exist, and business groups, through political ties, can act as rent-seeking devices under the protection of government. In this case, business groups are not forced to compete externally or to acquire and develop technology (as they were in South Korea and Taiwan), but may instead prevent competition and stifle technological progress.

In summary, business groups appear to emerge for a variety of reasons and can play a positive or negative role in economic and technological development. After all, stage and pattern of development, business group organizational cultures, possible alternatives forms, and the nature of firm–government relations all appear to play their part in shaping the developmental role of business groups. Business groups ultimately embody and combine both advantages and disadvantages over other business forms. They may facilitate innovative activities by providing innovation infrastructure, which brings private benefits to their affiliated firms. They also bring public benefits to the overall economy, as long as they positively support national development when there is a need for a powerful early stage resource mobilization. So long as market imperfections remain in an economy, and even in maturing economic environments where key resources for innovation remain in the hands of business groups, business groups will continue to play a significant role in innovation. Business groups may generate public costs to the economies, if they hinder innovation by erecting various entry barriers to independent firms that embody new and diverse ideas and breakthroughs. The pros and cons of business groups in late-industrializing economies are not predetermined, but are contingent on the effective internal mechanism for innovation. It is through these mechanisms that they mobilize and utilize their accumulated resources and capabilities, which can be instrumental to the enhancement of the innovative capabilities of national economies as well as to the profitability of the business group entities.

REFERENCES

AMSDEN, A. H. (1989). *Asia's Next Giant: South Korea and Late Industrialization.* New York: Oxford University Press.

AMSDEN, A. H. (1995). "Like the Rest: South-East Asia's 'Late' Industrialization," *Journal of International Development,* 7/5: 791–9.

AMSDEN, A. H., and HIKINO, T. (1994). "Project Execution Capability, Organizational Know-How and Conglomerate Corporate Growth in Late Industrialization," *Industrial and Corporate Change,* 3: 111–48.

BARNEY, J. (1991). "Firm Resources and Sustained Competitive Advantage," *Journal of Management,* 17/1: 99–120.

BONAGLIA, F., COLPAN, A. M., and GOLDSTEIN, A. (2008). "Innovation and Internationalization in the White Goods GVC: The Case of Arcelik," *International Journal of Technological Learning, Innovation and Development,* Special Issue on "Global Value Chains & Innovation Networks: Prospects for Industrial Upgrading in Developing Countries," 1/4: 520–35.

CHANDLER, A. D. (1962). *Strategy and Structure: Chapters in the History of the American Industrial Enterprise*. Cambridge, MA: MIT Press.

CHANDLER, A. D. (1990). *Scale and Scope: The Dynamics of Industrial Capitalism*. Cambridge, MA: Bellknap Press.

CHANG, S. J. (2003). *Financial Crisis and the Transformation of the Korean Business Groups: The Rise and Fall of the Chaebols*. Cambridge: Cambridge University Press.

CHANG, S. J., CHUNG, C., and MAHMOOD, I. P. (2006). "When and How Does Business Group Affiliation Promote Firm Innovation? A Tale of Two Emerging Economies," *Organization Science*, 17/5: 637–56.

GERSCHENKRON, A. (1962). *Economic Backwardness in Historical Perspective*. Cambridge, MA: Harvard University Press.

GRANOVETTER, M. (1985). "Economic Action and Social Structure: The Problem of Embeddedness," *American Journal of Sociology*, 91/3: 481–510.

HAGGARD, S. (1990). *Pathways from the Periphery: The Politics of Growth in the Newly Industrializing Countries*. London: Cornell University Press.

HOBDAY, M. (1995). *Innovation in East Asia: The Challenge to Japan*. Aldershot: Edward Elgar.

HOBDAY, M., RUSH, H., and BESSANT, J. (2004). "Approaching the Innovation Frontier in Korea: The Transition Phase to Leadership," *Research Policy*, 33: 1433–57.

INTARAKUMNERD, P. (2000). "The Telecommunication Business Groups: An Analysis of the Factors Shaping the Direction of their Growth Paths." Unpublished DPhil thesis, SPRU, University of Sussex.

KHANNA, T., and PALEPU, K. (1997). "Why Focused Strategies May be Wrong for Emerging Markets," *Harvard Business Review* (July–Aug.), 41–51.

KHANNA, T., and RIVKIN, J. W. (2001). "Estimating the Performance Effects of Business Groups in Emerging Markets," *Strategic Management Journal*, 22/1: 45–7.

KIM, L. (1997). *Imitation to Innovation: The Dynamics of Korea's Technological Learning*. Boston: Harvard Business School Press.

LEFF, N. (1978). "Industrial Organization and Entrepreneurship in Developing Countries: The Economic Groups," *Economic Development and Cultural Change*, 26: 661–75.

MAHMOOD, I. P., and MITCHELL, W. (2004). "Two Faces: Effects of Business Groups on Innovation in Emerging Economies," *Management Science*, 50/10: 1348–65.

MORCK, R., and YEUNG, B. (2003). "Agency Problems in Large Family Business Groups," *Entrepreneurship Theory and Practice*, 27/4: 367–82.

PENROSE, E. (1959). *The Theory of the Growth of the Firm*. Oxford: Oxford University Press.

PENROSE, E. (1960). "The Growth of the Firm: A Case Study: The Hercules Powder Company," *Business History Review*, 34/1 (Spring).

RAJAN, R., and ZINGALES L. (2001). "The Great Reversals: The Politics of Financial Development in the 20th Century." National Bureau of Economic Research Working Paper No. 8178.

SERVAES, H. (1996). "The Value of Diversification during the Conglomerate Merger Wave," *Journal of Finance*, 51: 227–52.

VARGAS, A. T. (2004). "Growth Paths of Large Firms in Late Industrialising Countries: The Case of Mexican Business Groups 1890s-1990s." Unpublished DPhil thesis, SPRU, University of Sussex.

VOGEL, E. F. (1991). *The Four Little Dragons: The Spread of Industrialization in East Asia*. Cambridge. MA: Harvard University Press.

YUAN, L. T., and LOW, L. (1990). *Local Entrepreneurship in Singapore: Private and State*. Singapore: The Institute of Policy Studies, Times Academy Press.

INDEX